W9-COB-313

AND JOBS ACT

James F. Fegen, Jr.
Senior Vice President,
Product Operations

Laurie Asch
(LL.M., NY Bar)
Director, Core Federal Tax

Christine Carr
Senior Director,
Data Management

Mark Sheiner
Senior Product Manager

Stanley V. Baginski
(LL.M., NY Bar)
Managing Editor

Kersten Behrens
(J.D., NY, NJ Bar)
Managing Editor

John G. Clark
(LL.M., NY Bar)
Managing Editor

Elyce Friedfeld
(LL.M., NY Bar)
Managing Editor

Lesli S. Laffie
(LL.M., NY, NJ Bar)
Managing Editor

Thomas Long
(LL.M., NY, NJ Bar)
Managing Editor

Dennis P.
McMahon
(LL.M., NY,
MA Bar)
Managing Editor

Jeffrey N.
Pretsfelder
(J.D., C.P.A., NJ,
NY Bar)
Managing Editor

Suzanne Baillie
Schmitt
(LL.M., NY Bar
(Retired))
Managing Editor

Gary S. Bronstein
(LL.M., CA,
MA Bar)
Senior Editor

Steve Brylski
(LL.M., NY Bar)
Senior Editor

Min Soo Kim
(LL.M., CA, NY
Bar)
Senior Editor

Carla M. Martin
(LL.M., AL, FL Bar)
Senior Editor

Catherine E.
Murray
(LL.M., NY Bar)
Senior Editor

Karen A. Rennie
(LL.M., NY Bar)
Senior Editor

Marian Rosenberg
(LL.M., NY Bar)
Senior Editor

E.H. Rubinsky
(LL.M., NY Bar)
Senior Editor

Simon Schneebalg
(LL.M., NY Bar)
Senior Editor

Richard H.
Sternberg
(LL.M., NY Bar)
Senior Editor

Natalie Tal
(LL.M., NY Bar)
Senior Editor

Anne Wagenbrenner
(LL.M., NY, CT
Bar)
Senior Editor

Scott E. Weiner
(J.D., NY Bar)
Senior Editor

Harris Abrams
(LL.M., PA Bar)
Senior Project Editor

Rosemary
Saldan-Pawson
(J.D., NY, KS Bar)
Senior Project Editor

James A. Chapman
(LL.M., MI Bar)

Gregory J. Evanella
(J.D., NJ Bar)

Rachel Glatt
(J.D., NY Bar)

Vikram Gosain
(J.D., C.P.A., AZ,
CA Bar)

Robert O. Heroux
(LL.M., C.P.A.,
NY, CT Bar)

Kevin Ledig
(J.D., NY, NJ Bar)

Michael A. Levin
(J.D., NY Bar)

Gwenn Lukas
(LL.M., IL, WI Bar)

Elizabeth McLeod
(J.D., NY Bar)

John Melazzo
(J.D., NJ Bar)

Chris Migliaccio
(J.D., NY Bar)

Cara O'Brien
(LL.M., NY Bar)

Richard O'Donnell
(LL.M., NJ Bar
(Retired))

Peter Ogrodnik
(LL.M., NJ Bar)

Michael E. Overton
(LL.M., NY,
VA Bar)

Tola Ozim
(J.D., NY Bar)

S. Scott Pierce
(J.D., NJ, PA Bar)

Karen E. Rodrigues
(LL.M., TX Bar)

Julie S. Rose
(J.D., CT Bar)

Robert Rywick
(J.D., NY Bar)

James Seidel
(LL.M., NY Bar)

Dara R. Siegel
(J.D., NY Bar)

Ralph M. Silberman
(J.D., VA, DC Bar)

David Simonetti
(LL.M., NY Bar)

Kristina G. Smith
(J.D., NY, DC,
WY Bar)

Michael A.
Sonnenblick
(LL.M., NY Bar)

Nicholas Stevens
(LL.M., NY, CA
Bar)

Robert Trinz
(M.A., M.S. (Tax))

Jabari M. Vaughn
(LL.M., NY Bar)

Data Management

Naveen Bhaskar
Manager

Kurt Coffman
Manager

Taji Mabra
Manager

Laurie Mitchell
Manager

Shashikanth Ainapur
Assistant Manager

Madhu Sandepudi
Team Lead

Sachidananda Swain
Team Lead

Sridhar B.
Ravindranath
Chillagattu
Peggy Frank

Madhu Babu
Jellarapu
Sanath Kaspa
Gurunadha Sarma
Konkapaka
Jyothirmai
Kothireddy
Venu Masna
Zarina Mohammed
Jyothi Nenavath
Ruth Russell
Sirisha Sunkaranam

June Babb
Supervisor

Dino Colacito
Michael Gonzalez
Angel Morales
Brian Spach
Norine Wright

Ruby Charles
Supervisor

Akinsheye Babb
Jon Benson
Lourdes Chin
Edward Mack
Mimoza Osmanaj
Torodd Taylor

Judy Cosme
Supervisor

Christopher Barbieri
Lisa Crater
Geneva Gittens
Henry Rodgers
Xiomara Tejeda

Dan Danquah
Supervisor

Charlene Brown
Craig Clark
Vijay Jagdeo
Ciara Larkin
Anthony Kibort

Michael Paci
Luke Sims

Eric Encinareal
Supervisor

Nicole Gattone

Robert Gleason
Supervisor

Joan Baselice
John Harrison
Margaret Taylor
Volpe

Gregg Reed Harris
Supervisor

Raymond Au-Yeung
Natalie Buckley
Anissa Esquina
Anthony Guglielmo
Caroline Koch
Marcia Sam

Helen McFarlane
Supervisor

Melissa Acquafredda
Marie Rivera
Carol Watson
Brett Whitmoyer

Rahul K.
Manudhanya
Team Lead

Praveen Kumar
Dandu
Kishore G
Srikanth Kukunoor
Jaya Krishna
Miriyala
Sriram Sampoorna
Ramya Tipirishetty
Nalini Mallacheri

Vamsikrishna
Penumacha
Team Lead

Renuka Lakshmi
Kaki
Shanmuka Kurella
Sirisha Sannidhanam
Nidhi Tiwari

Tushar Shetty
Supervisor

Grant Gordils
Michelle Harmon
Edward Huang
Cindy Sotero
Jonathan Thayer

Sue Ellen Sobel
Supervisor

Alexis Brown
Ron Gittens
Jennifer Huber
Amelia Massiah

Vikram Vuppula
Team Lead

Maria Aarthi
Srikanth Gaddam
Avanth
Ganamanpalli
Adnan Raza
Mohammad
J C S Nikhilesh
Chirag Kishor
Ravrani
Pavan S
Mubeen Mohd
Shareeful
Santosh Tiruvakour

Jay Kwon
*Lead Production
Analyst*

Melanie Thomas
*Senior Data
Support Coordinator*

Paralegals

Joann Casanova
Catherine Daleo
Monica Grier
Danny Wang

**Legal Resource
Center & Indexing**

Peter Durham
Manager

Thomas Adewolu
Bernie Bayless
Pierre Calixte
Andrea Leal
Patricia Link
Michael Stanton
Arlene Verderber
Holly Yue

Janet Mazefsky
*Assistant Manager,
Indexing*

Linda Lao
Claudie Peterfreund
Deirdre Simmons

Jeff Carlson
Supervisor

Salina Janifer
William Lesesne

**Tax Practitioner
Segment**

Betsy Hussin
*Senior Vice
President*

Alan Cohen
*Vice President,
International
Markets*

Perry Townes
*Vice President,
Global Platform
Strategy & Strategic
Customers*

Bill Burke
Senior Director

Jonathan Davis
Director

Christopher
Dimenna
Director

Nicole Severson
*Senior Product
Manager,
Checkpoint*

Mark Sheiner
*Senior Product
Manager*

Audrey Bohler
Product Manager

Karen Gibney
Product Manager

Adam Gretz
Product Manager

Michele Henderlong
Product Manager

**Content
Technology**

Tim Rendulic
*Vice President,
Head of Technology*

Jason Rapaccuiolo
Director

Alanna Dixon
Manager

Mohammad Nadeem
Khan
Manager

Randall Rodakowski
Manager

Nagakumari Akveti
Assistant Manager

Dave Bantel
Mohan
Bhairavabhatla
Sebastian C M
Tracey Cruz
Suresh Babu
Damodaran
Bryan Daneman
Debasis Das
Andy Dreistadt
John Fletcher K
Puneeth Prashanth
Ganapuram
Terri Ganssley
Nadine Graham
Steven Haber
Bandhu Himabindu
David Hoskin
Krishna Chaitanya
Kakarala
Farid Khan
Darren Kocur
Srilaxmi Kota
Reena Kumari
Anjaneyulu
Medarametla
David McInerney
Scott Murphy
Praveen Myakala
William Peake
Steve Pitamber
Phani Kumar
Ponugupati
Abesh Rajasekharan
Srikanth Samala
Sravanthi
Sreeramoju
Christopher Stryshak

Kundena Sudhakar
Shafin Thiyam
Vamshi Krishna
Thota
Aniwesh Vatsal
Sreedhar Vengal
Connie Wang
Karen Wharton
Travis Wright
Praveen Yarraguntla
Hongtu Zhang
Teresa Zhang

**Manufacturing &
Fulfillment Services**

Rick Bivona
Director

Anthony Scribano
*Scheduling and
Fulfillment Manager*

Rachel Hassenbein
*Associate
Fulfillment Manager*

John Disposti
*Senior Production
Associate*

Greg Miller
*Associate Production
Manager*

Bryan Gardner
*Senior Production
Associate*

Lourdes Barba
Jace Bersin
Jennifer Kalison

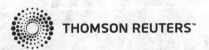

COMPLETE ANALYSIS OF THE

TAX CUTS AND JOBS ACT

An Act to provide for reconciliation pursuant to titles II and V of the concurrent resolution on the budget for fiscal year 2018

Table of Contents

¶

Organization of this Book 1

Contents 2

Analysis of Provisions Under the Following Headings:
Income Tax Rates 100
Inflation Adjustments 200
Alternative Minimum Tax.............................. 300
ACA Individual Mandate 400
Individuals: Deductions And Personal Credits 500
Individuals: Income And Exclusions 600
Qualified Business Income 700
S Corporations 800
Partnerships 900
Business Deductions And Credits 1000
Section 179 Expensing 1100
Bonus Depreciation.................................. 1200
Depreciation 1300
Tax Accounting 1400
Capital Gains 1500
Able Programs And 529 Plans 1600
Bonds and Development Incentives 1700
2016 Disaster Area Relief............................. 1800
Modified Territorial System 1900
Subpart F Inclusion For Global Intangible Low-Taxed Income 2000
Other Changes To Subpart F 2100
Anti-Base Erosion And Profit-Shifting Provisions........... 2200
Other Foreign Provisions 2300
Insurance 2400
Tax-Exempt Organizations 2500
Compensation 2600
Retirement Plans.................................... 2700
Estate And Gift Taxes 2800
Excise Taxes....................................... 2900
Procedure And Administration 3000
Miscellaneous 3100
Client Letters 3200

Act Section Cross Reference Table 6000

Code Section Cross Reference Table 6001

Code Sections Amended by Act 6002

Act Sections Amending Code 6003

FTC 2nd ¶ s Affected by Act 6004

USTR ¶ s Affected by Act 6005

Pension Analysis ¶ s Affected by Act 6006

Pension & Benefits Explanations ¶ s Affected by Act 6007

Estate Planning Analysis ¶ s Affected by Act 6008

Catalyst ¶ s Affected by Act 6009

Table of Action Alert Items 6010

Committee Report Finding Table 6011

Index... p. 805

¶ 1. Organization of the Book

Complete Analysis of the Tax Cuts and Jobs Act

The following sections contain the Complete Analysis of PL 115-97, 12/22/ 2017, "An Act to provide for reconciliation pursuant to titles II and V of the concurrent resolution on the budget for fiscal year 2018," which was passed by Congress on Dec. 20, 2017 and signed by the President on Dec. 22, 2017. This legislation is commonly known as the "Tax Cuts and Jobs Act" and is referred to as such in the Complete Analysis.

The original title for the legislation was "Tax Cuts and Jobs Act." That title was used by both the House of Representatives and the Senate as the bill made its way through Congress. The title was changed after the Senate parliamentarian ruled it violated Senate rules for legislation enacted under budget reconciliation procedures.

Please go to the Thomson Reuters Checkpoint product support page for the Complete Analysis of the Tax Cuts and Jobs Act at http://support.checkpoint.thomsonreuters.com/taxcutsandjobsact to access PDF copies of:

- the official statutory language contained in P.L. 115-97, 12/22/2017 (the Tax Cuts and Jobs Act), and
- Conf Rept. No. 115-466, the Committee Report accompanying P.L. 115-97.

The Complete Analysis provides an Analysis of the tax provisions of the Tax Cuts and Jobs Act, arranged in topical order. Each Analysis paragraph starts with a boldface title. That is followed by a list of Highlights: the Code sections amended, added, affected, repealed by or related to the change, the Act section that caused the change, and the generally effective date for the change. Each Analysis paragraph discusses the background for the change, the new law change, and the effective date for that change. Analysis paragraphs may include (1) illustrations and observations providing practical insight into the effects of the change, (2) recommendations explaining how to take advantage of opportunities presented by the law change, (3) cautions explaining how to avoid pitfalls created by the law change, and (4) viewpoints providing commentary from outside experts. The Analysis is reproduced at ¶ 100 *et seq.*

The Analysis also includes numerous client letters highlighting the changes made by the Tax Cuts and Jobs Act. They are located at ¶ 3201 *et seq.*

The Complete Analysis of the Tax Cuts and Jobs Act includes cites to Conf Rept. No 115-466. Each Analysis paragraph includes a numbered "Com Rept ¶ " reference to the specific official Committee Report language that relates to the Act provision discussed in that Analysis paragraph. A PDF copy of Conf Rept. No. 115-466 is available on the Thomson Reuters Checkpoint product support page at http://support.checkpoint.thomsonreuters.com/taxcutsandjobsact.

The finding table at ¶ 6011 contains a full listing of Com Rept paragraphs cited in the Complete Analysis. Each Com Rept paragraph entry corresponds to a specific Tax Cuts and Jobs Act section and title, and shows the official page range in the PDF copy where the Com Rept paragraph language can be found. You can use the PDF copy in conjunction with the finding table to access the official Committee Report language you need.

HIGHLIGHTS OF THE TAX CUTS AND JOBS ACT

New income tax rates & brackets

For tax years beginning after Dec. 31, 2017 and before Jan. 1, 2026, seven tax rates apply for individuals: 10%, 12%, 22%, 24%, 32%, 35%, and 37%. The Tax Cuts and Jobs Act also provides four tax rates for estates and trusts: 10%, 24%, 35%, and 37%. For analysis, see ¶ 101, ¶ 104, and ¶ 1501.

Standard deduction increased

For tax years beginning after Dec. 31, 2017 and before Jan. 1, 2026, the standard deduction is increased to $24,000 for married individuals filing a joint return, $18,000 for head-of-household filers, and $12,000 for all other taxpayers. These amounts are adjusted for inflation in tax years beginning after 2018. No changes are made to the current-law additional standard deduction for the elderly and blind. For analysis, see ¶ 501.

Personal exemptions suspended

For tax years beginning after Dec. 31, 2017 and before Jan. 1, 2026, the deduction for personal exemptions is effectively suspended because the statutory exemption amount is reduced to zero. A number of corresponding changes are made throughout the Code where specific provisions contain references to the statutory personal exemption amount; in each of these instances, the dollar amount to be used is $4,150, as adjusted by inflation. These include Code Sec. 642(b)(2)(C),(Code Sec. 642(b)(2)(C)) (exemption deduction for qualified disability trusts), Code Sec. 3402 (wage withholding exception for 2018), and Code Sec. 6334(d) (property exempt from levy). For analysis, see ¶ 502.

New measure of inflation provided

For tax years beginning after Dec. 31, 2017 (Dec. 31, 2018 for figures that are newly provided under the Act for 2018 and thus won't be reset until after that year, e.g., the tax brackets), dollar amounts that were previously indexed using CPI-U will instead be indexed using chained CPI-U (C-CPI-U). This change, unlike many provisions in the Act, is permanent. For analysis, see ¶ 201, ¶ 202.

Combat zone treatment extended to Egypt's Sinai Peninsula

The Act provides that a "qualified hazardous duty area" is treated as a combat zone for purposes of the various tax benefits under the Code for members of the U.S. Armed Forces serving in a combat zone. A "qualified hazardous duty area" is defined as the Sinai Peninsula of Egypt if, as of Dec. 22, 2017, any member of the U.S. Armed Forces is entitled to special pay under section 310 of title 37, United States Code (relating to special pay; duty subject to hostile fire or imminent danger) for services performed in that This benefit lasts only during the period the entitlement is in effect. For analysis, see ¶ 605.

Repeal of ACA individual mandate

Under pre-Act law, the Affordable Care Act (also called the ACA or Obamacare) required individuals who were not covered by a health plan that provided at least minimum essential coverage to pay a "shared responsibility payment" (also referred to as a penalty) with their federal tax return, for any month the individual did not have minimum essential coverage. This provision is commonly known as the "Individual Mandate."

The Act permanently repeals the Individual Mandate by providing that for months beginning after Dec. 31, 2018, the amount of the individual shared responsibility payment is reduced to zero. For analysis, see ¶ 401.

Individual AMT retained, with higher AMT exemption amounts

For tax years beginning after Dec. 31, 2017 and before Jan. 1, 2026, the Act increases the amount of an individuals alternative minimum taxable income (AMTI) that is exempt from AMT—the "AMT exemption" amounts—as follows:

> ... For joint returns and surviving spouses, $109,400;

> ... For single taxpayers, $70,300;

> ... For marrieds filing separately, $54,700.

The above AMT exemption amounts are reduced (not below zero) to an amount equal to 25% of the amount by which the individual's AMTI exceeds a phase-out amount, increased as follows:

> ... For joint returns and surviving spouses, $1 million.

> ... For all other taxpayers (other than estates and trusts), $500,000.

For trusts and estates, the base figure of $22,500 and phase-out amount of $75,000 remain unchanged. All of these amounts will be adjusted for inflation after 2018 under the new C-CPI-U inflation measure (see above). For analysis, see ¶ 301.

ABLE account changes

For tax years beginning after Dec. 22, 2017 and before Jan. 1, 2026, the ABLE account contribution limitation for contributions made by the designated beneficiary is increased, and other changes are in effect as described below. After the overall limitation on contributions is reached (i.e., the annual gift tax exemption amount; for 2018, $15,000), an ABLE account's designated beneficiary can contribute an additional amount, up to the lesser of (a) the federal poverty line for a one-person household; or (b) the individual's compensation for the tax year.

The Act allows the designated beneficiary of an ABLE account to claim the saver's credit under Code Sec. 25B for contributions made to his or her ABLE account.

The Act also requires that a designated beneficiary (or person acting on the beneficiary's behalf) maintain adequate records for ensuring compliance with the above limitations. For analysis of the above changes, see ¶ 1601, ¶ 1602.

Coordination with QTPs. For distributions after Dec. 22, 2017, amounts from qualified tuition programs (QTPs, also known as 529 accounts) may be rolled over to an ABLE account without penalty, provided that the ABLE account is owned by the designated beneficiary of that 529 account, or a member of his or her family. The rolled-over amounts are counted towards the overall limitation on amounts that can be contributed to an ABLE account within a tax year, and any amount rolled over in excess of this limitation is includible in the gross income of the distributee. For analysis, see ¶ 1603.

Student loan discharged on death or disability

For discharges of indebtedness after Dec. 31, 2017 and before Jan. 1, 2026, certain student loans that are discharged on account of death or total and permanent disability of the student are excluded from gross income. For analysis, see ¶ 604.

Certain self-created property not treated as capital asset

For dispositions after Dec. 31, 2017, patents, inventions, models or designs (whether or not patented), and secret formulas or processes, which are held either by the taxpayer who created the property or by a taxpayer with a substituted or transferred basis from the taxpayer who created the property (or for whom the property was created), are specifically excluded from the definition of a "capital asset." For analysis, see ¶ 1504.

Estate and gift tax retained, with increased exemption amount

For estates of decedents dying and gifts made after Dec. 31, 2017 and before Jan. 1, 2026, the Act doubles the base estate and gift tax exemption amount from $5 million to $10 million. The $10 million amount is indexed for inflation occurring after 2011 and is expected to be approximately $11.2 million in 2018 ($22.4 million per married couple). For analysis, see ¶ 2407.

Time to contest IRS levy extended

For levies made after Dec. 22, 2017 and for certain levies made before Dec. 23, 2017, the nine-month period during which IRS may return the monetary proceeds from the sale of property that has been wrongfully levied upon is extended to two years. The period for bringing a civil action for wrongful levy is similarly extended from nine months to two years. For analysis, see ¶ 3002.

Due diligence requirements for claiming head of household filing status

For tax years beginning after Dec. 31, 2017, the Act expands the due diligence requirements for paid preparers to cover determining eligibility for a taxpayer to file as head of household. A penalty of $500 (adjusted for inflation) is imposed for each failure to meet these requirements. For analysis, see ¶ 3001.

Business Tax Changes

Corporate tax rates reduced

For tax years beginning after Dec. 31, 2017, the corporate tax rate is a flat 21% rate. For analysis, see ¶ 102, ¶ 1309.

Dividends-received deduction percentages reduced

For tax years beginning after Dec. 31, 2017, the 70% dividends-received deduction is reduced to 50% and the 80% dividends-received deduction for 20% or more owned corporations is reduced to 65%. For analysis, see ¶ 103.

Corporate alternative minimum tax repealed

For tax years beginning after Dec. 31, 2017, the corporate AMT is repealed. For analysis, see ¶ 303.

For tax years beginning after 2017 and before 2022, the AMT credit is refundable and can offset regular tax liability in an amount equal to 50% (100% for tax years beginning in 2021) of the excess of the minimum tax credit for the tax year over the amount of the credit allowable for the year against regular tax liability. Accordingly, the full amount of the minimum tax credit will be allowed in tax years beginning before 2022. For analysis, see ¶ 304.

Increased Code Section 179 expensing

For property placed in service in tax years beginning after Dec. 31, 2017, the maximum amount a taxpayer may expense under Code Sec. 179 is increased to $1 million, and the phase-out threshold amount is increased to $2.5 million.

For tax years beginning after 2018, these amounts (as well as the $25,000 sport utility vehicle limitation) are indexed for inflation.

Qualified real property. The definition of Code Sec. 179 property is expanded to include certain personal property even though it is used predominantly to furnish lodging or in connection with furnishing lodging. The definition of qualified real property eligible for Code Sec. 179 expensing is also expanded to include the following improvements to nonresidential real property after the date such property was first placed in service: roofs; heating, ventilation, and air-conditioning property; fire protection and alarm systems; and security systems. Also any other building improvements to nonresidential real property that aren't elevators or escalators, building enlargements or attributable to internal structural framework are Code Sec. 179 property. For analysis, see ¶ 1101, ¶ 1102, ¶ 1103, ¶ 1104.

Temporary 100% cost recovery of qualifying business assets

A 100% first-year deduction for the adjusted basis is allowed for qualified property acquired and placed in service after Sept. 27, 2017, and before Jan. 1, 2023 (after Sept. 27, 2017 and before Jan. 1, 2024 for certain aircraft and property with longer production periods). Thus, the phase-down of the 50% allowance to zero that occurs for property placed in service during 2018, 2019 and 2020 (2019, 2020 and 2021 for certain aircraft and property with a long production period) is repealed. The additional first-year depreciation deduction is allowed for new and used property.

> *caution:* The Act refers to the new 100% depreciation deduction in the placed-in-service year as "100% expensing," but the tax break should not be confused with expensing under Code Sec. 179, which is subject to entirely separate rules (see above).

In later years, the first-year bonus depreciation deduction phases down, as follows:

- 80% for property placed in service after Dec. 31, 2022 and before Jan. 1, 2024.
- 60% for property placed in service after Dec. 31, 2023 and before Jan. 1, 2025.
- 40% for property placed in service after Dec. 31, 2024 and before Jan. 1, 2026.
- 20% for property placed in service after Dec. 31, 2025 and before Jan. 1, 2027.

For certain property with longer production periods, the beginning and end dates in the list above are increased by one year. For example, bonus first-year depreciation is 80% for long-production-period property placed in service after Dec. 31, 2023 and before Jan. 1, 2025.

First-year bonus depreciation sunsets after 2026.

For productions placed in service after Sept. 27, 2017, qualified property eligible for a 100% first-year depreciation allowance includes qualified film, television and live theatrical productions. A production is considered placed in service at the time of initial release, broadcast, or live staged performance.

For trees and vines bearing fruit or nuts and certain other specified plants planted or grafted after Sept. 27, 2017, and before Jan. 1, 2027, the 100% first-year deduction is also available subject to phase out rules similar to those above.

For the first tax year ending after Sept. 27, 2017, a taxpayer can elect to claim 50% bonus first-year depreciation (instead of claiming a 100% first-year depreciation allowance). For analysis, see ¶ 1201, ¶ 1202, ¶ 1203, ¶ 1204, ¶ 1205, ¶ 1206, ¶ 1207.

Luxury automobile depreciation limits increased

For passenger automobiles placed in service after Dec. 31, 2017 for which the additional first-year depreciation deduction under Code Sec. 168(k) is not claimed, the maximum amount of allowable depreciation is increased to: $10,000 for the year in which the vehicle is placed in service, $16,000 for the second year, $9,600 for the third year, and $5,760 for the fourth and later years in the recovery period. For passenger automobiles placed in service after 2018, these dollar limits are indexed for inflation. For passengers autos eligible for bonus first-year depreciation, the additional first-year depreciation allowance remains at $8,000. For analysis, see ¶ 1307.

Computers removed from listed property

Computer or peripheral equipment is removed from the definition of listed property, and so isn't subject to the heightened substantiation requirements and possible slower cost recovery that apply to listed property. For analysis, see ¶ 1308.

Changes to farming cost recovery

For property placed in service after Dec. 31, 2017, the cost recovery period is shortened from seven to five years for any machinery or equipment (other than any grain bin, cotton ginning asset, fence, or other land improvement) used in a farming business, the original use of which commences with the taxpayer.

In addition, taxpayers can use the 200% declining balance method--the 150% declining balance depreciation method is no longer required--for property used in a farming business (i.e., for 3-, 5-, 7-, and 10-year property). The 150%

declining balance method continues to apply to any 15-year or 20-year property used in the farming business to which the straight-line method does not apply and to property for which the taxpayer elects to use the 150% declining balance method. For analysis, see ¶ 1304, ¶ 1305.

For tax years beginning after Dec. 31, 2017, an electing farming business—i.e., a farming business electing out of the limitation on the deduction for interest—must use ADS to depreciate any property with a recovery period of 10 years or more (e.g., a single purpose agricultural or horticultural structures, trees or vines bearing fruit or nuts, farm buildings, and certain land improvements). For analysis, see ¶ 1306

Recovery period for certain real property improvements is shortened

For property placed in service after Dec. 31, 2017, the separate definitions of qualified leasehold improvement, qualified restaurant, and qualified retail improvement property are eliminated, and a general 15-year recovery period and straight-line depreciation are provided for qualified improvement property (generally a less restrictive category than the aggregate of the three categories that it replaces). A 20-year ADS recovery period is provided for such property.

Thus, qualified improvement property placed in service after Dec. 31, 2017, is generally depreciable over 15 years using the straight-line method and half-year convention.

For property placed in service after Dec. 31, 2017, the ADS recovery period for residential rental property is shortened from 40 years to 30 years.

For tax years beginning after Dec. 31, 2017, an electing real property trade or business—i.e., a real property trade or business electing out of the limitation on the deduction for interest—must use ADS to depreciate any buildings or qualified improvement property.

For analysis, see ¶ 1301, ¶ 1302, ¶ 1303.

Costs of replanting citrus plants lost due to casualty

For replanting costs paid or incurred after Dec. 22, 2017, but no later than Dec. 22, 2027, for citrus plants lost or damaged due to casualty, the costs may also be deducted by a person other than the taxpayer if (1) the taxpayer has an equity interest of not less than 50% in the replanted citrus plants at all times during the tax year in which the replanting costs are paid or incurred and such other person holds any part of the remaining equity interest, or (2) such other person acquires all of the taxpayer's equity interest in the land on which the lost or damaged citrus plants were located at the time of such loss or damage, and the replanting is on such land. For analysis, see ¶ 1411.

Limits on deduction of business interest

For tax years beginning after Dec. 31, 2017, every business, regardless of its form, is generally subject to a disallowance of a deduction for net interest expense in excess of 30% of the business's adjusted taxable income. The business interest limitation generally applies at the taxpayer level. However, for partnerships and S corporations, the limitation applies at the entity level.

For tax years beginning after Dec. 31, 2017 and before Jan. 1, 2022, adjusted taxable income is computed without regard to deductions allowable for depreciation, amortization, or depletion and without the former Code Sec. 199 domestic production activities deduction (which is repealed effective Dec. 31, 2017).

Under a small business exception, the business interest limitation doesn't apply to taxpayers (other than tax shelters) for a tax year if the taxpayer's average annual gross receipts for the three-tax year period ending with the prior tax year don't exceed $25 million. The business interest limitation also doesn't apply to certain regulated public utilities and electric cooperatives. Real property trades or businesses can elect out of the limitation if they use ADS to depreciate applicable real property used in a trade or business. Farming businesses can also elect out if they use ADS to depreciate certain property used in the farming business. There is also an exception for interest on floor plan financing (i.e., indebtedness used to finance the acquisition of motor vehicles, boats or farm machinery for sale or lease, and secured by such inventory). For analysis, see ¶ 1003.

Modification of net operating loss (NOL) deduction

For NOLs arising in tax years ending after Dec. 31, 2017, the two-year carryback and the special carryback provisions are repealed, but a two-year carryback applies for certain losses incurred in the trade or business of farming.

NOLs generally can be carried forward indefinitely. For analysis, see ¶ 1002.

For losses arising in tax years beginning after Dec. 31, 2017, the NOL deduction is generally limited to 80% of taxable income (determined without regard to the NOL deduction). Carryovers to other years are adjusted to take account of this limitation. For analysis, see ¶ 1001.

NOLs of property and casualty insurance companies can be carried back two years and carried forward 20 years to offset 100% of taxable income in those years. For analysis, see ¶ 1002, ¶ 1001

Domestic production activities deduction repealed

For tax years beginning after Dec. 31, 2017, the Code Sec. 199 domestic production activities deduction (DPAD) is repealed for non-corporate taxpayers.

For tax years beginning after Dec. 31, 2018, the DPAD is repealed for C corporations. For analysis, see ¶ 1004.

Like-kind exchange treatment limited

Generally effective for transfers after Dec. 31, 2017, the rule allowing the deferral of gain on like-kind exchanges is modified to allow for like-kind exchanges only with respect to real property that is not held primarily for sale. However, under a transition rule, the pre-Act like-kind exchange rules apply to exchanges of personal property if the taxpayer has either disposed of the relinquished property or acquired the replacement property on or before Dec. 31, 2017. For analysis, see ¶ 1503.

Five-year write-off of specified research or experimentation expenses

For amounts paid or incurred in tax years beginning after Dec. 31, 2021, "specified R&E expenses" must be capitalized and amortized ratably over a 5-year period (15 years if conducted outside of the U.S.), beginning with the midpoint of the tax year in which the specified R&E expenses were paid or incurred.

Specified R&E expenses subject to capitalization include expenses for software development, but not expenses for land or for depreciable or depletable property used in connection with the research or experimentation (but do include the depreciation and depletion allowances of such property). Also excluded are exploration expenses incurred for ore or other minerals (including oil and gas). In the case of retired, abandoned, or disposed property with respect to which specified R&E expenses are paid or incurred, any remaining basis may not be recovered in the year of retirement, abandonment, or disposal, but instead must continue to be amortized over the remaining amortization period.

Use of this provision is treated as a change in the taxpayer's accounting method under Code Sec. 481, initiated by the taxpayer, and made with IRS's consent. For R&E expenditures paid or incurred in tax years beginning after Dec. 31, 2025, the provision is applied on a cut-off basis (so there is no adjustment under Code Sec. 481(a) for R&E paid or incurred in tax years beginning before Jan. 1, 2026). For analysis, see ¶ 1408.

Employer's deduction for fringe benefit expenses limited

For amounts paid or incurred after Dec. 31, 2017, deductions for entertainment expenses are disallowed, eliminating the subjective determination of whether such expenses are sufficiently business related; the current 50% limit on the deductibility of business meals is expanded to meals provided through an in-house cafeteria or otherwise on the premises of the employer; and deductions for employee transportation fringe benefits (e.g., parking and mass transit) are denied, but the exclusion from income for such benefits received by an employee is retained. In addition, no deduction is allowed for transportation expenses that are the equivalent of commuting for employees (e.g., between the employee's home and the workplace), except as provided for the safety of the employee.

For tax years beginning after Dec. 31, 2025, the Act will disallow an employer's deduction for expenses associated with meals provided for the convenience of the employer on the employer's business premises, or provided on or near the employer's business premises through an employer-operated facility that meets certain requirements. For analysis, see ¶ 1005, ¶ 1006, ¶ 1007.

Nondeductible penalties and fines

For amounts generally paid or incurred after Dec. 21, 2017, no deduction is allowed for any otherwise deductible amount paid or incurred (whether by suit, agreement, or otherwise) to, or at the direction of, a government or specified nongovernmental with respect to the violation or potential violation of any law. There is an exception for payments the taxpayer establishes are either restitution (including remediation of property) or amounts required to come into compliance with the law at issue. An exception also applies to any amount paid or incurred as taxes due.

Restitution for failure to pay any tax, that is assessed as restitution under the Code, is deductible only to the extent it would have been allowed as a deduction if it had been timely paid.

Government agencies (or entities treated as such) must report to IRS and to the taxpayer the amount of each settlement agreement or order entered into where the aggregate amount required to be paid or incurred at the direction of the government is at least $600.

These rules generally don't apply to amounts paid or incurred under any binding order or agreement entered into before Dec. 22, 2017. For analysis, see ¶ 1009, ¶ 1008.

No deduction for amounts paid for sexual harassment subject to nondisclosure agreement

For amounts paid or incurred after Dec. 22, 2017, no deduction is allowed for any settlement, payout, or attorney fees related to sexual harassment or sexual abuse if such payments are subject to a nondisclosure agreement. For analysis, see ¶ 1010.

Employee achievement awards

For amounts paid or incurred after Dec. 31, 2017, "tangible personal property" that can be excludible employee achievement awards doesn't include cash or cash equivalents; gifts cards, coupons, or certificates; vacations, meals or lodging; or certain other non-tangible personal property. For analysis, see ¶ 2605.

Limitation on excessive employee compensation

For tax years beginning after Dec. 31, 2017, the exceptions to the $1 million deduction limitation for commissions and performance-based compensation are repealed. The definition of "covered employee" is revised to include the principal executive officer, the principal financial officer, and the three other highest paid officers. If an individual is a covered employee with respect to a corporation for a tax year beginning after Dec. 31, 2016, the individual remains a covered employee for all future years.

Under a transition rule, the changes do not apply to any remuneration under a written binding contract that was in effect on Nov. 2, 2017 and that was not modified in any material respect after that date. Compensation paid pursuant to a plan qualifies for this exception if the right to participate in the plan is part of a written binding contract with the covered employee in effect on Nov. 2, 2017. For analysis, see ¶ 2601, ¶ 2602, ¶ 2603

Deduction for local lobbying expenses eliminated

For amounts paid or incurred after Dec. 21, 2017, the deduction for lobbying expenses with respect to legislation before local government bodies (including Indian tribal governments) is eliminated. For analysis, see ¶ 1011.

Orphan drug credit modified

For amounts paid or incurred after Dec. 31, 2017, the Code Sec. 45C orphan drug credit is limited to 25% (down from 50%) of qualified clinical testing expenses for the tax year. Taxpayers can elect a reduced credit in lieu of reducing otherwise allowable deductions in a manner similar to the research credit. For analysis, see ¶ 1015, ¶ 1016.

Rehabilitation credit limited

For amounts paid or incurred after Dec. 31, 2017, the 10% credit for qualified rehabilitation expenditures with respect to a pre-'36 building is repealed. A 20% credit is provided for qualified rehabilitation expenditures with respect to a certified historic structure, which can be claimed ratably over a five-year period beginning in the tax year in which a qualified rehabilitated structure is placed in service. Transition rules apply. For analysis, see ¶ 1014.

New credit for employer-paid family and medical leave

For wages paid in tax years beginning after Dec. 31, 2017, but not beginning after Dec. 31, 2019, businesses can claim a general business credit equal to 12.5% of the amount of wages paid to qualifying employees during any period in which the employees are on Family and Medical Leave (FMLA) if the rate of payment is 50% of the wages normally paid to the employees. The credit is increased by 0.25 percentage points (but not above 25%) for each percentage point by which the payment rate exceeds 50%. All qualifying full-time employees have to be given at least two weeks of annual paid family and medical leave (all less-than-full-time qualifying employees have to be given a commensurate amount of leave on a *pro rata* basis). For analysis, see ¶ 1013.

Accounting method changes

Tax year of inclusion: AFS conformity rule

Generally for tax years beginning after Dec. 31, 2017, a taxpayer is required to recognize income no later than the tax year in which the income is taken into account as income on an applicable financial statement (AFS) or another financial statement under rules specified by IRS (subject to an exception for long-term contract income under Code Sec. 460).

The Act also codifies the current deferral method of accounting for advance payments for goods and services provided by Rev Proc 2004-34, to allow taxpayers to defer the inclusion of income associated with certain advance payments to the end of the tax year following the tax year of receipt if the income also is deferred for financial statement purposes. In addition, it directs taxpayers to apply the revenue recognition rules under Code Sec. 452 before applying the Code Sec. 1272 original issue discount (OID) rules..

For any taxpayer required by this provision to change its accounting method for its first tax year beginning after Dec. 31, 2017, the change is treated as initiated by the taxpayer and made with IRS's consent.

Under a special effective date provision, the AFS conformity rule applies for OID for tax years beginning after Dec. 31, 2018, and the adjustment period is six years.

For analysis, see ¶ 2105, ¶ 1407.

Cash method of accounting

For tax years beginning after Dec. 31, 2017, the cash method of accounting may be used by taxpayers (other than tax shelters) that satisfy a $25 million gross receipts test, regardless of whether the purchase, production, or sale of merchandise is an income-producing factor. This means that taxpayers with annual average gross receipts that do not exceed $25 million (indexed for inflation for tax years beginning after Dec. 31, 2018) for the three prior tax years are allowed to use the cash method.

As under pre-Act law, qualified personal service corporations, partnerships without C corporation partners, S corporations, and other pass-through entities are allowed to use the cash method without regard to whether they meet the $25 million gross receipts test, so long as the use of the method clearly reflects income.

An accounting method change under this rule is a change in the taxpayer's accounting method for purposes of Code Sec. 481.

For analysis, see ¶ 1404, ¶ 1403, ¶ 1405, ¶ 1401, ¶ 1402.

Accounting for inventories

For tax years beginning after Dec. 31, 2017, taxpayers that meet the $25 million gross receipts test are not required to account for inventories under Code Sec. 471, but rather may use an accounting method for inventories that either (1) treats inventories as non-incidental materials and supplies, or (2) conforms to the taxpayer's financial accounting treatment of inventories.

An accounting method change under this rule is a change in the taxpayer's accounting method for purposes of Code Sec. 481. For analysis, see ¶ 1404, ¶ 1403, ¶ 1405, ¶ 1401, ¶ 1402.

Capitalization and inclusion of certain expenses in inventory costs

For tax years beginning after Dec. 31, 2017, any producer or re-seller that meets the $25 million gross receipts test is exempt from the application of the Code Sec. 263A UNICAP rules. An accounting method change under this rule is a change in the taxpayer's accounting method for purposes of Code Sec. 481. For analysis, see ¶ 1404, ¶ 1403, ¶ 1405, ¶ 1401, ¶ 1402.

Accounting for long-term contracts

For contracts entered into after Dec. 31, 2017 in tax years ending after that date, the exception for small construction contracts from the requirement to use the percentage of completion method (PCM) is expanded to apply to contracts for the construction or improvement of real property if the contract: (1) is expected (at the time the contract is entered into) to be completed within two years of commencement of the contract and (2) is performed by a taxpayer that (for the tax year in which the contract was entered into) meets the $25 million gross receipts test.

Use of this PCM exception for small construction contracts is applied on a cut-off basis for all similarly classified contracts (so there is no adjustment under Code Sec. 481(a) for contracts entered into before Jan. 1, 2018). For analysis, see ¶ 1404, ¶ 1403, ¶ 1405, ¶ 1401, ¶ 1402.

Exclusions from tax-free contributions to capital

For contributions made after Dec. 22, 2017, the contributions to a corporation's capital that are tax-free capital contributions do not include--in addition to contributions in aid of construction (CIACs) or other contributions as a customer or potential customer-- contributions by a governmental entity or civic group (other than a contribution by a shareholder as such).

This provision does not apply to any contribution made after Dec. 22, 2017 by a governmental entity pursuant to a master development plan that had been approved before Dec. 22, 2017. For analysis, see ¶ 3101.

Repeal of tax-free rollover of publicly traded securities gain into specialized small business investment companies

For sales after Dec. 31, 2017, the Act repeals the tax-free rollover of gain from the sale of publicly traded securities into specialized small business investment companies. For analysis, see ¶ 1507.

Tax incentives for investment in Qualified Opportunity Zones

The Act allows for the designation of certain low-income community population census tracts as Qualified Opportunity Zones (QO Zones). The designation remains in effect from the designation date through the end of the 10th calendar year that begins on or after the designation date.

The Act also provides for Qualified Opportunity Funds (QO Funds). A QO Fund is an investment vehicle organized as a corporation or a partnership for the purpose of investing in QO Zone property (other than another QO Fund), that holds at least 90% of its assets in QO Zone property. QO Zone property includes QO Zone stock, QO Zone partnership interests, and QO Zone business property.

Effective on Dec. 22, 2017, temporary deferral applies for capital gains that are re-invested in a QO Zone Fund. The maximum amount of the deferred gain equals the amount the taxpayer invested in a QO Fund during the 180-day period beginning on the date of sale of the asset to which the deferral pertains. Capital gains that exceed the maximum deferral amount are recognized and included in gross income.

Post-acquisition capital gains apply for a sale or exchange of an investment in QO Funds that are held for at least 10 years. For analysis, see ¶ 1704, ¶ 1703.

Pass-Throughs

New deduction for pass-through income

For tax years beginning after Dec. 31, 2017 and before Jan. 1, 2026, the Act adds a new deduction for noncorporate taxpayers for qualified business income—also referred to as the "pass-through deduction." The deduction reduces taxable income, rather than adjusted gross income (AGI), but is available to taxpayers who take the standard deduction. For analysis, see ¶ 701.

The deduction is generally 20% of a taxpayer's qualified business income (QBI) from a partnership, S corporation, or sole proprietorship. QBI is defined as the net amount of items of income, gain, deduction, and loss with respect to the trade or business. Certain types of investment-related items are excluded from QBI, e.g., capital gains or losses, dividends, and interest income (unless the interest is properly allocable to the business), as are employee compensation and guaranteed payments to a partner.

Taxpayers in service related businesses, such as healthcare professionals, law, accounting, actuarial science, performing artists, consulting, athletics, financial services, brokerage services, including investing and investment management, trading, or dealing in securities, partnership interests, or commodities, and any trade or business whose principal asset is the reputation or skill of one or more of its employees are eligible. However, the deduction with respect to service businesses is phased out if the taxpayer's taxable income exceeds the threshold amount of $157,500 ($315,000 in the case of a joint return). For analysis, see ¶ 702, ¶ 703.

Taxpayers whose taxable income exceeds the threshold amount of $157,500 ($315,000 in the case of a joint return) are also subject to limitations based on the W-2 wages and the adjusted basis in acquired qualified property, see ¶ 702.

For partnerships and S corporations, the deduction is taken at the partner or shareholder level. Trusts and estates are eligible for the deduction, subject to apportionment between the trust or estate and the beneficiaries. For analysis, see ¶ 704.

QBI from sources within Puerto Rico is eligible for the deduction if all the income is subject to tax in the U.S. For analysis, see ¶ 705.

Partnerships

Repeal of partnership technical termination

For partnership tax years beginning after Dec. 31, 2017, the Act repeals the "technical termination" rule of Code Sec. 708(b)(1)(B)—i.e., the rule that a partnership is considered as terminated if there is a sale or exchange of 50% or more of the total interest in partnership capital and profits within any 12-month period. For analysis, see ¶ 901.

Look-through rule applied to gain on sale of partnership interest

For sales and exchanges after Nov. 26, 2017, gain or loss from the sale or exchange of a partnership interest is effectively connected with a U.S. trade or business ("effectively connected") to the extent that the transferor would have had effectively connected gain or loss had the partnership sold all of its assets at fair market value as of the date of the sale or exchange. Any gain or loss from this hypothetical asset sale by the partnership must be allocated to interests in the partnership in the same manner as non-separately stated income and loss.

For sales, exchanges, and dispositions after Dec. 31, 2017, if any gain on the disposition of a partnership interest is treated as "effectively connected" under the above rule, the transferee must withhold 10% of the amount realized on the disposition, unless the transferor certifies that it's not a foreign person. For analysis, see ¶ 2304.

Partnership "substantial built-in loss" modified

For transfers of partnership interests after Dec. 31, 2017, the definition of a substantial built-in loss is modified for purposes of Code Sec. 743(d), affecting transfers of partnership interests. In addition to the present-law definition, a substantial built-in loss also exists if the transferee would be allocated a net loss in excess of $250,000 upon a hypothetical disposition by the partnership of all partnership's assets in a fully taxable transaction for cash equal to the assets' fair market value, immediately after the transfer of the partnership interest. For analysis, see ¶ 902.

Charitable contributions and foreign taxes in partner's share of loss

For partnership tax years beginning after Dec. 31, 2017, a partner's distributive shares of partnership charitable contributions and taxes paid or accrued to foreign countries or U.S. possessions are taken into account in determining the amount of a partner's loss. However, for charitable contributions of property with a fair market value that exceeds its adjusted basis, the partner's distributive share of the excess is not taken into account. For analysis, see ¶ 903.

S corporations

Treatment of S corporation converted to C corporation

If an S corporation converts to a C corporation, cash distributions made by the C corporation to its shareholders during a post-termination transition period (PTTP) are—to the extent of the amount in the corporation's accumulated adjustments account (AAA)—tax-free to the shareholders and reduce the adjusted basis of the stock, to the extent of the amount in the accumulated adjustment account. The Act provides that distributions made after Dec. 22, 2017 from an "eligible terminated S corporation" are treated as paid from its AAA and from its earnings and profits on a pro rata basis. Resulting adjustments are taken into account ratably over a 6-year period. An eligible terminated S corporation is any C corporation that (i) was an S corporation on Dec. 21, 2017, (ii) revokes its S corporation election during the 2-year period beginning on Dec. 22, 2017, and (iii) had the same owners on Dec. 22, 2017 and on the revocation date (in the same proportion). For analysis, see ¶ 801.

Tax-exempt organizations

Excise tax on excess tax-exempt organization executive compensation

For tax years beginning after Dec. 31, 2017, a tax-exempt organization is subject to a tax at the corporate tax rate (21% under the Act) on the sum of: (1) the remuneration (other than an excess parachute payment) in excess of $1 million paid to a covered employee by an applicable tax-exempt organization for a tax year; and (2) any excess parachute payment (as newly defined) paid by the applicable tax-exempt organization to a covered employee. A covered employee is an employee (including any former employee) of an applicable tax-exempt organization if the employee is one of the five highest compensated employees of the organization for the tax year or was a covered employee of the organization (or a predecessor) for any preceding tax year beginning after Dec. 31, 2016. Remuneration is treated as paid when there is no substantial risk of forfeiture of the rights to such remuneration. For analysis, see ¶ 2501.

Excise tax on investment income of private colleges and universities

For tax years beginning after Dec. 31, 2017, an excise tax equal to 1.4% is imposed on the net investment income of certain private colleges and universities. This applies to private colleges and universities with at least 500 students, more than 50% of the students of which are located in the U.S., and with assets (other than those used directly in carrying out the institution's exempt purpose) of at least $500,000 per student. The number of students is based on the daily average number of full-time equivalent students. For analysis, see ¶ 2502.

UBTI separately computed for each trade or business activity

For tax years beginning after Dec. 31, 2017 (subject to an exception for net operating losses (NOLs) arising in a tax year beginning before Jan. 1, 2018, that are carried forward), tax-exempt organizations may not use losses from one unrelated trade or business to offset income derived from another unrelated trade or business. Gains and losses have to be calculated and applied separately. For analysis, see ¶ 2503.

Electing small business trusts (ESBTs)

Qualifying beneficiaries of an ESBT

Effective on Jan. 1, 2018, a nonresident alien individual can be a potential current beneficiary of an ESBT. For analysis, see ¶ 802.

Charitable contribution deduction for ESBTs

For tax years beginning after Dec. 31, 2017, an ESBT's charitable contribution deduction is determined by the rules applicable to individuals, rather than the rules for trusts. Thus, the percentage limitations and carryforward provisions applicable to individuals apply to charitable contributions made by the portion of an ESBT holding S corporation stock. For analysis, see ¶ 803.

Retirement plans

Repeal of the rule allowing recharacterization of Roth IRA contributions

Under pre-Act law, an individual could elect to recharacterize a contribution made to one type of IRA (traditional or Roth) as made to the other type of IRA in a so-called "conversion contribution" by making a trustee-to-trustee transfer to the other type of IRA. The Act provides that for years beginning after Dec. 31, 2017, the rule allowing recharactization of IRA contributions does not apply to a conversion contribution to a Roth IRA. Thus, recharacterization can't be used to unwind a Roth conversion. For analysis, see ¶ 2701.

Length of service award programs for public safety volunteers

For tax years beginning after Dec. 31, 2017, the Act increases the aggregate amount of length of service awards that may accrue for a bona fide volunteer with respect to any year of service to $6,000 (from $3,000) and provides for cost-of-living adjustments. For analysis, see ¶ 2703.

Extended rollover period for rollover of plan loan offset amounts

For plan loan offset amounts that are treated as distributed in tax years beginning after Dec. 31, 2017, the Act provides that the period during which a qualified plan loan offset amount may be contributed to an eligible retirement plan as a rollover contribution is extended from 60 days after the offset date, to the federal income tax return due date (including extensions) for the tax year in which the plan loan offset occurs—that is, the tax year in which the amount is treated as distributed from the plan. For analysis, see ¶ 2702.

Bond provisions

Repeal of advance refunding bonds

For advance refunding bonds issued after Dec. 31, 2017, the exclusion from gross income for interest on a bond issued to advance refund another bond is repealed. For analysis, see ¶ 1701.

Tax-credit bonds repealed

For bonds issued after Dec. 31, 2017, the authority to issue tax-credit bonds and direct-pay bonds is prospectively repealed. For analysis, see ¶ 1702.

Foreign provisions

Deduction for foreign-source portion of dividends

For tax years of foreign corporations beginning after Dec. 31, 2017, and for tax years of U.S. shareholders in which or with which such tax years of foreign corporations end, the current-law system of taxing U.S. corporations on the foreign earnings of their foreign subsidiaries when these earnings are distributed is replaced. The Act provides for an exemption (referred to here as a deduction for dividends received, or DRD) for certain foreign income. This exemption is provided for by means of a 100% deduction for the "foreign-source portion" of dividends received from specified 10% owned foreign corporations (generally, any foreign corporation other than a passive foreign investment company (PFIC) that is not also a controlled foreign corporation (CFC), with respect to which any domestic corporation is a U.S. shareholder) by domestic corporations that are U.S. shareholders of those foreign corporations within the meaning of Code Sec. 951(b). The foreign-source portion of such a dividend is the amount bearing the same ratio to the dividend that the specified 10%-owned foreign corporation's undistributed foreign earnings bears to its total undistributed earnings. The allowance of the DRD is subject to a holding period requirement.

No foreign tax credit or deduction is allowed for any taxes paid or accrued with respect to a dividend that qualifies for the DRD.

The DRD is available only to C corporations that are not regulated investment companies (RICs) or real estate investment trusts (REITs).

For analysis, see ¶ 1901, ¶ 1902.

Sales or transfers involving specified 10%-owned foreign corporations

For sales or exchanges after Dec. 31, 2017, by a domestic corporation of stock in a foreign corporation held for one year or more, any amount received by the domestic corporation that is treated as a dividend for purposes of Code Sec. 1248 is treated as a dividend for purposes of applying the new foreign-source portion DRD rule described above. For analysis, see ¶ 1904.

For dividends received in tax years beginning after Dec. 31 2017, a domestic corporate shareholder's adjusted basis in the stock of a "specified 10-percent owned foreign corporation" is reduced by an amount equal to the portion of any dividend received with respect to such stock from such foreign corporation that was not taxed by reason of the new foreign-source portion DRD described above in any tax year of such domestic corporation, but only for the purpose of determining losses on sales and exchanges of the foreign corporation's stock. For analysis, see ¶ 1903.

If, after Dec. 31 2017, a U.S. corporation transfers substantially all of the assets of a foreign branch to a foreign subsidiary corporation, the "transferred loss" amount (i.e., the losses incurred by the foreign branch over certain taxable income earned by the foreign branch) must generally be included in the U.S. corporation's gross income. For analysis, see ¶ 1905.

Treatment of deferred foreign income upon transition to new participation exemption system—deemed repatriation

U.S. shareholders owning at least 10% of a foreign subsidiary must include in income for the subsidiary's last tax year beginning before 2018, the shareholder's pro rata share of the subsidiary's undistributed, non-previously-taxed post-1986 foreign earnings. The inclusion amount is reduced by any aggregate foreign earnings and profits deficits, and a partial deduction is allowed so that a shareholder's effective tax rate is 15.5% on his aggregate foreign cash position and 8% otherwise. The net tax liability can be spread over a period of up to eight years. Special rules apply for S corporation shareholders and for RICs and REITs.

For analysis, see ¶ 1906, ¶ 1907, ¶ 1908, ¶ 1909, ¶ 1910, ¶ 1911, ¶ 1912, ¶ 1913.

Current inclusion of global intangible low-taxed income (GILTI)

For tax years of foreign corporations beginning after Dec. 31, 2017, and for tax years of U.S. shareholders in which or with which such tax years of foreign corporations end, a U.S. shareholder of any CFC has to include in gross income its global intangible low-taxed income (GILTI)–i.e., the excess of the shareholder's "net CFC tested income" over the shareholder's "net deemed tangible income return" (10% of the aggregate of the shareholder's pro rata share of the qualified business asset investment of each CFC with respect to which it is a U.S. shareholder). The GILTI is treated as an inclusion of Subpart F income for the shareholder. Only an 80% foreign tax credit is available for amounts included in income as GILTI, and no carryback or carryforward is allowed. For analysis, see ¶ 2001, ¶ 2003, ¶ 2004.

Deduction for foreign-derived intangible income and GILTI

For tax years beginning after Dec. 31, 2017 and before Jan. 1, 2026, in the case of a domestic corporation, a deduction is allowed equal to the sum of (i) 37.5% of its foreign-derived intangible income (FDII) for the year, plus (ii) 50% of the GILTI amount included in gross income, see above. Generally, FDII is the amount of a corporation's deemed intangible income that is attributable to sales of property to foreign persons for use outside the U.S. or the performance of services for foreign persons or with respect to property outside the U.S. Coupled with the 21% tax rate for domestic corporations, these deductions result in effective tax rates of 13.125% on FDII and of 10.5% on GILTI. The deduction rates are reduced for tax years after 2025. For analysis, see ¶ 2002.

Repeal of foreign base company oil-related income rule

For tax years of foreign corporations beginning after Dec. 31, 2017 and for tax years of U.S. shareholders in which or with which such tax years of foreign subsidiaries end, the Act eliminates foreign base company oil-related income as a category of foreign base company income FBCI includible as subpart F income. For analysis, see ¶ 2104.

Repeal of rule taxing income when CFC decreases investment

For tax years of foreign corporations beginning after Dec. 31, 2017, and for tax years of U.S. shareholders within which or with which such tax years of foreign corporations end, the Act repeals Code Sec. 955. As a result, a U.S. shareholder in a CFC that invested its previously excluded subpart F income in qualified foreign base company shipping operations is no longer required to include in income a pro rata share of the previously excluded subpart F income when the CFC decreases such investments. For analysis, see ¶ 2105.

Modification of CFC status attribution rules

For the last tax year of a foreign corporation beginning before Jan. 1, 2018, for all later tax years of a foreign corporation, and for the tax years of a U.S. shareholder with or with which such tax years end, the Act amends the constructive ownership rules so that certain stock of a foreign corporation owned by a foreign person is attributed to a related U.S. person for purposes of determining whether the related U.S. person is a U.S. shareholder of the foreign corporation and, therefore, whether the foreign corporation is a CFC. For analysis, see ¶ 2102.

Expansion of definition of "U.S. Shareholder"

For the last tax year of foreign corporations beginning before Jan. 1, 2018, and for tax years of U.S. shareholders with or within which such tax years of foreign corporations end, the Act expands the definition of "U.S. shareholder" to include any U.S. person who owns 10% or more of the *total value* (not just voting power) of all classes of stock of a foreign corporation. For analysis, see ¶ 2101.

Elimination of 30-day minimum holding period for CFC status

For tax years of foreign corporations beginning after Dec. 31, 2017, and for tax years of U.S. shareholders in which or with which such tax years of foreign subsidiaries end, a foreign corporation is not required to be a CFC for an uninterrupted period of 30 days or more during the tax, for its Subpart F income to be taxed to its U.S. shareholders. For analysis, see ¶ 2103.

Prevention of base erosion

Base erosion and anti-abuse tax

The Act establishes a base erosion minimum tax to prevent companies from stripping earnings out of the U.S. through payments to foreign affiliates that are deductible for U.S. tax purposes. The tax is structured as an alternative minimum tax that applies when a multinational company reduces its regular U.S. tax liability to less than a specified percentage of its taxable income, after adding back deductible base eroding payments and a percentage of tax losses claimed that were carried from another year. The tax applies to deductible payments to foreign affiliates from domestic corporations, as well as to foreign corporations engaged in a U.S. trade or business in computing the tax on their effectively connected income (ECI). For analysis, see ¶ 2201.

Limitations on income shifting through intangible property transfers

For transfers in tax years beginning after Dec. 31, 2017, the Act addresses recurring definitional and methodological issues that have arisen in controversies in transfers of intangible property for purposes of Code Sec. 367(d) and Code Sec. 482, both of which use the statutory definition of "intangible property" in Code Sec. 936(h)(3)(B). The Act revises that definition and confirms IRS's authority to require certain valuation methods. It does not modify the basic approach of the existing transfer pricing rules with regard to income from intangible property. Workforce in place, goodwill (both foreign and domestic), and going concern value are intangible property, as is the residual category of "any similar item" the value of which is not attributable to tangible property or the services of an individual. For analysis, see ¶ 2202.

Denial of deduction for certain related party payments

For tax years beginning after Dec. 31, 2017, the Act denies a deduction for any disqualified related party amount paid or accrued pursuant to a hybrid transaction or by, or to, a hybrid entity. A disqualified related party amount is any interest or royalty paid or accrued to a related party to the extent that: (1) there is no corresponding inclusion to the related party under the tax law of the country of which the related party is a resident for tax purposes, or (2) the related party is allowed a deduction for that amount under that country's tax law. In general, a hybrid transaction is one that involves payment of interest or royalties that are not treated as such by the country of residence of the foreign recipient. And, in general, a hybrid entity is an entity that is treated as fiscally transparent for federal income purposes but not so treated for purposes of the tax law of the foreign country, or vice versa. For analysis, see ¶ 2204.

Surrogate foreign corporation dividends aren't qualified

For dividends paid in tax years beginning after Dec. 31, 2017, any dividend received by an individual shareholder from a corporation that is a surrogate foreign corporation as defined in Code Sec. 7874(a)(2)(B) (other than a foreign corporation treated as a domestic corporation under Code Sec. 7874(b)), and that first became a foreign surrogate corporation after Dec. 22, 2017, is not entitled to the lower tax rates on qualified dividends provided by Code Sec. 1(h). For analysis, see ¶ 2206.

Repeal of indirect foreign tax credits; change to CFC shareholder deemed-paid credit

For tax years of foreign corporations beginning after Dec. 31, 2017 and for tax years of U.S. shareholders in which or with which such tax years of foreign subsidiaries end, no foreign tax credit or deduction is allowed for any taxes (including withholding taxes) paid or accrued with respect to any dividend to which the deduction for foreign-source portion of dividends (see above) applies.

A foreign tax credit is allowed for any subpart F income that is included in the income of the U.S. shareholder on a current year basis. For analysis, see ¶ 2301.

Separate foreign tax credit limitation basket for foreign branch income

For tax years beginning after Dec. 31, 2017, foreign branch income must be allocated to a specific foreign tax credit basket. Foreign branch income is the business profits of a U.S. person that are attributable to one or more qualified business units in one or more foreign countries. For analysis, see ¶ 2303.

Change in rule for sourcing income from sales of inventory

For tax years that beginning after Dec. 31, 2017, gains, profits, and income from the sale or exchange of inventory property produced partly in, and partly outside, the U.S. must be allocated and apportioned on the basis of the location of production with respect to the property. For example, income derived from the sale of inventory property to a foreign jurisdiction is sourced wholly within the U.S. if the property was produced entirely in the U.S., even if title passage occurred elsewhere. For analysis, see ¶ 2305.

Election with respect to foreign tax credit limitation

Under pre-Act law, for purposes of the limitation on the foreign tax credit, if a taxpayer sustains an overall domestic loss for any tax year, then, for each succeeding year, an amount of U.S. source taxable income equal to the lesser of:

...the full amount of the loss to the extent not carried back to prior tax years; or

...50% of the taxpayer's U.S. source taxable income for that succeeding tax year,

is recharacterized as foreign source income.

The Act provides that for any tax year of the taxpayer beginning after Dec. 31, 2017 and before Jan. 1, 2028, the taxpayer may, with respect to pre-2018 unused overall domestic losses, elect to substitute, for the above 50% amount, a percentage greater than 50% but not greater than 100%. For analysis, see ¶ 2302.

Other international reforms

Restriction on insurance business exception to PFIC rules

Under pre-Act law, U.S. shareholders of a passive foreign investment company (PFIC) are taxed currently on the PFIC's earnings, subject to an exception for certain income derived in the active conduct of an insurance business. For tax years beginning after Dec. 31, 2017, the Act replaces the test based on whether a corporation is predominantly engaged in an insurance business with a test based on the corporation's insurance liabilities. For analysis, see ¶ 2411.

Repeal of fair market value of interest expense apportionment

For tax years beginning after Dec. 31, 2017, for purposes of determining U.S. source and foreign source income, members of a U.S. affiliated group have to allocate interest expense with respect to assets based on the adjusted tax basis of the assets, and not based on their fair market values. For analysis, see ¶ 2306.

Stock compensation of insiders in expatriated corporations

For corporations first becoming expatriated corporations after Dec. 22, 2017, the excise tax imposed on the value of specified stock compensation held by "disqualified individuals" if a corporation expatriates in an inversion transaction is increased from 15% to 20%. For analysis, see ¶ 2205.

Client Letters

The Analysis includes Client Letters highlighting the tax changes made by the Tax Cuts and Jobs Act. The Client Letters are located at ¶ 3201 *et seq.*

Act Section Cross-Reference Table

Arranged in Act section order, this table shows substantive Code section(s) amended, added, affected, repealed by or related to the Tax Cuts and Jobs Act section, the topic involved, the generally effective date of the amendment, the relevant paragraph number for the Analysis and the paragraph where the relevant Committee Reports are reproduced. The table is reproduced at ¶ 6000.

Code Section Cross-Reference Table

Arranged in Code section order, this table shows the Tax Cuts and Jobs Act section(s) that amend, add, affect, repeal or relate to the Code Section, the topic involved, the generally effective date of the amendment, the relevant paragraph number for the Analysis and the paragraph where the relevant Committee Reports are reproduced. The table is reproduced at ¶ 6001.

Code Sections Amended by Act

Arranged in Code section order, this table shows all changes to the Internal Revenue Code made by the Tax Cuts and Jobs Act, including conforming amendments. The table is reproduced at ¶ 6002.

Act Sections Amending Code

Arranged in Act section order, this table shows all changes to the Internal Revenue Code made by the Tax Cuts and Jobs Act including conforming amendments. The table is reproduced at ¶ 6003.

Federal Tax Coordinator 2d ¶s Affected by Act

Arranged in FTC 2d ¶ order, this table shows the FTC 2d paragraphs that have been affected by the Tax Cuts and Jobs Act. The table is reproduced at ¶ 6004 .

United States Tax Reporter ¶s Affected by Act

Arranged in USTR ¶ order, this table shows the USTR paragraphs that have been affected by the Tax Cuts and Jobs Act. The table is reproduced at ¶ 6005.

Pension Analysis ¶s Affected by Act

Arranged in Pension Analysis ¶ order, this table shows the Pension Analysis paragraphs that have been affected by the Tax Cuts and Jobs Act. The table is reproduced at ¶ 6006.

Pension and Benefits Explanations ¶s Affected by Act

Arranged in Pension and Benefits Explanations ¶ order, this table shows the Benefits Explanations paragraphs that have been affected by the Tax Cuts and Jobs Act. The table is reproduced at ¶ 6007.

Estate Planning Analysis ¶s Affected by Act

Arranged in Estate Planning Analysis ¶ order, this table shows the Estate Planning Analysis paragraphs that have been affected by the Tax Cuts and Jobs Act. The table is reproduced at ¶ 6008.

Catalyst ¶s Affected by Act

Arranged in Catalyst ¶ order, this table shows the Catalyst paragraphs that have been affected by the Tax Cuts and Jobs Act. The table is reproduced at ¶ 6009.

Kiddie tax modified

For tax years beginning after Dec. 31, 2017, the tax on certain children with unearned income (the "kiddie tax") is imposed as follows: the child's taxable income attributable to earned income is taxed under the rates for single individuals, and the child's taxable income attributable to net unearned income is taxed according to the brackets applicable to trusts and estates. This rule applies to the child's ordinary income and his or her income taxed at preferential rates. For analysis, see ¶ 105.

Capital gains provisions conformed

The Act generally retains present-law 0%, 15%, and 20% tax rates on net capital gains and qualified dividends. It also retains the pre-Act law breakpoints at which the 15% and 20% tax rates begin to apply, but indexes them for inflation using C-CPI-U in tax years after Dec. 31, 2017. For 2018, the 15% breakpoint is $77,200 for joint returns and surviving spouses, $51,700 for heads of household, $38,600 for single taxpayers, $38,600 for married taxpayers filing separately, and $2,600 for trusts and estates. The 20% breakpoint is $479,000 for joint returns and surviving spouses, $452,400 for heads of household, $425,800 for single files, $239,500 for married taxpayers filing separately, and $12,700 for estates and trusts. For analysis, see ¶ 1501.

Carried interests—new holding period requirement

For tax years beginning after Dec. 31, 2017, the Act effectively imposes a 3-year holding period requirement in order for certain partnership interests received in connection with the performance of services ('carried interests") to be taxed as long-term capital gain. If the 3-year holding period is not met with respect to an applicable partnership interest held by the taxpayer, the taxpayer's gain will be treated as short-term gain taxed at ordinary income rates. For analysis, see ¶ 1502.

New limitations on "excess business loss"

For tax years beginning after Dec. 31, 2017 and before Jan. 1, 2026, the Act provides that the excess farm loss limitation doesn't apply. Instead, a noncorporate taxpayer's "excess business loss" for a tax year is disallowed, and the disallowed loss is carried forward and treated as part of the taxpayer's net operating loss (NOL) carryforward in later tax years. This limitation applies *after* the application of the passive loss rules. For analysis, see ¶ 1409.

Deduction for personal casualty & theft losses suspended

For tax years beginning after Dec. 31, 2017 and before Jan. 1, 2026, the personal casualty and theft loss deduction is suspended, except for personal casualty losses incurred in a federally-declared disaster. Special rules apply where a taxpayer has personal casualty gains. For analysis, see ¶ 508.

Gambling loss limitation modified

For tax years beginning after Dec. 31, 2017 and before Jan. 1, 2026, the limitation on wagering losses under Code Sec. 165(d) is modified to provide that *all* deductions for expenses incurred in carrying out wagering transactions, and not just gambling losses, are limited to the extent of gambling winnings. For analysis, see ¶ 509.

Child tax credit increased; partial credit for non-child dependents

For tax years beginning after Dec. 31, 2017 and before Jan. 1, 2026, the child tax credit is increased to $2,000. The income levels at which the credit phases out are increased to $400,000 for married taxpayers filing jointly ($200,000 for all other taxpayers) (not indexed for inflation). The amount of the credit that is refundable is increased to $1,400 per qualifying child, and this amount is indexed for inflation, up to the base $2,000 base credit amount. The earned income threshold for the refundable portion of the credit is decreased from $3,000 to $2,500. No credit will be allowed to a taxpayer with respect to any qualifying child unless the taxpayer provides the child's SSN. In addition, a $500 nonrefundable credit is provided for certain non-child dependents. For analysis, see ¶ 516, ¶ 517, ¶ 518.

State and local tax (SALT) deduction limited

For tax years beginning after Dec. 31, 2017 and before Jan. 1, 2026, except as described below, state, local, and foreign property taxes, and state and local sales taxes, are deductible only when paid or accrued in carrying on a trade or business or an activity described in Code Sec. 212 (generally, for the production of income). State and local income, war profits, and excess profits are not allowable as a deduction.

However, a taxpayer may claim an itemized deduction of up to $10,000 ($5,000 for married taxpayers filing separately) for the *aggregate* of (i) state and local property taxes *not* paid or accrued in carrying on a trade or business or activity described in Code Sec. 212; and (ii) state and local income, war profits, and excess profits taxes (or sales taxes in lieu of income, etc. taxes) paid or accrued in the tax year. Foreign real property taxes may not be deducted.

An amount paid in a tax year beginning before Jan. 1, 2018, for a state or local income tax imposed for a tax year beginning after Dec. 31, 2017, is treated as paid on the last day of the tax year for which such tax is so imposed, for purposes of applying the above limits. In other words, a taxpayer who, in 2017, pays an income tax that is imposed for a tax year after 2017, can't claim an itemized deduction in 2017 for that prepaid income tax. For analysis, see ¶ 506.

Mortgage interest deduction limited

For tax years beginning after Dec. 31, 2017 and before Jan. 1, 2026, the deduction for home mortgage interest is limited to interest on up to $750,000 ($375,000 for married taxpayers filing separately) of acquisition indebtedness and the deduction for interest on home equity indebtedness is suspended. For tax years beginning after Dec. 31, 2025, the pre-Act $1 million/$500,000 acquisition indebtedness limitations are restored and apply regardless of when the indebtedness was incurred, and the suspension for home equity indebtedness interest ends.

The new lower limit doesn't apply to acquisition indebtedness incurred before Dec. 15, 2017.

A taxpayer who entered into a binding written contract before Dec. 15, 2017 to close on the purchase of a principal residence before Jan. 1, 2018, and who purchases the residence before Apr. 1, 2018, is considered to incur acquisition indebtedness before Dec. 15, 2017.

The pre-Act acquisition indebtedness limitations continue to apply to taxpayers who refinance existing qualified residence indebtedness that was incurred before Dec. 15, 2017, provided the resulting indebtedness doesn't exceed the amount of the refinanced indebtedness. For analysis, see ¶ 507.

Medical expense deduction threshold temporarily reduced

For tax years beginning after Dec. 31, 2016 and ending before Jan. 1, 2019, the threshold on medical expense deductions is reduced to 7.5% of adjusted gross income (AGI) for all taxpayers. In addition, the 10%-of-AGI threshold that applied under pre-Act law for alternative minimum tax (AMT) purposes doesn't apply to tax years beginning after Dec. 31, 2016 and ending before Jan. 1, 2019. For analysis, see ¶ 505.

Individual charitable contribution deduction limitation increased

For contributions made in tax years beginning after Dec. 31, 2017 and before Jan. 1, 2026, the 50% limitation under Code Sec. 170(b) for an individual's cash contributions to public charities and certain private foundations is increased to 60%. Contributions exceeding the 60% limitation are generally allowed to be carried forward and deducted for up to five years, subject to the later year's ceiling. For analysis, see ¶ 512.

And, for contributions made in tax years beginning after Dec. 31, 2016, the Code Sec. 170(f)(8)(D) donee-reporting exemption from the contemporaneous written acknowledgment requirement is repealed. For analysis, see ¶ 515.

No deduction for amounts paid for college athletic seating rights

For contributions made in tax years beginning after Dec. 31, 2017, no charitable deduction is allowed for any payment to an institution of higher education in exchange for which the payor receives the right to purchase tickets or seating at an athletic event. For analysis, see ¶ 513.

Alimony deduction by payor/inclusion by payee suspended

For any divorce or separation agreement executed after Dec. 31, 2018 (or executed on or before Dec. 31, 2018 but modified later if the modification expressly provides that the Act rules apply), alimony and separate maintenance payments are not deductible by the payor spouse and are not included in the income of the payee spouse. For analysis, see ¶ 510.

Miscellaneous itemized deductions suspended

For tax years beginning after Dec. 31, 2017 and before Jan. 1, 2026, the deduction for miscellaneous itemized deductions that are subject to the 2%-of-AGI floor is suspended. For analysis, see ¶ 503.

Overall limitation ("Pease" limitation) on overall itemized deductions suspended

For tax years beginning after Dec. 31, 2017 and before Jan. 1, 2026, the "Pease limitation" on overall itemized deductions (also referred to as the "3%/80% rule) is suspended. For analysis, see ¶ 504.

Qualified bicycle commuting exclusion suspended

For tax years beginning after Dec. 31, 2017 and before Jan. 1, 2026, the exclusion from gross income and wages for qualified bicycle commuting reimbursements is suspended. For analysis, see ¶ 602.

Exclusion for moving expense reimbursements suspended

For tax years beginning after Dec. 31, 2017 and before Jan. 1, 2026, the exclusion for qualified moving expense reimbursements is suspended, except for members of the Armed Forces on active duty (and their spouses and dependents) who move pursuant to a military order and incident to a permanent change of station. For analysis, see ¶ 602.

Moving expenses deduction suspended

For tax years beginning after Dec. 31, 2017 and before Jan. 1, 2026, the deduction for moving expenses is suspended, except for members of the Armed Forces on active duty who move pursuant to a military order and incident to a permanent change of station. For analysis, see ¶ 514.

Deduction for living expenses of members of Congress eliminated

For tax years beginning after Dec. 22, 2017, members of Congress cannot deduct living expenses when they are away from home. For analysis, see ¶ 511.

Table of Action Alert Items

This table shows the items for which the taxpayer must take certain actions (e.g., make an election, file an amended return, file a statement with IRS, complete a transaction, etc.) by a specified date, with cross-references to the Analysis paragraph that discusses the Act rule requiring the action. The table is reproduced at ¶ 6010.

Committee Report Finding Table

Arranged in Act section order, this table shows Committee Report paragraph numbers and corresponding Conf Rept. No. 115-466 pages for each Act section. A PDF copy of Conf Rept. No. 115-466 is accessible on the Thomson Reuters Checkpoint product support page at http://support.checkpoint.thomsonreuters.com/taxcutsandjobsact.

Index

A detailed index, which directs the reader to the appropriate Analysis paragraph, is reproduced immediately after the aforementioned Tables for the Complete Analysis.

¶ 2. Contents

¶

INCOME TAX RATES 100

Individual income tax rate structure replaced with 10%, 12%, 22%, 24%, 32%, 35%, and 37% tax brackets 101

Reduction of corporate tax rates 102

Reduction in corporate dividends received deduction 103

Estates and trusts income tax rate structure replaced with 10%, 24%, 35%, and 37% tax brackets 104

Kiddie tax modified to effectively apply estates' and trusts' ordinary and capital gains rates to child's net unearned income 105

INFLATION ADJUSTMENTS 200

Inflation adjustment of income tax brackets to be made based on chained CPI-U (C-CPI-U), instead of the CPI-U 201

Chained CPI-U (C-CPI-U) replaces CPI-U in inflation adjustments of various tax parameters under the Code 202

ALTERNATIVE MINIMUM TAX 300

Alternative minimum tax exemption amounts for individuals increased 301

AMT adjustment for standard deduction is made retroactively inapplicable to in 2016 and 2017 to net disaster losses from 2016 disaster areas 302

Alternative minimum tax on corporations is repealed 303

Corporate minimum tax credit (MTC) may offset regular tax liability for any tax year, and is refundable for 2018–2021 304

ACA INDIVIDUAL MANDATE 400

Shared responsibility payment requirement eliminated after 2018 401

INDIVIDUALS: DEDUCTIONS AND PERSONAL CREDITS 500

Standard deduction is almost doubled, inflation adjustment is modified 501

Deduction for personal exemptions for taxpayer, spouse, and dependents is suspended; return-filing and withholding requirements are modified 502

Miscellaneous itemized deductions are disallowed 503

Overall limitation on itemized deductions ("Pease limitation" or "3%/80% rule") is suspended 504

7.5%-of-AGI floor for medical expense deduction is retroactively extended through 2018 and applied to all taxpayers — 505

Itemized deduction is limited to $10,000 for combined state/local property, state/local/foreign income, and (if elected) general sales taxes — 506

Mortgage interest deduction acquisition debt maximum is lowered to $750,000, deduction for home equity interest is suspended — 507

Personal casualty losses are nondeductible unless attributable to a federally declared disaster — 508

Gambling loss limitation is broadened: deduction for *any* expense incurred in gambling—not just gambling losses—is limited to gambling winnings — 509

Alimony won't be deductible by the payor or includible by the recipient for post-2018 divorce or separation instruments — 510

$3,000 deduction for living expenses of members of Congress is eliminated — 511

Limit on an individual's contributions of cash to charitable organizations is increased from 50% to 60% of donor's contribution base — 512

Charitable deduction is denied for contributions to a college or university in exchange for athletic event seating rights — 513

Moving expense deduction eliminated, except for certain armed forces members — 514

Donee-reporting exception to substantiation requirement for charitable contributions is retroactively repealed — 515

Child tax credit is increased to $2,000 and expanded for tax years beginning after 2017 — 516

Refundable portion of the child tax credit is increased to $1,400 for tax years beginning after 2017 — 517

Qualifying child's social security number is required to claim child tax credit — 518

INDIVIDUALS: INCOME AND EXCLUSIONS — **600**

Exceptions to life insurance transfer-for-value rule don't apply to life settlement transactions — 601

Exclusion for qualified moving expense reimbursements suspended, except for armed forces — 602

Exclusion for qualified bicycle commuting reimbursement suspended — 603

Exclusion for discharge of certain student loans is broadened to include discharges on account of death or disability — 604

Special "combat zone" benefits extended retroactively to members of the armed forces performing services in the Sinai Peninsula of Egypt 605

QUALIFIED BUSINESS INCOME 700

Overview of qualified business income deduction 701

20% deduction for qualified business income 702

Qualified business income defined 703

Application of qualified business income deduction to entities 704

Treatment of qualified business income from Puerto Rico sources 705

S CORPORATIONS 800

Treatment of revocations of S corporation elections 801

Expansion of qualifying beneficiaries of Electing Small Business Trusts (ESBTs) 802

Charitable deductions of Electing Small Business Trusts (ESBTs) 803

PARTNERSHIPS 900

Repeal of partnership technical termination rule 901

Mandatory basis adjustment upon transfers of partnership interests amended 902

Basis reduction for partnership charitable contributions amended 903

BUSINESS DEDUCTIONS AND CREDITS 1000

NOL deduction is limited to 80% of taxable income 1001

NOLs can't be carried back, but can be carried forward indefinitely 1002

Deduction for net business interest is limited to 30% of adjusted taxable income, with indefinite carryover 1003

Domestic production activity deduction (DPAD) is repealed 1004

Business deduction is denied for entertainment expenses 1005

Expenses for employer-operated eating facilities are only 50% deductible through 2025, then become nondeductible 1006

Employers can't deduct cost of providing qualified transportation fringes and other transportation benefits 1007

Denial of deduction for fines, penalties, etc., is broadened 1008

Information reporting requirements are added for government and other agencies that receive fines, penalties, etc., of $600 or more for law violations 1009

Business expense deduction is barred for settlement of sexual abuse or harassment suit that's subject to nondisclosure agreement — 1010

Business expense deduction for lobbying local government is repealed — 1011

Deduction of FDIC premiums is phased out for banks with assets over $10 billion, eliminated at $50 billion — 1012

Employers are allowed a credit for paid family and medical leave — 1013

Credit for qualified rehabilitation expenditures is limited to certified historic structures and has to be taken ratably over 5 years — 1014

Orphan drug credit is reduced to 25% of qualified clinical testing expenses — 1015

Reduced orphan drug credit election is available to avoid having to reduce any deduction or charge to capital account for qualified clinical testing expenses — 1016

Limitation on aggregate business credits is conformed to the repeal of the corporate AMT — 1017

SECTION 179 EXPENSING — **1100**

Pre-adjustment Code Sec. 179 limits raised to $1 million (annual limit on expensing) and $2.5 million (annual phase-down threshold based on investment) — 1101

More building improvements are made eligible to be section 179 property — 1102

Otherwise-qualifying residential property no longer excluded from section 179 property — 1103

$25,000 per-vehicle limit on Code Sec. 179 expensing of SUVs is made adjustable for inflation — 1104

BONUS DEPRECIATION — **1200**

Overview—Bonus depreciation is increased to 100% ("full expensing") and is extended and modified — 1201

Bonus depreciation and other benefits for qualified property are extended — 1202

Bonus depreciation increased to 100% (full expensing) with phase down generally deferred from 2018 to 2023 — 1203

Elective form of bonus depreciation for specified plants is extended and increased to 100% (full expensing) with phase down deferred from 2018 to 2023 — 1204

Used property is allowed 100% bonus depreciation (full expensing) — 1205

Qualified film, television and live theatrical productions added to "qualified property" eligible for 100% bonus depreciation (full expensing) 1206

Property used in certain businesses exempt from business interest limitations is excluded from 100% bonus depreciation (full expensing) 1207

Qualified improvement property made no longer eligible for bonus depreciation 1208

$8,000 increase for "qualified property" in the first-year depreciation cap for passenger autos is extended 1209

Placed-in-service deadline for disregard of some bonus depreciation-eligible property under the percentage of completion method is extended 1210

Corporate election trading bonus and accelerated depreciation for otherwise-deferred AMT credits is ended (conforming to repeal of corporate AMT) 1211

DEPRECIATION **1300**

Real Property Depreciation

Eligibility of building improvements for a 15-year recovery period is expanded 1301

ADS recovery period for residential rental property is shortened to 30 years 1302

ADS depreciation for buildings (and improvements) if election is made to exempt a real property business from the business interest deduction limit 1303

Farm Depreciation

Most new farming equipment and machinery is made 5-year MACRS property 1304

200% declining balance method of MACRS depreciation is made available for many types of MACRS farming property 1305

ADS depreciation required for 10-year-or-more MACRS property if election made to exempt farming from the business interest deduction limitation 1306

Cars And Listed Property

Annual caps on depreciation of passenger automobiles are raised 1307

Treatment of computer equipment as listed property is ended 1308

Public Utility Property

Normalization requirements for public utility property 1309

TAX ACCOUNTING   1400

Gross receipts limit for cash-method use by C corporations (and certain partnerships) raised to $25 million, related rules changed   1401

Gross receipts limits for cash-method use by farming C corporations (and certain partnerships) are raised to a uniform $25 million and some related rules are changed   1402

Alternatives to inventory accounting are made available to most small businesses meeting a $25 million gross receipts test   1403

Small business exception to UNICAP rules is expanded to apply to producers and resellers meeting the $25 million gross receipts test   1404

Gross receipts limit to qualify for small construction contract exception to percentage of completion method is raised to $25 million   1405

Income inclusion for tax purposes can't be later than when included for certain financial reporting purposes   1406

Accrual basis taxpayers may defer inclusion of advance payments in income to the end of year after year of receipt if so deferred for financial reporting   1407

Code Sec. 174 research and experimental expenditures paid or incurred in tax years starting after 2021 are to be amortized over 5 years   1408

Excess business loss disallowance rule replaces limitation on excess farm loss for non-corporate taxpayers for tax years beginning after Dec. 31, 2017   1409

Production period for beer, wine, distilled spirits won't include their aging period for UNICAP interest capitalization rule purposes for the next 2 calendar years   1410

Minority and subsequent owners can expense certain costs of replanting citrus plants lost by reason of casualty   1411

CAPITAL GAINS   1500

Breakpoints for imposition of 15% and 20% capital gains/qualified dividends rates are set as statutory dollar amounts, adjusted for inflation   1501

Certain gains from partnership profits interests held in connection with performance of investment services are short-term capital gains if held for 3 years or less   1502

Like-kind exchanges are limited to exchanges of real estate   1503

Patents, inventions, certain models or designs, and secret formulas or processes are excluded from the definition of a capital asset   1504

Contents

Cost of insurance adjustment to the basis of life insurance or annuity contracts is retroactively eliminated — 1505

Tax reporting requirements added for policy sales and death benefits paid under life insurance contracts — 1506

Tax-free rollover of publicly traded securities gain into "specialized small business investment companies" is repealed — 1507

ABLE PROGRAMS AND 529 PLANS — 1600

ABLE account contribution limit is increased for contributions by account's designated beneficiary — 1601

Saver's credit is allowed for ABLE account contributions by designated beneficiary — 1602

Tax-free 60-day rollovers from 529 plan accounts to ABLE accounts are permitted — 1603

$10,000 per year of 529 plan account funds may be used for elementary or secondary school tuition — 1604

BONDS AND DEVELOPMENT INCENTIVES — 1700

Exclusion of interest on advance refunding bonds is repealed — 1701

New tax-credit and direct-pay bonds may not be issued — 1702

Gains invested in a Qualified Opportunity Fund can be temporarily deferred and permanently excluded if the investment in the Fund is held for 10 years — 1703

Chief executive officers of a state can designate low-income communities as Qualified Opportunity Zones — 1704

2016 DISASTER AREA RELIEF — 1800

10%-of-AGI casualty loss threshold is retroactively made inapplicable in 2016 and 2017 to net disaster losses from 2016 disaster areas — 1801

$100 per-casualty floor on deduction is retroactively raised to $500 in 2016 and 2017 for net disaster losses from 2016 disaster areas — 1802

Non-itemizers are retroactively allowed to deduct net disaster losses from 2016 disaster areas in 2016 and 2017, via enhanced standard deduction — 1803

Favorable tax treatment provided for qualified 2016 disaster area plan distributions — 1804

Qualified 2016 disaster distributions to be included in gross income ratably over three years — 1805

Penalty-free early retirement plan withdrawals may be made for 2016 disaster area victims — 1806

Recontributions of qualified 2016 disaster distributions and continued deferral of tax on amounts previously distributed permitted   1807

Period of time is provided, during which qualified retirement plans and IRAs can provide 2016 disaster relief before adopting retroactive 2016 disaster relief amendments   1808

MODIFIED TERRITORIAL SYSTEM   **1900**

Deduction allowed for dividends received by a corporate U.S. shareholder from a specified 10% owned foreign corporation under participation exemption system   1901

Dividends allowed as a Code Sec. 245A DRD are not treated as foreign source income for purposes of the FTC limitation   1902

Basis of stock in specified 10% owned foreign corporation reduced to the extent of Code Sec. 245A DRD in determining loss on disposition   1903

Amounts treated as dividends under Code Sec. 1248 and Code Sec. 964(e) are treated as dividends for purposes of the Code Sec. 245A DRD   1904

Transferred loss amount included in income upon transfer of foreign branch assets to a specified 10% owned foreign corporation   1905

Mandatory Inclusion On Deemed Repatriation Of Accumulated Foreign Earnings

Pre-2018 accumulated deferred foreign income must be included in Subpart F income upon transition to a participation exemption system   1906

Foreign E&P deficits reduce the pre-2018 accumulated deferred foreign income included in Subpart F   1907

Deduction for pre-2018 accumulated deferred foreign income; disallowance of foreign tax credit for deducted portion; recapture for expatriated entities   1908

A U.S. shareholder may elect to pay the net tax liability for pre-2018 accumulated deferred foreign income in installments   1909

S corporation shareholders may elect to defer net tax liability for accumulated deferred foreign income until a triggering event   1910

Six year statute of limitation for assessment of net tax liability due to pre-2018 accumulated deferred foreign income   1911

Pre-2018 accumulated deferred foreign income excluded for purposes of REIT gross income tests; election provided to include that amount in REIT income over eight years   1912

Election not to take pre-2018 accumulated deferred foreign income into account for NOL purposes — 1913

SUBPART F INCLUSION FOR GLOBAL INTANGIBLE LOW-TAXED INCOME — **2000**

U.S. shareholders of CFCs must include their global intangible low-taxed income (GILTI) in gross income — 2001

Domestic corporations allowed deduction for foreign-derived intangible income and global intangible low-taxed income — 2002

80% deemed paid foreign tax credit available for global intangible low-taxed income — 2003

Separate foreign tax credit basket for global intangible low-taxed income (GILTI) — 2004

OTHER CHANGES TO SUBPART F — **2100**

Definition of U.S. shareholder of a controlled foreign corporation expanded to include 10% owner by value — 2101

Subpart F constructive attribution rules allow downward attribution from foreign persons to related U.S. persons — 2102

Requirement that corporation must be controlled for 30 days before Subpart F inclusions apply is eliminated — 2103

Foreign base company oil-related income not included in foreign base company income — 2104

Previously excluded Subpart F income withdrawn from a qualified shipping investment no longer included in U.S. shareholder's income — 2105

ANTI-BASE EROSION AND PROFIT-SHIFTING PROVISIONS — **2200**

Base erosion minimum tax added on payments to foreign related parties. — 2201

Limitations imposed on income shifting through intangible property transfers — 2202

Repeal of active trade or business exception under Code Sec. 367 — 2203

Deduction is disallowed for certain related party amounts paid or accrued in hybrid transactions or with hybrid entities — 2204

Excise tax on stock compensation of insiders in expatriated corporations increased — 2205

Surrogate foreign corporation shareholders aren't eligible for reduced dividends rate — 2206

OTHER FOREIGN PROVISIONS   2300

Changes To The Foreign Tax Credit

Repeal of Code Sec. 902 and other adjustments to the foreign tax credit to account for participation exemption   2301

Taxpayers who sustain a pre-2018 overall domestic loss can elect to recharacterize as much as 100% of U.S. source income as foreign source income   2302

Addition of separate foreign tax credit basket for foreign branch income   2303

Source Of Income And Expense Allocation

Treatment of gain or loss of foreign person from sale or exchange of partnership interests   2304

Source of income from sales of inventory determined solely on basis of production activities   2305

Fair market value method of interest expense allocation or apportionment repealed after 2017   2306

INSURANCE   2400

Life Insurance Companies

Definition of "company's share" and "policyholder's share" amended for determining insurance company dividends received deduction and reserves   2401

Operations loss deduction for life insurance companies repealed   2402

Small life insurance company deduction repealed   2403

Amortization period for insurance companies' capitalized policy acquisition expenses increased to 15 years from 10 years   2404

Repeal of ten-year spread for life insurance companies' reserve changes   2405

Rules on computation of life insurance tax reserves amended   2406

Tax on distributions to stock life insurance company shareholders from a pre-1984 policyholders surplus account is repealed; phased inclusion of remaining balance of policyholders surplus account is provided   2407

Property And Casualty Insurance Companies

Increase from 15% to 25% of the proration rules for property and casualty insurance companies   2408

Modification of discounting rules for unpaid losses when determining property and casualty insurance companies' income   2409

Industry-Wide Provisions

Elective deduction of discounted loss reserve amounts for insurance companies—and related special estimated tax payment rules—are repealed 2410

Active insurance business exception to passive foreign investment company rules requires minimum insurance liabilities amount 2411

TAX-EXEMPT ORGANIZATIONS 2500

Excise tax imposed on tax-exempt organizations that pay excess compensation 2501

New excise tax imposed on investment income of private colleges and universities 2502

Tax-exempt organizations' unrelated business taxable income calculated separately for each trade or business 2503

Tax-exempt organizations' unrelated business taxable income increased by disallowed fringe benefit expenses 2504

COMPENSATION 2600

Performance-based compensation and commissions are subject to $1 million deduction limit 2601

Definition of "publicly held corporation" subject to $1 million compensation deduction limit is expanded 2602

Definition of "covered employee" who's subject to $1 million compensation deduction limit is expanded 2603

Employees can elect to defer income from option or RSU stock for up to five years after vesting 2604

Cash, gift cards, and certain other property don't qualify as employee achievement awards 2605

Form W-2 must include information about deferrals and inclusions under Code Sec. 83(i) 2606

Withholding is required at highest individual rate when stock subject to Code Sec. 83(i) election is included in income 2607

Penalty imposed for employer's failure to notify employee that stock is eligible for Code Sec. 83(i) election 2608

RETIREMENT PLANS 2700

Special rule allowing recharacterization of Roth IRA contributions and traditional IRA contributions does not apply to conversion contributions to a Roth IRA 2701

Rollover period for plan loan offset amounts is extended from 60 days, to tax return due date 2702

Accrual limit for length of service award plans is increased from $3,000 to $6,000 2703

ESTATE AND GIFT TAXES 2800

Estate tax basic exclusion amount increased from $5 million to $10 million 2801

EXCISE TAXES 2900

Payments for aircraft management services are exempted from excise taxes on taxable air transportation 2901

PROCEDURE AND ADMINISTRATION 3000

Head of household filing status added to paid preparer due diligence requirements 3001

Extension of time limit for contesting IRS levy and for third party suits challenging levies 3002

MISCELLANEOUS 3100

Contributions by a customer or potential customer, or by a governmental entity or civic group in a capacity other than as a shareholder, are not nontaxable contributions to capital 3101

Assignments not included in income, and contribution deductions allowed, for Alaska Native Settlement Trusts 3102

CLIENT LETTERS 3200

Overview of provisions of the TCJA affecting individuals 3201

Overview of the business tax changes in the Tax Cuts and Jobs Act ("TCJA") 3202

Overview of the provisions in the TCJA on partnerships, S corporations, and pass-through income 3203

Overview of the foreign tax provisions in the TCJA 3204

Overview of the retirement plan changes in the TCJA 3205

TCJA provisions on tax-exempt organizations 3206

Provisions that sunset under the TCJA 3207

TCJA drops corporate income tax rate to 21% and modifies individual rate brackets 3208

TCJA repeals corporate AMT and temporarily eases individual AMT 3209

TCJA puts $10,000 aggregate limit on state and local tax deduction 3210

Contents

TCJA eliminates the ACA "individual mandate" starting in 2019 for individuals failing to maintain minimum essential health care coverage ... 3211

TCJA greatly eases rules for bonus depreciation, Code Sec. 179 expensing and regular depreciation ... 3212

New 20% deduction for "qualified business income" ("pass-through" income) under the TCJA ... 3213

TCJA expands use of cash basis accounting method and ties income inclusion reporting for tax purposes to reporting for financial purposes ... 3214

TCJA doubles estate and gift tax exemption to $11.2 million per person ... 3215

TCJA lowers the maximum debt on which home mortgage interest is deductible, and eliminates the deduction for home equity loan interest ... 3216

TCJA limits like-kind exchange nonrecognition rules to real estate ... 3217

TCJA provides tax benefits for investments in Qualified Opportunity Funds ... 3218

TCJA business credit changes include a new employer credit for paid family and medical leave ... 3219

TCJA will end alimony-payer deduction and payee's income inclusion for post-2018 divorces and separations ... 3220

TCJA doubles the child tax credit and allows a new lower credit for other dependents ... 3221

TCJA severely cuts personal casualty and theft loss deductions ... 3222

TCJA allows $10,000 per year of 529 plan account funds to be used for elementary or secondary school tuition ... 3223

TCJA adds new ABLE account advantages ... 3224

¶ 100. Income Tax Rates

¶ 101. Individual income tax rate structure replaced with 10%, 12%, 22%, 24%, 32%, 35%, and 37% tax brackets

Code Sec. 1(j)(1), as amended by Tax Cuts and Jobs Act §11001(a)
Code Sec. 1(j)(2)(A), as amended by Tax Cuts and Jobs Act §11001(a)
Code Sec. 1(j)(2)(B), as amended by Tax Cuts and Jobs Act §11001(a)
Code Sec. 1(j)(2)(C), as amended by Tax Cuts and Jobs Act §11001(a)
Code Sec. 1(j)(2)(D), as amended by Tax Cuts and Jobs Act §11001(a)
Code Sec. 1(j)(2)(F), as amended by Tax Cuts and Jobs Act §11001(a)
Code Sec. 1(j)(3), as amended by Tax Cuts and Jobs Act §11001(a)
Code Sec. 1(j)(6), as amended by Tax Cuts and Jobs Act §11001(a)
Generally effective: Tax years beginning after 2017 and before 2026
Committee Reports, see ¶ 5001

To determine regular tax liability, an individual uses the appropriate tax rate schedule (or IRS-issued income tax tables for taxable income of less than $100,000) to compute tax liability. The Code provides four (statutory) tax rate schedules for individuals based on filing status, i.e., single, married filing jointly/surviving spouse, married filing separately, and head of household. Each schedule is divided into income ranges ("tax brackets"), which are taxed at progressively higher marginal tax rates as income increases. The same marginal tax rates apply to all individual taxpayers, but the bracket amounts (income ranges) to which the rates apply differ based on the taxpayer's filing status.

Under pre-Tax Cuts and Jobs Act law, the rate schedules (the statutory schedules, as modified by Code Sec. 1(i)) were divided into seven tax brackets—10%, 15%, 25%, 28%, 33%, 35%, and 39.6%. Each year, IRS adjusts the bracket amounts for each schedule for inflation (generally, for inflation since 1992), and IRS's inflation-adjusted rate schedules are the ones used to compute tax. (FTC 2d/FIN ¶ A-1100, ¶ A-1101, ¶ A-1102, ¶ A-1103; USTR ¶ 14, ¶ 14.08)

The inflation-adjusted rate schedules for individuals for 2017 were as follows:

FTC 2d References are to Federal Tax Coordinator 2d
FIN References are to RIA's Analysis of Federal Taxes: Income (print)
USTR References are to United States Tax Reporter
Catalyst References are to Checkpoint Catalyst
PCA References are to Pension Analysis (print and electronic)
PBE References are to Pension & Benefits Explanations
BCA References are to Benefits Analysis (electronic)
BC References are to Benefits Coordinator (print)
EP References are to Estate Planning Analysis (print and electronic)

2017 Single Individuals Income Tax Rates

If taxable income is:	The tax is:
Not over $9,325	10% of taxable income
Over $9,325 but not over $37,950	$932.50 plus 15% of the excess over $9,325
Over $37,950 but not over $91,900	$5,226.25 plus 25% of the excess over $37,950
Over $91,900 but not over $191,650	$18,713.75 plus 28% of the excess over $91,900
Over $191,650 but not over $416,700	$46,643.75 plus 33% of the excess over $191,650
Over $416,700 but not over $418,400	$120,910.25 plus 35% of the excess over $416,700
Over $418,400	$121,505.25 plus 39.6% of the excess over $418,400

2017 Married Filing Jointly and Surviving Spouse Income Tax Rates

If taxable income is:	The tax is:
Not over $18,650	10% of taxable income
Over $18,650 but not over $75,900	$1,865 plus 15% of the excess over $18,650
Over $75,900 but not over $153,100	$10,452.50 plus 25% of the excess over $75,900
Over $153,100 but not over $233,350	$29,752.50 plus 28% of the excess over $153,100
Over $233,350 but not over $416,700	$52,222.50 plus 33% of the excess over $233,350
Over $416,700 but not over $470,700	$112,728 plus 35% of the excess over $416,700
Over $470,700	$131,628 plus 39.6% of the excess over $470,700

2017 Married Filing Separate Income Tax Rates

If taxable income is:	The tax is:
Not over $9,325	10% of taxable income
Over $9,325 but not over $37,950	$932.50 plus 15% of the excess over $9,325
Over $37,950 but not over $76,550	$5,226.25 plus 25% of the excess over $37,950
Over $76,550 but not over $116,675	$14,876.25 plus 28% of the excess over $76,550
Over $116,675 but not over $208,350	$26,111.25 plus 33% of the excess over $116,675
Over $208,350 but not over $235,350	$56,364 plus 35% of the excess over $208,350
Over $235,350	$65,814 plus 39.6% of the excess over $235,350

2017 Head of Household Income Tax Rates

If taxable income is:	The tax is:
Not over $13,350	10% of taxable income
Over $13,350 but not over $50,800	$1,335 plus 15% of the excess over $13,350
Over $50,800 but not over $131,200	$6,952.50 plus 25% of the excess over $50,800
Over $131,200 but not over $212,500	$27,052.50 plus 28% of the excess over $131,200

Over $212,500 but not over $416,700	$49,816.50 plus 33% of the excess over $212,500
Over $416,700 but not over $444,550	$117,202.50 plus 35% of the excess over $416,700
Over $444,550	$126,950 plus 39.6% of the excess over $444,550

New Law. For tax years beginning after Dec. 31, 2017, and before Jan. 1, 2026 (Code Sec. 1(j)(1) as amended by Tax Cuts and Jobs Act §11001(a)), the Tax Cuts and Jobs Act provides that the statutory individual income tax rate tables (as modified by Code Sec. 1(i)) don't apply (Code Sec. 1(j)(1)(A)) and are temporarily replaced (Com Rept, see ¶ 5001) with the following new rate tables (Code Sec. 1(j)(1)(B)):

Single Individuals Income Tax Rates

If taxable income is:	The tax is:
Not over $9,525	10% of taxable income
Over $9,525 but not over $38,700	$952.50 plus 12% of the excess over $9,525
Over $38,700 but not over $82,500	$4,453.50 plus 22% of the excess over $38,700
Over $82,500 but not over $157,500	$14,089.50 plus 24% of the excess over $82,500
Over $157,500 but not over $200,000	$32,089.50 plus 32% of the excess over $157,500
Over $200,000 but not over $500,000	$45,689.50 plus 35% of the excess over $200,000
Over $500,000	$150,689.50 plus 37% of the excess over $500,000

(Code Sec. 1(j)(2)(C))

Married Filing Jointly and Surviving Spouse Income Tax Rates

If taxable income is:	The tax is:
Not over $19,050	10% of taxable income
Over $19,050 but not over $77,400	$1,905 plus 12% of the excess over $19,050
Over $77,400 but not over $165,000	$8,907 plus 22% of the excess over $77,400
Over $165,000 but not over $315,000	$28,179 plus 24% of the excess over $165,000
Over $315,000 but not over $400,000	$64,179 plus 32% of the excess over $315,000
Over $400,000 but not over $600,000	$91,379 plus 35% of the excess over $400,000
Over $600,000	$161,379 plus 37% of the excess over $600,000

(Code Sec. 1(j)(2)(A))

Married Filing Separate Income Tax Rates

If taxable income is:	The tax is:
Not over $9,525	10% of taxable income
Over $9,525 but not over $38,700	$952.50 plus 12% of the excess over $9,525
Over $38,700 but not over $82,500	$4,453.50 plus 22% of the excess over $38,700
Over $82,500 but not over $157,500	$14,089.50 plus 24% of the excess over $82,500

Over $157,500 but not over $200,000	$32,089.50 plus 32% of the excess over $157,500
Over $200,000 but not over $300,000	$45,689.50 plus 35% of the excess over $200,000
Over $300,000	$80,689.50 plus 37% of the excess over $300,000

(Code Sec. 1(j)(2)(D))

Head of Household Income Tax Rates

If taxable income is:	The tax is:
Not over $13,600	10% of taxable income
Over $13,600 but not over $51,800	$1,360 plus 12% of the excess over $13,600
Over $51,800 but not over $82,500	$5,944 plus 22% of the excess over $51,800
Over $82,500 but not over $157,500	$12,698 plus 24% of the excess over $82,500
Over $157,500 but not over $200,000	$30,698 plus 32% of the excess over $157,500
Over $200,000 but not over $500,000	$44,298 plus 35% of the excess over $200,000
Over $500,000	$149,298 plus 37% of the excess over $500,000

(Code Sec. 1(j)(2)(B))

observation: Thus, for tax years 2018–2025, individuals' taxable income will be subject to the seven tax brackets described above, taxed at 10%, 12%, 22%, 24%, 32%, 35% and 37% marginal tax rates.

But, barring further legislation, the Tax Cuts and Jobs Act changes will expire (sunset) after 2025, and the pre-Tax Cuts and Jobs Act brackets and rates (i.e., 10%, 15%, 25%, 28%, 33%, 35% and 39.6%) will once again be in effect.

observation: The Tax Cuts and Jobs Act changes to the income tax brackets will lower tax rates at many income levels. But, determining whether a particular household will actually see a decrease or increase in tax liability under the new rate structure will be dependent on the impact on that household of the other Tax Cuts and Jobs Act changes to suspend personal exemptions (see ¶ 502) and suspend/or limit many itemized deductions (including limiting the deduction for state and local taxes to $10,000, see ¶ 507 *et seq.*), and to increase the standard deduction (see ¶ 501) and the child tax credit (see ¶ 516). Reduced tax rates could still produce a higher tax liability or a household that ends up with more income subject to tax because of the loss/or reduction of exemptions and deductions.

One category of taxpayers certain to benefit from the rate structure changes are those in the highest tax bracket. Since higher income taxpayers were barred from claiming personal exemptions and itemized deductions under pre-Tax Cuts Act and Jobs Act law (under phase-out rules), the suspension/or limitation of those items doesn't result in an increase in their taxable income (from 2017 levels). Instead, taxpayers in the top bracket will benefit from both (i) lowering their taxable income—either by claiming the increased standard deduction, or a higher itemized deduction now that the itemized deduction phase-out rules have been suspended (see ¶ 504)—*and* (ii) the reduced tax rates and bracket changes.

Taxpayers most likely to see a tax increase under the new tax rate structure are those who could take large itemized deductions (e.g., for state and local income taxes) under pre-Tax Cuts and Jobs Act law, but who won't be able to itemize at all under the Tax Cuts and Jobs Act, due to the suspension and/or limitation of various deductions. Having to take a standard deduction (instead of a larger itemized deduction), coupled with the loss of personal exemptions, will increase the amount of income on which these taxpayers pay tax.

observation: The reduction in the tax rates and changes to the bracket ranges for 2018 offer a saving opportunity for some taxpayers who are able to defer income to a later year. A taxpayer whose income will fall into a lower tax bracket(s) in 2018 could benefit from deferring income from 2017 to 2018.

Further, a taxpayer in the top tax bracket in both 2017 and 2018 would benefit from this strategy due to reduction of the top tax rate. For example, a single taxpayer making over $500,000 would save 2.6% in tax (the difference between a top rate of 39.6% and 37%) on income he or she defers from 2017 to 2018, e.g., a $50,000 bonus deferred to 2018 would result in a tax saving of $1,300.

observation: A taxpayer who's able to defer income to 2018 from a "pass-through" business (an S corporation, partnership, sole proprietorship, or LLC) may also be able to benefit from the deferral due to the new 20% deduction for qualified business income that takes effect in 2018 (see ¶ 701).

For Tax Cuts and Jobs Act changes to:

... the income tax rates on estates and trusts, see ¶ 104;

... the taxation of the unearned income of children (i.e., modification of the "kiddie tax rules"), see ¶ 105; and

... the inflation adjustment of the rate breakpoints at which tax on capital gains and ordinary dividends are imposed, see ¶ 1501.

Annual inflation adjustment of the tax rate schedules; "marriage penalty" relief. The Code Sec. 1(j)(2) individuals tax tables above (and estates' and trusts' income tax table at ¶ 104) won't be adjusted for inflation for tax years beginning in 2018. (Code Sec. 1(j)(3)(A) as amended by Tax Cuts and Jobs Act §11001(a))

> **⚫️** *observation:* That is, the Code Sec. 1(j)(2) statutory tables above (and at ¶ 104) are the ones that will apply for 2018.

For tax years beginning after 2018, IRS must issue tax rate schedules annually to apply in lieu of the statutory (i.e., Code Sec. 1(j)(2)) tables above. These tables are to be prescribed in the same manner as required under Code Sec. 1(f)(1) and Code Sec. 1(f)(2)—i.e., generally, by increasing the minimum and maximum dollar amount for each rate bracket for which tax is imposed by the cost-of-living (inflation) adjustment (COLA) provided in Code Sec. 1(f)(3)—but, without the special adjustments required just for the pre-Tax Cuts and Jobs Act statutory tax tables (i.e., "the permanent tax tables") under Code Sec. 1(f)(2)(A)(i) and Code Sec. 1(f)(2)(A)(ii), described at ¶ 201. (Code Sec. 1(j)(3)(B))

> **⚫️** *observation:* The direction in Code Sec. 1(j)(3)(B) above to IRS, to prescribe the inflation-adjusted tables to apply in lieu of the Code Sec. 1(j)(2) tables—in the same manner as required under Code Sec. 1(f)(1) and Code Sec. 1(f)(2) (except as otherwise provided below)—appears to incorporate the general rounding rule required under Code Sec. 1(f)(7)(A) (Code Sec. 1(f)(6)(A) before redesignated by Tax Cuts and Jobs Act §11002(b). That is, any COLA increase to the minimum and maximum dollar amount for each rate bracket that isn't a multiple of $50 must be rounded to the next lowest multiple of $50 (see FTC 2d/FIN ¶ A-1103). (But, see special rounding rule below.)

However, in prescribing the annual inflation-adjusted tax rate schedules to apply in lieu of the Code Sec. 1(j)(2) tables above, IRS must (Code Sec. 1(j)(3)(B)):

. . . apply the Code Sec. 1(f)(3) inflation adjustment provisions (see ¶ 201) by substituting "calendar year 2017," for "calendar year 2016" in Code Sec. 1(f)(3)(A)(ii) (Code Sec. 1(j)(3)(B)(i));

. . . apply the special rounding rule in Code Sec. 1(f)(7)(B) to *any unmarried individual other than a surviving spouse or head of household.* That is, for any unmarried individual other than a surviving spouse or head of household, any COLA increase to the minimum and maximum dollar amount for each rate bracket that isn't a multiple of $25 must be rounded to the next lowest multiple of $25. (Code Sec. 1(j)(3)(B)(ii)); and

. . . not apply the special rules under Code Sec. 1(f)(8) requiring adjustments to eliminate the "marriage penalty" in the 15% bracket. (Code Sec. 1(j)(3)(B)(iii))

> ⓇⒾⒶ *observation:* A "marriage penalty" exists whenever the tax on a couple's joint return is more than the combined taxes each spouse would pay if they weren't married and if each filed a single or head of household return (see FTC 2d/FIN ¶ A-1102). The Tax Cuts and Jobs Act sets the statutory tax brackets for marrieds filing jointly—through the 32% bracket—at twice the amount of the corresponding tax brackets for singles (see Code Sec. 1(j)(2)(A) and Code Sec. 1(j)(2)(C) above, respectively), thus eliminating any marriage penalty effect through the 32% bracket. Because the 35% bracket for marrieds filing jointly isn't twice the amount of the singles 35% bracket—the marriage penalty effect will still apply to joint filers whose income falls in that bracket, specifically to joint filers with income between $600,000 and $1,000,000 (when the 37% bracket begins). Thus, the most the marriage penalty may be under the new rate structure is $8,000 (i.e., the last $400,000 of income for which singles [at $200,000 each] would be taxed at 35%, but joint filers will be taxed at 37%).

> Under pre-Tax Cuts and Jobs Act law, only the 10% and 15% married filing jointly brackets were set at twice that of the singles bracket, and so the marriage penalty effect applied in the brackets above the 15% bracket (see FTC 2d/FIN ¶ A-1102).

For the Tax Cuts and Jobs Act changes to how the Code Sec. 1(f)(3) inflation adjustment is computed for purposes of the income tax brackets, and many other tax calculations under the Code, see ¶ 201.

Changes to withholding tax rates "tied" to the income tax rates. Certain withholding requirements are tied to (based on) the income tax rates imposed under Code Sec. 1 on individual taxpayers. So, the Tax Cuts and Jobs Act changes to the Code Sec. 1 rates for 2018−2025, may also change these tied rates for 2018−2025.

The Tax Cuts and Jobs Act provides that any reference under the Internal Revenue Code to a rate of tax under Code Sec. 1(c) (the pre-Tax Cuts and Jobs Act tax rate schedule for single individuals) will be treated as a reference to the corresponding rate bracket under Code Sec. 1(j)(2)(C) (the Tax Cuts and Jobs Act tax rate schedule for single individuals), except that the reference in Code Sec. 3402(q)(1) (providing the withholding rate on gambling winnings, see FTC 2d/FIN ¶ J-8600, ¶ J-8600.1, ¶ J-8602; USTR ¶ 34,024.26) to the "third lowest rate of tax applicable under Code Sec. 1(c)" will be treated as a reference to the "fourth lowest rate of tax under Code Sec. 1(j)(2)(C)." (Code Sec. 1(j)(2)(F))

> ⓇⒾⒶ *observation:* The result of the rule above is to reduce the withholding tax rate on gambling winnings for 2018−2025 to 24% (from 25%).

🅡🅘🅐 *observation:* Additional withholding rates tied to the Code Sec. 1 individual rates that are reduced for 2018–2025 due to the Tax Cuts and Jobs Act tax rate reductions for individuals include:

. . . *Backup withholding rate on reportable payments.* This rate equals the "fourth lowest tax rate imposed on single filers" ((FTC 2d/FIN ¶ J-9000, ¶ J-9001; USTR ¶ 34,064)), and so is reduced to 24% (from 28%);

. . . *Mandatory flat rate withholding for supplemental wage payments by any one employer to an employee during the calendar year that exceed $1 million.* The mandatory flat rate withholding for these payments is equal to the maximum rate of tax in effect under Code Sec. 1 for tax years beginning in that calendar year ((FTC 2d/FIN ¶ H-4530, ¶ H-4542; USTR ¶ 34,024.13)), and so is reduced to 37% (from 39.6%);

. . . *Voluntary withholding rates on social security and other specified federal payments.* The permitted rates for this voluntary withholding— withholding requested by the taxpayer—are: (1) 7%; (2) any rate equal to one of the three lowest income tax rates for single filers; or (3) any other rate permitted under regs ((FTC 2d/FIN ¶ H-4475, ¶ H-4483; USTR ¶ 34,024.25))—and so option (2) is reduced to 10%, 12%, or 22% (from 10%, 15%, or 25%).

. . . *Withholding rate on Indian casino profits distributed to tribal members.* The withholding rate used to compute the "annualized tax" withheld on Indian casino profits paid to tribal members is no rate in excess of the fourth lowest income tax rate for single filers (see (FTC 2d/FIN ¶ J-8600, ¶ J-8617; USTR ¶ 34,024.26))—and so is reduced to no rate higher than 24% (from no rate higher than 28%).

For Tax Cuts and Jobs Act required income tax withholding at the highest rate in effect under Code Sec. 1 for qualified stock for which a Code Sec. 83(i) election is made, see ¶ 2607.

Rate reductions don't require straddle computations. When a tax rate change occurs during a taxpayer's tax year, the tax must be computed using straddle computations that take into account the different rates applicable to portions of the year (see FTC 2d/FIN ¶ A-1115; USTR ¶ 154). The straddle computation rules are made inapplicable to any change in a rate of tax by reason of Tax Cuts and Jobs Act §11001(a) discussed above (and at ¶ 104). (Code Sec. 1(j)(6))

Sunset. The above-described changes to the individuals income tax rate structure don't apply for tax years beginning after Dec. 31, 2025. (Code Sec. 1(j)(1))

☐ **Effective:** For tax years beginning after Dec. 31, 2017 (Tax Cuts and Jobs Act §11001(c)), and before Jan. 1, 2026. (Code Sec. 1(j)(1))

¶ 102. Reduction of corporate tax rates

Code Sec. 11(b), as amended by Tax Cuts and Jobs Act §13001(a)
Code Sec. 1445(e), as amended by Tax Cuts and Jobs Act §13001(b)(3)
Generally effective: Tax years beginning after Dec. 31, 2017
Committee Reports, see ¶ 5032

Under pre-Tax Cuts and Jobs Act law, corporations were subject to graduated rates that resulted in a 35% corporate rate for income over $10 million, with a phase out of the lower rates.

The income tax rate imposed on ordinary corporations was:

... 15% on the first $50,000 of its taxable income,

... 25% on any amount in excess of $50,000 and up to $75,000,

... 34% on any amount in excess of $75,000 and up to $10,000,000, and

... 35% on any amount in excess of $10,000,000.

The graduated rates for corporations were phased out as follows: if a corporation has taxable income in excess of $100,000, then the tax as determined under the above graduated rate schedule was increased by 5% of the excess, or $11,750, whichever is less and if a corporation had taxable income in excess of $15,000,000, the amount of the tax was further increased by an additional amount equal to the lesser of 3% of such excess, or $100,000.

Under these rules, the following rates applied:

Taxable income over—	But not over—	The tax is:	Of the amount over—
0	$50,000	15%	0
$50,000	75,000	$7,500 + 25%	$50,000
75,000	100,000	13,750 + 34%	75,000
100,000	335,000	22,250 + 39%	100,000
335,000	10,000,000	113,900 + 34%	335,000
10,000,000	15,000,000	3,400,000 + 35%	10,000,000
15,000,000	18,333,333	5,150,000 + 38%	15,000,000
18,333,333	—	35%	0

Personal service corporations (defined in Code Sec. 448(d)(2) (see FTC 2d/FIN ¶ G-2058; USTR ¶ 4484.02) did not have the advantage of the lower rates and were taxed at a flat 35% rate. (FTC 2d/FIN ¶ D-1000, ¶ D-1003; USTR ¶ 114.01; Catalyst ¶ 502:162)

New Law. The Tax Cuts and Jobs Act reduces the corporate tax rate to a flat 21% rate. (Code Sec. 11(b) as amended by Tax Cuts and Jobs Act §13001(a))

The Tax Cuts and Jobs Act similarly reduces the withholding rate on dispositions of U.S. real property interests (USRPIs) from 35% as follows:

• the withholding rate on dispositions of USRPIs by domestic partnerships, trusts, or estates (FTC 2d/FIN ¶ O-13000, ¶ O-13035; USTR ¶ 14,454.02) is determined by multiplying the gain by the highest corporate tax rate (Code Sec. 1445(e)(1) as amended by Tax Cuts and Jobs Act §13001(b)(3)(A));

• the withholding rate on distributions of USRPIs by foreign corporations in recognition transactions (FTC 2d/FIN ¶ O-13039; USTR ¶ 14,454.02) is determined by multiplying the gain by the highest corporate tax rate; (Code Sec. 1445(e)(2) as amended by Tax Cuts and Jobs Act §13001(b)(3)(B)); and

• the withholding rate on distributions of USRPIs by regulated investment companies (RICs) or real estate investment trusts (REITs) (FTC 2d/FIN ¶ O-13055; USTR ¶ 14,454.02) is determined by multiplying the gain by the highest corporate tax rate. (Code Sec. 1445(e)(6) as amended by Tax Cuts and Jobs Act §13001(b)(3)(C))

Conforming amendments eliminate:

• the alternative capital gains rate for corporations (FTC 2d/FIN ¶ I-5100, ¶ I-5117; USTR ¶ 12,014) (Code Sec. 1201 as repealed by Tax Cuts and Jobs Act §13001(b)(2)(A)); (Com Rept, see ¶ 5032); and

• the disallowance of graduated rates and accumulated earnings credit in the case of corporate transfers of property to a controlled transferee corporation (FTC 2d/FIN ¶ E-10200, ¶ E-10201; USTR ¶ 15,514.01) (Code Sec. 1551 as repealed by Tax Cuts and Jobs Act §13001(b)(5)(A)); and

• the rule that a RIC that is a personal holding company or that fails to comply with regs for the purpose of ascertaining the actual ownership of its stock is taxed at the highest corporate tax rate. (FTC 2d/FIN ¶ E-6100, ¶ E-6102; USTR ¶ 8524.10) (Code Sec. 852(b)(1) as amended by Tax Cuts and Jobs Act §13001(b)(4))

> **☝ observation:** The alternative capital gains rate didn't apply under pre-Tax Cuts and Jobs Act law, except for qualified timber gains for tax years beginning in 2016, see FTC 2d/FIN ¶ I-5518.1; USTR ¶ 12,014.01.

In addition, the limitations on multiple tax benefits in the case of certain controlled corporations are amended to eliminate the application of these rules to the pre-Tax Cuts and Jobs Act graduated corporate rates and the alternative minimum tax (AMT), with the result that they apply only to limit the accumulated earnings tax credit to $250,000 ($150,000 in the case of certain services corporations). (FTC 2d/FIN ¶ E-10300, ¶ E-10301; USTR ¶ 15,614) (Code Sec. 1561 as amended by Tax Cuts and Jobs Act §13001(b)(6))

References to the alternative capital gains rate are eliminated for purposes of:

- the interest on the Code Sec. 453A deferred tax liability in certain installments sales (FTC 2d/FIN ¶ G-6000, ¶ G-6317; USTR ¶ 453A4) (Code Sec. 527(b) as amended by Tax Cuts and Jobs Act §13001(b)(2)(C));

- the tax on the net capital gain of Code Sec. 527 political organizations (FTC 2d/FIN ¶ D-5000, ¶ D-5008; USTR ¶ 5274) (Code Sec. 527(b) as amended by Tax Cuts and Jobs Act §13001(b)(2)(D));

- the alternative tax on mutual savings banks conducting life insurance businesses (FTC 2d/FIN ¶ E-3300, ¶ E-3328) (Code Sec. 594(a) as amended by Tax Cuts and Jobs Act §13001(b)(2)(E));

- the estate tax deduction for taxes imposed on income in respect of a decedent (FTC 2d/FIN ¶ C-9500, ¶ C-9563; USTR ¶ 6914.07) (Code Sec. 691(c)(4) as amended by Tax Cuts and Jobs Act §13001(b)(2)(F))

- the tax on the net capital gain of life insurance companies (FTC 2d/FIN ¶ E-4800, ¶ E-4801; USTR ¶ 8014) (Code Sec. 801(a) as amended by Tax Cuts and Jobs Act §13001(b)(2)(G));

- the tax on the net capital gain of nonlife insurance companies (FTC 2d/FIN ¶ E-5500, ¶ E-5501) (Code Sec. 831(e) as amended by Tax Cuts and Jobs Act §13001(b)(2)(H));

- the determination of insurance company taxable income (FTC 2d/FIN ¶ E-5605; USTR ¶ 8324.02) (Code Sec. 832(c)(5) as amended by Tax Cuts and Jobs Act §13001(b)(2)(I)) and the determination of taxable investment income (FTC 2d/FIN ¶ E-5504; USTR ¶ 8344) (Code Sec. 834(b)(1)(D) as amended by Tax Cuts and Jobs Act §13001(b)(2)(I));

- the tax on the net capital gain over the deduction for dividends paid determined by reference solely to capital gain dividends of regulated investment companies (FTC 2d/FIN ¶ E-6100, ¶ E-6102; USTR ¶ 8524.10) (Code Sec. 852(b)(3)(A) as amended by Tax Cuts and Jobs Act §13001(b)(2)(J));

- the tax on the net capital gain over the deduction for dividends paid determined by reference solely to capital gain dividends of REITs. The Tax Cuts and Jobs Act defines this amount as the REIT's undistributed capital gain. (FTC 2d/FIN ¶ E-6600, ¶ E-6609; USTR ¶ 8574.01) (Code Sec. 857(b)(3) as amended by Tax Cuts and Jobs Act §13001(b)(2)(K));

- the tax on the net capital gain of income of foreign corporations connected with a U.S. business (FTC 2d/FIN ¶ O-10600, ¶ O-10602; USTR ¶ 8824) (Code Sec. 882(a)(1) as amended by Tax Cuts and Jobs Act §13001(b)(2)(L));

- the Code Sec. 904 limitation of the foreign tax credit (FTC 2d/FIN ¶ O-4400, ¶ O-4404.6; USTR ¶ 9044.01). (Code Sec. 904(b)(2)(C) as amended by Tax Cuts and Jobs Act §13001(b)(2)(M)(i)) Instead, the limitation provides that there is a capital gain differential if the Code Sec. 1(h) rate applies for the tax year (Code Sec. 904(b)(3)(D) as amended by Tax Cuts and Jobs Act §13001(b)(2)(M)(ii)) and the rate differential portion of foreign source net capital gain, net capital gain, or the excess of net capital gain from U.S. sources over net capital gain, as the case may be, is the same proportion of the amount as (i) the excess of the highest tax rate under Code Sec. 1(a), Code Sec. 1(b),Code Sec. 1(c), Code Sec. 1(d), or Code Sec. 1(e)(whichever applies) over the Code Sec. 1(h) alternative capital gain tax rate bears to (ii) the Code Sec. 1(h) alternative capital gain tax rate. (Code Sec. 904(b)(3)(E) as amended by Tax Cuts and Jobs Act §13001(b)(2)(M)(iii))

• the S corporation built-in gains tax on net capital gains (FTC 2d/FIN ¶ D-1640, ¶ D-1657; USTR ¶ 13,744.01) (Code Sec. 1374(b) as amended by Tax Cuts and Jobs Act §13001(b)(2)(N));

• the tax on the net capital gain of farmers' cooperatives (FTC 2d/FIN ¶ E-1000, ¶ E-1001; USTR ¶ 13,814) (Code Sec. 1381(b) as amended by Tax Cuts and Jobs Act §13001(b)(2)(O)); and

• corporate estimated tax overpayments (FTC 2d/FIN ¶ T-6600, ¶ T-6605.1; USTR ¶ 64,254) and the corporate estimated tax penalty (FTC 2d/FIN ¶ S-5320, ¶ S-5325; USTR ¶ 66,554). (Code Sec. 6425(c)(1)(A) as amended by Tax Cuts and Jobs Act §13001(b)(2)(P)); (Code Sec. 6655(g)(1)(A)(i) as amended by Tax Cuts and Jobs Act §13001(b)(2)(P))

• the tax on corporate withdrawals out of capital gain accounts from Merchant Marine capital construction funds (FTC 2d/FIN ¶ J-1335, ¶ J-1360; USTR ¶ 75,184) (Code Sec. 7518(g)(6)(A) as amended by Tax Cuts and Jobs Act §13001(b)(2)(Q)); (Code Sec. 7518(g)(6)(A) as amended by Tax Cuts and Jobs Act §13001(b)(7))

For the normalization requirement for public utilities whose tax rates are reduced, see ¶ 1309.

☐ **Effective:** Tax years beginning after Dec. 31, 2017. (Tax Cuts and Jobs Act §13001(c)(1)) However, the lower withholding rates for distributions of USRPIs apply for distributions after Dec. 31, 2017. (Tax Cuts and Jobs Act §13001(c)(2)) In addition, the limitations on multiple tax benefits in the case of certain controlled corporations apply for transfers after Dec. 31, 2017. (Tax Cuts and Jobs Act §13001(c)(3))

observation: While the Code Sec. 1 changes to the individual tax rates are specifically excepted from the Code Sec. 15 straddle computation rules (see ¶ 101), the Code Sec. 11 changes to the corporate tax rates are not. Under Code Sec. 15, when tax rates change during a taxpayer's tax year (straddle year), the taxpayer's tax for the straddle year is computed using a blended tax rate. That is, the taxpayer (i) calculates two tentative taxes for the straddle year by applying each tax rate to the taxpayer's income for the year, (ii) multiplies each tentative tax by the proportion of the straddle year to which each tax rate applies, and (iii) adds the results of the two calculations, see FTC 2d ¶ A-1116; USTR

¶ 154.01. Thus, it appears that corporations with fiscal years ending after Dec. 31, 2017, when the new corporate tax rate comes into effect, would have to perform this calculation to determine their taxes for the year.

¶ 103. Reduction in corporate dividends received deduction

Code Sec. 243, as amended by Tax Cuts and Jobs Act §13002(a)
Code Sec. 245(c)(1)(B), as amended by Tax Cuts and Jobs Act §13002(b)
Code Sec. 246(b)(3), as amended by Tax Cuts and Jobs Act §13002(c)
Code Sec. 246A(a)(1), as amended by Tax Cuts and Jobs Act §13002(d)
Generally effective: Tax years beginning after Dec. 31, 2017.
Committee Reports, see ¶ 5032

As described at ¶ 102, the Tax Cuts and Jobs Act reduced the corporate tax rate to a flat 21% rate. Under pre-Tax Cuts and Jobs Act law, corporations were entitled to a 70% (80% for 20% or more owned, by vote or value, corporations) dividends received deduction. (FTC 2d/FIN ¶ D-2200, ¶ D-2201, ¶ D-2205; USTR ¶ 2434.01; Catalyst ¶ 107:190; Catalyst ¶ 108:210; Catalyst ¶ 109:100; Catalyst ¶ 112:100; Catalyst ¶ 112:110; Catalyst ¶ 114:204; Catalyst ¶ 142:174; Catalyst ¶ 2103:121)

The maximum tax rate on dividends eligible for the 70% dividends received deduction was 10.5%. (Com Rept, see ¶ 5032)

New Law. The Tax Cuts and Jobs Act:

• reduces the 70% dividends received deduction to 50% (Code Sec. 243(a)(1) as amended by Tax Cuts and Jobs Act §13002(a)(1)), and

• reduces the 80% dividends received deduction for 20% or more owned corporations to 65% (Code Sec. 243(c)(1) as amended by Tax Cuts and Jobs Act §13002(a)(2))

> *observation:* The maximum tax on dividends is 10.5% (50% of 21%); 7.35% (35% of 21%) for 20% or more owned corporations.

The Tax Cuts and Jobs Act includes the following conforming amendments:

• the 70% (80% for 20% or more owned corporations) dividends received deductions for dividends out of earnings and profits attributable to effectively connected income received or accrued by the other corporation while the other corporation was a foreign sales corporation (FSC) (FTC 2d/FIN ¶ O-1660, ¶ O-1661; USTR ¶ 2434.03) is reduced to 50% (65% for 20% or more owned corporations). (Code Sec. 245(c)(1)(B) as amended by Tax Cuts and Jobs Act §13002(b))

• the 70% (80% for 20% or more owned corporations) taxable income limitation on the dividends received deductions (FTC 2d/FIN ¶ D-2253; USTR ¶ 2434.04) is amended to apply a 50% (65% for 20% or more owned corporations) dividend limitation. (Code Sec. 246(b)(3) as amended by Tax Cuts and Jobs Act §13002(c))

• the percentage reduction of deduction for dividends from debt-financed portfolio stock (FTC 2d/FIN ¶ D-2255; USTR ¶ 2434.05) is amended to reduce the 50% (65% for 20% or more owned corporations) deduction. (Code Sec. 246A(a)(1) as amended by Tax Cuts and Jobs Act §13002(d))

• the rule treating dividends from a foreign corporation as foreign source income for foreign tax credit purposes only to the extent that they exceed 100/70ths (100/80ths for dividends from a 20% owned corporation) of the dividends received deduction allowable for the dividend. (FTC 2d/FIN ¶ O-10900, ¶ O-10928; USTR ¶ 8614.11) is amended to apply only to the extent that they exceed 100/50ths (100/65ths for dividends from a 20% owned corporation) of the dividends received deduction allowable for the dividend. (Code Sec. 861(a)(2)(B) as amended by Tax Cuts and Jobs Act §13002(e))

☐ **Effective:** Tax years beginning after Dec. 31, 2017. (Tax Cuts and Jobs Act §13002(f))

¶ 104. Estates and trusts income tax rate structure replaced with 10%, 24%, 35%, and 37% tax brackets

Code Sec. 1(j)(1), as amended by Tax Cuts and Jobs Act §11001(a)
Code Sec. 1(j)(2)(E), as amended by Tax Cuts and Jobs Act §11001(a)
Code Sec. 1(j)(3)(A), as amended by Tax Cuts and Jobs Act §11001(a)
Generally effective: Tax years beginning after 2017 and before 2026
Committee Reports, see ¶ 5001

The income tax liability of estates and trusts is computed using a tax rate schedule applicable only for estates and trusts. The tax rate schedule is divided into income ranges (tax brackets), which are taxed at progressively higher marginal tax rates as the income brackets increase.

Under pre-Tax Cuts and Jobs Act law, the rate schedule for estates and trusts (the statutory schedule as modified by Code Sec. 1(i)) was divided into five tax brackets: 15%, 25%, 28%, 33%, and 39.6%. Each year IRS adjusts each bracket (income range) for inflation (computed from 1992), and IRS's inflation-adjusted rate schedule is the one used to compute tax. (FTC 2d/FIN ¶ C-1000, ¶ C-1003, ¶ C-1005, ¶ C-7000, ¶ C-7002, ¶ C-7004; USTR ¶ 14.13)

The inflation-adjusted rate schedule for estates and trusts income for 2017 was as follows:

2017 Estates and Trusts Income Tax Rates

If taxable income is:	The tax is:
Not over $2,550	15% of taxable income
Over $2,550 but not over $6,000	$382.50 plus 25% of the excess over $2,550
Over $6,000 but not over $9,150	$1,245 plus 28% of the excess over $6,000
Over $9,150 but not over $12,500	$2,127 plus 33% of the excess over $9,150
Over $12,500	$3,232.50 plus 39.6% of the excess over $12,500

New Law. For tax years beginning after Dec. 31, 2017, and before Jan. 1, 2026 (Code Sec. 1(j)(1) as amended by Tax Cuts and Jobs Act §11001(a)), the Tax Cuts and Jobs Act provides that the statutory income tax rate table for estates and trusts (as modified by Code Sec. 1(i)) doesn't apply (Code Sec. 1(j)(1)(A)) and is temporarily replaced (Com Rept, see ¶ 5001) with the following new tax rate table (Code Sec. 1(j)(1)(B))

Estates and Trusts Income Tax Rates

If taxable income is:	The tax is:
Not over $2,550	10% of taxable income
Over $2,550 but not over $9,150	$255 plus 24% of the excess over $2,550
Over $9,150 but not over $12,500	$1,839 plus 35% of the excess over $9,150
Over $12,500	$3,011.50 plus 37% of the excess over $12,500

(Code Sec. 1(j)(2)(E))

observation: Thus, for tax years 2018–2025, estates' and trusts' taxable income will be subject to the four tax brackets described above, taxed at 10%, 24%, 35% and 37% marginal tax rates.

But, barring further legislation, the Tax Cuts and Jobs Act changes will expire (sunset) after 2025, and the pre-Tax Cuts and Jobs Act five tax brackets and rates for estates and trusts (i.e., 15%, 25%, 28%, 33%, and 39.6%) will once again be in effect.

The Code Sec. 1(j)(2) tax tables (i.e., the estates and trusts income tax table above (and the individual income tax tables at ¶ 101) won't be adjusted for inflation for tax years beginning in 2018. (Code Sec. 1(j)(3)(A) as amended by Tax Cuts and Jobs Act §11001(a))

observation: That is, the Code Sec. 1(j)(2)(E) statutory table above is the one that will apply for 2018.

For the inflation adjustment of all of the Code Sec. 1(j)(2) tax tables (i.e., including the Code Sec. 1(j)(2)(E) statutory table above) for tax years beginning after 2018, see ¶ 101.

And, for rule providing that the Tax Cuts and Jobs Act rate reductions above don't trigger the Code Sec. 15 straddle computation rules, see ¶ 101.

For Tax Cuts and Jobs Act changes to:

. . . the income tax rates for individuals, see ¶ 101;

. . . the inflation adjustment of the rate breakpoints at which capital gains and qualified dividend tax is imposed, see ¶ 1501; and

. . . how the Code Sec. 1(f)(3) inflation adjustment is computed for purposes of the income tax brackets, and many other tax calculations under the Code, see ¶ 201.

Sunset. The above-described changes to the estates and trusts income tax rate structure don't apply for tax years beginning after Dec. 31, 2025. (Code Sec. 1(j)(1))

☐ **Effective:** For tax years beginning after Dec. 31, 2017 (Tax Cuts and Jobs Act §11001(c)), and before Jan. 1, 2026. (Code Sec. 1(j)(1))

¶ 105. Kiddie tax modified to effectively apply estates' and trusts' ordinary and capital gains rates to child's net unearned income

Code Sec. 1(j)(1), as amended by Tax Cuts and Jobs Act §11001(a)
Code Sec. 1(j)(4), as amended by Tax Cuts and Jobs Act §11001(a)
Generally effective: Tax years after 2017 and before 2026
Committee Reports, see ¶ 5001

The tax on certain children with unearned income (the "kiddie tax") applies (under Code Sec. 1(g)) to the net unearned income of any child who: (i) is under age 19 by the close of the tax year, or is a full-time student under age 24; (ii) has at least one living parent at the close of the tax year; (iii) has unearned income of more than $2,100 (for 2017); and (iv) doesn't file a joint return. The kiddie tax applies regardless of whether the child may be claimed as a dependent by either or both parents. For children over age 17, the kiddie tax applies only to children whose earned income doesn't exceed one-half of the amount of their support.

Unearned income for these purposes is income other than wages, salaries, professional fees, other amounts received as compensation for personal services actually rendered, and distributions from qualified disability trusts. In general, a child is eligible to use the preferential tax rates for qualified dividends and capital gains.

Under the kiddie tax rules, children are taxed at the normally applicable rates on their earned income, and on their investment income ("unearned income") up to a prescribed amount (which is adjusted annually for inflation, $2,100 for 2017). For children who have more than the prescribed amount of unearned income for the tax year, that income is taxed to the child, but at the rate that would apply if that income were included in the parents' return, if that rate is higher than what the child would otherwise pay.

Specifically, under pre-Tax Cuts and Jobs Act law, the tax on the income of a child who was subject to the kiddie tax rules, was the greater of:

(1) the tax that would be imposed if the kiddie tax didn't apply; or

(2) the sum of: (i) the tax that would be imposed if the kiddie tax rules didn't apply and if the child's taxable income for the tax year were reduced by the child's net unearned income (investment income minus twice the minimum basic standard deduction allowed to dependents, i.e., for 2017, $2,100), plus (ii) the child's share of the "allocable parental tax" (the tax on the child's net unearned income that would be imposed if that net unearned income were included in the parents' return). (Special allocation rules applied where parent had more than one child subject to kiddie tax.) (FTC 2d/FIN ¶ A-1300, ¶ A-1301 et seq.; USTR ¶ 14.09)

New Law. The Tax Cuts and Jobs Act modifies the kiddie tax to effectively apply the estates' and trusts' ordinary and capital gains rates to the net unearned income of a child. As under pre-Tax Cuts and Jobs Act law, the child's taxable income attributable to earned income is taxed according to an unmarried taxpayer's brackets and rates. Thus, under the Tax Cuts and Jobs Act changes, the child's tax will no longer be affected by the tax situation of the child's parent or the unearned income of any siblings. (Com Rept, see ¶ 5001)

Specifically, for tax years beginning after Dec. 31, 2017 and before Jan. 1, 2026 (Code Sec. 1(j)(1) as amended by Tax Cuts and Jobs Act §11001(a)), the Tax Cuts and Jobs Act provides that in the case of a child to whom the Code Sec. 1(g) kiddie tax applies for the tax year, the rules at (A) and (B) below apply in lieu of the above-described kiddie tax computations. (Code Sec. 1(j)(4)(A) as amended by Tax Cuts and Jobs Act §11001(a))

(A) In determining the amount of tax imposed on the child, the income tax table otherwise applicable under Code Sec. 1(j) to the child (i.e., the applicable individual tax rate schedule provided under the Tax Cuts and Jobs Act, see ¶ 101) is applied with the following modifications (Code Sec. 1(j)(4)(B)):

. . . the maximum taxable income taxed at a rate below 24% can't be more than the sum of (Code Sec. 1(j)(4)(B)(i)): (i) the child's earned taxable income (Code Sec. 1(j)(4)(B)(i)(I)), plus (ii) the minimum taxable income for the 24% bracket in the Estates and Trusts Income Tax Table (as adjusted for inflation) for the tax year (Code Sec. 1(j)(4)(B)(i)(II))(i.e., for 2018, $2,550, see ¶ 104);

. . . the maximum taxable income taxed at a rate below 35% can't be more than the sum of (Code Sec. 1(j)(4)(B)(ii)): (i) the child's earned taxable income (Code Sec. 1(j)(4)(B)(ii)(I)), plus (ii) the minimum taxable income for the 35% bracket in the Estates and Trusts Income Tax Table (as adjusted for inflation) for the tax year (Code Sec. 1(j)(4)(B)(ii)(II)) (i.e., for 2018, $9,150, see ¶ 104); and

... the maximum taxable income taxed at a rate below 37% can't be more than the sum of (Code Sec. 1(j)(4)(B)(iii)): (i) the child's earned taxable income (Code Sec. 1(j)(4)(B)(iii)(I)), plus (ii) the minimum taxable income for the 37% bracket in the Estates and Trusts Income Tax Table (as adjusted for inflation) for the tax year (Code Sec. 1(j)(4)(B)(iii)(II)) (i.e., for 2018, $12,500, see ¶ 104).

> *observation:* That is, under rule (A) above:
>
> ... the maximum amount of taxable income taxed at rates below 24% can't exceed the child's earned taxable income + (for 2018) $2,550;
>
> ... the maximum amount of taxable income taxed at rates below 35% can't exceed the child's earned taxable income + (for 2018) $9,150; and
>
> ... the maximum taxable income taxed at a rate below 37% can't exceed the child's earned taxable income + (for 2018) $12,500.

(B) For purposes of applying the Code Sec. 1(h) capital gains rates (as modified by the Tax Cuts and Jobs Act, see ¶ 1501) (Code Sec. 1(j)(4)(C)):

... the maximum zero rate amount can't be more than the sum of (Code Sec. 1(j)(4)(C)(i)): (i) the child's earned taxable income (Code Sec. 1(j)(4)(C)(i)(I)), plus (ii) the maximum zero rate amount for estates and trusts in effect for the tax year (Code Sec. 1(j)(4)(C)(i)(II)) (i.e., for 2018, $2,600, see ¶ 1501); and

... the maximum 15% rate amount can't be more than the sum of (Code Sec. 1(j)(4)(C)(ii)): (i) the child's earned taxable income (Code Sec. 1(j)(4)(C)(ii)(I)), plus (ii) the maximum 15% rate amount for estates and trusts in effect for the tax year (Code Sec. 1(j)(4)(C)(ii)(II)) (i.e., for 2018, $12,700, see ¶ 1501).

> *observation:* That is, under rule (B) above:
>
> ... the maximum amount of capital gains taxed at a zero rate can't exceed the child's earned taxable income + (for 2018) $2,600; and
>
> ... the maximum amount of capital gains taxed at a 15% rate can't exceed the child's earned taxable income + (for 2018) $12,700.

> *observation:* Applying the estate and trust tax rates under the kiddie tax rules will produce a higher tax bill because, as described above, the income ranges under the estate and trust tax schedule are much smaller than those for individuals. For example, the top 37% income tax rate applies to married joint filers at $600,000 (see ¶ 101), but it applies to an estate or trust (and now also under the kiddie tax) at $12,500.

For purposes of the Tax Cuts and Jobs Act rules above, "earned taxable income" means, for any child for any year, the child's taxable income reduced (but not below zero) by the child's net unearned income (as defined in Code Sec. 1(g)(4) under the pre-Tax Cuts and Jobs Act kiddie tax rules above). (Code Sec. 1(j)(4)(D))

> **☯️** *observation:* The Tax Cuts and Jobs Act doesn't change the definition of a child subject to the kiddie tax for purposes of the above-described modified kiddie tax rules in effect for 2018−2025.

Sunset. The above-described changes to the kiddie tax rules don't apply for tax years beginning after Dec. 31, 2025. (Code Sec. 1(j)(1))

☐ **Effective:** For tax years beginning after Dec. 31, 2017 (Tax Cuts and Jobs Act §11001(c)) and before Jan. 1, 2026. (Code Sec. 1(j)(1))

¶ 200. Inflation Adjustments

¶ 201. Inflation adjustment of income tax brackets to be made based on chained CPI-U (C-CPI-U), instead of the CPI-U

Code Sec. 1(f)(3), as amended by Tax Cuts and Jobs Act §11002(a)
Code Sec. 1(f)(6), as amended by Tax Cuts and Jobs Act §11002(b)
Code Sec. 1(f)(2)(A), as amended by Tax Cuts and Jobs Act §11002(c)
Code Sec. 1(i)(1)(C), as amended by Tax Cuts and Jobs Act §11002(c)(2)(A)
Code Sec. 1(i)(3)(C), as amended by Tax Cuts and Jobs Act §11002(c)(2)(B)
Generally effective: Tax years beginning after 2017
Committee Reports, see ¶ 5002

The tax bracket amounts (income ranges) provided in the statutory income tax rate schedules are adjusted upwards annually to reflect inflation. IRS must, by Dec. 15 of each year, prescribe new income tax rate schedules for tax years beginning in the next calendar year, to apply in place of the (un-inflation-adjusted) statutory tax rate schedules provided in Code Sec. 1(a) (for marrieds filing jointly), Code Sec. 1(b) (heads of households), Code Sec. 1(c) (single filers), Code Sec. 1(d) (marrieds filing separately), and Code Sec. 1(e) (estates and trusts)—as modified by Code Sec. 1(i) (see ¶ 101 and ¶ 104). With certain exceptions, IRS must (as provided in Code Sec. 1(f)) adjust these statutory rate schedules by increasing the minimum and maximum dollar amounts for each bracket provided in the statutory rate schedules by a cost-of-living adjustment (COLA) for the calendar year provided under Code Sec. 1(f)(3).

Under pre-Tax Cuts and Jobs Act law, with certain exceptions, Code Sec. 1(f)(3) provided that the COLA for a calendar year was the percentage (if any) by which:

(1) the consumer price index (CPI) for the preceding calendar year, exceeded

(2) the CPI for calendar year '92 (the permanent base year).

FTC 2d References are to Federal Tax Coordinator 2d
FIN References are to RIA's Analysis of Federal Taxes: Income (print)
USTR References are to United States Tax Reporter
Catalyst References are to Checkpoint Catalyst
PCA References are to Pension Analysis (print and electronic)
PBE References are to Pension & Benefits Explanations
BCA References are to Benefits Analysis (electronic)
BC References are to Benefits Coordinator (print)
EP References are to Estate Planning Analysis (print and electronic)

Some special rules applied in computing inflation adjustment of the 10% (lowest) and 39.6% (highest) brackets, and to eliminate the "marriage penalty" effect under the 15% bracket.

Increases resulting from the COLAs above were rounded to the next lowest multiple of $50 ($25 for married individuals filing separate returns).

The CPI for a calendar year was defined as the average of the Consumer Price Index as of the 12-month period ending on Aug. 31. For this purpose, the "Consumer Price Index" was the last CPI for "all-urban consumers" published by the Department of Labor (DOL) (i.e., the "CPI-U"). The CPI revision that was most consistent with the CPI for calendar year '86 was used. (FTC 2d/FIN ¶ A-1100, ¶ A-1103, ¶ C-1000, ¶ C-1005, ¶ C-7000, ¶ C-7004)

New Law. The Tax Cuts and Jobs Act requires the use of chained CPI-U (i.e., "C-CPI-U"), instead of CPI-U, in indexing the income tax brackets for inflation (see ¶ 101 and ¶ 104). The C-CPI-U, like the CPI-U, is a measure of the average change over time in prices paid by urban consumers. But, the C-CPI-U differs from the CPI-U in that it accounts for the ability of individuals to alter their consumption patterns in response to relative price changes. (Com Rept, see ¶ 5002)

> *observation:* The C-CPI-U reflects people's ability to lessen the impact of inflation by buying fewer goods or services that have risen in price and buying more goods and services whose price have risen less, or not at all. Thus, C-CPI-U is a slower-growing method of calculating COLAs. Using a lower rate of inflation to calculate future tax brackets means taxpayers will more quickly slip into the next higher tax bracket (often called "bracket creep"), and so will pay more in taxes over time.

Specifically, the Tax Cuts and Jobs Act provides that for purposes of applying the Code Sec. 1(f) adjustments to the statutory tax rate tables (as described at ¶ 101) (Code Sec. 1(f)(3) as amended by Tax Cuts and Jobs Act §11002(a)), the COLA for any calendar year is the percentage (if any) by which (Code Sec. 1(f)(3)(A)):

(a) the C-CPI-U for the preceding calendar year, exceeds (Code Sec. 1(f)(3)(A)(i))

(b) the CPI for calendar year 2016, multiplied by an "amount determined" under Code Sec. 1(f)(3)(B) (see below). (Code Sec. 1(f)(3)(A)(ii))

The "amount determined" for rule (b) above is computed by dividing (Code Sec. 1(f)(3)(B))

(i) the C-CPI-U for calendar year 2016, by (Code Sec. 1(f)(3)(B)(i))

(ii) the CPI for calendar year 2016. (Code Sec. 1(f)(3)(B)(ii))

Thus, the Tax Cuts and Jobs Act changes above apply the inflation indexing under Code Sec. 1(f)(3) as if CPI-U applies through 2017, and C-CPI-U applies for years thereafter. (Com Rept, see ¶ 5002) But, see the special rule below for inflation adjustments for the tax parameters that were reset for 2018 by the Tax Cuts and Jobs Act.

> *observation:* Code Sec. 1(f)(3) doesn't provide any specific rule for rounding of COLA adjustment computed based on C-CPI-U. As discussed at ¶ 101, it appears that, for purposes of adjusting the tax brackets imposed under the Tax Cuts and Jobs Act for inflation (after 2018), that the rounding rules under Code Sec. 1(f)(7) apply, i.e., generally, that COLA increases to the minimum and maximum dollar amount for each rate bracket that isn't a multiple of $50—is rounded to the next lowest multiple of $50.

For purposes of the rules above (Code Sec. 1(f)(6) as amended by Tax Cuts and Jobs Act §11002(b)), "C-CPI-U" means the Chained Consumer Price Index for All Urban Consumers (as published by the Bureau of Labor Statistics of the DOL). The values of the C-CPI-U taken into account for purposes of determining the COLA for any calendar year under Code Sec. 1(f) are the latest values so published as of the date on which the Bureau of Labor Statistics publishes the initial value of the C-CPI-U for Aug. for the preceding calendar year. (Code Sec. 1(f)(6)(A))

The C-CPI-U for any calendar year is the average of the C-CPI-U as of the close of the 12-month period ending on Aug. 31 of that calendar year. (Code Sec. 1(f)(6)(B))

> *observation:* Many other tax parameters under the Code are indexed for inflation by reference to the above-described Code Sec. 1(f)(3) inflation adjustment rules. Often those provisions apply the Code Sec. 1(f)(3) inflation computation, but with an adjustment to the base year from which inflation is to be measured.
>
> See ¶ 202, for Tax Cuts and Jobs Act conforming changes to make above-described C-CPI-U inflation indexing applicable to various other tax parameters under the Code.

Special rule for inflation adjustment of tax brackets in effect for 2018-2025, inflation adjustments with base years after 2016. As discussed at ¶ 101 and ¶ 104, the Tax Cuts and Jobs Act temporarily replaces (for tax years 2018−2025) the individual and estate and trust income tax rate structure (under the Code Sec. 1(a)−Code Sec. 1(e) "the permanent tables," as modified by Code Sec. 1(i)) with a new rate structure (under Code Sec. 1(j)(2)). The Act changes the tax rates imposed, and resets the tax bracket amounts (income ranges). Those reset tax bracket amounts are first indexed for inflation for tax years after 2018, and, in computing that inflation adjustment, IRS must apply the rule of Code Sec. 1(f)(3)(A)(ii) above—by substituting "calendar year 2017" for "calendar year 2016" (see ¶ 101)

The Tax Cuts and Jobs Act provides, for purposes of any Code provision which provides for the substitution of a *year after 2016* for "2016" in Code Sec. 1(f)(3)(A)(ii), that Code Sec. 1(f)(3)(A) must be applied by substituting "the C-CPI-U for calendar year 2016" for "the CPI for calendar year 2016, multiplied by an amount determined under Code Sec. 1(f)(3)(B)." (Code Sec. 1(f)(3)(C))

> ⚫*observation:* Thus, under the special rule above, tax parameters reset by the Tax Cuts and Jobs Act for 2018 and first indexed for inflation after 2018 (such as the tax brackets at ¶ 101 and ¶ 104 and the increased standard deductions at ¶ 501), are indexed for inflation solely based on the C-CPI-U.

> ⚫*illustration:* So, for the income tax brackets that apply under the Tax Cuts and Jobs Act for 2018−2025 described at ¶ 101 and ¶ 104, the COLA for any calendar year after 2018 is the percentage (if any) by which:
>
> (a) the C-CPI-U for the preceding calendar year, exceeds
>
> (b) the C-CPI-U for calendar year 2016.

Application of C-CPI-U inflation indexing to Code's permanent tax tables. As discussed at ¶ 101 and ¶ 104, the Tax Cuts and Jobs Act's tax rate schedules (under Code Sec. 1(j)(2)) don't apply (i.e., sunset) for tax years after 2025, and the Code's "permanent tax tables" (under Code Sec. 1(a)−Code Sec. 1(e), and the modifications to those tables under Code Sec. 1(i)) are once again in effect.

The Tax Cuts and Jobs Act provides that in prescribing the COLA adjusted tax tables to be used in lieu of the Code Sec. 1(a)−Code Sec. 1(e) statutory tables, IRS must:

. . . except as otherwise provided under Code Sec. 1(f)(8) (special rule to eliminate marriage penalty in the 15% bracket), increase the minimum and maximum dollar amount for each rate bracket for which tax is imposed under the table, by a COLA for the calendar year, determined by substituting "1992" for "2016" in Code Sec. 1(f)(3)(A)(ii) above; and

. . . in the case of adjustments to the dollar amounts at which the 36% bracket or at which the 39.6% bracket begins, by substituting "1993" for "2016" in Code Sec. 1(f)(3)(A)(ii) above. (Code Sec. 1(f)(2)(A) as amended by Tax Cuts and Jobs Act §S11002(c)(1))

In addition, the Tax Cuts and Jobs Act makes conforming changes to the Code Sec. 1(i) provisions (which modify the brackets and rates provided in Code Sec. 1(a)–Code Sec. 1(e)) to provide that:

. . . the Code Sec. 1(i), 10% maximum bracket amounts be adjusted for inflation under Code Sec. 1(f)(3) by substituting "2002" for "2016" in Code Sec. 1(f)(3)(A)(ii) above (Code Sec. 1(i)(1)(C) as amended by Tax Cuts and Jobs Act §11002(c)(2)(A)); and

. . . the Code Sec. 1(i), 39.6% minimum bracket (threshold) amounts be adjusted for inflation under Code Sec. 1(f)(3) by substituting "2012" for "2016" in Code Sec. 1(f)(3)(A)(ii) above. (Code Sec. 1(i)(3)(C) as amended by Tax Cuts and Jobs Act §11002(c)(2)(B))

> *observation:* Thus, the C-CPI-U inflation indexing also applies to the tax rate brackets that will be in effect after the Tax Cuts and Jobs Act tax brackets expire (sunset) after 2025, but inflation will be measured for purposes of those brackets based on earlier base years, as described above.

☐ **Effective:** For tax years beginning after Dec. 31, 2017. (Tax Cuts and Jobs Act §11002(c))

¶ 202. Chained CPI-U (C-CPI-U) replaces CPI-U in inflation adjustments of various tax parameters under the Code

Various tax parameters under the Code are adjusted for inflation to protect taxpayers from the effects of rising prices. Most of these adjustments are based on annual changes in the level of the Consumer Price Index for all Urban Consumers ("CPI-U'). In many cases, the inflation computations are based on the Code Sec. 1(f)(3) inflation adjustment (cost-of-living adjustment (COLA)) rules for the regular income tax brackets, but with an adjustment to the base year from which inflation should be measured.

Under pre-Tax Cuts and Jobs Act law, the Code Sec. 1(f)(3) inflation adjustment computation was based on annual changes in the level of the Consumer Price Index for all Urban Consumers (i.e., the "CPI-U"), an index that measures prices paid by typical urban consumers on a broad range of products, developed and published by the Department of Labor (DOL). But, as described at ¶ 201, effective for tax years beginning after 2017, the Tax Cuts and Jobs Act modifies the Code Sec. 1(f)(3) inflation adjustment computation rules to require use of chained CPI-U (i.e., "C-CPI-U"), instead of CPI-U, to index the income tax brackets for inflation. The C-CPI-U, like the CPI-U, is a measure of the average change over time in prices paid by urban consumers. But, the C-CPI-U differs from the CPI-U in that it accounts for the ability of individuals to alter their consumption patterns in response to relative price changes. (Com Rept, see ¶ 5002)

New Law. The Tax Cuts and Jobs Act requires the use of the C-CPI-U to index the tax parameters under the Code that are currently indexed by the CPI-U. (Com Rept, see ¶ 5002)

The following provisions are modified (conformed) to require inflation adjustments be based on the C-CPI-U, instead of the CPI-U:

• Adoption credit dollar amounts (see FTC 2d/FIN ¶ A-4400, ¶ A-4417; USTR ¶ 234). (Code Sec. 23(h)(2) as amended by Tax Cuts and Jobs Act §11002(d)(1)(A))

• Lifetime learning credit phase-out (see FTC 2d/FIN ¶ A-4500, ¶ A-4517.1; USTR ¶ 25A4.02) (Code Sec. 25A(h)(2)(A)(ii) as amended by Tax Cuts and Jobs Act §11002(d)(1)(B)), and former Hope credit dollar limitations and phase-out (see FTC 2d/FIN ¶ A-4501; USTR ¶ 25A4). (Code Sec. 25A(h)(1)(A)(ii) as amended by Tax Cuts and Jobs Act §11002(d)(1)(B); Code Sec. 25A(h)(2)(A)(ii) as amended by Tax Cuts and Jobs Act §11002(d)(1)(B))

• Saver's credit adjusted gross income (AGI) limits (see FTC 2d/FIN ¶ A-4450, ¶ A-4451.1; USTR ¶ 25B4). (Code Sec. 25B(b)(3)(B) as amended by Tax Cuts and Jobs Act §11002(d)(1)(C)) (Also see ¶ 1602, for Tax Cuts and Jobs Act changes to the saver's credit for 2018−2025.)

• Earned income credit (EIC) earned income, phase-out, and disqualified income dollar amounts (see FTC 2d/FIN ¶ A-4200, ¶ A-4226; USTR ¶ 324.01). (Code Sec. 32(b)(2)(B)(ii)(II) as amended by Tax Cuts and Jobs Act §11002(d)(1)(D); Code Sec. 32(j)(1)(B)(i) as amended by Tax Cuts and Jobs Act §11002(d)(1)(D); Code Sec. 32(j)(1)(B)(ii) as amended by Tax Cuts and Jobs Act §11002(d)(1)(D))

• Repayment cap on excess advance payments of the premium tax credit (PTC) (see FTC 2d/FIN ¶ A-4240, ¶ A-4248.1; USTR ¶ 36B4.06). (Code Sec. 36B(f)(2)(B)(ii)(II) as amended by Tax Cuts and Jobs Act §11002(d)(1)(E))

• Credit for basic research expenses, determination of "maintenance-of-effort amount" (see FTC 2d/FIN ¶ L-15500, ¶ L-15511; USTR ¶ 414.02). (Code Sec. 41(e)(5)(C)(i) as amended by Tax Cuts and Jobs Act §11002(d)(1)(F); Code Sec. 41(e)(5)(C)(ii) as amended by Tax Cuts and Jobs Act §11002(d)(2))

• Low-income housing credit qualified contract rule, adjusted investor equity, qualified-contract COLA (see FTC 2d/FIN ¶ L-15700, ¶ L-15722). (Code Sec. 42(h)(6)(G)(i)(II) as amended by Tax Cuts and Jobs Act §11002(d)(3)(A); Code Sec. 42(h)(6)(G)(ii) as amended by Tax Cuts and Jobs Act §11002(d)(3)(B))

• Low-income housing credit rehabilitation expenditures (see FTC 2d/FIN ¶ L-15700, ¶ L-15727; USTR ¶ 424.50) and population component of state housing credit ceiling amount (see FTC 2d/FIN ¶ L-16000, ¶ L-16006.2; USTR ¶ 424.76). (Code Sec. 42(e)(3)(D)(ii) as amended by Tax Cuts and Jobs Act §11002(d)(1)(G); Code Sec. 42(h)(3)(H)(i)(II) as amended by Tax Cuts and Jobs Act §11002(d)(1)(G))

• Small employer health insurance credit, average annual wages for dollar limitation for eligible small employers and credit phase-out (see FTC 2d/FIN ¶ L-15680, ¶ L-15689.2; USTR ¶ 45R4.02). (Code Sec. 45R(d)(3)(B)(ii) as amended by Tax Cuts and Jobs Act §11002(d)(1)(H))

• Alternative minimum tax (AMT) for noncorporate taxpayers (individuals, estates and trusts), statutory dollar amounts in tentative minimum tax calculation, AMT exemption amounts, and exemption phase-out thresholds (see FTC 2d/FIN ¶ A-8100, ¶ A-8101, ¶ A-8162, ¶ A-8164; USTR ¶ 554, ¶ 554.01). (Code Sec. 55(d)(4)(A)(ii) as amended by Tax Cuts and Jobs Act §11002(d)(1)(I); (Code Sec. 55(d)(3)(A)(ii) as redesignated by Tax Cuts and Jobs Act §12001(b)(5)(A))) (Also see ¶ 301, for Tax Cuts and Jobs Act changes to the AMT for noncorporate taxpayers for 2018−2025.)

• AMT exemption amount for child subject to the "kiddie tax" (see FTC 2d/FIN ¶ A-8160, ¶ A-8163; USTR ¶ 594). (Code Sec. 59(j)(2)(B) as amended by Tax Cuts and Jobs Act §11002(d)(4)) (Also see ¶ 105, for Tax Cuts and Jobs Act changes to the kiddie tax rules for 2018−2025.)

• Educator's classroom expense deduction dollar amount (see FTC 2d/FIN ¶ A-2600, ¶ A-2611.2; USTR ¶ 624.02). (Code Sec. 62(d)(3)(B) as amended by Tax Cuts and Jobs Act §11002(d)(1)(J))

• Standard deduction (see FTC 2d/FIN ¶ A-2800, ¶ A-2809; USTR ¶ 634). (Code Sec. 63(c)(4)(B) as amended by Tax Cuts and Jobs Act §11002(d)(1)(K)) (Also see ¶ 501, for Tax Cuts and Jobs Act changes to the standard deduction for 2018−2025.)

• Overall limitation on itemized deductions, AGI phase-out amounts (see FTC 2d/FIN ¶ A-2730, ¶ A-2731; USTR ¶ 684). (Code Sec. 68(b)(2)(B) as amended by Tax Cuts and Jobs Act §11002(d)(2)) (Also see ¶ 504, for Tax Cuts and Jobs Act suspension of the overall limitation on itemized deductions for 2018−2025.)

• Health flexible spending arrangement (health FSA) salary reduction contributions under cafeteria plan, annual limit (see FTC 2d/FIN ¶ H-2400, ¶ H-2461.3; USTR ¶ 1254.05). (Code Sec. 125(i)(2)(B) as amended by Tax Cuts and Jobs Act §11002(d)(1)(L))

• Qualified transportation fringe exclusion, dollar limitations (see FTC 2d/FIN ¶ H-2200, ¶ H-2217.1; USTR ¶ 1324.08). (Code Sec. 132(f)(6)(A)(ii) as amended by Tax Cuts and Jobs Act §11002(d)(5))

• Qualified savings bond interest exclusion phase-out (see FTC 2d/FIN ¶ J-3050, ¶ J-3053; USTR ¶ 1254.05). (Code Sec. 135(b)(2)(B)(ii) as amended by Tax Cuts and Jobs Act §11002(d)(1)(M))

• Adoption assistance exclusion dollar amounts and phaseout (see FTC 2d/FIN ¶ H-1450, ¶ J-1451, ¶ H-1453, ¶ H-1464; USTR ¶ 1374). (Code Sec. 137(f)(2) as amended by Tax Cuts and Jobs Act §11002(d)(1)(N))

• State ceiling for volume caps on qualified bonds, per resident and maximum limits (see FTC 2d/FIN ¶ J-3150, ¶ J-3155; USTR ¶ 1464.01). (Code Sec. 146(d)(2)(B) as amended by Tax Cuts and Jobs Act §11002(d)(1)(O))

• Qualified bond land acquisition limitations, first-time farmer exception (see FTC 2d/FIN ¶ J-3150, ¶ J-3186; USTR ¶ 1474.01). (Code Sec. 147(c)(2)(H)(ii) as amended by Tax Cuts and Jobs Act §11002(d)(1)(P))

• Personal exemption deduction amount (see FTC 2d/FIN ¶ J-3500, ¶ J-3506; USTR ¶ 1514). (Code Sec. 151(d)(4)(B) as amended by Tax Cuts and Jobs Act §11002(d)(1)(Q)) (Also see ¶ 502, for Tax Cuts and Jobs Act suspension of the deduction for personal exemptions for 2018−2025.)

• Rural mail carriers exclusion for qualified reimbursements (see FTC 2d/FIN ¶ L-1900, ¶ L-1911; USTR ¶ 1624.157). (Code Sec. 162(o)(3) as amended by Tax Cuts and Jobs Act §11002(d)(6))

• Code Sec. 179 expensing dollar limit and phase-out (see FTC 2d/FIN ¶ L-9900, ¶ L-9907.1; USTR ¶ 1794.01). (Code Sec. 179(b)(6)(A)(ii) as amended by Tax Cuts and Jobs Act §11002(d)(1)(R)) (Also see ¶ 1101, for other Tax Cuts and Jobs Act changes to the Code Sec. 179 expensing rules.)

• Medical expenses deduction for qualified long-term care insurance premiums, age-defined dollar amounts (see FTC 2d/FIN ¶ K-2100, ¶ K-2141.1; USTR ¶ 2134.075). (Code Sec. 213(d)(10)(B) as amended by Tax Cuts and Jobs Act §11002(d)(7)) (Also see ¶ 505, for Tax Cuts and Jobs Act changes to medical expense deduction.)

• Individual retirement account (IRA) deductible contribution limit (see FTC 2d/FIN ¶ H-12200, ¶ H-12215, ¶ H-12290.7; USTR ¶ 2194.01, and reduced limit for nonparticipant spouse of active participant (see FTC 2d/FIN ¶ H-12217, ¶ H-12217.2; USTR ¶ 2194.02) (Code Sec. 219(b)(5)(C)(i)(II) as amended by Tax Cuts and Jobs Act §11002(d)(1)(S); Code Sec. 219(g)(8)(B) as amended by Tax Cuts and Jobs Act §11002(d)(1)(S)

• Archer medical savings account (Archer MSA) annual deductible and out-of-pocket expense amounts (see FTC 2d/FIN ¶ H-1326, ¶ H-1332.1; USTR ¶ 2204.01). (Code Sec. 220(g)(2) as amended by Tax Cuts and Jobs Act §11002(d)(1)(T))

• Student loan interest deduction phaseout (see FTC 2d/FIN ¶ K-5500, ¶ K-5502; USTR ¶ 2214.01). (Code Sec. 221(f)(1)(B) as amended by Tax Cuts and Jobs Act §11002(d)(1)(U))

• Health savings account (HSA) dollar limits for high deductible health plans, and monthly deductible contribution limits (see FTC 2d/FIN ¶ H-1350, ¶ H-1350.14; USTR ¶ 2234.03). (Code Sec. 223(g)(1)(B) as amended by Tax Cuts and Jobs Act §11002(d)(1)(V))

• Limitation on depreciation for luxury automobiles, automobile price inflation adjustment (see FTC 2d/FIN ¶ L-10000, ¶ L-10004; USTR ¶ 280F4). (Code Sec. 280F(d)(7)(B) as amended by Tax Cuts and Jobs Act §11002(d)(8)) (Also see ¶ 1307, for Tax Cuts and Jobs Act changes to annual cap on depreciation of automobiles.)

• Roth IRA dollar amounts for AGI limits (see FTC 2d/FIN ¶ H-12290, ¶ H-12290.10; USTR ¶ 408A4). (Code Sec. 408A(c)(3)(D)(ii) as amended by Tax Cuts and Jobs Act §11002(d)(1)(W))

• Installment acceleration amounts for 2008-2011 amortization elections by defined benefit plan sponsors, excess employee compensation (see FTC 2d/FIN ¶ H-7750, ¶ H-7751.2H; USTR ¶ 4304.03). (Code Sec. 430(c)(7)(D)(vii)(II) as amended by Tax Cuts and Jobs Act §11002(d)(1)(X))

• Agricultural and horticultural organization dues exempted from unrelated business income tax (UBIT) (see FTC 2d/FIN ¶ D-6800, ¶ D-6847; USTR ¶ 5124). (Code Sec. 512(d)(2)(B) as amended by Tax Cuts and Jobs Act §11002(d)(1)(Y))

• Low-cost articles exempted from unrelated business income tax (UBIT) (see FTC 2d/FIN ¶ D-6800, ¶ D-6845). (Code Sec. 513(h)(2)(C)(ii) as amended by Tax Cuts and Jobs Act §11002(d)(1)(Z))

• Limit on nonlife insurance companies permitted to elect to be taxed only on taxable investment income (see FTC 2d/FIN ¶ E-5500, ¶ E-5503; USTR ¶ 8314). (Code Sec. 831(b)(2)(D)(ii) as amended by Tax Cuts and Jobs Act §11002(d)(1)(AA))

• Exclusion of gain upon expatriation (see FTC 2d/FIN ¶ O-11650, ¶ O-11652; USTR ¶ 877A4). (Code Sec. 877A(a)(3)(B)(i)(II) as amended by Tax Cuts and Jobs Act §11002(d)(1)(BB))

• Foreign earned income exclusion, exclusion amount (see FTC 2d/FIN ¶ O-1100, ¶ O-1102; USTR ¶ 9114.12). (Code Sec. 911(b)(2)(D)(ii)(II) as amended by Tax Cuts and Jobs Act §11002(d)(9))

• Debt instruments issued for property in seller-financed transactions, cash method election, debt's stated principal amount (see FTC 2d/FIN ¶ J-4100, ¶ J-4163; USTR ¶ 12,714.03). (Code Sec. 1274A(d)(2) as amended by Tax Cuts and Jobs Act §11002(d)(10))

• Applicable exclusion amount for unified credit against estate tax (see FTC 2d ¶ R-7100, ¶ R-7101; USTR Estate & Gift Taxes ¶ 20,104). (Code Sec. 2010(c)(3)(B)(ii) as amended by Tax Cuts and Jobs Act §11002(d)(1)(CC)) (Also see ¶ 2801, for Tax Cuts and Jobs Act changes to the estate and gift tax exemption for 2018−2025.)

• Special use valuation, limitation on decrease in value of qualified real property (see FTC 2d ¶ R-5200, ¶ R-5204; USTR Estate & Gift Taxes ¶ 20,32A4). (Code Sec. 2032A(a)(3)(B) as amended by Tax Cuts and Jobs Act §11002(d)(1)(DD))

• Gift tax annual exclusion (see FTC 2d ¶ Q-5000, ¶ Q-5002; USTR Estate & Gift Taxes ¶ 25,034). (Code Sec. 2503(b)(2)(B) as amended by Tax Cuts and Jobs Act §11002(d)(1)(EE))

• Manufacturers excise tax rate on arrow shafts (see FTC 2d ¶ W-2750, ¶ W-2752; USTR Excise Taxes ¶ 41,614). (Code Sec. 4161(b)(2)(C)(i)(II) as amended by Tax Cuts and Jobs Act §11002(d)(11))

• Air transportation of persons excise tax, domestic segment and international departure dollar amounts (see FTC 2d ¶ W-5100, ¶ W-5101, ¶ W-5103; USTR Excise Taxes ¶ 42,614.01). (Code Sec. 4261(e)(4)(A)(ii) as amended by Tax Cuts and Jobs Act §11002(d)(1)(FF))

• Post-2019 excise tax on high-cost employer-sponsored health coverage, annual limit (see FTC 2d/FIN ¶ H-1225, ¶ H-1231; USTR ¶ 49,80I4). (Code Sec. 4980I(b)(3)(C)(v)(II) as amended by Tax Cuts and Jobs Act §11002(d)(12))

• Failure to maintain health insurance coverage penalty (the "individual mandate"), applicable dollar amounts (see FTC 2d/FIN ¶ V-3900, ¶ V-3907; USTR ¶ 50,00A4.2). (Code Sec. 5000A(c)(3)(D)(ii) as amended by Tax Cuts and Jobs Act §11002(d)(1)(GG)) (For the Tax Cuts and Jobs Act repeal of the individual mandate after 2018, see ¶ 401.)

• Reporting threshold for gifts from foreign persons (see FTC 2d/FIN ¶ S-3584.1, ¶ S-3649.5; USTR ¶ 60,39F4). (Code Sec. 6039F(d) as amended by Tax Cuts and Jobs Act §11002(d)(13))

• Protection of purchaser in casual sale against filed tax lien, sale price limit, and priority against tax liens for small mechanics liens on residential property (see FTC 2d/FIN ¶ V-6400, ¶ V-6440, ¶ V-6445; USTR ¶ 63,234.16). (Code Sec. 6323(i)(4)(B) as amended by Tax Cuts and Jobs Act §11002(d)(1)(HH))

• Exemption from IRS levy for fuel, provisions, furniture, etc., and exemption from IRS levy for books and tool's of taxpayer's trade, etc., dollar limitations (see FTC 2d/FIN ¶ V-5200, ¶ V-5232, ¶ V-5233; USTR ¶ 63,314.05). (Code Sec. 6334(g)(1)(B) as amended by Tax Cuts and Jobs Act §11002(d)(1)(II))

• Rate of interest on estate tax deferred under Code Sec. 6166, taxable value (see FTC 2d/FIN ¶ S-6000, ¶ S-6009; USTR ¶ 66,014). (Code Sec. 6601(j)(3)(B) as amended by Tax Cuts and Jobs Act §11002(d)(1)(JJ))

• Minimum failure to pay penalty on income tax returns filed more than 60 days late (see FTC 2d/FIN ¶ V-1750, ¶ V-1752; USTR ¶ 66,514.01). (Code Sec. 6651(i)(1) as amended by Tax Cuts and Jobs Act §11002(d)(1)(KK))

• Penalties for exempt organizations' failure to file certain information returns, registration requirement, etc., or make certain disclosures (see FTC 2d/FIN ¶ V-2530, ¶ V-2538, ¶ V-2700, ¶ V-2716, ¶ V-2717, ¶ V-2718, ¶ V-2719; USTR ¶ 66,524). (Code Sec. 6652(c)(7)(A) as amended by Tax Cuts and Jobs Act §11002(d)(1)(LL))

• Penalty on return preparer for negotiating a client's tax check (see FTC 2d/FIN ¶ V-2630, ¶ V-2671; USTR ¶ 66,954). (Code Sec. 6695(h)(1) as amended by Tax Cuts and Jobs Act §11002(d)(1)(MM))

• Penalty for failure to file complete partnership return on time (see FTC 2d/FIN ¶ V-1750, ¶ V-1762; USTR ¶ 66,984). (Code Sec. 6698(e)(1) as amended by Tax Cuts and Jobs Act §11002(d)(1)(NN))

• Penalty for failure to file complete S corporation return on time (see FTC 2d/FIN ¶ V-1750, ¶ V-1763.2; USTR ¶ 66,994). (Code Sec. 6699(e)(1) as amended by Tax Cuts and Jobs Act §11002(d)(1)(OO))

• Penalty for failure to file correct information returns (see FTC 2d/FIN ¶ V-1800, ¶ V-1805, ¶ V-1811; USTR ¶ 67,214). (Code Sec. 6721(f)(1) as amended by Tax Cuts and Jobs Act §11002(d)(1)(PP))

• Penalty for failure to furnish correct payee statements (see FTC 2d/FIN ¶ V-1800, ¶ V-1816, ¶ V-1818; USTR ¶ 67,224). (Code Sec. 6722(f)(1) as amended by Tax Cuts and Jobs Act §11002(d)(1)(QQ))

• Revocation of passport for taxpayer with seriously delinquent tax debt, debt amount (see FTC 2d/FIN ¶ V-3500, ¶ V-3507; USTR ¶ 73,454). (Code Sec. 7345(f)(2) as amended by Tax Cuts and Jobs Act §11002(d)(1)(RR))

• Limitations on maximum hourly rate awardable as attorney's fees (see FTC 2d/FIN ¶ U-1267, ¶ U-1268; USTR ¶ 74,304.01). (Code Sec. 7430(c)(1) as amended by Tax Cuts and Jobs Act §11002(d)(1)(SS))

• Dollar loan limitation for exception to below market interest rate rules for certain qualified continuing care facilities—before 2006 (see FTC 2d/FIN ¶ J-2900, ¶ J-2989; USTR ¶ 78,724.201). (Code Sec. 7872(g)(5) as amended by Tax Cuts and Jobs Act §11002(d)(14))

• Qualified small employer health saving arrangements (HRAs), maximum dollar limitations (see FTC 2d/FIN ¶ H-1349, ¶ H-1349.20; USTR ¶ 98,314). (Code Sec. 9831(d)(2)(D)(ii)(II) as amended by Tax Cuts and Jobs Act §11002(d)(1)(TT))

☐ **Effective:** For tax years beginning after Dec. 31, 2017. (Tax Cuts and Jobs Act §11002(e))

¶ 300. Alternative Minimum Tax

¶ 301. Alternative minimum tax exemption amounts for individuals increased

Code Sec. 55(d)(4), as amended by Tax Cuts and Jobs Act §12003(a)
Code Sec. 55(d)(4)(A)(ii), as amended by Tax Cuts and Jobs Act §11002(d)(1)(I)
Generally effective: Tax years beginning after 2017 and before 2026
Committee Reports, see ¶ 5029

In addition to income tax imposed under subtitle A of the Code, taxpayers are subject to a second tax system—the alternative minimum tax (AMT). The taxpayer's *total* tax liability for the year equals the sum of (i) the taxpayer's regular tax liability, plus (ii) the taxpayer's AMT liability for the year. The AMT is intended to reduce a taxpayer's ability to avoid taxes by using certain deductions and other tax benefit items. For the Tax Cuts and Jobs Act repeal of the AMT on corporations, see ¶ 303.

The AMT equals the amount by which the taxpayer's "tentative minimum tax" exceeds the taxpayer's regular income tax for the tax year. To compute a taxpayer's tentative minimum tax, the taxpayer's "alternative minimum taxable income" (AMTI) must be determined.

AMTI is computed by adding or subtracting AMT adjustments and adding AMT preferences to the taxpayer's regular taxable income for the tax year. (See FTC 2d/FIN ¶ A-8101; USTR ¶ 554.01.) AMT adjustments or preference items fall into one of two categories—deferral items (items that affect more than one tax year, and cause a timing difference between regular tax and AMT), or exclusion items (items that affect one tax year and are taken away entirely for AMT purposes). (See FTC 2d/FIN ¶s A-8191 *et seq.*, A-8201 *et seq.*, A-8301 *et seq.*; USTR ¶s 564 *et seq.*, 574, 584).

Next, the AMT exemption amount (a statutory amount, adjusted annually for inflation) is subtracted from the taxpayer's AMTI. The result is the "taxable excess." But, the exemption amounts are phased out by an amount equal to 25% of the amount by which the individual's AMTI exceeded certain levels (statutory amounts also adjusted annually for inflation).

FTC 2d References are to Federal Tax Coordinator 2d
FIN References are to RIA's Analysis of Federal Taxes: Income (print)
USTR References are to United States Tax Reporter
Catalyst References are to Checkpoint Catalyst
PCA References are to Pension Analysis (print and electronic)
PBE References are to Pension & Benefits Explanations
BCA References are to Benefits Analysis (electronic)
BC References are to Benefits Coordinator (print)
EP References are to Estate Planning Analysis (print and electronic)

Additionally, marrieds filing separately had to add the lesser of the following amounts to their AMTI: (a) 25% of AMTI (determined without regard to this adjustment) over the minimum amount of income at which the exemption is completely phased out, or (b) the exemption amount.

A noncorporate taxpayer's (i.e., an individual's, estate's, or trust's) tentative minimum tax will equal:

(1) the sum of:

. . . 26% of the taxable excess that doesn't exceed a $175,000 statutory amount, adjusted for inflation (for 2017, $187,800; $93,900 for married filing separately), plus

. . . 28% of the taxable excess over the statutory amount as adjusted for inflation (i.e., for 2017, $187,800; $93,900 for married filing separately), minus

(2) the taxpayer's AMT foreign tax credit, if any, for the tax year. (See (FTC 2d/FIN ¶ A-8101 *et seq.*; USTR ¶ 554.01).)

Under pre-Tax Cuts and Jobs Act law, the above-described exemption amounts were:

(a) $78,750 for marrieds filing jointly/surviving spouses ($84,500 for 2017, as adjusted for inflation);

(b) $50,600 for other unmarried individuals ($54,300 for 2017, as adjusted for inflation);

(c) 50% of the marrieds-filing-jointly amount for marrieds filing separately, i.e., $39,375 ($42,250 for 2017, as adjusted for inflation); and

(d) $22,500 for estates and trusts ($24,100 for 2017, as adjusted for inflation).

And, those exemption amounts were reduced (phased out) by an amount equal to 25% of the amount by which the individual's AMTI exceeded:

(i) $150,000 for marrieds filing jointly and surviving spouses ($160,900 for 2017, as adjusted for inflation, completely phased out at AMTI of $498,900);

(ii) $112,500 for unmarried individuals ($120,700 for 2017, as adjusted for inflation; completely phased out at AMTI of $337,900); and

(iii) 50% of the marrieds-filing-jointly amount for marrieds filing separately, or an estate or trust, i.e., $75,000 ($80,450 for 2017, as adjusted for inflation; completely phased out at AMTI of $249,450). (FTC 2d/FIN ¶ A-8160, ¶ A-8162, ¶ A-8163, ¶ A-8164; USTR ¶ 554.01; Catalyst ¶ 142:102; Catalyst ¶ 502:163)

New Law. For tax years beginning after Dec. 31, 2017 and before Jan. 1, 2026, the Tax Cuts and Jobs Act (Code Sec. 55(d)(4)(A) as amended by Tax Cuts and Jobs Act §12003(a)) temporarily increases (Com Rept, see ¶ 5029) the statutory AMT exemption amounts (Code Sec. 55(d)(4)(A)(i)):

(A) for marrieds filing jointly/surviving spouses—to $109,400 (from $78,750); and (Code Sec. 55(d)(4)(A)(i)(I))

(B) for other unmarrieds—to $70,300 (from $50,600). (Code Sec. 55(d)(4)(A)(i)(II))

> **observation:** Because the Code sets the AMT exemption amount for marrieds filing separately at 50% of the marrieds-filing-jointly amount, the changes above also increase the statutory AMT exemption amount for marrieds filing separately—to $54,700 (from $39,375).
>
> The Tax Cuts and Jobs Act doesn't increase the statutory ($22,500) AMT exemption amount for estates and trusts.

Also, for tax years beginning after Dec. 31, 2017 and before Jan. 1, 2026, the Tax Cuts and Jobs Act (Code Sec. 55(d)(4)(A)) temporarily increases (Com Rept, see ¶ 5029) the statutory AMTI threshold amounts for phase-out of the exemption amounts (Code Sec. 55(d)(4)(A)(ii)):

(I) for marrieds filing jointly/surviving spouses—to $1,000,000 (from $150,000) (Code Sec. 55(d)(4)(A)(ii)(I)); and

(II) for other unmarrieds (Code Sec. 55(d)(4)(A)(ii)(II)) (but, not for estates or trusts) (Code Sec. 55(d)(4)(A)(ii)(III))—to 50% of the amount in (I) above, i.e., $500,000 (from $112,500). (Code Sec. 55(d)(4)(A)(ii)(II))

> **observation:** Because the Code sets the AMTI exemption phase-out threshold amount for marrieds filing separately at 50% of the marrieds-filing-jointly amount, the changes above also increase the statutory AMTI exemption phase-out threshold amount for marrieds filing separately—to $500,000 (from $75,000).
>
> And, because the provision specifically doesn't increase the statutory AMTI exemption phase-out threshold amount for estates and trusts, that amount remains $75,000 (adjusted annually for inflation, see below).

For tax years after 2018 (Code Sec. 55(d)(4)(B)(i)), the above-described $109,400 and $70,300 statutory AMT exemption amounts, and $1,000,000 statutory AMTI exemption phase-out threshold amount (Code Sec. 55(d)(4)(B)(ii))) will each be increased by an amount equal to (Code Sec. 55(d)(4)(B)(i)):

(i) that dollar amount × (Code Sec. 55(d)(4)(B)(i)(I))

(ii) the cost-of living adjustment (COLA) under Code Sec. 1(f)(3) (the inflation adjustment for the income tax rate schedules modified under the Tax Cuts And Jobs Act, see ¶ 201) for the calendar year in which the tax year begins, but determined by substituting "calendar year 2017" for "calendar year 2016" in Code Sec. 1(f)(3)(A)(ii). (Code Sec. 55(d)(4)(B)(i)(II))

Any increased amount determined under these rules will be rounded to the nearest multiple of $100. (Code Sec. 55(d)(4)(B)(iii))

For any tax year to which the above-described Tax Cuts and Jobs Act increased AMT exemption and AMTI phase-out amounts apply (i.e., 2018−2025), no adjustment is made to any of those increased dollar amounts under Code Sec. 55(d)(3) (as redesignated by Tax Cuts and Jobs Act §12001(b)(5)(A) (the inflation adjustment rules that apply to the statutory amounts in effect after the increased Tax Cuts and Jobs Act statutory exemption and phase-out amounts expire [sunset]). (Code Sec. 55(d)(4)(B)(iv))

observation: Thus, the increased AMT exemption amounts, and AMTI exemption phase-out threshold amounts for marrieds filing jointly and other unmarrieds described above, are the amounts that will apply in 2018. But for later tax years, those amounts will be adjusted for inflation under the rules of Code Sec. 1(f)(3) (as modified, as described above).

observation: So, for 2018, the AMT exemption amounts for individuals will be:

. . . $109,400 for marrieds filing jointly/surviving spouses;

. . . $70,300 for other unmarrieds; and

. . . $54,700 for marrieds filing separately.

And, for 2018, the AMTI exemption phase-out threshold amounts for individuals will be:

. . . $1,000,000 for marrieds filing jointly/surviving spouses; and

. . . $500,000 for all other taxpayers (other than estates and trusts)

observation: So, under the AMTI exemption phase-out rule, for 2018—the AMT exemptions for individuals will completely phase out at AMTI of:

. . . $1,437,600 for marrieds filing jointly/surviving spouses (i.e., $1,000,000 + $437,600 [4 × $109,400]);

. . . $781,200 for other unmarrieds (i.e., $500,000 + $281,200 [4 × $70,300]); and

. . . $718,800 for marrieds filing separately (i.e., $500,000 + $218,800 [4 × $54,700]).

observation: The increased AMT exemption amounts (and higher income levels for phase-out of the exemptions) mean that fewer people will be subject to the AMT in 2018−2025.

observation: However, in prior years, many taxpayers ended up subject to the AMT because of multiple personal exemptions and/or large itemized deductions for state and local taxes (preference items excluded in computing AMTI). For these taxpayers, the increased exemption and exemption phase-out amounts for 2018−2025 aren't needed to provide relief from AMT liability, as the Tax Cuts and Jobs Act's suspension of personal exemptions (see ¶ 502), and limitation on itemized deduction for state and local taxes to $10,000 (see ¶ 506) for those same tax years—already assured that these taxpayers wouldn't be subject to the AMT.

Another provision of the Tax Cuts and Jobs Act modifies the inflation adjustment rules for the statutory AMT exemption and AMTI exemption phase-out threshold amounts for estates and trusts, and for individuals, as in effect after 2025 when the Tax Cuts and Jobs Act increased amounts expire (sunset). Specifically, for tax years beginning after 2017, these statutory amounts are increased by an amount equal to:

(a) the specific statutory dollar amount ×

(b) the COLA under Code Sec. 1(f)(3) (see ¶ 201) for the calendar year in which the tax year begins, but determined by substituting "calendar year 2011" for "calendar year 2016" in Code Sec. 1(f)(3)(A)(ii). (Code Sec. 55(d)(4)(A)(ii) as amended by Tax Cuts and Jobs Act §11002(d)(1)(I); Code Sec. 55(d)(3)(A)(ii) as redesignated by Tax Cuts and Jobs Act §12001(b)(5)(A))

observation: So, the Code Sec. 1(f)(3) inflation adjustment rules described at ¶ 201 (as modified, as described above) will apply to the statutory exemption and AMTI exemption phase-out threshold amounts for estates and trusts for 2018 and later years.

And, after 2025, when the above-described increased AMT exemption and AMTI exemption threshold phase-out amounts for individuals expire, and the pre-Tax Cuts and Jobs Act statutory amounts are once again in effect, those amounts will also be adjusted for inflation under the Code Sec. 1(f)(3) inflation adjustment rules described at ¶ 201 (as modified, as described above).

observation: So, for estates and trusts for 2018:

. . . the AMT exemption amount will be $22,500 (adjusted for inflation as described above); and

. . . the AMTI exemption phase-out threshold amount will be $75,000 (adjusted for inflation as described above).

Sunset. The above-described increased AMT exemption and AMTI exemption phase-out threshold amounts for individuals, and the inflation adjustment of those increased amounts, won't apply for tax years beginning after Dec. 31, 2025. (Code Sec. 55(d)(4)(A))

☐ **Effective:** Except as otherwise provided below, for tax years beginning after Dec. 31, 2017 (Tax Cuts and Jobs Act §12003(b)) and before Jan. 1, 2026 (Code Sec. 55(d)(4)(A))

For inflation adjustment of the exemption and exemption phase-out threshold amounts for estates and trusts, and for individuals after expiration of the pre-Tax Cuts and Jobs Act increased amounts, for tax years beginning after Dec. 31, 2017. (Tax Cuts and Jobs Act §11002(e))

¶ 302. AMT adjustment for standard deduction is made retroactively inapplicable in 2016 and 2017 to net disaster losses from 2016 disaster areas

Code Sec. 56(b)(1)(E), Tax Cuts and Jobs Act §11028(c)(1)(D)
Generally effective: Tax years beginning after Dec. 31, 2015, and before
    Jan. 1, 2018
Committee Reports, see ¶ 5012

The standard deduction isn't allowed for purposes of the alternative minimum tax (AMT). Thus, a taxpayer who has taken the standard deduction for regular tax purposes must add back the amount of the deduction in computing alternative minimum taxable income (AMTI). (FTC 2d/FIN ¶ A-8300, ¶ A-8305; USTR ¶ 564.02)

The Tax Cuts and Jobs Act allows individuals who claim the standard deduction in 2016 and 2017, to increase the standard deduction by any net disaster loss, see ¶ 1803.

New Law. The Tax Cuts and Jobs Act provides that, if an individual has a net disaster loss (defined at ¶ 1803) for any tax year beginning after Dec. 31, 2015, and before Jan. 1, 2018 (Tax Cuts and Jobs Act §11028(c)(1)), the AMT adjustment for the standard deduction doesn't apply to the increase in the standard deduction that is attributable to the net disaster loss. (Tax Cuts and Jobs Act §11028(c)(1)(D))

> *observation:* Thus, while the standard deduction is generally disallowed under the AMT rules, the portion of the standard deduction attributable to a net disaster loss is allowed for AMT purposes.

> *illustration:* In 2017, a single taxpayer has a $1,000 net disaster loss, but no other itemized deductions. His standard deduction for 2017

would normally be $6,350, but because of the net disaster loss rules, this is increased to $7,350 (see ¶ 1803).

In determining the AMT, the taxpayer can't take the standard deduction. But, because of the Tax Cuts and Jobs Act, the taxpayer can deduct the $1,000 net disaster loss when determining his AMTI.

☐ **Effective:** Tax years beginning after Dec. 31, 2015, and before Jan. 1, 2018. (Tax Cuts and Jobs Act §11028(c)(1))

¶ 303. Alternative minimum tax on corporations is repealed

Code Sec. 55(a), as amended by Tax Cuts and Jobs Act §12001(a)
Code Sec. 55(b)(1), as amended by Tax Cuts and Jobs Act §12001(b)(3)(A)
Code Sec. 55(b)(3), as amended by Tax Cuts and Jobs Act §12001(b)(3)(B)
Code Sec. 55(c)(1), as amended by Tax Cuts and Jobs Act §12001(b)(4)
Code Sec. 55(d)(2), as amended and redesignated by Tax Cuts and Jobs Act §12001(b)(5)
Code Sec. 55(d)(3), as amended and redesignated by Tax Cuts and Jobs Act §12001(b)(5)
Code Sec. 55(e), as amended by Tax Cuts and Jobs Act §12001(b)(6)
Code Sec. 56(b)(2)(C), as amended and redesignated by Tax Cuts and Jobs Act §12001(b)(7)
Code Sec. 56(c), as amended by Tax Cuts and Jobs Act §12001(b)(8)(A)
Code Sec. 56(g), as amended by Tax Cuts and Jobs Act §12001(b)(8)(A)
Code Sec. 58(a)(3), as amended and redesignated by Tax Cuts and Jobs Act §12001(b)(9)
Code Sec. 59(a)(1)(C), as amended by Tax Cuts and Jobs Act §12001(b)(3)(C)(i)
Code Sec. 59(a)(2), as amended by Tax Cuts and Jobs Act §12001(b)(3)(C)(ii)
Code Sec. 59(b), as amended by Tax Cuts and Jobs Act §12001(b)(10)
Code Sec. 59(f), as amended by Tax Cuts and Jobs Act §12001(b)(10)
Generally effective: Tax years beginning after 2017
Committee Reports, see ¶ 5029

Under pre-Tax Cuts and Jobs Act law, in addition to income tax imposed under subtitle A of the Code, a second tax system, the alternative minimum tax (AMT), applied (under part VI of subchapter A of chapter 1 of the Code, i.e., Code Sec. 55–Code Sec. 59) to noncorporate and corporate taxpayers. The taxpayer's *total* tax liability for the year was equal to the sum of (i) the taxpayer's regular tax liability, plus (ii) the taxpayer's AMT liability for the year. The AMT was designed to reduce a taxpayer's ability to avoid taxes by using certain deductions and other tax benefit items. For Tax Cuts and Jobs Act changes to the AMT on noncorporate taxpayers (individuals, trusts, and estates), see ¶ 301.

AMT was imposed on a corporation to the extent that the corporation's "tentative minimum tax" exceeded its regular income tax for the tax year. (FTC 2d/FIN ¶ A-8100, ¶ A-8103 *et seq.*, ¶ A-8130, ¶ A-8131 *et seq.*; USTR ¶ 554, ¶ 554.01; Catalyst ¶ 142:100; Catalyst ¶ 142:110; Catalyst ¶ 142:120; Catalyst ¶ 142:130; Catalyst ¶ 142:140; Catalyst ¶ 142:150; Catalyst ¶ 142:160; Catalyst ¶ 142:170; Catalyst ¶ 142:180; Catalyst ¶ 142:190; Catalyst ¶ 124:200; Catalyst ¶ 142:210; Catalyst ¶ 142:220; Catalyst ¶ 142:230; Catalyst ¶ 406:250; Catalyst ¶ 502:161; Catalyst ¶ 502:198)

A corporation's tentative minimum tax equalled 20% of the corporation's "alternative minimum taxable income" (AMTI) in excess of an exemption amount, minus the corporation's AMT foreign tax credit. (FTC 2d/FIN ¶ A-8103; USTR ¶ 554.01) The exemption amount was $40,000, but that was phased out by an amount equal to 25% of the amount that the corporation's AMTI exceeded $150,000. (FTC 2d/FIN ¶ A-8160, ¶ A-8161; USTR ¶ 554.01)

A corporation's AMTI was computed by taking the taxpayer's regular taxable income for the tax year and (i) adding or subtracting AMT adjustments, and (ii) adding AMT preferences. Among the most significant adjustments and preferences for corporations were adjustments for depreciation, adjusted current earnings (ACE), depletion, and intangible drilling costs. (FTC 2d/FIN ¶ A-8190, ¶ A-8191 *et seq.*:, ¶ A-8200, ¶ A-8201 *et seq.*; USTR ¶ 564, ¶ 564.01, ¶ 564.03) Most corporate taxpayers had to include the ACE adjustment to AMTI, which increased AMTI for items excluded from regular tax such as tax-exempt interest, certain dividends received deductions, the difference between LIFO and FIFO inventory, and a portion of the deferred gain on installment sales. (FTC 2d/FIN ¶ A-8400, ¶ A-8401 *et seq.*; USTR ¶ 564.03)

Certain "small" corporations—those whose average annual gross receipts for the prior three years didn't exceed $7.5 million—were exempt from the AMT. And, for the corporation's first three-year period (or portion of a period), the limit was $5 million instead of $7.5 million. (FTC 2d/FIN ¶ A-8140, ¶ A-8141 *et seq.*; USTR ¶ 554.01)

A taxpayer's net operating loss (NOL) deduction, generally, couldn't reduce a taxpayer's AMTI by more than 90% of the AMTI (determined without regard to the NOL deduction). (FTC 2d/FIN ¶ A-8140, ¶ A-8141 *et seq.*; USTR ¶ 564.01)

New Law. The Tax Cuts and Jobs Act repeals the AMT on corporations (Com Rept, see ¶ 5029) by modifying Code Sec. 55(a) to provide that the AMT is imposed only on taxpayers other than corporations (Code Sec. 55(a) as amended by Tax Cuts and Jobs Act §S12001(a)) and by eliminating references to corporate taxpayers and rules applicable only to corporate taxpayers under the AMT provisions, specifically, under:

... Code Sec. 55, on imposition of the AMT (Code Sec. 55(b)(1) as amended by Tax Cuts and Jobs Act §12001(b)(3)(A); Code Sec. 55(b)(3) as amended by Tax Cuts and Jobs Act §12001(b)(3)(B); Code Sec. 55(c)(1) as amended by Tax Cuts and Jobs Act §12001(b)(4); Code Sec. 55(d)(2) as amended and redesignated by Tax Cuts and Jobs Act §12001(b)(5); Code Sec. 55(d)(3) as amended and redesignated by Tax Cuts and Jobs Act §12001(b)(5); Code Sec. 55(e) as amended by Tax Cuts and Jobs Act §12001(b)(6); Code Sec. 1561(a) as amended by Tax Cuts and Jobs Act §12001(b)(16));

... Code Sec. 56, on adjustments in computing AMTI (Code Sec. 56(b)(2)(C) as amended and redesignated by Tax Cuts and Jobs Act §12001(b)(7); Code Sec. 56(c) as amended by Tax Cuts and Jobs Act §12001(b)(8)(A); Code Sec. 56(g) as amended by Tax Cuts and Jobs Act §12001(b)(8)(A));

... Code Sec. 58, on denial of certain losses for AMT purposes (Code Sec. 58(a)(3) as amended and redesignated by Tax Cuts and Jobs Act §12001(b)(9)), and

... Code Sec. 59, providing other definitions and special rules. (Code Sec. 59(a)(1)(C) as amended by Tax Cuts and Jobs Act §12001(b)(3)(C)(i); Code Sec. 59(a)(2) as amended by Tax Cuts and Jobs Act §12001(b)(3)(C)(ii); Code Sec. 59(b) as amended by Tax Cuts and Jobs Act §12001(b)(10); Code Sec. 59(f) as amended by Tax Cuts and Jobs Act §12001(b)(10))

For changes to corporation's minimum tax credit (MTC/AMT credit) to allow offset against regular tax liability for any tax year, and to make the credit refundable for 2018−2021, see ¶ 304.

> *observation:* The Tax Cuts and Jobs Act also reduces the top corporate tax rate to 21% (see ¶ 102). Elimination of the corporate AMT makes it possible for some businesses to lower their effective tax rates below 21% with various deductions, the benefit of which would otherwise have been reduced or eliminated if the AMT applied.

The Tax Cuts and Jobs Act also makes conforming changes to various other Code provisions to reflect the repeal of the corporate AMT, including:

... limits on the general business credit (Code Sec. 38(c)(6)(E) as amended by Tax Cuts and Jobs Act §12001(b)(1)), see discussion at ¶ 1017;

... tax on foreign corporations engaged in U.S. business (see FTC 2d/FIN ¶ A-8130, ¶ A-8134; USTR ¶ 114.02) (Code Sec. 11(d) as amended by Tax Cuts and Jobs Act §12001(b)(11); Code Sec. 882(a)(1) as amended by Tax Cuts and Jobs Act §12001(b)(14));

... adjustments for corporation's overpayment of estimated income tax (see FTC 2d/FIN ¶ T-6600, ¶ T-6605.1; USTR ¶ 64,254) (Code Sec. 6425(c)(1)(A) as amended by Tax Cuts and Jobs Act §12001(b)(17)); and

... penalty for corporation's failure to pay estimated tax (see FTC 2d/FIN ¶ S-5320, ¶ S-5325, ¶ S-5342; USTR ¶ 66,554, ¶ 66,554.02) (Code Sec. 6655(e)(2) as amended by Tax Cuts and Jobs Act §12001(b)(18); Code Sec. 6655(g)(1)(A) as amended by Tax Cuts and Jobs Act §12001(b)(19))

☐ **Effective:** For tax years beginning after Dec. 31, 2017. (Tax Cuts and Jobs Act §12001(c))

¶ 304. Corporate minimum tax credit (MTC) may offset regular tax liability for any tax year, and is refundable for 2018–2021

Code Sec. 53(e), as amended by Tax Cuts and Jobs Act §12002(a)
Code Sec. 53(d)(3), as amended by Tax Cuts and Jobs Act §12002(b)
Code Sec. 53(d)(2), as amended by Tax Cuts and Jobs Act §12001(b)(2)
Code Sec. 1374(b)(3)(B), as amended by Tax Cuts and Jobs Act §12002(c)
Code Sec. 168(k)(4), as amended by Tax Cuts and Jobs Act §12001(b)(13)
Generally effective: Tax years beginning after Dec. 31, 2017
Committee Reports, see ¶ 5029

Under pre-Tax Cuts and Jobs Act law, an alternative minimum tax (AMT), which applied to the extent that the taxpayer's "tentative minimum tax" liability exceeded the taxpayer's regular income tax liability for the tax year, was imposed on noncorporate and corporate taxpayers. But as discussed at ¶ 303, the Tax Cuts and Jobs Act repeals the AMT on corporations for tax years beginning after 2017.

Under Code Sec. 53, a taxpayer who was subject to the AMT in an earlier year may be entitled to carryforward a "minimum tax credit" (MTC) (also called the "AMT credit"), against the taxpayer's regular tax. For this purpose, Code Sec. 53(b) provides, subject to the limitation below, that the MTC for a tax year equals the excess, if any, of:

(1) the adjusted net minimum tax ("ANMT") imposed for all earlier tax years beginning after '86, over

(2) the amount allowable as an MTC for those earlier years.

That is, each year the aggregate ANMT is available for credit against regular tax, to the extent it hasn't been used as a credit against regular tax in earlier years.

The amount of the ANMT is determined differently for noncorporate and corporate taxpayers. A noncorporate taxpayer's ANMT for a tax year is determined by taking the amount of the taxpayer's AMT for the year, and then subtracting the amount of AMT that the taxpayer would have had if the only applicable AMT preferences and adjustments were "exclusion preferences" (see ¶ 301). A corporate taxpayer's ANMT for a tax year equals the AMT paid for that tax year.

Under pre-Tax Cuts and Jobs Act law, Code Sec. 53(c) provided that the MTC was limited to the excess of:

(a) the taxpayer's regular tax liability for the year to which the credit was being carried, reduced by the sum of the taxpayer's allowable credits under subparts A, B, D, E and F of part IV, subchapter A, Chapter 1, Subtitle A (i.e., all personal and business related income credits, other than the subpart C refundable credits), over

(b) the tentative minimum tax (i.e., AMT before deducting the regular tax) for that year.

The MTC was nonrefundable (except for certain individual taxpayers for tax years before 2013).

Unused MTCs could be carried forward indefinitely, but couldn't be carried back.

And, corporations were allowed to claim a limited amount of MTCs in lieu of bonus depreciation (see ¶ 1210). (FTC 2d/FIN ¶ A-8800, ¶ A-8801 *et seq.*; USTR ¶ 534; Catalyst ¶ 142:210)

New Law. Under the Tax Cuts and Jobs Act, in the case of a corporation, the MTC may offset regular tax liability for any tax year. The MTC is refundable for any tax year beginning after 2017 and before 2022 in an amount equal to 50% (100% for tax years beginning in 2021) of the excess MTC for the tax year, over the amount of the credit allowable for the year against regular tax liability. Thus, the full amount of the corporation's MTC will be allowed in tax years beginning before 2022. (Com Rept, see ¶ 5029)

The Tax Cuts and Jobs Act accomplishes this by providing that, for any tax year of a corporation beginning in 2018, 2019, 2020, or 2021, the above-described Code Sec. 53(c) limitation is increased by the AMT refundable credit amount (defined below) for that tax year. (Code Sec. 53(e)(1) as amended by Tax Cuts and Jobs Act §12002(a))

> *observation:* Increasing the Code Sec. 53(c) limitation operates to increase (by the AMT refundable credit amount) the amount of MTC the corporation may claim for the tax year.

For this purpose, the "AMT refundable amount" is an amount equal to 50% (100% for a tax year beginning in 2021) of the excess (if any) of (Code Sec. 53(e)(2)):

(A) the MTC for the tax year determined under Code Sec. 53(b) (i.e., the excess (if any) of the ANMT imposed for all earlier tax years beginning after '86, over the amount allowable as an MTC for those earlier years), over (Code Sec. 53(e)(2)(A))

(B) the credit allowed under Code Sec. 53(a) for the tax year (before application of Code Sec. 53(e) above, i.e., before increase of the Code Sec. 53(c) limitation by the refundable credit amount) (Code Sec. 53(e)(2)(B)), i.e., the amount of the credit allowable for the year against regular tax liability. (Com Rept, see ¶ 5029)

For purposes of the Code (other than the Code Sec. 53 MTC), the MTC allowed by reason of Code Sec. 53(e) above will be treated as a credit allowed under subpart C of part IV, subchapter A, Chapter 1, Subtitle A (i.e., as a refundable credit) (and not as a credit under subpart G, i.e., a nonrefundable credit). (Code Sec. 53(e)(3))

For any tax year of less than 365 days (i.e., a "short tax year"), the AMT refundable credit amount for that tax year will equal the amount that bears the same ratio to the amount determined without regard to this short tax year rule, as the number of days in the short tax year bears to 365. (Code Sec. 53(e)(4))

> **⟨RIA⟩** *observation:* That is, the AMT refundable credit amount for a short tax year will equal the AMT refundable credit amount × the number of days in the short tax year ÷ 365.

In the case of a corporation, any reference under the Code Sec. 53 MTC rules to Code Sec. 55 (imposing the AMT), Code Sec. 56 (providing for the adjustments used in computing alternative minimum taxable income (AMTI) for purposes of computing AMT), or Code Sec. 57 (providing preference items for purposes of computing AMT), is treated as a reference to that section as in effect before the amendments made by the Tax Cuts and Jobs Act to those provisions (Code Sec. 53(d)(3) as amended by Tax Cuts and Jobs Act §12002(b)) (i.e., changes made to reflect the repeal of the corporate AMT, see ¶ 303).

The Tax Cuts and Jobs Act also makes these conforming changes to reflect the impact of the repeal of the corporate AMT on MTC rules:

. . . modification of the definition of tentative minimum tax under the MTC, to provide that, for a corporation, tentative minimum tax will be treated as zero (Code Sec. 53(d)(2) as amended by Tax Cuts and Jobs Act §12001(b)(2));

. . . elimination of the carryover of MTC carryforwards earned in C corporation tax years for purposes of the S corporation built-in gains tax (FTC 2d/FIN ¶ D-1640, ¶ D-1665; USTR ¶ 13,744.01) (Code Sec. 1374(b)(3)(B) as amended by Tax Cuts and Jobs Act §12002(c)), for tax years after 2021 (see below).

. . . elimination of the rule permitting corporations to claim a limited amount of MTCs in lieu of bonus depreciation (Code Sec. 168(k)(4) as amended by Tax Cuts and Jobs Act §12001(b)(13)), see ¶ 1210.

☐ **Effective:** Except as provided below, for tax years beginning after 2017. (Tax Cuts and Jobs Act §12002(d)(1); Tax Cuts and Jobs Act §12001(c))

Conforming change to Code Sec. 1374(b)(3)(B) (S corporation built in gains rule), is effective for tax years beginning after Dec. 31, 2021. (Tax Cuts and Jobs Act §12002(d)(2))

¶ 400. ACA Individual Mandate

¶ 401. Shared responsibility payment (penalty) eliminated after 2018

Code Sec. 5000A(c), as amended by Tax Cuts and Jobs Act §11081
Generally effective: Months beginning after Dec. 31, 2018.
Committee Reports, see ¶ 5028

Under the Affordable Care Act, nonexempt individuals must either see that they and any of their nonexempt dependents have minimum essential coverage for the month, or pay a monthly shared responsibility payment (penalty). Exempt individuals include, among other categories, nonresident aliens, low-income individuals, persons subject to hardship and members of certain religious groups. Minimum essential coverage includes government-sponsored programs, eligible employer-sponsored plans, plans in the individual market, grandfathered group health plans and grandfathered health insurance coverage, and other coverage as recognized by the Secretaries of Health and Human Services and the Treasury. (FTC 2d ¶ A-6400 *et seq.*; USTR ¶ 50,00A4 *et seq.*)

Under pre-Tax Cuts and Jobs Act law, for each tax year, the shared responsibility payment (penalty) imposed on a taxpayer was the lesser of (a) the sum of the monthly penalty amounts, or (b) the sum of the monthly national average bronze plan premiums for the shared responsibility family plan. The monthly penalty amount for any taxpayer for any month during which a failure occurred was equal to 1/12 of the greater of the flat dollar amount or the excess income amount. The flat dollar amount was generally equal to the lesser of (1) the sum of the applicable dollar amounts (see below) for all individuals included in the taxpayer's shared responsibility family, or (2) 300% of the applicable dollar amount for the calendar year with or within which the tax year ends. The excess income amount was the product of the excess of the taxpayer's household income over the taxpayer's applicable filing threshold multiplied by 2.5% for tax years beginning after 2015. The applicable dollar amount for individuals aged 18 or over was $695 multiplied by a cost-of-living adjustment. (FTC 2d ¶ V-3900, ¶ V-3901, ¶ V-3905, ¶ V-3906, ¶ V-3907; USTR ¶ 50,00A4.2)

New Law. The Tax Cut and Jobs Act eliminates the shared responsibility payment by reducing the percentage, by which the excess of the taxpayer's

---

FTC 2d References are to Federal Tax Coordinator 2d
FIN References are to RIA's Analysis of Federal Taxes: Income (print)
USTR References are to United States Tax Reporter
Catalyst References are to Checkpoint Catalyst
PCA References are to Pension Analysis (print and electronic)
PBE References are to Pension & Benefits Explanations
BCA References are to Benefits Analysis (electronic)
BC References are to Benefits Coordinator (print)
EP References are to Estate Planning Analysis (print and electronic)

household income over the taxpayer's applicable filing threshold is multiplied, to zero (Code Sec. 5000A(c)(2)(B)(iii) as amended by Tax Cuts and Jobs Act §11081(a)(1)) and by setting the applicable dollar amount to zero. (Code Sec. 5000A(c)(3) as amended by Tax Cuts and Jobs Act §11081(a)(2)(A)) The Act also eliminates the cost of living adjustments to the applicable dollar amount. (Code Sec. 5000A(c)(3)(D) as repealed by Tax Cuts and Jobs Act §11081(a)(2)(B))

> *observation:* The net result of these changes is that no shared responsibility payment will be required after 2018, nor will there be any penalty imposed for failing to maintain minimum essential coverage.

☐ **Effective:** Months beginning after Dec. 31, 2018. (Tax Cuts and Jobs Act §11081(b))

¶ 500. Individuals: Deductions And Personal Credits

¶ 501. Standard deduction is almost doubled, inflation adjustment is modified

Code Sec. 63(c)(7), as amended by Tax Cuts and Jobs Act §11021(a)
Generally effective: Tax years beginning after Dec. 31, 2017, and before Jan. 1, 2026
Committee Reports, see ¶ 5005

Taxpayers who don't itemize deductions may reduce adjusted gross income (AGI) by the amount of the applicable standard deduction in arriving at taxable income. The standard deduction is the sum of an inflation-adjusted (statutory) basic standard deduction plus, if applicable, an inflation-adjusted (statutory) additional standard deduction for the elderly and blind. The basic standard deduction varies depending on the taxpayer's filing status. (FTC 2d ¶ A-2800 *et seq.*; USTR ¶ 634 *et seq.*)

Basic standard deduction. Under pre-Tax Cuts and Jobs Act law, for 2017, the inflation-adjusted basic standard deduction was $12,700 for joint filers and surviving spouses (computed as 200% of the single filers' amount); $9,350 for heads of household; and $6,350 for singles and marrieds filing separately. (FTC 2d/FIN ¶ A-2800, ¶ A-2803; USTR ¶ 634)

Inflation indexing. Under pre-Tax Cuts and Jobs Act law, the statutory basic standard deduction dollar amounts were indexed annually for inflation (under Code Sec. 63(c)(4)) by increasing those dollar amounts by an amount equal to: (i) the particular dollar amount, multiplied by (ii) the percentage by which the Consumer Price Index for all-urban consumers (the "CPI-U") for the preceding calendar year, exceeded the CPI-U for calendar year '87. (FTC 2d/FIN ¶ A-2800, ¶ A-2809; USTR ¶ 634)

New Law. Basic standard deduction almost doubled through 2025. Under the Tax Cuts and Jobs Act, for tax years beginning after Dec. 31, 2017, and before Jan. 1, 2026 (Code Sec. 63(c)(7) as amended by Tax Cuts and Jobs Act §11021(a)), the standard deduction dollar amounts are increased to:

FTC 2d References are to Federal Tax Coordinator 2d
FIN References are to RIA's Analysis of Federal Taxes: Income (print)
USTR References are to United States Tax Reporter
Catalyst References are to Checkpoint Catalyst
PCA References are to Pension Analysis (print and electronic)
PBE References are to Pension & Benefits Explanations
BCA References are to Benefits Analysis (electronic)
BC References are to Benefits Coordinator (print)
EP References are to Estate Planning Analysis (print and electronic)

(a) $24,000 for joint filers and surviving spouses (computed as 200% of the single filers' amount below) (Code Sec. 63(c)(2)(A); Code Sec. 63(c)(7)(A)(ii));

(b) $18,000 for heads of household (Code Sec. 63(c)(7)(A)(i)); and

(c) $12,000 for singles and marrieds filing separately. (Code Sec. 63(c)(7)(A)(ii))

So, the Tax Cuts and Jobs Act temporarily—i.e., beginning in 2018 and continuing through Dec. 31, 2025, when the provision sunsets—increases the basic standard deduction for individuals across all filing statuses, as discussed above. (Com Rept, see ¶ 5005)

The additional standard deduction for the elderly and the blind is unchanged. (Com Rept, see ¶ 5005)

> **illustration:** In 2018, T, a single taxpayer, qualifies for an additional standard deduction because he is 70 years old. So T's standard deduction for 2018 is $13,600 ($12,000, the 2018 standard deduction for unmarrieds, plus $1,600, the 2018 additional standard deduction for singles who are over 65 or blind).

> **illustration:** In 2018, A and her spouse, B, who are joint filers, both qualify for an additional standard deduction because they are both over 65. So A and B's standard deduction for 2018 is $26,600 ($24,000, the 2018 standard deduction for joint filers, plus 2 × $1,300, the 2018 additional standard deduction for married persons who are over 65 or blind).

> **observation:** The Tax Cuts and Jobs Act also suspends the deduction for personal exemptions (see ¶ 502), and suspends or limits other itemized deductions (see ¶ 503 *et seq.*), but generally cuts individual tax rates, through 2025 (see ¶ 101).

Inflation indexing uses chained CPI-U. The Tax Cuts and Jobs Act provides that the increased standard deduction dollar amounts above aren't adjusted for inflation under Code Sec. 63(c)(4) (as described above). (Code Sec. 63(c)(7)(B)(i))

Instead, for a tax year beginning after 2018, the $18,000 and $12,000 standard deduction dollar amounts are each increased by an amount equal to (Code Sec. 63(c)(7)(B)(ii)):

(i) that dollar amount, multiplied by (Code Sec. 63(c)(7)(B)(ii)(I))

(ii) the cost-of-living adjustment (COLA) determined under Code Sec. 1(f)(3) (i.e., based on chained CPI-U ("C-CPI-U"), see ¶ 201) for the calendar year in which the tax year begins, but determined by substituting "2017" for "2016" in Code Sec. 1(f)(3)(A)(ii). (Code Sec. 63(c)(7)(B)(ii)(II))

If any increase under the above rule isn't a multiple of $50, that increase must be rounded to the next lowest multiple of $50. (Code Sec. 63(c)(7)(B)(ii))

Thus, for tax years beginning after 2018, the above-described standard deduction dollar amounts are indexed for inflation using the C-CPI-U, instead of the CPI-U used under prior law. (Com Rept, see ¶ 5005)

> **🅡🅘🅐** *observation:* For tax years beginning after 2025, the standard deduction dollar amounts in effect after the Tax Cuts and Jobs Act's increased amounts above expire (sunset) will also be indexed for inflation based on C-CPI-U, see ¶ 202.

Sunset. The increased standard deduction amounts discussed above won't apply after Dec. 31, 2025. (Code Sec. 63(c)(7))

☐ **Effective:** Tax years beginning after Dec. 31, 2017 (Tax Cuts and Jobs Act §11021(b)), and before Jan. 1, 2026 (Code Sec. 63(c)(7)).

¶ 502. Deduction for personal exemptions for taxpayer, spouse, and dependents is suspended; return-filing and withholding requirements are modified

Code Sec. 151(d)(5), as amended by Tax Cuts and Jobs Act §11041(a)(2)
Code Sec. 151(d)(4), as amended by Tax Cuts and Jobs Act §11041(a)(2)
Code Sec. 642(b)(2)(C)(iii), as amended by Tax Cuts and Jobs Act §11041(b)
Code Sec. 3402(a)(2), as amended by Tax Cuts and Jobs Act §11041(c)(1)
Code Sec. 3402(f)(1), as amended by Tax Cuts and Jobs Act §11041(c)(2)(B)
Code Sec. 6334(d)(4), as amended by Tax Cuts and Jobs Act §11041(d)
Code Sec. 6012(f), as amended by Tax Cuts and Jobs Act §11041(e)
Generally effective: Tax years beginning after Dec. 31, 2017, and before Jan. 1, 2026
Committee Reports, see ¶ 5015

Personal exemption deductions for taxpayer, spouse, and dependents. Under pre-Tax Cuts and Jobs Act law, in determining taxable income, an individual reduced adjusted gross income (AGI) by any personal exemption deductions (allowed under Code Sec. 151) and by either the applicable standard deduction or itemized deductions. Personal exemptions generally were allowed for the taxpayer, the taxpayer's spouse, and any dependents. The exemption equalled a statutory amount (under Code Sec. 151(d)), indexed annually for inflation. No personal exemption was allowed to a dependent if a deduction was allowed to another taxpayer.

For 2017, the (inflation-adjusted) amount deductible for each personal exemption was $4,050. (FTC 2d/FIN ¶ A-3500, ¶ A-3500.1; USTR ¶ 1514)

Trusts and estates exemption deductions. Instead of the deduction for personal exemptions, an estate is allowed a deduction of $600. (FTC 2d ¶ C-7207; USTR ¶ 6424.01)

The deduction for the personal exemption for a trust, other than a trust that's required to distribute all of its income currently and a qualified disability trust (see below), is $100; the deduction for a trust that's required to distribute all of its income currently is $300. (FTC 2d ¶ C-2206; USTR ¶ 6424.01)

A *qualified disability trust* (FTC 2d/FIN ¶ C-2206.1; USTR ¶ 6424.01) was allowed an amount equal to an individual's personal exemption. (FTC 2d/FIN ¶ C-2200, ¶ C-2206 *et seq.*; USTR ¶ 6424.01)

Withholding rules. Every employer that pays wages must deduct and withhold tax determined under tables or computational procedures prescribed by IRS. The tables or procedures: (1) apply to the "amount of wages" paid during specified periods that IRS prescribes; and (2) provide for amounts to be deducted and withheld from the wages.

Under pre-tax Cuts and Jobs Act law, for purposes of applying these tables or procedures, the term "the amount of wages" meant the amount by which the wages exceeded the number of withholding exemptions claimed, multiplied by the amount of one exemption. The amount of each withholding exemption was equal to the amount of one personal exemption prorated to the payroll period. (FTC 2d/FIN ¶ H-4485, ¶ H-4492; USTR ¶ 1514)

For purposes of the withholding rules, an employee was entitled to an exemption amount for each item listed in Code Sec. 3402(f)(1). These items provided for exemptions for: (a) the employee; (b) the employee's spouse; (c) the employee's dependents; (d) whether the employee was entitled to any additional allowance under Code Sec. 3402(m) (additional allowances based on itemized deductions, etc.); and (e) a standard deduction allowance that was equal to one exemption unless (i) the employee was married and the spouse was an employee receiving wages subject to withholding, or (ii) the employee had withholding exemption certificates in effect for more than one employer. (FTC 2d/FIN ¶ H-4485, ¶ H-4505 *et seq.*; USTR ¶ 1514)

Determining property exempt from levy. Under pre-Tax Cuts and Jobs Act law, subject to exceptions, for levies issued on wages, salary, or other income of an individual who was paid or received all wages, salary, or other income on a weekly basis, the amount exempt from levy was the amount equal to the taxpayer's standard deduction and personal exemptions allowable for the tax year in which the levy occurred, divided by 52. If the taxpayer didn't supply a written and properly verified statement specifying the facts necessary for IRS to determine the proper exempt amount, then the exempt amount was determined using the standard deduction for a married individual filing separately and one personal exemption. (FTC 2d/FIN ¶ V-5200, ¶ V-5236; USTR ¶ 63,314.05)

Filing requirements for individuals. Under pre-Tax Cuts and Jobs Act law, an unmarried individual had to file a return for the tax year if, in that year, the individual had income that equaled or exceeded the exemption amount, plus the standard deduction for that individual. An individual entitled to file a joint return had to do so, unless that individual's gross income, when combined with the spouse's gross income for the tax year, was less than the sum of twice the exemption amount, plus the basic standard deduction for a joint return, as long as the individual and spouse, at the end of the tax year, had the same household as their home. (FTC 2d/FIN ¶ S-1700 *et seq.*; USTR ¶ 60,124)

New Law. **Deduction for personal exemptions suspended for 2018– 2025.** The Tax Cuts and Jobs Act provides that, for tax years beginning after Dec. 31, 2017, and before Jan. 1, 2026, the exemption amount under Code Sec. 151 is zero (Code Sec. 151(d)(5)(A) as amended by Tax Cuts and Jobs Act §11041(a)(2)) (and the regular exemption inflation adjustments rules don't apply). (Code Sec. 151(d)(4) as amended by Tax Cuts and Jobs Act §11041(a)(1)) Thus, the deduction for personal exemptions is suspended (Com Rept, see ¶ 5015) for tax years 2018–2025.

> **observation:** The Tax Cuts and Jobs Act also suspends or limits many itemized deductions (see ¶ 503 *et seq.*), but it nearly doubles the standard deduction (¶ 501), and generally cuts individual tax rates, through 2025 (see ¶ 101).

But, for purposes of any other Code provision, the above reduction of the Code Sec. 151 exemption amount to zero won't be taken into account in determining whether a deduction for personal exemptions is allowed or allowable, or whether a taxpayer is entitled to a deduction for personal exemptions. (Code Sec. 151(d)(5)(B))

Congress says that the rule above is intended to clarify that, for purposes of tax years in which the personal exemption is reduced to zero, that should not alter the operation of those provisions of the Code that refer to a taxpayer allowed a deduction (or an individual with respect to whom a taxpayer is allowed a deduction) under Code Sec. 151. Thus, for instance, Code Sec. 24(a) allows a credit against tax for each qualifying child of the taxpayer for which the taxpayer is allowed a deduction under Code Sec. 151. A qualifying child defined under Code Sec. 152(c) remains eligible for the credit, notwithstanding that the deduction under Code Sec. 151 has been reduced to zero. (Com Rept, see ¶ 5015)

Qualified disability trust's exemption for tax years 2018–2025; inflation adjustment. Under the Tax Cuts and Jobs Act, for any tax year in which the exemption amount under Code Sec. 151(d) is zero (i.e., for tax years 2018–

2025, as described above), the amount of a qualified disability trust's exemption is $4,150.(Code Sec. 642(b)(2)(C)(iii)(I) as amended by Tax Cuts and Jobs Act §11041(b)) For calendar years beginning after 2018, the $4,150 amount is increased in the same manner as provided in Code Sec. 6334(d)(4)(C). (Code Sec. 642(b)(2)(C)(iii)(II)), i.e., by an amount equal to the dollar amount of the exemption, multiplied by the cost-of-living adjustment (COLA) determined under Code Sec. 1(f)(3) (i.e., based on chained CPI-U (C-CPI-U), see ¶ 201) for the calendar year in which the tax year begins, determined by substituting "2017" for "2016" in Code Sec. 1(f)(3)(A)(ii). (Code Sec. 6334(d)(4)(C) as amended by Tax Cuts and Jobs Act §11041(d)) If any increase determined under these rules isn't a multiple of $100, then that increase must be rounded to the next lowest multiple of $100. (Code Sec. 6334(d)(4)(C))

> ⓡⁱᵃ*observation:* For tax years beginning after Dec. 31, 2025 (i.e., after the deduction for personal exemptions is once again in effect), the inflation adjustment of the personal exemption amount—and, therefore, the inflation adjustment for the qualified disability trust's exemption—will also be based on C-CPI-U, see ¶ 202.

> ⓡⁱᵃ*observation:* The estate's $600 deduction, as well as the $100 or $300 deductions allowable to a trust, aren't affected by the Tax Cuts and Jobs Act.

Determining withholding under the Tax Cuts and Jobs Act.   Under the Tax Cuts and Jobs Act, for tax years beginning after Dec. 31, 2017 (Tax Cuts and Jobs Act §11041(f)(1)), for purposes of applying withholding tables or computational procedures prescribed by IRS, the "amount of wages" means the amount by which the wages exceed the taxpayer's withholding allowance, prorated to the payroll period. (Code Sec. 3402(a)(2) as amended by Tax Cuts and Jobs Act §11041(c)(1))

And, for purposes of the withholding rules, under rules determined by IRS, instead of being entitled to an "exemption" for each item listed in Code Sec. 3402(f)(1), the employee is entitled to a "withholding allowance" that's determined based on (Code Sec. 3402(f)(1) as amended by Tax Cuts and Jobs Act §11041(c)(2); Code Sec. 3402(f)(2)):

(A) whether the employee is an individual for whom a deduction is allowable with respect to another taxpayer under Code Sec. 151 (Code Sec. 3402(f)(1)(A));

(B) if the employee is married, whether the employee's spouse is entitled to an allowance, or would be so entitled if the spouse were an employee receiving wages, under (A) (above) or (D) (below), but only if the spouse doesn't have in effect a withholding allowance certificate claiming the allowance (Code Sec. 3402(f)(1)(B));

(C) the number of individuals for whom, on the basis of facts existing at the beginning of the day, there may reasonably be expected to be allowable a credit under Code Sec. 24(a) (i.e., a child tax credit, see FTC 2d ¶ A-4050 *et seq.*; USTR ¶ 244 *et seq.*, and see ¶ 516 for Tax Cuts and Jobs Act changes) for the tax year for amounts deducted and withheld under Chapter 1 of the Code in the calendar year in which the day falls are allowed as a credit. (Code Sec. 3402(f)(1)(C))

> *observation:* Under pre-Tax Cuts and Jobs Act law, instead of factor (C) above, a portion of the withholding allowance was based on the number of a taxpayer's dependent exemptions.

(D) any additional amounts the employee elects to take into account under Code Sec. 3402(m) (additional withholding allowances), but only if the employee's spouse doesn't have in effect a withholding allowance certificate making the election (Code Sec. 3402(f)(1)(D));

(E) the standard deduction allowable to the employee (one-half of the standard deduction for an employee who is married (as determined under Code Sec. 7703, see FTC 2d ¶ A-1600 *et seq.*; USTR ¶ 77,034 *et seq.*) and whose spouse is an employee receiving wages subject to withholding (Code Sec. 3402(f)(1)(E)); and

> *observation:* Under pre-Tax Cuts and Jobs Act law, instead of factor (E) above, the portion of the withholding allowance that provided a standard deduction allowance, equalled one exemption.

(F) Whether the employee has withholding allowance certificates in effect for more than one employer. (Code Sec. 3402(f)(1)(F))

> *observation:* Under pre-Tax Cuts and Jobs Act law, instead of being a separate factor, (F) above was a factor in determining the amount of the standard deduction allowance allowed to the employee.

Transitional rule for IRS issuance of withholding tables and procedures. But, IRS may administer the withholding rules under Code Sec. 3402 for tax years beginning before Jan. 1, 2019, without regard to the above-described changes to the withholding rules or the above-described suspension of personal exemptions. (Tax Cuts and Jobs Act §11041(f)(2)) That is, at IRS's discretion, wage withholding rules for 2018 may remain the same as under pre-Tax Cuts and Jobs Act law. (Com Rept, see ¶ 5015)

Rules for determining amount of property exempt from levy, tax years 2018–2025; inflation adjustment; verified statement. For any tax year in which the Code Sec. 151(d) exemption amount is zero (i.e., for tax years 2018–2025, as described above), for levies issued on wages, etc., of an individual who is paid or receives all wages, etc., on a weekly basis, the amount exempt from levy is equal to (Code Sec. 6334(d)(4)(A) as amended by Tax Cuts and Jobs Act §11041(d)):

(1) the sum of: (i) $4,150 times the number of the taxpayer's dependents for the tax year in which the levy occurs, plus (ii) the standard deduction, divided by (Code Sec. 6334(d)(4)(A)(i); Code Sec. 6334(d)(4)(B));

(2) 52. (Code Sec. 6334(d)(4)(A)(ii))

For tax years beginning in calendar years after 2018, the $4,150 amount is increased under the same inflation-adjustment rules discussed under "Qualified disability trust's exemption for tax years 2018 − 2025; inflation adjustment," above. (Code Sec. 6334(d)(4)(C))

If the taxpayer doesn't supply a written and properly verified statement specifying the facts necessary for IRS to determine the proper exempt amount, then the exempt amount (under (1) and (2), above) is determined using the standard deduction for a married individual filing separately and one personal exemption. (Code Sec. 6334(d)(4)(D))

Filing requirements based solely on standard deduction for tax years 2018–2025. For tax years beginning after Dec. 31, 2017, and before Jan. 1, 2026, the filing requirement rules of Code Sec. 6012(a) (based on exemption amount and standard deduction, see prior law discussion, above) don't apply. And, every individual who has gross income for the tax year must file an income tax return, except (Code Sec. 6012(f) as amended by Tax Cuts and Jobs Act §11041(e)):

(a) an unmarried individual (as determined under Code Sec. 7703), who has gross income for the tax year that doesn't exceed the standard deduction for that individual for that tax year (for the Tax Cuts and Jobs Act increased standard deductions, see ¶ 501) (Code Sec. 6012(f)(1)); or

(b) an individual entitled to file jointly if: (i) the individual's gross income, when combined with the spouse's gross income, doesn't exceed, for the tax year, the standard deduction that would apply to the taxpayer for the tax year if the individual and spouse filed jointly (Code Sec. 6012(f)(2)(A)); (ii) the individual and spouse have the same household as their home at the end of the tax year (Code Sec. 6012(f)(2)(B)); (iii) the spouse doesn't file separately (Code Sec. 6012(f)(2)(C)); and (iv) neither the individual nor spouse is an individual for whom a dependency deduction may be claimed by another taxpayer, who has income (other than earned income) in excess of the limited deduction allowed for dependents. (Code Sec. 6012(f)(2)(D))

Thus, for an unmarried individual, that individual must file a return if the taxpayer's gross income for the tax year exceeds the applicable standard deduction. Married individuals must file a return if the individual's gross income, when combined with the individual's spouse's gross income, for the tax year is more than the standard deduction that applies for a joint return, as long as: (i) the individual and spouse, at the close of the tax year, had the same household as their home; (ii) the spouse does not file separately; and (iii) neither the individual nor the spouse is a dependent of another taxpayer who has income (other than earned income) in excess of the limited deduction allowed for dependents (for 2017, $1,050). (Com Rept, see ¶ 5015)

Sunset. The suspension of the deduction for personal exemptions for a taxpayer, the taxpayer's spouse, and any dependents won't apply for tax years beginning after Dec. 31, 2025. (Code Sec. 151(d)(5)(A))

☐ **Effective:** The suspension of the deduction for personal exemptions applies for tax years beginning after Dec. 31, 2017 (Tax Cuts and Jobs Act §11041(f)(1)) and before Jan. 1, 2026. (Code Sec. 151(d)(5)(A))

Other changes discussed above apply for tax years beginning after Dec. 31, 2017. (Tax Cuts and Jobs Act §11041(f)(1))

But, IRS may administer the withholding rules under Code Sec. 3402 for tax years beginning before Jan. 1, 2019, without regard to the above-described changes made to the withholding rules or the suspension of personal exemptions. (Tax Cuts and Jobs Act §11041(f)(2))

¶ 503. Miscellaneous itemized deductions are disallowed

Code Sec. 67(g), as amended by Tax Cuts and Jobs Act §11045(a)
Generally effective: Tax years beginning after Dec. 31, 2017, and before
   Jan. 1, 2026
Committee Reports, see ¶ 5019

Under pre-Tax Cuts and Jobs Act law, individuals who itemized their deductions could deduct certain miscellaneous itemized deductions to the extent that the aggregate of those deductions exceeded 2% of adjusted gross income (AGI). "Miscellaneous itemized deductions" meant the itemized deductions other than those listed in Code Sec. 67(b). (FTC 2d/FIN ¶ A-2710 *et seq.*; USTR ¶ 674; Catalyst ¶ 253:157; Catalyst ¶ 762:208)

The miscellaneous itemized deductions to which the 2%-of-AGI floor applied included the following:

• unreimbursed employee business expenses. (FTC 2d/FIN ¶ A-2722 *et seq.*; USTR ¶ 674)

• unreimbursed vehicle expenses of rural mail carriers. (FTC 2d/FIN ¶ A-2724.1; USTR ¶ 674)

• investment expenses and expenses for the production or collection of income. (FTC 2d/FIN ¶ A-2725; USTR ¶ 674)

• tax determination expenses. (FTC 2d/FIN ¶ A-2726; USTR ¶ 674)

- expenses allowed under the "hobby loss" rules of Code Sec. 183. (FTC 2d/ FIN ¶ A-2721; USTR ¶ 674)

Miscellaneous itemized deductions are reported on Form 1040, Schedule A. (FTC 2d/FIN ¶ A-2711)

New Law. Miscellaneous itemized deductions aren't allowed under the Tax Cuts and Jobs Act for any tax year beginning after Dec. 31, 2017, and before Jan. 1, 2026. (Code Sec. 67(g) as amended by Tax Cuts and Jobs Act §11045(a))

> *observation:* Certain other miscellaneous deductions aren't subject to the 2%-of-AGI floor and are reported on Line 28 of Schedule A (Form 1040), Itemized Deductions. These include amortizable bond premium, estate tax on income in respect of a decedent (IRD), impairment-related work expenses, and repayments of more than $3,000 under a claim of right. These aren't miscellaneous itemized deductions for purposes of Code Sec. 67 and so are unaffected by this provision.

Sunset. The disallowance of miscellaneous itemized deductions won't apply in tax years beginning after Dec. 31, 2025. (Code Sec. 67(g))

☐ **Effective:** Tax years beginning after Dec. 31, 2017 (Tax Cuts and Jobs Act §11045(b)) and before Jan. 1, 2026. (Code Sec. 67(g))

¶ 504. Overall limitation on itemized deductions ("Pease limitation" or "3%/80% rule") is suspended

Code Sec. 68(f), as amended by Tax Cuts and Jobs Act §11046(a)
Generally effective: Tax years beginning after Dec. 31, 2017, and before
   Jan. 1, 2026
Committee Reports, see ¶ 5019

Under pre-Tax Cuts and Jobs Act law, the overall limitation on itemized deductions (also called the "Pease limitation" or "3%/80% rule") limited the total amount of otherwise allowable itemized deductions paid during the tax year for certain higher-income taxpayers (see adjusted gross income [AGI] thresholds, below). The overall limitation was applied last, after application of any other limitations on itemized deductions. It didn't apply to medical expenses, investment interest, casualty, theft, or wagering losses, and charitable contributions up to the amount of any "qualified contributions" (i.e., certain cash contributions paid after Aug. 22, 2017, and before Jan. 1, 2018, for relief efforts in the Hurricane Harvey, Hurricane Irma, or Hurricane Maria disaster areas). (FTC 2d/FIN ¶ A-2730, ¶ A-2731; USTR ¶ 684)

Under the pre-Tax Cuts and Jobs Act overall limitation, the otherwise allowable total amount of itemized deductions was reduced by 3% of the amount by which the taxpayer's AGI exceeded a threshold amount. For 2017, this threshold amount was: (1) $261,500 for single individuals; (2) $313,800 for joint filers and surviving spouses; (3) $287,650 for heads of household; and (4) $156,900 for marrieds filing separately. But the overall limitation didn't reduce itemized deductions by more than 80%. (FTC 2d/FIN ¶ A-2730, ¶ A-2731; USTR ¶ 684)

New Law. The Tax Cuts and Jobs Act suspends (Com Rept, see ¶ 5020) the overall limitation on itemized deductions for tax years beginning after Dec. 31, 2017 and before Jan. 1, 2026. (Code Sec. 68(f) as amended by Tax Cuts and Jobs Act §11046(a))

> **🖊️ *observation:*** That is, the overall limitation won't apply for tax years 2018–2025.

> **🖊️ *observation:*** The Tax Cuts and Jobs Act also suspends the deduction for personal exemptions (¶ 502), and suspends or limits other itemized deductions (see ¶ 503 *et seq.*), but generally cuts individual tax rates through 2025 (see ¶ 101), and nearly doubles the standard deduction, through 2025 (see ¶ 501).

Sunset. The suspension of the overall limitation, as described above, won't apply for tax years beginning after Dec. 31, 2025. (Code Sec. 68(f))

☐ **Effective:** Tax years beginning after Dec. 31, 2017 ((Tax Cuts and Jobs Act §11046(b))), and before Jan. 1, 2026. (Code Sec. 68(f))

¶ 505. 7.5%-of-AGI floor for medical expense deduction is retroactively extended through 2018 and applied to all taxpayers

Code Sec. 213(f), as amended by Tax Cuts and Jobs Act §11027(a)
Code Sec. 56(b)(1)(B), as amended by Tax Cuts and Jobs Act §11027(b)
Generally effective: Tax years beginning after Dec. 31, 2016, and ending before Jan. 1, 2019
Committee Reports, see ¶ 5011

A deduction is allowed for the expenses paid during the tax year for the medical care of the taxpayer, the taxpayer's spouse, and the taxpayer's dependents to the extent the expenses exceed a threshold amount. To be deductible, the expenses may not be reimbursed by insurance or otherwise. If the medical expenses are reimbursed, then they must be reduced by the reimbursement before the AGI floor is applied. (FTC 2d/FIN ¶ K-2000 *et seq.*; USTR ¶ 2134 *et seq.*)

Under pre-Tax Cuts and Jobs Act law, the threshold was generally 10% of adjusted gross income (AGI). But for tax years beginning after Dec. 31, 2012, and ending before Jan. 1, 2017, a 7.5%-of-AGI floor for medical expenses applied if a taxpayer or the taxpayer's spouse had reached age 65 before the close of the tax year. (FTC 2d/FIN ¶ K-2002; USTR ¶ 2134.14)

> **observation:** This temporary break for senior citizens expired at the end of 2016. Before the enactment of the Tax Cuts and Jobs Act, it was uncertain as to whether this break would be left expired, further extended, or made permanent.

Under pre-Tax Cuts and Jobs Act law, the regular Code Sec. 213 medical expense deduction rules applied for alternative minimum tax (AMT) purposes, except that medical expenses were deductible only to the extent they exceeded 10% of AGI. So, taxpayers couldn't take advantage of the lower 7.5% threshold for AMT purposes, even if they qualified for it for regular tax purposes. (FTC 2d/FIN ¶ A-8307; USTR ¶ 564.02)

New Law. For tax years beginning after Dec. 31, 2016, and ending before Jan. 1, 2019, the Tax Cuts and Jobs Act provides that any taxpayer may deduct medical expenses to the extent they exceed 7.5% of the taxpayer's AGI. (Code Sec. 213(f)(2) as amended by Tax Cuts and Jobs Act §11027(a))

> **observation:** In other words, the Tax Cuts and Jobs Act retroactively extends the tax break through 2018, and also retroactively makes it available to *any* individual taxpayer regardless of age for 2017–2018.

In addition, the rule limiting medical expense deduction for AMT purposes to 10% of AGI doesn't apply to tax years beginning after Dec. 31, 2016, and ending before Jan. 1, 2019. (Code Sec. 56(b)(1)(B) as amended by Tax Cuts and Jobs Act §11027(b))

> **observation:** This means that for medical expenses of individuals, the 7.5% (rather than 10%) threshold applies for AMT (as well as regular tax) purposes for 2017–2018.

> **illustration:** During 2017, Individual C had AGI of $200,000, unreimbursed hospital expenses of $35,000, and $5,000 of prescription drug expenses. C had a total of $40,000 in medical expenses; and 7.5% of her AGI is $15,000. She may deduct, as medical expenses on her 2017 returns, the excess of $40,000 over $15,000, or $25,000.

> **observation:** For tax years ending after Dec. 31, 2018, medical expenses will be subject to the 10% floor for both regular tax and AMT purposes.

☐ **Effective:** Tax years beginning after Dec. 31, 2016 (Tax Cuts and Jobs Act §11027(c)), and ending before Jan. 1, 2019 (Code Sec. 213(f)(2); Code Sec. 56(b)(1)(B)).

¶ 506. Itemized deduction is limited to $10,000 for SALT— combined state/local property, state/local/foreign income, and (if elected) general sales taxes

Code Sec. 164(b)(6), as amended by Tax Cuts and Jobs Act §11042(a)
Generally effective: Tax years beginning after Dec. 31, 2017, and before
    Jan. 1, 2026
Committee Reports, see ¶ 5016

Under pre-Tax Cuts and Jobs Act law, individual taxpayers were allowed an itemized deduction for the following state and local taxes (SALT) and foreign taxes, even though not incurred in a taxpayer's trade or business (FTC 2d/FIN ¶ K-4000, ¶ K-4001 *et seq.*; USTR ¶ 1644 *et seq.*):

(1) state, local, and foreign real property taxes (FTC 2d/FIN ¶ K-4500, ¶ K-4504 *et seq.*; USTR ¶ 1644 *et seq.*);

(2) state and local personal property taxes (FTC 2d/FIN ¶ K-4500, ¶ K-4502 *et seq.*; USTR ¶ 1644 *et seq.*); and

(3) state, local, and foreign income, war profits, and excess profits taxes. (FTC 2d/FIN ¶ K-4500, ¶ K-4506 *et seq.*, ¶ K-4700, ¶ K-4701 *et seq.*; USTR ¶ 1644 *et seq.*)

Taxpayers could elect an itemized deduction for state and local general sales taxes, instead of the itemized deduction for state and local income taxes. (FTC 2d/FIN ¶ K-4500, ¶ K-4504 *et seq.*; USTR ¶ 1644 *et seq.*)

New Law. Under the Tax Cuts and Jobs Act, for individual taxpayers, for tax years beginning after Dec. 31, 2017, and before Jan. 1, 2026 (Code Sec. 164(b)(6) as amended by Tax Cuts and Jobs Act §11042(a))—

(A) foreign real property tax may not be deducted (Code Sec. 164(b)(6)(A)), other than taxes paid or accrued in carrying on a trade or business or in an activity described in Code Sec. 212 (deduction for expenses incurred for the production or collection of income, etc., FTC 2d ¶ L-1400 *et seq.*; USTR ¶ 2124 *et seq.*) (Code Sec. 164(b)(6)); and

(B) the aggregate deduction for state and local real property taxes, state and local personal property taxes, state and local, and foreign, income, war profits, excess profits taxes, and general sales taxes (if elected) for any tax year is limited to $10,000 ($5,000 for marrieds filing separately), (Code Sec. 164(b)(6)(B)) except as otherwise provided below.

But, the $10,000 aggregate limitation rule in (B) above, doesn't apply to: (i) foreign income, war profits, excess profits taxes; (ii) state and local, and foreign, real property taxes; and (iii) state and local personal property taxes, if these taxes are paid or accrued in carrying on a trade or business or in an activity described in Code Sec. 212. (Code Sec. 164(b)(6)) So, deductions for state, local, and foreign property taxes, and sales taxes, that are deductible in computing income on an individual's Schedule C, Schedule E, or Schedule F on the individual's tax return, are allowed. (Com Rept, see ¶ 5016)

> *Illustration (1):* An individual may deduct state, local, and foreign property taxes, and sales taxes, if these taxes are imposed on business assets (such as residential rental property). (Com Rept, see ¶ 5016)

For individuals, state and local income, war profits, and excess profits taxes are not allowed as a deduction (other than under the $10,000 aggregate limitation discussed above). (Com Rept, see ¶ 5016)

Under the $10,000 aggregate limitation rule above, a taxpayer may claim an itemized deduction of up to $10,000 ($5,000 for marrieds filing separately) for the aggregate of (a) state and local property taxes not paid or accrued in carrying on a trade or business or an activity described in Code Sec. 212, and (b) state and local income, war profits, and excess profits taxes (or sales taxes in lieu of income, etc. taxes) paid or accrued in the tax year. Foreign real property taxes may not be deducted under the $10,000 aggregate limitation rule. (Com Rept, see ¶ 5016)

> **⍱** *observation:* In light of the above $10,000 limitation, practitioners may want to advise taxpayers to pay the final (4th quarter) installment of 2017 state and local estimated income tax no later than Dec. 31, 2017, rather than on the 2018 due date.

Pre-payment in 2017 of 2018 and later year income taxes is barred. For purposes of the $10,000 aggregate limitation rule above, an amount paid in a tax year beginning before Jan. 1, 2018, for a state or local income tax imposed for a tax year beginning after Dec. 31, 2017, is treated as paid on the last day of the tax year for which the tax is imposed. (Code Sec. 164(b)(6))

That is, an individual may not claim an itemized deduction in 2017 on a pre-payment of income tax for a future tax year in order to avoid the $10,000 aggregate limitation rule applicable for tax years beginning after 2017. (Com Rept, see ¶ 5016)

> **⍱** *observation:* Because the rule above barring pre-payments doesn't apply to property taxes, taxpayers may want to consider prepayment of a 2018 property tax installment on or before Dec. 31, 2017, to increase their 2017 itemized deduction for state and local taxes. See "Prepay-

ment of property tax, IRS guidance," below, for IRS's rules on prepayment of property tax in 2017.

observation: Practitioners may also want to advise clients to consider paying prior years' (past-due) state and local taxes before the end of 2017, to increase their 2017 itemized deduction.

observation: But, before any strategy to increase a taxpayer's 2017 itemized deduction for state and local tax is implemented, possible exposure to the AMT for 2017, based on those larger deductions, must be considered.

Prepayment of property tax—IRS guidance. Under IRS guidance in IR-2017-210, 12/27/2017, for prepaid state or local property tax to be deductible in 2017:

(i) the taxpayer must make the payment in 2017, and

(ii) the real property taxes must be *assessed* before 2018. (IR-2017-210, 12/27/2017)

A prepayment of anticipated real property taxes that have not been assessed before 2018 isn't deductible in 2017. State or local law determines whether and when a property tax is assessed, which is generally when the taxpayer becomes liable for the property tax imposed (i.e., presumably, when the notification of the assessment is sent to the taxpayer, see Illustrations 2 and 3, below). (IR-2017-210, 12/27/2017)

illustration (2): County A assesses property tax on July 1, 2017, for the period July 1, 2017 − June 30, 2018. On July 31, 2017, County A sends notices to residents notifying them of the assessment, and billing the property tax in two installments, with the first installment due Sept. 30, 2017 and the second installment due Jan. 31, 2018. After paying the first installment in 2017, if the taxpayer pays the second installment on or before Dec. 31, 2017, the taxpayer can deduct this prepayment on the taxpayer's 2017 return. (IR-2017-210, 12/27/2017)

illustration (3): County B (like County A, above) assesses and bills its residents for property taxes on July 1, 2017, for the period July 1, 2017 − June 30, 2018. County B intends to make the usual assessment in July 2018 for the period July 1, 2018 − June 30, 2019. But because county residents wish to prepay their 2018-2019 property taxes in 2017, County B changes its computer systems so that they will accept prepayment of property taxes for the 2018-2019 property tax year in 2017. But County B doesn't actually send the assessment notification for the 2018-2019 taxes until July 1, 2018. Taxpayers who prepay their 2018-2019 property taxes in 2017 can't deduct this prepayment on their

2017 federal returns, because the county doesn't assess the property tax for the 2018-2019 tax year until July 1, 2018. (IR-2017-210, 12/27/2017)

Sunset. The above-described suspension of the deduction of foreign real property taxes, and $10,000 aggregate limitation on income, property, and (if elected) sales tax itemized deductions, won't apply for tax years beginning after Dec. 31, 2025. (Code Sec. 164(b)(6))

sample client letter: A sample client letter explaining the limitation on the SALT deduction appears in ¶ 3210.

☐ **Effective:** For tax years beginning after Dec. 31, 2016. (Tax Cuts and Jobs Act §11042(b)) But, as described above, the suspension of the deduction of foreign real property taxes, and $10,000 aggregate limitation on income, property, and (if elected) sales tax itemized deductions, is specifically made to apply for tax years beginning after Dec. 31, 2017, and before Jan. 1, 2026. (Code Sec. 164(b)(6))

observation: Presumably, the "tax years beginning after Dec. 31, 2016" effective date in Tax Cuts and Jobs Act §11042(b) above is intended to make effective the Code Sec. 164(b)(6) rule barring the pre-payment in 2017 of 2018 or later years income taxes.

Because the language of Code Sec. 164(b)(6) itself limits the suspension of the deduction of foreign real property tax and the $10,000 aggregate limitation on income, property, and (if elected) sales tax itemized deductions for individuals, to tax years beginning after Dec. 31, 2017, and before Jan. 1, 2026, the Tax Cuts and Jobs Act §11042(b) doesn't change the dates of applicability for those rules.

¶ 507. Mortgage interest deduction acquisition debt maximum is lowered to $750,000, deduction for home equity interest is suspended

Code Sec. 163(h)(3)(F), as amended by Tax Cuts and Jobs Act §11043(a)
Generally effective: Tax years beginning after Dec. 31, 2017, and before
   Jan. 1, 2026
Committee Reports, see ¶ 5017

Taxpayers may claim an itemized deduction for "qualified residence interest" (QRI) (the "mortgage interest deduction"). Deductible QRI is interest that's paid or accrued during the tax year on acquisition indebtedness that's secured by a qualified residence, or, under pre-Tax Cuts and Jobs Act law, it also included home equity indebtedness that was secured by a qualified residence. (FTC 2d/FIN ¶ K-5470, ¶ K-5471, ¶ K-5490; USTR ¶ 1634.052)

Under pre-Tax Cuts and Jobs Act law, for this purpose, the maximum amount treated as acquisition indebtedness was $1 million ($500,000 for marrieds filing separately). (FTC 2d/FIN ¶ K-5470, ¶ K-5471 *et seq.*, ¶ K-5485; USTR ¶ 1634.052)

Acquisition indebtedness also includes indebtedness from the refinancing of other acquisition indebtedness, but only to the extent of the amount (and term) of the refinanced indebtedness. (FTC 2d/FIN ¶ K-5470, ¶ K-5471 *et seq.*, ¶ K-5488; USTR ¶ 1634.052)

Under pre-Tax Cuts and Jobs Act law, home equity indebtedness was indebtedness (other than acquisition indebtedness) secured by a qualified residence, regardless of how the proceeds of the indebtedness were used. The amount of home equity indebtedness couldn't exceed $100,000 ($50,000 for a married individual filing separately) and couldn't exceed the fair market value of the residence, reduced by the acquisition indebtedness. (FTC 2d/FIN ¶ K-5470, ¶ K-5471 *et seq.*, ¶ K-5490 *et seq.*; USTR ¶ 1634.052)

New Law. For tax years beginning after Dec. 31, 2017, and before Jan. 1, 2026, the Tax Cuts and Jobs Acts modifies the mortgage interest deduction rules, as follows (Code Sec. 163(h)(3)(F)(i) as amended by Tax Cuts and Jobs Act §11043(a)):

- **Deduction for home equity interest is suspended for 2018−2025.** The deduction for QRI paid on home equity indebtedness doesn't apply. (Code Sec. 163(h)(3)(F)(i)(I)) That is, for tax years beginning after Dec. 31, 2017 and before Jan. 1, 2026, taxpayers may not claim a deduction for interest on home equity indebtedness. (Com Rept, see ¶ 5017)

- **Maximum acquisition debt is limited to $750,000 ($375,000 for marrieds filing separately) for 2018−2025.** The aggregate amount treated as acquisition indebtedness can't exceed $750,000 ($375,000 for marrieds filing separately). (Code Sec. 163(h)(3)(F)(i)(II)) That is, for tax years beginning after Dec. 31, 2017 and before Jan. 1, 2026, a taxpayer may treat no more than $750,000 as acquisition indebtedness ($375,000 for married filing separately). (Com Rept, see ¶ 5017)

- **Debt incurred on or before Dec. 15, 2017 is subject to $1,000,000 ($500,000 for marrieds filing separately) acquisition debt limit.** The Tax Cuts and Jobs Act's $750,000/$375,000 limit on acquisition indebtedness above, doesn't apply to any indebtedness incurred on or before Dec. 15, 2017. (Code Sec. 163(h)(3)(F)(i)(III)) That is, for acquisition indebtedness incurred before Dec. 15, 2017, the limitation is $1,000,000 ($500,000 for marrieds filing separately). (Com Rept, see ¶ 5017)

In applying the $750,000/$375,000 acquisition debt limit above to any indebtedness incurred after Dec. 15, 2017, the $750,000/$375,000 limit must be reduced (but not below zero) by the amount of any indebtedness incurred on or before Dec. 15, 2017 that's treated as acquisition indebtedness for purposes of the deduction for QRI for the tax year. (Code Sec. 163(h)(3)(F)(i)(III))

• **Pre-Dec. 15, 2017 binding contract exception to $750,000/$375,000 acquisition debt limit.** For a taxpayer who enters into a written binding contract before Dec. 15, 2017 to close on the purchase of a principal residence before Jan. 1, 2018, and who purchases that residence before Apr. 1, 2018, the special rule above for debt incurred on or before Dec. 15, 2017 (limiting acquisition indebtedness to $1,000,000/$500,000) applies, by substituting "Apr. 1, 2018" for "Dec. 15, 2017." (Code Sec. 163(h)(3)(F)(i)(IV))

> *observation:*   That is, a taxpayer who has entered into a binding written contract before Dec. 15, 2017 to close on the purchase of a principal residence before Jan. 1, 2018, and who purchases that residence before Apr. 1, 2018, is treated as having incurred acquisition indebtedness before Dec. 15, 2017 under the special rule above, and, so, may apply the $1,000,000/$500,000 limit.

After 2025, $1,000,000/$500,000 acquisition debt limit applies, regardless of when debt is incurred. For tax years beginning after Dec. 31, 2025, the limitation on the amount of indebtedness (under Code Sec. 163(h)(3)(B)(ii), i.e., the $1,000,000/$500,000 limitation) is applied to the taxpayer's aggregate amount of acquisition indebtedness, without regard to the tax year in which the indebtedness was incurred. (Code Sec. 163(h)(3)(F)(ii))

That is, for tax years beginning after Dec. 31, 2025, a taxpayer may treat up to $1,000,000 ($500,000 for married separate filers) of indebtedness as acquisition indebtedness, regardless of when the indebtedness was incurred. (Com Rept, see ¶ 5017)

Treatment of debt refinancings. For any indebtedness that's incurred to refinance indebtedness, the refinanced indebtedness is treated, for purposes of the special rule above for debt incurred on or before Dec. 15, 2017 (limiting acquisition indebtedness to $1,000,000/$500,000) as incurred on the date the original indebtedness was incurred, to the extent the amount of the indebtedness resulting from the refinancing doesn't exceed the amount of the refinanced indebtedness. (Code Sec. 163(h)(3)(F)(iii)(I))

Thus, the $1,000,000/$500,000 limit applies to any indebtedness incurred on or after Dec. 15, 2017, to refinance QRI incurred before that date, to the extent the amount of the indebtedness resulting from the refinancing doesn't exceed the amount of the refinanced indebtedness. The maximum dollar amount that may be treated as principal residence acquisition indebtedness doesn't decrease by reason of a refinancing. (Com Rept, see ¶ 5017)

But the above rule (applying the $1,000,000/$500,000 limit) doesn't apply to any indebtedness after the expiration of the term of the original indebtedness or, if the principal of the original indebtedness is not amortized over its term, the expiration of the term of the first refinancing of the indebtedness (or if earlier, the date that is 30 years after the date of the first refinancing). (Code Sec. 163(h)(3)(F)(iii)(II))

Coordination with income exclusion rules for pre-2017 discharge of mortgage debt. Code Sec. 108(h)(2) (excluding from income, pre-2017 discharges of up to $2 million of mortgage debt on a taxpayer's main home, see FTC 2d ¶ J-7417; USTR ¶ 1084.01) must be applied without regard to the Code Sec. 163(h)(3)(F) rules described above. (Code Sec. 163(h)(3)(F)(iv))

Sunset. The Tax Cuts and Jobs Act changes described above won't apply for tax years beginning after Dec. 31, 2025. (Code Sec. 163(h)(3)(F)(i))

sample client letter: A sample client letter explaining these mortgage interest deduction rules appears in ¶ 3216.

☐ **Effective:** Tax years beginning after Dec. 31, 2017 (Tax Cuts and Jobs Act §11043(b)), and before Jan. 1, 2026. (Code Sec. 163(h)(3)(F)(i))

¶ 508. Personal casualty losses are nondeductible unless attributable to a federally declared disaster

Code Sec. 165(h)(5), as amended by Tax Cuts and Jobs Act §11044(a)
Generally effective: Losses incurred in tax years beginning after Dec. 31, 2017, and before Jan. 1, 2026
Committee Reports, see ¶ 5018

Personal casualty and theft losses. Under pre-Tax Cuts and Jobs Act law, for individuals, losses of property not connected with a trade or business or a transaction entered into for profit were deductible as personal casualty losses if the losses were the result of fire, storm, shipwreck, or other casualty, or of theft. (FTC 2d/FIN ¶ M-1600 *et seq.*, ¶ M-2100 *et seq.*; USTR ¶ 1654.300 *et seq.*, ¶ 1654.350 *et seq.*; Catalyst ¶ 406:234; Catalyst ¶ 510:104)

Personal casualty or theft losses are deductible only to the extent they exceed $100 per casualty or theft. In addition, aggregate net casualty and theft losses are deductible only to the extent they exceed 10% of an individual's adjusted gross income (AGI). The 10%-of-AGI threshold is applied after the per-casualty floor. (FTC 2d/FIN ¶ M-1900 *et seq.*, ¶ M-1901, ¶ M-1907; USTR ¶ 1654.304)

Personal casualty gains. A personal casualty gain is the recognized gain from any involuntary conversion of nonbusiness, not-for-profit property arising from fire, storm, shipwreck, or other casualty, or from theft, such as where the taxpayer receives an insurance payment or other reimbursement that exceeds the taxpayer's adjusted basis in the destroyed, damaged, or stolen property. (FTC 2d ¶ M-1908; USTR ¶ 1654.304)

If personal casualty losses exceed personal casualty gains for a tax year, the losses are allowed only to the extent of the sum of the amount of the personal casualty gains for the tax year, plus so much of the excess of personal casualty losses over personal casualty gains as exceeds 10% of the taxpayer's AGI. (FTC 2d ¶ M-1907; USTR ¶ 1654.304)

Federally declared disasters. A "federally declared disaster"—a term used in the Code for the election to claim a disaster loss in the preceding tax year and for other tax rules relating to disasters—is a disaster determined by the President to warrant federal assistance under the Robert T. Stafford Disaster Relief and Emergency Assistance Act. (FTC 2d ¶ M-2002; USTR ¶ 1654.520)

New Law. The Tax Cuts and Jobs Act provides that, for tax years beginning after Dec. 31, 2017, and before Jan. 1, 2026, personal casualty and theft losses of an individual are deductible only to the extent they're attributable to a federally declared disaster ("federal disaster losses"). (Code Sec. 165(h)(5)(A) as amended by Tax Cuts and Jobs Act §11044(a)) The loss deduction is subject to the $100-per-casualty and 10%-of-AGI limitations described above. (Com Rept, see ¶ 5018)

Exception for taxpayers with casualty gains. An exception to the rule that disallows a deduction for personal casualty losses other than federal disaster losses applies where a taxpayer has personal casualty gains for the tax year. (Code Sec. 165(h)(5)(B))

In that case, a taxpayer may deduct the portion of the personal casualty loss not attributable to a federally declared disaster (a "nonfederal casualty loss") to the extent the loss doesn't exceed the personal casualty gains. (Code Sec. 165(h)(5)(B)(i))

In applying the 10%-of-AGI floor to federal disaster losses, the amount of the individual's personal casualty gains for a tax year available to offset against federal disaster losses is reduced by the amount of personal casualty gains for the year offset against nonfederal casualty losses. (Code Sec. 165(h)(5)(B)(ii))

> *observation:* So, where an individual has both personal casualty gains and personal casualty losses for a tax year, the individual first reduces the amount of personal casualty gains by the amount of nonfederal casualty losses. Any remaining personal casualty gains are then used to reduce the amount of the taxpayer's deductible federal disaster losses. Any remaining federal disaster losses are deductible to the extent they exceed the 10%-of-AGI floor.

illustration: Individual X has AGI of $100,000 for the current tax year. After applying the $100-per-casualty limit, X also has $20,000 of nonfederal casualty losses, $30,000 of federal disaster losses, and $25,000 of personal casualty gains for the year. The nonfederal casualty losses are offset against personal casualty gains and reduce the amount of personal casualty gains to be applied against X's federal disaster losses to $5,000 ($25,000 − $20,000).

Now, X determines how much of the federal disaster losses are deductible. First, X may deduct $5,000 of federal disaster losses to offset the remaining personal casualty gains. Next, X applies the 10%-of-AGI limit. 10% of X's $100,000 AGI is $10,000. So, of X's remaining $25,000 in federal disaster losses, X may deduct $15,000 ($25,000 − $10,000).

Sunset. The limitation of deductible personal casualty and theft losses to those losses attributable to a federally declared disaster won't apply to losses incurred in tax years after Dec. 31, 2025. (Code Sec. 165(h)(5)(A))

☐ **Effective:** Losses incurred in tax years beginning after Dec. 31, 2017 (Tax Cuts and Jobs Act §11044(b)), and before Jan. 1, 2026. (Code Sec. 165(h)(5)(A))

¶ 509. Gambling loss limitation is broadened: deduction for *any* expense incurred in gambling—not just gambling losses—is limited to gambling winnings

Code Sec. 165(d), as amended by Tax Cuts and Jobs Act §11050
Generally effective: Tax years beginning after Dec. 31, 2017, and before
  Jan. 1, 2026
Committee Reports, see ¶ 5024

Under Code Sec. 165(d), losses sustained from wagering transactions are allowed only to the extent of the gains from those transactions. (FTC 2d ¶ M-6100 *et seq.*; USTR ¶ 1654.500)

Pre-Tax Cuts and Jobs Act case law (the 2011 Tax Court decision in *Mayo*) provided that the nonwagering expenses (e.g., the expenses of transportation, meals and entertainment, and admission fees) of a gambling business weren't included in "gambling losses," so these expenses weren't subject to the rule limiting gambling losses to gambling gains, and were deductible business expenses. IRS acquiesced in the result reached in *Mayo*. (FTC 2d ¶ M-6100 *et seq.*, ¶ M-6102.1; USTR ¶ 1654.500)

observation: The holding in *Mayo* didn't allow gambling-related nonwagering expenses to be deducted by individuals who weren't in the trade or business of gambling; the decision applied to those who were in the trade or business of gambling.

New Law. The Tax Cuts and Jobs Act provides that for tax years beginning after Dec. 31, 2017, and before Jan. 1, 2026, for purposes of the limit on wagering losses, the term "losses from wagering transactions" includes any deduction otherwise allowable under the Code incurred in carrying on any wagering transaction. (Code Sec. 165(d) as amended by Tax Cuts and Jobs Act §11050(a))

The Tax Cuts and Jobs Act clarifies the scope of "losses from wagering transactions" as that term is used in the Code Sec. 165(d) limitation on gambling losses. The term includes any deduction otherwise allowable under the Code that's incurred in carrying on any wagering transaction. The provision is intended to clarify that the gambling loss limitation applies not only to the actual costs of wagers incurred by an individual, but to other expenses incurred by the individual in connection with the conduct of that individual's gambling activity. Thus, for instance, an individual's otherwise deductible expenses in traveling to or from a casino are subject to the Code Sec. 165(d) limitation. The provision reverses the result in *Mayo*. (Com Rept, see ¶ 5024)

> **RIA** *observation:* Thus, under the Tax Cuts and Jobs Act, those in the trade or business of gambling may no longer deduct non-wagering expenses, such as travel expenses or fees, to the extent those expenses exceed gambling gains.

Sunset. The above rule won't apply to tax years beginning after Dec. 31, 2025. (Code Sec. 165(d))

☐ **Effective:** Tax years beginning after Dec. 31, 2017 (Tax Cuts and Jobs Act §11050(b)), and before Jan. 1, 2026. (Code Sec. 165(d)).

¶ 510. Alimony won't be deductible by the payor or includible by the recipient for post-2018 divorce or separation instruments

Code Sec. 61(a)(8), as amended by Tax Cuts and Jobs Act §11051(b)(1)(A)
Code Sec. 62(a)(10), as amended by Tax Cuts and Jobs Act §11051(b)(2)(A)
Code Sec. 71, as repealed by Tax Cuts and Jobs Act §11051(b)(1)(B)
Code Sec. 215, as repealed by Tax Cuts and Jobs Act §11051(a)
Code Sec. 682, as repealed by Tax Cuts and Jobs Act §11051(b)(1)(C)
Generally effective: Divorce or separation instruments executed after Dec. 31, 2018
Committee Reports, see ¶ 5025

Under pre-Tax Cuts and Jobs Act law, individuals could deduct an amount equal to the alimony or separate maintenance payments paid during the individual's tax year. (FTC 2d/FIN ¶ K-6000, ¶ K-6001 *et seq.*; USTR ¶ 2154 *et seq.*) These payments were "above-the-line." (FTC 2d/FIN ¶ A-2600, ¶ A-2621; USTR ¶ 624.04)

And, alimony and separate maintenance payments were includible in the gross income of the recipient spouse. (FTC 2d/FIN ¶ J-1410, ¶ J-1413 *et seq.*; USTR ¶ 714 *et seq.*) The income from an alimony or "pre-divorce" trust was includible in the income of the beneficiary/recipient. (FTC 2d/FIN ¶ C-5400, ¶ C-5433 *et seq.*; USTR ¶ 6824)

New Law. Under the Tax Cuts and Jobs Act, generally, for divorce or separation instruments executed after Dec. 31, 2018 (but see special effective date rules below):

. . . the deduction for payment of alimony won't apply (Code Sec. 215 as repealed by Tax Cuts and Jobs Act §11051(a); Code Sec. 62(a)(10) as amended by Tax Cuts and Jobs Act §11051(b)(2)(A)); and

. . . the inclusion in gross income for receipt of alimony payments won't apply, whether the recipient receives the alimony payments, or is the beneficiary of an alimony trust. (Code Sec. 61(a)(8) as amended by Tax Cuts and Jobs Act §11051(b)(1)(A); Code Sec. 71 as repealed by Tax Cuts and Jobs Act §11051(b)(1)(B); Code Sec. 682 as repealed by Tax Cuts and Jobs Act §11051(b)(1)(C))

Thus, alimony and separate maintenance payments will not be deductible by the payor spouse. And, because of the elimination of the Code provisions specifying that alimony and separate maintenance payments are included in income, income used for alimony payments will be taxed at the rates that apply to the payor spouse, rather than those that apply to the recipient spouse. (Com Rept, see ¶ 5025)

> *observation:* The Tax Cuts and Jobs Act also suspends other deductions (¶ 503 *et seq.*), but it generally cuts individual tax rates (see ¶ 101).

> *sample client letter:* A sample client letter explaining the changed tax treatment of alimony appears in ¶ 3220.

> *observation:* The tax rules for *child support*—i.e., that payers of child support don't get a deduction, and recipients of child support don't have to pay tax on those amounts—weren't changed by the Tax Cuts and Jobs Act.

☐ **Effective:** For any divorce or separation instrument (as defined in Code Sec. 71(b)(2) as in effect before Dec. 22, 2017) that's:

(i) executed after Dec. 31, 2018 (Tax Cuts and Jobs Act §11051(c)(1)), or

(ii) executed on or before Dec. 31, 2018, and modified after Dec. 31, 2018, if the modification expressly provides that the amendments made by Tax Cuts and Jobs Act §11051 above (i.e., repealing the alimony deduction, and the inclusion in gross income of alimony), apply to the modification. (Tax Cuts and Jobs Act §11051(c)(2))

¶ 511. $3,000 deduction for living expenses of members of Congress is eliminated

Code Sec. 162(a), as amended by Tax Cuts and Jobs Act §13311(a)
Generally effective: Tax years beginning after Dec. 22, 2017
Committee Reports, None

Subject to limitations, taxpayers can deduct away-from-home travel costs if the costs qualify as deductible business or investment-related expenses. (FTC 2d/FIN ¶ L-1700 *et seq.*; USTR ¶ 1624.114) Individuals engaged in occupations that involve extended overnight travel have far more travel expense problems to face than those who occasionally leave home on business. (FTC 2d/FIN ¶ L-2000 *et seq.*)

The tax home of a member of Congress (including a delegate from a U.S. territory or the Resident Commissioner of Puerto Rico) is the member's place of residence in the state, congressional district, or possession that the member represents. The member is therefore away from home while in Washington on Congressional business.

Under pre-Tax Cuts and Jobs Act law, members of Congress were allowed to deduct up to $3,000 of living expenses when they were away from home (such as expenses connected with maintaining a residence in Washington, D.C.) in any tax year. (FTC 2d/FIN ¶ L-2014 *et seq.*; USTR ¶ 1624.141)

New Law. The Tax Cuts and Jobs Act prohibits members of Congress from deducting living expenses when they are away from home, eliminating the $3,000 allowance. (Code Sec. 162(a) as amended by Tax Cuts and Jobs Act §13311(a))

☐ **Effective:** Tax years beginning after Dec. 22, 2017. (Tax Cuts and Jobs Act §13311(b))

¶ 512. Limit on an individual's contributions of cash to charitable organizations is increased from 50% to 60% of donor's contribution base

Code Sec. 170(b)(1)(G), as amended by Tax Cuts and Jobs Act §11023(a)
Generally effective: Contributions made in tax years beginning after Dec. 31,
2017, and before Jan. 1, 2026
Committee Reports, see ¶ 5007

The deduction for an individual's charitable contributions is limited to prescribed percentages of the taxpayer's "contribution base." Under pre-Tax Cuts and Jobs Act law, the applicable percentages were 50%, 30%, or 20%, and depended only on the type of organization to which the contribution was made, whether the contribution was made "to" or merely "for the use of" the donee organization, and whether the contribution consisted of capital gain property. (FTC 2d/FIN ¶ K-3670 *et seq.*; USTR ¶ 1704.05 *et seq.*)

An individual's contribution base is adjusted gross income (AGI), but without deducting any net operating loss (NOL) carryback to that year. (FTC 2d/FIN ¶ K-3672; USTR ¶ 1704.06) In some cases, a taxpayer may elect an increased ceiling for capital gain property contributions by reducing the amount of the contributions. (FTC 2d/FIN ¶ K-3689; USTR ¶ 1704.11)

Under pre-Tax Cuts and Jobs Act law, an individual could take an itemized deduction up to 50% of the individual's contribution base (the "50% limit") for contributions to (as opposed to for the use of) 50% charities. (FTC 2d/FIN ¶ K-3670, ¶ K-3671; USTR ¶ 1704.05) These are charitable organizations such as (1) churches, (2) educational organizations, (3) foundations for the benefit of state colleges or universities, (4) hospitals and medical research organizations, (5) agricultural research organizations, (6) governmental bodies, (7) publicly supported organizations, (8) certain membership and other broadly supported organizations, (9) supporting organizations, and (10) certain private foundations. (FTC 2d/FIN ¶ K-3720 *et seq.*; USTR ¶ 1704.07)

Charities that aren't 50% charities are 30% charities. Individuals may deduct up to 30% of their contribution bases (the "30% limit") for charitable contributions to or for the use of 30% charities and contributions for the use of 50% charities. (FTC 2d/FIN ¶ K-3685; USTR ¶ 1704.10)

If an individual's charitable contributions exceed the applicable contribution-base percentage limit, then the excess may be carried forward and deducted for up to five years under Code Sec. 170(d)(1). Any contribution carried to a future year remains in its percentage limitation category, and can only be deducted after any contributions made in that category in that future year, subject to the limitations applicable to that year. The carryforward is available even if the individual didn't itemize deductions in the contribution year. (FTC 2d/FIN ¶ K-3700 *et seq.*; USTR ¶ 1704.13)

New Law. The Tax Cuts and Jobs Act increases the contribution-base percentage limit for tax years beginning after Dec. 31, 2017, and before Jan. 1, 2026, for deductions of *cash* contributions by individuals to 50% charities from 50% to 60% (the "60% limit"). (Code Sec. 170(b)(1)(G)(i) as amended by Tax Cuts and Jobs Act §11023(a)) As Congress believes that a robust charitable sector is vital to the U.S. economy, and that charitable giving is critical to ensuring that the sector thrives, it is desirable to provide additional incentives for taxpayers to provide monetary and volunteer support to charities. Increasing the charitable percentage limit for cash contributions to public charities is intended to encourage taxpayers to provide essential monetary support to front-line charities. (Com Rept, see ¶ 5007)

> *observation:* Although the Tax Cuts and Jobs Act increases the percentage limit for cash contributions to charities, other provisions reduce charitable giving incentives. Perhaps most significantly, more taxpayers are expected to take advantage of the increased standard deduction (¶ 501) rather than itemizing deductions. Taxpayers who no longer itemize won't be able to deduct any of their charitable contributions.

Cash contributions that are taken into account under the 60% limit aren't taken into account for purposes of applying the 50% limit. (Code Sec. 170(b)(1)(G)(iii)(I)) But the 30% and 50% limits are applied for a tax year by reducing the aggregate contribution limit allowed for that year by the aggregate cash contributions allowed under the 60% limit for the year. (Code Sec. 170(b)(1)(G)(iii)(II))

> *illustration (1):* Individual X has a contribution base of $180,000. She contributes $50,000 to a 50% charity and an automobile worth $10,000 *for the use of* the 50% charity. X's limit for cash contributions is $108,000 ($180,000 × 60%). X's limit on contributions for the use of a charity is $54,000 ($180,000 × 30%), but this amount must be reduced by X's $50,000 cash contribution, to yield a contribution limit of $4,000. X may deduct $4,000 of the automobile's value in the current tax year but must carry the remaining $6,000 foreword to subsequent tax years.

If the aggregate amount of an individual's cash contributions to 50% charities for the year exceeds 60% of the individual's contribution base, then the excess is carried forward and is treated as a deductible charitable contribution in each of the five succeeding tax years. The carryover's deductible for a year in the carryover period to the extent it, plus the taxpayer's contributions for the year, don't exceed 60% of the individual's contribution base under the Code Sec. 170(d)(1) rules. (Code Sec. 170(b)(1)(G)(ii)) *illustration (2):* Individual Y has a contribution base of $100,000 in Year 1 and contributes $65,000 in cash to a 50% charity. Y can deduct $60,000 in Year 1 (60% of $100,000), and carry over $5,000. In Year 2, Y's contribution base is also $100,000, and she contributes $59,000 to the charity. Y can deduct $60,000 (60% of $100,000) in Year 2. So, in addition to deducting the $59,000 contribution, Y may deduct $1,000 of the carryover from Year 1 and carry the other $4,000 over to Year 3.

Sunset. The increased 60%-of-contribution-base limit won't apply to contributions made in tax years after Dec. 31, 2025. (Code Sec. 170(b)(1)(G)(i))

☐ **Effective:** Contributions made in tax years beginning after Dec. 31, 2017 (Tax Cuts and Jobs Act §11023(b)), and before Jan. 1, 2026. (Code Sec. 170(b)(1)(G)(i))

¶ 513. Charitable deduction is denied for contributions to a college or university in exchange for athletic event seating rights

Code Sec. 170(l)(1), as amended by Tax Cuts and Jobs Act §13704(a)
Generally effective: Contributions in tax years beginning after Dec. 31, 2017
Committee Reports, see ¶ 5007

Under pre-Tax Cuts and Jobs Act law, if a taxpayer made a payment to or for the benefit of a college or university that would have been allowable as a charitable deduction but for the fact that, as a result, the taxpayer received (directly or indirectly) the right to buy tickets for seating at an athletic event in the institution's athletic stadium, 80% of the payment was treated as a charitable contribution. The 80% rule applied whether or not tickets would have been readily available to the taxpayer without making the payment, and even if the seating was located in a special viewing area within the athletic stadium (e.g., a skybox). (FTC 2d/FIN ¶ K-3000 *et seq.*, ¶ K-3100; USTR ¶ 1704.38)

If a part of a payment was for the purchase of the tickets, then that part was treated as a separate amount under pre-Tax Cuts and Jobs Act law. The 80% deduction rule above didn't apply if the taxpayer received tickets or seating, rather than the right to buy tickets or seating, in return for the payment. (FTC 2d/FIN ¶ K-3100; USTR ¶ 1704.38)

observation: Allowing 80% of the contributions to be deducted was an exception to the requirement that a charitable contribution not be made in exchange for a benefit to the donor commensurate with the money or property transferred. (FTC 2d ¶ K-3032; USTR ¶ 1704.38)

New Law. Under the Tax Cuts and Jobs Act, no charitable deduction is allowed for a payment to a college or university in exchange for which the contributor receives the right to purchase tickets or seating at an athletic event. (Code Sec. 170(l)(1) as amended by Tax Cuts and Jobs Act §13704(a)) Congress believes that taxpayers should only be permitted a charitable deduction commensurate with the value of assets given to charity. (Com Rept, see ¶ 5007)

> **illustration:** Individual Y contributes $10,000 to University on Dec. 31, 2017, in exchange for the right to buy season tickets in premium seating for University's football team. Y may deduct $8,000 (80%) of the contribution. If Y waits until Jan. 1, 2018, to make the contribution, the Tax Cuts and Jobs Act eliminates Y's ability to deduct any amount of the $10,000 as a charitable deduction.

☐ **Effective:** Contributions made in tax years beginning after Dec. 31, 2017. (Tax Cuts and Jobs Act §13704(b))

¶ 514. Moving expense deduction eliminated, except for certain armed forces members

Code Sec. 217, as amended by Tax Cuts and Jobs Act §11049(a)
Generally effective: Tax years beginning after Dec. 31, 2017, and before
    Jan. 1, 2026
Committee Reports, see ¶ 5023

Code Sec. 217 allows an above-the-line deduction for moving expenses paid or incurred during the tax year in connection with the commencement of work by a taxpayer as an employee or as a self-employed individual at a new principal place of work. These expenses are deductible only if the move meets certain conditions related to distance from the taxpayer's previous residence and the taxpayer's status as a full-time employee in the new location. Special rules apply in the case of a member of the Armed Forces of the U.S. In the case of any such individual who is on active duty, who moves pursuant to a military order and incident to a permanent change of station, the limitations related to distance from the taxpayer's previous residence and status as a full-time employee in the new location don't apply. (FTC 2d ¶ L-3600FTC 2d/FIN ¶ L-3630; USTR ¶ 2174; Catalyst ¶ 425:140)

New Law. The Tax Cuts and Jobs Act temporarily suspends the moving expense deduction for tax years beginning after Dec. 31, 2017, and before Jan. 1, 2026, except in the case of a member of the Armed Forces of the United States on active duty who moves pursuant to a military order and incident to a permanent change of station. (Code Sec. 217(k) as amended by Tax Cuts and Jobs Act §11049(a))

For the Tax Cuts and Jobs Act's suspension of the exclusion for qualified moving expense reimbursements from 2018 through 2025, except for members of the armed forces, see ¶ 602.

Sunset. The above rule won't apply to tax years beginning after Dec. 31, 2025. (Code Sec. 217(k))

☐ **Effective:** Tax years beginning after Dec. 31, 2017 (Tax Cuts and Jobs Act §11049(b)), and before Jan. 1, 2026. (Code Sec. 217(k))

¶ 515. Donee-reporting exception to substantiation requirement for charitable contributions is retroactively repealed

Code Sec. 170(f)(8)(D), as amended by Tax Cuts and Jobs Act §13705(a)
Generally effective: Contributions made in tax years beginning after Dec. 31, 2016
Committee Reports, see ¶ 5007

No charitable deduction is allowed for contributions of $250 or more unless the donor substantiates the contribution by a contemporaneous written acknowledgment (CWA) from the donee organization. (FTC 2d/FIN ¶ K-3900; USTR ¶ 1704)

Under pre-Tax Cuts and Jobs Act law, IRS was authorized to issue regs that exempted donors from this substantiation requirement if the donee organization filed a return that contained the same information required on the CWA. (FTC 2d/FIN ¶ K-3938; USTR ¶ 1704.50)

In 2015, IRS issued proposed regs that would have provided for donee reporting. But it later withdrew those regs because of concerns about having donee organizations collect and maintain the taxpayer identification numbers (TINs) of donors.

Because IRS hadn't issued final regs, the donee-reporting exception from the CWA requirement didn't apply. IRS's rulemaking authority was discretionary, and the donee-reporting exception wasn't self-executing in the absence of regs. So, for example, a Form 990 filed by a donee organization couldn't be used as a substitute for donor substantiation. (FTC 2d/FIN ¶ K-3938; USTR ¶ 1704.50)

New Law. The Tax Cuts and Jobs Act repeals the donee-reporting exception from the CWA requirement. (Code Sec. 170(f)(8)(D) as amended by Tax Cuts and Jobs Act §13705(a))

☐ **Effective:** Contributions made in tax years beginning after Dec. 31, 2016. (Tax Cuts and Jobs Act §13705(b))

¶ 516. Child tax credit is increased to $2,000 and expanded and a partial credit is allowed for certain non-child dependents

Code Sec. 24(h), as amended by Tax Cuts and Jobs Act §11022(a)
Generally effective: Tax years beginning after Dec. 31, 2017, and before
   Jan. 1, 2026
Committee Reports, see ¶ 5006

Under pre-Tax Cuts and Jobs Act law, individuals could have claimed a maximum child tax credit (CTC) of $1,000 for each qualifying child under the age of 17. (FTC 2d/FIN ¶ A-4050, ¶ A-4051; USTR ¶ 244)

The CTC was phased-out for taxpayers with modified adjusted gross income (MAGI) above certain threshold amounts ($110,000 for joint filers, $75,000 for single filers and heads of household, and $55,000 for married taxpayers filing separately). The CTC allowable under Code Sec. 24 was reduced (but not below zero) by $50 for each $1,000 (or fraction thereof) by which the taxpayer's MAGI exceeded the applicable threshold amount. In other words, if the excess wasn't a multiple of $1,000, it was treated as the next higher multiple of $1,000. (FTC 2d/FIN ¶ A-4050, ¶ A-4052; USTR ¶ 244)

> *illustration (1):* H and W have one qualifying child. H and W's MAGI for the year is $113,001, which exceeds the $110,000 phaseout threshold for joint filers (see above) by $3,001. Thus, H and W must reduce the amount of their CTC credit by $200 ($50 × 4), to $800 ($1,000 − $200). If H and W's MAGI had been $113,000, they would only have had to reduce the CTC by $150 ($50 × 3), to $850.

New Law. For a tax year beginning after Dec. 31, 2017, and before Jan. 1, 2026, (Code Sec. 24(h)(1) as amended by Tax Cuts and Jobs Act §11022(a)) the Tax Cuts and Jobs Act modifies the CTC by increasing the credit amount (discussed below), increasing the threshold amounts for the phaseout (discussed below), and allowing a partial credit for dependents who don't qualify for a full CTC (discussed below).

For changes to the refundable portion of the CTC made by the Tax Cuts and Jobs Act, see ¶ 517.

For the requirement under the Tax Cuts and Jobs Act that a qualifying child's social security number is needed to claim the CTC, see ¶ 518.

Increase in the credit amount. For a tax year beginning after Dec. 31, 2017, and before Jan. 1, 2026, (Code Sec. 24(h)(1)) the Tax Cuts and Jobs Act substitutes "$2,000" for the "$1,000" credit amount under Code Sec. 24(a). (Code Sec. 24(h)(2)) Thus, the Tax Cuts and Jobs Act temporarily increases the CTC to $2,000 per child. (Com Rept, see ¶ 5006)

Increase in the threshold amount for phaseout. In lieu of the threshold amount determined under Code Sec. 24(b)(2), the threshold amount for applying the phaseout is $400,000 for a joint return ($200,000 for all other returns) (Code Sec. 24(h)(3)), for a tax year beginning after Dec. 31, 2017, and before Jan. 1, 2026. (Code Sec. 24(h)(1)) In other words, the CTC begins to phase out for taxpayers with adjusted gross income in excess of $400,000 (for married taxpayers filing a joint return) and $200,000 (for all other taxpayers). (Com Rept, see ¶ 5006)

> *observation:* If a taxpayer who does not file a joint return has one qualifying child, the CTC is completely phased out if the taxpayer's MAGI is (or exceeds) $240,000. If that taxpayer has two qualifying children, the CTC is completely phased out if the taxpayer's MAGI is (or exceeds) $280,000.

> *illustration (2):* T, a single taxpayer, has one qualifying child. T's MAGI is $240,000. Thus, T's CTC of $2,000 is reduced to zero ($\frac{(\$240,000 - \$200,000)}{1,000} \times \$50$).

> *illustration (3):* The facts are the same as in illustration (2) except that T has two qualifying children. T's MAGI is $280,000. Thus, T's $4,000 CTC is reduced to zero ($\frac{(\$280,000 - \$200,000)}{1,000} \times \$50$).

> *illustration (4):* H and W have one qualifying child. H and W's MAGI for the year is $403,001, which exceeds the $400,000 phaseout threshold for joint filers (see above) by $3,001. Thus, H and W must reduce the amount of their CTC credit by $200 ($50 × 4), to $1800 ($2,000 − $200). If H and W's MAGI had been $403,000, they would only have had to reduce the CTC by $150 ($50 × 3), to $1850.

> *observation:* Under the Tax Cuts and Jobs Act, married filing separately taxpayers are subject to the same phaseout threshold as other taxpayers who do not file a joint return (single and head of household taxpayers). Thus, the threshold for a taxpayer filing as married filing separately is increased from $55,000 (under pre-Tax Cuts and Jobs Act law) to $200,000.

The threshold amount is not indexed for inflation. (Com Rept, see ¶ 5006)

Partial credit allowed for certain other dependents. For a tax year beginning after Dec. 31, 2017, and before Jan. 1, 2026, (Code Sec. 24(h)(1)) a taxpayer's credit determined under Code Sec. 24(a) (as increased to $2,000 per qualifying child, see above) is increased by $500 for each dependent of the taxpayer (as defined in Code Sec. 152, see FTC 2d/FIN ¶ A-3601 *et seq.*; USTR ¶ 1524 *et seq.*) other than a qualifying child. (Code Sec. 24(h)(4)(A)) Thus, the CTC is modified to temporarily provide for a $500 non-refundable credit for qualifying dependents other than qualifying children and generally retains the Code Sec. 152 definition of a dependent. (Com Rept, see ¶ 5006)

> *observation:* For purposes of the partial credit, a qualifying dependent who isn't a qualifying child presumably includes a child over age of 17 (the age limit applicable to a qualifying child for purposes of the CTC, see FTC 2d ¶ A-4053; USTR ¶ 244). Thus, the partial credit might apply to a child under 19, a full-time student under age 24, or a disabled child of any age, see FTC 2d ¶ A-3605.4; USTR ¶ 1524. The partial credit may also apply to other qualifying (non-child) relatives if all requirements are met, see FTC 2d/FIN ¶ A-3605.6 *et seq.*; USTR ¶ 1524. In addition, the dependent must be a U.S. citizen, a U.S. national, or a U.S. resident. See below and FTC 2d/FIN ¶ A-4053; A-3605.2; USTR ¶ 244; 1524 *et seq.*

Exception for certain noncitizens. The partial credit for dependents who aren't qualifying children doesn't apply to an individual who isn't a dependent if Code Sec. 152(b)(3)(A) was applied without the reference to a country contiguous to the U.S. (Code Sec. 24(h)(4)(B))

> *observation:* In other words, an individual must be a U.S. citizen, a U.S. national, or a U.S. resident in order to be eligible for the $500 partial credit allowed for dependents who aren't qualifying children. Thus, residents of Canada or Mexico don't qualify for the partial credit unless they are U.S. citizens or U.S. nationals. See FTC 2d/FIN ¶ A-4053; USTR ¶ 244 et seq.

Qualifying children without social security numbers. If a qualifying child isn't allowed a CTC under Code Sec. 24 because of the rule under Code Sec. 24(h)(7) (i.e., because the child doesn't have an SSN, see ¶ 518), that child is treated as a dependent to whom the partial credit applies under Code Sec. 24(h)(4)(A) (discussed above). (Code Sec. 24(h)(4)(C))

> *observation:* Thus, a taxpayer can claim the partial credit amount ($500) if a qualifying child doesn't have an SSN. In that case, qualifying children without SSNs are treated the same as dependents who aren't qualifying children.

☐ **Effective:** For tax years beginning after Dec. 31, 2017 (Tax Cuts and Jobs Act §11022(b); Code Sec. 24(h)(1)), and ending before Jan. 1, 2026. (Code Sec. 24(h)(1))

¶ 517. Refundable portion of the child tax credit is increased to $1,400 for tax years beginning after 2017

Code Sec. 24(h), as amended by Tax Cuts and Jobs Act §11022(a)
Generally effective: Tax years beginning after Dec. 31, 2017, and before
  Jan. 1, 2026
Committee Reports, see ¶ 5006

Under pre-Tax Cuts and Jobs Act law, individuals could have claimed a maximum child tax credit (CTC) of $1,000 for each qualifying child under the age of 17. (FTC 2d/FIN ¶ A-4050, ¶ A-4051; USTR ¶ 244) The CTC was phased-out for taxpayers with modified adjusted gross income (MAGI) above certain threshold amounts ($110,000 for joint filers, $75,000 for single filers and heads of household, and $55,000 for married taxpayers filing separately). (FTC 2d/FIN ¶ A-4050, ¶ A-4052; USTR ¶ 244).

For the increase in the CTC and threshold amounts, and the expansion of a partial CTC to dependents who are not qualifying children under the Tax Cuts and Jobs Act, see ¶ 516.

For all taxpayers with qualifying children (regardless of how many), the CTC was refundable to the extent of the lesser of the $1,000 credit or 15% of the taxpayer's earned income in excess of $3,000. Neither the $1,000 limit nor the $3,000 earned income threshold was adjusted for inflation. (FTC 2d/FIN ¶ A-4050, ¶ A-4055; USTR ¶ 244.02).

> *illustration (1):* H and W, joint filers, had earned income of $15,500 and one qualifying child. Under pre-Tax Cuts and Jobs Act law, H and W's $1,000 CTC was fully refundable, because 15% of the excess of H and W's earned income ($15,500) over $3,000 is $1,875 [($15,500 − $3,000) × 15% = $1,875], which was greater than the $1,000 CTC to which they were entitled.

> *illustration (2):* Assume the facts are the same as in illustration (1), except that H and W have earned income of $8,500. Under pre-Tax Cuts and Jobs Act law, only $825 of H and W's CTC is refundable (15% × (8,500 − $3,000).

For the requirement under the Tax Cuts and Jobs Act that a qualifying child's social security number is needed to claim the CTC, see ¶ 518.

New Law. The Tax Cuts and Jobs Act provides that, for a tax year beginning after Dec. 31, 2017, and before Jan. 1, 2026, (Code Sec. 24(h)(1) as amended by Tax Cuts and Jobs Act §11022(a)) the amount determined under Code Sec. 24(d)(1)(A) (i.e., the refundable portion of the credit) for any qualifying child cannot exceed $1,400, and Code Sec. 24(h)(4) (which allows for a partial credit for dependents who aren't qualifying children, see ¶ 516) is disregarded when applying Code Sec. 24(d)(1)(A). (Code Sec. 24(h)(5)(A))

> **observation:** In other words, only the CTC under Code Sec. 24(a) can be refunded (up to the limit of $1,400, as adjusted for inflation). The partial credit, under Code Sec. 24(h)(4), for dependents who aren't qualifying children is *nonrefundable*, see ¶ 516.

Inflation adjustment. For tax years beginning after 2018, the $1,400 limit on the amount of the refundable portion of the CTC under Code Sec. 24(h)(5)(A) (discussed above) is increased by an amount equal to: (Code Sec. 24(h)(5)(B))

. . . that dollar amount (i.e., $1,400), multiplied by (Code Sec. 24(h)(5)(B)(i))

. . . the cost-of-living adjustment (COLA) determined under Code Sec. 1(f)(3) (inflation adjustments for income tax rate brackets, see FTC 2d/FIN ¶ A-1103; USTR ¶ 14.08) for the calendar year in which the tax year begins, determined by substituting "2017" for "2016" in Code Sec. 1(f)(3)(A)(ii). (Code Sec. 24(h)(5)(B)(ii))

Any increase determined under this inflation adjustment rule is rounded to the next highest multiple of $100. (Code Sec. 24(h)(5)(B))

For the changes made by the Tax Cuts and Jobs Act to the inflation adjustment of income tax brackets, see ¶ 201.

Earned income threshold for refundable credit. Under the Tax Cuts and Jobs Act, Code Sec. 24(d)(1)(B)(i) (the earned income threshold for determining the refundable portion of the credit) is applied by substituting "$2,500" for "$3,000" (Code Sec. 24(h)(6)) for a tax year beginning after Dec. 31, 2017, and before Jan. 1, 2026. (Code Sec. 24(h)(1)) Thus, the Tax Cuts and Jobs Act temporarily lowers the earned income threshold for the refundable child tax credit to $2,500. (Com Rept, see ¶ 5006)

> **observation:** Lowering the threshold from $3,000 to $2,500 means that the refundable portion of the credit will be a larger amount.

> **illustration (3):** H and W, who file a joint return, have earned income of $8,500. Under Tax Cuts and Jobs Act law, $900 of H and W's CTC is refundable (15% x ($8,500 − $2,500), as compared to only $825 under pre-Tax Cuts and Jobs Act law (15% × (8,500 − $3,000).

☐ **Effective:** For tax years beginning after Dec. 31, 2017 (Tax Cuts and Jobs Act §11022(b); Code Sec. 24(h)(1)), and ending before Jan. 1, 2026. (Code Sec. 24(h)(1))

¶ 518. Qualifying child's social security number is required to claim child tax credit

Code Sec. 24(h), as amended by Tax Cuts and Jobs Act §11022(a)
Generally effective: Tax years beginning after Dec. 31, 2017, and before Jan. 1, 2026
Committee Reports, see ¶ 5006

Under pre-Tax Cuts and Jobs Act law, individuals could have claimed a maximum child tax credit (CTC) of $1,000 for each qualifying child under the age of 17. (FTC 2d/FIN ¶ A-4050, ¶ A-4051; USTR ¶ 244) The CTC was phased-out for taxpayers with modified adjusted gross income (MAGI) above certain threshold amounts ($110,000 for joint filers, $75,000 for single filers and heads of household, and $55,000 for married taxpayers filing separately). (FTC 2d/FIN ¶ A-4050, ¶ A-4052; USTR ¶ 244).

For the increase in the CTC and threshold amounts, and the expansion of a partial CTC to dependents who are not qualifying children under the Tax Cuts and Jobs Act, see ¶ 516.

Under pre-Tax Cuts and Jobs Act law, the CTC wasn't allowed to a taxpayer for any qualifying child unless the taxpayer included the qualifying child's name and taxpayer identification number (TIN) on the tax return for the year. Also, the qualifying child's TIN had to be issued on or before the due date for the filing of the return (including extensions). (FTC 2d/FIN ¶ A-4050, ¶ A-4059; USTR ¶ 244)

For this purpose, a TIN included a social security number (SSN), an individual taxpayer identification number (ITIN), or an adoption taxpayer identification number (ATIN), see FTC 2d/FIN ¶ S-1501; USTR ¶ 61,094. In other words, a taxpayer was still *eligible* for the CTC if the taxpayer didn't include a valid SSN for a qualifying child on the taxpayer's return as long as the taxpayer included an ITIN or ATIN for the child. (FTC 2d/FIN ¶ A-4050, ¶ A-4059; USTR ¶ 244)

For the changes to the refundable portion of the CTC made by the Tax Cuts and Jobs Act, see ¶ 517.

New Law. For a tax year beginning after Dec. 31, 2017, and before Jan. 1, 2026, (Code Sec. 24(h)(1) as amended by Tax Cuts and Jobs Act §11022(a)) no CTC is allowed under Code Sec. 24 to a taxpayer for any qualifying child unless the taxpayer includes the SSN of that child on the tax return for the tax year. (Code Sec. 24(h)(7))

An SSN is an SSN issued to an individual by the Social Security Administration, but only if the SSN is issued: (Code Sec. 24(h)(7))

. . . to a citizen of the U.S. or under 42 USC §205(c)(2)(B)(i)(I) or 42 USC §205(c)(2)(B)(i)(III) (to the extent it relates to subclause (I)) of the Social Security Act, and (Code Sec. 24(h)(7)(A))

. . . before the date of the return. (Code Sec. 24(h)(7)(B))

> **⊘** *observation:* Section 205(c)(2)(B)(i)(I) of the Social Security Act provides that the Commissioner of Social Security will assure that SSNs are assigned to aliens when they are lawfully admitted to the U.S. either for permanent residence or under a law permitting them to be employed in the U.S., and to other aliens at the time their status is changed to make it lawful for them to be employed in the U.S.
>
> Section 205(c)(2)(B)(i)(III), in part, allows the Commissioner to assign an SSN to any other individual when it appears that he could have been (but wasn't) assigned an SSN under the provisions of subclause (I), but only after investigation to establish the identity of the individual, the fact that an SSN hasn't already been assigned, and the fact that the individual is a citizen or a noncitizen who isn't prohibited from engaging in employment as a result of his alien status.

Thus, in order to receive the CTC (i.e., both the refundable and non-refundable portion), a taxpayer must include an SSN for each *qualifying child* for whom the credit is claimed on the tax return. The SSN requirement doesn't apply to a non-child dependent for whom the $500 non-refundable credit (discussed at ¶ 516) is claimed. (Com Rept, see ¶ 5006)

> **⊘** *observation:* Similar to pre-Tax Cuts and Jobs Act law, there is no requirement that the taxpayer provide his or her SSN or be a U.S. citizen, U.S. national, or U.S. resident in order to claim the CTC. The only requirements are that the taxpayer provide: (1) the qualifying child's SSN and (2) the taxpayer's TIN issued on or before the due date for the return. This means illegal immigrants with ITINs, who have U.S.-born qualifying children, will remain eligible to claim the CTC (including the refundable portion).

☐ **Effective:** For tax years beginning after Dec. 31, 2017 (Tax Cuts and Jobs Act §11022(b); Code Sec. 24(h)(1)), and ending before Jan. 1, 2026. (Code Sec. 24(h)(1))

¶ 600. Individuals: Income And Exclusions

¶ 601. Exceptions to life insurance transfer-for-value rule don't apply to life settlement transactions

Code Sec. 101(a), as amended by Tax Cuts and Jobs Act §13522(a)
Code Sec. 101(a)(1), as amended by Tax Cuts and Jobs Act §13522(b)
Generally effective: Transfers after Dec. 31, 2017
Committee Reports, see ¶ 5075

Amounts received under a life insurance contract by reason of the insured's death generally aren't included in the recipient's gross income. (FTC 2d/FIN ¶ J-4700; USTR ¶ 1014)

But if a life insurance contract is transferred for valuable consideration, the death benefits paid on the life insurance contract are excludable only to the extent of the actual value of the consideration paid, plus any premiums or other amounts paid by the transferee after the transfer. (FTC 2d/FIN ¶ J-4730 *et seq.*; USTR ¶ 1014.02)

Under an exception to this transfer-for-value rule, the entire proceeds are excluded when the transferee's basis is determined in whole or in part by reference to the transferor's basis—for example, when a policy is transferred from one corporation to another in a tax-free reorganization. (FTC 2d/FIN ¶ J-4742; USTR ¶ 1014.02)

Under another exception, the full exclusion is allowed for proceeds of a policy that has been transferred to the insured, to a partner of the insured, to a partnership in which the insured's a partner, or to a corporation in which the insured's a shareholder or officer. (FTC 2d/FIN ¶ J-4737 *et seq.*; USTR ¶ 1014.02)

Under pre-Tax Cuts and Jobs Act law, these two exceptions applied to life settlement transactions, *i.e.*, to sales of life insurance policies to third-party investors in a commercial context, as well as to other transfers.

☑ *observation:* Under the pre-Tax Cuts and Jobs Act transfer-for-value rule, it was possible for investors to structure a life settlement transac-

---

FTC 2d References are to Federal Tax Coordinator 2d
FIN References are to RIA's Analysis of Federal Taxes: Income (print)
USTR References are to United States Tax Reporter
Catalyst References are to Checkpoint Catalyst
PCA References are to Pension Analysis (print and electronic)
PBE References are to Pension & Benefits Explanations
BCA References are to Benefits Analysis (electronic)
BC References are to Benefits Coordinator (print)
EP References are to Estate Planning Analysis (print and electronic)

tion to avoid paying income tax on the profit realized when the insured died.

New Law. The Tax Cuts and Jobs Act provides that the exceptions to the transfer-for-value rule don't apply to a transfer of a life insurance contract, or any interest in a life insurance contract, in a reportable policy sale. (Code Sec. 101(a)(3)(A) as amended by Tax Cuts and Jobs Act §13522(a)) Thus, some part of the death benefit ultimately payable under such a contract may be includible in income. (Com Rept, see ¶ 5075)

The term "reportable policy sale" means the acquisition of an interest in a life insurance contract, directly or indirectly, if the acquirer has no substantial family, business, or financial relationship with the insured apart from the acquirer's interest in the life insurance contract. (Code Sec. 101(a)(3)(B))

An indirect acquisition includes the acquisition of an interest in a partnership, trust, or other entity that holds an interest in the life insurance contract. (Code Sec. 101(a)(3)(B))

> **observation:** This provision applies to life insurance transfers that take place in a commercial context, *i.e.,* life settlement transactions. The purpose is to make sure that the transfer-for-value rule applies to those transactions, so that the party that receives the insurance proceeds pays some tax.

For reporting requirements for reportable policy sales, see ¶ 1506.

☐ **Effective:** Transfers after Dec. 31, 2017. (Tax Cuts and Jobs Act §13522(c))

¶ 602. Exclusion for qualified moving expense reimbursements suspended, except for armed forces

Code Sec. 132(g), as amended by Tax Cuts and Jobs Act §11048
Generally effective: Tax years beginning after Dec. 31, 2017, and before
Jan. 1, 2026
Committee Reports, see ¶ 5022

Code Sec. 132(a)(6) provides that gross income doesn't include any fringe benefit that qualifies as a "qualified moving expense reimbursement." Code Sec. 132(g) provides that "qualified moving expense reimbursement" means any amount received (directly or indirectly) by an individual from an employer as a payment for (or a reimbursement of) expenses that would be deductible moving expenses under Code Sec. 217 (see FTC 2d ¶ L-3600; USTR ¶ 1324.09; PBE ¶ 132-4.09; BC ¶ 28,005; BCA ¶ 128,005) if directly paid or incurred by the individual. Code Sec. 132(g) further provides that "qualified moving expense reimbursement" doesn't include any payment for (or reimbursement of) an expense actually deducted by the individual in an earlier tax year.

New Law. The Tax Cuts and Jobs Act temporarily suspends the exclusion from income of qualified moving expense reimbursements for tax years beginning after Dec. 31, 2017, and before Jan. 1, 2026, except in the case of a member of the U.S. Armed Forces on active duty who moves pursuant to a military order and incident to a permanent change of station. (Code Sec. 132(g) as amended by Tax Cuts and Jobs Act §11048(a))

Sunset. The above rules suspending the exclusion from income of qualified moving expense reimbursement sunset for tax years beginning after Dec. 31, 2025. (Code Sec. 132(g))

For the suspension of the deduction for moving expenses, see ¶ 514.

☐ **Effective:** Tax years beginning after Dec. 31, 2017 (Tax Cuts and Jobs Act §11048(b)) and before Jan. 1, 2026. (Code Sec. 132(g)(2))

¶ 603. Exclusion for qualified bicycle commuting reimbursement suspended

Code Sec. 132(f)(8), as amended by Tax Cuts and Jobs Act §11047(a)
Generally effective: Tax years beginning after Dec. 31, 2017 and before Jan. 1, 2026
Committee Reports, see ¶ 5021

Under pre-Tax Cuts and Jobs Act law, employees receiving any fringe benefit that met the requirements for a "qualified transportation fringe" could exclude that benefit from income, up to the amount of a monthly dollar limit. A "qualified transportation fringe" included any of the following provided by an employer to an employee: (1) commuter transportation in a "commuter highway vehicle," including van pools, (2) transit passes, (3) qualified parking, and (4) qualified bicycle commuting reimbursement.

The amount of the qualified bicycle commuting reimbursement could not exceed $20 per month, multiplied by the number of qualified bicycle commuting months during the year. Thus, the maximum amount of the reimbursement was $240 per employee per year. (FTC 2d/FIN ¶ H-2205, ¶ H-2215.1; USTR ¶ 1324.08; PBE ¶ 132-4.08; BC ¶ 24,653; BCA ¶ 124,653)

New Law. The Tax Cuts and Jobs Act suspends the exclusion for qualified bicycle commuting reimbursements for tax years beginning after Dec. 31, 2017 and through tax years beginning before Jan. 1, 2026. (Code Sec. 132(f)(8) as amended by Tax Cuts and Jobs Act §11047(a))

Sunset. The above rules suspending the exclusion from income of qualified bicycle commuting reimbursements sunset for tax years beginning after Dec. 31, 2025. (Code Sec. 132(f)(8))

☐ **Effective:** Tax years beginning after Dec. 31, 2017 (Tax Cuts and Jobs Act §11047(b)) and before Jan. 1, 2026. (Code Sec. 132(f)(8))

¶ 604. Exclusion for discharge of certain student loans is broadened to include discharges on account of death or disability

Code Sec. 108(f)(5), as amended by Tax Cuts and Jobs Act §11031(a)
Generally effective: Discharges of indebtedness after Dec. 31, 2017 and
before Jan. 1, 2026
Committee Reports, see ¶ 5013

Exclusion for discharge of certain student loans. Under an exception to the general rule that the discharge of a taxpayer's indebtedness is included in gross income, amounts from the forgiveness (in whole or in part) of certain student loans are excluded from gross income, as long as the forgiveness is contingent on the student's working for a certain period of time in certain professions for any of a broad class of employers. (FTC 2d ¶ J-7508 *et seq.*; USTR ¶ 1084.04 *et seq.*)

Student loan defined for exclusion for discharge of certain student loans. For the discharge to qualify for the exclusion, Code Sec. 108(f)(2) provides that the loan must be made to an individual to assist the individual in attending an educational organization described in Code Sec. 170(b)(1)(A)(ii) (i.e., that has a regular faculty and curriculum and a regularly enrolled body of students in attendance where its education activities are regularly carried on, see FTC 2d ¶ K-3724; USTR ¶ 1704.42), and by:

(1) the U.S. or an instrumentality or agency of the U.S.;

(2) a state, territory, or possession of the U.S. or the District of Columbia or any political subdivision thereof;

(3) a public benefit corporation that's tax-exempt under Code Sec. 501(c)(3) (i.e., a religious, charitable, etc. organization) and that has assumed control over a state, county, or municipal hospital, and whose employees have been deemed to be public employees under state law; or

(4) an educational organization described in Code Sec. 170(b)(1)(A)(ii), if the loan is made: (a) under an agreement with any entity described in (1), (2), or (3), above, under which the funds from which the loan was made were provided to the educational organization, or (b) under a program of the educational organization that's designed to encourage the organization's students to serve in occupations with unmet needs or in areas with unmet needs, as long as the ser-

vices provided by the students (or former students) are for or under the direction of a governmental unit or a Code Sec. 501(c)(3) organization that's exempt from tax under Code Sec. 501(a). (See FTC 2d ¶ J-7509; USTR ¶ 1084.04.)

Under pre-Tax Cuts and Jobs Act law, there was no provision for exclusion for discharges of student loans due to death or disability. (FTC 2d/FIN ¶ J-7500, ¶ J-7508 *et seq.*; USTR ¶ 1084.04)

New Law. The Tax Cuts and Jobs Act modifies the student loan discharge exclusion rules to include certain discharges on account of death or disability. (Com Rept, see ¶ 5013)

Specifically, for discharges after Dec. 31, 2017 and before Jan. 1, 2026, an individual's gross income doesn't include any amount that (but for this exclusion) would be includible in gross income for the tax year by reason of the discharge (in whole or in part) of any loan that meets the definition below, if the discharge was (Code Sec. 108(f)(5)(A) as amended by Tax Cuts and Jobs Act §11031(a)):

(a) under section 437(a) or 437(d) of the Higher Education Act of '65 or under the parallel benefit under part D of title IV of that Act (relating to the repayment of loan liability) (Code Sec. 108(f)(5)(A)(i));

(b) under section 464(c)(1)(F) of the Act in (a) above (Code Sec. 108(f)(5)(A)(ii)); or

(c) otherwise discharged on account of the death or total and permanent disability of the student. (Code Sec. 108(f)(5)(A)(iii))

A loan meets the definition for this exclusion if the loan is (Code Sec. 108(f)(5)(B)):

(i) a student loan as defined in Code Sec. 108(f)(2) (see above) (Code Sec. 108(f)(5)(B)(i)); or

(ii) a private education loan (as defined in section 140(7) of the Consumer Credit Protection Act (15 U.S.C. 25 1650(7)). (Code Sec. 108(f)(5)(B)(ii))

Sunset. The above exclusion won't apply for discharges after Dec. 31, 2025. (Code Sec. 108(f)(5)(A))

☐ **Effective:** Discharges of indebtedness after Dec. 31, 2017 (Tax Cuts and Jobs Act §11031(b)) and before Jan. 1, 2026. (Code Sec. 108(f)(5)(A))

¶ 605. Special "combat zone" benefits extended retroactively to members of the armed forces performing services in the Sinai Peninsula of Egypt

Code Sec. 2(a)(3), Tax Cuts and Jobs Act §11026(a)(1)
Code Sec. 112, Tax Cuts and Jobs Act §11026(a)(2)

Code Sec. 692, Tax Cuts and Jobs Act §11026(a)(3)
Code Sec. 2201, Tax Cuts and Jobs Act §11026(a)(4)
Code Sec. 3401(a)(1), Tax Cuts and Jobs Act §11026(a)(5)
Code Sec. 4253(d), Tax Cuts and Jobs Act §11026(a)(6)
Code Sec. 6013(f)(1), Tax Cuts and Jobs Act §11026(a)(7)
Code Sec. 7508, Tax Cuts and Jobs Act §11026(a)(8)
Generally effective: June 9, 2015, except for the rule related to Code
  Sec. 3401(a)(1), which applies to remuneration paid after Dec. 22, 2017
Committee Reports, see ¶ 5010

Members of the Armed Forces serving in a "combat zone" are afforded a number of tax benefits. (Com Rept, see ¶ 5010) "Combat zone" means any area the President designates by executive order as an area in which U.S. Armed Forces are engaged in combat. For this purpose, a qualified hazardous duty area is treated as if it were a combat zone. (FTC 2d/FIN ¶ H-3100, ¶ H-3109; USTR ¶ 1124)

Before the enactment of the Tax Cuts and Jobs Act, the special combat benefits provided in the below provisions did not apply to members of the Armed Forces serving in the Sinai Peninsula of Egypt because it had not been officially designated a qualified hazardous duty area:

• Spouses of military personnel and government employees in "missing status" (missing in action (MIA), prisoner of war (POW), etc.) as a result of service in a combat zone, and who are otherwise eligible for "surviving spouse status," can qualify as surviving spouses and compute their tax using the married-filing-jointly tax rate schedule from the earlier of (1) the officially determined date of death, or (2) if no official determination is made, generally the date that is two years after the official termination of combat activities. (FTC 2d/FIN ¶ A-1700, ¶ A-1703; USTR ¶ 24.02)

⚓ observation: The surviving-spouse filing status is only available for two years following the year of death of the taxpayer's spouse, see FTC 2d/FIN ¶ S-1808; USTR ¶ 24.02.

• Certain military pay received for any month during which an Armed Forces member serves in a "combat zone," or is hospitalized as a result of serving in a combat zone, is excluded from gross income. (FTC 2d/FIN ¶ H-3100, ¶ H-3106, ¶ H-3109, ¶ H-3109.1, ¶ H-3112; USTR ¶ 1124)

• If a member of the Armed Forces dies while in active service or at any place as a result of wounds, disease or injury incurred while serving in the combat zone, the decedent's federal income tax liability is cancelled for the tax year in which death occurred and for any earlier tax year ending on or after the first day of service in a combat zone. (FTC 2d/FIN ¶ C-9650, ¶ C-9651; USTR ¶ 6924)

• When death occurs in a combat zone, the estate of an Armed Forces member is entitled to compute its estate tax liability under an estate tax rate schedule that contains rates lower than the rates in the generally applicable Code Sec. 2201(c) rate schedule. (FTC 2d/FIN ¶ R-7000, ¶ R-7011; USTR ¶ 22,014)

• While withholding is generally required from taxable payments to members of the Armed Forces, there is no withholding on any remuneration for active service as a member of the Armed Forces performed in any month during which the recipient is entitled, under Code Sec. 112, to the exclusion of "combat zone compensation" from gross income (see above), to the extent that the remuneration is excluded from gross income under that provision. (FTC 2d/FIN ¶ H-4425, ¶ H-4447; USTR ¶ 34,014.17)

• Communications excise tax isn't imposed on any payment received for any telephone service that originates within a combat zone from a member of the Armed Forces who is performing service in the combat zone. (FTC 2d/FIN ¶ W-5000, ¶ W-5033; USTR ¶ 42,534.08)

• Spouses of persons in the Armed Forces and government employees in "missing" status as a result of service in a combat zone can elect to file a joint return for any year which begins on or before the day that is two years after the date of termination of combatant activities in that zone, if the spouse is otherwise entitled to file a joint return. (FTC 2d/FIN ¶ S-1800, ¶ S-1808; USTR ¶ 60,134.01)

• Individuals serving in the Armed Forces in a combat zone, or when deployed outside the U.S. away from the individual's permanent duty station while participating in a contingency operation (as defined in 10 USC 101(a)(13)) or that became such a contingency operation by operation of law, are entitled to extra time in which to perform certain duties under the internal revenue laws. These service personnel may disregard the period of such combat zone service plus any period of hospitalization abroad, resulting from injury in that service, and the next 180 days. The period during which IRS can perform certain acts relating to the determination, assessment and collection of their tax liability is likewise extended. (FTC 2d/FIN ¶ S-8000, ¶ S-8007; USTR ¶ 75,084)

Previous Acts, such as Sec. 1(b), PL 104-117, 3/20/1996, related to services performed in Bosnia and Herzegovina, Croatia, or Macedonia, and Sec. 1(b), PL 106-21, 4/19/1999, related to services performed in any area of the Federal Republic of Yugoslavia (Serbia/Montenegro), Albania, the Adriatic Sea, and the northern Ionian Sea, have defined other qualified hazardous duty areas. (FTC 2d/FIN ¶ H-3100, ¶ H-3109.1; USTR ¶ 75,084)

New Law. The Tax Cuts and Jobs Act retroactively provides that, with respect to the "applicable period" (see below), a qualified hazardous duty area is treated in the same manner as if it were a combat zone under Code Sec. 112

(see above) for purposes of the following Internal Revenue Code provisions: (Tax Cuts and Jobs Act §11026(a))

(1) Code Sec. 2(a)(3) (providing that spouses of military personnel and government employees in "missing status" as a result of service in a combat zone can qualify as surviving spouses and compute their tax using the married-filing-jointly tax rate schedule from the earlier of (1) the officially determined date of death of the spouse who was in missing status, or (2) if no official determination is made, generally the date that is two years after the official termination of combat activities in that zone, if the spouse otherwise qualifies for surviving spouse filing status); (Tax Cuts and Jobs Act §11026(a)(1))

(2) Code Sec. 112 (providing for the exclusion of certain combat pay of members of the Armed Forces); (Tax Cuts and Jobs Act §11026(a)(2))

(3) Code Sec. 692 (providing for the cancellation of the decedent Armed Forces member's income tax liability for the tax year in which death occurred and for any earlier tax year ending on or after the first day of service in a combat zone); (Tax Cuts and Jobs Act §11026(a)(3))

(4) Code Sec. 2201 (providing an estate tax rate break to estates of members of the Armed Forces who die in a combat zone or by reason of combat-zone-incurred wounds, etc.); (Tax Cuts and Jobs Act §11026(a)(4))

(5) Code Sec. 3401(a)(1) (providing for an exception from withholding on any remuneration for active service as a member of the Armed Forces performed in any month during which the recipient is entitled, under Code Sec. 112, to the exclusion of "combat zone compensation" from gross income); (Tax Cuts and Jobs Act §11026(a)(5))

(6) Code Sec. 4253(d) (providing for the non-imposition of communications excise tax on payments for phone service originating from a combat zone from members of the Armed Forces); (Tax Cuts and Jobs Act §11026(a)(6))

(7) Code Sec. 6013(f)(1) (providing that spouses of persons in the Armed Forces and government employees in "missing status" as a result of service in a combat zone can elect to file a joint return for any year that begins on or before the day that is two years after the date of termination of combatant activities in that zone, if the spouse otherwise qualifies to file a joint return); (Tax Cuts and Jobs Act §11026(a)(7))

(8) Code Sec. 7508 (time for performing certain acts postponed by reason of service in combat zone). (Tax Cuts and Jobs Act §11026(a)(8))

Sinai Peninsula of Egypt as qualified hazardous duty area. "Qualified hazardous duty area" means the Sinai Peninsula of Egypt, if as of Dec. 22, 2017, any member of the U.S. Armed Forces is entitled to special pay under section 310 of title 37, U.S.C. (relating to special pay; duty subject to hostile fire or imminent danger), for services performed in that location. The term includes that location only during the period that entitlement is in effect. (Tax Cuts and Jobs Act §11026(b))

Sunset. *Applicable period.* Except as provided in Tax Cuts and Jobs Act §11026(a)(5) (see (5) above), the applicable period is the portion of the first tax year ending after June 9, 2015, which begins on that date, and (Tax Cuts and Jobs Act §11026(c)(1)(A)) any subsequent tax year beginning before Jan. 1, 2026. (Tax Cuts and Jobs Act §11026(c)(1)(B)). For purposes of (5) above, the applicable period is the portion of the first tax year ending after Dec. 22, 2017 which begins on that date, and (Tax Cuts and Jobs Act §11026(c)(2)(A)) any subsequent tax year beginning before Jan. 1, 2026. (Tax Cuts and Jobs Act §11026(c)(2)(B)).

☐ **Effective:** Except as provided in Tax Cuts and Jobs Act §11026(a)(5), June 9, 2015. (Tax Cuts and Jobs Act §11026(d)(1)) Tax Cuts and Jobs Act §11026(a)(5) applies to remuneration paid after Dec. 22, 2017. (Tax Cuts and Jobs Act §11026(d)(2))

recommendation: The retroactive application of "qualified hazard duty area" status to activities in the Sinai Peninsula in Egypt creates re-fund possibilities for taxpayers who would have been eligible for any of the benefits listed above for tax years ending after June 9, 2015. These taxpayers should consider filing an amended return to claim a refund for overpayments made.

¶ 700. Qualified Business Income

¶ 701. Overview of qualified business income deduction

Under pre-Tax Cuts and Jobs Act law, there was no special deduction for qualified business income (QBI).

New Law. The Tax Cuts and Jobs Act adds a new deduction for noncorporate taxpayers for qualified business income. The deduction is also referred to as the "pass-through deduction." The deduction reduces taxable income, rather than adjusted gross income, but is available to taxpayers who take the standard deduction. In general, the deduction cannot exceed 20% of the excess of the taxpayer's taxable income over net capital gain, see ¶ 702.

The deduction is generally 20% of a taxpayer's qualified business income (QBI) from a partnership, S corporation, or sole proprietorship, defined as the net amount of items of income, gain, deduction, and loss with respect to the trade or business, see ¶ 702. Certain types of investment-related items are excluded from QBI, e.g., capital gains or losses, dividends, and interest income (unless the interest is properly allocable to the business). Employee compensation and guaranteed payments to a partner are also excluded, see ¶ 703.

Taxpayers in service related businesses, such as healthcare professionals, law, accounting, actuarial science, performing artists, consulting, athletics, financial services, brokerage services, including investing and investment management, trading, or dealing in securities, partnership interests, or commodities, and any trade or business where the principal asset of such trade or business is the reputation or skill of one or more of its employees are eligible. However, the deduction for taxpayers in service businesses is phased out if the taxpayer's taxable income exceeds the threshold amount of $157,500 ($315,000 in the case of a joint return), see ¶ 703.

Taxpayers whose taxable income exceeds the threshold amount of $157,500 ($315,000 in the case of a joint return) are also subject to limitations based on the W-2 wages and the adjusted basis in acquired qualified property, see ¶ 702.

The deduction is taken for partnerships and S corporations at the partner or shareholder level. Trusts and estates are eligible for the deduction. W-2 wages and the adjusted basis in acquired qualified property are apportioned between

---

FTC 2d References are to Federal Tax Coordinator 2d
FIN References are to RIA's Analysis of Federal Taxes: Income (print)
USTR References are to United States Tax Reporter
Catalyst References are to Checkpoint Catalyst
PCA References are to Pension Analysis (print and electronic)
PBE References are to Pension & Benefits Explanations
BCA References are to Benefits Analysis (electronic)
BC References are to Benefits Coordinator (print)
EP References are to Estate Planning Analysis (print and electronic)

the trust or estate and the beneficiaries. Specified agricultural or horticultural cooperatives are also eligible for the deduction under special rules, see ¶ 704.

Qualified business income includes only income effectively connected with a U.S. trade or business, see ¶ 703. However, qualified business income from sources within Puerto Rico is eligible for the deduction if all the income is subject to tax in the U.S., see ¶ 705.

The deduction will not apply to tax years beginning after Dec. 31, 2025, see ¶ 702.

The deduction is intended to reduce the tax rate on qualified business income to a rate that is closer to the corporate tax rate described at ¶ 102. (Com Rept, see ¶ 5003)

¶ 702. 20% deduction for qualified business income

Code Sec. 199A(a), as added by Tax Cuts and Jobs Act §11011(a)
Code Sec. 199A(b), as added by Tax Cuts and Jobs Act §11011(a)
Code Sec. 199A(e), as added by Tax Cuts and Jobs Act §11011(a)
Code Sec. 199A(f), as added by Tax Cuts and Jobs Act §11011(a)
Code Sec. 62(a), as amended by Tax Cuts and Jobs Act §11011(b)(1)
Code Sec. 63, as amended by Tax Cuts and Jobs Act §11011(b)
Code Sec. 3402(m)(1), as amended by Tax Cuts and Jobs Act §11011(b)(4)
Code Sec. 6662(d)(1)(C), as amended by Tax Cuts and Jobs Act §11011(c)
Generally effective: Tax years beginning after Dec. 31, 2017 and before Jan. 1, 2026
Committee Reports, see ¶ 5003

Under pre-Tax Cuts and Jobs Act law, there was no special deduction for qualified business income (QBI).

New Law. The Tax Cuts and Jobs Act adds a new deduction for noncorporate taxpayers for QBI. The deduction is generally 20% of a taxpayer's qualified business income from a partnership, S corporation, or sole proprietorship, defined as the net amount of items of income, gain, deduction, and loss with respect to the trade or business, The amount of the deduction is specifically calculated as the sum of:

(1) the lesser of (i) the combined qualified business income amount described at ¶ 703 of the taxpayer for the tax year (Code Sec. 199A(a)(1)(A) as added by Tax Cuts and Jobs Act §11011(a)) or (ii) the sum of 20% of the excess (if any) of the taxpayer's taxable income for the tax year (Code Sec. 199A(a)(1)(B)(i)) (determined without regard to this deduction (Code Sec. 199A(e)(1))) over the sum of (a) the taxpayer's Code Sec. 1(h) net capital gain (see FTC 2d ¶ I-5100; USTR ¶ 14.08) for the tax year and (b) the taxpayer's aggregate amount of the qualified cooperative dividends (described below) for the tax year (Code Sec. 199A(a)(1)(B)(ii)), plus

(2) the lesser of (A) 20% of the aggregate amount of the qualified cooperative dividends of the taxpayer for the tax year (Code Sec. 199A(a)(2)(A)), or (B) the taxpayer's taxable income (minus the taxpayer's net capital gain) for the tax year. (Code Sec. 199A(a)(2)(B))

However, the total amount cannot exceed the taxpayer's taxable income (minus the taxpayer's net capital gain) for the tax year. (Code Sec. 199A(a))

A taxpayer's combined qualified business income amount for a tax year is equal to:

• the sum of the deductible amounts determined below for each qualified trade or business described at ¶ 703 carried on by the taxpayer (Code Sec. 199A(b)(1)(A)), plus

• 20% of the aggregate amount of the qualified REIT dividends and qualified publicly traded partnership income of the taxpayer for the tax year. (Code Sec. 199A(b)(1)(B))

A qualified REIT dividend is any dividend from a real estate investment trust received during the tax year that is not a Code Sec. 857(b)(3) capital gain dividend (see FTC 2d ¶ E-6609; USTR ¶ 8574.01) (Code Sec. 199A(e)(3)(A)) and is not Code Sec. 1(h)(11) qualified dividend income (see FTC 2d ¶ E-6619.1; USTR ¶ 8574.02). (Code Sec. 199A(e)(3)(B))

A qualified cooperative dividend is any Code Sec. 1388(a) patronage dividend (see FTC 2d ¶ E-1104; USTR ¶ 13,814.05), any Code Sec. 1388(f) per-unit retain allocation (see FTC 2d ¶ E-1126; USTR ¶ 13,814.14), any Code Sec. 1388(c) qualified written notice of allocation (see FTC 2d ¶ E-1121; USTR ¶ 13,814.02), or any similar amount received from an organization governed by the rules applicable to cooperatives before the enactment of subchapter T that (i) is includible in gross income (Code Sec. 199A(e)(4)(A)), and (ii) is received from an organization described in Code Sec. 501(c)(12) (see FTC 2d ¶ D-6101; USTR ¶ 5014.21) or Code Sec. 1381(a) (see FTC 2d ¶ E-1003; USTR ¶ 13,814) (Code Sec. 199A(e)(4)(B)(i)), or an organization governed by the rules applicable to cooperatives before the enactment of subchapter T. (Code Sec. 199A(e)(4)(B)(ii))

Qualified publicly traded partnership income for any qualified trade or business of the taxpayer is the sum of:

• the net amount of the taxpayer's allocable share of each qualified item of income gain deduction and loss (described at ¶ 703 and determined after excluding reasonable compensation, guaranteed payments and other payments for services as described at ¶ 703) from a Code Sec. 7704 publicly traded partnership that is not treated as a corporation for tax purposes (see FTC 2d ¶ D-1363; USTR ¶ 77,044) (Code Sec. 199A(e)(5)(A)) and

• any gain recognized by the taxpayer upon the disposition of its interest in such a partnership to the extent that the gain is treated as amount realized from a sale or exchange of property other than a capital asset under Code Sec. 751(a) (see FTC 2d ¶ B-3901; USTR ¶ 7514.01). (Code Sec. 199A(e)(5)(B))

Unless the taxpayer is below the threshold amounts described below, the deductible amount for a qualified trade or business is the lesser of:

(a) 20% of the taxpayer's qualified business income from the qualified trade or business (Code Sec. 199A(b)(2)(A)) or

(b) the greater of (I) 50% of the W-2 wages relating to the qualified trade or business (Code Sec. 199A(b)(2)(B)(i)) or (II) the sum of (i) 25% of the W-2 wages relating to the qualified trade or business and (ii) 2.5% percent of the unadjusted basis immediately after acquisition of all qualified property. (Code Sec. 199A(b)(2)(B)(ii))

> *Illustration:* A taxpayer who is subject to the limit does business as a sole proprietorship conducting a widget-making business. The business buys a widget-making machine for $100,000 and places it in service in 2020. The business has no employees in 2020. The limitation in 2020 is the greater of (a) 50% of W-2 wages, or $0 and (b) the sum of 25% of W-2 wages ($0) plus 2.5% of the unadjusted basis of the machine immediately after its acquisition: $100,000 x .025 = $2,500. Thus, the amount of the limitation on the taxpayer's deduction is $2,500.(Com Rept, see ¶ 5003)

A person's W-2 wages for a tax year is the total of the wages described in Code Sec. 6051(a)(3) and the Code Sec. 6051(a)(8) elective deferrals (see FTC 2d ¶ S-3152; USTR ¶ 60,514) paid by the person for employment of employees during the calendar year ending during the tax year (Code Sec. 199A(b)(4)(A)), but only for amounts properly allocable to qualified business income. (Code Sec. 199A(b)(4)(B)) In addition, amounts that are not properly included in a return filed with the Social Security Administration on or before the 60th day after the due date (including extensions) for such return are excluded. (Code Sec. 199A(b)(4)(C)) IRS is directed to issue regs regarding how wages and adjusted basis of qualified property are determined in cases of a short tax year or where the taxpayer acquires or disposes of, the major portion of a trade or business or the major portion of a separate unit of a trade or business during the tax year. (Code Sec. 199A(b)(5))

Qualified property relating to a qualified trade or business for a tax year is tangible property of a character subject to a Code Sec. 167 depreciation allowance that:

(A) is held by, and available for use in, the qualified trade or business at the close of the tax year (Code Sec. 199A(b)(6)(A)(i))

(B) is used at any point during the taxable year in the production of qualified business income (Code Sec. 199A(b)(6)(A)(ii)), and

(C) the depreciable period for which has not ended before the close of the tax year. (Code Sec. 199A(b)(6)(A)(iii))

The depreciable period for qualified property of a taxpayer is the period beginning on the date the property was first placed in service by the taxpayer and ending on the later of (i) the date that is 10 years after that date (Code Sec. 199A(b)(6)(B)(i)), or (ii) the last day of the last full year in the applicable recovery period that would apply to the property under Code Sec. 168 (MACRS, see FTC 2d ¶ L-8100; USTR ¶ 1684), without regard to the Code Sec. 168(g) alternative depreciation system (see FTC 2d ¶ L-9400; USTR ¶ 1684.03). (Code Sec. 199A(b)(6)(B)(ii))

However, the wage limitation doesn't apply for taxpayers below the threshold amount (Code Sec. 199A(b)(3)(A)) of $157,500 ($315,000 in the case of a joint return). (Code Sec. 199A(e)(2)(A)) For tax years beginning after 2018, this amount is increased for inflation by an amount equal to (i) the threshold amount times (ii) the Code Sec. 1(f)(3) cost-of-living adjustment (see FTC 2d ¶ A-1103; USTR ¶ 14.08) for the calendar year in which the tax year begins determined by substituting "calendar year 2017" for "calendar year 2016" in Code Sec. 1(f)(3)(A)(ii) (see ¶ 201). If the increased amount is not a multiple of $50, the amount is rounded to the next lowest multiple of $50. (Code Sec. 199A(e)(2)(B))

> *observation:* Because of the threshold amounts, certain married taxpayers may find it beneficial to file separate returns.

> *illustration:* H has a qualified business which produces $150,000 of qualified business income. W is employed and her taxable income is $200,000. If H and W file joint returns, their $350,000 joint income will exceed their $315,000 threshold amount and they will be subject to the limitation. In contrast, if H files a separate return, his $150,000 taxable income will be below his threshold amount and he will not be subject to the limitation.

If (i) the taxable income of a taxpayer for any tax year exceeds the threshold amount, by less than $50,000 ($100,000 in the case of a joint return) (Code Sec. 199A(b)(3)(B)(i)(I)) and (ii) the amount in item (b) in the above list (determined without regard to this rule) is less than 20% of the taxpayer's qualified business income from the qualified trade or business (Code Sec. 199A(b)(3)(B)(i)(II)), then the item (b) limitation will not apply. Instead, the 20% of the taxpayer's qualified business income from the qualified trade or business amount will be reduced by (1) 20% of the taxpayer's qualified business income from the qualified trade or business (determined without regard to this rule) (Code Sec. 199A(b)(3)(B)(iii)(I)) minus (2) the amount in item (b) in the above list (determined without regard to this rule) (the excess amount) (Code Sec. 199A(b)(3)(B)(iii)(II)) multiplied by (I) the amount by which the taxpayer's taxable income for the tax year exceeds the threshold amount (Code Sec. 199A(b)(3)(B)(ii)(I)) and divided by (II) $50,000 ($100,000 in the case of a joint return). (Code Sec. 199A(b)(3)(B)(ii)(II))

Application of the deduction for qualified business income The deduction applies only for income tax purposes. (Code Sec. 199A(f)(3))

For purposes of determining Code Sec. 55 alternative minimum taxable income (see FTC 2d ¶ A-8101; USTR ¶ 554.01), qualified business income is determined without regard to any adjustments under Code Sec. 56 through Code Sec. 59 (see FTC 2d ¶ A-8200 *et seq.*; USTR ¶s 564, 574, 584, 594) (Code Sec. 199A(f)(2))

IRS is directed to prescribe regs that are necessary to carry out the purposes of the deduction including regs (i) requiring or restricting the allocation of items and wages for purposes of the deduction, (ii) requiring reporting as IRS determines appropriate (Code Sec. 199A(f)(4)(A)), and (iii) applying the deduction in the case of tiered entities. (Code Sec. 199A(f)(4)(B))

IRS is directed (i) to apply rules similar to Code Sec. 179(d)(2) (see FTC 2d ¶ L-9226; USTR ¶ 1794.01) in order to prevent the manipulation of the depreciable period of qualified property using transactions between related parties (Code Sec. 199A(h)(1)), and (ii) to prescribe rules for determining the unadjusted basis immediately after acquisition of qualified property acquired in like-kind exchanges or involuntary conversions. (Code Sec. 199A(h)(2)) This guidance may also apply to sale-leaseback transactions. (Com Rept, see ¶ 5003)

The deduction isn't taken into account in determining adjusted gross income (see FTC 2d/FIN ¶ A-2600, ¶ A-2601; USTR ¶ 624) (Code Sec. 62(a) as amended by Tax Cuts and Jobs Act §11011(b)(1)) However, the deduction can be taken by taxpayers who don't itemize their deductions (see FTC 2d/FIN ¶ A-2500, ¶ A-2501; USTR ¶ 634) (Code Sec. 63(b)(3) as amended by Tax Cuts and Jobs Act §11011(b)(2)), is not subject to the limitations on itemized deductions (see FTC 2d/FIN ¶ A-2700, ¶ A-2701; USTR ¶ 634) (Code Sec. 63(d)(3) as amended by Tax Cuts and Jobs Act §11011(b)(3)), and may be taken into account in determining withholding allowances (see FTC 2d/FIN ¶ H-4485, ¶ H-4511; USTR ¶ 34,024.10). (Code Sec. 3402(m)(1) as amended by Tax Cuts and Jobs Act §11011(b)(4))

The deduction will not apply to tax years beginning after Dec. 31, 2025. (Code Sec. 199A(i))

Where a taxpayer claims the deduction for a tax year, the accuracy penalty for substantial understatements of income tax applies if the amount of the understatement is 5% (instead of the usual 10%, see FTC 2d/FIN ¶ V-2150, ¶ V-2159; USTR ¶ 66,624.03). (Code Sec. 6662(d)(1)(C) as amended by Tax Cuts and Jobs Act §11011(c))

For the application of the deduction to partnerships, S corporations, trusts, estates and agricultural and horticultural cooperatives, see ¶ 704.

Conforming amendments The Act includes the following conforming amendments:

• net operating losses (FTC 2d/FIN ¶ M-4100, ¶ M-4109; USTR ¶ 1724.12) are determined without regard to this deduction (Code Sec. 172(d)(8) as amended by Tax Cuts and Jobs Act §11011(d)(1));

• the taxable income limitation on the dividends received deductions (FTC 2d/FIN ¶ D-2201, ¶ D-2251; USTR ¶ 2434.04) is determined without regard to this deduction (Code Sec. 246(b)(1) as amended by Tax Cuts and Jobs Act §11011(d)(2)); and

• the allowance of the small producers' percentage depletion deduction (FTC 2d/FIN ¶ N-2403; USTR ¶ 613A4) (Code Sec. 613A(a) as amended by Tax Cuts and Jobs Act §11011(d)(3)) and the taxable income limitation on small producers' percentage depletion deductions (FTC 2d/FIN ¶ N-2446; USTR ¶ 613A4) are determined without regard to this deduction. (Code Sec. 613A(d)(1)(C) as amended by Tax Cuts and Jobs Act §11011(d)(4))

• the corporate 10% of taxable income charitable deduction limitation (FTC 2d/FIN ¶ K-3830, ¶ K-3832; USTR ¶ 1704.06) is determined without regard to this deduction (Code Sec. 170(b)(2)(D) as amended by Tax Cuts and Jobs Act §11011(e)(5));

☐ **Effective:** Tax years beginning after Dec. 31, 2017 (Tax Cuts and Jobs Act §11011(e)) and before Jan. 1, 2026. (Code Sec. 199A(i))

¶ 703. Qualified business income defined

Code Sec. 199A(c), as added by Tax Cuts and Jobs Act §11011(a)
Code Sec. 199A(d), as added by Tax Cuts and Jobs Act §11011(a)
Generally effective: Tax years beginning after Dec. 31, 2017 and before Jan. 1, 2026
Committee Reports, see ¶ 5003

Under pre-Tax Cuts and Jobs Act law, there was no special deduction for qualified business income (QBI).

New Law. As described at ¶ 702, the Tax Cuts and Jobs Act adds a new deduction for noncorporate taxpayers based on QBI.

The qualified business income for a tax year is the net amount of qualified items of income, gain, deduction, and loss relating to any qualified trade or business of the taxpayer. It doesn't include any qualified REIT dividends, qualified cooperative dividends or qualified publicly traded partnership income (see ¶ 702). (Code Sec. 199A(c)(1) as added by Tax Cuts and Jobs Act §11011(a)) If the net amount of qualified income, gain, deduction, and loss relating to qualified trade or businesses of the taxpayer for any tax year is less than zero, the amount is carried over as a loss from a qualified trade or business in the succeeding tax year. (Code Sec. 199A(c)(2))

For this purpose, qualified items of income, gain, deduction, and loss are items of income, gain, deduction, and loss to the extent these items are:

• effectively connected with the conduct of a trade or business within the U.S. under Code Sec. 864(c) (see FTC 2d ¶ O-10603; USTR ¶ 8644.02) (applied by substituting "qualified trade or business" (described below) for "nonresident alien individual or a foreign corporation" or for a "foreign corporation" each place it appears) (Code Sec. 199A(c)(3)(A)(i)), and

• included or allowed in determining taxable income for the tax year. (Code Sec. 199A(c)(3)(A)(ii))

For the treatment of qualified business income from sources in Puerto Rico, see ¶ 705.

> *Illustration (1):* A qualified business has $100 of ordinary income from inventory sales, and makes a $25 expenditure that must be capitalized and amortized over five years. The business income is $95 ($100 minus $5 current-year ordinary amortization deduction). (Com Rept, see ¶ 5003)

> *Illustration (2):* Taxpayer has qualified business income of $20,000 from qualified business A and a qualified business loss of $50,000 from qualified business B in Year 1. Taxpayer is not permitted a deduction for Year 1 and has a carryover qualified business loss of $30,000 to Year 2. In Year 2, Taxpayer has qualified business income of $20,000 from qualified business A and qualified business income of $50,000 from qualified business B. To determine the deduction for Year 2, Taxpayer reduces the 20% deductible amount determined for the qualified business income of $70,000 from qualified businesses A and B by 20% of the $30,000 carryover qualified business loss. (Com Rept, see ¶ 5003)

However, the following investment items are not taken into account as a qualified item of income, gain, deduction, or loss:

(1) Any item of short-term capital gain, short-term capital loss, long-term capital gain, or long-term capital loss (Code Sec. 199A(c)(3)(B)(i));

(2) Any dividend, income equivalent to a dividend, or Code Sec. 954(c)(1)(G) payment in lieu of dividends (see FTC 2d ¶ O-2531; USTR ¶ 9544.02) (Code Sec. 199A(c)(3)(B)(ii));

(3) Any interest income other than interest income that is properly allocable to a trade or business (Code Sec. 199A(c)(3)(B)(iii));

(4) Any Code Sec. 954(c)(1)(C) commodity transaction gain or loss or Code Sec. 954(c)(1)(D) foreign currency gain or loss (applied by substituting qualified trade or business for controlled foreign corporation) (Code Sec. 199A(c)(3)(B)(iv));

(5) Any item of income, gain, deduction, or loss relating to Code Sec. 954(c)(1)(F) notional principal contracts (determined without regard to the rules coordinating the notional principal contract rules with other categories of foreign personal holding company income and excluding items attributable to notional principal contracts entered into in Code Sec. 1221(a)(7) hedging transactions (see FTC 2d ¶ I-6231; USTR ¶ 12,214.80) (Code Sec. 199A(c)(3)(B)(v));

(6) Any amount received from an annuity that is not received in connection with the trade or business (Code Sec. 199A(c)(3)(B)(vi)); and

(7) Any item of deduction or loss properly allocable to an amount described in any of the preceding items in this list (Code Sec. 199A(c)(3)(B)(vii))

In addition, qualified business income doesn't include:

(a) reasonable compensation paid to the taxpayer by any qualified trade or business of the taxpayer for services rendered for the trade or business (Code Sec. 199A(c)(4)(A)),

(b) any Code Sec. 707(c) guaranteed payment (see FTC 2d ¶ B-2005; USTR ¶ 7074.04) paid to a partner for services rendered for the trade or business (Code Sec. 199A(c)(4)(B)), and

(c) to the extent provided in regs, any Code Sec. 707(a) payment to a partner outside of his partner capacity (see FTC 2d ¶ B-2001; USTR ¶ 7074.01) for services rendered for the trade or business. (Code Sec. 199A(c)(4)(C))

> *observation:* Although qualified business income passes through from partnerships and S corporations to the partners or shareholders, in the case of an S corporation, IRS requires that a shareholder receive reasonable compensation from the S corporation for his services, see FTC 2d ¶ H-4329. Similarly, in the case of a partnership interest received by gift, the Code requires that the donor partner receives reasonable compensation from the partnership for his services, see FTC 2d ¶ B-3423; USTR ¶ 7044.13. Thus, where a business is conducted through a partnership or an S corporation, a portion of its income may have to be treated as compensation, which is not qualified business income. In contrast, in the case of a business conducted by a sole propri-

etor or a single member LLC that is treated as a disregarded entity, all of the business's income can be qualified business income.

For this purpose, a qualified trade or business is any trade or business other than a specified service trade or business or the business of performing services as an employee. (Code Sec. 199A(d)(1))

> **observation:** It appears that a "trade or business" would be defined by reference to Code Sec. 162, see FTC 2d ¶ L-1100; USTR ¶ 1624.002.

> **observation:** The rules for distinguishing employees from independent contractors are described at FTC 2d ¶ H-4250; USTR ¶ 14,024.09.

A specified service trade or business is:

(A) any trade or business involving the performance of services described in Code Sec. 1202(e)(3)(A) other than engineering or architecture (see FTC 2d ¶ I-9105; USTR ¶ 12,024.02) or which would be so described if the term "employee owners" were substituted for "employees" in that section (Code Sec. 199A(d)(2)(A)); or

(B) any trade or business which involves performance of services that consist of investing and investment management, trading, or dealing in securities described in Code Sec. 475(c)(2) (see FTC 2d ¶ I-7657; USTR ¶ 4754), partnership interests, or commodities described in Code Sec. 475(e)(2) (see FTC 2d ¶ I-7668; USTR ¶ 4754.01). (Code Sec. 199A(d)(2)(B))

Services described above include health (i.e., medical services by physicians, nurses, dentists, and other similar healthcare professionals, but not services not directly related to healthcare, such as the operation of spas and health clubs), law, accounting, actuarial science, performing arts (but not services by persons other than performing artists, such as promoters or broadcasters), consulting, athletics, financial services, brokerage services, including investing and investment management, trading, or dealing in securities, partnership interests, or commodities, and any trade or business where the principal asset of such trade or business is the reputation or skill of one or more of its employees. (Com Rept, see ¶ 5003)

However, if for any tax year, the taxable income of any taxpayer is less than the sum of the $157,500 ($315,000 in the case of a joint return) threshold amount described at ¶ 702 plus $50,000 ($100,000 in the case of a joint return), the exclusion for specified service trades or businesses of the taxpayer for the tax year will not apply. (Code Sec. 199A(d)(3)(A)(i)) Instead, the qualified items of income, gain, deduction, loss, W-2 wages, and unadjusted basis immediately after the acquisition of qualified property of the taxpayer allocable to the specified service trades or businesses will be taken into account in computing the qualified business income, W-2 wages, and unadjusted basis of the taxpayer for the tax year, but only to the extent of the applicable percentage of the qualified items of income, gain, deduction, loss, W-2 wages, and unadjusted basis of the taxpayer allocable to the specified service trades or businesses. (Code Sec. 199A(d)(3)(A)(ii)) The applicable percentage for any tax year is 100% reduced (not below zero) by the percentage equal to (i) the taxable income of the taxpayer for the tax year in excess of the threshold amount (Code Sec. 199A(d)(3)(B)(i)) divided by (ii) $50,000 ($100,000 in the case of a joint return). (Code Sec. 199A(d)(3)(B)(ii))

> **✏️ illustration:** A is a lawyer who files a joint return. He and his wife have taxable income from his law practice of $365,000 and no other income. Since A is a lawyer, the items relating to his law practice will be taken into account only to the extent of the applicable percentage of those amounts. The applicable percentage will be 50% ($50,000 (taxable income of $340,000 minus the threshold amount of $315,000) divided by $100,000).

☐ **Effective:** Tax years beginning after Dec. 31, 2017 (Tax Cuts and Jobs Act §11011(e)) and before Jan. 1, 2026. (Code Sec. 199A(i))

¶ 704. Application of qualified business income deduction to entities

Code Sec. 199A(f), as added by Tax Cuts and Jobs Act §11011(a)
Code Sec. 199A(g), as added by Tax Cuts and Jobs Act §11011(a)
Generally effective: Tax years beginning after Dec. 31, 2017 and before Jan. 1, 2026
Committee Reports, see ¶ 5003

Under pre-Tax Cuts and Jobs Act law, there was no special deduction for qualified business income (QBI).

New Law. As described at ¶ 702, the Tax Cuts and Jobs Act adds a new deduction for noncorporate taxpayers based on QBI.

The qualified business income deduction for noncorporate taxpayers described at ¶ 702 is applied to partnerships and S corporations at the partner or shareholder level. (Code Sec. 199A(f)(1)(A)(i)) Thus, each partner or shareholder must take into account his allocable share of each qualified item of income, gain, deduction, and loss (Code Sec. 199A(f)(1)(A)(ii)), and is treated as having W-2 wages for the tax equal to his allocable share of the W-2 wages of the partnership or S corporation for the tax year (as determined under IRS regs). (Code Sec. 199A(f)(1)(A)(iii)) A partner's or shareholder's allocable share of W-2 wages is determined in the same manner as the partner's or shareholder's allocable share of wage expenses and a partner's or shareholder's allocable share of the unadjusted basis of qualified property immediately after acquisition of qualified property is determined in the same manner as the partner's or shareholder's allocable share of depreciation. In the case of an S corporation, an allocable share is the shareholder's pro rata share of an item. (Code Sec. 199A(f)(1)(A))

> *observation:* It would appear that partnerships have the flexibility to cause specific partners to be allocated W-2 wages and unadjusted basis, by making special allocations of wage expenses and depreciation deductions.

Rules similar to the pre-Tax Cuts and Jobs Act (Code Sec. 199(d)(1)(B)(i) as repealed by Tax Cuts and Jobs Act §13305(a)) (see ¶ 1004; FTC 2d ¶ L-4376.1; USTR ¶ 1994.110) apply to apportion W-2 wages and unadjusted basis immediately after the acquisition of qualified property among trusts, estates, and beneficiaries for purposes of the deduction. (Code Sec. 199A(f)(1)(B))

Application of deduction to agricultural or horticultural cooperatives For any tax year of a specified agricultural or horticultural cooperative beginning after Dec. 31, 2017, a deduction is allowed to the extent of the lesser of:

(A) 20% of the excess (if any) of (i) the gross income of the specified agricultural or horticultural cooperative (Code Sec. 199A(g)(1)(A)(i)) over the qualified cooperative dividends of the taxpayer paid during the tax year for the tax year (Code Sec. 199A(g)(1)(A)(ii)), or

(B) the greater of (I) 50% of the W-2 wages of the cooperative relating to the qualified trade or business (Code Sec. 199A(g)(1)(B)(i)) or (II) the sum of (i) 25% of the W-2 wages relating to the qualified trade or business and (ii) 2.5% percent of the unadjusted basis immediately after acquisition of all qualified property of the cooperative. (Code Sec. 199A(g)(1)(B)(ii))

However, the total amount cannot exceed the specified agricultural or horticultural cooperative's taxable income for the tax year. (Code Sec. 199A(g)(2))

A specified agricultural or horticultural cooperative is an organization subject to part I of subchapter T (Code Sec. 1381 through Code Sec. 1383) that is engaged in:

(1) manufacturing, producing, growing, or extracting, in whole or significant part any agricultural or horticultural product (Code Sec. 199A(g)(3)(A));

(2) marketing agricultural or horticultural products that its patrons have manufactured, produced, grown, or extracted (Code Sec. 199A(g)(3)(B)); or

(3) providing supplies, equipment, or services to farmers or to organizations described in items (1) or (2). (Code Sec. 199A(g)(3)(C))

☐ **Effective:** Tax years beginning after Dec. 31, 2017 (Tax Cuts and Jobs Act §11011(e)) and before Jan. 1, 2026. (Code Sec. 199A(i))

¶ 705. Treatment of qualified business income from Puerto Rico sources

Code Sec. 199A(f), as added by Tax Cuts and Jobs Act §11011(a)
Generally effective: Tax years beginning after Dec. 31, 2017 and before Jan. 1, 2026
Committee Reports, see ¶ 5003

Under pre-Tax Cuts and Jobs Act law, there was no special deduction for qualified business income (QBI).

New Law. As described at ¶ 702, the Tax Cuts and Jobs Act adds a new deduction for noncorporate taxpayers based on QBI.

Although the qualified business income deduction described at ¶ 702 applies only to qualified business income that is effectively connected with the conduct of a trade or business within the U.S. (see ¶ 703), in the case of any taxpayer with qualified business income from sources within Puerto Rico, if all the income is taxable in the U.S. under Code Sec. 1 for the tax year, then the taxpayer's qualified business income for the tax is determined by treating Puerto Rico as part of the U.S. (Code Sec. 199A(f)(1)(C)(i)) In the case of any taxpayer subject to this rule, the W-2 wages of the taxpayer relating to any qualified trade or business conducted in Puerto Rico are determined without regard to the Code Sec. 3401(a)(8) exclusion for remuneration paid for services in Puerto Rico (see FTC 2d ¶ H-4446; USTR ¶ 31,014.23). (Code Sec. 199A(f)(1)(C)(ii))

☐ **Effective:** Tax years beginning after Dec. 31, 2017 (Tax Cuts and Jobs Act §11011(e)) and before Jan. 1, 2026. (Code Sec. 199A(h))

¶ 800. S Corporations

¶ 801. Treatment of revocations of S corporation elections

Code Sec. 481(d), as amended by Tax Cuts and Jobs Act §13543(a)
Code Sec. 1371(f), as amended by Tax Cuts and Jobs Act §13543(b)
Generally effective: Dec. 22, 2017
Committee Reports, see ¶ 5083

observation: Because the Tax Cuts and Jobs Act reduces corporate tax rates, it is expected that some S corporations will terminate their S corporation status and convert to C corporations.

A C corporation, a partnership that has a C corporation as a partner, or a tax-exempt trust or corporation with unrelated business income generally may not use the cash method of accounting. Exceptions are made for farming businesses, qualified personal service corporations, and the above entities to the extent their average annual gross receipts do not exceed $5 million for all prior years (including the prior tax years of any predecessor of the entity) (the "gross receipts test"). However, the cash method generally may not be used if the purchase, production, or sale of merchandise is an income producing factor. Where the purchase, production, or sale of merchandise is an income producing factor, the taxpayer is generally required to keep inventories and use an accrual method with respect to inventory items. (see FTC 2d ¶ G-2054; USTR ¶ 4484)

IRS permission is generally required before making a change in accounting method. (FTC 2d ¶ G-2101; USTR ¶ 4464.21)

Code Sec. 481 prescribes the rules to be followed in computing taxable income when changing accounting methods in order to prevent items of income or expense from being duplicated or omitted. Under IRS guidance, net adjustments that decrease taxable income generally are taken into account entirely in the year of change, and net adjustments that increase taxable income generally are taken into account ratably during the four-taxable-year period beginning with the year of change. (FTC 2d/FIN ¶ G-2185; USTR ¶ 4464.225)

The one-year period after which a corporation's S election terminates is generally the post-termination transition period (PTTP). (see FTC 2d ¶ D-1788;

FTC 2d References are to Federal Tax Coordinator 2d
FIN References are to RIA's Analysis of Federal Taxes: Income (print)
USTR References are to United States Tax Reporter
Catalyst References are to Checkpoint Catalyst
PCA References are to Pension Analysis (print and electronic)
PBE References are to Pension & Benefits Explanations
BCA References are to Benefits Analysis (electronic)
BC References are to Benefits Coordinator (print)
EP References are to Estate Planning Analysis (print and electronic)

USTR ¶ 13,774) Distributions of money made by a former S corporation in the PTTP reduce the adjusted basis of stock to the extent that the amount distributed doesn't exceed the amount of the accumulated adjustments account, unless the corporation elects to have the distributions treated as dividends. These distributions are nontaxable distributions, rather than normal C corporation distributions. (FTC 2d/FIN ¶ D-1800, ¶ D-1846; USTR ¶ 13,714.04; Catalyst ¶ 251:100; Catalyst ¶ 251:160; Catalyst ¶ 252:190; Catalyst ¶ 252:200; Catalyst ¶ 252:220; Catalyst ¶ 252:230; Catalyst ¶ 254:180)

New Law. The Tax Cuts and Jobs Act provides special rules for taking into account adjustments under Code Sec. 481 that are attributable to the revocation of S corporation elections of an eligible terminated S corporation during the two-year period described below. Under these rules, the adjustments are taken into account ratably over a six-tax year period beginning with the year of change. (Code Sec. 481(d)(1) as amended by Tax Cuts and Jobs Act §13543(a))

An eligible terminated S corporation is a C corporation that:

(1) on Dec. 21, 2017 was an S corporation on the day that revoked its S corporation election (see FTC 2d ¶ D-1901; USTR ¶ 13,624.02) during the two-year period beginning on Dec. 22, 2017 (Code Sec. 481(d)(2)(A)); and

(2) the owners of the stock of the corporation on the date the revocation is made, are the same owners (and in identical proportions) as on Dec. 22, 2017. (Code Sec. 481(d)(2)(B))

> ⚫*observation:* Thus, if a corporation has to change from the cash method to the accrual method because it changes from being an S corporation to being a C corporation, the corporation can take any tax increases into account ratably over a six-tax year period beginning with the year of change.

In addition, if an eligible terminated S corporation makes a cash distribution after the PTTP, the accumulated adjustments account is allocated to the distribution, and the distribution is chargeable to accumulated earnings and profits, in the same ratio as the amount that the accumulated adjustments account bears to the amount of such accumulated earnings and profits. (Code Sec. 1371(f) as amended by Tax Cuts and Jobs Act §13543(b))

> ⚫*observation:* Thus, instead of being charged first to any accumulated earnings and profits and being taxed as a C corporation dividend, the cash distribution is allocated between the accumulated earnings and profits and the accumulated adjustments account.

> ⚫*observation:* It appears that the benefits of these rules will apply only if the S corporation election is terminated by a revocation, not by a termination. Thus, it is necessary to revoke the election, rather than terminate it by disqualifying the corporation from S corporation status.

observation: It appears that the benefits of these rules will apply even if shares of the S corporation are transferred, provided that a later transaction causes the stock ownership on the revocation date (i.e., the first date of the taxable year if the revocation is made on or before the 15th day of the third month of the tax year; otherwise the first day of the next tax year, see FTC 2d ¶ D-1903; USTR ¶ 13,624.02) to be identical to that on Dec. 22, 2017.

☐ **Effective:** Dec. 22, 2017. (Com Rept, see ¶ 5083)

¶ 802. Expansion of qualifying beneficiaries of Electing Small Business Trusts (ESBTs)

Code Sec. 1361(c)(2)(B)(v), as amended by Tax Cuts and Jobs Act §13541(a)
Generally effective: Jan. 1, 2018
Committee Reports, see ¶ 5081

ESBTs are trusts that are permitted to be shareholders of S corporations. Under pre-Tax Cuts and Jobs Act law, if an ESBT held shares of an S corporation, each potential current beneficiary of the ESBT was treated as a shareholder. This meant that each potential current beneficiary of the ESBT had to be eligible to be an S corporation shareholder. Thus, a nonresident alien couldn't be a potential current beneficiary of an ESBT. (FTC 2d/FIN ¶ D-1455, ¶ D-1482; USTR ¶ 13,614.03; Catalyst ¶ 252:160; Catalyst ¶ 254:102)

New Law. The Tax Cuts and Jobs Act provides that the rule treating each potential current beneficiary of an ESBT as an S corporation shareholder doesn't apply for purposes of the rule that disqualifies nonresident aliens from being S corporation shareholders. (Code Sec. 1361(c)(2)(B)(v) as amended by Tax Cuts and Jobs Act §13541(a)) Thus, nonresident aliens may be potential current beneficiaries of an ESBT. (Com Rept, see ¶ 5081)

☐ **Effective:** Jan. 1, 2018. (Tax Cuts and Jobs Act §13541(b))

¶ 803. Charitable deductions of Electing Small Business Trusts (ESBTs)

Code Sec. 641(c)(2)(E), as amended by Tax Cuts and Jobs Act §13542(a)
Generally effective: Tax years beginning after Dec. 31, 2017
Committee Reports, see ¶ 5082

ESBTs that are permitted to be shareholders of S corporations are subject to tax on their portion of the S corporation's items at the trust level at the highest noncorporate tax rate. (FTC 2d/FIN ¶ C-5700, ¶ C-5701; USTR ¶ 6414.08) Individuals are allowed charitable contribution deductions that are limited to certain percentages of adjusted gross income generally with a five-year carryforward of amounts in excess of this limitation. (FTC 2d/FIN ¶ K-3670, ¶ K-3671, ¶ K-3672; USTR ¶ 1704.05) Under pre-Tax Cuts and Jobs Act law, ESBTs were treated as trusts. Thus, ESBTs were allowed a charitable contribution deduction for amounts of gross income, without limitation, which under the terms of the governing instrument were paid for a charitable purpose. No carryover of excess contributions was allowed. (FTC 2d/FIN ¶ C-2300, ¶ C-2301; USTR ¶ 6424.02)

New Law. The Tax Cuts and Jobs Act provides that the trust rules regarding the charitable deduction limitation don't apply for ESBTs. (Code Sec. 641(c)(2)(E)(i) as amended by Tax Cuts and Jobs Act §13542(a)) Instead, ESBTs are subject to the limitation applicable to individuals. (Com Rept, see ¶ 5082) The ESBT's contribution base, for purposes of the charitable deduction limitation, is determined by computing adjusted gross income in the same manner as that of an individual, except that the deductions for costs that are paid or incurred in connection with the administration of the trust and which would not have been incurred if the property were not held in such trust are deductible in determining adjusted gross income. (Code Sec. 641(c)(2)(E)(ii))

☐ **Effective:** Tax years beginning after Dec. 31, 2017. (Tax Cuts and Jobs Act §13542(b))

¶ 900. Partnerships

¶ 901. Repeal of partnership technical termination rule

Code Sec. 708(b)(1), as amended by Tax Cuts and Jobs Act §13504(a)
Generally effective: Partnership tax years beginning after Dec. 31, 2017
Committee Reports, see ¶ 5065

Under pre-Tax Cuts and Jobs Act law, a partnership was terminated if (i) no part of any business, financial operation, or venture of the partnership continued to be carried on by any of its partners in a partnership or (ii) if within any 12-month period, there was a sale or exchange of 50% or more of the total interest in partnership capital and profits (a technical termination). Under regulations, the technical termination gave rise to a deemed contribution of all the partnership's assets and liabilities to a new partnership in exchange for an interest in the new partnership, followed by a deemed distribution of interests in the new partnership to the purchasing partners and the other remaining partners. As a result of a technical termination, (1) some of the tax attributes of the old partnership terminated, (2) the partnership's taxable year closed, potentially resulting in short tax years, (3) partnership-level elections generally ceased to apply, and (4) the partnership depreciation recovery periods restarted. (FTC 2d/FIN ¶ B-4300, ¶ B-4301, ¶ B-4305, ¶ G-1200, ¶ G-1224, ¶ L-10400, ¶ L-10401; USTR ¶ 7084, ¶ 1684.072, ¶ 7064.02; Catalyst ¶ 203:134; Catalyst ¶ 204:164; Catalyst ¶ 205:117; Catalyst ¶ 209:135; Catalyst ¶ 210:140; Catalyst ¶ 217:156; Catalyst ¶ 218:100; Catalyst ¶ 402:145; Catalyst ¶ 508:175)

New Law. The Tax Cuts and Jobs Act law eliminates the technical termination rule. (Com Rept, see ¶ 5065) Thus, a partnership is terminated only if no part of any business, financial operation, or venture of the partnership continues to be carried on by any of its partners in a partnership. (Code Sec. 708(b)(1) as amended by Tax Cuts and Jobs Act §13504(a))

Conforming amendments have eliminated:

• the rule restarting the depreciation period upon a technical termination (Code Sec. 168(i)(7)(B) as amended by Tax Cuts and Jobs Act §13504(b)(1)); and

---

FTC 2d References are to Federal Tax Coordinator 2d
FIN References are to RIA's Analysis of Federal Taxes: Income (print)
USTR References are to United States Tax Reporter
Catalyst References are to Checkpoint Catalyst
PCA References are to Pension Analysis (print and electronic)
PBE References are to Pension & Benefits Explanations
BCA References are to Benefits Analysis (electronic)
BC References are to Benefits Coordinator (print)
EP References are to Estate Planning Analysis (print and electronic)

• the rule excepting technical terminations from the effects of the loss disallowance rule applicable to investment partnerships. (FTC 2d/FIN ¶ B-4009.3; USTR ¶ 7434.01) (Code Sec. 743(e) as amended by Tax Cuts and Jobs Act §13540(b)(2))

☐ **Effective:** Partnership tax years beginning after Dec. 31, 2017. (Tax Cuts and Jobs Act §13504(c))

¶ 902. Mandatory basis adjustment upon transfers of partnership interests amended

Code Sec. 743(d)(1), as amended by Tax Cuts and Jobs Act §13502(a)
Generally effective: Transfers of partnership interests after Dec. 31, 2017
Committee Reports, see ¶ 5063

Under pre-Tax Cuts and Jobs Act law, the basis of partnership property was not adjusted as a result of a transfer of a partnership interest unless the partnership made a Code Sec. 754 basis adjustment election or there was a substantial built-in loss with respect to the transfer of a partnership interest. The partnership had a substantial built-in loss with respect to a transfer of a partnership interest if the partnership's adjusted basis in the partnership property exceeded by more than $250,000 the fair market value of the property. (FTC 2d/FIN ¶ B-4000, ¶ B-4009, ¶ B-4009.1; USTR ¶ 7434.01; Catalyst ¶ 210:130)

New Law. The Tax Cuts and Jobs Act provides that a partnership has a substantial built-in loss with respect to a transfer of a partnership interest if either:

(1) the partnership's adjusted basis in the partnership property exceeds by more than $250,000 the fair market value of the property (Code Sec. 743(d)(1)(A) as amended by Tax Cuts and Jobs Act §13502(a)), or

(2) the transferee partner would be allocated a loss of more than $250,000 if the partnership assets were sold for cash equal to their fair market value immediately after the transfer. (Code Sec. 743(d)(1)(B))

> *Illustration:* A partnership that has three taxable partners (A, B, and C) and that didn't make a Code Sec. 754 election has two assets: Asset X, with a built-in gain of $1 million and Asset Y, with a built-in loss of $900,000. Under the partnership agreement, any gain on sale or exchange of Asset X is specially allocated to partner A, while the three partners share equally in all other partnership items, including in the built-in loss in Asset Y. Each of partner B and partner C has a net built-in loss of $300,000 (one third of the $900,000 loss attributable to asset Y). Nevertheless, the partnership does not have an overall built-in loss, but a net built-in gain of $100,000 ($1 million minus $900,000). Partner C sells his partnership interest to another person, D, for

$33,333. Under the above rules, the test for a substantial built-in loss applies both at the partnership level and at the transferee partner level. If the partnership were to sell all its assets for cash at their fair market value immediately after the transfer to D, D would be allocated a loss of $300,000 (one third of the built-in loss of $900,000 in Asset Y). Since a substantial built-in loss exists under the partner-level test, the mandatory basis adjustment applies even though the partnership does not have a substantial built-in loss. (Com Rept, see ¶ 5063)

☐ **Effective:** Transfers of partnership interests after Dec. 31, 2017. (Tax Cuts and Jobs Act §13502(b))

¶ 903. Basis reduction for partnership charitable contributions amended

Code Sec. 704(d), as amended by Tax Cuts and Jobs Act §13503(a)
Generally effective: Partnership tax years beginning after Dec. 31, 2017.
Committee Reports, see ¶ 5064

A partner's basis in his partnership interest is increased by its distributive share of income (including tax exempt income) and is decreased (but not below zero) by distributions by the partnership and its distributive share of partnership losses and expenditures of the partnership not deductible in computing partnership taxable income and not properly chargeable to capital account. In the case of a charitable contribution, a partner's basis is reduced by the partner's distributive share of the adjusted basis of the contributed property. (FTC 2d ¶ B-1507 B-1510; USTR ¶ 7054)

Under pre-Tax Cuts and Jobs Act law, a partner was allowed to deduct his distributive share of partnership loss only to the extent of the adjusted basis of the partner's interest in the partnership at the end of the partnership year in which such loss occurred. The excess of the loss over the basis was allowed as a deduction at the end of the partnership year in which the excess was repaid to the partnership. However, in applying the basis limitation on partner losses, the regs didn't take into account the partner's share of partnership charitable contributions and foreign taxes paid or accrued. IRS took the position in a private letter ruling that the basis limitation on partner losses didn't apply to limit the partner's deduction for its share of the partnership's charitable contributions. While the regs relating to the loss limitation didn't mention the foreign tax credit, a taxpayer could have chosen the foreign tax credit in lieu of deducting foreign taxes. (FTC 2d/FIN ¶ B-3500, ¶ B-3501, ¶ B-3503; USTR ¶ 7044.10; Catalyst ¶ 203:170; Catalyst ¶ 209:120)

New Law. The Tax Cuts and Jobs Act provides that in determining the amount of the partner's loss, the partner's distributive shares under Code Sec. 702(a) of partnership charitable contributions and taxes paid or accrued to foreign countries or U.S. possessions are taken into account. (Code Sec. 704(d)(3)(A) as amended by Tax Cuts and Jobs Act §13503(a)(3)) However, in the case of a charitable contribution of property with a fair market value that exceeds its adjusted basis, the partner's distributive share of the excess is not taken into account. (Code Sec. 704(d)(3)(B))

> **(RIA) observation:** This rule is somewhat similar to a rule providing that an S corporation shareholder's basis is reduced as a result of a charitable contribution by the S corporation only to the extent of the basis of the property contributed (see FTC 2d ¶ D-1864; USTR ¶ 13,674).

☐ **Effective:** Partnership tax years beginning after Dec. 31, 2017. (Tax Cuts and Jobs Act §13503(b))

¶ 1000. Business Deductions And Credits

¶ 1001. NOL deduction is limited to 80% of taxable income

Code Sec. 172(a), as amended by Tax Cuts and Jobs Act §13302(a)(1)
Code Sec. 172(b)(2), as amended by Tax Cuts and Jobs Act §13302(a)(2)
Code Sec. 172(d)(6)(C), as amended by Tax Cuts and Jobs Act §13302(a)(3)
Code Sec. 172(f), as amended by Tax Cuts and Jobs Act §13302(d)(2)
Generally effective: Losses arising in tax years beginning after Dec. 31, 2017
Committee Reports, see ¶ 5045

A net operating loss (NOL) deduction is allowed in computing taxable income for a tax year in an amount equal to the aggregate of the NOL carryovers and NOL carrybacks to that year.

Under pre-Tax Cuts and Jobs Act law, the NOL deduction wasn't subject to a limitation based on taxable income. (FTC 2d/FIN ¶ M-4400, ¶ M-4401; USTR ¶ 1724; Catalyst ¶ 142:180)

Intervening year computations. Under Code Sec. 172(b)(2), if an NOL isn't absorbed in the first year to which it's carried, the amount of loss then carried to a second year must be reduced not only by the first carryover year's taxable income but also by certain modifications attributable to that first year. If the loss is carried to more than two years, modifications must be made to each of the years to which it's carried ("intervening years") other than the last one.

The portion of an NOL that's carried to any tax year after the first year to which it's carried is the excess of the NOL over the sum of the taxable incomes of all the tax years that precede that later year, as modified. (FTC 2d/FIN ¶ M-4200, ¶ M-4200.1; USTR ¶ 1724.20)

New Law. The Tax Cuts and Jobs Act limits the NOL deduction to 80% of taxable income, determined without regard to the NOL deduction itself. Carryovers to other years are adjusted to take account of the 80% limitation. (Com Rept, see ¶ 5045)

FTC 2d References are to Federal Tax Coordinator 2d
FIN References are to RIA's Analysis of Federal Taxes: Income (print)
USTR References are to United States Tax Reporter
Catalyst References are to Checkpoint Catalyst
PCA References are to Pension Analysis (print and electronic)
PBE References are to Pension & Benefits Explanations
BCA References are to Benefits Analysis (electronic)
BC References are to Benefits Coordinator (print)
EP References are to Estate Planning Analysis (print and electronic)

Specifically, under the Tax Cuts and Jobs Act, a deduction is allowed for the tax year for an amount equal to the lesser of (Code Sec. 172(a) as amended by Tax Cuts and Jobs Act §13302(a)(1)):

(1) the aggregate of the NOL carryovers to that year, plus the NOL carrybacks to that year; or (Code Sec. 172(a)(1))

(2) 80% of taxable income, computed without regard to the NOL deduction. (Code Sec. 172(a)(2))

> **observation:** This provision limits the value of NOLs, because they can no longer completely eliminate the taxable income in the year to which they're carried. Although the unused NOL deduction can be carried forward indefinitely (see ¶ 1002), the carryover is worth less than a current deduction.

> **illustration:** In 2018, a calendar-year taxpayer has a $90,000 NOL. It has no other NOL carryovers. It carries forward the NOL to 2019, a year in which it has taxable income of $100,000. The taxpayer's 2019 NOL deduction is limited to $80,000 ($100,000 × 80%). The remaining $10,000 can't be deducted in 2019, but can be carried forward indefinitely.

Intervening year computations. For purposes of computing the taxable income of tax years to which an NOL is carried, which is needed to determine the amount of the NOL absorbed in those years, taxable income can't exceed the amount computed under Code Sec. 172(a)(2)—80% of taxable income, computed without regard to the NOL deduction—for those intervening years. (Code Sec. 172(b)(2)(C) as amended by Tax Cuts and Jobs Act §13302(a)(2))

REITs. For any year in which a taxpayer qualifies as a real estate investment trust (REIT), "taxable income" for purposes of the 80% limitation is the REIT's real estate investment trust taxable income (see Catalyst ¶ 552:121; FTC 2d/FIN ¶ E-6607; USTR ¶ 8574.01), computed without regard to the deduction for dividends paid (see Catalyst ¶ 552:105; FTC 2d/FIN ¶ E-6608; USTR ¶ 8574.01). (Code Sec. 172(d)(6)(C) as amended by Tax Cuts and Jobs Act §13302(a)(3))

Property and casualty insurance companies. For an insurance company (as defined in Code Sec. 816(a)) other than a life insurance company (Code Sec. 172(f) as amended by Tax Cuts and Jobs Act §13302(d)(2)), the NOL deduction is the aggregate of the NOL carryovers to the tax year, plus the NOL carrybacks to that tax year. (Code Sec. 172(f)(1)) Code Sec. 172(b)(2)(C) (above) doesn't apply. (Code Sec. 172(f)(2))

Thus, the 80%-of-taxable-income limit doesn't apply to NOLs of property and casualty insurance companies. (Com Rept, see ¶ 5045)

For Tax Cuts and Jobs Act changes in the NOL carryback and carryforward periods, see ¶ 1002.

☐ **Effective:** Losses arising in tax years beginning after Dec. 31, 2017. (Tax Cuts and Jobs Act §13302(e)(1))

> *observation:* This effective date means that losses that arose in tax years that began before Jan. 1, 2018, won't be subject to the 80%-of-taxable-income limit. Taxpayers will have to distinguish between the two types of losses when computing the NOL deduction.

> *observation:* Taxpayers with fiscal tax years won't be subject to the 80%-of-taxable-income limit for the year that began in 2017 and ends in 2018, but will be subject to the limit for the year that begins in 2018.

¶ 1002. NOLs can't be carried back, but can be carried forward indefinitely

Code Sec. 172(b)(1)(A), as amended by Tax Cuts and Jobs Act §13302(b)(1)
Code Sec. 172(b)(1), as amended by Tax Cuts and Jobs Act §13302(b)(2)
Code Sec. 172(b)(1)(B), as amended by Tax Cuts and Jobs Act §13302(c)(1)
Code Sec. 172, as amended by Tax Cuts and Jobs Act §13302(c)(2)(A)
Code Sec. 172(b)(1)(C), as amended by Tax Cuts and Jobs Act §13302(d)(1)
Generally effective: NOLs arising in tax years ending after Dec. 31, 2017
Committee Reports, see ¶ 5045

Under pre-Tax Cuts and Jobs Act law, a net operating loss (NOL) for any tax year was generally carried back two years, and then carried forward 20 years. (FTC 2d/FIN ¶ M-4301; USTR ¶ 1724.30; Catalyst ¶ 135:171; Catalyst ¶ 135:382; Catalyst ¶ 136:102; Catalyst ¶ 502:182) Taxpayers could elect to forego the carryback. (FTC 2d/FIN ¶ M-4304; USTR ¶ 1724.33)

The entire amount of the NOL for a tax year is carried to the earliest of the tax years to which it may be carried, then carried to the next earliest of those tax years, etc. (FTC 2d/FIN ¶ M-4300; USTR ¶ 1724.31; Catalyst ¶ 136:211; Catalyst ¶ 136:351; Catalyst ¶ 142:181)

Special carryback or carryover periods applied in certain cases. Specified liability losses (SLLs) could be carried back 10 years. (FTC 2d/FIN ¶ M-4331; USTR ¶ 1724.42; Catalyst ¶ 142:181) Farming losses could be carried back five years. (FTC 2d/FIN ¶ M-4311; USTR ¶ 1724.437; Catalyst ¶ 142:181)

There was a three-year carryback of an individual's NOL attributable to a casualty or disaster (FTC 2d/FIN ¶ M-4307; USTR ¶ 1724.434) and of a small business or farm NOL (that wasn't a farming loss) attributable to a federally declared disaster. (FTC 2d/FIN ¶ M-4308; USTR ¶ 1724.436)

NOLs attributable to corporate equity reduction interest losses (CERILs) were subject to the usual NOL carryback and carryover rules, but couldn't be carried back to a tax year before the corporate equity reduction transaction (CERT) occurred. (FTC 2d/FIN ¶ M-4314; USTR ¶ 1724.35; Catalyst ¶ 136:351)

A real estate investment trust (REIT) couldn't carry back a NOL for a REIT year to any tax year preceding the year of loss. (FTC 2d/FIN ¶ M-4330; USTR ¶ 1724.39; Catalyst ¶ 552:121)

New Law. The Tax Cuts and Jobs Act repeals the general two-year NOL carryback and the special carryback provisions, but provides a two-year carryback for certain losses incurred in a farming trade or business. The Act also provides that NOLs may be carried forward indefinitely. (Com Rept, see ¶ 5045)

For a provision that limits the NOL deduction to 80% of taxable income, see ¶ 1001.

Repeal of NOL carryback. The Tax Cuts and Jobs Act provides that an NOL can't be carried back to any tax year, except as otherwise provided for farming losses and insurance companies (see below). (Code Sec. 172(b)(1)(A)(i) as amended by Tax Cuts and Jobs Act §13302(b)(1)(A))

> **⊘ observation:** The two-year carryback provided a way for profitable businesses that had suffered a down year to receive a much-needed cash infusion, particularly when the taxpayer applied for a quick carryback refund (FTC 2d/FIN ¶ T-6500; USTR ¶ 64,114). Under the Tax Cuts and Jobs Act, a taxpayer will have to wait at least one year to receive a tax benefit from its loss.

Indefinite carryforward of NOLs. Under the Tax Cuts and Jobs Act, an NOL for any tax year is an NOL carryover to each tax year, rather than to just the next 20 tax years. (Code Sec. 172(b)(1)(A)(ii) as amended by Tax Cuts and Jobs Act §13302(b)(1)(B))

Two-year farming loss carryback allowed. Under an exception to the no-carryback rule, any part of an NOL for the tax year that's a farming loss of the taxpayer can be carried back to each of the two tax years preceding the tax year of the loss. (Code Sec. 172(b)(1)(B)(i) as amended by Tax Cuts and Jobs Act §13302(c)(1))

A "farming loss" is the lesser of (Code Sec. 172(b)(1)(B)(ii)):

(1) the amount that would be the NOL for the tax year if only income and deductions attributable to farming businesses are taken into account, or (Code Sec. 172(b)(1)(B)(ii)(I))

(2) the amount of the NOL for the tax year. (Code Sec. 172(b)(1)(B)(ii)(II))

"Farming business" is defined as in Code Sec. 263A(e)(4) for purposes of the uniform capitalization (UNICAP) rules (see FTC 2d/FIN ¶ N-1073; USTR ¶ 263A4.15). (Code Sec. 172(b)(1)(B)(ii)(I))

In applying Code Sec. 172(b)(2), which provides the order in which NOLs are absorbed, a farming loss for any tax year is treated as a separate NOL for that tax year and is taken into account after the remaining part of that year's NOL. (Code Sec. 172(b)(1)(B)(iii))

Election to forego farming loss carryback. A taxpayer entitled to a two-year carryback of a farming loss may elect to forego the carryback. The election is made in the manner prescribed by IRS and must be made by the due date (including extensions) for filing the taxpayer's return for the tax year of the NOL. The election is irrevocable for the tax year for which it was made. (Code Sec. 172(b)(1)(B)(iv))

> *observation:* This election is generally made when the NOL deduction is expected to be worth more in future years because the taxpayer's income was taxed at a lower rate in the previous two years. Because the Tax Cuts and Jobs Act generally lowers individual and corporate tax rates (see ¶ 101 and ¶ 102), the election may not prove beneficial in the first two years that it's in effect.

Insurance companies get two-year carryback, 20-year carryforward. For an insurance company (as defined in Code Sec. 816(a)) other than a life insurance company, *i.e.*, a property and casualty insurance company (Com Rept, see ¶ 5045), the NOL for any tax year (Code Sec. 172(b)(1)(C) as amended by Tax Cuts and Jobs Act §13302(d)(1)) can be:

. . . carried back to each of the two tax years preceding the tax year of the loss (Code Sec. 172(b)(1)(C)(i)), and

. . . carried forward to each of the 20 tax years following the tax year of the loss. (Code Sec. 172(b)(1)(C)(ii))

Conforming changes to other NOL rules. As a result of the above changes, the following pre-Tax Cuts and Jobs Act rules are eliminated:

. . . the special rules for REITs (Code Sec. 172(b)(1) as amended by Tax Cuts and Jobs Act §13302(b)(2));

. . . the ten-year carryback for SLLs (Code Sec. 172(b)(1) as amended by Tax Cuts and Jobs Act §13302(b)(2); Code Sec. 172(f) as amended by Tax Cuts and Jobs Act §13302(c)(2)(A));

. . . the rules for CERILs (Code Sec. 172(b)(1) as amended by Tax Cuts and Jobs Act §13302(b)(2); Code Sec. 172(g) as amended by Tax Cuts and Jobs Act §13302(c)(2)(A));

. . . the three-year carryback for casualty or disaster losses (Code Sec. 172(b)(1) as amended by Tax Cuts and Jobs Act §13302(b)(2));

. . . the five-year carryback for farming losses (replaced by the two-year carryback discussed above). (Code Sec. 172(b)(1) as amended by Tax Cuts and Jobs Act §13302(b)(2); Code Sec. 172(h) as amended by Tax Cuts and Jobs Act §13302(c)(2)(A))

☐ **Effective:** NOLs arising in tax years ending after Dec. 31, 2017. (Tax Cuts and Jobs Act §13302(e)(2))

> *observation:* This effective date means that NOLs that arose in tax years that ended before Jan. 1, 2018, will be subject to the two-year carryback/20-year carryforward rule and the special rules that applied under pre-Tax Cuts and Jobs Act law. Taxpayers will have to distinguish between the two types of NOLs when computing the NOL deduction.

> *observation:* Taxpayers with fiscal tax years will be subject to the no-carryback/indefinite carryforward rule for the year that began in 2017 and ends in 2018.

¶ 1003. Deduction for net business interest is limited to 30% of adjusted taxable income, with indefinite carryover

Code Sec. 163(j), as amended by Tax Cuts and Jobs Act §13301(a)
Code Sec. 381(c)(20), as amended by Tax Cuts and Jobs Act §13301(b)(1)
Code Sec. 382(d)(3), as amended by Tax Cuts and Jobs Act §13301(b)(2)
Code Sec. 382(k)(1), as amended by Tax Cuts and Jobs Act §13301(b)(3)
Generally effective: Tax years beginning after Dec. 31, 2017
Committee Reports, see ¶ 5044

Interest paid or accrued during the tax year on indebtedness is generally deductible, but the deduction is subject to a number of limitations. (FTC 2d/FIN ¶ K-5000 *et seq.*; USTR ¶ 1634)

Noncorporate taxpayers may not deduct personal interest. For this purpose, personal interest doesn't include interest on debt properly allocable to a trade or business, other than the trade or business of being an employee. (FTC 2d/FIN ¶ K-5512; USTR ¶ 1634.054)

Earnings stripping. A corporation's payment of deductible interest to a related person who pays no U.S. tax on the corresponding income is referred to as earnings stripping. To prevent earnings stripping, pre-Tax Cuts and Jobs Act law denied a corporation's interest deduction for "disqualified interest" to the extent of the corporation's "excess interest expense" in any year that the corporation had a debt-to-equity ratio greater than 1.5 to 1. (FTC 2d/FIN ¶ K-5360 *et seq.*; USTR ¶ 1634.058; Catalyst ¶ 106:200)

New Law. The Tax Cuts and Jobs Act repeals the earnings stripping rules and replaces them with a limitation on the deduction of business interest. (Code Sec. 163(j)(1) as amended by Tax Cuts and Jobs Act §13301(a))

Under this limitation, the deduction allowed for business interest for any tax year can't exceed the sum of (Code Sec. 163(j)(1)):

(1) the taxpayer's business interest income for the tax year; (Code Sec. 163(j)(1)(A))

(2) 30% of the taxpayer's adjusted taxable income for the tax year; plus (Code Sec. 163(j)(1)(B))

(3) the taxpayer's floor plan financing interest for the tax year. (Code Sec. 163(j)(1)(C))

The amount at (2), above (30% of adjusted taxable income), can't be less than zero. (Code Sec. 163(j)(1))

Floor plan financing interest is fully deductible under this provision. The deduction for net interest expense (less floor plan financing interest) is limited to 30% of adjusted taxable income. (Com Rept, see ¶ 5044)

illustration (1): For 2018, Corporation X has $100,000 of adjusted taxable income, $2,000 of business interest income, and $12,000 of business interest expense. It has no floor plan financing interest.

X can deduct all $12,000 of its business interest expense, because that's less than the sum of its $2,000 of business interest income plus 30% of its adjusted taxable income (30% × $100,000 = $30,000).

observation: Because the business interest limitation ties the amount of deductible business interest to the taxpayer's adjusted taxable income, it can hurt a business that has had an unsuccessful year. The reduction in the taxpayer's adjusted taxable income in the off year will reduce the amount of interest that the taxpayer can deduct in that year. This effect is partly, but not fully, mitigated by the carryforward of disallowed interest (see below).

illustration (2): In 2019, Corporation X in *RIA illustration (1)* has only $10,000 of adjusted taxable income and again has $2,000 of business interest income and $12,000 of business interest expense.

Here, X's deduction for business interest is limited to $5,000—its $2,000 of business interest income plus 30% of its adjusted taxable income (30% × $10,000 = $3,000). The $7,000 of disallowed interest can be carried forward indefinitely (see below under "Carryforward of disallowed interest").

ⓥ *illustration (3):* Assume that in 2019, Corporation X in *RIA illustration (1)* had adjusted taxable income of ($20,000), $2,000 of business interest income, and $12,000 of business interest expense.

Because X's adjusted taxable income is negative, it is deemed to be zero for purposes of the business interest limitation. X can deduct $2,000 of its business interest, an amount equal to its $2,000 of business interest income. The $10,000 of disallowed interest can be carried forward indefinitely.

The business interest limitation applies at the taxpayer level. For an affiliated group of corporations that file a consolidated return, it applies at the consolidated tax return filing level. (Com Rept, see ¶ 5044)

Carryforward of disallowed interest. Any business interest that isn't deductible because of the business interest limitation is treated as business interest paid or accrued in the following tax year (Code Sec. 163(j)(2)), and may be carried forward indefinitely, subject to the restrictions applicable to partnerships described below. (Com Rept, see ¶ 5044)

Small business exception. The business interest limitation doesn't apply to a taxpayer that meets the $25 million gross receipts test of Code Sec. 448(c) (see ¶ 1401) for any tax year. (Code Sec. 163(j)(3)) This test is met if the taxpayer's average annual gross receipts for the three-tax-year period ending with the prior tax year don't exceed $25 million. (Com Rept, see ¶ 5044)

For a taxpayer that isn't a corporation or a partnership (*i.e.,* a sole proprietorship (Com Rept, see ¶ 5044)), the gross receipts test is applied as if the taxpayer were a corporation or partnership. (Code Sec. 163(j)(3))

The small business exception doesn't apply to tax shelters that are prohibited from using the cash method of accounting under Code Sec. 448(a)(3) (see Catalyst ¶ 754:135; FTC 2d/FIN ¶ G-2054; USTR ¶ 4484). (Code Sec. 163(j)(3))

Exceptions for certain trades or businesses. As is discussed below, for purposes of the business interest limitation, the term "trade or business" doesn't include the trade or business of performing services as an employee, an electing real property trade or business, an electing farming business, and certain trades or businesses of regulated public utilities. (Code Sec. 163(j)(7)(A))

Employee. The trade or business of performing services as an employee isn't a "trade or business" for purposes of the business interest limitation. (Code Sec. 163(j)(7)(A)(i)) Thus, an employee's wages aren't counted in the taxpayer's adjusted taxable income for purposes of determining the limitation. (Com Rept, see ¶ 5044) *observation:* If an individual earns wages as an employee and also does business as a sole proprietor, the wages can't be used to increase the deduction for business interest allocable to the proprietorship.

Electing real property trade or business. An electing real property trade or business isn't a "trade or business" for purposes of the business interest limitation. (Code Sec. 163(j)(7)(A)(ii))

An "electing real property trade or business" is any trade or business:

... that is described in Code Sec. 469(c)(7)(C) (for purposes of qualifying as real estate professional under the passive loss rules, see Catalyst ¶ 762:164; FTC 2d/FIN ¶ M-5175; USTR ¶ 4694.63) and

... that makes an election under Code Sec. 163(j)(7)(B). (Code Sec. 163(j)(7)(B))

The Code Sec. 163(j)(7)(B) election must be made at the time and in the manner that IRS prescribes. Once made, the election is irrevocable. (Code Sec. 163(j)(7)(B))

Making the election requires the electing real property trade or business to use the alternative depreciation system (ADS) to depreciate any of its non-residential real property, residential rental property, and qualified improvement property, see ¶ 1303.

A trade or business described in Code Sec. 469(c)(7)(C) is a real property development, redevelopment, construction, reconstruction, acquisition, conversion, rental, operation, management, leasing, or brokerage trade or business. At the taxpayer's election, the business interest limitation doesn't apply to such trades or businesses. (Com Rept, see ¶ 5044)

This definition is intended to include real property trades or businesses conducted by a corporation or a real estate investment trust (REIT). It's also intended that operating or managing a lodging facility is a real property operation or management trade or business. (Com Rept, see ¶ 5044)

The definition of a real property trade or business refers only to the description in Code Sec. 469(c)(7)(C). It doesn't refer to other rules of Code Sec. 469, such as Code Sec. 469(a) (limitation on passive activity losses) or Code Sec. 469(c)(2) (passive activities include rental activities). Therefore, those other rules aren't made applicable to the business interest limitation by the reference to Code Sec. 469(c)(7)(C). (Com Rept, see ¶ 5044)

Electing farming business. An electing farming business isn't a "trade or business" for purposes of the business interest limitation. (Code Sec. 163(j)(7)(A)(iii))

An "electing farming trade or business" is:

. . . a farming business, as defined in Code Sec. 263A(e)(4) (see FTC 2d/FIN ¶ N-1073; USTR ¶ 263A4.15), that makes an election under Code Sec. 163(j)(7)(C) (Code Sec. 163(j)(7)(C)(i)); or

. . . a trade or business of a specified agricultural or horticultural cooperative, as defined in Code Sec. 199A(g)(2) (see ¶ 704), for which the cooperative makes an election under Code Sec. 163(j)(7)(C). (Code Sec. 163(j)(7)(C)(ii))

The election must be made at the time and in the manner that IRS prescribes. Once made, the election is irrevocable. (Code Sec. 163(j)(7)(C))

Making the election requires the electing farming business to use the alternative depreciation system (ADS) to depreciate any property used in the farming business with a recovery period of ten years or more, see ¶ 1306.

Regulated public utility. The trade or business of the furnishing or sale of:

. . . electrical energy, water, or sewage disposal services, (Code Sec. 163(j)(7)(A)(iv)(I))

. . . gas or steam through a local distribution system, or (Code Sec. 163(j)(7)(A)(iv)(II))

. . . transportation of gas or steam by pipeline (Code Sec. 163(j)(7)(A)(iv)(III))

isn't a "trade or business" for purposes of the business interest limitation if the rates for the furnishing or sale have been established or approved by:

. . . a state or political subdivision of a state,

. . . a U.S. agency or instrumentality,

. . . a public service or public utility commission or other similar body of a state or political subdivision of a state, or

. . . an electric cooperative's governing or ratemaking body. (Code Sec. 163(j)(7)(A)(iv))

Thus, the business interest limitation doesn't apply to these regulated public utilities. (Com Rept, see ¶ 5044)

Property used in a regulated public utility trade or business described in Code Sec. 163(j)(7)(A)(iv) is excluded from 100% bonus depreciation (full expensing), see ¶ 1207.

Business interest. "Business interest" means any interest paid or accrued on indebtedness properly allocable to a trade or business. (Code Sec. 163(j)(5)) Any amount treated as interest under the Code is interest for purposes of the business interest limitation. (Com Rept, see ¶ 5044).

Business interest doesn't include investment interest within the meaning of Code Sec. 163(d) (see FTC 2d/FIN ¶ K-5312; USTR ¶ 1634.053). (Code Sec. 163(j)(5))

Business interest income. "Business interest income" means the amount of interest includible in the taxpayer's gross income for the tax year that's properly allocable to a trade or business. The term doesn't include investment income within the meaning of Code Sec. 163(d) (see FTC 2d/FIN ¶ K-5315; USTR ¶ 1634.053). (Code Sec. 163(j)(6))

Corporation's interest income and expense. Because the Code Sec. 163(d) investment interest limitation doesn't apply to corporations, a corporation has neither investment interest nor investment income within the meaning of Code Sec. 163(d). Thus, a corporation's interest income and interest expense is properly allocable to a trade or business, unless the trade or business is otherwise excluded from the application of the business interest limitation. (Com Rept, see ¶ 5044)

Adjusted taxable income. "Adjusted taxable income" means the taxpayer's taxable income (Code Sec. 163(j)(8)), computed without regard to (Code Sec. 163(j)(8)(A)):

. . . any item of income, gain, deduction, or loss that isn't properly allocable to a trade or business; (Code Sec. 163(j)(8)(A)(i))

. . . any business interest or business interest income; (Code Sec. 163(j)(8)(A)(ii))

. . . the amount of any net operating loss (NOL) deduction under Code Sec. 172 (see FTC 2d/FIN ¶ M-4000 *et seq.*; USTR ¶ 1724 *et seq.*); (Code Sec. 163(j)(8)(A)(iii))

. . . the amount of any qualified business income deduction allowed under Code Sec. 199A (added by the Tax Cuts and Jobs Act, see ¶ 702); and (Code Sec. 163(j)(8)(A)(iv))

. . . for tax years beginning before Jan. 1, 2022, any deduction allowable for depreciation, amortization, or depletion. (Code Sec. 163(j)(8)(A)(v))

Because the Tax Cuts and Jobs Act repeals the Code Sec. 199 domestic production activities deduction (see ¶ 1004), effective for tax years beginning after Dec. 31, 2017, adjusted taxable income is computed without regard to that deduction. (Com Rept, see ¶ 5044)

IRS may provide for other adjustments to be made in computing adjusted taxable income. (Code Sec. 163(j)(8)(B))

Floor plan financing interest. "Floor plan financing interest" means interest paid or accrued on floor plan financing indebtedness. (Code Sec. 163(j)(9)(A))

"Floor plan financing indebtedness" means indebtedness (Code Sec. 163(j)(9)(B)):

. . . used to finance the acquisition of motor vehicles held for sale or lease, and (Code Sec. 163(j)(9)(B)(i))

... secured by the inventory so acquired. (Code Sec. 163(j)(9)(B)(ii))

The term "motor vehicle" means a motor vehicle that's any of the following (Code Sec. 163(j)(9)(C)):

- any self-propelled vehicle designed for transporting persons or property on a public street, highway, or road. (Code Sec. 163(j)(9)(C)(i))
- a boat. (Code Sec. 163(j)(9)(C)(ii))
- farm machinery or equipment. (Code Sec. 163(j)(9)(C)(iii))

Property used in a trade or business that has had floor plan financing indebtedness is excluded from 100% bonus depreciation (full expensing), see ¶ 1207.

Partnerships. The business interest limitation applies to partnerships at the partnership level. Any deduction for business interest is taken into account in determining the partnership's nonseparately stated taxable income or loss. (Code Sec. 163(j)(4)(A)(i)) This amount is the "Ordinary business income or loss" reflected on Form 1065 (U.S. Return of Partnership Income). (Com Rept, see ¶ 5044)

Each partner's adjusted taxable income is determined without regard to the partner's distributive share of any of the partnership's items of income, gain, deduction, or loss. (Code Sec. 163(j)(4)(A)(ii)(I)) This rule is intended to prevent double counting. Without such a rule, the same dollars of adjusted taxable income of a partnership could generate additional interest deductions as the income is passed through to the partners. (Com Rept, see ¶ 5044)

> *Illustration (4):* ABC is a partnership owned 50-50 by XYZ Corporation and an individual. ABC generates $200 of noninterest income. Its only expense is $60 of business interest.
>
> ABC's deduction for business interest is limited to 30% of its adjusted taxable income, which is $60 (30% × $200). ABC deducts $60 of business interest and reports ordinary business income of $140.
>
> XYZ's distributive share of ABC's ordinary business income is $70. XYZ has net taxable income of zero from its other operations, without regard to its business interest expense of $25. None of XYZ's income is interest income.
>
> In the absence of a double-counting rule, the $70 of taxable income from XYZ's distributive share of ABC's income would allow XYZ to deduct up to an additional $21 of interest (30% × $70). As a result, XYZ's $100 share of ABC's adjusted taxable income would generate $51 of interest deductions, well in excess of the intended 30% limitation. If XYZ were a pass-through entity rather than a corporation, additional deductions might be available to its partners as well, and so on.
>
> The double-counting rule prevents this result by providing that XYZ's adjusted taxable income is computed without regard to its $70

distributive share of ABC's nonseparately stated income. As a result, XYZ has adjusted taxable income of $0. XYZ's deduction for business interest is limited to 30% × $0, which is $0, resulting in a deduction disallowance of $25. (Com Rept, see ¶ 5044)

Each partner's adjusted taxable income is increased by the partner's distributive share of the partnership's excess taxable income. (Code Sec. 163(j)(4)(A)(ii)(II)) A partnership's "excess taxable income" is the amount that bears the same ratio to the partnership's adjusted taxable income as (Code Sec. 163(j)(4)(C)):

... the excess (if any) of (Code Sec. 163(j)(4)(C)(i)) 30% of the partnership's adjusted taxable income over (Code Sec. 163(j)(4)(C)(i)(I)) the amount (if any) by which the partnership's business interest, reduced by any floor plan financing interest, exceeds its business interest income, bears to (Code Sec. 163(j)(4)(C)(i)(II))

... 30% of the partnership's adjusted taxable income. (Code Sec. 163(j)(4)(C)(ii))

This rule allows a partner to deduct additional interest expense the partner may have paid or incurred to the extent the partnership could have deducted more business interest. (Com Rept, see ¶ 5044)

For this purpose, a partner's distributive share of partnership excess taxable income is determined in the same manner as the partner's distributive share of the partnership's nonseparately stated taxable income or loss. (Code Sec. 163(j)(4)(A)(ii))

> *Illustration (5):* The facts are the same as in *Illustration (4)*, except that ABC has only $40 of business interest. As in *Illustration (4)*, ABC has a limit of $60 on its interest deduction. The excess of this limit over the partnership's business interest is $20 ($60 − $40). ABC's excess taxable income is $66.67 [($20 ÷ $60) × $200]. XYZ's distributive share of the excess taxable income from ABC partnership is $33.33. XYZ's deduction for business interest is limited to 30% of the sum of its adjusted taxable income plus its $10 distributive share of the excess taxable income from ABC partnership [30% × ($0 + $33.33)]. As a result of the rule, XYZ may deduct $10 of business interest and has an interest deduction disallowance of $15. (Com Rept, see ¶ 5044)

S corporations and shareholders. Rules similar to those under "Partnerships," above, apply to an S corporation and its shareholders. (Code Sec. 163(j)(4)(D))

Partnership carryforwards. The general carryforward rule of Code Sec. 163(j)(2) (see "Carryforward of disallowed interest," above) doesn't apply to partnerships. (Com Rept, see ¶ 5044) Instead, any business interest that isn't deductible by a partnership for any tax year because of the business interest limitation isn't treated as business interest paid or accrued by the partnership in the next tax year. (Code Sec. 163(j)(4)(B)(i)(I)) Rather, it's treated as excess business interest that's allocated to each partner in the same manner as the partnership's nonseparately stated taxable income or loss. (Code Sec. 163(j)(4)(B)(i)(II))

Any excess business interest that's allocated to a partner from a partnership under this rule for any tax year is treated as business interest paid or accrued by the partner in the next succeeding tax year in which the partner is allocated excess taxable income from the partnership, but only to the extent of the excess taxable income. (Code Sec. 163(j)(4)(B)(ii)(I))

Thus, the partner may deduct its share of the partnership's excess business interest in any future year, but only against excess taxable income attributed to the partner by the partnership whose activities gave rise to the excess business interest carryforward. Any such deduction requires a corresponding reduction in excess taxable income. (Com Rept, see ¶ 5044)

Any part of the excess business interest that remains after this carryover is treated as business interest paid or accrued in later tax years, subject to the same limitations. (Code Sec. 163(j)(4)(B)(ii)(II))

For this purpose, excess taxable income allocated to a partner from a partnership for any tax year isn't taken into account for any business interest other than excess business interest from the partnership until all of the excess business interest for that tax year and all preceding tax years has been treated as paid or accrued. (Code Sec. 163(j)(4)(B)(ii))

Partner's basis adjustments.   A partner's adjusted basis in a partnership interest is reduced (but not below zero) by the amount of excess business interest allocated to the partner (Code Sec. 163(j)(4)(B)(iii)(I)), even though the carryforward doesn't give rise to a partner deduction in the year of the basis reduction. However, the partner's deduction in a future year for interest carried forward doesn't reduce the partner's basis in the partnership interest. (Com Rept, see ¶ 5044)

If a partner disposes of a partnership interest, then the partner's adjusted basis in the partnership interest is increased immediately before the disposition by any excess of the amount of the basis reduction over the part of any excess business interest allocated to the partner that has previously been treated as business interest paid or accrued by the partner. This basis increase also applies where a partnership interest is transferred (including by reason of death) in a transaction in which gain isn't recognized in whole or in part. (Code Sec. 163(j)(4)(B)(iii)(II))

No deduction is allowed to the transferor or transferee for any excess business interest resulting in a basis increase. (Code Sec. 163(j)(4)(B)(iii)(II))

The above rules on carryforwards don't apply to S corporations and their shareholders. (Com Rept, see ¶ 5044)

Treatment of interest carryovers in corporate transactions. Carryovers of disallowed business interest to tax years ending after the date of distribution or transfer are included in the list of items that are carried over under Code Sec. 381 (FTC 2d/FIN ¶ F-7000, ¶ F-7001, ¶ F-7012; USTR ¶ 3814, ¶ 3814.01, ¶ 3814.02; Catalyst ¶ 135:160) to a distributee or transferee corporation for distributions in Code Sec. 332 liquidations or for certain transfers under Code Sec. 361. (Code Sec. 381(c)(20) as amended by Tax Cuts and Jobs Act §13301(b)(1))

But carryovers of disallowed interest are treated as items of pre-change loss that are subject to the Code Sec. 382 limitation (FTC 2d/FIN ¶ F-7200, ¶ F-7201, ¶ F-7363; Catalyst ¶ 136:211). (Code Sec. 382(d)(3) as amended by Tax Cuts and Jobs Act §13301(b)(2))

As a conforming change, a loss corporation (FTC 2d/FIN ¶ F-7203; USTR ¶ 3824.01; Catalyst ¶ 128:261; Catalyst ¶ 136:110; Catalyst ¶ 137:271; Catalyst ¶ 142:184) is defined to include a corporation with a carryover of disallowed interest. (Code Sec. 382(k)(1) as amended by Tax Cuts and Jobs Act §13301(b)(3))

☐ **Effective:** Tax years beginning after Dec. 31, 2017. (Tax Cuts and Jobs Act §13301(c))

¶ 1004. Domestic production activity deduction (DPAD) is repealed

Code Sec. 199, as repealed by Tax Cuts and Jobs Act §13305(a)
Generally effective: Tax years beginning after Dec. 31, 2017
Committee Reports, see ¶ 5048

Under pre-Tax Cuts and Jobs Act law, the domestic production activities deduction ("DPAD"), which was allowed for certain qualifying U.S.-based activities, was equal to 9% of the lesser of the taxpayer's qualified production activities income or the taxpayer's taxable income (determined without regard to the DPAD) for the tax year. (FTC 2d/FIN ¶ L-4325, ¶ L-4326 *et seq.*; USTR ¶ 1994 *et seq.*; Catalyst ¶ 108:105; Catalyst ¶ 142:194; Catalyst ¶ 403:105; Catalyst ¶ 403:212)

New Law. The Tax Cuts and Jobs Act repeals the DPAD. (Code Sec. 199 as repealed by Tax Cuts and Jobs Act §13305(a))

☐ **Effective:** Tax years beginning after Dec. 31, 2017. (Tax Cuts and Jobs Act §13305(c))

¶ 1005. Business deduction is denied for entertainment expenses

Code Sec. 274(a)(1)(A), as amended by Tax Cuts and Jobs Act §13304(a)(1)(A)
Code Sec. 274(a)(1), as amended by Tax Cuts and Jobs Act §13304(a)(1)(B)
Code Sec. 274(a)(2), as amended by Tax Cuts and Jobs Act §13304(a)(1)(C)
Code Sec. 274(d), as amended by Tax Cuts and Jobs Act §13304(a)(2)(A)(i)
Code Sec. 274(d), as amended by Tax Cuts and Jobs Act §13304(a)(2)(A)(ii)
Code Sec. 274(l), as amended by Tax Cuts and Jobs Act §13304(a)(2)(B)
Code Sec. 274(n), as amended by Tax Cuts and Jobs Act §13304(a)(2)(C)
Code Sec. 274(n)(1), as amended by Tax Cuts and Jobs Act §13304(a)(2)(D)
Code Sec. 274(n)(2), as amended by Tax Cuts and Jobs Act §13304(a)(2)(E)
Code Sec. 7701(b)(5)(A)(iv), as amended by Tax Cuts and Jobs Act §13304(a)(2)(F)
Generally effective: Amounts incurred or paid after Dec. 31, 2017
Committee Reports, see ¶ 5047

Under pre-Tax Cuts and Jobs Act law, no deduction was allowed for ordinary and necessary expenses for an activity of a type generally considered to be entertainment, amusement, or recreation, or for a facility used in connection with such an activity, unless the taxpayer established that the expense was directly related to or associated with the active conduct of the taxpayer's trade or business or income-producing activity. The deduction couldn't exceed the portion of the item that met the "directly related to or associated with" standard. (FTC 2d/FIN ¶ L-2100, ¶ L-2101; USTR ¶ 2744.01; Catalyst ¶ 105:120; Catalyst ¶ 108:104; Catalyst ¶ 154:130; Catalyst ¶ 758:170)

However, the restrictions on deducting entertainment expenses don't apply to nine types of expenses that are listed in Code Sec. 274(e), including the following:

. . . expenses for goods, services, and facilities that are treated as compensation to an employee on the employer's income tax return and as wages of the employee for withholding purposes. (FTC 2d/FIN ¶ L-2123; USTR ¶ 2744.015)

. . . expenses paid or incurred by the taxpayer, in connection with the performance of services for another person, under a reimbursement or other expense allowance arrangement, if the taxpayer accounts for the expenses to that person. (FTC 2d/FIN ¶ L-2124; USTR ¶ 2744.01)

... expenses for recreational, social, or similar activities (including related facilities) primarily for the benefit of the taxpayer's employees, other than highly-compensated employees. (FTC 2d/FIN ¶ L-2125; USTR ¶ 2744.01)

The bar on deducting expenses of an entertainment facility applied in the case of a club, unless the taxpayer established that the facility was used primarily for the furtherance of the taxpayer's trade or business and that the item was directly related to the active conduct of that trade or business. (FTC 2d/FIN ¶ L-2149; USTR ¶ 2744.01)

The deduction allowed for entertainment expenses was limited to 50% of the otherwise deductible amount of the expense. (FTC 2d/FIN ¶ L-2135; USTR ¶ 2744.01)

New Law. The Tax Cuts and Jobs Act repeals the rule that allowed a deduction for entertainment, amusement, or recreation expenses that were directly related to or associated with the active conduct of the taxpayer's trade or business. (Code Sec. 274(a)(1)(A) as amended by Tax Cuts and Jobs Act §13304(a)(1)(A))

The Tax Cuts and Jobs Act also repeals:

... the rule that limited the deduction to the portion of the item that met the "directly related to or associated with" standard. (Code Sec. 274(a)(1) as amended by Tax Cuts and Jobs Act §13304(a)(1)(B))

... the rule that allowed a deduction for a club if the taxpayer established that the facility was used primarily for the furtherance of the taxpayer's trade or business and that the item was directly related to the active conduct of that trade or business. (Code Sec. 274(a)(2) as amended by Tax Cuts and Jobs Act §13304(a)(1)(C))

... the 50% deduction limit on expenses for activities or facilities generally considered to be entertainment, amusement, or recreation. (Code Sec. 274(n) as amended by Tax Cuts and Jobs Act §13304(a)(2)(C); Code Sec. 274(n)(1) as amended by Tax Cuts and Jobs Act §13304(a)(2)(D))

Under the Tax Cuts and Jobs Act, no deduction is allowed for: (1) an activity generally considered to be entertainment, amusement, or recreation, (2) membership dues for any club organized for business, pleasure, recreation, or other social purposes, or (3) a facility used in connection with any of the above items. (Com Rept, see ¶ 5047)

> *observation:* Entertainment expenses are completely nondeductible, regardless of whether they are directly related to or associated with the taxpayer's business, unless one of the exceptions in Code Sec. 274(e) (discussed above) applies. Code Sec. 274(e) wasn't changed by the Tax Cuts and Jobs Act.

As under pre-Tax Cuts and Jobs Act law, taxpayers may still generally deduct 50% of the food and beverage expenses associated with operating their trade or business, such as meals consumed by employees on work travel. (Com Rept, see ¶ 5047)

To conform other provisions of Code Sec. 274 to the above changes, the Tax Cuts and Jobs Act repeals:

. . . the substantiation rules for activities or facilities generally considered to be entertainment, amusement, or recreation. (Code Sec. 274(d) as amended by Tax Cuts and Jobs Act §13304(a)(2)(A)(i): Code Sec. 274(d) as amended by Tax Cuts and Jobs Act §13304(a)(2)(A)(ii))

. . . the additional limitations on entertainment tickets for activities or facilities generally considered to be entertainment, amusement, or recreation. (Code Sec. 274(l) as amended by Tax Cuts and Jobs Act §13304(a)(2)(B))

. . . the exception to the 50% deduction limit that applied to expenses that were part of a package that included a ticket to attend certain charitable sporting events. (Code Sec. 274(n)(2) as amended by Tax Cuts and Jobs Act §13304(a)(2)(E))

The Tax Cuts and Jobs Act also makes a conforming change to the rule that treats a professional athlete as being present in the U.S. for purposes of the substantial presence test on any day that the athlete is temporarily in the U.S. to compete in a charitable sporting event. That rule made a cross-reference to now-repealed Code Sec. 274(l)(1)(B). (Code Sec. 7701(b)(5)(A)(iv) as amended by Tax Cuts and Jobs Act §13304(a)(2)(F))

For a 50% deduction limit on expenses for employer-operated eating facilities, see ¶ 1006.

For disallowance of a deduction for transportation benefits, see ¶ 1007.

☐ **Effective:** Amounts incurred or paid after Dec. 31, 2017. (Tax Cuts and Jobs Act §13304(e)(1))

¶ 1006. Expenses for employer-operated eating facilities are only 50% deductible through 2025, then become nondeductible

Code Sec. 274(n)(2), as amended by Tax Cuts and Jobs Act §13304(b)(1)
Code Sec. 274(o), as amended by Tax Cuts and Jobs Act §13304(d)(2)
Generally effective: Amounts incurred or paid after Dec. 31, 2017, and before Jan. 1, 2026
Committee Reports, see ¶ 5047

A deduction for any food or beverage expense is generally limited to 50% of the otherwise deductible amount. (FTC 2d/FIN ¶ L-2135; USTR ¶ 2744.01)

Under pre-Tax Cuts and Jobs Act law, this 50% limit didn't apply to expenses for food or beverages that were excludable from the recipient's gross income under Code Sec. 132(e) as a *de minimis* fringe benefit. (FTC 2d/FIN ¶ L-2141; USTR ¶ 2744.01)

Code Sec. 132(e)(1) defines a "de minimis fringe benefit" as any property or service whose value is so small that accounting for it would be unreasonable or administratively impracticable, taking into account the frequency with which the employer provides similar fringe benefits to other employees. (FTC 2d/FIN ¶ H-1802; USTR ¶ 1324.06)

Under Code Sec. 132(e)(2), the value of meals provided to employees at an employer-operated eating facility is an excludable *de minimis* fringe if:

(1) the facility is located on or near the employer's business premises;

(2) the facility's annual revenue equals or exceeds its direct operating costs; and

(3) for highly compensated employees, the facility is operated without discriminating in favor of such employees. (FTC 2d/FIN ¶ H-1821; USTR ¶ 1324.06)

Code Sec. 119 provides an exclusion from an employee's gross income for the value of meals furnished on the employer's business premises, for the convenience of the employer, to the employee, the employee's spouse, and any of the employee's dependent children. (FTC 2d/FIN ¶ H-1751 *et seq.*; USTR ¶ 1194 *et seq.*)

An employee entitled under Code Sec. 119 to exclude the value of a meal provided at an employer-operated eating facility is treated as having paid an amount for the meal equal to the facility's direct operating costs attributable to the meal for purposes of requirement (2), above. This makes those meals excludable as a *de minimis* fringe.

Thus, under pre-Tax Cuts and Jobs Act law, employers could fully deduct the cost of business meals that were excludable from the income of employees because they were provided at an employer-operated eating facility for the convenience of the employer. (FTC 2d/FIN ¶ H-1821; USTR ¶ 1324.06)

New Law. The Tax Cuts and Jobs Act provides that the 50% limit on deducting food or beverage expenses applies to an employer's expenses of providing food and beverages to employees at an eating facility that qualifies as a *de minimis* fringe benefit. (Code Sec. 274(n)(2) as amended by Tax Cuts and Jobs Act §13304(b)(1))

Expenses nondeductible after Dec. 31, 2025. The Tax Cuts and Jobs Act provides that, for amounts incurred or paid after Dec. 31, 2025 (Tax Cuts and Jobs Act §13304(e)(2)), no deduction will be allowed for (Code Sec. 274(o) as amended by Tax Cuts and Jobs Act §13304(d)(2)):

... any expense for the operation of an employer-operated eating facility described in Code Sec. 132(e)(2);

... any expense for food or beverages, including under Code Sec. 132(e)(1), associated with an employer-operated eating facility (Code Sec. 274(o)(1)); or

... any expense for meals described in Code Sec. 119(a). (Code Sec. 274(o)(2))

☐ **Effective:** The rule allowing a 50% deduction applies to amounts incurred or paid after Dec. 31, 2017 (Tax Cuts and Jobs Act §13304(e)(1)), and before Jan. 1, 2026. (Tax Cuts and Jobs Act §13304(e)(2)) Amounts incurred or paid after Dec. 31, 2025, will be nondeductible. (Tax Cuts and Jobs Act §13304(e)(2))

¶ 1007. Employers can't deduct cost of providing qualified transportation fringes and other transportation benefits

Code Sec. 274(a)(4), as amended by Tax Cuts and Jobs Act §13304(c)(1)(B)
Code Sec. 274(l), as amended by Tax Cuts and Jobs Act §13304(c)(2)
Generally effective: Amounts incurred or paid after Dec. 31, 2017
Committee Reports, see ¶ 5047

The value of a qualified transportation fringe benefit provided by an employer to an employee is excluded from the employee's income, subject to monthly limits. (FTC 2d/FIN ¶ H-2205; USTR ¶ 1324.08)

Code Sec. 132(f) defines a "qualified transportation fringe" as (FTC 2d/FIN ¶ H-2205; USTR ¶ 1324.08):

(1) transportation in a commuter highway vehicle for travel between the employee's residence and place of employment (FTC 2d/FIN ¶ H-2210; USTR ¶ 1324.08);

(2) transit passes (FTC 2d/FIN ¶ H-2212; USTR ¶ 1324.08);

(3) qualified parking (FTC 2d/FIN ¶ H-2213; USTR ¶ 1324.08); and

(4) qualified bicycle commuting reimbursement. (FTC 2d/FIN ¶ H-2215.1; USTR ¶ 1324.08)

The Tax Cuts and Jobs Act suspends the exclusion for qualified bicycle commuting reimbursements for tax years beginning after Dec. 31, 2017, and before Jan. 1, 2026, see ¶ 603.

Under pre-Tax Cuts and Jobs Act law, a deduction wasn't barred for the expenses of providing qualified transportation fringe benefits or other transportation or commuting benefits to an employee.

New Law. The Tax Cuts and Jobs Act provides that no deduction is allowed for the expense of a qualified transportation fringe, as defined in Code

Sec. 132(f), provided to an employee of the taxpayer. (Code Sec. 274(a)(4) as amended by Tax Cuts and Jobs Act §13304(c)(1)(B))

> **✔ observation:** Although the Tax Cuts and Jobs Act denies the employer a deduction for the qualified transportation fringe benefit, it doesn't change the employee's exclusion of the benefit from income under Code Sec. 132, except in the case of qualified bicycle commuting reimbursements.

The Tax Cuts and Jobs Act also provides that no deduction is allowed for any expense incurred for providing any transportation, or any payment or reimbursement, to an employee of the taxpayer for travel between the employee's residence and place of employment, except as necessary for ensuring the employee's safety. (Code Sec. 274(l)(1) as amended by Tax Cuts and Jobs Act §13304(c)(2))

However, this bar on deducting transportation expenses doesn't apply to any qualified bicycle commuting reimbursement, as described in Code Sec. 132(f)(5)(F) (see FTC 2d/FIN ¶ H-2215.1; USTR ¶ 1324.08), for amounts paid or incurred after Dec. 31, 2017, and before Jan. 1, 2026. (Code Sec. 274(l)(2))

> **✔ observation:** The period for which a deduction for qualified bicycle commuting reimbursements is allowed corresponds to the period for which the exclusion for those reimbursements is suspended, see ¶ 603.

☐ **Effective:** Amounts incurred or paid after Dec. 31, 2017. (Tax Cuts and Jobs Act §13304(e)(1)) The exception for qualified bicycle commuting reimbursements applies for amounts paid or incurred after Dec. 31, 2017, and before Jan. 1, 2026. (Code Sec. 274(l)(2))

¶ 1008. Denial of deduction for fines, penalties, etc., is broadened

Code Sec. 162(f), as amended by Tax Cuts and Jobs Act §13306(a)(1)
Generally effective: Amounts paid or incurred on or after Dec. 22, 2017
Committee Reports, see ¶ 5049

Under pre-Tax Cuts and Jobs Act law, no deduction was allowed under Code Sec. 162(a) (the deduction for ordinary and necessary expenses of a trade or business, see FTC 2d ¶ L-1200 *et seq.*; USTR ¶ 1624 *et seq.*) for any fine or similar penalty paid to a government for the violation of any law. (FTC 2d/FIN ¶ L-2700 *et seq.*; USTR ¶ 1624.388; Catalyst ¶ 154:125; Catalyst ¶ 154:133)

New Law. Under the Tax Cuts and Jobs Act, except as provided below, no otherwise allowable deduction is allowed under Chapter 1 of Subtitle A of the

Code (Code Sec. 1–Code Sec. 1400U-3) for any amount paid or incurred (whether by suit, agreement, or otherwise) to, or at the direction of, a government or governmental entity in relation to the violation of any law or the investigation or inquiry by such government or entity into the potential violation of any law. (Code Sec. 162(f)(1) as amended by Tax Cuts and Jobs Act §13306(a)(1)) This rule applies only where a government (or other entity treated in a manner similar to a government, see below) is a complainant or investigator with respect to the violation or potential violation of any law. (Com Rept, see ¶ 5049)

> **☯** *observation:* Thus, in addition to denying deductions for the payment of any fine, etc., to a government (as under prior law), the provision denies deductions for payments to, or at the direction of, a government or governmental entity (as this term has been expanded under the Tax Cuts and Jobs Act, as described below).

Exception for amounts constituting restitution. The Code Sec. 162(f)(1) deduction denial rule above doesn't apply to any amount that (Code Sec. 162(f)(2)(A)):

(A) the taxpayer shows (Code Sec. 162(f)(2)(A)(i))

. . . is restitution (which term includes the remediation of property) for damage or harm that was or may be caused by the violation of any law or the potential violation of any law, or (Code Sec. 162(f)(2)(A)(i)(I))

. . . is paid to come into compliance with any law that was violated or otherwise involved in the investigation or inquiry discussed above (Code Sec. 162(f)(2)(A)(i)(II));

(B) is identified as restitution, or as an amount paid to come into compliance with the law discussed in (A) above, in the court order or settlement agreement (Code Sec. 162(f)(2)(A)(ii)); and

(C) is restitution for failure to pay any tax imposed under the Code in the same manner as if that amount were that tax), would have been allowed as a deduction under Chapter 1 of Subtitle A of the Code if it had been timely paid. (Code Sec. 162(f)(2)(A)(iii))

The identification described under requirement (B) above, alone, isn't sufficient to make the showing required under requirement (A) above (Code Sec. 162(f)(2)(A)).

The exception for restitution above doesn't apply to any amount paid or incurred as reimbursement to the government or entity for the costs of any investigation or litigation. (Code Sec. 162(f)(2)(B))

The exception for restitution applies to payments that the taxpayer establishes are either restitution (including remediation of property) or amounts required to come into compliance with any law that was violated or involved in the investigation or inquiry and that are identified in the court order or settlement agreement as restitution, remediation, or amounts required to come into compliance. (Com Rept, see ¶ 5049)

For any amount of restitution for failure to pay any tax and assessed as restitution under the Code, the restitution is deductible only to the extent it would have been allowed as a deduction if it had been timely paid. IRS remains free to challenge the characterization of an amount so identified, but no deduction is allowed unless the identification is made. Restitution or included remediation of property doesn't include reimbursement of government investigative or litigation costs. (Com Rept, see ¶ 5049)

Exception for certain court-ordered amounts. The Code Sec. 162(f)(1) deduction denial rule above doesn't apply to any amount paid or incurred by reason of any order of a court in a suit in which no government or governmental entity is a party. (Code Sec. 162(f)(3))

Exception for taxes due. In addition, the Code Sec. 162(f)(1) deduction denial rule above doesn't apply to any amount paid or incurred as taxes due. (Code Sec. 162(f)(4))

Certain nongovernmental, regulatory entities treated as governmental entities. For purposes of the Code Sec. 162(f) deduction denial rules above, the following nongovernmental entities are treated as governmental entities (Code Sec. 162(f)(5)):

(i) any nongovernmental entity that exercises self-regulatory powers (including imposing sanctions) in connection with a qualified board or exchange (as defined in Code Sec. 1256(g)(7) (defining qualified board or exchange for the Code Sec. 1256 mark-to-market rules, see FTC 2d ¶ I-7613; USTR ¶ 12,564.01) (Code Sec. 162(f)(5)(A)); and

(ii) to the extent provided in regs, any nongovernmental entity that exercises self-regulatory powers (including imposing sanctions) as part of performing an essential governmental function. (Code Sec. 162(f)(5)(B))

For reporting requirements related to the above rules, see ¶ 1009.

☐ **Effective:** Amounts paid or incurred on or after Dec. 22, 2017, except for amounts paid or incurred under any binding order or agreement that's entered into before Dec. 22, 2017. But this exception doesn't apply to an order or agreement requiring court approval unless the approval was obtained before Dec. 22, 2017. (Tax Cuts and Jobs Act §13306(a)(2))

¶ 1009. Information reporting requirements are added for government and other agencies that receive fines, penalties, etc., of $600 or more for law violations

Code Sec. 6050X, as added by Tax Cuts and Jobs Act §13306(b)(1)
Generally effective: Amounts paid or incurred on or after Dec. 22, 2017
Committee Reports, see ¶ 5049

Under pre-Tax Cuts and Jobs Act law, fines and similar penalties paid to a government for the violation of any law are barred as business expense deductions for any tax year. For the Tax Cuts and Jobs Act's clarification of and exceptions to this rule in certain circumstances, e.g., for amounts constituting restitution or paid to come into compliance with law, for amounts paid or incurred as taxes due, or as a result of certain court orders, see ¶ 1008.

Under pre-Tax Cuts and Jobs Act law, no Code Sec. 162(a) deduction is allowed for any fine or similar penalty paid to:

(1) the government of the U.S., a state, a territory or possession of the U.S., the District of Columbia, or Puerto Rico;

(2) the government of a foreign country; or

(3) a political subdivision of, or corporation or other entity serving as an agency or instrumentality (see FTC 2d/FIN ¶ L-2701.1) of any of the governments in (1) and (2), above. (FTC 2d/FIN ¶ L-2700 *et seq.*; USTR ¶ 1624.388)

For treatment under the Tax Cuts and Jobs Act of certain non-governmental entities as governmental entities for purposes of the clarification and relaxation of the rule relating to the non-deductibility of fines, penalties and other amounts, see ¶ 1008.

> *observation:* Under pre-Tax Cuts and Jobs Act law, there were no information reporting requirements imposed on governments or other entities for their receipt of any amount of fines, penalties, or other amounts for violations of law.

New Law. The Tax Cuts and Jobs Act requires government agencies (or entities treated as such agencies) that are complainants or investigators with respect to a violation or potential violation of any law, to report to IRS and to the taxpayer the amount of each settlement agreement or order entered into where the aggregate amount required to be paid or incurred to or at the direction of the government is at least $600 (or such other amount as may be specified by IRS). (Com Rept, see ¶ 5049)

Specifically, the Tax Cuts and Jobs Act provides that the appropriate official of any government entity (or non-governmental entity described in Code

Sec. 162(f)(5), see ¶ 1008), which is involved in a suit or agreement described below, must file a return with IRS detailing—

(1) the amount required to be paid as a result of a suit or agreement to which Code Sec. 162(f)(1) applies (see analysis at ¶ 1008), (Code Sec. 6050X(a)(1)(A) as added by Tax Cuts and Jobs Act §13306(b)(1))

(2) any amount required to be paid as a result of the suit or agreement which constitutes restitution or remediation of property, and (Code Sec. 6050X(a)(1)(B))

(3) any amount required to be paid as a result of the suit or agreement for the purpose of coming into compliance with any law which was violated or was involved in the investigation or inquiry. (Code Sec. 6050X(a)(1)(C))

Thus, the report must separately identify any amounts that are for restitution or remediation of property, or correction of noncompliance. (Com Rept, see ¶ 5049)

> *observation:* It would appear that the reporting requirement targets amounts constituting restitution or paid to come into compliance with law, since these amounts could be deductible by the taxpayer under the relaxed rules of the Tax Cuts and Jobs Act, as described at ¶ 1008.

The reporting requirement applies—

. . . to a suit for a violation of any law over which the government or entity has authority and for which there has been a court order, or (Code Sec. 6050X(a)(2)(A)(i)(I))

. . . to an agreement which is entered into for a violation of any law over which the government or entity has authority, or for an investigation or inquiry by the government or entity into the potential violation of any law over which the government or entity has authority, (Code Sec. 6050X(a)(2)(A)(i)(II))

The requirement only applies if the aggregate amount involved in all court orders and agreements with respect to the violation, investigation, or inquiry is $600 or more. (Code Sec. 6050X(a)(2)(A)(ii)) IRS is required to adjust the $600 threshold whenever it is necessary to insure the efficient administration of the internal revenue laws. (Code Sec. 6050X(a)(2)(B))

Whenever a return has been filed with IRS under the above requirement, a written statement must also be furnished at the same time to each party to the suit or agreement, setting out the name of the government or entity and the information supplied to IRS under this section. (Code Sec. 6050X(b))

The officer or employee having control of the suit, investigation, or inquiry is the appropriate official to be responsible for filing the returns and statements required under this provision. (Code Sec. 6050X(c)) *observation:* The reporting requirement under the Tax Cuts and Jobs Act doesn't apply to payments made by one private party to another in a lawsuit between private parties, merely because a judge or jury acting in the capacity as a court directs the payment to be made. The fact that a court enters a judgment or directs a result in a private dispute doesn't cause the payment to be made "at the direction of a government" for purposes of Code Sec. 162(f). (Com Rept, see ¶ 5049)

For analysis of the deductibility of fines, penalties and amounts to governments and certain non-governmental entities under the Tax Cuts and Jobs Act, see ¶ 1008.

☐ **Effective:** Amounts paid or incurred on or after Dec. 22, 2017, except for amounts paid or incurred under any binding order or agreement entered into before that date. The exception doesn't apply to an order or agreement requiring court approval unless the approval was obtained before that date. (Tax Cuts and Jobs Act §13306(b)(3))

¶ 1010. Business expense deduction is barred for settlement of sexual abuse or harassment suit that's subject to nondisclosure agreement

Code Sec. 162(q), as amended by Tax Cuts and Jobs Act §13307(a)
Generally effective: Amounts paid or incurred after Dec. 22, 2017
Committee Reports, see ¶ 5050

Taxpayers may deduct ordinary and necessary business expenses paid or incurred in carrying on any trade or business, subject to certain exceptions, see FTC 2d ¶ L-1200 *et seq.*; USTR ¶ 1624 *et seq.* Payment of a judgment or settlement of a suit or claim arising out of a business matter is generally deductible as a business expense, see FTC 2d ¶ L-2500 *et seq.*; USTR ¶ 1624.040.

Under pre-Tax Cuts and Jobs Act law, there was no rule denying a business expense deduction for a payment to settle a sexual abuse or harassment suit subject to a nondisclosure agreement (NDA), or attorney's fees related to the settlement. (FTC 2d/FIN ¶ A-2500 *et seq.*; USTR ¶ 1624.040)

observation: An NDA—also known as a confidentiality agreement (CA), confidential disclosure agreement (CDA), or secrecy agreement (SA)—is a legal contract between at least two parties that outlines confidential information that the parties wish to restrict access to or by third parties.

New Law. Under the Tax Cuts and Jobs Act, no business expense deduction is allowed for: (1) any settlement or payment related to sexual harassment or sexual abuse, if the settlement or payment is subject to a nondisclosure agreement (Code Sec. 162(q)(1) as amended by Tax Cuts and Jobs Act §13307(a)); or (2) attorney's fees related to the settlement or payment in (1) (Code Sec. 162(q)(2)). In other words, the Tax Cuts and Jobs Act denies a deduction for any settlement, payout, or attorney fees related to sexual abuse or sexual harassment if the payments are subject to a nondisclosure agreement. (Com Rept, see ¶ 5050)

☐ **Effective:** Amounts paid or incurred after Dec. 22, 2017. (Tax Cuts and Jobs Act §13307(b))

¶ 1011. Business expense deduction for lobbying local governments is repealed

Code Sec. 162(e)(2), as amended by Tax Cuts and Jobs Act §13308(a)
Code Sec. 162(e)(7), as amended by Tax Cuts and Jobs Act §13308(a)
Generally effective: Amounts paid or incurred on or after Dec. 22, 2017
Committee Reports, see ¶ 5051

In general, no trade or business expense deduction is allowed for amounts paid or incurred in connection with influencing, or attempting to influence, legislation. (FTC 2d/FIN ¶ L-2401; USTR ¶ 1624.395) However, under pre-Tax Cuts and Jobs Act law, this rule didn't apply to legislation of a local council or similar governing body. Instead, a deduction was allowed for all ordinary and necessary expenses (including but not limited to, traveling expenses and the cost of preparing testimony) paid or incurred during the tax year in carrying on any trade or business in direct connection with:

. . . appearances before, submission of statements to, or sending communications to the committees or individual members of the council or body about legislation, or proposed legislation, of direct interest to the taxpayer; or

. . . communication of information between the taxpayer and an organization of which the taxpayer was a member relating to any legislation or proposed legislation that was of direct interest to the taxpayer and to the organization, and that part of dues paid or incurred with respect to any organization of which the taxpayer was a member that was attributable to the expenses of the above-described activities carried on by the organization.

An Indian tribal government was considered a "local council or similar governing body" for this purpose, and so business expenses for lobbying tribal governments were deductible. (FTC 2d/FIN ¶ L-2400, L-2407; USTR ¶ 1624.395)

New Law. The Tax Cuts and Jobs Act eliminates the trade or business expense deduction for lobbying a local council or similar governing body, including an Indian tribal government. (Code Sec. 162(e)(2) as amended by Tax Cuts and Jobs Act §13308(a)) So, the general disallowance rules applicable to lobbying and political expenditures apply to costs incurred related to such local legislation. (Com Rept, see ¶ 5051)

☐ **Effective:** Amounts paid or incurred on or after Dec. 22, 2017. (Tax Cuts and Jobs Act §13308(c))

¶ 1012. Deduction of FDIC premiums is phased out for banks with assets over $10 billion, eliminated at $50 billion

Code Sec. 162(r), as amended by Tax Cuts and Jobs Act §13531(a)
Generally effective: Tax years beginning after Dec. 31, 2017
Committee Reports, see ¶ 5079

The Federal Deposit Insurance Corporation ("FDIC") provides deposit insurance for banks and savings institutions. To maintain their status as insured depository institutions, banks must pay semiannual assessments, also known as premiums, into the deposit insurance fund ("DIF"). (Com Rept, see ¶ 5079)

Under pre-Tax Cuts and Jobs Act law, deposit insurance premiums were treated as ordinary and necessary business expenses and were fully deductible once the all-events test for the premium was satisfied. (Com Rept, see ¶ 5079)

New Law. Under the Tax Cuts and Jobs Act, no deduction is allowed for the applicable percentage of any FDIC premium paid or incurred by the taxpayer. (Code Sec. 162(r)(1) as amended by Tax Cuts and Jobs Act §13531(a))

Applicable percentage. The term "applicable percentage" means, for any taxpayer for any tax year, the ratio (expressed as a percentage) that the excess of the taxpayer's total consolidated assets over $10 billion bears to $40 billion. (Code Sec. 162(r)(3))

> *Illustration:* For a taxpayer with total consolidated assets of $20 billion, the deduction is disallowed for 25% of FDIC premiums [($20 billion − $10 billion) ÷ $40 billion = 25%] and allowed for 75%. (Com Rept, see ¶ 5079)

The applicable percentage can't exceed 100%. (Code Sec. 162(r)(3)) Thus, the applicable percentage is 100% for taxpayers with total consolidated assets of $50 billion or more [($50 billion − $10 billion) ÷ $40 billion = 100%]. (Com Rept, see ¶ 5079)

> *observation:* Taxpayers with total consolidated assets of $50 billion or more can't deduct any of their FDIC premiums.

The disallowance provision doesn't apply if the taxpayer's total consolidated assets of as of the close of the tax year don't exceed $10 billion. (Code Sec. 162(r)(2))

FDIC premium. "FDIC premium" means any assessment imposed under section 7(b) of the Federal Deposit Insurance Act (12 USC §1817(b)). (Code Sec. 162(r)(4))

Total consolidated assets. "Total consolidated assets" has the meaning given to that term under section 165 of the Dodd-Frank Wall Street Reform and Consumer Protection Act (12 USC §5365). (Code Sec. 162(r)(5)) Total consolidated assets are determined as of the close of the tax year. (Code Sec. 162(r)(3))

Expanded affiliated groups. Members of an expanded affiliated group are treated as a single taxpayer for purposes of determining a taxpayer's total consolidated assets. (Code Sec. 162(r)(6)(A))

An "expanded affiliated group" is an affiliated group as defined in Code Sec. 1504(a) (FTC 2d/FIN ¶ E-7601; USTR ¶ 15,024.17), but determined (Code Sec. 162(r)(6)(B)(i)):

. . . by substituting "more than 50%" for "at least 80%" each place it appears, and (Code Sec. 162(r)(6)(B)(i)(I))

. . . without the exceptions for insurance companies in Code Sec. 1504(b)(2) and for foreign corporations in Code Sec. 1504(b)(3) (FTC 2d/FIN ¶ E-7646; USTR ¶ 15,024.17). (Code Sec. 162(r)(6)(B)(i)(II))

> *observation:* In other words, the normal 80% vote and value test for affiliated groups (FTC 2d/FIN ¶ E-7606; USTR ¶ 15,024.17) becomes a more-than-50% test for purposes of the expanded affiliated group. In addition, the expanded affiliated group includes insurance companies and foreign corporations.

A partnership or other non-corporate entity is treated as a member of an expanded affiliated group if it's controlled by members of that group, including by any entity treated as a member of the group by reason of this rule. "Control" is defined for this purpose as under the Code Sec. 954(d)(3) controlled foreign corporation rules (Catalyst ¶ 2102:104; FTC 2d/FIN ¶ O-2533; USTR ¶ 9544.03). (Code Sec. 162(r)(6)(B)(ii))

☐ **Effective:** Tax years beginning after Dec. 31, 2017. (Tax Cuts and Jobs Act §13531(b))

¶ 1013. Employers are allowed a credit for paid family and medical leave

Code Sec. 38(b)(37), as amended by Tax Cuts and Jobs Act §13403(b)
Code Sec. 38(c)(4)(B)(ix), as amended by Tax Cuts and Jobs Act §13403(c)
Code Sec. 45S, as added by Tax Cuts and Jobs Act §13403(a)(1)
Code Sec. 280C(a), as amended by Tax Cuts and Jobs Act §13403(d)(1)
Code Sec. 6501(m), as amended by Tax Cuts and Jobs Act §13403(d)(2)
Generally effective: Wages paid in tax years beginning after Dec. 31, 2017
  and before Jan. 1, 2020
Committee Reports, see ¶ 5060

Taxpayers are entitled to a current year business credit (the Code Sec. 38 general business credit) equal to the sum of certain stated credits. Some (but not most) of the credits composing the business credit can be used to reduce a taxpayer's alternative minimum tax (AMT). (FTC 2d/FIN ¶ L-15200, ¶ L-15201; USTR ¶ 384.01)

> *observation:* Under pre-Tax Cuts and Jobs Act law, there was no employer tax credit for paid family and medical leave. Thus, that credit wasn't one of the credits composing the current year business credit, nor could it be used to reduce a taxpayer's AMT.

No deduction is allowed for that portion of wages or salaries paid or incurred for a tax year which is equal to the sum of the credits determined for the tax year under:

. . . Code Sec. 45A(a) (the Indian employment credit), FTC 2d ¶ L-15671; USTR ¶ 45A4

. . . Code Sec. 45P(a) (the employer wage credit for employees who are active duty members of the uniformed services), FTC 2d ¶ L-15676; USTR ¶ 45P4

. . . Code Sec. 51(a) (the work opportunity credit), FTC 2d ¶ L-17775; USTR ¶ 514

. . . Code Sec. 1396(a) (the empowerment zone employment credit), FTC 2d ¶ L-15631; USTR ¶ 13,964

. . . Code Sec. 1400P(b) (the employer credit for housing employees affected by Hurricane Katrina), FTC 2d ¶ L-17796; USTR ¶ 14,00P4.02 and

. . . Code Sec. 1400R (the employee retention credit for employers affected by Hurricane Katrina). FTC 2d ¶ L-17894; USTR ¶ 14,00R4.01

New Law. The Tax Cuts and Jobs Act allows a credit to certain employers for paid family and medical leave. (Code Sec. 45S(a) as added by Tax Cuts and Jobs Act §13403(a)(1))

The paid family and medical leave credit—

... is a component of the Code Sec. 38 general business credit, (Code Sec. 38(b)(37) as amended by Tax Cuts and Jobs Act §13403(b))

... can be used to reduce a taxpayer's AMT, and (Code Sec. 38(c)(4)(B)(ix) as amended by Tax Cuts and Jobs Act §13403(c))

... won't apply to wages paid in tax years beginning after Dec. 31, 2019. (Code Sec. 45S(i))

Amount of the credit. The Tax Cuts and Jobs Act provides that for purposes of the Code Sec. 38 general business credit, an eligible employer (defined below) is allowed the paid family and medical leave credit which is an amount equal to the applicable percentage of the amount of wages paid to qualifying employees during any period in which those employees are on family and medical leave. (Code Sec. 45S(a)(1)) The applicable percentage is 12.5% increased (but not above 25%) by 0.25 percentage points for each percentage point by which the rate of payment (as described under Code Sec. 45S(c)(1)(B) (discussed under "Eligible employer," below) exceeds 50%.(Code Sec. 45S(a)(2))

> *illustration (1):* Employer pays $10,000 of wages to qualifying employees during a period in which those employees are on family and medical leave. This amount is 50% of the wages normally paid to the employees for services rendered to the employer. Employer can claim a paid family and medical leave credit of 12.5% of $10,000, or $1,250.

> *illustration (2):* Employer pays $12,000 of wages to qualifying employees during a period in which those employees are on family and medical leave. This amount is 60% of the wages normally paid to the employees for services rendered to the employer. The 60% rate of payment exceeds 50% by 10%. As the applicable percentage of 12.5% used to determine the credit is increased (but not above 25%) by 0.25 percentage points for each percentage point by which the rate of payment exceeds 50%, Employer's credit is increased by 10 × 0.25%, or 2.5%. Employer can thus can claim a paid family and medical leave credit of 15% (12.5% plus 2.5%) of $12,000, or $1,800.

The credit allowed for any employee for any tax year can't exceed an amount equal to the product of the normal hourly wage rate of that employee for each hour (or fraction thereof) of actual services performed for the employer and the number of hours (or fraction thereof) for which family and medical leave is taken. (Code Sec. 45S(b)(1))

> *illustration (3):* Employee's normal hourly wage rate is $15.00 per hour. She takes family and medical leave for 40 hours. The credit allowed with respect to the employee therefore can't exceed $15.00 × 40, or $600.

observation: The percentage limitation of Code Sec. 45S(a) applies to wages paid to "qualifying employees"—that is, to the aggregate amount of wages paid to all of an employer's qualifying employees. The limitation of Code Sec. 45S(b)(1) (based on wage rate and hours of leave taken) applies with respect to each individual employee.

The wages of any employee who isn't paid on an hourly wage rate are prorated to an hourly wage rate under regs to be established by IRS. (Code Sec. 45S(b)(2))

The amount of family and medical leave that may be taken into account with respect to any employee in determining the credit for any tax year can't exceed 12 weeks. (Code Sec. 45S(b)(3))

Eligible employer. For purposes of the credit,(Code Sec. 45S(c)) an eligible employer is any employer who has in place a written policy that meets the following requirements:

(A) The policy provides:

(i) for a qualifying employee who is not a part-time employee (as defined in Code Sec. 4980E(d)(4)(B), which defines a "part-time employee" as any employee customarily employed for fewer than 30 hours per week), not less than two weeks of annual paid family and medical leave, and (Code Sec. 45S(c)(1)(A)(i))

(ii) for a qualifying employee who is a part-time employee, an amount of annual paid family and medical leave that is not less than an amount which bears the same ratio to the amount of annual paid family and medical leave that is provided to a qualifying employee described in clause (i) (above) as—(Code Sec. 45S(c)(1)(A)(ii))

(I) the number of hours the employee is expected to work during any week, bears to (Code Sec. 45S(c)(1)(A)(ii)(I))

(II) the number of hours an equivalent qualifying employee described in clause (i) is expected to work during the week. (Code Sec. 45S(c)(1)(A)(ii)(II))

(B) The policy requires that the rate of payment under the program is not less than 50% of the wages normally paid to that employee for services performed for the employer. (Code Sec. 45S(c)(1)(B))

Any determination as to whether an employer satisfies the applicable requirements for an eligible employer (as described in Code Sec. 45S(c)) is to be made by IRS based on such information, to be provided by the employer, as IRS determines to be necessary or appropriate. (Code Sec. 45S(f))

All persons treated as a single employer under Code Sec. 52(a) (members of the same controlled group of corporations) and Code Sec. 52(b) (trades or businesses, whether or not incorporated, which are under common control) are treated as a single taxpayer for purposes of the credit. (Code Sec. 45S(c)(3))

Nothing in the rules governing who is an eligible employer is to be construed as subjecting an employer to any penalty, liability, or other consequence (other than ineligibility for the paid family and medical leave credit or recapturing the benefit of that credit) for failure to comply with the requirements of those rules. (Code Sec. 45S(c)(5))

Added employers. An added employer (defined below) isn't treated as an eligible employer unless that employer provides paid family and medical leave in compliance with a written policy which ensures that the employer—(Code Sec. 45S(c)(2)(A))

(i) won't interfere with, restrain, or deny the exercise of, or the attempt to exercise, any right provided under the policy, and (Code Sec. 45S(c)(2)(A)(i))

(ii) won't discharge or in any other manner discriminate against any individual for opposing any practice prohibited by the policy. (Code Sec. 45S(c)(2)(A)(ii))

For these purposes, an added employer is an eligible employer (determined without regard to Code Sec. 45S(c)(2)), whether or not covered by title I of the Family and Medical Leave Act of 1993, as amended (FMLA), who offers paid family and medical leave to added employees. (Code Sec. 45S(c)(2)(B)(ii)) An added employee is a qualifying employee who is not covered by title I of that Act. (Code Sec. 45S(c)(2)(B)(i))

> *observation:* Title I of the Family and Medical Leave Act of 1993 generally applies to an employee who has been employed by the employer for at least 12 months, worked at least 1,250 hours over the past 12 months, and worked at a location where the company employs 50 or more employees within 75 miles.

Qualifying employees. A qualifying employee is any employee (as defined in section 3(e) of the Fair Labor Standards Act of 1938, as amended, which defines an employee as any individual employed by an employer (with some exceptions for public and agricultural employees)) who—(Code Sec. 45S(d))

... has been employed by the employer for one year or more, and (Code Sec. 45S(d)(1))

... for the preceding year, had compensation not in excess of an amount equal to 60% of the amount applicable for that year under Code Sec. 414(q)(1)(B)(i) (which provides the income threshold to determine who is a highly compensated employee for purposes of the retirement plan antidiscrimination rules). (Code Sec. 45S(d)(2))

For purposes of the credit, any determination as to whether an employee satisfies the applicable requirements for qualifying employee (as described in Code Sec. 45S(d)), is to be made by IRS based on such information, to be provided by the employer, as IRS determines to be necessary or appropriate. (Code Sec. 45S(f))

Family and medical leave defined. Except as provided in Code Sec. 45S(e)(2) (below), for purposes of the credit, "family and medical leave" means leave for any one or more of the purposes described under section 102(a)(1), subparagraphs (A) through (E), or section 102(a)(3) of the Family and Medical Leave Act of 1993, as amended (FMLA), whether the leave is provided under that Act or by a policy of the employer. (Code Sec. 45S(e)(1))

> *observation:* FMLA section 102(a)(1), subparagraphs (A) through (E), provides for leave for the following purposes:
>
> (A) Because of the birth of a son or daughter of the employee and to care for that son or daughter.
>
> (B) Because of the placement of a son or daughter with the employee for adoption or foster care.
>
> (C) To care for the spouse, or a son, daughter, or parent, of the employee, if that spouse, son, daughter, or parent has a serious health condition.
>
> (D) Because of a serious health condition that makes the employee unable to perform the functions of the position of that employee.
>
> (E) Because of any qualifying exigency (as determined by the Secretary of Labor) arising out of the fact that the spouse, or a son, daughter, or parent of the employee is on covered active duty (or has been notified of an impending call or order to covered active duty) in the Armed Forces.
>
> FMLA section 102(a)(3) provides for leave for an eligible employee who is the spouse, son, daughter, parent, or next of kin of a covered veteran or member of the Armed Forces.

However, if an employer provides paid leave as vacation leave, personal leave, or medical or sick leave (other than leave specifically for one or more of the purposes referred to in paragraph Code Sec. 45S(e)(1), above), that paid leave isn't considered to be family and medical leave under Code Sec. 45S(e)(1). (Code Sec. 45S(e)(2))

Any leave which is paid by a state or local government or required by state or local law isn't taken into account in determining the amount of paid family and medical leave provided by the employer. (Code Sec. 45S(c)(4))

"Vacation leave," "personal leave," and "medical or sick leave" mean those types of leave within the meaning of FMLA section 102(d)(2). (Code Sec. 45S(e)(3)) *observation:* FMLA section 102(d)(2) doesn't define "vacation leave," "personal leave," or "medical or sick leave." A technical correction may be needed to clarify what was intended by Code Sec. 45S(e)(3).

Wages. "Wages" for purposes of the paid family and medical leave credit has the meaning given that term by Code Sec. 3306(b) (determined without regard to any dollar limitation contained in that section). Wages don't include any amount taken into account for purposes of determining any other credit allowed under Code Sec. 38 through Code Sec. 45R. (Code Sec. 45S(g))

Election to have credit not apply. A taxpayer can elect to have the paid family and medical leave credit not apply for any tax year. (Code Sec. 45S(h)(1)) Rules similar to the rules of Code Sec. 51(j)(2) and Code Sec. 51(j)(3) apply for purposes of the election to have the credit not apply. (Code Sec. 45S(h)(2))

observation: Code Sec. 51(j)(2) and Code Sec. 51(j)(3) govern the election out of the work opportunity credit. Under those subsections:

. . . the election can be made (or revoked) at any time up to three years (without extensions) from the return due date, and

. . . the election is made simply by not claiming the credit (either on an original return or on an amended return) at any time before the expiration of the three year period (which begins on the last day allowed for filing the return, determined without regard to extensions).

The period to assess a deficiency attributable to an election not to take the credit (or any revocation of an election not to take the credit) won't expire before the date one year after the date IRS is notified of the election or the revocation. (Code Sec. 6501(m) as amended by Tax Cuts and Jobs Act §13403(d)(2))

Denial of double benefit. A taxpayer can't take both a credit and a deduction for amounts for which the paid family and medical leave credit is claimed. Thus, a taxpayer can't deduct that portion of the wages or salaries paid or incurred for the tax year which is equal to the sum of the credits determined for the tax year under Code Sec. 45A(a), Code Sec. 45P(a), Code Sec. 51(a), Code Sec. 1396(a), Code Sec. 1400P(b) *and* Code Sec. 45S. (Code Sec. 280C(a) as amended by Tax Cuts and Jobs Act §13403(d)(1))

☐ **Effective:** Wages paid in tax years beginning after Dec. 31, 2017 (Tax Cuts and Jobs Act §13403(e)) and before Jan. 1, 2020. (Code Sec. 45S(i))

¶ 1014. Credit for qualified rehabilitation expenditures is limited to certified historic structures and has to be taken ratably over 5 years

Code Sec. 47(a), as amended by Tax Cuts and Jobs Act §13402
Code Sec. 47(c)(1), as amended by Tax Cuts and Jobs Act §13402(b)(1)(A)
Code Sec. 47(c)(2)(B)(iv), as amended by Tax Cuts and Jobs Act
§13402(b)(1)(B)
Code Sec. None, Tax Cuts and Jobs Act §13402(c)
Generally effective: Amounts paid or incurred after Dec. 31, 2017
Committee Reports, see ¶ 5059

Pre-Tax Cuts and Jobs Act law provided a two-tier tax credit for qualified rehabilitation expenditures (QREs). The rehabilitation credit for any tax year was the sum of—

(1) 20% of the QREs with respect to a certified historic structure, i.e., any building that was listed in the National Register, or that was located in a registered historic district and certified by the Secretary of the Interior to the Secretary of the Treasury as being of historic significance to the district; and

(2) 10% of the QREs with respect to a qualified rehabilitated building other than a certified historic structure. (FTC 2d/FIN ¶ L-16100 *et seq.*; USTR ¶ 474)

> **✔️ *observation:*** The rehabilitation credit is part of the Code Sec. 46 investment credit, which is combined with other credits into one general business credit under Code Sec. 38 for purposes of determining each credit's allowance limitation for the tax year, see FTC 2d/FIN ¶ L-15201; USTR ¶ 384.01.

A qualified rehabilitated building is any depreciable and amortizable building (and its structural components) that has been substantially rehabilitated, and placed in service before the beginning of the rehabilitation. Under pre-Tax Cuts and Jobs Act law, buildings other than certified historic structures also had to have been placed in service before 1936, and in the rehabilitation process, they had to meet certain percentage requirements for the retention of existing external walls and the internal structural framework of the building. Specifically, in the rehabilitation process at least 50% of the building's existing external walls had to be retained in place as external walls, at least 75% of the building's existing external walls had to be retained in place as internal or external walls, and at least 75% of the building's existing internal structural framework had to be retained in place. (FTC 2d/FIN ¶ L-16100 *et seq.*, ¶ L-16103; USTR ¶ 474; Catalyst ¶ 403:209; Catalyst ¶ 406:182)

> **✔️ *observation:*** Thus, only certified historic structures are eligible for the rehabilitation credit no matter when they were first placed in service

and without regard to meeting certain minimum percentage wall and internal structural framework retention requirements in the rehabilitation process.

illustration: Taxpayer incurs $600,000 of QREs with respect to a qualified rehabilitated building that is a certified historic structure in Year 1, and places the building in service in the same year. Subject to the Code Sec. 38 credit allowance limitation for the tax year, Taxpayer is allowed a credit of $120,000 (20% of $600,000) with respect to the QREs, and can take the entire credit in Year 1 (the year the building is placed in service).

For rehabilitations not completed in phases, a building is treated as having been substantially rehabilitated only if the QREs during the 24-month period selected by the taxpayer (at the time and in the manner prescribed by regs) and ending with or within the tax year exceed the greater of:

. . . the adjusted basis of the building (and its structural components), or

. . . $5,000. (FTC 2d/FIN ¶ L-16106; USTR ¶ 474)

For rehabilitations completed in phases, if the rehabilitation may reasonably be expected to be completed in phases that are set forth in architectural plans and specifications that are completed before the rehabilitation begins, a 60-month period is substituted for the 24-month period in the above rule. Thus, for rehabilitations completed in phases, a building is treated as having been substantially rehabilitated only if the QREs during the *60-month* period selected by the taxpayer (at the time and in the manner prescribed by regs) and ending with or within the tax year exceed the greater of:

. . . the adjusted basis of the building (and its structural components), or

. . . $5,000. (FTC 2d/FIN ¶ L-16113; USTR ¶ 474)

Under pre-Tax Cuts and Jobs Act law, buildings in a registered historic district could qualify for the lower 10% rehabilitation credit if:

(1) the building wasn't a certified historic structure, and

(2) the Secretary of the Interior certified to IRS that the building wasn't of historic significance to the district.

There was a limited exception to the rule at (2) above, where a taxpayer could still have the rehabilitation treated as a qualified rehabilitation for purposes of the 10% credit, if the taxpayer certified to IRS that at the beginning of the rehabilitation the taxpayer in good faith was unaware of the "no historic significance" certification requirement. (FTC 2d/FIN ¶ L-16300 *et seq.*, ¶ L-16301; USTR ¶ 474)

New Law. The Tax Cuts and Jobs Act repeals the 10% credit for pre-1936 buildings (Com Rept, see ¶ 5059) and retains the 20% credit for QREs with respect to certified historic structures. However, the 20% credit is allowable ratably over a five-year period starting with the year the qualified rehabilitated building is placed in service. (Code Sec. 47(a) as amended by Tax Cuts and Jobs Act §13402(a))

> *observation:* As the Tax Cuts and Jobs Act provides that the 20% credit must be taken ratably over five years, what had been (under pre-Tax Cuts and Jobs Act law) a 20% credit available to taxpayers in the year a qualified rehabilitated building was placed in service has effectively been converted into a 4% credit taken in each of five years starting with the year the building is placed in service.

Specifically, the Tax Cuts and Jobs Act provides that for purposes of Code Sec. 46, for any tax year during the five-year period beginning in the tax year in which a qualified rehabilitated building is placed in service, the rehabilitation credit for that year is an amount equal to the ratable share (defined below) for that year. (Code Sec. 47(a)(1))

The ratable share for any tax year during the five-year period described above is the amount equal to 20% of the QREs with respect to the qualified rehabilitated building, as allocated ratably to each year during that period. (Code Sec. 47(a)(2))

> *illustration:* Taxpayer incurs $600,000 of QREs with respect to a qualified rehabilitated building that is a certified historic structure in Year 1, and places the building in service in the same year. Taxpayer is allowed a credit of $120,000 (20% of $600,000) with respect to the QREs. Subject to the Code Sec. 38 credit allowance limitation for each tax year, Taxpayer's ratable share (and, thus, the amount of the rehabilitation credit Taxpayer can claim for each year in the five-year period beginning in Year 1) is $120,000 allocated ratably to each year during that five-year period, or $24,000 per year.

> *observation:* Thus, although the 20% credit is retained for QREs with respect to certified historic structures, the fact that the 20% credit has to be taken ratably over five years, effectively reduces the credit allowable each year to 20% of 20%, or a 4% effective credit rate for each year.

The Tax Cuts and Jobs Act changes the definition of a qualified rehabilitated building by striking:

. . . the language "in the case of any building other than a certified historic structure, in the rehabilitation process— (I) 50% or more of the existing external walls of such building are retained in place as external walls, (II) 75% or more of the existing external walls of such building are retained in place as internal or external walls, and (III) 75% or more of the existing internal structural framework of such building is retained in place, and" and replacing it with "such building is a certified historic structure, and" (Code Sec. 47(c)(1)(A)(iii) as amended by Tax Cuts and Jobs Act §13402(b)(1)(A)(i)), and

. . . the requirement that the building must be first placed in service before 1936. (Code Sec. 47(c)(1)(B) as amended by Tax Cuts and Jobs Act §13402(b)(1)(A)(ii))

> **observation:** These changes reflect the repeal of the 10% rehabilitation credit for QREs for buildings other than certified historic structures.

> **observation:** Thus, under the Tax Cuts and Jobs Act, a qualified rehabilitated building is any building "and its structural components" if—

> (1) the building has been substantially rehabilitated,

> (2) the building was placed in service before the beginning of the rehabilitation,

> (3) *the building is a certified historic structure, and*

> (4) depreciation (or amortization in lieu of depreciation) is allowable for the building.

Conforming change. A QRE doesn't include any expenditure attributable to the rehabilitation of a qualified rehabilitated building unless the rehabilitation is a certified rehabilitation (within the meaning of Code Sec. 47(c)(2)(C)). (Code Sec. 47(c)(2)(B)(iv) as amended by Tax Cuts and Jobs Act §13402(b)(1)(B))

> **observation:** Under Code Sec. 47(c)(2)(C), "certified rehabilitation" means any rehabilitation of a certified historic structure.

> **observation:** Thus, the Tax Cuts and Jobs Act removes the pre-Tax Cut and Jobs Act rules that were formerly in Code Sec. 47(c)(2)(B)(iv) relating to buildings in registered historic districts that were not certified historic structures but could still qualify for the pre-Tax Cuts and Jobs Act 10% rehabilitation credit.

QRE doesn't include any expenditure attributable to the rehabilitation of a qualified rehabilitated building unless the rehabilitation is a certified rehabilitation (within the meaning of Code Sec. 47(c)(2)(C)). (Code Sec. 47(c)(2)(B)(iv) as amended by Tax Cuts and Jobs Act §13402(b)(1)(B))

> **observation:** Under Code Sec. 47(c)(2)(C), "certified rehabilitation" means any rehabilitation of a certified historic structure.

🄡ᴵᴬ *observation:* Thus, the Tax Cuts and Jobs Act removes the pre-Tax Cut and Jobs Act rules that were formerly in Code Sec. 47(c)(2)(B)(iv) relating to buildings in registered historic districts that were not certified historic structures but could still qualify for the pre-Tax Cuts and Jobs Act 10% rehabilitation credit.

Redesignations. The Tax Cuts and Jobs Act redesignates pre-Tax Cuts and Jobs Act Code Sec. 47(c)(1)(C) and Code Sec. 47(c)(1)(D) as Code Sec. 47(c)(1)(B) and Code Sec. 47(c)(1)(C), respectively. (Code Sec. 47(c)(1)(B) as redesignated by Tax Cuts and Jobs Act §13402(b)(1)(A)(iii), Code Sec. 47(c)(1)(C) as redesignated by Tax Cuts and Jobs Act §13402(b)(1)(A)(iii)).

☐ **Effective:** Amounts paid or incurred after Dec. 31, 2017. (Tax Cuts and Jobs Act §13402(c)(1))

Transition rule.　In the case of QREs with respect to any building—

(A) owned or leased by the taxpayer during the entirety of the period after Dec. 31, 2017 (Tax Cuts and Jobs Act §13402(c)(2)(A)), and

(B) with respect to which the 24-month period selected by the taxpayer under Code Sec. 47(c)(1)(B)(i) (as amended by Tax Cuts and Jobs Act §13402(b)) or the 60-month period applicable under Code Sec. 47(c)(1)(B)(ii) (as amended by Tax Cuts and Jobs Act §13402(b)), discussed above) begins not later than 180 days after Dec. 22, 2017 (Tax Cuts and Jobs Act §13402(c)(2)(B)),

the amendments made by Tax Cuts and Jobs Act §13402 discussed above will apply to these expenditures paid or incurred after the end of the tax year in which the 24-month period, or the 60-month period (as applicable), referred to in item (B), above, ends. (Tax Cuts and Jobs Act §13402(c)(2))

🄡ᴵᴬ *observation:* The 24-month and 60-month periods referred to in this rule are the periods, chosen by the taxpayer, in which QREs in excess of the greater of the adjusted basis of the building (and its structural components), or $5,000, must be made for a building to be treated as having been substantially rehabilitated. The 24-month period is used for rehabilitations not completed in phases, and the 60-month rule is used for rehabilitations which are completed in phases. Thus, if a taxpayer owns or leases a building at all times after Dec. 31, 2017, and selects a 24-month period (or a 60-month period, for a rehabilitation completed in phases) beginning not later than 180 days after Dec. 22, 2017, the changes made to the rehabilitation credit by the Tax Cuts and Jobs Act will apply only to QREs paid or incurred after the end of the tax year in which that 24-month period, or the 60-month period (as applicable), ends.

The transition rule applies both to QREs with respect to certified historic structures and with respect to pre-1936 buildings (i.e., buildings other than certified historic structures). (Com Rept, see ¶ 5059)

illustration (1): Taxpayer incurs $600,000 of QREs after Dec. 22, 2017 with respect to a qualified rehabilitated building that is a certified historic structure. The rehabilitation is not completed in phases, so the period in which the amount of QREs is measured to determine eligibility for the rehabilitation credit is 24 months rather than 60 months.

If Taxpayer selects a 24-month period beginning more than 180 days after Dec. 22, 2017, the changes made to the rehabilitation credit by the Tax Cuts and Jobs Act will determine the amount of Taxpayer's rehabilitation credit. Thus, Taxpayer is allowed a credit of $120,000 (20% of $600,000) with respect to the QREs. Taxpayer's ratable share (and, thus, the amount of the rehabilitation credit Taxpayer can claim for each year in the five-year period beginning in Year 1) is $120,000 allocated ratably to each year during that five-year period, or $24,000 per year.

However, if Taxpayer selects a 24-month period beginning 180 days or less after Dec. 22, 2017, the amount of Taxpayer's rehabilitation credit will be determined under pre-Tax Cuts and Jobs Act law. Thus, Taxpayer is allowed a credit of $120,000 (20% of $600,000) with respect to the QREs (assuming all the QREs are paid or incurred by the end of the tax year in which the 24-month period ends), and can take the entire credit in the tax year in which the property is placed in service.

illustration (2): Taxpayer incurs $600,000 of QREs after Dec. 22, 2017 with respect to a qualified rehabilitated building that is *not* a certified historic structure. The rehabilitation is not completed in phases, so the period in which the amount of QREs is measured to determine eligibility for the rehabilitation credit is 24 months rather than 60 months.

If Taxpayer selects a 24-month period beginning more than 180 days after Dec. 22, 2017, the 10% rehabilitation credit available under pre-Tax Cuts and Jobs Act law with respect to QREs for buildings other than certified historic structures won't be available to Taxpayer due to the repeal of that credit by the Tax Cuts and Jobs Act.

However, if Taxpayer selects a 24-month period beginning 180 days or less after Dec. 22, 2017, pre-Tax Cuts and Jobs Act law (under which the 10% credit was available) still applies. Thus, assuming all the QREs are paid or incurred by the end of the tax year in which the 24-month period ends, Taxpayer is allowed a credit of $60,000 (10% of

$600,000) with respect to the QREs, and can take the entire credit in the tax year in which the property is placed in service.

¶ 1015. Orphan drug credit is reduced to 25% of qualified clinical testing expenses

Code Sec. 45C(a), as amended by Tax Cuts and Jobs Act §13401(a)
Generally effective: Tax years beginning after Dec. 31, 2017
Committee Reports, see ¶ 5058

For purposes of the Code Sec. 38 general business credit, an elective credit (i.e., the "orphan drug" credit) is available for a percentage of qualified clinical testing expenses paid or incurred by the taxpayer during the tax year to get approval from the Food and Drug Administration (FDA) for the U.S. sale of drugs for rare diseases or conditions. Under pre-Tax Cuts and Jobs Act law, the credit was equal to *50%* of the qualified clinical testing expenses for the tax year. (FTC 2d/FIN ¶ L-15615*et seq.*, ¶ L-15617, ¶ L-15620; USTR ¶ 280C4, ¶ 414.04, ¶ 45C4*et seq.*)

Qualified clinical testing expenses are costs incurred to perform human clinical testing on an orphan drug after the drug has been approved for human testing by the Food and Drug Administration (FDA) but before the drug has been approved for sale by the FDA (or, if the drug is a biological product, before a license is issued).

> *observation:* Qualified clinical testing expenses are defined, with certain modifications, by reference to the Code Sec. 41 definition of expenses qualifying for the research credit, i.e. qualified research expenses. Amounts included in computing the orphan drug credit are excluded from the computation of the research credit, see FTC 2d/FIN ¶ L-15624; L-15624.2; L-15624.4; USTR ¶ 45C4.02.

New Law. The Tax Cuts and Jobs Act provides that for purposes of the Code Sec. 38 general business credit, the amount of the orphan drug credit equals *25%* of the qualified clinical testing expenses for the tax year. (Code Sec. 45C(a) as amended by Tax Cuts and Jobs Act §13401(a))

> *observation:* Thus, the Tax Cuts and Jobs Act cuts the available orphan drug credit in half from 50% of qualified clinical testing expenses under pre-Tax Cuts and Jobs Act law to 25% of qualified clinical testing expenses for tax years beginning in 2018 (see **Effective** below)

For the election added by the Tax Cuts and Jobs Act allowing a taxpayer to take a *reduced orphan drug credit* to avoid having to reduce a deduction or charge to its capital account for qualified clinical testing expenses allowable for the credit, see ¶ 1016.

☐ **Effective:** Tax years beginning after Dec. 31, 2017. (Tax Cuts and Jobs Act §13401(c))

¶ 1016. Reduced orphan drug credit election is available to avoid having to reduce any deduction or charge to capital account for qualified clinical testing expenses

Code Sec. 280C(b), as amended by Tax Cuts and Jobs Act §13401(b)
Generally effective: Tax years beginning after Dec. 31, 2017
Committee Reports, see ¶ 5058

An elective orphan drug credit, a component of the Code Sec. 38 general business credit, is available in an amount equal to a percentage of qualified clinical testing expenses paid or incurred by the taxpayer during the tax year. The Tax Cuts and Jobs Act reduced the pre-Tax Cuts and Jobs Act orphan drug credit amount by half to *25% of the qualified clinical testing expenses for the tax year*, see ¶ 1015.

Under pre-Tax Cuts and Jobs Act law, the amount of any otherwise allowable deduction for qualified clinical testing expenses must be reduced by the amount of the orphan drug credit *allowable* for these expenses without regard to the Code Sec. 38(c) tax liability limitations. And, if the taxpayer capitalizes, rather than deducts, the qualified clinical testing expenses otherwise allowable as a deduction for the tax year, the amount chargeable to the capital account for the tax year is reduced by the excess of the amount of the credit *allowable* (determined without regard to the Code Sec. 38(c) tax liability limitations) over the amount allowable as a deduction for qualified clinical testing expenses for the tax year. (FTC 2d/FIN ¶ L-15615*et seq.*, ¶ L-15617, ¶ L-15620; USTR ¶ 280C4, ¶ 414.04, ¶ 45C4*et seq.*)

> *illustration (1):* For a tax year in which the orphan drug credit under the Tax Cuts and Jobs Act is available (Year 1), a calendar year taxpayer incurs $200,000 of qualified clinical testing expenses. The allowable credit is $50,000 (i.e., 25% of $200,000). The $150,000 portion not allowable as a credit may either be fully deducted in Year 1, or may be capitalized in Year 1 and amortized over the four-year balance of the five-year amortization period (if the taxpayer so elects under Code Sec. 174) resulting in an amortization deduction of $37,500 for each of the next four tax years (i.e., Year 2 through Year 5).

> *observation:* A similar rule applies requiring a taxpayer to reduce any deduction for research expenses for a tax year by 100% of the Code Sec. 41 research credit determined for the year.

> *observation:* The reduced deduction or charge to capital account discussed above applies even if the taxpayer is unable to use the full or

any part of the orphan drug credit because of the Code Sec. 38(c) tax liability limitations.

Under pre-Tax Cuts and Jobs Act law, upon electing the orphan drug credit, a taxpayer could not avoid the reduction in either its deductions or capital account for qualified clinical testing expenses. (FTC 2d/FIN ¶ L-15615*et seq.*, ¶ L-15620; USTR ¶ 280C4)

> **☛** *observation:* However, this was contrary to the election available to take a reduced research credit under Code Sec. 41 to avoid any reduction in deductions or capital account charges for qualified research expenses, see FTC 2d/FIN ¶ L-15308.

New Law. The Tax Cuts and Jobs Act allows a taxpayer to elect to take a reduced orphan drug credit in lieu of reducing otherwise allowable deductions. (Com Rept, see ¶ 5058). Specifically, the Tax Cuts and Jobs Act provides that, for a tax year for which a reduced orphan drug credit election (see below) is made,(Code Sec. 280C(b)(3)(A) as amended by Tax Cuts and Jobs Act §13401(b)) Code Sec. 280C(b)(1) and Code Sec. 280C(b)(2) (i.e., the rules requiring the taxpayer to reduce the deduction or charge to capital by the amount of the orphan credit allowable for qualified clinical testing expenses) don't apply, and (Code Sec. 280C(b)(3)(A)(i)) the amount of the orphan drug credit is the amount determined under Code Sec. 280C(b)(3)(B) (i.e. for purposes of the reduced credit amount described below).(Code Sec. 280C(b)(3)(A)(ii))

> **☛** *observation:* This rule is similar to the election that is available to take a reduced research credit under Code Sec. 41 to avoid any reduction in deductions or capital account charges for qualified research expenses.(Com Rept, see ¶ 5058)

Amount of the reduced orphan drug credit. The reduced orphan drug credit amount for any tax year is the amount equal to the excess of—(Code Sec. 280C(b)(3)(B))

(1) the amount of credit determined under Code Sec. 45C(a), i.e., the orphan drug credit, without regard to Code Sec. 280C(b)(3) (i.e., before it is reduced), over (Code Sec. 280C(b)(3)(B)(i))

(2) the product of — (Code Sec. 280C(b)(3)(B)(ii))

the amount described in (1), and (Code Sec. 280C(b)(3)(B)(ii)(I)) the maximum rate of tax under Code Sec. 11(b) (i.e., the maximum corporate tax rate).(Code Sec. 280C(b)(3)(B)(ii)(II))

> **☛** *observation:* In other words, to compute the reduced orphan drug credit amount for the tax year, the taxpayer just subtracts the product of the allowable orphan drug credit amount (i.e., the un-reduced credit

amount) and the maximum corporate tax rate from the un-reduced credit amount.

illustration (2): Thus, with a maximum corporate tax rate of 21% under the Tax Cuts and Jobs Act, a taxpayer incurring $200,000 of qualified clinical testing expenses for its tax year beginning in 2018 and a potential $50,000 orphan drug credit for that year can avoid any reduction in any deduction or charge to its capital account for qualified clinical testing expenses by claiming a reduced orphan drug credit of $39,500 ($50,000 - $10,500 (i.e., $50,000 x .21)).

illustration (3): For a tax year for which the credit is available (Year 1), a calendar year taxpayer incurs $200,000 of qualified clinical testing expenses. Although the allowable credit is $50,000 (i.e., 25% of $200,000), the taxpayer elects to take the reduced credit amount of $39,500. By doing so, the $200,000 of qualified clinical testing expenses can be fully deducted in Year 1, or may be capitalized in Year 1 and amortized over the four-year balance of the five-year amortization period (if the taxpayer so elects under Code Sec. 174 (related to the deduction of research and experimental (R&E) expenditures) resulting in an amortization deduction of $50,000 for each of the next four tax years (i.e., Year 2 through Year 5).

For analysis of the Tax Cuts and Jobs Act's reduction of the maximum corporate income tax rate to 21%, see ¶ 102.

Making the reduced credit amount election. Under the Tax Cuts and Jobs Act, the reduced orphan drug credit amount election under Code Sec. 280C(b)(3) for any tax year is to be made on a tax return no later than the time for filing the return for that year (including extensions), and in the manner prescribed by IRS. The election, once made, is irrevocable.(Code Sec. 280C(b)(3)(C))

☐ **Effective:** Tax years beginning after Dec. 31, 2017. (Tax Cuts and Jobs Act §13401(c))

¶ 1017. Limitation on aggregate business credits is conformed to the repeal of the corporate AMT

Code Sec. 38(c)(6)(E), as amended by Tax Cuts and Jobs Act §12001(b)(1)
Generally effective: Tax years beginning after Dec. 31, 2017
Committee Reports, see ¶ 5029

Code Sec. 38 provides a tax credit (the general business credit) that consists of the component credits listed in Code Sec. 38(b), see FTC 2d/FIN ¶ L-15201; USTR ¶ 384.01.

Under Code Sec. 38(c)(1) (the tax liability limitation), the general business credit is limited to the excess, if any, of the taxpayer's "net income tax" (generally, the taxpayer's regular income tax and alternative minimum tax (AMT), reduced by most non-refundable credits other than the general business credit) over the greater of: (1) the taxpayer's tentative minimum tax for the tax year or (2) 25% of the portion of the taxpayer's "net regular tax liability" (generally, the regular income tax reduced by most non-refundable credits other than the general business credit) that exceeds $25,000. (FTC 2d/FIN ¶ L-15200, ¶ L-15202; USTR ¶ 384.02)

Under the above formula, various nonrefundable business credits allowed under the regular tax are not allowed against the AMT, but certain exceptions apply, see FTC 2d/FIN ¶ L-15202; USTR ¶ 384.02. (Com Rept, see ¶ 5029)

New Law. The Tax Cuts and Jobs Act provides, in the case of a corporation, that Code Sec. 38(c) is applied by treating the corporation as having a tentative minimum tax of zero. (Code Sec. 38(c)(6)(E) as amended by Tax Cuts and Jobs Act §12001(b)(1))

> *observation:* The above change leaves the tax liability limitation (above) unchanged as applied to individuals but negates the AMT as a limit on allowable business credits for corporations. Thus, under the Tax Cuts and Jobs Act corporations are allowed business credits for a tax year to the extent that they don't exceed 25% of the regular income tax (reduced by most non-refundable non-business credits) over $25,000. And the change reflects the Tax Cuts and Jobs Act's continuation, with modification, of the AMT for individuals (¶ 301) and the repeal of the AMT for corporations (¶ 303).

☐ **Effective:** Tax years beginning after Dec. 31, 2017. (Tax Cuts and Jobs Act §12001(c))

¶ 1100. Section 179 Expensing

¶ 1101. Pre-adjustment Code Sec. 179 limits raised to $1 million (annual limit on expensing) and $2.5 million (annual phase-down threshold based on investment)

Code Sec. 179(b)(1), as amended by Tax Cuts and Jobs Act §13101(a)(1)

Code Sec. 179(b)(2), as amended by Tax Cuts and Jobs Act §13101(a)(2)

Code Sec. 179(b)(6)(A), as amended by Tax Cuts and Jobs Act §13101(a)(3)(A)(i)

Code Sec. 179(b)(6)(A)(ii), as amended by Tax Cuts and Jobs Act §11002(d)(1)(R)

Code Sec. 179(b)(6)(A)(ii), as amended by Tax Cuts and Jobs Act §13101(a)(3)(A)(ii)

Generally effective: Property placed in service in tax years beginning after Dec. 31, 2017

Committee Reports, see ¶ 5034

Subject to overall amount limits (and, for each asset, reduction to the extent that the asset isn't used exclusively in a taxpayer's business (Com Rept, see ¶ 5034)), most taxpayers can elect to treat the cost of any section 179 property (see ¶ 1102) placed in service during the tax year as an expense which is not chargeable to capital account and, thus, allowed as a deduction for the tax year in which the section 179 property is placed in service, see FTC 2d/FIN ¶ L-9900 *et seq.*; USTR ¶ 1794 *et seq.*

Under pre-Tax Cuts and Jobs Act law, a taxpayer's annually allowable Code Sec. 179 expense couldn't exceed $500,000 as adjusted for inflation (the annual dollar limit). The dollar limit had to be reduced (i.e., phased down, but not below zero) by the amount by which the cost of section 179 property placed in service by the taxpayer during the tax year exceeded $2,000,000 adjusted for inflation (the annual beginning-of-phase-down threshold). (FTC 2d/FIN ¶ L-9900, ¶ L-9907; USTR ¶ 1794.01; Catalyst ¶ 403:115; Catalyst ¶ 403:130; Catalyst ¶ 406:120).

FTC 2d References are to Federal Tax Coordinator 2d
FIN References are to RIA's Analysis of Federal Taxes: Income (print)
USTR References are to United States Tax Reporter
Catalyst References are to Checkpoint Catalyst
PCA References are to Pension Analysis (print and electronic)
PBE References are to Pension & Benefits Explanations
BCA References are to Benefits Analysis (electronic)
BC References are to Benefits Coordinator (print)
EP References are to Estate Planning Analysis (print and electronic)

Under the inflation adjustment (see above), the $500,000 and $2 million figures were each increased for any tax year beginning after calendar year 2015 by an amount equal to—

... $500,000 (or $2 million), multiplied by

... the cost of living adjustment determined under Code Sec. 1(f)(3) (inflation adjustments for tax rate brackets, see FTC 2d/FIN ¶ A-1103; USTR ¶ 14.08) for the calendar year in which the tax year begins, but determined by substituting calendar year 2014 for calendar year 1992 in Code Sec. 1(f)(3)(B). (FTC 2d/FIN ¶ L-9900, ¶ L-9907.1; USTR ¶ 1794.01)

> *observation:* The cost of living adjustment determined under Code Sec. 1(f)(3), after substituting calendar year 2014 for calendar year 1992, was the percentage (if any) by which the CPI (consumer price index) for the year preceding the calendar year for which an adjusted figure was being calculated exceeded the CPI for calendar year 2014.

The amount of any increase was rounded to the nearest multiple of $10,000, see FTC 2d/FIN ¶ L-9907.01; USTR ¶ 1794.01.

New Law. The Tax Cuts and Jobs Act raises the pre-inflation-adjusted annual dollar limit from $500,000 to $1 million and the pre-inflation-adjusted annual beginning-of-phase-down threshold from $2 million to $2.5 million. (Code Sec. 179(b)(1) as amended by Tax Cuts and Jobs Act §13101(a)(1); Code Sec. 179(b)(2) as amended by Tax Cuts and Jobs Act §13101(a)(2))

> *observation:* The increase in the annual dollar limit and annual beginning-of-phase-down threshold, along with expansion of what is section 179 property (see ¶ 1102, ¶ 1103), considerably increases the availability of expensing under Code Sec. 179. However, the Tax Cuts and Jobs Act has, until the beginning of 2023, *all but eliminated the significance* of qualifying for expensing under Code Sec. 179. This is so because bonus depreciation, until the beginning in 2023 of its scheduled phase out, is available under the Tax Cuts and Jobs Act (1) at a 100% (instead of 50%) rate that is the equivalent of expensing (¶ 1203, ¶ 1204) and (2) as had previously only been the case for Code Sec. 179 expensing, for used property (¶ 1205).

> *observation:* For property placed in service in tax years beginning in calendar year 2018 (see **Effective** below) the inflation-adjusted figures had been scheduled to be $520,000 and $2.07 million, see FTC 2d/FIN ¶ L-9907; USTR ¶ 1794.01. But the figures for tax years beginning in 2018 will, under the Tax Cuts and Jobs Act, instead be $1 million and $2.5 million. (Inflation adjustment doesn't apply to tax years that begin in calendar year 2018, see below.)

The inflation adjustment formula is changed to provide that the above $1 million and 2.5 million figures are each increased for any tax year beginning after calendar *2018* (instead of 2015, see background above) by an amount equal to— (Code Sec. 179(b)(6)(A) as amended by Tax Cuts and Jobs Act §13101(a)(3)(A)(i))

. . . $1 million (or $2.5 million), multiplied by (Code Sec. 179(b)(6)(A)(i))

. . . the cost of living adjustment determined under Code Sec. 1(f)(3) (inflation adjustments for tax rate brackets, see the observation below) for the calendar year in which the tax year begins, but determined by substituting calendar year *2017* (instead of calendar year 2014, see background above) for calendar year *2016* (instead of calendar year 1992, see background above) in Code Sec. 1(f)(3)(B). (Code Sec. 179(b)(6)(A)(ii) as amended by Tax Cuts and Jobs Act §11002(d)(1)(R); Code Sec. 179(b)(6)(A)(ii) as amended by Tax Cuts and Jobs Act §13101(a)(3)(A)(ii))

> *observation:* The above change from calendar year 1992 to calendar year 2016 reflects one of the modifications to the formula for determining the cost of living adjustment under Code Sec. 1(f)(3) by the Tax Cuts and Jobs Act. For detailed discussion, see ¶ 201.

> *observation:* The nearest-multiple-of-$10,000 rule for the rounding of inflation increases (see background above) is unchanged by the Tax Cuts and Jobs Act.

For the inclusion of previously not-included types of building improvements as section 179 property, see ¶ 1102.

For the elimination of the rule that excluded most otherwise-qualifying residential property from being section 179 property, see ¶ 1103.

For the change from not making to making an inflation adjustment to the dollar limit on treating SUVs as section 179 property, see ¶ 1104.

☐ **Effective:** Property placed in service in tax years beginning after Dec. 31, 2017. (Tax Cuts and Jobs Act §13101(d))

¶ 1102. More building improvements are made eligible to be section 179 property

Code Sec. 179(d)(1)(B)(ii), as amended by Tax Cuts and Jobs Act §13101(b)(1)
Code Sec. 179(f), as amended by Tax Cuts and Jobs Act §13101(b)(2)
Generally effective: Property placed in service in tax years beginning after Dec. 31, 2017
Committee Reports, see ¶ 5034

Subject to overall amount limits (and, for each asset, reduction to the extent that the asset isn't used exclusively in a taxpayer's business (Com Rept, see ¶ 5034)), most taxpayers can elect to treat the cost of any section 179 property placed in service during the tax year as an expense which is not chargeable to capital account and, thus, allowed as a deduction for the tax year in which the section 179 property is placed in service, see FTC 2d/FIN ¶ L-9900 *et seq.*; USTR ¶ 1794 *et seq.*

Section 179 property must be acquired by purchase for use in the active conduct of a trade or business, not be subject to some general exclusions, and be of a qualifying type; the qualifying types are (1) tangible property which is both MACRS property (FTC 2d/FIN ¶ L-8201 *et seq.*; USTR ¶ 1684.01 *et seq.*) and Code Sec. 1245 property (FTC 2d/FIN ¶ I-10101 *et seq.*; USTR ¶ 12454.01), standards which are met by most types of tangible property, but not buildings or non-production-process land improvements, (2) non-customized ("off the shelf") computer software that is Code Sec. 1245 property, and (3) at the election of the taxpayer, certain building improvements and buildings ("qualified real property"), see FTC 2d/FIN ¶ L-9922 *et seq.*; USTR ¶ 1794.02.

Under pre-Tax Cuts and Jobs Act law, "qualified real property" consisted of (1) qualified leasehold improvement property (certain improvements to an existing building by a lessor or lessee of building space, see FTC 2d/FIN ¶ L-8208.1; USTR ¶ 1684.02), (2) qualified retail improvement property (certain improvements to an existing building for use in a retail business, see FTC 2d/ FIN ¶ L-8208.5; USTR ¶ 1684.02) and (3) qualified restaurant property (buildings and improvements to buildings, if, in either case, more than half of the footage was used as a restaurant, see FTC 2d/FIN ¶ L-8208.2; USTR ¶ 1684.02). (FTC 2d/FIN ¶ L-9900, ¶ L-9901.1, ¶ L-9922; USTR ¶ 1794.02; Catalyst ¶ 403:120; Catalyst ¶ 406:120)

Also, under pre-Tax Cuts and Jobs Act law, roofs, built-in heating, ventilation and air conditioning ("HVAC" property), built-in fire protection and alarm systems, and built-in security systems were almost always (in the case of roofs) or often considered building components, see FTC 2d/FIN ¶ L-8210 *et seq.*, and thus couldn't be section 179 property unless they were qualified real property; for this analysis as applied to heating and air conditioning property, see FTC 2d/FIN ¶ L-9923.1. (FTC 2d/FIN ¶ L-9900, ¶ L-9922, ¶ L-9923.1; USTR ¶ 1794.02)

New Law. The Tax Cuts and Jobs Act changes the definition of "qualified real property" (for which treatment as section 179 property can be elected, see background above) by (1) substituting "qualified improvement property" (see **Qualified improvement property** defined below) for "qualified leasehold improvement property," "qualified retail improvement property" and "qualified restaurant property" as property included in the definition of "qualified real property" and (2) adding, as included property, roofs; heating, ventilation and air-conditioning property (HVAC property); fire-protection and alarm systems;

and security systems (that meet the requirements described under **Certain structural components** below). (Code Sec. 179(d)(1)(B)(ii) as amended by Tax Cuts and Jobs Act §13101(b)(1); Code Sec. 179(f) as amended by Tax Cuts and Jobs Act §13101(b)(2))

⚓ *observation:* Except as discussed in the first caution below, the above changes to the definition of qualified real property are greatly expansive of what property qualifies because (1) **Qualified improvement property** (below) includes property without regard to what business it is used in or whether the improved space is leased space, (2) qualified leasehold improvement property and qualified retail improvement property had to be placed in service at least three years after the building that they improve was placed in service, see FTC 2d/FIN ¶s L-8208.1, L-8208.5; USTR ¶ 1794.02, and (3) qualifying roofs, HVAC property, fire protection and alarm systems and security systems that are structural components of buildings are treated as qualified real property even if they are not qualified improvement property (see **Certain structural components** below).

⚓ *caution:* The only way in which the Tax Cuts and Jobs Act definition of qualified real property is more restrictive than the definition under pre-Tax Cuts and Jobs Act law is in its exclusion of (A) restaurant buildings and (B) some restaurant improvements (specifically, building enlargements, elevators and escalators, and internal structural framework (see below) that weren't excluded under the definition of qualified restaurant property, see FTC 2d/FIN ¶ L-8208.2; USTR ¶ 1684.02).

⚓ *caution:* The election to treat qualified real property as section 179 property applies for purposes of both making the property eligible for Code Sec. 179 expensing and for purposes of the "investment limitation" under which, after the aggregate cost of all section 179 property placed in service by the taxpayer during the tax year exceeds a threshold amount, the annual dollar limitation on Code Sec. 179 expensing decreases by one dollar for each dollar of the excess, see ¶ 1101 and the illustration immediately below.

⚓ *illustration:* T, is a calendar year taxpayer and manufacturer that is required by business necessity to place into service in 2018 $2 million of section 179 property that is machinery, other equipment or off-the shelf software (see background above). T is also considering completing the following two projects in 2018—for Building A the making of $500,000 of building improvements that are **Qualified improvement property** (below) and for Building B the making of $500,000 of improvements that are described under **Certain structural components** below. If T proceeds with this plan and also makes a qualified real property election for 2018 T will be able to expense under Code Sec. 179 only some combination, totaling $500,000, of the Building A and Building B improvements, losing forever the ability to expense the other $500,000 worth or improvements. This is so because the $3 million of section 179 property that T would be placing into service would be $500,000 in excess of the $2.5 million threshold at which, for 2018, the investment limitation begins to require dollar-for-dollar decrease in the $1 million annual dollar limitation that applies for 2018, see ¶ 1101. Thus, the $1 million annual dollar limitation for 2018 is reduced by the $500,000 excess.

T's needs to invest in fixed assets and T's overall tax situation for 2018 cannot be determined with certainty, Nevertheless, it would appear that, if feasible, T would benefit from proceeding with either the Building A or Building B project in 2018 and deferring the other project until 2019 (a year in which it is at least possible to expense all or part of the $500,000 cost of the deferred project).

observation: In addition to substituting qualified improvement property for qualified leasehold improvement property, qualified retail improvement property and qualified restaurant property as property eligible to be section 179 property, the Tax Cuts and Jobs Act made the same substitution as to eligibility for a 15-year MACRS recovery period, see ¶ 1301.

Qualified improvement property. Qualified improvement property is as described in Code Sec. 168(e)(6). (Code Sec. 179(f)(1))

observation: Under Code Sec. 168(e)(6) as amended by the Tax Cuts and Jobs Act, see ¶ 1301, qualified improvement property is any improvement to an interior portion of a building *which is non-residential real property* if the improvement is placed in service after the date the building was first placed in service, except for any improvement for which the expenditure is attributable to: (1) enlargement of the building, (2) any elevator or escalator or (3) the internal structural framework of the building.

Certain structural components. Roofs, HVAC property, fire-protection and alarm systems, and security systems are qualified real property if they are improvements to *non-residential real property* that are placed in service after the date that the non-residential real property was placed in service. (Code Sec. 179(f)(2))

observation: Roofs are almost inevitably structural components of buildings and thus almost always need the qualified real property classification to qualify as section 179 property, see background above. However, HVAC property, fire-protection and alarm systems and security systems may or may not be considered building structural components, based on the highly fact-specific issues of (1) whether and how they are attached to the building and (2) how they are used, see FTC 2d/FIN ¶ L-8210 *et seq.* Thus, these items, both under pre-Tax Cuts and Jobs Act law and under the Act, can sometimes qualify as section 179 property without benefit of the qualified real property classification.

For the increase in the annual dollar limits (and annual threshold levels for their phase-down) applicable to expensing under Code Sec. 179, see ¶ 1101.

For the elimination of the rule that excluded most otherwise-qualifying residential property from being section 179 property, see ¶ 1103.

For the change from not making to making an inflation adjustment to the dollar limit on treating SUVs as section 179 property, see ¶ 1104.

☐ **Effective:** Property placed in service in tax years beginning after Dec. 31, 2017. (Tax Cuts and Jobs Act §13101(d))

¶ 1103. Otherwise-qualifying residential property no longer excluded from section 179 property

Code Sec. 179(d)(1), as amended by Tax Cuts and Jobs Act §13101(c)
Generally effective: Property placed in service in tax years beginning after Dec. 31, 2017
Committee Reports, see ¶ 5034

Subject to overall amount limits (and, for each asset, reduction to the extent that the asset isn't used exclusively in a taxpayer's business (Com Rept, see ¶ 5034)), most taxpayers can elect to treat the cost of any section 179 property placed in service during the tax year as an expense which is not chargeable to capital account and, thus, allowed as a deduction for the tax year in which the section 179 property is placed in service, see FTC 2d/FIN ¶ L-9900 *et seq.*; USTR ¶ 1794 *et seq.*

Section 179 property must be acquired by purchase for use in the active conduct of a trade or business and be of a qualifying type; the qualifying types are (1) tangible property which is both MACRS property (FTC 2d/FIN ¶ L-8201 *et seq.*; USTR ¶ 1684.01 *et seq.*) and Code Sec. 1245 property (FTC 2d/FIN ¶ I-10101 *et seq.*; USTR ¶ 12454.01), standards which are met by most types of tangible property, but not buildings or non-production-process land improvements, (2) non-customized ("off the shelf") computer software that is Code Sec. 1245 property, (3) at the election of the taxpayer, some building improvements, and (4) under pre-Tax Cuts and Jobs Act law, at the election of the tax-payer, restaurant buildings, see FTC 2d/FIN ¶ L-9922 et seq.; USTR ¶ 1794.02.

Also, under pre-Tax Cuts and Jobs Act law, otherwise-qualifying property was ineligible if it was included in any of the categories of property described in Code Sec. 50(b). (FTC 2d/FIN ¶ L-9900, ¶ L-9922, ¶ L-9922.1; USTR ¶ 1794.02; Catalyst ¶ 403:120; Catalyst ¶ 406:120)

The categories of property that are described in Code Sec. 50(b) and that are therefore ineligible for the investment credit provided by Code Sec. 46 (which is made up of the rehabilitation credit and certain energy-related credits, see FTC 2d/FIN ¶ L-16501) are as follows:

(1) most property used predominantly outside of the U.S.

(2) property used by tax-exempt organizations unless, generally, it is used predominantly in their unrelated trades or businesses.

(3) most property used by governmental entities or foreign individuals or entities.

(4) property used predominantly to furnish lodging (e.g., apartment buildings and dormitories) or in connection with furnishing of lodging, except for (A) energy property, (B) some expenditures for certified historic structures, (C) property used to lodge transients (e.g. hotels or motels with more than half of the living quarters normally rented for less than 30 days) and (D) nonlodging commercial facilities equally available to people using the lodging facilities and people who aren't (for example, restaurants, drug stores, grocery stores and vending machines), see FTC 2d/FIN ¶s L-17247, L-17249 et seq.; USTR ¶ 504.01.

Lobby furniture, office equipment, laundry facilities (but not coin-operated machines, see FTC 2d/FIN ¶ L-17249) and swimming pools are property used in connection with the furnishing of lodging, see FTC 2d/FIN ¶ L-17252.

However, whether furnished to management or tenants, electrical energy, water, sewage disposal services, gas, telephone service, or other similar services aren't treated as used in connection with the furnishing of lodging; examples of these items are gas and electric meters, telephone poles and lines, telephone station and switchboard equipment, and water and gas mains furnished by a public utility, FTC 2d/FIN ¶ L-17252.

New Law. The Tax Cuts and Jobs Act excepts property described in Code Sec. 50(b)(2) from the ineligibility of property described in Code Sec. 50(b) to be section 179 property. (Code Sec. 179(d)(1) as amended by Tax Cuts and Jobs Act §13101(c))

Thus, the change expands the definition of section 179 property to include certain depreciable tangible personal property used predominantly to furnish lodging or in connection with the furnishing of lodging (see item (4) above). Examples of this property are beds and other furniture, refrigerators, ranges, and other equipment used in the living quarters of a lodging facility such as an apartment house, dormitory, or any other facility (or part of a facility) where sleeping accommodations are provided and let. (Com Rept, see ¶ 5034) For additional discussion of property deemed described in Code Sec. 50(b)(2), see background above and FTC 2d/FIN ¶ L-17249 *et seq.*

> ⓇⒾⒶ*observation:* The Committee Report limits the residential property no longer excluded from being section 179 property to depreciable tangible personal property. This limitation is valid regarding the personal property limitation because (A) even as changed by the Tax Cuts and Jobs Act, building improvements eligible to be section 179 property don't include improvements to residential buildings (see ¶ 1102) and (B) related land improvements don't qualify as section 179 property (see background above).
>
> The limitation of property newly permitted by the Tax Cuts and Jobs Act to tangible property seems however less valid. For example, computer software used in a management office would have been ineligible under pre-Tax Cuts and Jobs Act law, see background above. But under the Tax Cuts and Jobs Act, "off the shelf" computer software that doesn't have to be capitalized as part of the cost of ineligible property would be eligible to be section 179 property, see FTC 2d/FIN ¶ L-9922; USTR ¶ 1794.02.

For the increase in the annual dollar limits (and annual threshold levels for their phase-down) applicable to expensing under Code Sec. 179, see ¶ 1101.

For the inclusion of previously not-included types of building improvements as section 179 property, see ¶ 1102.

For the change from not making to making an inflation adjustment to the dollar limit on treating SUVs as section 179 property, see ¶ 1104.

☐ **Effective:** Property placed in service in tax years beginning after Dec. 31, 2017. (Tax Cuts and Jobs Act §13101(d))

¶ 1104. $25,000 per-vehicle limit on Code Sec. 179 expensing of SUVs is made adjustable for inflation

Code Sec. 179(b)(6)(A), as amended by Tax Cuts and Jobs Act §13101(a)(3)(B)(i)
Code Sec. 179(b)(6)(B), as amended by Tax Cuts and Jobs Act §13101(a)(3)(B)(ii)
Generally effective: Property placed in service in tax years beginning after Dec. 31, 2017
Committee Reports, see ¶ 5034

Subject to overall amount limits (and, for each asset, a reduction to the extent that property isn't used exclusively in a taxpayer's business (Com Rept, see ¶ 5034)), most taxpayers can elect to treat the cost of any section 179 property (see ¶ 1102) placed in service during the tax year as an expense which is not chargeable to capital account and, thus, allowed as a deduction for the tax year in which the section 179 property is placed in service, see FTC 2d/FIN ¶ L-9900 *et seq.*; USTR ¶ 1794 *et seq.*

A taxpayer's annually allowable Code Sec. 179 expense is subject to a dollar limit (the annual dollar limit) and that dollar limit has to be reduced (i.e., phased down, but not below zero) by the amount by which the cost of section 179 property placed in service by the taxpayer during the tax year exceeds a threshold amount, see ¶ 1101.

In addition to being subject to the dollar limit and its possible phase-down, the cost of each sport utility vehicle (SUV) placed in service by a taxpayer is subject to a $25,000 limit, on a per-vehicle basis. on the amount that can be expensed under Code Sec. 179, see FTC 2d/FIN ¶ L-9907.2; USTR ¶ 1794.015.

For purposes of the $25,000 limitation an SUV is any 4-wheeled vehicle that—

. . . is primarily designed or which can be used to carry passengers over public streets, roads, or highways (except any vehicle operated exclusively on a rail or rails);

. . . is *not subject* to Code Sec. 280F (imposing annual dollar limits on depreciation and expensing for most autos rated at no more than 6,000 pounds unloaded gross vehicle weight and trucks or vans rated at 6,000 pounds loaded gross vehicle weight, see FTC 2d/FIN ¶ L-10003; USTR ¶ 280F4; for the Tax Cuts and Jobs Act's changes to the dollar limits, see ¶ 1307);

. . . is rated at not more than 14,000 pounds gross vehicle weight; and

. . . *does not have* certain bus-like or truck-like characteristics, see FTC 2d/FIN ¶ L-9907.2; USTR ¶ 1794.015.

Under pre-Tax Cuts and Jobs Act law, the $25,000 per-vehicle limit on SUV expensing under Code Sec. 179, unlike the dollar limit and threshold for phase-down under Code Sec. 179, wasn't adjusted for inflation. (FTC 2d/FIN ¶ L-9900, ¶ L-9907.1, ¶ L-9907.2; USTR ¶ 1794.01; Catalyst ¶ 403:134)

New Law. The Tax Cuts and Jobs Act makes adjustable for inflation the $25,000 pre-vehicle limit on the cost of an SUV eligible for Code Sec. 179. (Code Sec. 179(b)(6)(A) as amended by Tax Cuts and Jobs Act §13101(a)(3)(B)(i))

observation: Because of the above change Code Sec. 179(b)(6) applies the same inflation adjustment formula (except as discussed below for rounding) to the $25,000 per-SUV limit as it does to the $1 million annual dollar limit and $2.5 million beginning-of-phase-down threshold (see ¶ 1101 for discussion of the formula as applied to the $1 million and $2 million figures).

Under that formula, inflation adjustments are made to the $25,000 limit for *tax years that begin after calendar year 2018* in the following manner: the $25,000 figure is increased by an amount equal to—

... $1 million (or $2.5 million), multiplied by

... the cost of living adjustment determined under Code Sec. 1(f)(3) (inflation adjustments for tax rate brackets) for the calendar year in which the tax year begins, but determined by substituting calendar year 2017 for calendar year 2016 in Code Sec. 1(f)(3)(B).

The amount of any increase is rounded to the nearest multiple of $100. (Code Sec. 179(b)(6)(B) as amended by Tax Cuts and Jobs Act §13101(a)(3)(B)(ii))

observation: Increases in the $1 million annual dollar limit and $2.5 million beginning-of-phase-down threshold are rounded to the nearest $10,000, see ¶ 1101.

For the increase in the annual dollar limits (and annual threshold levels for their phase-down) applicable to expensing under Code Sec. 179, see ¶ 1101.

For the inclusion of previously not-included types of building improvements as section 179 property, see ¶ 1102.

For the elimination of the rule that excluded most otherwise-qualifying residential property from being section 179 property, see ¶ 1103.

☐ **Effective:** Property placed in service in tax years beginning after Dec. 31, 2017. (Tax Cuts and Jobs Act §13101(d))

¶ 1200. Bonus Depreciation

¶ 1201. Overview—Bonus depreciation is increased to 100% ("full expensing") and is extended and modified

caution: Before amendment by the Tax Cuts and Jobs Act, Code Sec. 168(k) said that "the depreciation deduction provided ... for the taxable year in which [qualified] property is placed in service shall include an allowance equal to 50 percent of the adjusted basis of the qualified property." As discussed below, and at ¶ 1203, the Act changes the 50 percent figure to 100 percent. Thus, the Act increases the tax benefit almost universally known as bonus depreciation from 50% bonus depreciation to 100% bonus depreciation.

However, the caption of Tax Cuts and Jobs Act §13201, which provides the 100% benefit is "Temporary 100-Percent Expensing For Certain Business Assets." This caption mustn't cause the practitioner to confuse the 100% bonus depreciation provided by Code Sec. 168(k) ("100% expensing" or "full expensing") with the expensing-in-lieu-of-depreciation that has been long provided by Code Sec. 179 and that has itself been increased and modified by the Tax Cuts and Jobs Act. For a discussion of the changes to Code Sec. 179 expensing, see ¶ 1101, ¶ 1102, ¶ 1104, and ¶ 1103.

The Tax Cuts and Jobs Act—

... extends the deadline for placing into service qualified property eligible for bonus depreciation and AMT relief from Dec. 31, 2019 (Dec. 31, 2020 for certain long-production-period property and aircraft) to Dec. 31, 2026 (Dec. 31, 2027 for certain long-production-period property and aircraft), see ¶ 1202.

... increases bonus depreciation for qualified property from 50% to 100% ("full expensing") but with a phase-down after Dec. 31, 2022 (Dec. 31, 2023 for certain long-production-period property and aircraft); the phase down in 2018 and 2019 for most qualified property (2019 and 2020 for certain long-production-period property and aircraft) is eliminated, ¶ 1203.

FTC 2d References are to Federal Tax Coordinator 2d
FIN References are to RIA's Analysis of Federal Taxes: Income (print)
USTR References are to United States Tax Reporter
Catalyst References are to Checkpoint Catalyst
PCA References are to Pension Analysis (print and electronic)
PBE References are to Pension & Benefits Explanations
BCA References are to Benefits Analysis (electronic)
BC References are to Benefits Coordinator (print)
EP References are to Estate Planning Analysis (print and electronic)

... makes changes, similar to those above, that increase to 100% (with post-2022 phase-down) and extend the bonus depreciation available under the elective rules for certain plants bearing fruits or nuts (specified plants), see ¶ 1204.

... expands qualified property to include used property, see ¶ 1205.

... expands qualified property to include, if otherwise qualifying, certain qualified film and television and certain qualified live theatrical productions, see ¶ 1206.

... excludes certain public utility property and vehicle dealer property from being qualified property see ¶ 1207.

... eliminates the phase down in 2018 and 2019 of the $8,000 increase, allowed to passenger automobiles that are qualified property, in the otherwise-applicable first-year passenger automobile depreciation cap, see ¶ 1208.

... to conform to the elimination of the AMT for corporations, eliminates the election available to corporations to exchange bonus depreciation and accelerated depreciation for a refund in an amount equal to certain otherwise-deferred credits of AMT against regular tax, see ¶ 1210.

Additionally, the disregard of some qualified property in the application of the percentage completion method is extended to conform to the extension of placed-in-service deadlines for qualified property, see ¶ 1209.

For discussion of the continuing eligibility of qualified improvement property to be qualified property notwithstanding the deletion of the rule that specifically provided that qualified improvement property satisfied the type-of-property requirement for being qualified property, see ¶ 1301.

As discussed in more detail at ¶ 1202, the above changes generally apply to property acquired and placed in service after Sept. 27, 2017 in tax years ending after that date, except that the changes to the elective rules for specified plants apply to specified plants planted or grafted after Sept. 27, 2017 in tax years ending after that date.

But the change from 50% to 100% bonus depreciation can be deferred to apply only to qualified property and specified plants placed in service after the first tax year ending after Sept. 27, 2017, see ¶ 1203 and ¶ 1204.

¶ 1202. Bonus depreciation and other benefits for qualified property are extended

Code Sec. 168(k)(2)(A)(iii), as amended by Tax Cuts and Jobs Act §13201(b)(1)(A)(i)

Code Sec. 168(k)(2)(B)(i)(II), as amended by Tax Cuts and Jobs Act §13201(b)(1)(A)(ii)(I)

Code Sec. 168(k)(2)(B)(i)(III), as amended by Tax Cuts and Jobs Act §13201(b)(1)(A)(i)

Code Sec. 168(k)(2)(B)(ii), as amended by Tax Cuts and Jobs Act §13201(b)(1)(A)(i)

Code Sec. 168(k)(2)(E)(i), as amended by Tax Cuts and Jobs Act §13201(b)(1)(A)(i)

Generally effective: Property placed in service and acquired after Sept. 27, 2017 and before Jan. 1, 2027

Committee Reports, see ¶ 5036

Under Code Sec. 168(k), a taxpayer that owns "qualified property" (see below) is allowed additional depreciation in the year that the property is placed in service (with corresponding reductions in basis and, thus, reductions of the regular depreciation deductions otherwise allowed in the placed-in-service year and in later years), see FTC 2d/FIN ¶ L-9310; USTR ¶ 1684.025.

Passenger automobiles are subject to annual dollar-caps on allowable depreciation, but for passenger automobiles that are qualified property, the first year depreciation cap is increased, see FTC 2d/FIN ¶s L-10004.1A, L-10004.4; USTR ¶s 1684.0281, 280F4.

Additionally, qualified property is exempt from the alternative minimum tax (AMT) depreciation adjustment, see FTC 2d/FIN ¶ A-8221; USTR ¶ 1684.029, which is the adjustment that requires that certain property depreciated on the 200% declining balance method for regular income tax purposes must be depreciated on the 150% declining balance method for AMT purposes, see FTC 2d/FIN ¶ A-8220; USTR ¶ 564.01.

The bonus depreciation and increased passenger automobile first-year depreciation cap don't apply to classes of property for which the taxpayer elects to not accept the benefits (an "election-out"), see FTC 2d/FIN ¶ L-9318; USTR ¶ 1684.0291.

Also, under pre-Tax Cuts and Jobs Act law, see ¶ 1211, corporations could elect for qualified property to (1) decline bonus depreciation and the increased passenger automobile first-year cap and (2) depreciate the qualified property under the straight-line method in exchange for receiving as a refundable credit certain Code Sec. 53 alternative minimum tax credits (against the regular income tax) that would continue to be otherwise deferred, see FTC 2d/FIN ¶ L-15213; USTR ¶ 1684.0293.

One of several requirements for being qualified property is a timely placed-in-service requirement, see FTC 2d/FIN ¶ L-9312; USTR ¶ 1684.026.

Under pre-Tax Cuts and Jobs Act law the timely-placed-in-service requirement was that the property had to be placed in service by the taxpayer before Jan. 1, 2020, except for certain aircraft and certain long-production-period property that had to be placed in service before Jan. 1, 2021 (the pre-2021 deadline). To be eligible for the pre-2021 deadline, the aircraft and long-production period property had to be acquired before Jan. 1, 2020 or under a written contract entered into before Jan. 1, 2020 (the acquisition requirement). For property manu-factured, constructed or produced by the taxpayer for the taxpayer's own use, the acquisition requirement was met if the taxpayer began manufacture, con-struction or production before Jan. 1, 2020 (the self-constructed property rule). (FTC 2d/FIN ¶ L-9310, ¶ L-9312, ¶ L-9315, ¶ L-9316 *et seq.*; USTR ¶ 1684.026, ¶ 1684.027; Catalyst ¶ 403:100; Catalyst ¶ 403:180; Catalyst ¶ 403:190; Catalyst ¶ 403:200; Catalyst ¶ 403:210; Catalyst ¶ 403:220; Catalyst ¶ 406:123) Long-production-period property could qualify for the pre-2021 deadline only to the extent of adjusted basis attributable to manufacture, con-struction or production before Jan. 1, 2020 (the progress expenditure rule). (FTC 2d/FIN ¶ L-9310, ¶ L-9316.1; USTR ¶ 1684.027)

New Law. The Tax Cuts and Jobs Act extends the bonus depreciation de-duction (Com Rept, see ¶ 5036) by changing the timely-placed-in-service re-quirement (above) to provide that qualified property has to be placed in service by the taxpayer before *Jan. 1, 2027*, except that the aircraft (by cross reference from Code Sec. 168(k)(2)(C)(i)) and long-production-period property discussed above have to be placed in service before *Jan. 1, 2028* (the pre-2028 deadline). (Code Sec. 168(k)(2)(A)(iii) as amended by Tax Cuts and Jobs Act §13201(b)(1)(A)(i); Code Sec. 168(k)(2)(B)(i)(II) as amended by Tax Cuts and Jobs Act §13201(b)(1)(A)(ii)(I))

For an overview that lists the extension of bonus depreciation and the other changes made to bonus depreciation by the Tax Cuts and Jobs Act, see ¶ 1201.

In a conforming change, the timely acquisition requirement (see background above) for the aircraft (by cross reference from Code Sec. 168(k)(2)(C)(i)) and long-production-period property is changed to provide that to qualify for the pre-2028 deadline the property must be acquired before *Jan. 1, 2027* or under a written contract entered into before *Jan. 1, 2027.* (Code Sec. 168(k)(2)(B)(i)(III) as amended by Tax Cuts and Jobs Act §13201(b)(1)(A)(i))

Additionally, the progress expenditures rule for long-production period prop-erty (see background above) is conformed to provide that long-production-period property can qualify for the pre-2028 deadline only to the extent of adjusted basis attributable to manufacture, construction or produc-tion before *Jan. 1, 2027.* (Code Sec. 168(k)(2)(B)(ii) as amended by Tax Cuts and Jobs Act §13201(b)(1)(A)(i))

Also, the self-constructed property rule (see background above) for aircraft (by cross reference from Code Sec. 168(k)(2)(C)(i)) and long-production period property is conformed to provide that the taxpayer must begin manufacture, construction or production before *Jan. 1, 2027.* (Code Sec. 168(k)(2)(E)(i) as amended by Tax Cuts and Jobs Act §13201(b)(1)(A)(i))

For the extension of the bonus depreciation available under elective rules for "specified plants," see ¶ 1204.

☐ **Effective:** Property that is both (1) acquired and placed in service after Sept. 27, 2017 (Tax Cuts and Jobs Act §13201(h)(1)) and (2) placed in service before Jan. 1, 2027 (Code Sec. 168(k)(2)(A)(iii)) (before Jan. 1, 2028 in the case of certain long-production-period property and aircraft (Code Sec. 168(k)(2)(b)(i)(II); Code Sec. 168(k)(2)(C)(i)).

Property won't be treated as acquired after Sept. 27, 2017 if a written binding contract for its acquisition was entered into before Sept. 28, 2017. (Tax Cuts and Jobs Act §13201(h)(1))

> *observation:* IRS, in regs and other guidance, has issued detailed guidance as to when property is considered to be acquired for bonus depreciation purposes, see FTC 2d/FIN ¶ L-9315 *et seq.*; USTR ¶ 1684.026.

¶ 1203. Bonus depreciation increased to 100% (full expensing) with phase down generally deferred from 2018 to 2023

Code Sec. 168(k)(1)(A), as amended by Tax Cuts and Jobs Act §13201(a)(1)(A)
Code Sec. 168(k)(6), as amended by Tax Cuts and Jobs Act §13201(a)(2)
Code Sec. 168(k)(8), as amended by Tax Cuts and Jobs Act §13201(a)(3)(B)
Code Sec. 168(k)(10), as amended by Tax Cuts and Jobs Act §13201(e)
Generally effective: Property placed in service and acquired after Sept. 27, 2017 and before Jan. 1, 2027
Committee Reports, see ¶ 5036

Under pre-Tax Cuts and Jobs Act law, under Code Sec. 168(k), a taxpayer that owned "qualified property" (see below) was allowed, subject to the phase-down rules discussed below, additional depreciation at a 50% rate (bonus depreciation) in the year that the property was placed in service (with corresponding reductions in basis and, thus, reductions of the regular depreciation deductions otherwise allowed in the placed-in-service year and in later years), see FTC 2d/FIN ¶ L-9310; USTR ¶ 1684.025. For discussion of other benefits available for qualified property, see ¶ 1202 , ¶ 1208, ¶ 1209 and ¶ 1210.

One of several requirements for being qualified property is a timely-placed-in-service requirement, see FTC 2d/FIN ¶ L-9312; USTR ¶ 1684.026.

Under pre-Tax Cuts and Jobs Act law the timely-placed-in-service requirement was that the property had to be placed in service by the taxpayer before Jan. 1, 2020, except for certain aircraft and, to the extent of pre-2020 costs, certain long-production-period property that had to be placed in service before Jan.

1, 2021 (the pre-2021 deadline), see FTC 2d/FIN ¶s L-9312, L-9315, L-9316 *et seq.*; USTR ¶s 1684.026, 1684.027.

Under pre-Tax Cuts and Jobs Act law, phase-down rules provided that qualified property (other than the aircraft and long-production period property discussed above) was allowed only 40% bonus depreciation if placed in service in 2018 and only 30% bonus depreciation if placed in service in 2019. The aircraft and long-production-period property discussed above were allowed only 40% bonus depreciation if placed in service in 2019 and 30% bonus depreciation if placed in service in 2020. IRS interpreted additional phase-down rules in the Code relating to aircraft and long-production-period property placed in service in 2019 as requiring, subject to technical correction, that (1) both types of property could qualify for 40% (instead of 30%) bonus depreciation only if they satisfied the acquisition requirement before Jan. 1, 2019 instead of before Jan. 1, 2020 and (2) the progress expenditure rule applies so as to permit 40% (instead of 30%) bonus depreciation only for adjusted basis attributable to manufacture, construction or production before Jan. 1, 2019. (FTC 2d/FIN ¶ L-9310, ¶ L-9311.1; USTR ¶ 1684.0253; Catalyst ¶ 403:100; Catalyst ¶ 403:180; Catalyst ¶ 403:190; Catalyst ¶ 403:210; Catalyst ¶ 403:220; Catalyst ¶ 406:123)

For the bonus depreciation available (and phase down) under elective rules for "specified plants," see ¶ 1204.

New Law. The Tax Cuts and Jobs Act (1) raises the bonus depreciation rate to 100% for all qualified property and (2) cancels the phase down that was to begin in 2018 for most qualified property and in 2019 for property described in Code Sec. 168(k)(2)(B) (the long-production-period property discussed above) and in Code Sec. 168(k)(2)(C) (the aircraft discussed above). (Code Sec. 168(k)(1)(A) as amended by Tax Cuts and Jobs Act §13201(a)(1)(A); Code Sec. 168(k)(6)(A) as amended by Tax Cuts and Jobs Act §13201(a)(2); Code Sec. 168(k)(6)(A)(i); Code Sec. 168(k)(6)(B); Code Sec. 168(k)(6)(B)(i)) However, phase down is instead scheduled to begin (see the schedules below) in 2023 for most qualified property (2024 for property described in Code Sec. 168(k)(2)(B) and Code Sec. 168(k)(2)(C)). (Code Sec. 168(k)(6)(A); Code Sec. 168(k)(6)(B))

For an election to briefly defer the change from 50% to 100% expensing, see **Deferral election** below.

For an overview that lists the changes above and below and the other changes made to bonus depreciation by the Tax Cuts and Jobs Act, see ¶ 1201.

> *caution:* The caption of Tax Cuts and Jobs Act §13201 is "Temporary 100-Percent Expensing For Certain Business Assets." This caption must not cause the practitioner to confuse the 100% bonus depreciation provided by Code Sec. 168(k) ("100% expensing" or "full expensing") with the expensing-in-lieu-of-depreciation for small businesses that has been long provided by Code Sec. 179 and that has been increased and

modified by the Tax Cuts and Jobs Act. For a discussion of the changes to Code Sec. 179, see ¶ 1101, ¶ 1102, ¶ 1104, and ¶ 1103.

caution: No bonus depreciation is available for qualified property, other than property described in Code Sec. 168(k)(2)(B) (the long production period property discussed above) and Code Sec. 168(k)(2)(C) (the aircraft discussed above) that is placed in service after Dec. 31, 2026, see ¶ 1202.

No bonus depreciation is available for property described in Code Sec. 168(k)(2)(B) and Code Sec. 168(k)(2)(C) that is placed in service after Dec. 31, 2027, see ¶ 1202.

Bonus depreciation phase-down schedule for most qualified property. For qualified property other than property described in Code Sec. 168(k)(2)(B) (the long production period property discussed above) and Code Sec. 168(k)(2)(C) (the aircraft discussed above) the applicable percentages are as follows:

. . . 100% for property placed in service after Sept. 27, 2017 and before Jan. 1, 2023;

. . . 80% for property placed in service during calendar year 2023;

. . . 60% for property placed in service during calendar year 2024;

. . . 40% for property placed in service during calendar year 2025;

. . . 20% for property placed in service during calendar year 2026. (Code Sec. 168(k)(6)(A)) For property placed in service after 2026, see the caution above.

Bonus depreciation phase down schedule for certain long-production period property and aircraft. For qualified property that is property described in Code Sec. 168(k)(2)(B) (the long production period property discussed above) or Code Sec. 168(k)(2)(C) (the aircraft discussed above) the applicable percentages are as follows:

. . . 100% for property placed in service after Sept. 27, 2017 and before Jan. 1, 2024;

. . . 80% for property placed in service during calendar year 2024;

. . . 60% for property placed in service during calendar year 2025;

. . . 40% for property placed in service during calendar year 2026;

. . . 20% for property placed in service during calendar year 2027. (Code Sec. 168(k)(6)(B)) For property placed in service after 2027, see the caution above.

Deferral election. A taxpayer can elect, for property placed in service in the taxpayer's first tax year ending after Sept. 27, 2017, to apply a 50% bonus depreciation rate to the property. The election also applies to the bonus depreciation available under elective rules for "specified plants" (as discussed at

¶ 1204). (Code Sec. 168(k)(9)(A) as amended by Tax Cuts and Jobs Act §13201(d))

The election is to be made in the time, form and manner instructed by IRS. (Code Sec. 168(k)(9))

Preservation of phase-down in 2018, 2019 and 2020.

The Tax Cuts and Jobs Act applies the pre-Tax Cuts and Jobs Act phase-down of bonus depreciation for property acquired before Sept. 28, 2017. (Com Rept, see ¶ 5036)

> *observation:* Note that because of the effective date rule, which provides that, generally, property must be both the placed in service *and acquired* after Sept. 27, 2017 for changes to bonus depreciation to apply, see **Effective** below, the rules immediately below are arguably not necessary to preserve the phase-down for property acquired before Sept. 28, 2017.
>
> However, a benefit of the rules, is that they don't include the additional phase-down rules that as discussed in the background above caused IRS to (1) require aircraft and long-production-period property placed in service in 2019 to satisfy a pre-2019 acquisition requirement if they were to be eligible for 40% (instead of 30%) bonus depreciation and (2) apply to long-production period property placed in service in 2019 a progress expenditure rule that permitted 40% (instead of 30%) bonus depreciation only for adjusted basis attributable to manufacture, construction or production before Jan. 1, 2019.

Under the Tax Cuts and Jobs Act the pre-Tax Cuts and Jobs Act phase-down rules (see background above) apply only to qualified property acquired before Sept. 28, 2017 (pre-Sept. 28, 2017/50% qualified property). (Code Sec. 168(k)(8) as amended by Tax Cuts and Jobs Act §13201(a)(3)(B))

For pre-Sept. 28, 2017/50% qualified property *other than* property described in Code Sec. 168(k)(2)(B) (the long-production-period property discussed in background above) or in Code Sec. 168(k)(2)(C) (the aircraft discussed in background above), bonus depreciation is— (Code Sec. 168(k)(8))

. . . 50% for property placed in service before 2018. (Code Sec. 168(k)(8)(A)(i))

. . . 40% for property placed in service in 2018. (Code Sec. 168(k)(8)(B)(i))

. . . 30% for property placed in service in 2019. (Code Sec. 168(k)(8)(C)(i))

. . . 0% for property placed in service after 2019. (Code Sec. 168(k)(8)(D)(i))

And for pre-Sept. 28, 2017/50% qualified property *that is* property described in Code Sec. 168(k)(2)(B) or in Code Sec. 168(k)(2)(C), bonus depreciation is— (Code Sec. 168(k)(8))

. . . 50% for property placed in service in 2018. (Code Sec. 168(k)(8)(A)(ii))

... 40% for property placed in service in 2019. (Code Sec. 168(k)(8)(B)(ii))

... 30% for property placed in service in 2020. (Code Sec. 168(k)(8)(C)(ii))

... 0% for property placed in service after 2020. (Code Sec. 168(k)(8)(D)(ii))

For the increase to 100% and phase-down rules for the bonus depreciation available under elective rules for "specified plants," see ¶ 1204.

☐ **Effective:** Property that is both (1) acquired and placed in service after Sept. 27, 2017 (Tax Cuts and Jobs Act §13201(h)(1)) and (2) placed in service before Jan. 1, 2027 (Code Sec. 168(k)(2)(A)(iii)) (before Jan. 1, 2028 in the case of certain long-production-period property and aircraft (Code Sec. 168(k)(2)(b)(i)(II); Code Sec. 168(k)(2)(C)(i)).

Property won't be treated as acquired after Sept. 27, 2017 if a written binding contract for its acquisition was entered into before Sept. 28, 2017. (Tax Cuts and Jobs Act §13201(h)(1))

¶ 1204. Elective form of bonus depreciation for specified plants is extended and increased to 100% (full expensing) with phase down deferred from 2018 to 2023

Code Sec. 168(k)(5), as amended by Tax Cuts and Jobs Act §13201(a)(3)(A)
Code Sec. 168(k)(5)(A), as amended by Tax Cuts and Jobs Act §13201(b)(1)(B)
Code Sec. 168(k)(5)(A)(i), as amended by Tax Cuts and Jobs Act §13201(a)(1)(B)
Code Sec. 168(k)(6)(C), as amended by Tax Cuts and Jobs Act §13201(a)(2)
Code Sec. 168(k)(10), as amended by Tax Cuts and Jobs Act §13201(e)
Generally effective: Plants planted or grafted after Sept. 27, 2017 and before Jan. 1, 2027
Committee Reports, see ¶ 5036

Under pre-Tax Cuts and Jobs Act law, under Code Sec. 168(k), a taxpayer that owned "qualified property" was allowed 50% additional depreciation (bonus depreciation) in the year that the property was placed in service (with corresponding reductions in basis and, thus, reductions of the regular depreciation deductions otherwise allowed in the placed-in-service year and in later years), see FTC 2d/FIN ¶ L-9310 *et seq.*; USTR ¶ 1684.025 *et seq.* For discussion of other benefits available for qualified property, see ¶ 1202, ¶ 1208, ¶ 1209 and ¶ 1210. For the Tax Cuts and Jobs Act's extension of the period for which the bonus depreciation is available, increase of the bonus depreciation rate to 100% rate and deferral of when the bonus depreciation must be phased down, see ¶ 1202 and ¶ 1203.

Also, under pre-Tax Cuts and Jobs Act law, under elective rules with some differences from those for qualifying property, 50% bonus depreciation and relief from alternative minimum tax depreciation adjustments were available for certain fruit-bearing or nut-bearing plants (specified plants). Solely for bonus depreciation purposes the plants were considered to be placed in service when planted or grafted rather than, as is the case for general depreciation purposes, when the plants became income-producing. Specified plants had to be planted, or grafted to another plant, before Jan. 1, 2020 (and after Dec. 31, 2015 (Com Rept, see ¶ 5036)). Additionally, under phase-down rules, bonus depreciation was only 40% if the plant was planted or grafted in 2018 and only 30% if in 2019. (FTC 2d/FIN ¶ L-9310, ¶ L-9311.1A; USTR ¶ 1684.0254; Catalyst ¶ 403:187)

New Law. The Tax Cuts and Jobs Act allows the elective form of bonus depreciation for specified plants if the plants are planted, or grafted to another plant, before Jan. 1, 2027 (instead of before Jan. 1, 2020 as was the rule under pre-Tax Cuts and Jobs Act law, see above). Code Sec. 168(k)(5)(A) as amended by Tax Cuts and Jobs Act §13201(b)(1)(B)

The Tax Cuts and Jobs Act also raises the depreciation rate to 100% (full expensing) for specified plants to which the elective bonus depreciation rules for specified plants apply and cancels the phase down of the bonus depreciation rate that was to begin in 2018 (discussed above). (Code Sec. 168(k)(5)(A)(i) as amended by Tax Cuts and Jobs Act §13201(a)(1)(B); Code Sec. 168(k)(5) as amended by Tax Cuts and Jobs Act §13201(a)(3)) For an election to briefly defer the 100% rate, see **Deferral election** below.

Phase down is instead scheduled to begin in 2023 under the below schedule of applicable bonus depreciation percentages. (Code Sec. 168(k)(6)(C) as amended by Tax Cuts and Jobs Act §13201(a)(2))

The applicable percentages are as follows:

. . . 100% for plants planted or grafted after Sept. 27, 2017 and before Jan. 1, 2023;

. . . 80% for plants planted or grafted during calendar year 2023;

. . . 60% for plants planted or grafted during calendar year 2024;

. . . 40% for plants planted or grafted during calendar year 2025;

. . . 20% for plants planted or grafted during calendar year 2026. (Code Sec. 168(k)(6)(C))

For an overview that lists the above changes and the other changes made to bonus depreciation by the Tax Cuts and Jobs Act, see ¶ 1201.

Deferral election. For specified plants placed in service (i.e., planted or grafted, see background above) in the taxpayer's first tax year ending after Sept. 27, 2017, a taxpayer can elect to apply, under the elective bonus depreciation rules for specified plants, a 50% bonus depreciation rate. The election also applies to the bonus depreciation available for qualified property (as discussed at ¶ 1203). (Code Sec. 168(k)(10)(A) as amended by Tax Cuts and Jobs Act §13201(e))

The election is to be made in the time, form and manner instructed by IRS. (Code Sec. 168(k)(10)(B))

For an overview that includes the above changes and the other changes made to bonus depreciation by the Tax Cuts and Jobs Act, see ¶ 1201.

□ **Effective:** Plants that are both (1) planted or grafted after Sept. 27, 2017 in a tax year that ends after Sept. 27, 2017 (Tax Cuts and Jobs Act §13201(h)(2)) and (2) planted or grafted before Jan. 1, 2027. (Code Sec. 168(k)(5)(A))

¶ 1205. Used property is allowed 100% bonus depreciation (full expensing)

Code Sec. 168(k)(2)(A)(ii), as amended by Tax Cuts and Jobs Act §13201(c)(1)
Code Sec. 168(k)(2)(E)(ii), as amended by Tax Cuts and Jobs Act §13201(c)(2)
Code Sec. 168(k)(2)(E)(iii)(I), as amended by Tax Cuts and Jobs Act §13201(c)(3)
Generally effective: Property both acquired and placed in service after Sept. 27, 2017 and before Jan. 1, 2027
Committee Reports, see ¶ 5036

Under Code Sec. 168(k), a taxpayer that owns "qualified property" (see below) is, generally, allowed additional depreciation (bonus depreciation) in the year that the property is placed in service (with corresponding reductions in basis and, thus, reductions of the regular depreciation deductions otherwise allowed in the placed-in-service year and in later years), see FTC 2d ¶ L-9310; USTR ¶ 1684.025. For additional discussion of tax benefits for qualified property under pre-Tax Cuts and Jobs Act Law, see ¶ 1202, ¶ 1208, ¶ 1209, and ¶ 1210.

Under pre-Tax Cuts and Jobs Act law qualified property had to satisfy the following requirements:

. . . the property had to be of a qualifying type; i.e., generally, most machinery, equipment or other tangible property except buildings; most computer software; and, notwithstanding the exception for buildings, certain building improvements;

. . . the property couldn't be property that must be depreciated under the alternative depreciation system;

. . . the property had to be placed in service by the taxpayer before Jan. 1, 2020, except that certain aircraft and, to the extent of pre-Jan. 1, 2020 costs, certain long-production-period property were allowed to be placed in service before Jan. 1, 2021, see FTC 2d/FIN ¶ L-9312 *et seq.*; USTR ¶ 1684.026 *et seq.*; TaxDesk ¶ 269,342 *et seq.*.

Additionally, under pre-Tax Cuts and Jobs Act law, the original use of qualified property had to begin with the taxpayer (the original use requirement). (FTC 2d/FIN ¶ L-9310, ¶ L-9314; USTR ¶ 1684.026)

Also, if property (1) was originally placed in service by a person, and (2) was sold and leased back by that person within three months after the date that property was originally placed in service, the property was treated as originally placed in service not earlier than the date on which the property was used under the leaseback (the sale-leaseback rule). (FTC 2d/FIN ¶ L-9310, ¶ L-9314; USTR ¶ 1684.026)

And, if (1) property was originally placed in service by the lessor, (2) the property was sold by the lessor or any later purchaser within 3 months after the date it was placed in service (for multiple units of property subject to the same lease, within three months after the final unit was placed in service, so long as the period during which all units were placed in service was no more than 12 months) and (3) the user of the property after the last sale during the 3-month period remained the same as when the property was originally placed in service, the property was treated as placed in service no earlier than the date of the last sale (the syndication rule). (FTC 2d/FIN ¶ L-9310, ¶ L-9314.1; USTR ¶ 1684.026)

For additional discussion of qualified property requirements, see ¶ 1202, ¶ 1206, and ¶ 1207.

New Law. The Tax Cuts and Jobs Act eliminates the requirement that original use of qualified property *must* begin with the taxpayer (the original use requirement, see above), thus allowing purchases of both used and new items (Com Rept, see ¶ 5036), by providing instead that property either—

. . . meet the original use requirement, *or*

. . . meet the requirement (the acquisition requirement) described immediately below. (Code Sec. 168(k)(2)(A)(ii) as amended by Tax Cuts and Jobs Act §13201(c)(1))

For an overview that lists the above change and the other changes made to bonus depreciation by the Tax Cuts and Jobs Act (including changes to the requirements for qualified property), see ¶ 1201.

Property meets the acquisition requirement if—(Code Sec. 168(k)(2)(E)(ii) as amended by Tax Cuts and Jobs Act §13201(c)(2))

. . . the property wasn't used by the taxpayer at any time before the acquisition, *and* (Code Sec. 168(k)(2)(E)(ii)(I))

. . . the acquisition of the property meets the requirements of Code Sec. 179(d)(2)(A), Code Sec. 179(d)(2)(B), Code Sec. 179(d)(2)(C), and Code Sec. 179(d)(3). (Code Sec. 168(k)(2)(E)(ii)(II))

observation: Code Sec. 179(d)(2)(A), Code Sec. 179(d)(2)(B) and Code Sec. 179(d)(2)(C) require that an asset not be acquired in certain types of transactions as a condition of qualifying for expensing-in-lieu-of-depreciation under Code Sec. 179 (section 179 property).

By reference to Code Sec. 179(d)(2)(A) an asset won't be qualified property for Code Sec. 168(k) purposes if the transaction is between certain related persons, see FTC 2d/FIN ¶ L-9926; USTR ¶ 1794.02.

By reference to Code Sec. 179(d)(2)(B) an asset won't be qualified property for Code Sec. 168(k) purposes if the transaction is between members of the same controlled group, see FTC 2d/FIN ¶ L-9927; USTR ¶ 1794.02.

By reference to Code Sec. 179(d)(2)(C) an asset won't be qualified property for Code Sec. 168(k) purposes if the transaction is one in which basis of the property acquired is determined (1) in whole or in part by reference to the adjusted basis of the property in the hands of the person from whom acquired (carryover basis transactions) (for example, gifts (Com Rept, see ¶ 5036)) or (2) under Code Sec. 1014(a) (property acquired from a decedent, for example, under a will or by intestacy), see FTC 2d/FIN ¶ L-9929; USTR ¶ 1794.02.

observation: Code Sec. 179(d)(3) requires that in transactions in which the basis of property is determined by reference to the basis of other property held at any time by the acquiring person (substituted basis transactions), the substituted basis portion of the acquisition cost not qualify as section 179 property, see FTC 2d/FIN ¶ L-9929; USTR ¶ 1794.02.

For the Tax Cuts and Jobs Act's restriction of tax-free like-kind exchanges to only real estate transactions, see ¶ 1503.

Sale-leaseback rule eliminated. The Tax Cuts and Jobs Act eliminated the sale-leaseback rule (see background discussion above). (Code Sec. 168(k)(2)(ii))

observation: Presumably, the sale-leaseback rule was eliminated because under Code Sec. 168(k)(2)(ii) as amended by the The Tax Cuts and Jobs Act (see above) the lessor doesn't have to be the original user of the property in order for the property to be qualified property in the lessor's hands.

Syndication rule conformed. The Tax Cuts and Jobs Act changes element (1) of the syndication rule (see background discussion above) to require that property is used by the lessor of the property and the use is the lessor's first use of the property. (Code Sec. 168(k)(2)(E)(iii)(I) as amended by Tax Cuts and Jobs Act §13201(c)(3))

> **⚫✓observation:** Because, under pre-Tax Cuts and Jobs Act law, element (1) of the syndication rule (see the observation below) required that property was originally placed in service by the lessor, the change in element (1) to read as immediately above conforms the syndication rule to the Tax Cuts and Jobs Act broadening of qualified property to include, as discussed above, used property.

☐ **Effective:** Property that is both (1) acquired and placed in service after Sept. 27, 2017 (Tax Cuts and Jobs Act §13201(h)(1)) and (2) placed in service before Jan. 1, 2027 (Code Sec. 168(k)(2)(A)(iii)) (before Jan. 1, 2028 in the case of certain long-production-period property and aircraft (Code Sec. 168(k)(2)(b)(i)(II); Code Sec. 168(k)(2)(C)(i)).

Property won't be treated as acquired after Sept. 27, 2017 if a written binding contract for its acquisition was entered into before Sept. 28, 2017. (Tax Cuts and Jobs Act §13201(h)(1))

¶ 1206. Qualified film, television and live theatrical productions added to "qualified property" eligible for 100% bonus depreciation (full expensing)

Code Sec. 168(k)(2)(A)(i), as amended by Tax Cuts and Jobs Act §13201(g)(1)(C)

Code Sec. 168(k)(2)(H), as amended by Tax Cuts and Jobs Act §13201(g)(2)

Generally effective: Property placed in service and acquired after Sept. 27, 2017 and before Jan. 1, 2027

Committee Reports, see ¶ 5036

Under Code Sec. 168(k), a taxpayer that owns "qualified property" (see below) is, generally, allowed additional depreciation (bonus depreciation) in the year that the property is placed in service (with corresponding reductions in basis and, thus, reductions of the regular depreciation deductions otherwise allowed in the placed-in-service year and in later years), see FTC 2d ¶ L-9310; USTR ¶ 1684.025. For additional discussion of tax benefits for qualified property under pre-Tax Cuts and Jobs Act Law, see ¶ 1202, ¶ 1208, ¶ 1209 and ¶ 1210.

Under pre-Tax Cuts and Jobs Act law qualified property had to satisfy the following requirements:

(1) the property had to be of a qualifying type (see below);

(2) the property couldn't be property that must be depreciated under the alternative depreciation system;

(3) the property's original use had to begin with the taxpayer;

(4) the property had to be placed in service by the taxpayer before Jan. 1, 2020, except that certain aircraft and, to the extent of pre-Jan. 1, 2020 costs, certain long-production-period property were allowed to be placed in service before Jan. 1, 2021, see FTC 2d/FIN ¶ L-9312 *et seq.*; USTR ¶ 1684.026 *et seq.*

Under pre-Tax Cuts and Jobs Act law, the types of property that satisfied requirement (1) above were, generally, most tangible property excluding buildings, most computer software; and, as an exception to the exclusion of buildings, certain building improvements. (FTC 2d/FIN ¶ L-9310, ¶ L-9312; USTR ¶ 1684.026; Catalyst ¶ 403:190)

For additional discussion of qualified property requirements, see ¶ 1202, ¶ 1205, and ¶ 1207.

New Law. The Tax Cuts and Jobs Act adds (Com Rept, see ¶ 5036) certain qualified film or television productions (defined below) and certain qualified live theatrical productions (defined below) to the types of property that meet the type of property requirement (see above) for being "qualified property." (Code Sec. 168(k)(2)(A)(i) as amended by Tax Cuts and Jobs Act §13201(g)(1)(C))

For an overview that lists the above change and the other changes made to bonus depreciation by the Tax Cuts and Jobs Act (including changes to the requirements for qualified property), see ¶ 1201.

Eligible qualified film or television productions. A qualified film or television production meets the type-of-property requirement for being qualified property if—

. . . it is a qualified film or television production as defined in Code Sec. 181(d) (generally a film or television production 75% of the total compensation of which is paid to actors, production personnel, directors and producers for services performed in the U.S., FTC 2d/FIN ¶s L-3142, L-3143; USTR ¶s 1814.07, 1814.09), and

. . . it is a qualified film or television production for which a deduction would have been allowable under Code Sec. 181 (see FTC 2d/FIN ¶ L-3140 *et seq.*; USTR ¶ 1814 *et seq.*) without regard to Code Sec. 181(a)(2) (dollar limits, see FTC 2d/FIN ¶ L-3144; USTR ¶ 1814.01) and Code Sec. 181(g) (the sunset provision that doesn't allow elective expensing under Code Sec. 181 for productions commencing after Dec. 31, 2016, see FTC 2d/FIN ¶ L-3141; USTR ¶ 1814). (Code Sec. 168(k)(2)(A)(i)(IV))

Eligible qualified live theatrical production. A qualified live theatrical production meets the type-of-property requirement for being qualified property if—

... it is a qualified live theatrical production as defined in Code Sec. 181(e) (generally a live staged production 75% of the total compensation of which is paid to actors, production personnel, directors and producers for services performed in the U.S., FTC 2d/FIN ¶s L-3142.1, L-3143; USTR ¶s 1814.08, 1814.09), and

... it is a qualified theatrical production for which a deduction would have been allowable under Code Sec. 181 (see FTC 2d/FIN ¶ L-3140 *et seq.*; USTR ¶ 1814 *et seq.*) without regard to Code Sec. 181(a)(2) (dollar limits, see FTC 2d/FIN ¶ L-3144; USTR ¶ 1814.01) and Code Sec. 181(g) (the sunset provision that doesn't allow elective expensing under Code Sec. 181 for productions commencing after Dec. 31, 2016, see FTC 2d/FIN ¶ L-3141; USTR ¶ 1814). (Code Sec. 168(k)(2)(A)(i)(V))

Placed-in-service rule. For purposes of determining whether the production satisfies the placed-in-service requirement for qualified property (see background above and observation below)—

... a qualified film or television production is considered to be placed in service at the time of initial release or broadcast, and

... a qualified live theatrical production is considered to be placed in service at the time of the initial live staged performance. (Code Sec. 168(k)(2)(H) as amended by Tax Cuts and Jobs Act §13201(g)(2))

(RIA) *observation:* As changed by the Tax Cuts and Jobs Act, the placed-in-service deadline for qualified property is Dec. 31, 2026 (Dec. 31, 2027 for certain aircraft and the pre-Jan. 1, 2027 costs of certain long-production-period property, see ¶ 1202).

(RIA) *observation:* Because the bonus depreciation available under the Tax Cuts and Jobs Act is without dollar limits some taxpayers who previously made an election to expense production costs under Code Sec. 181 might consider revoking the election, see FTC 2d/FIN ¶ L-3146.2; USTR ¶ 1814.13.

☐ **Effective:** Property that is both (1) acquired and placed in service after Sept. 27, 2017 (Tax Cuts and Jobs Act §13201(h)(1)) and (2) placed in service before Jan. 1, 2027 (Code Sec. 168(k)(2)(A)(iii))

Property won't be treated as acquired after Sept. 27, 2017 if a written binding contract for its acquisition was entered into before Sept. 28, 2017. (Tax Cuts and Jobs Act §13201(h)(1))

¶ 1207. Property used in certain businesses exempt from business interest limitations is excluded from 100% bonus depreciation (full expensing)

Code Sec. 168(k)(9), as amended by Tax Cuts and Jobs Act §13201(d)
Generally effective: Property acquired and placed in service after Sept. 27,
   2017 and before Jan. 1, 2027
Committee Reports, see ¶ 5036

Under Code Sec. 168(k), a taxpayer that owns "qualified property" (see below) is, generally, allowed additional depreciation (bonus depreciation) in the year that the property is placed in service (with corresponding reductions in basis and, thus, reductions of the regular depreciation deductions otherwise allowed in the placed-in-service year and in later years), see FTC 2d ¶ L-9310; USTR ¶ 1684.025. For additional discussion of tax benefits for qualified property, see ¶ 1202, ¶ 1209 and ¶ 1210.

Under pre-Tax Cuts and Jobs Act law qualified property had to satisfy the following requirements:

. . . the property had to be of a qualifying type; i.e., generally, most tangible property excluding buildings; most computer software; and, as an exception to the exclusion of buildings, certain building improvements;

. . . the property couldn't be property that must be depreciated under the alternative depreciation system;

. . . the property's original use had to begin with the taxpayer;

. . . the property had to be placed in service by the taxpayer before Jan. 1, 2020, except that certain aircraft and, to the extent of pre-Jan. 1, 2020 costs, certain long-production-period property were allowed to be placed in service before Jan. 1, 2021, see FTC 2d/FIN ¶ L-9312 *et seq.*; USTR ¶ 1684.026 *et seq.*

There was no rule that excepted property from qualified property status based on the property's use in an ineligible trade or business. (FTC 2d/FIN ¶ L-9310, ¶ L-9312; USTR ¶ 1684.026; Catalyst ¶ 403:190)

For additional discussion of qualified property requirements, see ¶ 1202, ¶ 1205, and ¶ 1206.

New Law. The Tax Cuts and Jobs Act excludes from "qualified property" (above) (Code Sec. 168(k)(9) as amended by Tax Cuts and Jobs Act §13201(d)) (1) any property which is primarily used in a trade or business described in Code Sec. 163(j)(7)(A)(iv) (see **Public utility property exclusion** below) (Code Sec. 168(k)(9)(A)) and (2) certain businesses that have floor plan financing indebtedness (see **Vehicle dealer property exclusion**). (Code Sec. 168(k)(9)(B))

For an overview that lists the above change and the other changes made to bonus depreciation by the Tax Cuts and Jobs Act (including changes to the requirements for qualified property), see ¶ 1201.

Public utility property exclusion. Businesses described in Code Sec. 163(j)(7)(A)(iv) include certain regulated public utilities, i.e., trades or businesses that furnish or sell (1) electrical energy, water, or sewage disposal services, (2) gas or steam through a local distribution system, or (3) transportation of gas or steam by pipeline, if the rates for the furnishing or sale, as the case may be, have been established or approved by a State or political subdivision thereof, by any agency or instrumentality of the United States, or by a public service or public utility commission or other similar body of any State or political subdivision thereof. This definition is the definition of public utility property in Code Sec. 163(i)(10) but without regard to Code Sec. 163(i)(10)(C). (Com Rept, see ¶ 5036)

> *observation:* Code Sec. 163(i)(10) defines public utility property for purposes of the MACRS depreciation rules. Code Sec. 163(i)(10)(C) refers to certain telecommunication property. Thus, the public utility property exclusion doesn't apply to that telecommunications property. For authorities analyzing whether property is covered by the definition in Code Sec. 163(i)(10) in specific situations, see Code Sec. L-9302.

> *observation:* The public utility property described in Code Sec. 163(j)(7)(A)(iv) is one of the categories of property that is excepted from the limitations, provided by the Tax Cuts and Jobs Act, on the deduction of business interest.

Note also that, except for the vehicle dealer property discussed below, other categories of businesses that are excepted from the business interest deductions limitations—for example an electing real property trade or business—aren't excluded, on that basis, from bonus depreciation. For full discussion of the limitations on business interest deductions, see ¶ 1003.

Vehicle dealer property exclusion. Excluded from being qualified property is any property used in a trade or business that has had floor plan financing indebtedness (as defined in Code Sec. 163(j)(9)) if the floor plan financing interest related to that indebtedness is taken into account under Code Sec. 163(j)(1)(C). (Code Sec. 168(k)(9)(B))

> *observation:* Under the Tax Cuts and Jobs Act, floor plan financing indebtedness as defined in Code Sec. 163(j)(9) is certain debt incurred by retail dealers of vehicles that, when taken into account under Code Sec. 163(j)(1)(C), reduces the amount of interest deductions disallowed under the business interest deductions limitations provided by the Tax

Cuts and Jobs Act. The effect is that floor plan financing interest isn't subject to the limitations on business interest deductions, see ¶ 1003.

The exclusion doesn't apply if the taxpayer isn't a tax shelter prohibited from using the cash method of accounting and is exempt from the limitations on business interest deductions provided by the Tax Cuts and Jobs Act by meeting the small business gross receipts test of Code Sec. 448(c). (Com Rept, see ¶ 5036)

observation: The reason that the exclusion doesn't apply in the situation described in the Committee Report excerpt immediately above is as follows: (1) though not clear from the wording of the excerpt, not being a tax shelter prohibited from using the cash method of accounting and meeting the small business gross receipts test of Code Sec. 448(c) are *both* conditions of satisfying the exemption for small business from the business interest deduction limitations, see ¶ 1003, and (2) a small business that is exempt from the business interest deduction limitations can never accrue interest that is subject to being taken into account under Code Sec. 163(j)(1)(C).

☐ **Effective:** Property that is both (1) acquired and placed in service after Sept. 27, 2017 (Tax Cuts and Jobs Act §13201(h)(1)) and (2) placed in service before Jan. 1, 2027 (Code Sec. 168(k)(2)(A)(iii)) (before Jan. 1, 2028 in the case of certain long-production-period property and aircraft (Code Sec. 168(k)(2)(b)(i)(II); Code Sec. 168(k)(2)(C)(i)).

Property won't be treated as acquired after Sept. 27, 2017 if a written binding contract for its acquisition was entered into before Sept. 28, 2017. (Tax Cuts and Jobs Act §13201(h)(1))

¶ 1208. $8,000 increase for "qualified property" in the first-year depreciation cap for passenger autos is extended

Code Sec. 168(k)(2)(A)(iii), as amended by Tax Cuts and Jobs Act §13201(b)(1)(A)(i)
Code Sec. 168(k)(2)(F)(iii), as amended by Tax Cuts and Jobs Act §13201(f)
Generally effective: Property both acquired and placed in service after Sept. 27, 2017 and before Jan. 1, 2027
Committee Reports, see ¶ 5036

Code Sec. 280F(a) imposes dollar limits on the depreciation deductions (including deductions under the Code Sec. 179 expensing election) that can be claimed with respect to "passenger automobiles," see FTC 2d/FIN ¶ L-10003; USTR ¶ 280F4. The dollar limits are adjusted annually from a base amount to reflect changes in the automobile component of the Consumer Price Index (CPI). Generally, for passenger automobiles placed in service in 2017, the adjusted first-year limit is $3,160, see FTC 2d/FIN ¶ L-10004; USTR ¶ 280F4. For passenger automobiles built on a truck chassis ("qualifying trucks and vans") a different CPI component is used, and for 2017 the adjusted first-year limit is $3,560, see FTC 2d/FIN ¶ L-10004.4; USTR ¶ 280F4.

For any passenger automobile that is "qualified property" and which *isn't* subject to a taxpayer election to *decline* the bonus depreciation otherwise available for "qualified property" under Code Sec. 168(k) (see FTC 2d/FIN ¶ L-9318; USTR ¶ 1684.0291), the above rules apply, except that the applicable first-year depreciation limit is increased in an amount not indexed for inflation (the increase amount), see FTC 2d/FIN ¶ L-10004.1A, ¶ L-10004.4; USTR ¶ 1684.0281, ¶ 280F4; Catalyst ¶ 403:207.

The increase amount is $8,000 and under pre-Tax Cuts and Jobs Act law was phased-down to $6,400 for passenger automobiles placed in service in calendar year 2018 and $4,800 for passenger automobiles placed in service in 2019. (FTC 2d/FIN ¶ L-10000, ¶ L-10004.1A, ¶ L-10004.4; USTR ¶ 1684.0281, ¶ 280F4; Catalyst ¶ 403:207)

Under pre-Tax Cuts and Jobs Act law, qualified property didn't include property placed in service after Dec. 31, 2019, except for certain aircraft and, to the extent of pre-Jan. 1, 2020 costs, certain long-production-period property that had, instead, a Dec. 31, 2020 placed-in-service deadline, see FTC 2d/FIN ¶ L-9310, ¶ L-9312, ¶ L-9316 *et seq.*; USTR ¶ 1684.026, ¶ 1684.027.

> **🅡🅘🅐** *observation:* The Dec. 31, 2020 deadline provided under pre-Tax Cuts and Jobs Act law for certain aircraft and long-production period property wasn't available for passenger automobiles. Passenger automobiles aren't aircraft, and passenger automobiles couldn't qualify as long-production-period property because one of the requirements for being long-production-period property was that the property either have at least a 10 year MACRS recovery period or be used in the trade or business of transporting persons or property. Passenger automobiles have a recovery period of only five years, see FTC 2d/FIN ¶ L-8205; USTR ¶ 1684.01, and a vehicle used in the trade or business of transporting persons or property isn't treated as a passenger automobile, see FTC 2d/FIN ¶ L-10003; USTR ¶ 280F4.

New Law.

Extension of $8,000 increase. The Tax Cuts and Jobs Act provides that the placed-in-service deadline for "qualified property" is Dec. 31, 2026 (Dec. 31, 2027 for the aircraft and long-production-period property discussed above). (Code Sec. 168(k)(2)(A)(iii) as amended by Tax Cuts and Jobs Act §13201(b)(1)(A)(i))

For an overview that lists the changes discussed above and below and the other changes made to bonus depreciation by the Tax Cuts and Jobs Act, see ¶ 1201.

observation: Thus, for a passenger automobile that satisfies the other requirements (see below) for qualified property and for which the taxpayer doesn't elect to decline bonus depreciation, the Tax Cuts and Jobs Act extends the placed-in-service deadline for the $8,000 increase in the otherwise applicable first-year depreciation limit from Dec. 31, 2019 to Dec. 31, 2026. The Dec. 31, 2027 deadline that applies to the aircraft and long-production-period property discussed above isn't available for passenger automobiles for the reasons discussed above concerning the Dec. 31, 2020 deadline under pre-Tax Cuts and Jobs Act law.

observation: Property is "qualified property" if it satisfies the definitional requirements and isn't subject to certain ineligibility rules, see ¶ 1202, ¶ 1205 , ¶ 1206, and ¶ 1207. As applied to passenger automobiles, the effect of these requirements and ineligibility rules is that in most instances a passenger automobile that satisfies the Dec. 31, 2026 placed-in-service deadline will be eligible for the increase in the first-year depreciation limit if it is predominantly used by the taxpayer in his business.

illustration (1): On Oct. 15, 2017, T, a calendar year taxpayer, acquired and places into service a passenger automobile in his business. Assume that the vehicle is "qualified property" (and an election to decline 100% bonus depreciation doesn't apply to the vehicle). T is allowed first-year depreciation for 2017 of no more than $11,160 (the $3,160 amount discussed above plus $8,000).

observation: The Tax Cuts and Jobs Act considerably increased in the dollar caps on passenger automobile depreciation for vehicles placed in service after Dec. 31, 2017 and made the caps inflation adjustable for vehicles placed in service after Dec. 31, 2018, see ¶ 1307.

illustration (2): The facts are the same as in illustration (1) except that T places the passenger automobile into service during calendar year 2018. T is allowed first-year depreciation for 2018 of no more than $18.000 (the $10,000 first year depreciation cap for passenger automobiles placed in service during calendar year 2018, see the observation immediately above).

illustration (3): The facts are the same as in illustration (1) except that the passenger automobile that T places into service is a "qualifying truck or van" (see above). T is allowed first-year depreciation for 2017 of no more than $11,560 (the $3,560 amount discussed above plus $8,000).

illustration (4): The facts are the same as in illustration (1), except that in 2017 T uses the passenger automobile 80% for business and 20% for personal activities. Because the passenger auto depreciation limits are proportionally reduced to the extent that a vehicle isn't exclusively used in business, see FTC 2d/FIN ¶ L-10004; USTR ¶ 280F4, T is allowed first-year depreciation for 2017 of no more than $8,929 (80% × $111,160).

observation: When 100% bonus depreciation for qualified property was last in effect, i.e., generally for property acquired after Sept. 8, 2010 and placed in service before Jan. 1, 2011, IRS, in Rev Proc 2011-26, took the position, based on its literal interpretation of certain language in Code Sec. 280F, that to the extent that the unadjusted depreciable basis of a passenger automobile exceeded the enhanced first-year depreciation cap, no additional depreciation was allowable during the 5-year (six tax years) recovery period for the vehicle (and the amount was deductible after the recovery period to the extent that the depreciation cap for post-recovery period years permitted, see FTC 2d/FIN ¶ L-10008), see FTC 2d/FIN ¶ L-10004.1B.

IRS provided what it called a safe-harbor to mitigate the harsh and anomalous result of its interpretation, but the safe harbor required a complicated calculation, see FTC 2d/FIN ¶ L-10004.1B.

Practitioners should look for what administrative approach IRS will take under the 100% bonus depreciation provided by the Tax Cuts and Jobs Act.

Preservation of 2018 and 2019 phase-down. The Tax Cuts and Jobs Act applies the pre-Tax Cuts and Jobs Act phase-down of the increase amount discussed above. (Com Rept, see ¶ 5036)

observation: Thus, for vehicles acquired before Sept. 28, 2017, the below amendment of Code Sec. 168(k)(F)(2)(iii) by the Tax Cuts and Jobs Act preserves (1) the pre-Tax Cuts and Jobs Act $8,000 increase in the first year depreciation cap for vehicles placed in service in 2017 (see above) and (2) the pre-Tax Cuts and Jobs Act phase-down for vehicles placed in service in calendar years 2018 and 2019 of the $8,000 cap increase (see above).

Note that because of the effective date rule, which provides that, generally, property must be both the placed in service *and acquired* after Sept. 27, 2017 for changes to bonus depreciation to apply, see **Effective** below, the same results could have been achieved by simply striking Code Sec. 168(k)(F)(2)(iii) (which provides the phase-down).

For passenger automobiles placed in service after Sept. 27, 2017, but acquired before Sept. 28, 2017, the increases in the first year depreciation cap are as follows:

. . . $8,000 for passenger autos placed in service in during 2017;

. . . $6,400 for passenger autos placed in service in during 2018; and

. . . $4,800 for passenger autos placed in service in during 2019. (Code Sec. 168(k)(2)(F)(iii) as amended by Tax Cuts and Jobs Act §13201(f))

> *observation:* To the benefit of taxpayers, the Tax Cuts and Jobs Act didn't substitute a rule that would have made the $8,000 increase subject to the post-2022 phase-down (post-2023 for the aircraft and long-production period property discussed above) that, as discussed at ¶ 1203, applies to 100% bonus depreciation itself.

For an overview that lists the changes discussed above and below and the other changes made to bonus depreciation by the Tax Cuts and Jobs Act, see ¶ 1201.

☐ **Effective:** Property that is both (1) acquired and placed in service after Sept. 27, 2017 (Tax Cuts and Jobs Act §13201(h)(1)) and (2) placed in service before Jan. 1, 2027. (Code Sec. 168(k)(2)(A)(iii))

Property won't be treated as acquired after Sept. 27, 2017 if a written binding contract for its acquisition was entered into before Sept. 28, 2017. (Tax Cuts and Jobs Act §13201(h)(1))

¶ 1209. Placed-in-service deadline for disregard of some bonus depreciation-eligible property under the percentage of completion method is extended

Code Sec. 460(c)(6)(B)(ii), as amended by Tax Cuts and Jobs Act §13201(b)(2)(A)
Generally effective: Property placed in service and acquired after Sept. 27, 2017 and before Jan. 1, 2027
Committee Reports, see ¶ 5036

Under the percentage of completion method of accounting (PCM) for a long term contract, the taxpayer includes in gross income the percentage of the total estimated revenue from the contract that corresponds to the "completion percentage." The completion percentage is determined by comparing costs allocated to the contract and incurred before the close of the tax year with the estimated total contract costs. The completion percentage is then multiplied by the total estimated revenue to obtain the cumulative gross receipts, and the gross receipts for the current year are then determined by subtracting the cumulative gross receipts for the immediately preceding tax year. Thus, as the taxpayer incurs allocable contract costs, it includes the contract price in gross income, see FTC 2d/FIN ¶ G-3123; USTR ¶ 4604.001.

Costs are allocated to a contract under a regular PCM method or under an alternative simplified method. Under both methods, depreciation, amortization and cost recovery allowances on equipment and facilities used to perform the contract are taken into account as costs under the contract, see FTC 2d/FIN ¶s G-3125.1, G-3138, G-3142, G-3143; USTR ¶ 4604.001.

> *observation:* Thus, an increased depreciation deduction for a tax year increases the percentage of completion for that year and the amount of gross receipts taken into account as gross income for the year. Similarly, a decreased depreciation decreases the amount of gross receipts taken into account as gross income for the year.

Under Code Sec. 168(k), "qualified property," see FTC 2d/FIN ¶ L-9312 *et seq.*; USTR ¶ 1684.026 *et seq.*, unless a taxpayer elects otherwise, is allowed additional first year depreciation deductions (bonus depreciation) in the year that the property is placed in service (with corresponding reductions in basis and, thus, reductions of the regular depreciation deductions otherwise allowed in the placed-in-service year and in later years), see FTC 2d/FIN ¶ L-9311; USTR ¶ 1684.025. For additional discussion of tax benefits for qualified property under pre-Tax Cuts and Jobs Act Law and under Tax Cuts and Jobs Act Law, see ¶ 1202, ¶ 1208 and ¶ 1210.

For purposes of determining the completion percentage (see above), certain qualified property isn't taken into account. The qualified property to which the exclusion applies is property that (1) has an MACRS recovery period of seven years or less (the recovery period requirement) and (2) is placed in service (the timing requirement) before, under pre-Tax Cuts and Jobs Act law, Jan. 1, 2020 (before Jan. 1, 2021, to the extent of pre-Jan. 1, 2020 costs, for qualified property described in Code Sec. 168(k)(2)(B) (certain property with a long production period, see FTC 2d/FIN ¶ L-9316.1; USTR ¶ 1684.027)). (FTC 2d/FIN ¶ G-3100, ¶ G-3143; USTR ¶ 4604.001; Catalyst ¶ 758:170)

> *observation:* Not taking certain qualified property into account generally defers the allocable contract costs taken into account from year to year and, thus, defers the gross income taken into account under the PCM, see the observation above.

New Law. The Tax Cuts and Jobs Act extends (Com Rept, see ¶ 5036) the deadline in the timing requirement for disregard of certain qualified property (with a MACRS recovery property of seven years or less, see above) under the percentage of completion method (above) to provide that property must be placed in service before *Jan. 1, 2027* (before *Jan. 1, 2028* for property described in Code Sec. 168(k)(2)(B), i.e. certain long-production-period property, see above). (Code Sec. 460(c)(6)(B)(ii) as amended by Tax Cuts and Jobs Act §13201(b)(2)(A))

For an overview that lists the above change and other bonus deprecia-tion-related changes made by the Tax Cuts and Jobs Act, see ¶ 1201.

> *observation:* The seven year extension of the placed-in-service dead-lines imposed by the timing requirement conforms to the seven year ex-tension of bonus depreciation discussed at ¶ 1202.

> *observation:* One of the requirements for being property described in Code Sec. 168(k)(2)(B) is that it either have a MACRS recovery period of at least 10 years or be used in the trade or business of transporting persons or property (transportation property), see FTC 2d/FIN ¶ L-9316.1; USTR ¶ 1684.027. Property with a recovery period of at least 10 years can't qualify for the disregard of qualified property for percentage of completion method purposes because property must have a MACRS recovery period of seven years or less to be eligible for the disregard, see above. On the other hand an example of transportation property that can qualify is commercial aircraft, which have a recovery period of seven years, see ¶ L-8206

☐ **Effective:** Property that is both (1) acquired and placed in service after Sept. 27, 2017 (Tax Cuts and Jobs Act §13201(h)(1)) and (2) placed in service before Jan. 1, 2027 (Code Sec. 168(k)(2)(A)(iii)) (before Jan. 1, 2028 in the case of certain long-production-period property and aircraft (Code Sec. 168(k)(2)(b)(i)(II); Code Sec. 168(k)(2)(C)(i))).

Property won't be treated as acquired after Sept. 27, 2017 if a written binding contract for its acquisition was entered into before Sept. 28, 2017. (Tax Cuts and Jobs Act §13201(h)(1))

¶ 1210. Corporate election trading bonus and accelerated depreciation for otherwise-deferred AMT credits is ended (conforming to repeal of corporate AMT)

Code Sec. 168(k), as amended by Tax Cuts and Jobs Act §12001(b)(13)
Generally effective: Tax years beginning after Dec. 31, 2017
Committee Reports, see ¶ 5029, 5036

Under pre-Tax Cuts and Jobs Act law, corporations could elect for qualified property to decline bonus depreciation (see ¶ 1202 *et seq.*), other accelerated de-preciation and the increased passenger automobile first-year depreciation cap

(¶ 1209) in exchange for receiving as a refundable credit certain Code Sec. 53 alternative minimum tax credits (against the regular income tax) that would otherwise continue to be deferred. (FTC 2d/FIN ¶ L-15200, ¶ L-15213; USTR ¶ 1684.0293)

The amount of the refundable credit was (1) limited to 20% of the bonus depreciation for qualified property that could be claimed as a deduction for the tax year and then (2) further limited for a tax year to the lesser of (A) 50% of the alternative minimum tax credit (AMT credit) for the first tax year ending after Dec. 31, 2015 (determined before the application of any tax liability limitation) or (B) the AMT credit for the tax year allocable to the adjusted net minimum tax imposed for tax years ending before Jan. 1, 2016 (determined before the application of any tax liability limitation and determined on a first-in, first-out basis), see FTC 2d/FIN ¶ L-15213A; USTR ¶ 1684.0293. (Com Rept, see ¶ 5036)

New Law. The Tax Cuts and Jobs Act repeals former Code Sec. 168(k)(4) (which provided the election to trade depreciation benefits for a refund of otherwise-deferred AMT credits as discussed above). (Code Sec. 168(k) as amended by Tax Cuts and Jobs Act §12001(b)(13))

The election was repealed as an amendment conforming to the repeal of the corporate AMT by the Tax Cuts and Jobs Act (see ¶ 303). (Com Rept, see ¶ 5036)

☐ **Effective:** Tax years beginning after Dec. 31, 2017. (Tax Cuts and Jobs Act §12001(c))

¶ 1300. Depreciation

Real Property Depreciation

¶ 1301. Eligibility of building improvements for a 15-year recovery period is expanded

Code Sec. 168(b)(3), as amended by Tax Cuts and Jobs Act §13204(a)(2)(A)

Code Sec. 168(b)(3)(G), as amended by Tax Cuts and Jobs Act §13204(a)(2)(B)

Code Sec. 168(e)(3)(E), as amended by Tax Cuts and Jobs Act §13204(a)(1)(A)(i)

Code Sec. 168(e), as amended by Tax Cuts and Jobs Act §13204(a)(1)(B)

Code Sec. 168(e)(6), as amended by Tax Cuts and Jobs Act §13204(a)(4)(B)

Code Sec. 168(g)(3)(B), as amended by Tax Cuts and Jobs Act §13204(a)(3)(B)(i)

Code Sec. 168(g)(3)(B), as amended by Tax Cuts and Jobs Act §13204(a)(3)(B)(ii)

Code Sec. 168(k)(2)(A)(i), as amended by Tax Cuts and Jobs Act §13204(a)(4)(A)

Generally effective: Property placed in service after Dec. 31, 2017

Committee Reports, see ¶ 5039

For most tangible property, the depreciation deduction allowed for the exhaustion of property used in a trade or business, or for the production of income, is determined under the modified accelerated cost recovery system (MACRS) of Code Sec. 168, see FTC 2d/FIN ¶ L-8101; USTR ¶ 1684.

The rules that, in most situations, assign a recovery period (i.e., depreciation period) to a type of MACRS property are known as the General Depreciation System (GDS). The assignment of a recovery period is usually made by reference to that type of property's "class life," as listed in Rev Proc 87-56, and determined under the "class life" system, see FTC 2d/FIN ¶ L-8203; USTR ¶ 1684.

However, under the GDS, the Code also sometimes specifically assigns a recovery period to a type of property without reference to class life. Thus, under pre-Tax Cuts and Jobs Act law, three types of building improvements—quali-

---

FTC 2d References are to Federal Tax Coordinator 2d
FIN References are to RIA's Analysis of Federal Taxes: Income (print)
USTR References are to United States Tax Reporter
Catalyst References are to Checkpoint Catalyst
PCA References are to Pension Analysis (print and electronic)
PBE References are to Pension & Benefits Explanations
BCA References are to Benefits Analysis (electronic)
BC References are to Benefits Coordinator (print)
EP References are to Estate Planning Analysis (print and electronic)

fied leasehold improvement property, qualified restaurant property and qualified retail improvement property—had a 15-year recovery period. (FTC 2d/FIN ¶ L-8200, ¶ L-8208, ¶ L-8208.1, ¶ L-8208.2, ¶ L-8208.5; USTR ¶ 1684.02; Catalyst ¶ 402:195)

The MACRS GDS rules also provide for the method under which various types of property are depreciated—a 200% declining balance method, a 150% declining balance method, or the straight-line method, see FTC 2d/FIN ¶ L-8902 *et seq.*; USTR ¶ 1684 *et seq.*

Under pre-Tax Cuts and Jobs Act law, qualified leasehold improvement property, qualified restaurant property and qualified retail improvement property were depreciated under the straight-line method. (FTC 2d/FIN ¶ L-8900, ¶ L-8917; USTR ¶ 1684.02; Catalyst ¶ 402:205; Catalyst ¶ 406:144)

Alternative depreciation system. Taxpayers are sometimes required to (because of certain triggers such as tax-exempt financing, see FTC 2d/FIN ¶ L-9400, ¶ L-9402; USTR ¶ 1684.03), and can elect to, depreciate MACRS property under an alternative depreciation system (ADS) instead of under the general depreciation rules, see FTC 2d/FIN ¶ L-9401; USTR ¶ 1684.03.

For most MACRS property, the ADS requires (1) a recovery period (generally longer than under the GDS) equal to the property's class life (assigned by Code Sec. 168(g)(3)(B) if not assigned by Rev Proc 87-56 (above)), and (2) the straight-line method of depreciation, see FTC 2d/FIN ¶ L-9403; USTR ¶ 1684.03.

Under pre-Tax Cuts and Jobs Act law, the ADS provided a recovery period of 39 years for qualified leasehold improvement property, qualified restaurant property and qualified retail improvement property. (FTC 2d/FIN ¶ L-9400, ¶ L-9403; USTR ¶ 1684.03)

New Law. The Tax Cuts and Jobs Act eliminates (see **Removal of other improvement categories** below) the separate definitions (above) of qualified leasehold improvement property, qualified restaurant property and qualified retail improvement property. (Com Rept, see ¶ 5039)

Also, according to the Joint Explanatory Statement accompanying the conference agreement, the Tax Cuts and Jobs Act provides a general 15-year recovery period for qualified improvement property. (Com Rept, see ¶ 5039)

> *caution:* The 15-year recovery period for qualified improvement property that the Joint Explanatory Statement indicates is provided by the Tax Cuts and Jobs Act isn't reflected in the actual statutory language, even though the text does provide straight-line depreciation for qualified improvement property (below), as well as a definition of qualified improvement property (below).
>
> In response to an inquiry by Thomson Reuters Tax and Accounting, a Ways and Means spokesperson stated that the Joint Explanatory

Statement reflects the intent of House/Senate conferees and that the absence of legislative text is an error that will be addressed in future technical corrections.

Presumably, any correction of the omission of the 15-year recovery period rule will be effective for property placed in service after Dec. 31, 2017 (see **Effective** below).

caution: In a related omission, the text of the Tax Cuts and Jobs Act failed to provide an ADS recovery period for the 15-year qualified improvement property. Instead, Code Sec. 168(g)(3)(B) as amended by Tax Cuts and Jobs Act §13204(a)(3)(B)(i) provides an ADS recovery period (20 years) for property described in Code Sec. 168(e)(3)(D)(v). Code Sec. 168(e)(3)(D)(v) is the number of the Code section that under the Senate bill would have provided a *10 year* recovery for qualified improvement property.

Straight-line method. Qualified improvement property is depreciated on the straight-line method. (Code Sec. 168(b)(3)(G) as amended by Tax Cuts and Jobs Act §13204(a)(2)(B))

Qualified improvement property defined. "Qualified improvement property" is any improvement to an interior portion of a building that is nonresidential real property if the improvement is placed in service after the date the building was first placed in service (Code Sec. 168(e)(6)(A) as amended by Tax Cuts and Jobs Act §13204(a)(4)(B)) *except* for any improvement for which the expenditure is attributable to (1) enlargement of the building, (2) any elevator or escalator, or (3) the internal structural framework of the building. (Code Sec. 168(e)(6)(B))

observation: The substitution of qualified improvement property for qualified leasehold improvement, qualified restaurant property and qualified retail improvement property as property that receives preferred MACRS depreciation treatment is greatly expansive of what property qualifies because (1) "qualified improvement property" includes property without regard to what business it is used in or whether the improved space is leased space; (2) qualified leasehold improvement property and qualified retail improvement property must be placed in service at least three years after the building that they improve was placed in service, see FTC 2d/FIN ¶s L-8208.1, L-8208.5; USTR ¶ 1794.02 and (3) the only way in which the definition of qualified improvement property is more restrictive than the three definitions provided under pre-Tax Cuts and Jobs Act law is in its exclusion of restaurant buildings and some restaurant improvements. For example, the definition of qualified restaurant property didn't exclude building enlargements, see FTC 2d/FIN ¶ L-8208.2; USTR ¶ 1684.02.

observation: The Tax Cuts and Jobs Act, in addition to assigning a 15 year MACRS recovery period to qualified improvement property, instead of the 39 year period that applies to other non-residential real property, see FTC 2d/FIN ¶ L-8210; USTR ¶ 1684.02, substituted qualified improvement property for qualified leasehold improvement, qualified restaurant property and qualified retail improvement property as improvement property eligible for expensing under Code Sec. 179 (¶ 1102).

Conforming change. The Tax Cuts and Jobs Act eliminates specific mention of qualified improvement property as a type of property that, if other requirements are satisfied, is qualified property eligible for bonus depreciation (but see caution immediately below). (Code Sec. 168(k)(2)(A)(i) as amended by Tax Cuts and Jobs Act §13204(a)(4)(A))

caution: The elimination of qualified improvement property as a type of property specifically mentioned as a type of property that can qualify, if otherwise eligible, for bonus depreciation is in fact a conforming change and not a substantive change. This is so because the Tax Cuts and Jobs Act's assignment of a 15-year MACRS recovery period to qualified improvement property means that qualified improvement property satisfies the type-of-requirement for qualified property by being property with a no-more-tham-20-year MACRS recovery period, see FTC 2d/FIN ¶ L-9300, ¶ L-9312; USTR ¶ 1684.026.

Removal of other improvement categories. The Tax Cuts and Jobs Act removes former Code Sec. 168(e)(3)(E)(iv), former Code Sec. 168(e)(3)(E)(v) and former Code Sec. 168(e)(3)(E)(ix) which provided a 15-year recovery period for, respectively, qualified leasehold improvement, qualified restaurant property and qualified retail improvement property (see background above). (Code Sec. 168(e)(3)(E) as amended by Tax Cuts and Jobs Act §13204(a)(1)(A)(i))

Also, the Tax Cuts and Jobs Act removes former Code Sec. 168(e)(6), former Code Sec. 168(e)(7) and former Code Sec. 168(e)(8) which provided the definitions of, respectively, qualified leasehold improvement, qualified restaurant property and qualified retail improvement property (see background above). (Code Sec. 168(e) as amended by Tax Cuts and Jobs Act §13204(a)(1)(B))

And, the Tax Cuts and Jobs Act removes former Code Sec. 168(b)(3)(G), former Code Sec. 168(b)(3)(H) and former Code Sec. 168(B)(3)(I) which provided straight-line depreciation for, respectively, qualified leasehold improvement, qualified restaurant property and qualified retail improvement property (see background above). (Code Sec. 168(b)(3) as amended by Tax Cuts and Jobs Act §13204(a)(2)(A))

Additionally, the Tax Cuts and Jobs Act removes from Code Sec. 168(g)(B)(3) the table entries that provided a 39-year ADS recovery period for qualified leasehold improvement, qualified restaurant property and qualified retail improvement property (see background above). (Code Sec. 168(g)(3)(B) as amended by Tax Cuts and Jobs Act §13204(a)(3)(B)(ii))

Redesignations. The Tax Cuts and Jobs Act redesignates former Code Sec. 168(e)(3)(E)(vi), former Code Sec. 168(e)(3)(E)(vii) and former Code Sec. 168(e)(3)(E)(viii) as Code Sec. 168(e)(3)(E)(iv), Code Sec. 168(e)(3)(E)(v) and Code Sec. 168(e)(3)(E)(vi) (because of the removal of the 15-year recovery period rules for qualified leasehold improvement, qualified restaurant property and qualified retail improvement property, see above). (Code Sec. 168(e)(3)(E)(iv) as amended by Tax Cuts and Jobs Act §13204(a)(1)(A)(iv); Code Sec. 168(e)(3)(E)(v) as amended by Tax Cuts and Jobs Act §13204(a)(1)(A)(iv); Code Sec. 168(e)(3)(E)(vi) as amended by Tax Cuts and Jobs Act §13204(a)(1)(A)(iv))

☐ **Effective:** Property placed in service after Dec. 31, 2017 (Tax Cuts and Jobs Act §13204(b)(1)).

¶ 1302. ADS recovery period for residential rental property is shortened to 30 years

Code Sec. 168(g)(2)(C), as amended by Tax Cuts and Jobs Act §13204(a)(3)(C)
Generally effective: Property placed in service after Dec. 31, 2017
Committee Reports, see ¶ 5039

For most tangible property, the depreciation deduction allowed for the exhaustion of property used in a trade or business, or for the production of income, is determined under the modified accelerated cost recovery system (MACRS) of Code Sec. 168, see FTC 2d/FIN ¶ L-8101; USTR ¶ 1684.

The rules that, in most situations, assign a recovery period (i.e., depreciation period) to a type of MACRS property are known as the General Depreciation System (GDS). The assignment of a recovery period is usually made by reference to that type of property's "class life," as listed in Rev Proc 87-56, and determined under the "class life" system, see FTC 2d/FIN ¶ L-8203; USTR ¶ 1684.

However, under the GDS, the Code also sometimes specifically assigns a recovery period to a type of property without reference to class life. Thus, nonresidential real property (buildings, and their structural components, other than residential rental property) have a 39-year recovery period, see FTC 2d/FIN ¶ L-8210; USTR ¶ 1684.02, and residential rental property (apartment buildings and their structural components) have a 27.5 year recovery period, see FTC 2d/ FIN ¶ L-8211; USTR ¶ 1684.02.

The MACRS GDS rules also provide for the method under which various types of property are depreciated—a 200% declining balance method, a 150% declining balance method, or the straight-line method, see FTC 2d/FIN ¶ L-8902 *et seq.*; USTR ¶ 1684 *et seq.*

Under the GDS, nonresidential real property and residential rental property are both depreciated under the straight-line method, see FTC 2d/FIN ¶ L-8917; USTR ¶ 1684.02

Alternative depreciation system. Taxpayers are sometimes required to (because of certain triggers such as tax-exempt financing, see FTC 2d/FIN ¶ L-9402; USTR ¶ 1684.03, and can elect to, depreciate MACRS property under an alternative depreciation system (ADS) instead of under the general depreciation rules, see FTC 2d/FIN ¶ L-9401; USTR ¶ 1684.03.

For most MACRS property, the ADS requires (1) a recovery period (generally longer than under the GDS) equal to the property's class life (assigned by Code Sec. 168(g)(3)(B) if not assigned by Rev Proc 87-56 (above)), and (2) the straight-line method of depreciation, see FTC 2d/FIN ¶ L-9403; USTR ¶ 1684.03.

However, under pre-Tax Cuts and Jobs Act law, the ADS provided a recovery period, without regard to class life, of 40 years for both nonresidential real property and residential rental property. (FTC 2d/FIN ¶ L-9400, ¶ L-9403; USTR ¶ 1684.03; Catalyst ¶ 402:313; Catalyst ¶ 406:170)

New Law. Under The Tax Cuts and Jobs Act, the alternative depreciation system (ADS) recovery period is 40 years for nonresidential real property and 30 years for residential rental property. (Code Sec. 168(g)(2)(C) as amended by Tax Cuts and Jobs Act §13204(a)(3)(C))

Thus, the ADS recovery period for residential rental property is shortened to 30 years. (Com Rept, see ¶ 5039)

    observation: The ADS recovery period for nonresidential rental property remains 40 years.

For the preferential MACRS depreciation rules, including a 15-year recovery period, for some building improvements as changed by the Tax Cuts and Jobs Act, see ¶ 1301.

For mandatory ADS depreciation for nonresidential real property, residential rental property and qualified improvement property if a taxpayer elects to not apply the business interest deduction limitations to a real property trade or business, see ¶ 1303.

☐ **Effective:** Property placed in service after Dec. 31, 2017. (Tax Cuts and Jobs Act §13204(b)(1))

¶ 1303. ADS depreciation for buildings (and improvements) if election is made to exempt a real property business from the business interest deduction limit

Code Sec. 168(g)(1)(F), as amended by Tax Cuts and Jobs Act §13204(a)(3)(A)(i)

Code Sec. 168(g)(8), as amended by Tax Cuts and Jobs Act §13204(a)(3)(A)(ii)

Generally effective: Tax years beginning after Dec. 31, 2017

Committee Reports, see ¶ 5039

For most tangible property, the depreciation deduction allowed for the exhaustion of property used in a trade or business, or for the production of income, is determined under the modified accelerated cost recovery system (MACRS) of Code Sec. 168, see FTC 2d/FIN ¶ L-8101; USTR ¶ 1684.

The rules that, in most situations, assign a recovery period (i.e., depreciation period) to a type of MACRS property are known as the General Depreciation System (GDS). The assignment of a recovery period is usually made by reference to that type of property's "class life," as listed in Rev Proc 87-56, and determined under the "class life" system, see FTC 2d/FIN ¶ L-8203; USTR ¶ 1684.

The MACRS general depreciation also provides for the method under which the property is depreciated, see FTC 2d/FIN ¶ L-8902 *et seq.*; USTR ¶ 1684 *et seq.*

Some MACRS property is depreciated on the straight-line method, see FTC 2d/FIN ¶ L-8917; USTR ¶ 1684.01 *et seq.*

However, unless a taxpayer elects otherwise, other MACRS property, with exceptions, is depreciable on the more accelerated 200% declining balance method, FTC 2d/FIN ¶ L-8909; USTR ¶ 1684.01 *et seq.*, and the excepted property is depreciated under the 150% declining balance method, see FTC 2d/FIN ¶ L-8912; USTR ¶ 1684.01 *et seq.*

Alternative depreciation system. Taxpayers are sometimes required to (because of certain triggers such as tax-exempt financing, see FTC 2d/FIN ¶ L-9400, ¶ L-9402; USTR ¶ 1684.03), and can elect to, depreciate MACRS property under an alternative depreciation system (ADS) instead of under the general depreciation rules, see FTC 2d/FIN ¶ L-9401; USTR ¶ 1684.03.

For most MACRS property, the ADS requires (1) a recovery period (generally longer than under the GDS) equal to the property's class life (assigned by Code Sec. 168(g)(3)(B) if not assigned by Rev Proc 87-56 (above)), and (2) the straight-line method of depreciation, see FTC 2d/FIN ¶ L-9403; USTR ¶ 1684.03.(; Catalyst ¶ 402:310; Catalyst ¶ 406:170)

New Law. The Tax Cuts and Jobs Act requires depreciation under the MACRS alternative depreciation system (ADS, see background above) for any nonresidential real property, residential rental property and qualified improvement property held by an electing real property trade or business, as defined in Code Sec. 163(j)(7)(B) (see ¶ 1003 and below). (Code Sec. 168(g)(1)(F) as amended by Tax Cuts and Jobs Act §13204(a)(3)(A)(i); Code Sec. 168(g)(8) as amended by Tax Cuts and Jobs Act §13204(a)(3)(A)(ii))

Thus, the Tax Cuts and Jobs Act allows an electing real property trade or business to not apply the Act's limitations on business interest deductions (see ¶ 1003), but the election requires the electing real property trade or business to use the alternative depreciation system to depreciate any of its non-residential real property, residential rental property and qualified improvement property. (Com Rept, see ¶ 5039)

> *observation:* If a real property trade or business passes an average-of-no-more-than-$25-million-gross-receipts test and isn't a tax shelter, the business isn't subject to the business interest deduction limitations. Thus, the taxpayer that owns it doesn't have to decide whether or not to be make the election for that real property trade or business.

> *observation:* In deciding whether to make what is an irrevocable election, ¶ 1003, a taxpayer with a real property trade or business must, of course, compare the extent to which the limitations, as discussed at ¶ 1003, will affect (i.e., defer) interest deductions and the extent to which the taxpayer will have to claim depreciation deductions at a decelerated rate and over a longer period.

> In this regard, the following are the affects of the ADS on the depreciation of nonresidential real property, residential rental property and qualified improvement property:

> . . . nonresidential real property (nonresidential buildings depreciated and improvements to them other than qualified improvement property, see below) is depreciated on the straight-line method under both the MACRS general depreciation system (GDS), see FTC 2d/FIN ¶ L-8917; USTR ¶ 1684.02, and the ADS, and under the ADS its depreciation period is increased from 39 years to 40 years, see ¶ 1302.

> . . . residential rental property (residential buildings and any improvements to them) is depreciated on the straight-line method under both the general depreciation system (GDS), see FTC 2d/FIN ¶ L-8917; USTR ¶ 1684.02, and the ADS, but under the ADS its depreciation period is increased from 27.5 years to 30 years, see ¶ 1302.

... qualified improvement property (certain improvements to nonresidential real property) is depreciated on the straight-line method under both the GDS and the ADS, but under the ADS its depreciation period is increased from 15 years to 20 years, see ¶ 1301.

☐ **Effective:** Tax years beginning after Dec. 31, 2017. (Tax Cuts and Jobs Act §13204(b)(2))

Farm Depreciation

¶ 1304. Most new farming equipment and machinery is made 5-year MACRS property

Code Sec. 168(e)(3)(B)(vii), as amended by Tax Cuts and Jobs Act §13203(a)
Generally effective: Property placed in service after Dec. 31, 2017
Committee Reports, see ¶ 5038

For most tangible property, the depreciation deduction allowed for the exhaustion of property used in a trade or business, or for the production of income, is determined under the modified accelerated cost recovery system (MACRS) of Code Sec. 168, see FTC 2d/FIN ¶ L-8101; USTR ¶ 1684.

The rules that, in most situations, assign a recovery period (i.e., depreciation period) to a type of MACRS property are known as the General Depreciation System (GDS). The assignment of a recovery period is usually made by reference to that type of property's "class life," as listed in Rev Proc 87-56, 1987-2 CB 674, and determined under the "class life" system, see FTC 2d/FIN ¶ L-8203; USTR ¶ 1684.

However, under the GDS, the Code also specifically assigns a recovery period to some types of property without reference to class life. Thus, property with a 7-year recovery period includes property with a class life of 10 or more years but less than 16 years, but also includes (1) certain other types of property specified in the Code and (2) property with no specified class life, see FTC 2d/FIN ¶ L-8206; USTR ¶ 1684.01. Similarly, property with a 5 recovery period includes property with a class life of 4 or more years but less than 10 years, also includes certain other types of property specified in the Code, see FTC 2d/FIN ¶ L-8205; USTR ¶ 1684.01.

Under pre-Tax Cuts and Jobs Act law, machinery and equipment used in a farming business had a 7-year recovery period (Com Rept, see ¶ 5038), based on a class life of 10 years (see above). (FTC 2d/FIN ¶ L-8200, ¶ L-8206; USTR ¶ 1684.01; Catalyst ¶ 402:190; Catalyst ¶ 406:150)

However, the Code assigned a 5-year recovery period to items of machinery and equipment placed in service during calendar year 2009 and used in a farming business, as defined in Code Sec. 263A(e)(4), see FTC 2d/FIN ¶ N-1073; USTR ¶ 263A4.15, if (1) the item's original use began with the taxpayer and (2) the item wasn't a grain bin, cotton ginning asset, fence or other land improvement. (FTC 2d/FIN ¶ N-1360, ¶ N-1362; USTR ¶ 1684.01)

Alternative depreciation system. Taxpayers are in some circumstances required to, and can always elect to, depreciate MACRS property under an alternative depreciation system (ADS) instead of under the GDS, see FTC 2d/FIN ¶ L-9401; USTR ¶ 1684.03.

For most MACRS property, other than buildings, the ADS requires (1) a recovery period equal to the property's class life (which is often longer than the GDS recovery period), and (2) the straight-line method of depreciation, see FTC 2d/FIN ¶ L-9403; USTR ¶ 1684.03.

Under the general rule matching the ADS recovery period to an asset's class life, farming equipment and machinery (except cotton ginning assets) have a recovery period under the alternative depreciation system (ADS) of 10 years (and for cotton ginning assets, 12 years), see FTC 2d/FIN ¶ N-1361; USTR ¶ 1684.03.

And for the farming machinery equipment placed in service in calendar year 2009 to which the Code assigned a 5-year recovery, the Code specifically assigned the same 10 year ADS recovery period that generally applies to farming equipment and machinery (except cotton ginning assets). (FTC 2d/FIN ¶ N-1361; USTR ¶ 1684.03)

New Law. The Tax Cuts and Jobs Act removes from the rule that provides a 5-year recovery period for certain farming machinery and equipment the language that limited the 5-year recovery period to property placed in service in calendar year 2009. Code Sec. 168(e)(3)(B)(vii) as amended by Tax Cuts and Jobs Act §13203(a)

> *observation:* Thus, the The Tax Cuts and Jobs Act applies, without a limited placed-in-service window, a 5-year MACRS recovery period to items of machinery and equipment used in a farming business, as defined in Code Sec. 263A(e)(4) (see FTC 2d/FIN ¶ N-1073; USTR ¶ 263A4.15), if (1) the item's original use began with the taxpayer and (2) the item isn't a grain bin, cotton ginning asset, fence or other land improvement. For the 7-year recovery period that applies to other farming machinery and equipment, see the background above

> *observation:* The rule that assigned an ADS recovery period of 10 years to farm property to which the 5-year recovery period for property placed in service in calendar year 2009 applied did so by a reference to Code Sec. 168(e)(3)(B)(vii) with no specific mention of the calendar

year 2009 limitation. Thus, the Tax Cuts and Jobs Act didn't have to amend that rule to provide a 10 year ADS recovery period for property to which a 5-year general depreciation recovery period applies under the Tax Cuts and Jobs Act (see above)

And for farm machinery and equipment to which a 7-year recovery period applies, a 10-year recovery period (12 years for cotton ginning assets) continues to apply under the rule that matches ADS recovery period to class life, see background above.

For the Tax Cuts and Jobs Acts expansion of the availability of the 200% declining balance depreciation method to many types of farming property, see ¶ 1305.

For the mandatory use of the alternative depreciation system for certain farming property used in a farming business for which a taxpayer elects to not apply the Tax Cuts and Jobs Act's business interest deduction limitations, see ¶ 1306.

☐ **Effective:** Property that is placed in service after Dec. 31, 2017 in a tax year that ends after Dec. 31, 2017. (Tax Cuts and Jobs Act §13203(c))

¶ 1305. 200% declining balance method of MACRS depreciation is made available for many types of MACRS farming property

Code Sec. 168(b)(2), as amended by Tax Cuts and Jobs Act §13203(b)
Generally effective: Property placed in service after Dec. 31, 2017
Committee Reports, see ¶ 5038

For most tangible property, the depreciation deduction allowed for the exhaustion of property used in a trade or business, or for the production of income, is determined under the modified accelerated cost recovery system (MACRS) of Code Sec. 168, see FTC 2d/FIN ¶ L-8101; USTR ¶ 1684.

The MACRS rules assign various depreciation periods (recovery periods) to various types of property, see FTC 2d/FIN ¶ L-8202 *et seq.*; USTR ¶ 1684 *et seq.*, and provide depreciation conventions that provide for how property is depreciated in the first year and last year that the taxpayer is eligible to depreciate the property, see FTC 2d/FIN ¶ L-8701 *et seq.*; USTR ¶ 1684 *et seq.*

The MACRS rules also provide for the method under which the property is depreciated, see FTC 2d/FIN ¶ L-8902 *et seq.*; USTR ¶ 1684 *et seq.*

Some MACRS property—i.e. most buildings (including, with exceptions, building improvements), water utility property, railroad gradings and tunnel bores, trees or vines bearing fruits or nuts, and property for which a taxpayer makes an election—is depreciated on the straight-line method, see FTC 2d/FIN ¶ L-8917; USTR ¶ 1684.01 *et seq.*

However, unless a taxpayer elects otherwise, other MACRS property, with exceptions, is depreciable on the more accelerated 200% declining balance method, FTC 2d/FIN ¶ L-8909; USTR ¶ 1684.01 *et seq.*

Under pre-Tax Cuts and Jobs Act law, the excepted property, which had to be depreciated under the 150% declining balance method, was (1) property with a MACRS recovery period of 15 or 20 years, (2) certain electric metering and grid property, (3) property for which the taxpayer elected to have the 150% declining balance method apply instead of the 200% declining method and (4) property used in a farming business as defined in Code Sec. 263A(e)(4) (the definition is discussed at FTC 2d/FIN ¶ N-1073; USTR ¶ 263A4.15). (FTC 2d/FIN ¶ L-8900, ¶ L-8912; USTR ¶ 1684.01; Catalyst ¶ 402:200; Catalyst ¶ 406:140)

Thus, under pre-Tax Cuts and Jobs Act law, all MACRS farming property was depreciated under the 150% declining balance method except for buildings, trees or vines bearing fruits or nuts (which had to be depreciated under the straight line method as discussed above) and farming property subject to the alternative depreciation system (see below). (Com Rept, see ¶ 5038)

Alternative depreciation system. Taxpayers are in some circumstances required to, and can always elect to, depreciate MACRS property under an alternative depreciation system (ADS) instead of under the general depreciation rules, see FTC 2d/FIN ¶ L-9401; USTR ¶ 1684.03.

For most MACRS property, other than buildings, the ADS requires (1) a recovery period equal to the property's class life (which is often longer than the regular recovery period), and (2) the straight-line method of depreciation, see FTC 2d/FIN ¶ L-9403; USTR ¶ 1684.03.

New Law. The Tax Cuts and Jobs Act removes the rule (above) that requires that property used in a farming business, as defined in Code Sec. 263A(e)(4) (FTC 2d/FIN ¶ N-1073; USTR ¶ 263A4.15), be depreciated on the 150% declining balance method. (Code Sec. 168(b)(2) as amended by Tax Cuts and Jobs Act §13203(b))

> *observation:* Thus, under the Tax Cuts and Jobs Act, MACRS farming property is depreciated under the 200% declining balance method except for (1) buildings and trees or vines bearing fruits or nuts (to which the straight-line method applies, see background above), (2) property for which the taxpayer elects either the straight-line method or 150% declining balance method (see background above), (3) 15 year or 20 year MACRS property that has to be depreciated under the 150% declining balance method (see background above), and (4) property subject to the alternative depreciation system (see the caution below).

One category of property included as 15-year property is land improvements other than buildings, see FTC 2d/FIN ¶ L-8208; USTR ¶s 1684.01, 1684.02. However, fences and grain bins have a 7-year recovery period, see FTC 2d/FIN ¶ L-8206, and single purpose agricultural or horticultural structures (e.g., greenhouses, specialized housing for livestock) have a 10-year recovery period, see FTC 2d/FIN ¶ L-8207.1; USTR ¶ 1684.01.

20-year MACRS property includes "farm buildings", which are certain structures that are neither conventional buildings nor single purpose agricultural or horticultural structures; these include tobacco barn uses for curing and further processing, through boxing, of tobacco leaves, see FTC 2d/FIN ¶ L-8209.

caution: As discussed in the background above, if property is subject to the alternative depreciation system (ADS) either electively or mandatorily, the property must be depreciated over its class-life and on the straight-line method.

Under pre-Tax Cuts and Jobs Act law, the circumstance most likely to trigger mandatory ADS for a farming business was an election to deduct pre-productive period expenses in lieu of subjecting them to the uniform capitalization rules; i.e., the ADS was required for all farming assets if the taxpayer made an election, see FTC 2d/FIN ¶s N-1084, N-1090; USTR ¶ 263A4.155.

And, the ADS is mandatory for certain property used in a taxpayer's farming business if the taxpayer makes the election, available under the Tax Cuts and Jobs Act, to not apply the Act's business interest limitation deduction rules to that business, see ¶ 1306.

For a five-year MACRS recovery period for most new farming machinery and equipment, see ¶ 1305.

☐ **Effective:** Property that is placed in service after Dec. 31, 2017 in a tax year that ends after Dec. 31, 2017. (Tax Cuts and Jobs Act §13203(c))

¶ 1306. ADS depreciation required for 10-year-or-more MACRS property if election made to exempt farming from the business interest deduction limitation

Code Sec. 168(g)(1)(G), as amended by Tax Cuts and Jobs Act §13205(a)
Generally effective: Tax years beginning after Dec. 31, 2017
Committee Reports, see ¶ 5040

For most tangible property, the depreciation deduction allowed for the exhaustion of property used in a trade or business, or for the production of income, is determined under the modified accelerated cost recovery system (MACRS) of Code Sec. 168, see FTC 2d/FIN ¶ L-8101; USTR ¶ 1684.

The rules that, in most situations, assign a recovery period (i.e., depreciation period) to a type of MACRS property are known as the General Depreciation System (GDS). The assignment of a recovery period is usually made by reference to that type of property's "class life," as listed in Rev Proc 87-56, and determined under the "class life" system, see FTC 2d/FIN ¶ L-8203; USTR ¶ 1684.

The MACRS general depreciation also provides for the method under which the property is depreciated, see FTC 2d/FIN ¶ L-8902 *et seq.*; USTR ¶ 1684 *et seq.*

Some MACRS property is depreciated on the straight-line method, see FTC 2d/FIN ¶ L-8917; USTR ¶ 1684.01 *et seq.*

However, unless a taxpayer elects otherwise, other MACRS property, with exceptions, is depreciable on the more accelerated 200% declining balance method, FTC 2d/FIN ¶ L-8909; USTR ¶ 1684.01 *et seq.*, and the excepted property is depreciated under the 150% declining balance method, see FTC 2d/FIN ¶ L-8912; USTR ¶ 1684.01 *et seq.*

Alternative depreciation system. Taxpayers are sometimes required to (because of certain triggers such as tax-exempt financing, see FTC 2d/FIN ¶ L-9400, ¶ L-9402; USTR ¶ 1684.03), and can elect to, depreciate MACRS property under an alternative depreciation system (ADS) instead of under the general depreciation rules, see FTC 2d/FIN ¶ L-9401; USTR ¶ 1684.03.

For most MACRS property, the ADS requires (1) a recovery period (generally longer than under the GDS) equal to the property's class life (assigned by Code Sec. 168(g)(3)(B) if not assigned by Rev Proc 87-56 (above)), and (2) the straight-line method of depreciation, see FTC 2d/FIN ¶ L-9403; USTR ¶ 1684.03.(; Catalyst ¶ 402:310; Catalyst ¶ 406:170)

New Law. The Tax Cuts and Jobs Act requires depreciation under the alternative depreciation system (see background above) of any MACRS property with a recovery period of 10 years or more that is held by an electing farming business, as defined in Code Sec. 163(j)(7) (see ¶ 1003 and below). (Code Sec. 168(g)(1)(G) as amended by Tax Cuts and Jobs Act §13205(a))

Thus, the Tax Cuts and Jobs Act allows an electing farming business to not apply the Act's limitations on business interest deductions (see ¶ 1003), but the election requires the electing farming business to use the alternative depreciation system to depreciate any property used in the farming business with a recovery period of ten years or more. (Com Rept, see ¶ 5040)

⊘*observation:* If a farming business passes an average-of-no-more-than-$25-million-gross-receipts test and isn't a tax shelter, the business isn't subject to the business interest deduction limitations. Thus, the taxpayer that owns it doesn't have to decide whether or not to be make the election for that farming business.

⊘*observation:* In deciding whether to make what is an irrevocable election, ¶ 1003, a taxpayer with a non-exempt farming business must, of course, compare the extent to which the limitations, as discussed at ¶ 1003, will affect (i.e., defer) interest deductions and the extent to which the taxpayer will have to claim depreciation deductions at a decelerated rate and over a longer period.

In this regard, the following is a list of the property types most likely to be subject to the ADS aspect of the election and the affects of the ADS on their depreciation:

. . . non-residential real property (buildings). These are depreciated on the straight-line method under both the general depreciation system (GDS), see FTC 2d/FIN ¶ L-8917; USTR ¶ 1684.02, and the ADS, and under the ADS their depreciation period is increased from 39 years to 40 years, see FTC 2d/FIN ¶ L-8210; USTR ¶ 1684.03.

. . . qualified improvement property (certain improvements to non-residential buildings). This property is depreciated on the straight-line method under both the GDS and the ADS, but under the ADS the depreciation period is increased from 10 years to 20 years, see ¶ 1301.

. . . fruit or nut-bearing trees and vines. These are depreciated on the straight-line method under both the GDS and the ADS, but under the ADS the depreciation period is increased from 10 years to 20 years, see FTC 2d/FIN ¶s L-8207, L-9403; USTR ¶s 1684.01, 1684.03.

. . . single purpose agricultural or horticultural structures (for example, greenhouses and specialized structures for housing livestock). These are depreciated on the 200% declining balance method under the GDS, see ¶ 1305, and the straight-line method under the ADS, and under the ADS their depreciation period is increased from 10 years to 15 years, see FTC 2d/FIN ¶s L-8207.1, L-9403; USTR ¶s 1684.01, 1684.03.

. . . certain specialized farm buildings not mentioned above (for example tobacco curing barns). These are depreciated on the 150% declining balance method under the GDS, see FTC 2d/FIN ¶ L-8912; USTR ¶ 1684.01, and the straight-line method under the ADS, and under the ADS their depreciation period is increased from 20 years to 25 years, see FTC 2d/FIN ¶s L-8209, L-9403; USTR ¶s 1684.01, 1684.03.

. . . most land improvements other than fences and storage bins, see FTC 2d/FIN ¶ L-8206, and items mentioned above. These are depreciated on the 150% declining balance method under the GDS, see FTC 2d/FIN ¶ L-8912; USTR ¶ 1684.01, and the straight-line method under the ADS, and under the ADS their depreciation period is increased from 15 years to 20 years, FTC 2d/FIN ¶s L-8208, L-9403; USTR ¶s 1684.02, 1684.03.

For a five-year MACRS recovery period, under the Tax Cuts and Jobs Act, for most new farming machinery and equipment, see ¶ 1304.

For the availability, under the Tax Cuts and Jobs Act, of the 200% declining balance depreciation method for many types of farming property, see ¶ 1305.

☐ **Effective:** Tax years beginning after Dec. 31, 2017. (Tax Cuts and Jobs Act §13205(b))

Cars and Listed Property

¶ 1307. Annual caps on depreciation of passenger automobiles are raised

Code Sec. 280F(a)(1)(A), as amended by Tax Cuts and Jobs Act §13202(a)(1)
Code Sec. 280F(a)(1)(B), as amended by Tax Cuts and Jobs Act §13202(a)(2)(A)
Code Sec. 280F(d)(7)(B)(i), as amended by Tax Cuts and Jobs Act §13202(a)(2)(B)(i)
Code Sec. 280F(d)(7)(B)(i), as amended by Tax Cuts and Jobs Act §11002(d)(8)
Code Sec. 280F(d)(7)(B)(i)(II), as amended by Tax Cuts and Jobs Act §13202(a)(2)(B)(ii)
Code Sec. 280F(d)(7)(B)(ii), as amended by Tax Cuts and Jobs Act §11002(d)(8)
Generally effective: Property placed in service after Dec. 31, 2017
Committee Reports, see ¶ 5037

Code Sec. 280F(a) imposes dollar limits (caps) on the depreciation deductions, including deductions under the Code Sec. 179 expensing election, that can be claimed with respect to "passenger automobiles," see FTC 2d/FIN ¶ L-10003; USTR ¶ 280F4. Thus, the aggregate of any Code Sec. 179 expensing election and depreciation deductions otherwise allowable in the placed-in-service year isn't allowed to exceed the placed-in-service year dollar cap. (Com Rept, see ¶ 5037)

Under pre-Tax Cuts and Jobs Act law, the base amounts (to be adjusted as discussed below) for calculating the caps were $2,560 for the year the vehicle was placed in service, $4,100 for the second year in the recovery period, $2,450 for the third year in the recovery period, and $1,475 for the fourth, fifth and sixth years of the recovery period (passenger vehicles are 5-year MACRS property). (FTC 2d/FIN ¶ L-10004; USTR ¶ 280F4)

The base amount was also $1,475 for caps for years after the recovery period to the extent that one or more post-recovery years were needed to fully depreciate the vehicle. (FTC 2d/FIN ¶ L-10004; USTR ¶ 280F4)

Under pre-Tax Cuts and Jobs Act law, the CPI adjustment applied to passenger automobiles placed in service after 1988 and provided that each of the base amounts (above) were increased by the "automobile price inflation adjustment" for the calendar year in which the automobile is placed in service. The automobile price adjustment for any calendar year was the percentage (if any) by which (1) the CPI automobile component (of the CPI for all urban consumers as published by the Department of Labor) for Oct. of the preceding calendar year exceeded (2) the CPI component for Oct. 1987. (FTC 2d/FIN ¶ L-10004; USTR ¶ 280F4; Catalyst ¶ 402:282; Catalyst ¶ 403:207)

For example for passenger automobiles placed in service in calendar year 2017, the placed-in-service year limit is $3,160 see FTC 2d/FIN ¶ L-10004; USTR ¶ 280F4.

New Law. The Tax Cuts and Jobs Act provides that the base amounts of depreciation caps for a passenger automobile are as follows—

... $10,000 for the year that a vehicle is placed in service,

... $16,000 for the second year in the recovery period,

... $9,600 for the third year in the recovery period,

... $5,760 for the fourth, fifth and sixth year in the recovery period, (Code Sec. 280F(a)(1)(A) as amended by Tax Cuts and Jobs Act §13202(a)(1))

... and $5,760 for any years after the recovery period (see background above). (Code Sec. 280F(a)(1)(B) as amended by Tax Cuts and Jobs Act §13202(a)(2)(A))

> *observation:* The above limits are more than three times higher than the ones in place under pre-Tax Cuts and Jobs Act law. For example, as discussed in the background above, for passenger automobiles placed in service in calendar year 2017, the placed-in-service year limit is $3,160. The higher limits, will more truly restrict the effect of the limits to "luxury" vehicles (in keeping with the Code's caption of the depreciation caps provision).

◆observation: For passenger automobiles built on a truck chassis ("qualifying trucks and vans"), IRS provides that a different CPI component is used, generally resulting in slightly higher limits. For example for qualifying trucks and vans placed in service in calendar year 2017, the placed-in-service year limit is $3,560, see FTC 2d/FIN ¶ L-10004.4; USTR ¶ 280F4. Presumably, IRS will continue the use of the different CPI component for qualifying trucks and vans in determining the automobile price inflation adjustments that are scheduled for vehicles placed in service *after calendar year 2018,* see below.

◆observation: For vehicles that are qualifying property for which bonus depreciation is allowed, $8,000 is added to the otherwise-applicable placed-in-service year limit, see ¶ 1208.

The Tax Cuts and Jobs Act provides that the automobile price inflation adjustment for a calendar year (see immediately below) of the base amounts discussed above applies to passenger automobiles placed in service after *2018* (instead of 1988, see background above). (Code Sec. 280F(d)(7))(A)(i) as amended by Tax Cuts and Jobs Act §13202(a)(2)(B)(i))

Also, the definition of the automobile price adjustment for any calendar year (see background above) is changed to mean the percentage if any by which (1) the *C-CPI-U* automobile component (see below) for Oct. of the preceding calendar year exceeds (2) (A) the automobile component of the CPI *as defined in Code Sec. 1(f)(4)* (see FTC 2d/FIN ¶ A-1103) (Code Sec. 280F(d)(7)(B)(i) as amended by Tax Cuts and Jobs Act §11002(d)(8)) for Oct. *2017* (instead of 1987, see background above) (Code Sec. 280F(d)(7))(B)(i)(II) as amended by Tax Cuts and Jobs Act §13202(a)(2)(B)(ii)) (B) multiplied by the amount determined under Code Sec. 1(f)(3)(B) (see ¶ 201). (Code Sec. 280F(d)(7)(B)(i) as amended by Tax Cuts and Jobs Act §11002(d)(8))

The C-CPI-U automobile component is the automobile component of the Chained Consumer Price Index for All Urban Consumers as described in Code Sec. 1(f)(6) (see ¶ 201). Code Sec. 280F(d)(7)(B)(ii) as amended by Tax Cuts and Jobs Act §11002(d)(8)

◆observation: The Tax Cuts and Jobs Act didn't change the rule that provides that the calculated increase is rounded to the nearest $100 (rounded upward if the calculated increase is exactly $50), see FTC 2d/FIN ¶ L-10004; USTR ¶ 280F4.

☐ **Effective:** Property that is placed in service after Dec. 31, 2017 in a tax year that ends after Dec. 31, 2017. (Tax Cuts and Jobs Act §13202(c))

¶ 1308. Treatment of computer equipment as listed property is ended

Code Sec. 280F(d)(4)(A), as amended by Tax Cuts and Jobs Act §13202(b)(1)(B)
Code Sec. 280F(d)(4), as amended by Tax Cuts and Jobs Act §13202(b)(2)
Generally effective: Property placed in service after Dec. 31, 2017
Committee Reports, see ¶ 5037

Because of their potential for personal use, Code Sec. 280F categorizes certain types of property as listed property and subjects listed property to reduced, or possibly reduced, tax benefits and heightened substantiation requirements, see FTC 2d/FIN ¶ L-10001 *et seq.*; USTR ¶ 280F4 *et seq.*

Under pre-Tax Cuts and Jobs Act law, subject to exceptions, listed property included (1) passenger automobiles, (2) other property used as a means of transportation, (3) property of a type generally used for purposes of entertainment, recreation, or amusement, (4) computer or peripheral equipment, and (5) any other property of a type specified in regs. (FTC 2d/FIN ¶ L-10002; USTR ¶ 280F4)

Computer or peripheral equipment that was used exclusively at a regular business establishment and owned or leased by the person operating the establishment (including a home office) wasn't listed property. (FTC 2d/FIN ¶ L-10002; USTR ¶ 280F4; Catalyst ¶ 402:280)

Reduced or possibly reduced tax benefits. An employee who owns or leases listed property that he uses in his employment isn't allowed any depreciation deduction, expensing allowance, or deduction for lease payments for that use unless it's for the convenience of the employer and required as a condition of employment, see FTC 2d/FIN ¶ L-10022; USTR ¶ 280F4.

Also, unless listed property is used more-than-50% for business as determined under a qualified business use test that is stricter than the test that generally applies to determine deductible business use, the property must be depreciated under the alternative depreciation system (ADS, which requires use of the straight-line method and possibly longer depreciation periods, FTC 2d/FIN ¶ L-9401 *et seq.*; USTR ¶ 1684.03), see FTC 2d/FIN ¶s L-10001, L-10024 *et seq.*; USTR ¶ 280F4. And recapture rules apply if the property becomes non-compliant, FTC 2d/FIN ¶ L-10032; USTR ¶ 280F4.

Taxpayers who lease listed property must annually include in income, during the lease term, amounts prescribed by IRS that implement the requirement in the Code that the lessee's deductions for rentals or other payments for listed property be reduced; the lessor of the property isn't subject to the listed property rules, see FTC 2d/FIN ¶ L-10200 *et seq.*; USTR ¶ 280F4.01.

Also, independent of their status as listed property, Code Sec. 280F imposes on passenger automobiles annual limits (caps) on depreciation deductions, see FTC 2d/FIN ¶ L-10004 *et seq.*; USTR ¶ 280F4.

Substantiation requirements. Under Code Sec. 274(d) and regs issued under that section, no deduction or credit is allowed for an item of listed property unless the taxpayer substantiates, by adequate records or by the taxpayer's own statement supported by sufficient corroborating evidence, the following elements for the item: the amount of each separate expenditure for the item (e.g., the cost of buying it), the amount of each business or investment use of the item based on the appropriate measure (e.g., time), the total use of the item for the tax period, the date of each expenditure for or use of the item, and the business purpose for each expenditure for or use of the item, see FTC 2d/FIN ¶ L-4644; USTR ¶ 2744.10.

New Law. The Tax Cuts and Jobs Act ends the inclusion of computer and peripheral equipment as a type of property included in the definition of listed property. (Code Sec. 280F(d)(4)(A) as amended by Tax Cuts and Jobs Act §13202(b)(1)(B))

Computers and peripheral equipment are therefore no longer subject to the heightened substantiation requirements that apply to listed property (see background above). (Com Rept, see ¶ 5037)

> *observation:* Additionally, computers and peripheral equipment are no longer subject to the rules for listed property that limit, or may limit, tax benefits, see background above.

Conforming change. The exception (see background above) from listed property status for computer or peripheral equipment used exclusively at a regular business establishment and owned or leased by the person operating the establishment (including a home office) is removed. (Code Sec. 280F(d)(4) as amended by Tax Cuts and Jobs Act §13202(b)(2))

Redesignation. Because of the removal of former Code Sec. 280F(d)(4)(B) (which provided the exception from listed property status discussed immediately above), former Code Sec. 280F(d)(4)(C) (an exception concerning transportation property that is for hire, see FTC 2d/FIN ¶ L-10002; USTR ¶ 280F4) is redesignated as Code Sec. 280F(d)(4)(B). (Code Sec. 280F(d)(4)(B) as amended by Tax Cuts and Jobs Act §13202(b)(1)(C))

For the Tax Cuts and Jobs Act's raising of Code Sec. 280F's depreciation limits imposed on passenger automobiles, see ¶ 1307.

☐ **Effective:** Property that is placed in service after Dec. 31, 2017 in a tax year that ends after Dec. 31, 2017. (Tax Cuts and Jobs Act §13202(c))

Public Utility Property

¶ 1309. Normalization requirements for public utilities

Code Sec. None, as amended by Tax Cuts and Jobs Act §13001(d)
Generally effective: Tax years beginning after Dec. 31, 2017.
Committee Reports, see ¶ 5032

As described at ¶ 102, the Tax Cuts and Jobs Act reduced the corporate tax rate to a flat 21% rate. Public utilities are required, as a condition of using MACRS to use normalization accounting under which depreciation for ratemaking purposes doesn't reflect the accelerated depreciation under MACRS. (FTC 2d/FIN ¶ L-9300, ¶ L-9301; USTR ¶ 1684.01)

New Law. The Tax Cuts and Jobs Act provides that public utilities subject to the normalization method of accounting are not treated as applying the normalization method for any public utility property for purposes of Code Sec. 167 or Code Sec. 168 if they reduce their excess tax reserves resulting from the lower tax rate (see below) in computing their cost of service for ratemaking purposes and for purposes of reflecting operating results in their regulated books of account, more rapidly or to a greater extent than the amount the reserve would be reduced under the average rate assumption method. (Tax Cuts and Jobs Act §13001(d)(1))

For this purpose, the excess tax reserve is the reserve for deferred taxes described in Code Sec. 168(i)(9)(A)(ii) (see FTC 2d ¶ L-9304; USTR ¶ 1684.01) as in effect on the day before the rate reductions described at ¶ 102 take effect (Tax Cuts and Jobs Act §13001(d)(3)(A)(i)), minus the amount that would be the balance in the reserve if the amount of the reserve were determined by assuming that the Tax Cuts and Jobs Act corporate rate reductions were in effect for all prior periods. (Tax Cuts and Jobs Act §13001(d)(3)(A)(ii))

The average rate assumption method is the method under which the excess in the reserve for deferred taxes is reduced over the remaining lives of the property as used in its regulated books of account which gave rise to the reserve for deferred taxes. Under this method, if timing differences for the property reverse, the amount of the adjustment to the reserve for the deferred taxes is calculated by multiplying (1) the ratio of the aggregate deferred taxes for the property to the aggregate timing differences for the property as of the beginning of the period in question (Tax Cuts and Jobs Act §13001(d)(3)(B)(i)) by (2) the amount of the timing differences that reverse during the period. (Tax Cuts and Jobs Act §13001(d)(3)(B)(ii))

The reversal of timing differences generally occurs when the amount of the tax depreciation taken on the asset is less than the amount of the regulatory depreciation taken on the asset. To ensure that the deferred tax reserve, including the excess tax reserve, is reduced to zero at the end of the regulatory life of the asset that generated the reserve, the amount of the timing difference which reverses during a tax year is multiplied by the ratio of (1) the aggregate deferred taxes as of the beginning of the period in question to (2) the aggregate timing differences for the property as of the beginning of the period in question. (Com Rept, see ¶ 5032)

Illustration: A calendar year regulated utility placed property costing $100 million in service in 2016. For regulatory (book) purposes, the property is depreciated over 10 years on a straight line basis with a full year's allowance in the first year. For tax purposes, the property is depreciated over 5 years using the 200% declining balance method and a half-year placed in service convention.

Normalization calculation for corporate rate reduction
(Millions of dollars)
Year(s)

	2016	2017	2018	2019	2020	2021
Tax expense	20	32	19.2	11.52	11.52	5.76
Book depreciation	10	10	10	10	10	10
Timing difference	10	22	9.2	1.52	1.52	(4.24)
Tax rate	35%	35%	21%	21%	21%	31.1%
Annual adjustment to reserve	3.5	7.7	1.9	0.3	0.3	(1.3)
Cumulative deferred tax reserve	3.5	11.2	13.1	13.5	13.8	12.5
Annual adjustment at 21%						(0.9)
Annual adjustment at average rate						(1.3)
Excess tax reserve						0.4

Normalization calculation for corporate rate reduction
(Millions of dollars)
Year(s)

	2022	2023	2024	2025	Total
Tax expense	0	0	0	0	100
Book depreciation	10	10	10	10	100
Timing difference	(10)	(10)	(10)	(10)	0
Tax rate	31.1%	31.1%	31.1%	31.1%	
Annual adjustment to reserve	(3.1)	(3.1)	(3.1)	(3.1)	0
Cumulative deferred tax reserve	9.3	6.2	3.1	(0.0)	0
Annual adjustment at 21%	(2.1)	(2.1)	(2.1)	(2.1)	(9.3)
Annual adjustment at average rate	(3.1)	(3.1)	(3.1)	(3.1)	(13.8)
Excess tax reserve	1.0	1.0	1.0	1.0	4.5

The excess tax reserve as of Dec. 31, 2017, the day before the corporate rate reduction takes effect, is $4.5 million. The taxpayer will begin taking the excess tax reserve into account in the 2021 tax year, which is the first year in which the tax depreciation taken with respect to the property is less than the depreciation reflected in the regulated books of account. The annual adjustment to the deferred tax reserve for the 2021 through 2025 tax years is multiplied by 31.1% which is the ratio of the aggregate deferred taxes as of the beginning of 2021 ($13.8 million) to the aggregate timing differences for the property as of the beginning of 2021 ($44.2 million). (Com Rept, see ¶ 5032)

However, if, as of the first day of the tax year that includes Dec. 22, 2017, the taxpayer was required by a regulatory agency to compute depreciation for public utility property on the basis of an average life or composite rate method (Tax Cuts and Jobs Act §13001(d)(2)(A)), and the taxpayer's books and underlying records did not contain the vintage account data necessary to apply the average rate assumption method (Tax Cuts and Jobs Act §13001(d)(2)(B)), the taxpayer will be treated as using a normalization method of accounting if, with respect to the jurisdiction, the taxpayer uses the alternative method for public utility property that is subject to the regulatory authority of that jurisdiction.

The alternative method is the method in which the taxpayer computes the excess tax reserve on all public utility property included in the plant account on the basis of the weighted average life or composite rate used to compute depreciation for regulatory purposes (Tax Cuts and Jobs Act §13001(d)(3)(C)(i)), and reduces the excess tax reserve ratably over the remaining regulatory life of the property. (Tax Cuts and Jobs Act §13001(d)(3)(C)(ii))

If, for any tax year ending after Dec. 22, 2017, the taxpayer does not use a normalization method of accounting, the taxpayer's tax for the tax year is increased by the amount by which it reduces its excess tax reserve more rapidly than permitted under a normalization method of accounting (Tax Cuts and Jobs Act §13001(d)(4)(A)) and the taxpayer would not be treated as using a normalization method for purposes of the MACRS rules. (Tax Cuts and Jobs Act §13001(d)(4)(B))

☐ **Effective:** Tax years beginning after Dec. 31, 2017. (Com Rept, see ¶ 5032)

¶ 1400. Tax Accounting

¶ 1401. Gross receipts limit for cash-method use by C corporations (and certain partnerships) raised to $25 million, related rules changed

Code Sec. 448(b)(3), as amended by Tax Cuts and Jobs Act §13102(a)(2)
Code Sec. 448(c)(1), as amended by Tax Cuts and Jobs Act §13102(a)(1)
Code Sec. 448(c)(4), as amended by Tax Cuts and Jobs Act §13102(a)(3)
Code Sec. 448(d)(7), as amended by Tax Cuts and Jobs Act §13102(a)(4)
Generally effective: Tax years beginning after Dec. 31, 2017
Committee Reports, see ¶ 5035

There are several limits on the use of the cash method of accounting. (Com Rept, see ¶ 5035)

One limit is the rule that generally requires taxpayers to account for purchases and sales using the accrual method if the taxpayer must use an inventory method with respect to those purchases and sales, see FTC 2d/FIN ¶ G-2089; USTR ¶ 4464.07. However under pre-Tax Cuts and Jobs Act law, IRS guidance provided some exceptions to the requirement, see FTC 2d/FIN ¶s G-2089.1, G-5005.1, G-5005.4. For provisions in the Tax Cuts and Jobs Act concerning exemption from inventory use, see ¶ 1403. However under pre-Tax Cuts and Jobs Act law, taxpayers that satisfied a no-more-than-$1-million-in-gross-receipts test (and that weren't tax shelters) could choose to not use both the inventory method and the accrual method (though otherwise applicable), see FTC 2d/FIN ¶s G-2089.1, G-5005.1. And *certain* taxpayers that satisfied a no-more-than-$10-million-in-gross-receipts test could chose not to use either or both of the inventory method and the accrual method (though otherwise applicable), see FTC 2d/FIN ¶ G-5005.4. (For provisions in the Tax Cuts and Jobs Act concerning these rules, see ¶ 1403).

Code Sec. 448 provides other limits on the use of the cash method, see FTC 2d/FIN ¶ G-2054; USTR ¶ 4484.

Specifically, under Code Sec. 448 tax shelters aren't allowed to use the cash method, see FTC 2d/FIN ¶s G-2054, G-2056; USTR ¶ 4484.

FTC 2d References are to Federal Tax Coordinator 2d
FIN References are to RIA's Analysis of Federal Taxes: Income (print)
USTR References are to United States Tax Reporter
Catalyst References are to Checkpoint Catalyst
PCA References are to Pension Analysis (print and electronic)
PBE References are to Pension & Benefits Explanations
BCA References are to Benefits Analysis (electronic)
BC References are to Benefits Coordinator (print)
EP References are to Estate Planning Analysis (print and electronic)

And subject to exceptions (below) neither are C corporations and partnerships with a C corporation as a partner (the Code Sec. 448 C corporation restriction), see FTC 2d/FIN ¶ G-2054; USTR ¶ 4484. For purposes of this rule, both tax-exempt corporations and tax-exempt trusts are treated as C corporations with respect to their unrelated business taxable income, see FTC 2d/FIN ¶ G-2055; USTR ¶ 4484.

Excepted from the Code Sec. 448 C corporation restriction are (1) entities that engage in certain services and meet the other requirements for status as personal service corporations and (2) farming businesses, see FTC 2d/FIN ¶s G-2054, G-2057 *et seq.*; USTR ¶ 4484. But for the separate rule that under Code Sec. 447, requires C corporations (or partnerships with a C corporation as a partner) that have a farming business to use the accrual method, see ¶ 1402.

Under pre-Tax Cuts and Jobs Act law, the Code Sec. 448 C corporation restriction didn't apply for a tax year if, for *all prior* tax years beginning after Dec. 31, '85, the corporation or partnership (or a predecessor) met the following test (the gross receipts test): the average annual gross receipts of the entity for the three-tax-year period ending with the earlier tax year did not exceed $5,000,000 (unadjusted for inflation). (FTC 2d/FIN ¶ G-2050, ¶ G-2069; USTR ¶ 4484; Catalyst ¶ 753:110; Catalyst ¶ 754:102; Catalyst ¶ 754:130; Catalyst ¶ 755:103) In applying the test, gross receipts were aggregated among certain related taxpayers, and there were rules addressing short-tax years, certain receipts excluded from gross receipts, and taxpayers not in existence for the entire three-tax-year period, see FTC 2d/FIN ¶s G-2069, G-2070, G-2071; USTR ¶ 4484.

Under pre-Tax Cuts and Jobs Act law, Code Sec. 448 provided, for a change from the cash method required because of Code Sec. 448, that (1) the change is treated as initiated by the taxpayer, (2) the change is treated as made with IRS consent and (3) any required Code Sec. 481 adjustment is required to be taken into account over a period not to exceed four years (10 years in the case of a hospital). (FTC 2d/FIN ¶ G-2050, ¶ G-2073, ¶ G-2078; USTR ¶ 4484)

New Law. The Tax Cuts and Jobs Act expands the universe of taxpayers that can use the cash method of accounting. (Com Rept, see ¶ 5035)

> *observation:* Provisions in the Tax Cuts and Jobs Act that widen the availability of the cash method are (1) the provisions of Code Sec. 448 discussed below for C corporations (and partnerships with C corporations as partners), (2) the provisions of Code Sec. 447 specific to the farming businesses of C corporations (and partnerships with a C corporation as a partner), see background above and ¶ 1402, and (3) indirectly, the provisions concerning use of the inventory method, see background above and ¶ 1403.

Prior-year compliance not required. The Tax Cuts and Jobs Act amends Code Sec. 448(b)(3) to require that a C corporation (or partnership with a C corporation as a partner), or any predecessor, meet the gross receipts test *for the tax year* (rather than all prior tax years beginning after Dec. 31, '85, see the observation below) (Code Sec. 448(b)(3) as amended by Tax Cuts and Jobs Act §13102(a)(2)) and amends Code Sec. 448(c)(1), which provides the gross receipts test (see below), to refer to the tax year (rather than any prior tax year, see background above). (Code Sec. 448(c)(1) as amended by Tax Cuts and Jobs Act §13102(a)(1))

> *observation:* Thus, the gross receipts test must be satisfied, by meeting the three-prior-year-averaging-test discussed below, only for the tax year for which the taxpayer seeks to use the cash method and not, as under pre-Tax Cuts and Jobs Act law, for all earlier tax years that begin after 1985, see background above.

Three-year testing period moved. Under the Tax Cuts and Jobs Act, the gross-receipts test is satisfied for the tax year if the average annual gross receipts are under the prescribed dollar limit (dollar limit) for the three tax-year period ending with the tax year that *precedes* the tax year for which the taxpayer is being tested. (Code Sec. 448(c)(1))

> *observation:* The three year testing period ends with the tax year *before* the tax year for which the taxpayer is being tested and not, as under pre-Tax Cuts and Jobs Act law, with the tax year for which the taxpayer is being tested, see background above.

Dollar limit raised. The gross-receipts test is satisfied if, during the three-year testing period (above), average annual gross receipts doesn't exceed $25 million (Code Sec. 448(c)(1)), subject to adjustment for inflation for tax years beginning after Dec. 31, 2018 (see **Inflation adjustment** below). (Code Sec. 448(c)(4) as amended by Tax Cuts and Jobs Act §13102(a)(3))

> *observation:* Under pre-Tax Cuts and Jobs Act law, the dollar limit was $5 million and wasn't adjusted for inflation, see background above.

> *illustration:* T Corporation (T) is strictly a service provider (and isn't a tax shelter, see background above). But T, being neither a personal services corporation nor a farming business, doesn't qualify for the exemptions from Code Sec. 448 that apply to those categories (see background above).

However, even after taking into account aggregation rules (see background above), T has gross receipts of only $20 million in 2015, $25 million in Year 2016 and $30 million in 2017. Thus, because T's average gross receipts, for 2015, 2016 and 2017 don't exceed $25 million, Code Sec. 448 doesn't bar T's use of the cash method in 2018.

observation: Had T been in a farming business instead of being a service provider, T would have also been exempt from Code Sec. 447's required use of the accrual method by corporations (and partnerships to which they belong) that own a farming business, see background above and ¶ 1402.

Also, had T been, for example, a retailer instead of being a service provider, T, by satisfying one of two alternative conditions, would have been exempt from the inventory requirement (which, in turn, requires use of the accrual method), see background above and ¶ 1403.

Inflation adjustment. Under the inflation adjustment for tax years beginning after Dec. 31, 2018, the $25 million amount is increased by an amount equal to (Code Sec. 448(c)(4)) $25 million multiplied by (Code Sec. 448(c)(4)(A)) the cost-of-living adjustment (COLA) determined under Code Sec. 1(f)(3) for the calendar year in which the tax year begins by substituting "calendar year 2017" for "calendar year 2016" in Code Sec. 1(f)(3)(A)(ii) (see ¶ 201 for how a Code Sec. 1(f)(3) COLA is determined without the substitution of "calendar year 2017" for "calendar year 2016"). (Code Sec. 448(c)(4)(B))

If the increase amount isn't a multiple of $1,000,000 the amount is rounded to the nearest multiple of $1,000,000. (Code Sec. 448(c)(4))

Accounting method changes. The Tax Cuts and Jobs Act amends Code Sec. 448(d)(7) by providing that the accounting method change rules in Code Sec. 448(d)(7) apply to *any* change made under Code Sec. 448. (Code Sec. 448(d)(7) as amended by Tax Cuts and Jobs Act §13102(a)(4))

The Tax Cuts and Jobs Act also removes the Code Sec. 481(a) adjustment rules that were provided by Code Sec. 448(d)(7) under pre-Tax Cuts and Jobs Act law for changes to which the accounting method change rules in Code Sec. 448(d)(7) apply. (Code Sec. 448(d)(7))

observation: Thus, under Code Sec. 448(d)(7) as amended by the Tax Cuts and Jobs Act:

... accounting method changes covered by the rules in Code Sec. 448(d)(7) include both changes made because a taxpayer is prohibited *or no longer prohibited* by Code Sec. 448 from using the cash method, see background above.

... accounting method changes to which Code Sec. 448(d)(7) applies continue to be treated as initiated by the taxpayer, see background above; note that this rule relates merely to Code Sec. 481(a)(2), which is in substance a transitional rule concerning the enactment of the '54

Code and thus affects continually fewer taxpayers, see FTC 2d/FIN ¶s G-2073, G-2299; USTR ¶s 4484, 4814.

... accounting method changes to which Code Sec. 448(d)(7) applies continue to be treated as made with IRS consent, see background above; note that, as was true under pre-Tax Cuts and Jobs Act law, IRS will almost certainly nevertheless require that the taxpayer follow consent procedures to make the accounting method changes, see FTC 2d/FIN ¶s G-2073 *et seq.*, G-2205; USTR ¶ 4484.

... because Code Sec. 448(d)(7) no longer provides Code Sec. 481(a) adjustment rules specific to accounting method changes covered by Code Sec. 448(d)(7), general rules for Code Sec. 481(a) adjustments apply. The only significant effect of this is that the 10-year period over which hospitals are to take into account adjustments no longer applies, see background discussion above. The end of the hospitals rule is the only significant effect because the-up-to-4-year rule that applied under pre-Tax Cuts and Jobs Act law to other covered changes, see background above, was implemented by IRS regs that provided that the changes were subject to the general accounting method changes rules. And those general rules in most cases provide a four-year adjustment period for required adjustments that increase taxable income (positive adjustments) and a one year period for required adjustments that decrease taxable income (negative adjustments), see FTC 2d/FIN ¶s G-2074, G-2185, G-2205.

☐ **Effective:** Tax years beginning after Dec. 31, 2017. (Tax Cuts and Jobs Act §13102(e)(1))

¶ 1402. Gross receipts limits for cash-method use by farming C corporations (and certain partnerships) are raised to a uniform $25 million and some related rules are changed

Code Sec. 447(c), as amended by Tax Cuts and Jobs Act §13102(a)(5)(C)
Code Sec. 447(c), as amended by Tax Cuts and Jobs Act §13102(a)(5)(A)(i)
Code Sec. 447(c)(2), as amended by Tax Cuts and Jobs Act §13102(a)(5)(A)(ii)
Code Sec. 447(d), as amended by Tax Cuts and Jobs Act §13102(a)(5)(B)
Generally effective: Tax years beginning after Dec. 31, 2017
Committee Reports, see ¶ 5035

There are several limits on the use of the cash method of accounting. (Com Rept, see ¶ 5035)

One limit is the rule that generally requires taxpayers to account for purchases and sales using the accrual method if the taxpayer must use an inventory method with respect to those purchases and sales, see FTC 2d/FIN ¶ G-2089; USTR ¶ 4464.07. However under pre-Tax Cuts and Jobs Act law, IRS guidance provided some exceptions to the requirement, see FTC 2d/FIN ¶s G-2089.1, G-5005.1, G-5005.4. For provisions in the Tax Cuts and Jobs Act concerning exemption from inventory use, see ¶ 1403.

Code Sec. 448 provides other limits on the use of the cash method, see below. (For provisions in the Tax Cuts and Jobs Act concerning these rules, see ¶ 1401.)

Specifically, under Code Sec. 448 tax shelters aren't allowed to use the cash method, see FTC 2d/FIN ¶s G-2054, G-2056; USTR ¶ 4484.

And, subject to exceptions, neither are C corporations and partnerships with a C corporation as a partner (the Code Sec. 448 C corporation restriction), see FTC 2d/FIN ¶ G-2054; USTR ¶ 4484. For purposes of this rule both tax-exempt corporations and tax-exempt trusts are treated as C corporations with respect to their unrelated business taxable income, see FTC 2d/FIN ¶ G-2055; USTR ¶ 4484.

One of the exceptions from the Code Sec. 448 C corporation restriction is for farming businesses, see FTC 2d/FIN ¶ G-2057; USTR ¶ 4484.

However, Code Sec. 447 requires farming businesses owned by corporations other than S corporations (or partnerships with such a non-S corporation as a partner) to use the accrual method to account for the income from that business (the Code Sec. 447 C corporation restriction), see FTC 2d/FIN ¶ N-1036 et seq.; USTR ¶ 4474.

The Code Sec. 447 C corporation restriction doesn't apply to the business of operating a nursery or sod farm or of raising or harvesting trees (other than fruit or nut trees), FTC 2d/FIN ¶ N-1036 et seq.; USTR ¶ 4474.

And, under pre-Tax Cuts and Jobs Act law, there were two other exceptions to the Code Sec. 447 C corporation restriction.

Under one of the exceptions, the Code Sec. 447 C corporation restriction didn't apply for a tax year if for *each prior* tax year beginning *after Dec. 31, '75* the gross receipts of the corporation (or any predecessor) didn't exceed $1 million (unadjusted for inflation). In applying the test, all corporations that were members of the same consolidated group under Code Sec. 1563(a) were treated as one corporation (the $1 million aggregation rule). (FTC 2d/FIN ¶ N-1010, ¶ N-1036; USTR ¶ 4474)

Under the other exception, the Code Sec. 447 C corporation restriction didn't apply for a tax year if for *each prior* tax year beginning *after Dec. 31, '85* (1) the corporation (or a predecessor) was a family corporation and (2) its gross receipts didn't exceed $25 million (unadjusted for inflation). (FTC 2d/FIN

¶ N-1010, ¶ N-1040 *et seq.*; USTR ¶ 4474; Catalyst ¶ 754:130) And, under Code Sec. 447(d)(2)(B), (1) an aggregation rule different than the $1 million aggregation rule (above) applied, see FTC 2d/FIN ¶ N-1043; USTR ¶ 4474, and (2) there were attribution rules for the amount of a pass-thru entity's gross receipts to be taken into account if the corporation held an interest in the pass-through entity, see FTC 2d/FIN ¶ N-1044; USTR ¶ 4474. Family corporations were generally corporations controlled by one family, but certain corporations controlled by two or three families qualified under "grandfather" rules, see FTC 2d/FIN ¶s N-1040, N-1041; USTR ¶ 4474.

Under pre-Tax Cuts and Jobs Act law, Code Sec. 447 provided, for a taxpayer required to change to the accrual method because of Code Sec. 447, (1) that the change was treated as made with IRS consent, and (2) that under regs, the net amount of any required Code Sec. 481 adjustments was to be taken into account over the 10 years beginning with the year of change (or less than 10 years if there was a stated future life (of the entity) of less than 10 years). Also, for purposes of Code Sec. 481(a)(2), the change was treated as not initiated by the taxpayer (meaning that a taxpayer didn't take pre-'54 Code items into account in determining the amount of Code Sec. 481 adjustments, see FTC 2d/ FIN ¶ G-2299; USTR ¶ 4814). (FTC 2d/FIN ¶ N-1010, ¶ N-1039; USTR ¶ 4474)

New Law. The Tax Cuts and Jobs Act expands the universe of farming C corporations (and farming partnerships with a C corporation partner that can use the cash method. (Com Rept, see ¶ 5035)

> **RIA** *observation:* In addition to the provisions of Code Sec. 447 discussed below specific to the farming businesses of C corporations (and partnerships with a C corporation as a partner), provisions in the Tax Cuts and Jobs Act that widen the availability of the cash method are (1) the provisions of Code Sec. 448 that more generally apply to C corporations (and partnerships with C corporations as partners), see background above and ¶ 1401, and (2) indirectly, the provisions concerning use of the inventory method, see background above and ¶ 1403.

Under the Tax Cuts and Jobs Act, a corporation that meets the gross-receipts test of Code Sec. 448(c) isn't for the tax year treated as a corporation for purposes of Code Sec. 447(a) (the rule that requires that a corporation that has a farming business or is a partner in a partnership that has a farming business must use the accrual, method, see background above). (Code Sec. 447(c) as amended by Tax Cuts and Jobs Act §13102(a)(5)(A)(i); Code Sec. 447(c)(2) as amended by Tax Cuts and Jobs Act §13102(a)(5)(A)(ii)) And the Tax Cuts and Jobs Act removes Code Sec. 447(d), which included Code Sec. 447(d)(1) and Code Sec. 447(d)(2)—the provisions that under pre-Tax Cuts and Jobs Acts law provided the gross receipts test that applied instead of Code Sec. 448(c) to make corporations exempt from the application of Code Sec. 447(a). (Code Sec. 447 as amended by Tax Cuts and Jobs Act §13102(a)(5)(C)(i))

❡ observation: For C corporations that *aren't* family corporations, see background above, the above changes, by referencing Code Sec. 448(c), (1) raise the gross-receipts test dollar limit from $1 million to $25 million, (2) adjust the $25 million dollar limit for inflation and (3) change the gross-receipts test from a snapshot of gross-receipts solely for the year for which the cash method is to be used (the cash-method year) to a three-year averaging test ending with the year before the cash-method year, see background above and ¶ 1401. And other rules in Code Sec. 448(c) apply to the taxpayer—i.e., aggregation rules (adding gross receipts of certain related taxpayers to the taxpayer's), rules addressing short-tax years, rules allowing certain receipts to not be taken into account, and rules for taxpayers not in existence for the entire three-year averaging period, see FTC 2d/FIN ¶s G-2069, G-2070, G-2071; USTR ¶ 4484.

Also, under Code Sec. 447(c) (above), the gross receipts test must be satisfied only for the tax year for which the taxpayer seeks to use the cash method and not, as under pre-Tax Cuts and Jobs Act law, for all earlier tax years that begin after 1975, see background above.

❡ illustration (1): T Corporation (T) is engaged in farming and isn't a family corporation. After taking into account aggregation rules (see the observation above), T has gross receipts of only $20 million in 2015, $25 million in Year 2016 and $30 million in 2017. Thus, because T's average gross receipts, for 2015, 2016 and 2017 don't exceed $15 million, Code Sec. 447 doesn't require T's use of the accrual method in 2018.

❡ observation: For C corporations that *are* family corporations, see background above, the Tax Cuts and Jobs Act (1) adjusts the $25 million dollar limit for inflation for tax years ending after Dec. 31, 2018 (but doesn't raise it) and (2) changes the gross-receipts test from a snapshot of gross-receipts solely for the year for which the cash method is to be used (the cash-method year) to a three-year averaging test ending with the year before the cash-method year, see background above and ¶ 1401. And other rules in Code Sec. 448(c) apply to the taxpayer—i.e., aggregation rules (adding gross receipts of certain related taxpayers to the taxpayer's), rules addressing short-tax years, rules allowing certain receipts to not be taken into account, and rules for taxpayers not in existence for the entire three-year averaging period, see FTC 2d/FIN ¶s G-2069, G-2070, G-2071; USTR ¶ 4484.

Also, under Code Sec. 447(c) (above), the gross receipts test must be satisfied only for the tax year for which the taxpayer seeks to use the cash method and not, as under pre-Tax Cuts and Jobs Act law, for all earlier tax years that begin after 1985, see background above.

illustration (2): F Corporation (F) is engaged in farming and is a family corporation. After taking into account aggregation rules (see the observation above), F has gross receipts of only $20 million in 2015, $25 million in Year 2016 and $30 million in 2017. Thus, because F's average gross receipts, for 2015, 2016 and 2017 don't exceed $25 million, Code Sec. 447 doesn't require F's use of the accrual method in 2018.

observation: The use of an inventory method is optional for farmers, see Code Sec. 1.471-6. Thus, a farmer that doesn't use an inventory method (1) won't be subject to the rules that, subject to exceptions, require using an accrual method to account for purchases and sales if the taxpayer uses an inventory method with respect to those purchases and sales. Moreover, even if T or F in illustrations (1) and (2) had been using an inventory method, T or F, by satisfying the $25 million test and one of two additional conditions, could change from the inventory method (and, hence, the accrual method) under the exemption from the inventory method provided by the Tax Cuts and Jobs Act, see¶ 1403.

Accounting method changes. The Tax Cuts and Jobs Act replaces the pre-Tax Cuts and Jobs Act accounting method change rules in Code Sec. 447 (see background above) with a rule that states that any change made under Code Sec. 447 is treated for purposes of Code Sec. 481(a) as initiated by the taxpayer and made with IRS consent. (Code Sec. 447(d) as amended by Tax Cuts and Jobs Act §13102(a)(5)(B))

observation: One effect of the above change is that the rules in Code Sec. 447 concerning accounting method changes apply not just to taxpayers changing to the accrual method as required by Code Sec. 447 but also to taxpayers changing from the accrual method because they are no longer required to use it under Code Sec. 447.

Another effect is that the rule that provides an up-to-10-year period to take Code Sec. 481(a) adjustments into account, see background above, was removed, with the result that the general rules for the period for taking Code Sec. 481(a) adjustments into account apply. Usually, under the general rules the adjustments are taken into account in the year of change for adjustments that decrease taxable income (negative adjustments) and over a 4-year period beginning with the year of change for adjustments that increase taxable income (positive adjustments), see FTC 2d/FIN ¶ G-2185 *et seq.*

Also, the changes to which the accounting method change rules in Code Sec. 447 apply are treated as made with IRS consent rather than without IRS consent. This means that a few long-existing taxpayers must take pre-'54 Code items, if any, into account in determining the amount of Code Sec. 481 adjustments, see background above.

Provisions removed. As discussed above the Tax Cuts and Jobs Act removed Code Sec. 447(d)(1) and Code Sec. 447(d)(2)—provisions that under pre-Tax Cuts and Jobs Acts law provided the gross-receipts test that exempted corporations from the application of Code Sec. 447(a). Additionally, the Tax Cuts and Jobs Act removes the other provisions in Code Sec. 447(d) and all of Code Sec. 447(e), Code Sec. 447(h) and Code Sec. 447(i). (Code Sec. 447 as amended by Tax Cuts and Jobs Act §13102(a)(5)(C)(i))

> **🅡🅐 *observation:*** The other provisions in former 447(d) and all of the provisions in Code Sec. 447(e), Code Sec. 447(h) and Code Sec. 447(i) were removed because their only subject was the treatment of family corporations, a category that, as discussed above, is no longer treated differently than other corporations under Code Sec. 447.

Provisions redesignated. Because of the removal of provisions, former Code Sec. 447(f) is redesignated as Code Sec. 447(d) (the accounting method change rules discussed above), and former Code Sec. 447(g) is redesignated as Code Sec. 447(e) (concerning certain accounting methods grandfathered as permissible notwithstanding other rules in Code Sec. 447, see FTC 2d/FIN ¶ N-1049 *et seq.*; USTR ¶ 4474). Code Sec. 447 as amended by Tax Cuts and Jobs Act §13102(a)(5)(C)(ii)

☐ **Effective:** Tax years beginning after Dec. 31, 2017. (Tax Cuts and Jobs Act §13102(e)(1))

The removal of former Code Sec. 447(i) (see **Provisions removed** above) won't apply for any suspense account established under former Code Sec. 447(i) before Dec. 22, 2017, see FTC 2d/FIN ¶ N-1045 *et seq.*; USTR ¶ 4474.01. (Tax Cuts and Jobs Act §13102(e)(2))

¶ 1403. Alternatives to inventory accounting are made available to most small businesses meeting a $25 million gross receipts test

Code Sec. 471(c), as amended by Tax Cuts and Jobs Act §13102(c)
Generally effective: Tax years beginning after Dec. 31, 2017
Committee Reports, see ¶ 5035

If IRS determines that the use of inventories is necessary in order to clearly determine the income of any taxpayer, the taxpayer must use an inventory method. FTC 2d/FIN ¶ G-5001; USTR ¶ 4714. In any case where the use of an inventory method is necessary to clearly reflect income, the taxpayer must use the accrual method of accounting with regard to purchases and sales. FTC 2d/FIN ¶ G-2089 et seq.; USTR ¶ 4464 et seq.

Under pre-Tax Cuts and Jobs Act law, there were a number of exceptions under which taxpayers that would otherwise be required to account for inventories under Code Sec. 471 and, thus, would have been required to use the accrual method under Code Sec. 446, could instead treat merchandise as materials and supplies deductible as expenses in the year they were consumed and used. One exception was provided for taxpayers whose average annual gross receipts didn't exceed $1 million. A second exception was provided for taxpayers in certain industries whose average annual gross receipts didn't exceed $10 million and who weren't otherwise prohibited from using the cash method under Code Sec. 448. (FTC 2d/FIN ¶ G-5000, ¶ G-5005A et seq., ¶ G-2050, ¶ G-2089.1; USTR ¶ 4464.07, ¶ 4714.15)

New Law. The Tax Cuts and Jobs Act exempts certain taxpayers from the requirement to keep inventories (Com Rept, see ¶ 5035) by providing that if a taxpayer (other than a tax shelter prohibited from using the cash receipts and disbursements method of accounting under Code Sec. 448(a)(3)) meets the gross receipts test of Code Sec. 448(c) for any tax year (Code Sec. 471(c)(1) as amended by Tax Cuts and Jobs Act §13102(c)), Code Sec. 471(a) doesn't apply to that taxpayer for that tax year. (Code Sec. 471(c)(1)(A))

> *observation:* Code Sec. 448(c), as amended by the Tax Cuts and Jobs Act, provides that corporations and partnerships with a corporate partner are permitted to use the cash method only if they have average annual gross receipts of $25 million or less during the preceding three years, see ¶ 1401.

In addition, the taxpayer's method of accounting for inventory for that tax year won't be treated as failing to clearly reflect income if the method—(Code Sec. 471(c)(1)(B))

(1) treats inventory as non-incidental materials and supplies, or (Code Sec. 471(c)(1)(B)(i))

(2) conforms to the taxpayer's method of accounting reflected in an "applicable financial statement" (i.e., an AFS, defined below) of the taxpayer for that tax year or, if the taxpayer doesn't have any AFSs for the tax year, the taxpayer's books and records prepared in accordance with the taxpayer's accounting procedures. (Code Sec. 471(c)(1)(B)(ii))

In other words, taxpayers that meet the $25 million gross receipts test aren't required to account for inventories under Code Sec. 471, but rather may use a method of accounting for inventories that either (1) treats inventories as non-incidental materials and supplies, or (2) conforms to the taxpayer's financial accounting treatment of inventories. (Com Rept, see ¶ 5035)

For any taxpayer that isn't a corporation or a partnership, the gross receipts test of Code Sec. 448(c) must be applied in the same manner as if each trade or business of that taxpayer was a corporation or partnership. (Code Sec. 471(c)(3))

Applicable financial statement. The term "applicable financial statement" has the meaning of that term in Code Sec. 451(b)(3), see ¶ 1406. (Code Sec. 471(c)(2))

Accounting method changes. Any change in method of accounting made under Code Sec. 471(c) will be treated for purposes of Code Sec. 481 as initiated by the taxpayer and made with IRS's consent. (Code Sec. 471(c)(4))

> *observation:* The designation of an accounting method as "initiated by the taxpayer" relates to Code Sec. 481(a)(2) which states what is in substance a transitional rule, of significance to increasingly few taxpayers today, concerning the enactment of the 1954 Code, see FTC 2d/FIN ¶ G-2299; USTR ¶ 4814.

> *observation:* Where legislation designates an accounting method change as made with IRS's consent, IRS can nevertheless require, as part of its administration of accounting method rules, that the taxpayer follow consent procedures to make the change, see FTC 2d/FIN ¶ G-2202.2.

Redesignation. The Tax Cuts and Jobs Act redesignates pre-Tax Cuts and Jobs Act Code Sec. 471(c) as Code Sec. 471(d). (Code Sec. 471 as amended by Tax Cuts and Jobs Act §13102(c))

☐ **Effective:** Tax years beginning after Dec. 31, 2017. (Tax Cuts and Jobs Act §13102(e)(1))

¶ 1404. Small business exception to UNICAP rules is expanded to apply to producers and resellers meeting the $25 million gross receipts test

Code Sec. 263A(i), Tax Cuts and Jobs Act §13102(b)
Generally effective: Tax years beginning after Dec. 31, 2017
Committee Reports, see ¶ 5035

The Uniform Capitalization (UNICAP) rules provide that direct and certain indirect costs allocable to real or tangible personal property produced by a taxpayer must be capitalized into the basis of that property. For real or personal property acquired by a taxpayer for resale, Code Sec. 263A generally requires that direct and certain indirect costs allocable to that property be included in inventory. FTC 2d/FIN ¶ G-5452 et seq.; USTR ¶ 263A4 et seq.

Code Sec. 263A provides a number of exceptions to the general UNICAP requirements. Under pre-Tax Cuts and Jobs Act law, the UNICAP rules didn't apply to any **personal property** *acquired* during any tax year by a taxpayer *for resale* if the taxpayer's (or any predecessor's) average annual gross receipts for the immediately preceding three years didn't exceed *$10 million.* Those taxpayers (small resellers) weren't required to include additional Code Sec. 263A costs in inventory. (FTC 2d/FIN ¶ G-5450, ¶ G-5479; USTR ¶ 263A4)

> *observation:* This exception to the UNICAP rules didn't apply to small business taxpayers who *produced* personal property that was subject to Code Sec. 263A. (FTC 2d/FIN ¶ G-5450, ¶ G-5479.1; USTR ¶ 263A4.02)

For the Tax Cuts and Jobs Act's increase in the gross receipts test amount from *$10 million* to *$25 million,* see ¶ 1401.

New Law. The Tax Cuts and Jobs Act expands the exception for small taxpayers from the UNICAP rules (Com Rept, see ¶ 5035) by providing that, for any taxpayer (other than a tax shelter prohibited from using the cash receipts and disbursements method of accounting under Code Sec. 448(a)(3)) which meets the gross receipts test of Code Sec. 448(c) for any tax year, Code Sec. 263A won't apply with respect to the taxpayer for that tax year. (Code Sec. 263A(i)(1) as amended by Tax Cuts and Jobs Act §13102(b)(1))

> *observation:* Code Sec. 448(c) provides that corporations and partnerships with a corporate partner are permitted to use the cash method only if they have average annual gross receipts of *$25 million* or less during the preceding three years, see ¶ 1401.

In other words, any producer or reseller that meets the *$25 million* gross receipts test is exempted from the application of Code Sec. 263A. (Com Rept, see ¶ 5035)

> *observation:* Thus, the modified exception not only increases the dollar limitation, but it is also expanded to apply to both producers and resellers of both real and personal property.

> *observation:* The Tax Cuts and Jobs Act also clarifies that tax shelters prohibited from using the cash method of accounting cannot take advantage of the small business exception. That clarifying language didn't appear in pre-Tax Cuts and Jobs Act Code Sec. 263A(b)(2)(B),

i.e., the provision that contained the small business exception to the application of the UNICAP rules.

Application of gross receipts test to individuals, etc. For any taxpayer which isn't a corporation or a partnership, the gross receipts test of Code Sec. 448(c) will be applied in the same manner as if each trade or business of the taxpayer is a corporation or partnership. (Code Sec. 263A(i)(2))

Coordination with section 481. Any change in method of accounting made under Code Sec. 263A(i) will be treated for purposes of Code Sec. 481 as initiated by the taxpayer and made with IRS consent. (Code Sec. 263A(i)(3))

Conforming change. To conform with the above changes, the Tax Cuts and Jobs Act also provides that the uniform capitalization rules apply to real or personal property described in Code Sec. 1221(a)(1) which is acquired by the taxpayer for resale. (Code Sec. 263A(b)(2) as amended by Tax Cuts and Jobs Act §13102(b)(2))

☐ **Effective:** Tax years beginning after Dec. 31, 2017. (Tax Cuts and Jobs Act §13102(e)(1))

¶ 1405. Gross receipts limit to qualify for small construction contract exception to percentage of completion method is raised to $25 million

Code Sec. 460(e)(1)(B), as amended by Tax Cuts and Jobs Act §13102(d)(1)(A)
Code Sec. 460(e)(1)(B)(ii), as amended by Tax Cuts and Jobs Act §13102(d)(1)(B)
Code Sec. 460(e)(2), as amended by Tax Cuts and Jobs Act §13102(d)(2)
Generally effective: Contracts entered into after Dec. 31, 2017
Committee Reports, see ¶ 5035

In general, for a long-term contract, the taxable income from the contract is determined under the percentage-of-completion method. Under this method, the taxpayer must include in gross income for the tax year an amount equal to the product of:

... the gross contract price and

... the percentage of the contract completed during the tax year.

The percentage of the contract completed during the tax year is determined by comparing costs allocated to the contract and incurred before the end of the tax year with the estimated total contract costs. Costs allocated to the contract typically include all costs (including depreciation) that directly benefit or are incurred by reason of the taxpayer's long-term contract activities. The allocation of costs to a contract is made in accordance with regs. Costs incurred with respect to the long-term contract are deductible in the year incurred, subject to general accrual method of accounting principles and limitations. FTC 2d ¶ G-3123; USTR ¶ 4604.001

An exception from the requirement to use the percentage-of-completion method is provided for certain construction contracts ("small construction contracts"). Under pre-Tax Cuts and Jobs Act law, a contract for the construction or improvement of real property qualified for the exception if the contract was entered into by a taxpayer—

(1) who estimated (at the time the contract was entered into) that the contract would be completed within two years of commencement of the contract and

(2) whose average annual gross receipts for the prior three tax years did not exceed $10 million. Pre-Tax Cuts and Jobs Act law provided rules for determining a taxpayer's gross receipts for purposes of this rule.

Thus, long-term contract income from small construction contracts has to be reported consistently using the taxpayer's exempt contract method (the method of accounting that a taxpayer must use to account for all of its long-term contracts (and any portions of long-term contracts) that are exempt from the use of the percentage of completion method). Permissible exempt contract methods include the completed contract method, the exempt-contract percentage-of-completion method, the percentage-of-completion method, or any other permissible method. (FTC 2d ¶ G-3210; USTR ¶ 4604.12; Catalyst ¶ 103:106; Catalyst ¶ 756:194; Catalyst ¶ 758:122; Catalyst ¶ 758:211)

Code Sec. 448 provides other limits on the use of the cash method, see FTC 2d/FIN ¶ G-2054; USTR ¶ 4484. Specifically, under Code Sec. 448, C corporations and partnerships having a C corporation as a partner that don't meet a gross receipts test limit or other exception, can't use the cash method of accounting, and under no circumstances is a tax shelter allowed to use the cash method of accounting, see FTC 2d/FIN ¶s G-2054, G-2056; USTR ¶ 4484.

New Law. The Tax Cuts and Jobs Act expands the exception for small construction contracts from the requirement to use the percentage-of-completion method (Com Rept, see ¶ 5035) by providing that a contract qualifying for the exception from the requirement to use the percentage-of-completion method includes a construction contract that is—

(1) entered into by a taxpayer (other than a tax shelter, see below) who estimates (at the time the contract is entered into) that the contract will be completed within two years of commencement of the contract, and

(2) performed by a taxpayer who meets the gross receipts test of Code Sec. 448(c) for the tax year in which the contract is entered into. (Code Sec. 460(e)(1)(B)(ii) as amended by Tax Cuts and Jobs Act §13102(d)(1)(B))

observation: Under pre-Tax Cuts and Jobs Act law, Code Sec. 448(c) provided a *$5 million gross receipts test* limit that a C corporation or partnership having a C corporation partner had to satisfy to qualify for the exception from the general rule barring certain taxpayers from using the cash method of accounting. The exception was and is (see below) unavailable to tax shelters. (FTC 2d ¶ G-2069; USTR ¶ 4484) For analysis of the Tax Cuts and Jobs Act's raising of the gross receipts test limit for cash-method use by C corporations (and certain partnerships) to $25 million, see ¶ 1401.

observation: Thus, for purposes of the exception for small construction contracts from the requirement to use the percentage-of-completion method, the Tax Cuts and Jobs Act raises the *$10 million gross receipts test limit* to a *$25 million gross receipts test limit.*

For purposes of Code Sec. 460(e)(1)(B)(ii) (item (2), above), in the case of any taxpayer which is not a corporation or a partnership (e.g., an individual), the gross receipts test of Code Sec. 448(c) is applied in the same manner as if each trade or business of the taxpayer were a corporation or a partnership. Code Sec. 460(e)(2)(A) as amended by Tax Cuts and Jobs Act §13102(d)(2)

The Tax Cuts and Jobs act repeals the provisions providing rules for determining a taxpayer's gross receipts for purposes of item (2), above. (Code Sec. 460(e)(2) as amended by Tax Cuts and Jobs Act §13102(d)(2)), (Code Sec. 460(e)(3) as amended by Tax Cuts and Jobs Act §13102(d)(2))

observation: Since the Tax Cuts and Jobs Act in item (2), above, defines the gross receipts test with reference to Code Sec. 448(c), rather than with a stated dollar figure (as under pre-Tax Cuts and Jobs Act law), the pre-Tax Cuts and Jobs Act provisions providing rules in Code Sec. 460 for determining a taxpayer's gross receipts for these purposes are no longer necessary.

Certain tax shelters barred from using the exception. The Tax Cuts and Jobs Act provides that the exception from the requirement to use the percentage-of-completion method applies only to contracts for the construction or improvement of real property entered into by a taxpayer other than a tax shelter prohibited from using the cash receipts and disbursements method of accounting under Code Sec. 448(a)(3). (Code Sec. 460(e)(1)(B))

observation: Thus, tax shelters prohibited from using the cash receipts and disbursements method of accounting under Code Sec. 448(a)(3) can't take advantage of the exception from the requirement to use the percentage-of-completion method otherwise available for certain construction contracts.

Accounting method changes. Any change in method of accounting made under Code Sec. 460(e)(1)(B)(ii) (the gross receipts test, discussed above, which must be satisfied to qualify for the exception from the requirement to use the percentage-of-completion method) will be treated as initiated by the taxpayer and made with the consent of IRS. The change will be effected on a cut-off basis for all similarly classified contracts entered into on or after the year of change. Code Sec. 460(e)(2)(B)

> **✪** *observation:* The designation of an accounting method as "initiated by the taxpayer" relates to Code Sec. 481(a)(2) which states what is in substance a transitional rule, of significance to increasingly few taxpayers today, concerning the enactment of the 1954 Code, see FTC 2d/FIN ¶ G-2299; USTR ¶ 4814.

> **✪** *observation:* Where legislation designates an accounting method change as made with IRS's consent, IRS can nevertheless require, as part of its administration of accounting method rules, that the taxpayer follow consent procedures to make the change, see FTC 2d/FIN ¶ G-2202.2.

Redesignations. The Tax Cuts and Jobs Act redesignates pre-Tax Cuts and Jobs Act Code Sec. 460(e)(4) through Code Sec. 460(e)(6) as Code Sec. 460(e)(3) through Code Sec. 460(e)(5), respectively. (Code Sec. 460(e)(3) as redesignated by Tax Cuts and Jobs Act §13102(d)(2), Code Sec. 460(e)(4) as redesignated by Tax Cuts and Jobs Act §13102(d)(2), Code Sec. 460(e)(5) as redesignated by Tax Cuts and Jobs Act §13102(d)(2))

☐ **Effective:** Contracts entered into after Dec. 31, 2017, in tax years ending after that date. (Tax Cuts and Jobs Act §13102(e)(1))

¶ 1406. Income inclusion for tax purposes can't be later than when included for certain financial reporting purposes

Code Sec. 451(b), as amended by Tax Cuts and Jobs Act §13221(a)
Code Sec. None, Tax Cuts and Jobs Act §13221(d)
Code Sec. None, Tax Cuts and Jobs Act §13221(e)
Generally effective: Tax years beginning after Dec. 31, 2017.
Committee Reports, see ¶ 5043

In general, for a cash basis taxpayer, an amount is included in income when actually or constructively received. FTC 2d ¶ G-2411; USTR ¶ 4514.003 For an accrual basis taxpayer, however, an amount is included in income when all the events have occurred that fix the right to receive that income and the amount of that income can be determined with reasonable accuracy, unless an exception permits deferral or exclusion. (FTC 2d ¶ G-2471; USTR ¶ 4514.011)

✐ observation: Thus, under pre-Tax Cuts and Jobs Act law, when an amount is included in income for tax purposes is determined without regard to when it is included in income for financial accounting purposes.

The holder of a debt instrument with original issue discount (OID) generally accrues and includes the OID in gross income as interest over the term of the instrument, regardless of when the stated interest (if any) is paid. (FTC 2d ¶ J-4001; USTR ¶ 12,714)

New Law. The Tax Cuts and Jobs Act requires a taxpayer to recognize income no later than the tax year in which the income is taken into account as income on (1) an applicable financial statement (AFS) or (2) under rules specified by IRS, another financial statement. (Code Sec. 451(b) as amended by Tax Cuts and Jobs Act §13221(a))

✐ observation: This income recognition timing rule is also referred to as "the AFS conformity rule".

Specifically, the Tax Cuts and Jobs Act provides that, for an accrual basis taxpayer, the all-events test with respect to any item of gross income (or portion thereof) won't be treated as met any later than when that item (or portion thereof) is taken into account as revenue in (Code Sec. 451(b)(1)(A)):

(1) an applicable financial statement (AFS, defined below) of the taxpayer (Code Sec. 451(b)(1)(A)(i)), or

(2) such other financial statement as IRS may specify for purposes of Code Sec. 451(b). (Code Sec. 451(b)(1)(A)(ii))

Thus, the Tax Cuts and Jobs Act requires a taxpayer to recognize income no later than the tax year in which that income is taken into account as income on an applicable financial statement (AFS) or another financial statement under rules specified by IRS. For example, under the Tax Cuts and Jobs Act, any unbilled receivables for partially performed services must be recognized to the extent the amounts are taken into income for financial statement purposes. (Com Rept, see ¶ 5043)

This rule doesn't apply to:

(i) a taxpayer which doesn't have a financial statement described in items (1) or (2), above, for a tax year (Code Sec. 451(b)(1)(B)(i)), or

(ii) any item of gross income in connection with a mortgage servicing contract. (Code Sec. 451(b)(1)(B)(ii))

For purposes of Code Sec. 451, the all-events test is met with respect to any item of gross income if all the events have occurred which fix the right to receive that income and the amount of the income can be determined with reasonable accuracy. (Code Sec. 451(b)(1)(C))

Code Sec. 451(b)(1), discussed above, doesn't apply to any item of gross income for which the taxpayer uses a special method of accounting provided under any other provision of this Chapter 1 of the Internal Revenue Code (i.e., Code Sec. 1 through Code Sec. 1400U-3, governing normal income taxes and surtaxes, see FTC 2d/FIN ¶ G-2003; USTR ¶ 4464.01, other than any provision of part V of subchapter P (i.e., Code Sec. 1271 through Code Sec. 1288, covering special capital gain and loss rules for bonds and other debt instruments, see FTC 2d/FIN ¶ I-8001; USTR ¶ 12,714), except as provided in Code Sec. 451(b)(1)(B)(ii) (item (ii), above). (Code Sec. 451(b)(2))

Thus, the Tax Cuts and Jobs Act requires a taxpayer to recognize income no later than the tax year in which that income is taken into account as income on an applicable financial statement or another financial statement under rules specified by IRS, but provides an exception for long-term contract income to which Code Sec. 460 applies. For example, under the proposal, any unbilled receivables for partially performed services must be recognized to the extent the amounts are taken into income for financial statement purposes. (Com Rept, see ¶ 5043)

Applicable financial statement defined. For purposes of Code Sec. 451(b), an applicable financial statement (AFS) is (Code Sec. 451(b)(3)):

(A)   a financial statement which is certified as being prepared in accordance with generally accepted accounting principles (GAAP) and which is (Code Sec. 451(b)(3)(A)):

(i) a Form 10−K (or successor form), or annual statement to shareholders, required to be filed by the taxpayer with the U.S. Securities and Exchange Commission (Code Sec. 451(b)(3)(A)(i)),

(ii)   an audited financial statement of the taxpayer which is used for (Code Sec. 451(b)(3)(A)(ii)):

(I) credit purposes (Code Sec. 451(b)(3)(A)(ii)(I)),

(II) reporting to shareholders, partners, or other proprietors, or to beneficiaries (Code Sec. 451(b)(3)(A)(ii)(II)), or

(III) any other substantial nontax purpose,
but only if there is no statement of the taxpayer described in item (i), above, or (Code Sec. 451(b)(3)(A)(ii)(III))

(iii) filed by the taxpayer with any other federal agency for purposes other than federal tax purposes, but only if there is no statement of the taxpayer described in items (i) or (ii), above. (Code Sec. 451(b)(3)(A)(iii))

(B) a financial statement which is made on the basis of international financial reporting standards and is filed by the taxpayer with an agency of a foreign government which is equivalent to the U.S. Securities and Exchange Commission and which has reporting standards not less stringent than the standards required by that Commission, but only if there is no statement of the taxpayer described in item (A), above, or (Code Sec. 451(b)(3)(B))

(C) a financial statement filed by the taxpayer with any other regulatory or governmental body specified by IRS, but only if there is no statement of the taxpayer described in items (A) or (B), above. (Code Sec. 451(b)(3)(C))

> **observation:** This definition of an AFS differs from the definition of that term provided by Rev Proc 2004-34 (FTC 2d ¶ G-2548.1; USTR ¶ 4514.191) in the following ways:
>
> (1) Rev Proc 2004-34 requires an AFS described in item (A)(ii) to be certified and accompanied by the report of an independent CPA (or in the case of a foreign corporation, by the report of a similarly qualified independent professional);
>
> (2) Rev Proc 2004-34 limits an AFS described in item (A)(ii)(II) to a statement used for reporting to shareholders (rather than a statement used for reporting to shareholders, partners, or other proprietors, or to beneficiaries, as allowed by Code Sec. 451(b)(3)(A)(ii)(II));
>
> (3) Instead of the statements allowed by items (A)(iii) and (C), Rev Proc 2004-34 allows the use of a financial statement (other than a tax return) required to be provided to the federal or a state government or any federal or state agencies (other than the SEC or IRS); and
>
> (4) Rev Proc 2004-34 doesn't allow the use of a financial statement filed with an agency of a foreign government, as provided in item (B).

Allocation of transaction price. For purposes of these rules, in the case of a contract which contains multiple performance obligations, the allocation of the transaction price to each performance obligation is equal to the amount allocated to each performance obligation for purposes of including that item in revenue in the applicable financial statement (AFS) of the taxpayer. (Code Sec. 451(b)(4))

Group of entities. For purposes of Code Sec. 451(b)(1), discussed above, if the financial results of a taxpayer are reported on the applicable financial statement (as defined in Code Sec. 451(b)(3), see "applicable financial statement," above) for a group of entities, that statement may be treated as the applicable financial statement of the taxpayer. (Code Sec. 451(b)(5))

Accounting method change rules. The rules discussed below apply for a "qualified change in method of accounting" (Tax Cuts and Jobs Act §13221(d)(1)), defined as a change that is either required by the amendments discussed above made by the Tax Cuts and Jobs Act (Tax Cuts and Jobs Act §13221(d)(2)(A)) or was prohibited under the Code before those amendments and is permitted under the Code after those amendments. (Tax Cuts and Jobs Act §13221(d)(2)(B))

For the taxpayer's first tax year beginning after Dec. 31, 2017, a qualified change in method of accounting (Tax Cuts and Jobs Act §13221(d)(1))—

(A) is treated as initiated by the taxpayer (see the first observation below), and (Tax Cuts and Jobs Act §13221(d)(1)(A))

(B) as made with IRS's consent (see the second observation below). (Tax Cuts and Jobs Act §13221(d)(1)(B))

> ⓡ *observation:* The designation of an accounting method as "initiated by the taxpayer" relates to Code Sec. 481(a)(2), which states what is in substance a transitional rule, of significance to increasingly few taxpayers today, concerning the enactment of the 1954 Code, see FTC 2d/FIN ¶ G-2299; USTR ¶ 4814.

> ⓡ *observation:* Where legislation designates an accounting method change as made with IRS's consent, IRS can nevertheless require, as part of its administration of accounting method rules, that the taxpayer follow consent procedures to make the change, see FTC 2d/FIN ¶ G-2202.2.

Also, for any tax year, for income from a debt instrument having original issue discount (OID), the period for taking into account any adjustments under Code Sec. 481 ("Code Sec. 481(a) adjustments," FTC 2d/FIN ¶ G-2290 *et seq.*; USTR ¶ 4814) because of a "qualified change in method of accounting" (above) is six years. (Tax Cuts and Jobs Act §13221(e); Tax Cuts and Jobs Act §13221(e)(2)) For the effective date specific to OID income, see **Effective** below.

> ⓡ *observation:* The six-year period is an exception to the general rules that require that Code Sec. 481(a) adjustments are taken into account in the year of change if they reduce taxable income ("negative adjustments") and over a four-year period beginning with the year of change if they decrease taxable income ("positive adjustments"), see FTC 2d/FIN ¶ G-2185.

Advance payments. The Tax Cuts and Jobs Act also codifies and modifies IRS guidance on accounting for advance payment income, see ¶ 1407.

Redesignations. Pre-Tax Cuts and Jobs Act Code subsections 451(b) through 451(i) are redesignated as Code subsections 451(c) through 451(j), respectively. Tax Cuts and Jobs Act §13221(a) Those Code subsections (as redesignated by Tax Cuts and Jobs Act §13221(a)) are, in turn, redesignated as Code

Sec. 451(d) through Code Sec. 451(k), respectively, by Tax Cuts and Jobs Act §13221(b), see ¶ 1407.

☐ **Effective:** Tax years beginning after Dec. 31, 2017 (Tax Cuts and Jobs Act §13221(c)) but for income from a debt instrument having OID, tax years beginning after Dec. 31, 2018. (Tax Cuts and Jobs Act §13221(e); Tax Cuts and Jobs Act §13221(e)(1))

¶ 1407. Accrual basis taxpayers may defer inclusion of advance payments in income to the end of year after year of receipt if so deferred for financial reporting

Code Sec. 451(c), as amended by Tax Cuts and Jobs Act §13221(b)
Code Sec. None, Tax Cuts and Jobs Act §13221(d)
Generally effective: Tax years beginning after Dec. 31, 2017
Committee Reports, see ¶ 5043

In general, for a cash basis taxpayer, an amount is included in income when actually or constructively received. FTC 2d ¶ G-2411; USTR ¶ 4514.003 For an accrual basis taxpayer, however, an amount is included in income when all the events have occurred that fix the right to receive that income and the amount of that income can be determined with reasonable accuracy, unless an exception permits deferral or exclusion. (FTC 2d ¶ G-2471; USTR ¶ 4514.011)

    🅡 *observation:* Thus, under pre-Tax Cuts and Jobs Act law, when an amount is included in income for tax purposes is determined without regard to when it is included in income for financial accounting purposes.

An accrual-basis taxpayer that receives advance payments for services to be performed in the future generally must report those payments as income when received. However, a number of exceptions exist to permit deferral of income related to advance payments, i.e., payments received before the taxpayer provides goods or services to its customer. The exceptions often allow tax deferral to mirror financial accounting deferral (e.g., income is recognized as the goods are provided or the services are performed). (FTC 2d ¶ G-2540; USTR ¶ 4514.166) For example, under Rev Proc 2004-34, if the taxpayer has an applicable financial statement (AFS) and is able to determine the extent to which advance payments are recognized in revenues in its AFSs for the tax year of receipt, a taxpayer must (1) include the advance payment in gross income for the tax year of receipt to the extent recognized in revenues in its AFS for that tax year; and (2) include the remaining amount of the advance payment in gross income for the next succeeding tax year (i.e., the tax year immediately following the tax year in which the advance payment is received by the taxpayer). (FTC 2d ¶ G-2548.1; USTR ¶ 4514.191) And, under pre-Tax Cuts and Jobs Act law, if a taxpayer received advance payments under an agreement for the sale of inventoriable goods in one tax year, Reg §1.451-5(c) provided that all advance payments received under that agreement by the last day of the second tax year following the year in which substantial advance payments were received, had to be included in income in the second tax year to the extent not previously included in income in accordance with the taxpayer's accrual method of accounting. (FTC 2d ¶ G-2596; USTR ¶ 4514.166)

New Law. The Tax Cuts and Jobs Act codifies the deferral method of accounting for advance payments for goods and services provided by IRS under Rev Proc 2004-34 (Com Rept, see ¶ 5043) by providing that a taxpayer which computes taxable income under the accrual method of accounting and receives any advance payment (defined below) during the tax year, must: (Code Sec. 451(c)(1) as amended by Tax Cuts and Jobs Act §13221(b))

(A) except as provided in item (B), include the advance payment in gross income for that tax year (Code Sec. 451(c)(1)(A)), or

(B) if the taxpayer elects (under the procedures described below) the application of subparagraph Code Sec. 451(c)(1)(B) with respect to the category of advance payments to which the advance payment belongs, the taxpayer must (Code Sec. 451(c)(1)(B)):

(i) to the extent that any portion of the advance payment is required under Code Sec. 451(b) (see ¶ 1406), to be included in gross income in the tax year in which that payment is received, so include that portion (Code Sec. 451(c)(1)(B)(i)), and

(ii) include the remaining portion of the advance payment in gross income in the tax year following the tax year in which the payment is received. (Code Sec. 451(c)(1)(B)(ii))

Thus, the Tax Cuts and Jobs Act allows taxpayers to defer the inclusion of income associated with certain advance payments to the end of the tax year following the tax year of receipt if that income also is deferred for financial statement purposes. Moreover, it is intended to override the exception in Reg §1.451-5 for advance payment received for goods. (Com Rept, see ¶ 5043)

For analysis of the Tax Cuts and Jobs Act change that provides that income inclusion for tax purposes can't be later than when it is included for certain financial reporting purposes, see ¶ 1406.

Advance payment defined. An advance payment is any payment (Code Sec. 451(c)(4)(A)):

(i) the full inclusion of which in the gross income of the taxpayer for the tax year of receipt is a permissible method of accounting under Code Sec. 451 (determined without regard to Code Sec. 451(c)) (Code Sec. 451(c)(4)(A)(i)),

(ii) any portion of which is included in revenue by the taxpayer in a financial statement described in Code Sec. 451(b)(1)(A)(i) or Code Sec. 451(b)(1)(A)(ii) for a later tax year (Code Sec. 451(c)(4)(A)(ii)), and

(iii) which is for goods, services, or such other items as may be identified by IRS for these purposes. (Code Sec. 451(c)(4)(A)(iii))

Except as otherwise provided by IRS, an advance payment doesn't include:

(i) rent (Code Sec. 451(c)(4)(B)(i))

(ii) insurance premiums governed by subchapter L (Code Sec. 801 through Code Sec. 848, see FTC 2d ¶ E-4800; USTR ¶ 8014) (Code Sec. 451(c)(4)(B)(ii)),

(iii) payments with respect to financial instruments (Code Sec. 451(c)(4)(B)(iii)),

(iv) payments with respect to warranty or guarantee contracts under which a third party is the primary obligor (Code Sec. 451(c)(4)(B)(iv)),

(v) payments subject to:

. . . Code Sec. 871(a) (i.e., the tax on income of nonresident alien individuals not connected with a U.S. business),

. . . Code Sec. 881 (i.e., the tax on income of foreign corporations not connected with United States business),

. . . Code Sec. 1441 (i.e., the tax withheld on certain amounts paid to foreign persons), or

. . . Code Sec. 1442 (i.e., the tax withheld from income of foreign corporations)(Code Sec. 451(c)(4)(B)(v)),

(vi) payments in property to which Code Sec. 83 (taxation of property transferred in connection with the performance of services) applies (Code Sec. 451(c)(4)(B)(vi)), and

(vii) any other payment identified by IRS for purposes of Code Sec. 451(c)(4). (Code Sec. 451(c)(4)(B)(vii))

An item of gross income is received by the taxpayer if it's actually or constructively received, or if it's due and payable to the taxpayer. (Code Sec. 451(c)(4)(C)) For purposes of Code Sec. 451(c), in allocating the transaction price, rules similar to Code Sec. 451(b)(4), discussed in ¶ 1406, apply. (Code Sec. 451(c)(4)(D))

Taxpayer ceasing to exist during, or at end of, tax year. Except as otherwise provided by IRS, the election under Code Sec. 451(c)(1)(B), discussed above, doesn't apply with respect to advance payments received by the taxpayer during a tax year if the taxpayer ceases to exist during (or with the close of) that tax year. (Code Sec. 451(c)(3))

Making the Code Sec. 451(c)(1)(B) election and when it applies. Except as otherwise provided in Code Sec. 451(c)(2), the election under Code Sec. 451(c)(1)(B) must be made at the time, in the form and manner, and with respect to the categories of advance payments, as IRS may provide. (Code Sec. 451(c)(2)(A)) An election under Code Sec. 451(c)(1)(B) will be effective for the tax year with respect to which it is first made and for all later years, unless the taxpayer secures IRS's consent to revoke the election. For purposes of the Code, the computation of taxable income under an election made under Code Sec. 451(c)(1)(B) will be treated as a method of accounting. (Code Sec. 451(c)(2)(B))

Accounting method change rules. The rules discussed below apply for a "qualified change in method of accounting" (Tax Cuts and Jobs Act §13221(d)(1)), defined as a change that is either required by the amendments discussed above made by the Tax Cuts and Jobs Act (Tax Cuts and Jobs Act §13221(d)(2)(A)) or was prohibited under the Code before those amendments and is permitted under the Code after those amendments. (Tax Cuts and Jobs Act §13221(d)(2)(B))

For the taxpayer's first tax year beginning after Dec. 31, 2017, a qualified change in method of accounting— (Tax Cuts and Jobs Act §13221(d)(1))

(A) is treated as initiated by the taxpayer (see the first observation below), and (Tax Cuts and Jobs Act §13221(d)(1)(A))

(B) as made with IRS's consent (see the second observation below). (Tax Cuts and Jobs Act §13221(d)(1)(B))

> *observation:* The designation of an accounting method as "initiated by the taxpayer" relates to Code Sec. 481(a)(2) which states what is in substance a transitional rule, of significance to increasingly few taxpayers today, concerning the enactment of the 1954 Code, see FTC 2d/FIN ¶ G-2299; USTR ¶ 4814.

> *observation:* Where legislation designates an accounting method change as made with IRS's consent, IRS can nevertheless require, as part of its administration of accounting method rules, that the taxpayer follow consent procedures to make the change, see FTC 2d/FIN ¶ G-2202.2.

Redesignations. Pre-Tax Cuts and Jobs Act Code subsections 451(b) through 451(i), which are redesignated as Code subsections 451(c) through 451(j), respectively, by Tax Cuts and Jobs Act §13221(a) (see ¶ 1406), are, in turn, redesignated as Code Sec. 451(d) through Code Sec. 451(k), respectively. Tax Cuts and Jobs Act §13221(b)

☐ **Effective:** Tax years beginning after Dec. 31, 2017. (Tax Cuts and Jobs Act §13221(c))

¶ 1408. Code Sec. 174 research and experimental expenditures paid or incurred in tax years starting after 2021 are to be amortized over 5 years

Code Sec. 174, as amended by Tax Cuts and Jobs Act §13206(a)
Code Sec. 41(d)(1)(A), as amended by Tax Cuts and Jobs Act §13206(d)(1)
Code Sec. 280C(c)(1), as amended by Tax Cuts and Jobs Act §13206(d)(2)(A)
Code Sec. 280C(c)(2), as amended by Tax Cuts and Jobs Act §13206(d)(2)(B)
Code Sec. 280C(c)(2), as amended by Tax Cuts and Jobs Act §13206(d)(2)(D)
Generally effective: Amounts paid or incurred in tax years beginning after Dec. 31, 2021
Committee Reports, see ¶ 5041

Under pre-Tax Cuts and Jobs Act law, taxpayers could elect to deduct currently the amount of certain reasonable research or experimentation (R & E) expenditures paid or incurred in connection with a trade or business. (FTC 2d/FIN ¶ L-3100, ¶ L-3101, ¶ L-3117, ¶ L-3118, ¶ L-3119, ¶ L-3120; USTR ¶ 1744)

illustration (1): In Year 1, a tax year that begins before 2022, A pays $150,000 to B to undertake R & E work to create a particular product. Under pre-Tax Cuts and Jobs Act law, A can deduct the amount paid to B as a deduction under Code Sec. 174 in Year 1.

In lieu of a current deduction, taxpayers could capitalize R & E expenditures and amortize those expenditures ratably over the useful life of the research, but in no case over a period of less than 60 months (deferred expense election). The amortization period begins with the month in which the taxpayer first realizes benefits from the R & E expenditures. (FTC 2d/FIN ¶ L-3121, ¶ L-3122, ¶ L-3123, ¶ L-3124, ¶ L-3125, ¶ L-3126, ¶ L-3127; USTR ¶ 1744; Catalyst ¶ 425:150; Catalyst ¶ 753:145) If a project proves unsuccessful and is abandoned, a taxpayer can deduct capitalized R & E expenditures as a loss in that year. (FTC 2d/FIN ¶ L-3130; USTR ¶ 1744)

illustration (2): The facts are the same as in illustration (1) except that B makes the deferred expense election and the useful life of the research is 60 months. B capitalizes the $150,000 payment and amortizes that amount over 60 months at $2,500 per month beginning with the month in which B first realizes benefits from the R & E expenditures.

Taxpayers, alternatively, can elect to amortize their R & E expenditures over a period of 10 years. This election avoids AMT preferences and adjustments. For changes made to the AMT by the Tax Cuts and Jobs Act, see ¶ 303.

R & E expenditures deductible under Code Sec. 174 are not subject to capitalization under either the general capitalization rules under Code Sec. 263(a) (see FTC 2d/FIN ¶ L-5100; USTR ¶ 2634) or the uniform capitalization (UNICAP) rules under Code Sec. 263A(a) (see FTC 2d/FIN ¶ G-5450; USTR ¶ 263A4). Amounts defined as R & E expenditures under Code Sec. 174 generally include all costs incurred in the experimental or laboratory sense related to the development or improvement of a product. In particular, qualifying costs are those incurred for activities intended to discover information that would eliminate uncertainty concerning the development or improvement of a product (see FTC 2d/FIN ¶ L-3103; USTR ¶ 1744.02). In addition, IRS issued administrative guidance treating the costs of developing computer software similar to research expenditures. (FTC 2d/FIN ¶ L-5600, ¶ L-5613, ¶ L-5616, ¶ L-5618, ¶ L-5620, ¶ L-5621, ¶ L-5623; USTR ¶ 1674.033)

Generally, no current deduction under Code Sec. 174 is allowable for expenditures for the acquisition or improvement of land or of depreciable or depletable property used in connection with any research or experimentation. (FTC 2d/FIN ¶ L-3114; USTR ¶ 1744.02) In addition, no current deduction is allowed for research expenses incurred for the purpose of ascertaining the existence, location, extent, or quality of any deposit of ore or other mineral, including oil and gas. (FTC 2d/FIN ¶ L-3114.1; USTR ¶ 1744.02)

New Law. In the case of a taxpayer's specified R & E expenditures (defined below) for any tax year (Code Sec. 174(a) as amended by Tax Cuts and Jobs Act §13206(a)) that are paid or incurred in tax years beginning after Dec. 31, 2021: (Tax Cuts and Jobs Act §13206(e))

(1) except for the amortization deduction described in item (2), no deduction will be allowed for the R & E expenditures, and (Code Sec. 174(a)(1))

(2) the taxpayer will (Code Sec. 174(a)(2)) charge the expenditures to capital account, and (Code Sec. 174(a)(2)(A)) will be allowed an amortization deduction of the expenditures ratably over the five-year period beginning with the midpoint of the tax year in which the expenditures are paid or incurred. (Code Sec. 174(a)(2)(B)) For the amortization period that applies to expenditures for foreign research, see below.

> *illustration (3):* The facts are the same as in illustration (1) except that A pays the $150,000 to B in a tax year beginning after Dec. 31, 2021 and A uses the calendar year as its accounting period. Under the Tax Cuts and Jobs Act, B will amortize the amount paid to B ($150,000) over 60 months at $2,500 per month in Year 1. The amortization period will begin with the midpoint of the tax year in which B pays or incurs the expenses (July). B's deduction under Code Sec. 174 for the first year will be $15,000.

> *observation:* In many cases, the taxpayer's amortization period will begin earlier under Code Sec. 174(a)(2)(B) once it takes effect than it does under the deferred expense election under pre-Tax Cuts and Jobs Act law. Under Code Sec. 174(a)(2)(B), the amortization period under Code Sec. 174(a)(2)(B) begins at the midpoint of the tax year in which the payments are made. That date, in many cases, will be earlier than the month that the taxpayer first realized benefits from his R & E expenditures (the beginning of the amortization period under pre-Tax Cuts and Jobs Act law).

A 15-year period (instead of the five-year period in item (2) above) will apply in the case of any specified R & E expenditures which are attributable to foreign research (within the meaning of research credit rules under Code Sec. 41(d)(4)(F)). (Code Sec. 174(a)(2)(B))

> *observation:* Under Code Sec. 41(d)(4)(F), foreign research is any research conducted outside the U.S., Puerto Rico, or any U.S. possession, see FTC 2d/FIN ¶ L-15434.2; USTR ¶ 414.01. Under the Tax Cuts and Jobs Act, the R & E expenses attributable to foreign research will have to be amortized over 15 years or 180 months.

> *illustration (4):* The facts are the same as in illustration (3) except that A pays $150,000 to B for foreign research. B will amortize the amount paid to B ($150,000) over 15 years or 180 months at $833.33 per month. B's deduction under Code Sec. 174 for Year 1 will be $5,000.

Specified R & E expenditures defined. For amounts paid or incurred in tax years beginning after Dec. 31, 2021, (Tax Cuts and Jobs Act §13206(e)) specified R & E expenditures will be, with respect to any tax year, R & E expenditures which are paid or incurred by the taxpayer during the tax year in connection with the taxpayer's trade or business. (Code Sec. 174(b))

> *observation:* Presumably, specified R & E expenditures will encompass the same type of expenses that are subject to Code Sec. 174 under pre-Tax Cuts and Jobs Act definition. For a discussion of the trade or business requirement under pre-Tax Cuts and Jobs Act law, see FTC 2d/FIN ¶ L-3103 *et seq.*, USTR ¶ 1744.02

Land. The amortization of R & E expenditures under Code Sec. 174 will not apply:

. . . to any expenditure for the acquisition or improvement of land, or

. . . for the acquisition or improvement of property to be used in connection with the R & E and of a character which is subject to the allowance under Code Sec. 167 (relating to allowance for depreciation, etc.) or Code Sec. 611 (relating to allowance for depletion); but for purposes of Code Sec. 174 allowances under Code Sec. 167, and allowances under Code Sec. 611, will be considered as expenditures. (Code Sec. 174(c)(1))

In other words, specified R & E expenditures will not include expenditures for land or for depreciable or depletable property used in connection with the research and experimentation, but do include the depreciation and depletion allowances of the property. (Com Rept, see ¶ 5041)

> **⊘** *observation:* The same rule applies under pre-Tax Cuts and Jobs Act Code Sec. 174(c), see FTC 2d/FIN ¶ L-3114; USTR ¶ 1744.02.

Exploration expenditures. The amortization of R & E expenditures under Code Sec. 174 will not apply to any expenditure paid or incurred for the purpose of ascertaining the existence, location, extent, or quality of any deposit of ore or other mineral (including oil and gas). (Code Sec. 174(c)(2)) In other words, exploration expenditures incurred for ore or other minerals (including oil and gas) will be excluded from specified R & E expenditures. (Com Rept, see ¶ 5041)

> **⊘** *observation:* The same rule applies under pre-Tax Cuts and Jobs Act Code Sec. 174(d), see FTC 2d/FIN ¶ L-3114.1; USTR ¶ 1744.02.

Software development. For amounts paid or incurred in tax years beginning after Dec. 31, 2021, (Tax Cuts and Jobs Act §13206(e)) any amount paid or incurred in connection with the development of any software will be treated as a R & E expenditure for purposes of Code Sec. 174. (Code Sec. 174(c)(3)) Thus, specified R & E expenditures subject to capitalization will include expenditures for software development. (Com Rept, see ¶ 5041)

> **⊘** *observation:* Thus, the Tax Cuts and Jobs Act requires that amounts paid or incurred for software development costs in tax years beginning after Dec. 31, 2021 will have to be amortized over 5 years (15 years for expenses attributable to foreign research). This treatment changes pre-Tax Cuts and Jobs Act law in effect for tax years beginning before 2022 under which IRS permits taxpayers to deduct software development costs under Code Sec. 174 under Rev Proc 2000-50 and Rev Proc 69-21, see FTC 2d/FIN ¶ L-5613; USTR ¶ 1674.033.

Disposition, retirement, or abandonment of research. If any property with respect to which specified R & E expenditures are paid or incurred is disposed, retired, or abandoned during the period during which the expenditures are allowed as an amortization deduction, no deduction will be allowed with respect to the expenditures on account of the disposition, retirement, or abandonment and the amortization deduction will continue with respect to the expenditures.(Code Sec. 174(d)) Thus, in the case of retired, abandoned, or disposed property with respect to which specified R & E expenditures are paid or incurred, any remaining basis will not be recovered in the year of retirement, abandonment, or disposal, but instead will continue to be amortized over the remaining amortization period. (Com Rept, see ¶ 5041)

> **observation:** Some cases determined under pre-Tax Cuts and Jobs Act law have held that the amortization period terminates in the year that a project is abandoned. Code Sec. 174(d) clarifies that the amortization period will not terminate in the year of abandonment, etc. for amounts paid or incurred in tax years beginning after Dec. 31, 2021. (FTC 2d/FIN ¶ L-3130; USTR ¶ 1744)

Change in method of accounting. The changes to Code Sec. 174 by the Tax Cuts and Jobs Act will be treated as a change in method of accounting for purposes of Code Sec. 481 and (Tax Cuts and Jobs Act §13206(b)) the change will be:

(1) treated as initiated by the taxpayer, (Tax Cuts and Jobs Act §13206(b)(1))

(2) treated as made with IRS's consent, and (Tax Cuts and Jobs Act §13206(b)(2))

(3) applied only on a cut-off basis for any R & E expenditures paid or incurred in tax years beginning after Dec. 31, 2021, and no Code Sec. 481(a) adjustments will be made (Tax Cuts and Jobs Act §13206(b)(3)) for R & E expenditures paid or incurred in tax years beginning before Jan. 1, 2021. (Com Rept, see ¶ 5041)

> **observation:** The designation of an accounting method as "initiated by the taxpayer" relates to Code Sec. 481(a)(2) which states what is in substance a transitional rule, of significance to increasingly few taxpayers today, concerning the enactment of the 1954 Code, see FTC 2d/FIN ¶ G-2299; USTR ¶ 4814.

> **observation:** Where legislation designates an accounting method change as made with IRS's consent, IRS can nevertheless require, as part of its administration of accounting method rules, that the taxpayer follow consent procedures to make the change, see FTC 2d/FIN ¶ G-2202.2.

Effect on research credit. The Tax Cuts and Jobs Act strikes "expenses under Code Sec. 174" in Code Sec. 41(d)(1)(A) (relating to the requirement that research is treated as qualified research only if the expenditures for the research can be deductible under Code Sec. 174, see FTC 2d/FIN ¶ L-15400, ¶ L-15406, ¶ L-15407; USTR ¶ 414.01) and substitutes "specified R & E expenditures under Code Sec. 174." (Code Sec. 41(d)(1)(A) as amended by Tax Cuts and Jobs Act §13206(d)(1)) *observation:* The change described above updates Code Sec. 41(d)(1)(A) to use the term "specified R & E expenditures" added by the Tax Cuts and Jobs Act.

Conforming changes. If: (Code Sec. 280C(c)(1) as amended by Tax Cuts and Jobs Act §13206(d)(2)(A))

(1) the amount of the research credit determined for the tax year under Code Sec. 41(a)(1), exceeds (Code Sec. 280C(c)(1)(A))

(2) the amount allowable as a deduction for the tax year for qualified research expenses (QREs) or basic research expenses (see FTC 2d/FIN ¶ L-15400; USTR ¶ 414), (Code Sec. 280C(c)(1)(B))

the amount chargeable to capital account for the tax year for the expenses will be reduced by the amount of the excess. (Code Sec. 280C(c)(1))

illustration (5): In 2028, X has in the current year credit-eligible research expenditures totalling $1,000,000 and X's allowable research credit is $80,000. The amount that X will capitalize cannot exceed $920,000 (i.e., $1,000,000 − $80,000).

observation: The rule provided in Code Sec. 280C(c)(1) is similar to the rule provided in pre-Tax Cuts and Jobs Act Code Sec. 280C(c)(2).

For amounts paid or incurred in tax years beginning after Dec. 31, 2021, (Tax Cuts and Jobs Act §13206(e)) the Tax Cuts and Jobs Act strikes the rule provided in:

. . . Code Sec. 280C(c)(1) providing that no deduction is allowed for that portion of the qualified research expenses (FTC 2d/FIN ¶ L-15401; USTR ¶ 414.01) or basic research expenses (FTC 2d/FIN ¶ L-15404; USTR ¶ 414.02) otherwise allowable as a deduction for the tax year which is equal to the amount of the research credit determined for the tax year. (Code Sec. 280C(c)(1) as amended by Tax Cuts and Jobs Act §13206(d)(2)(A))

observation: The rule provided in pre-Tax Cuts and Jobs Act Code Sec. 280C(c)(1) will no longer be necessary for amounts paid or incurred in tax years beginning after Dec. 31, 2021 because all amounts will be capitalized and amortized.

. . . Code Sec. 280C(c)(2) providing for the reduction of capital account by the amount of the research credit, see FTC 2d/FIN ¶ L-3131; USTR ¶ 280C4. (Code Sec. 280C(c)(2) as amended by Tax Cuts and Jobs Act §13206(d)(2)(B)) The Tax Cuts and Jobs Act also deletes a reference in Code Sec. 280C(c)(2)(A)(i) to Code Sec. 280C(c)(2) to reflect the striking of that rule. (Code Sec. 280C(c)(2)(A)(i) as amended by Tax Cuts and Jobs Act §13206(d)(2)(D))

Redesignations. For amounts paid or incurred in tax years beginning after Dec. 31, 2021, (Tax Cuts and Jobs Act §13206(e)) the Tax Cuts and Jobs Act redesignates the rules applicable to:

... the election of a reduced research credit provided in pre-Tax Cuts and Jobs Act Code Sec. 280C(c)(3) (FTC 2d/FIN ¶ L-15300, ¶ L-15308; USTR ¶ 280C4) as Code Sec. 280C(c)(2). (Code Sec. 280C(c)(2) as redesignated by Tax Cuts and Jobs Act §13206(d)(2)(C))

... controlled groups provided in pre-Tax Cuts and Jobs Act Code Sec. 280C(c)(4) as Code Sec. 280C(c)(3) FTC 2d/FIN ¶ L-3100, ¶ L-3131; USTR ¶ 280C4. (Code Sec. 280C(c)(3) as redesignated by Tax Cuts and Jobs Act §13206(d)(2)(C))

☐ **Effective:** For amounts paid or incurred in tax years beginning after Dec. 31, 2021. (Tax Cuts and Jobs Act §13206(e))

¶ 1409. Excess business loss disallowance rule replaces limitation on excess farm loss for non-corporate taxpayers for tax years beginning after Dec. 31, 2017

Code Sec. 461(l), as amended by Tax Cuts and Jobs Act §11012(a)
Generally effective: Tax years beginning after Dec. 31, 2017 and ending
  before Jan. 1, 2026
Committee Reports, see ¶ 5004

Under pre-Tax Cuts and Jobs Act law, if a non-corporate taxpayer received any applicable subsidy for any tax year, the taxpayer's excess farm loss for the tax year wasn't allowed. Thus, the amount of losses that could be claimed by an individual, estate, trust, or partnership were limited to a threshold amount (discussed below) if the taxpayer had received an applicable subsidy. (FTC 2d/FIN ¶ N-1300, ¶ N-1331; USTR ¶ 4614.78)

For this purpose, an excess farm loss was the excess of the taxpayer's aggregate deductions that were attributable to *farming* businesses over the sum of the taxpayer's aggregate gross income or gain attributable to *farming* businesses plus a threshold amount. (FTC 2d/FIN ¶ N-1300, ¶ N-1333; USTR ¶ 4614.78) The threshold amount was the greater of (1) $300,000 ($150,000 for married individuals filing separately), or (2) for the five-consecutive-year period preceding the tax year, the excess of the aggregate gross income or gain attributable to the taxpayer's farming businesses over the aggregate deductions attributable to the taxpayer's farming businesses. (FTC 2d/FIN ¶ N-1300, ¶ N-1336 ; USTR ¶ 4614.78) Any excess farm loss was carried over to the next tax year. (FTC 2d/FIN ¶ N-1339.1; USTR ¶ 4614.78)

New Law. The Tax Cuts and Jobs Act provides that, for a tax year of a taxpayer other than a corporation beginning after Dec. 31, 2017 and before Jan.

1, 2026, (Code Sec. 461(l)(1) as amended by Tax Cuts and Jobs Act §11012(a)) the limitation on excess *farm* loss for non-corporate taxpayers under Code Sec. 461(j) (discussed above) doesn't apply. (Code Sec. 461(l)(1)(A)) Instead, the taxpayer's excess *business* loss (defined below), if any, for the tax year is disallowed. (Code Sec. 461(l)(1)(B)) Thus, for tax years beginning after Dec. 31, 2017 and before Jan. 1, 2026, excess business losses of a taxpayer other than a corporation are not allowed for the tax year. (Com Rept, see ¶ 5004)

> *observation:* In other words, the Tax Cuts and Jobs Act expands the limitation on excess farming loss to other non-corporate taxpayers engaged in any business. Also, Code Sec. 461(j) might apply to the excess business losses of a farmer who wasn't subject to Code Sec. 461(j) because the farmer didn't receive any applicable subsidies.

> *observation:* Although Code Sec. 461 contains two subsections (j) (the limitation on excess farm losses of certain taxpayers and the definition of a farming syndicate), it's clear that Congress intended that Code Sec. 461(l) should replace the limitation on excess farm losses of certain taxpayers.

> *observation:* Although the introductory language of Code Sec. 461(l) indicates that it applies to a taxpayer "other than a corporation," Code Sec. 461(l)(4) provides rules for applying Code Sec. 461(l) to S corporations. Presumably, the introductory language of Code Sec. 461(l) should have provided that it applies to a taxpayer other than a *C* corporation.

> *observation:* Code Sec. 461(l) can apply to the excess business loss of sole proprietorships, partnerships (see below), S corporations (see below), limited liability companies (LLCs), estates, and trusts.

For coordination of the excess business loss rules with the passive activity loss rules, see below.

Excess business loss. An "excess business loss" is the excess (if any) of (Code Sec. 461(l)(3)(A)) the taxpayer's aggregate deductions for the tax year that are attributable to trades or businesses of the taxpayer (determined without regard to whether or not the deductions are disallowed for that tax year under Code Sec. 461(l)(1)), over (Code Sec. 461(l)(3)(A)(i)) the sum of: (Code Sec. 461(l)(3)(A)(ii))

(i) the taxpayer's aggregate gross income or gain for the tax year which is attributable to those trades or businesses, plus (Code Sec. 461(l)(3)(A)(ii)(I))

(ii) $250,000 (200% of that amount for a joint return (i.e., $500,000)). (Code Sec. 461(l)(3)(A)(ii)(II))

For inflation adjustments to the thresholds, see below.

illustration (1): In 2018, T, a single taxpayer, has deductions of $500,000 from a business. T's gross income from the business is $200,000. T's excess business loss is $50,000 ($500,000 − ($200,000 + $250,000)). The $50,000 excess business loss is treated as part of the taxpayer's net operating loss (NOL) carryfoward in later years.

illustration (2): The facts are the same as in illustration (1) except that T is married and files a joint return. T doesn't have an excess business loss because the aggregate business deductions ($500,000) don't exceed the $200,000 of business income plus the $500,000 threshold for joint filers.

observation: In determining whether a taxpayer has an excess business loss, Code Sec. 461(l) applies to the aggregate income and deductions from all of a taxpayer's trades or businesses. Presumably, if a husband and wife have separate trades or businesses and the couple files a joint return, Code Sec. 461(l) applies to the aggregate income and deductions from all of the couple's trades or businesses.

illustration (3): The facts are the same as in illustration (2) except that T's spouse (S) also has a business that has deductions of $500,000 and gross income of $200,000. S and T's excess business loss is $100,000 ($1,000,000 − ($400,000 + $500,000).

observation: Code Sec. 461(l) limits the ability of non-corporate taxpayers to use trade or business losses against other sources of income (such as salaries, fees, interest, dividends and capital gains). The practical result is that the business losses of a non-corporate taxpayer for a tax year can offset no more than $500,000 (for married individuals filing jointly), or $250,000 (for other individuals), of a taxpayer's non-business income for that year. Note that if married taxpayers file a joint return, the losses (up to the $500,000 limit) of one spouse can also be used to offset the other spouse's non-business income. For how to coordinate the passive activity loss rules with the excess business loss rules, see below.

illustration (4): The facts are the same as in illustration (2) except that T's spouse (S) earns a salary of $150,000. Since T and S's aggregate deductions ($500,000) don't exceed T and S's aggregate income ($200,000 + $150,000 or $350,000) plus the $500,000 threshold for joint filers, T and S don't have an excess business loss. Thus, T's business losses can be used to offset S's income on their joint return.

Inflation adjustment of threshold amounts. For tax years beginning after Dec. 31, 2018, the $250,000 threshold amount (described above) is increased by an amount equal to: (Code Sec. 461(l)(3)(B))

. . . that dollar amount (i.e., $250,000), multiplied by (Code Sec. 461(l)(3)(B)(i))

. . . the cost-of-living adjustment (COLA) determined under Code Sec. 1(f)(3) (inflation adjustments for income tax rate brackets, see FTC 2d/FIN ¶ A-1103; USTR ¶ 14.08) for the calendar year in which the tax year begins, determined by substituting "2017" for "2016" in Code Sec. 1(f)(3)(A)(ii). (Code Sec. 461(l)(3)(B)(ii))

For the changes made by the Tax Cuts and Jobs Act to the inflation adjustment of income tax brackets, see ¶ 201.

If any amount as increased under the above rule isn't a multiple of $1,000, the amount will be rounded to the nearest multiple of $1,000. (Code Sec. 461(l)(3)(B)(ii))

Disallowed excess business loss treated as NOL. Any loss that is disallowed as an excess business loss is treated as an NOL carryover to the following tax year under Code Sec. 172. (Code Sec. 461(l)(2)) So, excess business losses are carried forward and treated as part of the taxpayer's NOL carryfoward in later tax years. Under the Tax Cuts and Jobs Act, NOL carryovers are generally allowed for a tax year up to the lesser of the carryover amount or 90% (80% for tax years beginning after 2022) of taxable income determined without regard to the deduction for NOLs. (Com Rept, see ¶ 5004) For the 90% limitation on NOL deductions under the Tax Cuts and Jobs Act, see ¶ 1001. For the repeal of the carryback and the addition of an indefinite carryforward for NOL deductions under the Tax Cuts and Jobs Act, see ¶ 1002.

> *observation:* The requirement that excess business loss be carried forward as part of an NOL forces taxpayers who have losses in excess of the thresholds (discussed below) to wait at least one year to get a tax refund in connection with those excess losses. For example, if a taxpayer has an excess business loss, that loss *must* be carried forward to the next year, even if the taxpayer has income from other sources that could have, in absence of this rule, been offset by the loss.

> *illustration (5):* The facts are the same as in illustration (1). T's excess business loss of $50,000 is treated as an NOL carryforward. T can't deduct the NOL until the next tax year. If T doesn't have income in the next year, T continues to carry forward the NOL.

Partnerships and S corporations. For partnerships or S corporations (Code Sec. 461(l)(4)) excess business loss limitation rules apply at the partner or shareholder level. (Code Sec. 461(l)(4)(A)) Each partner's or shareholder's allocable share of the items of income, gain, deduction, or loss of the partnership or

S corporation for any tax year from trades or businesses attributable to the partnership or S corporation is taken into account by the partner or shareholder in applying Code Sec. 461(l) to the partner's or shareholder's tax year with or within which the tax year of the partnership or S corporation ends. (Code Sec. 461(l)(4)(B)) For an S corporation, an allocable share is the shareholder's pro-rata share of an item. (Code Sec. 461(l)(4)) In other words, each partner's share and each S corporation shareholder's pro-rata share of items of income, gain, deduction or loss of the partnership or S corporation are taken into account in applying the limitation for the tax year of the partner or S corporation shareholder. (Com Rept, see ¶ 5004)

illustration (6): In 2017, X and Y quit their jobs in order to start a business, as equal partners. X is single and invests $500,000 of capital, and so does Y, who is married. The 2018 partnership tax return reports a net loss of $700,000. X's and Y's allocable share of the partnership's loss is $350,000 each, which they report on Schedule E of their respective 2018 individual tax returns.

Since the excess loss limitation applies at the partner level, X has an excess business loss of $100,000 ($350,000 less the $250,000 threshold for single) and Y has no excess business loss because his allocable share of $350,000 is less than the $500,000 married threshold.

illustration (7): The facts are the same as in illustration (6). In 2018, X received a salary of $300,000 before forming the partnership and had income from other sources of $50,000. Even though X has an excess business loss (see illustration (5)), X can use $250,000 (up to the threshold amount) of the losses from the partnership to offset X's other income. However, even though X has sufficient income in 2018 to offset the entire loss, X *must* treat the $100,000 excess business loss as an NOL carryforward. If the partnership is not profitable in 2018 and X has no other substantial sources of income, X must continue to carry forward the NOL.

IRS can issue regs that apply these rules to any other pass-through entity to the extent necessary to carry out the purposes of Code Sec. 461(l). (Com Rept, see ¶ 5004)

Coordination with passive activity loss rules. Code Sec. 461(l) applies after the application of the passive loss rules of Code Sec. 469. (Code Sec. 461(l)(6))

observation: Code Sec. 469 contains passive loss rules which limit deductions and credits from passive trades or business activities.FTC 2d/FIN ¶ M-4600 *et seq.*; USTR ¶ 4694 *et seq.*

observation: Thus, Code Sec. 461(l)(6) provides an ordering rule so that the passive loss limitation rules apply *before* the excess business loss rule. Presumably, if a loss is disallowed under the passive activity loss rules, any deductions or income from that passive activity would not be considered in the determination of whether a taxpayer has an excess business loss. However, in the determination of whether a taxpayer has an excess business loss, Code Sec. 461(l)(3)(A) doesn't limit the "aggregate deductions attributable to a trade or business " and the "aggregate gross income or gain attributable to those trades or businesses" to *active* trades or businesses. IRS may need to provide further guidance on the interaction between the passive activity loss rules and the excess business loss rules.

Additional reporting. IRS can require any additional reporting it considers necessary to carry out the purposes of Code Sec. 461(l). (Code Sec. 461(l)(5))

☐ **Effective:** Tax years beginning after Dec. 31, 2017 (Tax Cuts and Jobs Act §11012(b)) and ending before Jan. 1, 2026. (Code Sec. 461(l)(1))

¶ 1410. Production period for beer, wine, distilled spirits won't include their aging period under the UNICAP interest capitalization rules for the next 2 calendar years

Code Sec. 263A(f), as amended by Tax Cuts and Jobs Act §13801(a)
Generally effective: For interest costs paid or accrued in calendar years beginning after Dec. 31, 2017 and before Jan. 1, 2020
Committee Reports, see ¶ 5096

The Uniform Capitalization (UNICAP) rules provide that direct and certain indirect costs allocable to real or tangible personal property produced by a taxpayer or acquired for resale must be either capitalized into the basis of that property or included in inventory. FTC 2d/FIN ¶ G-5452 et seq.; USTR ¶ 263A4 et seq. For interest expense, a taxpayer must capitalize otherwise deductible interest that the taxpayer pays or incurs during the production period to the extent the interest is allocable to designated property that the taxpayer produces, see FTC 2d/FIN ¶ L-5915; USTR ¶ 263A4.11. For purposes of the interest capitalization rules, "designated property" includes tangible personal property that has an estimated production period exceeding two years or has an estimated production period exceeding one year and a cost exceeding $1 million dollars, see FTC 2d/FIN ¶ L-5920; USTR ¶ 263A4.11. The "production period" begins on the date the production begins on a unit of property and ends on the date it is ready to be placed in service or ready to be held for sale. (FTC 2d/FIN ¶ L-5900, ¶ L-5932; USTR ¶ 263A4.11)

Under pre-Tax Cuts and Jobs Act law, for property such as beer, wine, or distilled spirits that is aged before it is sold, the aging period was *included* in the production period. (FTC 2d/FIN ¶ L-5900, ¶ L-5932; USTR ¶ 263A4.11)

> **⚫️***observation:*** This rule had the potential to substantially increase the length of the production period for property that is customarily aged before it is sold, and resulted in capitalization of a larger portion of a taxpayer's interest expense for certain property merely due to the natural aging process of the property.

New Law. For purposes of the application of the UNICAP interest capitalization rules, the Tax Cuts and Jobs Act provides that the production period does *not* include the aging period for—(Code Sec. 263A(f)(4)(A) as amended by Tax Cuts and Jobs Act §13801(a)(2))

(i) beer (as defined in Code Sec. 5052(a)), (Code Sec. 263A(f)(4)(A)(i))

(ii) wine (as described in Code Sec. 5041(a)), or (Code Sec. 263A(f)(4)(A)(ii))

(iii) distilled spirits (as defined in Code Sec. 5002(a)(8)), except those spirits that are unfit for use for beverage purposes. (Code Sec. 263A(f)(4)(A)(iii))

In other words, the provision excludes the aging periods for beer, wine, and distilled spirits from the production period for purposes of the UNICAP interest capitalization rules. Thus, producers of beer, wine and distilled spirits are able to deduct interest expenses (subject to any other applicable limitation) attributable to a shorter production period. (Com Rept, see ¶ 5096)

> **⚫️***observation:*** The practical impact of this exclusion is that beer, wine, and distilled spirits won't be considered "designated property" if the production period (without taking into account any aging period) doesn't exceed two years (one year if it has a cost in excess of $1 million dollars). Thus, the UNICAP rules won't apply and these producers will be able to deduct their interest expenses instead of capitalizing them under the UNICAP rules.

> **⚫️***observation:*** However, if the beer, wine, or distilled spirits has a production period that exceeds two years (one year if it has a cost in excess of $1 million) *even without taking into consideration the aging period*, that property will still be considered "designated property" and the producer will have to capitalize interest in accordance with the UNICAP rules, albeit over a shorter time period.

Expiration of the exclusion. This exclusion won't apply to interest costs paid or accrued after Dec. 31, 2019. (Code Sec. 263A(f)(4)(B)) In other words, the exemption expires for tax years beginning after Dec. 31, 2019. (Com Rept, see ¶ 5096)

Redesignation and conforming change. The Tax Cuts and Jobs Act also:

. . . redesignates pre-Tax Cuts and Jobs Act Code Sec. 263A(f)(4) (which defines "production period") as Code Sec. 263A(f)(5). (Code Sec. 263A(f)(4) as redesignated by Tax Cuts and Jobs Act §13801(a)(1))

. . . amends the definition of production period under Code Sec. 263A(f)(5)(B)(ii) by adding "except as provided in paragraph (4)," before "ending on the date." (Code Sec. 263A(f)(5)(B)(ii) as amended by Tax Cuts and Jobs Act §13801(b))

☐ **Effective:** For interest paid or accrued in calendar years beginning after Dec. 31, 2017 (Tax Cuts and Jobs Act §13801(c)) and before Jan. 1, 2020. (Code Sec. 263A(f)(4)(B))

> 🅡 *observation:* Thus, the exclusion applies to interest paid or accrued after 2017 and expires for interest paid or accrued after 2019. For interest paid or accrued after Dec. 31, 2019, the production period with respect to beer, wine, and distilled spirits will, once again, include the aging period.

¶ 1411. Minority and subsequent owners can expense certain costs of replanting citrus plants lost by reason of casualty

Code Sec. 263A(d)(2)(C), as amended by Tax Cuts and Jobs Act §13207(a)
Generally effective: Amounts paid or incurred after Dec. 22, 2017 and
  before Dec. 23, 2027
Committee Reports, see ¶ 5042

If plants bearing an edible crop for human consumption were lost or damaged (while in the hands of the taxpayer) by reason of freezing temperatures, disease, drought, pests, or casualty, the uniform capitalization (UNICAP) rules do not apply to any costs of the taxpayer of replanting plants bearing the same type of crop. Thus, the uniform capitalization rules do not require the capitalization of the replanting costs, which may therefore be expensed. Replanting costs for this purpose generally include costs attributable to the replanting, cultivating, maintaining, and developing of the plants that were lost or damaged, but not the acquisition costs of replacement trees or seedlings (which thus must still be capitalized). (FTC 2d/FIN ¶ N-1081; USTR ¶ 263A4.157; Catalyst ¶ 756:186)

The above exception to the UNICAP rule applies whether the replanting occurs on the same parcel of land on which the lost or damaged plants were located or on any parcel of land of the same acreage in the U.S. (FTC 2d/FIN ¶ N-1081; USTR ¶ 263A4.157)

Although replanting costs generally must be incurred by the taxpayer that owned the property when the plants were lost or damaged, costs paid or incurred by a person other than the taxpayer owning the plants at the time of damage or loss qualify for the casualty loss exception discussed above if:

(a) the taxpayer who owned the plants when the damage or loss occurred owns an equity interest of more than 50% in the plants or crops at all times during the tax year in which the amounts (replanting costs) were paid or incurred; and

(b) the person other than the person who owned the plants at the time of damage or loss owns any portion of the remaining equity interest and materially participates in the replanting, maintenance, cultivation, or development of these plants during the tax year in which the amounts (replanting costs) were paid or incurred. (FTC 2d/FIN ¶ N-1082; USTR ¶ 263A4.157)

New Law. The Tax Cuts and Jobs Act provides a special temporary rule applying the exception to the UNICAP rules to certain costs of replanting citrus plants lost by reason of casualty. (Code Sec. 263A(d)(2)(C) as amended by Tax Cuts and Jobs Act §13207(a))

The exception to the UNICAP rules (and, thus, the ability to expense replanting costs) applies to amounts paid or incurred by a person (other than the taxpayer described in Code Sec. 263A(d)(2)(A), that is, other than the person who owned the plants at the time of the casualty) if:

(I) the taxpayer who owned the plants at the time of the casualty has an equity interest of not less than 50% in the replanted citrus plants at all times during the tax year in which those amounts were paid or incurred and the person who did not own the plants at the time of the casualty holds any part of the remaining equity interest, or (Code Sec. 263A(d)(2)(C)(i)(I))

(II) the person who did not own the plants at the time of the casualty acquired the entirety of the equity interest of the person who did own the plants at the time of the casualty in the land on which the lost or damaged citrus plants were located at the time of the loss or damage, and the replanting is on that land. (Code Sec. 263A(d)(2)(C)(i)(II))

> *observation:* The material participation requirement for expensing certain replanting costs under pre-Tax Cuts and Jobs Act law (item (b), above) doesn't apply to the exception to the UNICAP rules added by the Tax Cuts and Jobs Act.

> *observation:* The exception to the UNICAP rules for subsequent owners (in item (II), above) applies only if the replanting is done on the same land on which the lost or damaged citrus plants were located at the time of the loss or damage. This restriction doesn't apply where replanting is done by the person who owned the plants at the time of the

casualty. In that case, the pre-Tax Cuts and Jobs Act UNICAP exception (under which replanting can be done on any land in the U.S., provided that the land on which the replanting is done is of the same acreage as the land on which the plants were lost or damaged) still applies.

illustration (1): Taxpayer owns a minority interest in a grove of citrus plants destroyed by a hurricane in Year 1. The citrus plants are replanted in Year 2. Under the rule set forth in item (I), above, Taxpayer isn't required to capitalize the cost of replanting the citrus plants (and, thus, can expense that cost) if the person who owned the plants at the time of the hurricane has an equity interest of at least 50% in the replanted citrus plants at all times during Year 2.

illustration (2): Smith owns a grove of citrus plants and the land on which the plants are located. The plants are destroyed by a hurricane in Year 1. Jones acquires all of Smith's equity interest in the land on which the plants had been located, and replants citrus plants on that land. Under the rule set forth in item (II), above, Jones can expense the cost of replanting the citrus plants.

Sunset. The exception to the UNICAP rules for certain costs of replanting citrus plants lost by reason of casualty (discussed above) won't apply to any cost paid or incurred after Dec. 22, 2027 (the date 10 years after the enactment of the Tax Cuts and Jobs Act). (Code Sec. 263A(d)(2)(C)(ii))

☐ **Effective:** Amounts paid or incurred after Dec. 22, 2017 (Tax Cuts and Jobs Act §13207(b)) but not after Dec. 22, 2027, i.e., the date that is 10 years after Dec. 22, 2017. (Code Sec. 263A(d)(2)(C)(ii))

observation: Thus, the Tax Cuts and Jobs Act changes discussed above apply to amounts paid or incurred after Dec. 22, 2017 and before Dec. 23, 2027.

¶ 1500. Capital Gains

¶ 1501. Breakpoints for imposition of 15% and 20% capital gains/qualified dividends rates are set as statutory dollar amounts, adjusted for inflation

Code Sec. 1(j)(1), as amended by Tax Cuts and Jobs Act §11001(a)
Code Sec. 1(j)(5), as amended by Tax Cuts and Jobs Act §11001(a)
Generally effective: Tax years beginning after 2017 and before 2026
Committee Reports, see ¶ 5001

The adjusted net capital gain of a noncorporate taxpayer (i.e., an individual, estate, or trust) is taxed at maximum rates of 0%, 15%, or 20% (see FTC 2d/FIN ¶ I-5110; USTR ¶ 14.08).

"Adjusted net capital gain" is net capital gain plus qualified dividend income, minus specified types of long-term capital gain that are taxed at a maximum rate of 28% ("28%-percent rate gain"—i.e., gain on the sale of most collectibles and the unexcluded part of gain on Code Sec. 1202 small business stock) or 25% ("unrecaptured section 1250 gain"—i.e., gain attributable to real estate depreciation) (see FTC 2d/FIN ¶ I-5110.10; USTR ¶ 14.08). "Net capital gain" is the excess of net long-term capital gains (from sales or exchanges of capital assets held for over one year) over net short-term capital losses for a tax year (see FTC 2d/FIN ¶ I-5107; USTR ¶ 14.08). "Qualified dividend income" is income from dividends received from domestic corporations and qualified foreign corporations, subject to a holding period requirement and specified exclusions (see FTC 2d/FIN ¶ I-5115.1; USTR ¶ 14.085).

Under pre-Tax Cuts and Jobs Act law, the Code provided that:

... the 0% tax rate applied to adjusted net capital gain that otherwise would be taxed at a regular tax rate below the 25% rate (i.e., at the 10% or 15% ordinary income tax rates (15% tax rate for estates and trusts) in effect under pre-Tax Cuts and Jobs Act law, see ¶ 101);

... the 15% tax rate applied to adjusted net capital gain in excess of the amount taxed at the 0% rate, that otherwise would be taxed at a regular tax rate below the 39.6% (i.e., at the 25%, 28%, 33% or 35% ordinary income tax rates (25%,

FTC 2d References are to Federal Tax Coordinator 2d
FIN References are to RIA's Analysis of Federal Taxes: Income (print)
USTR References are to United States Tax Reporter
Catalyst References are to Checkpoint Catalyst
PCA References are to Pension Analysis (print and electronic)
PBE References are to Pension & Benefits Explanations
BCA References are to Benefits Analysis (electronic)
BC References are to Benefits Coordinator (print)
EP References are to Estate Planning Analysis (print and electronic)

28%, and 33% rates for estates and trusts) in effect under pre-Tax Cuts and Jobs Act law, see ¶ 101); and

... the 20% tax rate applied to adjusted net capital gain that exceeded the amounts taxed at the 0% and 15% rates. (FTC 2d/FIN ¶ I-5100, ¶ I-5110, ¶ I-5110.1, ¶ I-5110.2, ¶ I-5110.3; USTR ¶ 14.08; Catalyst ¶ 502:161; Catalyst ¶ 502:163)

> **observation:** Because the ordinary income tax brackets (income ranges taxed at progressively higher marginal rates) for each filing status are adjusted for inflation, the breakpoints at which each marginal tax rate applies change annually. For 2017, the maximum income subject to an ordinary income tax rate below 25% was: $75,900 for joint filers and surviving spouses; $50,800 for heads of household; $37,950 for single filers; $37,950 for married taxpayers filing separately (see ¶ 101); and $2,550 for estates and trusts (see ¶ 104).
>
> And, the maximum income subject to an ordinary income tax rate below 39.6% was: $470,700 for joint filers and surviving spouses; $444,550 for heads of household; $418,400 for single filers; $235,350 for married taxpayers filing separately (see ¶ 101); and $12,500 for estates and trusts (see ¶ 104).
>
> So, for 2017:
>
> ... the 0% tax rate applied to adjusted net capital gain up to $75,900 for joint filers and surviving spouses, $50,800 for heads of household, $37,950 for single filers, $37,950 for married taxpayers filing separately, and $2,550 for estates and trusts;
>
> ... the 15% tax rate applied to adjusted net capital gain over the amount subject to the 0% rate and up to $470,700 for joint filers and surviving spouses, $444,550 for heads of household, $418,400 for single filers, $235,350 for married taxpayers filing separately, and $12,500 for estates and trusts; and
>
> ... the 20% tax rate applied to adjusted net capital gain over $470,700 for joint filers and surviving spouses, $444,550 for heads of household, $418,400 for single filers, $235,350 for married taxpayers filing separately, and $12,500 for estates and trusts.

New Law. For tax years beginning after Dec. 31, 2017 and before Jan. 1, 2026 (Code Sec. 1(j)(1) as amended by Tax Cuts and Jobs Act §11001(a)), the Tax Cuts and Jobs Act provides that the capital gains rate rules above are to apply with the following modifications (Code Sec. 1(j)(5)(A) as amended by Tax Cuts and Jobs Act §11001(a)):

(1) the 0% rate is to apply to adjusted net capital gain that's below the "maximum zero rate amount" (instead of to the adjusted net capital gain that

otherwise would be taxed at a regular tax rate below the 25%). (Code Sec. 1(j)(5)(A)(i)) And, for this purpose (Code Sec. 1(j)(5)(B)), the "maximum zero rate amount" is (Code Sec. 1(j)(5)(B)(i)):

... for a joint return or surviving spouse, $77,200 (Code Sec. 1(j)(5)(B)(i)(I));

... for an individual who is a head of household (as defined in Code Sec. 2(b)), $51,700 (Code Sec. 1(j)(5)(B)(i)(II));

... for any other individual (other than an estate or trust), an amount equal to $1/2$ of the amount in effect for joint filers for the tax year (Code Sec. 1(j)(5)(B)(i)(III)); and

... for an estate or trust, $2,600. (Code Sec. 1(j)(5)(B)(i)(IV))

(2) the 15% rate is to apply to adjusted net capital gain that exceeds the amount subject to the 0% rate and that's below the "maximum 15% rate amount" (instead of to the amount that exceeds the amount subject to the 0% rate and that otherwise would be taxed at a regular tax rate below 39.6%). (Code Sec. 1(j)(5)(A)(ii)) And, for this purpose (Code Sec. 1(j)(5)(B)), the "maximum 15% rate amount" is (Code Sec. 1(j)(5)(B)(ii)):

... for a joint return or surviving spouse, $479,000 ($1/2$ that amount for marrieds filing separately) (Code Sec. 1(j)(5)(B)(ii)(I));

... for a head of household, $452,400 (Code Sec. 1(j)(5)(B)(ii)(II));

... for any other individual (other than an estate or trust), $425,800 (Code Sec. 1(j)(5)(B)(ii)(III)); and

... for an estate or trust, $12,700. (Code Sec. 1(j)(5)(B)(ii)(IV))

In addition, for any tax year beginning after 2018, each of the dollar amounts under rules (1) and (2) above must be increased by an amount equal to (Code Sec. 1(j)(5)(C)): (i) that dollar amount (Code Sec. 1(j)(5)(C)(i)) × (ii) the cost-of-living (inflation) adjustment determined under Code Sec. 1(f)(3) (see ¶ 201) for the calendar year in which the tax year begins, determined by substituting "calendar year 2017" for calendar year 2016' in Code Sec. 1(f)(3)(A)(ii). (Code Sec. 1(j)(5)(C)(ii)) If any increase under this rule isn't a multiple of $50, the increase must be rounded to the next multiple of $50. (Code Sec. 1(j)(5)(C))

> *observation:* Thus, the dollar amounts described in rules (1) and (2) above are the amounts in effect for 2018.
>
> So, for 2018:
>
> ... the 0% tax rate applies to adjusted net capital gain up to $77,200 for joint filers and surviving spouses, $51,700 for heads of household, $38,600 for single filers, $38,600 for married taxpayers filing separately, and $2,600 for estates and trusts;
>
> ... the 15% tax rate applies to adjusted net capital gain over the amount subject to the 0% rate, and up to $479,000 for joint filers and

surviving spouses, $452,400 for heads of household, $425,800 for single filers, $239,500 for married taxpayers filing separately, and $12,700 for estates and trusts; and

. . . the 20% tax rate applies to adjusted net capital gain over $479,000 for joint filers and surviving spouses, $452,400 for heads of household, $425,800 for single filers, $239,500 for married taxpayers filing separately, and $12,700 for estates and trusts.

Sunset. The rules above modifying the capital gains/qualified dividend computation rules don't apply for tax years beginning after Dec. 31, 2025. (Code Sec. 1(j)(1))

☐ **Effective:** For tax years beginning after Dec. 31, 2017 (Tax Cuts and Jobs Act §11001(c)), and before Jan. 1, 2026. (Code Sec. 1(j)(1))

¶ 1502. Certain gains from partnership profits interests held in connection with performance of investment services are short-term capital gains if held for 3 years or less

Code Sec. 1061, as added by Tax Cuts and Jobs Act §13309(a)
Generally effective: Tax years beginning after Dec. 31, 2017
Committee Reports, see ¶ 5052

A profits interest in a partnership is any interest other than a capital interest. A profits interest gives the holder the right to receive future profits and appreciation in value of assets of a partnership, but doesn't give the holder a share of the proceeds upon the immediate liquidation of the partnership. The receipt of a capital interest for services provided to a partnership results in taxable compensation for the recipient. However, under a safe harbor rule, the receipt of a profits interest in exchange for services provided is not a taxable event to the recipient if the profits interest entitles the holder to share only in gains and profits generated after the date of issuance (and certain other requirements are met). FTC 2d/FIN ¶ B-1408; USTR ¶ 7214.01

> **observation:** Thus, certain partnerships will issue profits interests to key service providers because they aren't taxable at grant, but the holder of the profits interest will be considered to be a partner from the time of vesting and will be eligible for long-term capital gain treatment upon a liquidity event *if the relevant holding period is met.*

> **observation:** Profits interests are commonly used in private investment funds and are often referred to as "carried interest" or "carry." In this context, carried interest is a share of the profits that the general partner (commonly a manager of a private equity fund, hedge fund, or

similar investment vehicle) receives as compensation (i.e., the percentage of an investment's gains that the manager takes as compensation), regardless of that partner's capital investment, if any.

🔵 *observation:* A carried interest is generally used to motivate the general partner (fund manager) to work toward improving the fund's performance. While fund managers usually receive a fixed management fee, the majority of their profits comes from carried interest that is contingent on the success of the underlying investments.

🔵 *observation:* The tax treatment of carried interest has for many years been a high-profile target for potential reform.

Although a partnership doesn't pay income tax, it is required to compute certain classes of income and deductions as separate items. These classes of income and deductions are then directly "passed through" to the partners, who take them into account for tax purposes by including their distributive share of each of these classes of income and deductions as separate items on their tax returns. In the hands of the partner, the character of any partnership item that must be "separately stated" is determined as if realized directly from the source from which the partnership realized it, or incurred in the same manner as the partnership incurred it. Thus, to determine the nature of an item of separately stated income, gain, loss, deduction or credit in the hands of the partnership and in the hands of the partner, the partnership is viewed as an entity, and the items are characterized from the viewpoint of the partnership rather than from the viewpoint of an individual partner. FTC 2d/FIN ¶ B-1900 *et seq.*; USTR ¶ 7024.02

🔵 *observation:* In other words, if the tax character of a "separately stated" partnership item must be determined, it is determined at the partnership level, and the item retains this character in the hands of the partners.

🔵 *observation:* Thus, if a partnership recognizes gain from the sale of a capital asset that it has held for more than one year, an individual partner who is allocated a share of the partnership's long-term capital gain will be taxed on that share at long-term capital gain rates.

Under pre-Tax Cuts and Jobs Act law, carried interest typically passed through an investment partnership as long-term capital gains and, thus, was taxed in the hands of the taxpayer at more favorable rates. (FTC 2d/FIN ¶ B-2140 *et seq.*, ¶ B-2141; USTR ¶ 7074.02; Catalyst ¶ 202:202; Catalyst ¶ 209:112; Catalyst ¶ 217:122)

The long-term capital gains rates under pre-Tax Cuts and Jobs Act law were as follows:

. . . 0% on adjusted net capital gain for taxpayers who fell into an income tax bracket below 25% for ordinary income.

. . . 15% on adjusted net capital gain for taxpayers who fell into an income tax bracket below 39.6% for ordinary income, and

. . . 20% on adjusted net capital gain for taxpayers who fell into the 39.6% income tax bracket (the highest marginal rate on ordinary income).

Thus, for the wealthiest citizens who fell into the 39.6% bracket, long-term capital gains were generally taxed at a rate of 20%. FTC 2d/FIN ¶ I-5110; USTR ¶ 14.08 However, there was also a 3.8% net investment income tax (NIIT). Because the NIIT applied to capital gains, the overall rate on long-term capital gains for some high-income taxpayers was 23.8% (20% plus the 3.8% NIIT). The NIIT applied to taxpayers whose modified adjusted gross income exceeded $250,000 for joint returns and surviving spouses, $125,000 for separate returns, and $200,000 in all other cases. FTC 2d/FIN ¶ A-6360 et seq.; USTR ¶ 14,114 et seq.

For a discussion of the Tax Cuts and Jobs Act changes to the income tax rates for individuals, see ¶ 101.

For a discussion of the interaction between the new income tax brackets and capital gains rates under the Tax Cuts and Jobs Act, see ¶ 1501

> *observation:* Historically, private equity funds were structured as limited partnerships, with the capital investors holding limited partner interests and the fund manager setting up a special purpose vehicle as the general partner. Although the general partner received the carried interest by contributing services, the general partner was subject to tax in the same manner as a partner who contributed capital. As a result, the general partner's allocable share of the fund income retained its character as it passed from the fund to the general partner.

> *observation:* Issuing carried interest was attractive in the context of investment services because a large percentage of the income of many funds consists of long-term capital gain, qualified dividend income, or other income subject to tax at preferential rates.

> *illustration (1):* A fund raised capital of $100 million and ultimately sold its investments for $150 million, resulting in a gain of $50 million. Assuming the manager (a profits interest partner) had a 20% carried interest, the manager was allocated $10 million of capital gain. At a maximum rate of 23.8% (20% capital gains rate plus the 3.8% NIIT, if applicable), the fund manager generated a net after-tax return of at least $7.62 million.

> Alternatively, if the manager wasn't a partner in the fund and received a management fee equal to 20% of gross profits rather than an

allocation of carried interest, the manager was taxed at ordinary income rates on the $10 million management fee; at a maximum federal rate of 39.6% (under pre-Tax Cuts and Jobs Act law), the fund manager generated a net after tax return of $6.04 million.

🅡🅐 *observation:* This was the crux of the perceived windfall that fund managers derived from carried interest. Outside of the partnership context, individuals typically are taxed at favorable capital gain rates only on gains generated from investments of their after-tax dollars. However, as a result of the partnership tax regime, carried interest passed through the partnership as long-term capital gain and fund managers were able to pay tax at a more favorable rate on gains derived from their efforts (i.e., services), which would have been ordinary income had it been paid as compensation for their services.

🅡🅐 *observation:* Many lawmakers view this treatment as inequitable, under the premise that long-term capital gains should apply to returns from the investment of capital, rather than compensation for the provision of services.

IRS issued proposed regs attempting to mitigate the perceived abuse with respect to carried interest. However, the proposed regs would only be effective for arrangements entered into or are modified after the date they are adopted and published as final regs, and, so, they don't currently apply. (FTC 2d/FIN ¶ B-2140 *et seq.,* ¶ B-2141, ¶ B-2142, ¶ B-2143; USTR ¶ 7074.02)

🅡🅐 *observation:* Under the proposed regs, an arrangement would be treated as a disguised payment for services if:

. . . a service provider performs services (either directly or through a delegate) to or for the benefit of a partnership, either as a partner or in anticipation of becoming a partner,

. . . there is a related direct or indirect allocation and distribution to the service provider, and

. . . the performance of services and the allocation and distribution, when viewed together, are properly characterized as a transaction between the partnership and the partner acting other than in his capacity as a partner (i.e., an outsider).

If applicable, the transaction would be treated as resulting in a compensation payment to an outsider, rather than an allocation of income, with the result that, where appropriate, the payment would have to be capitalized. In addition, the payment would be ordinary income to the partner receiving the payment as opposed to capital gain. (FTC 2d/FIN ¶ B-2140 et seq.; USTR ¶ 7074.02)

New Law. The Tax Cuts and Jobs Act changes the tax treatment of gains from a profits interest in a partnership (sometimes referred to a carried interest) held in connection with the performance of services (Com Rept, see ¶ 5052) by providing that if one or more "applicable partnership interests" (defined below) are held by a taxpayer at any time during the tax year, the excess (if any) of— (Code Sec. 1061(a) as added by Tax Cuts and Jobs Act §13309(a)(2))

(1) the taxpayer's net long-term capital gain with respect to those interests for that tax year, over (Code Sec. 1061(a)(1))

(2) the taxpayer's net long-term capital gain with respect to those interests for that tax year computed by applying Code Sec. 1222(3) and Code Sec. 1222(4) by substituting "3 years" for "1 year," (Code Sec. 1061(a)(2))

will be treated as short-term capital gain. This treatment applies notwithstanding Code Sec. 83 or any election in effect under Code Sec. 83(b). (Code Sec. 1061(a))

Thus, the Tax Cuts and Jobs Act provides for a three-year holding period in the case of certain net long-term capital gain with respect to any applicable partnership interest held by the taxpayer. Code Sec. 83 (relating to property transferred in connection with the performance of services) doesn't apply to the transfer of a partnership interest to which this provision applies. (Com Rept, see ¶ 5052)

The fact that an individual may have included an amount in income upon acquisition of an applicable partnership interest, or that an individual may have made a Code Sec. 83(b) election with respect to an applicable partnership interest, doesn't change the three-year holding period requirement for long-term capital gain treatment with respect to the applicable partnership interest. Thus, Code Sec. 1061(a) treats as short-term capital gain taxed at ordinary income rates the amount of the taxpayer's net long-term capital gain with respect to an applicable partnership interest for the tax year that exceeds the amount of such gain calculated as if a three-year (not one-year) holding period applies. In making this calculation, the provision takes account of long-term capital losses calculated as if a three-year holding period applies. (Com Rept, see ¶ 5052)

> *illustration (2):* Fund manager P holds a profits interest in a partnership that was received in connection with the performance of services. P's separately stated net long-term capital gain in connection with that interest is $200 million. However, only $150 million of that amount is attributable to underlying investments that have been held for more than three years. Thus, P will be treated as having received $150 million of long-term capital gain which will be taxed at capital gains rates, and $50 million of short-term capital gain which will be taxed at ordinary income tax rates.

observation: As noted above, short-term capital gains are taxed at the same rates as ordinary income. FTC 2d/FIN ¶ I-5100 *et seq.*; USTR ¶ 14.08. Under the Tax Cuts and Jobs Act, the highest marginal tax rate for ordinary income is 37%, see ¶ 101. Thus, the maximum rate at which carried interest attributable to underlying investments not held for more than 3 years can be taxed is 37%.

observation: The Tax Cuts and Jobs Act's holding period change from more than one to more than three years is imposed on individual profits partners in partnerships whose business is raising or returning capital, or investing in specified assets, including securities, commodities, cash or cash equivalents, and some real estate interests. Although the longer holding period seeks to reduce the amount of investment eligible for the lower 20% or 23.8% long-term capital gain rate, its impact may in fact be limited since the average holding period for private equity fund managers is greater than three years. Most private equity managers who buy companies, restructure and refinance them, and then sell them, and most real estate partnerships already hold their underlying assets for six or more years. Thus, Tax Cuts and Jobs Act's change to the holding period required for long-term capital gain treatment could affect some hedge fund managers who invest for shorter periods, but they can restructure their portfolios and practices to hold qualifying assets for more than three years and get the lower long-term capital gain rate.

observation: Although the Tax Cuts and Jobs Act imposes a more than three-year holding period requirement on the underlying investments in order for certain profits interests received for the performance of services to qualify as long term capital gain rather than ordinary income, profits partners in investment partnerships often have their profits interests redeemed. If there is a sale, exchange or redemption of a partner's interest, the three-year holding period requirement applies to the partner's holding period of the profits interest, not the underlying assets. Further, if the disposition of the profits interest is considered a transfer to a related party, the partner has all short term capital gain even if his holding period is longer than three years.

observation: Under Code Sec. 83, a service provider is taxed on property received "in connection with the performance of services" when the property is substantially vested (i.e., when the property isn't subject to a substantial risk of forfeiture, or is transferable to a third party free of risk). The service provider receiving the property can instead elect, under Code Sec. 83(b), to include the income from the transfer in gross income in the year in which the property is received (i.e., before it becomes substantially vested). FTC 2d/FIN ¶ H-2500; USTR ¶ 834 *et seq.*

✐ *observation:* As indicated above, the main objection to the carried interest "loophole" was that the "carry" (or percentage of investment gains) was really compensation for the performance of services and not that the underlying investments weren't being held for a long enough period of time.

IRS authority to limit scope of the change. IRS has the authority to provide that Code Sec. 1061(a) won't apply to income or gain attributable to any asset not held for portfolio investment on behalf of third party investors (defined below). (Code Sec. 1061(b)) Thus, IRS may issue regs or other guidance saying that Code Sec. 1061(a) doesn't apply to income or gain attributable to any asset that isn't held for portfolio investment on behalf of third party investors. (Com Rept, see ¶ 5052)

Applicable partnership interest defined. Unless an exception (discussed below) applies, an "applicable partnership interest" is any interest in a partnership which, directly or indirectly, is transferred to (or is held by) the taxpayer in connection with the performance of substantial services by the taxpayer, or any other related person, in any applicable trade or business. An interest held by an individual employed by another entity that is conducting a trade or business (which is not an applicable trade or business) and who provides services only to that other entity is *not* an applicable partnership interest. (Code Sec. 1061(c)(1))

It is intended that a partnership interest won't fail to be treated as transferred or held in connection with the performance of services merely because the taxpayer *also* made contributions to the partnership. IRS is directed to provide guidance implementing this intent. (Com Rept, see ¶ 5052)

Applicable trade or business defined. An "applicable trade or business" is any activity conducted on a regular, continuous, and substantial basis which, regardless of whether the activity is conducted in one or more entities, consists (in whole or part) of (Code Sec. 1061(c)(2)) raising or returning capital, and (Code Sec. 1061(c)(2)(A)) either— (Code Sec. 1061(c)(2)(B))

(i) investing in (or disposing of) specified assets (or identifying specified assets for such investing or disposition), or (Code Sec. 1061(c)(2)(B)(i))

(ii) developing specified assets. (Code Sec. 1061(c)(2)(B)(ii))

Developing specified assets takes place, for example, if it is represented to investors, lenders, regulators, or others that the value, price, or yield of a portfolio business may be enhanced or increased in connection with choices or actions of a service provider or of others acting in concert with or at the direction of a service provider. Services performed as an employee of an applicable trade or business are treated as performed in an applicable trade or business for purposes of this rule. However, merely voting shares owned doesn't amount to development; for example, a mutual fund that merely votes proxies received with respect to shares of stock it holds isn't engaged in development. (Com Rept, see ¶ 5052)

Specified asset defined. The term "specified asset" means securities (as defined in Code Sec. 475(c)(2) without regard to the last sentence thereof), commodities (as defined in Code Sec. 475(e)(2)), real estate held for rental or investment, cash or cash equivalents, options or derivative contracts with respect to any of the foregoing, and an interest in a partnership to the extent of the partnership's proportionate interest in any of the foregoing. (Code Sec. 1061(c)(3))

> *observation:* Code Sec. 475(c)(2) and Code Sec. 475(e)(2) define the terms securities and commodities, respectively, for purposes of the mark-to-market rules that apply to securities deals and certain commodities dealers. FTC 2d/FIN ¶ I-7650 *et seq.*; USTR ¶ 4754 *et seq.*

In other words, for this purpose:

. . . a security means any (1) share of corporate stock, (2) partnership interest or beneficial ownership interest in a widely held or publicly traded partnership or trust, (3) note, bond, debenture, or other evidence of indebtedness, (4) interest rate, currency, or equity notional principal contract, (5) interest in, or derivative financial instrument in, any such security or any currency (regardless of whether Code Sec. 1256 applies to the contract), and (6) position that is not such a security and is a hedge with respect to such a security and is clearly identified.

. . . a commodity means any (1) commodity that is actively traded, (2) notional principal contract with respect to such a commodity, (3) interest in, or derivative financial instrument in, such a commodity or notional principal contract, or (4) position that is not such a commodity and is a hedge with respect to such a commodity and is clearly identified.

. . . real estate held for rental or investment doesn't include, for example, real estate on which the holder operates an active farm.

. . . to determine the proportionate interest of a partnership in any specified asset, a partnership interest includes any partnership interest that isn't otherwise treated as a security for purposes of the provision (e.g., an interest in a partnership that isn't widely held or publicly traded). For example, assume that a hedge fund acquires an interest in an operating business conducted in the form of a non-publicly traded partnership that isn't widely held; the partnership interest is a specified asset for purposes of the provision. (Com Rept, see ¶ 5052)

Exceptions to the definition of applicable partnership interest. The term "applicable partnership interest" doesn't include— (Code Sec. 1061(c)(4))

. . . any interest in a partnership held by a corporation (directly or indirectly), or (Code Sec. 1061(c)(4)(A))

So, if two corporations form a partnership to conduct a joint venture for developing and marketing a pharmaceutical product, the partnership interests held by the two corporations aren't applicable partnership interests. (Com Rept, see ¶ 5052)

. . . any capital interest in a partnership which provides the taxpayer with a right to share in partnership capital commensurate with (Code Sec. 1061(c)(4)(B)) either (1) the amount of capital contributed (determined at the time the interest is received), or (Code Sec. 1061(c)(4)(B)(i)) (2) the value of the interest subject to tax under Code Sec. 83 upon the receipt or vesting of that interest. (Code Sec. 1061(c)(4)(B)(ii))

For example, if a partner receives a capital interest in the partnership for capital he or she contributed to the partnership, and the partnership agreement provides that the partner's share of partnership capital is commensurate with the amount of capital he or she contributed (as of the time the partnership interest was received) compared to total partnership capital, the partnership interest isn't an applicable partnership interest to that extent. (Com Rept, see ¶ 5052)

Third party investor defined. A "third party investor" is a person who— (Code Sec. 1061(c)(5))

. . . holds an interest in the partnership that doesn't constitute property held in connection with an applicable trade or business; and (Code Sec. 1061(c)(5)(A))

. . . isn't (and has never been) actively engaged, and isn't (and was never) related to a person engaged, in (directly or indirectly) providing substantial services described in Code Sec. 1061(c)(1) for that partnership or any applicable trade or business. (Code Sec. 1061(c)(5)(B))

Transfer of an applicable partnership interest to a related person. If a taxpayer transfers any applicable partnership interest, directly or indirectly, to a "related person" (defined below), the taxpayer must include in gross income (as short term capital gain) the excess (if any) of—(Code Sec. 1061(d)(1))

. . . the amount of taxpayer's long-term capital gain with respect to that interest for the tax year that is attributable to the sale or exchange of any asset held for not more than three years that is allocable to that interest, over (Code Sec. 1061(d)(1)(A))

. . . any amount treated as short-term capital gain under Code Sec. 1061(a) relating to the transfer of that interest. (Code Sec. 1061(d)(1)(B))

Thus, if a taxpayer transfers any applicable partnership interest, directly or indirectly, to a person related to the taxpayer, then the taxpayer includes in gross income as short-term capital gain as much of the taxpayer's net long-term capital gain attributable to the sale or exchange of an asset held for not more than three years as is allocable to the interest. The amount included as short-term capital gain on the transfer is reduced by the amount treated as short-term capital gain on the transfer for the tax year under Code Sec. 1061(a) (that is, amounts aren't double-counted). (Com Rept, see ¶ 5052)

Related person defined. A person is related to the taxpayer for these purposes if (Code Sec. 1061(d)(2)) the person is a member of the taxpayer's family within the meaning of Code Sec. 318(a)(1), or (Code Sec. 1061(d)(2)(A)) the person performed a service within the current calendar year (or the preceding three calendar years) in any applicable trade or business in or for which the taxpayer performed a service (Code Sec. 1061(d)(2)(B)) (i.e., a colleague). (Com Rept, see ¶ 5052)

> *observation:* Under Code Sec. 1061, the term "family" is defined using the constructive ownership rules of Code Sec. 318(a)(1). Thus, it includes, generally, the employee's spouse, children, grandchildren, and parents. FTC 2d/FIN ¶ F-11803; USTR ¶ 3184.02.

Reporting. IRS is directed to require reporting (at the time and in the manner prescribed by IRS) as is needed to carry out the purposes of Code Sec. 1061. (Code Sec. 1061(e)) The penalties otherwise applicable to a failure to report to partners under Code Sec. 6031(b) apply to a failure to report under this requirement. (Com Rept, see ¶ 5052)

Regs. IRS is directed to issue regs or other guidance as needed or appropriate to carry out the purposes of Code Sec. 1061. (Code Sec. 1061(f)) This guidance is to address prevention of the abuse of the purposes of the provision, including through the allocation of income to tax-indifferent parties. Guidance is also to provide for the application of the provision in the case of tiered structures of entities. (Com Rept, see ¶ 5052)

Redesignation. Pre-Tax Cuts and Jobs Act Code Sec. 1061 is redesignated as Code Sec. 1062. (Code Sec. 1062 as redesignated by Tax Cuts and Jobs Act §13309(a)(1))

☐ **Effective:** Tax years beginning after Dec. 31, 2017. (Tax Cuts and Jobs Act §13309(c))

¶ 1503. Like-kind exchanges are limited to exchanges of real estate

Code Sec. 1031(a)(1), as amended by Tax Cuts and Jobs Act §13303(a)
Code Sec. 1031(a)(2), as amended by Tax Cuts and Jobs Act §13303(b)(1)(A)
Code Sec. 1031(e), as amended by Tax Cuts and Jobs Act §13303(b)(2)
Code Sec. 1031(e), as amended by Tax Cuts and Jobs Act §13303(b)(3)
Code Sec. 1031(h), as amended by Tax Cuts and Jobs Act §13303(b)(4)
Code Sec. 1031(i), as amended by Tax Cuts and Jobs Act §13303(b)(1)(B)
Generally effective: Exchanges completed after Dec. 31, 2017

Committee Reports, see ¶ 5046

Under Code Sec. 1031, a taxpayer doesn't recognize gain or loss on an exchange of like-kind (see FTC 2d/FIN ¶ I-3059 *et seq.*; USTR ¶ 10,314.02) properties if both the relinquished property and the replacement property are held for productive use in a trade or business or for investment purposes, see FTC 2d/FIN ¶ I-3050 *et seq.*; USTR ¶ 10,314 *et seq.*

Under pre-Tax Cuts and Jobs Act law, property eligible to be exchanged in a tax-free like-kind exchange included real property and personal property, including intangible personal property such as patents and other intellectual property. (FTC 2d/FIN ¶ I-3050, ¶ I-3060, ¶ I-3065, ¶ I-3065.1, ¶ I-3065.2; USTR ¶ 10,314, ¶ 10,314.02; Catalyst ¶ 501:144; Catalyst ¶ 501:192; Catalyst ¶ 505:100; Catalyst ¶ 505:110) The like-kind exchange rules didn't apply to exchanges of stock in trade or other property held primarily for sale, stocks (other than shares in certain mutual ditch, reservoir, or irrigation companies, see FTC 2d/FIN ¶ I-3091.1; USTR ¶ 10,314.04), bonds, or notes, other securities, or evidences of indebtedness or interest; interests in a partnership; certificates of trust or beneficial interest, or choses in action. (FTC 2d/FIN ¶ I-3089, ¶ I-3090, ¶ I-3091, ¶ I-3092, ¶ I-3093, ¶ I-3094; USTR ¶ 10,314.04)

Under pre-Tax Cuts and Jobs Act law, depreciable tangible personal property could have been exchanged for like-kind property if the relinquished property and replacement property were of a like class if the properties were either within the same general asset class or within the same product class. (FTC 2d/FIN ¶ I-3060, ¶ I-3061, ¶ I-3062, ¶ I-3063, ¶ I-3064; USTR ¶ 10,314.02) But, personal property used predominantly in the U.S. was not like-kind with respect to personal property used predominantly outside the U.S. (FTC 2d/FIN ¶ I-3064.1; USTR ¶ 10,314.04) Similarly, livestock of different sexes weren't like-kind property. (FTC 2d/FIN ¶ I-3067; USTR ¶ 10,314.04)

Under pre-Tax Cuts and Jobs Act law, IRS provided safe harbors for like-kind exchange (LKE) programs involving multiple exchanges of 100 or more items of tangible personal property by taxpayers (for example, lessors of equipment or vehicles). (FTC 2d/FIN ¶ I-3067)

New Law. In light of the increased and expanded expensing under Code Sec. 168(k) (¶ 1201 *et seq.*) and Code Sec. 179 (¶ 1101 *et seq.*) for tangible personal property and certain building improvements, Congress believed that Code Sec. 1031 should be limited to exchanges of real property not held primarily for sale. (Com Rept, see ¶ 5046).

Specifically, no gain or loss is recognized on the exchange of *real* property held for productive use in a trade or business or for investment if the *real* property is exchanged solely for *real* property of like kind which is to be held either for productive use in a trade or business or for investment. (Code Sec. 1031(a)(1) as amended by Tax Cuts and Jobs Act §13303(a)) *observation:* Under the Tax Cuts and Jobs Act, exchanges of personal property and intangible property do not qualify as tax-free under Code Sec. 1031 for exchanges completed after Dec. 31, 2017. Thus, exchanges of machinery, equipment, vehicles, patents and other intellectual property, artwork, collectibles, and other intangible business assets do not qualify for nonrecognition of gain or loss as like-kind exchanges.

observation: In determining whether property was like-kind under Code Sec. 1031 under pre-Tax Cuts and Jobs Act law, the applicable state law generally determined the classification of property rights as real property or personal property. However, state law property classifications were not the sole basis for that determination and federal tax law could determine whether exchanged properties are like-kind, see FTC 2d/FIN ¶ I-3059.1; USTR ¶ 10,314.02. Presumably, a similar rule will apply in determining whether a property right is real property eligible to be exchanged in a tax-free like-kind exchange.

observation: Any taxpayer (such as a lessor of equipment or vehicles) who structured an ongoing LKE program of multiple exchanges of tangible personal property under the safe harbors provided in Rev Proc 2003-39 (FTC 2d/FIN ¶ I-3067; USTR ¶ 10,314.02) needs to reconsider these arrangements as a result of the Tax Cuts and Jobs Act.

Congress intended that real property eligible for like-kind exchange treatment under pre-Tax Cuts and Jobs Act law would continue to be eligible for like-kind exchange treatment. (Com Rept, see ¶ 5046)

observation: Under pre-Tax Cuts and Jobs Act law, a variety of partial interests in real property could be exchanged as like-kind and these interests presumably still are eligible for like-kind exchange treatment. These interests include certain partial interests in real property (see FTC 2d/FIN ¶s I-3072, I-3073; USTR ¶s 10.134.02, 10,134.03), remainder interests and life estates in real property (see FTC 2d/FIN ¶ I-3072; USTR ¶ 10,314.03), leaseholds of at least 30 years (see FTC 2d/FIN ¶ I-3076), perpetual water rights, coal and oil leases, royalty interests in oil, gas, and mineral rights (see FTC 2d/FIN ¶ I-3079; USTR ¶ 10,314.03), interests in certain trusts (such as Illinois land trusts and Delaware statutory trusts (DSTs), see FTC 2d/FIN ¶ I-3074 and FTC 2d/FIN ¶ I-3075), and undivided fractional interests in real property (see FTC 2d/FIN ¶ I-3092.1).

Also, Code Sec. 1031(a) does not apply to any exchange of real property held primarily for sale. (Code Sec. 1031(a)(2) as amended by Tax Cuts and Jobs Act §13303(b)(1)(A)) Thus, the Tax Cuts and Jobs Act limits the application of the like-kind exchange rules to real property that is not held primarily for sale. (Com Rept, see ¶ 5046)

> **⊘ observation:** The rule provided in Code Sec. 1031(a)(2) is similar to the pre-Tax Cuts Jobs Act law's exclusion of stock in trade or other property held primarily for sale from property eligible to be exchanged in a like-kind exchange, see FTC 2d/FIN ¶ I-3091; USTR ¶ 10,314.04. Presumably, similar rules will apply to determine whether real property is "held primarily for sale" under Code Sec. 1031(a)(2). In that case, "primarily" will presumably mean "of first importance" or "principally."

> **⊘ observation:** Presumably, under Code Sec. 1031(a)(2), neither the relinquished property nor the replacement property can be real property that is held primarily for sale.

The Tax Cuts and Jobs Act strikes rules providing that "stocks" (i.e., property ineligible for like-kind exchange treatment under pre-Tax Cuts and Jobs Act law) do not include shares in a mutual ditch, reservoir, or irrigation company if at the time of the exchange the mutual ditch, reservoir, or irrigation company is an organization described in (Code Sec. 501(c)(12)(A) (i.e., requirements for an organization to be exempt from income tax, see FTC 2d/FIN ¶ D-6101; USTR ¶ 5014.21) determined without regard to the percentage of its income that is collected from its members for the purpose of meeting losses and expenses), and the shares in the company have been recognized by the highest court of the state in which the company was organized or by applicable state statute as constituting or representing real property or an interest in real property. (Code Sec. 1031(i) as amended by Tax Cuts and Jobs Act §13303(b)(2)(B)) However, Congress intended that a like-kind exchange of real property includes an exchange of shares in a mutual ditch, reservoir, or irrigation company described in Code Sec. 501(c)(12)(A) if at the time of the exchange the shares have been recognized by the highest court or statute of the state in which the company is organized as constituting or representing real property or an interest in real property. (Com Rept, see ¶ 5046)

> **⊘ observation:** Under Code Sec. 501(c)(12)(A), a mutual ditch or irrigation company is exempt from income tax if at least 85% of its income consists of amounts collected from members for the sole purpose of meeting losses and expenses. However, the 85% test doesn't apply for purposes of determining whether the stock in the company is treated as real property. Thus, a mutual ditch or irrigation company doesn't have to be exempt from income tax in order for the stock in that company to be treated as real property for purposes of the like-kind exchange rules.

Partnerships that elect out of partnership treatment. For purposes of Code Sec. 1031, an interest in a partnership which has in effect a valid election under Code Sec. 761(a) (FTC 2d/FIN ¶ B-1201; USTR ¶ 7614.02) to be excluded from the application of all of the partnership rules provided in subchapter K of the Code is treated as an interest in each of the assets of the partnership and not as an interest in a partnership. (Code Sec. 1031(e) as amended by Tax Cuts and Jobs Act §13303(b)(3))

> *observation:* The rules provided in Code Sec. 1031(e) are the same as the rules that were provided in pre-Tax Cuts and Jobs Act Code Sec. 1031(a)(2).

Foreign real property. Real property located in the U.S. and real property located outside the U.S. are not property of a like kind. (Code Sec. 1031(h) as amended by Tax Cuts and Jobs Act §13303(b)(4))

> *observation:* The rule provided in Code Sec. 1031(h) is the same as those provided in pre-Tax Cuts and Jobs Act Code Sec. 1031(h)(1).

Livestock of different sexes. The Tax Cuts and Jobs Act repeals rules providing that livestock of different sexes are not property of like-kind (FTC 2d/FIN ¶ I-3067; USTR ¶ 10,314.04). (Tax Cuts and Jobs Act §13303(b)(2))

> *observation:* The rule provided in pre-Tax Cuts and Jobs Act Code Sec. 1031(e) is no longer necessary since livestock is personal property and any exchange of livestock can't be a tax-free exchange under Code Sec. 1031.

Property excluded from like-kind exchange rule The Tax Cuts and Jobs Act strikes the rules providing that exchanges of certain types of property (stock in trade or other property held primarily for sale, stocks, bonds, or notes, other securities, or evidences of indebtedness or interest; interests in a partnership; certificates of trust or beneficial interest, or choses in action) are excluded from nonrecognition under Code Sec. 1031(a). (Code Sec. 1031(a)(2) as amended by Tax Cuts and Jobs Act §13303(b)(1)(A))

> *observation:* The list of property excluded from nonrecognition treatment that was provided in pre-Tax Cuts and Jobs Act Code Sec. 1031(a)(2) is no longer necessary since all of the excluded property is personal property.

□ **Effective:** Except for the transition rule discussed immediately below, exchanges completed after Dec. 31, 2017. (Tax Cuts and Jobs Act §13303(c)(1))

But, the changes made by the Tax Cuts and Jobs Act do not apply to any exchange if (Tax Cuts and Jobs Act §13303(c)(2)) the property:

(1) disposed of by the taxpayer in the exchange is disposed of before Jan. 1, 2018, or (Tax Cuts and Jobs Act §13303(c)(2)(A))

(2) received by the taxpayer in the exchange is received before Jan. 1, 2018. (Tax Cuts and Jobs Act §13303(c)(2)(B))

> **𝕣/** *observation:* Under the transition rule, an exchange is subject to the pre-Tax Cuts and Jobs Act rules if a taxpayer disposes of the relinquished property in a forward exchange (item (1) above) or receives the replacement property in a reverse exchange (exchanges in which the replacement property is transferred before the relinquished property is transferred, see item (2) above) before Jan. 1, 2018. Thus, if the first step in either a forward exchange or a reverse exchange occurs before Jan. 1, 2018, an exchange of personal property can qualify as a tax-free like-kind exchange if the other requirements under Code Sec. 1031 are satisfied.

> **𝕣/** *illustration (1):* Under an exchange agreement, T transfers a painting (relinquished property) to a qualified intermediary (QI) on Dec. 30, 2017. The QI has to acquire a painting (replacement property) identified by T within 45 days (FTC 2d/FIN ¶ I-3100) and transfer the painting to T within 180 days after the transfer of the relinquished property. Thus, the exchange of personal property presumably will qualify as a tax-free like-kind exchange if the other requirements provided under pre-Tax Cuts and Jobs Act law are satisfied.

> **𝕣/** *illustration (2):* The facts are the same as in illustration (1) except that the exchange is a reverse exchange. If the QI transfers the replacement painting to T before Jan. 1, 2018, the exchange of personal property will qualify as tax-free like-kind exchange if the exchange satisfies the other requirements provided under pre-Tax Cuts and Jobs Act law.

¶ 1504. Patents, inventions, certain models or designs, and secret formulas or processes are excluded from the definition of a capital asset

Code Sec. 1221(a)(3), as amended by Tax Cuts and Jobs Act §13314(a)
Code Sec. 1231(b)(1)(C), as amended by Tax Cuts and Jobs Act §13314(b)
Generally effective: Dispositions after Dec. 31, 2017
Committee Reports, see ¶ 5057

Property held by a taxpayer (whether or not connected with his trade or business) is generally considered a capital asset. Certain assets, however, are specifically excluded from the definition of capital asset, see FTC 2d/FIN ¶ I-6001; USTR ¶ 12,214.

Under pre-Tax Cuts and Jobs Act law, Code Sec. 1221(a)(3) excluded certain self-created intangibles such as copyrights, literary, musical, or artistic compositions, letters or memoranda, or similar property from the definition of a capital asset if the asset is held either by the taxpayer who created the property, or (in the case of a letter, memorandum, or similar property) a taxpayer for whom the property was produced. For purpose of determining gain, a transferee with substituted or transferred basis property received from the transferor who created the intangible, or for whom the property was created, also is subject to the exclusion. (FTC 2d/FIN ¶ I-6600, ¶ I-6601; USTR ¶ 12,214.45; Catalyst ¶ 501:180; Catalyst ¶ 502:113; Catalyst ¶ 502:141)

Any self-created intangible that was excluded from the definition of a capital asset under Code Sec. 1221(a)(3) also was ineligible to be treated as a capital gain-ordinary loss asset (i.e., a trade or business asset) under Code Sec. 1231. (FTC 2d/FIN ¶ I-9000, ¶ I-9008; USTR ¶ 12,314.14; Catalyst ¶ 115:181; Catalyst ¶ 502:195)

New Law. The Tax Cuts and Jobs Act excludes a patent, invention, model or design (whether or not patented), and a secret formula or process which is held either by the taxpayer who created the property or a taxpayer with a substituted or transferred basis from the taxpayer who created the property (or for whom the property was created), from the definition of a capital asset. (Com Rept, see ¶ 5057) Specifically, the Tax Cuts and Jobs Act provides that a capital asset does not include (Code Sec. 1221(a)) *a patent, invention, model or design (whether or not patented), a secret formula or process,* a copyright, a literary, musical, or artistic composition, a letter or memorandum, or similar property, held by (Code Sec. 1221(a)(3) as amended by Tax Cuts and Jobs Act §13314(a)) a taxpayer

(1) whose personal efforts created the property, (Code Sec. 1221(a)(3)(A)) in the case of a letter, memorandum, or similar property, a taxpayer for whom the property was prepared or produced, or (Code Sec. 1221(a)(3)(B))

(2) who owns any property described in item (1) above, whose basis, for purposes of determining gain from a sale or exchange, is determined in whole or in part by reference to the basis of the property in the hands of a person who created the property through his personal efforts. (Code Sec. 1221(a)(3)(C))

Thus, gains or losses from the sale or exchange of a patent, invention, model or design (whether or not patented), or a secret formula or process which is held either by the taxpayer who created the property or a taxpayer with a substituted or transferred basis from the taxpayer who created the property (or for whom the property was created) do not receive capital gain treatment. (Com Rept, see ¶ 5057)

    observation: Even though patents are excluded from the definition of a capital asset under Code Sec. 1221(a)(3), certain transfers of patents by inventors and certain financial backers are treated as sales or exchange of long-term capital assets under Code Sec. 1235, see FTC 2d/FIN ¶ I-8300; USTR ¶ 12,354. But, capital gain treatment under Code Sec. 1235 is presumably not available for inventions, models or designs, secret formulas or processes that are not patented.

Conforming change for trade or business property. For purposes of the capital gain-ordinary loss rule under Code Sec. 1231, property used in a trade or business includes property that meets all of the following requirements: (1) it is used in a trade or business (FTC 2d/FIN ¶ I-9010; USTR ¶ 12,314); (2) it is held by the taxpayer for more than one year; (3) it is subject to depreciation under the general depreciation rules (FTC 2d/FIN ¶ L-7500; USTR ¶ 1684); and (4) it isn't a *patent, invention, model or design (whether or not patented), a secret formula or process,* a copyright, a literary, musical or artistic composition, a letter or memorandum or similar property held by a person described in Code Sec. 1221(a)(3). (Code Sec. 1231(b)(1)(C) as amended by Tax Cuts and Jobs Act §13314(b))

☐ **Effective:** Dispositions after Dec. 31, 2017. (Tax Cuts and Jobs Act §13314(c))

¶ 1505. Cost of insurance adjustment to the basis of life insurance or annuity contracts is retroactively eliminated

Code Sec. 1016(a)(1), Tax Cuts and Jobs Act §13521(a)
Generally effective: For transactions entered into after Aug. 25, 2009
Committee Reports, see ¶ 5075

The cost or other basis of property must be properly adjusted for any expenditure, or other item, properly chargeable to a capital account, see FTC 2d/FIN ¶ P-1801; USTR ¶ 10,164. The adjusted basis is then used for computing gain or loss on the disposition of the property and for computing additional depreciation, depletion and other deductions, see FTC 2d/FIN ¶ P-1700 et seq.; USTR ¶ 10,164.

Under pre-Tax Cuts and Jobs Act law, IRS determined, in Rev Rul 2009-13, that when an insured (seller) sold a life insurance contract, the seller's gain was the excess of the amount realized on the sale (sales price) over the seller's basis (total premiums less the cost of insurance). The reduction in basis for the cost of insurance charges was deemed necessary to account for the insurance protection the seller received before the sale. On the sale of a policy with a cash surrender value, the amount of the inside build-up under the contract (i.e., the excess of the cash surrender value of the contract over the aggregate premiums paid) was ordinary income under the "substitute for ordinary income doctrine."

Any gain in excess of the inside build-up was capital gain. (FTC 2d/FIN ¶ J-5300FTC 2d ¶ J-5307; USTR ¶ 10,164; Catalyst ¶ 504:131)

> *illustration:* Under the rules of Rev Rul 2009-13, if a policyholder paid $64,000 in premiums, of which $10,000 was consumed for cost of insurance, when the policyholder sold the policy to a third-party investor for $80,000, the policyholder's tax basis for computing gain on sale was only $54,000 ($64,000 in premiums paid less $10,000 cost of insurance). Thus, assuming the policyholder made no cash value withdrawals and didn't otherwise reduce the face amount of his policy, the gain on sale was $26,000 ($80,000 minus $54,000).

> *observation:* Before the issuance of Rev Rul 2009-13, most taxpayers took the position that a taxpayer's basis in a life insurance contract equaled total premiums paid to the insurer, less tax-free receipts under the contract. The basis reduction rule implemented by IRS in Rev Rul 2009-13 generally resulted in a greater gain (or smaller loss) on the sale of the policy because taxpayers weren't permitted to include the full amount of premiums paid in their basis. In addition, the gain was bifurcated between ordinary income and capital gain, even if the contract was a capital asset in the hands of the seller.

> *observation:* Contrary to its treatment of sales of life insurance contracts, in Rev Rul 2009-13 IRS held that there was no reduction in basis for "cost of insurance" for a complete surrender of a life insurance policy. However, IRS also clarified that the surrender of a life insurance contract results in ordinary income, not capital gain, even though life insurance contracts are "capital assets" for tax purposes.

> *observation:* The treatment of gain from the *sale* of a taxpayer's life insurance contract as both ordinary income and long-term capital gain differed from the treatment of gain from the complete *surrender* of a life insurance contract. Upon complete surrender, any taxable gain was treated as ordinary income regardless of the fact that the contract was a capital asset to the seller. Thus, under pre-Tax Cuts and Jobs Act law, if a taxpayer was considering disposing of a life insurance contract, the taxpayer had to be aware of the differences in tax consequences between a complete surrender of the contract and a sale of the contract.

New Law. Under the Tax Cuts and Jobs Act, no adjustment to basis is made for mortality, expense, or other reasonable charges incurred under an annuity or life insurance contract. (Code Sec. 1016(a)(1) as amended by Tax Cuts and Jobs Act §13521(a)) Thus, in determining the basis of a life insurance or annuity contract, no adjustment is made for mortality, expense, or other reasonable charges incurred under the contracts (known as "cost of insurance"). This reverses the position of IRS in Rev Rul 2009-13 that, on the sale of a cash value life insurance contract, the insured's (seller's) basis is reduced by the cost of insurance. (Com Rept, see ¶ 5075)

　　🅡🅘🅐 illustration: Under the Tax Cuts and Jobs Act, if a policyholder paid $64,000 in premiums, of which $10,000 represented the cost of insurance, when the policyholder sells the policy to a third-party investor for $80,000, the policyholder's tax basis for computing gain on sale is $64,000. Assuming the policyholder made no cash value withdrawals and didn't otherwise reduced the face amount of his policy, the gain on the sale is $16,000 ($80,000 minus $64,000). This reduces the gain over what it would have been under pre-Tax Cuts and Jobs Act law by $10,000 (i.e., the cost of insurance).

　　🅡🅘🅐 observation: Presumably, to the extent Rev Rul 2009-13 provides guidance with respect to the complete surrender of a life insurance contract, those rules still apply.

☐ **Effective:** For transactions entered into after Aug. 25, 2009. (Tax Cuts and Jobs Act §13521(b))

　　🅡🅘🅐 observation: The effective date coincides with the effective date of Rev Rul 2009-13. As a practical matter, this retroactively eliminates the reduction in basis for the cost of insurance on the sale of a life insurance contract and, thus, eliminates the necessity to bifurcate gain from the sale between ordinary income and capital gain. This will result in a smaller gain, but the entire gain will be ordinary income.

　　🅡🅘🅐 observation: Because the Tax Cuts and Jobs Act applies retroactively to transactions entered into after Aug. 25, 2009, for sales of insurance policies made within the statute of limitations for filing amended returns, taxpayers may want to consider filing an amended return to claim a refund for the amount of any additional tax they may have paid as a result of the application of Rev Rul 2009-13.

¶ 1506. Tax reporting requirements added for policy sales and death benefits paid under life insurance contracts

Code Sec. 6050Y, as added by Tax Cuts and Jobs Act §13520(a)
Code Sec. 6724(d), as amended by Tax Cuts and Jobs Act §13520(c)(1)
Code Sec. 6047(g), as amended by Tax Cuts and Jobs Act §13520(c)(2)
Generally effective: Reportable policy sales and reportable death benefits paid after Dec. 31, 2017
Committee Reports, see ¶ 5075

Although the proceeds of a life insurance contract that are payable by reason of the death of the insured generally aren't included in the gross income of the recipient, the transfer of a life insurance contract (or any interest in that contract), by assignment or otherwise, can affect the tax treatment of the proceeds paid by reason of the death of the insured if the transfer is made for valuable consideration. If that's the case, the death benefits paid on the life insurance contract are excludable only to the extent of the "actual value" of the consideration paid by the transferee to acquire the contract (or interest), plus any premiums or other amounts paid by the transferee after the transfer (see FTC 2d/FIN ¶s J-4700 *et seq.* , J-4701, J-4729, J-4730; USTR ¶s 1014, 1014.02).

For analysis of rules under the Tax Cuts and Jobs Act that clarify the adjustments made to the basis of life insurance or annuity contracts, see ¶ 1505.

For analysis of the modification under the Tax Cuts and Jobs Act of the applicability of these "transfer for value" rules to a transfer of an interest in a life insurance contract in a reportable policy sale, see ¶ 601.

For the definition of a reportable policy sale, see ¶ 601.

> **observation:** Under pre-Tax Cuts and Jobs Act law, there were no requirements to report any type of sale or transfer of a life insurance policy for valuable consideration to a third party.

New Law. The Tax Cuts and Jobs Act imposes reporting requirements in the case of the purchase of an existing life insurance contract in a reportable policy sale and imposes reporting requirements on the payor in the case of the payment of reportable death benefits. (Com Rept, see ¶ 5075)

Reporting requirements for payments under a life insurance contract. Under The Tax Cuts and Jobs Act, every person who acquires a life insurance contract or any interest in a life insurance contract in a reportable policy sale during any tax year is required to make a return for that tax year (at a time and manner prescribed by IRS) setting forth — (Code Sec. 6050Y(a)(1) as added by Tax Cuts and Jobs Act §13520(a))

(1) the name, address, and TIN of that person, (Code Sec. 6050Y(a)(1)(A))

(2) the name, address, and TIN of each recipient of payment in the reportable policy sale, (Code Sec. 6050Y(a)(1)(B))

(3) the date of the sale, (Code Sec. 6050Y(a)(1)(C))

(4) the name of the issuer of the life insurance contract sold and the policy number of that contract, and (Code Sec. 6050Y(a)(1)(D))

(5) the amount of each payment. (Code Sec. 6050Y(a)(1)(E))

The term "reportable policy sale" is defined in Code Sec. 101(a)(3)(B). (Code Sec. 6050Y(d)(2))

Every person required to make a return reporting payments under a life insurance contract must also furnish to each person whose name has to be set forth in the return a written statement that shows—(Code Sec. 6050Y(a)(2))

. . . the name, address, and phone number of the information contact of the person required to make the return, and (Code Sec. 6050Y(a)(2)(A))

. . . the information required to be shown on the return for that person, except that for an issuer of a life insurance contract, the statement is not required to include the information specified in Code Sec. 6050Y(a)(1)(E) (i.e., the amount of each payment, see (5) above). (Code Sec. 6050Y(a)(2)(B))

For any reportable policy sale (as defined in Code Sec. 101(a)(3)(B), see ¶ 601), the term "payment" means the amount of cash and the fair market value of any consideration transferred in the sale. (Code Sec. 6050Y(d)(1))

Reporting requirements for life insurance seller's basis in life insurance contracts. Upon receipt of a written statement required under Code Sec. 6050Y(a)(2), or upon notice of a transfer of a life insurance contract to a foreign person, an issuer of that life insurance contract must file a return (at a time and manner prescribed by IRS) setting forth— (Code Sec. 6050Y(b)(1))

. . . the name, address, and TIN of the seller who transfers any interest in a contract in such a sale, (Code Sec. 6050Y(b)(1)(A))

. . . the investment in the contract (as defined in Code Sec. 72(e)(6)) with respect to the seller, and (Code Sec. 6050Y(b)(1)(B))

. . . the policy number of the contract. (Code Sec. 6050Y(b)(1)(C))

An issuer of a life insurance contract required to make a return must also furnish to each person included in the return a written statement showing—(Code Sec. 6050Y(b)(2))

. . . the name, address, and phone number of the information contact of the person required to make such return, and (Code Sec. 6050Y(b)(2)(A))

. . . the information required to be shown on such return with respect to each seller whose name is required to be set forth in such return. (Code Sec. 6050Y(b)(2)(B))

An "issuer" is any life insurance company that bears the risk for a life insurance contract on the date any return or statement is required to be made under these reporting rules. (Code Sec. 6050Y(d)(3))

Reporting requirements for reportable death benefits. Every person who makes a payment of reportable death benefits during any tax year must file a return for the tax year (at a time and manner prescribed by IRS) setting forth— (Code Sec. 6050Y(c)(1))

... the name, address, and TIN of the person making the payment, (Code Sec. 6050Y(c)(1)(A))

... the name, address, and TIN of each recipient of the payment, (Code Sec. 6050Y(c)(1)(B))

... the date of each payment, (Code Sec. 6050Y(c)(1)(C))

... the gross amount of each payment, and (Code Sec. 6050Y(c)(1)(D))

... an estimate of the investment in the contract (defined in Code Sec. 72). (Code Sec. 6050Y(c)(1)(E))

Every person required to make a return for reportable death benefits must furnish to each person whose name must be set forth in the return a written statement showing—(Code Sec. 6050Y(c)(2))

... the name, address, and phone number of the information contact of the person required to make the return, and (Code Sec. 6050Y(c)(2)(A))

... the information required to be shown on such return with respect to each recipient of payment whose name is required to be set forth in such return. (Code Sec. 6050Y(c)(2)(B))

"Reportable death benefits" are amounts paid by reason of the death of the insured under a life insurance contract that has been transferred in a reportable policy sale. (Code Sec. 6050Y(d)(4))

Conforming changes. As a result of this change:

... the definition of "information return" for purposes of the penalty waiver for failure to meet magnetic media requirements under Code Sec. 6724 now includes returns under Code Sec. 6050Y. (Code Sec. 6724(d)(1)(B)(xxvi) as amended by Tax Cuts and Jobs Act §13520(c)(1)(A))

... the definition of "payee statement" for purposes of the penalty waiver for failure to meet magnetic media requirements under Code Sec. 6724 now includes returns under Code Sec. 6050Y(a)(2), Code Sec. 6050Y(b)(2) and Code Sec. 6050Y(c)(2). (Code Sec. 6724(d)(2)(JJ) as amended by Tax Cuts and Jobs Act §13520(c)(1)(B))

... Code Sec. 6047 (information relating to certain trusts and annuity plans) does not apply for any information which is required to be reported under Code Sec. 6050Y relating to life insurance contract transactions. (Code Sec. 6047(g) as amended by Tax Cuts and Jobs Act §13520(c)(2)(B))

☐ **Effective:** For (1) reportable policy sales (as defined in Code Sec. 6050Y(d)(2) as added by Tax Cuts and Jobs Act §13520(a)) after Dec. 31, 2017, and (Tax Cuts and Jobs Act §13520(d)(1)) (2) reportable death benefits (as defined in Code Sec. 6050Y(d)(4) (as added by Tax Cuts and Jobs Act §13520(a)) paid after Dec. 31, 2017. (Tax Cuts and Jobs Act §13520(d)(2))

¶ 1507. Tax-free rollover of publicly traded securities gain into "specialized small business investment companies" is repealed

Code Sec. 1044, as repealed by Tax Cuts and Jobs Act §13313(a)
Code Sec. 1016(a)(23), as amended by Tax Cuts and Jobs Act §13313(b)
Generally effective: For sales after Dec. 31, 2017
Committee Reports, see ¶ 5056

Under pre-Tax Cuts and Jobs Act law, a corporation or individual could elect to not recognize gain on the sale of publicly traded securities to the extent the proceeds were invested in stock of (or a partnership interest in) a "specialized small business investment company" (SSBIC). If the election was made, the amount of gain recognized on the sale was limited to the excess of the amount realized on the sale over:

. . . the cost of any common stock or partnership interest in the SSBIC purchased by the taxpayer during the 60-day period beginning on the day of the sale, reduced by:

. . . any portion of that cost previously taken into account under the above rule. (FTC 2d/FIN ¶ I-3790 *et seq.*; USTR ¶ 10,444 *et seq.*; Catalyst ¶ 504:135; Catalyst ¶ 511:100; Catalyst ¶ 511:163)

> *observation:* SSBICs were created to invest in small businesses owned by individuals who were socially or economically disadvantaged, especially minorities. While the program was repealed in 1996, SSBICs that were licensed before Oct. 1, 1996 were grandfathered.

> *observation:* The rule applied to sales, but not exchanges of public securities. Thus, a transfer of publicly traded securities for money or a promise to pay money would qualify, but a transfer for other property did not qualify.

Generally, the amount of gain that an individual could elect to roll over under pre-Tax Cuts and Jobs Act Code Sec. 1044 for a tax year was limited to the lesser of (1) $50,000 or (2) $500,000 reduced by the gain previously excluded under this rule. For married taxpayers filing separately, these amounts were $25,000 and $250,000, respectively. (FTC 2d/FIN ¶ I-3790, ¶ I-3792; USTR ¶ 10,444 *et seq.*) For corporations, these limits were $250,000 and $1 million, respectively. (FTC 2d/FIN ¶ I-3790, ¶ I-3793; USTR ¶ 10,444 *et seq.*)

Any gain not recognized under this rule reduced the taxpayer's basis in any SSBIC investment made during the 60-day period. Where the taxpayer made more than one SSBIC investment during the 60-day period, the bases of those investments were reduced in the order they were acquired.

> ●*observation:* As a result of the fact that the law provided for an exclusion of gain and a corresponding reduction in the basis of the SSBIC investment, the effect of the law was to "roll over" the gain.

However, basis in SSBIC common stock wasn't reduced for purposes of calculating the gain eligible for exclusion under Code Sec. 1202 for certain qualified small business stock gains. (FTC 2d/FIN ¶ I-3790, ¶ I-3791; USTR ¶ 10,444 *et seq.*)

> ●*observation:* Thus, important tax implications could have arisen from the interplay between Code Sec. 1044 and Code Sec. 1202. Under Code Sec. 1202, noncorporate taxpayers that hold "qualified small business stock" (QSBS) for more than five years may exclude from gross income certain specified percentages (i.e., generally 100%, 75% or 50%, depending on when the stock was acquired) of the gain realized on the sale or exchange of the QSBS, see FTC 2d/FIN ¶ I-9100 *et seq.*; USTR ¶ 12,024 *et seq.* Individual taxpayers who sold shares in an SSBIC could qualify for gain exclusion under Code Sec. 1202. However, because the basis in SSBIC stock was *not* reduced by gain not recognized under the rollover rule, a lesser amount of gain would qualify for the exclusion under Code Sec. 1202.

New Law. The Tax Cuts and Jobs Act repeals the tax-free rollover of publicly traded securities gain into "specialized small business investment companies" by striking pre-Tax Cuts and Jobs Act Code Sec. 1044. (Code Sec. 1044 as repealed by Tax Cuts and Jobs Act §13313(a)) Thus, the Tax Cuts and Jobs Act repeals the election (described above) to roll over, tax free, gain realized on the sale of publicly traded securities. (Com Rept, see ¶ 5056)

> ●*observation:* The Tax Cuts and Jobs Act made no changes to Code Sec. 1202, so those rules still apply. However, as noted above, any gain deferred under Code Sec. 1044 that is realized on the sale of those shares isn't eligible for exclusion from gross income under Code Sec. 1202.

Conforming change. The Tax Cuts and Jobs Act also amends Code Sec. 1016(a)(23) by eliminating references to Code Sec. 1044, and Code Sec. 1044(d). (Code Sec. 1016(a)(23) as amended by Tax Cuts and Jobs Act §13313(b))

☐ **Effective:** For sales after Dec. 31, 2017. (Tax Cuts and Jobs Act §13313(c))

¶ 1600. Able Programs And 529 Plans

¶ 1601. ABLE account contribution limit is increased for contributions by account's designated beneficiary

Code Sec. 529A(b)(2)(B), as amended by Tax Cuts and Jobs Act §11024(a)(1)

Code Sec. 529A(b)(2), as amended by Tax Cuts and Jobs Act §11024(a)(2)

Code Sec. 529A(b)(7), as amended by Tax Cuts and Jobs Act §11024(a)(3)

Generally effective: Tax years beginning after Dec. 22, 2017, for contributions before Jan. 1, 2026

Committee Reports, see ¶ 5008

States may create qualified ABLE programs, under which qualified ABLE accounts may be established for designated beneficiaries who are disabled or blind. Only one account is allowed per beneficiary. Contributions are nondeductible, but earnings on account balances accumulate on a tax-deferred basis. Distributions are tax-free up to the amount of the designated beneficiary's qualified disability expenses. (FTC 2d/FIN ¶ A-4740; USTR ¶ 529A4)

Under pre-Tax Cuts and Jobs Act law, a qualified ABLE program had to provide that no contribution to an ABLE account would be accepted if it would result in the aggregate contributions from all contributors to the ABLE account for the tax year (other than rollovers from another account) exceeding the amount of the annual gift tax exclusion for that tax year ($14,000 for 2017, $15,000 for 2018). (FTC 2d/FIN ¶ A-4744.2; USTR ¶ 529A4)

New Law. The Tax Cuts and Jobs Act temporarily increases the contribution limitation to ABLE accounts for contributions made by the account's designated beneficiary. Under the provision, after the general limitation on contributions (equal to the annual gift tax exclusion) is reached, an ABLE account's designated beneficiary may contribute an additional amount, up to the lesser of (a) the beneficiary's compensation for the tax year or (b) the federal poverty line for a one-person household. (Com Rept, see ¶ 5008)

The Tax Cuts and Jobs Act allows a qualified ABLE program to accept, in addition to an amount equal to the annual gift tax exclusion for that tax year (Code Sec. 529A(b)(2)(B)(i) as amended by Tax Cuts and Jobs Act

FTC 2d References are to Federal Tax Coordinator 2d
FIN References are to RIA's Analysis of Federal Taxes: Income (print)
USTR References are to United States Tax Reporter
Catalyst References are to Checkpoint Catalyst
PCA References are to Pension Analysis (print and electronic)
PBE References are to Pension & Benefits Explanations
BCA References are to Benefits Analysis (electronic)
BC References are to Benefits Coordinator (print)
EP References are to Estate Planning Analysis (print and electronic)

§11024(a)(1)), an additional contribution to an ABLE account before Jan. 1, 2026, by a designated beneficiary who meets the requirements described below. (Code Sec. 529A(b)(2)(B)(ii))

Limit on additional contribution. The amount of the additional contribution can't exceed the lesser of (Code Sec. 529A(b)(2)(B)(ii)):

(1) compensation includible in the designated beneficiary's gross income for the tax year, or (Code Sec. 529A(b)(2)(B)(ii)(I))

(2) an amount equal to the poverty line for a one-person household, as determined for the calendar year preceding the calendar year in which the tax year begins. (Code Sec. 529A(b)(2)(B)(ii)(II))

"Compensation" (in (1), above) is defined as in Code Sec. 219(f)(1) for purposes of the individual retirement account (IRA) deduction limits (see FTC 2d/FIN ¶H-12226; USTR ¶2194.01). (Code Sec. 529A(b)(2)(B)(ii)(I))

"Poverty line" (in (2), above) has the meaning given to that term by section 673 of the Community Services Block Grant Act (42 USC §9902). (Code Sec. 529A(b)(7)(B) as amended by Tax Cuts and Jobs Act §11024(a)(3))

> *observation:* For 2017, the federal poverty line for a one-person household was $12,060 for the 48 contiguous states and the District of Columbia. That figure will apply for contributions in calendar year 2018 under (2), above.

> *observation:* A designated beneficiary's additional contributions for 2018 can't exceed the federal poverty line of $12,060. The full $12,060 can be contributed if the beneficiary's 2018 compensation is at least that much. If the designated beneficiary's compensation is less than $12,060, the additional contributions are limited to the amount of the compensation.

Designated beneficiaries who may make additional contribution. To qualify to make an additional contribution, a designated beneficiary must be an employee, including a self-employed individual within the meaning of Code Sec. 401(c) (FTC 2d/FIN ¶H-9501; USTR ¶4014.24), for whom (Code Sec. 529A(b)(7)(A) as amended by Tax Cuts and Jobs Act §11024(a)(3)):

... no contribution's made for the tax year to a defined contribution plan (within the meaning of Code Sec. 414(i), FTC 2d/FIN ¶H-5204; USTR ¶4144.16) for which the requirements of Code Sec. 401(a) or Code Sec. 403(a) are met (Code Sec. 529A(b)(7)(A)(i)),

... no contribution's made for the tax year to an annuity contract described in Code Sec. 403(b) (a 403(b) annuity for employees of tax-exempt organizations or public schools, FTC 2d/FIN ¶H-12451; USTR ¶4034.08), and (Code Sec. 529A(b)(7)(A)(ii))

. . . no contribution's made for the tax year to an eligible deferred compensation plan described in Code Sec. 457(b) (an "eligible deferred compensation plan" of a state and local government or tax-exempt organization), FTC 2d/FIN ¶ H-3301; USTR ¶ 4574). (Code Sec. 529A(b)(7)(A)(iii))

> *observation:* Contributions up to the annual gift tax exclusion can be made by any person (FTC 2d/FIN ¶ A-4744; USTR ¶ 529A4), including the designated beneficiary. Additional contributions up to the lesser of compensation or the one-person federal poverty line can be made only by the designated beneficiary and only if the beneficiary's an employee or self-employed person for whom none of the contributions described above have been made.

> *observation:* Total contributions to an ABLE account for 2018 can be as much as $27,060 if the designated beneficiary qualifies to make $12,060 of additional contributions ($15,000 of regular contributions plus $12,060 of additional contributions).

> *illustration:* Individual X is a disabled individual who's the designated beneficiary of an ABLE account. In 2018, X is employed, earns $20,000, and has no retirement contributions made on X's behalf.
>
> In 2018, X's parents contribute $15,000 to X's ABLE account, which is equal to the annual gift tax exclusion for 2018. X can make an additional contribution to X's own ABLE account of up to $12,060. That's the lesser of (i) X's compensation for the tax year ($20,000) or (ii) the federal poverty line for a one-person household for the previous year ($12,060).

Designated beneficiary is responsible for recordkeeping. A designated beneficiary, or a person acting on the designated beneficiary's behalf, must maintain adequate records for purposes of ensuring, and is responsible for ensuring, that the requirements for the additional contribution are met. (Code Sec. 529A(b)(2) as amended by Tax Cuts and Jobs Act §11024(a)(2))

> *sample client letter:* A sample client letter explaining the additional ABLE account contributions and other ABLE account changes appears in ¶ 3219.

For a provision allowing the saver's credit for ABLE account contributions made by the designated beneficiary, see ¶ 1602.

For a provision allowing 60-day rollovers from a 529 account to an ABLE account, see ¶ 1603.

Sunset. The provision won't apply to contributions after Dec. 31, 2025. (Code Sec. 529A(b)(2)(B)(ii))

☐ **Effective:** Tax years beginning after Dec. 22, 2017. (Tax Cuts and Jobs Act §11024(c)) The provision won't apply to contributions after Dec. 31, 2025. (Code Sec. 529A(b)(2)(B)(ii))

¶ 1602. Saver's credit is allowed for ABLE account contributions by designated beneficiary

Code Sec. 25B(d)(1)(D), as amended by Tax Cuts and Jobs Act §11024(b)
Generally effective: Tax years beginning after Dec. 22, 2017, for contributions made before Jan. 1, 2026
Committee Reports, see ¶ 5008

ABLE accounts. States may create qualified ABLE programs, under which qualified ABLE accounts may be established for designated beneficiaries who are disabled or blind. Only one account is allowed per beneficiary. Contributions are nondeductible, but earnings on account balances accumulate on a tax-deferred basis. Distributions are tax-free up to the amount of the designated beneficiary's qualified disability expenses. (FTC 2d/FIN ¶ A-4740; USTR ¶ 529A4)

Saver's credit. An eligible lower-income taxpayer can claim a nonrefundable credit (the "saver's credit") for a percentage of up to $2,000 of qualified retirement savings contributions. The applicable percentage (50%, 20%, or 10%) depends on filing status and adjusted gross income (AGI). (FTC 2d/FIN ¶ A-4450; USTR ¶ 25B4)

> **⟨RIA⟩ observation:** The maximum saver's credit is $1,000 ($2,000 contribution × 50% credit percentage).

The credit's available for elective contributions to a Code Sec. 401(k) plan (including a SIMPLE 401(k)), Code Sec. 403(b) annuity, Code Sec. 457 plan, contributions to a traditional or Roth individual retirement account (IRA); SIMPLE IRA plan, or salary reduction simplified employee pension (SEP); contributions to a traditional or Roth IRA; and voluntary after-tax employee contributions to a qualified retirement plan or Code Sec. 403(b) annuity. (FTC 2d/FIN ¶ A-4453; USTR ¶ 25B4)

Under pre-Tax Cuts and Jobs Act law, the saver's credit wasn't available for contributions to an ABLE account.

New Law. The Tax Cuts and Jobs Act provides that the saver's credit may be claimed for the amount of contributions made before Jan. 1, 2026, by an individual to the ABLE account of which the individual is the designated beneficiary. (Code Sec. 25B(d)(1)(D) as amended by Tax Cuts and Jobs Act §11024(b))

So a designated beneficiary can claim the saver's credit for contributions made to the designated beneficiary's ABLE account. (Com Rept, see ¶ 5008)

observation: Although any person can make a contribution to an ABLE account (FTC 2d/FIN ¶ A-4744; USTR ¶ 529A4), only contributions by the account's designated beneficiary qualify for the saver's credit. The credit can reduce the cost to the designated beneficiary of contributing to the ABLE account.

observation: Because the saver's credit is nonrefundable (FTC 2d/FIN ¶ A-4455; USTR ¶ 25B4), it will only be of value to a designated beneficiary who has a tax liability that can be offset by the credit.

sample client letter: A sample client letter explaining the saver's credit for ABLE account contributions and other ABLE account changes appears in ¶ 3219.

For a provision increasing the amount of ABLE account contributions that can be made by the designated beneficiary, see ¶ 1601.

For a provision allowing 60-day rollovers from a 529 account to an ABLE account, see ¶ 1603.

Sunset. The provision won't apply to ABLE account contributions made after Dec. 31, 2025. (Code Sec. 25B(d)(1)(D))

☐ **Effective:** Tax years beginning after Dec. 22, 2017. (Tax Cuts and Jobs Act §11024(c)) The provision won't apply to ABLE account contributions made after Dec. 31, 2025. (Code Sec. 25B(d)(1)(D))

¶ 1603. Tax-free 60-day rollovers from 529 plan accounts to ABLE accounts are permitted

Code Sec. 529(c)(3)(C)(i)(III), as amended by Tax Cuts and Jobs Act §11025(a)
Generally effective: Distributions after Dec. 22, 2017, for transfers made before Jan. 1, 2026
Committee Reports, see ¶ 5009

529 accounts. Under Code Sec. 529, a person can make nondeductible cash contributions to a qualified tuition program (QTP, or 529 plan) on behalf of a designated beneficiary (a student or future student). The earnings on the contributions build up tax-free, and distributions from the 529 account are excludable to the extent used to pay qualified higher education expenses. (FTC 2d/FIN ¶ A-4700; USTR ¶ 5294)

Distributions that aren't used for qualified higher education expenses are includible in the distributee's gross income under the Code Sec. 72 annuity rules. (FTC 2d/FIN ¶ A-4709; USTR ¶ 5294.02) A 10% penalty tax is imposed on these taxable distributions. (FTC 2d/FIN ¶ A-4720; USTR ¶ 5294.02)

However, tax-free treatment is allowed to the part of any distribution from a 529 account that's transferred (rolled over) within 60 days to:

. . . another 529 account for the benefit of the same designated beneficiary; or

. . . to the credit of another designated beneficiary under a 529 account who's a member of the family of the designated beneficiary with respect to which the distribution was made. (FTC 2d/FIN ¶ A-4721; USTR ¶ 5294.02)

For this purpose, a "member of the family" means the designated beneficiary's: (1) spouse; (2) child or descendant of a child; (3) brother, sister, stepbrother, or stepsister; (4) father, mother, or ancestor of either; (5) stepfather or stepmother; (6) niece or nephew; (7) aunt or uncle; (8) in-law; (9) the spouse of any individual described in (2)–(8); and (10) any first cousin of the designated beneficiary. (FTC 2d/FIN ¶ A-4723; USTR ¶ 5294)

ABLE accounts. A qualified ABLE account is a tax-advantaged savings vehicle, similar in many ways to a 529 account, that can be used to pay the qualified disability expenses of a designated beneficiary who's disabled or blind. (FTC 2d/FIN ¶ A-4740; USTR ¶ 529A4) Total annual contributions by all contributors to an ABLE account can't exceed the gift tax exclusion amount for that year ($14,000 for 2017, $15,000 for 2018). (See ¶ 1601 for an increase in this limit.) Tax-free rollovers from another ABLE account don't count toward this limit. (FTC 2d/FIN ¶ A-4744.2; USTR ¶ 529A4)

Pre-Tax Cuts and Jobs Act law didn't provide for tax-free 60-day rollovers from a 529 account to an ABLE account.

New Law. The Tax Cuts and Jobs Act provides that a distribution from a 529 account is tax-free if, within 60 days of the distribution, it is transferred before Jan. 1, 2026, to an ABLE account of the same designated beneficiary or a member of the family of the designated beneficiary. (Code Sec. 529(c)(3)(C)(i)(III) as amended by Tax Cuts and Jobs Act §11025(a))

The provision allows for amounts from 529 accounts to be rolled over to an ABLE account without penalty, provided that the ABLE account is owned by the designated beneficiary of that 529 account or a member of that designated beneficiary's family. "Member of the family" includes the ten relationships listed above. (Com Rept, see ¶ 5009)

> *observation:* This provision is useful when the designated beneficiary of a 529 account doesn't need the account balance to pay for qualified higher education expenses and either the beneficiary or a member of the beneficiary's family is disabled or blind. Funds can be rolled

over from the 529 account to an ABLE account for the benefit of the disabled or blind individual. The tax deferral will continue, and distributions from the ABLE account will be tax-free if used for the designated beneficiary's qualified disability expenses.

Limitation. Tax-free rollover treatment doesn't apply to the part of a distribution that, when added to all other contributions made to the ABLE account for the tax year, exceeds the contribution limitation under Code Sec. 529A(b)(2)(B)(i) (which is equal to the annual gift tax exclusion for the tax year). (Code Sec. 529(c)(3)(C)(i))

So amounts rolled over from a 529 account to an ABLE account count towards the overall limitation on amounts that can be contributed to an ABLE account within a tax year. Any amount rolled over that's in excess of this limitation is includible in the distributee's gross income under the Code Sec. 72 annuity rules. (Com Rept, see ¶ 5009)

> *illustration:* An individual receives a $10,000 distribution from a 529 account in 2018 and rolls it over within 60 days to an ABLE account for his niece's benefit. The niece's account also received $8,000 of other contributions during 2018. The ABLE account contribution limit for 2018 under Code Sec. 529A(b)(2)(B)(i) is $15,000.
>
> The $10,000 rolled-over distribution, when added to the $8,000 of other contributions made to the ABLE account for 2018, exceeds the $15,000 contribution limit by $3,000. Therefore, only $7,000 of the distribution ($10,000 − $3,000) qualifies as a tax-free rollover to the ABLE account. The other $3,000 is includible in the distributee's income and is taxed under the annuity rules.

> *sample client letter:* A sample client letter explaining 60-day rollovers from 529 plan accounts to ABLE accounts and other ABLE account changes appears in ¶ 3219.

For a provision increasing the amount of ABLE account contributions that can be made by the designated beneficiary, see ¶ 1601.

For a provision allowing the saver's credit for ABLE account contributions made by the designated beneficiary, see ¶ 1602.

Sunset. The provision won't apply to transfers made after Dec. 31, 2025. (Code Sec. 529(c)(3)(C)(i)(III))

☐ **Effective:** Distributions after Dec. 22, 2017. (Tax Cuts and Jobs Act §11025(b)) The provision won't apply to transfers made after Dec. 31, 2025. (Code Sec. 529(c)(3)(C)(i)(III))

¶ 1604. $10,000 per year of 529 plan account funds may be used for elementary or secondary school tuition

Code Sec. 529(c)(7), as amended by Tax Cuts and Jobs Act §11032(a)(1)
Code Sec. 529(e)(3)(A), as amended by Tax Cuts and Jobs Act §11032(a)(2)
Generally effective: Distributions made after Dec. 31, 2017
Committee Reports, see ¶ 5014

Nondeductible cash contributions can be made to a qualified tuition program ("QTP," also commonly known as a "529 plan") on behalf of a designated beneficiary (a student or future student). The earnings on the contributions build up tax-free. (See FTC 2d ¶ A-4700 *et seq.*; USTR ¶ 5294 *et seq.*)

A distribution under a 529 plan that doesn't exceed the "qualified higher education expenses" of the designated beneficiary generally isn't includible in gross income (i.e., is a tax-free distribution) (see FTC 2d ¶ A-4709 *et seq.*; USTR ¶ 5294.02). For this purpose, the term "qualified higher education expenses" includes tuition, fees, books, etc., required for the enrollment or attendance of a designated beneficiary at an "eligible educational institution" (see FTC 2d ¶ A-4711 *et seq.*; USTR ¶ 5294.02).

Under pre-Tax Cuts and Jobs Act law, an "eligible educational institution" didn't include an elementary or secondary school, and so tuition required for enrollment or attendance at an elementary or secondary school didn't qualify as "qualified higher education expenses," and designated beneficiaries who paid such expenses couldn't receive tax-free 529 plan distributions. (FTC 2d/FIN ¶ A-4700, ¶ A-4711; USTR ¶ 5294.02)

New Law. Qualified higher education expenses include elementary school and secondary school tuition. For purposes of the 529 plan rules, the Tax Cuts and Jobs Act provides that qualified higher education expenses include (Code Sec. 529(c)(7) as amended by Tax Cuts and Jobs Act §11032(a)(1)) expenses for tuition in connection with enrollment or attendance at an elementary or secondary public, private, or religious school. (Code Sec. 529(c)(7))

Per-beneficiary limitation on amount of distributions. Under the Tax Cuts and Jobs Act, the amount of cash distributions from all 529 plans with respect to a beneficiary during any tax year can't, in the aggregate, include more than $10,000 in above-described expenses (i.e., elementary school and secondary school tuition) incurred during the tax year. (Code Sec. 529(e)(3)(A) as amended by Tax Cuts and Jobs Act §11032(a)(2))

That is, the above limitation applies on a per-student basis, rather than a per-account basis. So, although an individual may be the designated beneficiary of multiple 529 accounts, that individual may receive a maximum of $10,000 in tax-free distributions for elementary or secondary school tuition, regardless of whether the funds are distributed from multiple accounts. Any excess distributions received by the individual would be treated as a distribution subject to tax under the general rules of Code Sec. 529. (Com Rept, see ¶ 5014)

> ® *sample client letter:* A sample client letter explaining these 529 plan changes appears in ¶ 3223.

☐ **Effective:** Distributions made after Dec. 31, 2017. (Tax Cuts and Jobs Act §11032(b))

¶ 1700. Bonds and Development Incentives

¶ 1701. Exclusion of interest on advance refunding bonds is repealed

Code Sec. 149(d)(1), as amended by Tax Cuts and Jobs Act §13532(a)
Code Sec. 149(d)(2), as amended by Tax Cuts and Jobs Act §13532(b)(1)
Code Sec. 149(d)(3), as amended by Tax Cuts and Jobs Act §13532(b)(1)
Code Sec. 149(d)(4), as amended by Tax Cuts and Jobs Act §13532(b)(1)
Code Sec. 149(d)(6), as amended by Tax Cuts and Jobs Act §13532(b)(1)
Generally effective: Advance refunding bonds issued after Dec. 31, 2017
Committee Reports, see ¶ 5080

Under Code Sec. 103, interest received on state or local bonds isn't included in gross income if certain requirements are met. State and local bonds can be either governmental bonds or private activity bonds. (FTC 2d ¶ J-3000 *et seq.*; USTR ¶ 1034 *et seq.*) The proceeds of governmental bonds are used to finance governmental facilities, or the debt is repaid with governmental funds. For private activity bonds (FTC 2d ¶ J-3100 *et seq.*; USTR ¶ 1414 *et seq.*), the state or local government serves as a conduit for bonds that provide financing to private businesses, 501(c)(3) organizations (qualified 501(c)(3) bonds, see FTC 2d ¶ J-3300 *et seq.*; USTR ¶ 1454 *et seq.*), or individuals.

The exclusion from gross income for interest on state and local bonds applies to interest on a bond issued to refund a state and local bond (a "refunding bond"). A refunding bond is any bond of which the proceeds are used to pay principal, interest, or redemption price on a prior bond issue (the refunded bond).

There's no statutory limit on the number of times tax-exempt bonds may be currently refunded, but pre-Tax Cuts and Jobs Act law limited advance refundings. A current refunding bond is one for which the refunded bond is redeemed within 90 days of issuance of the refunding bond. An advance refunding bond, on the other hand, is one for which the refunding bond is issued more than 90 days before the redemption of the refunded bond. (FTC 2d/FIN ¶ J-3650, ¶ J-3660 *et seq.*; USTR ¶ 1494.03)

FTC 2d References are to Federal Tax Coordinator 2d
FIN References are to RIA's Analysis of Federal Taxes: Income (print)
USTR References are to United States Tax Reporter
Catalyst References are to Checkpoint Catalyst
PCA References are to Pension Analysis (print and electronic)
PBE References are to Pension & Benefits Explanations
BCA References are to Benefits Analysis (electronic)
BC References are to Benefits Coordinator (print)
EP References are to Estate Planning Analysis (print and electronic)

The ability to issue advance refunding bonds allowed state and local governments to issue and have outstanding two sets of federally subsidized debt associated with the same activity. (Com Rept, see ¶ 5080)

Under pre-Tax Cuts and Jobs Act law, generally, governmental bonds and qualified 501(c)(3) bonds could only be advance refunded one time. (FTC 2d/FIN ¶ J-3650, ¶ J-3661; USTR ¶ 1494.03) Private activity bonds (other than qualified 501(c)(3) bonds) couldn't be advance refunded at all. In addition, certain provisions of the arbitrage bond rules applied to advance refunding bonds. (FTC 2d/FIN ¶ J-3650, ¶ J-3660 *et seq.*; USTR ¶ 1494.03)

New Law. The Tax Cuts and Jobs Act provides that there is no income-tax exemption for interest on any bond issued to advance refund another bond. (Code Sec. 149(d)(1) as amended by Tax Cuts and Jobs Act §13532(a))

Thus, the Tax Cuts and Jobs Act repeals the exclusion from gross income for interest on a bond issued to advance refund another bond. (Com Rept, see ¶ 5080)

For this purpose, a bond is issued to advance refund another bond if it is issued more than 90 days before the redemption of the refunded bond. (Code Sec. 149(d)(2) as redesignated by Tax Cuts and Jobs Act §13532(a))

> *observation:* Thus, the definition of advance refunding remains the same as under pre-Tax Cuts and Jobs Act law.

Congress believes that a single activity should have a maximum of only one set of federally subsidized debt, and so believes removing the ability to issue tax-advantaged advance refunding bonds is appropriate. (Com Rept, see ¶ 5080)

> *observation:* Current refunding bonds continue to be tax-exempt.

☐ **Effective:** Advance refunding bonds issued after Dec. 31, 2017. (Tax Cuts and Jobs Act §13532(c))

> *observation:* Thus, interest on advance refunding bonds issued on or before Dec. 31, 2017 is subject to pre-Tax Cut and Jobs Act rules.

¶ 1702. New tax-credit and direct-pay bonds may not be issued

Code Sec. 54, as repealed by Tax Cuts and Jobs Act §13404(a)
Code Sec. 54A, as repealed by Tax Cuts and Jobs Act §13404(a)
Code Sec. 54B, as repealed by Tax Cuts and Jobs Act §13404(a)
Code Sec. 54C, as repealed by Tax Cuts and Jobs Act §13404(a)
Code Sec. 54D, as repealed by Tax Cuts and Jobs Act §13404(a)
Code Sec. 54E, as repealed by Tax Cuts and Jobs Act §13404(a)
Code Sec. 54F, as repealed by Tax Cuts and Jobs Act §13404(a)

Code Sec. 54AA, as repealed by Tax Cuts and Jobs Act §13404(a)
Code Sec. 6431, as repealed by Tax Cuts and Jobs Act §13404(b)
Code Sec. 1397E, as repealed by Tax Cuts and Jobs Act §13404(c)(1)
Generally effective: Bonds issued after Dec. 31, 2017
Committee Reports, see ¶ 5061

Tax-credit bonds (TCBs) are bonds in which the holder receives a tax credit in lieu of a prescribed portion of interest on the bond. The borrowing subsidy generally is measured by reference to the credit rate set by the Treasury Department. (Com Rept, see ¶ 5061)

Under pre-Tax Cuts and Jobs Act law, TCBs could be issued for a variety of projects. Except for Build America Bonds (BABs, see below), each TCB was issued for a separate purpose or type of project, the bonds for each of which were subject to either an annual or cumulative limitation on the dollar amount of bonds that could be issued. Unused annual volume limitations could be carried forward to subsequent years. (FTC 2d ¶ L-15530 *et seq.*, ¶ L-16480 *et seq.*; USTR ¶ 544 *et seq.*)

Qualified tax-credit bonds. Taxpayers who hold qualified tax-credit bonds (QTCBs) on specified dates during the year are entitled to a nonrefundable credit equal to a portion of the bonds' outstanding face amount. The credit may be claimed against regular income tax and alternative minimum tax (AMT) liability. The credit is includible in gross income, and is treated as interest income. A QTCB is one of a number of types of bond (see below) that is part of an issue that meets certain requirements relating to expenditures, reporting, arbitrage, maturity, and financial conflicts of interest. There are no restrictions on the type of investor who can purchase QTCBs. (FTC 2d ¶ L-15530 *et seq.*; USTR ¶ 54A4 *et seq.*)

Under pre-Tax Cuts and Jobs Act law, the following types of QTCBs could be issued:

... Qualified forestry conservation bonds (QFCBs), subject to a $500 million volume limitation. (FTC 2d ¶ L-15550 *et seq.*; USTR ¶ 54B4 *et seq.*)

... New clean renewable energy bonds (new CREBs), subject to a $2.4 billion volume limitation. (FTC 2d ¶ L-15560 *et seq.*; USTR ¶ 54C4 *et seq.*)

... Qualified energy conservation bonds (QECBs), subject to a $3.2 billion volume limitation. (FTC 2d ¶ L-15570 *et seq.*; USTR ¶ 54D4 *et seq.*)

... Qualified zone academy bonds (QZABs), subject to a $400 million bond limitation for each of calendar years 2008 and 2011−2016 and a $1.4 billion limit for calendar years 2009 and 2010. (FTC 2d ¶ L-15580 *et seq.*; USTR ¶ 54E4 *et seq.*) The volume cap for years after 2016 is $0, but issuers could still issue bonds if they had remaining amounts under the limitations from years before 2017. (FTC 2d ¶ L-15586; USTR ¶ 54E4.01)

. . . Qualified school construction bonds (QSCBs), subject to a volume cap of $11 billion for each of 2009 and 2010. (FTC 2d ¶ L-15590 *et seq.*; USTR ¶ 54F4) The volume cap for years after 2010 is $0, but issuers could still issue bonds if they had remaining amounts under the limitations from years before 2011. (FTC 2d ¶ L-15593; USTR ¶ 54F4)

Old CREBs. Taxpayers who hold clean renewable energy bonds (old CREBs) on specified dates during a year are entitled to a nonrefundable tax credit equal to a portion of the bond's outstanding face amount. Old CREBs aren't QTCBs. Unlike holders of most QTCBs, issuers of old CREBs couldn't choose to receive refundable credits (see below). Old CREBs were issued through Dec. 31, 2009 and were subject to a $1.2 billion dollar volume cap. (FTC 2d ¶ L-16480 *et seq.*; USTR ¶ 544 *et seq.*)

Build America bonds. For 2009 and 2010, state and local governments could issue BABs, otherwise tax-exempt bonds used to finance capital projects that the issuer elected to treat as taxable governmental bonds. At the issuer's option, either the holder of the BAB could accrue a tax credit equal to 35% of the interest payable on the interest payment dates of the bond during the calendar year, or the issuer itself could claim a refundable credit equal to 35% of each interest payment made under the bond (see below). BABs weren't subject to a volume cap. (FTC 2d ¶ L-15590 *et seq.*; USTR ¶ 54AA4)

Direct-pay bonds. For state and local bonds that were qualified bonds, the issuer could elect to receive a refundable tax credit in the form of a direct payment from IRS in lieu of any credit otherwise allowed to the holder of the bond. Qualified bonds included BABs and QTCBs other than QZABs issued using allocations or carryforwards of national bond limitations for years after 2010. Old CREBs and QZABs issued under post-2010 limitations weren't qualified bonds. (FTC 2d ¶ L-15547 *et seq.*, ¶ L-15607 *et seq.*; USTR ¶ 64,314 *et seq.*)

New Law. The Tax Cuts and Jobs Act repeals the provisions of the Code authorizing issuance of tax-credit bonds and the provision allowing direct-pay bonds. (Com Rept, see ¶ 5061)

Specifically, the Tax Cuts and Jobs Act repeals the following Code sections:

. . . Credit to holders of clean renewable energy bonds. (Code Sec. 54 as repealed by Tax Cuts and Jobs Act §13404(a))

. . . Credit to holders of qualified tax credit bonds. (Code Sec. 54A as repealed by Tax Cuts and Jobs Act §13404(a))

. . . Qualified forestry conservation bonds. (Code Sec. 54B as repealed by Tax Cuts and Jobs Act §13404(a))

. . . New clean renewable energy bonds. (Code Sec. 54C as repealed by Tax Cuts and Jobs Act §13404(a))

. . . Qualified energy conservation bonds. (Code Sec. 54D as repealed by Tax Cuts and Jobs Act §13404(a))

. . . Qualified zone academy bonds. (Code Sec. 54E as repealed by Tax Cuts and Jobs Act §13404(a))

. . . Qualified school construction bonds. (Code Sec. 54F as repealed by Tax Cuts and Jobs Act §13404(a))

. . . Build America bonds. (Code Sec. 54AA as repealed by Tax Cuts and Jobs Act §13404(a))

. . . Credit for qualified bonds allowed to issuer. (Code Sec. 6431 as repealed by Tax Cuts and Jobs Act §13404(b))

. . . Credit to holders of qualified zone academy bonds. (Code Sec. 1397E as repealed by Tax Cuts and Jobs Act §13404(c)(1))

Congress believes that some tax-credit bond programs allowed for financing of activities that were of questionable value to taxpayers. In any case, sufficient time had passed to allow full use of the allocations provided for under tax-credit bond programs, and terminating the issuance of new tax-credit bonds was appropriate. (Com Rept, see ¶ 5061)

☐ **Effective:** Bonds issued after Dec. 31, 2017. (Tax Cuts and Jobs Act §13404(c))

> *observation:* No new tax-credit bonds may be issued after 2017, but current rules continue to apply to tax-credit bonds that were issued before Jan. 1, 2018.

¶ 1703. Gains invested in a Qualified Opportunity Fund can be temporarily deferred and permanently excluded if the investment in the Fund is held for 10 years

Code Sec. 1400Z-2, as added by Tax Cuts and Jobs Act §13823(a)
Code Sec. 1016(a)(38), as amended by Tax Cuts and Jobs Act §13823(b)
Generally effective: Dec. 22, 2017
Committee Reports, see ¶ 5106

The Tax Cuts and Jobs Act authorizes the designation of certain low-income communities as Qualified Opportunity Zones (QO Zones), see ¶ 1704.

New Law. The Tax Cuts and Jobs Act provides for the temporary deferral of inclusion in gross income for capital gains reinvested in a Qualified Opportunity Fund (QO Fund) and the permanent exclusion of certain capital gains from the sale or exchange of an investment in the QO Fund. (Com Rept, see ¶ 5106)

In the case of gain from the sale to, or exchange with, an unrelated person (defined below) of any property held by the taxpayer, at the election of the taxpayer: (Code Sec. 1400Z-2(a)(1) as added by Tax Cuts and Jobs Act §13823(a))

(1) gross income for the tax year does *not* include so much of the gain as does not exceed the aggregate amount invested by the taxpayer in a QO Fund (defined below) during the 180-day period beginning on the date of the sale or exchange (the temporary deferral election). (Code Sec. 1400Z-2(a)(1)(A))

> *illustration (1):*   T sells property and realizes a gain of $1 million on Dec. 1, 2021. On Dec. 31, 2021 (i.e., a date within the 180-day period beginning on Dec. 1, 2021), T invests all of the $1 million gain in a QO Fund. If T makes the temporary deferral election, T does not include the $1 million of realized gain in his gross income for the 2021 tax year.

> *observation:*   Although the Committee Report indicates that the temporary deferral election applies to "capital gains" reinvested in a QO Fund (see above), Code Sec. 1400Z-2(a) applies to gains from a sale or exchange of "any property" and isn't expressly limited to gains from the sale or exchange of a capital asset.

> *observation:*   There's no dollar limitation on the amount of gain that can be deferred under the temporary deferral election.

> *observation:*   For purposes of determining the 180-day period, the period presumably expires on the 180th day following the date of the sale or exchange even if that day is a holiday, Saturday, or Sunday.

> *observation:*   Presumably, the taxpayer must actually acquire ownership of the investment in the QO Fund before the expiration of the 180-day period. It presumably would not be sufficient to have entered into a contract to acquire an interest in a QO Fund before the expiration of the 180-day period.

> *observation:*   Although the Tax Cuts and Jobs Act provides no indication that extensions of the 180-day period for acquiring the investment in the QO Fund would be available, it would appear that IRS could allow a postponement of the 180-day deadline for taxpayers serving in the U.S. Armed Forces or taxpayers affected by a Presidentially declared disaster, terrorist or military actions under the rules discussed in FTC 2d/FIN ¶s S-8012, S-8502; USTR ¶ 75,08A4.

> *observation:*   If the sale or exchange occurs in the second half of the tax year, the 180-day period may span two tax years. If a taxpayer hasn't reinvested the gain in a QO Fund by the unextended due date of his income tax return for the tax year of the sale or exchange, the tax-

payer may want to request an extension and delay filing his return for the year of the sale or exchange until the taxpayer has (or hasn't) made the investment in a QO Fund.

(2) the amount of gain excluded under item (1) (i.e., the temporary deferral election under Code Sec. 1400Z-2(a)(1)(A)) is included in gross income as provided by Code Sec. 1400Z-2(b) (discussed below). (Code Sec. 1400Z-2(a)(1)(B))

observation: Thus, if a taxpayer makes the temporary deferral election under item (1) with respect to gain that the taxpayer reinvests in a QO Fund, he has to include the deferred gain in gross income at the end of the deferral period (determined under item (2)).

(3) the permanent exclusion of certain gain from the investment is determined under Code Sec. 1400Z-2(c) (the permanent exclusion election). (Code Sec. 1400Z-2(a)(1)(C))

observation: It appears that any taxpayer (individual, estate, trust, corporation, partnership, etc.) can make the temporary deferral election or the permanent exclusion election under Code Sec. 1400Z-2(a). For how Code Sec. 1400Z-2 applies to decedents, see below.

observation: Presumably, IRS will provide instructions for making the temporary deferral election and the permanent exclusion election.

When elections can't be made. No election can be made under Code Sec. 1400Z-2(a)(1) (discussed above at items (1), (2), and (3)) (Code Sec. 1400Z-2(a)(2)) with respect to a sale or exchange if an election previously made with respect to the sale or exchange is in effect. (Code Sec. 1400Z-2(a)(2)(A))

observation: Thus, only one election can be made with respect to any sale or exchange. But, the one-election-limitation does not appear to prevent a taxpayer from making the temporary deferral election under Code Sec. 1400Z-2(a)(1)(A) and the permanent exclusion election under Code Sec. 1400Z-2(a)(1)(C) because those two elections would be made with respect to different sales. The temporary deferral election is made with respect to gains from the sale or exchange of any property that are invested in a QO Fund and the permanent exclusion election is made with respect to gain from the sale or exchange of an investment in the QO Fund.

observation: The one-election-limitation would presumably prevent a taxpayer from making successive temporary deferral elections with respect to the reinvestment of part of any gains from a sale or exchange in a QO Fund and the later reinvestment of another part of the gains from that same sale or exchange in the same or a different QO Fund. That is, in that case, the second reinvestment in a QO Fund of any gains from the same sale or exchange is ineligible for the temporary deferral election under Code Sec. 1400Z-2(a)(1)(A).

observation: The one-sale-limitation also might apply to a taxpayer, who sold property on an installment basis and made a temporary deferral election applicable to gain recognized in the year of sale. In that case, the one-election-limitation might prevent that taxpayer from making a second temporary deferral election with respect to an investment in a QO Fund of gain recognized from an installment payment received after the tax year of the sale because the two elections would relate to gain from the same sale.

Also, no election can be made under Code Sec. 1400Z-2(a)(1) (discussed above at items (1), (2), and (3)) (Code Sec. 1400Z-2(a)(2)) with respect to any sale or exchange after Dec. 31, 2026. (Code Sec. 1400Z-2(a)(2)(B)) According to the Committee Report, there is no gain deferral available with respect to any sale or exchange made after Dec. 31, 2026. (Com Rept, see ¶ 5106)

observation: This date corresponds with the latest date that the deferral period ends, see below.

Recognition of deferred gain at the end of the deferral period.

Inclusion of deferred gain. Gain to which Code Sec. 1400Z-2(a)(1)(B) applies (i.e., gain excluded under the temporary deferral election) is included in income in the tax year which includes the *earlier* of: (Code Sec. 1400Z-2(b)(1))

(a) the date on which the investment is sold or exchanged, or (Code Sec. 1400Z-2(b)(1)(A))

(b) Dec. 31, 2026. (Code Sec. 1400Z-2(b)(1)(B))

observation: Presumably, the "investment" referred to in Code Sec. 1400Z-2(b)(1)(A) (item (a) immediately above) and throughout Code Sec. 1400Z-2 is the investment in the QO Fund.

observation: The temporary deferral period ends on Dec. 31, 2026 unless the taxpayer sells or exchanges the investment in a QO Fund before that date.

illustration (2): The facts are the same as in illustration (1). If T holds the investment in the QO Fund until Dec. 31, 2026, T has to include the deferred gain in gross income in 2026. For the amount of the gain, see illustration (3) below.

observation: As discussed at ¶ 1704, the designation of a QO Zone remains in effect until the end of the 10th calendar year beginning on or after the date of the designation (i.e., Dec. 31, 2028). But, the deferral period ends two years earlier (i.e., on Dec. 31, 2026 unless a sale or exchange causes the period to end before Dec. 31, 2026). Thus, the temporary deferral election presumably isn't available for investments in QO Funds during the entire period that the QO Zone designation is in effect.

Amount of deferred gain included in gross income. The amount of gain included in gross income under *Code Sec. 1400Z-2(a)(1)(A)* (see observation below) is the *excess* of: (Code Sec. 1400Z-2(b)(2)(A))

observation: The reference to Code Sec. 1400Z-2(a)(1)(A) appears to be incorrect because Code Sec. 1400Z-2(a)(1)(A) provides for the temporary deferral of gains (rather than an inclusion in gross income). Presumably, the reference should be to Code Sec. 1400Z-2(a)(1)(B).

(a) the *lesser* of the amount of gain excluded under *Code Sec. 1400Z-2(b)(1)* (see observation below) or the fair market value (FMV) of the investment as determined as of the date described in Code Sec. 1400Z-2(b)(1) (i.e., the end of the deferral period), *over* (Code Sec. 1400Z-2(b)(2)(A)(i))

observation: In item (a), the reference to the "amount of gain excluded under Code Sec. 1400Z-2(b)(1)" appears to be incorrect since Code Sec. 1400Z-2(b)(1) contains rules for determining when a taxpayer includes the income previously deferred by the reinvestment in the QO Fund. Presumably, the reference should be to Code Sec. 1400Z-2(a)(1)(A) (discussed above).

observation: If a taxpayer's investment in the QO Fund has depreciated (i.e., the FMV of the investment is less than the amount of the deferred gain), the FMV (instead of the deferred gain) is used to compute the amount of gain recognized when the deferral period ends.

(b) the taxpayer's basis in the investment (defined immediately below). (Code Sec. 1400Z-2(b)(2)(A)(ii))

illustration (3): The facts are the same as in illustrations (1) and (2) except that T's basis in the investment is $100,000 (see illustration (4) below) and the FMV of the investment is $1.5 million. The amount that T has to include in income is $900,000 ($1 million − $100,000).

Basis in the investment. Except for the increases to basis discussed below or in Code Sec. 1400Z-2(c) (discussed below), the taxpayer's basis in the investment is zero. (Code Sec. 1400Z-2(b)(2)(B)(i))

Basis increases. In the case of any investment held for at least *five* years, the basis of the investment is increased by an amount equal to 10% of the amount of gain temporarily deferred under Code Sec. 1400Z-2(a)(1)(A) (discussed above). (Code Sec. 1400Z-2(b)(2)(B)(iii))

> ⚑ *illustration (4):* The facts are the same as in illustrations (1), (2), and (3). Since T held the investment for five years, T's basis in the investment is increased by $100,000 (10% of the deferred gain of $1 million). Since T had a zero basis in the investment (before the increase) under Code Sec. 1400Z-2(b)(2)(B)(i) (discussed above), T's basis in the investment is $100,000.

In the case of any investment held by the taxpayer for at least *seven* years, in addition to any basis adjustment made under Code Sec. 1400Z-2(b)(2)(B)(iii) for an investment held more than five years (discussed immediately above), the basis of the property is increased by an amount equal to 5% of the amount of gain deferred by reason of Code Sec. 1400Z-2(a)(1). (Code Sec. 1400Z-2(b)(2)(B)(iv))

> ⚑ *observation:* The 10% basis increase provided in Code Sec. 1400Z-2(b)(2)(B)(iii) applies to the basis in the "investment" while the basis increase under Code Sec. 1400Z-2(b)(2)(B)(iv) applies to the basis of the "property." Presumably, both increases are intended to apply to the basis in the investment and could result in an increase equal to 15% of the deferred gain to the basis if the investment is held for seven years.

The basis in the investment is increased by the amount of gain recognized when the temporary deferral period ends under Code Sec. 1400Z-2(a)(1)(B) with respect to the property. (Code Sec. 1400Z-2(b)(2)(B)(ii)) Thus, if the investment is held by the taxpayer until at least Dec. 31, 2026, the basis in the investment increases by the remaining 85% of the deferred gain. (Com Rept, see ¶ 5106)

> ⚑ *observation:* Presumably, Code Sec. 1400Z-2(b)(2)(B)(ii) is intended to apply only when a taxpayer recognizes gain when the temporary deferral period ends on Dec. 31, 2026 (i.e., when there has not been a sale or exchange of the investment before that date).

> ⚑ *observation:* In the case of a sale or exchange of the investment before Dec. 31, 2026 (that causes the deferral period to end and gain to be recognized), the inclusion of any gain recognized in the basis in the investment would result in a circular computation. Under that computation, the basis in the investment is used to calculate the amount of gain recognized at the end of the deferral period (see item (b) above) and

the amount of any gain recognized would be needed to compute the basis in the investment.

Investments with mixed funds. In the case of any investment in a QO Fund only a portion of which consists of investments of gain to which an election under Code Sec. 1400Z-2(a) is in effect: (Code Sec. 1400Z-2(e)(1))

. . . the investment is treated as two separate investments, consisting of (Code Sec. 1400Z-2(e)(1)(A))

(1) one investment that only includes amounts to the election under Code Sec. 1400Z-2(a) applies, and (Code Sec. 1400Z-2(e)(1)(A)(i))

(2) a separate investment consisting of other amounts, and (Code Sec. 1400Z-2(e)(1)(A)(ii))

. . . the temporary deferral election rules under Code Sec. 1400Z-2(a), the gain inclusion rules under Code Sec. 1400Z-2(b), and, the permanent exclusion election rules under Code Sec. 1400Z-2(c) only apply to the investment described in item (1). (Code Sec. 1400Z-2(e)(1)(B))

> *illustration (5):* The facts are the same as in illustration (1) except that T only invested $ 750,000 of the $1 million gain in the QO Fund at first in a transaction for which T made the temporary deferral election. A few weeks later T invested the remaining $250,000 of the gain in the same QO Fund for which a temporary deferral election couldn't be available by reason of the one-election-limitation discussed above. T's total investment in the QO Fund is treated as two separate investments under item (1) above. One investment consists of $750,000 (the amount subject to the temporary deferral election) and the other investment consists of the $250,000 (the amount not eligible for the temporary deferral election).

> *illustration (6):* The facts are the same as in illustration (1) except that T initially invested $1.25 million (comprised of T's $1 million gain on the sale of property and T's $250,000 in savings) in the QO Fund. Since T's investment in the QO Fund exceeds T's $1 million gain on the sale of property, T's investment in the QO Fund is treated as two separate investments under item (1) above. One investment consists of $1 million (the amount subject to the temporary deferral election) and the other investment consists of T's savings of $250,000 (the amount not eligible for the temporary deferral election even if it was commingled with T's $1 million gain on the sale of property when it was invested in a single transaction in the QO Fund.

Decedents. In the case of a decedent, amounts recognized under Code Sec. 1400Z-2 are, if not properly includible in the decedent's gross income, included in gross income as provided under the rules for determining income with respect to the decedent under (FTC 2d/FIN ¶ C-9501; USTR ¶ 6914). (Code Sec. 1400Z-2(e)(3))

Permanent exclusion election for investments in QO Funds held for at least 10 years. In the case of any investment held by the taxpayer for at least ten years and with respect to which the taxpayer makes an election under Code Sec. 1400Z-2(c), the basis of the property equals the fair market value of the investment on the date that the investment is sold or exchanged. (Code Sec. 1400Z-2(c)) Under the permanent exclusion, any post-acquisition capital gains on investments in QO Funds that are held for at least ten years are excluded from gross income. (Com Rept, see ¶ 5106)

> *observation:* Since the basis of the property equals the fair market value of the investment (i.e., the investment in the QO Fund), there's no gain or loss realized on a sale or exchange of the investment subject to the election.

> *observation:* As explained above, taxpayers who made the temporary deferral election have to recognize any deferred gain on Dec. 31, 2026 (unless a sale or exchange causes the period to end before Dec. 31, 2026). Since the end of the deferral period on Dec. 31, 2026 will occur before any taxpayer could have held his investment for ten years, the permanent exclusion election won't protect a taxpayer from recognizing any deferred gain. Thus, if the taxpayer holds his investment for ten years, the permanent exclusion election presumably will only exclude gain in excess of the deferred gain (that has already been recognized).

> *observation:* Although Code Sec. 1400Z-2(c) uses the term "any investment," the election is presumably limited to an investment in a QO Fund.

Related persons. For purposes of Code Sec. 1400Z-2, persons are related to each other if the persons are described in the constructive ownership rules under Code Sec. 267(b) (FTC 2d/FIN ¶ I-3504; USTR ¶ 2674.03) or Code Sec. 707(b)(1) (FTC 2d/FIN ¶ B-2016; USTR ¶ 7074.03), determined by substituting "20%" for "50%" each place it occurs in Code Sec. 267(b) and Code Sec. 707(b)(1). (Code Sec. 1400Z-2(e)(2))

Losses on investments in QO Funds. Taxpayers can recognize losses associated with investments in QO Funds. (Com Rept, see ¶ 5106)

> *observation:* Unless a taxpayer's basis in the investment in a QO Fund qualifies for a basis increase under the rules discussed above (for example, the increase for holding the investment for five or seven years), the taxpayer will have a zero basis in his investment. Thus, it

may be unlikely that a taxpayer will even realize a loss on any sale or exchange of the investment that could be recognized.

QO Fund. For purposes of Code Sec. 1400Z-2, (Code Sec. 1400Z-2(d)) a QO Fund is any investment vehicle:

... that is organized as a corporation or a partnership for the purpose of investing in QO Zone property (defined below) (other than another QO Fund)

... that holds at least 90% of its assets in QO Zone property (defined below), determined by the average of the percentage of QO Zone property held in the QO fund as measured: (Code Sec. 1400Z-2(d)(1))

• on the last day of the first six-month period of the tax year of the QO Fund, and (Code Sec. 1400Z-2(d)(1)(A))

• on the last day of the tax year of the QO Fund. (Code Sec. 1400Z-2(d)(1)(B))

> **⟪RIA⟫** *observation:* Thus, a QO Fund can't be organized for the purpose of investing in other QO Funds or be a fund holding only QO Funds.

IRS can prescribe the regs as may be necessary or appropriate to carry out the purposes of Code Sec. 1400Z-2, including rules: (Code Sec. 1400Z-2(e)(4))

... for the certification of QO Funds. (Code Sec. 1400Z-2(e)(4)(A)) Congress intends that the certification process for a QO Fund will be done by the Treasury Dept.'s Community Development Financial Institutions Fund (CDFI) in a manner similar to the process for allocating the new markets tax credit. (Com Rept, see ¶ 5106)

... to ensure a QO Fund has a reasonable period of time to reinvest the return of capital from investments in QO Zone stock and QO Zone partnership interests, and to reinvest proceeds received from the sale or disposition of QO Zone property. (Code Sec. 1400Z-2(e)(4)(B))

For the penalty that applies to a QO Fund that doesn't meet the 90% requirement, see below.

QO Zone property. A QO Zone property is property which is: (Code Sec. 1400Z-2(d)(2)(A))

... QO Zone stock (defined below), (Code Sec. 1400Z-2(d)(2)(A)(i))

... QO Zone partnership interest (defined below), or (Code Sec. 1400Z-2(d)(2)(A)(ii))

... QO Zone business property (defined below). (Code Sec. 1400Z-2(d)(2)(A)(iii))

> **⟪RIA⟫** *observation:* The definition of QO Zone property is similar to the definition of a DC Zone asset (FTC 2d/FIN ¶ I-8752; USTR

¶ 14,00B4.01) for purposes of the zero capital gain rate and the definition of qualified community assets (FTC 2d/FIN ¶ I-8803; USTR ¶ 14,00F4.01) for purposes of the income exclusion for gain from certain renewal community assets.

QO Zone stock. Except as discussed below, QO Zone stock is any stock in a domestic corporation if: (Code Sec. 1400Z-2(d)(2)(B)(i))

. . . the stock is acquired by the QO Fund after Dec. 31, 2017, at its original issue (directly or through an underwriter) from the corporation solely in exchange for cash, (Code Sec. 1400Z-2(d)(2)(B)(i)(I))

. . . as of the time the stock was issued, the corporation was a QO Zone business (defined below) (or, in the case of a new corporation, the corporation was being organized for purposes of being a QO Zone business), and (Code Sec. 1400Z-2(d)(2)(B)(i)(II))

. . . during substantially all of the QO Fund's holding period for the stock, the corporation qualified as a QO Zone business. (Code Sec. 1400Z-2(d)(2)(B)(i)(III))

> **✔** *observation:* The definition of QO Zone stock is very similar to the definition of a DC Zone business stock (FTC 2d/FIN ¶ I-8753; USTR ¶ 14,00B4.01) for purposes of the zero capital gain rate and qualified community stock (FTC 2d/FIN ¶ I-8803; USTR ¶ 14,00F4.01) for purposes of the income exclusion for certain renewal community assets.

> **✔** *observation:* Code Sec. 1400Z-2 doesn't define the term "substantially all" used in Code Sec. 1400Z-2(d)(2)(B)(i)(III) for purposes of the definition of a QO Zone stock.

A rule similar to the rule of Code Sec. 1202(c)(3) (rules related to purchases by a corporation of its own stock for purposes of the gain exclusion from small business stock, see FTC 2d/FIN ¶ I-9102; USTR ¶ 12,024) applies for purposes of the definition of QO Zone stock. (Code Sec. 1400Z-2(d)(2)(B)(ii))

> **✔** *observation:* Thus, the purpose of the requirement in Code Sec. 1400Z-2(d)(2)(B)(ii) (that rules similar to the rules in Code Sec. 1202(c)(3) apply) is to prevent avoidance of the original issuance requirement. For example, if these anti-avoidance rules didn't apply, a corporation could redeem a substantial amount of its stock. and a few months later issue stock. In that case, the stock issuance would have the form of an "original issue" of stock, but, in substance would resemble a mere reissuance of stock.

QO Zone partnership interest. A QO Zone partnership interest is any capital or profits interest in a domestic partnership if: (Code Sec. 1400Z-2(d)(2)(C))

. . . the interest is acquired by the QO Fund after Dec. 31, 2017, from the partnership solely in exchange for cash, (Code Sec. 1400Z-2(d)(2)(C)(i))

. . . as of the time the interest was acquired, the partnership was a QO Zone business (defined below) (or, in the case of a new partnership, the partnership was being organized for purposes of being a QO Zone business), and (Code Sec. 1400Z-2(d)(2)(C)(ii))

. . . during substantially all of the QO Fund's holding period for the interest, the partnership qualified as a QO Zone business. (Code Sec. 1400Z-2(d)(2)(C)(iii))

> *observation:* The definition of QO Zone partnership interest is very similar to the definition of a DC Zone partnership interest stock (FTC 2d/FIN ¶ I-8754; USTR ¶ 14,00B4.01) for purposes of the zero capital gain rate and qualified community partnership interest (FTC 2d/FIN ¶ I-8803.2; USTR ¶ 14,00F4.01) for purposes of the income exclusion for certain renewal community assets.

> *observation:* Code Sec. 1400Z-2 doesn't define the term "substantially all" used in Code Sec. 1400Z-2(d)(2)(C)(iii) for purposes of the definition of a QO Zone partnership interest.

QO Zone business property. A QO Zone business property is tangible property used in a trade or business of the taxpayer if these three requirements are satisfied: (Code Sec. 1400Z-2(d)(2)(D)(i))

(i) the property was acquired by the QO Zone by purchase (as defined in Code Sec. 179(d)(2)) after Dec. 31, 2017. (Code Sec. 1400Z-2(d)(2)(D)(i)(I))

(ii) the original use of the property in the QO Zone commences with the QO Fund or the QO Fund substantially improves the property. (Code Sec. 1400Z-2(d)(2)(D)(i)(II)) For this purpose, property is treated as substantially improved by the taxpayer only if, during any 30-month period beginning after the date of acquisition of the property, additions to basis with respect to the property in the QO Fund's hands exceed an amount equal to the adjusted basis of the property at the beginning of the 30-month period in the taxpayer's hands. (Code Sec. 1400Z-2(d)(2)(D)(ii))

(iii) during substantially all of the QO Fund's holding period for the property, substantially all of the use of the property was in a QO Zone. (Code Sec. 1400Z-2(d)(2)(D)(i)(III))

> *observation:* Since Code Sec. 1400Z-2(d)(2)(D)(i) limits QO Zone business property to tangible property, intangible property can't be QO Zone business property.

> *observation:* Under Code Sec. 179(d)(2) (referred to in item (i)), a "purchase" is any acquisition of property other than an acquisition (1)

from a person related to the taxpayer; (2) from another member of a controlled group of corporations; or (3) in which the basis of the acquiring person in the property is (a) in whole or part, a carryover basis, or (b) determined under Code Sec. 1014(a) (concerning property acquired from a decedent), see FTC 2d/FIN ¶ L-9925; USTR ¶ 1794.04.

❤️ observation: The definition of QO Zone business property is very similar to the definition of a DC Zone business property (FTC 2d/FIN ¶ I-8755; USTR ¶ 14,00B4.01) for purposes of the zero capital gain rate and qualified community business property (FTC 2d/FIN ¶ I-8804; USTR ¶ 14,00F4.01) for purposes of the income exclusion for certain renewal community assets.

❤️ observation: Code Sec. 1400Z-2 doesn't define the term "substantially all" for purposes of the definition of a QO Zone business property under Code Sec. 1400Z-2(d)(2)(D)(i)(III) (item (iii) above).

Related party. For purposes of *Code Sec. 1400Z-2(d)(2)(A)(i)* (see observation below), the related person rule of Code Sec. 179(d)(2) is applied under *Code Sec. 1400Z-2(d)(8)* (see observation below) in lieu of the application of the rule in Code Sec. 179(d)(2)(A). (Code Sec. 1400Z-2(d)(2)(D)(iii))

❤️ observation: There appear to be drafting errors in Code Sec. 1400Z-2(d)(2)(D)(iii).

The reference to Code Sec. 1400Z-2(d)(2)(A)(i) is to the listing of QO Zone stock as a type of QO Zone property and that rule doesn't appear to require a definition of related parties. Presumably, the reference should be to Code Sec. 1400Z-2(d)(2)(D)(i)(I) (rule incorporating Code Sec. 179(d)(2) by reference, see item (i) above).

Also, the reference to Code Sec. 1400Z-2(d)(8) presumably is incorrect because Code Sec. 1400Z-2(d)(8) does not exist.

QO Zone business. A QO Zone business is a trade or business: (Code Sec. 1400Z-2(d)(3)(A))

. . . in which substantially all of the tangible property owned or leased by the taxpayer is QO Zone business property (determined by substituting "QO Zone business" for "QO Fund" each place it appears in Code Sec. 1400Z-2(d)(2)(D), see above),

. . . which satisfies the requirements of Code Sec. 1397C(b)(2) (rule relating to the definition of an enterprise zone business that requires at least 50% of a qualified business entity's total gross income be derived from the active conduct of a qualified business, see FTC 2d/FIN ¶ L-9955; USTR ¶ 13,97A4), Code Sec. 1397C(b)(4) (requirement under the definition of a qualified business entity requiring that a substantial portion of the entity's intangible property is used in the active conduct of the business, see FTC 2d/FIN ¶ L-9955; USTR ¶ 13,97A4), and Code Sec. 1397C(b)(8) (rule providing that less than 5% of the average unadjusted basis of qualified business entity's property is attributable to nonqualified financial property, see FTC 2d/FIN ¶ L-9955; USTR ¶ 13,97A4). (Code Sec. 1400Z-2(d)(3)(A)(ii)) and

. . . which is *not* described in Code Sec. 144(c)(6)(B) (i.e., property other than any private or commercial golf course, country club, massage parlor, hot tub facility, suntan facility, racetrack or other facility used for gambling, or any store the principal business of which is the sale of alcoholic beverages for consumption off premises, see FTC 2d/FIN ¶ J-3299; USTR ¶ 1444.02). (Code Sec. 1400Z-2(d)(3)(A)(iii))

> **RIA** *observation:* Based on the context, it appears that the term "taxpayer" in Code Sec. 1400Z-2(d)(3)(A)(i) may refer to the corporation, etc. operating the QO Zone business. But, in Code Sec. 1400Z-2(a), the term "taxpayer" presumably is used to refer to the person who invested any gain from a sale or exchange in the QO Fund. Since the same term is used to refer to different persons or entities in Code Sec. 1400Z-2, it would appear that a technical correction may be necessary to clarify the rules.

For purposes of the definition of a QO Zone business under Code Sec. 1400Z-2(d)(3)(A), tangible property that ceases to be a QO Zone business property continues to be treated as a QO Zone business property for the *lesser* of: (Code Sec. 1400Z-2(d)(3)(B))

(a) five years after the date on which the tangible property ceases to be so qualified, or (Code Sec. 1400Z-2(d)(3)(B)(i))

(b) the date on which the tangible property is no longer held by the QO Zone business. (Code Sec. 1400Z-2(d)(3)(B)(ii))

Anti-abuse regs. IRS can prescribe the regs as may be necessary or appropriate to carry out the purposes of Code Sec. 1400Z-2, including (Code Sec. 1400Z-2(e)(4)) rules to prevent abuse. (Code Sec. 1400Z-2(e)(4)(C))

Penalty for failure of a QO Fund to maintain the 90% investment standard. If a QO Fund fails to meet the 90% requirement of *Code Sec. 1400Z-2(c)(1)* (see observation below), the QO Fund has to pay a penalty for each month it fails to meet the requirement in an amount equal to the product of: (Code Sec. 1400Z-2(f)(1))

> **RIA** *observation:* The reference to Code Sec. 1400Z-2(c)(1) appears to be incorrect because the requirement to hold 90% of the QO Fund's assets in QO Zone property is provided in Code Sec. 1400Z-2(d)(1).

• the excess of: (Code Sec. 1400Z-2(f)(1)(A))

. . . the amount equal to 90% of its aggregate assets, over (Code Sec. 1400Z-2(f)(1)(A)(i))

. . . the aggregate amount of QO Zone property held by the fund, multiplied by (Code Sec. 1400Z-2(f)(1)(A)(ii))

• the underpayment rate established under Code Sec. 6621(a)(2) (see FTC 2d/ FIN ¶ V-1101; USTR ¶ 66,214) for the month. (Code Sec. 1400Z-2(f)(1)(B))

Partnerships. If the QO Fund is a partnership, the penalty is taken into account proportionately as part of the distributive share of each partner of the partnership. (Code Sec. 1400Z-2(f)(2))

Reasonable cause exception. No penalty is imposed under Code Sec. 1400Z-2(f) with respect to any failure if it is shown that the failure is due to reasonable cause. (Code Sec. 1400Z-2(f)(3))

Basis adjustment. The Tax Cuts and Jobs Act adds a basis adjustment to the extent provided in Code Sec. 1400Z-2(b)(2) (increase to basis of an investment held for five years and seven years, see above) and Code Sec. 1400Z-2(c) (determination of basis under the permanent deferral election, see above) to the list of proper basis adjustments that must be made under Code Sec. 1016(a), see (FTC 2d/FIN ¶ P-1700; USTR ¶ 10,164). (Code Sec. 1016(a)(38) as amended by Tax Cuts and Jobs Act §13823(b))

> **RIA** *observation:* Code Sec. 1016(a)(38) doesn't cause the increases to basis made under Code Sec. 1400Z-2 (discussed above) to be repeated under Code Sec. 1016. Instead, the main effect of being added to the list of items requiring basis adjustments in Code Sec. 1016(a) is to make the increases under Code Sec. 1400Z-2 subject to Code provisions that cross-refer to Code Sec. 1016 and require that adjustments be made under Code Sec. 1016.

☐ **Effective:** Dec. 22, 2017. (Tax Cuts and Jobs Act §13823(d))

¶ 1704. Chief executive officers of a state can designate low-income communities as Qualified Opportunity Zones

Code Sec. 1400Z-1, as added by Tax Cuts and Jobs Act §13823(a)
Generally effective: Dec. 22, 2017
Committee Reports, see ¶ 5106

For tax benefits available for investments in Qualified Opportunity Zones (QO Zones, defined below), see ¶ 1703.

New Law. The Tax Cuts and Jobs Act allows for the designation of certain low-income community (defined below) population census tracts as Qualified Opportunity Zones (QO Zones, defined below). (Com Rept, see ¶ 5106) A QO Zone is:

... a population census tract that

... is a low-income community that

... is designated as a QO Zone. (Code Sec. 1400Z-1(a) as added by Tax Cuts and Jobs Act §13823(a))

Designation. For purposes of Code Sec. 1400Z-1(a) (discussed immediately above), a population census tract that is a low-income community is designated as a QO Zone if these two requirements are satisfied: (Code Sec. 1400Z-1(b)(1))

(1) not later than the end of the determination period (defined below), the chief executive officer of the state (defined below) in which the tract is located: (Code Sec. 1400Z-1(b)(1)(A))

• nominates the tract for designation as a QO Zone, and (Code Sec. 1400Z-1(b)(1)(A)(i))

• notifies IRS in writing of the nomination. (Code Sec. 1400Z-1(b)(1)(A)(ii)) A determination period is the 90-day period beginning on the Dec. 22, 2017, as extended under Code Sec. 1400Z-1(b)(2) (discussed below). (Code Sec. 1400Z-1(c)(2)(B))

> **action alert:** If a chief executive officer of a state doesn't request a 30-day extension (see below), the chief executive officer has until Mar. 22, 2018 to nominate a census tract as a QO Zone and to notify IRS.

> **observation:** The chief executive officer of a state includes a governor of a state as well as the mayor of D.C. (see below).

(2) IRS certifies the nomination and designates the tract as a QO Zone before the end of the consideration period. (Code Sec. 1400Z-1(b)(1)(B)) A consideration period is the 30-day period beginning on the date on which IRS receives notice under Code Sec. 1400Z-1(b)(1)(A)(ii) (discussed above), as extended under Code Sec. 1400Z-1(b)(2) (discussed below). (Code Sec. 1400Z-1(c)(2)(A))

Extensions. A chief executive officer of a state can request that IRS extend either the determination or consideration period, or both (determined without regard to the extension rule), for an additional 30 days. (Code Sec. 1400Z-1(b)(2))

> **observation:** If IRS grants a chief executive officer's request for a 30-day extension of both the determination period (i.e., 90-day period

beginning on the Dec. 22, 2017) and the consideration period (30-day period beginning on the date on which IRS receives notice under Code Sec. 1400Z-1(b)(1)(A)(ii)), the determination period as extended would be the 120-day period beginning on Dec. 22, 2017 and the consideration period as extended would be the 60-day period beginning on the date that IRS receives the notice. Thus, if both extensions are granted, any designation will have to be made within the 180-day period beginning on Dec. 22, 2017.

Number of designations. Except for states with less than 100 low-income communities (discussed in the next sentence), the number of population census tracts in a state that can be designated as QO Zones can not exceed 25% of the number of low-income communities in the state. (Code Sec. 1400Z-1(d)(1)) But, if the number of low-income communities in a state is less than 100, then a total of 25 of the tracts can be designated as QO Zones. (Code Sec. 1400Z-1(d)(2))

Designation of tracts contiguous with low-income communities. A population census tract that is not a low-income community can be designated as a QO Zone if: (Code Sec. 1400Z-1(e)(1))

... the tract is contiguous with the low-income community that is designated as a QO Zone, and (Code Sec. 1400Z-1(e)(1)(A))

... the median family income of the tract does not exceed 125% of the median family income of the low-income community with which the tract is contiguous. (Code Sec. 1400Z-1(e)(1)(B))

But, under Code Sec. 1400Z-1(e)(1) (discussed immediately above), no more than 5% of the population census tracts designated in a state as a QO Zone can be tracts contiguous with low-income communities. (Code Sec. 1400Z-1(e)(2))

Definitions.

Low-income communities. The term "low-income community" has the same meaning as when used in Code Sec. 45D(e) for purposes of the new markets tax credit (see FTC 2d/FIN ¶ L-17926; USTR ¶ 45D4.04). (Code Sec. 1400Z-1(c)(1))

> *observation:* For purposes of the new markets credit, a low-income community includes (a) any population census tract with a poverty rate of at least 20%, or (b) in the case of a tract not located within a metropolitan area, the median family income for the tract doesn't exceed 80% of statewide median family income, (85% if the tract is located within a "high migration rural county") or (c) in the case of a tract located within a metropolitan area, the median family income for the tract doesn't exceed 80% (85% if the tract is located within a "high migration rural county") of the greater of statewide median family income or

the metropolitan area median family income. See FTC 2d/FIN ¶ L-17926; USTR ¶ 45D4.04.

State. For purposes of Code Sec. 1400Z-1, a state includes any possession of the U.S. (Code Sec. 1400Z-1(c)(3)) For this purpose, Congress indicated that a state includes the District of Columbia (D.C.) and that the mayor of D.C. can also submit nominations. (Com Rept, see ¶ 5106)

> *observation:* Thus, a population census tract that is a low-income community in a U.S. possession (such as Puerto Rico or the Virgin Islands) can be designated as a QO Zone.

According to the Committee Report, each population census tract in each U.S. possession that is a low-income community is considered certified and designated as a QO Zone effective on Dec. 22, 2017. (Com Rept, see ¶ 5106)

Period for which designation is in effect. A designation as a QO Zone remains in effect for the period beginning on the date of the designation and ending at the close of the 10th calendar year beginning on or after the date of designation. (Code Sec. 1400Z-1(f))

> *observation:* As discussed above, any QO Zone designation will have to be made before the expiration of the 180-day period beginning on Dec. 22, 2017 or in calendar 2018. Thus, a designation would remain in effect until the end of the 10th calendar year beginning on or after the date of the designation (i.e., Dec. 31, 2028).

☐ **Effective:** Dec. 22, 2017. (Tax Cuts and Jobs Act §13823(d))

¶ 1800. 2016 Disaster Area Relief

¶ 1801. 10%-of-AGI casualty loss threshold is retroactively made inapplicable in 2016 and 2017 to net disaster losses from 2016 disaster areas

Code Sec. 165(h)(2)(A)(ii), Tax Cuts and Jobs Act §11028(c)(1)(A)
Generally effective: Tax years beginning after Dec. 31, 2015, and before Jan. 1, 2018
Committee Reports, see ¶ 5012

The deduction for casualty and theft losses of personal-use property is subject to two limitations: the per-casualty floor (FTC 2d ¶ M-1901 *et seq.*; USTR ¶ 1654.304) and the 10%-of-adjusted-gross-income (AGI) threshold (FTC 2d ¶ M-1907 *et seq.*; USTR ¶ 1654.304).

For the Tax Cuts and Jobs Act's changes to the per-casualty floor for certain net disaster losses, see ¶ 1802. For the Tax Cuts and Jobs Act's increase to the standard deduction for net disaster losses from 2016 disasters, see ¶ 1803. For the Tax Cuts and Jobs Act's allowance of the portion of the standard deduction attributable to the net disaster loss for alternative minimum tax (AMT) purposes, see ¶ 302.

Under the 10%-of-AGI threshold, if personal casualty losses for a tax year exceed personal casualty gains for that tax year, the losses are allowed for the tax year only to the extent of the sum of: (1) the amount of the personal casualty gains for the tax year, plus (2) so much of the excess as exceeds 10% of the taxpayer's AGI. The 10%-of-AGI threshold is applied after the per-casualty floor. (FTC 2d/FIN ¶ M-1900FTC 2d ¶ M-1907; USTR ¶ 1654.304)

New Law. The Tax Cuts and Jobs Act provides that, if an individual has a net disaster loss (defined at ¶ 1802) for any tax year beginning after Dec. 31, 2015, and before Jan. 1, 2018 (Tax Cuts and Jobs Act §11028(c)(1)), then the amount determined under (2) above is the sum of (Tax Cuts and Jobs Act §11028(c)(1)(A)):

(i) the net disaster loss, and (Tax Cuts and Jobs Act §11028(c)(1)(A)(i))

FTC 2d References are to Federal Tax Coordinator 2d
FIN References are to RIA's Analysis of Federal Taxes: Income (print)
USTR References are to United States Tax Reporter
Catalyst References are to Checkpoint Catalyst
PCA References are to Pension Analysis (print and electronic)
PBE References are to Pension & Benefits Explanations
BCA References are to Benefits Analysis (electronic)
BC References are to Benefits Coordinator (print)
EP References are to Estate Planning Analysis (print and electronic)

(ii) so much of the excess of personal casualty losses for the tax year over personal casualty gains for that tax year (reduced by the net disaster loss) as exceeds 10% of the individual's AGI. (Tax Cuts and Jobs Act §11028(c)(1)(A)(ii))

Thus, the requirement that personal casualty losses exceed 10% of AGI to qualify for a deduction doesn't apply to the net disaster loss, i.e., to the individual's net personal casualty loss arising in the 2016 disaster areas described in Tax Cuts and Jobs Act §11028(a) after Dec. 31, 2015, and which are attributable to the events giving rise to the Presidential declaration described in Tax Cuts and Jobs Act §11028(a) which was applicable to that area. (Com Rept, see ¶ 5012)

> **🅡🅘🅐 *illustration:*** In 2017, T has $100,000 of AGI. He has a personal casualty loss (unrelated to any net disaster losses) of $1,000 and a net disaster loss (relating back to a 2016 disaster area) of $5,000. Without the above provision, because of the $100 per-casualty floor (see ¶ 1802 for Tax Cuts and Jobs Act change) the $1,000 loss would be reduced to $900, and the net disaster loss would be reduced to $4,900, for a total of $5,800. But because $5,800 is less than 10% of the taxpayer's AGI, no deductible loss would be allowed.
>
> As a result of the Tax Cuts and Jobs Act, the personal casualty loss is reduced by $100 to $900 and the net disaster loss is reduced by $500 to $4,500 (see ¶ 1802). The deductible loss allowed is (1) $4,500 plus (2) the excess of $900 (the personal casualty loss reduced by the net disaster loss) over $10,000 (10% of AGI). Since $900 is less than $10,000, (2) is $0. So the total loss deduction allowed is $4,500.

☐ **Effective:** Tax years beginning after Dec. 31, 2015, and before Jan. 1, 2018. (Tax Cuts and Jobs Act §11028(c)(1))

¶ 1802. $100 per-casualty floor on deduction is retroactively raised to $500 in 2016 and 2017 for net disaster losses from 2016 disaster areas

Code Sec. 165(h)(1), Tax Cuts and Jobs Act §11028(c)(1)(B)
Generally effective: Tax years beginning after Dec. 31, 2015, and before
*   Jan. 1, 2018*
Committee Reports, see ¶ 5012

The deduction for casualty and theft losses of personal-use property is subject to two limitations: the per-casualty floor (FTC 2d ¶ M-1901 *et seq.*; USTR ¶ 1654.304) and the 10%-of-adjusted-gross-income (AGI) threshold (FTC 2d ¶ M-1907 *et seq.*; USTR ¶ 1654.304).

For the Tax Cuts and Jobs Act's changes to the 10%-of-AGI threshold for net disaster losses from 2016 disaster areas, see ¶ 1801. For the Tax Cuts and Jobs Act's increase to the standard deduction for net disaster losses from 2016 disasters, see ¶ 1803. For the Tax Cuts and Jobs Act's allowance of the portion of the standard deduction attributable to the net disaster loss for alternative minimum tax (AMT) purposes, see ¶ 302.

Under the per-casualty floor, any casualty or theft loss with respect to an individual taxpayer's property that isn't connected with a trade or business or a transaction entered into for profit is allowed only to the extent the amount of the loss from each casualty or theft exceeds $100. (FTC 2d/FIN ¶ M-1900, ¶ M-1901; USTR ¶ 1654.304)

New Law. The Tax Cuts and Jobs Act provides that, if an individual has a net disaster loss (defined below) for any tax year beginning after Dec. 31, 2015, and before Jan. 1, 2018 (Tax Cuts and Jobs Act §11028(c)(1)), the $100-per-casualty floor is increased to $500. (Tax Cuts and Jobs Act §11028(c)(1)(B))

Thus, in order to be deductible, the losses must exceed $500 per casualty. Additionally, such losses may be claimed in addition to the standard deduction. (Com Rept, see ¶ 5012)

> *observation:* The increase in the per-casualty floor from $100 to $500 works to the taxpayer's disadvantage. However, this is more than offset by the Tax Cuts and Jobs Act provision at ¶ 1801, making the 10%-of-AGI threshold inapplicable to net disaster losses. For a comprehensive illustration showing the effect of both provisions, see ¶ 1801.

"Net disaster loss" defined. A "net disaster loss" is the excess of:

... qualified disaster-related personal casualty losses (defined below) over

... personal casualty gains (defined below). (Tax Cuts and Jobs Act §11028(c)(2))

"Qualified disaster-related personal casualty losses" defined. "Qualified disaster-related personal casualty losses" are losses described in Code Sec. 165(c)(3) (FTC 2d ¶ M-1601; USTR ¶ 1654.301), i.e., casualty losses of property not connected with a trade or business or a transaction entered into for profit, that arise in a 2016 disaster area described in Tax Cuts and Jobs Act §11028(a) after Dec. 31, 2015, and that are attributable to the events giving rise to the Presidential declaration described in Tax Cuts and Jobs Act §11028(a) that applied to that area. (Tax Cuts and Jobs Act §11028(c)(3))

"2016 disaster area" defined. For purposes of these provisions, the term "2016 disaster area" means any area with respect to which a major disaster was declared by the President during calendar year 2016 under section 401 of the

Robert T. Stafford Disaster Relief and Emergency Assistance Act. (Tax Cuts and Jobs Act §11028(a))

"Personal casualty gains" defined. "Personal casualty gains" are defined as in Code Sec. 165(h)(3)(A). (Tax Cuts and Jobs Act §11028(c)(2)) Thus, the term means the recognized gain from any involuntary conversion of nonbusiness, not-for-profit property arising from a casualty, see FTC 2d ¶ M-1908; USTR ¶ 1654.304.

☐ **Effective:** Tax years beginning after Dec. 31, 2015, and before Jan. 1, 2018. (Tax Cuts and Jobs Act §11028(c)(1))

¶ 1803. Non-itemizers are retroactively allowed to deduct net disaster losses from 2016 disaster areas in 2016 and 2017, via enhanced standard deduction

Code Sec. 63(c), Tax Cuts and Jobs Act §11028(c)(1)(C)
Generally effective: Tax years beginning after Dec. 31, 2015, and before Jan. 1, 2018
Committee Reports, see ¶ 5012

Standard deduction. Individuals who don't elect to itemize deductions for the tax year can instead deduct a standard deduction in determining taxable income. The standard deduction is the sum of: (a) the basic standard deduction and (b) the additional standard deduction for individuals aged 65 or over and/or blind. (FTC 2d/FIN ¶ A-2800, ¶ A-2801; USTR ¶ 634)

For the Tax Cuts and Jobs Act's *post-2017* changes to the standard deduction, see ¶ 501.

Casualty losses. A taxpayer generally may claim a deduction for any loss sustained during the tax year and not compensated by insurance or otherwise. (FTC 2d/FIN ¶ M-1900, ¶ M-1901; USTR ¶ 1654.304)

For individuals, a personal loss from a casualty is deductible only as an itemized deduction. Generally, no personal casualty loss deductions are available to individuals who claimed the standard deduction. (FTC 2d/FIN ¶ A-2800, ¶ A-2801; USTR ¶ 634).

New Law. The Tax Cuts and Jobs Act provides that, if an individual has a net disaster loss (defined below) for any tax year beginning after Dec. 31, 2015, and before Jan. 1, 2018 (Tax Cuts and Jobs Act §11028(c)(1)), the standard deduction is increased by the net disaster loss. (Tax Cuts and Jobs Act §11028(c)(1)(C)) *observation:* This rule allows an individual to claim a net casualty loss arising in the 2016 disaster areas even if the individual elects to take the standard deduction in 2016 or 2017, instead of itemizing.

illustration: In 2017, A, a single individual, incurred a $2,000 net disaster loss as a result of an event attributable to a 2016 disaster area. A had only $1,000 of other itemized deductions for 2017.

The standard deduction for singles for 2017 is $6,350, which is greater than A's total itemized deductions of $3,000. Without the above Tax Cuts and Jobs Act provision, A's standard deduction would be limited to $6,350.

As a result of the Tax Cuts and Jobs Act, A can deduct a standard deduction of $8,350 ($6,350 regular standard deduction + $2,000 net disaster loss).

"Net disaster loss" defined. A "net disaster loss" is the excess of:

... qualified disaster-related personal casualty losses (defined below) over

... personal casualty gains (defined below). (Tax Cuts and Jobs Act §11028(c)(2))

"Qualified disaster-related personal casualty losses" defined. "Qualified disaster-related personal casualty losses" are losses described in Code Sec. 165(c)(3) (FTC 2d ¶ M-1601; USTR ¶ 1654.301), i.e., casualty losses of property not connected with a trade or business or a transaction entered into for profit, that arise in a 2016 disaster area described in Tax Cuts and Jobs Act §11028(a) after Dec. 31, 2015, and that are attributable to the events giving rise to the Presidential declaration described in Tax Cuts and Jobs Act §11028(a) that applied to that area. (Tax Cuts and Jobs Act §11028(c)(3))

"2016 disaster area" defined. For purposes of these provisions, the term "2016 disaster area" means any area with respect to which a major disaster was declared by the President during calendar year 2016 under section 401 of the Robert T. Stafford Disaster Relief and Emergency Assistance Act. (Tax Cuts and Jobs Act §11028(a))

"Personal casualty gains" defined. "Personal casualty gains" are defined as in Code Sec. 165(h)(3)(A). (Tax Cuts and Jobs Act §11028(c)(2)) Thus, the term means the recognized gain from any involuntary conversion of nonbusiness, not-for-profit property arising from a casualty, see FTC 2d ¶ M-1908; USTR ¶ 1654.304.

Other net disaster loss Tax Cuts and Jobs Act provisions. The following special tax rules also apply to a net disaster losses:

... the portion of the standard deduction attributable to the loss is allowed for alternative minimum tax (AMT) purposes (see ¶ 302),

... the $100-per-casualty floor on the casualty loss deduction is increased to $500 (see ¶ 1802), and

... the loss isn't subject to the 10%-of-adjusted-gross-income (AGI) threshold for the casualty loss deduction (see ¶ 1801).

☐ **Effective:** Tax years beginning after Dec. 31, 2015, and before Jan. 1, 2018. (Tax Cuts and Jobs Act §11028(c)(1))

¶ 1804. Favorable tax treatment provided for qualified 2016 disaster area plan distributions

Code Sec. None, Tax Cuts and Jobs Act §11028(a)
Code Sec. None, Tax Cuts and Jobs Act §11028(b)(1)(B)
Code Sec. None, Tax Cuts and Jobs Act §11028(b)(1)(D)
Code Sec. 401(a)(31), Tax Cuts and Jobs Act §11028(b)(1)(F)
Code Sec. 402(f), Tax Cuts and Jobs Act §11028(b)(1)(F)
Code Sec. 3405, Tax Cuts and Jobs Act §11028(b)(1)(F)
Generally effective: Dec. 22, 2017, for distributions made on or after Jan. 1, 2016, and before Jan. 1, 2018
Committee Reports, see ¶ 5012

Qualified plans place restrictions on when amounts can be distributed to plan participants. Typically, these restrictions provide that distributions aren't permitted before severance from employment, death, disability, or reaching age 59-1/2 (70-1/2 for section 457 plans). However, these plans can provide that amounts may be distributed before these events occur for financial hardship, or unforeseeable emergency (in the case of section 457 plans). Similarly, IRAs can allow for early distributions under a variety of situations, including hardship. (FTC 2d ¶ H-3327, ¶ H-9211, ¶ H-11400, ¶ H-11406.3; USTR ¶ 4014.172, ¶ 4034.04, ¶ 4084.03; PCA ¶ 28,512, ¶ 32,807.3; PBE ¶ 401-4.172, ¶ 403-4.04, ¶ 408-4.03)

All or part of an eligible rollover distribution from a qualified plan can be rolled over to another qualified plan or IRA within 60 days, tax-free. IRS has the discretion to waive the 60-day rollover requirement for distributions where an individual suffers a casualty, disaster, or other event beyond his reasonable control, and where not waiving the 60-day requirement would be against equity or good conscience. (FTC 2d ¶ H-11472; USTR ¶ 4024.04; PCA ¶ 32,873; PBE ¶ 402-4.04)

Because hardship distributions aren't "eligible rollover distributions," all assets distributed as a hardship withdrawal, including assets attributable to employee elective deferrals and those attributable to employer matching or nonelective contributions, are ineligible for rollover. Thus, these amounts cannot be recontributed to the plan. (FTC 2d ¶ H-11406.3; USTR ¶ 4024.04; PCA ¶ 32,807.3; PBE ¶ 402-4.04)

Ordinarily, eligible rollover distributions from qualified plans that aren't rolled over in a trustee-to-trustee ("direct") transfer, are subject to 20% withholding. (FTC 2d ¶ J-8576; USTR ¶ 34,054; PCA ¶ 55,676; PBE ¶ 3405-4)

New Law. Under the Tax Cuts and Jobs Act, the favorable tax treatment of "qualified 2016 disaster distributions" from "eligible retirement plans" that "qualified individuals" may receive includes:

- the reduction of the tax on a qualified 2016 disaster distribution by including it in income ratably over three years, see ¶ 1805;
- the inapplicability of the Code Sec. 72(t) 10% additional tax on early distributions, see ¶ 1806; and
- the continued deferral of the income realized from a qualified 2016 disaster distribution, for amounts that are recontributed to an eligible retirement plan, see ¶ 1807.

2016 disaster area. For purposes of these provisions, the term "2016 disaster area" means any area with respect to which a major disaster has been declared by the President under section 401 of the Robert T. Stafford Disaster Relief and Emergency Assistance Act during calendar year 2016. (Tax Cuts and Jobs Act §11028(a))

Qualified 2016 disaster distributions. A "qualified 2016 disaster distribution" is any distribution:

(1) from an "eligible retirement plan" (see below),

(2) made on or after January 1, 2016, and before Jan. 1, 2018,

(3) to an individual whose principal place of abode at any time during calendar year 2016 was in the 2016 disaster area, and

(4) who sustained an economic loss by reason of that 2016 disaster. (Tax Cuts and Jobs Act §11028(b)(1)(D)(i))

An "eligible retirement plan," in turn, is defined under Code Sec. 402(c)(8)(B). (Tax Cuts and Jobs Act §11028(b)(1)(D)(ii)) Thus, for purposes of the definition of a "qualified 2016 disaster distribution," an "eligible retirement plan" is:

(A) an IRA,

(B) an individual retirement annuity under Code Sec. 408(b), other than an endowment contract,

(C) a Code Sec. 401(a) qualified trust,

(D) a Code Sec. 403(a) qualified annuity plan,

(E) a Code Sec. 457(b) eligible deferred compensation plan maintained by a governmental employer, and

(F) a Code Sec. 403(b) annuity contract.

In addition, if any portion of an eligible rollover distribution is attributable to distributions from a Code Sec. 402A designated Roth account, then for that portion, an eligible retirement plan includes only another designated Roth account and a Roth IRA.

> **⊘** *observation:* Distributions from section 457 plans sponsored by non-governmental organizations don't qualify as qualified 2016 disaster distributions.

Aggregate distributions may not exceed $100,000. For purposes of these rules, the aggregate amount of eligible retirement plan distributions received by an individual that may be treated as qualified 2016 disaster distributions for any tax year can't exceed the excess (if any) of (i) $100,000, over (ii) the aggregate amounts treated as qualified 2016 disaster distributions received by the individual for all prior tax years. (Tax Cuts and Jobs Act §11028(b)(1)(B)(i))

> **⊘** *observation:* Thus, the total amount that an individual can receive in qualified 2016 disaster distributions cannot exceed $100,000. Amounts over that figure will be subject to the Code Sec. 72(t) 10% tax on early withdrawals (unless another exception applies, such as payments on account of disability).

Distributions up to $100,000 won't disqualify plan. If a distribution made to an individual because of 2016 disasters (without regard to the $100,000 limit, above) would be a qualified 2016 disaster distribution, the plan won't be treated as violating any Code requirements merely because the plan treats the distribution as a qualified 2016 disaster distribution—unless the aggregate amount of qualified 2016 disaster distributions from all plans maintained by the employer (and any member of any controlled group that includes the employer) to an individual exceeds $100,000. (Tax Cuts and Jobs Act §11028(b)(1)(B))

For purposes of the $100,000 limit on qualified 2016 disaster distributions, "controlled group" means any group treated as a single employer under the:

(I) Code Sec. 414(b) rules for controlled groups of corporations,

(II) Code Sec. 414(c) rules for groups of partnerships, proprietorships, etc., under common control, and

(III) Code Sec. 414(m) and Code Sec. 414(o) rules for affiliated service groups and certain separate organizations or arrangements. (Tax Cuts and Jobs Act §11028(b)(1)(B)(iii))

A qualified 2016 disaster distribution is treated as meeting the limitations on distributions from:

• 401(k) plans (under Code Sec. 401(k)(2)(B)(i)),

• tax-deferred annuity custodial accounts (under Code Sec. 403(b)(7)(A)(ii)),

• tax deferred annuity salary reduction agreements (under Code Sec. 403(b)(11)), and

• section 457 plans (under Code Sec. 457(d)(1)(A)). (Tax Cuts and Jobs Act §11028(b)(1)(F)(ii))

No withholding on distributions. The Tax Cuts and Jobs Act provides that qualified 2016 disaster distributions aren't "eligible rollover distributions" under the:

• Code Sec. 401(a)(31) rules regarding direct transfers of eligible rollover distributions,

• Code Sec. 402(f) rules for requiring that written explanations of the direct rollover rules be provided to recipients of distributions, and

• Code Sec. 3405 rules regarding 20% withholding on eligible rollover distributions that aren't directly rolled over. (Tax Cuts and Jobs Act §11028(b)(1)(F)(i))

> **⊘** *illustration:* Long, 50 years old, worked as a chef at the Texas Inn restaurant in Marshall, Texas. Because of damage to the restaurant caused by Mississippi River Delta floods, Texas Inn's owners decided to close indefinitely, and Long was terminated. On Oct. 1, 2016, Long took a $20,000 qualified 2016 disaster distribution from Texas Inn's 401(k) plan. Ordinarily, due to mandatory 20% withholding on such distributions, Long should have only received $16,000. But, since this was a qualified 2016 disaster distribution, Long should receive the full $20,000, with no amounts being withheld.

☐ **Effective:** Dec. 22, 2017, for distributions made on or after Jan. 1, 2016, and before Jan. 1, 2018. (Tax Cuts and Jobs Act §11028(b)(1)(D))

¶ 1805. Qualified 2016 disaster distributions to be included in gross income ratably over three years

Code Sec. None, Tax Cuts and Jobs Act §11028(b)(1)(E)
Generally effective: Dec. 22, 2017, for distributions made on or after Jan. 1, 2016, and before Jan. 1, 2018
Committee Reports, see ¶ 5012

Any amount actually distributed to any distributee by a qualified plan is taxable to the distributee in the taxable year in which distributed. So, as a general rule, a distribution from any qualified plan has to be included in the distributee's gross income for the year in which the distribution is received. (FTC 2d ¶ H-11000; USTR ¶ 4024.02, ¶ 4034.04, ¶ 4024.03; PCA ¶ 32,101; PBE ¶ 402-4.02, ¶ 402-4.03, ¶ 403-4.04)

New Law. The Tax Cuts and Jobs Act provides that a "qualified 2016 disaster distribution" (see ¶ 1804) is included in a taxpayer's gross income ratably over the three-tax year period beginning with the tax year the distribution is received.

This three-year ratable inclusion rule applies unless the taxpayer elects not to have it apply. (Tax Cuts and Jobs Act §11028(b)(1)(E)(i))

observation: Taxation of a qualified 2016 disaster distribution would continue to be deferred if the amount paid out from a qualified retirement plan is timely recontributed under the rules explained at ¶ 1807.

observation: Due to the tremendous economic dislocation caused by 2016 disasters, including loss of jobs, the three-year ratable inclusion of income (an "income averaging" of sorts) will help prevent taxpayers from having artificially high income in one year—and a concomitant increase in federal tax liability—due to a qualified 2016 disaster distribution, and much lower income (and tax liability) in later years.

observation: The Tax Cuts and Jobs Act does not state how a taxpayer would opt out of the three-year ratable inclusion of income for qualified 2016 disaster distributions. Presumably, this would be done by including the entire amount of the distribution in income for the tax year it's received from the qualified retirement plan.

illustration (1): Bruce worked on as on oil rigger for Smallco, a small oil producer in Marshall, Texas. Because of damage to the rig caused by Mississippi River Delta floods, Smallco determines that it will be off-line indefinitely, and places Bruce on indefinite leave. In 2017, Bruce, realizing his income will be limited for the foreseeable future, takes a $75,000 qualified hurricane distribution from Smallco's 401(k) plan. Unless he elects to recognize the entire $75,000 distribution in income for his 2017 tax year, Bruce must recognize $25,000 in each of his 2017, 2018, and 2019 tax years.

Special Roth IRA rules apply. The Tax Cuts and Jobs Act provides that rules similar to those of Code Sec. 408A(d)(3)(E) apply for purposes of the three-year ratable inclusion of income rules. (Tax Cuts and Jobs Act §11028(b)(1)(E)(ii)) *observation:* Thus, if an individual who receives a qualified 2016 disaster distribution dies before the full taxable amount of the distribution has been included in gross income, then the remainder must be included in gross income for the tax year that includes the individual's death.

illustration (2): In Illustration (1), above, in 2019, Bruce returns to full-time work. Realizing that he no longer needs the full qualified 2016 disaster distribution of $75,000 that he took from Smallco's 401(k) plan, Bruce recontributes $30,000 to the plan in 2018. Thus, only $45,000 of the distribution ($75,000 − $30,000) is taxable. The $30,000 amount that is recontributed is treated as a direct rollover of $30,000 of the distribution.

☐ **Effective:** Dec. 22, 2017, distributions made on or after Jan. 1, 2016, and before Jan. 1, 2018. (Tax Cuts and Jobs Act §11028(b)(1)(D))

¶ 1806. Penalty-free early retirement plan withdrawals may be made for 2016 disaster area victims

Code Sec. 72(t), Tax Cuts and Jobs Act §11028(b)(1)(A)
Generally effective: Dec. 22, 2017
Committee Reports, see ¶ 5012

In addition to being subject to regular income tax, early distributions from qualified plans and IRAs may also be subject to the 10% tax under Code Sec. 72(t), unless an exception is met. The following distributions are not subject to this early withdrawal tax:

(1) distributions which are part of a series of substantially equal periodic payments (not less frequently than annually) made for the life (or life expectancy) of the employee or the joint lives (or joint life expectancies) of the employee and his designated beneficiary,

(2) distributions made to an employee after separation from service after reaching age 55. This rule does not apply to distributions from IRAs;

(3) distributions which are dividends paid with respect to stock of a corporation which are described in Code Sec. 404(k) (ESOPs) (but this exception from the 10% tax does not apply to dividends that are reinvested in qualifying employer securities pursuant to a participant's election);

(4) withdrawals from a qualified plan or IRA due to IRS levy,

(5) distributions made to the employee (other than those described in (1) through (4), above, and in (6) and (7), below) to the extent allowable as a medical expense deduction for amounts paid during the tax year for the employee's medical care;

(6) any distribution made to an alternate payee under a qualified domestic relations order. This exception does not apply to IRA distributions;

(7) early distributions from an IRA to certain unemployed individuals to pay for health insurance premiums;

(8) early withdrawals of up to $10,000 in IRA funds for "first-time homebuyers," so long as the distribution is used within 120 days, i.e., before the close of the 120th day after the day on which the payment or distribution is received;

(9) early withdrawal of IRA funds to pay higher education expenses;

(10) the transfer of assets of a terminated defined benefit plan (participants' interests in which have been fully vested) to a Code Sec. 401(k) plan maintained by the same employer, which is not considered an actual distribution from the terminated plan;

(11) tax-free eligible rollover distributions, since the additional tax on early distributions applies only to the portion of a distribution that is includible in income;

(12) contributions and trust income that are treated under regulations as having been applied to the purchase of life insurance protection for a plan participant, even though the contributions and income are includible in income; and

(13) distributions of elective deferrals and employee contributions in excess of Code Sec. 415 limits. (FTC 2d ¶ H-11102; USTR ¶ 724.22; PCA ¶ 32,203; PBE ¶ 72-4.22)

Further, for the first-time homebuyer's exception (item (8), above), amounts withdrawn from an IRA can be recontributed to that IRA, or another IRA, up to 120 days after distribution, if the home purchase can't be completed. (FTC 2d ¶ H-11110; USTR ¶ 724.22; PCA ¶ 32,211; PBE ¶ 72-4.22)

New Law. For 2016 disaster victims, the Tax Cuts and Jobs Act provides that the Code Sec. 72(t) 10% tax on early withdrawals from qualified retirement plans, governmental section 457 plans, and IRAs, does not apply to any "qualified 2016 disaster distribution." (Tax Cuts and Jobs Act §11028(b)(1)(A))

> *observation:* "Qualified 2016 disaster distributions" are defined at ¶ 1804. These are not subject to the Code Sec. 72(t) 10% tax for early withdrawals, but are still subject to tax if not timely recontributed under the rules explained at ¶ 1807. For three-year ratable inclusion in income of amounts received as qualified disaster-relief distributions, see ¶ 1805.

☐ **Effective:** Dec. 22, 2017.

¶ 1807. Recontributions of qualified 2016 disaster distributions and continued deferral of tax on amounts previously distributed permitted

Code Sec. None, Tax Cuts and Jobs Act §11028(b)(1)(C)
Generally effective: Dec. 22, 2017
Committee Reports, see ¶ 5012

Qualified plans place restrictions on when amounts can be distributed to plan participants. Ordinarily, these restrictions provide that distributions aren't permitted before severance from employment, death, disability, or reaching age 59-1/2 (70-1/2 for section 457 plans). However, these plans can provide that amounts may be distributed before a plan participant's severance from service or attainment of age 59-1/2 (70-1/2 for section 457 plans) for financial hardship, or unforeseeable emergency (in the case of section 457 plans). Similarly, IRAs can allow for early distributions under a variety of situations, including hardship. (FTC 2d ¶ H-3327, ¶ H-9211, ¶ H-11406.3; USTR ¶ 4014.172, ¶ 4034.04, ¶ 4084.03; PCA ¶ 28,512, ¶ 32,807.3; PBE ¶ 401-4.172, ¶ 403-4.04, ¶ 408-4.03)

All or part of an eligible rollover distribution from a qualified plan can be rolled-over to another qualified plan or IRA within 60 days, tax-free. IRS has the discretion to waive the 60-day rollover requirement for distributions where an individual suffers a casualty, disaster, or other event beyond his reasonable control, and where not waiving the 60-day requirement would be against equity or good conscience. (FTC 2d ¶ H-11472; USTR ¶ 4024.04; PCA ¶ 32,873; PBE ¶ 402-4.04)

Because hardship distributions aren't "eligible rollover distributions," all assets distributed as a hardship withdrawal, including assets attributable to employee elective deferrals and those attributable to employer matching or nonelective contributions, are ineligible for rollover. Thus, these amounts cannot be recontributed to the plan. (FTC 2d ¶ H-11406.3; USTR ¶ 4024.04; PCA ¶ 32,807.3; PBE ¶ 402-4.04)

New Law. The Tax Cuts and Jobs Act provides that any individual who receives a qualified 2016 disaster distribution (as defined at ¶ 1804) at any time during the three-year period beginning on the day after the date of the distribution, may make one or more repayment contributions to an "eligible retirement plan" (as defined in Code Sec. 402(c)(8)(B), see ¶ 1804) in which he or she is a beneficiary, and to which a rollover contribution could be made under Code Sec. 402(c), Code Sec. 403(a)(4), Code Sec. 403(b)(8), Code Sec. 408(d)(3), or Code Sec. 457(e)(16), as the case may be. However, the aggregate amount of these repayment contributions can't exceed the amount of the qualified 2016 disaster distribution. (Tax Cuts and Jobs Act §11028(b)(1)(C)(i)) *observation:* Because distributions from nongovernmental section 457 plans are not qualified 2016 disaster distributions (see ¶ 1804), the provisions allowing repayment of qualified 2016 disaster distributions don't apply to distributions from section 457 plans maintained by charities and other nongovernmental organizations.

illustration: The Interfaith Charity Nursing Home, a tax-exempt entity, sponsors a section 457 plan for its employees. The nursing home was seriously damaged by Mississippi River Delta floods, and must close. Although nursing home employees otherwise meet the criteria for receiving "qualified 2016 disaster distributions" from the nursing home's section 457 plan, because the plan is maintained by a nongovernmental entity, there is no tax break for recontributions of 2016 disaster distributions.

Repayments treated as direct rollovers. If a repayment (i.e., a "recontribution") of a qualified 2016 disaster distribution from an eligible retirement plan (other than an IRA) is made within the three-year period, then, to the extent of the amount of the recontribution, the taxpayer is treated:

(1) as having received the qualified 2016 disaster distribution in an eligible rollover distribution (as defined in Code Sec. 402(c)(4), i.e., a distribution of all or part of the balance to the employee's credit in a qualified trust), and

(2) as having transferred the repayment amount to the eligible retirement plan in a direct trustee-to-trustee transfer within 60 days of the distribution. (Tax Cuts and Jobs Act §11028(b)(1)(C)(ii))

observation: Thus, a qualified 2016 disaster distribution is tax-free up to the amount that is recontributed to an eligible retirement plan.

Similarly, if a repayment contribution is made for a qualified 2016 disaster distribution from an IRA, then, to the extent of the amount of the contribution, the qualified 2016 disaster distribution is treated as a Code Sec. 408(d)(3) rollover distribution (see below), and is treated as having been transferred to the eligible retirement plan in a direct trustee-to-trustee transfer within 60 days of the distribution. (Tax Cuts and Jobs Act §11028(b)(1)(C)(iii))

A Code Sec. 408(d)(3) distribution is any amount paid or distributed out of an IRA or individual retirement annuity to the individual for whose benefit the account or annuity is maintained if:

(a) the entire amount received (including money and any other property) is paid into an IRA or individual retirement annuity (other than an endowment contract) for the benefit of the individual no later than the 60th day after the day on which he receives the payment or distribution; or

(b) the entire amount received (including money and any other property) is paid into an eligible retirement plan for the benefit of the individual no later than the 60th day after the date on which the payment or distribution is received, except that the maximum amount which may be paid into the plan may not exceed the portion of the amount received that's includible in gross income.

☐ **Effective:** Dec. 22, 2017.

¶ 1808. Period of time is provided, during which qualified retirement plans and IRAs can provide 2016 disaster relief before adopting retroactive 2016 disaster relief amendments

Code Sec. None, Tax Cuts and Jobs Act §11028(b)(2)
Generally effective: From Dec. 22, 2017 to last day of 2018 plan year
Committee Reports, see ¶ 5012

For a retirement plan to be tax-qualified, it must be operated in accordance with its written terms. A change in the law may oblige a plan to change its operations, but compliance with the law change won't satisfy the qualification requirements if the plan's operations are contrary to the plan's terms. The failure to amend the plan to reflect the law changes results in an "operational failure," that, if not corrected under IRS's Employee Plans Compliance Resolution System—Voluntary Correction Program, can result in the plan's being disqualified (with loss of its tax-exempt status). A plan does not have an operational failure if it is amended retroactively either (i) during the Code Sec. 401(b) "remedial amendment period," or (ii) under another statutory provision, to reflect the plan's operations. See FTC 2d ¶ H-8750; T-10592; USTR ¶ 4014.01; 4014.08; PCA ¶ 13,103; 27,301; PBE ¶ 401-4.01; 401-4.08.

New Law. The Tax Cuts and Jobs Act provides that if its provisions involving employee retirement plans and IRAs apply to any plan or annuity contract, the plan or contract is treated as being operated in accordance with the plan's or contract's own terms (i.e., as if the plan had actually been amended to reflect these new provisions) during the time period discussed below. (Tax Cuts and Jobs Act §11028(b)(2)(A))

> 🅡 *observation:* This provision allows a plan to implement any changes in the law or regulations governing qualified plans and IRAs without first having to be amended.

For the retroactive amendment relief to apply, a subsequent amendment to the plan or annuity contract must be made:

(A) in accordance with any amendment made by the Tax Cuts and Jobs Act, or any IRS or Dept. of Labor regulation pursuant to the Tax Cuts and Jobs Act, and

(B) on or before the last day of the first plan year beginning on or after Jan. 1, 2018, or any later date that IRS may prescribe. (Tax Cuts and Jobs Act §11028(b)(2)(B)(i))

For a governmental plan (as defined in Code Sec. 414(d)), the amendment period (in item (B), above) is two years after the date that would otherwise apply. (Tax Cuts and Jobs Act §11028(b)(2)(B)(i))

> *observation:* In effect, qualified plans and annuity contracts would have until at least the last day of the first plan year beginning on or after Jan. 1, 2018 to make conforming amendments to the Tax Cuts and Jobs Act's legislative or regulatory changes. And a governmental plan would have until at least the last day of the first plan year beginning on or after Jan. 1, 2020 to adopt these amendments.

Time period and special rules. These rules allowing plans to follow the Tax Cuts and Jobs Act's legislative or regulatory changes before being properly amended do not apply to any amendment unless the plan or contract is operated as if the amendment were in effect, and the amendment applies retroactively during the period:

(a) beginning on the date that the Tax Cuts and Jobs Act, or a regulation issued under the Act, takes effect (or for a plan or contract amendment not required by the Act or regulation, the effective date specified by the plan), and

(b) ending on or before the last day of the first plan year beginning on or after Jan. 1, 2018 (or Jan. 1, 2020, in the case of governmental plans), or any later date that IRS may prescribe (or, if earlier, the date the plan or contract amendment is adopted). (Tax Cuts and Jobs Act §11028(b)(2)(B)(ii))

> *observation:* The legislative amendment's effective date would be Dec. 22, 2017—the Tax Cuts and Jobs Act's date of enactment.

> *observation:* Thus, a plan amendment adopted to conform with the Tax Cuts and Jobs Act's legislative or regulatory changes would have to have a retroactive effective date.

> *illustration:* To provide relief to its employees from the ravages of Mississippi River Delta flooding, Smallco, a small oil producer, allows them to take "qualified 2016 disaster distributions" from its calendar year 401(k) plan, even though the plan does not yet provide for these distributions. As long as the Smallco plan is retroactively amended by Dec. 31, 2018, the plan won't be disqualified.

☐ **Effective:** Dec. 22, 2017, during the time period discussed above.

¶ 1900. Modified Territorial System

¶ 1901. Deduction allowed for dividends received by a corporate U.S. shareholder from a specified 10% owned foreign corporation under participation exemption system

Code Sec. 245A, as added by Tax Cuts and Jobs Act §14101(a)
Code Sec. 246(c)(1), as amended by Tax Cuts and Jobs Act §14101(b)(1)
Code Sec. 246(c)(5), as amended by Tax Cuts and Jobs Act §14101(b)(2)
Generally effective: Distributions made after Dec. 31, 2017
Committee Reports, see ¶ 5107

Under pre-Tax Cuts and Jobs Act law, the U.S. employed a worldwide tax system, under which U.S. corporations were generally taxed on all income, whether derived in the U.S. or abroad. Foreign income earned by U.S. corporate shareholders through foreign corporations was generally subject to U.S. tax only when the income was distributed as a dividend to the U.S. corporate shareholders. However, under the Subpart F rules, U.S. shareholders of a controlled foreign corporation (CFC) are required to include in income their pro rata share of the CFC's Subpart F income whether or not the income is distributed to the shareholders. For Subpart F income purposes, a U.S. shareholder is a U.S. person who is a 10% owner (see ¶ 2101) of a foreign corporation. Subpart F income includes investment income (e.g., dividends, interest), insurance income and foreign based company sales and services income. FTC 2d/FIN ¶s O-2300 *et seq.*, O-2400 *et seq.*, O-2470 *et seq.*, O-2520 *et seq.*, O-2710 *et seq.*; USTR ¶s 9514, 9524, 9544

Under pre-Tax Cuts and Jobs Act law, a foreign tax credit was generally available to offset, in whole or in part, the U.S. tax owed on foreign-source income, whether earned directly by the domestic corporation, repatriated as a dividend from a foreign subsidiary, or included in income under Subpart F. FTC 2d ¶ O-4000 *et seq.*; USTR ¶s 9014, 9024, 9604

No dividends-received deduction is allowed under Code Sec. 243 (dividends from domestic corporations) or Code Sec. 245 (U.S. source dividends from foreign corporations) for any dividend on any share of stock that is held by the

---

FTC 2d References are to Federal Tax Coordinator 2d
FIN References are to RIA's Analysis of Federal Taxes: Income (print)
USTR References are to United States Tax Reporter
Catalyst References are to Checkpoint Catalyst
PCA References are to Pension Analysis (print and electronic)
PBE References are to Pension & Benefits Explanations
BCA References are to Benefits Analysis (electronic)
BC References are to Benefits Coordinator (print)
EP References are to Estate Planning Analysis (print and electronic)

taxpayer for 45 days or less during the 91-day period beginning on the date that is 45 days before the date on which the stock becomes ex-dividend as to that dividend. (FTC 2d/FIN ¶ D-2200, ¶ D-2263; USTR ¶ 2434.04; Catalyst ¶ 107:193)

New Law. The Tax Cuts and Jobs Act allows a domestic corporation that is a U.S. shareholder of a specified 10% owned foreign corporation to take a deduction in an amount equal to the foreign-source portion of any dividend received from the specified 10% owned foreign corporation (hereafter the Code Sec. 245A DRD). (Code Sec. 245A(a) as added by Tax Cuts and Jobs Act §14101(a))

> **☙observation:** Code Sec. 245A uses the term U.S. shareholder but does not define that term. However, the Committee Report states that the Code Sec. 245A DRD is allowed to a domestic corporation that is a U.S. shareholder of the foreign corporation within the meaning of Code Sec. 951(b) (i.e., a U.S. shareholder that owns 10% of a foreign corporation, see ¶ 2101). (Com Rept, see ¶ 5107).

A *specified 10% owned foreign corporation* is any foreign corporation as to which a domestic corporation is a U.S. shareholder, other than a passive foreign investment company (PFIC) that is not a CFC. (Code Sec. 245A(b))

The *foreign-source portion of any dividend* from a specified 10% owned foreign corporation is an amount which bears the same ratio to the dividend as the undistributed foreign earnings of the specified 10% owned foreign corporation bears to the total undistributed earnings of that specified 10% owned foreign corporation. (Code Sec. 245A(c)(1))

The *undistributed earnings* are the amount of the earnings and profits (E&P) of the specified 10% owned foreign corporation (computed under Code Sec. 964(a) and Code Sec. 986) as of the close of the tax year of the specified 10% owned foreign corporation in which the dividend is distributed, and without diminution by reason of dividends distributed during that tax year. (Code Sec. 245A(c)(2))

The *undistributed foreign earnings* are the portion of the undistributed earnings which is attributable to neither (i) income of the foreign corporation which is effectively connected with the conduct of a U.S. trade or business and subject to U.S. income tax, nor (ii) any dividend received (directly or through a wholly owned foreign corporation) from a domestic corporation at least 80% of the stock of which (by vote and value) is owned (directly or through that wholly owned foreign corporation) by the foreign corporation (determined without regard to whether the domestic corporation is a RIC or a REIT). (Code Sec. 245A(c)(3))

The term "dividend received" is intended to be interpreted broadly, consistently with the meaning of the phrases "amount received as dividends" and "dividends received" under Code Sec. 243 and Code Sec. 245. In addition, the Code Sec. 245 DRD is available only to C corporations that are not registered investment companies or real estate investment trusts. A CFC treated as a domestic corporation for purposes of computing its taxable income may be eligible for the Code Sec. 245 DRD with respect to that income.(Com Rept, see ¶ 5107)

Foreign tax credit disallowed. No foreign tax credit under Code Sec. 901 or deduction is allowed for any taxes paid or accrued (or treated as paid or accrued) as to any dividend for which the Code Sec. 245A DRD is allowed. (Code Sec. 245A(d))

Exception for hybrid dividend. The Code Sec. 245A DRD doesn't apply to any dividend received by a U.S. shareholder from a CFC if the dividend is a hybrid dividend. (Code Sec. 245A(e)(1))

If a CFC with respect to which a domestic corporation is a U.S. shareholder receives a hybrid dividend from any other CFC with respect to which the domestic corporation is also a U.S. shareholder, then, notwithstanding any other Code provision, the hybrid dividend is treated for purposes of Code Sec. 951(a)(1)(A) as Subpart F income of the receiving CFC for the tax year of the CFC in which the dividend was received, and the U.S. shareholder includes in gross income an amount equal to that shareholder's pro rata share (determined in the same manner as under Code Sec. 951(a)(2)) of that Subpart F income. (Code Sec. 245A(e)(2))

No foreign tax credit or deduction is allowed for any hybrid dividend received by, or any amount included in the gross income of a U.S. shareholder under the above rule. (Code Sec. 245A(e)(3))

A *hybrid dividend* is an amount received from a CFC:

• for which a Code Sec. 245A DRD would be allowed but for this hybrid dividend exception, and

• for which the CFC received a deduction (or other tax benefit) with respect to any income, war profits, or excess profits taxes imposed by any foreign country or U.S. possession. (Code Sec. 245A(e)(4))

Exception for purging distribution of PFICs. Any amount that a shareholder of a PFIC that has made a qualifying electing fund (QEF) election treats as a deemed dividend under Code Sec. 1291(d)(2)(B) is not treated as a dividend for purposes of the Code Sec. 245A DRD. (Code Sec. 245A(f))

> *observation:* While a PFIC that is a CFC qualifies as a specified 10% owned foreign corporation for purposes of the Code Sec. 245A DRD, a purging distribution of that PFIC under Code Sec. 1291(d)(2)(B) does not qualify for the deduction.

IRS is authorized to issue regulations or other guidance necessary or appropriate to carry out the above provisions, including regulations for the treatment of U.S. shareholders owning stock of a specified 10% owned foreign corporation through a partnership. (Code Sec. 245A(g))

Required holding period. The Code Sec. 245A DRD is available only to U.S. shareholders who have held shares of the specified 10% owned foreign corporation for more than 365 days during a 731 day period (beginning on the date which is one year before the date on which the shares become ex-dividend with respect to the dividend), provided the specified 10% owned foreign corporation is a specified 10% owned foreign corporation at all times during that period, and the taxpayer is a U.S. shareholder of the specified 10% owned foreign corporation at all times during that period. The rule for preference dividends under Code Sec. 246(c)(2) does not apply for purposes of the Code Sec. 245A DRD. (Code Sec. 246(c)(5) as amended by Tax Cuts and Jobs Act §14101(b)(2))

The Code Sec. 245A DRD is not allowed to the extent that the taxpayer is under an obligation (under a short sale or otherwise) to make related payments as to positions in substantially similar or related property. (Code Sec. 246(c)(1) as amended by Tax Cuts and Jobs Act §14101(b)(1))

☐ **Effective:** Distributions made after Dec. 31, 2017. (Tax Cuts and Jobs Act §14101(f))

¶ 1902. Dividends allowed as a Code Sec. 245A DRD are not treated as foreign source income for purposes of the FTC limitation

Code Sec. 904(b)(5), as amended by Tax Cuts and Jobs Act §14101(d)
Generally effective: Deductions for tax years ending after Dec. 31, 2017
Committee Reports, see ¶ 5107

The U.S. taxes U.S. persons on their worldwide income. A U.S. taxpayer is allowed a credit for foreign taxes paid in order to prevent double taxation of the same income. FTC 2d/FIN ¶s O-1000 *et seq.*, O-4000 *et seq.*; USTR ¶ 9014

In order to prevent U.S. taxpayers from claiming a credit in excess of the amount of U.S. income tax effectively imposed on foreign-source income, a limitation is imposed on the foreign tax credit (FTC). The limitation is calculated by multiplying the taxpayer's pre-credit U.S. tax liability on its worldwide income by the ratio of its income from sources outside the U.S. to its entire taxable income for the tax year (the FTC limitation). FTC 2d/FIN ¶ O-4400 *et seq.*; USTR ¶ 9044; Catalyst ¶ 107:193; Catalyst ¶ 2110:100

New Law. Under the Tax Cuts and Jobs Act, if a domestic corporation that is a U.S. shareholder of a 10% owned specified foreign corporation receives a dividend from that foreign corporation, a deduction is allowed for the foreign-source portion of the dividend (hereafter the Code Sec. 245A DRD, see ¶ 1901).

> **☑ observation:** Code Sec. 245A uses the term U.S. shareholder but does not define that term. However, the Committee Report states that the Code Sec. 245A DRD is allowed to a domestic corporation that is a U.S. shareholder of the foreign corporation within the meaning of Code Sec. 951(b) (i.e., a U.S. shareholder that owns 10% of a foreign corporation, see ¶ 2101). (Com Rept, see ¶ 5107).

For purposes of determining the FTC limitation, in the case of a domestic corporation which is a U.S. shareholder of a specified 10% owned foreign corporation, the shareholder's taxable income from sources outside the U.S. (and entire taxable income) is determined without regard to:

(i) the foreign-source portion of any dividend received from that foreign corporation, and

(ii) any deductions properly allocable or apportioned to

• income (other than amounts includible as Subpart F income under Code Sec. 951(a)(1) or as global intangible low-taxed income under Code Sec. 951A(a), see ¶ 2001) with respect to stock of that specified 10% owned foreign corporation, or

• that stock to the extent income with respect to the stock is other than amounts includible in Subpart F income or global intangible low-taxed income. (Code Sec. 904(b)(5) as amended by Tax Cuts and Jobs Act §14101(d))

Any terms defined in Code Sec. 245A (see ¶ 1901) have the same meaning for purposes of this rule. (Code Sec. 904(b)(5))

☐ **Effective:** Deductions for tax years ending after Dec. 31, 2017. (Tax Cuts and Jobs Act §14101(f))

¶ 1903. Basis of stock in specified 10% owned foreign corporation reduced to the extent of Code Sec. 245A DRD in determining loss on disposition

Code Sec. 961(d), as amended by Tax Cuts and Jobs Act §14102(b)(1)
Generally effective: Distributions made after Dec. 31, 2017
Committee Reports, see ¶ 5108

Under the Subpart F rules, a U.S. shareholder of a controlled foreign corporation (CFC) increases the basis of its stock in the CFC by an amount equal to the amount of the CFC's earnings that are included in the U.S. shareholder's income under Subpart F. For Subpart F income purposes, a U.S. shareholder is a U.S. person who is a 10% owner (see ¶ 2101) of a foreign corporation. Correspondingly, the U.S. shareholder reduces its basis by an amount equal to any distributions on that stock that are excluded from its income as previously taxed income under Subpart F. (FTC 2d ¶ O-2400, ¶ O-2422; USTR ¶ 9614.02)

Under Code Sec. 1059, a corporation that receives an extraordinary dividend as to any share of stock, that has not been held for more than two years before the dividend announcement date, reduces its basis in that stock (but not below zero) by the non-taxed portion of the extraordinary dividend. FTC 2d ¶ P-5100 *et seq.*; USTR ¶ 10,594

New Law. Under the Tax Cuts and Jobs Act, if a corporation, that is a U.S. shareholder of a 10% owned specified foreign corporation, receives a dividend from that foreign corporation, a deduction is allowed for the foreign- source portion of the dividend (hereafter the Code Sec. 245A DRD, see ¶ 1901).

Under the Tax Cuts and Jobs Act, if a domestic corporation receives a dividend from a specified 10% owned foreign corporation in any tax year, solely for purposes of determining loss on any disposition of stock of that foreign corporation in that tax year or any subsequent tax year, the basis of the domestic corporation in that stock is reduced (but not below zero) by the amount of the Code Sec. 245A DRD allowable to the domestic corporation on that stock. (Code Sec. 961(d) as amended by Tax Cuts and Jobs Act §14102(b)(1))

However, no reduction in basis is required to the extent the basis in the specified 10% owned foreign corporation's stock was already reduced under Code Sec. 1059. (Code Sec. 961(d))

> *observation:* Although Code Sec. 961 itself does not define a U.S. shareholder, it is part of Subpart F and thus incorporates the Code Sec. 951(b) definition of U.S. shareholder.

☐ **Effective:** Distributions made after Dec. 31, 2017. (Tax Cuts and Jobs Act §14102(b)(2))

¶ 1904. Amounts treated as dividends under Code Sec. 1248 and Code Sec. 964(e) are treated as dividends for purposes of the Code Sec. 245A DRD

Code Sec. 1248, as amended by Tax Cuts and Jobs Act §14102(a)
Code Sec. 964(e)(4), as amended by Tax Cuts and Jobs Act §14102(c)
Generally effective: Sales or exchanges after Dec. 31, 2017
Committee Reports, see ¶ 5108

Under the Subpart F rules, U.S. shareholders of a controlled foreign corporation (CFC) are required to include in income their pro rata share of the CFC's

Subpart F income whether or not the income is distributed to the shareholders. For Subpart F income purposes, a U.S. shareholder is a U.S. person who is a 10% owner (see ¶ 2101) of a foreign corporation (hereafter a U.S. Shareholder). In order to prevent U.S. Shareholders from repatriating CFC earnings at favorable capital gains rates instead of as dividends, gain on a sale of CFC stock by a Code Sec. 1248 shareholder is recharacterized as dividend income to the extent of the untaxed E&P attributable to that stock (the Code Sec. 1248 amount). A Code Sec. 1248 shareholder is a U.S. person who owned 10% of a foreign corporation at any time during the 5 year period ending on the date of the sale, exchange, or distribution of that stock. (FTC 2d/FIN ¶ O-2800 *et seq.*; USTR ¶ 12,484 *et seq.*; Catalyst ¶ 104:199; Catalyst ¶ 107:222; Catalyst ¶ 113:120; Catalyst ¶ 113:130; Catalyst ¶ 113:160; Catalyst ¶ 113:170; Catalyst ¶ 113:210; Catalyst ¶ 118:180; Catalyst ¶ 122:190; Catalyst ¶ 129:260; Catalyst ¶ 129:300; Catalyst ¶ 132:110; Catalyst ¶ 2106:140; Catalyst ¶ 2106:160; Catalyst ¶ 2106:170)

Further, gain recognized by a CFC from the sale or exchange of stock in a foreign corporation is treated as a dividend to the same extent that it would have been so treated (see above) had the CFC been a U.S. person. (FTC 2d/FIN ¶ O-4800, ¶ O-4816.1; USTR ¶ 9644.05)

New Law. Under the Tax Cuts and Jobs Act, if a corporation, that is a U.S. shareholder of a 10% owned specified foreign corporation, receives a dividend from that foreign corporation, a deduction is allowed for the foreign-source portion of the dividend (hereafter the Code Sec. 245A DRD, see ¶ 1901).

In the case of the sale or exchange by a domestic corporation of stock in a foreign corporation held for one year or more, any amount received by the domestic corporation which is treated as a dividend by reason of Code Sec. 1248 is treated as a dividend for purposes of applying the Code Sec. 245A DRD rules. (Code Sec. 1248(j) as amended by Tax Cuts and Jobs Act §14102(a))

Under the Tax Cuts and Jobs Act, if, for any tax year of a CFC beginning after Dec. 31, 2017, any amount is treated as a dividend under Code Sec. 964(e)(1) by reason of a sale or exchange by the CFC of stock in another foreign corporation held for one year or more, then, notwithstanding any other provision of the Code:

(i) the foreign-source portion of the dividend is treated for purposes of Code Sec. 951(a)(1)(A) as Subpart F income of the selling CFC for the tax year,

(ii) a U.S. Shareholder with respect to the selling CFC includes in gross income for the tax year of the shareholder with or within which the tax year of the CFC ends an amount equal to the shareholder's pro rata share (determined in the same manner as under Code Sec. 951(a)(2)) of the amount treated as Subpart F income under item (i), and

(iii) the Code Sec. 245A DRD is allowable to the U.S. Shareholder with respect to the Subpart F income included in gross income under item (ii) in the same manner as if the Subpart F income were a dividend received by the shareholder from the selling CFC. (Code Sec. 964(e)(4)(A) as amended by Tax Cuts and Jobs Act §14102(c))

In the case of a sale or exchange by a CFC of stock in another foreign corporation in a tax year of the selling CFC beginning after Dec. 31, 2017, rules similar to the rules of Code Sec. 961(d) (see ¶ 1903) apply. (Code Sec. 964(e)(4)(B))

The foreign-source portion of any amount treated as a dividend under Code Sec. 964(e)(1) is determined in the same manner as under Code Sec. 245A(c) (see ¶ 1901). (Code Sec. 964(e)(4)(C))

☐ **Effective:** Sales or exchanges after Dec. 31, 2017. (Tax Cuts and Jobs Act §14102(a)(2)); (Tax Cuts and Jobs Act §14102(c)(2))

¶ 1905. Transferred loss amount included in income upon transfer of foreign branch assets to a specified 10% owned foreign corporation

Code Sec. 91, as added by Tax Cuts and Jobs Act §14102(d)(1)
Generally effective: Transfers after Dec. 31, 2017
Committee Reports, see ¶ 5108

Various loss recapture provisions address instances where a taxpayer may deduct losses from foreign branch operations against U.S. taxable income and then incorporate the branch when it becomes profitable. For example, under pre-Tax Cuts and Jobs Act law, if a U.S. person transferred any assets of a foreign branch to a foreign corporation, the transferor had to recognize gain to the extent of net losses incurred by the foreign branch that were deducted by the U.S. transferor, and amounts recognized due to the recapture of overall foreign losses (OFLs). (FTC 2d/FIN ¶ F-6128, ¶ F-6129 *et seq.*; USTR ¶ 3674.02)

Under the OFL provisions, if property which has been used in a trade or business predominantly outside the U.S. is disposed of during any tax year, the taxpayer is treated as having received and recognized foreign taxable income in the tax year of the disposition in an amount equal to the lesser of the excess of the fair market value of the property over the taxpayer's adjusted basis in the property or the remaining amount of the OFL not previously recaptured. (FTC 2d/FIN ¶ O-4700 *et seq.*, ¶ O-4706; USTR ¶ 9044.01; Catalyst ¶ 104:201; Catalyst ¶ 118:115; Catalyst ¶ 127:163; Catalyst ¶ 129:190; Catalyst ¶ 2110:190)

New Law. Under the Tax Cuts and Jobs Act, if a domestic corporation transfers substantially all of the assets of a foreign branch (within the meaning of Code Sec. 367(a)(3)(C) in effect before enactment of Dec. 22, 2017) to a specified 10% owned foreign corporation (¶ 1901) with respect to which it is a U.S. shareholder after the transfer, the domestic corporation includes in gross income for the tax year which includes the transfer an amount equal to the transferred loss amount for the transfer. (Code Sec. 91(a) as added by Tax Cuts and Jobs Act §14102(d)(1))

> *observation:* Code Sec. 245A uses the term U.S. shareholder of a specified 10% owned foreign corporation but does not define the term. However, the Committee Report states that a U.S. shareholder of such a foreign corporation is a U.S. shareholder within the meaning of Code Sec. 951(b) (see ¶ 2101). (Com Rept, see ¶ 5107).

The *transferred loss amount* is, for any transfer of substantially all of the assets of a foreign branch, the excess (if any) of:

(1) the sum of losses:

(i) which were incurred by the foreign branch after Dec. 31, 2017, and before the transfer, and

(ii) with respect to which a deduction was allowed to the taxpayer, over

(2) the sum of:

(i) any taxable income of the branch for a tax year after the tax year in which the loss was incurred and through the close of the tax year of the transfer, and

(ii) any amount which is recognized due to the recapture of OFLs under Code Sec. 904(f)(3) on account of the transfer. (Code Sec. 91(b))

The transferred loss amount is reduced (but not below zero) by the amount of gain recognized by the taxpayer on account of the transfer (other than amounts recognized due to the recapture of OFLs). (Code Sec. 91(c))

Amounts included in gross income are treated as derived from U.S. sources. (Code Sec. 91(d))

Consistent with IRS regulations or other prescribed guidance, proper adjustments must be made in the adjusted basis of the taxpayer's stock in the specified 10% owned foreign corporation to which the transfer is made, and in the transferee's adjusted basis in the property transferred, to reflect amounts included in gross income under Code Sec. 91. (Code Sec. 91(e))

> *observation:* This recapture provision essentially replaces the Code Sec. 367(a)(3)(C) loss recapture provision which was eliminated as part of the removal of the active trade or business exception, see ¶ 2203.

Transition rule. The amount of gain taken into account under Code Sec. 91(c) must be reduced by the amount of gain which would be recognized under Code Sec. 367(a)(3)(C) (determined without regard to the repeal of Code

Sec. 367(a), see ¶ 2203) with respect to losses incurred before Jan. 1, 2018. (Tax Cuts and Jobs Act §14102(d)(4))

☐ **Effective:** Transfers made after Dec. 31, 2017. (Tax Cuts and Jobs Act §14102(d)(3))

Mandatory Inclusion On Deemed Repatriation Of Accumulated Foreign Earnings

¶ 1906. Pre-2018 accumulated deferred foreign income must be included in Subpart F income upon transition to a participation exemption system

Code Sec. 965(a), as amended by Tax Cuts and Jobs Act §14103(a)
Code Sec. 965(d), as amended by Tax Cuts and Jobs Act §14103(a)
Code Sec. 965(e), as amended by Tax Cuts and Jobs Act §14103(a)
Code Sec. 965(o), as amended by Tax Cuts and Jobs Act §14103(a)
Generally effective: Last tax year of a deferred income corporation begin-
ning before Jan. 1, 2018
Committee Reports, see ¶ 5109

Under pre-Tax Cuts and Jobs Act law, the U.S. employed a worldwide tax system, under which U.S. persons were generally taxed on all income, whether derived in the U.S. or abroad. Foreign income earned by U.S. shareholders through foreign corporations is generally subject to U.S. tax only when the income is distributed as a dividend to the U.S. shareholder. Under the Subpart F rules, U.S. shareholders of a controlled foreign corporation (CFC) are required to include in income their pro rata share of the CFC's Subpart F income whether or not the income is distributed to the shareholders. For Subpart F income purposes, a U.S. shareholder is a U.S. person who is a 10% owner (see ¶ 2101) of a foreign corporation (hereafter a U.S. Shareholder). However, actual distributions are tax-free where the amounts distributed were previously taken into income of a U.S. Shareholder as Subpart F income. Subpart F income includes investment income (e.g., dividends, interest), insurance income and foreign based company sales and services income. (FTC 2d/FIN ¶ O-2300 *et seq.*, ¶ O-2400 *et seq.*, ¶ O-2470 *et seq.*, ¶ O-2520 *et seq.*, ¶ O-2710 *et seq.*; USTR ¶ 9514, ¶ 9524, ¶ 9544; Catalyst ¶ 2101:100; Catalyst ¶ 2101:130; Catalyst ¶ 2101:140; Catalyst ¶ 2101:160; Catalyst ¶ 2102:100; Catalyst ¶ 2103:100; Catalyst ¶ 2104:100)

New Law. Under the Tax Cuts and Jobs Act, in the last tax year of a deferred foreign income corporation (defined below) which begins before Jan. 1, 2018, the Subpart F income of the foreign corporation (as otherwise determined for the tax year under Code Sec. 952) is increased by the greater of (i) the accumulated post-1986 deferred foreign income (defined below) of the corporation determined as of Nov. 2, 2017, or (ii) the accumulated post-1986 deferred foreign income of the corporation determined as of Dec. 31, 2017 (hereafter the mandatory inclusion). (Code Sec. 965(a) as amended by Tax Cuts and Jobs Act §14103(a))

Thus, a U.S. Shareholder in a deferred foreign income corporation must include in income its pro rata share of the undistributed, non-previously-taxed post-1986 foreign earnings of the corporation. (Com Rept, see ¶ 5109)

> *observation:* In contrast to the Code Sec. 245A DRD for post-2018 foreign earnings (see ¶ 1901), which is available only to corporate U.S. shareholders, the mandatory inclusion of pre-2018 accumulated deferred foreign earnings applies to all U.S. shareholders within the meaning of Code Sec. 951(b). (Com Rept, see ¶ 5109). Note that although Code Sec. 965 itself does not define a U.S. shareholder, it is part of Subpart F and thus incorporates the Code Sec. 951(b) definition of U.S. shareholder (see ¶ 2101).

The post-1986 E&P taken into consideration in computing the mandatory inclusion generally is reduced by foreign E&P deficits that are properly allocated to the U.S. Shareholder, see ¶ 1907.

A deduction for a portion of the mandatory inclusion is allowed for domestic corporations, but no foreign tax credit is available as to that portion, see ¶ 1908.

A *deferred foreign income corporation* is, as to any U.S. Shareholder, any specified foreign corporation (defined below) of the U.S. Shareholder which has accumulated post-1986 deferred foreign income (as of the close of the tax year referred to in Code Sec. 965(a)(1) or (2) (above) greater than zero. (Code Sec. 965(d)(1))

The *accumulated post-1986 deferred foreign income* is the post-1986 earnings and profits (E&P), except to the extent the earnings:

(A) are attributable to income of the specified foreign corporation which is effectively connected with the conduct of a U.S. trade or business and subject to U.S. income tax, (Code Sec. 965(d)(2)(A)) or

(B) in the case of a CFC, if distributed, would be excluded from the gross income of a U.S. Shareholder as previously taxed earnings under Code Sec. 959. (Code Sec. 965(d)(2)(B))

To the extent provided in regulations or other IRS guidance, in the case of any CFC which has shareholders which are not U.S. Shareholders, accumulated post-1986 deferred foreign income must be appropriately reduced by amounts which would be described in item (B) above if the shareholders were U.S. Shareholders. (Code Sec. 965(d)(2))

Post-1986 E&P is the E&P of the foreign corporation (computed under Code Sec. 964(a) and Code Sec. 986, and by only taking into account periods when the foreign corporation was a specified foreign corporation) accumulated in tax years beginning after Dec. 31, 1986, and determined:

(A) as of the date of the tax year referred to in Code Sec. 965(a)(1) or (2) (see above), whichever is applicable to the foreign corporation, and

(B) without diminution by reason of dividends distributed during that tax year as a mandatory inclusion other than dividends distributed to another specified foreign corporation. (Code Sec. 965(d)(3))

In order to avoid double-counting and double non-counting of earnings, IRS may provide guidance to adjust the amount of post-1986 E&P of a specified foreign corporation to ensure that a single item of a specified foreign corporation is taken into account only once in determining the income of a U.S. Shareholder subject to this rule. (Com Rept, see ¶ 5109)

A *specified foreign corporation* is (i) any CFC, and (ii) any foreign corporation as to which one or more domestic corporations is a U.S. Shareholder. (Code Sec. 965(e)(1)) For purposes of Code Sec. 951 (Subpart F income inclusions) and Code Sec. 961 (CFC basis adjustments), a foreign corporation (see item (ii)) is treated as a CFC solely for purposes of taking into account the Subpart F income of the corporation under Code Sec. 965(a) (and for purposes of applying Code Sec. 965(f)). (Code Sec. 965(e)(2)) A specified foreign corporation does not include any corporation which is a PFIC with respect to the shareholder and which is not a CFC. (Code Sec. 965(e)(3))

IRS may prescribe regulations or other guidance as may be necessary or appropriate to carry out these provisions including regulations or other guidance to provide appropriate basis adjustments, and to prevent the avoidance of the purposes of these provisions, including through a reduction in E&P, changes in entity classification, changes in accounting methods, or otherwise. (Code Sec. 965(o))

For an election to pay net tax liability arising from a mandatory inclusion in eight installments, see ¶ 1909.

For an election that allows an S corporation to defer net tax liability arising from a mandatory inclusion, see ¶ 1910.

For the six-year statute of limitation on assessment of net tax liability, see ¶ 1911.

For the exclusion of pre-2018 accumulated deferred foreign income for purposes of the REIT gross income test, and an election to include deferred foreign income in REIT income over a period of eight years, see ¶ 1912.

For an election not to take pre-2018 accumulated deferred foreign income into account for NOL purposes, see ¶ 1913.

☐ **Effective:** Last tax year of a deferred income corporation beginning before Jan. 1, 2018. (Code Sec. 965(a) as amended by Tax Cuts and Jobs Act §14103(a))

> *observation:* The Committee Report adds effective date language to the effect that this provision applies to U.S. Shareholders, for the tax years in which or with which the tax years of the foreign corporations end. (Com Rept, see ¶ 5109)

¶ 1907. Foreign E&P deficits reduce the pre-2018 accumulated deferred foreign income included in Subpart F

Code Sec. 965(b), as amended by Tax Cuts and Jobs Act §14103(a)
Code Sec. 965(f), as amended by Tax Cuts and Jobs Act §14103(a)
Generally effective: Last tax year of a deferred income corporation beginning before Jan. 1, 2018
Committee Reports, see ¶ 5109

Under pre-Tax Cuts and Jobs Act law, the U.S. employed a worldwide tax system, under which U.S. persons were generally taxed on all income, whether derived in the U.S. or abroad. Foreign income earned by U.S. shareholders through foreign corporations was generally subject to U.S. tax only when the income was distributed as a dividend to the U.S. shareholder. Under the Subpart F rules, U.S. shareholders of a controlled foreign corporation (CFC) are required to include in income their pro rata share of the CFC's Subpart F income whether or not the income is distributed to the shareholders. For Subpart F income purposes, a U.S. shareholder is a U.S. person who is a 10% owner (see ¶ 2101) of a foreign corporation (hereafter a U.S. Shareholder). However, actual distributions are tax-free where the amounts distributed were previously taken into income of a U.S. Shareholder as Subpart F income. Subpart F income includes investment income (e.g., dividends, interest), insurance income, and foreign based company sales and services income. (FTC 2d/FIN ¶ O-2300 *et seq.*, ¶ O-2400 *et seq.*, ¶ O-2470 *et seq.*, ¶ O-2520 *et seq.*, ¶ O-2710 *et seq.*; USTR ¶ 9514, ¶ 9524, ¶ 9544; Catalyst ¶ 2101:100; Catalyst ¶ 2101:130; Catalyst ¶ 2101:140; Catalyst ¶ 2101:160; Catalyst ¶ 2102:100; Catalyst ¶ 2103:100; Catalyst ¶ 2104:100; Catalyst ¶ 2104:110)

New Law. Under the Tax Cuts and Jobs Act, in a specified foreign corporation's last tax year before the transition to the participation exemption system (see ¶ 1901), the corporation's Subpart F income is increased by its accumulated deferred foreign income (¶ 1906), and its U.S. Shareholders must include in income their pro rata share of that Subpart F income (hereafter the mandatory inclusion, see ¶ 1906).

observation: In contrast to the Code Sec. 245A DRD for post-2018 foreign earnings (see ¶ 1901), which is available only to corporate U.S. shareholders, the mandatory inclusion of pre-2018 accumulated deferred foreign earnings applies to all U.S. shareholders within the meaning of Code Sec. 951(b). (Com Rept, see ¶ 5109). Note that although Code Sec. 965 itself does not define a U.S. shareholder, it is part of Subpart F and thus incorporates the Code Sec. 951(b) definition of U.S. shareholder (see ¶ 2101).

However, in the case of a taxpayer that is a U.S. Shareholder as to at least one deferred foreign income corporation (¶ 1906) and at least one E&P deficit foreign corporation (defined below), the amount that would (but for this rule) be taken into account as a mandatory inclusion consisting of that U.S. Shareholder's pro rata share of the Subpart F income of each deferred foreign income corporation is reduced by the amount of the U.S. Shareholder's aggregate foreign E&P deficit (defined below) which is allocated to the deferred foreign income corporation (hereafter the deficit reduction). (Code Sec. 965(b)(1) as amended by Tax Cuts and Jobs Act §14103(a))

The determination of any U.S. Shareholder's pro rata share of any amount with respect to any specified foreign corporation is determined under rules similar to the rules of Code Sec. 951(a)(2) by treating the amount in the same manner as Subpart F income (and by treating the specified foreign corporation as a CFC). (Code Sec. 965(f)(1))

The portion which is included in the income of a U.S. Shareholder under Code Sec. 951(a)(1) as a mandatory inclusion which is equal to the deduction allowed (¶ 1908)

(i) is treated as income exempt from tax for purposes of Code Sec. 705(a)(1)(B) and Code Sec. 1367(a)(1)(A), and

(ii) is not treated as income exempt from tax for purposes of determining whether an adjustment must be made to an accumulated adjustment account under Code Sec. 1368(e)(1)(A). (Code Sec. 965(f)(2))

Allocation of aggregate foreign E&P deficit. The aggregate foreign E&P deficit of any U.S. Shareholder is allocated among the deferred foreign income corporations of the U.S. Shareholder in an amount which bears the same proportion to the aggregate as:

(i) the U.S. Shareholder's pro rata share of the accumulated post-1986 deferred foreign income (¶ 1906) of each deferred foreign income corporation, bears to

(ii) the aggregate of the U.S. Shareholder's pro rata share of the accumulated post-1986 deferred foreign income of all of the U.S. shareholder's deferred foreign income corporations. (Code Sec. 965(b)(2))

The *aggregate foreign E&P deficit* is, as to any U.S. Shareholder, the lesser of:

(1) the aggregate of that shareholder's pro rata shares of the specified E&P deficits of that shareholders' E&P deficit foreign corporations, or

(2) the amount determined under item (ii) above. (Code Sec. 965(b)(3)(A)(i))

If the amount described in item (2) above is less than the amount described in item (1) above, then the shareholder must designate, in the form and manner as IRS determines:

(a) the amount of the specified E&P deficit which is to be taken into account for each E&P deficit corporation as to the taxpayer, and

(b) in the case of an E&P deficit corporation which has a qualified deficit (as defined in Code Sec. 952), the portion (if any) of the deficit taken into account under item (a) which is attributable to a qualified deficit, including the qualified activities to which the portion is attributable. (Code Sec. 965(b)(3)(A)(ii))

The deficits (including hovering deficits) of a foreign subsidiary that accumulated while it was a specified foreign corporation may be taken into account in determining the aggregate foreign E&P deficit of a U.S. Shareholder. (Com Rept, see ¶ 5109)

An *E&P deficit foreign corporation* is, as to any taxpayer, any specified foreign corporation (¶ 1906) with respect to which the taxpayer is a U.S. Shareholder, if, as of Nov. 2, 2017:

(i) the specified foreign corporation has a deficit in post-1986 E&P, and

(ii) the corporation was a specified foreign corporation, and the taxpayer was a U.S. Shareholder of that corporation. (Code Sec. 965(b)(3)(B))

The *specified E&P deficit* is, with respect to any E&P deficit foreign corporation, the amount of the deficit referred to in the definition of E&P deficit foreign corporation. (Code Sec. 965(b)(3)(C))

Treatment of E&P in later years. For purposes of applying Code Sec. 959 (previous taxed income rules) in any tax year beginning with the tax year described in Code Sec. 965(a), with respect to any U.S. Shareholder of a deferred foreign income corporation, an amount equal to the shareholder's deficit reduction (defined above) that is allocated to the deferred foreign income corporation is treated as an amount that was included in the U.S. shareholder's gross income under Code Sec. 951(a). (Code Sec. 965(b)(4)(A))

For any tax year beginning with the tax year described in Code Sec. 965(a), a U.S. Shareholder's pro rata share of the E&P of any E&P deficit foreign corporation is increased by the amount of the specified E&P deficit of the corporation taken into account by the shareholder as a deficit reduction (defined above), and, for purposes of Code Sec. 952, the increase is attributable to the same activity to which the deficit so taken into account was attributable. (Code Sec. 965(b)(4)(B))

Netting among U.S. Shareholders in an affiliated group. In the case of any affiliated group that includes at least one E&P net surplus shareholder and one E&P net deficit shareholder, the amount which would (but for this rule) be taken into account under Code Sec. 951(a)(1) as a mandatory inclusion (see ¶ 1906) by each E&P net surplus shareholder is reduced (but not below zero) by the shareholder's applicable share of the affiliated group's aggregate unused E&P deficit. (Code Sec. 965(b)(5)(A))

An *E&P net surplus shareholder* is any U.S. Shareholder that would (determined without regard to this rule) take into account an amount greater than zero under Code Sec. 951(a)(1) as a mandatory inclusion. (Code Sec. 965(b)(5)(B))

An *E&P net deficit shareholder* is any U.S. Shareholder if:

(i) the aggregate foreign E&P deficit with respect to the shareholder (as defined above without regard to Code Sec. 965(b)(3)(A)(i)(II)), exceeds

(ii) the amount that would (but for Code Sec. 965(b)) be taken into account by the shareholder under Code Sec. 951(a)(1) as a mandatory inclusion. (Code Sec. 965(b)(5)(C))

An *aggregate unused E&P deficit* is, with respect to any affiliated group, the lesser of (i) the sum of the excesses described in the definition of E&P net deficit shareholder (above), determined with respect to each E&P net deficit shareholder in the group, or (ii) the amount determined under item (ii) of the definition of applicable share (below). (Code Sec. 965(b)(5)(D)(i))

If the group ownership percentage of any E&P net deficit shareholder is less than 100%, the amount of the excess described in the definition of E&P net deficit shareholder (above) that is taken into account under item (i) of the definition of aggregate unused E&P deficit (above) with respect to the E&P net deficit shareholder is the group ownership percentage of that amount. (Code Sec. 965(b)(5)(D)(ii))

An *applicable share* is, with respect to any E&P net surplus shareholder in any affiliated group, the amount that bears the same proportion to the group's aggregate unused E&P deficit as:

(i) the product of the shareholder's group ownership percentage, multiplied by the amount that would (but for Code Sec. 965(b)(5)) be taken into account under Code Sec. 951(a)(1) as a mandatory inclusion by the shareholder, bears to

(ii) the aggregate amount determined under item (i) with respect to all E&P net surplus shareholders in the group. (Code Sec. 965(b)(5)(E))

The *group ownership percentage* is, with respect to any U.S. Shareholder in any affiliated group, the percentage of the value of the stock of the U.S. Shareholder that is held by other includible corporations in the affiliated group. Notwithstanding the preceding sentence, the group ownership percentage of the common parent of the affiliated group is 100%. Any term used in this definition which is also used in Code Sec. 1504 has the same meaning as when used therein. (Code Sec. 965(b)(5)(F))

It is expected that IRS will exercise its authority under the consolidated return provisions to appropriately limit the netting across chains of ownership within a group of related parties, in the application of Code Sec. 965. In addition, it is recognized that basis adjustments (increases or decreases) may be necessary with respect to both the stock of the deferred foreign income corporation and the E&P deficit foreign corporation; IRS is authorized to provide for such basis adjustments or other adjustments, as may be appropriate. For example, with respect to the stock of the deferred foreign income corporation, IRS may determine that a basis increase is appropriate in the tax year of the Code Sec. 951A inclusion or, alternatively, IRS may modify the application of Code Sec. 961(b)(1) with respect to that stock. Moreover, with respect to the stock of the E&P deficit corporation, IRS may require a reduction in basis for the tax year in which the U.S. Shareholder's pro rata share of the earnings of the E&P deficit corporation are increased. (Com Rept, see ¶ 5109)

> *Illustration (1): Reduction of amounts included in income of U.S. Shareholder of foreign corporations with E&P deficits.* Z, a domestic corporation, is a U.S. Shareholder of specified foreign corporations A, B, C and D. Z owns: 60% of Corporation A which has a post-1986 deficit of ($1,000); 10% of Corporation B which has a post-1986 deficit of ($200); 70% of Corporation C which has a post-1986 profit of $2,000; and 100% of Corporation D which has a post-1986 profit of $1000. Z's pro rata share of the profit/deficit of Corporation A is ($600), B is ($20), (C) is $1,400, and D is $1,000. Corporation A and B are E&P deficit foreign corporations.

> The aggregate foreign E&P deficit of the U.S. Shareholder is ($620), and the aggregate share of accumulated post-1986 deferred foreign income is $2,400. Thus, the portion of the aggregate foreign E&P deficit allocable to Corporation C is ($362) ($620 x 1400/2400). The remainder of the aggregate foreign E&P deficit is allocable to Corporation D. The U.S. Shareholder has a net surplus of E&P in the amount of $1,780. (Com Rept, see ¶ 5109)

> *Illustration (2):* A U.S. corporation has two domestic subsidiaries, X and Y, each of which it owns 100% and 80%, respectively. If X has a $1,000 net E&P surplus, and Y has $1,000 net E&P deficit, X is an E&P net surplus shareholder, and Y is an E&P net deficit shareholder. The net E&P surplus of X is reduced by the net E&P deficit of Y to the extent of the group's ownership percentage in Y, which is 80%.

The remaining net E&P deficit of Y is unused. If the U.S. Shareholder Z is also a wholly owned subsidiary of the same U.S. parent as X and Y, the group ownership percentage of Y is unchanged, and the surpluses of X and Z are reduced ratably by $800 of the net E&P deficit of Y. (Com Rept, see ¶ 5109)

Illustration (3): Hovering deficit. A foreign corporation organized after Dec. 31, 1986 has $100 of accumulated E&P as of Nov. 2, 2017, and Dec. 31, 2017 (determined without diminution by reason of dividends distributed during the tax year and after any increase for qualified deficits), which consist of $120 general limitation E&P and a $20 passive limitation deficit, the foreign corporation's post-1986 E&P would be $100, even if the $20 passive limitation deficit was a hovering deficit. Foreign income taxes related to the hovering deficit, however, would not generally be deemed paid by the U.S. Shareholder recognizing an incremental income inclusion. (Com Rept, see ¶ 5109)

It is expected that IRS may issue guidance to provide that, solely for purposes of calculating the amount of foreign income taxes deemed paid by the U.S. Shareholder with respect to an inclusion under Code Sec. 965, a hovering deficit may be absorbed by current year E&P and the foreign income taxes related to the hovering deficit may be added to the specified foreign corporation's post-1986 foreign income taxes in that separate category on a pro rata basis in the year of inclusion. (Com Rept, see ¶ 5109)

☐ **Effective:** Last tax year of a deferred income corporation beginning before Jan. 1, 2018. (Code Sec. 965(a) as amended by Tax Cuts and Jobs Act §14103(a))

🖉 *observation:* The Committee Report adds effective date language to the effect that this provision applies to U.S. Shareholders, for the tax years in which or with which the tax years of the foreign corporations end. (Com Rept, see ¶ 5109)

¶ 1908. Deduction for pre-2018 accumulated deferred foreign income; disallowance of foreign tax credit for deducted portion; recapture for expatriated entities

Code Sec. 965(c), as amended by Tax Cuts and Jobs Act §14103(a)
Code Sec. 965(g), as amended by Tax Cuts and Jobs Act §14103(a)
Code Sec. 965(l), as amended by Tax Cuts and Jobs Act §14103(a)
Generally effective: Last tax year of a deferred income corporation beginning before Jan. 1, 2018
Committee Reports, see ¶ 5109

Under pre-Tax Cuts and Jobs Act law, the U.S. employed a worldwide tax system, under which U.S. persons were generally taxed on all income, whether derived in the U.S. or abroad. Foreign income earned by U.S. corporate shareholders through foreign corporations was generally subject to U.S. tax only when the income was distributed as a dividend to the U.S. corporate shareholder. However, under the Subpart F rules, U.S. shareholders of a controlled foreign corporation (CFC) are required to include in income their pro rata share of the CFC's Subpart F income whether or not the income is distributed to the shareholders. For Subpart F income purposes, a U.S. shareholder is a U.S. person who is a 10% owner (see ¶ 2101) of a foreign corporation (hereafter a U.S. Shareholder). Subpart F income includes investment income (e.g., dividends, interest), insurance income and foreign based company sales and services income.

Foreign tax credit. Under pre-Tax Cuts and Jobs Act, a foreign tax credit was generally available to offset, in whole or in part, the U.S. tax owed on foreign-source income, whether earned directly by the domestic corporation, repatriated as a dividend from a foreign subsidiary, or included in income under Subpart F. If a domestic corporation claims a credit for foreign taxes, it must include in income an amount equal to the foreign income taxes deemed paid by it. (FTC 2d/FIN ¶ O-4000 *et seq.*; USTR ¶ 9014, ¶ 9024, ¶ 9604, ¶ 784; Catalyst ¶ 2101:170; Catalyst ¶ 2110:100)

Expatriation. The taxable income of an expatriated entity for any tax year for U.S. tax purposes is no less than the inversion gain of the entity for the tax year. An expatriated entity is a domestic corporation as to which a foreign corporation is a surrogate foreign corporation. A surrogate foreign corporation is a foreign corporation that has acquired substantially all of the properties held by the domestic corporation. The inversion rules apply if, after the acquisition, at least 60% of the stock of the foreign corporation is held by the former shareholders of the domestic corporation. But if the domestic corporation's shareholders hold 80% or more (by either vote or value) of the foreign corporation's stock after the acquisition, the foreign corporation is simply treated as a domestic corporation for U.S. income tax purposes. (FTC 2d/FIN ¶ F-5700 *et seq.*; USTR ¶ 78,744; Catalyst ¶ 118:200; Catalyst ¶ 120:120; Catalyst ¶ 122:150; Catalyst ¶ 124:270; Catalyst ¶ 127:190; Catalyst ¶ 129:200; Catalyst ¶ 132:130)

New Law. Under the Tax Cuts and Jobs Act, in a specified foreign corporation's last tax year before the transition to the participation exemption system (see ¶ 1901), the corporation's Subpart F income is increased by its accumulated deferred foreign income (see ¶ 1906), and its U.S. Shareholders must include in income their pro rata share of that Subpart F income (hereafter the mandatory inclusion, see ¶ 1906 & ¶ 1907).

> **RIA** *observation:* In contrast to the Code Sec. 245A DRD for post-2018 foreign earnings (see ¶ 1901), which is available only to corporate U.S. shareholders, the mandatory inclusion of pre-2018 accumulated deferred foreign earnings applies to all U.S. shareholders within the meaning of

Code Sec. 951(b). (Com Rept, see ¶ 5109). Note that although Code Sec. 965 itself does not define a U.S. shareholder, it is part of Subpart F and thus incorporates the Code Sec. 951(b) definition of U.S. shareholder (see ¶ 2101).

However, a U.S. Shareholder of a deferred foreign income corporation is allowed a deduction for the tax year in which a mandatory inclusion is included in the gross income of the U.S. Shareholder in an amount equal to the sum of:

(i) the U.S. Shareholder's 8% rate equivalent percentage of the excess (if any) of:

(a) the amount so included as gross income, over

(b) the amount of the U.S. Shareholder's aggregate foreign cash position, plus

(ii) the U.S. Shareholder's 15.5% rate equivalent percentage of so much of the amount described in item (i)(b) (above) as does not exceed the amount described in item (i)(a) (above). (Code Sec. 965(c)(1) as amended by Tax Cuts and Jobs Act §14103(a))

The *8% rate equivalent percentage* is, as to any U.S. Shareholder for any tax year, the percentage which would result in the amount to which that percentage applies being subject to a 8% rate of tax determined by only taking into account a deduction equal to that percentage of the amount and the highest rate of tax specified in Code Sec. 11 for the tax year. In the case of any tax year of a U.S. Shareholder to which Code Sec. 15 applies, the highest rate of tax under Code Sec. 11 before the effective date of the change in rates and the highest rate of tax under Code Sec. 11 after the effective date of the change is each taken into account under the preceding sentence in the same proportions as the portion of the tax year which is before and after the effective date, respectively. (Code Sec. 965(c)(2)(A))

The *15.5% rate equivalent percentage* is, with respect to any U.S. Shareholder for any tax year, the percentage determined under the 8% equivalent percentage definition applied by substituting a 15.5% rate of tax for the 8% rate of tax. (Code Sec. 965(c)(2)(B))

The calculation of the Code Sec. 965(c) deduction is based on the highest rate of tax applicable to corporations in the tax year of inclusion, even if the U.S. Shareholder is an individual. The use of rate equivalent percentages is intended to ensure that the rates of tax imposed on the deferred foreign income is similar for all U.S. Shareholders, regardless of the year in which Code Sec. 965 gives rise to an income inclusion. Individual U.S. Shareholders, and the investors in U.S. Shareholders that are pass-through entities generally can elect application of corporate rates for the year of inclusion. (Com Rept, see ¶ 5109)

The *aggregate foreign cash position* is, for any U.S. Shareholder, the greater of:

(1) the aggregate of the U.S. Shareholder's pro rata share of the cash position of each specified foreign corporation (¶ 1906) of the U.S. Shareholder determined as of the close of the last tax year of the specified foreign corporation beginning before Jan. 1, 2018, (Code Sec. 965(c)(3)(A)(i)) or

(2) one half of the sum of:

(i) the aggregate described in item (1) determined as of the close of the last tax year of each specified foreign corporation which ends before Nov. 2, 2017, plus

(ii) the aggregate described in item (1) determined as of the close of the tax year of each specified foreign corporation which precedes the tax year referred to in item (1). (Code Sec. 965(c)(3)(A)(ii))

The *cash position* of any specified foreign corporation is the sum of:

(i) cash held by the foreign corporation,

(ii) the net accounts receivable of the foreign corporation, plus

(iii) the fair market value of the following assets held by the corporation:

(I) personal property which is of a type that is actively traded and for which there is an established financial market (actively traded personal property),

(II) commercial paper, certificates of deposit, the securities of the Federal government and of any State or foreign government,

(III) any foreign currency,

(IV) any obligation with a term of less than one year, and

(V) any asset which IRS identifies as being economically equivalent to any of the above assets. (Code Sec. 965(c)(3)(B))

Net accounts receivable is, with respect to any specified foreign corporation, the excess (if any) of the corporation's accounts receivable, over the corporation's accounts payable (determined consistent with the rules of Code Sec. 461). (Code Sec. 965(c)(3)(C))

Cash positions of a specified foreign corporation that are net accounts receivable of the foreign corporation, actively traded personal property, or any obligation with a term of less than one year are not taken into account by a U.S. Shareholder in determining its aggregate foreign cash position to the extent that the U.S. Shareholder demonstrates to the satisfaction of IRS that the amount is taken into account by the U.S. Shareholder with respect to another specified foreign corporation. (Code Sec. 965(c)(3)(D))

Non-corporate entities. An entity (other than a corporation) is treated as a specified foreign corporation of a U.S. Shareholder for purposes of determining the U.S. Shareholder's aggregate foreign cash position if any interest in that entity is held by a specified foreign corporation of the U.S. Shareholder (determined after application of this rule) and the entity would be a specified foreign corporation of the U.S. Shareholder if that entity were a foreign corporation. (Code Sec. 965(c)(3)(E))

If IRS determines that a principal purpose of any transaction was to reduce the aggregate foreign cash position taken into account under these rules, the transaction is disregarded for these purposes. (Code Sec. 965(c)(3)(F))

> *illustration:* If a U.S. Shareholder owns a 5% interest in a partnership, the balance of which is held by a specified foreign corporation as to which the shareholder is a U.S. Shareholder, the partnership is treated as a specified foreign corporation as to the U.S. Shareholder, and the cash or cash equivalents held by the partnership are includible in the aggregate cash position of the U.S. Shareholder on a look-through basis. It is expected that IRS will provide guidance for taking into account only the specified foreign corporation's share of the partnership's cash position, and not the 5% interest directly owned by the U.S. Shareholder. (Com Rept, see ¶ 5109)

Disallowance of foreign tax credit or deduction. No foreign tax credit (FTC) is allowed under Code Sec. 901 for the applicable percentage of any taxes paid or accrued (or treated as paid or accrued) with respect to any amount for which the deduction (described above) is allowed. (Code Sec. 965(g)(1))

The *applicable percentage* is the amount (expressed as a percentage) equal to the sum of:

(A) 0.771 multiplied by the ratio of:

(i) the excess to which Code Sec. 965(c)(1)(A) applies, divided by

(ii) the sum of the excess plus the amount to which Code Sec. 965(c)(1)(B) applies, plus

(B) 0.557 multiplied by the ratio of:

(i) the amount to which Code Sec. 965(c)(1)(B) applies, divided by

(ii) the sum described in item (A)(ii) above. (Code Sec. 965(g)(2))

No deduction is allowed for any tax for which a credit is not allowable under Code Sec. 901 under the above rule (determined by treating the taxpayer as having elected to take the foreign tax credit). (Code Sec. 965(g)(3))

With respect to the taxes treated as paid or accrued by a domestic corporation as to amounts which are includible in gross income of the domestic corporation as a mandatory inclusion, Code Sec. 78 applies only to so much of the taxes as bears the same proportion to the amount of the taxes as:

(A) the excess of

(i) the amounts which are includible in gross income of the domestic corporation as a mandatory inclusion, over

(ii) the Code Sec. 965(c) deduction allowed with respect to those amounts, bears to

(B) those amounts. (Code Sec. 965(g)(4))

Recapture for expatriated entities. If a Code Sec. 965(c) deduction is allowed to a U.S. Shareholder and the shareholder first becomes an expatriated entity at any time during the 10-year period beginning on Dec. 22, 2017 (with respect to a surrogate foreign corporation which first becomes a surrogate foreign corporation during that period), then:

(A) the income tax is increased for the first tax year in which the taxpayer becomes an expatriated entity by an amount equal to 35% of the amount of the Code Sec. 965(c) deduction allowed, and

(B) no credits are allowed against the increase in tax described in item (A). (Code Sec. 965(l)(1))

An *expatriated entity* has the meaning given that term in Code Sec. 7874(a)(2), except it doesn't include an entity if the surrogate foreign corporation with respect to the entity is treated as a domestic corporation. (Code Sec. 965(l)(2))

A *surrogate foreign corporation* has the meaning given that term in Code Sec. 7874(a)(2)(B). (Code Sec. 965(l)(3))

Although the amount due under the recapture provision is computed by reference to the year in which the deemed Subpart F income was originally reported, the additional tax arises and is assessed for the tax year in which the U.S. Shareholder becomes an expatriated entity. No foreign tax credits are permitted with respect to the additional tax due as a result of the recapture rule. (Com Rept, see ¶ 5109)

☐ **Effective:** Last tax year of a deferred income corporation beginning before Jan. 1, 2018. (Code Sec. 965(a) as amended by Tax Cuts and Jobs Act §14103(a))

> *observation:* The Committee Report adds effective date language to the effect that this provision applies to U.S. Shareholders, for the tax years in which or with which the tax years of the foreign corporations end. (Com Rept, see ¶ 5109)

¶ 1909. A U.S. shareholder may elect to pay the net tax liability for pre-2018 accumulated deferred foreign income in installments

Code Sec. 965(h), as amended by Tax Cuts and Jobs Act §14103(a)
Generally effective: Last tax year of a deferred income corporation beginning before Jan. 1, 2018
Committee Reports, see ¶ 5109

Under pre-Tax Cuts and Jobs Act law, the U.S. employed a worldwide tax system, under which U.S. persons were generally taxed on all income, whether derived in the U.S. or abroad. Foreign income earned by U.S. shareholders through foreign corporations was generally subject to U.S. tax only when the income was distributed as a dividend to the U.S. shareholder. However, under the Subpart F rules, U.S. shareholders of a controlled foreign corporation (CFC) are required to include in income their pro rata share of the CFC's Subpart F income whether or not the income is distributed to the shareholders. For Subpart F income purposes, a U.S. shareholder is a U.S. person who is a 10% owner (see ¶ 2101) of a foreign corporation (hereafter a U.S. Shareholder). Subpart F income includes investment income (e.g., dividends, interest), insurance income, and foreign based company sales and services income. (FTC 2d/FIN ¶ O-2300 *et seq.*, ¶ O-2400 *et seq.*, ¶ O-2470 *et seq.*, ¶ O-2520 *et seq.*, ¶ O-2710 *et seq.*; USTR ¶ 9414, ¶ 9524, ¶ 9544; Catalyst ¶ 2101:100; Catalyst ¶ 2101:130; Catalyst ¶ 2101:140; Catalyst ¶ 2101:160; Catalyst ¶ 2102:100; Catalyst ¶ 2103:100; Catalyst ¶ 2104:100; Catalyst ¶ 2104:110)

New Law. Under the Tax Cuts and Jobs Act, in a specified foreign corporation's last tax year before the transition to the participation exemption system (see ¶ 1901), the corporation's Subpart F income is increased by its accumulated deferred foreign income (¶ 1906), and its U.S. Shareholders must include in income their pro rata share of that Subpart F income (hereafter the mandatory inclusion, see ¶ 1906 & ¶ 1907) reduced by a specified deduction (see ¶ 1908).

> **🅡🅘🅐** *observation:* In contrast to the Code Sec. 245A DRD for post-2018 foreign earnings (see ¶ 1901), which is available only to corporate U.S. shareholders, the mandatory inclusion of pre-2018 accumulated deferred foreign earnings applies to all U.S. shareholders within the meaning of Code Sec. 951(b). (Com Rept, see ¶ 5109). Note that although Code Sec. 965 itself does not define a U.S. shareholder, it is part of Subpart F and thus incorporates the Code Sec. 951(b) definition of U.S. shareholder (see ¶ 2101).

A U.S. Shareholder of a deferred foreign income corporation may elect to pay the net tax liability (defined below) under Code Sec. 965 in eight installments as follows:

(A) 8% of the net tax liability in the case of each of the first five install-ments,

(B) 15% of the net tax liability in the case of the sixth installment,

(C) 20% of the net tax liability in the case of the seventh installment, and

(D) 25% of the net tax liability in the case of the eighth installment. (Code Sec. 965(h)(1) as amended by Tax Cuts and Jobs Act §14103(a))

Due date of payment. If an election is made, the first installment must be paid on the due date (determined without regard to any extension of time for filing the return) for the tax return for the last tax year of a deferred income foreign corporation beginning before Jan. 1, 2018, and each succeeding install-ment must be paid on the due date (as so determined) for the return for the tax year following the tax year as to which the preceding installment was made. (Code Sec. 965(h)(2))

Acceleration of payment. If there is an addition to tax for failure to timely pay any required installment, a liquidation or sale of substantially all the assets of the taxpayer (including in a title 11 bankruptcy or similar case), a cessation of business by the taxpayer, or any similar circumstance, then the unpaid por-tion of all remaining installments is due on the date of that event (or in the case of a title 11 bankruptcy or similar case, the day before the petition is filed). This rule does not apply to the sale of substantially all the assets of a taxpayer to a buyer if the buyer enters into an agreement with IRS under which the buyer is liable for the remaining installments due in the same manner as if the buyer were the taxpayer. (Code Sec. 965(h)(3))

Proration of deficiency to installments. If an election is made to pay the net tax liability in installments and a deficiency has been assessed as to the net tax liability, the deficiency must be prorated to the installments payable. The part of the deficiency so prorated to any installment the date for payment of which has not arrived must be collected at the same time as, and as a part of, the install-ment. The part of the deficiency so prorated to any installment the date for pay-ment of which has arrived must be paid upon notice and demand from IRS. This rule does not apply if the deficiency is due to negligence, to intentional disregard of rules and regulations, or to fraud with intent to evade tax. (Code Sec. 965(h)(4))

Election. Any election to pay in installments must be made not later than the due date for the return of tax for the last tax year of the deferred income for-eign corporation which begins before Jan. 1, 2018, and must be made in the manner provide by IRS. (Code Sec. 965(h)(5))

The *net tax liability* of any U.S. Shareholder is the excess (if any) of:

(i) the taxpayer's net income tax for the tax year in which an amount is in-cluded in the gross income of the U.S. Shareholder under Subpart F as a mandatory inclusion, over

(ii) the taxpayer's net income tax for the tax year determined:

(I)   without regard to the mandatory inclusion provisions and

(II) without regard to any income or deduction properly attributable to a dividend received by the U.S. Shareholder from any deferred foreign income corporation. (Code Sec. 965(h)(6)(A))

The *net income tax* is the regular tax liability reduced by nonrefundable personal credits, refundable credits, business-related and other credits. (Code Sec. 965(h)(6)(B))

☐ **Effective:** Last tax year of a deferred income corporation beginning before Jan. 1, 2018. (Code Sec. 965(a) as amended by Tax Cuts and Jobs Act §14103(a))

> *observation:* The Committee Report adds effective date language to the effect that this provision applies to U.S. Shareholders, for the tax years in which or with which the tax years of the foreign corporations end. (Com Rept, see ¶ 5109)

¶ 1910. S corporation shareholders may elect to defer net tax liability for accumulated deferred foreign income until a triggering event

Code Sec. 965(i), as amended by Tax Cuts and Jobs Act §14103(a)
Code Sec. 965(j), as amended by Tax Cuts and Jobs Act §14103(a)
Generally effective: Last tax year of a deferred income corporation beginning before Jan. 1, 2018
Committee Reports, see ¶ 5109

Under pre-Tax Cuts and Jobs Act law, the U.S. employed a worldwide tax system, under which U.S. persons were generally taxed on all income, whether derived in the U.S. or abroad. Foreign income earned by U.S. shareholders through foreign corporations was generally subject to U.S. tax only when the income was distributed as a dividend to the U.S. shareholder. However, under the Subpart F rules, U.S. shareholders of a controlled foreign corporation (CFC) are required to include in income their pro rata share of the CFC's Subpart F income whether or not the income is distributed to the shareholders. For Subpart F income purposes, a U.S. shareholder is a U.S. person who is a 10% owner (see ¶ 2101) of a foreign corporation (hereafter a U.S. Shareholder). Subpart F income includes investment income (e.g., dividends, interest), insurance income, and foreign based company sales and services income. FTC 2d/FIN ¶s O-2300 *et seq.*, O-2400 *et seq.*, O-2470 *et seq.*, O-2520 *et seq.*, O-2710 *et seq.*; USTR ¶s 9514, 9524, 9544

An S corporation is generally not subject to tax but passes through its items of income, gain, deduction and loss to its shareholders who pay tax on their pro-rata share of the S corporation's income. FTC 2d/FIN ¶ D-1640 *et seq.*; USTR ¶ 13,664

New Law. Under the Tax Cuts and Jobs Act, in a specified foreign corporation's last tax year before the transition to the participation exemption system (see ¶ 1901), the corporation's Subpart F income is increased by its accumulated deferred foreign income (¶ 1906), and its U.S. Shareholders must include in income their pro rata share of that Subpart F income (the mandatory inclusion, see ¶ 1906 & ¶ 1907), reduced by a specified deduction (see ¶ 1908).

> *observation:* In contrast to the Code Sec. 245A DRD for post-2018 foreign earnings (see ¶ 1901), which is available only to corporate U.S. shareholders, the mandatory inclusion of pre-2018 accumulated deferred foreign earnings applies to all U.S. shareholders within the meaning of Code Sec. 951(b). (Com Rept, see ¶ 5109). Note that although Code Sec. 965 itself does not define a U.S. shareholder, it is part of Subpart F and thus incorporates the Code Sec. 951(b) definition of U.S. shareholder (see ¶ 2101).

In the case of any S corporation which is a U.S. Shareholder of a deferred foreign income corporation (¶ 1906), each shareholder of the S corporation may elect to defer payment of the shareholder's net tax liability (defined below) with respect to the S corporation until the shareholder's tax year which includes the triggering event (defined below) for the liability (hereafter the deferral election). Any net tax liability payment which is deferred is assessed on the tax return as an addition to tax in the shareholder's tax year which includes the triggering event. (Code Sec. 965(i)(1) as amended by Tax Cuts and Jobs Act §14103(a))

Triggering event. In the case of any shareholder's net tax liability under Code Sec. 965 with respect to any S corporation, the triggering event for the liability is whichever of the following occurs first:

(i) the corporation ceases to be an S corporation (determined as of the first day of the first tax year that the corporation is not an S corporation),

(ii) a liquidation or sale of substantially all the assets of the S corporation (including in a title 11 bankruptcy or similar case), a cessation of business by the S corporation, the S corporation ceases to exist, or any similar circumstance,

(iii) a transfer of any share of stock in the S corporation by the taxpayer (including by reason of death, or otherwise). (Code Sec. 965(i)(2)(A))

In the case of a transfer of less than all of the taxpayer's shares of stock in the S corporation, the transfer is only the triggering event for so much of the taxpayer's net tax liability with respect to the S corporation as is properly allocable to that stock. (Code Sec. 965(i)(2)(B))

A transfer described in item (iii) above is not treated as a triggering event if the transferee enters into an agreement with IRS under which the transferee is liable for net tax liability on the stock in the same manner as if the transferee were the taxpayer. (Code Sec. 965(i)(2)(C))

A shareholder's *net tax liability* as to any S corporation is the net tax liability as determined under Code Sec. 965(h)(6) (see ¶ 1909) if the only Subpart F income taken into account by the shareholder by reason of Code Sec. 965 were allocations from the S corporation. (Code Sec. 965(i)(3))

Election to pay deferred liability in installments. In the case of a taxpayer which elects to defer payment:

(A) the Code Sec. 965(h) election to pay the liability in installments (see ¶ 1909) is applied separately to the liability for which the deferral election applies,

(B) the Code Sec. 965(h) election for the liability is treated as timely made if made not later than the due date for the tax return for the tax year in which the triggering event as to the liability occurs,

(C) the first installment under the Code Sec. 965(h) election for the liability is paid not later than the due date (but determined without regard to any extension of time for filing the return), and

(D) if the triggering event as to any net tax liability is a liquidation or sale of substantially all the assets, a cessation of business by the S corporation, the S corporation ceasing to exist, or any similar circumstance (see item (ii) above), a Code Sec. 965(h) election for the liability may be made only with consent of IRS. (Code Sec. 965(i)(4))

If any shareholder of an S corporation elects to defer payment, the S corporation is jointly and severally liable for the payment and any penalty, addition to tax, or additional amount attributable thereto. (Code Sec. 965(i)(5))

Any limitation on the time period for the collection of a liability deferred under the above provision may not be treated as beginning before the date of the triggering event with respect to the liability. (Code Sec. 965(i)(6))

Shareholder reporting of tax liability. Any shareholder of an S corporation which makes a deferral election must report the amount of the shareholder's deferred net tax liability on the shareholder's tax return for the tax year for which the election is made and on the tax return for each tax year thereafter until the amount has been fully assessed on the returns. (Code Sec. 965(i)(7)(A))

The *deferred net tax liability* is, for any tax year, the amount of net tax liability payment of which has been deferred by means of a deferral election and which has not been assessed on a return for any earlier tax year. (Code Sec. 965(i)(7)(B))

In the case of any failure to report any amount required to be reported under Code Sec. 965(i)(7)(A) for any tax year before the due date for the return for the tax year, there is assessed on the return as an addition to tax 5% of that amount. (Code Sec. 965(i)(7)(C))

Election. Any deferral election:

(A) must be made by the shareholder of the S corporation not later than the due date for the shareholder's return for the tax year which includes the close of the tax year of the S corporation in which the mandatory inclusion amount is taken into account, and

(B) must be made in the manner IRS provides. (Code Sec. 965(i)(8))

Reporting by S corporation. Each S corporation which is a U.S. Shareholder of a specified foreign corporation (¶ 1906) must report in its tax return the amount includible in its gross income for the tax year by reason of the mandatory inclusion (see ¶ 1906) and the amount of the deduction allowable under Code Sec. 965(c) (see ¶ 1908). Any copy provided to a shareholder must include a statement of the shareholder's pro rata share of the amounts. (Code Sec. 965(j))

☐ **Effective:** Last tax year of a deferred income corporation beginning before Jan. 1, 2018. (Code Sec. 965(a) as amended by Tax Cuts and Jobs Act §14103(a))

> *observation:* The Committee Report adds effective date language to the effect that this provision applies to U.S. Shareholders, for the tax years in which or with which the tax years of the foreign corporations end. (Com Rept, see ¶ 5109)

¶ 1911. Six year statute of limitation for assessment of net tax liability due to pre-2018 accumulated deferred foreign income

Code Sec. 965(k), as amended by Tax Cuts and Jobs Act §14103(a)
Generally effective: Last tax year of a deferred income corporation beginning before Jan. 1, 2018
Committee Reports, see ¶ 5109

A three-year statute of limitations generally applies to income tax returns under Code Sec. 6501, so that IRS may not assess taxes more than three years after the return was filed (or, if later, the due date of the return). A six-year statute of limitations applies when a return contains a substantial omission of gross income. (FTC 2d/FIN ¶ T-4000 *et seq.*, ¶ T-4200 *et seq.*; USTR ¶ 65,014; Catalyst ¶ 2101:100; Catalyst ¶ 2101:130; Catalyst ¶ 2101:140; Catalyst

¶ 2101:160; Catalyst ¶ 2102:100; Catalyst ¶ 2103:100; Catalyst ¶ 2104:100; Catalyst ¶ 2104:110)

New Law. Under the Tax Cuts and Jobs Act, in a specified foreign corporation's last tax year before the transition to the participation exemption system (see ¶ 1901), the corporation's Subpart F income is increased by its accumulated deferred foreign income (¶ 1906), and its U.S. shareholders must include in income their pro rata share of that Subpart F income (the mandatory inclusion, see ¶ 1906 & ¶ 1907), reduced by a specified deduction (see ¶ 1908). The net tax liability arising from this mandatory inclusion can be paid over a period of eight years (see ¶ 1909).

> ⓡ *observation:* In contrast to the Code Sec. 245A DRD for post-2018 foreign earnings (see ¶ 1901), which is available only to corporate U.S. shareholders, the mandatory inclusion of pre-2018 accumulated deferred foreign earnings applies to all U.S. shareholders within the meaning of Code Sec. 951(b). (Com Rept, see ¶ 5109). Note that although Code Sec. 965 itself does not define a U.S. shareholder, it is part of Subpart F and thus incorporates the Code Sec. 951(b) definition of U.S. shareholder (see ¶ 2101).

Under the Tax Cuts and Jobs Act, the statute of limitations for the assessment of the net tax liability (as defined in Code Sec. 965(h)(6), see ¶ 1909) doesn't expire before the date that is six years after the return for the tax year described in Code Sec. 965(h)(6) was filed. (Code Sec. 965(k) as amended by Tax Cuts and Jobs Act §14103(a))

☐ **Effective:** Last tax year of a deferred income corporation beginning before Jan. 1, 2018. (Code Sec. 965(a) as amended by Tax Cuts and Jobs Act §14103(a))

> ⓡ *observation:* The Committee Report adds effective date language to the effect that this provision applies to U.S. shareholders, for the tax years in which or with which the tax years of the foreign corporations end. (Com Rept, see ¶ 5109)

¶ 1912. Pre-2018 accumulated deferred foreign income excluded for purposes of REIT gross income tests; election provided to include that amount in REIT income over eight years

Code Sec. 965(m), as amended by Tax Cuts and Jobs Act §14103(a)
Generally effective: Last tax year of a deferred income corporation beginning before Jan. 1, 2018
Committee Reports, see ¶ 5109

Under pre-Tax Cuts and Jobs Act law, the U.S. employed a worldwide tax system, under which U.S. persons were generally taxed on all income, whether derived in the U.S. or abroad. Foreign income earned by U.S. shareholders through foreign corporations was generally subject to U.S. tax only when the income was distributed as a dividend to the U.S. shareholders. However, under the Subpart F rules, U.S. shareholders of a controlled foreign corporation (CFC) are required to include in income their pro rata share of the CFC's Subpart F income whether or not the income is distributed to the shareholders. For Subpart F income purposes, a U.S. shareholder is a U.S. person who is a 10% owner (see ¶ 2101) of a foreign corporation (hereafter a U.S. Shareholder). Subpart F income includes investment income (e.g., dividends, interest), insurance income and foreign based company sales and services income. FTC 2d/FIN ¶s O-2300 *et seq.*, O-2400 *et seq.*, O-2470 *et seq.*, O-2520 *et seq.*, O-2710 *et seq.*; USTR ¶s 9514, 9524, 9544

Real estate investment trusts (REITs) are pass-through entities that are allowed a deduction for dividends paid to shareholders. As a result, REITs do not generally pay tax if they distribute their income (the distribution requirement), instead the income is taxed to the REIT shareholders. To qualify as a REIT the entity must limit its operations to the ownership of real estate assets and the provision of certain services to tenants and meet certain asset and income tests. Under the income tests, at least 95% of the entity's gross income must be derived from passive sources in real estate and securities, and 75% of its gross income must be from certain real estate sources, including rents from real property and gain from the sale or other dispositions of real property. (FTC 2d/FIN ¶ E-6520 *et seq.*, ¶ E-6600 *et seq.*; USTR ¶ 8564, ¶ 8574; Catalyst ¶ 552:113)

New Law. Under the Tax Cuts and Jobs Act, in a specified foreign corporation's last tax year before the transition to the participation exemption system (see ¶ 1901), the corporation's Subpart F income is increased by its accumulated deferred foreign income (¶ 1906), and its U.S. Shareholders must include in income their pro rata share of that Subpart F income (hereafter the mandatory inclusion, see ¶ 1906 & ¶ 1906), reduced by a specified deduction (see ¶ 1908).

> *observation:* In contrast to the Code Sec. 245A DRD for post-2018 foreign earnings (see ¶ 1901), which is available only to corporate U.S. shareholders, the mandatory inclusion of pre-2018 accumulated deferred foreign earnings applies to all U.S. shareholders within the meaning of Code Sec. 951(b). (Com Rept, see ¶ 5109). Note that although Code Sec. 965 itself does not define a U.S. shareholder, it is part of Subpart F and thus incorporates the Code Sec. 951(b) definition of U.S. shareholder (see ¶ 2101).

Mandatory inclusion not taken into account for gross income tests. If a REIT is a U.S. Shareholder in one or more deferred foreign income corporations (¶ 1906) any amount required to be taken into account as a mandatory inclusion is not taken into account as gross income of the REIT for purposes of applying the REIT gross income tests under Code Sec. 856(c)(2) and Code Sec. 856(c)(3) to any tax year for which the amount is taken into account under Code Sec. 951(a)(1). (Code Sec. 965(m)(1)(A) as amended by Tax Cuts and Jobs Act §14103(a))

Election to take income into account over an eight-year period. If a REIT so elects, notwithstanding Code Sec. 965(a), for purposes of the computation of REIT taxable income under Code Sec. 857(b), any amount required to be taken into account as a mandatory inclusion is not included in income in the tax year in which it would otherwise be included in gross income. Instead, it is included in gross income as follows:

(i) 8% of the amount in the case of each of the tax years in the five tax year period beginning with the tax year in which the amount would otherwise be included,

(ii) 15% of the amount in the case of the first tax year following that period,

(iii) 20% of the amount in the case of the second tax year following that period,

(iv) 25% of the amount in the case of the third tax year following that period. (Code Sec. 965(m)(1)(B))

Thus, REITs are permitted to elect to meet their distribution requirement with respect to pre-2018 accumulated deferred foreign income over an eight-year period under this installment schedule. (Com Rept, see ¶ 5109)

Any election must be made not later than the due date for the first tax year in the five tax year period beginning with the tax year in which the amount would otherwise be included, and must be made in the manner provided by IRS. (Code Sec. 965(m)(2)(A))

For purposes of determining the portion of the accumulated deferred foreign income that may be deducted under Code Sec. 965(c)(1) (see ¶ 1908) when this election is in effect:

(i) the aggregate amount of gross income and foreign cash position to which Code Sec. 965(c)(1)(A) and Code Sec. 965(c)(1)(B) respectively apply (see ¶ 1908) must be determined without regard to the election, (Code Sec. 965(m)(2)(B)(i)(I))

(ii) each aggregate amount is allocated to each tax year in the eight-year period in the same proportion as the amount included in the gross income of the U.S. Shareholder under Subpart F as a mandatory inclusion is allocated to each tax year, (Code Sec. 965(m)(2)(B)(i)(II))

(iii) the REIT cannot make an election to pay its net tax liability in installments (see ¶ 1909) for any such tax year. (Code Sec. 965(m)(2)(B)(i)(III))

> ⓇⒾⒶ *observation:* Code Sec. 965(m)(2)(B)(i)(III) provides that a REIT may not make an election under Code Sec. 965(g). Presumably technical corrections will amend this provision to reference the installment payment election under Code Sec. 965(h).

Triggering event. If there is a liquidation or sale of substantially all the assets of the REIT (including in a title 11 bankruptcy or similar case), a cessation of business by the REIT, or any similar circumstance, then any amount not yet included in gross income under the above rules must be included in gross income as of the day before the date of that event and the unpaid portion of any tax liability as to the inclusion is due on the date of that event (or in the case of a title 11 bankruptcy or similar case, the day before the petition is filed). (Code Sec. 965(m)(2)(B)(ii))

☐ **Effective:** Last tax year of a deferred income corporation beginning before Jan. 1, 2018. (Code Sec. 965(a) as amended by Tax Cuts and Jobs Act §14103(a))

> ⓇⒾⒶ *observation:* The Committee Report adds effective date language to the effect that this provision applies to U.S. Shareholders, for the tax years in which or with which the tax years of the foreign corporations end. (Com Rept, see ¶ 5109)

¶ 1913. Election not to take pre-2018 accumulated deferred foreign income into account for NOL purposes

Code Sec. 965(n), as amended by Tax Cuts and Jobs Act §14103(a)
Generally effective: Last tax year of a deferred income corporation beginning before Jan. 1, 2018
Committee Reports, see ¶ 5109

Under pre-Tax Cuts and Jobs Act law, the U.S. employed a worldwide tax system, under which U.S. persons were generally taxed on all income, whether derived in the U.S. or abroad. Foreign income earned by U.S. shareholders through foreign corporations was generally subject to U.S. tax only when the income was distributed as a dividend to the U.S. shareholder. However, under the Subpart F rules, U.S. shareholders of a controlled foreign corporation (CFC) are required to include in income their pro rata share of the CFC's Subpart F income whether or not the income is distributed to the shareholders. For Subpart F income purposes, a U.S. shareholder is a U.S. person who is a 10% owner (see ¶ 2101) of a foreign corporation (hereafter a U.S. Shareholder). Subpart F income includes investment income (e.g., dividends, interest), insurance income, foreign based company sales and services income. FTC 2d/FIN ¶s O-2300 *et seq.*, O-2400 *et seq.*, O-2470 *et seq.*, O-2520 *et seq.*, O-2710 *et seq.*; USTR ¶s 9514, 9524, 9544

Under pre-Tax Cuts and Jobs Act law, a foreign tax credit was generally available to offset, in whole or in part, the U.S. tax owed on foreign-source income, whether earned directly by the domestic corporation, repatriated as a dividend from a foreign subsidiary, or included in income under Subpart F. Under Code Sec. 78, if a domestic corporation claims a credit for foreign taxes, it must include in income an amount equal to the foreign income taxes deemed paid by it. (FTC 2d ¶ O-4000 *et seq.*; USTR ¶s 9014, 9024, 9604, 784)

A net operating loss (NOL) is the excess of a taxpayer's deductions over gross income. A deduction is allowed in computing taxable income for any tax year in an amount equal to NOL carrybacks and carryovers to that year. FTC 2d/FIN ¶ M-4400 *et seq.*; USTR ¶ 1724

New Law. Under the Tax Cuts and Jobs Act, in a specified foreign corporation's last tax year before the transition to the participation exemption system (see ¶ 1901), the corporation's Subpart F income is increased by its accumulated deferred foreign income (¶ 1906), and its U.S. shareholders must include in income their pro rata share of that Subpart F income (hereafter the mandatory inclusion, see ¶ 1906 & ¶ 1907), reduced by a specified deduction (see ¶ 1908).

> *observation:* In contrast to the Code Sec. 245A DRD for post-2018 foreign earnings (see ¶ 1901), which is available only to corporate U.S. shareholders, the mandatory inclusion of pre-2018 accumulated deferred foreign earnings applies to all U.S. shareholders within the meaning of Code Sec. 951(b). (Com Rept, see ¶ 5109). Note that although Code Sec. 965 itself does not define a U.S. shareholder, it is part of Subpart F and thus incorporates the Code Sec. 951(b) definition of U.S. shareholder (see ¶ 2101).

If a U.S. Shareholder of a deferred foreign income corporation (¶ 1906) elects the application of this rule for the last tax year of a deferred income corporation which begins before Jan. 1, 2018, then the Code Sec. 965(n)(2) amount (defined below) is not taken into account:

(1) in determining the amount of the NOL deduction under Code Sec. 172 of the shareholder for the tax year, or

(2) in determining the amount of taxable income for the tax year which may be reduced by NOL carryovers or carrybacks to that tax year under Code Sec. 172 (see ¶ 1001). (Code Sec. 965(n)(1) as amended by Tax Cuts and Jobs Act §14103(a))

The *Code Sec. 965(n)(2) amount* is the sum of:

(A) the amount required to be taken into account under Subpart F as a mandatory inclusion (determined after taking the Code Sec. 965(c) deduction, see ¶ 1908), plus

(B) in the case of a domestic corporation that takes a foreign tax credit for the tax year, the taxes deemed to be paid by that corporation under Code Sec. 960(a) and Code Sec. 960(b) for that tax year with respect to the amount described in item (A) which are treated as a dividend under Code Sec. 78. (Code Sec. 965(n)(2))

This election must be made no later than the due date (including extensions) for filing the return of tax for the tax year, and must be made in the manner prescribed by IRS. (Code Sec. 965(n)(3))

☐ **Effective:** Last tax year of a deferred income corporation beginning before Jan. 1, 2018. (Code Sec. 965(a) as amended by Tax Cuts and Jobs Act §14103(a))

> ⓇⒾⒶ *observation:* The Committee Report adds effective date language to the effect that this provision applies to U.S. Shareholders, for the tax years in which or with which the tax years of the foreign corporations end. (Com Rept, see ¶ 5109)

¶ 2000. Subpart F Inclusion For Global Intangible Low-Taxed Income

¶ 2001. U.S. shareholders of CFCs must include their global intangible low-taxed income (GILTI) in gross income

Code Sec. 951A, as added by Tax Cuts and Jobs Act §14201(a)

Generally effective: Tax years of foreign corporations beginning after Dec. 31, 2017

Committee Reports, see ¶ 5110

Under pre-Tax Cuts and Jobs Act law, foreign income earned by U.S. persons through foreign corporations was generally subject to tax only when that income was distributed to the U.S. shareholder as a dividend. However, under the Subpart F rules, U.S. persons who are 10% shareholders of a controlled foreign corporation (CFC) (hereafter U.S. Shareholders) are required to include in income their pro rata share of the CFC's Subpart F income whether or not this income is distributed to the shareholders. (FTC 2d/FIN ¶ O-2300 *et seq.*, ¶ O-2400 *et seq.*, ¶ O-2470 *et seq.*; USTR ¶ 9514, ¶ 9524; Catalyst ¶ 2101:101; Catalyst ¶ 2101:141; Catalyst ¶ 2102:102; Catalyst ¶ 2103:102; Catalyst ¶ 2104:102)

New Law. Under the Tax Cuts and Jobs Act, each person who is a U.S. Shareholder of any CFC for any tax year of the U.S. Shareholder must include in gross income the shareholder's global intangible low-taxed income (GILTI) for the tax year. (Code Sec. 951A(a) as added by Tax Cuts and Jobs Act §14201(a))

> **⚫observation:** Under the Tax Cuts and Jobs Act, foreign income earned by a U.S. corporation through a foreign subsidiary is generally exempt from U.S. tax under the participation exemption system (see ¶ 1901). The imposition of a tax on foreign-source intangible income aims to counteract the incentive created by the participation exemption to shift profits abroad. (Com Rept, see ¶ 5110)

Treatment of GILTI as Subpart F income for certain purposes. Any GILTI included in gross income under the above rule is treated in the same

---

FTC 2d References are to Federal Tax Coordinator 2d
FIN References are to RIA's Analysis of Federal Taxes: Income (print)
USTR References are to United States Tax Reporter
Catalyst References are to Checkpoint Catalyst
PCA References are to Pension Analysis (print and electronic)
PBE References are to Pension & Benefits Explanations
BCA References are to Benefits Analysis (electronic)
BC References are to Benefits Coordinator (print)
EP References are to Estate Planning Analysis (print and electronic)

manner as an amount included under Code Sec. 951(a)(1)(A) for purposes of applying Code Sec. 168(h)(2)(B), Code Sec. 535(b)(10), Code Sec. 851(b), Code Sec. 904(h)(1), Code Sec. 959, Code Sec. 961, Code Sec. 962, Code Sec. 993(a)(1)(E), Code Sec. 996(f)(1), Code Sec. 1248(b)(1), Code Sec. 1248(d)(1), Code Sec. 6501(e)(1)(C), Code Sec. 6654(d)(2)(D), and Code Sec. 6655(e)(4). IRS may provide for the application of this rule to other income tax provisions in any case in which the determination of Subpart F income is required to be made at the level of the CFC. (Code Sec. 951A(f)(1))

For purposes of the Code sections cited to above, with respect to any CFC any pro rata amount from which is taken into account in determining the GILTI included in gross income of a U.S. Shareholder, the portion of the GILTI which is treated as being with respect to that CFC is:

(A) in the case of a CFC with no tested income, zero, and

(B) in the case of a CFC with tested income, the portion of the GILTI which bears the same ratio to the GILTI as the U.S. Shareholder's pro rata amount of the tested income of the CFC bears to the aggregate amount described in item (A) of the definition of net CFC tested income (below) with respect to the U.S. Shareholder. (Code Sec. 951A(f)(2))

GILTI is, with respect to any U.S. Shareholder for any tax year of the U.S. Shareholder, the excess (if any) of:

(A) the shareholder's net CFC tested income for the tax year, over

(B) the shareholder's net deemed tangible income return for the tax year. (Code Sec. 951A(b)(1))

The *net deemed tangible income return* is, with respect to any U.S. Shareholder for any tax year, the excess of:

(A) 10% of the aggregate of the shareholder's pro rata share of the qualified business asset investment of each CFC with respect to which the shareholder is a U.S. Shareholder for the tax year (determined for each tax year of each CFC which ends in or with the tax year of the U.S. Shareholder), over

(B) the amount of interest expense taken into account under Code Sec. 951A(c)(2)(A)(ii) in determining the shareholder's net CFC tested income for the tax year to the extent the interest income attributable to the expense is not taken into account in determining the shareholder's net CFC tested income. (Code Sec. 951A(b)(2))

The *net CFC tested income* is, with respect to any U.S. Shareholder for any tax year of the U.S. Shareholder, the excess (if any) of:

(A) the aggregate of the shareholder's pro rata share of the tested income of each CFC with respect to which the shareholder is a U.S. Shareholder for the tax year of the U.S. Shareholder (determined for each tax year of the CFC which ends in or with that tax year of the U.S. Shareholder), over

(B) the aggregate of the shareholder's pro rata share of the tested loss of each CFC with respect to which the shareholder is a U.S. Shareholder for the tax year of the U.S. Shareholder (determined for each tax year of the CFC which ends in or with that tax year of the U.S. Shareholder). (Code Sec. 951A(c)(1))

The *pro rata shares* for purposes of the above rules are determined under the rules of Code Sec. 951(a)(2) in the same manner as that provision applies to Subpart F income and are taken into account in the tax year of the U.S. Shareholder in which or with which the tax year of the CFC ends. A person is treated as a U.S. Shareholder of a CFC for any tax year only if that person owns (within the meaning of Code Sec. 958(a)) stock in the foreign corporation on the last day in the tax year of the foreign corporation on which the foreign corporation is a CFC. A foreign corporation is treated as a CFC for any tax year if the foreign corporation is a CFC at any time during that tax year. (Code Sec. 951A(e))

The *tested income* is, with respect to any CFC for any tax year of the CFC, the excess (if any) of:

(i) the gross income of the corporation determined without regard to:

(I) any item of income described in Code Sec. 952(b),

(II) any gross income taken into account in determining the Subpart F income of the corporation,

(III) any gross income excluded from the foreign base company income (as defined in Code Sec. 954) and the insurance income (as defined in Code Sec. 953) of the corporation by reason of Code Sec. 954(b)(4),

(IV) any dividend received from a related person (as defined in Code Sec. 954(d)(3)), and

(V) any foreign oil and gas extraction income (as defined in Code Sec. 907(c)(1)) of the corporation, over

(ii) the deductions (including taxes) properly allocable to that gross income under rules similar to the rules of Code Sec. 954(b)(5) (or to which the deductions would be allocable if there were that gross income). (Code Sec. 951A(c)(2)(A))

The *tested loss* is, with respect to any CFC for any tax year of the CFC, the excess (if any) of the amount described in item (ii) above over the amount described in item (i) above. Code Sec. 952(c)(1)(A) is applied by increasing the earnings and profits of the CFC by the tested loss of the corporation. (Code Sec. 951A(c)(2)(B)) *observation:* Code Sec. 952(c)(1)(A) limits the Subpart F income of any CFC for any tax year to the earnings and profits of the CFC for the tax year.

The *qualified business asset investment* is, with respect to any CFC for any tax year, the average of the corporation's aggregated adjusted bases as of the close of each quarter of that tax year in specified tangible property:

(A) used in a trade or business of the corporation, and

(B) of a type with respect to which a deduction is allowable under Code Sec. 167. (Code Sec. 951A(d)(1))

Specified tangible property is any tangible property used in the production of tested income. However, in the case of property used both in the production of tested income and income which is not tested income, the property is treated as specified tangible property in the same proportion that the gross income described in Code Sec. 951A(c)(1)(A) (item (A) of the definition of net CFC tested income (above)) produced with respect to the property bears to the total gross income produced with respect to the property. (Code Sec. 951A(d)(2))

For purposes of determining the qualified business asset investment, notwithstanding any other provision which is enacted after Dec. 22, 2017, the adjusted basis in any property is determined by using the alternative depreciation system under Code Sec. 168(g), and by allocating the depreciation deduction with respect to the property ratably to each day during the period in the tax year to which the depreciation relates. (Code Sec. 951A(d)(3))

For purposes of the qualified business asset investment rules, if a CFC holds an interest in a partnership at the close of the tax year of the CFC, the CFC must take into account under Code Sec. 951A(d)(1) the CFC's distributive share of the aggregate of the partnership's adjusted bases (determined as of that date in the hands of the partnership) in tangible property held by the partnership to the extent the property:

(A) is used in the trade or business of the partnership,

(B) is of a type with respect to which a deduction is allowable under Code Sec. 167, and

(C) is used in the production of tested income (determined with respect to the CFC's distributive share of income with respect to the property).

The CFC's distributive share of the adjusted basis of any property is the CFC's distributive share of income with respect to the property. (Code Sec. 951A(d)(3))

caution: There appears to be an error in the numbering of Code Sec. 951A(d), with Code Sec. 951A(d)(3) appearing twice. Presumably technical corrections will be issued to address this.

IRS may issue regulations or other guidance to prevent the avoidance of the purposes of the qualified business asset investment rules, including guidance which provides for the treatment of property if that property is transferred, or held, temporarily, or if the avoidance of the purposes of these rules is a factor in the transfer or holding of the property. (Code Sec. 951A(d)(4))

Non-economic transactions intended to affect tax attributes of CFCs and their U.S. Shareholders (including amounts of tested income and tested loss, tested foreign income taxes, net deemed tangible income return, and qualified business asset investment) to minimize tax under the above rules should be disregarded. For example, IRS is expected to prescribe regulations to address transactions that occur after the measurement date of post-1986 earnings and profits under Code Sec. 965 (see ¶ 1906), but before the first tax year for which Code Sec. 951A applies, if those transactions are undertaken to increase a CFC's qualified business asset investment. (Com Rept, see ¶ 5110)

An 80% deemed paid foreign tax credit is available for GILTI (see ¶ 2003) and a separate foreign tax credit basket applies for it, see ¶ 2004.

A domestic corporation is allowed a deduction for a portion of its GILTI, see ¶ 2002.

☐ **Effective:** Tax years of foreign corporations beginning after Dec. 31, 2017, and tax years of U.S. Shareholders in which or with which those tax years of foreign corporations end. (Tax Cuts and Jobs Act §14201(d))

¶ 2002. Domestic corporations allowed deduction for foreign-derived intangible income and global intangible low-taxed income

Code Sec. 250, as added by Tax Cuts and Jobs Act §14202(a)
Generally effective: Tax years beginning after Dec. 31, 2017
Committee Reports, see ¶ 5111

Under pre-Tax Cuts and Jobs Act law, the U.S. employed a worldwide tax system, under which U.S. persons were generally taxed on all income, whether derived in the U.S. or abroad. Foreign income earned by U.S. corporate shareholders through foreign corporations was generally subject to U.S. tax only when the income was distributed as a dividend to the U.S. corporate shareholder. However, under the Subpart F rules, U.S. persons who are 10% shareholders of a controlled foreign corporation (CFC) (hereafter U.S. Shareholders) are required to include in income their pro rata share of the CFC's Subpart F income whether or not the income is distributed to the shareholders. (FTC 2d/ FIN ¶ O-2300 *et seq.*, ¶ O-2400 *et seq.*, ¶ O-2470 *et seq.*; USTR ¶ 9514, ¶ 9524)

New Law. Under the Tax Cuts and Jobs Act, in the case of a domestic corporation for any tax year, a deduction is allowed in an amount equal to the sum of:

(A) 37.5% of the foreign-derived intangible income (FDII) of the domestic corporation for the tax year, plus

(B) 50% of (i) the global intangible low-taxed income (GILTI, see ¶ 2001) amount (if any) which is included in the gross income of the domestic corporation under Code Sec. 951A for the tax year, and (ii) the amount treated as a dividend received by the corporation under Code Sec. 78 which is attributable to the amount described in item (i) (see ¶ 2301). (Code Sec. 250(a)(1) as added by Tax Cuts and Jobs Act §14202(a))

Coupled with the 21% tax rate for domestic corporations (see ¶ 102), these deductions result in effective tax rates of 13.125% on FDII and of 10.5% on GILTI (with respect to domestic corporations) for tax years beginning after Dec. 31, 2017, and before Jan. 1, 2026. Because only 80% of foreign tax credits are allowed to offset U.S. tax on GILTI (see ¶ 2003), the minimum foreign tax rate, with respect to GILTI, at which no U.S. residual tax is owed by a domestic corporation is 13.125% (80% of that foreign rate equals the 10.5% U.S. rate on GILTI). If the foreign tax rate on GILTI is 0%, then the U.S. residual tax rate on GILTI is 10.5%. Therefore, as foreign tax rates on GILTI range between 0% and 13.125%, the total combined foreign and U.S. tax rate on GILTI ranges between 10.5% and 13.125%. At foreign tax rates greater than or equal to 13.125%, there is no residual U.S. tax owed on GILTI, so that the combined foreign and U.S. tax rate on GILTI equals the foreign tax rate. (Com Rept, see ¶ 5111)

The deduction for FDII and GILTI is available only to C corporations that are not RICs or REITs because of Code Sec. 852(b)(2)(C) and Code Sec. 857(b)(2)(A) respectively. (Com Rept, see ¶ 5111)

Limitation based on taxable income. If, for any tax year, the sum of the FDII and the GILTI amount otherwise taken into account by the domestic corporation under the above rule, exceeds the taxable income of the domestic corporation (determined without regard to this provision), then the FDII and the GILTI amount so taken into account are reduced as follows:

(i) FDII is reduced by an amount which bears the same ratio to the excess as the FDII bears to the sum described above, and

(ii) the GILTI amount is reduced by the remainder of the excess. (Code Sec. 250(a)(2))

Deduction is reduced for tax years after 2025. In the case of any tax year beginning after Dec. 31, 2025, the allowed deduction will decrease to (i) 21.875% of the FDII of the domestic corporation for the tax year (item (A) above), and (ii) 37.5% of the GILTI amount included in the gross income of the domestic corporation for the tax year and the amount treated as a dividend received by the corporation under Code Sec. 78 which is attributable to the amount (item (B) above). (Code Sec. 250(a)(3))

For domestic corporations in taxable years beginning after Dec. 31, 2025, the effective tax rate on FDII is 16.406% and the effective U.S. tax rate on GILTI is 13.125%. The minimum foreign tax rate, with respect to GILTI, at which no U.S. residual tax is owed is 16.406%. If the foreign tax rate on GILTI is 0%, then the U.S. residual tax rate on GILTI is 13.125%. Therefore, as foreign tax rates on GILTI range between 0% and 16.406%, the total combined foreign and U.S. tax rate on GILTI ranges between 13.125% and 16.406%. At foreign tax rates greater than or equal to 16.406%, there is no residual U.S. tax on GILTI, and the combined foreign and U.S. tax rate on GILTI equals the foreign tax rate. (Com Rept, see ¶ 5111)

The *foreign-derived intangible income (FDII)* of any domestic corporation is the amount which bears the same ratio to the deemed intangible income of the corporation as:

(A) the foreign-derived deduction eligible income of the corporation, bears to

(B) the deduction eligible income of the corporation. (Code Sec. 250(b)(1))

The *deemed intangible income* is the excess (if any) of:

(i) the deduction eligible income of the domestic corporation, over

(ii) the deemed tangible income return of the corporation. (Code Sec. 250(b)(2)(A))

The *deemed tangible income return* is, with respect to any corporation, an amount equal to 10% of the corporation's qualified business asset investment (as defined in Code Sec. 951A(d) (see ¶ 2001), determined by substituting "deduction eligible income" for "tested income" in Code Sec. 951A(d)(2) and without regard to whether the corporation is a CFC) . (Code Sec. 250(b)(2)(B))

The *deduction eligible income* is, with respect to any domestic corporation, the excess (if any) of:

(i) gross income of the corporation determined without regard to:

... the Subpart F income of the corporation determined under Code Sec. 951(a)(1),

... the GILTI determined under Code Sec. 951A,

... any financial services income (as defined in Code Sec. 904(d)(2)(D)) of the corporation,

... any dividend received from a corporation which is a CFC of the domestic corporation,

. . . any domestic oil and gas extraction income of the corporation (i.e., income described in Code Sec. 907(c)(1), determined by substituting "within the U.S." for "without the U.S."), and

. . . any foreign branch income (as defined in Code Sec. 904(d)(2)(J)),
over

(ii) the deductions (including taxes) properly allocable to that gross income. (Code Sec. 250(b)(3))

Foreign-derived deduction eligible income is, with respect to any taxpayer for any tax year, any deduction eligible income of the taxpayer which is derived in connection with:

(A) property which is sold by the taxpayer to any person who is not a U.S. person, and which the taxpayer establishes to IRS's satisfaction is for a foreign use, or

(B) services provided by the taxpayer which the taxpayer establishes to IRS's satisfaction are provided to any person, or with respect to property, not located within the U.S. (Code Sec. 250(b)(4))

Foreign use means any use, consumption, or disposition which is not within the U.S. (Code Sec. 250(b)(5)(A))

If a taxpayer sells property to another person (other than a related party) for further manufacture or other modification within the U.S., the property is not treated as sold for a foreign use even if the other person subsequently uses the property for a foreign use. Similarly, if a taxpayer provides services to another person (other than a related party) located within the U.S., the services are not treated as described in Code Sec. 250(b)(4)(B) (item (B) above) even if that other person uses the services in providing services which are so described. (Code Sec. 250(b)(5)(B))

If property is sold to a related party who is not a U.S. person, the sale isn't treated as for a foreign use unless the property is ultimately sold by a related party or used by a related party in connection with property which is sold or the provision of services, to another person who is an unrelated party who is not a U.S. person, and the taxpayer establishes to IRS's satisfaction that the property is for a foreign use. A sale of property is treated as a sale of each component of the property. (Code Sec. 250(b)(5)(C)(i))

If a service is provided to a related party who is not located in the U.S., the service is not treated as described in Code Sec. 250(b)(5)(A)(ii) unless the taxpayer established to IRS's satisfaction that the service is not substantially similar to services provided by the related party to persons located within the U.S. (Code Sec. 250(b)(5)(C)(ii))

☂️ observation: The reference to Code Sec. 250(b)(5)(A)(ii) appears to be a mistake since there is no such provision. It is possible that the reference is meant to be to Code Sec. 250(b)(4)(B).

A *related party* is any member of an affiliated group as defined in Code Sec. 1504(a), determined by substituting "more than 50%" for "at least 80%" each place it appears, and without regard to the provisions excluding insurance companies and foreign companies. Any person (other than a corporation) is treated as a member of the group if that person is controlled by members of the group (including any entity treated as a member of the group by reason of this sentence) or controls any such member. For purposes of the preceding sentence, control is determined under the rules of Code Sec. 954(d)(3). (Code Sec. 250(b)(5)(D))

Sold, sells, and sale include any lease, license, exchange, or other disposition. (Code Sec. 250(b)(5)(E))

IRS may prescribe regs or other guidance as may be necessary or appropriate to carry out the above provisions. (Code Sec. 250(c))

☐ **Effective:** Tax years beginning after Dec. 31, 2017. (Tax Cuts and Jobs Act §14202(c))

¶ 2003. 80% deemed paid foreign tax credit available for global intangible low-taxed income

Code Sec. 960(d), as amended by Tax Cuts and Jobs Act §14201(b)(1)
Generally effective: Tax years of foreign corporations beginning after Dec. 31, 2017
Committee Reports, see ¶ 5110

The U.S. taxes U.S. persons on both foreign and U.S. income. In order to mitigate the possibility of U.S. persons being taxed on their foreign-sourced income by both the U.S. and the country in which that income was earned, the U.S. provides a credit against U.S. tax liability on a taxpayer's foreign-source income (the foreign tax credit). FTC 2d/FIN ¶ O-4000 *et seq.*; USTR ¶ 9014 A domestic corporation taxed on the Subpart F earnings of a CFC is allowed to take a deemed-paid credit for foreign taxes paid by the CFC on the portion of the CFC's earnings that the U.S. Shareholder is required to include in income under Subpart F. (FTC 2d/FIN ¶ O-4900 *et seq.*; USTR ¶ 9604; Catalyst ¶ 2101:171; Catalyst ¶ 2110:104)

New Law. Under the Tax Cuts and Jobs Act, for purposes of the CFC provisions, if any amount is includible in the gross income of a domestic corporation as global intangible low-taxed income (GILTI) (see ¶ 2001), that domestic corporation is deemed to have paid foreign income taxes equal to 80% of the product of (i) the domestic corporation's inclusion percentage multiplied by (ii) the aggregate tested foreign income taxes paid or accrued by CFCs. (Code Sec. 960(d)(1) as amended by Tax Cuts and Jobs Act §14201(b)(1))

> **☙ observation:** Allowing a "deemed paid" foreign tax credit for GILTI is consistent with the treatment of Subpart F income. However unlike in the case of Subpart F income, the credit is limited to 80% of the foreign taxes paid.

The *inclusion percentage* is, with respect to any domestic corporation, the ratio (expressed as a percentage) of:

(A) the corporation's GILTI, divided by

(B) the aggregate amount of the domestic corporation's pro rata share of each CFC's tested income (see ¶ 2001) with respect to the corporation. (Code Sec. 960(d)(2))

The *tested foreign income taxes* are, with respect to any domestic corporation which is a U.S. shareholder of a CFC, the foreign income taxes paid or accrued by the foreign corporation which are properly attributable to the tested income of the foreign corporation taken into account by the domestic corporation under Code Sec. 951A. (Code Sec. 960(d)(3))

The taxes deemed to have been paid are treated as an increase in GILTI for purposes of Code Sec. 78, determined by taking into account 100% of the aggregate tested foreign income taxes, see ¶ 2301.

A separate foreign tax credit basket is used for the GILTI credit, see ¶ 2004.

☐ **Effective:** Tax years of foreign corporations beginning after Dec. 31, 2017, and tax years of U.S. shareholders in which or with which those tax years of foreign corporations end. (Tax Cuts and Jobs Act §14201(d))

¶ 2004. Separate foreign tax credit basket for global intangible low-taxed income (GILTI)

Code Sec. 904(d)(1), as amended by Tax Cuts and Jobs Act §14201(b)(2)(A)
Code Sec. 904(d)(2)(A)(ii), as amended by Tax Cuts and Jobs Act §14201(b)(2)(B)
Code Sec. 904(c), as amended by Tax Cuts and Jobs Act §14201(b)(2)(C)
Generally effective: Tax years of foreign corporations beginning after Dec. 31, 2017
Committee Reports, see ¶ 5110

In order to mitigate the possibility of U.S. persons being taxed on their foreign-sourced income by both the U.S. and the country in which that income was earned, the U.S. provides a credit against U.S. tax liability on a taxpayer's foreign-source income (the foreign tax credit). FTC 2d/FIN ¶ O-4000 *et seq.*; USTR ¶ 9014 The foreign tax credit is limited to the U.S. tax on foreign source income. This ensures that the credit only mitigates double taxation of foreign source income without offsetting U.S. tax on U.S. source income. The foreign tax credit limitation is calculated separately for certain categories (or "baskets") of income. Under pre-Tax Cuts and Jobs Act law, there were two such baskets: income was either passive category income or general category income (defined as income other than passive category income). The amount of foreign taxes paid or accrued which exceeded the foreign tax credit limitation for a tax year could be carried forward 10 years or carried back one year. (FTC 2d/FIN ¶ O-4300 *et seq.*; USTR ¶ 9044; Catalyst ¶ 104:200; Catalyst ¶ 118:115; Catalyst ¶ 406:279; Catalyst ¶ 2106:134; Catalyst ¶ 2110:106; Catalyst ¶ 2110:130)

New Law. The Tax Cuts and Jobs Act requires U.S. shareholders of CFCs to include in gross income their global intangible low-taxed income (GILTI) for the tax year in a similar manner to Subpart F income (see ¶ 2001).

The Tax Cuts and Jobs Act adds any amount includible in gross income as GILTI (other than passive category income) as a third foreign tax credit basket. (Code Sec. 904(d)(1)(A) as amended by Tax Cuts and Jobs Act §14201(b)(2)(A))

In addition, the Act amends the definition of general category income to carve out both passive category income and amounts includible in gross income under Code Sec. 951A. (Code Sec. 904(d)(2)(A)(ii) as amended by Tax Cuts and Jobs Act §14201(b)(2)(B))

Finally, the Tax Cuts and Jobs Act denies a carryforward and a carryback for taxes paid or accrued with respect to amounts in the Code Sec. 951A income basket. (Code Sec. 904(c) as amended by Tax Cuts and Jobs Act §14201(b)(2)(C))

For the 80% deemed paid foreign tax credit available for GILTI, see ¶ 2003.

☐ **Effective:** Tax years of foreign corporations beginning after Dec. 31, 2017, and tax years of U.S. shareholders in which or with which those tax years of foreign corporations end. (Tax Cuts and Jobs Act §14201(d))

¶ 2100. Other Changes To Subpart F

¶ 2101. Definition of U.S. shareholder of a controlled foreign corporation expanded to include 10% owner by value

Code Sec. 951(b), as amended by Tax Cuts and Jobs Act §14214(a)
Generally effective: Tax years of foreign corporations beginning after Dec. 31, 2017
Committee Reports, see ¶ 5115

Under Subpart F, 10% U.S. shareholders of a controlled foreign corporation (CFC) (hereafter U.S. Shareholders) are required to include in income their pro rata share of the CFC's Subpart F income whether or not this income is distributed to them. FTC 2d/FIN ¶s O-2300 *et seq.*, O-2400 *et seq.*, O-2470 *et seq.*; USTR ¶s 9514, 9524

Under pre-Tax Cuts and Jobs Act law, a U.S. Shareholder was a U.S. person who owned, directly or by attribution, at least 10% of the total combined *voting power* of all classes of a foreign corporation's stock that were entitled to vote. (FTC 2d/FIN ¶ O-2300, ¶ O-2303; USTR ¶ 9514.01; Catalyst ¶ 2101:101; Catalyst ¶ 2101:111; Catalyst ¶ 2102:101; Catalyst ¶ 2103:101; Catalyst ¶ 2104:101; Catalyst ¶ 2110:141)

New Law. The Tax Cuts and Jobs Act expands the definition of U.S. Shareholder to include U.S. persons who own 10% or more of the *total value* of shares of all classes of stock of the foreign corporation. (Code Sec. 951(b) as amended by Tax Cuts and Jobs Act §14214(a))

☐ **Effective:** Tax years of foreign corporations beginning after Dec. 31, 2017, and tax years of U.S. Shareholders with or within which those tax years of foreign corporations end. (Tax Cuts and Jobs Act §14214(b))

¶ 2102. Subpart F constructive attribution rules allow downward attribution from foreign persons to related U.S. persons

Code Sec. 958(b), as amended by Tax Cuts and Jobs Act §14213(a)
Generally effective: The last tax year of foreign corporations beginning
  before Jan. 1, 2018
Committee Reports, see ¶ 5114

Under Subpart F, U.S. persons who are 10% shareholders of a controlled foreign corporation (CFC) (hereafter U.S. Shareholders) are required to include in income their pro rata share of the CFC's Subpart F income whether or not this income is distributed to the shareholders. Subpart F income includes foreign base company income (FBCI). Constructive attribution rules apply to determine whether (i) a U.S. person is a U.S. Shareholder, (ii) a person is related to the CFC for purposes of the FBCI rules, (iii) the stock of a domestic corporation is treated as owned by a U.S. Shareholder, and (iv) a foreign corporation is treated as a CFC. FTC 2d/FIN ¶s O-2300 *et seq.*, O-2400 *et seq.*, O-2470 *et seq.*, O-2520 *et seq.*; USTR ¶s 9524, 9544, 9564

The constructive attribution rules attribute (i) stock owned, directly or indirectly, by or for a partner or a beneficiary of an estate to the partnership or estate, (ii) stock owned, directly or indirectly, by or for a beneficiary or owner of a trust to the trust, and (iii) stock owned, directly or indirectly, by of for a 50% or more shareholder of a corporation to the corporation (hereafter the downward attribution rules). However, under pre-Tax Cuts and Jobs Act law, those rules could not be applied so as to consider a U.S. person as owning stock which was owned by a foreign person. (FTC 2d/FIN ¶ O-2300, ¶ O-2331 *et seq.*; USTR ¶ 9584.01; Catalyst ¶ 105:183)

New Law. Under the Tax Cuts and Jobs Act, stock owned by a foreign person can be treated as owned by a U.S. person in applying the downward attribution rules. (Code Sec. 958(b) as amended by Tax Cuts and Jobs Act §14213(a))

This change renders ineffective transactions effectuating "de-control" of a foreign subsidiary by taking advantage of the rule that effectively turned off the constructive stock ownership rules which otherwise would have resulted in a U.S. person being treated as owning stock owned by a foreign person. This converted former CFCs to non-CFCs, despite continuous ownership by U.S. shareholders. (Com Rept, see ¶ 5114)

☐ **Effective:** The last tax year of foreign corporations beginning before Jan. 1, 2018, and each subsequent tax year of the foreign corporations, and tax years of U.S. Shareholders in which or with which those tax years of foreign corporations end. (Tax Cuts and Jobs Act §14213(b))

¶ 2103. Requirement that corporation must be controlled for 30 days before Subpart F inclusions apply is eliminated

Code Sec. 951(a)(1), as amended by Tax Cuts and Jobs Act §14215(a)
Generally effective: Tax years of foreign corporations beginning after Dec. 31, 2017
Committee Reports, see ¶ 5116

Under Subpart F, U.S. persons who are 10% shareholders of a controlled foreign corporation (CFC) (hereafter U.S. Shareholders) are required to include in income their pro rata share of the CFC's Subpart F income whether or not this income is distributed to the shareholders. FTC 2d/FIN ¶s O-2300 *et seq.*, O-2400 *et seq.*, O-2470 *et seq.*; USTR ¶s 9514, 9524

However, under pre-Tax Cuts and Jobs Act law, a foreign corporation was required to be a CFC for an uninterrupted period of 30 days or more during the tax year for its Subpart F income to be taxed to its U.S. Shareholders. (FTC 2d/FIN ¶ O-2400, ¶ O-2404; USTR ¶ 9514; Catalyst ¶ 2101:102; Catalyst ¶ 2101:141; Catalyst ¶ 2102:102; Catalyst ¶ 2103:102; Catalyst ¶ 2104:102)

New Law. The Tax Cuts and Jobs Act eliminates the rule requiring a foreign corporation to be a CFC for an uninterrupted period of 30 days or more during the tax year for its Subpart F income to be taxed to its U.S. Shareholders. (Code Sec. 951(a)(1) as amended by Tax Cuts and Jobs Act §14215(a))

☐ **Effective:** Tax years of foreign corporations beginning after Dec. 31, 2017, and tax years of U.S. Shareholders with or within which those tax years of foreign corporations end. (Tax Cuts and Jobs Act §14215(b))

¶ 2104. Foreign base company oil-related income not included in foreign base company income

Code Sec. 954(a)(5), as amended by Tax Cuts and Jobs Act §14211(a)(3)
Code Sec. 954(g), as amended by Tax Cuts and Jobs Act §14211(b)(3)
Generally effective: Tax years of foreign corporations beginning after Dec. 31, 2017
Committee Reports, see ¶ 5112

Under Subpart F, U.S. persons who are 10% shareholders of a controlled foreign corporation (CFC) (hereafter U.S. Shareholders) are required to include in income their pro rata share of the CFC's Subpart F income whether or not this income is distributed to the shareholders. Subpart F income includes foreign base company income (FBCI). FTC 2d/FIN ¶s O-2300 *et seq.*, O-2400 *et seq.*, O-2470 *et seq.*, O-2520 *et seq.*; USTR ¶s 9524, 9544

Under pre-Tax Cuts and Jobs Act law, foreign base company oil related income was included in the Subpart F income of U.S. Shareholders as a category of FBCI. (FTC 2d/FIN ¶ O-2660 *et seq.*; USTR ¶ 9544, ¶ 9544.05; Catalyst ¶ 2101:132)

New Law. The Tax Cuts and Jobs Act eliminates foreign base company oil related income as a category of FBCI. (Code Sec. 954(a)(5) as amended by Tax Cuts and Jobs Act §14211(a)(3); Code Sec. 954(g) as amended by Tax Cuts and Jobs Act §14211(b)(3))

☐ **Effective:** Tax years of foreign corporations beginning after Dec. 31, 2017, and tax years of U.S. Shareholders with or within which those tax years of foreign corporations end. (Tax Cuts and Jobs Act §14211(c))

¶ 2105. Previously excluded Subpart F income withdrawn from a qualified shipping investment no longer included in U.S. shareholder's income

Code Sec. 955, as repealed by Tax Cuts and Jobs Act §14212(a)
Generally effective: Tax years of foreign corporations beginning after Dec. 31, 2017
Committee Reports, see ¶ 5113

Under Subpart F, U.S. persons who are 10% shareholders of a controlled foreign corporation (CFC) (hereafter U.S. Shareholders) are required to include in income their pro rata share of the CFC's Subpart F income whether or not this income is distributed to the shareholders. Subpart F income includes foreign base company income (FBCI). For pre-2005 tax years, FBCI included foreign base company shipping income (FBCSI). FBCSI generally included income derived from the use of any aircraft or vessel in foreign commerce, the performance of services directly related to the use of any aircraft or vessel, the sale or other disposition of any aircraft or vessel, and certain space or ocean activities. FTC 2d/FIN ¶s O-2300 *et seq.*, O-2400 *et seq.*, O-2470 *et seq.*, O-2520 *et seq.*, O-2710 *et seq.*; USTR ¶s 9524, 9544

Prior to the '86 Tax Reform Act, FBCSI that was reinvested in the shipping operations of a CFC (a qualified shipping investment) was not included in Subpart F income. FTC 2d/FIN ¶ O-10621 The previously excluded income was then recaptured if and when it was subsequently withdrawn from the qualified shipping investment. Although the '86 Tax Reform Act repealed the exclusion for qualified shipping investments, the recapture provision was retained. (FTC 2d/FIN ¶ O-2740 *et seq.*; USTR ¶ 9554 *et seq.*; Catalyst ¶ 2101:145)

New Law. The Tax Cuts and Jobs Act repeals the provision that required that previously excluded Subpart F income withdrawn from a qualified shipping investment be recaptured. (Code Sec. 955 as repealed by Tax Cuts and Jobs Act §14212(a)) *observation:* As a result, a U.S. Shareholder in a CFC that invested its previously excluded Subpart F income in a qualified shipping investment is no longer required to include in income a pro rata share of the previously excluded Subpart F income when the CFC decreases the investment.

☐ **Effective:** Tax years of foreign corporations beginning after Dec. 31, 2017, and tax years of U.S. Shareholders in which or with which those tax years of foreign corporations end. (Tax Cuts and Jobs Act §14212(c))

¶ 2200. Anti-Base Erosion And Profit-Shifting Provisions

¶ 2201. Base erosion minimum tax added on payments to foreign related parties

Code Sec. 59A, as added by Tax Cuts and Jobs Act §14401(a)

Code Sec. 6038A(b), as amended by Tax Cuts and Jobs Act §14401(b)

Code Sec. 26(b)(2), as amended by Tax Cuts and Jobs Act §14401(c)

Code Sec. 882(a), as amended by Tax Cuts and Jobs Act §14401(d)(2)

Code Sec. 6425(c)(1)(A), as amended by Tax Cuts and Jobs Act §14401(d)(3)

Code Sec. 6655, as amended by Tax Cuts and Jobs Act §14401(d)(4)

Generally effective: Base erosion payments paid or accrued in tax years beginning after Dec. 31, 2017

Committee Reports, see ¶ 5124

Under pre-Tax Cuts and Jobs Act law, a multinational corporation resident in the U.S. was subject to U.S. tax on its worldwide income—active foreign earnings were subject to U.S. tax only when they were repatriated to a domestic parent. This system created incentives for multinational companies to shift income away from the U.S. to lower-tax jurisdictions and to defer the repatriation of active foreign source earnings. The Tax Cuts and Jobs Act generally establishes a hybrid territorial system by providing for a participation exemption (i.e., a 100% deduction for the foreign-source portion of dividends received from 10%-owned foreign corporations, see ¶ 1901). Because the deduction for dividends received can eliminate additional domestic tax on foreign profits, corporations with foreign operations may be more likely to use deductible payments to erode the U.S. tax base and shift income to foreign affiliates in lower-tax jurisdictions.

New Law. The Tax Cuts and Jobs Act establishes a base erosion minimum tax to prevent companies from stripping earnings out of the U.S. through payments to foreign affiliates that are deductible for U.S. tax purposes. The tax is structured as an alternative minimum tax that applies when a multinational company reduces its regular U.S. tax liability to less than a specified percentage of its taxable income, after adding back deductible base eroding payments and a

FTC 2d References are to Federal Tax Coordinator 2d
FIN References are to RIA's Analysis of Federal Taxes: Income (print)
USTR References are to United States Tax Reporter: Income
Catalyst References are to Checkpoint Catalyst
PCA References are to Pension Analysis (print and electronic)
PBE References are to Pension & Benefits Explanations
BCA References are to Benefits Analysis (electronic)
BC References are to Benefits Coordinator (print)
EP References are to Estate Planning Analysis (print and electronic)

percentage of tax losses claimed that were carried from another year. The tax applies to deductible payments to foreign affiliates from domestic corporations, as well as on foreign corporations engaged in a U.S. trade or business in computing the tax on their effectively connected income (ECI). (Code Sec. 59A as added by Tax Cuts and Jobs Act §14401(a))

Applicable taxpayers and related parties   The base erosion minimum tax provision applies to corporations, other than RICs, REITs, and S corporations (Code Sec. 59A(e)(1)(A)), that have average annual gross receipts of at least $500,000,000 for the three-tax year period ending with the preceding tax year (Code Sec. 59A(e)(1))(B)) and a "base erosion percentage" of at least 3%(Code Sec. 59A(e)(1)(C)) ("applicable taxpayers") (except that, as discussed below, an increased rate and lower base erosion percentage applies for certain banks and securities dealers). In the case of a foreign corporation engaged in a U.S. trade or business, only gross receipts taken into account in determining effectively connected income (ECI) are counted. (Code Sec. 59A(e)(2)(A)) A foreign taxpayer and a U.S. person that are treated as a single employer under Code Sec. 52(a) are treated as a single person for purposes of determining the base erosion percentage, except that in applying Code Sec. 1563, the exception excluding certain foreign corporations in Code Sec. 1563(b)(2) is disregarded. (Code Sec. 59A(e)(3))·

The gross receipts for any tax year of less than 12 months are annualized by multiplying the short-period gross receipts for the short period by 12, and dividing the result by the number of months in the short period. Gross receipts for any particular year are reduced by returns and allowances of that year, and gross receipts of any predecessors of the taxpayer are considered in applying the three-year test. In determining gross receipts, several of the rules of Code Sec. 448(c)(3) apply, specifically that gross receipts for short tax years are annualized, gross receipts for a tax year are reduced by returns and allowances, and the receipts of a predecessor entity are considered. (Code Sec. 59A(e)(2)(B)) Payments for cost of goods sold (COGS) are not base erosion payments—such payments are reductions to income rather than deductions. (Com Rept, see ¶ 5124).

A "related party" with respect to an applicable taxpayer is any "25% owner" (Code Sec. 59A(g)(1)(A)), any person related to the taxpayer or 25% owner under Code Sec. 267(b) or Code Sec. 707(b)(1) (Code Sec. 59A(g)(1)(B)), and any other person who is related to the taxpayer under Code Sec. 482(Code Sec. 59A(g)(1)(C)). A "25% owner" is a person that owns 25% of the total voting power of all classes of stock of a corporation entitled to vote (Code Sec. 59A(g)(2)(A)) or 25% of the total value of all classes of the corporation's stock (Code Sec. 59A(g)(2)(B)). The constructive ownership rules of Code Sec. 318 apply, with 10% substituted for 50% in Code Sec. 318(a)(2)(C) (attribution from a corporation to a shareholder) (Code Sec. 59A(g)(3)(A)) and with the caveat that Code Sec. 318(a)(3) will not apply to treat a U.S. person as owning stock which is owned by a non-U.S. person (Code Sec. 59A(g)(3)(B)).

A foreign person is defined as in Code Sec. 6038A(c)(3). (Code Sec. 59A(f))

Base erosion minimum tax amount   An applicable taxpayer is required to pay a tax equal to the "base erosion minimum tax amount" for the tax year. (Code Sec. 59A(a)) This amount is the excess of 10% of the taxpayer's "modified taxable income" (5% in tax years beginning in calendar year 2018, (Code Sec. 59A(b)(1)(A))) over its regular tax liability (as defined in Code Sec. 26(b)) reduced (although not below zero) by any excess of the credits allowed against the taxpayer's regular tax liability (Code Sec. 59A(b)(1)(B)(i)) over the sum of (1) the credit allowed under Code Sec. 38 for the tax year properly allocable to the research credit determined under Code Sec. 41(a) Code Sec. 59A(b)(1)(B)(ii)(I) plus (2) the portion of its applicable regular tax liability credits ("the applicable Section 38 credits") not in excess of 80% of the lesser of (a) the applicable Section 38 credits amount or (b) the base erosion minimum tax amount determined without this adjustment (Code Sec. 59A(b)(1)(B)(ii)(I)). Applicable Section 38 credits are (1) the low-income housing credit determined under Code Sec. 42(a) (Code Sec. 59A(b)(4)(A)), (2) the renewable electricity production credit under Code Sec. 45(a) (Code Sec. 59A(b)(4)(B)), and the investment credit determined under Code Sec. 46 to the extent allocable to the energy credit determined under Code Sec. 48 (Code Sec. 59A(b)(4)(C)).

> *observation:* The minimum base erosion tax is intended to apply to companies that significantly reduce their U.S. tax liability with base erosion payments to foreign affiliates. A taxpayer that reduces its tax liability to an amount that is less than 10% of its modified taxable income (generally, taxable income after adding back deductible payments to foreign affiliates) has to pay the alternative tax. Credits are taken into account in computing the taxpayer's regular tax liability, increasing the likelihood that the minimum tax will apply, except that the base erosion tax can be offset by a taxpayer's research credits and 80% of its renewable electricity production credits, low-income housing credits, and investment credits allocable to the energy credit (the applicable Section 38 credits). This means that a taxpayer that would otherwise reduce its tax liability to zero with credits cannot do so, and is instead subject to tax on a minimum of 20% of 10% of modified taxable income (or 2% of modified taxable income). And, the absence of a carryover for excess credits potentially eliminates the 20% of applicable Section 38 credits benefits. This also means that investors will not be able to calculate the value of their credits until they compute their modified taxable income for any particular year. It remains to be seen how the limitation on the ability to claim a portion of the credit will impact the associated industries with respect to existing and new projects, especially when combined with the fact that, as discussed below, the excep-

tion allowing research credits and a portion of the applicable Section 38 credits is eliminated for tax years beginning after December 31, 2025.

illustration: A U.S. parented multinational group (USC) has a regular tax liability for the year of $21,000. USC claims $2,000 in research credits, $1,000 of renewable electricity production credits (an applicable Section 38 credit), and $1,500 of other tax credits.

In the absence of Code Sec. 59A, USC would have a regular tax liability of $16,500 ($21,000 (tax liability) - $4,500 (total credits)). For purposes of the base erosion minimum tax, however, USC increases its regular tax liability by eliminating the benefit of its tax credits, but then adding back the research credit and 80% of the applicable Section 38 credits. USC's tax liability, as adjusted for this purpose, is $19,300 [$21,000 - ($4,500 - ($2,000 + (80% × $1,000)) = $21,000 - $1,700 = $19,300]. That is, USC benefits from a net addback of $2,800.

The base erosion minimum tax amount is the amount by which 10% of the taxpayer's modified taxable income exceed its regular tax liability as adjusted for credits. With an adjusted tax liability of $19,300, USC will owe a base erosion minimum tax amount to the extent its modified taxable income exceeds $193,000. With taxable income of $100,000, USC will have to pay tax if it deducts more than $93,000 in base erosion tax benefits.

observation: As shown in Illustration (1), Code Sec. 59A generally allows up to 80% of a taxpayer's applicable Section 38 credits to offset base erosion minimum tax liability, but the benefit of these credits is eliminated when the base erosion minimum tax amount, unadjusted for the applicable Section 38 credits, is less than 80% of the taxpayer's applicable Section 38 credits. In the example, the taxpayer is subject to tax with modified taxable income of $193,000 because its base erosion minimum tax unadjusted for the applicable Section 38 credits ($19,300 − ($21,000 - ($4500 − $2000)) = $800) is less than its applicable Section 38 credits ($1,000). The taxpayer would be subject to tax so long as its modified taxable income is more than $18,500 (and 10% of its modified taxable income is more than $1,850), i.e., the point at which the base erosion minimum tax amount without the adjustment for the applicable Section 38 credits is zero ($21,000 - ($4,500 - $2,000)) = $18,500).

For tax years beginning after December 31, 2025, the taxpayer's base will be increased from 10% to 12.5% of modified taxable income (Code Sec. 59A(b)(2)(A)) and the taxpayer's regular tax liability will be reduced by the aggregate amount of credits allowed to the taxpayer with no other adjustments (Code Sec. 59A(b)(2)(B)).

In the case of a taxpayer that is a member of an affiliated group (defined in Code Sec. 1504(a)(1)) that includes a bank as defined in Code Sec. 581 (Code Sec. 59A(b)(3)(B)(i)) or a registered securities dealer defined in section 15(a) of the Securities Exchange Act of 1934 (Code Sec. 59A(b)(3)(A)), the rates are 6% instead of 5%, 11% instead of 10%, and 13.5% instead of 12.5% (Code Sec. 59A(b)(3)(B)(ii)).

A corporation's "modified taxable income" for a year is (1) its taxable income, determined without regard to any "base erosion tax benefit" from any "base erosion payment" (Code Sec. 59A(c)(1)(A)) or (2) the "base erosion percentage" of any allowable net operating loss deduction allowed under Code Sec. 172 for the tax year (Code Sec. 59A(c)(1)(B)).

Base erosion payments A "base erosion payment" is any amount paid or accrued by the taxpayer to a foreign related party for which a deduction is allowable. (Code Sec. 59A(d)(1)) This includes the purchase from a foreign related party of property that is subject to an allowance for depreciation or amortization. (Code Sec. 59A(d)(2)) A reinsurance payment (including any premium or other consideration paid or accrued) to a foreign person related party is also a base erosion payment if it creates either a reduction in gross premiums and other consideration under Code Sec. 803(a)(1)(B) or a deduction from gross premiums written on insurance contracts under Code Sec. 832(b)(4). (Code Sec. 59A(d)(3))

While base erosion payments generally do not include amounts that constitute a reduction in a taxpayer's gross receipts (Code Sec. 59A(d)(4)(A)), a payment to a related party that becomes a "surrogate foreign corporation" after Nov. 9, 2017 that results in a reduction of the taxpayer's gross receipts is a base erosion payment (Code Sec. 59A(d)(4)(B)(i)) , as is a payment to a member of the "expanded affiliate group" of the surrogate foreign corporation (Code Sec. 59A(d)(4)(B)(ii)). The term "surrogate foreign corporation" is defined as it is in Code Sec. 7874(a)(2) except that it does not include a corporation treated as a domestic corporation under Code Sec. 7874(b). (Code Sec. 59A(d)(4)(C)(i)) The term "expanded affiliate group" has the meaning given in Code Sec. 7874(c)(1). (Code Sec. 59A(d)(4)(C)(ii))

Two type of otherwise deductible payments are not base erosion payments. First, an amount paid or accrued to a related party for services is not a base erosion payment if it satisfies the requirements for using the services cost method under Code Sec. 482 and Reg §1.482-9 (determined without regard to the requirement that the services do not contribute significantly to fundamental risks of business success or failure) (Code Sec. 59A(d)(5)(A)) (FTC 2d/FIN ¶ G-4201; USTR ¶ 4824.065; Catalyst ¶ 2001:191) and the payment is for total services costs with no markup component (Code Sec. 59A(d)(5)(B)).

⚫*observation:* This add-back is unlikely to be of much practical value. The services cost method is an elective simplified method for valuing low-margin support-type services, and payments for covered services generally include low benchmarked markups without violating transfer pricing or base erosion principles.

The second exception is for "qualified derivative payments" (Code Sec. 59A(h)(1)) when the taxpayer annually marks to market the underlying derivative. Specifically, a "qualified derivative payment" is any payment made by a taxpayer pursuant to a derivative if the taxpayer (1) recognizes gain or loss as if the derivative were sold for fair market value on the last business day of the tax year (Code Sec. 59A(h)(2)(A)(i)), (2) treats any gain or loss as ordinary (Code Sec. 59A(h)(2)(A)(ii)), and (3) treats all items of income, deduction, gain, or loss with respect to a payment pursuant to the derivative as ordinary Code Sec. 59A(h)(2)(A)(iii). This exception is limited strictly to derivative payments and does not apply to payments on other components of a derivative contract. It does not apply to payments that would be treated as base erosion payments if they were not made pursuant to a derivative (including any interest, royalty, or service payment) (Code Sec. 59A(h)(3)(A))and it does not apply if the contract has derivative and nonderivative components and the payment is properly allocable to the non-derivative component (Code Sec. 59A(h)(3)(B)). Qualified derivative payment treatment is only available if the taxpayer includes the information necessary to identify the payments to be so treated and such other information as IRS determines necessary to carry out the exception in the information required to be reported under Code Sec. 6038B(b)(2) with respect to the tax year. (Code Sec. 59A(h)(2)(B))

⚫*observation:* It is likely that the intention here was to reference Code Sec. 6038A(b), which includes the reporting requirements relating to Code Sec. 59A.

A derivative, for these purposes, means any contract (including an option, forward contract, futures contract, short position, swap, or similar contract) in which the value, or payment under it, is determined by reference to one or more of the following: (1) any share of stock in a corporation (Code Sec. 59A(h)(4)(A)(i)), (2) any evidence of indebtedness (Code Sec. 59A(h)(4)(A)(ii)), (3) any commodity which is actively traded (Code Sec. 59A(h)(4)(A)(iii)), (4) any currency (Code Sec. 59A(h)(4)(A)(iv)), or (5) any rate, price, amount, index, formula, or algorithm Code Sec. 59A(h)(4)(A)(v). However, the term "derivative" does not include any of the reference items itself. The term "derivative" also does not include "any insurance, annuity or endowment contract issued by an insurance company to which subchapter L applies (or any foreign corporation which would be subject to subchapter L if it were a domestic corporation). (Code Sec. 59A(h)(4)(C)) Unless regulations provide otherwise, American depository receipts (ADRs) and similar instruments with respect to shares of stock in foreign corporations are treated as shares of stock in foreign corporations.(Code Sec. 59A(h)(4)(B))

A "base erosion tax benefit" is (1) any deduction relating to a base erosion payment (Code Sec. 59A(c)(2)(A)(i)), (2) any depreciation or amortization on property acquired with a base erosion payment (Code Sec. 59A(c)(2)(A)(ii)), (3) any reduction under Code Sec. 803(a)(1)(B) in the gross amount of premiums and other consideration on insurance and annuity contracts for premiums and other consideration arising out of indemnity insurance and any deduction under Code Sec. 832(b)(4)(A) from the amount of gross premiums written on insurance contracts during the tax year for premiums paid for reinsurance (Code Sec. 59A(c)(2)(A)(iii)), and (4) any reduction in gross receipts from a payment to an expatriated entity in computing gross income of the taxpayer for the tax year (Code Sec. 59A(c)(2)(A)(iv)). However, base erosion tax benefits associated with base erosion payments that are subject to tax under Code Sec. 871 or Code Sec. 881, and with respect to which tax has been deducted and withheld under Code Sec. 1441 or Code Sec. 1442, are not taken into account in computing modified taxable income. (Code Sec. 59A(c)(2)(B)(i)) The amount not taken into account in computing modified taxable income is reduced under rules similar to the rules in Code Sec. 163(j)(5)(B) as in effect before December 22, 2017. (Code Sec. 59A(c)(2)(B)(ii)) A reduction in allowable interest deduction as a result of Code Sec. 163(j) (¶ 1003) is allocated first to payments to unrelated parties and then to payments to related parties. (Code Sec. 59A(c)(3))

> *observation:* Payments to related foreign parties that are actually taxed do not have to be added back to modified taxable income. Presumably, a proportionate part of a base erosion payment that is subject to a lower rate of tax under a treaty will be added back to modified taxable income and the portion of the payment treated as not subject to tax will be determined using a ratio equal to the reduction in the rate under the treaty over the full tax rate that would have applied in the absence of the treaty. Deductions for reinsurance payments to a foreign insurance company attributable to U.S. risks that are subject to tax under Code Sec. 4371 are not excluded from the definition of base erosion tax benefits.

A taxpayer's "base erosion percentage" for any tax year is the aggregate amount of base erosion tax benefits for the tax year (Code Sec. 59A(c)(4)(A)(i)) divided by (1) the aggregate deductions allowable to the taxpayer for the tax year, including base erosion payments and depreciation or amortization for property acquired with a base erosion payment (Code Sec. 59A(c)(4)(A)(ii)(I)), plus (2) the base erosion tax benefits relating to reinsurance payments and cost of goods sold payment to surrogate foreign corporations (Code Sec. 59A(c)(4)(A)(ii)(II)). The aggregate amount of deductions allowed to the taxpayer does not take into account deductions under Code Sec. 172, Code Sec. 245A, or Code Sec. 250 (Code Sec. 59A(c)(4)(B)(i)), any deduction for payments for services that satisfy the requirements for using the services cost method under Reg §1.482-9 and qualify for the exception in Code Sec. 59A(d)(5) from treatment as a base erosion payment (Code Sec. 59A(c)(4)(B)(ii)), and any deduction for a qualified derivative payment which is not treated as a base erosion payment (Code Sec. 59A(c)(4)(B)(iii)).

The base erosion percentage required for certain banks and securities dealers to be treated as an applicable taxpayer is reduced to 2%. (Code Sec. 59A(b)(3)(B); Code Sec. 59A(e)(1)(C))

IRS is authorized to prescribe regulations or other guidance as necessary or appropriate, including regulations (1) providing for adjustments to prevent avoidance, including through (a) the use of unrelated persons, conduit transactions, or other intermediaries (Code Sec. 59A(i)(1)(A)), or (b) transactions or arrangements designed (in whole or in part) to characterize payments subject to Code Sec. 59A as not subject to it (Code Sec. 59A(i)(1)(B)(i)), or to substitute payments not subject to Code Sec. 59A for payments subject to it (Code Sec. 59A(i)(1)(B)(ii)). IRS is also authorized to issue regulations implementing the related party rules including regulations to prevent avoidance of the exceptions to the Code Sec. 318 constructive ownership rules under Code Sec. 59A(g)(3). (Code Sec. 59A(i)(2))

Information Reporting Requirements The Tax Cuts and Jobs Act adds reporting requirements related to Code Sec. 59A to Code Sec. 6038A. (Code Sec. 6038A as amended by Tax Cuts and Jobs Act §14401(b)(1)) A corporation that is domestic and 25% foreign owned must report the name, principal place of business, nature of business, and country or countries in which it is organized or resident of each person which is a related party to the reporting corporation (Code Sec. 6038A(b)(1)(A)(i)) that had any transaction with the reporting corporation during its tax year (Code Sec. 6038A(b)(1)(A)(ii)), as well as the manner in which the reporting corporation is related (Code Sec. 6038A(b)(1)(B)) and the transactions between the reporting corporation and each foreign person which is a related party to the reporting corporation (Code Sec. 6038A(b)(1)(C)). A reporting corporation or a foreign corporation subject to Code Sec. 6038C that is an applicable taxpayer also has to report information that IRS determine is necessary to determine the base erosion minimum tax amount, base erosion payments, and base erosion tax benefits for the tax year (Code Sec. 6038(b)(2)(A)) and whatever other information the IRS prescribes to carry out the provisions of Code Sec. 59A (Code Sec. 6038(b)(2)(B)).

The penalties in Code Sec. 6038A(d)(1) and Code Sec. 6038A(d)(2) for a failure by a 25% foreign-owned corporation to furnish information or maintain records on transactions with related parties is increased from $10,000 to $25,000. (Code Sec. 6038A as amended by Tax Cuts and Jobs Act §14401(b)(2))

Code Sec. 26(b)(2) is amended to disallow credits against the base erosion and anti-abuse tax. (Code Sec. 26 as amended by Tax Cuts and Jobs Act §14401(c)) Code Sec. 882(a)(1) is amended to add Code Sec. 59A to the list of provisions taxing foreign persons. (Code Sec. 882(a) as amended by Tax Cuts and Jobs Act §14401(d)(2))Conforming amendments include tax under Code Sec. 59A in Code Sec. 6425(c)(1)(A), which defines income tax liability (Code Sec. 6425(c)(1)(A) as amended by Tax Cuts and Jobs Act §14401(d)(3)), and in Code Sec. 6655(g)(1)(A)(ii), which defines tax generally. (Code Sec. 6655(g)(1)(A) as amended and redesignated by Tax Cuts and Jobs Act §14401(d)(4)(A)). In circumstances where tax is required to be paid in installments, "modified taxable income," as defined in Code Sec. 59A(e)(1), is added as a measure of the required installments in Code Sec. 6655(e)(2)(A)(i) and Code Sec. 6655(e)(2)(B)(i). (Code Sec. 6655(e)(2) as amended and redesignated by Tax Cuts and Jobs Act §14401(d)(4)(B))

☐ **Effective:** This provision applies to base erosion payments paid or accrued in tax years beginning after December 31, 2017. (Tax Cuts and Jobs Act §14401(e))

¶ 2202. Limitations imposed on income shifting through intangible property transfers

Code Sec. 936(h)(3)(B), as amended by Tax Cuts and Jobs Act §14221(a)
Code Sec. 367(d)(2), as amended by Tax Cuts and Jobs Act §14221(b)(1)
Code Sec. 482, as amended by Tax Cuts and Jobs Act §14221(b)(2)
Generally effective: Transfers in tax years beginning after Dec. 31, 2017
Committee Reports, see ¶ 5117

Under Code Sec. 367(d), a U.S. person that transfers intangible property—as defined in Code Sec. 936(h)(3)(B)—to a foreign corporation in a transaction that would otherwise qualify for nonrecognition treatment is generally treated as having sold the intangible property in exchange for payments contingent on the property's productivity, use, or disposition. In these cases, the U.S. transferor includes an amount in income each year over the useful life of the property. The appropriate amounts of the imputed payments is determined using Code Sec. 482 transfer pricing principles, which require that the imputed payments be "commensurate with the income" attributable to the intangible property. Reg §1.482-4(f)(2) (FTC 2d ¶ G-4554; USTR ¶ 4824.04; Catalyst ¶ 2001:145).

Treatment of Code Sec. 936(h)(3)(B) Intangible Property Under Code Sec. 367 Former Code Sec. 936(h)(3)(B) identified several categories of intangible property, none of which specifically included goodwill or going concern value, although there was a catch-all category for "similar items." (FTC 2d/FIN ¶ O-1546)

When Code Sec. 367(d) was enacted, Congress did not view foreign goodwill and going concern value as creating the kind of avoidance issues associated with other kinds of intangible property. In fact, former temporary regulations issued in 1986 exempted outbound transfers of foreign goodwill and going concern value from gain recognition under Code Sec. 367(d). (Reg. § 1.367(d)-1T(b) before removed by TD 9803, 12/15/2016) Foreign goodwill and going concern value was defined in the Code Sec. 367(a) regulations as the residual value of a business operation conducted outside the U.S. after all other tangible and intangible assets were identified and valued. (Reg. § 1.367(a)-1T(d)(5)(iii) before amend by TD 9803, 12/15/2016)

Rather than rely on the exception in the Code Sec. 367(d) regulations, some taxpayers claimed that foreign goodwill and going concern value were not Code Sec. 936(h)(3)(B) intangible property, and thus were wholly outside the scope of Code Sec. 367(d). These taxpayers then relied on the exemption in former Code Sec. 367(a)(3) for transfers of property to a foreign corporation for use in an active trade or business outside the U.S. TD 9803, 12/15/2016. The Tax Cuts and Jobs Act repealed former Code Sec. 367(a)(3) (see ¶ 2203).

Over the years, however, IRS began to reconsider the exception for outbound transfers of foreign goodwill and going concern value. The share of business value attributable to intangibles had generally increased significantly, and other statutory and regulatory changes (such as the enactment of Code Sec. 197, the check-the-box regulations, and the subpart F look-through rule in Code Sec. 954(c)(6)) incentivized valuation strategies that overstated the value of goodwill and going concern value, and, in turn, minimized the inclusion under either Code Sec. 367(a) or Code Sec. 367(d).

In 2016, new regulations eliminated nonrecognition treatment for foreign goodwill and going concern value by both narrowing the former Code Sec. 367(a)(3) foreign trade or business exception and removing the exception under the Code Sec. 367(d) regulations for transfers of foreign goodwill and going concern value. These regulations did not, however, specifically categorize foreign goodwill and going concern value as Code Sec. 936(h)(3)(B) intangible property, which would have subjected all outbound transfers of foreign goodwill and going concern value to Code Sec. 367(d) (and eliminated the incentive to overvalue foreign goodwill and going concern value). As a result, gain on the outbound transfer of foreign goodwill and going concern value became subject either to immediate tax under Code Sec. 367(a) or deferred tax under Code Sec. 367(d) depending, in part, on whether the transferred foreign goodwill and going concern value was considered Code Sec. 936(h)(3)(B) intangible property. A transfer of foreign goodwill and going concern value that was not Code Sec. 936(h)(3)(B) intangible property was subject to immediate tax under Code Sec. 367(a) unless the taxpayer elected to defer the tax under Code Sec. 367(d). On the other hand, when Code Sec. 367(d) applied to a transfer of foreign goodwill and going concern value (either because the transferred foreign goodwill and going concern value was Code Sec. 936(h)(3)(B) intangible property or because the taxpayer elected to treat it as Code Sec. 936(h)(3)(B) intangible property) Code Sec. 482 principles generally required gain recognition over the useful life of the property. (FTC 2d/FIN ¶ F-6500 *et seq.*; USTR ¶ 3674.03; Catalyst ¶ 104:140; Catalyst ¶ 118:140; Catalyst ¶ 122:220; Catalyst ¶ 124:210; Catalyst ¶ 127:140; Catalyst ¶ 129:170)

Treatment of Code Sec. 936(h)(3)(B) Intangible Property Under Code Sec. 482 IRS can allocate income among commonly controlled businesses under Code Sec. 482 to prevent evasion of taxes or to clearly reflect income. The regulations under Code Sec. 482 implement the clear reflection of income principle by subjecting controlled transactions to an "arm's length" standard, which is satisfied if the results of a controlled transaction are "consistent with the results that would have been realized if uncontrolled taxpayers had engaged in the same transaction under the same circumstances (arm's length result)." (FTC 2d/FIN ¶ G-4018; USTR ¶ 4824.01; Catalyst ¶ 2001:102) The arm's length standard is intended to preserve the U.S. tax base by ensuring that tax-payers do not shift income properly attributable to the U.S. to a related company in another taxing jurisdiction through non-arm's length pricing. Recent amendments to the Code Sec. 482 regulations coordinate the application of the arm's-length standard and best method rule of Code Sec. 482 with other Code provisions, including Code Sec. 367(d). In particular, the Code Sec. 482 regulations provide that the combined effect of two or more separate transactions could be considered in the aggregate if the transactions, taken as a whole, are so interrelated that an aggregate analysis results in the most reliable measure of an arm's-length result. Reg §1.482-1T(f)(2)(i)(B) The idea was that viewing related transactions separately for transfer pricing and valuation purposes could fail to account for synergies among the related transactions that should be reflected in the appropriate arm's-length consideration, which could allow a taxpayer to shift value between related parties. TD 9738, 9/17/2015; see Reg §1.482-1T(f)(2)(i)(B). (FTC 2d/FIN ¶ G-4051; Catalyst ¶ 104:146; Catalyst ¶ 118:148; Catalyst ¶ 122:228; Catalyst ¶ 124:219; Catalyst ¶ 129:176; Catalyst ¶ 2001:111)

New Law.

The Tax Cuts and Jobs Act amends the definition of intangible property in Code Sec. 936(h)(3)(B) to include goodwill (foreign and domestic), going concern value, and workforce in place (including its composition and terms and conditions (contractual or otherwise) of its employment). (Code Sec. 936(h)(3)(B)(vi) as amended by Tax Cuts and Jobs Act §14221(a)(2)) The definition of intangible property also includes a residual category of "any similar item, the value or potential value of which is not attributable to tangible property or the services of any individual." (Code Sec. 936(h)(3)(B)(vii)) The requirement that an item "have substantial value independent of the services of any individual" to be treated as "intangible property" under Code

Sec. 936(b)(3)(H) was removed (Tax Cuts and Jobs Act §14221(a)(3)) to make clear that the source or amount of value of intangible property is not relevant to whether property that is one of the specified types of intangible property is within the scope of the provision. (Com Rept, see ¶ 5117)

> **℞ observation:** Transfers of goodwill, going concern value, or workforce in place are, as Code Sec. 936(h)(3)(B) intangible property, subject to the commensurate with income standard under Code Sec. 367(d) and Code Sec. 482. The Tax Court in *Amazon.com Inc. v. Commissioner*, 148 T.C. 8 (2017) had held that the definition of intangible property under Code Sec. 936(h)(3)(B) did not allow the IRS to use a valuation method that includes goodwill or going concern value because they did not qualify as "any similar item" that has substantial value independent of the services of an individual.

The Tax Cuts and Jobs Act grants IRS authority to specify the method to be used to determine the value of intangible property, both with respect to outbound restructurings of U.S. operations under Code Sec. 367(d) and intercompany pricing allocations under Code Sec. 482. For transfers of intangible property, including intangible property transferred with other property or services, aggregate-basis valuation is allowed for purposes of Code Sec. 367(d) if it results in a more reliable valuation than an asset-by-asset valuation. (Code Sec. 367(d)(2)(D)(i) as amended by Tax Cuts and Jobs Act §14221(b)(2)) Alternatively, IRS may value transferred intangible property on the basis of the realistic alternatives to the transfer (Code Sec. 367(d)(2)(D)(ii)), if this achieves a more reliable result than an asset-by-asset approach. (Code Sec. 367(d)(2)(D))This is consistent with the position that additional value that results from the interrelation of intangible assets (e.g., goodwill and going concern value) can be properly attributed to the aggregate underlying intangible assets when it yields a more reliable result, and with Tax Court decisions outside of the Code Sec. 482 context in which collections of multiple, related intangible assets were treated as an aggregate. It is also consistent with rules governing cost-sharing arrangements under the Code Sec. 482 regulations. (Com Rept, see ¶ 5117)

For purposes of the Code Sec. 482 allocations, the IRS is instructed to issue regulations requiring the valuation of transfers of intangible property (including intangible property transferred with other property or services) on an aggregate basis or on the basis of the realistic alternatives to the transfer if it determines that such basis is the most reliable means of valuation. (Code Sec. 482 as amended by Tax Cuts and Jobs Act §14221(b)(1)) The amendment thus codifies the use of the realistic alternative principles to determine valuation with respect to intangible property transactions, which assumes that a taxpayer will only enter into a particular transaction if none of its realistic alternatives is economically preferable to the transaction under consideration. For example, under the regulations, the IRS can determine an arm's-length price by reference to a transaction (such as the owner of intangible property using it to make a product itself) that is different from the transaction that was actually completed (such as the owner of that same intangible property licensing the manufacturing rights and then buying the product from the licensee). (Com Rept, see ¶ 5117)

☐ **Effective:** Transfers in tax years beginning after December 31, 2017. (Tax Cuts and Jobs Act §14221(c)(1))

Nothing in Tax Cuts and Jobs Act §14221(a) is to be construed to create any inference with respect to the application Code Sec. 936(h)(3) or with Treasury's authority to issue regulations applying to tax years beginning before January 1, 2018 . (Tax Cuts and Jobs Act §14221(c)(2))

¶ 2203. Repeal of active trade or business exception under Code Sec. 367

Code Sec. 367(a)(3), as amended by Tax Cuts and Jobs Act §14102(e)(1)
Generally effective: Transfers after Dec. 31, 2017
Committee Reports, see ¶ 5108

If a U.S. person transfers property to a foreign corporation in connection with certain exchanges that would otherwise be tax-free, the foreign corporation is not treated as a corporation for purposes of determining the extent to which gain is recognized on the transfer. Thus, gain is recognized when U.S. persons transfer property to foreign corporations under regular income tax rules. FTC 2d/FIN ¶ F-6000 *et seq.*; USTR ¶ 3674 *et seq.*

Under pre-Tax Cuts and Jobs Act law, this gain recognition rule did not apply to transfers of any eligible property to a foreign corporation for use by the foreign corporation in the active conduct of a trade or business outside of the U.S., provided certain reporting requirements were met (the active trade or business exception). (FTC 2d/FIN ¶ F-6100 *et seq.*; USTR ¶ 3674.02; Catalyst ¶ 118:110; Catalyst ¶ 122:120; Catalyst ¶ 122:130; Catalyst ¶ 124:120; Catalyst ¶ 124:130; Catalyst ¶ 127:110; Catalyst ¶ 127:120; Catalyst ¶ 129:150)

New Law. The Tax Cuts and Jobs Act eliminates the active trade or business exception. (Code Sec. 367(a) as amended by Tax Cuts and Jobs Act §14102(e)(1))

> *observation:* The Code Sec. 367(a)(3)(C) loss recapture provision which was eliminated as part of the removal of the active trade or business exception was essentially replaced by the Code Sec. 91 loss recapture provision, see ¶ 1905.

☐ **Effective:** Transfers after Dec. 31, 2017 (Tax Cuts and Jobs Act §14102(e)(3)).

¶ 2204. Deduction is disallowed for certain related party amounts paid or accrued in hybrid transactions or with hybrid entities

Code Sec. 267A, as added by Tax Cuts and Jobs Act §14222(a)
Generally effective: Tax years beginning after Dec. 31, 2017
Committee Reports, see ¶ 5118

> **observation:** Multinational companies can often take advantage of differences between how the U.S. and other jurisdictions treat certain entities and instruments for tax purposes and lower their overall tax liability on cross-border investments. For example, an entity can be set up that is treated as fiscally transparent for U.S. federal tax purposes but as an entity in the country in which it is resident or subject to tax. Such an entity is referred to as a hybrid entity—an entity that is treated as fiscally transparent for foreign tax purposes but not for U.S. tax purposes is a hybrid entity known as a reverse hybrid. Similarly, an instrument may be treated as debt in one country but not in another, in which case a payment under the instrument may be deductible interest expense in the payor's jurisdiction but as an exempt dividend in the recipient's country.
>
> Taxing authorities, including IRS, have taken the position that arrangements involving hybrids are abusive to the extent that they result in double non-taxation. For example, hybrid entities can be used so that interest on a loan between foreign corporations is disregarded for U.S. tax purposes because the loan and interest payment both take place within a single entity. Similarly, a payment that is treated as deductible interest or royalties in the U.S. may not be includible by the recipient under the laws of the country in which it is resident or subject to tax, for example because the payment is treated as an exempt dividend in that country.

Under pre-Tax Cuts and Jobs Act law, there was no explicit disallowance of a deduction for any disqualified related party amount paid or accrued under a hybrid transaction or by, or to, a hybrid entity.

New Law. The Tax Cuts and Jobs Act prohibits a deduction for any disqualified related party amount (defined below) paid or accrued under a hybrid transaction or by, or to, a hybrid entity. (Code Sec. 267A(a) as added by Tax Cuts and Jobs Act §14222(a))

Disqualified related party amount. A disqualified related party amount is any interest or royalty paid or accrued to a related party to the extent that:

(a) that amount isn't included in the income of the related party under the tax law of the country of which the related party is a resident for tax purposes or is subject to tax, or (Code Sec. 267A(b)(1)(A))

(b) the related party is allowed a deduction for that amount under the tax law of that country. (Code Sec. 267A(b)(1)(B))

A disqualified related party amount doesn't include any payment to the extent the payment is included in the gross income of a U.S. shareholder under Code Sec. 951(a). (Code Sec. 267A(b)(1))

Related party. A related party is a related person as defined in Code Sec. 954(d)(3), except that that section is applied to the person making the payment of the disqualified related party amount in lieu of the controlled foreign corporation otherwise referred to in Code Sec. 954(d)(3). (Code Sec. 267A(b)(2))

> *observation:* Code Sec. 954(d)(3) provides that a person is a related person with respect to a controlled foreign corporation (CFC) if:
>
> . . . that person is an individual, corporation, partnership, trust, or estate which controls, or is controlled by, the CFC, or
>
> . . . that person is a corporation, partnership, trust, or estate which is controlled by the same person or persons which control the CFC. Catalyst ¶ 2102:104; FTC 2d ¶ O-2533; USTR ¶ 9544.02
>
> Thus, for purposes of Code Sec. 267A, a person is a related person with respect to the person making the payment of the disqualified related party amount if:
>
> . . . that person is an individual, corporation, partnership, trust, or estate which controls, or is controlled by, the person making the payment of the disqualified related party amount, or
>
> . . . that person is a corporation, partnership, trust, or estate which is controlled by the same person or persons which control the person making the payment of the disqualified related party amount.

Hybrid transaction. For this purpose, a hybrid transaction is any transaction, series of transactions, agreement, or instrument one or more payments with respect to which are treated as interest or royalties for purposes of Chapter 1 of the Internal Revenue Code (Code Sec. 1 through Code Sec. 1400U-3) and which aren't so treated for purposes the tax law of the foreign country of which the recipient of the payment is resident for tax purposes or is subject to tax. (Code Sec. 267A(c))

> *observation:* Presumably Congress intended the phrase "which aren't so treated for purposes the tax law of the foreign country . . ." to

read "which aren't so treated for purposes *of* the tax law of the foreign country . . ." A technical correction may be required to address this.

Hybrid entity. For this purpose, a hybrid entity is any entity which is either: (Code Sec. 267A(d))

(1) treated as fiscally transparent for purposes of Chapter 1 of the Code but not so treated for purposes of the tax law of the foreign country of which the entity is resident for tax purposes or is subject to tax, or (Code Sec. 267A(d)(1))

(2) treated as fiscally transparent for purposes of that tax law but not so treated for purposes of Chapter 1 of the Code. (Code Sec. 267A(d)(2))

IRS must issue regs or other guidance as may be necessary or appropriate to carry out the purposes of Code Sec. 267A, including regs or other guidance providing for: (Code Sec. 267A(e))

(1) rules for treating certain conduit arrangements which involve a hybrid transaction or a hybrid entity as subject to Code Sec. 267A(a), (Code Sec. 267A(e)(1))

(2) rules for the application of Code Sec. 267A to foreign branches or domestic entities, (Code Sec. 267A(e)(2))

(3) rules for treating certain structured transactions as subject to Code Sec. 267A(a), (Code Sec. 267A(e)(3))

(4) rules for treating a tax preference as an exclusion from income for purposes of applying Code Sec. 267A(b)(1) if that tax preference has the effect of reducing the generally applicable statutory rate by 25% or more, (Code Sec. 267A(e)(4))

(5) rules for treating the entire amount of interest or royalty paid or accrued to a related party as a disqualified related party amount if that amount is subject to a participation exemption system or other system which provides for the exclusion or deduction of a substantial portion of that amount, (Code Sec. 267A(e)(5))

(6) rules for determining the tax residence of a foreign entity if the entity is otherwise considered a resident of more than one country or of no country, (Code Sec. 267A(e)(6))

(7) exceptions from Code Sec. 267A(a) with respect to:

(A) cases in which the disqualified related party amount is taxed under the laws of a foreign country other than the country of which the related party is a resident for tax purposes, and (Code Sec. 267A(e)(7)(A))

(B) other cases which IRS determines do not present a risk of eroding the federal tax base, and (Code Sec. 267A(e)(7)(B))

(8) requirements for recordkeeping and information reporting in addition to any requirements imposed by Code Sec. 6038A. (Code Sec. 267A(e)(8))

IRS must issue regs or other guidance as may be necessary or appropriate to carry out the purposes of the provision for branches (domestic or foreign) and domestic entities (item (2), above), even if these branches or entities do not meet the statutory definition of a hybrid entity.(Com Rept, see ¶ 5118)

☐ **Effective:** Tax years beginning after Dec. 31, 2017. (Tax Cuts and Jobs Act §14222(c))

¶ 2205. Excise tax on stock compensation of insiders in expatriated corporations increased

Code Sec. 4985(a)(1), as amended by Tax Cuts and Jobs Act §13604
Generally effective: Corporations first becoming expatriated corporations after Dec. 22, 2017
Committee Reports, see ¶ 5087

An excise tax is imposed on the value of the specified stock compensation held by disqualified individuals if a corporation expatriates and gain on any stock in the expatriated corporation is recognized by any shareholder in the expatriation transaction. Under pre-Tax Cuts and Jobs Act law, the excise tax was applied at the 15% Code Sec. 1(h)(1)(C) rate to the value of the specified stock compensation (i.e., payments with a value that is based on (or determined by reference to) the value (or change in value) of stock in the corporation) held (directly or indirectly) by or for the benefit of the individual or a member of the individual's family during the twelve-month period beginning six months before the expatriation date. (FTC 2d/FIN ¶ F-5730, ¶ F-5731; USTR ¶ 49,854, ¶ 49,854.01; Catalyst ¶ 120:130; Catalyst ¶ 124:280)

New Law. The Tax Cuts and Jobs Act amends the excise tax so that it is applied at the 20% Code Sec. 1(h)(1)(D) rate to the value of the specified stock compensation held (directly or indirectly) by or for the benefit of the individual or a member of the individual's family during the twelve-month period beginning six months before the expatriation date. (Code Sec. 4985(a)(1) as amended by Tax Cuts and Jobs Act §13604(a))

☐ **Effective:** Corporations first becoming expatriated corporations after Dec. 22, 2017. (Tax Cuts and Jobs Act §13604(b))

¶ 2206. Surrogate foreign corporation shareholders aren't eligible for reduced dividends rate

Code Sec. 1(h)(11)(C)(iii), as amended by Tax Cuts and Jobs Act §14223(a)(3)
Generally effective: Dividends received after Dec. 22, 2017
Committee Reports, see ¶ 5119

Qualified dividend income is taxed at capital gain, rather than ordinary income, rates. Generally, qualified dividend income includes dividends received during the tax year from domestic corporations and qualified foreign corporations. (FTC 2d/FIN ¶ I-5115.1; USTR ¶ 14.085)

Subject to several exceptions, a qualified foreign corporation is any foreign corporation if—

(1) the corporation is incorporated in a U.S. possession; or

(2) the corporation is eligible for benefits of a comprehensive income tax treaty with the U.S. that IRS determines is satisfactory for purposes of the Code's qualified dividend income rules and that includes an exchange-of-information program. (FTC 2d/FIN ¶ I-5115.5 *et seq.*; USTR ¶ 14.085)

Under the corporate expatriation rules (FTC 2d/FIN ¶ F-5700 *et seq.*; USTR ¶ 78,744 *et seq.*), a domestic corporation or partnership (or related U.S. persons) with respect to which a foreign corporation is a surrogate foreign corporation (an expatriated entity) is taxed on its inversion gain (FTC 2d/FIN ¶ F-5724 *et seq.*; USTR ¶ 78,744.03).

A foreign corporation is treated as a surrogate foreign corporation if, under a plan (see below) or series of related transactions:

(1) the entity completes after Mar. 4, 2003, the direct or indirect acquisition of substantially all of the properties held directly or indirectly by a domestic corporation or substantially all of the properties constituting a trade or business of a domestic partnership (a domestic entity acquisition);

(2) after the acquisition at least 60% of the foreign entity (by vote or value) is held:

(a) in the case of an acquisition of a domestic corporation, by former shareholders of the domestic corporation (defined below) by reason of holding stock in the domestic corporation, or

(b) in the case of an acquisition of a domestic partnership, by former partners of the partnership (defined below) by reason of holding a capital or profits interest in the partnership (the ownership percentage), and

(3) after the acquisition, the expanded affiliated group (EAG) (defined below) that includes the foreign entity doesn't have substantial business activities in the foreign country in which or under the laws of which the entity is created or organized when compared to the total business activities of the EAG. (FTC 2d/FIN ¶ F-5701 *et seq.*; USTR ¶ 78,744.01)

An EAG is an affiliated group as defined in Code Sec. 1504(a) but without excluding foreign corporations and substituting "more than 50%" for "at least 80%" each place it appears in Code Sec. 1504(a). A member of the affiliated group is an entity included in the affiliated group. Under the regs, an EAG is, as to a domestic entity acquisition, an affiliated group that includes the foreign acquiring corporation, determined as of the completion date. A member of the EAG is an entity included in the EAG. (FTC 2d/FIN ¶ F-5706; USTR ¶ 78,744.01)

If 80% of the foreign corporation is owned by the shareholders or partners of the domestic corporation or partnership by reason of holding an ownership interest in the domestic corporation or partnership, the foreign corporation is treated as a domestic corporation and not as a surrogate foreign corporation for purposes determining whether a domestic inverted entity is an expatriated entity. (FTC 2d/FIN ¶ F-5701 ; USTR ¶ 78,744.01) (; Catalyst ¶ 107:185; Catalyst ¶ 118:200; Catalyst ¶ 120:120; Catalyst ¶ 122:150; Catalyst ¶ 124:270; Catalyst ¶ 127:190; Catalyst ¶ 129:200; Catalyst ¶ 132:130; Catalyst ¶ 2106:100)

New Law. The reduced rate on dividends is denied to dividends from any corporation that becomes a surrogate foreign corporation after Dec. 22, 2017, other than a foreign corporation that's treated as a domestic corporation under the corporate expatriation rules. (Code Sec. 1(h)(11)(C)(iii) as amended by Tax Cuts and Jobs Act §14223(a)(3))

Thus, any individual shareholder who receives a dividend from a surrogate foreign corporation, other than a foreign corporation that's treated as a domestic corporation, isn't entitled to the lower rates on qualified dividends provided for in Code Sec. 1(h). (Com Rept, see ¶ 5119)

> *illustration (1):* Foreign Corporation acquires substantially all the assets of a domestic corporation after Dec. 22, 2017 in a transaction that results in Foreign Corporation becoming a surrogate foreign corporation not treated as a domestic corporation. Dividends paid by the Foreign Corporation aren't qualified dividends eligible for reduced rates.

> *illustration (2):* The same facts as in *RIA illustration (1)*, except that the transaction occurred on June 10, 2017. As Foreign Corporation became a surrogate foreign corporation before the Tax Cuts and Jobs Act was enacted, it is grandfathered in, and the dividends it pays may be qualified dividends if other requirements are met.

☐ **Effective:** Dividends received after Dec. 22, 2017. (Tax Cuts and Jobs Act §14223(b))

¶ 2300. Other Foreign Provisions

Changes To The Foreign Tax Credit

¶ 2301. Repeal of Code Sec. 902 and other adjustments to the foreign tax credit to account for participation exemption

Code Sec. 902, as repealed by Tax Cuts and Jobs Act §14301(a)
Code Sec. 960, as amended by Tax Cuts and Jobs Act §14301(b)(1)
Code Sec. 78, as amended by Tax Cuts and Jobs Act §14301(c)(1)
Generally effective: Tax years of foreign corporations beginning after Dec. 31, 2017
Committee Reports, see ¶ 5120

Deemed-paid credit. Under pre-Tax Cuts and Jobs Act law, a U.S. corporation that owned at least 10% of the voting stock of a foreign corporation was allowed a deemed-paid credit for foreign income taxes paid by the foreign corporation that the U.S. corporation was treated as having paid when the income on which the foreign tax was paid was distributed to the shareholder as a dividend. The amount of the foreign corporation's foreign taxes deemed paid was the foreign corporation's foreign income taxes multiplied by the ratio of the (1) amount of the dividend (determined without regard to the gross-up for taxes) to (2) the foreign subsidiary's undistributed earnings. (FTC 2d/FIN ¶ O-4800 *et seq.*; USTR ¶ 9024 *et seq.*)

Deemed-paid credit as applicable to U.S. Shareholders of CFCs. A 10% shareholder in a controlled foreign corporation (CFC) (a U.S. Shareholder) is allowed to take a deemed-paid credit for foreign taxes paid by the CFC on the portion of the CFC's earnings that the U.S. Shareholder is required to include in income under Subpart F. No credit is allowed upon a subsequent actual distribution of this previously taxed income (PTI), unless the foreign taxes associated with the income have not yet been deemed paid by the domestic corporation. The amount of the foreign corporation's foreign taxes deemed paid is the foreign income tax multiplied by the ratio of the (1) amount of Subpart F inclusion (without gross-up) to (2) the undistributed earnings. (FTC 2d/FIN ¶ O-4900 *et seq.*; USTR ¶ 9604)

FTC 2d References are to Federal Tax Coordinator 2d
FIN References are to RIA's Analysis of Federal Taxes: Income (print)
USTR References are to United States Tax Reporter: Income
Catalyst References are to Checkpoint Catalyst
PCA References are to Pension Analysis (print and electronic)
PBE References are to Pension & Benefits Explanations
BCA References are to Benefits Analysis (electronic)
BC References are to Benefits Coordinator (print)
EP References are to Estate Planning Analysis (print and electronic)

The deemed paid credit was also available for foreign taxes paid by lower-tier foreign corporations that were members of the domestic corporation's qualified group which included first- through sixth-tier foreign subsidiaries, provided Code Sec. 902(a) and Code Sec. 902(b) ownership requirements were met. (FTC 2d/FIN ¶ O-4800, ¶ O-4804 *et seq.*, ¶ O-4900, ¶ O-4903; USTR ¶ 9024.02 *et seq.*; Catalyst ¶ 113:100; Catalyst ¶ 113:121; Catalyst ¶ 113:135; Catalyst ¶ 113:172; Catalyst ¶ 113:212; Catalyst ¶ 113:216; Catalyst ¶ 406:279; Catalyst ¶ 2101:171; Catalyst ¶ 2106:130; Catalyst ¶ 2106:146; Catalyst ¶ 2110:100; Catalyst ¶ 2110:116; Catalyst ¶ 2110:142; Catalyst ¶ 2110:153; Catalyst ¶ 2110:224)

Under pre-Tax Cuts and Jobs Act law, the foreign income taxes deemed paid by a domestic corporation for any year by reason of a lower-tier CFC's holdings of U.S. property could not exceed the amount of taxes that would have been deemed paid if the amount invested in U.S. property had been distributed through a chain of foreign corporations to the U.S. parent (the limitation on Code Sec. 956 inclusions). (FTC 2d/FIN ¶ O-4900, ¶ O-4904 *et seq.*; USTR ¶ 9604.03)

Gross-up for foreign taxes deemed paid. If a domestic corporation claims a deemed-paid credit for foreign taxes, it must include in income an amount equal to the foreign income taxes deemed paid by it. (FTC 2d/FIN ¶ O-4900, ¶ O-4907; USTR ¶ 784)

New Law. Deemed-paid credit. The Tax Cuts and Jobs Act repeals the deemed-paid credit with respect to dividends received by a domestic corporation that owns 10% or more of the voting stock of a foreign corporation. (Code Sec. 902 as repealed by Tax Cuts and Jobs Act §14301(a))

> **⊘** *observation:* In a tax system under which 100% of dividends received by 10% corporate U.S. shareholders of certain foreign corporations are exempt from U.S. tax (see ¶ 1901), it would not be appropriate to continue to allow credits for taxes deemed paid on those tax-free dividends. Such a tax system would result in a double benefit to the U.S. shareholder by first allowing a dividend to be recognized in income that is not subject to U.S. tax, and by then reducing the U.S. tax liability with a credit for taxes paid on the foreign source income.

Deemed-paid credit as applicable to U.S. Shareholders of CFCs. The Tax Cuts and Jobs Act amends the deemed-paid credit as applicable to U.S. Shareholders of CFCs as follows:

If a domestic corporation takes into income a Subpart F inclusion as to a CFC in which it is a U.S. Shareholder, the domestic corporation is deemed to have paid so much of the foreign corporation's foreign income taxes as are properly attributable to that income. (Code Sec. 960(a) as amended by Tax Cuts and Jobs Act §14301(b)(1))

If any portion of a distribution from a CFC to its corporate U.S. Shareholder is excluded from gross income as previously taxed income under Code Sec. 959(a), the domestic corporation is treated as having paid so much of the foreign corporation's foreign income taxes as (i) are properly attributable to that portion, and (ii) have not been deemed to have been paid by the domestic corporation under Code Sec. 960 for the tax year or any earlier tax year. (Code Sec. 960(b)(1))

The limitation on Code Sec. 956 inclusions is eliminated from Code Sec. 960. (Code Sec. 960)

Distributions made through tiered-CFCs. If Code Sec. 959(b) applies to any portion of a distribution from a CFC to another CFC, that CFC is treated as having paid so much of the other CFC's foreign income taxes as (i) are properly attributable to that portion, and (ii) have not been deemed to have been paid by a domestic corporation under Code Sec. 960 for the tax year or any earlier tax year. (Code Sec. 960(b)(2))

Foreign income taxes are any income, war profits, or excess profits taxes paid or accrued to any foreign country or U.S. possession. (Code Sec. 960(e))

IRS is authorized to publish regulations or other guidance as may be necessary or appropriate to carry out these provisions. (Code Sec. 960(f))

Gross-up for foreign taxes deemed paid. Under Tax Cuts and Jobs Act law, if a domestic corporation chooses to take a foreign tax credit for any tax year, an amount equal to the taxes deemed to be paid by that corporation under Code Sec. 960(a), Code Sec. 960(b) and Code Sec. 960(d) (determined without regard to the phrase "80%" in Code Sec. 960(d)(1), see ¶ 2003) for that tax year are treated for income tax purposes (other than Code Sec. 245 and Code Sec. 245A, see ¶ 1901) as a dividend received by that domestic corporation from the foreign corporation. (Code Sec. 78 as amended by Tax Cuts and Jobs Act §14301(c)(1))

☐ **Effective:** Tax years of foreign corporations beginning after Dec. 31, 2017, and tax years of U.S. Shareholders in which or with which the tax years of foreign corporations end. (Tax Cuts and Jobs Act §14301(d))

¶ 2302. Taxpayers who sustain a pre-2018 overall domestic loss can elect to recharacterize as much as 100% of U.S. source income as foreign source income

Code Sec. 904(g), as amended by Tax Cuts and Jobs Act §14304(a)
Generally effective: Tax years beginning after Dec. 31, 2017 and before Jan. 1, 2028
Committee Reports, see ¶ 5123

The U.S. imposes tax on the worldwide income of its citizens and residents, regardless of whether the income is U.S. or foreign source and regardless of where the economic activities that produced the income occurred. The U.S. provides relief to a taxpayer from the double tax imposed on foreign source income by providing an election to claim a dollar-for-dollar credit against its U.S. tax liability for the amount of its foreign taxes (the "foreign tax credit" (FTC)). FTC 2d/FIN ¶s O-1000 *et seq.*, O-4000 *et seq.*; USTR ¶ 9014

The FTC is limited to ensure that foreign taxes paid at rates higher than the U.S. rate will not reduce the taxpayer's U.S. tax on its U.S. source income. The amount of foreign tax allowed as a credit against a taxpayer's U.S. tax liability for the tax year is limited to the amount of U.S. tax that otherwise would be imposed on the taxpayer's foreign source income (the Code Sec. 904 limitation). FTC 2d/FIN ¶ O-4400 *et seq.*; USTR ¶ 9044

> *observation:* By limiting the credit in this manner, a taxpayer avoids being subject to double taxation on foreign source income, but still pays U.S. tax equal to the U.S. tax rate multiplied by the taxpayer's U.S. source income.

Under pre-Tax Cuts and Jobs Act law, taxpayers who sustained an overall domestic loss (ODL) for any tax year could recharacterize an amount of U.S. source taxable income as foreign source for each succeeding tax year in an amount that was equal to the lesser of—

- the full amount of the loss to the extent not carried back to prior tax years, or
- 50% of the taxpayer's U.S. source taxable income for that succeeding tax year. (FTC 2d/FIN ¶ O-4700, ¶ O-4720, ¶ O-4721; USTR ¶ 9044.01)

> *illustration:* A taxpayer generates a $100 U.S. source loss and earns $100 of foreign source income in Year 1 (Y1), and pays $30 of foreign tax on the $100 of foreign source income. Because the taxpayer has no net taxable income in Y1, no foreign tax credit can be claimed in Y1 for the $30 of foreign taxes.
>
> Under pre-Tax Cuts and Jobs Act law, if the taxpayer earned $100 of U.S. source income and $100 foreign source income in Year 2 (Y2), then $50 of the U.S. source income was recharacterized as foreign source income to reflect the fact that the previous year's $100 U.S. source loss reduced taxpayer's ability to claim a foreign tax credit. The remainder of the overall domestic loss ($50) was available for recapture in later taxable years.

> *observation:* This recharacterization of U.S. source income as foreign source income results in an increase in the taxpayer's foreign tax credit limitation.

An ODL—

• for a *qualified tax year* is the U.S. source loss for that tax year to the extent the loss offsets taxable income from foreign sources for that tax year or for any prior qualified tax year by reason of a carryback; and

• for *any other tax year* is the U.S. source loss for that tax year to the extent that loss offsets taxable income from foreign sources for any prior qualified tax year by reason of a carryback. (FTC 2d/FIN ¶ O-4700, ¶ O-4720, ¶ O-4721; USTR ¶ 9044.01; Catalyst ¶ 2110:180)

New Law. The Tax Cuts and Jobs Act provides that with respect to pre-2018 unused ODLs taken into account under Code Sec. 904(g)(1) for any applicable tax year, a taxpayer may elect to substitute a percentage greater than 50% but not greater than 100% for 50% in Code Sec. 904(g)(1)(B). (Code Sec. 904(g)(5)(A) as amended by Tax Cuts and Jobs Act §14304(a))

Pre-2018 unused ODL is any overall domestic loss which—

• arises in a qualified tax year beginning before Jan. 1, 2018, and

• has not been used under Code Sec. 904(g)(1) for any tax year beginning before Jan. 1, 2018. (Code Sec. 904(g)(5)(B))

An *applicable tax year* is any tax year of the taxpayer beginning after Dec. 31, 2017 and before Jan. 1, 2028. (Code Sec. 904(g)(5)(C))

☐ **Effective:** Tax years beginning after Dec. 31, 2017. (Tax Cuts and Jobs Act §14304(b)), and before Jan. 1, 2028 (Code Sec. 904(g)(5)(C))

> *illustration:* Under the Tax Cuts and Jobs Act, assume the same facts as in the above illustration except Y1 is a pre-2018 tax year, and the Y1 loss otherwise qualifies as a Pre-2018 ODL. In this example in Y2 when the taxpayer earns $100 of U.S. source income and $100 foreign source income, the taxpayer may elect to have as much as $100 of the U.S. source income recharacterized as foreign source income (compared to the $50 amount under pre-Tax Cuts and Jobs Act law).

> *observation:* By increasing the amount of U.S. source income that may be recharacterized as foreign source income, the Tax Cuts and Jobs Act provision makes it possible for taxpayers to ultimately apply more of their ODLs to obtain a larger FTC more quickly.

¶ 2303. Addition of separate foreign tax credit basket for foreign branch income

Code Sec. 904(d)(1), as amended by Tax Cuts and Jobs Act §14302(a)
Code Sec. 904(d)(2)(J), as amended by Tax Cuts and Jobs Act §14302(b)(1)
Generally effective: Tax years beginning after Dec. 31, 2017

Committee Reports, see ¶ 5121

The U.S. taxes U.S. persons on their worldwide income. In order to mitigate the possibility of U.S. persons being taxed on their foreign-sourced income by both the U.S. and the country in which that income was earned, the U.S. provides a credit against U.S. tax liability on a taxpayer's foreign-source income (the foreign tax credit). FTC 2d/FIN ¶ O-4000 *et seq.*; USTR ¶ 9014 The foreign tax credit is limited to the U.S. tax on foreign source income. This ensures that the credit only mitigates double taxation of foreign source income without offsetting U.S. tax on U.S. source income. The foreign tax credit limitation is calculated separately for certain categories (or "baskets") of income. Under pre-Tax Cuts and Jobs Act law, there were two such baskets: income was either passive category income or general category income. (FTC 2d ¶ O-4300; USTR ¶ 9044.01; Catalyst ¶ 118:115; Catalyst ¶ 406:279; Catalyst ¶ 2106:134; Catalyst ¶ 2110:100; Catalyst ¶ 2110:130)

New Law. The Tax Cuts and Jobs Act requires foreign branch income to be allocated to a separate foreign tax credit basket. (Code Sec. 904(d)(1)(B) as amended by Tax Cuts and Jobs Act §14302(a))

Foreign branch income is the business profits of a U.S. person which are attributable to one or more qualified business units (QBUs, as defined in Code Sec. 989(a)) in one or more foreign countries. The amount of business profits attributable to a QBU will be determined under IRS regulations. Foreign branch income does not include passive income. (Code Sec. 904(d)(2)(J) as amended by Tax Cuts and Jobs Act §14302(b)(1))

☐ **Effective:** Tax years beginning after Dec. 31, 2017. (Tax Cuts and Jobs Act §14302(c))

Source Of Income And Expense Allocation

¶ 2304. Treatment of gain or loss of foreign person from sale or exchange of partnership interests

Code Sec. 864(c)(8), as amended by Tax Cuts and Jobs Act §13501(a)
Code Sec. 1446(f), as amended by Tax Cuts and Jobs Act §13501(b)
Generally effective: Sales and exchanges after Nov. 26, 2017.
Committee Reports, see ¶ 5062

Under pre-Tax Cuts and Jobs Act law, the IRS in Rev Rul 91-32 took the position that gain or loss of a foreign partner from a disposition of an interest in a partnership that conducts a trade or business through a fixed place of business or has a permanent establishment in the U.S. is treated as gain or loss effectively connected with the U.S. trade or business or is gain or loss attributable to the permanent establishment. However, the Tax Court, in rejected the IRS position and held that a foreign corporation's gain on the sale of an interest in a partnership that engaged in a U.S. trade or business wasn't U.S. source income and wasn't effectively connected with a U.S. trade or business. (FTC 2d/FIN ¶ O-10600, ¶ O-10610)

New Law. The Tax Cuts and Jobs Act provides that notwithstanding any tax rules, if a nonresident alien individual or foreign corporation owns, directly or indirectly, an interest in a partnership that is engaged in any trade or business in the U.S., gain or loss on the sale or exchange of all (or any portion of) the interest is treated as effectively connected with the conduct of the trade or business to the extent the gain or loss does not exceed the amount described below. (Code Sec. 864(c)(8)(A) as amended by Tax Cuts and Jobs Act §13501(a))

The amount for any partnership interest sold or exchanged subject to these rules is:

(1) (a) gain on the sale or exchange of the partnership interest, to the extent of the portion of the partner's distributive share of the amount of gain that would have been effectively connected with the conduct of a U.S. trade or business if the partnership had sold all of its assets at their fair market value as of the date of the sale or exchange of the interest, and (b) zero, if no gain on the deemed sale would have been effectively connected with the conduct of a U.S. trade or business (Code Sec. 864(c)(8)(B)(i)), and

(2) (a) loss on the sale or exchange of the partnership interest, to the extent of the portion of the partner's distributive share of the loss on the sale that would have been treated as gain that is effectively connected with the conduct of a U.S. trade or business if gain, rather than loss, had been realized, and (b) zero, if no loss on the deemed sale would have been effectively connected with the conduct of a U.S. trade or business. (Code Sec. 864(c)(8)(B)(ii))

For this purpose, a partner's distributive share of gain or loss on the deemed sale is determined in the same manner as the partner's distributive share of the non-separately stated taxable income or loss of such partnership. (Code Sec. 864(c)(8)(B))

If a partnership subject to the above rules holds any U.S. real property interests described in Code Sec. 897(c) (see FTC 2d/FIN ¶ O-10735; USTR ¶ 8974) at the time of the sale or exchange of the partnership interest, the gain or loss treated as effectively connected income is reduced by the amount treated as effectively connected with the conduct of a U.S. trade or business because of the U.S. real property interests. (Code Sec. 864(c)(8)(C))

For this purpose, a sale or exchange includes any sale, exchange or disposition. (Code Sec. 864(c)(8)(D)) IRS is directed to issue regs that it determines appropriate to apply these rules including regs providing that the above rules apply to nonrecognition exchanges under Code Sec. 332 (see FTC 2d/FIN ¶ F-13200; USTR ¶ 3324), Code Sec. 351 (see FTC 2d/FIN ¶ F-1000; USTR

¶ 3514), Code Sec. 354 (see FTC 2d/FIN ¶ F-4000; USTR ¶ 3544), Code Sec. 355 (see FTC 2d/FIN ¶ F-4500; USTR ¶ 3554), Code Sec. 356 (see FTC 2d/FIN ¶ F-4017; USTR ¶ 3564) or Code Sec. 361 (see FTC 2d/FIN ¶ F-4100; USTR ¶ 3614). (Code Sec. 864(c)(8)(E))

Except as described below, if any portion of the gain on any disposition of an interest in a partnership would be treated under the above rules as effectively connected with the conduct of a U.S. trade or business, the transferee must deduct and withhold a tax equal to 10% of the amount realized on the disposition. (Code Sec. 1446(f)(1) as amended by Tax Cuts and Jobs Act §13501(b))

This guidance may, for example, provide that if an interest in a publicly traded partnership is sold by a foreign partner through a broker, the broker may deduct and withhold the 10% tax on behalf of the transferee. (Com Rept, see ¶ 5062)

However, no withholding is required if the transferor furnishes its affidavit to the transferee stating, under penalty of perjury, the transferor's U.S. taxpayer identification number and that the transferor is not a foreign person. (Code Sec. 1446(f)(2)(A)) This exemption doesn't apply for a disposition if:

- the transferee has actual knowledge that the affidavit is false, or the transferee receives a notice (as described in Code Sec. 1445(d), see FTC 2d ¶ O-13014; USTR ¶ 15,454.01) from a transferor's agent or transferee's agent that the affidavit or statement is false (Code Sec. 1446(f)(2)(B)(i)), or

- IRS by regs requires the transferee to furnish a copy of the affidavit or statement to IRS and the transferee fails to furnish a copy of the affidavit or statement to IRS at the time and in the manner required by the regs. (Code Sec. 1446(f)(2)(B)(ii))

The Code Sec. 1445(d) rules that apply to dispositions of a U.S. real property interest shall similarly apply to a transferor's agent or transferee's agent with regard to any affidavit described above. (Code Sec. 1446(f)(2)(C)) Terms used in these rules that are also used in Code Sec. 1445 will have the same meaning as when used in Code Sec. 1445. (Code Sec. 1446(f)(5))

At the request of the transferor or transferee, IRS may prescribe a reduced amount to be withheld if IRS determines that the reduced amount will not jeopardize the collection of the tax imposed on the gain treated as effectively connected with the conduct of a trade or business in the U.S. under the above rules. (Code Sec. 1446(f)(3))

If a transferee fails to withhold any amount that has to be withheld under the above rules, the partnership must deduct and withhold from distributions to the transferee a tax in an amount equal to the amount the transferee failed to withhold, plus interest. (Code Sec. 1446(f)(4))

IRS is directed to issue regs that may be necessary to carry out the purposes of the withholding rules, including regs providing for exceptions from the with-holding rules. (Code Sec. 1446(f)(6))

☐ **Effective:** Sales, exchanges, and dispositions after Nov. 26, 2017. (Tax Cuts and Jobs Act §13501(c)(1)) However, the withholding requirements apply to sales, exchanges or dispositions after Dec. 31, 2017. (Tax Cuts and Jobs Act §13501(c)(2))

¶ 2305. Source of income from sales of inventory determined solely on basis of production activities

Code Sec. 863(b), as amended by Tax Cuts and Jobs Act §14303(a)
Generally effective: Tax years beginning after Dec. 31, 2017
Committee Reports, see ¶ 5122

Income from the sale of personal property is usually sourced to the seller's residence. However, this rule doesn't apply to income from the sale of inventory. FTC 2d/FIN ¶s O-10962, O-10948, O-10957; USTR ¶ 8654

Under pre-Tax Cuts and Jobs Act law, gains, profits, and income from the sale or exchange of inventory property produced (in whole or in part) by the taxpayer within in the U.S. and sold or exchanged without the U.S., or vice versa, was sourced partly to the place of production and partly to the place of sale pursuant to apportionment methods specified in the regs. (FTC 2d/FIN ¶ O-10900, ¶ O-10962 et seq.; USTR ¶ 8634.02; Catalyst ¶ 501:182)

New Law.

Under the Tax Cuts and Jobs Act, in determining source of income, gains, profits, and income from the sale or exchange of inventory property that is pro-duced (in whole or in part) within the U.S. and sold or exchanged without the U.S. (or vice versa) are allocated and apportioned between sources within and without the U.S. solely on the basis of the production activities with respect to the property. (Code Sec. 863(b) as amended by Tax Cuts and Jobs Act §14303(a))

For example, income derived from the sale of inventory property to a foreign jurisdiction is sourced wholly within the U.S. if the property was produced en-tirely in the U.S., even if title passage occurred elsewhere. Likewise, income derived from inventory property sold in the U.S., but produced entirely in an-other country, is sourced in that country even if title passage occurs in the U.S. If the inventory property is produced partly in, and partly outside, the U.S., however, the income derived from its sale is sourced partly in the U.S. (Com Rept, see ¶ 5122)

☐ **Effective:** Tax years beginning after Dec. 31, 2017. (Tax Cuts and Jobs Act §14303(b))

¶ 2306. Fair market value method of interest expense allocation or apportionment repealed after 2017

Code Sec. 864(e)(2), as amended by Tax Cuts and Jobs Act §14502(a)
Generally effective: Tax years beginning after Dec. 31, 2017
Committee Reports, see ¶ 5126

Prior Law. It is necessary to determine both income from U.S. sources and income from foreign sources for a number of different tax purposes. In doing so, it is necessary to either allocate or apportion various expenses including interest expense between income from U.S. sources and income from foreign sources. Under pre-Tax Cuts and Jobs Act law, with the exception of qualified nonrecourse indebtedness, allocations and apportionments of interest expense had to be allocated or apportioned on the basis of assets rather than gross income. The regs allowed taxpayers to determine the value of their assets either on the basis of the tax book value or the fair market value of their assets. The tax book value was generally the asset's adjusted basis for U.S. tax purposes. Under the fair market method, a taxpayer had to establish the fair market value of its assets to the satisfaction of IRS. Once a taxpayer used the fair market value method for purposes of asset apportionment, the taxpayer had to continue to use that method unless expressly authorized to change methods by IRS. (FTC 2d/FIN ¶ O-11100, ¶ O-11108, ¶ O-11119).

New Law. Under the Tax Cuts and Jobs Act, allocations and apportionments of interest expense must be determined using the adjusted bases of the assets rather than the fair market value of the assets or gross income. (Code Sec. 864(e)(2) as amended by Tax Cuts and Jobs Act §14502(a))

> *observation:* Under the Tax Cuts and Jobs Act, taxpayers may expense 100% of the cost of qualified property (¶ 1203) and the small business expensing limitation under Code Sec. 179 has been increased to $1,000,000 (¶ 1101). The effect of these changes will tend to sharply reduce the adjusted basis of U.S. assets. Thus, the U.S. assets will often have a fair market value that is greater than their tax book value. The repeal of the fair market value alternative, will, therefore, tend to reduce the amount of interest allocated to U.S. source income.

☐ **Effective:** Tax years beginning after Dec. 31, 2017. (Tax Cuts and Jobs Act §14502(b))

¶ 2400. Insurance

Life Insurance Companies

¶ 2401. Definition of "company's share" and "policyholder's share" amended for determining insurance company dividends received deduction and reserves

Code Sec. 812, as amended by Tax Cuts and Jobs Act §13518(a)
Generally effective: Tax years beginning after Dec. 31, 2017
Committee Reports, see ¶ 5073

A corporate shareholder is entitled to a deduction for dividends received from a domestic corporation subject to income tax under Chapter 1 of the Code.

The dividends-received deductions for dividends from domestic corporations or from certain foreign corporations are allowed to a life insurance company for purposes of (1) the 100% dividends-received deduction, and (2) the life insurance company's share of the dividends received (other than 100% dividends). FTC 2d ¶ E-4821; USTR ¶ 8124

Under pre-Tax Cuts and Jobs Act law, the rules for allocating items of investment yield between the company and the policyholders provided that the policyholder's share of any item was 100% of the item less the company's share. Under Code Sec. 812(a)(1), the company's share was the percentage obtained by dividing the company's share of net investment income by total net investment income. FTC 2d ¶ E-4824; USTR ¶ 8054

Under pre-Tax Cuts and Jobs Act law, Code Sec. 812(c) defined "net investment income" as 90% of gross investment income or, for gross investment income attributable to assets held in segregated asset accounts under variable contracts, 95% of gross investment income. FTC 2d ¶ E-4825; USTR ¶ 8124

Under pre-Tax Cuts and Jobs Act law, Code Sec. 812(d) defined "gross investment income" as the sum of the following: (1) interest, including tax-exempt interest, (2) dividends, (3) rent, (4) royalties, (5) income from a lease, mortgage or other instrument or agreement, (6) income from altering or terminating such an instrument or agreement, (7) the increase for any tax year in the policy cash values of life insurance policies and annuity and endowment

---

FTC 2d References are to Federal Tax Coordinator 2d
FIN References are to RIA's Analysis of Federal Taxes: Income (print)
USTR References are to United States Tax Reporter
Catalyst References are to Checkpoint Catalyst
PCA References are to Pension Analysis (print and electronic)
PBE References are to Pension & Benefits Explanations
BCA References are to Benefits Analysis (electronic)
BC References are to Benefits Coordinator (print)
EP References are to Estate Planning Analysis (print and electronic)

contracts, (8) the excess of net short-term capital gain over net long-term capital loss, and (9) certain noninsurance trade or business income. FTC 2d ¶ E-4826; USTR ¶ 8124

Under pre-Tax Cuts and Jobs Act law, in determining life insurance company reserves under Code Sec. 807, there was a decrease in reserves if the closing balance of reserve items, reduced by: (1) the amount of policyholders' allocated share of tax-exempt interest (2) the amount of the policyholders' share of the increase for the tax year in policy cash values of life insurance policies and annuity and endowment contracts to which Code Sec. 264(f) applied, and (3) certain deductions that applied only to mutual life insurance companies, and only for tax years beginning in 2004, was less than the opening balance of the reserve items for the tax year. FTC 2d ¶ E-4954; USTR ¶ 8074

New Law. The Tax Cuts and Jobs Act rewrites Code Sec. 812 to provide only two definitions. First, for purposes of Code Sec. 805(a)(4), the term "company's share" means—for any tax year beginning after Dec. 31, 2017—70%. (Code Sec. 812(a) as amended by Tax Cuts and Jobs Act §13518(a))

> *observation:* Thus, the "company's share," rather than varying based on the percentage determined by dividing an insurance company's share of net investment income by total net investment income, is now a fixed percentage—70%.

Second, for purposes of Code Sec. 807, the term "policyholder's share" means—for any tax year beginning after Dec. 31, 2017—30%. (Code Sec. 812(b) as amended by Tax Cuts and Jobs Act §13518(a))

> *observation:* Thus, the "policyholder's share," rather than varying based on the insurance company's share, is a fixed percentage—30%.

> *observation:* As a result of the re-write of Code Sec. 812, the remainder of Code Sec. 812, before amendment by the Tax Cuts and Jobs Act (former Code Sec. 812(b) through former Code Sec. 812(f)), is removed.

☐ **Effective:** Tax years beginning after Dec. 31, 2017. (Tax Cuts and Jobs Act §13518(c))

¶ 2402. Operations loss deduction for life insurance companies repealed

Code Sec. 381(d), as amended by Tax Cuts and Jobs Act §13511(b)(3)
Code Sec. 805(a)(4)(B)(ii), as amended by Tax Cuts and Jobs Act §13511(b)(4)
Code Sec. 805(a)(5), as amended by Tax Cuts and Jobs Act §13511(b)(5)
Code Sec. 805(b)(4), as amended by Tax Cuts and Jobs Act §13511(a)

Code Sec. 810, as repealed by Tax Cuts and Jobs Act §13511(b)(1)
Code Sec. 844, as repealed by Tax Cuts and Jobs Act §13511(b)(2)
Code Sec. 953(b)(1)(B), as amended by Tax Cuts and Jobs Act §13511(b)(7)
Generally effective: For losses arising in tax years beginning after Dec. 31, 2017
Committee Reports, see ¶ 5066

Under pre-Tax Cuts and Jobs Act law, life insurance companies were not allowed to take a deduction for net operating losses under Code Sec. 172, the general provision allowing deductions for net operating losses (NOLs). (FTC 2d ¶ E-4807)

Instead, these insurance companies could deduct their losses from operations ("operations loss deductions") under Code Sec. 810. The operations loss deduction was the excess of the life insurance company deductions for any tax year over the life insurance company gross income for that year. (FTC 2d ¶ E-4831; USTR ¶ 8104; Catalyst ¶ 135:310)

In general, operational losses could have been carried back three years and carried forward 15 years. A new life insurance company was allowed to carry forward losses for 18 years. (FTC 2d ¶ E-4831; USTR ¶ 8104)

New Law. The Tax Cuts and Jobs Act repeals the operations loss deduction for life insurance companies. (Code Sec. 810 as repealed by Tax Cuts and Jobs Act §13511(b)(1))

The Act also removes the prohibition on life insurance companies deducting their NOLs under Code Sec. 172. (Code Sec. 805(b)(4) as amended by Tax Cuts and Jobs Act §13511(a)) Further, the Act repeals the special loss carryover rules for these insurers. (Code Sec. 844 as repealed by Tax Cuts and Jobs Act §13511(b)(2))

According to Congress, this change puts losses of life insurance companies on the same footing as losses of property and casualty insurance companies, and of other corporations. Thus, the Act provides that: (a) these insurers' NOL deduction will be limited to 90% of taxable income (determined without regard to the deduction), (b) provides that carryovers to other years are adjusted to take account of this limit and that the losses may be carried forward indefinitely with interest, and (d) repeals the three-year carryback. (Com Rept, see ¶ 5066)

The Tax Cuts and Jobs Act also makes the following conforming changes to the Code:

Code Sec. 381(d) is repealed to eliminate a reference to repealed Code Sec. 810. (Code Sec. 381(d) as amended by Tax Cuts and Jobs Act §13511(b)(3))

Code Sec. 805(a)(4)(B)(ii) is amended to replace a reference to the repealed Code Sec. 810 operating loss deduction with the phrase "the deduction allowed under section 172.' (Code Sec. 805(a)(4)(B)(ii) as amended by Tax Cuts and Jobs Act §13511(b)(4))

Code Sec. 805(a) is further amended to eliminate paragraph (5), which referenced the repealed Code Sec. 810 operating loss deduction. (Code Sec. 805(a)(5) as amended by Tax Cuts and Jobs Act §13511(b)(5)).

Code Sec. 953(b)(1)(B), regarding insurance income, is amended to replace a reference to repealed Code Sec. 805(a)(5) with a reference to Code Sec. 172. (Code Sec. 953(b)(1)(B) as amended by Tax Cuts and Jobs Act §13511(b)(6))

☐ **Effective:** For losses arising in tax years beginning after Dec. 31, 2017. (Tax Cuts and Jobs Act §13511(c))

¶ 2403. Small life insurance company deduction repealed

Code Sec. 806, as repealed by Tax Cuts and Jobs Act §13512(a)
Code Sec. 453B(e)(3), as amended by Tax Cuts and Jobs Act §13512(b)(1)
Generally effective: Tax years beginning after Dec. 31, 2017
Committee Reports, see ¶ 5067

Under pre-Tax Cuts and Jobs Act law, small life insurance companies were entitled to a small life insurance company deduction. The amount of the deduction was 60% of tentative life insurance company taxable income (LICTI) up to a maximum of $3 million. The deduction was reduced, but not below zero, by 15% of the amount of tentative LICTI that exceeded $3 million. FTC 2d ¶ E-4838; USTR ¶ 8064

The small life insurance company deduction was only available to life insurance companies with assets of less than $500 million (FTC 2d ¶ E-4800, ¶ E-4838, ¶ E-4841; USTR ¶ 8064; Catalyst ¶ 2104:110; Catalyst ¶ 2104:130)

For purposes of the deduction, the amount of the tentative LICTI for any tax year was determined without regard to any items attributable to noninsurance businesses. And the term "noninsurance business" meant any activity which was not an insurance business.

Further, for purposes of determining which activities were "noninsurance business," any activity that was not an insurance business was nonetheless treated as an insurance business if the business—

(1) was of a type traditionally carried on by life insurance companies for investment purposes, but only if the carrying on of this activity (other than in the case of real estate) did not constitute the active conduct of a trade or business, or

(2) involved the performance of administrative services in connection with plans providing life insurance, pension, or accident and health benefits. (FTC 2d ¶ E-4841, ¶ E-4842)

In addition, under Code Sec. 453B, a special rule applied to a transfer of an installment obligation by any person other than a life insurance company, to a life insurance company or to a partnership of which a life insurance company was a partner. In either case, none of the income tax provisions providing for nonrecognition of gain applied to any gain resulting from the transfer of the installment obligation. (FTC 2d ¶ G-6450, ¶ G-6498; USTR ¶ 453B4)

The rule for transfers of installment obligations to insurance companies did not apply to any transfer, or deemed transfer, of an installment obligation if the life insurance company elected to determine its LICTI:

(a) by returning the income on the installment obligation under the installment method, and

(b) as if the income were an item attributable to a noninsurance business (as defined in items (1) and (2), above). (FTC 2d ¶ G-6501; USTR ¶ 453B4)

> ⓡ *observation:* Under pre-Tax Cuts and Jobs Act law, the term "noninsurance business" was defined in the then existing Code Sec. 806(b)(3).

New Law. The Tax Cuts and Jobs Act eliminates the small life insurance company deduction by repealing Code Sec. 806. (Code Sec. 806 as repealed by Tax Cuts and Jobs Act §13512(a))

> ⓡ *observation:* The small life insurance company deduction may have served as a transition rule effectively providing a corporate tax rate reduction to small life insurers in connection with 1984 changes to the rules governing life insurance company taxation. However, in light of the reduction of the corporate income tax rate to 21%, Congress may have felt that relief was no longer necessary.

The Tax Cuts and Jobs Act makes a conforming change to Code Sec. 453B(e)(2)(B) by removing a reference to repealed Code Sec. 806, and by adding a new paragraph defining "noninsurance business." (Code Sec. 453B(e) as amended by Tax Cuts and Jobs Act §13512(b)(1))

Thus, for purposes of determining LICTI, the Act provides that the term "noninsurance business" means any activity that is not an insurance business. In defining "noninsurance business," the Act provides that any activity that is not an insurance business must be treated as an insurance business if the activity:

(i) is of a type traditionally carried on by life insurance companies for investment purposes, but only if the carrying on of this activity (other than in the case of real estate) does not constitute the active conduct of a trade or business, or

(ii) involves the performance of administrative services in connection with plans providing life insurance, pension, or accident and health benefits. (Code Sec. 453B(e)(3) as amended by Tax Cuts and Jobs Act §13512(b)(1)(B))

> **⊘** *observation:* In effect, the Tax Cuts and Jobs Act transfers the definition of "noninsurance business" from former Code Sec. 806(b)(3), verbatim, to Code Sec. 453B(e)(3),

☐ **Effective:** Tax years beginning after Dec. 31, 2017. (Tax Cuts and Jobs Act §13512(c))

¶ 2404. Amortization period for insurance companies' capitalized policy acquisition expenses increased to 15 years from 10 years

Code Sec. 848(a)(2), as amended by Tax Cuts and Jobs Act §13519(a)(1)
Code Sec. 848(b)(1), as amended by Tax Cuts and Jobs Act §13519(b)
Code Sec. 848(c)(1), as amended by Tax Cuts and Jobs Act §13519(a)(2)
Code Sec. 848(c)(2), as amended by Tax Cuts and Jobs Act §13519(a)(3)
Code Sec. 848(c)(3), as amended by Tax Cuts and Jobs Act §13519(a)(4)
Generally effective: Net premiums for tax years beginning after Dec. 31, 2017
Committee Reports, see ¶ 5074

The policy acquisition expenses incurred in any tax year by a property and casualty insurance company for specified insurance contracts are not currently deductible in that year. Instead, under pre-Tax Cuts and Jobs Act law, the expenses had to be capitalized and amortized on a straight-line basis over a period of 120 months (unless a shorter period applied) beginning with the first month in the second half of the tax year in which the expenses were incurred. FTC 2d ¶ E-5609; USTR ¶ 8484(; Catalyst ¶ 404:182)

Under a special rule, an insurance company had a shorter amortization period of 60 months, rather than the generally applicable 120-month period, to amortize its first $5 million of policy acquisition expenses for any tax year. The availability of the 60-month period was phased out ratably on a dollar-for-dollar basis as the company's amortizable policy acquisition expenses increase from $10 million to $15 million. Thus, if a company's amortizable expenses for the tax year are $11 million, only $4 million could be amortized over the shorter period. FTC 2d ¶ E-5103; USTR ¶ 8484

For any tax year, the specified policy acquisition expenses that an insurance company had to amortize was the sum of the percentages listed below of the net premiums on the three categories of specified insurance contracts. However, the amount of specified policy acquisition expenses for a tax year may not exceed the amount of the insurance company's general deductions for that tax year.

Under pre-Tax Cuts and Jobs Act law, the percentages for the specified contract categories were:

(1) annuity contracts—1.75% of net premiums;

(2) group life insurance contracts—2.05% of net premiums; and

(3) other specified insurance contracts—7.70% of net premiums. FTC 2d ¶ E-5110; USTR ¶ 8484

New Law. The Tax Cuts and Jobs Act increases the amortization period for policy acquisition costs to 180 months from 120 months. (Code Sec. 848(a)(2) as amended by Tax Cuts and Jobs Act §13519(a)); (Code Sec. 848(b)(1) as amended by Tax Cuts and Jobs Act §13519(a))

> *observation:* Thus—except for the $5 million in policy acquisition expenses subject to 5-year (60-month) amortization—policy acquisition expenses must be amortized over 15 years (180 months) instead of over 10 years (120 months).

> *observation:* The extension of the policy acquisition cost amortization period to 15 years will increase insurance company taxable income because a smaller amortization amount will be determined for each tax year.

The Tax Cuts and Jobs Act also increases the percentages of the net premiums that make up the policy acquisition expenses that must be amortized, as follows:

(i) annuity contracts—2.09% of net premiums, up from 1.75%; (Code Sec. 848(c)(1) as amended by Tax Cuts and Jobs Act §13519(a)(2));

(ii) group life insurance contracts—2.45% of net premiums, up from 2.05%; (Code Sec. 848(c)(2) as amended by Tax Cuts and Jobs Act §13519(a)(3))and

(iii) other specified insurance contracts—9.2% of net premiums, up from 7.7%. (Code Sec. 848(c)(3) as amended by Tax Cuts and Jobs Act §13519(a)(4))

> *observation:* Tax Cuts and Jobs Act §13519(a)(2) through Tax Cuts and Jobs Act §13519(a)(4), discussed in items (i) through (iii), above, refer to Code Sec. 848(c)(1) through Code Sec. 848(c)(3), respectively. However, as the premium percentages referred to are in Code Sec. 848(c)(1)(A) through Code Sec. 848(c)(1)(C), and as there is no Code Sec. 848(c)(3), it appears that Congress intended to amend Code Sec. 848(c)(1)(A) through Code Sec. 848(c)(1)(C). A technical correction may be required to address this discrepancy.

☐ **Effective:** Net premiums for tax years beginning after Dec. 31, 2017. (Tax Cuts and Jobs Act §13519(c)(1))

Transition rule. The Tax Cuts and Jobs Act provides that specified policy acquisition expenses that were first required to be capitalized in a tax year beginning before Jan. 1, 2018, will continue to be allowed as a deduction ratably over the 120-month period beginning with the first month in the second half of that tax year. (Tax Cuts and Jobs Act §13519(c)(2))

> *observation:* Thus, the changes made to the amortization period for specified policy acquisition expenses by the Tax Cuts and Jobs Act do not apply to these expenses if they were required to be capitalized in a pre-Jan. 1, 2018 tax year.

¶ 2405. Repeal of ten-year spread for life insurance companies' reserve changes

Code Sec. 807(f)(1), as amended and redesignated by Tax Cuts and Jobs Act §13513(a)
Generally effective: Tax years after Dec. 31, 2017
Committee Reports, see ¶ 5068

Under pre-Tax Cuts and Jobs Act law, if a life insurance company's basis for determining reserve items changes during the course of a tax year, and that basis affects the reserves for contracts issued in an earlier year, then the amount of reserve change could have been taken into account over a ten-year period.

If the change was an increase, under the so-called the ten-year spread rule, one-tenth of the total increase was deducted from life insurance company taxable income as an increase in reserves each year for ten years, starting in the year of the change. And if the change was a decrease, one-tenth of the total decrease was added to gross income as a decrease in reserves each year for ten years, starting in the year of the change. (FTC 2d/FIN ¶ E-4950, ¶ E-4982; USTR ¶ 8074; Catalyst ¶ 135:312)

New Law. Under the Tax Cuts and Jobs Act, the ten-year spread rule is repealed. Instead, reserve changes are to be taken into account under Code Sec. 481's general rule for making tax accounting method changes as adjustments attributable to changes initiated by the taxpayer with IRS consent. (Code Sec. 807(f)(1) as amended by Tax Cuts and Jobs Act §13513(a))

Thus, income or loss resulting from a change in method of computing life insurance company reserves is taken into account consistent with IRS procedures, generally ratably over a four-year period, instead of over a ten-year period. (Com Rept, see ¶ 5068)

☐ **Effective:** Tax years beginning after Dec. 31, 2017. (Tax Cuts and Jobs Act §13513(b))

¶ 2406. Rules on computation of life insurance tax reserves amended

Code Sec. 807(c), as amended by Tax Cuts and Jobs Act §13517(a)(1)
Code Sec. 807(d), as amended by Tax Cuts and Jobs Act §13517(a)(2)
Code Sec. 807(e), as amended by Tax Cuts and Jobs Act §13517(a)(3)
Code Sec. 7702, as amended by Tax Cuts and Jobs Act §13517(a)(4)
Generally effective: Tax years beginning after Dec. 31, 2017
Committee Reports, see ¶ 5072

Under pre-Tax Cuts and Jobs Act law, for purposes of the rules relating to life insurance company reserves, the discounted amounts needed to satisfy insurance claims or annuity contracts that weren't life, accident or health contingencies were calculated by using the highest rate of interest of (1) the applicable federal interest rate, (2) the prevailing state assumed interest rate, or (3) the rate the company assumed when it issued the contract. The interest rate was determined at the time the contracts first did not involve life, accident, or health contingencies. (FTC 2d/FIN ¶ E-4950, ¶ E-4953; USTR ¶ 8074)

Under pre-Tax Cuts and Jobs Act law, the amount of life insurance reserves for any contract was the greater of (a) the net surrender value of the contract, or (b) the federally prescribed reserve. The amount of the federally prescribed reserve was computed actuarially by using: (1) the tax reserve method applicable to the particular type of contract; (2) the greater of the applicable federal interest rate or the prevailing state assumed interest rate; and (3) the prevailing commissioners' standard tables for mortality or morbidity. In addition, among other things, the definition of the applicable tax reserve method made reference to the reserve method covering a contract as of the date of the contract's issuance, and there was a special rule providing that the issue date for group contracts was the date the master plan was issued. (FTC 2d/FIN ¶ E-4956, ¶ E-4958, ¶ E-4959; USTR ¶ 8074)

Under special rules for the computation of the reserve for supplemental benefits, the reserve was the same as that used on the National Association of Insurance Commissioners (NAIC) approved annual statement, i.e., the statutory reserve, except as provided otherwise by regulations. (FTC 2d/FIN ¶ E-4973; USTR ¶ 8074)

The reserve for a qualified substandard risk was computed as though the risk is contained in a separate contract. (FTC 2d/FIN ¶ E-4975; USTR ¶ 8074)

Mortality tables for computing guideline single premium under life insurance rules. Under pre-Tax Cuts and Jobs Act law, for purposes of the life insurance contract rules, the "guideline single premium" that is required to fund future benefits under the contract was actuarially computed based on, among other things, mortality charges that, under regulations, were reasonable and that, unless otherwise permitted, did not exceed the mortality charges specified in the prevailing commissioners' standard tables used in computing the issuing company's statutory reserves as of the time the contract was issued. (FTC 2d/FIN ¶ J-4800, ¶ J-4812; USTR ¶ 77,024.05; Catalyst ¶ 2104:131)

New Law. Under the Tax Cuts and Jobs Act, the appropriate rate of interest to be used for purposes of the rules relating to life insurance company reserves is the highest rate or rates permitted to be used to discount the obligations by the NAIC as of the date the reserve is determined. (Code Sec. 807(c) as amended by Tax Cuts and Jobs Act §13517(a)(1))

In addition, under the Tax Cuts and Jobs Act, the amount of life reserves for a contract—other than a variable contract—is the greater of (a) the net surrender value of the contract, or (b) 92.81% of the federally prescribed reserve. (Code Sec. 807(d)(1)(A) as amended by Tax Cuts and Jobs Act §13517(a)(2)(C))

For a variable contract, the amount of the life insurance reserves for a variable contract is equal to the sum of:

(i) the greater of:

(I) the net surrender value of the contract, or

(II) the portion of the reserve that is separately accounted for under Code Sec. 817, plus

(ii) 92.81% of the excess (if any) of the reserve determined under Code Sec. 807(d)(2) (see below) over the amount in item (i) above. (Code Sec. 807(d)(1)(B))

In no event will the reserves as determined under the rules in items (i) and (ii), above, for any contract as of any time exceed the amount which would be taken into account with respect to the contract as of that time in determining statutory reserves (as defined inCode Sec. 807(d)(4) (see below). (Code Sec. 807(d)(1)(C))

In addition, in no event can any amount or item be taken into account more than once in determining any reserve. (Code Sec. 807(d)(1)(D)) Under this no-double-counting rule, for example, an amount taken into account in determining a loss reserve under Code Sec. 807 may not be taken into account again in determining a loss reserve under Code Sec. 832. Similarly, a loss reserve determined under the tax reserve method—whether the Commissioners Reserve Valuation Method, the Commissioner's Annuity Reserve Valuation Method, a principles-based reserve method, or another method developed in the future, that is prescribed for a type of contract by the NAIC—may not again be taken into account in determining the portion of the reserve that is separately accounted for under Code Sec. 817, or be included also in determining the net surrender value of a contract. (Com Rept, see ¶ 5072)

Under the Tax Cuts and Jobs Act, the federally prescribed reserve for any life insurance contract is determined by using the tax reserve method applicable to the contract. (Code Sec. 807(d)(2)) In addition, instead of referencing the methods in effect as of the date of issuance of a contract, the definition of the applicable tax reserve method references the method as of the date the reserve is determined. (Code Sec. 807(d)(3))

Also, the special rules for determining the issuance date for group contracts, and for computing reserves for qualified substandard risks, are eliminated. (Code Sec. 807(e) as amended by Tax Cuts and Jobs Act §13517(a)(3)(A))

With respect to qualified supplemental benefits, under the Tax Cuts and Jobs Act, the requirement that the reserve be the same as that used on the NAIC approved annual statement is eliminated. (Code Sec. 807(e)(2)(A) as amended by Tax Cuts and Jobs Act §13517(a)(3)(C))

Under the Tax Cuts and Job Act, IRS must require reporting (at such time and in such manner as IRS prescribes) with respect to the opening balance and closing balance of reserves and with respect to the method of computing reserves for purposes of determining income. (Code Sec. 807(e)(6) as amended by Tax Cuts and Jobs Act §13517(a)(3)(D)) For this purpose, IRS may issue guidance requiring a life insurance company (including an affiliated group filing a consolidated return that includes a life insurance company) to report each of the line item elements of each separate account by combining them with each such item from all other separate accounts and the general account, and to report the combined amounts on a line-by-line basis on the taxpayer's return. Similarly, IRS may, in such guidance, provide that reporting on a separate account by separate account basis is generally not permitted. Under existing regulatory authority, if IRS determines it is necessary in order to carry out and enforce this provision, IRS may require e-filing or comparable filing of the return on magnetic media or other machine readable form, and may require that the taxpayer provide its annual statement via a link, electronic copy, or other similar means. (Com Rept, see ¶ 5072)

Mortality tables for computing guideline single premium under life insurance rules. Under the Tax Cuts and Job Act, the guideline single premium under life insurance rules must be computed by, among other things, reasonable mortality charges which meet the requirements prescribed in regulations to be promulgated by IRS, or that do not exceed the mortality charges specified in the "prevailing commissioners' standard tables." (Code Sec. 7702(c)(3)(B)(i) as amended by Tax Cuts and Jobs Act §13517(a)(4)(A))

For these purposes, the "prevailing commissioners' standard tables" means the most recent commissioners' standard tables prescribed by the NAIC which are permitted to be used in computing reserves for that type of contract under the insurance laws of at least 26 states when the contract was issued. If the prevailing commissioners' standard tables as of the beginning of any calendar year ("year of change") are different from the prevailing commissioners' standard tables as of the beginning of the preceding calendar year, the issuer may use the prevailing commissioners' standard tables as of the beginning of the preceding calendar year with respect to any contract issued after the change and before the close of the three-year period beginning on the first day of the year of change. (Code Sec. 7702(f)(10) as amended by Tax Cuts and Jobs Act §13517(a)(4)(B))

Transition rule. Under the Tax Cut and Jobs Act, for the first tax year beginning after Dec. 31, 2017, the reserve with respect to any contract (as determined under Code Sec. 807(d)) at the end of the preceding tax year, must be determined as if the amendments discussed above had applied to the reserve in such preceding tax year. (Tax Cuts and Jobs Act §13517(c)(2))

Transition relief. If

(i) the reserve determined under Code Sec. 807(d) (determined after application of the transition rule) with respect to any contract as of the close of the year preceding the first tax year beginning after Dec. 31, 2017, differs from

(ii) the reserve which would have been determined with respect to that contract as of the close of that tax year under Code Sec. 807(d) determined without regard to Code Sec. 807(d)(2),

then the difference between the amount of the reserve described in item (i) and the amount of the reserve described in item (ii), must be taken into account using the following method:

(A) If the amount determined under item (i) exceeds the amount determined under item (ii), 1/8 of the excess must be taken into account, for each of the eight succeeding tax years, as a deduction under Code Sec. 805(a)(2) or Code Sec. 832(c)(4), as applicable.

(B) If the amount determined under item (ii) exceeds the amount determined under item (i), 1/8 of the excess must be included in gross income, for each of the eight succeeding tax years, Code Sec. 803(a)(2) or Code Sec. 832(b)(1)(C), as applicable. (Tax Cuts and Jobs Act §13517(c)(3))

☐ **Effective:** Tax years beginning after Dec. 31, 2017. (Tax Cuts and Jobs Act §13517(c)(1))

¶ 2407. Tax on distributions to stock life insurance company shareholders from a pre-1984 policyholders' surplus account is repealed; phased inclusion of remaining balance of policyholders' surplus account is provided

Code Sec. 815, as repealed by Tax Cuts and Jobs Act §13514(a)
Code Sec. 801(c), as amended by Tax Cuts and Jobs Act §13514(b)

Code Sec. None, Tax Cuts and Jobs Act §13514(d)
Generally effective: Tax years beginning after Dec. 31, 2017
Committee Reports, see ¶ 5069

Under Code Sec. 801(a), life insurance companies are taxed on their life insurance company taxable income (LICTI), which includes capital gains, under the rates that apply to corporations. Under Code Sec. 801(b), "LICTI" is defined as life insurance company gross income, minus life insurance deductions. Under pre-Tax Cuts and Jobs Act law, Code Sec. 801(c) imposed a tax on distributions to shareholders from a pre-1984 policyholders' surplus account, as provided under Code Sec. 815. Thus, LICTI was increased by distributions to shareholders from a pre-'84 policyholders' surplus account. (FTC 2d/FIN ¶ E-4801; USTR ¶ 8014)

Under the law in effect from 1959 through 1983 ("pre-1984 law"), a life insurance company was subject to a three-phase computation of taxable income. In phase I, a company was taxed on the lesser of its gain from operations, or its taxable investment income. In phase II, if a company's gain from operations exceeded its taxable investment income, it was taxed on 50% of the excess. In phase III, tax on the other 50% of the gain from operations was deferred, and was accounted for as part of a policyholder's surplus account, and (subject to certain limitations) taxed only when distributed to stockholders, or upon corporate dissolution.

To determine the amount that had been distributed to shareholders under pre-1984 law, a company maintained a shareholders surplus account, which generally included the company's previously taxed income that would be available for distribution to shareholders. The order of distributions to shareholders was treated as: (i) first out of the shareholders surplus account, (ii) then out of the policyholders' surplus account, and (iii) finally, out of other accounts.

The Deficit Reduction Act of 1984 (Sec. 211(a), PL 98-369, 7/18/1984) included provisions that—for 1984 and following years—eliminated further deferral of tax on amounts that previously would have been deferred under the three-phase system. Although for tax years after 1983, life insurance companies could not enlarge their policyholders' surplus account, under pre-Tax Cuts and Jobs Act law, life insurance companies were not taxed on previously deferred amounts, unless those amounts were treated as distributed to shareholders, or subtracted from the policyholders' surplus account.

Further, under pre-Tax Cuts and Jobs Act law, any direct, or indirect, distribution to shareholders from an "existing policyholders' surplus account" (defined under Code Sec. 815 to mean any policyholders' surplus account which had a balance as of the close of Dec. 31, 1983) was subject to tax at the corporate rate in the tax year of the distribution. Also, as under pre-1984 law, any distribution to shareholders was treated under pre-Tax Cuts and Jobs Act law as made (1) first out of the shareholders surplus account, to the extent thereof, (2) then out of the policyholders' surplus account, to the extent thereof, and (3) finally, out of other accounts.

For tax years beginning after Dec. 31, 2004, and before Jan. 1, 2007, the application of the rules imposing income tax on distributions to shareholders from the policyholders' surplus account of a life insurance company were suspended. Distributions in those years were treated as first made out of the policyholders' surplus account, to the extent thereof, and then out of the shareholders surplus account, and lastly, out of other accounts. (FTC 2d/FIN ¶ E-5300; USTR ¶ 8154; Catalyst ¶ 135:313)

New Law. The Tax Cuts and Jobs Act repeals Code Sec. 815 (Code Sec. 815 as repealed by Tax Cuts and Jobs Act §13514(a)) and strikes Code Sec. 801(c). (Code Sec. 801(c) as amended by Tax Cuts and Jobs Act §13514(b)) Thus, for a stock life insurance company, income tax is not imposed on distributions to shareholders from a pre-1984 policyholders' surplus account. (Com Rept, see ¶ 5069)

Phased inclusion of remaining balance of policyholders' surplus accounts. For any stock life insurance company which has a balance (determined as of the close of the company's last tax year beginning before Jan. 1, 2018, and referred to below as the "remaining balance") in an "existing policyholders' surplus account" (as defined in Code Sec. 815 before it was repealed; see above), the tax imposed by Code Sec. 801 for the first eight tax years beginning after Dec. 31, 2017, is the amount that would be imposed by Code Sec. 801 for that year on the sum of:

(1) LICTI (as described under Code Sec. 801, but not less than zero); plus

(2) $1/8$th of the remaining balance. (Tax Cuts and Jobs Act §13514(d))

Thus, for any stock life insurance company with an existing policyholders' surplus account, a tax is imposed on the remaining balance of the account as of Dec. 31, 2017. A life insurance company is required to pay tax on the balance of the account ratably over the first eight tax years beginning after Dec. 31, 2017. Specifically, the tax imposed on a life insurance company is the tax on the sum of LICTI for the tax year (but not less than zero), plus $1/8$th of the balance of the existing policyholders' surplus account as of Dec. 31, 2017. Thus, life insurance company losses are not allowed to offset the amount of the policyholders' surplus account balance subject to tax. (Com Rept, see ¶ 5069)

☐ **Effective:** Tax years beginning after Dec. 31, 2017. (Tax Cuts and Jobs Act §13514(c))

Property And Casualty Insurance Companies

¶ 2408. Increase from 15% to 25% of the proration rules for property and casualty insurance companies

Code Sec. 832(b)(5)(B), as amended by Tax Cuts and Jobs Act §13515(a)
Generally effective: Tax years after Dec. 31, 2017
Committee Reports, see ¶ 5070

Under pre-Tax Cuts and Jobs Act law, deductions are limited or disallowed in certain circumstances if they are related to the receipt of exempt income. Under so-called "proration" rules that reflect the fact that reserves generally are funded in part by certain untaxed income, property and casualty insurance companies were required to reduce reserve deductions for losses incurred by 15% of tax-exempt interest received, 15% of the aggregate amount of deductions taken for dividends received, and 15% of the increase for the tax year in policy cash values. (FTC 2d/FIN ¶ E-4950, ¶ E-5598; USTR ¶ 8324.01; Catalyst ¶ 152:143)

New Law. Under the Tax Cuts and Jobs Act, the 15% reduction in the reserve deduction for property and casualty insurance companies is replaced by a variable rate—specifically to 5.25% divided by the highest percentage in effect under Code Sec. 11(b). (Code Sec. 832(b)(5)(B) as amended by Tax Cuts and Jobs Act §13515(a))

As the top corporate tax rate is 21% for 2018 and thereafter (see ¶ 102), the percentage reduction is 25% under the proration rule for property and casualty insurance companies. (Com Rept, see ¶ 5070)

☐ **Effective:** Tax years beginning after Dec. 31, 2017. (Tax Cuts and Jobs Act §13515(b))

¶ 2409. Modification of discounting rules for unpaid losses when determining property and casualty insurance companies' income

Code Sec. 846(c)(2), as amended by Tax Cuts and Jobs Act §13523(a)
Code Sec. 846(d)(3), as amended by Tax Cuts and Jobs Act §13523(b)
Code Sec. 846(e), as amended by Tax Cuts and Jobs Act §13523(c)
Code Sec. 846, Tax Cuts and Jobs Act §13523(e)
Generally effective: Tax years beginning after Dec. 31, 2017
Committee Reports, see ¶ 5078

Under Code Sec. 831(a), a property and casualty insurance company generally is subject to tax on its taxable income. (FTC 2d/FIN ¶ E-5501; USTR ¶ 8314)

Code Sec. 832 provides that the taxable income of a property and casualty insurance company is the sum of its underwriting income and investment income (as well as gains and other income items), reduced by allowable deductions. Among the items that are deductible in calculating underwriting income are additions to reserves for losses incurred and expenses incurred. (FTC 2d/FIN ¶ E-5501; USTR ¶ 8324)

Before the enactment of the Tax Cuts and Jobs Act, Code Sec. 846(c)(2) provided that all property and casualty loss reserves (unpaid losses and unpaid loss adjustment expenses) for each line of business (as shown on the annual statement) were required to be discounted using the applicable Federal mid-term rate ("mid-term AFR"). The discount rate was the average of the mid-term AFRs effective at the beginning of each month over the 60-month period preceding the calendar year for which the determination was made. (FTC 2d/FIN ¶ E-5500, ¶ E-5566; USTR ¶ 8464; Catalyst ¶ 404:182; Catalyst ¶ 2103:173; Catalyst ¶ 2104:131; Catalyst ¶ 2104:134)

Also, when a taxpayer had to determine the period over which the reserves were discounted before the enactment of the Tax Cuts and Jobs Act, a prescribed loss payment pattern applied as set forth in Code Sec. 846(d)(3)(B) through Code Sec. 846(d)(3)(G). The prescribed length of time was either the accident year and the following three calendar years, or the accident year and the following 10 calendar years, depending on the line of business.

For certain "long-tail" lines of business, the 10-year period was extended, but not by more than five additional years. Thus, before the enactment of the Tax Cuts and Jobs Act, the maximum duration of any loss payment pattern was limited to the accident year and the following 15 years.

IRS had been directed to determine a loss payment pattern for each line of business by reference to the historical loss payment pattern for that line of business using aggregate experience reported on the annual statements of insurance companies, and was required to make this determination every five years, starting with 1987. (FTC 2d/FIN ¶ E-5500, ¶ E-5569; USTR ¶ 8464)

Before the enactment of the Tax Cuts and Jobs Act, Code Sec. 846(e) provided for an election under the discounting rules that permitted a taxpayer to use its own (rather than an industry-wide) historical loss payment pattern with respect to all lines of business, provided that applicable requirements were met. (FTC 2d/FIN ¶ E-5500, ¶ E-5570; USTR ¶ 8464)

New Law. The Tax Cuts and Jobs Act provides that the annual rate determined by IRS under Code Sec. 846(c) for any calendar year must be a rate determined on the basis of the corporate bond yield curve (as defined in Code Sec. 430(h)(2)(D)(i), determined by substituting "60-month period" for "24-month period" as set forth therein). (Code Sec. 846(c)(2) as amended by Tax Cuts and Jobs Act §13523(a))

In addition, the rules in Code Sec. 846(d)(3)(B) through Code Sec. 846(d)(3)(G) (see above) are removed. Instead, for any line of business not described in Code Sec. 846(d)(3)(A)(ii) (relating to auto liability, other liability, medical malpractice, workers' compensation, and multiple peril lines), losses paid after the first year following the accident year must be treated as paid equally in the second and third year following the accident year. (Code Sec. 846(d)(3)(B)(i) as amended by Tax Cuts and Jobs Act §13523(b))

The Tax Cuts and Jobs Act also provides that the period taken into account under Code Sec. 846(d)(3)(A)(ii) must be extended to the extent required by Code Sec. 846(d)(3)(A)(ii)(II) (see below). (Code Sec. 846(d)(3)(B)(ii)(I))

For purposes of determining the extended period permitted by Code Sec. 846(d)(3)(ii)(I), the amount of losses which would have been treated as paid in the 10th year after the accident year must be treated as paid in that 10th year and each following year in an amount equal to the amount of the average of the losses treated as paid in the seventh, eighth, and ninth years after the accident year (or, if lesser, the portion of the unpaid losses not theretofore taken into account). To the extent these unpaid losses have not been treated as paid before the 24th year after the accident year, they must be treated as paid in that 24th year. (Code Sec. 846(d)(3)(B)(ii)(II))

Thus, the pre-Tax Cuts and Jobs Act law three-year period for discounting certain lines of business other than long-tail lines of business was not modified. However, the previous-law 10-year period for certain long tail lines of business is extended for a maximum of 14 more years. Similarly, for lines of business to which the 10-year period applies, the amount of losses that would have been treated as paid in the 10th year following the accident year is treated as paid in that year and each following year in an amount equal to the average of the amounts treated as paid in the seventh, eighth, and ninth years (or if less, the remaining amount). To the extent these unpaid losses have not been treated as paid before the 25th year after the accident year, they are treated as paid in that 25th year. (Com Rept, see ¶ 5078)

The Tax Cuts and Jobs Act also eliminates the election (see above) provided for by Code Sec. 846(e). (Code Sec. 846(e) as amended by Tax Cuts and Jobs Act §13523(c)) Thus, the election permitting a taxpayer to use its own, rather than an aggregate industry-experience-based, historical loss payment pattern with respect to all lines of business has been repealed. (Com Rept, see ¶ 5078)

☐ **Effective:** For tax years beginning after Dec. 31, 2017. (Tax Cuts and Jobs Act §13523(d)) However, a transitional rule provided by the Tax Cuts and Jobs Act, for the first tax year beginning after Dec. 31, 2017:

(1) the unpaid losses and the expenses unpaid (as defined in Code Sec. 832(b)(5)(B), relating to the reduction in deductions applicable for determining insurance company taxable income, and Code Sec. 832(b)(6), relating to the expenses incurred as shown on the annual statement approved by the Na-

tional Association of Insurance Commissioners (NAIC)) at the end of the preceding tax year; and

(2) the unpaid losses as defined in Code Sec. 807(c)(2) (relating to unearned
premiums and unpaid losses included in total reserves), and Code Sec. 805(a)(1)
(relating to deductions for death benefits) at the end of the preceding tax year;

must be determined as if the amendments made by the Tax Cuts and Jobs Act
had applied to the unpaid losses and expenses unpaid in the preceding tax year,
and by using the interest rate and loss payment patterns applicable to accident
years ending with calendar year 2018, and any adjustment must be taken into
account ratably in the first tax year and the seven succeeding tax years. For following tax years, these amendments must be applied with respect to the unpaid
losses and expenses unpaid by using the interest rate and loss payment patterns
applicable to accident years ending with calendar year 2018. (Tax Cuts and Jobs
Act §13523(e))

Thus, any adjustment is spread over eight tax years, i.e., the adjustment is included in the taxpayer's gross income ratably in the first tax year beginning in
2018 and the seven succeeding taxable years. For tax years following the first
tax year beginning in 2018, the provision applies to the unpaid losses and expenses unpaid (i.e., unpaid losses and expenses unpaid at the end of the tax year
preceding the first tax year beginning in 2018) by using the interest rate and
loss payment patterns applicable to accident years ending with calendar year
2018. (Com Rept, see ¶ 5078)

Industry-Wide Provisions

¶ 2410. Elective deduction of discounted loss reserve amounts for insurance companies—and related special estimated tax payment rules—are repealed

Code Sec. 847, as repealed by Tax Cuts and Jobs Act §13516(a)
Generally effective: Tax years beginning after Dec. 31, 2017
Committee Reports, see ¶ 5071

Under pre-Tax Cuts and Jobs Act law, insurance companies were permitted
under Code Sec. 847 to elect to claim an additional deduction equal to the difference between (1) the amount of reserves computed on a discounted basis,
and (2) the amount computed on an undiscounted basis. Companies that made
this election were required to make a special estimated tax payment equal to the
tax benefit attributable to the deduction. In addition, the deductions were added
to a special loss discount account and, as losses were paid in future years,
amounts were subtracted from the account, and made subject to tax (net of any
earlier special estimated tax payments). Amounts added to the special loss discount account were automatically subtracted from the account, and made subject
to tax if those amounts had not already been subtracted after 15 years.

To the extent that a special estimated tax payment wasn't used to offset additional tax due for any of the intervening 15 years, the payment was treated for the 16th year as a regular estimated tax payment under Code Sec. 6655. If the amount of that deemed Code Sec. 6655 payment—together with the taxpayer's other payments credited against tax liability for the 16th year—exceeded the tax liability for that year, then the excess (up to the amount of the deemed Code Sec. 6655 payment) could have been refunded to the taxpayer. (FTC 2d/FIN ¶ E-5500; USTR ¶ 8474)

New Law. The Tax Cuts and Jobs Act repeals Code Sec. 847 (Code Sec. 847 as repealed by Tax Cuts and Jobs Act §13516(a)) Thus, the election to apply Code Sec. 847, the additional deduction, the special loss discount account, the special estimated tax payment, and the refundable amount rules, are eliminated. (Com Rept, see ¶ 5071)

☐ **Effective:** Tax years beginning after Dec. 31, 2017. (Tax Cuts and Jobs Act §13516(b))

For the first tax year beginning after 2017, the entire balance of an existing account is included in the income of the taxpayer, and the entire amount of existing special estimated tax payments are applied against the amount of additional tax attributable to that inclusion. Any special estimated tax payments in excess of that amount are treated as estimated tax payments under Code Sec. 6655. (Com Rept, see ¶ 5071)

¶ 2411. Active insurance business exception to passive foreign investment company rules requires minimum insurance liabilities amount

Code Sec. 1297(b)(2)(B), as amended by Tax Cuts and Jobs Act §14501(a)
Code Sec. 1297(f), as amended by Tax Cuts and Jobs Act §14501(b)
Generally effective: Tax years beginning after Dec. 31, 2017
Committee Reports, see ¶ 5125

Under the passive foreign investment company (PFIC) rules, a foreign corporation meeting certain thresholds for passive income or assets is treated as a PFIC. U.S. shareholders of a PFIC may choose between (i) current taxation on the income of the PFIC or (ii) deferral of such income subject to a deemed tax and interest regime. FTC 2d/FIN ¶ O-2200 *et seq.* Under pre-Tax Cuts and Jobs Act law, passive income did not include any income derived in the active conduct of an insurance business by a corporation that was predominantly engaged in an insurance business and that would be subject to tax under subchapter L (Code Sec. 801 through Code Sec. 848) if it were a domestic corporation. In applying this exception, IRS analyzed whether risks assumed under contracts issued by a foreign company organized as an insurer truly were insurance risks, whether the risks were limited under the terms of the contract, and the status of the company as an insurance company. (FTC 2d ¶ O-2200, ¶ O-2202; USTR ¶ 12,974; Catalyst ¶ 2107:114)

New Law. The Tax Cuts and Jobs Act eliminates the "predominantly engaged in an insurance business" test and instead provides that passive income does not include any income derived in the active conduct of an insurance business by a qualifying insurance corporation. (Code Sec. 1297(b)(2)(B) as amended by Tax Cuts and Jobs Act §14501(a))

A qualifying insurance corporation is for any tax year a foreign corporation (i) which would be subject to tax under subchapter L if it were a domestic corporation and (ii) the applicable insurance liabilities of which constitute more than 25% of its total assets, determined on the basis of those liabilities and assets as reported on the corporation's applicable financial statement for the last year ending with or within the tax year. (Code Sec. 1297(f)(1) as amended by Tax Cuts and Jobs Act §14501(b))

If a corporation fails to qualify as a qualified insurance corporation solely because its applicable insurance liabilities constitute 25% or less of its total assets, a U.S. person who owns stock in the corporation may elect to treat that stock as stock of a qualifying insurance corporation if:

(1) the corporation's applicable insurance liabilities constitute at least 10% of its total assets, and

(2) under IRS regulations, based on the applicable facts and circumstances,

(i) the corporation is predominantly engaged in an insurance business, and

(ii) its failure to qualify under the 25% threshold is due solely to run-off-related or rating-related circumstances involving the insurance business. (Code Sec. 1297(f)(2))

These circumstances include, for example, the fact that the company is in run-off, that is, it is not taking on new insurance business (and consequently has little or no premium income), and is using its remaining assets to pay off claims with respect to pre-existing insurance risks on its books. These circumstances also include, for example, the application to the company of specific requirements with respect to capital and surplus relating to insurance liabilities imposed by a rating agency as a condition of obtaining a rating necessary to write new insurance business for the current year. (Com Rept, see ¶ 5125)

Applicable insurance liabilities are, with respect to any life or property and casualty insurance business, (i) loss and loss adjustment expenses, and (ii) reserves (other than deficiency, contingency, or unearned premium reserves) for life and health insurance risks and life and health insurance claims with respect to contracts providing coverage for mortality or morbidity risks. The amount of any applicable insurance liability may not exceed the lesser of the amount (1) as reported to the applicable insurance regulatory body in the applicable financial statement (or, if less, the amount required by applicable law or regulation), or (2) as determined under IRS regulations. (Code Sec. 1297(f)(3))

An applicable financial statement is a statement for financial reporting purposes which:

(1) is made on the basis of generally accepted accounting principles (GAAP),

(2) is made on the basis of international financial reporting standards, but only if there is no statement that meets the requirements of item (1), or

(3) except as otherwise provided by IRS regulations, is the annual statement required to be filed with the applicable insurance regulatory body, but only if there is no statement that meets the requirements of items (1) or (2). (Code Sec. 1297(f)(4)(A))

An applicable insurance regulatory body is, with respect to any insurance business, the entity established by law to license, authorize, or regulate the insurance business and to which the applicable financial statement is provided. (Code Sec. 1297(f)(4)(B))

☐ **Effective:** Tax years beginning after Dec. 31, 2017. (Tax Cuts and Jobs Act §14501(c))

¶ 2500. Tax-Exempt Organizations

¶ 2501. Excise tax imposed on tax-exempt organizations that pay excess compensation

Code Sec. 4960, as added by Tax Cuts and Jobs Act §13602(a)
Generally effective: For tax years beginning after Dec. 31, 2017
Committee Reports, see ¶ 5085

Under pre-Tax Cuts and Jobs Act law, no deduction is allowed to a publicly held corporation for any remuneration paid to a "covered employee" that exceeds $1 million. (FTC 2d ¶ H-3776; USTR ¶ 1624.0091)

Also under pre-Tax Cuts and Jobs Act law, no deduction is allowed to any publicly held corporation for any parachute payment that is an "excess parachute payment." (FTC 2d ¶ H-3826; USTR ¶ 280G4) Further, there is a 20% excise tax on the amount of an "excess parachute payment" that is imposed on the recipient of that payment. (FTC 2d ¶ H-3003; USTR ¶ 280G4)

> *observation:* Under pre-Tax Cuts and Jobs Act law, there are reasonableness requirements, and a prohibition against private inurement, for the executive compensation for tax-exempt entities. However, no parallel limitation currently applies to tax-exempt organizations with respect to executive compensation and excess parachute payments.

A "covered employee" is either the chief executive officer (CEO) of the corporation, or one of the corporation's four highest paid officers (other than the CEO), whose compensation must be reported to the shareholders of the corporation. (FTC 2d ¶ H-3780; USTR ¶ 1624.0091)

For purposes of determining excess remuneration, wages include all remuneration for services performed by an employee for the employer, except for fees paid to a public official, and other specifically excluded types of remuneration. (FTC 2d ¶ H-4326; USTR ¶ 34,014.01)

A parachute payment is any payment that:

. . . is in the nature of compensation;

. . . is made to (or for the benefit of) a disqualified individual;

FTC 2d References are to Federal Tax Coordinator 2d
FIN References are to RIA's Analysis of Federal Taxes: Income (print)
USTR References are to United States Tax Reporter
Catalyst References are to Checkpoint Catalyst
PCA References are to Pension Analysis (print and electronic)
PBE References are to Pension & Benefits Explanations
BCA References are to Benefits Analysis (electronic)
BC References are to Benefits Coordinator (print)
EP References are to Estate Planning Analysis (print and electronic)

. . . is contingent on a change in ownership or control, i.e., a change in the ownership or effective control of a corporation, or a change in the ownership of a substantial part of the assets of a corporation; and

. . . has, together with the items listed above, an aggregate present value of at least three times the individual's "base amount." (FTC 2d ¶ H-3830; USTR ¶ 280G4)

Under Code Sec. 457(f)(3)(B), the rights of a person to compensation are subject to a substantial risk of forfeiture if that person's rights to the compensation are conditioned upon the future performance of substantial services by any individual. FTC 2d ¶ H-3307; USTR ¶ 4574

An "excess parachute payment" is the amount equal to the excess of any parachute payment over the portion of the "base amount" allocated to the parachute payment. (FTC 2d ¶ H-3874; USTR ¶ 280G4)

The "base amount" is an employee's annualized includible compensation for the base period. (FTC 2d ¶ H-3869; USTR ¶ 280G4) The portion of the base amount allocated to any parachute payment is the amount which bears the same ratio to the base amount as the present value of the parachute payment bears to the aggregate present value of all parachute payments. (FTC 2d ¶ H-3875; USTR ¶ 280G4)

A parachute payment does not include any payment made to or from a qualified plan, such as:

. . . a Code Sec. 401(a) qualified pension, profit-sharing or stock bonus plan, which includes a trust exempt from tax under Code Sec. 501(a),

. . . a Code Sec. 403(a) qualified annuity plan,

. . . a Code Sec. 408(k) simplified employee pension plan, or

. . . a Code Sec. 408(p) simple retirement account. (FTC 2d ¶ H-3839; USTR ¶ 280G4)

Under Code Sec. 414(q), a "highly compensated employee," for purposes of the nondiscrimination requirements applicable to qualified pension, profit-sharing, and stock bonus plans, is any employee who:

. . . was a 5% owner at any time during the year or the preceding year, or

. . . for the preceding year, received compensation from the employer in excess of $80,000 (as adjusted for cost-of-living increases), and, if the employer elects, was in the top-paid group of employees for the preceding year. (FTC 2d ¶ H-6702; USTR ¶ 4144.21)

A designated Roth contribution is any elective deferral that would be excludable from an employee's gross income in the absence of Code Sec. 402A, but which has been designated by the employee as not excludable from his or her gross income. (FTC 2d ¶ H-12295.5; USTR ¶ 4014.1745)

A transfer of property is treated as a payment for purposes of determining a parachute payment. (FTC 2d ¶ H-3832; USTR ¶ 280G4)

Further, for purposes of determining a parachute payment, the calculation of the present value of the contingent compensatory payments requires the use of a discount rate. The rate used is equal to 120% of the applicable federal rate (AFR), as determined under Code Sec. 1274(d), compounded semiannually. (FTC 2d ¶ H-3867; USTR ¶ 280G4)

New Law. Under the Tax Cuts and Jobs Act, an excise tax will be imposed on "covered employees" of "applicable tax-exempt organizations" whose "remuneration" exceeds $1 million, or who receive "excess parachute payments." (Code Sec. 4960 as added by Tax Cuts and Jobs Act §13602(a))

> *observation:* This new Code Sec. 4960, which would impose an excise tax on covered employees of applicable tax-exempt organizations, applies some of the rules described above, but also provides additional definitions that may differ from the terms defined above.

Specifically, a tax, equal to the product of the rate of tax under Code Sec. 11 (relating to the rate used to calculate the tax on the income of corporations), will be imposed on:

(1) "remuneration" (excluding any "excess parachute payment") paid in any tax year by an "applicable tax-exempt organization" to a "covered employee" that exceeds $1 million, plus

(2) any "excess parachute payment" paid by an "applicable tax-exempt organization" to any "covered employee." (Code Sec. 4960(a))

> *observation:* Since the Tax Cuts and Jobs Act provides that the corporate income tax rate is 21%, the new Code Sec. 4960 excise tax is 21%.

Remuneration is treated as paid when there is not a substantial risk of forfeiture (within the meaning of Code Sec. 457(f)(3)(B), see above) of the rights to that remuneration. (Code Sec. 4960(a))

Code Sec. 457(f)(3)(B) (see above) applies to ineligible deferred compensation subject to section Code Sec. 457(f). Thus, the tax imposed by Code Sec. 4960(a) can apply to the value of remuneration that is vested (and any increases in that value or vested remuneration), even if it is not yet received. (Com Rept, see ¶ 5085)

The applicable tax-exempt organization employer will be liable for any excise tax imposed on excess remuneration or "excess parachute payment." (Code Sec. 4960(b))

Remuneration that exceeds $1 million. For purposes of this excise tax, an "applicable tax-exempt organization" is any organization, which, for the tax year, is:

. . . exempt from tax under Code Sec. 501(a);

. . . a farmer's cooperative organization under Code Sec. 521(b)(1);

. . . has income excluded from tax under Code Sec. 115(1) (referring to income from states, municipalities, etc.); or

. . . a political organization under Code Sec. 527(e)(1). (Code Sec. 4960(c)(1))

For purposes of this excise tax, "remuneration" is considered to be wages (as defined under Code Sec. 3401(a), see above), but not including any designated Roth contribution. (Code Sec. 4960(c)(3)(A))

Remuneration also includes amounts required to be included in gross income under Code Sec. 457(f) (relating to ineligible deferred compensation plans). (Code Sec. 4960(c)(3)(A))

Remuneration does not include the portion of any remuneration paid to a licensed medical professional (which includes veterinarians) for medical or veterinary services performed by that professional. (Code Sec. 4960(c)(3)(B)) However, remuneration paid to such a medical professional in any other capacity (other than for the performance of medical or veterinary services) is taken into account. (Com Rept, see ¶ 5085)

A "covered employee" is any current or former employee of an applicable tax-exempt organization if the employee is (a) one of the five highest compensated employees of the organization for the tax year, or (b) was a covered employee of the organization, or any predecessor of the organization, for any tax year after Dec. 31, 2016. (Code Sec. 4960(c)(2))

Any remuneration for which a deduction under Code Sec. 162(m) is not allowed is not included in remuneration used to calculate this excise tax. (Code Sec. 4960(c)(6))

Remuneration of a covered employee paid by an applicable tax-exempt organization includes any remuneration paid for employment to a covered employee by a related person or government entity. (Code Sec. 4960(c)(4)(A)) A person or government entity is considered to be related to an applicable tax-exempt organization if the person or entity:

. . . controls, or is controlled by, the applicable tax-exempt organization;

. . . is controlled by a person, or persons, that control the organization;

. . . is a supported organization under Code Sec. 509(f)(3);

. . . is a supporting organization under Code Sec. 509(a)(3); or

... if the organization is a voluntary employees' beneficiary association (VEBA) under Code Sec. 509(c)(9), establishes, maintains, or makes contributions to that VEBA. (Code Sec. 4960(c)(4)(B))

If remuneration from more than one employer is used to calculate the excise tax, then each employer will be liable for the amount determined by the following ratio:

... the amount of remuneration paid by the employer to the employee; over

... the total amount of remuneration paid by all such employers to the employee. (Code Sec. 4960(c)(4)(C))

Excess parachute payments. For purposes of this excise tax, an "excess parachute payment" is the amount that exceeds the excess of any "parachute payment" over the "base amount" allocated to the payment. (Code Sec. 4960(c)(5)(A))

A "parachute payment" is any payment made as compensation to, or for the benefit of, a covered employee if (i) the payment is contingent on the employee's separation from employment with the employer, and (ii) the aggregate present value of the compensation payments to, or for the benefit of, the employee is equal to, or greater than, three times the base amount. (Code Sec. 4960(c)(5)(B))

However, a parachute payment does not include any payment:

(i) described in Code Sec. 280G(b)(6) (relating to the exemption for payments under qualified plans),

(ii) made under or to an annuity contract under Code Sec. 403(b), or a Code Sec. 457(b) plan,

(iii) made to a licensed medical professional (including veterinarians) to the extent that the payment is for services performed by that medical professional, or

(iv) made to an individual who is not considered a highly compensated employee under Code Sec. 414(q) (see above). (Code Sec. 4960(c)(5)(C))

For these purposes, the "base amount" is determined in the same manner as under Code Sec. 280G(b)(3) (relating to the base amount for a golden parachute payment). (Code Sec. 4960(c)(5)(D))

For purposes of determining an excess parachute payment, the rules of Code Sec. 280G(d)(3) and Code Sec. 280G(d)(3) apply. (Code Sec. 4960(c)(5)(E))

> 💡 *observation:* Thus, in determining an excess parachute payment, a property transfer would be treated as a payment, and the present value of a contingent compensation payment would be determined using a discount rate equal to 120% of the AFR.

IRS is directed to prescribe regulations that may be necessary to prevent the avoidance of the excise tax, including regulations preventing employees from being misclassified as contractors, or from being compensated through a pass-through or other entity to avoid such tax. (Code Sec. 4960(d))

☐ **Effective:** For tax years beginning after Dec. 31, 2017. (Tax Cuts and Jobs Act §13602(c))

¶ 2502. New excise tax imposed on investment income of private colleges and universities

Code Sec. 4968, as added by Tax Cuts and Jobs Act §13701(a)
Generally effective: Tax years beginning after Dec. 31, 2017
Committee Reports, see ¶ 5091

Under Code Sec. 511(a)(2)(B), any college or university that's an agency or instrumentality of any government or political subdivision, or that's owned or operated by a government, political subdivision, or related agency or instrumentality, is subject to the tax on unrelated business income (UBTI). The UBTI tax also applies to any corporation wholly owned by one or more of such colleges or universities. (FTC 2d/FIN ¶ D-6802; USTR ¶ 5114)

Under Code Sec. 4940(c), net investment income is the amount by which the sum of gross investment income and capital gain net income exceeds allowable deductions. Tax-exempt interest and related deductions are excluded from this computation. (FTC 2d/FIN ¶ D-7507; USTR ¶ 49,404)

Before the enactment of the Tax Cuts and Jobs Act, there was no excise tax on investment income of private colleges and universities.

New Law. The Tax Cuts and Jobs Act imposes on each "applicable educational institution" (see below) for the tax year, a tax equal to 1.4% of the applicable educational institution's "net investment income" (see below) for the tax year. (Code Sec. 4968(a) as added by Tax Cuts and Jobs Act §13701(a))

Private colleges and universities have had dramatic increases in their endowment balances, while at the same time college tuition has risen at rates in excess of the rate of inflation. Thus, a modest excise tax on an on the endowment's investment income from the endowment has been imposed where the endowment of the private college or university has grown so large that is not commensurate with the scope of the institution's activities in educating students. (Com Rept, see ¶ 5091)

An "applicable educational institution" is an eligible educational institution (as defined in Code Sec. 25A(f)(2), relating to all accredited public, nonprofit, and proprietary postsecondary institutions):

(A) which had at least 500 students during the preceding taxable year;

(B) more than 50% of the students of the eligible educational institution are located in the U.S.;

(C) which is not described in the first sentence of Code Sec. 511(a)(2)(B) (relating to state colleges and universities, see above); and

(D) the aggregate fair market value of the assets of which at the end of the preceding tax year (other than those assets which are used directly in carrying out the institution's exempt purpose) is at least $500,000 per student of the institution. (Code Sec. 4968(b)(1))

The number of students (see item (A), above) of an eligible educational institution must be based on the daily average number of full-time students attending the institution (with part-time students taken into account on a full-time student equivalent basis). (Code Sec. 4968(b)(2))

For purposes of these rules, "net investment income" (see above) is determined under rules similar to the rules of Code Sec. 4940(c) (see above). (Code Sec. 4968(c))

For purposes of item (C) (see above), and Code Sec. 4968(c) (see above), the assets and net investment income of any "related organization" (see below) with respect to an educational institution, must be treated as the assets and net investment income, respectively, of the eligible educational institution (see above), except that:

(i) no such amount is taken into account with respect to more than one educational institution; and

(ii) unless the organization is controlled by the institution, or is described in Code Sec. 509(a)(3) (relating to the definition of a private foundation) with respect to the institution for the taxable year, assets and net investment income which are not intended or available for the use or benefit of the educational institution must not be taken into account. (Code Sec. 4968(d)(1))

A related organization is, with respect to an eligible educational institution, any organization which:

(1) controls, or is controlled by, the eligible educational institution;

(2) is controlled by one or more persons that control the eligible educational institution; or

(3) is a supported organization (as defined in Code Sec. 509(f)(3)), or an organization described in Code Sec. 509(a)(3) (relating to the definition of a private foundation), during the tax year with respect to the eligible educational institution. (Code Sec. 4968(d)(2))

☐ **Effective:** For tax years beginning after Dec. 31, 2017. (Tax Cuts and Jobs Act §13701(c))

¶ 2503. Tax-exempt organizations' unrelated business taxable income calculated separately for each trade or business

Code Sec. 512(a)(6), as amended by Tax Cuts and Jobs Act §13702(a)
Generally effective: For tax years beginning after Dec. 31, 2017
Committee Reports, see ¶ 5092

Unrelated business taxable income (UBTI) is the gross income derived by any tax-exempt organization from any unrelated trade or business regularly carried on by the organization, less allowable deductions. (FTC 2d/FIN ¶ D-6804; USTR ¶ 5124; Catalyst ¶ 552:140)

An unrelated trade or business is any trade or business the conduct of which isn't substantially related to the exercise or performance by the organization of its exempt purpose. (FTC 2d ¶ D-6804; USTR ¶ 5134)

A net operating loss (NOL) deduction is allowed in the computation of unrelated business taxable income. However, no income or deduction that is excluded from the scope of the unrelated business income tax is taken into account in determining the amount of a NOL for a tax year, the amount of a carryover or carryback to any tax year, or the amount of the net operating loss deduction. FTC 2d ¶ D-6922; USTR ¶ 5124

Under Code Sec. 512(b)(12), in computing unrelated business taxable income, a specific deduction of $1,000 is allowed, except for purposes of computing the net operating loss deduction, and except with respect to certain local church units which file a separate return. For a diocese, province of a religious order, or a convention or association of churches, the specific deduction allowed with respect to each parish, individual church, district, or other local unit is the lower of:

... $1,000 or

... the gross income derived from any unrelated trade or business regularly carried on by the local unit. FTC 2d ¶ D-6921; USTR ¶ 5124

New Law. Under the Tax Cuts and Jobs Act, an organization that has more than one unrelated trade or business will compute UBTI, including for purposes of determining any NOL deduction, separately for each unrelated trade or business, and without regard to Code Sec. 512(b)(12) (see above). (Code Sec. 512(a)(6) as amended by Tax Cuts and Jobs Act §13702(a))

Specifically, for tax-exempt organizations that have more than one unrelated trade or business, UBTI is calculated under the following rules:

(A) UBTI, including for purposes of determining any net operating loss deduction, is computed separately with respect to each separate unrelated trade or business, and not including the specific deduction that applies for dioceses, religious orders, or conventions or associations of churches under Code Sec. 512(b)(12). (Code Sec. 512(a)(6)(A))

(B) The organization's UBTI is the sum of the UBTI so computed with respect to each unrelated trade or business, less the specific deduction under Code Sec. 512(b)(12) (see above). (Code Sec. 512(a)(6)(B))

(C) For purposes item (B), above, the UBTI for any such trade or business must not be less than zero. (Code Sec. 512(a)(6)(C))

> *observation:* Thus, losses from one unrelated trade or business may not be used to offset the income derived from another unrelated trade or business. Gains and losses must be calculated and applied separately.

☐ **Effective:** For tax years beginning after Dec. 31, 2017 (Tax Cuts and Jobs Act §13702(b)(1)), except where there is a NOL carryover. Specifically, if a NOL that has arisen in a tax year beginning before Jan. 1, 2018 is carried over to a tax year on or after Jan. 1, 2018, then:

. . . Code Sec. 512(c)(6)(A), as discussed above, must not apply to that NOL, and

. . . the organization's UBTI, after applying Code Sec. 512(c)(6)(B), as discussed above, must be reduced by the amount of the NOL. (Tax Cuts and Jobs Act §13702(b)(2))

¶ 2504. Tax-exempt organizations' unrelated business taxable income increased by disallowed fringe benefit expenses

Code Sec. 512(a)(7), as amended by Tax Cuts and Jobs Act §13703(a)
Generally effective: For amounts paid or incurred after Dec. 31, 2017
Committee Reports, see ¶ 5093

An organization may be tax exempt if it is both organized and operated exclusively for exempt purposes. (FTC 2d ¶ D-4101; USTR ¶ 5014)

Unrelated business taxable income (UBTI) is the gross income derived by any tax-exempt organization from any unrelated trade or business regularly carried on by the organization, less allowable deductions. (FTC 2d/FIN ¶ D-6804; USTR ¶ 5124)

An unrelated trade or business is any trade or business the conduct of which isn't substantially related to the exercise or performance by the organization of its exempt purpose. (FTC 2d/FIN ¶ D-6804; USTR ¶ 5134)

Under Code Sec. 274, no deduction is allowed for expenditures for goods, services, and facilities in connection with entertainment, amusement, or recreation—unless the taxpayer proves that the expenditure is "directly related to," or "associated with," the taxpayer's trade or business or investment-related activities. (FTC 2d ¶ L-2102; USTR ¶ 2744)

Entertainment expenses are considered to be "directly related to" the business where the entertainment:

. . . involves an active discussion aimed at obtaining immediate revenue,

. . . occurs in a clear business setting, or

. . . is reported as compensation for services performed by an individual other than an employee. (FTC 2d ¶ L-2112; USTR ¶ 2744)

Entertainment is considered to be "associated with" the active conduct of the taxpayer's trade or business if there is a clear business purpose for the expenditure, such as to get new business or to encourage the continuation of an existing business relationship. (FTC 2d ¶ L-2118; USTR ¶ 2744)

The amount an employee receives as a fringe benefit must be included in income, based on its fair market value. But any fringe benefit that qualifies as a "qualified transportation fringe" is excluded from income up to the amount of a monthly dollar limitation. (FTC 2d ¶ H-2205; USTR ¶ 614.027)

Under Code Sec. 132(f), a "qualified transportation fringe" is considered to be any of the following provided by an employer to an employee:

(A) commuter transportation (between the employee's home and place of employment) in a commuter highway vehicle, including van pools;

(B) transit passes;

(C) qualified parking; and

(D) qualified bicycle commuting reimbursement. (FTC 2d ¶ H-2205; USTR ¶ 1324.08)

Under Code Sec. 132(f)(5)(C), "qualified parking" means parking provided to an employee on or near the business premises of the employer, or on or near a location from which the employee commutes to work by transportation described in Code Sec. 132(f)(5)(A) (relating to "transit passes," see below), in a commuter highway vehicle, or by carpool. Qualified parking does not include any parking on or near property used by the employee for residential purposes. (FTC 2d ¶ H-2213; USTR ¶ 1324.08)

A "transit pass" is any pass, token, farecard, voucher, or similar item that entitles a person to transportation (or transportation at a reduced price) (a) on mass transit facilities (such as rail, bus, and ferry, whether or not publicly owned, or (b) provided by any person in the business of transporting persons for compensation or hire, if this transportation is in a highway vehicle with a seating capacity of at least six adults (excluding the driver). (FTC 2d ¶ H-2212; USTR ¶ 1324.08)

Under Code Sec. 132(j)(4)(B), an "on premises athletic facility" is any gym or other athletic facility (such as a swimming pool, tennis court or golf course) which is:

. . . located on the premises of the employer;

. . . operated by the employer; and

. . . used, with substantial exclusivity, by the employer's employees, their spouses and their dependent children. (FTC 2d ¶ H-1951; USTR ¶ 1324.07)

For purposes of determining an on premises athletic facility, a dependent child is any child (1) that is a dependent of the employee, or (2) both of whose parents are deceased and who is not yet 25 years old. (FTC 2d ¶ H-1885; USTR ¶ 1324.07)

New Law. Under the Tax Cuts and Jobs Act, a tax-exempt organization includes as UBTI any amount (i) for which a deduction is not allowed under Code Sec. 274 (see above), and (ii) which is paid by the organization for any qualified transportation fringe (as defined in Code Sec. 132(f), see above), any parking facility used in connection with qualified parking (as defined in Code Sec. 132(f)(5)(C), see above), or any on-premises athletic facility (as defined in Code Sec. 132(j)(4)(B), see above).

However, UBTI does not include the amounts described above to the extent the amount paid or incurred is directly connected with an unrelated trade or business which is regularly carried on by the organization.

IRS may issue regulations or other guidance as may be necessary or appropriate to carry out the purposes of the rules above, including regulations or other guidance providing for the appropriate allocation of depreciation and other costs with respect to facilities used for parking or for on-premises athletic facilities. (Code Sec. 512(a)(7) as amended by Tax Cuts and Jobs Act §13703(a))

☐ **Effective:** For amounts paid or incurred after Dec. 31, 2017. (Tax Cuts and Jobs Act §13703(b))

¶ 2600. Compensation

¶ 2601. Performance-based compensation and commissions are made subject to $1 million deduction limit

Code Sec. 162(m)(4), as amended by Tax Cuts and Jobs Act §13601(a)(1)
Generally effective: Tax years beginning after Dec. 31, 2017
Committee Reports, see ¶ 5084

An employer generally may deduct reasonable compensation for personal services as an ordinary and necessary business expense. (Catalyst ¶ 114:153; FTC 2d/FIN ¶ H-3600.1; USTR ¶ 1624.205) But a publicly held corporation (see ¶ 2602) can't deduct applicable employee remuneration in excess of $1 million per year paid to a covered employee (see ¶ 2603). (FTC 2d/FIN ¶ H-3776; USTR ¶ 1624.0091; Catalyst ¶ 114:153; Catalyst ¶ 115:205)

Under pre-Tax Cuts and Jobs Act law, performance-based compensation was exempt from the $1 million deduction limit, *i.e.*, it wasn't applicable employee remuneration. Compensation qualified for this exception if:

(1) it was payable solely on account of performance goals having been reached;

(2) the performance goals were preestablished and objective;

(3) the performance goals stated the method of computing compensation in an objective formula;

(4) the objective compensation formula precluded discretion to increase the amount payable upon reaching the goal;

(5) the performance goals were set by a compensation committee consisting solely of two or more outside directors;

(6) the performance goals were approved by shareholders; and

(7) before any remuneration was paid, the company's compensation committee certified that the performance goals had been reached. (FTC 2d/FIN ¶ H-3783 *et seq.*; USTR ¶ 1624.0092)

In addition, under pre-Tax Cuts and Jobs Act law, commission payments that were based solely on income that was generated directly by the employee's in-

FTC 2d References are to Federal Tax Coordinator 2d
FIN References are to RIA's Analysis of Federal Taxes: Income (print)
USTR References are to United States Tax Reporter
Catalyst References are to Checkpoint Catalyst
PCA References are to Pension Analysis (print and electronic)
PBE References are to Pension & Benefits Explanations
BCA References are to Benefits Analysis (electronic)
BC References are to Benefits Coordinator (print)
EP References are to Estate Planning Analysis (print and electronic)

dividual performance were exempt from the $1 million deduction limit. (FTC 2d/FIN ¶ H-3782; USTR ¶ 1624.0092; Catalyst ¶ 115:205)

New Law. The Tax Cuts and Jobs Act eliminates the exceptions for performance-based compensation and commissions from the definition of "applicable employee remuneration" that is subject to the $1 million deduction limit. (Code Sec. 162(m)(4) as amended by Tax Cuts and Jobs Act §13601(a)(1))

As a result, performance-based compensation and commissions are taken into account in determining the amount of compensation with respect to a covered employee for a tax year that exceeds $1 million and so isn't deductible as a business expense. (Com Rept, see ¶ 5084)

illustration: In 2018, corporation X, a publicly held corporation, pays its principal executive officer (PEO) salary of $750,000 and a bonus of $5 million that would qualify as performance-based. X can deduct $1 million of the compensation, while $4.75 million is nondeductible.

observation: The impact of the loss of this deduction is somewhat softened by the reduction in the corporate tax rate to a flat 21% rate (see ¶ 102), a change that reduces the value of corporate tax deductions.

observation: Even though there will no longer be a tax advantage in paying performance-based compensation, it's likely that companies will continue to favor this type of compensation as a matter of good compensation policy. Proxy advisory firms such as Institutional Shareholder Services (ISS) will continue to consider the alignment of pay with performance when making their voting recommendations. However, except where compensation is grandfathered under the transition rule discussed below, companies won't have to worry that technical failures to qualify compensation as performance-based will make the compensation nondeductible.

viewpoint: Arthur Kohn, Esq., a partner at Cleary Gottlieb Steen & Hamilton LLP, notes the following:

Companies that obtained shareholder approval of performance-based plans in the past should consider whether to notify shareholders that there is no longer a tax reason to comply with the technical requirements of the qualified performance-based compensation exception and that compensation plan design and practices may change as a result.

Without such a notice, shareholders might infer that individual limits, prohibition of positive discretion, and other provisions that were intended to permit compliance with the qualified performance-based compensation exception will continue to apply, even though the reason for those limitations was eliminated. The extent of the concern may be affected by a company's historical public disclosure related to Code Sec. 162(m).

Before amending any plan to reflect the foregoing, companies should consider whether the amendment would require shareholder approval pursuant to applicable listing requirements or the terms of the relevant plan or by reason of prior shareholder communications.

observation: The only exceptions to the $1 million deduction limit that remain after this change are those for:

... remuneration paid under a written binding contract that was in effect on Feb. 17, '93;

... payments to or on behalf of an employee or beneficiary from or under certain qualified retirement plans; and

... employee benefits that are reasonably believed to be excludable by the employee. (FTC 2d/FIN ¶ H-3781.1; USTR ¶ 1624.0092)

For an expansion of the definition of "publicly held corporation" that is subject to the $1 million compensation deduction limit, see ¶ 2602.

For an expansion of the definition of a "covered employee" who is subject to the $1 million compensation deduction limit, see ¶ 2603.

Transition rule. Under a transition rule, the above change and the other changes made by Tax Cuts and Jobs Act §13601 (see ¶ 2602 and ¶ 2603) won't apply to remuneration that's provided pursuant to a written binding contract that was in effect on Nov. 2, 2017, and that wasn't modified in any material respect on or after that date. (Tax Cuts and Jobs Act §13601(e)(2))

For purposes of the transition rule, compensation paid pursuant to a plan qualifies for this exception if the right to participate in the plan is part of a written binding contract with the covered employee in effect on Nov. 2, 2017. The fact that a plan was in existence on Nov. 2, 2017, isn't by itself sufficient to qualify the plan for the exception. (Com Rept, see ¶ 5084)

Illustration: XYZ Corporation hired a covered employee on Oct. 2, 2017. One term of the written employment contract is that the executive is eligible to participate in the XYZ Corporation Executive Deferred Compensation Plan in accordance with the plan terms. The plan provides for participation after six months of employment.

Amounts payable under the plan aren't subject to discretion. The corporation doesn't have the right to materially amend or terminate the plan, except on a prospective basis before any services are performed for the applicable period for which the compensation is to be paid.

Provided that the other conditions of the binding contract exception are met (*e.g.*, the plan is in writing), payments under the plan are grandfathered, even though the employee wasn't actually a participant in the plan on Nov. 2, 2017. (Com Rept, see ¶ 5084)

The exception doesn't apply to new contracts entered into or renewed after Nov. 2, 2017. For purposes of this rule, any contract that was entered into on or before Nov. 2, 2017, and is renewed after that date is treated as a new contract entered into on the day the renewal takes effect. (Com Rept, see ¶ 5084)

A contract that's terminable or cancelable unconditionally at will by either party to the contract without the other party's consent, or by both parties to the contract, is treated as a new contract entered into on the date that any termination or cancellation, if made, would be effective. However, a contract isn't treated as terminable or cancelable if it can be terminated or cancelled only by terminating the covered employee's employment relationship. (Com Rept, see ¶ 5084)

The exception for remuneration paid pursuant to a written binding contract ceases to apply to amounts paid after there has been a material modification to the terms of the contract. (Com Rept, see ¶ 5084)

observation: Companies should review their contracts and plans for performance-based compensation to determine whether they meet the written binding contract exception. Where that is the case, companies will want to take care not to make a material modification that will cause them to lose the benefit of the grandfather rule.

viewpoint: Arthur Kohn, Esq., a partner at Cleary Gottlieb Steen & Hamilton LLP, notes the following:

Most bonus plans allow the company negative discretion to pay less than the maximum compensation to which the executive would be entitled under the plan. Companies should consider whether the authority to exercise discretion over the amount of compensation to be paid would disqualify a contract or plan from transition relief.

In considering that issue, companies should note that Reg §1.162-27(h)(1)(i), which addressed the transition relief provided upon the enactment of Code Sec. 162(m) in 1993, stated that the relief "does not apply unless, under applicable state law, the corporation is obligated to pay the compensation if the employee performs services."

Companies should also note that the *Illustration* above, taken from the Conference Committee report (H. Rept. 115-466), assumes that "amounts payable under the plan aren't subject to discretion." However, it is unclear how important that assumption, or the illustration, will be to the application of the transition rule, particularly since the illustration concerns a deferred compensation plan rather than a perform-ance-based incentive plan.

☐ **Effective:** Tax years beginning after Dec. 31, 2017. (Tax Cuts and Jobs Act §13601(e)(1)) However, the amendments made by this provision don't apply to remuneration that's provided pursuant to a written binding contract that was in effect on Nov. 2, 2017, and that wasn't modified in any material respect on or after that date. (Tax Cuts and Jobs Act §13601(e)(2))

¶ 2602. Definition of "publicly held corporation" subject to $1 million compensation deduction limit is expanded

Code Sec. 162(m)(2), as amended by Tax Cuts and Jobs Act §13601(c)
Generally effective: Tax years beginning after Dec. 31, 2017
Committee Reports, see ¶ 5084

A publicly held corporation can't deduct compensation in excess of $1 million per year paid to a covered employee (see ¶ 2603). (FTC 2d/FIN ¶ H-3776; USTR ¶ 1624.0091; Catalyst ¶ 114:153; Catalyst ¶ 115:205)

Under pre-Tax Cuts and Jobs Act law, a "publicly held corporation" meant any corporation issuing any class of common equity securities required to be registered under section 12 of the Securities Exchange Act of 1934 (the "Exchange Act").

Registration is required under section 12 if: (1) the securities are listed on a national securities exchange or (2) the corporation has (a) $10 million or more of assets and (b) either (i) 2,000 or more shareholders or (ii) 500 or more shareholders who aren't "accredited investors." (FTC 2d/FIN ¶ H-3777; USTR ¶ 1624.0091)

All U.S. publicly traded companies are subject to registration under section 12, including their foreign affiliates. A foreign company publicly traded through American depository receipts ("ADRs") is also subject to this registration requirement, but only if more than 50% of the issuer's outstanding voting securities are held, directly or indirectly, by U.S. residents and either (i) the majority of the executive officers or directors are U.S. citizens or residents, (ii) more than 50% of the issuer's assets are located in the U.S., or (iii) the issuer's business is administered principally in the U.S. (Com Rept, see ¶ 5084)

New Law. The Tax Cuts and Jobs Act defines the term "publicly held corporation" as any corporation that's an issuer, as defined in section 3 of the Exchange Act (15 USC §78c):

. . . whose securities are required to be registered under section 12 of the Exchange Act (15 USC §78l), or

... that's required to file reports under section 15(d) of the Exchange Act (15 USC §78o(d)). (Code Sec. 162(m)(2) as amended by Tax Cuts and Jobs Act §13601(c))

> **observation:** Section 15(d) of the Exchange Act imposes reporting obligations on an issuer that filed a registration statement for debt or equity securities under the Securities Act of 1933, even though the securities aren't listed on an exchange.

So the applicability of the $1 million deduction limit is extended to all foreign companies publicly traded through ADRs as well as to all domestic publicly traded corporations. The expanded definition may include certain corporations that aren't publicly traded, such as large private C or S corporations. (Com Rept, see ¶ 5084)

> **viewpoint:** Arthur Kohn, Esq., a partner at Cleary Gottlieb Steen & Hamilton LLP, notes the following:
>
> While the Tax Cuts and Jobs Act extends Code Sec. 162(m)'s deductibility limitation to apply to certain additional companies, the limit remains relevant only for companies who seek to take a U.S. federal income deduction for compensation paid to their most senior executives. For foreign companies headquartered outside the U.S., the extended scope of the term "publicly held corporation" may not be relevant.

Transition rule. Under a transition rule, the above change and the other changes made by Tax Cuts and Jobs Act §13601 (see ¶ 2601 and ¶ 2603) won't apply to remuneration that's provided pursuant to a written binding contract that was in effect on Nov. 2, 2017, and that wasn't modified in any material respect on or after that date. (Tax Cuts and Jobs Act §13601(e)(2)) For further discussion of this transition rule, see ¶ 2601.

☐ **Effective:** Tax years beginning after Dec. 31, 2017. (Tax Cuts and Jobs Act §13601(e)(1)) However, the amendments made by this provision don't apply to remuneration that's provided pursuant to a written binding contract that was in effect on Nov. 2, 2017, and that wasn't modified in any material respect on or after that date. (Tax Cuts and Jobs Act §13601(e)(2))

¶ 2603. Definition of "covered employee" who's subject to $1 million compensation deduction limit is expanded

Code Sec. 162(m)(3)(A), as amended by Tax Cuts and Jobs Act §13601(b)(1)
Code Sec. 162(m)(3)(B), as amended by Tax Cuts and Jobs Act §13601(b)(2)

Code Sec. 162(m)(3)(C), as amended by Tax Cuts and Jobs Act §13601(b)(3)
Code Sec. 162(m)(4), as amended by Tax Cuts and Jobs Act §13601(d)
Generally effective: Tax years beginning after Dec. 31, 2017
Committee Reports, see ¶ 5084

A publicly held corporation (see ¶ 2602) can't deduct compensation in excess of $1 million per year paid to a covered employee. (FTC 2d/FIN ¶ H-3776; USTR ¶ 1624.0091; Catalyst ¶ 114:153; Catalyst ¶ 115:205)

The statutory definition of a "covered employee" is found in Code Sec. 162(m)(3) and is based on the executive compensation reporting required under the Securities Exchange Act of 1934 (the "Exchange Act"). Under this statutory rule, a "covered employee" was any employee who was: (1) the corporation's chief executive officer (CEO), or an individual acting in that capacity, as of the close of the tax year or (2) one of the corporation's four highest compensated officers (other than the CEO) for the tax year whose total compensation must be reported to shareholders under the Exchange Act.

However, because of changes in the reporting requirements, IRS said in Notice 2007-49 that it would interpret the term "covered employee" under Code Sec. 162(m) to mean any employee if:

. . . as of the close of the tax year, the employee was the principal executive officer (PEO) of the taxpayer (or an individual acting in that capacity); or

. . . the employee's total compensation for that tax year was required to be reported to shareholders under the Exchange Act because the employee was one of the three highest compensated officers for the tax year other than the PEO or principal financial officer (PFO). (FTC 2d/FIN ¶ H-3780; USTR ¶ 1624.0091)

> **observation:** Under Notice 2007-49, a company's PFO wasn't a covered employee under either prong of the definition.

So under pre-Tax Cuts and Jobs Act law, only four employees of a corporation were covered employees for any tax year. (Com Rept, see ¶ 5084)

New Law. The Tax Cuts and Jobs Act redefines the term "covered employee" to mean any employee of the taxpayer if:

(1) the employee is the PEO or PFO of the taxpayer at any time during the tax year, or was an individual acting in that capacity (Code Sec. 162(m)(3)(A) as amended by Tax Cuts and Jobs Act §13601(b)(1)),

(2) the employee's total compensation for the tax year must be reported to shareholders under the Exchange Act because the employee was one of the three highest compensated officers for the tax year other than the PEO or PFO (Code Sec. 162(m)(3)(B) as amended by Tax Cuts and Jobs Act §13601(b)(2)), or

(3) the employee was a covered employee of the taxpayer (or any predecessor) for any earlier tax year that began after Dec. 31, 2016. (Code Sec. 162(m)(3)(C) as amended by Tax Cuts and Jobs Act §13601(b)(3))

So the Tax Cuts and Jobs Act revises the definition of "covered employee" in the following ways:

. . . Both the corporation's PEO and its PFO are covered employees. (Com Rept, see ¶ 5084)

. . . An individual who holds the position of PEO or PFO at any time during the tax year is a covered employee. (Com Rept, see ¶ 5084)

> *illustration (1):*   Individual A was the PEO of corporation X, a publicly held corporation, at the start of 2018. But A resigned from the position during the tax year and was replaced by individual B, who held the position until the end of the year. Both A and B are covered employees of X.

. . . If an individual is a covered employee of a corporation for a tax year beginning after Dec. 31, 2016, then the individual remains a covered employee for all future years, including years during which the individual's no longer employed by the corporation and years after the individual's death (see below for compensation paid to beneficiaries). (Com Rept, see ¶ 5084)

> *illustration (2):*   Individual C was the PEO of corporation Y, a publicly held corporation, for all of 2018. In 2020, C remains employed by Y, but is no longer the CEO and isn't the CFO or one of the three most highly compensated officers. Compensation paid to C in 2020 remains subject to the $1 million deduction limit.

> *illustration (3):*   In 2024, individual C in *RIA illustration (2)* is no longer employed by corporation Y, but receives nonqualified deferred compensation (NQDC) that would otherwise be deductible by Y in 2024. That compensation is subject to the $1 million deduction limit.

> *observation:* Under the Tax Cuts and Jobs Act, a company will have at least five covered employees for any tax year—the PEO, the PFO, and the three other most highly compensated officers. Further, the number of covered employees is potentially unlimited, because part-year PEOs and PFOs and former covered employees are also included. However, an individual's status as a covered employee is relevant only if compensation is paid with respect to the individual that would otherwise be deductible by the company in that tax year.

> *viewpoint:* Arthur Kohn, Esq., a partner at Cleary Gottlieb Steen & Hamilton LLP, notes the following:

The extension of the covered employee definition raises an issue under the Code Sec. 409A plan failure rules concerning payments that have been deferred under the special rule for payments subject to Code Sec. 162(m) in Reg §1.409A-2(b)(7)(i) (see FTC 2d/FIN ¶ H-3200.82).

Under that rule, payments may be delayed at the election of an employer, without violating the Code Sec. 409A rules on permissible payment events and redeferral elections, to the extent that the employer reasonably anticipates that the payment would not be deductible under Code Sec. 162(m). The payments must be delayed until the employee's separation from service or to a year in which the payments would be deductible. Payments to all similarly situated employees are required to be treated on a reasonably consistent basis.

It is not clear how the change in the covered employee definition impacts payments that, under the special deferral provision, are not permitted to be paid until they would be deductible. The Tax Cuts and Jobs Act provides no transition rule related to this provision.

Companies not required to file proxy statements. The Tax Cuts and Jobs Act expanded the definition of a "publicly held corporation" to include some companies that aren't required to file a proxy statement (see ¶ 2602). For those companies, the term "covered employee" includes the three most highly compensated officers (item (2) above) whose compensation would have to be reported to shareholders if this reporting were required. (Code Sec. 162(m)(3) as amended by Tax Cuts and Jobs Act §13601(b)(3))

The definition of "covered employee" also includes officers of a publicly traded corporation that would otherwise have been required to file a proxy statement for the year, such as where the corporation would have been required to file a proxy statement but for the fact that the corporation delisted its securities or underwent a transaction that caused it be exempt from the proxy statement requirement. (Com Rept, see ¶ 5084)

> *observation:* Companies in these situations must identify their three most highly compensated officers for purposes of the $1 million deduction limit using the same rules that apply to companies that file a proxy statement.

Compensation paid to beneficiaries, ex-spouses, etc. Compensation doesn't fail to be "applicable employee remuneration" that's subject to the $1 million deduction limit merely because the compensation is includible in the income of, or paid to, a person other than the covered employee, including after the covered employee's death. (Code Sec. 162(m)(4)(F) as amended by Tax Cuts and Jobs Act §13601(d))

This rule encompasses compensation paid to a beneficiary after the employee's death or to a former spouse under a domestic relations order. (Com Rept, see ¶ 5084)

    illustration (4): In 2028, individual C in *RIA illustration (2)* is deceased, but C's beneficiary receives NQDC that would otherwise be deductible by corporation Y in 2028. That compensation is subject to the $1 million deduction limit.

Transition rule. Under a transition rule, the above change and the other changes made by Tax Cuts and Jobs Act §13601 (see ¶ 2601 and ¶ 2602) won't apply to remuneration that's provided pursuant to a written binding contract that was in effect on Nov. 2, 2017, and that wasn't modified in any material respect on or after that date. (Tax Cuts and Jobs Act §13601(e)(2)) For further discussion of this transition rule, see ¶ 2601.

☐ **Effective:** Tax years beginning after Dec. 31, 2017. (Tax Cuts and Jobs Act §13601(e)(1)) However, the amendments made by this provision don't apply to remuneration that's provided pursuant to a written binding contract that was in effect on Nov. 2, 2017, and that wasn't modified in any material respect on or after that date. (Tax Cuts and Jobs Act §13601(e)(2))

¶ 2604. Employees can elect to defer income from option or RSU stock for up to five years after vesting

Code Sec. 83(i), as amended by Tax Cuts and Jobs Act §13603(a)
Code Sec. 422(b), as amended by Tax Cuts and Jobs Act §13603(c)(1)(A)
Code Sec. 423(b)(5), as amended by Tax Cuts and Jobs Act §13603(c)(1)(B)(i)
Code Sec. 423(d), as amended by Tax Cuts and Jobs Act §13603(c)(1)(B)(ii)
Code Sec. 409A(d)(7), as amended by Tax Cuts and Jobs Act §13603(c)(2)
Generally effective: Stock attributable to options exercised, or restricted stock units settled, after Dec. 31, 2017
Committee Reports, see ¶ 5086

Code Sec. 83 governs the amount and timing of income inclusion for property, including employer stock, transferred to an employee in connection with the performance of services. (Catalyst ¶ 114:152; FTC 2d ¶ H-2501; USTR ¶ 834) Under Code Sec. 83(a), an employee must generally recognize income for the tax year in which the employee's right to the stock is transferable or isn't subject to a substantial risk of forfeiture ("substantially vested"). (Catalyst ¶ 114:152; FTC 2d ¶ H-2518; USTR ¶ 834) The amount includible in income is the excess of the stock's fair market value (FMV) at the time of substantial vesting over the amount, if any, paid by the employee for the stock. (Catalyst ¶ 114:152; FTC 2d ¶ H-2532; USTR ¶ 834)

These rules don't apply to the grant to an employee of a nonqualified (*i.e.*, nonstatutory) stock option unless the option has a readily ascertainable FMV. (Catalyst ¶ 114:152; FTC 2d ¶ H-2859; USTR ¶ 834.07) Instead, these rules apply to the employee's receipt of employer stock on exercise of the option. If the stock is substantially vested on receipt, then income is recognized in the tax year of receipt. If not, then the timing of income inclusion is determined under the rules applicable to the receipt of nonvested stock. In either case, the amount includible in income by the employee is the excess of the FMV of the stock as of the time of income inclusion, less the exercise price paid by the employee and the amount, if any, paid by the employee for the option. (Catalyst ¶ 114:153; FTC 2d ¶ H-2861; USTR ¶ 834.07) The employer's deduction is also determined under these rules. (Catalyst ¶ 114:152; FTC 2d ¶ H-2883; USTR ¶ 834.04)

In some cases, employer stock may be transferred to an employee in settlement of restricted stock units (RSUs). An RSU is an arrangement under which an employee has the right to receive at a specified future time an amount determined by reference to the value of one or more shares of employer stock. The receipt of employer stock in settlement of an RSU is subject to the same rules as other receipts of employer stock with respect to the timing and amount of income inclusion by the employee and the employer's deduction. (Com Rept, see ¶ 5086)

> *observation:* Income from the receipt of employer stock may result in a substantial tax liability, sometimes greater than the tax on the employee's regular salary. If the employer's stock is publicly traded, the employee may sell some of the stock to cover the tax liability. But often that isn't possible for employees of closely-held companies that restrict the transferability of their stock. This may cause some employees to let options lapse rather than incur the tax.

New Law. The Tax Cuts and Jobs Act allows a qualified employee to elect to defer the inclusion in income of the amount of income attributable to qualified stock transferred to the employee by the employer. (Com Rept, see ¶ 5086)

Specifically, the Tax Cuts and Jobs Act provides that, if qualified stock (defined below) is transferred to a qualified employee (defined below), and the employee makes an election under Code Sec. 83(i) with respect to the stock, then the income determined under Code Sec. 83(a) with respect to the stock is included in the employee's income in the tax year determined below, instead of the tax year described in Code Sec. 83(a). (Code Sec. 83(i)(1)(A) as amended by Tax Cuts and Jobs Act §13603(a))

Tax year of inclusion. If a Code Sec. 83(i) election (also called an inclusion deferral election) is made, then the tax year of inclusion is the employee's tax year that includes the earliest of (Code Sec. 83(i)(1)(B)):

(1) the first date the qualified stock becomes transferable (including, solely for this purpose, becoming transferable to the employer) (Code Sec. 83(i)(1)(B)(i));

(2) the date the employee first becomes an excluded employee (defined below) (Code Sec. 83(i)(1)(B)(ii));

(3) the first date on which any stock of the corporation that issued the qualified stock becomes readily tradable on an established securities market (Code Sec. 83(i)(1)(B)(iii));

(4) the date that's five years after the first date the employee's rights in the stock are transferable or aren't subject to a substantial risk of forfeiture, whichever occurs earlier (Code Sec. 83(i)(1)(B)(iv)); or

(5) the date on which the employee revokes (at the time and in the manner that IRS provides) the Code Sec. 83(i) election with respect to the stock. (Code Sec. 83(i)(1)(B)(v))

IRS is to determine the meaning of an "established securities market" in item (3), above. However, the term can't include any market that isn't recognized as an established securities market for purposes of a Code provision other than Code Sec. 83(i). (Code Sec. 83(i)(1)(B)(iii))

It's intended that the limited circumstances outlined in Code Sec. 83(c)(3) and applicable regs apply in determining when stock first becomes transferable or is no longer subject to a substantial risk of forfeiture (see Catalyst ¶ 114:152; FTC 2d/FIN ¶ H-2530 *et seq.*; USTR ¶ 834.02). For example, income inclusion can't be delayed due to a lock-up period as a result of an initial public offering (IPO). (Com Rept, see ¶ 5086)

> *viewpoint:* Arthur Kohn, Esq., a partner at Cleary Gottlieb Steen & Hamilton LLP, notes the following:
>
> While an election under new Code Sec. 83(i) defers the timing of income recognition, the amount of income inclusion is generally based on the fair market value of the stock received. Accordingly, if an employee makes a Code Sec. 83(i) election in connection with the exercise of an option to acquire vested stock, the amount of income required to be included at the end of the deferral period will be based on the value of the stock at the time of exercise, notwithstanding that the value of the stock may have declined during the deferral period. Accordingly, the tax liability could exceed the value of the stock at the end of the deferral period.

If no Code Sec. 83(i) election is made, then the income is includible for the tax year in which the qualified employee's right to the qualified stock is substantially vested under the regular Code Sec. 83(a) rules. (Com Rept, see ¶ 5086)

For income tax withholding when stock subject to a Code Sec. 83(i) election is included in income, see ¶ 2607. For information reporting to employees who have made a Code Sec. 83(i) election, see ¶ 2606.

Employer's deduction. If an employee makes a Code Sec. 83(i) election, then the employer's deduction of the amount of income attributable to the qualified stock is deferred until the employer's tax year in which or with which ends the tax year of the employee for which the amount is included in the employee's income as described in (1)–(5), above. (Com Rept, see ¶ 5086)

"Qualified employee" defined. A qualified employee (who may make a Code Sec. 83(i) election, see above) is an individual who isn't an excluded employee (Code Sec. 83(i)(3)(A)(i)) and who agrees, in the Code Sec. 83(i) election, to meet the requirements, to be determined by IRS, that are necessary to ensure the employer corporation's income tax withholding requirements with respect to the qualified stock are met. (Code Sec. 83(i)(3)(A)(ii))

An excluded employee is, for any corporation, any individual (Code Sec. 83(i)(3)(B)):

(1) who is a 1% owner within the meaning of the Code Sec. 416(i)(1)(B)(ii) top-heavy plan rules (FTC 2d ¶ H-8021; USTR ¶ 4164) at any time during the calendar year, or who was such a 1% owner at any time during the 10 preceding calendar years (Code Sec. 83(i)(3)(B)(i));

(2) who is or has been at any earlier time (Code Sec. 83(i)(3)(B)(ii)) the corporation's chief executive officer (CEO) or an individual acting in that capacity (Code Sec. 83(i)(3)(B)(ii)(I)), or the corporation's chief financial officer (CFO) or an individual acting in that capacity (Code Sec. 83(i)(3)(B)(ii)(II));

(3) who bears a relationship described in the Code Sec. 318(a)(1) family attribution rules (Catalyst ¶ 105:132; FTC 2d ¶ F-11803; USTR ¶ 3184) to an individual described in (2), above (Code Sec. 83(i)(3)(B)(iii)); or

(4) who is one of the four highest compensated officers of the corporation for the tax year, or was one of the four highest compensated officers of the corporation for any of the 10 preceding tax years, determined for each tax year on the basis of the shareholder disclosure rules for compensation under the Securities Exchange Act of 1934 (as if those rules applied to the corporation). (Code Sec. 83(i)(3)(B)(iv))

An excluded employee includes an individual who first becomes a 1% owner (item (1)) or one of the four highest compensated officers (item (4)) in a tax year, notwithstanding that the individual may not have been among such categories for the 10 preceding tax years. (Com Rept, see ¶ 5086)

"Qualified stock" defined. Qualified stock (that may be the subject of a Code Sec. 83(i) election, see above) is, for any qualified employee, any stock in a corporation that's the employer of that employee, if (Code Sec. 83(i)(2)(A)):

- the stock is received (Code Sec. 83(i)(2)(A)(i)):

. . . in connection with the exercise of an option (Code Sec. 83(i)(2)(A)(i)(I)); or

. . . in settlement of an RSU (Code Sec. 83(i)(2)(A)(i)(II)); and

- the corporation granted the option or RSU (Code Sec. 83(i)(2)(A)(ii)):

. . . in connection with the performance of services as an employee (Code Sec. 83(i)(2)(A)(ii)(I))); and

. . . during a calendar year in which the corporation was an eligible corporation (defined below). (Code Sec. 83(i)(2)(A)(ii)(II))

But qualified stock doesn't include any stock if the employee may sell the stock to, or otherwise receive cash in lieu of stock from, the corporation at the time that the employee's rights in the stock first become transferable or not subject to a substantial risk of forfeiture. (Code Sec. 83(i)(2)(B))

Other than Code Sec. 83(i), no part of Code Sec. 83, including Code Sec. 83(b), applies to RSUs. (Code Sec. 83(i)(7))

"Eligible corporation" defined. For purposes of determining whether stock is qualified stock (Code Sec. 83(i)(2)(C)), a corporation is an eligible corporation for a calendar year if (Code Sec. 83(i)(2)(C)(i)):

(a) no stock of the corporation (or any predecessor of the corporation) is readily tradable on an established securities market (as determined under Code Sec. 83(i)(1)(B)(iii), discussed above) during any preceding calendar year (Code Sec. 83(i)(2)(C)(i)(I)); and

(b) the corporation has a written plan under which, in that calendar year, not less than 80% of all employees who provide services to the corporation in the U.S. (or any U.S. possession) are granted stock options, or are granted RSUs, with the same rights and privileges to receive qualified stock. (Code Sec. 83(i)(2)(C)(i)(II))

It's intended that the requirement that 80% of all applicable employees be granted stock options or be granted RSUs apply consistently to eligible employees, whether they are new hires or existing employees. (Com Rept, see ¶ 5086)

Requirement (a), above, continues to apply up to the time a Code Sec. 83(i) election is made. (Com Rept, see ¶ 5086) So a Code Sec. 83(i) election can't be made if any stock of the corporation is readily tradable on an established securities market at any time before the election is made. (Code Sec. 83(i)(4)(B)(ii))

For purposes of (b), above, the determination of rights and privileges with respect to stock is made in a similar manner as under the Code Sec. 423(b)(5) rule for employee stock purchase plans (ESPPs) (FTC 2d ¶ H-2973; USTR ¶ 4234). (Code Sec. 83(i)(2)(C)(ii)(I)) However:

. . . employees won't fail to be treated as having the same rights and privileges to receive qualified stock solely because the number of shares available to all employees isn't equal in amount, so long as more than a *de minimis* number of shares is available to each employee. (Code Sec. 83(i)(2)(C)(ii)(II))

. . . rights and privileges with respect to the exercise of an option aren't treated as the same as rights and privileges with respect to the settlement of a RSU. (Code Sec. 83(i)(2)(C)(ii)(III))

The requirement that 80% of all applicable employees be granted stock options or RSUs with the same rights and privileges can't be satisfied in a tax year by granting a combination of stock options and RSUs. Rather, all such employees must either be granted stock options or be granted RSUs for that year. (Com Rept, see ¶ 5086)

For purposes of (b), above, the term "employee" doesn't include any part-time employee, as described in Code Sec. 4980E(d)(4) (*i.e.*, an employee who's customarily employed for fewer than 30 hours per week, FTC 2d/FIN ¶ H-1350.25), or any excluded employee (defined above). (Code Sec. 83(i)(2)(C)(iii))

> **🅡🅘🅐 *viewpoint:*** Arthur Kohn, Esq., a partner at Cleary Gottlieb Steen & Hamilton LLP, notes the following:
>
> While part-time employees are thus excludible from the 80% calculation, it appears that seasonal and other temporary full-time employees may not be excludible.

For calendar years beginning before Jan. 1, 2018, (b), above, is applied without regard to whether the rights and privileges with respect to the qualified stock are the same. (Code Sec. 83(i)(2)(C)(iv))

> **🅡🅘🅐 *observation:*** An employer may be reluctant to establish a plan to allow Code Sec. 83(i) elections because it will be required to offer options or RSUs to at least 80% of its full-time, U.S.-based employees, when it really wants to reward a smaller number of employees. But employers don't have to offer all 80% the same amount of stock, as long as 80% of the employees receive more than a *de minimis* amount. The employer is free to offer a smaller group of employees substantially more stock-based compensation.

> **🅡🅘🅐 *observation:*** The Code doesn't provide a definition or safe harbor for what's more than a *de minimis* amount of shares. IRS regs or other guidance will be needed to flesh out this concept.

> **🅡🅘🅐 *viewpoint:*** Arthur Kohn, Esq., a partner at Cleary Gottlieb Steen & Hamilton LLP, notes the following:

Broad-based offerings and sales of stock by privately-held corporations require registration, or an exemption from registration, under state securities laws. In California (and perhaps other states), securities laws treat a grant of stock (*e.g.,* pursuant to an RSU) in consideration for services as an offering and sale.

Time for making Code Sec. 83(i) election. A Code Sec. 83(i) election must be made no later than 30 days after the first date the employee's rights in the qualified stock are transferable or aren't subject to a substantial risk of forfeiture, whichever occurs earlier. (Code Sec. 83(i)(4)(A))

How Code Sec. 83(i) election is made. A Code Sec. 83(i) election must be made in a manner similar to the manner in which a Code Sec. 83(b) election is made (Catalyst ¶ 114:152; FTC 2d/FIN ¶ H-2540; USTR ¶ 834.03). (Code Sec. 83(i)(4)(A)) So the employee must provide the employer with a copy of the election. (Com Rept, see ¶ 5086)

Code Sec. 83(i) election can't be made if Code Sec. 83(b) election was made. A Code Sec. 83(i) election can't be made for qualified stock for which the employee has made a Code Sec. 83(b) election to report income in the year nonvested property is received (Catalyst ¶ 114:152; FTC 2d/FIN ¶ H-2540; USTR ¶ 834.03). (Code Sec. 83(i)(4)(B)(i))

So Code Sec. 83(i) doesn't apply to income with respect to nonvested stock that's includible as a result of an Code Sec. 83(b) election. (Com Rept, see ¶ 5086)

Corporate stock redemptions may bar Code Sec. 83(i) election. An employee may not make a Code Sec. 83(i) election for a year with respect to qualified stock if the corporation purchased any of its outstanding stock in the preceding calendar year, unless (Code Sec. 83(i)(4)(B)(iii))

. . . at least 25% of the total dollar amount of the stock so purchased is deferral stock (Code Sec. 83(i)(4)(B)(iii)(I)), *i.e.,* stock for which a Code Sec. 83(i) election is in effect (Code Sec. 83(i)(4)(C)(i)), and

. . . the determination of the individuals from whom deferral stock is purchased is made on a reasonable basis. (Code Sec. 83(i)(4)(B)(iii)(II))

This requirement is met if the corporation purchases all of its outstanding deferral stock. (Code Sec. 83(i)(4)(C)(iii))

For this purpose, stock purchased by a corporation from an individual isn't treated as deferral stock if, immediately after the purchase, the individual holds any deferral stock for which a Code Sec. 83(i) election has been in effect for a longer period than the election with respect to the stock purchased by the corporation. (Code Sec. 83(i)(4)(C)(ii)) So an individual's deferral stock with respect to which a Code Sec. 83(i) election has been in effect for the longest periods must generally be purchased first. (Com Rept, see ¶ 5086)

A corporation that has outstanding deferral stock as of the beginning of any calendar year and that purchases any of its outstanding stock during that calendar year must include on its tax return for the tax year in which, or with which, that calendar year ends the total dollar amount of its outstanding stock that it purchased during that calendar year. It must also include any other information that IRS requires for purposes of administering the rules on deferral stock. (Code Sec. 83(i)(4)(C)(iv))

Controlled group members treated as one corporation. For Code Sec. 83(i) election purposes, all persons that are treated as the same employer under Code Sec. 414(b) (because they're members of a controlled group of corporations, FTC 2d ¶ H-7901; USTR ¶ 4144.02) are treated as one corporation. (Code Sec. 83(i)(5))

Employer's notifications to employee. A corporation that transfers qualified stock to a qualified employee must, at the time that (or a reasonable period before) an amount attributable to the stock would (but for the Code Sec. 83(i) election) first be includible in the employee's gross income, certify to the employee that the stock is qualified stock. (Code Sec. 83(i)(6)(A))

The corporation must notify the employee (Code Sec. 83(i)(6)(B)):

... that the employee may elect to defer income on the stock under Code Sec. 83(i) (Code Sec. 83(i)(6)(B)(i));

... that, if the employee makes the Code Sec. 83(i) election, then the income recognized at the end of the deferral period will be based on the stock's value when the employee's rights in the stock first become transferable or not subject to substantial risk of forfeiture, whether or not the stock has declined in value during the deferral period (Code Sec. 83(i)(6)(B)(ii)(I));

... that the amount of the income recognized at the end of the deferral period will be subject to withholding under Code Sec. 3401(i) at the rate determined under Code Sec. 3402(t) (see ¶ 2607). (Code Sec. 83(i)(6)(B)(ii)(II))

The corporation must also notify the employee of the employee's responsibilities (as determined by IRS under Code Sec. 83(i)(3)(A)(ii)) with respect to the withholding. (Code Sec. 83(i)(6)(B)(ii)(III))

For the penalty for failure to provide this notice, see ¶ 2608.

Coordination with statutory stock option rules. A qualified employee may make a Code Sec. 83(i) election with respect to qualified stock attributable to a statutory option—an incentive stock option (ISO, see Catalyst ¶ 114:151; FTC 2d/FIN ¶ H-2753; USTR ¶ 4224) or an option granted under an employee stock purchase plan (ESPP, see FTC 2d/FIN ¶ H-2704; USTR ¶ 4214.01). (Com Rept, see ¶ 5086)

In that case, the option isn't treated as a statutory option and the rules relating to statutory options and related stock don't apply. Nonstatutory option treatment applies for Federal Insurance Contribution Act (FICA) purposes as well as for income tax purposes. (Com Rept, see ¶ 5086)

Thus, the Tax Cuts and Jobs Act provides that an option isn't treated as an ISO if a Code Sec. 83(i) election is made with respect to the stock received in connection with the exercise of the option. (Code Sec. 422(b) as amended by Tax Cuts and Jobs Act §13603(c)(1)(A))

Similarly, an option for which a Code Sec. 83(i) election is made with respect to the stock received in connection with its exercise isn't considered as granted under an ESPP. (Code Sec. 423(d) as amended by Tax Cuts and Jobs Act §13603(c)(1)(B)(ii))

For purposes of the requirement that an ESPP provide employees with the same rights and privileges (see FTC 2d/FIN ¶ H-2973; USTR ¶ 4234.02), the rules of Code Sec. 83(i) apply in determining which employees have the right to make a Code Sec. 83(i) election with respect to stock received under the ESPP. (Code Sec. 423(b)(5) as amended by Tax Cuts and Jobs Act §13603(c)(1)(B)(i))

Coordination with plan failure rules. An arrangement under which an employee may receive qualified stock isn't treated with respect to that employee as a nonqualified deferred compensation (NQDC) plan that is subject to the Code Sec. 409A plan failure rules (see Catalyst ¶ 754:122; FTC 2d/FIN ¶ H-3200 *et seq.*; USTR ¶ 409A4) solely because of an employee's Code Sec. 83(i) election, or ability to make the election. (Code Sec. 409A(d)(7) as amended by Tax Cuts and Jobs Act §13603(c)(2))

> *observation:* Nonqualified options on employer stock may be structured so as not to be considered NQDC, and so not subject to the Code Sec. 409A plan failure rules. (FTC 2d/FIN ¶ H-3200.29; USTR ¶ 409A4.02) The availability of a Code Sec. 83(i) election won't, in and of itself, make a stock option plan subject to Code Sec. 409A, with its attendant restrictions and harsh tax consequences for plan failures.

> *observation:* An arrangement providing RSUs is considered an NQDC plan and is subject to the Code Sec. 409A plan failure rules.

The exception from treatment as a NQDC plan for Code Sec. 409A purposes applies solely with respect to an employee who may receive qualified stock. (Com Rept, see ¶ 5086)

No effect on FICA and FUTA taxes. A Code Sec. 83(i) election applies only for income tax purposes. (Code Sec. 83(i)(1)) Therefore, it has no effect on the application of social security and Medicare taxes under FICA (Catalyst ¶ 656:104; FTC 2d ¶ H-4546; USTR ¶ 31,114) and unemployment taxes under the Federal Unemployment Tax Act (FUTA) (Catalyst ¶ 656:104; FTC 2d ¶ H-4726; USTR ¶ 33,014). (Com Rept, see ¶ 5086)

Transition rule. Until IRS issues regs or other guidance to implement the 80% requirement of Code Sec. 83(i)(2)(C)(i)(II) or the notice requirement of Code Sec. 83(i)(6), a corporation is treated as being in compliance with those requirements if it complies with a reasonable good-faith interpretation of the requirements. (Tax Cuts and Jobs Act §13603(g))

However, this transition rule isn't intended to be expanded beyond those two items. (Com Rept, see ¶ 5086)

☐ **Effective:** Stock attributable to options exercised, or RSUs settled, after Dec. 31, 2017. (Tax Cuts and Jobs Act §13603(f)(1))

¶ 2605. Cash, gift cards, and other nontangible personal property don't qualify as employee achievement awards

Code Sec. 274(j)(3)(A), as amended by Tax Cuts and Jobs Act §13310(a)
Generally effective: Amounts paid or incurred after Dec. 31, 2017
Committee Reports, see ¶ 5053

An "employee achievement award" is an item of tangible personal property that an employer transfers to an employee for a length-of-service or safety achievement. It must be awarded as part of a meaningful presentation and under conditions and circumstances that don't create a significant likelihood that the payment is disguised compensation. (FTC 2d/FIN ¶ L-2313; USTR ¶ 2744.09)

The employer's deduction for the cost of all employee achievement awards made to an employee in a tax year is limited to $400 if the award isn't a qualified plan award, and $1,600 if it is a qualified plan award. (FTC 2d/FIN ¶ L-2312; USTR ¶ 2744.09)

A "qualified plan award" is an employee achievement award that is awarded under an established written plan or program that doesn't discriminate in favor of highly-compensated employees as to eligibility or benefits. The average cost of all employee achievement awards provided by the employer during the year that would otherwise be qualified plan awards can't exceed $400. (FTC 2d/FIN ¶ L-2317; USTR ¶ 2744.09)

An employee generally includes in gross income the fair market value of any award received from the employer. However, an employee can exclude the value of an employee achievement award if the cost of the award to the employer doesn't exceed the deductible amount. (FTC 2d/FIN ¶ J-1219; USTR ¶ 744.02) *observation:* Employee achievement awards are a tax-advantaged way of rewarding employees for length-of-service or safety achievement. The employer can deduct the cost of the award within limits, but the employee doesn't include the value of the award in income.

Proposed regs issued in 1989 provided that the "tangible personal property" that can be given as an employee achievement award doesn't include cash or a certificate, other than a nonnegotiable certificate conferring only the right to receive tangible personal property. Other items that weren't considered tangible personal property under the proposed regs included vacations, meals, lodging, tickets to theater and sporting events, and stocks, bonds, and other securities. (FTC 2d/FIN ¶ L-2300, ¶ L-2316; USTR ¶ 2744.09)

However, under pre-Tax Cuts and Jobs Act law, the Code didn't define "tangible personal property" for purposes of employee achievement awards.

New Law. The Tax Cuts and Jobs Act provides that, for purposes of the definition of an "employee achievement award," the term "tangible personal property" doesn't include (Code Sec. 274(j)(3)(A)(ii) as amended by Tax Cuts and Jobs Act §13310(a)(3)):

. . . cash, cash equivalents, gift cards, gift coupons, or gift certificates; or (Code Sec. 274(j)(3)(A)(ii)(I))

. . . vacations, meals, lodging, tickets to theater or sporting events, stocks, bonds, other securities, and other similar items. (Code Sec. 274(j)(3)(A)(ii)(II))

observation: Because awards of these items aren't employee achievement awards, they can't be excluded as such by the employee who receives them.

However, arrangements that confer only the right to select and receive tangible personal property from a limited array of items pre-selected or pre-approved by the employer qualify as tangible personal property. (Code Sec. 274(j)(3)(A)(ii)(I))

illustration: For his 30th anniversary with Employer, Employee was allowed to choose a gift from a selection of tangible items, such as electronics, jewelry, and housewares. This arrangement can qualify as an employee achievement award.

No inference is intended that this is a change from pre-Tax Cuts and Jobs Act law and guidance. (Com Rept, see ¶ 5053)

observation: The Tax Cuts and Jobs Act provision is very similar to the 1989 proposed regs and to the position taken at p. 7 of IRS Pub No. 15-B, Employer's Tax Guide to Fringe Benefits (2017).

☐ **Effective:** Amounts paid or incurred after Dec. 31, 2017. (Tax Cuts and Jobs Act §13310(b))

¶ 2606. Form W-2 must include information about deferrals and inclusions under Code Sec. 83(i)

Code Sec. 6051(a)(16), as amended by Tax Cuts and Jobs Act §13603(d)
Code Sec. 6051(a)(17), as amended by Tax Cuts and Jobs Act §13603(d)
Generally effective: Stock attributable to options exercised, or restricted stock units settled, after Dec. 31, 2017
Committee Reports, see ¶ 5086

An employer must furnish to each employee a written statement on Form W-2 reporting the amount of the employee's wages and the amount of tax withheld on those wages. (FTC 2d/FIN ¶ S-3150; USTR ¶ 60,514)

The information reported on Form W-2 must include the items listed in Code Sec. 6051(a). (FTC 2d/FIN ¶ S-3152; USTR ¶ 60,514)

The Tax Cuts and Jobs Act added Code Sec. 83(i), which allows qualified employees to elect to defer recognition of income attributable to qualified stock received on exercise of an option or settlement of a restricted stock unit (RSU), see ¶ 2604.

Code Sec. 83(i)(1)(A) provides that if a Code Sec. 83(i) election is made, the income attributable to the qualified stock, as determined under the regular Code Sec. 83(a) rules on property received in connection with the performance of services (Catalyst ¶ 114:152; FTC 2d/FIN ¶ H-2532; USTR ¶ 834.01), is included in the employee's income in the tax year determined under Code Sec. 83(i)(1)(B)—*i.e.,* the employee's tax year that includes the earliest of:

- the first date the qualified stock becomes transferable (including, solely for this purpose, becoming transferable to the employer);

- the date the employee first becomes an excluded employee (as defined at ¶ 2604);

- the first date on which any stock of the corporation that issued the qualified stock becomes readily tradable on an established securities market;

- the date that's five years after the first date that the employee's rights in the stock became transferable or weren't subject to a substantial risk of forfeiture, whichever occurred earlier; or

- the date on which the employee revokes the Code Sec. 83(i) election.

See ¶ 2604, under "Tax year of inclusion."

New Law. The Tax Cuts and Jobs Act requires employers to report on Form W-2:

. . . the amount includible in gross income under Code Sec. 83(i)(1)(A) with respect to an event described in Code Sec. 83(i)(1)(B) that occurs in the calendar year. (Code Sec. 6051(a)(16) as amended by Tax Cuts and Jobs Act §13603(d))

. . . the aggregate amount of income that's being deferred under Code Sec. 83(i) elections, determined as of the close of the calendar year. (Code Sec. 6051(a)(17) as amended by Tax Cuts and Jobs Act §13603(d))

So the employer must report on Form W-2 the amount of income covered by a Code Sec. 83(i) election for (1) the year of deferral, and (2) the year the income's required to be included in income by the employee. (Com Rept, see ¶ 5086)

In addition, for any calendar year, the employer must report on Form W-2 the aggregate amount of income covered by Code Sec. 83(i) elections, determined as of the close of the calendar year. (Com Rept, see ¶ 5086)

> **⊘ observation:** As a result of these rules, an employee will receive a Form W-2 with information about the employee's Code Sec. 83(i) election for each year starting from the year when the election is made until the year when the stock's value must be included in the employee's income.

> **⊘ observation:** Even though the employee is responsible for paying the tax on the shares, the employer must keep track of any Code Sec. 83(i)(1)(B) event in order to include this information on Form W-2.

☐ **Effective:** Stock attributable to options exercised, or RSUs settled, after Dec. 31, 2017. (Tax Cuts and Jobs Act §13603(f)(1))

¶ 2607. Withholding is required at highest individual rate when stock subject to Code Sec. 83(i) election is included in income

Code Sec. 3401(i), as amended by Tax Cuts and Jobs Act §13603(b)(1)
Code Sec. 3402(t), as amended by Tax Cuts and Jobs Act §13603(b)(2)
Generally effective: Stock attributable to options exercised, or restricted stock units settled, after Dec. 31, 2017
Committee Reports, see ¶ 5086

Employers must withhold income tax on wages paid to employees, whether provided in cash or in property, including employer stock. (FTC 2d ¶s H-4326, H-4327; USTR ¶ 34,014.09) The tax must ordinarily be deducted and withheld when the wages are paid to the employee, either actually or constructively. (FTC 2d ¶ H-4487; USTR ¶ 34,024.01)

Withholding is based on graduated rates set out in IRS tables. (FTC 2d ¶ H-4486; USTR ¶ 34,024.02) Special withholding rates apply to payments that vary from payroll period to payroll period (supplemental wages), such as commissions, tips, and bonuses. The amount and method of withholding on supplemental wages, such as the aggregation method or the flat-rate method, depend in part on whether tax has been withheld from the employee's regular wages. (FTC 2d ¶ H-4531; USTR ¶ 34,024.13)

Code Sec. 3501(b) requires tax to be withheld on non-cash fringe benefits at the time and in the manner prescribed by IRS regs. Until final regs are issued, taxpayers can rely on IRS guidelines for withholding on non-cash fringe benefits. (FTC 2d ¶ H-4402; USTR ¶ 35,014)

The IRS guidelines require fringe benefits to be treated as paid at least annually. So a benefit provided in a calendar year must be treated as paid by Dec. 31 of that year. An employer may elect to treat fringe benefits as paid on a pay-period, quarterly, semiannual, annual, or other basis. The employer may also treat a fringe benefit as paid in installments, even if the entire benefit is paid at once. (FTC 2d ¶ H-4403; USTR ¶ 35,014)

Under pre-Tax Cuts and Jobs Act law, an employee's receipt of stock or restricted stock units (RSUs) was taxable when the employee's right to the stock was transferable or wasn't subject to a substantial risk of forfeiture.

The Tax Cuts and Jobs Act added Code Sec. 83(i), which allows employees to elect to defer recognition of income attributable to stock received on exercise of an option or settlement of an RSU until an opportunity to sell some of the stock arises, but in no event longer than five years from the date that the employee's right to the stock becomes substantially vested. See ¶ 2604.

New Law. The Tax Cuts and Jobs Act provides that qualified stock for which a Code Sec. 83(i) election is made is treated as wages received on the earliest date described in Code Sec. 83(i)(1)(B) (see ¶ 2604). (Code Sec. 3401(i)(1) as amended by Tax Cuts and Jobs Act §13603(b)(1))

The amount of wages received is equal to the amount included in income under Code Sec. 83 for the tax year that includes that date. (Code Sec. 3401(i)(2))

> *observation:* Code Sec. 83(i)(1)(B) lists five events that trigger inclusion in income of the value of qualified stock for which an employee has made a Code Sec. 83(i) election. These events are:
>
> • the first date the qualified stock becomes transferable (including, solely for this purpose, becoming transferable to the employer);
>
> • the date the employee first becomes an excluded employee (as defined at ¶ 2604);

- the first date on which any stock of the corporation that issued the qualified stock becomes readily tradable on an established securities market;

- the date that is five years after the first date that the employee's rights in the stock became transferable or weren't subject to a substantial risk of forfeiture, whichever occurred earlier; or

- the date on which employee revokes the Code Sec. 83(i) election.

See ¶ 2604 under "Tax Year of Inclusion."

Withholding rate. The income tax withholding rate for any qualified stock for which a Code Sec. 83(i) election is made can't be less than the maximum income tax rate in effect under Code Sec. 1. (Code Sec. 3402(t)(1) as amended by Tax Cuts and Jobs Act §13603(b)(2)) For the highest individual rate under the Tax Cuts and Jobs Act, see ¶ 101.

Stock treated as non-cash fringe benefit. Qualified stock for which a Code Sec. 83(i) election is made must be treated as a non-cash fringe benefit for purposes of the Code Sec. 3501(b) rules on the time and manner of income tax withholding. (Code Sec. 3402(t)(2))

☐ **Effective:** Stock attributable to options exercised, or RSUs settled, after Dec. 31, 2017. (Tax Cuts and Jobs Act §13603(f)(1))

¶ 2608. Penalty imposed for employer's failure to notify employee that stock is eligible for Code Sec. 83(i) election

Code Sec. 6652(p), as amended by Tax Cuts and Jobs Act §13603(e)
Generally effective: Failures after Dec. 31, 2017
Committee Reports, see ¶ 5086

The Tax Cuts and Jobs Act added Code Sec. 83(i), which allows qualified employees to elect to defer recognition of income attributable to qualified stock received on exercise of an option or settlement of a restricted stock unit (RSU) until an opportunity to sell the stock arises, but in no event longer than five years from the date that the employee's right to the stock becomes substantially vested. See ¶ 2604.

Under Code Sec. 83(i)(6), a corporation that transfers qualified stock to a qualified employee must provide a notice to the qualified employee at the time that (or a reasonable period before) an amount attributable to the stock would, but for Code Sec. 83(i) election, first be includible in the employee's gross income.

The notice must (1) certify to the employee that the stock is qualified stock, and (2) notify the employee that (a) the employee may elect to defer income inclusion with respect to the stock, and (b) if the employee makes the election, then the amount of income to be included at the end of the deferral period will be based on the stock's value when the employee's right to the stock is substantially vested, even if the value has declined during the deferral period.

The notice must also inform the employee that the amount of income to be included at the end of the deferral period will be subject to withholding and describe the employee's responsibilities with respect to the withholding. See ¶ 2604 under "Employer's notifications to employee."

New Law. The Tax Cuts and Jobs Act imposes a penalty on a person who fails to provide the notice required by Code Sec. 83(i)(6) on a timely basis. The amount of the penalty is $100 per failure, up to a maximum penalty of $50,000 for all failures by a person during a calendar year. (Code Sec. 6652(p) as amended by Tax Cuts and Jobs Act §13603(e))

The penalty won't be imposed for a failure that's shown to be due to reasonable cause and not to willful neglect. (Code Sec. 6652(p))

The penalty is paid in the same manner as tax, on notice and demand by IRS. (Code Sec. 6652(p))

☐ **Effective:** Failures after Dec. 31, 2017. (Tax Cuts and Jobs Act §13603(f)(2))

¶ 2700. Retirement Plans

¶ 2701. Special rule allowing recharacterization of Roth IRA contributions and traditional IRA contributions does not apply to conversion contributions to a Roth IRA

Code Sec. 408A(d)(6)(B)(iii), as amended by Tax Cuts and Jobs Act §13611(a)

Generally effective: Tax years after Dec. 31, 2017

Committee Reports, see ¶ 5088

Under pre-Tax Cuts and Jobs Act law, the Roth IRA rules allowed an individual to elect to "recharacterize" an IRA contribution—i.e., elect to treat a contribution made to one type of IRA as made to a different type of IRA in a so-called "conversion contribution"—by (a) transferring the contribution (or a portion of the contribtuion) from the first IRA to the second IRA in a trustee-to-trustee transfer, and (b) meeting specific requirements regarding the transfer. (FTC 2d/FIN ¶ H-12290, ¶ H-12290.22; USTR ¶ 408A4; PCA ¶ 35,223; PBE ¶ 408A4)

New Law. Under the Tax Cuts and Jobs Act, the provision allowing taxpayers to recharacterize Roth IRA contributions and traditional IRA contributions does not apply to a conversion contribution to a Roth IRA. (Code Sec. 408A(d)(6)(B)(iii) as amended by Tax Cuts and Jobs Act §13611(a))

Thus, recharacterization cannot be used to unwind a Roth conversion. However, recharacterization is still permitted with respect to other contributions. For example, an individual may make a contribution for a year to a Roth IRA and, before the due date for the individual's income tax return for that year, recharacterize it as a contribution to a traditional IRA. In addition, an individual may still make a contribution to a traditional IRA and convert the traditional IRA to a Roth IRA, but the provision precludes the individual from later unwinding the conversion through a recharacterization. (Com Rept, see ¶ 5088)

☐ **Effective:** Tax years beginning after Dec. 31, 2017. (Tax Cuts and Jobs Act §13611(b))

FTC 2d References are to Federal Tax Coordinator 2d
FIN References are to RIA's Analysis of Federal Taxes: Income (print)
USTR References are to United States Tax Reporter: Income
Catalyst References are to Checkpoint Catalyst
PCA References are to Pension Analysis (print and electronic)
PBE References are to Pension & Benefits Explanations
BCA References are to Benefits Analysis (electronic)
BC References are to Benefits Coordinator (print)
EP References are to Estate Planning Analysis (print and electronic)

¶ 2702. Rollover period for plan loan offset amounts is extended from 60 days, to tax return due date

Code Sec. 402(c)(3), as amended by Tax Cuts and Jobs Act §13613
Generally effective: Tax years beginning after Dec. 31, 2017
Committee Reports, see ¶ 5090

A distribution from a qualified plan is generally includible in gross income, except for a qualified distribution from a designated Roth account, or to the extent the distribution is a recovery of basis under the plan, or the distribution is contributed to another such plan or an IRA (referred to as "eligible retirement plans") in a tax-free rollover. For a distribution from a plan to an employee under age 59½, the distribution (other than a distribution from a governmental section 457(b) plan) is also subject to a 10% early distribution tax, unless an exception applies. (FTC 2d/FIN ¶ H-11006; H-11101; H-11402; USTR ¶ 4024; 724.21; 4024.04; PCA ¶ 32,107; 32,202; 32,803; PBE ¶ 4024; 724.21; 4024.04)

Tax-free rollovers. Under Code Sec. 402(c)(1), a distribution from a qualified plan to an employee that is rolled over to another plan is not includible in income (i.e., the distribution is tax-free) for the tax year in which the distribution is paid, if:

(1) any portion of the balance of an employee's credit in a qualified plan is distributed to the employee in an "eligible rollover distribution;"

(2) the employee transfers (i.e., rolls over) any portion of the property received in the distribution to an eligible retirement plan; and

(3) for a distribution of property other than money, the amount transferred (in item (2), above) consists of the property distributed (in item (1), above).

A tax-free rollover may be either:

. . . a direct rollover; or

. . . a contribution of an eligible rollover distribution to an eligible retirement plan that satisfies the Code Sec. 402(c)(3)(A) 60-day rollover requirement. (FTC 2d/FIN ¶ H-11402; USTR ¶ 4024.04; PCA ¶ 32,803; PBE ¶ 4024.04)

Under the Code Sec. 402(c)(3)(A) 60-day rollover requirement, a distribution from a qualified plan rolled over after the 60th day following the day on which the distributee receives the property, will not qualify as a tax-free rollover, except in the case of hardship. Under the hardship exception (provided under Code Sec. 402(c)(3)(B)), IRS has the authority to waive the 60-day rule, where the failure to waive the rule would be against equity or good conscience. Thus, unless an exception applies, a tax-free rollover must be transferred within 60 days (sometimes referred to as the "60-day rule"). (FTC 2d/FIN ¶ H-11452; USTR ¶ 4024.04; PCA ¶ 32,853; PBE ¶ 4024.04)

An "eligible rollover distribution," which is excludable from income if rolled over under the rules described above, is any distribution to an employee:

... of all, or any portion, of the balance of the employee's interest in a qualified plan;

... that is not excluded from eligible rollover distribution status. (FTC 2d/FIN ¶ H-11406; USTR ¶ 4024.04; PCA ¶ 32,807; PBE ¶ 4024.04)

Plans loans taxable as distributions. Under Code Sec. 72(p)(1), a loan from a "qualified employer plan" to an employee is treated as a plan distribution (referred to as a "deemed distribution") which may be taxable, unless the following conditions (described in Code Sec. 72(p)(2)), are met:

(a) the loan is required to be repaid within five years, except for certain home loans;

(b) the plan loan is amortized in substantially level payments, made not less frequently than quarterly;

(c) the amount of the loan, when added to the balance of all other plan loans to the employee, does not exceed a certain limit; and

(d) the loan is evidenced by a legally enforceable agreement. (FTC 2d/FIN ¶ H-11065; H-11066; USTR ¶ 724.23; PCA ¶ 32,166; 32,167; PBE ¶ 724.23)

A deemed distribution is not eligible for rollover to another eligible retirement plan.

Under Code Sec. 72(p)(4), a "qualified employer plan" means:

(i) a Code Sec. 401(a) qualified plan;

(ii) a Code Sec. 403(a) qualified annuity plan;

(iii) a plan under which amounts are contributed by an employer for the purchase of a Code Sec. 403(b) annuity contract;

(iv) a governmental plan, whether or not qualified; and

(v) any plan which was (or was determined to be) a qualified employer plan or a government plan, (i.e., a plan that once was described in items (i) through (iv) above). (FTC 2d/FIN ¶ H-11065.1; USTR ¶ 724.23; PCA ¶ 32,166.1; PBE ¶ 724.23)

Plan loan offsets. A plan may provide that, in certain circumstances (for example, if an employee terminates employment), an employee's obligation to repay a loan is accelerated and, if the loan is not repaid, the loan is cancelled and the amount in the employee's account balance is offset by the amount of the unpaid loan balance (referred to as a "loan offset"). A loan offset is treated as an actual distribution from the plan equal to the unpaid loan balance (rather than a deemed distribution), and (unlike a deemed distribution) the amount of the distribution is eligible for tax-free rollover to another eligible retirement plan.

Under pre-Tax Cuts and Jobs Act law, the rollover period during which a qualified plan loan offset amount had to be contributed to an eligible retirement plan in order to qualify as a tax-free rollover, was through the 60th day following the date of the offset. (FTC 2d/FIN ¶ H-11415; USTR ¶ 4024.04; PCA ¶ 32,816; PBE ¶ 4024.04)

New Law. The Tax Cuts and Jobs Act provides that the Code Sec. 402(c)(1) tax-free rollover rule does not apply to any transfer of a "qualified plan loan offset amount" made after the due date (including extensions) for filing the tax return for the tax year in which that amount is treated as distributed from a "qualified employer plan." (Code Sec. 402(c)(3)(C)(i) as amended by Tax Cuts and Jobs Act §13613(a))

> *observation:* Put another way, if the transfer of a qualified plan loan offset amount is made *before* the due date (including extensions) for filing the tax return for the tax year in which that amount is treated as distributed, then the transfer is considered a tax-free rollover under Code Sec. 402(c)(1).

> *observation:* Since the tax return due date may occur more than 60 days following the date of the offset, the Tax Cuts and Jobs Act is effectively providing an exception to the 60-day rollover requirement by allowing tax-free rollovers of qualified plan loan offset amounts more than 60 days following the date of the offset.

Thus, under the Tax Cuts and Jobs Act, the period during which a qualified plan loan offset amount may be contributed to an eligible retirement plan as a tax-free rollover contribution is extended from 60 days after the date of the offset, to the due date (including extensions) for filing the federal income tax return for the tax year in which the plan loan offset occurs, that is, the taxable year in which the amount is treated as distributed from the plan. (Com Rept, see ¶ 5090) So, in addition to the hardship exception (as provided under pre-Tax Cuts and Jobs Act law), the Act provides that the 60-day rollover requirement won't apply to transfers of certain plan loan offset amounts (see below). (Code Sec. 402(c)(3)(A))

For purposes of the plan loan offset exception to the 60-day rule, a "qualified plan loan offset amount" means a "plan loan offset amount" which is treated as distributed from a "qualified employer plan" to a participant or beneficiary solely by reason of:

(I) the termination of the qualified employer plan; or

(II) the failure to meet the repayment terms of the loan from the plan because of the participant's "severance from employment." (Code Sec. 402(c)(3)(C)(ii))

A "severance from employment" (sometimes also referred to as a "separation from service," and presumed to have the same meaning as a "severance from employment" for purposes of the rules above) may be due to layoff, cessation of business, termination of employment, or otherwise. (Com Rept, see ¶ 5090)

> *observation:* Thus, the failure to repay a loan for any reason other than as described in items (I) and (II), above—including financial hardship—does not constitute a "qualified plan loan offset amount." So, unless the Code Sec. 402(c)(3)(B) hardship exception applies (under which the failure to waive the 60-day rule would be against equity or good conscience, see above), the participant would have to roll over the transfer within 60 days of the date of the offset (as provided under pre-Tax Cuts and Jobs Act law) to avoid being taxed on the offset amount.

A "plan loan offset amount" means the amount by which the participant's accrued benefit under the plan is reduced in order to repay a loan from the plan. (Code Sec. 402(c)(3)(C)(iii))

The plan loan offset exception does not apply to any plan loan offset amount, unless the plan loan offset amount relates to a loan to which Code Sec. 72(p)(1) (see above) does not apply by reason of Code Sec. 72(p)(2) (see above). (Code Sec. 402(c)(3)(C)(iv))

> *observation:* Thus, to qualify for the plan loan offset exception from the 60-day rule, the plan loan offset amount must relate to a plan loan that satisfies at least one of the Code Sec. 72(p)(2) conditions described above, so that the loan is not otherwise treated as a taxable deemed distribution under Code Sec. 72(p)(1).

A "qualified employer plan" is defined under Code Sec. 72(p)(4) (see above). (Code Sec. 402(c)(3)(C)(v))

☐ **Effective:** For plan loan offset amounts which are treated as distributed in tax years beginning after Dec. 31, 2017. (Tax Cuts and Jobs Act §13613(c))

¶ 2703. Accrual limit for length of service award plans is increased from $3,000 to $6,000

Code Sec. 457(e)(11)(B), as amended by Tax Cuts and Jobs Act §13612
Generally effective: Tax years beginning after Dec. 31, 2017
Committee Reports, see ¶ 5089

Under Code Sec. 457, special rules apply to deferred compensation plans of state and local governments, and tax-exempt organizations. However, an exception to those rules applies for a plan paying solely length of service awards to bona fide volunteers (or their beneficiaries), on account of qualified services performed by the volunteers. For this purpose, qualified services consist of fire fighting and fire prevention services, emergency medical services, and ambulance services. An individual is treated as a bona fide volunteer for this purpose if the only compensation received by the individual for performing qualified services is in the form of either:

(1) reimbursement, or a reasonable allowance, for reasonable expenses incurred in the performance of those services; or

(2) reasonable benefits (including length of service awards), and nominal fees for the services, customarily paid in connection with the performance of those services by volunteers.

For a length of service award plan, the exception from application of Code Sec. 457 applies only if the aggregate amount of length of service awards accruing for a bona fide volunteer for any year of service does not exceed a certain amount (referred to as the "accrual limit"). Under pre-Tax Cuts and Jobs Act law, the accrual limit was $3,000, and there was no provision allowing for cost of living adjustments. (FTC 2d/FIN ¶ H-3339.1; USTR ¶ 4574; PCA ¶ 40,440.1; PBE ¶ 4574)

New Law. The Tax Cuts and Jobs Act increases the accrual limit from $3,000 to $6,000 (Code Sec. 457(e)(11)(B)(ii) as amended by Tax Cuts and Jobs Act §13612(a)), and provides for cost-of-living adjustments (see below). Thus, the Tax Cuts and Jobs Act increases the aggregate amount of length of service awards that may accrue for a bona fide volunteer for any year of service to $6,000, and adjusts that amount to reflect changes in cost-of-living. (Com Rept, see ¶ 5089)

In addition, if the length of service award plan is a defined benefit plan, then the accrual limit applies to the actuarial present value of the aggregate amount of length of service awards accruing for any year of service. Actuarial present value for any year is calculated using reasonable actuarial assumptions and methods, assuming payment will be made under the most valuable form of payment under the plan, with payment beginning at the later of:

(a) the earliest age at which unreduced benefits are payable under the plan; or

(b) the participant's age at the time of the calculation. (Code Sec. 457(e)(11)(B)(iv))

Cost of living adjustments. For tax years beginning after Dec. 31, 2017, IRS must adjust the $6,000 accrual amount (see above) at the same time, and in the same manner, as under the Code Sec. 415(d) cost-of-living adjustments for defined benefit plans, except that the base period to be used is the calendar quarter beginning July 1, 2016, and any increase that is not a multiple of $500 must be rounded to the next lowest multiple of $500. (Code Sec. 457(e)(11)(B)(iii))

> *observation:* Code Sec. 457(e)(11)(B)(iii) provides that cost of living adjustments are to be made for tax years beginning after Dec. 31, 2017 (see above). Technically, this means that for a calendar year plan, for example, a cost of living adjustment has to be made for the 2018 tax year, which is the *first* year that the provision described above is effective (see below). The committee report, however, states that cost of living adjustments are to be made for years *after* the first year the provision is effective (Com Rept, see ¶ 5089). This would mean that for a calendar year plan, the cost of living adjustment would have to be made for the 2019 tax year. Thus, with respect to when cost of living adjustments have to begin, there is a discrepancy between Code Sec. 457(e)(11)(B)(iii) and the committee report. Although the Code is the law, and the committee report is not, it seems that the committee report is accurate while the statutory language is not. Thus, a technical correction to the statutory language appears necessary.

☐ **Effective:** For tax years beginning after Dec. 31, 2017. (Tax Cuts and Jobs Act §13612(d))

¶ 2800. Estate And Gift Taxes

¶ 2801. Estate tax basic exclusion amount increased from $5 million to $10 million

Code Sec. 2010(c)(3)(C), as amended by Tax Cuts and Jobs Act §11061(a)
Code Sec. 2001(g), as amended by Tax Cuts and Jobs Act §11061(b)
Generally effective: For estates of decedents dying and gifts made after Dec. 31, 2017, and before Jan. 1, 2026.
Committee Reports, see ¶ 5026

A unified credit of the "applicable credit amount" is allowed against the estate tax imposed on the estates of U.S. citizens and residents. The "applicable credit amount" is the amount of tentative tax that would be determined if the amount with respect to which the tentative tax is to be computed were equal to the "applicable exclusion amount." (FTC 2d/FIN ¶ R-7101; USTR ¶ 20,104eg; EP ¶ 45,102)

The 2010 Tax Relief Act (Sec. 303, PL 111-312, 12/17/2010) provided that, for estates of decedents dying after 2009, the "applicable exclusion amount" is the sum of (1) the "basic exclusion amount" (defined below) and (2) in the case of a surviving spouse, the "deceased spousal unused exclusion amount" (the DSUE amount). For estates of decedents dying after Dec. 31, 2010, the "basic exclusion amount" was $5 million. (FTC 2d/FIN ¶ R-7101; USTR ¶ 20,104eg; EP ¶ 45,102; Catalyst ¶ 219:171)

observation: A credit of $1,730,800 exempted $5 million from tax.

For estates of decedents dying after 2011, the basic exclusion amount is increased by an amount equal to:

. . . $5 million, multiplied by

. . . the cost-of-living adjustment determined under Code Sec. 1(f)(3) for the year of the decedent's death by substituting "calendar year 2010" for "calendar year 1992" in Code Sec. 1(f)(3)(B). (Code Sec. 2010(c)(3)(B))

If any amount as adjusted under the above formula is not a multiple of $10,000, the amount is rounded to the nearest multiple of $10,000. (Code Sec. 2010(c)(3)) (FTC 2d/FIN ¶ R-7101; USTR ¶ 20,104eg; EP ¶ 45,102)

FTC 2d References are to Federal Tax Coordinator 2d
FIN References are to RIA's Analysis of Federal Taxes: Income (print)
USTR References are to United States Tax Reporter: Income
Catalyst References are to Checkpoint Catalyst
PCA References are to Pension Analysis (print and electronic)
PBE References are to Pension & Benefits Explanations
BCA References are to Benefits Analysis (electronic)
BC References are to Benefits Coordinator (print)
EP References are to Estate Planning Analysis (print and electronic)

The basic exclusion amount for estates of decedents dying, generation-skipping transfers, and gifts made, in 2018 was $5.6 million. (FTC 2d/FIN ¶ R-7101; USTR ¶ 20,104eg; EP ¶ 45,102)

For the surviving spouse of a deceased spouse, the DSUE amount is the unused portion of a decedent's applicable exclusion amount to the extent that this amount does not exceed the basic exclusion amount in effect in the year of the decedent's death. (FTC 2d/FIN ¶ R-7107; USTR ¶ 20,104eg; EP ¶ 45,108)

> *observation:* The rules allowing the unused unified credit of the deceased spouse to be carried over and used by the estate of the surviving spouse are described as providing for the "portability" of the unified credit between spouses. Under pre-Tax Cuts and Jobs Act law, portability allowed a married couple $11.2 million in applicable exclusion amount in 2018.

For generation-skipping transfer (GST) tax purposes, every individual is allowed a GST exemption for any calendar year equal to the basic exclusion amount for the calendar year. Thus, the GST tax exemption amount for 2018 was $5.6 million under pre-Tax Cuts and Jobs Act law. (FTC 2d/FIN ¶ R-9551; USTR ¶ 26,314eg; EP ¶ 46,092)

The 2010 Tax Relief Act clarified the rules on the computation of estate and gift taxes, to reflect differences in the unified credit resulting from different tax rates. For purposes of computing the amount by which a decedent's tentative estate tax is reduced for the gift tax on the decedent's post-'76 gifts, the Code Sec. 2001(c) tax rates in effect at the decedent's death (instead of the tax rates in effect at the time of the gifts) are used to compute both (a) the gift tax imposed on the gifts, and (b) the gift tax unified credit. (FTC 2d/FIN ¶ R-7009; USTR ¶ 20,014.01eg; EP ¶ 44,910)

New Law. Under the Tax Cuts and Jobs Act, the basic exclusion amount is increased from $5 million to $10 million for estates of decedents dying and gifts made after 2017, and before 2026. (Code Sec. 2010(c)(3)(C) as amended by Tax Cuts and Jobs Act §11061(a))

The $10 million amount is indexed for inflation occurring after 2011. (Com Rept, see ¶ 5026)

> *observation:* Thus, the basic exclusion amount would presumably be $11.2 million for 2018.

> *observation:* The language in the Tax Cuts and Jobs Act does not mention generation-skipping transfers, but because the GST exemption amount is based on the basic exclusion amount, generation-skipping transfers will also see an increased exclusion amount.

💞 *observation:* The GST tax exemption would continue to be the basic exclusion amount, which presumably, would be $11.2 million for generation-skipping transfers made in 2018.

💞 *viewpoint:* Michael S. Strauss, of Strauss & Malk LLP in Northbrook, Illinois, who concentrates his practice in estate and trust planning and administration, wealth protection and succession, and technology related matters, and who is the current author of Post Mortem Estate Planning (RIA TAPS Title 40) and a co-author of Post Mortem Tax Planning (Thomson Reuters/WG&L and Estate and Gift Planning for the Business Owner (RIA TAPS Title 10), notes the following:

The doubling of the basic exclusion amount will cause many estates to no longer be subject to federal estate taxation. Before adjusting a client's estate planning, however, consider whether the client will be subject to state estate tax. Illinois, for example, has a $4 million per person exemption, and while such a tax is deductible against the federal estate tax, if no federal estate tax is due the state estate tax is effectively increased.

The increased GST exemption may be an opportunity to address existing irrevocable trusts. For clients who have created any irrevocable trusts that have inclusion ratios greater than zero and where assets may ultimately pass to skip persons (either by design or due to changed facts), consider making a late allocation of GST exemption where appropriate to cause such trusts to have inclusion ratios of zero.

While the increased basic exclusion amount under the Tax Cuts and Jobs Act is scheduled to sunset on December 31, 2025, Congress could change the Act prior to its sunset. Consider making any appropriate lifetime gifts and allocations of GST exemption sooner rather than later.

Regarding modifications to the estate tax payable to reflect different basic exclusion amounts, IRS is directed to prescribe regulations that may be necessary so that Code Sec. 2001(g) may be carried out with respect to any difference between:

... the basic exclusion amount in effect at the time of the decedent's death, and

... the basic exclusion amount applicable with respect to any gifts made by the decedent. (Code Sec. 2001(g) as amended by Tax Cuts and Jobs Act §11061(b))

Sunset. The increased basic exclusion amount discussed above will not apply to estates of decedents dying and gifts made after Dec. 31, 2025. (Code Sec. 2010(c)(3)(C) §11061(b))

💞 *viewpoint:* Howard M. Zaritsky, J.D., Rapidan, Virginia, independent estate planning consultant and author of many articles and flagship treatises in the estate planning area, including Tax Planning for Wealth Transfer During Life and Tax Planning for Family Wealth Transfers At Death, notes the following:

Doubling of the applicable exclusion amount and GST exemption for transfers in 2018 − 2025 is, for most clients, the most important estate planning change under the new law. For clients who do not feel confident of their ability to die before 2026, this should be viewed as an increase in the gift tax applicable exclusion amount, more than in the estate tax applicable exclusion amount, because there is no certainty that these increases will be preserved after 2025.

For very wealthy clients, the best plan is to make in 2018 an additional $5 million ($10 million for a married client) irrevocable gift to one or more generation-skipping trusts. This will shift future appreciation and lock-in the use of the added applicable exclusion amount and GST exemption.

Relatively few clients will be willing and able to make such large additional gifts; most will be reluctant to part irrevocably with such large sums. Such reluctant clients will want to preserve their continued benefit from the transferred funds, either as a primary or secondary beneficiary. For such clients, there are two possible solutions.

First, a client can create a self-settled spendthrift trust in which he or she remains a discretionary beneficiary. At common law, a grantor's creditors can compel the trustee to distribute to the grantor the maximum amount that the trust permits the trustee to distribute. Thus, such transfers are incomplete for gift and estate tax purposes. Rev. Rul. 77-378, 1977-2 C.B. 347; Rev. Rul. 76-103, 1976-1 C.B. 293; Herzog v. Comm'r, 41 BTA 509 (1940), aff'd, 116 F2d 591 (2d Cir. 1941); Paolozzi v. Comm'r, 23 TC 182 (1954), acq. 1962-2 CB 5.

In 16 states, however, statutes vary the common law and permit the creation of self-settled spendthrift trusts. See Alas. Stat. §§ 34.40.010 to 34.40.130; 12 Del. Code §§ 3570 to 3576; Haw. Rev. Stat. §§ 554G-1 to 554G-12; Mich. Comp. Laws §§ 700.1041 − 700.1050; Miss. Code §§ 91-9-701 to 91-9-723, 91-9-503, 91-9-505, 91-9-507; Mo. Rev. Stat. §§ 456.5−505; Nev. Rev. Stat. §§ 166.010 to 166.170; NH Rev. Stat. § 564-D:1-18; Ohio Rev. Code §§ 5816.01 to 5816.14; R.I. Gen. Laws §§ 18-9.2-1 to 18-9.2-7); S.D. Cod. Laws §§ 55-16-1 to 55-16-17; Tenn. Code Ann. § 35-16-101; Utah Code § 25-6-14; Va. Code § 64-2-745.1; W.Va. Code §§ 44D-5-503a−44D-5-503c; and Wyo. Stat. §§ 4-1-505, 4-10-510 to 4-10-523. There is little case law on point, but it is reasonable to believe that a trust created under a domestic self-settled spendthrift trust statute by a grantor residing in such a state and with assets situated in such a state should be a completed transfer for wealth transfer tax purposes. Individuals who do not reside in one of these states should also be able to create an effective self-settled spendthrift trust in one of these states, though it is likely that a court would carefully examine the transaction to determine that the trust assets truly have adequate contacts with the state whose law controls to avoid creating an incomplete transfer. See also discussion of domestic asset protection trusts in Zaritsky, *Tax Planning for Family Wealth Transfers During Life: Analysis with Forms*, & 8.06; Esperti, Peterson, & Keebler, *Irrevocable Trusts: Analysis with Forms*, ch. 14; Spero, *Asset Protection: Legal Planning & Strategies*, ch. 6.

Second, a client can create a trust for the benefit of his or her spouse. Obviously, this provides a benefit to the client only as long as the marriage continues to be harmonious. A healthy dose of social realism is useful in such cases; one should assume that the client's marriage will be no more successful and enduring than those of a majority of other married couples, and that such a gift could easily divert assets from the client's control.

This problem can be overcome by having each spouse create a trust for the other spouse's benefit. This invites the government to apply the reciprocal trust doctrine, under which each grantor is treated as having retained over the trust he or she created those powers or interests granted the other spouse over that same trust. Estate of Grace v. United States, 395 US 316 (1969). This rule can be avoided, however, if the trust terms are sufficiently different that they are not treated as reciprocal. Such trusts are sometimes referred to as nonreciprocal spousal benefit trusts. See also Zaritsky, *Practical Estate Planning in 2011 and 2012*, & 4.02; Katzenstein & Simantob, "Painless Giving Techniques That Achieve Transfer Tax Savings," 30 Est. Plan. 3 (July 2003); Mahon, "Spousal Access Trusts Makes Use of Enlarged Gift Tax Exemption," 39 Est. Plan. 22 (Aug. 2012).

☐ **Effective:** For estates of decedents dying and gifts made after Dec. 31, 2017 (Tax Cuts and Jobs Act §11061(c)), and before Jan. 1, 2026 (Tax Cuts and Jobs Act §11061(a)).

¶ 2900. Excise Taxes

¶ 2901. Payments for aircraft management services are exempted from excise taxes on taxable air transportation

Code Sec. 4261(e)(5), as amended by Tax Cuts and Jobs Act §13822(a)
Generally effective: For amounts paid after Dec. 22, 2017
Committee Reports, see ¶ 5105

Air transportation excise taxes are imposed under Code Sec. 4261 and Code Sec. 4271—a 7.5% tax on domestic air passenger tickets, a domestic segment tax, a tax on international departures and arrivals by air, and a 6.25% tax on domestic air transportation of property—on amounts paid for "taxable transportation" by air, see FTC 2d ¶s W-5101, W-5103, W-5201; USTR Excise ¶s 42,614.01, 42,714.

"Taxable transportation" generally means transportation by air which begins and ends in the U.S. IRS, in determining whether a flight is taxable transportation and whether the amounts paid for that transportation are subject to excise tax, has looked to who has "possession, command, and control" of the aircraft under the relevant facts and circumstances, see FTC 2d ¶s W-5113, W-5201; USTR Excise ¶s 42,624, 42,724.

Generally, aircraft management services companies manage aircraft owned by other corporations or individuals ("aircraft owners'), and provide aircraft owners with, among other things, administrative and support services (e.g., scheduling, flight planning, and weather forecasting), aircraft maintenance services, pilots and crew, and compliance with regulatory standards. Aircraft owners generally pay these companies a monthly fee to cover the fixed expenses of maintaining the aircraft (e.g., insurance, maintenance, and recordkeeping) and a variable fee to cover the cost of using the aircraft (e.g., pilots, crew, and fuel).

In Mar. 2012, IRS issued informal guidance (Chief Counsel Advice 201210026) in which it determined that a management company—providing services to the aircraft owner under a typical aircraft maintenance service agreement—had provided all of the essential elements necessary for providing transportation by air, and that the owner had relinquished possession, command and

---

FTC 2d References are to Federal Tax Coordinator 2d
FIN References are to RIA's Analysis of Federal Taxes: Income (print)
USTR References are to United States Tax Reporter: Income
Catalyst References are to Checkpoint Catalyst
PCA References are to Pension Analysis (print and electronic)
PBE References are to Pension & Benefits Explanations
BCA References are to Benefits Analysis (electronic)
BC References are to Benefits Coordinator (print)
EP References are to Estate Planning Analysis (print and electronic)

control to the management company. So the aircraft management company was determined to be providing taxable transportation to the owner, and was required to collect air transportation excise tax from the aircraft owner and remit it to IRS. (FTC 2d ¶ W-5100, ¶ W-5131, ¶ W-5134)

Chief Counsel Advice 201210026 resulted in increased audit activity by IRS on aircraft management companies. But, in May 2013, IRS suspended assessment of the federal excise tax with respect to aircraft management services while it developed guidance on the tax treatment of aircraft management issues. And, in 2017 IRS, after losing a case challenging imposition of the 7.5% ticket tax on aircraft management firms (see *Net Jets Large Aircraft Inc., DC OH,* FTC 2d ¶ W-5148), decided not to pursue examination of the issue of whether amounts paid to aircraft companies by the owners or lessors of the aircraft are taxable until further guidance was made available. (Com Rept, see ¶ 5105)

> **❤️observation:** Commentators argued that the air transportation ticket taxes were designed to apply to commercial flights, not "general aviation" flights—like chartered and private planes—and that the excise tax scheme intends for private jet owners to pay higher fuel taxes than commercial airlines, but not ticket taxes. In their view, IRS's position in Chief Counsel Advice 201210026, improperly expanded the scope of the air transportation taxes by imposing ticket taxes on private flights operated through management companies.

New Law. The Tax Cuts and Jobs Act exempts certain payments related to the management of private aircraft from the excise taxes imposed on taxable transportation by air. (Com Rept, see ¶ 5105)

Specifically, the Tax Cuts and Jobs Act provides that no tax will be imposed under Code Sec. 4261 or Code Sec. 4271 on any amounts paid by an aircraft owner for aircraft management services related to (Code Sec. 4261(e)(5)(A) as amended by Tax Cuts and Jobs Act §13822(a)):

. . . maintenance and support of the aircraft owner's aircraft; or (Code Sec. 4261(e)(5)(A)(i))

. . . flights on the aircraft owner's aircraft. (Code Sec. 4261(e)(5)(A)(ii))

> **❤️observation:** The Tax Cuts and Jobs Act changes above ensure that the air transportation ticket taxes aren't imposed on private flights operated through management companies.

Payments for flight services are exempt under the rule above only to the extent they are attributable to flights on an aircraft owner's *own aircraft.* Thus, if an aircraft owner makes a payment to a management company for the provision of a pilot and the pilot provides his or her services on the aircraft owner's aircraft, the payment will be exempt from excise tax on taxable transportation by air. But, if the pilot provides his or her services to the aircraft owner on an aircraft other than the aircraft owner's (for instance, on an aircraft that's part of a fleet of aircraft available for third-party charter services), then the payment will be subject to excise tax on taxable transportation by air. (Com Rept, see ¶ 5105)

Congress says that examples of arrangements that can't qualify a person as an "aircraft owner" include ownership of stock in a commercial airline and participation in a fractional ownership aircraft program. (Com Rept, see ¶ 5105)

Congress also says that a business arrangement seeking to circumvent the Code Sec. 4043 surtax on fuel used in fractional ownership aircraft (see FTC 2d ¶ W-3301; USTR Excise ¶ 40,434exc) by operating outside of subpart K of Part 91 of title 14 of the Code of Federal Regulations (see FTC 2d ¶ W-3302; USTR Excise ¶ 40,434exc), allowing an aircraft owner the right to use any of a fleet of aircraft—be it through an aircraft interchange agreement, through holding of nominal shares in a fleet of aircraft, or any other arrangement that doesn't reflect true tax ownership of the aircraft being flown upon—isn't considered ownership for purposes of the above-described exemption. (Com Rept, see ¶ 5105)

For purposes of the exemption, "aircraft management services" include (Code Sec. 4261(e)(5)(B)):

(a) assisting an aircraft owner with administrative and support services, such as scheduling, flight planning, and weather forecasting (Code Sec. 4261(e)(5)(B)(i));

(b) getting insurance (Code Sec. 4261(e)(5)(B)(ii));

(c) maintaining and storing, and fueling of, aircraft (Code Sec. 4261(e)(5)(B)(iii));

(d) hiring and training of, and providing, pilots and crew (Code Sec. 4261(e)(5)(B)(iv));

(e) establishing and complying with safety standards; and (Code Sec. 4261(e)(5)(B)(v)); and

(f) other services that are necessary to support flights operated by an aircraft owner. (Code Sec. 4261(e)(5)(B)(vi))

Lessee treated as aircraft owner. Also for purposes of the exemption, the term "aircraft owner" includes a person who leases the aircraft other than under a disqualified lease. (Code Sec. 4261(e)(5)(C)(i)) A disqualified lease means a lease from a person providing aircraft management services with respect to the aircraft (or a related person—within the meaning of Code Sec. 465(b)(3)(C) under the at-risk rules, see FTC 2d/FIN ¶ M-4566; USTR ¶ 4654—to the person providing the services), if the lease is for a term of 31 days or less. (Code Sec. 4261(e)(5)(C)(ii))

Pro rata allocation of exemption. Where amounts paid to any person that (but for the Code Sec. 4261(e)(5) exemption above) is subject to the 7.5% tax on domestic air passenger tickets [under Code Sec. 4261(a)], a part of which consists of above-described aircraft management services, the Code Sec. 4261(e)(5) exemption will apply on a pro rata basis only to the part that consists of aircraft management services. (Code Sec. 4261(e)(5)(D))

That is, the pro rata allocation rule applies where a monthly payment made to a management company is allocated in part to exempt services and flights on the aircraft owner's aircraft, and in part to flights on aircraft other than the aircraft owner's. In these circumstances, excise tax would have to be collected on the part of the payment attributable to flights on aircraft not owned by the aircraft owner. (Com Rept, see ¶ 5105)

☐ **Effective:** For amounts paid after Dec. 22, 2017. (Tax Cuts and Jobs Act §13822(b))

¶ 3000. Procedure And Administration

¶ 3001. Head of household filing status added to paid preparer due diligence requirements

Code Sec. 6695(g), as amended by Tax Cuts and Jobs Act §11001(b)
Generally effective: Tax years beginning after Dec. 31, 2017
Committee Reports, see ¶ 5001

Under pre-Tax Cuts and Jobs Act law, any person who is a tax return preparer for any return or claim for refund who fails to comply with due diligence requirements imposed by IRS regs with regard to determining the eligibility for, or the amount of, a child tax credit, an American Opportunity tax credit, or an earned income tax credit must pay a penalty of $500 (as adjusted for inflation) for each failure. (FTC 2d ¶ S-1100, ¶ S-1106.1 *et seq.*, ¶ V-2630, ¶ V-2677.1; USTR ¶ 66,954.01)

New Law. The Tax Cuts and Jobs Act expands the penalty to apply to each failure of a tax return preparer for any return or claim for refund who fails to comply with due diligence requirements imposed by IRS regs with regard to determining the eligibility to file as a head of household, as described at ¶ 101. (Code Sec. 6695(g) as amended by Tax Cuts and Jobs Act §11001(b))

☐ **Effective:** Tax years beginning after Dec. 31, 2017. (Tax Cuts and Jobs Act §11001(c))

¶ 3002. Extension of time limit for contesting IRS levy and for third party suits challenging levies

Code Sec. 6343(b), as amended by Tax Cuts and Jobs Act §11071(a)
Code Sec. 6532(c)(1), as amended by Tax Cuts and Jobs Act §11071(b)
Generally effective: Levies made after Dec. 22, 2017 and certain levies
made before Dec. 23, 2017
Committee Reports, see ¶ 5027

If IRS determines that property has been wrongfully levied upon, IRS may return the specific property seized, the amount of money levied upon, or where property has already been sold, the amount of money IRS received from the

FTC 2d References are to Federal Tax Coordinator 2d
FIN References are to RIA's Analysis of Federal Taxes: Income (print)
USTR References are to United States Tax Reporter: Income
Catalyst References are to Checkpoint Catalyst
PCA References are to Pension Analysis (print and electronic)
PBE References are to Pension & Benefits Explanations
BCA References are to Benefits Analysis (electronic)
BC References are to Benefits Coordinator (print)
EP References are to Estate Planning Analysis (print and electronic)

sale of the property. Under pre-Tax Cuts and Jobs Act law, an amount equal to the money levied upon or the money received from a sale of the property may be returned within nine months from the date of the levy. (FTC 2d/FIN ¶ V-5100, ¶ V-5127; USTR ¶ 63,354.06)

Similarly, under pre-Tax Cuts and Jobs Act law, (i) a suit by someone other than the taxpayer for the return of property wrongfully levied on, (ii) an injunction against the enforcement of a levy or a sale of the seized property, or (iii) for the return of the proceeds from the sale of seized property had to be started within nine months from the date of the original levy or agreement giving rise to the action. This nine-month period was extended if a timely request for the return of property wrongfully levied was made under Code Sec. 6343(b) for a period of 12 months from the date of filing of the request or for a period of six months from the date IRS rejects the request, whichever comes first. (FTC 2d/FIN ¶ V-5126; USTR ¶ 65,324.04)

New Law. The Tax Cuts and Jobs Act extends the period so that an amount equal to the money levied upon or the money received from a sale of the property may be returned within two years from the date of the levy. (Code Sec. 6343(b) as amended by Tax Cuts and Jobs Act §11071(a))

Similarly, the period for a suit by someone other than the taxpayer for (i) the return of property wrongfully levied on, (ii) an injunction against the enforcement of a levy or a sale of the seized property, or (iii) for the return of the proceeds from the sale of seized property is extended so that the suit must be started within two years from the date of the original levy or agreement giving rise to the action. (Code Sec. 6532(c)(1) as amended by Tax Cuts and Jobs Act §11071(b)(1)) This two-year period is extended if a timely request for the return of property wrongfully levied on was made under Code Sec. 6343(b), for a period of 12 months from the date of filing of the request or for a period of six months from the date IRS rejects the request, whichever comes first. (Code Sec. 6532(c)(2) as amended by Tax Cuts and Jobs Act §11071(b)(2))

☐ **Effective:** Levies made after Dec. 22, 2017 and levies made before Dec. 23, 2017 if the nine-month period under pre-Tax Cuts and Jobs Act law had not expired as of Dec. 22, 2017. (Tax Cuts and Jobs Act §11071(c))

¶ 3100. Miscellaneous

¶ 3101. Contributions by a customer or potential customer, or by a governmental entity or civic group in a capacity other than as a shareholder, are not nontaxable contributions to capital

Code Sec. 118, as amended by Tax Cuts and Jobs Act §13312(a)
Generally effective: Contributions made after Dec. 22, 2017
Committee Reports, see ¶ 5055

Cash or other property contributed to the capital of a corporation is not income to the corporation, whether contributed as a shareholder or a nonshareholder. Under pre-Tax Cuts and Jobs Act law, a contribution to capital did not include any contribution in aid of construction (CIAC) or any other contribution by a customer or potential customer. Thus, a CIAC could not be excluded from the corporation's gross income as a capital contribution. However, the value of land or other property contributed to a corporation by a governmental unit or by a civic group for the purpose of inducing the corporation to locate its business in a particular community, or to enable the corporation to expand its operating facilities, was treated as a tax-free contribution to capital by a nonshareholder, rather than as a CIAC. In addition, an exception applied, under which money or property received as a CIAC from any person (whether or not a shareholder) by a regulated public utility that provided water or sewerage disposal services treated was nontaxable, provided that certain requirements were met. However, no deduction could be taken by the contributor and the basis of property contributed as a nontaxable CIAC was zero. (FTC 2d/FIN ¶ F-1900, ¶ F-1908, ¶ F-1909, ¶ F-1909.1, ¶ F-1918.1; USTR ¶ 1184, ¶ 1184.01)

Under pre-Tax Cuts and Jobs Act law, the statute of limitations was extended with regard to a CIAC to a regulated public utility if the CIAC was treated as a nontaxable contribution to capital. (FTC 2d/FIN ¶ T-4200, ¶ T-4221.1; USTR ¶ 1184)

New Law. The Tax Cuts and Jobs Act broadens the exceptions from the tax-free capital contribution rule. Thus, (i) a CIAC or any other contribution as a customer or potential customer (Code Sec. 118(b)(1) as amended by Tax Cuts

---

FTC 2d References are to Federal Tax Coordinator 2d
FIN References are to RIA's Analysis of Federal Taxes: Income (print)
USTR References are to United States Tax Reporter: Income
Catalyst References are to Checkpoint Catalyst
PCA References are to Pension Analysis (print and electronic)
PBE References are to Pension & Benefits Explanations
BCA References are to Benefits Analysis (electronic)
BC References are to Benefits Coordinator (print)
EP References are to Estate Planning Analysis (print and electronic)

and Jobs Act §13312(a)(3)) and (ii) any contribution by any governmental entity or civic group (other than contribution made by a shareholder in that capacity) (Code Sec. 118(b)(2)) are excluded from the tax-free capital contribution rule.

> ⓡ*observation:* Thus, property contributed to a corporation by a governmental unit or by a civic group for the purpose of inducing the corporation to locate its business in a particular community, or to enable the corporation to expand its operating facilities, is taxable to the corporation.

In addition, the regulated public utility exception and the special statute of limitations period are repealed. (Code Sec. 118(c) as amended by Tax Cuts and Jobs Act §13312(a)(1), Code Sec. 118(d) as amended by Tax Cuts and Jobs Act §13312(a)(1))

However, contributions in exchange for fair market value (determined without regard to discounts for lack of control and the effect of limited liquidity on valuation) and pro rata contributions by shareholders that are made without the issuance of additional stock are not taxable. In addition, a municipal tax abatement for locating a business in a particular municipality is not a contribution and is not taxable. (Com Rept, see ¶ 5055)

IRS is directed to issue regs or other guidance as may be necessary or appropriate to implement these rules, including regs or other guidance for determining whether any contribution is a CIAC. (Code Sec. 118(c))

☐ **Effective:** Contributions made after Dec. 22, 2017. (Tax Cuts and Jobs Act §13312(b)(1)). However, the changes don't apply to any contribution, made after Dec. 22, 2017 by a governmental entity under a master development plan that has been approved before Dec. 22, 2017 by a governmental entity. (Tax Cuts and Jobs Act §13312(b)(2))

¶ 3102. Assignments not included in income, and contribution deductions allowed, for Alaska Native Settlement Trusts

Code Sec. 139G, as added by Tax Cuts and Jobs Act §13821(a)
Code Sec. 247, as added by Tax Cuts and Jobs Act §13821(b)
Code Sec. 6039H, as amended by Tax Cuts and Jobs Act §13821(c)
Generally effective: For tax years beginning after Dec. 31, 2016
Committee Reports, see ¶ 5104

Under the Alaska Native Claims Settlement Act of 1971 (ANCSA), all Alaska natives who qualified under ANCSA's terms were able to receive stock in one of the Alaska Native Settlement Corporations (Native Corporation), and in the one local village corporation (Village Corporation), created to receive assets transferred from the federal government. ANCSA allowed the Native Corporations to convey certain assets to state-chartered settlement trusts (Alaska Native Settlement Trusts, or Settlement Trusts). The Settlement Trusts may not operate as a business nor make a later transfer of land or interests therein except for a reconveyance to the transferor corporation, if such a reconveyance is authorized in the trust instrument. FTC 2d ¶ C-1026; USTR ¶ 6464

Under Code Sec. 646(h), a Settlement Trust has the meaning provided under ANCSA (43 U.S.C. §1602(t)); *i.e.*, generally, a trust established and registered by a Native Corporation under Alaska law, pursuant to a shareholder resolution, which is designed to preserve native heritage and culture, and to promote the health, education, and economic welfare of its beneficiaries. (FTC 2d ¶ C-1037; USTR ¶ 6464) Further, a Native Corporation has the meaning provided under the ANCSA (43 U.S.C. §1602(m)); *i.e.*, a village corporation, an urban corporation, or a group corporation. (FTC 2d ¶ C-1035; USTR ¶ 6464)

Under the Economic Growth and Tax Relief Reconciliation Act of 2001 (EGTRA), Settlements Trusts were provided with special tax treatment. For contributions made to electing Settlement Trusts (see below for the election), the Settlement Trust's taxable income, other than its net capital gain, is subject to tax at the lowest rate specified in Code Sec. 1(c) (the lowest rate that applies to unmarried individuals). For a Settlement Trust with a net capital gain for the tax year, a tax is imposed on that gain at the rate of tax which would apply to the gain if the taxpayer were subject to a tax on his or her other taxable income at only the lowest rate under Code Sec. 1(c). (FTC 2d ¶ C-1026; USTR ¶ 6464)

EGTRA also provided that a Settlement Trust may have elected to have Code Sec. 646 apply to the trust and to its beneficiaries. This election had to have been made on or before the Settlement Trusts's due date (including extensions) for filing its tax return for the first tax year ending after June 7, 2001. Form 1041-N is used (i) to make the election, (ii) to report the Settlement Trust's income, deductions, gains, losses, etc., and (iii) to satisfy the information reporting requirements that apply to electing Settlement Trusts. (FTC 2d ¶ C-1027; USTR ¶ 6464) A Settlement Trust that has made this election is considered to be an "electing Settlement Trust." (FTC 2d ¶ C-1034; USTR ¶ 6464)

For an electing Settlement Trust, no amount is includible in the gross income of a trust beneficiary due to the sponsoring Native Corporation's contribution to the trust. (FTC 2d ¶ C-1028; USTR ¶ 6464)

Under pre-Tax Cuts and Jobs Act law, there were no Code Sections that specifically addressed assignments made to Settlement Trusts, or deductions for contributions made to Settlement Trusts.

New Law.

Assignments to Settlement Trusts. A Native Corporation's gross income does not include the value of any payments that would otherwise be made, or treated as being made, to the Native Corporation pursuant to, or as required by, any provision of the ANCSA, including any payment that would otherwise be made to a Village Corporation pursuant to section 7(j) of the ANCSA, provided that any such payments:

(a) are assigned in writing to a Settlement Trust, and

(b) were not received by the Native Corporation before the assignment. (Code Sec. 139G(a) as added by Tax Cuts and Jobs Act §13821(a))

> *observation:* Thus, a Native Corporation may assign certain payments to a Settlement Trust without having to recognize those payments as income.

If a Settlement Trust is assigned payments (as described in item (a), above), the Settlement Trust's gross income includes those payments when they are received by the Settlement Trust, under the assignment, and have the same character as if the payments were received by the Native Corporation. (Code Sec. 139G(b))

The written assignment must describe the amount and scope of the assignment with reasonable particularity. The description may either be in a percentage of one or more payments or in a fixed dollar amount. (Code Sec. 139G(c)) The assignment also must indicate whether the term of the assignment is in perpetuity or for a period of time, and whether the assignment is revocable. (Code Sec. 139G(d))

Notwithstanding Code Sec. 247 (see below), a Native Corporation is not allowed a deduction for any amount assigned as per Code Sec. 139G(a) (above). (Code Sec. 139G(e))

For purposes of the rules above, a Native Corporation and a Settlement Trust have the same meaning given to these terms under Code Sec. 646(h) (see above). (Code Sec. 139G(f))

Deduction of contributions to Settlement Trusts. Deductions are allowed for contributions made by a Native Corporation to a Settlement Trust (regardless of whether the Settlement Trust has elected to become an "electing Settlement Trust" via Code Sec. 646), if an annual election has been made as per Code Sec. 247(e) (see below). (Code Sec. 247(a) as added by Tax Cuts and Jobs Act §13821(b))

Election. For each tax year, a Native Corporation may elect to use this deduction (and have Code Sec. 247 apply) on the income tax return or an amendment or supplement to the return of the Native Corporation, with the election to be in effect only for that tax year. Any such election made by a Native Corporation may be revoked by a timely filed amendment or supplement to the income tax return of the Native Corporation. (Code Sec. 247(e))

Amount of deduction. The amount of the deduction is:

... for a cash contribution (regardless of the method of payment, including currency, coins, money order, or check), the amount of such contribution, or

... for a non-cash contribution, the lesser of:

(A) the Native Corporation's adjusted basis in the property contributed, or

(B) the fair market value of the property contributed. (Code Sec. 247(b))

The deduction allowed for any tax year must not be greater than the taxable income (as determined without regard to such deduction) of the Native Corporation for the tax year in which the contribution was made. (Code Sec. 247(c)(1)) However, if the aggregate amount of contributions for any tax year is greater than the tax income of the Native Corporation for the tax year in which the contribution was made, the excess amount is treated as a contribution described in Code Sec. 247(a) in each of the 15 following years, in order of time. (Code Sec. 247(c)(2)) Thus, the Native Corporation's deduction is limited to the amount of its taxable income for that year, and any unused deduction may be carried forward 15 additional years. (Com Rept, see ¶ 5104)

Notwithstanding Code Sec. 646(d)(2) (relating to a Settlement Trust's earnings not being reduced because of contributions), where a Native Corporation claims this deduction for any tax year, the earnings and profits of the Native Corporation for that tax year is reduced by the amount of the deduction. (Code Sec. 247(f)(1)) Also, the Native Corporation may not recognize any gain or loss with respect to a contribution of property for which a deduction is allowed. (Code Sec. 247(f)(2))

Subject to the rules in Code Sec. 247(g) (see below), a Settlement Trust must include in income the amount of any deduction allowed under Code Sec. 247 in the tax year in which the Settlement Trust actually receives that contribution. (Code Sec. 247(f)(3))

The Settlement Trust's holding period under Code Sec. 1223 (for purposes of determining any gain or loss) includes any time that the property was held by the Native Corporation. (Code Sec. 247(f)(4))

The Settlement Trust's basis for which a deduction is allowed is the lesser of (A) the adjusted basis of the Native Corporation in the property immediately before the contribution, or (B) the fair market value of the property immediately before the contribution. (Code Sec. 247(f)(5))

No deduction is allowed under Code Sec. 247 with respect to any contributions made to a Settlement Trust which are in violation of subsection (a)(2) or (c)(2) of section 39 of the ANCSA (relating to subsurface estate and timber resource restrictions). (Code Sec. 247(f)(6))

Deferring recognition of income. For a contribution which consists of property other than cash, a Settlement Trust may elect to defer recognition of any income related to the property until the sale or exchange of the property is made, in whole or in part, by the Settlement Trust. (Code Sec. 247(g)(1)) For this type of non-cash contribution, any income or gain realized on the sale or exchange of the property is treated as:

. . . for the amount of the income or gain that is equal to or less than the amount of income which would be included in income at the time of contribution under Code Sec. 247(f)(3) but for the taxpayer's election—as ordinary income; (Code Sec. 247(g)(2)(A)) and

. . . for any amounts of the income or gain which are greater than the amount of income which would be included in income at the time of contribution under Code Sec. 247(f)(3) but for the taxpayer's election—having the same character as if Code Sec. 247(g)(2) did not apply. (Code Sec. 247(g)(2)(B))

For each tax year, a Settlement Trust may elect to apply Code Sec. 247(g) for any property that is not cash, which was contributed during the year. Any property to which this deferral election applies must be identified and described with reasonable particularity on the income tax return, or an amendment or supplement to the return of the Settlement Trust, with the election to be in effect only for that tax year. (Code Sec. 247(g)(3)(A))

Any deferral election made by a Settlement Trust under Code Sec. 247(g) may be revoked by a timely filed amendment or supplement to the income tax return of such Settlement Trust. (Code Sec. 247(g)(3)(B))

For any property for which a deferral election is in effect under Code Sec. 247(g), and which is disposed of within the first tax year following the tax year in which the property was contributed to the Settlement Trust:

(I) Code Sec. 247 is applied as if the deferral election had not been made (Code Sec. 247(g)(3)(C)(i)(I)),

(II) any income or gain which would have been included in the year of contribution under Code Sec. 247(f)(3) (see above, upon receipt of the contribution) but for the taxpayer's deferral election under Code Sec. 247(g), must be included in income for the tax year of the contribution (Code Sec. 247(g)(3)(C)(i)(II)), and

(III) the Settlement Trust must pay any increase in tax resulting from such inclusion, including any applicable interest, plus 10% of the amount of such increase with interest. (Code Sec. 247(g)(3)(C)(i)(III)).

Notwithstanding the statute of limitations for tax assessments provided under Code Sec. 6501(a), any amount described in item (III), above, may be assessed, or a proceeding in court with respect to such amount may be initiated without assessment, within four years after the date on which the return making the election for such property was filed. (Code Sec. 247(g)(3)(C)(ii)) Thus, this provision provides for a four year assessment period in which to assess the tax, interest, and penalty amounts. (Com Rept, see ¶ 5104)

For purposes of this deduction, a Native Corporation and a Settlement Trust have the same meaning given to these terms under Code Sec. 646(h) (see above). (Code Sec. 247(d))

Information reporting for deductible contributions Any Native Corporation (as defined under subsection (m) of section 3 of the ANSCA) that has made a contribution to a Settlement Trust to which an election to deduct contributions under Code Sec. 247(e) (see above) applies, must provide the Settlement Trust with a statement regarding that election not later than Jan. 31 of the calendar year following the calendar year in which the contribution was made. (Code Sec. 6039H(e)(1) as amended by Tax Cuts and Jobs Act §13821(c))

> *observation:* Thus, if a Native Corporation has elected to deduct its contributions to a Settlement Trust, the Native Corporation must provide a statement to the Settlement Trust and include the information listed below, on or before the Jan. 31 of the year following the contribution. So if a contribution was made on May 12, 2017, the statement must be provided to the Settlement Trust on or before Jan. 31, 2018.

The statement must include:

(A) the total amount of contributions to which the election under Code Sec. 247(e) (see above) applies,

(B) for each contribution, whether such contribution was in cash,

(C) for each contribution which consists of property other than cash, the date that such property was acquired by the Native Corporation, and the adjusted basis and fair market value of such property on the date such property was contributed to the Settlement Trust,

(D) the date on which each contribution was made to the Settlement Trust, and

(E) any information that IRS determines may be necessary or appropriate for the identification of each contribution, and the accurate inclusion of income relating to such contributions by the Settlement Trust. (Code Sec. 6039H(e)(2))

☐ **Effective:** The new Code Sec. 139G rules discussed above apply retroactively for tax years beginning after Dec. 31, 2016. (Tax Cuts and Jobs Act §13821(a)(3))

The new Code Sec. 247 rule discussed above applies for tax years for which the statute of limitations on refund or credit under Code Sec. 6511 has not expired. (Tax Cuts and Jobs Act §13821(b)(3)(A))

> *observation:* A claim for credit or refund must be filed within the later of three years from the time a tax return was filed, or two years from the time the tax was paid. If no return was filed by the taxpayer, a

claim for credit or refund must be filed within two years from the time the tax was paid.

If the statute of limitations on a credit or refund expires before the end of the one-year period beginning on Dec. 22, 2017, a refund or credit of any overpayment may, nevertheless, be made or allowed if the claim is filed before the end of the one-year period. (Tax Cuts and Jobs Act §13821(b)(3)(B))

The changes to the Code Sec. 6039H(e) rules discussed above apply retroactively for tax years beginning after Dec. 31, 2016. (Tax Cuts and Jobs Act §13821(c)(3))

> *observation:* Generally, in situations where there are retroactive dates as discussed above, taxpayers may consider filing an amended return for refund under Code Sec. 6402 to take advantage of the changes made to the law.

¶ 3200. Client Letters

¶ 3201. Overview of provisions of the TCJA affecting individuals

> **To the practitioner:** You can use the following letter to provide clients with an overview of these tax provisions in the Tax Cuts and Jobs Act (TCJA) that have an impact on individuals. For analysis of the income tax rates beginning in 2018, see ¶ 105. For analysis of the new standard deduction, see ¶ 501. For analysis of the elimination of personal exemptions, see ¶ 502. For analysis of the new deduction for "qualified business income," see ¶ 702. For analysis of the child and family tax credit, see ¶ 516. For analysis of the new rules for deducting state and local income and property taxes, see ¶ 506. For analysis of the revised mortgage interest deduction, see ¶ 507. For analysis of the elimination of the miscellaneous itemized deduction, see ¶ 503. For analysis of the medical expense deduction, see ¶ 505. For analysis of the casualty and theft loss deduction, see ¶ 508. For analysis of the elimination of the overall limitation on itemized deductions, see ¶ 504. For analysis of the elimination of the moving expense deduction, see ¶ 514. For analysis of the elimination of the deduction for alimony paid, see ¶ 510. For analysis of the elimination of the health care individual mandate starting in 2019, see ¶ 401. For analysis of the increased estate and gift tax exemption, see ¶ 2801. For analysis of the increased alternative minimum tax exemption, see ¶ 301.

Dear Client,

The recently enacted Tax Cuts and Jobs Act (TCJA) is a sweeping tax package. Here's a look at some of the more important elements of the new law that have an impact on individuals. Unless otherwise noted, the changes are effective for tax years beginning in 2018 through 2025.

• *Tax rates.* The new law imposes a new tax rate structure with seven tax brackets: 10%, 12%, 22%, 24%, 32%, 35%, and 37%. The top rate was reduced from 39.6% to 37% and applies to taxable income above $500,000 for single taxpayers, and $600,000 for married couples filing jointly. The rates applicable to net capital gains and qualified dividends were not changed. The "kiddie tax" rules were simplified. The net unearned income of a child subject to the rules will be taxed at the capital gain and ordinary income rates that apply to trusts and estates. Thus, the child's tax is unaffected by the parent's tax situation or the unearned income of any siblings.

• *Standard deduction.* The new law increases the standard deduction to $24,000 for joint filers, $18,000 for heads of household, and $12,000 for

---

FTC 2d References are to Federal Tax Coordinator 2d
FIN References are to RIA's Analysis of Federal Taxes: Income (print)
USTR References are to United States Tax Reporter
Catalyst References are to Checkpoint Catalyst
PCA References are to Pension Analysis (print and electronic)
PBE References are to Pension & Benefits Explanations
BCA References are to Benefits Analysis (electronic)
BC References are to Benefits Coordinator (print)
EP References are to Estate Planning Analysis (print and electronic)

singles and married taxpayers filing separately. Given these increases, many taxpayers will no longer be itemizing deductions. These figures will be indexed for inflation after 2018.

• *Exemptions.* The new law suspends the deduction for personal exemptions. Thus, starting in 2018, taxpayers can no longer claim personal or dependency exemptions. The rules for withholding income tax on wages will be adjusted to reflect this change, but IRS was given the discretion to leave the withholding unchanged for 2018.

• *New deduction for "qualified business income."* Starting in 2018, taxpayers are allowed a deduction equal to 20 percent of "qualified business income," otherwise known as "pass-through" income, i.e., income from partnerships, S corporations, LLCs, and sole proprietorships. The income must be from a trade or business within the U.S. Investment income does not qualify, nor do amounts received from an S corporation as reasonable compensation or from a partnership as a guaranteed payment for services provided to the trade or business. The deduction is not used in computing adjusted gross income, just taxable income. For taxpayers with taxable income above $157,500 ($315,000 for joint filers), (1) a limitation based on W-2 wages paid by the business and depreciable tangible property used in the business is phased in, and (2) income from the following trades or businesses is phased out of qualified business income: health, law, consulting, athletics, financial or brokerage services, or where the principal asset is the reputation or skill of one or more employees or owners.

• *Child and family tax credit.* The new law increases the credit for qualifying children (i.e., children under 17) to $2,000 from $1,000, and increases to $1,400 the refundable portion of the credit. It also introduces a new (nonrefundable) $500 credit for a taxpayer's dependents who are not qualifying children. The adjusted gross income level at which the credits begin to be phased out has been increased to $200,000 ($400,000 for joint filers).

• *State and local taxes.* The itemized deduction for state and local income and property taxes is limited to a total of $10,000 starting in 2018.

• *Mortgage interest.* Under the new law, mortgage interest on loans used to acquire a principal residence and a second home is only deductible on debt up to $750,000 (down from $1 million), starting with loans taken out in 2018. And there is no longer any deduction for interest on home equity loans, regardless of when the debt was incurred.

• *Miscellaneous itemized deductions.* There is no longer a deduction for miscellaneous itemized deductions which were formerly deductible to the extent they exceeded 2 percent of adjusted gross income. This category included items such as tax preparation costs, investment expenses, union dues, and unreimbursed employee expenses.

• *Medical expenses.* Under the new law, for 2017 and 2018, medical expenses are deductible to the extent they exceed 7.5 percent of adjusted gross income for all taxpayers. Previously, the AGI "floor" was 10% for most taxpayers.

• *Casualty and theft losses.* The itemized deduction for casualty and theft losses has been suspended except for losses incurred in a federally declared disaster.

• *Overall limitation on itemized deductions.* The new law suspends the overall limitation on itemized deductions that formerly applied to taxpayers whose adjusted gross income exceeded specified thresholds. The itemized deductions of such taxpayers were reduced by 3% of the amount by which AGI exceeded the applicable threshold, but the reduction could not exceed 80% of the total itemized deductions, and certain items were exempt from the limitation.

• *Moving expenses.* The deduction for job-related moving expenses has been eliminated, except for certain military personnel. The exclusion for moving expense reimbursements has also been suspended.

• *Alimony.* For post-2018 divorce decrees and separation agreements, alimony will not be deductible by the paying spouse and will not be taxable to the receiving spouse.

• *Health care "individual mandate."* Starting in 2019, there is no longer a penalty for individuals who fail to obtain minimum essential health coverage.

• *Estate and gift tax exemption.* Effective for decedents dying, and gifts made, in 2018, the estate and gift tax exemption has been increased to roughly $11.2 million ($22.4 million for married couples).

• *Alternative minimum tax (AMT) exemption.* The AMT has been retained for individuals by the new law but the exemption has been increased to $109,400 for joint filers ($54,700 for married taxpayers filing separately), and $70,300 for unmarried taxpayers. The exemption is phased out for taxpayers with alternative minimum taxable income over $1 million for joint filers, and over $500,000 for all others.

As you can see from this overview, the new law affects many areas of taxation. If you wish to discuss the impact of the law on your particular situation, please give me a call.

Very truly yours,

¶ 3202. Overview of the business tax changes in the Tax Cuts and Jobs Act ("TCJA")

> **To the practitioner:** You can use the following letter to provide clients with an overview of the business tax changes in the Tax Cuts and Jobs Act ("TCJA"). For analysis of the corporate tax rate cut, see ¶ 102. For analysis of changes to the dividends-received deduction, see ¶ 103. For analysis of the repeal of the corporate alternative minimum tax, see ¶ 303. For analysis of the minimum tax credit rules, see ¶ 304. For analysis of changes to the treatment of net operating losses, see ¶ 1001 and ¶ 1002. For analysis of the limit on the business interest deduction, see ¶ 1003. For analysis of the repeal of the domestic production activities deduction, see ¶ 1004. For analysis of the new fringe benefit rules, see ¶ 1005, ¶ 1006, and ¶ 1007. For analysis of the new rules on deducting penalties and fines, see ¶ 1008. For analysis of the rules on sexual harassment settlements, see ¶ 1010. For analysis of the rules on lobbying expenses, see ¶ 1011. For analysis of the new family and medical leave credit, see ¶ 1013. For analysis of the reduced qualified rehabilitation credit, see ¶ 1014. For analysis of the reduced orphan drug credit, see ¶ 1015. For analysis of changes to the Code Sec. 179 expense election, see ¶ 1101 and ¶ 1102. For analysis of the bonus depreciation rules, see ¶ 1204. For analysis of the rules on depreciating qualified improvement property, see ¶ 1301 and ¶ 1302. For analysis of the rules on farming equipment and machinery, see 1304 and 1305. For analysis of the increased luxury automobile depreciation allowances, see ¶ 1307. For analysis of the rules removing computers and peripheral equipment from treatment as listed property, see ¶ 1308. For analysis of the new rules on research and experimentation expenses, see ¶ 1408. For analysis of the changes to the like-kind exchange rules, see ¶ 1503. For analysis of the rules on excessive employee compensation, see ¶ 2601, ¶ 2602, and ¶ 2603. For analysis of the rules on employee achievement awards, see ¶ 2605.

Dear Client,

The recently enacted Tax Cuts and Jobs Act ("TCJA") is a sweeping tax package. Here's an overview of some of the more important business tax changes in the new law. Unless otherwise noted, the changes are effective for tax years beginning in 2018.

- *Corporate tax rates reduced.* One of the more significant new law provisions cuts the corporate tax rate to a flat 21%. Before the new law, rates were graduated, starting at 15% for taxable income up to $50,000, with rates at 25% for income between 50,001 and $75,000, 34% for income between $75,001 and $10 million, and 35% for income above $10 million.

- *Dividends-received deduction.* The dividends-received deduction available to corporations that receive dividends from other corporations has

FTC 2d References are to Federal Tax Coordinator 2d
FIN References are to RIA's Analysis of Federal Taxes: Income (print)
USTR References are to United States Tax Reporter
Catalyst References are to Checkpoint Catalyst
PCA References are to Pension Analysis (print and electronic)
PBE References are to Pension & Benefits Explanations
BCA References are to Benefits Analysis (electronic)
BC References are to Benefits Coordinator (print)
EP References are to Estate Planning Analysis (print and electronic)

been reduced under the new law. For corporations owning at least 20% of the dividend-paying company, the dividends-received deduction has been reduced from 80% to 65% of the dividends. For corporations owning under 20%, the deduction is reduced from 70% to 50%.

• *Alternative minimum tax repealed for corporations.* The corporate alternative minimum tax (AMT) has been repealed by the new law.

• *Alternative minimum tax credit.* Corporations are allowed to offset their regular tax liability by the AMT credit. For tax years beginning after 2017 and before 2022, the credit is refundable in an amount equal to 50% (100% for years beginning in 2021) of the excess of the AMT credit for the year over the amount of the credit allowable for the year against regular tax liability. Thus, the full amount of the credit will be allowed in tax years beginning before 2022.

• *Net Operating Loss ("NOL") deduction modified.* Under the new law, generally, NOLs arising in tax years ending after 2017 can only be carried forward, not back. The general two-year carryback rule, and other special carryback provisions, have been repealed. However, a two-year carryback for certain farming losses is allowed. These NOLs can be carried forward indefinitely, rather than expiring after 20 years. Additionally, under the new law, for losses arising in tax years beginning after 2017, the NOL deduction is limited to 80% of taxable income, determined without regard to the deduction. Carryovers to other years are adjusted to take account of the 80% limitation.

• *Limit on business interest deduction.* Under the new law, every business, regardless of its form, is limited to a deduction for business interest equal to 30% of its adjusted taxable income. For pass-through entities such as partnerships and S corporations, the determination is made at the entity, i.e., partnership or S corporation, level. Adjusted taxable income is computed without regard to the repealed domestic production activities deduction and, for tax years beginning after 2017 and before 2022, without regard to deductions for depreciation, amortization, or depletion. Any business interest disallowed under this rule is carried into the following year, and, generally, may be carried forward indefinitely. The limitation does not apply to taxpayers (other than tax shelters) with average annual gross receipts of $25 million or less for the three-year period ending with the prior tax year. Real property trades or businesses can elect to have the rule not apply if they elect to use the alternative depreciation system for real property used in their trade or business. Certain additional rules apply to partnerships.

• *Domestic production activities deduction ("DPAD") repealed.* The new law repeals the DPAD for tax years beginning after 2017. The DPAD formerly allowed taxpayers to deduct 9% (6% for certain oil and gas activities) of the lesser of the taxpayer's (1) qualified production activities income ("QPAI") or (2) taxable income for the year, limited to 50% of the W-2 wages paid by the taxpayer for the year. QPAI was the taxpayer's receipts, minus expenses allocable to the receipts, from property manufactured, produced, grown, or extracted within the U.S.; qualified film productions; production of electricity, natural gas, or potable water; construction activities performed in the U.S.; and certain engineering or architectural services.

• *New fringe benefit rules.* The new law eliminates the 50% deduction for business-related entertainment expenses. The pre-Act 50% limit on deductible business meals is expanded to cover meals provided via an in-house cafeteria or otherwise on the employer's premises. Additionally, the deduction for transportation fringe benefits (e.g., parking and mass transit) is denied to employers, but the exclusion from income for such benefits for employees continues. However, bicycle commuting reimbursements are deductible by the employer but not excludable by the employee. Last, no deduction is allowed for transportation expenses that are the equivalent of commuting for employees except as provided for the employee's safety.

• *Penalties and fines.* Under pre-Act law, deductions are not allowed for fines or penalties paid to a government for the violation of any law. Under the new law, no deduction is allowed for any otherwise deductible amount paid or incurred by suit, agreement, or otherwise to or at the direction of a government or specified nongovernmental entity in relation to the violation of any law or the investigation or inquiry by the government or entity into the potential violation of any law. An exception applies to any payment the taxpayer establishes is either restitution (including remediation of property), or an amount required to come into compliance with any law that was violated or involved in the investigation or inquiry, that is identified in the court order or settlement agreement as such a payment. An exception also applies to an amount paid or incurred as taxes due.

• *Sexual harassment.* Under the new law, effective for amounts paid or incurred after Dec. 22, 2017, no deduction is allowed for any settlement, payout, or attorney fees related to sexual harassment or sexual abuse if the payments are subject to a nondisclosure agreement.

• *Lobbying expenses.* The new law disallows deductions for lobbying expenses paid or incurred after the date of enactment with respect to lobbying expenses related to legislation before local governmental bodies (including Indian tribal governments). Under pre-Act law, such expenses were deductible.

• *Family and medical leave credit.* A new general business credit is available for tax years beginning in 2018 and 2019 for eligible employers equal to 12.5% of wages they pay to qualifying employees on family and medical leave if the rate of payment is 50% of wages normally paid to the employee. The credit increases by 0.25% (up to a maximum of 25%) for each percent by which the payment rate exceeds 50% of normal wages. For this purpose, the maximum leave that may be taken into account for any employee for any year is 12 weeks. Eligible employers are those with a written policy in place allowing qualifying full-time employees at least two weeks of paid family and medical leave a year, and less than full-time employees a pro-rated amount of leave. A qualifying employee is one who has been employed by the employer for one year or more, and who, in the preceding year, had compensation not above 60% of the compensation threshold for highly compensated employees. Paid leave provided as vacation leave, personal leave, or other medical or sick leave is not considered family and medical leave.

• *Qualified rehabilitation credit.* The new law repeals the 10% credit for qualified rehabilitation expenditures for a building that was first placed in service before 1936, and modifies the 20% credit for qualified rehabilitation expenditures for a certified historic structure. The 20% credit is allowable during the five-year period starting with the year the building was placed in service in an amount that is equal to the ratable share for that year. This is 20% of the qualified rehabilitation expenditures for the building, as allocated ratably to each year in the five-year period. It is intended that the sum of the ratable shares for the five years not exceed 100% of the credit for qualified rehabilitation expenditures for the building. The repeal of the 10% credit and modification of the 20% credit take effect starting in 2018 (subject to a transition rule for certain buildings owned or leased at all times after 2017).

• *Orphan drug credit reduced and modified.* The new law reduces the business tax credit for qualified clinical testing expenses for certain drugs for rare diseases or conditions, generally known as "orphan drugs," from 50% to 25% of qualified clinical testing expenses for tax years beginning after 2017. These are costs incurred to test an orphan drug after it has been approved for human testing by the FDA but before it has been approved for sale. Amounts used in computing this credit are excluded from the computation of the separate research credit. The new law modifies the credit by allowing a taxpayer to elect to take a reduced orphan drug credit in lieu of reducing otherwise allowable deductions.

• *Increased Code Sec. 179 expensing.* The new law increases the maximum amount that may be expensed under Code Sec. 179 to $1 million. If more than $2.5 million of property is placed in service during the year, the $1 million limitation is reduced by the excess over $2.5 million. Both the $1 million and the $2.5 million amounts are indexed for inflation after 2018. The expense election has also been expanded to cover (1) certain depreciable tangible personal property used mostly to furnish lodging or in connection with furnishing lodging, and (2) the following improvements to nonresidential real property made after it was first placed in service: roofs; heating, ventilation, and air-conditioning property; fire protection and alarm systems; security systems; and any other building improvements that aren't elevators or escalators, don't enlarge the building, and aren't attributable to internal structural framework.

• *Bonus depreciation.* Under the new law, a 100% first-year deduction is allowed for qualified new and used property acquired and placed in service after September 27, 2017 and before 2023. Pre-Act law provided for a 50% allowance, to be phased down for property placed in service after 2017. Under the new law, the 100% allowance is phased down starting after 2023.

• *Depreciation of qualified improvement property.* The new law provides that qualified improvement property is depreciable using a 15-year recovery period and the straight-line method. Qualified improvement property is any improvement to an interior portion of a building that is nonresidential real property placed in service after the building was placed in service. It does not include expenses related to the enlargement of the building, any elevator or escalator, or the internal structural framework. There are no longer separate requirements for leasehold improvement property or restaurant property.

• *Depreciation of farming equipment and machinery.* Under the new law, subject to certain exceptions, the cost recovery period for farming equipment and machinery the original use of which begins with the taxpayer is reduced from 7 to 5 years. Additionally, in general, the 200% declining balance method may be used in place of the 150% declining balance method that was required under pre-Act law.

• *Luxury auto depreciation limits.* Under the new law, for a passenger automobile for which bonus depreciation (see above) is not claimed, the maximum depreciation allowance is increased to $10,000 for the year it's placed in service, $16,000 for the second year, $9,000 for the third year, and $5,760 for the fourth and later years in the recovery period. These amounts are indexed for inflation after 2018. For passenger autos eligible for bonus first year depreciation, the maximum additional first year depreciation allowance remains at $8,000 as under pre-Act law.

• *Computers and peripheral equipment.* The new law removes computers and peripheral equipment from the definition of listed property. Thus, the heightened substantiation requirements and possibly slower cost recovery for listed property no longer apply.

• *New rules for post-2021 research and experimentation ("R & E") expenses.* Under the new law, specified R & E expenses paid or incurred after 2021 in connection with a trade or business must be capitalized and amortized ratably over a 5-year period (15 years if conducted outside the U.S.). These include expenses for software development, but not expenses for land, or depreciable or depletable property used in connection with the R & E (but do include the depreciation and depletion allowance for such property). Under pre-TCJA law, i.e., for R&E expenses paid or incurred before 2022, these expenses are deductible currently or may be capitalized and recovered over the useful life of the research (not to exceed 60 months), or over a ten-year period, at the taxpayer's election.

• *Like-kind exchange treatment limited.* Under the new law, the rule allowing the deferral of gain on like-kind exchanges of property held for productive use in a taxpayer's trade or business or for investment purposes is limited to cover only like-kind exchanges of real property not held primarily for sale. Under a transition rule, the pre-TCJA law applies to exchanges of personal property if the taxpayer has either disposed of the property given up or obtained the replacement property before 2018.

• *Excessive employee compensation.* Under pre-Act law, a deduction for compensation paid or accrued with respect to a covered employee of a publicly traded corporation is deductible only up to $1 million per year. Exceptions applied for commissions, performance-based pay, including stock options, payments to a qualified retirement plan, and amounts excludable from the employee's gross income. The new law repealed the exceptions for commissions and performance-based pay. The definition of "covered employee" is revised to include the principal executive officer, principal financial officer, and the three highest-paid officers. An individual who is a covered employee for a tax year beginning after 2016 remains a covered employee for all future years.

• *Employee achievement awards clarified.* An employee achievement award is tax free to the extent the employer can deduct its cost, generally limited to $400 for one employee or $1,600 for a qualified plan award. An employee achievement award is an item of tangible personal property given to an employee in recognition of length of service or a safety achievement and presented as part of a meaningful presentation. The new law defines "tangible personal property" to exclude cash, cash equivalents, gift cards, gift coupons, gift certificates (other than from an employer pre-selected limited list), vacations, meals, lodging, theater or sports tickets, stocks, bonds, or similar items, and other non-tangible personal property.

If you wish to discuss any of these provisions, please give me a call.

Very truly yours,

¶ 3203. Overview of the provisions in the TCJA on partnerships, S corporations, and pass-through income

> **To the practitioner:** You can use the following letter to provide clients with an overview of these provisions in the TCJA affecting the tax treatment of pass-though entities and pass-through income. For analysis of the new deduction for pass-through income, see ¶ 701. For analysis of the changed rules for S corporation conversions, see ¶ 801. For analysis of the repeal of the partnership termination rule, see ¶ 901. For analysis of the change to the partnership loss limitation rule, see ¶ 903. For analysis of the look-through rule on the sale of a partnership interest, see ¶ 2304.

Dear Client,

Here's a look at some of the more important elements of the new tax law that have an impact on partnerships, S corporations, and pass-through income. In general, they are effective starting in 2018.

• *New deduction for pass-through income.* The new law provides a 20% deduction for "qualified business income," defined as income from a trade or business conducted within the U.S. by a partnership, S corporation, or sole proprietorship. Investment items, reasonable compensation paid by an S corporation, and guaranteed payments from a partnership are excluded. The deduction reduces taxable income but not adjusted gross income. For taxpayers with taxable income above $157,500 ($315,000 for joint filers), (1) a limitation based on W-2 wages paid by the business and the basis of acquired depreciable tangible property used in the business is phased in, and (2) the deduction is phased out for income from certain service related trades or businesses, such as health, law, consulting, athletics, financial or brokerage services, or where the principal asset is the reputation or skill of one or more employees or owners.

• *S corporation conversion to C corporation.* Under the new law, on the date of its enactment, any Code Section 481(a) adjustment of an "eligible terminated S corporation" attributable to the revocation of its S corporation election (i.e., a change from the cash method to the accrual method) is taken into account ratably during the 6-tax-year period starting with the year of change. An "eligible terminated S corporation" is any regular (C)

FTC 2d References are to Federal Tax Coordinator 2d
FIN References are to RIA's Analysis of Federal Taxes: Income (print)
USTR References are to United States Tax Reporter
Catalyst References are to Checkpoint Catalyst
PCA References are to Pension Analysis (print and electronic)
PBE References are to Pension & Benefits Explanations
BCA References are to Benefits Analysis (electronic)
BC References are to Benefits Coordinator (print)
EP References are to Estate Planning Analysis (print and electronic)

corporation which meets the following tests: (1) it was an S corporation the day before the enactment of the new law, (2) during the 2-year period beginning on the date of enactment it revokes its S corporation election, and (3) all of the owners on the date the election is revoked are the same owners (in identical proportions) as the owners on the date of enactment. If money is distributed by the eligible corporation after the post-termination transition period, the distribution will be allocated between the accumulated adjustment account and the accumulated earnings and profits, in the same ratio as the amount in the accumulated adjustments account bears to the amount of the accumulated earnings and profits.

• *Partnership "technical termination" rule repealed.* Before the new law, partnerships experienced a "technical termination" if, within any 12-month period, there was a sale or exchange of at least 50% of the total interest in partnership capital and profits. This resulted in a deemed contribution of all partnership assets and liabilities to a new partnership in exchange for an interest in it, followed by a deemed distribution of interests in the new partnership to the purchasing partners and continuing partners from the terminated partnership. Some of the tax attributes of the old partnership terminated, its tax year closed, partnership-level elections ceased to apply, and depreciation recovery periods restarted. This often imposed unintended burdens and costs on the parties. The new law repeals this rule. A partnership termination is no longer triggered if within a 12-month period, there is a sale or exchange of 50% or more of total partnership capital and profits interests. A partnership termination will still occur only if no part of any business, financial operation, or venture of the partnership continues to be carried on by any of its partners in a partnership.

• *Partnership loss limitation rule.* A partner can only deduct his share of partnership loss to the extent of his basis in his partnership interest as of the end of the partnership tax year in which the loss occurred. IRS has ruled, however, that this loss limitation rule should not apply to limit a partner's deduction for his share of partnership charitable contributions. Additionally, while the regulations under the loss limitation rules do not address the foreign tax credit, taxpayers may elect the credit instead of deducting foreign taxes, thus avoiding a basis adjustment. The new law addresses these issues by providing that the rule limiting a partner's losses to his basis in his partnership interest is applied by reducing his basis by his share of partnership charitable contributions and foreign taxes paid. However, in the case of partnership charitable contributions of property with a fair market value that exceeds its adjusted basis, the partner's basis reduction is limited to his share of the basis of the contributed property.

• *Look-through rule on sale of partnership interest.* Under the new law, gain or loss on the sale of a partnership interest is effectively connected with a U.S. business to the extent the selling partner would have had effectively connected gain or loss had the partnership sold all of its assets on the date of sale. Such hypothetical gain or loss must be allocated as non-separately stated partnership income or loss is. Unless the selling partner certifies that he is not a nonresident alien or foreign corporation, the buying partner must withhold 10% of the amount realized on the sale. This rule applies to transfers on or after 11/27/2017 and will cause gain or loss on the sale of an interest in a partnership engaged in a U.S. trade or business by a foreign person to be foreign source.

If you wish to discuss how the new law may affect your particular situation, please give me a call.

Very truly yours,

¶ 3204. Overview of the foreign tax provisions in the TCJA

> **To the practitioner:** You can use the following letter to provide clients with an overview of these foreign tax provisions in the TCJA. For analysis of the deduction for foreign-source portion of dividends, see ¶ 1901. For analysis of the new rule on sales of stock in a foreign corporation, see ¶ 1904. For analysis of the rule on the incorporation of a foreign branch, see ¶ 1905. For analysis of the deemed repatriation rules, see ¶ 1906. For analysis of the rules taxing global intangible low-taxed income (GILTI), see ¶ 2001. For analysis of the deduction for foreign-derived intangible income and GILTI, see ¶ 2002. For analysis of Subpart F changes, see ¶ 2101. For analysis of the base erosion prevention rules, see ¶ 2201. For analysis of the rules on intangible property transfers, see ¶ 2202. For analysis of the rules on related party payments in hybrid transactions, see ¶ 2204. For analysis of the rules on dividends received from surrogate foreign corporations, see ¶ 2206. For analysis of the modifications to the foreign tax credit system, see ¶ 2301

Dear Client,

Here's a look at some of the more important elements of the new tax law that have an impact on foreign taxation. In general, they are effective starting in 2018.

• *Deduction for foreign-source portion of dividends.* The new law provides a 100% deduction for the foreign source portion of dividends received from specified 10%-owned foreign corporations by domestic corporations that are 10% shareholders of those foreign corporations. No foreign tax credit is allowed for any taxes paid and accrued as to any dividend for which the deduction is allowed, and those amounts are not treated as foreign source income for purposes of the foreign tax limitation. In addition, if there is a loss on any disposition of stock of the specified 10%-owned foreign corporation, the basis of the domestic corporation in that stock is reduced (but not below zero) by the amount of the allowable deduction.

• *Sales or exchanges of stock in foreign corporations.* Under this new law provision, if a domestic corporation sells or exchanges stock in a foreign corporation held for over a year, any amount it receives which is treated as a dividend for Code Sec. 1248 purposes, will be treated as a dividend for purposes of the deduction for dividends received discussed above. Similarly, any gain recognized by a CFC from the sale or exchange of stock in a foreign corporation that is treated as a dividend under Code

---

FTC 2d References are to Federal Tax Coordinator 2d
FIN References are to RIA's Analysis of Federal Taxes: Income (print)
USTR References are to United States Tax Reporter
Catalyst References are to Checkpoint Catalyst
PCA References are to Pension Analysis (print and electronic)
PBE References are to Pension & Benefits Explanations
BCA References are to Benefits Analysis (electronic)
BC References are to Benefits Coordinator (print)
EP References are to Estate Planning Analysis (print and electronic)

Sec. 964 to the same extent that it would have been so treated had the CFC been a U.S. person is also treated as a dividend for purposes of the deduction for dividends received.

• *Incorporation of foreign branches.* Under the new law, if a U.S. corporation transfers substantially all of the assets of a foreign branch to a foreign sub, the transferred loss amount must generally be included in the U.S. corporation's gross income.

• *Deemed repatriation.* Under the new law, U.S. shareholders owning at least 10% of a foreign sub must include in income for the sub's last tax year beginning before 2018, the shareholder's pro-rata share of the undistributed, non-previously-taxed post-1986 foreign earnings of the corporation. The inclusion amount is reduced by any aggregate foreign earnings and profits deficits, and a partial deduction is allowed such that a shareholder's effective tax rate is 15.5% on his aggregate foreign cash position and 8% otherwise. The net tax liability can be spread over a period of up to 8 years. Special rules apply for S corporation shareholders and for RICs and REITs.

• *Global intangible low-taxed income (GILTI).* Under the new law, a U.S. shareholder of any CFC has to include in gross income its global intangible low-taxed income (GILTI), i.e., the excess of the shareholder's net CFC tested income over the shareholder's net deemed tangible income return (10% of the aggregate of the shareholder's pro rata share of the qualified business asset investment of each CFC with respect to which it is a U.S. shareholder). The GILTI is treated as an inclusion of Subpart F income for the shareholder. Only an 80% foreign tax credit is available for amounts included in income as GILTI.

• *Deduction for foreign-derived intangible income and GILTI.* Under the new law, in the case of a domestic corporation, a deduction is allowed equal to the sum of (i) 37.5% of its foreign-derived intangible income (FDII) for the year, plus (ii) 50% of the GILTI amount included in gross income, see above. Generally, FDII is the amount of a corporation's deemed intangible income that is attributable to sales of property to foreign persons for use outside the U.S. or the performance of services for foreign persons or with respect to property outside the U.S. Coupled with the 21% tax rate for domestic corporations, these deductions result in effective tax rates of 13.125% on FDII and of 10.5% on GILTI. The deduction rates are reduced for tax years after 2025.

• *Subpart F changes.* The new law made several changes to the taxation of subpart F income of U.S. shareholders of CFCs. Among other things, the new law expands the definition of U.S. shareholder to include U.S. persons who own 10% or more of the total value (not just vote) of shares of all classes of stock of the foreign corporation. In addition, the requirement that a corporation must be controlled for 30 days before Subpart F inclusions apply has been eliminated.

• *Base erosion prevention.* To prevent companies from stripping earnings out of the U.S. through payments to foreign affiliates that are deductible for U.S. tax purposes, a base erosion minimum tax applies to corporations, other than RICs, REITs, and S corporations, with average annual gross receipts of $500 million or more that made deductible payments to foreign affiliates that are at least 3% (2% in the case of banks and certain security dealers) of the corporation's total deductions for the year. The tax is structured as an alternative minimum tax and applies to domestic corporations, as well as on foreign corporations engaged in a U.S. trade or business in computing the tax on their effectively connected income.

• Other new law provisions limit income shifting via intangible property transfers, deny deductions for related party payments in hybrid transactions or with hybrid entities, and deny qualified dividend status to dividends received by individuals from surrogate foreign corporations. Finally, the new law introduces a series of modifications to the foreign tax credit system, as well as a number of other international reforms.

If you would like to discuss how these changes may affect your particular tax situation, please give me a call.

Very truly yours,

¶ 3205. Overview of the retirement plan changes in the TCJA

To the practitioner: You can use the following letter to provide clients with an overview of the changes affecting retirement plans in the Tax Cut and Jobs Act ('TCJA"). For analysis of the rule disallowing recharacterization of Roth IRA contributions and traditional IRA contributions for conversion contributions to a Roth IRA, see ¶ 2701. For analysis of the extended rollover period for loan offsets, see ¶ 2702. For analysis of the rule on length of service awards, see ¶ 2703. For an overview of the rules allowing favorable tax treatment provided for qualified 2016 disaster area plan distributions, see ¶ 1804. For analysis of the rule allowing qualified 2016 disaster distributions to be spread over three years, see ¶ 1805. For analysis of the rule relieving qualified 2016 disaster distributions from the 10% early withdrawal penalty, see ¶ 1806. For analysis of the rule allowing recontributions of qualified 2016 disaster distributions, see ¶ 1807. For analysis of the rule extending the period for amending qualified plans and IRAs for new law changes, see ¶ 1808.

Dear Client,

Here's a look at some of the more important changes in the TCJA that affect retirement plans. Except with regard to the disaster-related provisions (which contain special effective dates), the changes are effective for tax years beginning in 2018.

• *Recharacterization of IRA contributions.* An individual who makes a contribution to a regular or Roth IRA can recharacterize it as made to the other type of IRA via a trustee-to-trustee transfer before the due date of the return for the contribution year. Under the new law, however, once a contribution to a regular IRA has been converted into a contribution to a Roth IRA, it can no longer be converted back into a contribution to a regular IRA, i.e., a recharacterization cannot be used to "unwind" a Roth conversion.

• *Extended rollover period for plan loan offset amounts.* If an employee's loan from his qualified retirement plan, Code Sec. 403(b) plan, or Code Sec. 457(b) plan is treated as distributed from the plan due to the plan's termination or the employee's failure to meet the repayment terms due to his separation from service, the employee may roll over the deemed distribution to an eligible retirement plan. The new law allows the rollover to be made any time up to the due date (including extensions) of the em-

FTC 2d References are to Federal Tax Coordinator 2d
FIN References are to RIA's Analysis of Federal Taxes: Income (print)
USTR References are to United States Tax Reporter
Catalyst References are to Checkpoint Catalyst
PCA References are to Pension Analysis (print and electronic)
PBE References are to Pension & Benefits Explanations
BCA References are to Benefits Analysis (electronic)
BC References are to Benefits Coordinator (print)
EP References are to Estate Planning Analysis (print and electronic)

ployee's tax return for the year of the deemed distribution. Pre-Act law allowed the employee only 60 days from the date of the distribution.

• *Length of service awards to public safety volunteers.* Under pre-Act law, a plan that only provides length of service awards to bona fide volunteers or their beneficiaries for qualified services performed, is not treated as a deferred compensation plan for Code Sec. 457 purposes. Qualified services are fire fighting and prevention services, emergency medical services, and ambulance services, including services performed by dispatchers, mechanics, ambulance drivers, and certified instructors. The new law increases the limit on the aggregate amount of length of service awards that can accrue in a year of service for a bona fide volunteer from $3,000 to $6,000, to be adjusted annually for inflation. For a defined benefit plan, the limit applies to the actuarial present value of the aggregate amount of awards accruing for any year of service.

• *Qualified disaster distributions taxable over three-year period.* Under the new law, a "qualified 2016 disaster distribution" will be included in a taxpayer's gross income ratably over a three-year period starting with the year it is received, unless the taxpayer elects to have the distribution fully taxed in the year it is received. A "qualified 2016 disaster distribution" is a distribution received from an "eligible retirement plan" in 2016 or 2017 by an individual whose place of abode was in a Presidentially declared disaster area at any time during 2016, and who sustained an economic loss from the disaster. An eligible plan is an IRA, individual retirement annuity, qualified plan, Code Sec. 403(a) qualified annuity plan, Code Sec. 403(d) plan, governmental Code Sec. 457(b) plan, or Code Sec. 403(b) annuity contract. There is a $100,000 aggregate limit on qualifying distributions for these purposes.

• *Qualified 2016 disaster distributions not subject to 10% early withdrawal penalty.* In general, unless an exception applies, withdrawals from qualified plans and IRAs before age 59 and a half are subject to a 10% penalty in addition to regular taxation. Under the new law, a "qualified 2016 disaster distribution," defined above, will not be subject to the 10% penalty on early withdrawals from qualified plans and IRAs.

• *Three-year period to recontribute qualified 2016 disaster distributions.* In general, eligible distributions from qualified plans and IRAs can be rolled over into eligible plans within 60 days to avoid being taxed. Under the law new, qualified 2016 disaster distributions, defined above, can be recontributed to a qualified plan or IRA in which the taxpayer is a beneficiary up to three years beginning the day after the date of distribution and avoid taxation. A recontribution is treated as a direct trustee-to-trustee rollover.

• *Period to amend qualified plans and IRAs for new law changes extended.* Under the new law, a qualified plan or IRA can be amended for new law changes retroactively any time up to the last day of the first plan year beginning after 2017 without losing its qualified status for actions taken in compliance with the law changes. Thus, e.g., a qualified plan can make a qualified 2016 disaster distribution in 2017 without first amending the plan to allow such a distribution, as long as the amendment is made retroactively before the end of the extension period. For governmental plans, the amendment may be made up to the last day of the first plan year beginning after 2019.

If you would like to discuss how any of these provisions may impact you, please contact me at your earliest convenience.

Very truly yours,

¶ 3206. TCJA provisions on tax-exempt organizations

To the practitioner: You can use the following letter to inform your clients of the provisions in the Tax Cut and Jobs Act ('TCJA") that have an impact on tax-exempt organizations. For analysis of the new excise tax on an exempt organization's excessive compensation, see ¶ 2501. For analysis of the excise tax on private college investment income, see ¶ 2502. For analysis of the change on computing an exempt organization's UBTI, see ¶ 2503. For analysis of the rule adding disallowed fringe benefit costs to an exempt organization's UBTI, see ¶ 2504.

Dear Client,

Here's a look at some of the more important elements of the new tax law that have an impact on tax-exempt organizations. In general, the provisions involved are effective starting in 2018.

• *Excise tax on exempt organization's excessive compensation.* Before the new law, executive compensation paid by tax-exempt entities was subject to reasonableness requirements and a prohibition against private inurement. The new law adds an excise tax that is imposed on compensation in excess of $1 million paid by an exempt organization to a "covered" employee. The tax rate is set at 21%, which is the new corporate tax rate. Compensation for these purposes is the sum of (1) remuneration (other than an excess parachute payment) over $1 million paid to a covered employee by a tax-exempt organization for a tax year; plus (2) any excess parachute payment paid by the organization to a covered employee. A covered employee is an employee or former employee of the organization who is one of its five highest compensated employees for the tax year, or was a covered employee of the organization or its predecessor for any preceding tax year beginning after 2016. Remuneration is treated as paid when there is no substantial risk of forfeiture of the rights to the remuneration.

• *Excise tax on private college's investment income.* Before the new law, private colleges and universities were generally treated as public charities, as opposed to private foundations, and were therefore not subject to the private foundation excise tax on their net investment income. The new law imposes an excise tax on the net investment income of colleges and

---

FTC 2d References are to Federal Tax Coordinator 2d
FIN References are to RIA's Analysis of Federal Taxes: Income (print)
USTR References are to United States Tax Reporter
Catalyst References are to Checkpoint Catalyst
PCA References are to Pension Analysis (print and electronic)
PBE References are to Pension & Benefits Explanations
BCA References are to Benefits Analysis (electronic)
BC References are to Benefits Coordinator (print)
EP References are to Estate Planning Analysis (print and electronic)

universities meeting specified size and asset requirements. The excise tax rate is 1.4% of the institution's net investment income, and applies only to private colleges and universities with at least 500 students, more than half of whom are in the U.S., and with assets of at least $500,000 per student. For this purpose, assets used directly in carrying out the institution's exempt purpose are not counted. The number of students is based on a daily average of "full-time equivalent" students, i.e., two students carrying half loads would count as a single full-time equivalent student. For purposes of the excise tax, net investment income is the institution's gross investment income minus expenses incurred to produce it, but without the use of accelerated depreciation or percentage depletion.

• *Exempt organization's UBTI computed separately for separate businesses.* Before the new law, a tax-exempt organization computed its unrelated business taxable income (UBTI) by subtracting deductions directly connected with the unrelated trade or business from its gross income from the unrelated trade or business. If the organization had more than one unrelated trade or business, the organization combined its income and deductions from all of the trades or businesses. Under that approach, a loss from one trade or business could offset income from another unrelated trade or business, thus reducing overall UBTI. Under the new law, an exempt organization cannot use losses from one unrelated trade or business to offset income from another one. Gains and losses are calculated and applied to each unrelated trade or business separately. There is an exception for net operating losses from pre-2018 tax years that are carried forward.

• *Exempt organization's UBTI to include disallowed fringe benefit costs.* Under the new law, an exempt organization's unrelated business taxable income (UBTI) is to include any nondeductible entertainment expenses, and costs incurred for any qualified transportation fringe, parking facility used in connection with qualified parking, or any on-premises athletic facility. However, UBTI is not to include any such amount to the extent it is directly connected with an unrelated trade or business regularly carried on by the organization.

If you wish to discuss any of these provisions, please don't hesitate to contact me.

Very truly yours,

¶ 3207. Provisions that sunset under the TCJA

> **To the practitioner:** You can use the following letter to provide clients with an overview of provisions in the Tax Cuts and Jobs Act (TCJA) that have a definite sunset (expiration) date. For complete analysis of:

. . . the income tax rates beginning in 2018, see ¶ 101;

. . . the new standard deduction, see ¶ 501;

. . . the reduction of personal exemptions to $0, see ¶ 502;

. . . the new limitation on "excess business loss," see ¶ 1409;

. . . the curtailment of the deduction for personal casualty & theft losses, see ¶ 508;

. . . the modification of the gambling loss limitation, see ¶ 509;

. . . the increase in the child tax credit, see ¶ 516;

. . . the limit on the state and local tax deduction, see ¶ 506;

. . . the limit on the mortgage and home equity indebtedness interest deduction, see ¶ 507;

. . . the temporary reduction in the medical expense deduction threshold, see ¶ 505;

. . . the increase in the charitable contribution deduction limitation, see ¶ 512;

. . . the suspension of the miscellaneous itemized deduction, see ¶ 503;

. . . the suspension of the overall limitation ("Pease" Limitation) on itemized deductions, see ¶ 504;

. . . the suspension of the qualified bicycle commuting exclusion, see ¶ 603;

. . . the suspension of the exclusion for moving expense reimbursements, see ¶ 602;

. . . the suspension of the moving expenses deduction, see ¶ 514;

. . . the retention of AMT, but with higher exemption amounts, see ¶ 301;

. . . changes to ABLE accounts, see ¶ 1601;

. . . discharges of student loans on death or disability, see ¶ 604;

FTC 2d References are to Federal Tax Coordinator 2d
FIN References are to RIA's Analysis of Federal Taxes: Income (print)
USTR References are to United States Tax Reporter
Catalyst References are to Checkpoint Catalyst
PCA References are to Pension Analysis (print and electronic)
PBE References are to Pension & Benefits Explanations
BCA References are to Benefits Analysis (electronic)
BC References are to Benefits Coordinator (print)
EP References are to Estate Planning Analysis (print and electronic)

. . . the retention of the estate and gift tax, but with an increased exemption amount, see ¶ 2801;

. . . the temporary 100% cost recovery of qualifying business assets, see ¶ 1204;

. . . the new credit for employer-paid family and medical leave, see ¶ 1013;

. . . the new deduction for pass-through income, see ¶ 701 and ¶ 702;

. . . the deduction for foreign-derived intangible income and GILTI, see ¶ 2002; and

. . . the election with respect to the foreign tax credit limitation, see ¶ 2302.

Dear Client,

The Tax Cuts and Jobs Act (TCJA, or Act) makes substantial changes to the Internal Revenue Code. In order to comply with certain budgetary constraints, the TCJA contains a "sunset," or an expiration date, for many of its provisions—e.g. they apply for tax years beginning before Jan. 1, 2026. Accordingly, many of the TCJA provisions are temporary. This letter provides an overview of the Act's sunsetting provisions.

Unless otherwise noted, the provisions discussed below are effective for tax years beginning after Dec. 31, 2017 and before Jan. 1, 2026. For calendar-year taxpayers (nearly all individuals), this means that the provisions are effective for 2018-2025.

New income tax rates & brackets. Seven tax rates apply for individuals: 10%, 12%, 22%, 24%, 32%, 35%, and 37%. The Act also provides four tax rates for estates and trusts: 10%, 24%, 35%, and 37%.

Standard deduction increased. The standard deduction is increased to $24,000 for married individuals filing a joint return, $18,000 for head-of-household filers, and $12,000 for all other taxpayers, adjusted for inflation in the 2019-2025 tax years. No changes are made to the current-law additional standard deduction for the elderly and blind.

Personal exemption set to $0. The deduction for personal exemptions is effectively eliminated for 2018-2025 by reducing the exemption amount to zero.

New limitation on "excess business loss." The Act provides that excess business losses aren't allowed for the tax year but are instead carried forward and treated as part of the taxpayer's net operating loss (NOL) carryforward in subsequent tax years. A taxpayer has an excess business loss if the taxpayer's losses from all trades or businesses exceeds income from the trades or businesses by more than $250,000 ($500,000 for taxpayers who file joint returns). The $250,000/$500,000 amount is adjusted for inflation in years after 2018.

Deduction for personal casualty & theft losses not allowed. The personal casualty and theft loss deduction isn't allowed, except for personal casualty losses incurred in a federally declared disaster. However, where a taxpayer has personal casualty gains, personal casualty losses can still be offset against those gains, even if the losses aren't incurred in a federally declared disaster.

Gambling loss limitation modified. The limitation on wagering losses is modified to provide that *all* deductions for expenses incurred in carrying out wagering transactions, and not just gambling losses, are limited to the extent of gambling winnings.

Child tax credit increased. The child tax credit is increased to $2,000, and other changes are made to phase-outs and refundability during this same period. In addition, taxpayers are allowed a $500 credit for each dependent who isn't a qualifying child.

State and local tax deduction limited. Subject to the exception described below, state, local, and foreign property taxes, and state and local sales taxes, are deductible only when paid or accrued in carrying on a trade or business or income-producing activity. State and local income, war profits, and excess profits aren't allowable as a deduction. However, a taxpayer may claim an itemized deduction of up to $10,000 ($5,000 for a married taxpayer filing a separate return) for the *aggregate* of (i) state and local property taxes *not* paid or accrued in carrying on a trade or business or income-producing activity; and (ii) state and local income, war profits, and excess profits taxes (or sales taxes in lieu of income, etc. taxes) paid or accrued in the tax year. Foreign real property taxes may not be deducted.

Mortgage & home equity indebtedness interest deduction limited. The deduction for interest on home equity indebtedness is eliminated for 2018-2025, and the deduction for interest on "acquisition indebtedness" is limited to underlying indebtedness of up to $750,000 ($375,000 for married taxpayers filing separately). Acquisition indebtedness is generally debt a taxpayer incurred in acquiring, constructing or substantially improving the taxpayer's home or second residence. Congress ultimately didn't adopt a proposal to eliminate the mortgage interest deduction for mortgages on a taxpayer's second residence.

There is a grandfather clause for acquisition indebtedness taken out before Dec. 16, 2017, and the higher limits continue to apply to that debt. The grandfather clause also applies when a buyer has a written binding contract before Dec. 15, 2017, to close on the purchase of a *principal residence* (but not a second home) before Jan. 1, 2018, and ultimately closes before Apr. 1, 2018. The grandfather clause doesn't apply to home equity indebtedness.

For tax years beginning after Dec. 31, 2025, the prior $1 million/$500,000 limitations are restored, and a taxpayer may treat up to these amounts as acquisition indebtedness regardless of when the indebtedness was incurred. The prohibition on deducting home equity indebtedness interest also ends for tax years beginning after Dec. 31, 2025.

Medical expense deduction threshold temporarily reduced. For tax years beginning after Dec. 31, 2016 and ending before Jan. 1, 2019, the threshold on medical expense deductions is reduced to 7.5% of adjusted gross income (AGI) for all taxpayers (from 10%).

Charitable contribution deduction limitation increased. The 50% limitation under Code Sec. 170(b) for cash contributions to public charities and certain private foundations is increased to 60%. Contributions exceeding the 60% limitation are generally allowed to be carried forward and deducted for up to five years, subject to the later year's ceiling.

Miscellaneous itemized deductions not allowed. The deduction for miscellaneous itemized deductions (which had previously been subject to the 2%-of-AGI "haircut") isn't allowed.

Overall limitation ("Pease" Limitation) on itemized deductions not applicable. The "Pease limitation" on itemized deductions doesn't apply.

Qualified bicycle commuting exclusion not applicable. The exclusion from gross income and wages for qualified bicycle commuting reimbursements doesn't apply.

Exclusion for moving expense reimbursements not applicable. The exclusion for qualified moving expense reimbursements doesn't apply, except for members of the Armed Forces on active duty (and their spouses and dependents) who move pursuant to a military order and incident to a permanent change of station.

Moving expenses deduction not applicable. The deduction for moving expenses doesn't apply, except for members of the Armed Forces on active duty who move pursuant to a military order and incident to a permanent change of station.

AMT retained, with higher exemption amounts. The Act increases the alternative minimum tax (AMT) exemption amounts for individuals as follows:

- For joint returns and surviving spouses, $109,400.
- For single taxpayers, $70,300.

- For married couples filing separately, $54,700.

Under the Act, the above exemption amounts are reduced (not below zero) to an amount equal to 25% of the amount by which the alternative taxable income of the taxpayer exceeds the phase-out amounts, increased as follows:

- For joint returns and surviving spouses, $1 million.
- For all other taxpayers (other than estates and trusts), $500,000.

These amounts will be adjusted for inflation for the 2019-2025 tax years.

For trusts and estates, the base figure of $22,500 and phase-out amount of $75,000 remain unchanged.

ABLE account changes. Effective for tax years beginning after Dec. 22, 2017 (the enactment date of the TCJA) and before Jan. 1, 2026, the contribution limitation to ABLE accounts with respect to contributions made by the designated beneficiary is increased, and other changes are in effect. After the overall limitation on contributions is reached (i.e., the annual gift tax exemption amount; for 2018, $15,000), an ABLE account's designated beneficiary can contribute an additional amount, up to the lesser of (a) the federal poverty line for a one-person household; or (b) the individual's compensation for the tax year.

Student loan discharged on death or disability. Certain student loans that are discharged on account of death or total and permanent disability of the obligor are excluded from gross income.

Estate and gift tax retained, with increased exemption amount. For estates of decedents dying and gifts made after Dec. 31, 2017 and before Jan. 1, 2026, the Act doubles the base estate and gift tax exemption amount from $5 million to $10 million.

Temporary 100% cost recovery of qualifying business assets. A 100% first-year deduction for the adjusted basis is allowed for qualified property acquired and placed in service after Sept. 27, 2017, and before Jan. 1, 2023 (after Sept. 27, 2017, and before Jan. 1, 2024, for certain property with longer production periods). The additional first-year depreciation deduction is allowed for new and used property.

New credit for employer-paid family and medical leave. For wages paid in tax years beginning after Dec. 31, 2017, but not beginning after Dec. 31, 2019, the Act allows businesses to claim a general business credit equal to 12.5% of the amount of wages paid to qualifying employees during any period in which such employees are on family and medical leave (FMLA) if the rate of payment is 50% of the wages normally paid to an employee. The credit is increased by 0.25 percentage points (but not above 25%) for each percentage point by which the rate of payment exceeds 50%. All qualifying full-time employees have to be given at least two weeks of annual paid family and medical leave (all less-than-full-time qualifying employees have to be given a commensurate amount of leave on a pro rata basis).

New deduction for pass-through income. Generally for tax years beginning after Dec. 31, 2017 and before Jan. 1, 2026, the Act adds a new section, Code Sec. 199A, "Qualified Business Income," under which a non-corporate taxpayer, including a trust or estate, who has qualified business income (QBI) from a partnership, S corporation, or sole proprietorship is generally allowed a deduction equal to the lesser of 20% of QBI (not including net capital gains) or 50% of W-2 wages paid by the partnership, S corporation, or sole proprietorship. But the deduction can't exceed the taxpayer's taxable income, reduced by net capital gain.

Deduction for foreign-derived intangible income and GILTI. In the case of a domestic corporation, a deduction is allowed in an amount equal to the sum of: (i) 37.5% of the foreign-derived intangible income (FDII) of the domestic corporation for the tax year, plus (ii) 50% of the global intangible low-taxed income (GILTI) amount (if any) which is included in the gross income of the domestic corporation under Code Sec. 951A for the tax year. For tax years beginning after Dec. 31, 2025, those amounts are reduced to 21.875% and 37.5%, respectively. FDII of a domestic corporation is the amount which bears the same ratio to the corporation's deemed intangible income as its foreign-derived deduction eligible income bears to its deduction eligible income. The deduction is intended to partially offset the provision in the TCJA including FDII and GILTI in income.

Election with respect to foreign tax credit limitation. Under pre-TCJA law, for purposes of the limitation on the foreign tax credit, if a taxpayer sustains an overall domestic loss for any tax year, then, for each succeeding year, an amount of U.S. source taxable income, equal to the lesser of either the full amount of the loss to the extent not carried back to prior tax years or 50% of the taxpayer's U.S. source taxable income for that succeeding tax year, is recharacterized as foreign source income. For any tax year of a taxpayer that begins after Dec. 31, 2017 and before Jan. 1, 2028, the taxpayer may, with respect to pre-2018 unused overall domestic losses, elect to substitute, for 50% of the taxpayer's U.S. source taxable income for that succeeding tax year, a percentage greater than 50% but not greater than 100%.

As you can see from this overview of sunsetting TCJA provisions, the new law affects many areas of taxation. If you wish to discuss the impact of the law on your particular situation, please give me a call.

Very truly yours,

¶ 3208. TCJA drops corporate income tax rate to 21% and modifies individual rate brackets

> **To the practitioner:** You can use the following letter to inform your clients about the changes to both individual and corporate tax rates made by the Tax Cuts and Jobs Act (TCJA). For detailed analysis of changes to individual tax rates, see ¶ 101 *et seq.* For details about changes to the corporate tax income rate see ¶ 102 *et seq.*

Dear Client,

I am writing to inform you about changes to the individual and corporate income tax rates that take effect beginning in 2018 under the major piece of tax legislation called the Tax Cuts and Jobs Act (TCJA).

Rate changes for individuals. Individuals are subject to income tax on "ordinary income," such as compensation, and most retirement and interest income, at increasing rates that apply to different ranges of income depending on their filing status (single; married filing jointly, including surviving spouse; married filing separately; and head of household). Currently those rates are 10%, 15%, 25%, 28%, 33%, 35%, and 39.6%.

New rates. Beginning with the 2018 tax year and continuing through 2025, there will still be seven tax brackets for individuals, but their percentage rates will change to: 10%, 12%, 22%, 24%, 32%, 35%, and 37%. The following tables show the dollar ranges of these new brackets.

Single Individuals' 2018 Income Tax Rates

If taxable income is:	The tax is:
Not over $9,525	10% of taxable income
Over $9,525 but not over $38,700	$952.50 plus 12% of the excess over $9,525
Over $38,700 but not over $82,500	$4,453.50 plus 22% of the excess over $38,700
Over $82,500 but not over $157,500	$14,089.50 plus 24% of the excess over $82,500
Over $157,500 but not over $200,000	$32,089.50 plus 32% of the excess over $157,500
Over $200,000 but not over $500,000	$45,689.50 plus 35% of the excess over $200,000
Over $500,000	$150,689.50 plus 37% of the excess over $500,000

FTC 2d References are to Federal Tax Coordinator 2d
FIN References are to RIA's Analysis of Federal Taxes: Income (print)
USTR References are to United States Tax Reporter
Catalyst References are to Checkpoint Catalyst
PCA References are to Pension Analysis (print and electronic)
PBE References are to Pension & Benefits Explanations
BCA References are to Benefits Analysis (electronic)
BC References are to Benefits Coordinator (print)
EP References are to Estate Planning Analysis (print and electronic)

Married Filing Jointly and Surviving Spouse 2018 Income Tax Rates

If taxable income is:	The tax is:
Not over $19,050	10% of taxable income
Over $19,050 but not over $77,400	$1,905 plus 12% of the excess over $19,050
Over $77,400 but not over $165,000	$8,907 plus 22% of the excess over $77,400
Over $165,000 but not over $315,000	$28,179 plus 24% of the excess over $165,000
Over $315,000 but not over $400,000	$64,179 plus 32% of the excess over $315,000
Over $400,000 but not over $600,000	$91,379 plus 35% of the excess over $400,000
Over $600,000	$161,379 plus 37% of the excess over $600,000

Married Filing Separate 2018 Income Tax Rates

If taxable income is:	The tax is:
Not over $9,525	10% of taxable income
Over $9,525 but not over $38,700	$952.50 plus 12% of the excess over $9,525
Over $38,700 but not over $82,500	$4,453.50 plus 22% of the excess over $38,700
Over $82,500 but not over $157,500	$14,089.50 plus 24% of the excess over $82,500
Over $157,500 but not over $200,000	$32,089.50 plus 32% of the excess over $157,500
Over $200,000 but not over $300,000	$45,689.50 plus 35% of the excess over $200,000
Over $300,000	$80,689.50 plus 37% of the excess over $300,000

Head of Household 2018 Income Tax Rates

If taxable income is:	The tax is:
Not over $13,600	10% of taxable income
Over $13,600 but not over $51,800	$1,360 plus 12% of the excess over $13,600
Over $51,800 but not over $82,500	$5,944 plus 22% of the excess over $51,800
Over $82,500 but not over $157,500	$12,698 plus 24% of the excess over $82,500
Over $157,500 but not over $200,000	$30,698 plus 32% of the excess over $157,500
Over $200,000 but not over $500,000	$44,298 plus 35% of the excess over $200,000
Over $500,000	$149,298 plus 37% of the excess over $500,000

Bottom line. While these changes will lower rates at many income levels, determining the overall impact on any particular individual or family will depend on a variety of other changes made by the Tax Cuts and Jobs Act, including increases in the standard deduction, loss of personal and dependency exemptions, a dollar limit on itemized deductions for state and local taxes, and changes to the child tax credit and the taxation of a child's unearned income, known as the Kiddie Tax.

Capital gain rates. Three tax brackets currently apply to net capital gains, including certain kinds of dividends, of individuals and other noncorporate taxpayers: 0% for net capital gain that would be taxed at the 10% or 15% rate if it were ordinary income; 15% for gain that would be taxed above 15% and below 39.6% if it were ordinary income, or 20% for gain that would be taxed at the 39.6% ordinary income rate.

The TCJA, generally, keeps the existing rates and breakpoints on net capital gains and qualified dividends. For 2018, the 15% breakpoint is: $77,200 for joint returns and surviving spouses (half this amount for married taxpayers filing separately), $51,700 for heads of household, and $38,600 for other unmarried individuals. The 20% breakpoint is $479,000 for joint returns and surviving spouses (half this amount for married taxpayers filing separately), $452,400 for heads of household, and $425,800 for any other individual (other than an estate or trust).

Important: These new tax rates will not affect your tax on the return you will soon file for 2017, however they will almost immediately affect the amount of your wage withholding and the amount, if any, of estimated tax that you may need to pay.

A related change is that the future annual indexing of the rate brackets (and many other tax amounts) for inflation, which helps to prevent "bracket creep" and the erosion of the value of a variety of deductions and credits due solely to inflation, will be done in a way that understates inflation more than the current method does. While it won't be very recognizable immediately, over the years this will push some additional income into higher brackets and reduce the value of many tax breaks.

Corporate income tax rate drop. C corporations currently are subject to graduated tax rates of 15% for taxable income up to $50,000, 25% (over $50,000 to $75,000), 34% (over $75,000 to $10,000,000), and 35% (over $10,000,000). Personal service corporations pay tax on their entire taxable income at the rate of 35%. (The benefit of lower rate brackets was phased out at higher income levels.)

Beginning with the 2018 tax year, the TCJA makes the corporate tax rate a flat 21%. It also eliminates the corporate alternative minimum tax.

I hope this information helps you understand these changes. Please call me if you wish to discuss how they or any of the many other changes in the TCJA could affect your particular tax situation, and the possible planning steps you might consider in response to them.

Very truly yours,

¶ 3209. TCJA repeals corporate AMT and temporarily eases individual AMT

> **To the practitioner:** You can use the following letter to inform your clients about the Alternative Minimum Tax (AMT) changes made by the Tax Cuts and Jobs Act (TCJA). For detailed analysis of the repeal of the corporate AMT and related changes, see ¶ 303, and ¶ 304 for the credit for prior-year minimum tax liability. For additional details about the temporary changes to the individual AMT, see ¶ 301.

Dear Client,

I am writing to inform you about changes to the Alternative Minimum Tax (AMT) that take effect beginning in 2018 under the major piece of tax legislation called the Tax Cuts and Jobs Act (TCJA).

Before the TCJA, a second tax system called the alternative minimum tax (AMT) applied to both corporate and noncorporate taxpayers. The AMT was designed to reduce a taxpayer's ability to avoid taxes by using certain deductions and other tax benefit items. The taxpayer's tax liability for the year was equal to the sum of (i) the regular tax liability, plus (ii) the AMT liability for the year.

A corporation's tentative minimum tax equalled 20% of the corporation's "alternative minimum taxable income" (AMTI) in excess of a $40,000 exemption amount, minus the corporation's AMT foreign tax credit. AMTI was figured by subtracting various AMT adjustments and adding back AMT preferences. The $40,000 exemption amount gradually phased out at a rate of 25% of AMTI above $150,000. "Small" corporations— those whose average annual gross receipts for the prior three years didn't exceed $7.5 million ($5 million for startups)—were exempt from the AMT. A taxpayer's net operating loss (NOL) deduction, generally, couldn't reduce a taxpayer's AMTI by more than 90% of the AMTI (determined without regard to the NOL deduction). Very complex rules applied to the deductibility of minimum tax credits (MTCs). All-in-all, the AMT was a very complicated system that added greatly to corporate tax compliance chores.

Corporate AMT repeal. The TCJA repealed the AMT on corporations. Conforming changes also simplified dozens of other tax code sections that

---

FTC 2d References are to Federal Tax Coordinator 2d
FIN References are to RIA's Analysis of Federal Taxes: Income (print)
USTR References are to United States Tax Reporter
Catalyst References are to Checkpoint Catalyst
PCA References are to Pension Analysis (print and electronic)
PBE References are to Pension & Benefits Explanations
BCA References are to Benefits Analysis (electronic)
BC References are to Benefits Coordinator (print)
EP References are to Estate Planning Analysis (print and electronic)

were related to the corporate AMT. The TCJA also allows corporations to offset regular tax liability by any minimum tax credit they may have for any tax year. And, a corporation's MTC is refundable for any tax year beginning after 2017 and before 2022 in an amount equal to 50% (100% for tax years beginning in 2021) of the excess MTC for the tax year, over the amount of the credit allowable for the year against regular tax liability. Thus, the full amount of the corporation's MTC will be allowed in tax years beginning before 2022.

Temporary easing of individual AMT. The TCJA doesn't repeal the AMT for individuals, but it does increase its exemption amounts for tax years 2018 through 2025, making it less likely to hit at lower income levels. Before the TCJA, individual AMT exemptions for 2018 (as adjusted for inflation) would have been $86,200 for marrieds filing jointly and surviving spouses; $55,400 for other unmarried individuals; $43,100 for marrieds filing separately. Those exemption amounts would have been reduced by 25% of the amount by which the individual's AMTI exceeded:

. . . $164,100 for marrieds filing jointly and surviving spouses (completely phased out at $508,900);

. . . $123,100 for unmarried individuals (completely phased out at $344,700); and

. . . $82,050 for marrieds filing separately (completely phased out at $254,450, with an additional add-back to discourage separate filing by marrieds)

Exemption increases and higher phaseouts. The TCJA increases the individual AMT exemption amounts for tax years 2018 through 2025 to $109,400 for marrieds filing jointly and surviving spouses; $70,300 for single filers; and $54,700 for marrieds filing separately. These increased exemption amounts are reduced (not below zero) by 25% of the amount of the taxpayer's alternative taxable income above $1 million for joint returns and surviving spouses, and $500,000 for other taxpayers except estates and trusts. All of these amounts will be indexed for inflation after 2018 under a new measure of inflation that will result in smaller increases than under the method previously used.

For trusts and estates, the base figure AMT exemption of $22,500, and phase-out threshold of $75,000, remain unchanged.

If you were subject to the individual AMT in the past, you may be able to reduce your wage withholding or pay reduced amounts of estimated taxes going forward due to the exemption increases and higher phaseout levels.

I hope this information gives you a basic understanding of these big AMT changes. Please call me if you wish to discuss how they or any of the many other new tax rules in the TCJA might affect your particular situation, and the planning steps you might consider in response to them.

Very truly yours,

¶ 3210. TCJA puts $10,000 aggregate limit on state and local tax deduction

> **To the practitioner:** You can use the following letter to inform your clients about the new temporary limits placed on individuals' itemized deductions of state, local and foreign taxes by the Tax Cuts and Jobs Act (TCJA) effective beginning in the 2018 tax year. For detailed analysis of this provision, see ¶ 506.

Dear Client,

I am writing to inform you about the new limit placed on individuals' itemized deductions of various kinds of nonbusiness taxes, which was made by the massive Tax Cuts and Jobs Act (TCJA), effective beginning with the 2018 tax year.

Before the changes were effective, individuals were permitted to claim the following types of taxes as itemized deductions, even if they were not business related:

(1) state, local, and foreign real property taxes;

(2) state and local personal property taxes; and

(3) state, local, and foreign income, war profits, and excess profits taxes.

Taxpayers could elect to deduct state and local general sales taxes in lieu of the itemized deduction for state and local income taxes.

Tax deduction cuts. For tax years 2018 through 2025, TCJA limits deductions for taxes paid by individual taxpayers in the following ways:

. . . It limits the aggregate deduction for state and local real property taxes; state and local personal property taxes; state and local, and foreign, income, war profits, and excess profits taxes; and general sales taxes (if elected) for any tax year to $10,000 ($5,000 for marrieds filing separately). *Important exception:* The $10,000 limit doesn't apply to: (i) foreign income, war profits, excess profits taxes; (ii) state and local, and foreign, real property taxes; and (iii) state and local personal property taxes if those taxes are paid or accrued in carrying on a trade or business or in an activity engaged in for the production of income.

FTC 2d References are to Federal Tax Coordinator 2d
FIN References are to RIA's Analysis of Federal Taxes: Income (print)
USTR References are to United States Tax Reporter
Catalyst References are to Checkpoint Catalyst
PCA References are to Pension Analysis (print and electronic)
PBE References are to Pension & Benefits Explanations
BCA References are to Benefits Analysis (electronic)
BC References are to Benefits Coordinator (print)
EP References are to Estate Planning Analysis (print and electronic)

. . . It completely eliminates the deduction for foreign real property taxes unless they are paid or accrued in carrying on a trade or business or in an activity engaged in for profit.

To prevent avoidance of the $10,000 deduction limit by prepayment in 2017 of future taxes, the TCJA treats any amount paid in 2017 for a state or local income tax imposed for a tax year beginning in 2018 as paid on the last day of the 2018 tax year. So an individual may not claim an itemized deduction in 2017 on a pre-payment of income tax for a future tax year in order to avoid the $10,000 aggregate limitation.

I hope this information helps you understand these changes. Please call me if you wish to discuss how they or any of the many other changes in the TCJA could affect your particular tax situation, and the planning steps you might consider in response to them.

Very truly yours,

¶ 3211. TCJA eliminates the ACA "individual mandate" starting in 2019 for individuals failing to maintain minimum essential health care coverage

> **To the practitioner:** You can use the following to alert clients to the elimination of the health care "individual mandate" starting in 2019. For analysis of the TCJA provision, see ¶ 401.

Dear Client,

I am writing to let you know that, starting in 2019, the TCJA has eliminated the shared responsibility payment, more commonly known as the "individual mandate," that penalizes individuals who are not covered by a health care plan that provides at least minimum essential coverage, as outlined in the Affordable Care Act of 2010 (ACA). Since this penalty is only eliminated starting in 2019, you still need to take account of it in making your health care decisions for 2018.

For individuals who do not have the required health coverage in 2018, the minimum annual penalty is $695 per adult and $347.50 for each child under 18. The maximum annual penalty can be substantially higher based on household income. The penalty applies for each month for which the required coverage is not in place, and is based on 1/12 of the annual penalty amount. Certain individuals may be exempt based on household income or other factors. (If you would like me to determine the penalty that would apply in your particular situation, or whether you qualify for an exemption, please give me a call.)

Please be sure to consider the application of the individual mandate in making your health care decisions for 2018. If you elect to forgo minimal essential health coverage, the money you save in premiums will be reduced by the applicable penalty. Starting in 2019, the individual mandate should no longer be a factor in your health care planning.

Please give me a call if you wish to discuss this issue.

Very truly yours,

FTC 2d References are to Federal Tax Coordinator 2d
FIN References are to RIA's Analysis of Federal Taxes: Income (print)
USTR References are to United States Tax Reporter
Catalyst References are to Checkpoint Catalyst
PCA References are to Pension Analysis (print and electronic)
PBE References are to Pension & Benefits Explanations
BCA References are to Benefits Analysis (electronic)
BC References are to Benefits Coordinator (print)
EP References are to Estate Planning Analysis (print and electronic)

¶ 3212. TCJA greatly eases rules for bonus depreciation, Code Sec. 179 expensing and regular depreciation

> **To the practitioner:** You can use the following letter to inform all clients that own property used in a business (including as an employee) or in other income-producing activity about the Tax Cuts and Jobs Act's (TCJA's) changes to the rules for bonus depreciation and other cost recovery. Some of the rules were effective as early as Sept. 28, 2017. For detailed analysis of these changes, see ¶ 1101 *et seq.*

Dear Client,

I'm writing with good news. The Tax Cuts and Jobs Act (TCJA) has effectively lowered the cost of acquiring capital assets by making substantial changes to the income tax rules for bonus depreciation and other "cost recovery." There's a lot to discuss, but please bear with me. One or more of these changes will almost surely change your tax bill.

Bonus depreciation. Before the TCJA, taxpayers were allowed to deduct in the year that an asset was placed in service 50% of the cost of most new tangible property other than buildings and, with the exception of qualified improvement property, building improvements. Most new computer software was also eligible for the 50% deduction. Because of the deduction in the year placed in service, there was adjustment of the regular depreciation allowed in that year and later years. The "50% bonus depreciation" was to be phased down to 40% for property placed in service in calendar year 2018, 40% in 2019 and 0% in 2020 and afterward. The phase down was to begin a year later for certain private aircraft and long-production period property.

For property placed in service and acquired after Sept. 27, 2017 (with no written binding contract for acquisition in effect on Sept. 27, 2017), the TCJA has raised the 50% rate to 100%. (Appropriately, 100% bonus depreciation is also called "full expensing" or "100% expensing".)

Additionally, under the TCJA the post-Sept. 27, 2017 property eligible for bonus depreciation can be new *or used.* Also, certain film, television and live theatrical productions are now eligible. On the other hand, the TCJA excluded from bonus depreciation public utility property and property owned by certain vehicle dealerships.

FTC 2d References are to Federal Tax Coordinator 2d
FIN References are to RIA's Analysis of Federal Taxes: Income (print)
USTR References are to United States Tax Reporter
Catalyst References are to Checkpoint Catalyst
PCA References are to Pension Analysis (print and electronic)
PBE References are to Pension & Benefits Explanations
BCA References are to Benefits Analysis (electronic)
BC References are to Benefits Coordinator (print)
EP References are to Estate Planning Analysis (print and electronic)

The 2018/2019/2020 phase down (above) doesn't apply to post-Sept 27, 2017 property. Instead, 100% depreciation is decreased to 80% for property placed in service in calendar year 2023, 60% in 2024, 40% in 2025, 20% in 2026 and 0% in 2027 and afterward (with phase down beginning a year later for certain private aircraft and long-production period property).

Code Sec. 179 expensing. Before the TCJA, most smaller taxpayers could elect, on an asset-by-asset basis, to immediately deduct the entire cost of section 179 property up to an annual limit of $500,000 adjusted for inflation. For assets placed in service in tax years that begin in 2018, the scheduled adjusted limit was $520,000. The annual limit was reduced by one dollar for every dollar that the cost of all section 179 property placed in service by the taxpayer during the tax year exceeded a $2 million inflation-adjusted threshold. For assets placed in service in tax years that begin in 2018, the scheduled threshold was $2,070,000.

The TCJA substitutes as the annual dollar limit $1 million (inflation-adjusted for tax years beginning *after* 2018) and $2.5 million as the phase down threshold (similarly inflation adjusted).

Before the TCJA, section 179 property included tangible personal property as well as non-customized computer software. The only buildings or other non-production-process land improvements that qualified did so because the taxpayer elected to treat "qualified real property" as section 179 property, for purposes of both the dollar limit and the phase down threshold. Qualified real property included restaurant buildings and certain improvements to leased space, retail space and restaurant space.

For tax years beginning after 2017, those buildings and improvements are eliminated as types of qualified real property and there is substituted a far broader group of improvements made to any building other than a residential rental building: (1) any building improvement other than elevators, escalators, building enlargements or changes to internal structural framework, and (2) building components that are roofs; heating, ventilation and air conditioning property; fire protection and alarm systems; or security systems.

Also, for tax years beginning after 2017, items (for example, non-affixed appliances) used in connection with residential buildings (but not the buildings or improvements to them) are section 179 property.

Other rules for real property depreciation. If placed in service after 2017, qualified improvement property, in addition to being eligible for bonus depreciation and being newly eligible as section 179 property, has a 15 year depreciation period (rather than the usual 39 year period for non-residential buildings).

Apartment buildings and other residential rental buildings placed in service after 2017 generally continue to be depreciated over a 27.5 period, but should the alternative depreciation system (ADS) apply to a building either under an election or because the building is subject to one of the conditions (for example, tax-exempt financing) that make ADS mandatory, the ADS depreciation period is 30 years instead of the pre-TCJA 40 years.

For tax years beginning after 2017, if a taxpayer in a real property trade or business "elects out" of the TCJA's limits on business interest deductions, the taxpayer must depreciate all buildings and qualified improvement property under the ADS.

Vehicles. The TCJA triples the annual dollar caps on depreciation (and Code Sec. 179 expensing) of passenger automobiles and small vans and trucks. Also, because of the extension of bonus depreciation, the increase, for vehicles allowed bonus depreciation, of $8,000 in the otherwise-applicable first year cap is extended through 2026 (with no phase-down).

Computers and peripheral equipment. Under the TCJA, computer or peripheral equipment placed in service after 2017 isn't treated as "listed property" whether or not used in a business establishment (or home office) and whether or not, in the case of an employee, the use is for employer convenience. So an item no longer has to pass a more-than-50%-qualifed-business-use test to be eligible for Code Sec. 179 expensing and to avoid mandatory use of the ADS.

Farm property. For items placed in service after 2017, the TCJA shortens the depreciation period for most farming equipment and machinery from seven years to five and allows many types of farm property to be depreciated under the 200% (instead of 150%) declining balance method.

For tax years beginning after 2017, if a taxpayer elects to not subject a farming business to the TCJA's limits on business interest deductions, the taxpayer must depreciate under the ADS the business's buildings and other assets that have a depreciation period of 10 years or more.

Elective rules that sometimes make it easier for fruit-or-nut-bearing plants to qualify for bonus depreciation continue to apply.

Alternative minimum tax. Property eligible for bonus depreciation continues to be exempt from the unfavorable depreciation adjustments that apply under the AMT. However, the corporate AMT has been repealed; accordingly the election that corporations could make to give up bonus and other accelerated depreciation for bonus-depreciation-eligible property in exchange for a refund of otherwise-deferred AMT credits was eliminated.

I welcome a call at your convenience to talk about the above changes and the other changes made by the TCJA that almost surely change planning for your business and personal affairs.

Very truly yours,

¶ 3213. New 20% deduction for "qualified business income" ("pass-through" income) under the TCJA

> **To the practitioner:** You can use the following to let your clients know about a new deduction provided by the TCJA for "qualified business income," sometimes referred to as "pass-through income." The deduction should be a substantial benefit to your clients who have income from partnerships, S corporations, LLCs, or sole proprietorships. For analysis of the TCJA provision, see ¶ 701 *et seq.*

Dear Client,

I am writing to inform you of a significant new tax deduction taking effect in 2018 under the new tax law. It should provide a substantial tax benefit to individuals with "qualified business income" from a partnership, S corporation, LLC, or sole proprietorship. This income is sometimes referred to as "pass-through" income.

The deduction is 20% of your "qualified business income (QBI)" from a partnership, S corporation, or sole proprietorship, defined as the net amount of items of income, gain, deduction, and loss with respect to your trade or business. The business must be conducted within the U.S. to qualify, and specified investment-related items are not included, e.g., capital gains or losses, dividends, and interest income (unless the interest is properly allocable to the business). The trade or business of being an employee does not qualify. Also, QBI does not include reasonable compensation received from an S corporation, or a guaranteed payment received from a partnership for services provided to a partnership's business.

The deduction is taken "below the line," i.e., it reduces your taxable income but not your adjusted gross income. But it is available regardless of whether you itemize deductions or take the standard deduction. In general, the deduction cannot exceed 20% of the excess of your taxable income over net capital gain. If QBI is less than zero it is treated as a loss from a qualified business in the following year.

Rules are in place (discussed below) to deter high-income taxpayers from attempting to convert wages or other compensation for personal services into income eligible for the deduction.

FTC 2d References are to Federal Tax Coordinator 2d
FIN References are to RIA's Analysis of Federal Taxes: Income (print)
USTR References are to United States Tax Reporter
Catalyst References are to Checkpoint Catalyst
PCA References are to Pension Analysis (print and electronic)
PBE References are to Pension & Benefits Explanations
BCA References are to Benefits Analysis (electronic)
BC References are to Benefits Coordinator (print)
EP References are to Estate Planning Analysis (print and electronic)

For taxpayers with taxable income above $157,500 ($315,000 for joint filers), an exclusion from QBI of income from "specified service" trades or businesses is phased in. These are trades or businesses involving the performance of services in the fields of health, law, consulting, athletics, financial or brokerage services, or where the principal asset is the reputation or skill of one or more employees or owners. Here's how the phase-in works: If your taxable income is at least $50,000 above the threshold, i.e., $207,500 ($157,500 + $50,000), all of the net income from the specified service trade or business is excluded from QBI. (Joint filers would use an amount $100,000 above the $315,000 threshold, viz., $415,000.) If your taxable income is between $157,500 and $207,500, you would exclude only that percentage of income derived from a fraction the numerator of which is the excess of taxable income over $157,500 and the denominator of which is $50,000. So, e.g., if taxable income is $167,500 ($10,000 above $157,500), only 20% of the specified service income would be excluded from QBI ($10,000/$50,000). (For joint filers, the same operation would apply using the $315,000 threshold, and a $100,000 phase-out range.)

Additionally, for taxpayers with taxable income more than the above thresholds, a limitation on the amount of the deduction is phased in based either on wages paid or wages paid plus a capital element. Here's how it works: If your taxable income is at least $50,000 above the threshold, i.e., $207,500 ($157,500 + $50,000), your deduction for QBI cannot exceed the greater of (1) 50% of taxpayer's allocable share of the W-2 wages paid with respect to the qualified trade or business, or (2) the sum of 25% of such wages plus 2.5% of the unadjusted basis immediately after acquisition of tangible depreciable property used in the business (including real estate). So if your QBI were $100,000, leading to a deduction of $20,000 (20% of $100,000), but the greater of (1) or (2) above were only $16,000, your deduction would be limited to $16,000, i.e., it would be reduced by $4,000. And if your taxable income were between $157,500 and $207,500, you would only incur a percentage of the $4,000 reduction, with the percentage worked out via the fraction discussed in the preceding paragraph. (For joint filers, the same operations would apply using the $315,000 threshold, and a $100,000 phase-out range.)

Other limitations may apply in certain circumstances, e.g., for taxpayers with qualified cooperative dividends, qualified real estate investment trust (REIT) dividends, or income from publicly traded partnerships.

Obviously, the complexities surrounding this substantial new deduction can be formidable, especially if your taxable income exceeds the threshold discussed above. If you wish to work through the mechanics of the deduction with me, with particular attention to the impact it can have on your specific situation, please give me a call.

Very truly yours,

¶ 3214. TCJA expands use of cash basis accounting method and ties income inclusion reporting for tax purposes to reporting for financial purposes

To the practitioner: You can use the following letter to inform your clients about the changes to the rules governing tax accounting methods made by the Tax Cuts and Jobs Act (TCJA). For analysis of the provision expanding the exception from the UNICAP rules for small taxpayers, see ¶ 1404. For analysis of the provision increasing the gross receipts limit for the exception from the requirement to use inventories to account for goods sold (and, thus, to use the accrual method of accounting), see ¶ 1403. For analysis of the provision raising the gross receipts limit to qualify for the small construction contract exception to required use of the percentage of completion method, see ¶ 1405. For analysis of the provision raising the gross receipts limit for cash-method use by C corporations and partnerships having a C corporation as a partner, see ¶ 1401. For analysis of the provision raising the gross receipts limits for cash-method use by farming businesses owned by C corporations (or by partnerships with a C corporation as a partner), see ¶ 1402. For analysis of the provision requiring that income must be included for tax purposes no later than for certain financial reporting purposes, see ¶ 1406. For analysis of the provision allowing accrual basis taxpayers to defer inclusion of advance payments in income to the end of the year after the year of receipt if so deferred for financial reporting purposes, see ¶ 1407.

Dear Client,

The recently enacted Tax Cuts and Jobs Act (TCJA) includes a number of changes to the rules governing the choice of accounting methods by tax-payers.

In certain situations, the Act raises the gross receipts limit used to determine which taxpayers can use the cash method of accounting:

• The exception from the uniform capitalization (UNICAP) rules for small taxpayers is expanded for tax years beginning after Dec. 31, 2017, to apply to taxpayers whose average annual gross receipts for the immediately preceding three years didn't exceed *$25 million* (up from $10 million under pre-TCJA law), and is made available to both producers and resellers of both real and personal property, rather than just resellers (as under pre-TCJA law).

• The TCJA provides that, for tax years beginning after Dec. 31, 2017, taxpayers that have average annual gross receipts of *$25 million* or less during the preceding three years (up from $10 million under pre-TCJA law) aren't required to account for the cost of goods sold using inventories under Code Sec. 471 (and, thus, aren't required to use the accrual method of accounting), but rather may use a method of accounting for inventories that either (1) treats inventories as non-incidental materials and supplies, or (2) conforms to the taxpayer's financial accounting treatment of inventories.

• The TCJA provides that, in tax years beginning after Dec. 31, 2017, corporations and partnerships that have a corporation as a partner satisfy the gross receipts test for the tax year if the taxpayer's average annual gross receipts are under *$25 million* for the three tax-year period ending with the tax year *that precedes* the tax year for which the taxpayer is being tested. The $25 million limit is adjusted for inflation for tax years beginning after 2018. Under pre-Tax Cuts and Jobs Act law, the three-year testing period ended with the tax year *before* the tax year for which the taxpayer was being tested, and a corporation or partnership having a corporation as a partner didn't satisfy the gross receipts test unless the average annual gross receipts of the entity for the three-tax-year period ending with the earlier tax year did not exceed $5 million (unadjusted for inflation).

• The TCJA provides that, in tax years beginning after Dec. 31, 2017, a farming business owned by a C corporation (or partnerships with such a C corporation as a partner) is exempt from the rule requiring such corporations to use the accrual method if the corporation meets an inflation-adjusted *$25 million* gross receipts test for the tax year. This limit replaces both the non-inflation-adjusted $25 million limit for family corporations and the $1 million limit for non-family corporations in effect before the TCJA.

The Act requires (or allows) taxpayers in certain circumstances to recognize income for tax purposes no later than the year in which it's recognized for financial reporting purposes:

• The TCJA provides that, for an accrual basis taxpayer, the all events test with respect to any item of gross income (or portion thereof) in tax years beginning after Dec. 31, 2017, won't be treated as met any later than (and, thus, these taxpayers must recognize income no later than) the tax year in which the income is taken into account as income on (1) an applicable financial statement (AFS) or (2) under rules specified by IRS, another financial statement.

• The TCJA allows taxpayers in tax years beginning after Dec. 31, 2017, to defer the inclusion of income associated with certain advance payments to the end of the tax year following the tax year of receipt if that income also is deferred for financial statement purposes.

These changes may have an impact on your choice of accounting method, and cause you to want you to review and, possibly, revise those choices.

I hope this information helps you understand these changes. Please call me if you wish to discuss how they or any of the many other changes in the TCJA could affect your particular tax situation, and the possible planning steps you might consider in response to it.

Very truly yours,

¶ 3215. TCJA doubles estate and gift tax exemption to $11.2 million per person

> **To the practitioner:** You can use the following letter to inform your clients about the doubling of the estate and gift tax exemption that was made by the Tax Cuts and Jobs Act (TCJA) effective beginning in 2018. For detailed analysis of this provision, see ¶ 2801.

Dear Client,

I am writing to inform you about changes to the estate and gift tax exemption made by the massive Tax Cuts and Jobs Act (TCJA) effective beginning in 2018 that will result in many fewer estates being subject to the 40% tax, and larger estates owing less tax.

Before the TCJA, the first $5 million (as adjusted for inflation in years after 2011) of transferred property was exempt from estate and gift tax. For estates of decedents dying and gifts made in 2018, this "basic exclusion amount" as adjusted for inflation would have been $5.6 million, or $11.2 million for a married couple with proper planning and estate administration allowing the unused portion of a deceased spouse's exclusion to be added to that of the surviving spouse (known as "portability").

Exclusion doubled. The new law temporarily doubles the amount that can be excluded from these transfer taxes. For decedents dying and gifts made from 2018 through 2025, the TCJA doubles the base estate and gift tax exemption amount from $5 million to $10 million. Indexing for post-2011 inflation, brings this amount to approximately $11.2 million for 2018, and $22.4 million per married couple, with some basic portability techniques.

A related transfer tax called the generation-skipping transfer (GST) tax is designed to prevent avoidance of estate and gift taxes by skipping transfers to the next successive generation. The TCJA doesn't specifically mention generation-skipping transfers, but since the GST exemption amount is based on the basic exclusion amount, generation-skipping transfers will also benefit from the post-2017 increased exclusion.

FTC 2d References are to Federal Tax Coordinator 2d
FIN References are to RIA's Analysis of Federal Taxes: Income (print)
USTR References are to United States Tax Reporter
Catalyst References are to Checkpoint Catalyst
PCA References are to Pension Analysis (print and electronic)
PBE References are to Pension & Benefits Explanations
BCA References are to Benefits Analysis (electronic)
BC References are to Benefits Coordinator (print)
EP References are to Estate Planning Analysis (print and electronic)

This increased exclusion amount may have an impact on your current estate plan and cause you to consider the need to redraft some important documents, including wills and trusts.

I hope this information helps you understand this change. Please call me if you wish to discuss how it, or any of the many other changes in the TCJA, could affect your particular tax situation, and the planning steps you might consider in response.

Very truly yours,

¶ 3216. TCJA lowers the maximum debt on which home mortgage interest is deductible, and eliminates the deduction for home equity loan interest

To the practitioner: You can use the following letter to alert clients to the changes made by the TCJA to the rules for deducting qualified residential (home mortgage) interest. For analysis of the TCJA provision, see ¶ 507.

Dear Client,

I am writing to let you know about changes in the rules for deducting qualified residential interest, i.e., interest on your home mortgage, under the Tax Cuts and Jobs Act (TCJA).

Under the pre-TCJA rules, you could deduct interest on up to a total of $1 million of mortgage debt used to acquire your principal residence and a second home, i.e., acquisition debt. For a married taxpayer filing separately, the limit was $500,000. You could also deduct interest on home equity debt, i.e., debt secured by the qualifying homes. Qualifying home equity debt was limited to the lesser of $100,000 ($50,000 for a married taxpayer filing separately), or the taxpayer's equity in the home or homes (the excess of the value of the home over the acquisition debt). The funds obtained via a home equity loan did not have to be used to acquire or improve the homes. So you could use home equity debt to pay for education, travel, health care, etc.

Under the TCJA, starting in 2018, the limit on qualifying acquisition debt is reduced to $750,000 ($375,000 for a married taxpayer filing separately). However, for acquisition debt incurred before December 15, 2017, the higher pre-TCJA limit applies. The higher pre-TCJA limit also applies to debt arising from refinancing pre-December 15, 2017 acquisition debt, to the extent the debt resulting from the refinancing does not exceed the original debt amount. This means you can refinance up to $1 million of pre-December 15, 2017 acquisition debt in the future and not be subject to the reduced limitation.

And, importantly, starting in 2018, there is no longer a deduction for interest on home equity debt. This applies regardless of when the home equity

FTC 2d References are to Federal Tax Coordinator 2d
FIN References are to RIA's Analysis of Federal Taxes: Income (print)
USTR References are to United States Tax Reporter
Catalyst References are to Checkpoint Catalyst
PCA References are to Pension Analysis (print and electronic)
PBE References are to Pension & Benefits Explanations
BCA References are to Benefits Analysis (electronic)
BC References are to Benefits Coordinator (print)
EP References are to Estate Planning Analysis (print and electronic)

debt was incurred. Accordingly, if you are considering incurring home equity debt in the future, you should take this factor into consideration. And if you currently have outstanding home equity debt, be prepared to lose the interest deduction for it, starting in 2018. (You will still be able to deduct it on your 2017 tax return, filed in 2018.)

Lastly, both of these changes last for eight years, through 2025. In the absence of intervening legislation, the pre-TCJA rules come back into effect in 2026. So beginning in 2026, interest on home equity loans will be deductible again, and the limit on qualifying acquisition debt will be raised back to $1 million ($500,000 for married separate filers).

If you would like to discuss how these changes affect your particular situation, and any planning moves you should consider in light of them, please give me a call.

Very truly yours,

¶ 3217. TCJA limits like-kind exchange nonrecognition rules to real estate

> **To the practitioner:** You can use the following letter to provide clients with a summary of the rules in the Tax Cuts and Jobs Act (TCJA) that limit like-kind exchanges to exchanges of real property. For analysis of this provision, see ¶ 1503.

Dear Client,

I thought you should be aware of one of the changes made by the recently enacted Tax Cuts and Jobs Act (TCJA) that relates to like-kind exchanges.

In a like-kind exchange, a taxpayer doesn't recognize gain or loss on an exchange of like-kind properties if both the relinquished property and the replacement property are held for productive use in a trade or business or for investment purposes. For exchanges completed after Dec. 31, 2017, the TCJA limits tax-free exchanges to exchanges of real property that is not held primarily for sale (real property limitation). Thus, exchanges of personal property and intangible property can't qualify as tax-free like-kind exchanges.

Although the real property limitation applies to exchanges completed after Dec. 31, 2017, transition rules provide relief for certain exchanges. Specifically, the real property limitation doesn't apply to an exchange if the relinquished property is disposed before Jan. 1, 2018, or the replacement property is received by the taxpayer before Jan. 1, 2018. If the transition rules apply and all other requirements for a tax-free exchange are satisfied, an exchange of personal property or intangible property that is completed after Dec. 31, 2017 can qualify as a tax-free like-kind exchange.

If you wish to discuss the effect of the real property limitation on your business activities, please give me a call.

Very truly yours,

FTC 2d References are to Federal Tax Coordinator 2d
FIN References are to RIA's Analysis of Federal Taxes: Income (print)
USTR References are to United States Tax Reporter
Catalyst References are to Checkpoint Catalyst
PCA References are to Pension Analysis (print and electronic)
PBE References are to Pension & Benefits Explanations
BCA References are to Benefits Analysis (electronic)
BC References are to Benefits Coordinator (print)
EP References are to Estate Planning Analysis (print and electronic)

¶ 3218. TCJA provides tax benefits for investments in Qualified Opportunity Funds

> **To the practitioner:** You can use the following letter to provide clients with a summary of the tax benefits under the Tax Cuts and Jobs Act (TCJA) that are related to an investment in a Qualified Opportunity (QO) Fund. For analysis of the rules for designating a Qualified Opportunity Zone (QO Zone), see ¶ 1704. For analysis of the rules related to an investment in a QO Fund, see ¶ 1703.

Dear Client,

The recently enacted Tax Cuts and Jobs Act (TCJA) introduces two elections, one to defer gain from the sale of property that is reinvested in an investment in a Qualified Opportunity (QO) Fund and another to permanently exclude gain from the sale or exchange of the investment in the QO Fund. These elections can provide substantial tax benefits for taxpayers who can satisfy the detailed and quite complex set of rules.

Designation of a QO Zone. Under the TCJA, a state's chief executive officer (CEO) (generally, a governor or the mayor of the District of Columbia) can designate certain census tracts that are low-income communities as Qualified Opportunity Zones (QO Zones). The state's CEO has 90 days (plus, another 30 days under an extension) after Dec. 22, 2017 to nominate a tract by notifying IRS in writing of the nomination. IRS then has to certify the nomination and designate the tract as a QO Zone within 30 days (plus, another 30 days under an extension) after receiving the notice. Thus, the designation has to occur in 2018 and will remain in effect for ten calendar years.

QO Funds. A QO Fund is an investment vehicle organized as a corporation or a partnership for the purpose of investing in a QO Zone. The QO Fund can't invest in another QO Fund and has to hold at least 90% of its assets in QO Zone property (i.e., any QO Zone stock, any QO Zone partnership interest, and any QO Zone business property). A QO Zone property has to meet many requirements, including that substantially all of the entity's business property is used in a QO Zone. A penalty can apply to the QO Fund if it fails to meet the 90% requirement.

FTC 2d References are to Federal Tax Coordinator 2d
FIN References are to RIA's Analysis of Federal Taxes: Income (print)
USTR References are to United States Tax Reporter
Catalyst References are to Checkpoint Catalyst
PCA References are to Pension Analysis (print and electronic)
PBE References are to Pension & Benefits Explanations
BCA References are to Benefits Analysis (electronic)
BC References are to Benefits Coordinator (print)
EP References are to Estate Planning Analysis (print and electronic)

Temporary gain deferral election. If a taxpayer invests gains from the sale or exchange of property with an unrelated person in a QO Fund within the 180-day period beginning on the date of the sale or exchange, the taxpayer can elect to defer the gain from the sale or exchange.

Recognition of deferred gain. The taxpayer defers the gain until the later of the date on which the investment is sold or exchanged, or Dec. 31, 2026. At that time, the taxpayer includes the excess of (1) the gain over the *lesser* of the amount of deferred gain or the fair market value of the investment as determined on that date *over* (2) the taxpayer's basis in the investment.

Basis in the investment. A taxpayer's basis in the investment is zero unless any of the following increases apply: (a) 15% of the deferred gain if the investment is held for five years, (b) 10% of the deferred gain if the investment is held for seven years; and (c) any deferred gain recognized at the end of the deferral period.

Permanent gain exclusion election. At the taxpayer's election, a taxpayer can exclude any post-acquisition capital gains on an investment in a QO Fund if the investment in the QO Fund has been held for ten years.

When elections can't be made. A taxpayer can't make either election if there's already an election in effect with respect to the same sale or exchange. Also, a taxpayer can't make a temporary deferral election with respect to any sale or exchange after Dec. 31, 2026.

I hope that you found this brief description of the rules relating to investments interesting. If an investment in a QO Fund sounds like an attractive opportunity that you would like to hear more about, please give me a call.

Very truly yours,

¶ 3219. TCJA business credit changes include a new employer credit for paid family and medical leave

> **To the practitioner:** You can use the following letter to alert clients to the new employer credit for paid family and medical leave created by the Tax Cuts and Jobs Act (TCJA), as well as the Act's changes to the rehabilitation credit and the orphan drug credit. For analysis of the credit for paid family and medical leave, see ¶ 1013. For analysis of the credit for qualified rehabilitation expenditures, see ¶ 1014. For analysis of the orphan drug credit for clinical testing expenses for certain rare drugs or diseases, see ¶ 1015 and ¶ 1016.

Dear Client,

I am writing to inform you that Tax Cuts and Jobs Act (TCJA) makes changes to the general business credit by adding a new component credit for paid family and medical leave, and changing two current component credits, i.e., the rehabilitation credit and the orphan drug credit.

First, the Act introduces a new component credit for paid family and medical leave, i.e. the *paid family and medical leave credit*, which is available to eligible employers for wages paid to qualifying employees on family and medical leave. The credit is available as long as the amount paid to employees on leave is at least 50% of their normal wages and the leave payments are made in employer *tax years beginning in 2018 and 2019*. That is, under the Act, the new credit is temporary and won't be available for employer tax years beginning in 2020 or later unless Congress extends it further.

For leave payments of 50% of normal wage payments, the credit amount is 12.5% of wages paid on leave. If the leave payment is more than 50% of normal wages, then the credit is raised by .25% for each 1% by which the rate is more than 50% of normal wages. So, if the leave payment rate is 100% of the normal rate, i.e. is equal to the normal rate, then the credit is raised to 25% of the on leave payment rate. The maximum leave allowed for any employee for any tax year is 12 weeks.

Eligible employers are those with a written policy in place allowing (1) qualifying full-time employees at least two weeks of paid family and medical leave a year, and (2) less than full-time employees a pro-rated amount of

---

FTC 2d References are to Federal Tax Coordinator 2d
FIN References are to RIA's Analysis of Federal Taxes: Income (print)
USTR References are to United States Tax Reporter
Catalyst References are to Checkpoint Catalyst
PCA References are to Pension Analysis (print and electronic)
PBE References are to Pension & Benefits Explanations
BCA References are to Benefits Analysis (electronic)
BC References are to Benefits Coordinator (print)
EP References are to Estate Planning Analysis (print and electronic)

leave. On that note, qualifying employees are those who have (1) been employed by the employer for one year or more, and (2) who, in the preceding year, had compensation not above 60% of the compensation threshold for highly compensated employees. Paid leave provided as vacation leave, personal leave, or other medical or sick leave is not considered family and medical leave.

Second, the Act changes the *rehabilitation credit* for qualified rehabilitation *expenditures paid or incurred starting in 2018* by eliminating the 10% credit for expenditures for qualified rehabilitation buildings placed in service before 1936, and retaining the 20% credit for expenditures for certified historic structures, but reducing its value by requiring taxpayers to take the credit ratably over five years starting with the date the structure is placed in service. Formerly, a taxpayer could take the entire credit in the year the structure was placed in service. The Act also provides for a transition rule for buildings owned or leased at all times on and after Jan. 1, 2018.

Third, the Act also makes significant changes to another component credit of the general business credit, i.e., the *orphan drug credit* for clinical testing expenses for certain drugs for rare diseases or conditions. For clinical testing expense *amounts paid or incurred in tax years beginning in 2018*, the former 50% credit is cut in half to 25%. Taxpayers that claim the full credit have to reduce the amount of any otherwise allowable deduction for the expenses regardless of limitations under the general business credit. Similarly, taxpayers that capitalize, rather than deduct, their expenses have to reduce the amount charged to a capital account. The credit has been reduced and now equals 25 percent of qualifying clinical testing expenses. However, the Act gives taxpayers the option of taking a *reduced orphan drug credit* that if elected allows taxpayers to avoid reducing otherwise allowable deductions or charges to their capital account. The election for the reduced credit for any tax year must be made on a tax return no later than the time for filing the return for that year (including extensions) and in a manner prescribed by IRS. Once the reduced credit election is made, it is irrevocable.

I hope this information is helpful. If you wish to discuss any of these credits in more detail and the options you may have for your business, please give me a call.

Very truly yours,

¶ 3220. TCJA will end alimony-payer deduction and payee's income inclusion for post-2018 divorces and separations

---

To the practitioner: You can send the following letter to clients who are contemplating divorce or separation, or who are payers or recipients of alimony, so as to give them an overview of the Tax Cuts and Jobs Act's (TCJA's) changes to the tax treatment of alimony. For analysis of these changes, see ¶ 510.

Dear Client,

The Tax Cuts and Jobs Act (TCJA) has made changes to the tax treatment of alimony that you will be interested in. These changes take effect for divorces and legal separations *after 2018.*

Current rules. Under the current rules, an individual who pays alimony may deduct an amount equal to the alimony or separate maintenance payments paid during the year as an "above-the-line" deduction. (An "above-the-line" deduction, i.e., a deduction that a taxpayer need not itemize deductions to claim, is more valuable for the taxpayer than an itemized deduction.)

And, under current rules, alimony and separate maintenance payments are taxable to the recipient spouse (includible in that spouse's gross income).

Please note that the tax rules for *child support*—i.e., that payers of child support don't get a deduction, and recipients of child support don't have to pay tax on those amounts—is unchanged.

TCJA rules. Under the TCJA rules, there is no deduction for alimony for the payer. Furthermore, alimony is not gross income to the recipient. So for divorces and legal separations that are executed (i.e., that come into legal existence due to a court order) after 2018, the alimony-paying spouse won't be able to deduct the payments, and the alimony-receiving spouse doesn't include them in gross income or pay federal income tax on them.

TCJA rules don't apply to existing divorces and separations. It's important to emphasize that the current rules continue to apply to al-

---

FTC 2d References are to Federal Tax Coordinator 2d
FIN References are to RIA's Analysis of Federal Taxes: Income (print)
USTR References are to United States Tax Reporter
Catalyst References are to Checkpoint Catalyst
PCA References are to Pension Analysis (print and electronic)
PBE References are to Pension & Benefits Explanations
BCA References are to Benefits Analysis (electronic)
BC References are to Benefits Coordinator (print)
EP References are to Estate Planning Analysis (print and electronic)

ready-existing divorces and separations, as well as divorces and separations that are executed *before 2019*.

Some taxpayers may want the TCJA rules to apply to their existing divorce or separation. Under a special rule, if taxpayers have an existing (pre-2019) divorce or separation decree, and they have that agreement legally modified, then the new rules don't apply to that modified decree, unless the modification *expressly provides* that the TCJA rules are to apply. There may be situations where applying the TCJA rules voluntarily is beneficial for the taxpayers, such as a change in the income levels of the alimony payer or the alimony recipient.

If you wish to discuss the impact of these rules on your particular situation, please give me a call.

Very truly yours,

¶ 3221. TCJA doubles the child tax credit and allows a new lower credit for other dependents

> **To the practitioner:** You can use the following to alert clients to the enhancements made by the Tax Cuts and Jobs Act (TCJA) to the credit for children under 17 and the new credit for other dependents. For analysis of the TCJA provision, see ¶ 516, ¶ 517, and ¶ 518.

Dear Client

I am writing to let you know about improvements made by the Tax Cuts and Jobs Act (the "Act") to the child tax credit, i.e., the credit available for taxpayers with children under the age of 17 ("qualifying children"), and about a new credit for other dependents.

Under pre-Act law, the child tax credit was $1,000 per qualifying child, but it was reduced for married couples filing jointly by $50 for every $1,000 (or part of a $1,000) by which their adjusted gross income (AGI) exceeded $110,000. (The threshold was $55,000 for married couples filing separately, and $75,000 for unmarried taxpayers.) To the extent the $1,000-per-child credit exceeded your tax liability, it resulted in a refund up to 15% of your earned income (e.g., wages, or net self-employment income) above $3,000. For taxpayers with three or more qualifying children, the excess of the taxpayer's social security taxes for the year over the taxpayer's earned income credit for the year was refundable. In all cases the refund was limited to $1,000 per qualifying child.

Starting in 2018, the TCJA doubles the child tax credit to $2,000 per qualifying child under 17. It also allows a new $500 credit (per dependent) for any of your dependents who are not qualifying children under 17. There is no age limit for the $500 credit, but the tax tests for dependency must be met. Under the Act, the refundable portion of the credit is increased to a maximum of $1,400 per qualifying child. In addition, the earned threshold is decreased to $2,500 (from $3,000 under pre-Act law), which has the potential to result in a larger refund. The $500 credit for dependents other than qualifying children is nonrefundable.

The Act also substantially increases the "phase-out" thresholds for the credit. Starting in 2018, the total credit amount allowed to a married couple

FTC 2d References are to Federal Tax Coordinator 2d

FIN References are to RIA's Analysis of Federal Taxes: Income (print)

USTR References are to United States Tax Reporter

Catalyst References are to Checkpoint Catalyst

PCA References are to Pension Analysis (print and electronic)

PBE References are to Pension & Benefits Explanations

BCA References are to Benefits Analysis (electronic)

BC References are to Benefits Coordinator (print)

EP References are to Estate Planning Analysis (print and electronic)

filing jointly is reduced by $50 for every $1,000 (or part of a $1,000) by which their AGI exceeds $400,000 (up from the pre-Act threshold of $110,000). The threshold is $200,000 for all other taxpayers. So, if you were previously prohibited from taking the credit because your AGI was too high, you may now be eligible to claim the credit.

In order to claim the credit for a qualifying child, you *must* include that child's Social Security number (SSN) on your tax return. Under pre-Act law you could also use an individual taxpayer identification number (ITIN) or adoption taxpayer identification number (ATIN). If a qualifying child does not have an SSN, you will not be able to claim the $2,000 credit, but you can claim the $500 credit for that child using an ITIN or an ATIN. The SSN requirement does not apply for non-qualifying-child dependents, but you must provide an ITIN or ATIN for each dependent for whom you are claiming a $500 credit.

The changes made by the Act should make these credits more valuable and more widely available to many taxpayers.

If you have children under 17, or other dependents, and would like to determine if these changes can benefit you, please give me a call.

Very truly yours,

¶ 3222. TCJA severely cuts personal casualty and theft loss deductions

> **To the practitioner:** You can use the following letter to inform your clients about the severe new limits placed on individuals' itemized deductions of casualty and theft losses that were made by the Tax Cuts and Jobs Act (TCJA) effective beginning in the 2018 tax year. For detailed analysis of this provision, see ¶ 508.

Dear Client,

I am writing to inform you about the severe new limits placed on individuals' itemized deductions of casualty and theft losses that were made by the massive Tax Cuts and Jobs Act (TCJA) effective beginning in 2018.

Before the TCJA, individuals could claim as itemized deductions certain personal casualty losses, not compensated by insurance or otherwise, including losses arising from fire, storm, shipwreck, or other casualty, or from theft. There were two limitations to qualify for a deduction: (1) a loss had to exceed $100, and (2) aggregate losses could be deducted only to the extent they exceeded 10% of adjusted gross income.

Severe cutback. For tax years 2018 through 2025, the personal casualty and theft loss deduction isn't available, except for casualty losses incurred in a federally declared disaster. So a taxpayer who suffers a personal casualty loss from a disaster declared by the President under section 401 of the Robert T. Stafford Disaster Relief and Emergency Assistance Act still will be able to claim a personal casualty loss as an itemized deduction, subject to the $100-per-casualty and 10%-of-AGI limitations mentioned above. Also, where a taxpayer has personal casualty gains, personal casualty losses can still be offset against those gains, even if the losses aren't incurred in a federally declared disaster.

Insurance check needed. The casualty loss deduction helped to lessen the financial impact of casualty and theft losses on individuals. Now that the deduction generally won't be allowed, except for declared disasters, you may want to review your homeowner, flood, and auto insurance policies to determine if you need additional protection.

FTC 2d References are to Federal Tax Coordinator 2d
FIN References are to RIA's Analysis of Federal Taxes: Income (print)
USTR References are to United States Tax Reporter
Catalyst References are to Checkpoint Catalyst
PCA References are to Pension Analysis (print and electronic)
PBE References are to Pension & Benefits Explanations
BCA References are to Benefits Analysis (electronic)
BC References are to Benefits Coordinator (print)
EP References are to Estate Planning Analysis (print and electronic)

I hope this information helps you understand these changes. Please call me if you wish to discuss how this change or any of the many other changes in the TCJA could affect your particular tax situation, and the possible planning steps you might consider in response.

Very truly yours,

¶ 3223. TCJA allows $10,000 per year of 529 plan account funds to be used for elementary or secondary school tuition

> **To the practitioner:** You can use the following letter to provide clients with an overview of changes the Tax Cuts and Jobs Act (TCJA) makes to 529 plans. For analysis of these 529 plan changes, see ¶ 1604.

Dear Client,

The Tax Cuts and Jobs Act (TCJA) has made some changes to qualified tuition programs ("QTPs," also commonly known as "529 plans") that you might be interested in. These changes take effect for 529 plan distributions after 2017.

As you know, a 529 plan distribution is tax-free if it is used to pay "qualified higher education expenses" of the beneficiary (student). Before the TCJA made these changes, tuition for elementary or secondary schools wasn't a "qualified higher education expense," so students/529 beneficiaries who had to pay it couldn't receive tax-free 529 plan distributions.

The TCJA provides that qualified higher education expenses now include expenses for tuition in connection with enrollment or attendance at an elementary or secondary public, private, or religious school. Thus, tax-free distributions from 529 plans can now be received by beneficiaries who pay these expenses, effective for distributions from 529 plans after 2017.

There is a limit to how much of a distribution can be taken from a 529 plan for these expenses. The amount of cash distributions from all 529 plans per single beneficiary during any tax year can't, when combined, include more than $10,000 for elementary school and secondary school tuition incurred during the tax year.

As you can see, the new 529 plan rules might be beneficial to you. If you wish to discuss the impact of them on your particular situation, please give me a call.

Very truly yours,

FTC 2d References are to Federal Tax Coordinator 2d
FIN References are to RIA's Analysis of Federal Taxes: Income (print)
USTR References are to United States Tax Reporter
Catalyst References are to Checkpoint Catalyst
PCA References are to Pension Analysis (print and electronic)
PBE References are to Pension & Benefits Explanations
BCA References are to Benefits Analysis (electronic)
BC References are to Benefits Coordinator (print)
EP References are to Estate Planning Analysis (print and electronic)

¶ 3224. TCJA adds new ABLE account advantages

> **To the practitioner:** You can use the following letter to inform your clients about the changes to the rules on ABLE accounts made by the Tax Cuts and Jobs Act (TCJA). For detailed analysis of the additional ABLE contributions, see ¶ 1601. For the saver's credit for ABLE contributions, see ¶ 1602. For 60-day rollovers from 529 accounts to ABLE accounts, see ¶ 1603.

Dear Client,

I'm writing to let you know about three helpful changes in the rules affecting ABLE accounts that were made by the recent Tax Cuts and Jobs Act. These changes will take effect in 2018.

What is an ABLE account? An ABLE account is a tax-advantaged savings vehicle that can be established for a designated beneficiary who is disabled or blind. Only one account is allowed per beneficiary.

Contributions to an ABLE account aren't deductible, but amounts in the account grow on a tax-deferred basis. Distributions are tax-free up to the amount of the designated beneficiary's qualified disability expenses, a term that is broadly defined to include basic living expenses, such as housing, transportation, and education, as well as medical necessities.

In addition to the tax advantages of an ABLE account, there's a major non-tax advantage. The balance in an ABLE account and distributions used to pay qualified disability expenses are generally disregarded in determining eligibility for federal means-tested programs. This allows the beneficiary to save for the future without sacrificing current benefits.

Here are the three changes made by the Tax Cuts and Jobs Act:

Additional ABLE contributions are allowed. Contributions to an ABLE account can be made by the designated beneficiary or any other person. But until now, the total annual contributions by all persons couldn't exceed the amount of the gift tax exclusion for that year. For 2018, that figure is $15,000.

The Tax Cuts and Jobs Act allows the designated beneficiary (but no other person) to make additional contributions in excess of this limit. To be

FTC 2d References are to Federal Tax Coordinator 2d
FIN References are to RIA's Analysis of Federal Taxes: Income (print)
USTR References are to United States Tax Reporter
Catalyst References are to Checkpoint Catalyst
PCA References are to Pension Analysis (print and electronic)
PBE References are to Pension & Benefits Explanations
BCA References are to Benefits Analysis (electronic)
BC References are to Benefits Coordinator (print)
EP References are to Estate Planning Analysis (print and electronic)

eligible to make these contributions, the designated beneficiary must be employed or self-employed and must not be covered by an employer's retirement saving plan.

The additional contributions are limited to the lesser of (1) the previous year's poverty line for a one-person household or (2) the designated beneficiary's taxable compensation for the current year.

For 2017, the federal poverty line for a one-person household was $12,060 for the 48 contiguous states and the District of Columbia. So, the additional contributions for 2018 can't exceed that amount.

A designated beneficiary can contribute the full $12,060 for 2018 if the beneficiary's 2018 taxable compensation is at least that much. When added to the original $15,000, that allows a total of $27,060 in contributions.

If the beneficiary's compensation is less than $12,060, the additional contributions are limited to the amount of the compensation.

Saver's credit allowed for designated beneficiary's ABLE contributions. An eligible lower-income taxpayer can claim a nonrefundable saver's credit for a percentage of up to $2,000 of retirement savings contributions. The applicable percentage (50%, 20%, or 10%) depends on filing status and adjusted gross income. The maximum saver's credit is $1,000 ($2,000 contribution × 50% credit percentage).

The saver's credit is available for contributions to 401(k) plans, traditional or Roth IRAs, and certain other retirement plans. Until now, it wasn't available for contributions to an ABLE account.

The Tax Cuts and Jobs Act changed this by making ABLE account contributions by the designated beneficiary eligible for the saver's credit. A beneficiary who qualifies for this credit can have the ABLE contributions partly subsidized through a tax credit.

Tax-free rollovers from 529 accounts to ABLE accounts. In addition to ABLE accounts, the tax law also provides for qualified tuition programs, also known as 529 plans. These have tax features similar to ABLE accounts, but are used to pay for the education expenses of a designated beneficiary, who needn't be disabled.

It sometimes happens that the beneficiary of a 529 account has finished with school but still has funds remaining in the account. If the beneficiary takes a distribution of the balance, there will be a tax bill to pay that includes a 10% penalty tax.

One possible solution is to take a distribution from the 529 account and roll it over within 60 days to a 529 account for the benefit of a member of the designated beneficiary's family. The tax deferral will continue in the family member's account.

Until now, a distribution from a 529 account couldn't be rolled over to an ABLE account. The Tax Cuts and Jobs Act changes this rule, allowing a 60-day rollover from a designated beneficiary's 529 account to that same beneficiary's ABLE account. But this would only work if the beneficiary is disabled or blind and has an ABLE account.

Alternatively, a 60-day rollover is possible from a 529 account to the ABLE account of a member of the family of the 529 account's beneficiary. A family member is defined broadly for this purpose. It includes the designated beneficiary's spouse; child or descendant of a child; brother, sister, stepbrother, or stepsister; father, mother, or ancestor of either; stepfather or stepmother; niece or nephew; aunt or uncle; in-law; or the spouse of any of the above. It also includes a first cousin, but not a first cousin's spouse.

So, for example, a beneficiary who has no use for the balance in a 529 account can take a distribution from the account and roll it over within 60 days to an ABLE account for the beneficiary's niece who is disabled or blind. No tax is due on the distribution, and the tax deferral continues in the niece's ABLE account.

There's a dollar limit on the amount that can be rolled over in this way. The rollover amount, when added to other contributions to the ABLE account for the year, can't exceed the gift tax exclusion amount for the year, which is $15,000 for 2018.

I hope this information gives you a basic understanding of these ABLE account changes. Please call me if you wish to discuss how they or any of the many other new tax rules in the Tax Cuts and Jobs Act might affect your particular situation, and the planning steps you might consider in response to them.

Very truly yours,

¶ 6000. Act Section Cross Reference Table

Act §	Code §	Topic	Effective Date	Analysis ¶	Com Rep ¶
11001(a)	1(j)(1)	Breakpoints for imposition of 15% and 20% capital gains/ qualified dividends rates are set as statutory dollar amounts, adjusted for inflation	Tax years beginning after 2017 and before 2026	1501	5001
11001(a)	1(j)(1)	Estates and trusts income tax rate structure replaced with 10%, 24%, 35%, and 37% tax brackets	Tax years beginning after 2017 and before 2026	104	5001
11001(a)	1(j)(1)	Individual income tax rate structure replaced with 10%, 12%, 22%, 24%, 32%, 35%, and 37% tax brackets	Tax years beginning after 2017 and before 2026	101	5001
11001(a)	1(j)(1)	Kiddie tax modified to effectively apply estates' and trusts' ordinary and capital gains rates to child's net unearned income	Tax years after 2017 and before 2026	105	5001
11001(a)	1(j)(2)(A)	Individual income tax rate structure replaced with 10%, 12%, 22%, 24%, 32%, 35%, and 37% tax brackets	Tax years beginning after 2017 and before 2026	101	5001
11001(a)	1(j)(2)(B)	Individual income tax rate structure replaced with 10%, 12%, 22%, 24%, 32%, 35%, and 37% tax brackets	Tax years beginning after 2017 and before 2026	101	5001
11001(a)	1(j)(2)(C)	Individual income tax rate structure replaced with 10%, 12%, 22%, 24%, 32%, 35%, and 37% tax brackets	Tax years beginning after 2017 and before 2026	101	5001
11001(a)	1(j)(2)(D)	Individual income tax rate structure replaced with 10%, 12%, 22%, 24%, 32%, 35%, and 37% tax brackets	Tax years beginning after 2017 and before 2026	101	5001
11001(a)	1(j)(2)(E)	Estates and trusts income tax rate structure replaced with 10%, 24%, 35%, and 37% tax brackets	Tax years beginning after 2017 and before 2026	104	5001

Act §	Code §	Topic	Effective Date	Analy-sis ¶	Com Rep ¶
11001(a)	1(j)(3)	Individual income tax rate structure replaced with 10%, 12%, 22%, 24%, 32%, 35%, and 37% tax brackets	Tax years beginning after 2017 and before 2026	101	5001
11001(a)	1(j)(3)(A)	Estates and trusts income tax rate structure replaced with 10%, 24%, 35%, and 37% tax brackets	Tax years beginning after 2017 and before 2026	104	5001
11001(a)	1(j)(4)	Kiddie tax modified to effectively apply estates' and trusts' ordinary and capital gains rates to child's net unearned income	Tax years after 2017 and before 2026	105	5001
11001(a)	1(j)(5)	Breakpoints for imposition of 15% and 20% capital gains/qualified dividends rates are set as statutory dollar amounts, adjusted for inflation	Tax years beginning after 2017 and before 2026	1501	5001
11001(a)	1(j)(6)	Individual income tax rate structure replaced with 10%, 12%, 22%, 24%, 32%, 35%, and 37% tax brackets	Tax years beginning after 2017 and before 2026	101	5001
11001(b)	6695(g)	Head of household filing status added to paid preparer due diligence requirements	Tax years beginning after Dec. 31, 2017	3001	5001
11002(a)	1(f)(3)	Inflation adjustment of income tax brackets to be made based on chained CPI-U (C-CPI-U), instead of the CPI-U	Tax years beginning after 2017	201	5002
11002(b)	1(f)(6)	Inflation adjustment of income tax brackets to be made based on chained CPI-U (C-CPI-U), instead of the CPI-U	Tax years beginning after 2017	201	5002
11002(c)	1(f)(2)(A)	Inflation adjustment of income tax brackets to be made based on chained CPI-U (C-CPI-U), instead of the CPI-U	Tax years beginning after 2017	201	5002

Act §	Code §	Topic	Effective Date	Analy-sis ¶	Com Rep ¶
11002(c)(2)(A)	1(i)(1)(C)	Inflation adjustment of income tax brackets to be made based on chained CPI-U (C-CPI-U), instead of the CPI-U	Tax years beginning after 2017	201	5002
11002(c)(2)(B)	1(i)(3)(C)	Inflation adjustment of income tax brackets to be made based on chained CPI-U (C-CPI-U), instead of the CPI-U	Tax years beginning after 2017	201	5002
11002(d)(1)(A)	23(h)(2)	Chained CPI-U (C-CPI-U) replaces CPI-U in inflation adjustments of various tax parameters under the Code	Tax years beginning after Dec. 31, 2017	202	5002
11002(d)(1)(AA)	831(b)(2)(D)(ii)	Chained CPI-U (C-CPI-U) replaces CPI-U in inflation adjustments of various tax parameters under the Code	Tax years beginning after Dec. 31, 2017	202	5002
11002(d)(1)(B)	25A(h)(1)(A)(ii)	Chained CPI-U (C-CPI-U) replaces CPI-U in inflation adjustments of various tax parameters under the Code	Tax years beginning after Dec. 31, 2017	202	5002
11002(d)(1)(B)	25A(h)(2)(A)(ii)	Chained CPI-U (C-CPI-U) replaces CPI-U in inflation adjustments of various tax parameters under the Code	Tax years beginning after Dec. 31, 2017	202	5002
11002(d)(1)(BB)	877A(a)(3)(B)(i)(II)	Chained CPI-U (C-CPI-U) replaces CPI-U in inflation adjustments of various tax parameters under the Code	Tax years beginning after Dec. 31, 2017	202	5002
11002(d)(1)(C)	25B(b)(3)(B)	Chained CPI-U (C-CPI-U) replaces CPI-U in inflation adjustments of various tax parameters under the Code	Tax years beginning after Dec. 31, 2017	202	5002

Act §	Code §	Topic	Effective Date	Analy-sis ¶	Com Rep ¶
11002(d)(1)(CC)	2010(c)(3)(B)(ii)	Chained CPI-U (C-CPI-U) replaces CPI-U in inflation adjustments of various tax parameters under the Code	Tax years beginning after Dec. 31, 2017	202	5002
11002(d)(1)(D)	32(b)(2)(B)(ii)(II)	Chained CPI-U (C-CPI-U) replaces CPI-U in inflation adjustments of various tax parameters under the Code	Tax years beginning after Dec. 31, 2017	202	5002
11002(d)(1)(D)	32(j)(1)(B)(i)	Chained CPI-U (C-CPI-U) replaces CPI-U in inflation adjustments of various tax parameters under the Code	Tax years beginning after Dec. 31, 2017	202	5002
11002(d)(1)(D)	32(j)(1)(B)(ii)	Chained CPI-U (C-CPI-U) replaces CPI-U in inflation adjustments of various tax parameters under the Code	Tax years beginning after Dec. 31, 2017	202	5002
11002(d)(1)(DD)	2032A(a)(3)(B)	Chained CPI-U (C-CPI-U) replaces CPI-U in inflation adjustments of various tax parameters under the Code	Tax years beginning after Dec. 31, 2017	202	5002
11002(d)(1)(E)	36B(f)(2)(B)(ii)(II)	Chained CPI-U (C-CPI-U) replaces CPI-U in inflation adjustments of various tax parameters under the Code	Tax years beginning after Dec. 31, 2017	202	5002
11002(d)(1)(EE)	2503(b)(2)(B)	Chained CPI-U (C-CPI-U) replaces CPI-U in inflation adjustments of various tax parameters under the Code	Tax years beginning after Dec. 31, 2017	202	5002
11002(d)(1)(F)	41(e)(5)(C)(i)	Chained CPI-U (C-CPI-U) replaces CPI-U in inflation adjustments of various tax parameters under the Code	Tax years beginning after Dec. 31, 2017	202	5002

Act §	Code §	Topic	Effective Date	Analysis ¶	Com Rep ¶
11002(d)(1)(FF)	4261(e)(4)(A)(ii)	Chained CPI-U (C-CPI-U) replaces CPI-U in inflation adjustments of various tax parameters under the Code	Tax years beginning after Dec. 31, 2017	202	5002
11002(d)(1)(G)	42(e)(3)(D)(ii)	Chained CPI-U (C-CPI-U) replaces CPI-U in inflation adjustments of various tax parameters under the Code	Tax years beginning after Dec. 31, 2017	202	5002
11002(d)(1)(G)	42(h)(3)(H)(i)(II)	Chained CPI-U (C-CPI-U) replaces CPI-U in inflation adjustments of various tax parameters under the Code	Tax years beginning after Dec. 31, 2017	202	5002
11002(d)(1)(GG)	5000A(c)(3)(D)(ii)	Chained CPI-U (C-CPI-U) replaces CPI-U in inflation adjustments of various tax parameters under the Code	Tax years beginning after Dec. 31, 2017	202	5002
11002(d)(1)(H)	45R(d)(3)(B)(ii)	Chained CPI-U (C-CPI-U) replaces CPI-U in inflation adjustments of various tax parameters under the Code	Tax years beginning after Dec. 31, 2017	202	5002
11002(d)(1)(HH)	6323(i)(4)(B)	Chained CPI-U (C-CPI-U) replaces CPI-U in inflation adjustments of various tax parameters under the Code	Tax years beginning after Dec. 31, 2017	202	5002
11002(d)(1)(I)	55(d)(4)(A)(ii)	Alternative minimum tax exemption amounts for individuals increased	Tax years beginning after 2017 and before 2026	301	5029
11002(d)(1)(I)	55(d)(4)(A)(ii)	Chained CPI-U (C-CPI-U) replaces CPI-U in inflation adjustments of various tax parameters under the Code	Tax years beginning after Dec. 31, 2017	202	5002
11002(d)(1)(II)	6334(g)(1)(B)	Chained CPI-U (C-CPI-U) replaces CPI-U in inflation adjustments of various tax parameters under the Code	Tax years beginning after Dec. 31, 2017	202	5002

Act §	Code §	Topic	Effective Date	Analy-sis ¶	Com Rep ¶
11002(d)(1)(J)	62(d)(3)(B)	Chained CPI-U (C-CPI-U) replaces CPI-U in inflation adjustments of various tax parameters under the Code	Tax years beginning after Dec. 31, 2017	202	5002
11002(d)(1)(JJ)	6601(j)(3)(B)	Chained CPI-U (C-CPI-U) replaces CPI-U in inflation adjustments of various tax parameters under the Code	Tax years beginning after Dec. 31, 2017	202	5002
11002(d)(1)(K)	63(c)(4)(B)	Chained CPI-U (C-CPI-U) replaces CPI-U in inflation adjustments of various tax parameters under the Code	Tax years beginning after Dec. 31, 2017	202	5002
11002(d)(1)(KK)	6651(i)(1)	Chained CPI-U (C-CPI-U) replaces CPI-U in inflation adjustments of various tax parameters under the Code	Tax years beginning after Dec. 31, 2017	202	5002
11002(d)(1)(L)	125(i)(2)(B)	Chained CPI-U (C-CPI-U) replaces CPI-U in inflation adjustments of various tax parameters under the Code	Tax years beginning after Dec. 31, 2017	202	5002
11002(d)(1)(LL)	6652(c)(7)(A)	Chained CPI-U (C-CPI-U) replaces CPI-U in inflation adjustments of various tax parameters under the Code	Tax years beginning after Dec. 31, 2017	202	5002
11002(d)(1)(M)	135(b)(2)(B)(ii)	Chained CPI-U (C-CPI-U) replaces CPI-U in inflation adjustments of various tax parameters under the Code	Tax years beginning after Dec. 31, 2017	202	5002
11002(d)(1)(MM)	6695(h)(1)	Chained CPI-U (C-CPI-U) replaces CPI-U in inflation adjustments of various tax parameters under the Code	Tax years beginning after Dec. 31, 2017	202	5002

Act §	Code §	Topic	Effective Date	Analy-sis ¶	Com Rep ¶
11002(d)(1)(N)	137(f)(2)	Chained CPI-U (C-CPI-U) replaces CPI-U in inflation adjustments of various tax parameters under the Code	Tax years beginning after Dec. 31, 2017	202	5002
11002(d)(1)(O)	146(d)(2)(B)	Chained CPI-U (C-CPI-U) replaces CPI-U in inflation adjustments of various tax parameters under the Code	Tax years beginning after Dec. 31, 2017	202	5002
11002(d)(1)(OO)	6699(e)(1)	Chained CPI-U (C-CPI-U) replaces CPI-U in inflation adjustments of various tax parameters under the Code	Tax years beginning after Dec. 31, 2017	202	5002
11002(d)(1)(P)	147(c)(2)(H)(ii)	Chained CPI-U (C-CPI-U) replaces CPI-U in inflation adjustments of various tax parameters under the Code	Tax years beginning after Dec. 31, 2017	202	5002
11002(d)(1)(PP)	6721(f)(1)	Chained CPI-U (C-CPI-U) replaces CPI-U in inflation adjustments of various tax parameters under the Code	Tax years beginning after Dec. 31, 2017	202	5002
11002(d)(1)(Q)	151(d)(4)(B)	Chained CPI-U (C-CPI-U) replaces CPI-U in inflation adjustments of various tax parameters under the Code	Tax years beginning after Dec. 31, 2017	202	5002
11002(d)(1)(QQ)	6722(f)(1)	Chained CPI-U (C-CPI-U) replaces CPI-U in inflation adjustments of various tax parameters under the Code	Tax years beginning after Dec. 31, 2017	202	5002
11002(d)(1)(R)	179(b)(6)(A)(ii)	Chained CPI-U (C-CPI-U) replaces CPI-U in inflation adjustments of various tax parameters under the Code	Tax years beginning after Dec. 31, 2017	202	5002

Act §	Code §	Topic	Effective Date	Analysis ¶	Com Rep ¶
11002(d)(1)(R)	179(b)(6)(A)(ii)	Pre-adjustment Code Sec. 179 limits raised to $1 million (annual limit on expensing) and $2.5 million (annual phase-down threshold based on investment)	Property placed in service in tax years beginning after Dec. 31, 2017	1101	5034
11002(d)(1)(RR)	7345(f)(2)	Chained CPI-U (C-CPI-U) replaces CPI-U in inflation adjustments of various tax parameters under the Code	Tax years beginning after Dec. 31, 2017	202	5002
11002(d)(1)(S)	219(b)(5)(C)(i)(II)	Chained CPI-U (C-CPI-U) replaces CPI-U in inflation adjustments of various tax parameters under the Code	Tax years beginning after Dec. 31, 2017	202	5002
11002(d)(1)(S)	219(g)(8)(B)	Chained CPI-U (C-CPI-U) replaces CPI-U in inflation adjustments of various tax parameters under the Code	Tax years beginning after Dec. 31, 2017	202	5002
11002(d)(1)(SS)	7430(c)(1)	Chained CPI-U (C-CPI-U) replaces CPI-U in inflation adjustments of various tax parameters under the Code	Tax years beginning after Dec. 31, 2017	202	5002
11002(d)(1)(T)	220(g)(2)	Chained CPI-U (C-CPI-U) replaces CPI-U in inflation adjustments of various tax parameters under the Code	Tax years beginning after Dec. 31, 2017	202	5002
11002(d)(1)(TT)	9831(d)(2)(D)(ii)(II)	Chained CPI-U (C-CPI-U) replaces CPI-U in inflation adjustments of various tax parameters under the Code	Tax years beginning after Dec. 31, 2017	202	5002
11002(d)(1)(U)	221(f)(1)(B)	Chained CPI-U (C-CPI-U) replaces CPI-U in inflation adjustments of various tax parameters under the Code	Tax years beginning after Dec. 31, 2017	202	5002

Act §	Code §	Topic	Effective Date	Analysis ¶	Com Rep ¶
11002(d)(1)(V)	223(g)(1)(B)	Chained CPI-U (C-CPI-U) replaces CPI-U in inflation adjustments of various tax parameters under the Code	Tax years beginning after Dec. 31, 2017	202	5002
11002(d)(1)(W)	408A(c)(3)(D)(ii)	Chained CPI-U (C-CPI-U) replaces CPI-U in inflation adjustments of various tax parameters under the Code	Tax years beginning after Dec. 31, 2017	202	5002
11002(d)(1)(X)	430(c)(7)(D)(vii)(II)	Chained CPI-U (C-CPI-U) replaces CPI-U in inflation adjustments of various tax parameters under the Code	Tax years beginning after Dec. 31, 2017	202	5002
11002(d)(1)(Y)	512(d)(2)(B)	Chained CPI-U (C-CPI-U) replaces CPI-U in inflation adjustments of various tax parameters under the Code	Tax years beginning after Dec. 31, 2017	202	5002
11002(d)(1)(Z)	513(h)(2)(C)(ii)	Chained CPI-U (C-CPI-U) replaces CPI-U in inflation adjustments of various tax parameters under the Code	Tax years beginning after Dec. 31, 2017	202	5002
11002(d)(2)	41(e)(5)(C)(ii)	Chained CPI-U (C-CPI-U) replaces CPI-U in inflation adjustments of various tax parameters under the Code	Tax years beginning after Dec. 31, 2017	202	5002
11002(d)(2)	68(b)(2)(B)	Chained CPI-U (C-CPI-U) replaces CPI-U in inflation adjustments of various tax parameters under the Code	Tax years beginning after Dec. 31, 2017	202	5002
11002(d)(3)(A)	42(h)(6)(G)(i)(II)	Chained CPI-U (C-CPI-U) replaces CPI-U in inflation adjustments of various tax parameters under the Code	Tax years beginning after Dec. 31, 2017	202	5002

Act §	Code §	Topic	Effective Date	Analysis ¶	Com Rep ¶
11002(d)(3)(B)	42(h)(6)(G)(ii)	Chained CPI-U (C-CPI-U) replaces CPI-U in inflation adjustments of various tax parameters under the Code	Tax years beginning after Dec. 31, 2017	202	5002
11002(d)(4)	59(j)(2)(B)	Chained CPI-U (C-CPI-U) replaces CPI-U in inflation adjustments of various tax parameters under the Code	Tax years beginning after Dec. 31, 2017	202	5002
11002(d)(5)	132(f)(6)(A)(ii)	Chained CPI-U (C-CPI-U) replaces CPI-U in inflation adjustments of various tax parameters under the Code	Tax years beginning after Dec. 31, 2017	202	5002
11002(d)(6)	162(o)(3)	Chained CPI-U (C-CPI-U) replaces CPI-U in inflation adjustments of various tax parameters under the Code	Tax years beginning after Dec. 31, 2017	202	5002
11002(d)(7)	213(d)(10)(B)	Chained CPI-U (C-CPI-U) replaces CPI-U in inflation adjustments of various tax parameters under the Code	Tax years beginning after Dec. 31, 2017	202	5002
11002(d)(8)	280F(d)(7)(B)	Chained CPI-U (C-CPI-U) replaces CPI-U in inflation adjustments of various tax parameters under the Code	Tax years beginning after Dec. 31, 2017	202	5002
11002(d)(8)	280F(d)(7)(B)(i)	Annual caps on depreciation of passenger automobiles are raised	Property placed in service after Dec. 31, 2017	1307	5037
11002(d)(8)	280F(d)(7)(B)(ii)	Annual caps on depreciation of passenger automobiles are raised	Property placed in service after Dec. 31, 2017	1307	5037
11002(d)(9)	911(b)(2)(D)(ii)(II)	Chained CPI-U (C-CPI-U) replaces CPI-U in inflation adjustments of various tax parameters under the Code	Tax years beginning after Dec. 31, 2017	202	5002

Act §	Code §	Topic	Effective Date	Analy-sis ¶	Com Rep ¶
11002(d)(10)	1274A(d)(2)	Chained CPI-U (C-CPI-U) replaces CPI-U in inflation adjustments of various tax parameters under the Code	Tax years beginning after Dec. 31, 2017	202	5002
11002(d)(11)	4161(b)(2)(C)(i)(II)	Chained CPI-U (C-CPI-U) replaces CPI-U in inflation adjustments of various tax parameters under the Code	Tax years beginning after Dec. 31, 2017	202	5002
11002(d)(12)	4980I(b)(3)(C)(v)(II)	Chained CPI-U (C-CPI-U) replaces CPI-U in inflation adjustments of various tax parameters under the Code	Tax years beginning after Dec. 31, 2017	202	5002
11002(d)(13)	6039F(d)	Chained CPI-U (C-CPI-U) replaces CPI-U in inflation adjustments of various tax parameters under the Code	Tax years beginning after Dec. 31, 2017	202	5002
11002(d)(14)	7872(g)(5)	Chained CPI-U (C-CPI-U) replaces CPI-U in inflation adjustments of various tax parameters under the Code	Tax years beginning after Dec. 31, 2017	202	5002
11011(a)	199A(a)	20% deduction for qualified business income	Tax years beginning after Dec. 31, 2017 and before Jan. 1, 2026	702	5003
11011(a)	199A(b)	20% deduction for qualified business income	Tax years beginning after Dec. 31, 2017 and before Jan. 1, 2026	702	5003
11011(a)	199A(c)	Qualified business income defined	Tax years beginning after Dec. 31, 2017 and before Jan. 1, 2026	703	5003
11011(a)	199A(d)	Qualified business income defined	Tax years beginning after Dec. 31, 2017 and before Jan. 1, 2026	703	5003

Act §	Code §	Topic	Effective Date	Analysis ¶	Com Rep ¶
11011(a)	199A(e)	20% deduction for qualified business income	Tax years beginning after Dec. 31, 2017 and before Jan. 1, 2026	702	5003
11011(a)	199A(f)	20% deduction for qualified business income	Tax years beginning after Dec. 31, 2017 and before Jan. 1, 2026	702	5003
11011(a)	199A(f)	Application of qualified business income deduction to entities	Tax years beginning after Dec. 31, 2017 and before Jan. 1, 2026	704	5003
11011(a)	199A(f)	Treatment of qualified business income from Puerto Rico sources	Tax years beginning after Dec. 31, 2017 and before Jan. 1, 2026	705	5003
11011(a)	199A(g)	Application of qualified business income deduction to entities	Tax years beginning after Dec. 31, 2017 and before Jan. 1, 2026	704	5003
11011(b)	63	20% deduction for qualified business income	Tax years beginning after Dec. 31, 2017 and before Jan. 1, 2026	702	5003
11011(b)(1)	62(a)	20% deduction for qualified business income	Tax years beginning after Dec. 31, 2017 and before Jan. 1, 2026	702	5003
11011(b)(4)	3402(m)(1)	20% deduction for qualified business income	Tax years beginning after Dec. 31, 2017 and before Jan. 1, 2026	702	5003
11011(c)	6662(d)(1)(C)	20% deduction for qualified business income	Tax years beginning after Dec. 31, 2017 and before Jan. 1, 2026	702	5003

Act §	Code §	Topic	Effective Date	Analy-sis ¶	Com Rep ¶
11012(a)	461(l)	Excess business loss disallowance rule replaces limitation on excess farm loss for non-corporate taxpayers for tax years beginning after Dec. 31, 2017	Tax years beginning after Dec. 31, 2017 and ending before Jan. 1, 2026	1409	5004
11021(a)	63(c)(7)	Standard deduction is almost doubled, inflation adjustment is modified	Tax years beginning after Dec. 31, 2017, and before Jan. 1, 2026	501	5005
11022(a)	24(h)	Child tax credit is increased to $2,000 and expanded and a partial credit is allowed for certain non-child dependents	Tax years beginning after Dec. 31, 2017 and before Jan. 1, 2026	516	5006
11022(a)	24(h)	Qualifying child's social security number is required to claim child tax credit	Tax years beginning after Dec. 31, 2017 and before Jan. 1, 2026	518	5006
11022(a)	24(h)	Refundable portion of the child tax credit is increased to $1,400 for tax years beginning after 2017	Tax years beginning after Dec. 31, 2017 and before Jan. 1, 2026	517	5006
11023(a)	170(b)(1)(G)	Limit on an individual's contributions of cash to charitable organizations is increased from 50% to 60% of donor's contribution base	Contributions made in tax years beginning after Dec. 31, 2017, and before Jan. 1, 2026	512	5007
11024(a)(1)	529A(b)(2)(B)	ABLE account contribution limit is increased for contributions by account's designated beneficiary	Tax years beginning after Dec. 22, 2017, for contributions before Jan. 1, 2026	1601	5008
11024(a)(2)	529A(b)(2)	ABLE account contribution limit is increased for contributions by account's designated beneficiary	Tax years beginning after Dec. 22, 2017, for contributions before Jan. 1, 2026	1601	5008

Act §	Code §	Topic	Effective Date	Analy-sis ¶	Com Rep ¶
11024(a)(3)	529A(b)(7)	ABLE account contribution limit is increased for contributions by account's designated beneficiary	Tax years beginning after Dec. 22, 2017, for contributions before Jan. 1, 2026	1601	5008
11024(b)	25B(d)(1)(D)	Saver's credit is allowed for ABLE account contributions by designated beneficiary	Tax years beginning after Dec. 22, 2017, for contributions made before Jan. 1, 2026	1602	5008
11025(a)	529(c)(3)(C)(i)(III)	Tax-free 60-day rollovers from 529 plan accounts to ABLE accounts are permitted	Distributions after Dec. 22, 2017, for transfers made before Jan. 1, 2026	1603	5009
11026(a)(1)	2(a)(3)	Special "combat zone" benefits extended retroactively to members of the armed forces performing services in the Sinai Peninsula of Egypt	June 9, 2015	605	5010
11026(a)(2)	112	Special "combat zone" benefits extended retroactively to members of the armed forces performing services in the Sinai Peninsula of Egypt	June 9, 2015	605	5010
11026(a)(3)	692	Special "combat zone" benefits extended retroactively to members of the armed forces performing services in the Sinai Peninsula of Egypt	June 9, 2015	605	5010
11026(a)(4)	2201	Special "combat zone" benefits extended retroactively to members of the armed forces performing services in the Sinai Peninsula of Egypt	June 9, 2015	605	5010

Act §	Code §	Topic	Effective Date	Analy-sis ¶	Com Rep ¶
11026(a)(5)	3401(a)(1)	Special "combat zone" benefits extended retroactively to members of the armed forces performing services in the Sinai Peninsula of Egypt	Remuneration paid after Dec. 22, 2017	605	5010
11026(a)(6)	4253(d)	Special "combat zone" benefits extended retroactively to members of the armed forces performing services in the Sinai Peninsula of Egypt	June 9, 2015	605	5010
11026(a)(7)	6013(f)(1)	Special "combat zone" benefits extended retroactively to members of the armed forces performing services in the Sinai Peninsula of Egypt	June 9, 2015	605	5010
11026(a)(8)	7508	Special "combat zone" benefits extended retroactively to members of the armed forces performing services in the Sinai Peninsula of Egypt	June 9, 2015	605	5010
11027(a)	213(f)	7.5%-of-AGI floor for medical expense deduction is retroactively extended through 2018 and applied to all taxpayers	Tax years beginning after Dec. 31, 2016, and ending before Jan. 1, 2019	505	5011
11027(b)	56(b)(1)(B)	7.5%-of-AGI floor for medical expense deduction is retroactively extended through 2018 and applied to all taxpayers	Tax years beginning after Dec. 31, 2016, and ending before Jan. 1, 2019	505	5011
11028(a)	None	Favorable tax treatment provided for qualified 2016 disaster area plan distributions	Dec. 22, 2017, for distributions made on or after Jan. 1, 2016, and before Jan. 1, 2018	1804	5012

Act §	Code §	Topic	Effective Date	Analysis ¶	Com Rep ¶
11028(b)(1)(A)	72(t)	Penalty-free early retirement plan withdrawals may be made for 2016 disaster area victims	Dec. 22, 2017	1806	5012
11028(b)(1)(B)	None	Favorable tax treatment provided for qualified 2016 disaster area plan distributions	Dec. 22, 2017, for distributions made on or after Jan. 1, 2016, and before Jan. 1, 2018	1804	5012
11028(b)(1)(C)	None	Recontributions of qualified 2016 disaster distributions and continued deferral of tax on amounts previously distributed permitted	Dec. 22, 2017	1807	5012
11028(b)(1)(D)	None	Favorable tax treatment provided for qualified 2016 disaster area plan distributions	Dec. 22, 2017, for distributions made on or after Jan. 1, 2016, and before Jan. 1, 2018	1804	5012
11028(b)(1)(E)	None	Qualified 2016 disaster distributions to be included in gross income ratably over three years	Dec. 22, 2017, for distributions made on or after Jan. 1, 2016, and before Jan. 1, 2018	1805	5012
11028(b)(1)(F)	401(a)(31)	Favorable tax treatment provided for qualified 2016 disaster area plan distributions	Dec. 22, 2017, for distributions made on or after Jan. 1, 2016, and before Jan. 1, 2018	1804	5012
11028(b)(1)(F)	402(f)	Favorable tax treatment provided for qualified 2016 disaster area plan distributions	Dec. 22, 2017, for distributions made on or after Jan. 1, 2016, and before Jan. 1, 2018	1804	5012
11028(b)(1)(F)	3405	Favorable tax treatment provided for qualified 2016 disaster area plan distributions	Dec. 22, 2017, for distributions made on or after Jan. 1, 2016, and before Jan. 1, 2018 .	1804	5012

Act §	Code §	Topic	Effective Date	Analy-sis ¶	Com Rep ¶
11028(b)(2)	None	Period of time is provided, during which qualified retirement plans and IRAs can provide 2016 disaster relief before adopting retroactive 2016 disaster relief amendments	From Dec. 22, 2017 to last day of 2018 plan year	1808	5012
11028(c)(1)(A)	165(h)(2)(A)(ii)	10%-of-AGI casualty loss threshold is retroactively made inapplicable in 2016 and 2017 to net disaster losses from 2016 disaster areas	Tax years beginning after Dec. 31, 2015, and before Jan. 1, 2018	1801	5012
11028(c)(1)(B)	165(h)(1)	$100 per-casualty floor on deduction is retroactively raised to $500 in 2016 and 2017 for net disaster losses from 2016 disaster areas	Tax years beginning after Dec. 31, 2015, and before Jan. 1, 2018	1802	5012
11028(c)(1)(C)	63(c)	Non-itemizers are retroactively allowed to deduct net disaster losses from 2016 disaster areas in 2016 and 2017, via enhanced standard deduction	Tax years beginning after Dec. 31, 2015, and before Jan. 1, 2018	1803	5012
11028(c)(1)(D)	56(b)(1)(E)	AMT adjustment for standard deduction is made retroactively inapplicable to in 2016 and 2017 to net disaster losses from 2016 disaster areas	Tax years beginning after Dec. 31, 2015, and before Jan. 1, 2018	302	5012
11031(a)	108(f)(5)	Exclusion for discharge of certain student loans is broadened to include discharges on account of death or disability	Discharges of indebtedness after Dec. 31, 2017 and before Jan. 1, 2026	604	5013
11032(a)(1)	529(c)(7)	$10,000 per year of 529 plan account funds may be used for elementary or secondary school tuition	Distributions made after Dec. 31, 2017	1604	5014

Act §	Code §	Topic	Effective Date	Analysis ¶	Com Rep ¶
11032(a)(2)	529(e)(3)(A)	$10,000 per year of 529 plan account funds may be used for elementary or secondary school tuition	Distributions made after Dec. 31, 2017	1604	5014
11041(a)(2)	151(d)(4)	Deduction for personal exemptions for taxpayer, spouse, and dependents is suspended; return-filing and withholding requirements are modified	Tax years beginning after Dec. 31, 2017, and before Jan. 1, 2026	502	5015
11041(a)(2)	151(d)(5)	Deduction for personal exemptions for taxpayer, spouse, and dependents is suspended; return-filing and withholding requirements are modified	Tax years beginning after Dec. 31, 2017, and before Jan. 1, 2026	502	5015
11041(b)	642(b)(2)(C)(iii)	Deduction for personal exemptions for taxpayer, spouse, and dependents is suspended; return-filing and withholding requirements are modified	Tax years beginning after Dec. 31, 2017, and before Jan. 1, 2026	502	5015
11041(c)(1)	3402(a)(2)	Deduction for personal exemptions for taxpayer, spouse, and dependents is suspended; return-filing and withholding requirements are modified	Tax years beginning after Dec. 31, 2017, and before Jan. 1, 2026	502	5015
11041(c)(2)(B)	3402(f)(1)	Deduction for personal exemptions for taxpayer, spouse, and dependents is suspended; return-filing and withholding requirements are modified	Tax years beginning after Dec. 31, 2017, and before Jan. 1, 2026	502	5015

Act §	Code §	Topic	Effective Date	Analy-sis ¶	Com Rep ¶
11041(d)	6334(d)(4)	Deduction for personal exemptions for taxpayer, spouse, and dependents is suspended; return-filing and withholding requirements are modified	Tax years beginning after Dec. 31, 2017, and before Jan. 1, 2026	502	5015
11041(e)	6012(f)	Deduction for personal exemptions for taxpayer, spouse, and dependents is suspended; return-filing and withholding requirements are modified	Tax years beginning after Dec. 31, 2017, and before Jan. 1, 2026	502	5015
11042(a)	164(b)(6)	Itemized deduction is limited to $10,000 for SALT—combined state/local property, state/local/foreign income, and (if elected) general sales taxes	Tax years beginning after Dec. 31, 2017, and before Jan. 1, 2026	506	5016
11043(a)	163(h)(3)(F)	Mortgage interest deduction acquisition debt maximum is lowered to $750,000, deduction for home equity interest is suspended	Tax years beginning after Dec. 31, 2017, and before Jan. 1, 2026	507	5017
11044(a)	165(h)(5)	Personal casualty losses are nondeductible unless attributable to a federally declared disaster	Losses incurred in tax years beginning after Dec. 31, 2017, and before Jan. 1, 2026	508	5018
11045(a)	67(g)	Miscellaneous itemized deductions are disallowed	Tax years beginning after Dec. 31, 2017, and before Jan. 1, 2026	503	5019
11046(a)	68(f)	Overall limitation on itemized deductions ("Pease limitation" or "3%/80% rule") is suspended	Tax years beginning after Dec. 31, 2017, and before Jan. 1, 2026	504	5019

Act §	Code §	Topic	Effective Date	Analy-sis ¶	Com Rep ¶
11047(a)	132(f)(8)	Exclusion for qualified bicycle commuting reimbursement suspended	Tax years beginning after Dec. 31, 2017 and before Jan. 1, 2026	603	5021
11048	132(g)	Exclusion for qualified moving expense reimbursements suspended, except for armed forces	Tax years beginning after Dec. 31, 2017, and before Jan. 1, 2026	602	5022
11049(a)	217	Moving expense deduction eliminated, except for certain armed forces members	Tax year beginning after Dec. 31, 2017, and before Jan. 1, 2026	514	5023
11050	165(d)	Gambling loss limitation is broadened: deduction for *any* expense incurred in gambling—not just gambling losses—is limited to gambling winnings	Tax years beginning after Dec. 31, 2017, and before Jan. 1, 2026	509	5024
11051(a)	215	Alimony won't be deductible by the payor or includible by the recipient for post-2018 divorce or separation instruments	Divorce or separation instruments executed after Dec. 31, 2018	510	5025
11051(b)(1)(A)	61(a)(8)	Alimony won't be deductible by the payor or includible by the recipient for post-2018 divorce or separation instruments	Divorce or separation instruments executed after Dec. 31, 2018	510	5025
11051(b)(1)(B)	71	Alimony won't be deductible by the payor or includible by the recipient for post-2018 divorce or separation instruments	Divorce or separation instruments executed after Dec. 31, 2018	510	5025
11051(b)(1)(C)	682	Alimony won't be deductible by the payor or includible by the recipient for post-2018 divorce or separation instruments	Divorce or separation instruments executed after Dec. 31, 2018	510	5025

Act §	Code §	Topic	Effective Date	Analysis ¶	Com Rep ¶
11051(b)(2)(A)	62(a)(10)	Alimony won't be deductible by the payor or includible by the recipient for post-2018 divorce or separation instruments	Divorce or separation instruments executed after Dec. 31, 2018	510	5025
11061(a)	2010(c)(3)(C)	Estate tax basic exclusion amount increased from $5 million to $10 million	For estates of decedents dying and gifts made after Dec. 31, 2017, and before Jan. 1, 2026	2801	5026
11061(b)	2001(g)	Estate tax basic exclusion amount increased from $5 million to $10 million	For estates of decedents dying and gifts made after Dec. 31, 2017, and before Jan. 1, 2026	2801	5026
11071(a)	6343(b)	Extension of time limit for contesting IRS levy and for third party suits challenging levies	Levies made after Dec. 22, 2017 and certain levies made before Dec. 23, 2017	3002	5027
11071(b)	6532(c)(1)	Extension of time limit for contesting IRS levy and for third party suits challenging levies	Levies made after Dec. 22, 2017 and certain levies made before Dec. 23, 2017	3002	5027
11081	5000A(c)	Shared responsibility payment (penalty) eliminated after 2018	Months beginning after Dec. 31, 2018	401	5028
12001(a)	55(a)	Alternative minimum tax on corporations is repealed	Tax years beginning after 2017	303	5029
12001(b)(1)	38(c)(6)(E)	Limitation on aggregate business credits is conformed to the repeal of the corporate AMT	Tax years beginning after Dec. 31, 2017	1017	5029
12001(b)(2)	53(d)(2)	Corporate minimum tax credit (MTC) may offset regular tax liability for any tax year, and is refundable for 2018–2021	Tax years beginning after Dec. 31, 2017	304	5029
12001(b)(3)(A)	55(b)(1)	Alternative minimum tax on corporations is repealed	Tax years beginning after 2017	303	5029

Act §	Code §	Topic	Effective Date	Analysis ¶	Com Rep ¶
12001(b)(3)(B)	55(b)(3)	Alternative minimum tax on corporations is repealed	Tax years beginning after 2017	303	5029
12001(b)(3)(C)(i)	59(a)(1)(C)	Alternative minimum tax on corporations is repealed	Tax years beginning after 2017	303	5029
12001(b)(3)(C)(ii)	59(a)(2)	Alternative minimum tax on corporations is repealed	Tax years beginning after 2017	303	5029
12001(b)(4)	55(c)(1)	Alternative minimum tax on corporations is repealed	Tax years beginning after 2017	303	5029
12001(b)(5)	55(d)(2)	Alternative minimum tax on corporations is repealed	Tax years beginning after 2017	303	5029
12001(b)(5)	55(d)(3)	Alternative minimum tax on corporations is repealed	Tax years beginning after 2017	303	5029
12001(b)(6)	55(e)	Alternative minimum tax on corporations is repealed	Tax years beginning after 2017	303	5029
12001(b)(7)	56(b)(2)(C)	Alternative minimum tax on corporations is repealed	Tax years beginning after 2017	303	5029
12001(b)(8)(A)	56(c)	Alternative minimum tax on corporations is repealed	Tax years beginning after 2017	303	5029
12001(b)(8)(A)	56(g)	Alternative minimum tax on corporations is repealed	Tax years beginning after 2017	303	5029
12001(b)(9)	58(a)(3)	Alternative minimum tax on corporations is repealed	Tax years beginning after 2017	303	5029
12001(b)(10)	59(b)	Alternative minimum tax on corporations is repealed	Tax years beginning after 2017	303	5029
12001(b)(10)	59(f)	Alternative minimum tax on corporations is repealed	Tax years beginning after 2017	303	5029
12001(b)(13)	168(k)	Corporate election trading bonus and accelerated depreciation for otherwise-deferred AMT credits is ended (conforming to repeal of corporate AMT)	Tax years beginning after Dec. 31, 2017	1210	5029, 5036

Act §	Code §	Topic	Effective Date	Analysis ¶	Com Rep ¶
12001(b)(13)	168(k)(4)	Corporate minimum tax credit (MTC) may offset regular tax liability for any tax year, and is refundable for 2018−2021	Tax years beginning after Dec. 31, 2017	304	5029
12002(a)	53(e)	Corporate minimum tax credit (MTC) may offset regular tax liability for any tax year, and is refundable for 2018−2021	Tax years beginning after Dec. 31, 2017	304	5029
12002(b)	53(d)(3)	Corporate minimum tax credit (MTC) may offset regular tax liability for any tax year, and is refundable for 2018−2021	Tax years beginning after Dec. 31, 2017	304	5029
12002(c)	1374(b)(3)(B)	Corporate minimum tax credit (MTC) may offset regular tax liability for any tax year, and is refundable for 2018−2021	Tax years beginning after Dec. 31, 2017	304	5029
12003(a)	55(d)(4)	Alternative minimum tax exemption amounts for individuals increased	Tax years beginning after 2017 and before 2026	301	5029
13001(a)	11(b)	Reduction of corporate tax rates	Tax years beginning after Dec. 31, 2017	102	5032
13002(b)	245(c)(1)(B)	Reduction in corporate dividends received deduction	Tax years beginning after Dec. 31, 2017	103	5032
13001(b)(3)	1445(e)	Reduction of corporate tax rates	Tax years beginning after Dec. 31, 2017	102	5032
13002(c)	246(b)(3)	Reduction in corporate dividends received deduction	Tax years beginning after Dec. 31, 2017	103	5032
13002(d)	246A(a)(1)	Reduction in corporate dividends received deduction	Tax years beginning after Dec. 31, 2017	103	5032
13001(d)	None	Normalization requirements for public utilities	Tax years beginning after Dec. 31, 2017	1309	5032
13002(a)	243	Reduction in corporate dividends received deduction	Tax years beginning after Dec. 31, 2017	103	5032

Act §	Code §	Topic	Effective Date	Analysis ¶	Com Rep ¶
13101(a)(1)	179(b)(1)	Pre-adjustment Code Sec. 179 limits raised to $1 million (annual limit on expensing) and $2.5 million (annual phase-down threshold based on investment)	Property placed in service in tax years beginning after Dec. 31, 2017	1101	5034
13101(a)(2)	179(b)(2)	Pre-adjustment Code Sec. 179 limits raised to $1 million (annual limit on expensing) and $2.5 million (annual phase-down threshold based on investment)	Property placed in service in tax years beginning after Dec. 31, 2017	1101	5034
13101(a)(3)(A)(i)	179(b)(6)(A)	Pre-adjustment Code Sec. 179 limits raised to $1 million (annual limit on expensing) and $2.5 million (annual phase-down threshold based on investment)	Property placed in service in tax years beginning after Dec. 31, 2017	1101	5034
13101(a)(3)(A)(ii)	179(b)(6)(A)(ii)	Pre-adjustment Code Sec. 179 limits raised to $1 million (annual limit on expensing) and $2.5 million (annual phase-down threshold based on investment)	Property placed in service in tax years beginning after Dec. 31, 2017	1101	5034
13101(a)(3)(B)(i)	179(b)(6)(A)	$25,000 per-vehicle limit on Code Sec. 179 expensing of SUVs is made adjustable for inflation	Property placed in service in tax years beginning after Dec. 31, 2017	1104	5034
13101(a)(3)(B)(ii)	179(b)(6)(B)	$25,000 per-vehicle limit on Code Sec. 179 expensing of SUVs is made adjustable for inflation	Property placed in service in tax years beginning after Dec. 31, 2017	1104	5034
13101(b)(1)	179(d)(1)(B)(ii)	More building improvements are made eligible to be section 179 property	Property placed in service in tax years beginning after Dec. 31, 2017	1102	5034
13101(b)(2)	179(f)	More building improvements are made eligible to be section 179 property	Property placed in service in tax years beginning after Dec. 31, 2017	1102	5034

Act §	Code §	Topic	Effective Date	Analy- sis ¶	Com Rep ¶
13101(c)	179(d)(1)	Otherwise-qualifying residential property no longer excluded from section 179 property	Property placed in service in tax years beginning after Dec. 31, 2017	1103	5034
13102(a)(1)	448(c)(1)	Gross receipts limit for cash-method use by C corporations (and certain partnerships) raised to $25 million, related rules changed	Tax years beginning after Dec. 31, 2017	1401	5035
13102(a)(2)	448(b)(3)	Gross receipts limit for cash-method use by C corporations (and certain partnerships) raised to $25 million, related rules changed	Tax years beginning after Dec. 31, 2017	1401	5035
13102(a)(3)	448(c)(4)	Gross receipts limit for cash-method use by C corporations (and certain partnerships) raised to $25 million, related rules changed	Tax years beginning after Dec. 31, 2017	1401	5035
13102(a)(4)	448(d)(7)	Gross receipts limit for cash-method use by C corporations (and certain partnerships) raised to $25 million, related rules changed	Tax years beginning after Dec. 31, 2017	1401	5035
13102(a)(5)(A)(i)	447(c)	Gross receipts limits for cash-method use by farming C corporations (and certain partnerships) are raised to a uniform $25 million and some related rules are changed	Tax years beginning after Dec. 31, 2017	1402	5035
13102(a)(5)(A)(ii)	447(c)(2)	Gross receipts limits for cash-method use by farming C corporations (and certain partnerships) are raised to a uniform $25 million and some related rules are changed	Tax years beginning after Dec. 31, 2017	1402	5035

Act §	Code §	Topic	Effective Date	Analy- sis ¶	Com Rep ¶
13102(a)(5)(B)	447(d)	Gross receipts limits for cash-method use by farming C corporations (and certain partnerships) are raised to a uniform $25 million and some related rules are changed	Tax years beginning after Dec. 31, 2017	1402	5035
13102(a)(5)(C)	447(c)	Gross receipts limits for cash-method use by farming C corporations (and certain partnerships) are raised to a uniform $25 million and some related rules are changed	Tax years beginning after Dec. 31, 2017	1402	5035
13102(a)(5)(C)(ii)	447	Gross receipts limits for cash-method use by farming C corporations (and certain partnerships) are raised to a uniform $25 million and some related rules are changed	Tax years beginning after Dec. 31, 2017	1402	5035
13102(b)	263A(i)	Small business exception to UNICAP rules is expanded to apply to producers and resellers meeting the $25 million gross receipts test	Tax years beginning after Dec. 31, 2017	1404	5035
13102(c)	471(c)	Alternatives to inventory accounting are made available to most small businesses meeting a $25 million gross receipts test	Tax years beginning after Dec. 31, 2017	1403	5035
13102(d)(1)(A)	460(e)(1)(B)	Gross receipts limit to qualify for small construction contract exception to percentage of completion method is raised to $25 million	Contracts entered into after Dec. 31, 2017	1405	5035
13102(d)(1)(B)	460(e)(1)(B)(ii)	Gross receipts limit to qualify for small construction contract exception to percentage of completion method is raised to $25 million	Contracts entered into after Dec. 31, 2017	1405	5035

Act §	Code §	Topic	Effective Date	Analysis ¶	Com Rep ¶
13102(d)(2)	460(e)(2)	Gross receipts limit to qualify for small construction contract exception to percentage of completion method is raised to $25 million	Contracts entered into after Dec. 31, 2017	1405	5035
13201	168(k)	Overview—Bonus depreciation is increased to 100% ("full expensing") and is extended and modified	Property placed in service after Sept. 27, 2017	1201	5036
13201(a)(1)(A)	168(k)(1)(A)	Bonus depreciation increased to 100% (full expensing) with phase down generally deferred from 2018 to 2023	Property placed in service and acquired after Sept. 27, 2017 and before Jan. 1, 2027	1203	5036
13201(a)(1)(B)	168(k)(5)(A)(i)	Elective form of bonus depreciation for specified plants is extended and increased to 100% (full expensing) with phase down deferred from 2018 to 2023	Plants planted or grafted after Sept. 27, 2017 and before Jan. 1, 2027	1204	5036
13201(a)(2)	168(k)(6)	Bonus depreciation increased to 100% (full expensing) with phase down generally deferred from 2018 to 2023	Property placed in service and acquired after Sept. 27, 2017 and before Jan. 1, 2027	1203	5036
13201(a)(3)(A)	168(k)(5)	Elective form of bonus depreciation for specified plants is extended and increased to 100% (full expensing) with phase down deferred from 2018 to 2023	Plants planted or grafted after Sept. 27, 2017 and before Jan. 1, 2027	1204	5036
13201(a)(3)(B)	168(k)(8)	Bonus depreciation increased to 100% (full expensing) with phase down generally deferred from 2018 to 2023	Property placed in service and acquired after Sept. 27, 2017 and before Jan. 1, 2027	1203	5036

Act §	Code §	Topic	Effective Date	Analysis ¶	Com Rep ¶
13201(b)(1)(A)(i)	168(k)(2)(A)(iii)	$8,000 increase for "qualified property" in the first-year depreciation cap for passenger autos is extended	Property both acquired and placed in service after Sept. 27, 2017 and placed in service before Jan. 1, 2027	1208	5036
13201(b)(1)(A)(i)	168(k)(2)(A)(iii)	Bonus depreciation and other benefits for qualified property are extended	Property placed in service and acquired after Sept. 27, 2017 and before Jan. 1, 2027	1202	5036
13201(b)(1)(A)(i)	168(k)(2)(B)(i)(III)	Bonus depreciation and other benefits for qualified property are extended	Property placed in service and acquired after Sept. 27, 2017 and before Jan. 1, 2027	1202	5036
13201(b)(1)(A)(i)	168(k)(2)(B)(ii)	Bonus depreciation and other benefits for qualified property are extended	Property placed in service and acquired after Sept. 27, 2017 and before Jan. 1, 2027	1202	5036
13201(b)(1)(A)(i)	168(k)(2)(E)(i)	Bonus depreciation and other benefits for qualified property are extended	Property placed in service and acquired after Sept. 27, 2017 and before Jan. 1, 2027	1202	5036
13201(b)(1)(A)(ii)(I)	168(k)(2)(B)(i)(II)	Bonus depreciation and other benefits for qualified property are extended	Property placed in service and acquired after Sept. 27, 2017 and before Jan. 1, 2027	1202	5036
13201(b)(1)(B)	168(k)(5)(A)	Elective form of bonus depreciation for specified plants is extended and increased to 100% (full expensing) with phase down deferred from 2018 to 2023	Plants planted or grafted after Sept. 27, 2017 and before Jan. 1, 2027	1204	5036
13201(b)(2)(A)	460(c)(6)(B)(ii)	Overview—Bonus depreciation is increased to 100% ("full expensing") and is extended and modified	Property placed in service after Sept. 27, 2017	1201	5036

Act §	Code §	Topic	Effective Date	Analy-sis ¶	Com Rep ¶
13201(b)(2)(A)	460(c)(6)(B)(ii)	Placed-in-service deadline for disregard of some bonus depreciation-eligible property under the percentage of completion method is extended	Property placed in service and acquired after Sept. 27, 2017 and before Jan. 1, 2027	1209	5036
13201(c)(1)	168(k)(2)(A)(ii)	Used property is allowed 100% bonus depreciation (full expensing)	Property both acquired and placed in service after Sept. 27, 2017 and before Jan. 1, 2027	1205	5036
13201(c)(2)	168(k)(2)(E)(ii)	Used property is allowed 100% bonus depreciation (full expensing)	Property both acquired and placed in service after Sept. 27, 2017 and before Jan. 1, 2027	1205	5036
13201(c)(3)	168(k)(2)(E)(iii)(I)	Used property is allowed 100% bonus depreciation (full expensing)	Property both acquired and placed in service after Sept. 27, 2017 and before Jan. 1, 2027	1205	5036
13201(d)	168(k)(9)	Property used in certain businesses exempt from business interest limitations is excluded from 100% bonus depreciation (full expensing)	Property acquired and placed in service after Sept. 27, 2017 and before Jan. 1, 2027	1207	5036
13201(e)	168(k)(10)	Bonus depreciation increased to 100% (full expensing) with phase down generally deferred from 2018 to 2023	Property placed in service and acquired after Sept. 27, 2017 and before Jan. 1, 2027	1203	5036
13201(e)	168(k)(10)	Elective form of bonus depreciation for specified plants is extended and increased to 100% (full expensing) with phase down deferred from 2018 to 2023	Plants planted or grafted after Sept. 27, 2017 and before Jan. 1, 2027	1204	5036

Act §	Code §	Topic	Effective Date	Analysis ¶	Com Rep ¶
13201(f)	168(k)(2)(F)(iii)	$8,000 increase for "qualified property" in the first-year depreciation cap for passenger autos is extended	Property both acquired and placed in service after Sept. 27, 2017 and placed in service before Jan. 1, 2027	1208	5036
13201(g)(1)(C)	168(k)(2)(A)(i)	Qualified film, television and live theatrical productions added to "qualified property" eligible for 100% bonus depreciation (full expensing)	Property placed in service and acquired after Sept. 27, 2017 and before Jan. 1, 2027	1206	5036
13201(g)(2)	168(k)(2)(H)	Qualified film, television and live theatrical productions added to "qualified property" eligible for 100% bonus depreciation (full expensing)	Property placed in service and acquired after Sept. 27, 2017 and before Jan. 1, 2027	1206	5036
13202(a)(1)	280F(a)(1)(A)	Annual caps on depreciation of passenger automobiles are raised	Property placed in service after Dec. 31, 2017	1307	5037
13202(a)(2)(A)	280F(a)(1)(B)	Annual caps on depreciation of passenger automobiles are raised	Property placed in service after Dec. 31, 2017	1307	5037
13202(a)(2)(B)(i)	280F(d)(7)(B)(i)	Annual caps on depreciation of passenger automobiles are raised	Property placed in service after Dec. 31, 2017	1307	5037
13202(a)(2)(B)(ii)	280F(d)(7)(B)(i)(II)	Annual caps on depreciation of passenger automobiles are raised	Property placed in service after Dec. 31, 2017	1307	5037
13202(b)(2)	280F(d)(4)	Treatment of computer equipment as listed property is ended	Property placed in service after Dec. 31, 2017	1308	5037
13203(a)	168(e)(3)(B)(vii)	Most new farming equipment and machinery is made 5-year MACRS property	Property placed in service after Dec. 31, 2017	1304	5038

Act §	Code §	Topic	Effective Date	Analysis ¶	Com Rep ¶
13203(b)	168(b)(2)	200% declining balance method of MACRS depreciation is made available for many types of MACRS farming property	Property placed in service after Dec. 31, 2017	1305	5038
13204(a)(1)(A)(i)	168(e)(3)(E)	Eligibility of building improvements for a 15-year recovery period is expanded	Property placed in service after Dec. 31, 2017	1301	5039
13204(a)(1)(B)	168(e)	Eligibility of building improvements for a 15-year recovery period is expanded	Property placed in service after Dec. 31, 2017	1301	5039
13204(a)(3)(A)(i)	168(g)(1)(F)	ADS depreciation for buildings (and improvements) if election is made to exempt a real property business from the business interest deduction limit	Tax years beginning after Dec. 31, 2017	1303	5039
13204(a)(3)(A)(ii)	168(g)(8)	ADS depreciation for buildings (and improvements) if election is made to exempt a real property business from the business interest deduction limit	Tax years beginning after Dec. 31, 2017	1303	5039
13204(a)(3)(B)(i)	168(g)(3)(B)	Eligibility of building improvements for a 15-year recovery period is expanded	Property placed in service after Dec. 31, 2017	1301	5039
13204(a)(3)(C)	168(g)(2)(C)	ADS recovery period for residential rental property is shortened to 30 years	Property placed in service after Dec. 31, 2017	1302	5039
13204(a)(4)(A)	168(k)(2)(A)(i)	Overview—Bonus depreciation is increased to 100% ("full expensing") and is extended and modified	Property placed in service after Sept. 27, 2017	1201	5036
13204(a)(4)(B)	168(e)(6)	Eligibility of building improvements for a 15-year recovery period is expanded	Property placed in service after Dec. 31, 2017	1301	5039

Act §	Code §	Topic	Effective Date	Analy-sis ¶	Com Rep ¶
13205(a)	168(g)(1)(G)	ADS depreciation required for 10-year-or-more MACRS property if election made to exempt farming from the business interest deduction limitation	Tax years beginning after Dec. 31, 2017	1306	5040
13206(a)	174	Code Sec. 174 research and experimental expenditures paid or incurred in tax years starting after 2021 are to be amortized over 5 years	Amounts paid or incurred in tax years beginning after Dec. 31, 2021	1408	5041
13206(d)(1)	41(d)(1)(A)	Code Sec. 174 research and experimental expenditures paid or incurred in tax years starting after 2021 are to be amortized over 5 years	Amounts paid or incurred in tax years beginning after Dec. 31, 2021	1408	5041
13206(d)(2)(A)	280C(c)(1)	Code Sec. 174 research and experimental expenditures paid or incurred in tax years starting after 2021 are to be amortized over 5 years	Amounts paid or incurred in tax years beginning after Dec. 31, 2021	1408	5041
13206(d)(2)(B)	280C(c)(2)	Code Sec. 174 research and experimental expenditures paid or incurred in tax years starting after 2021 are to be amortized over 5 years	Amounts paid or incurred in tax years beginning after Dec. 31, 2021	1408	5041
13206(d)(2)(D)	280C(c)(2)	Code Sec. 174 research and experimental expenditures paid or incurred in tax years starting after 2021 are to be amortized over 5 years	Amounts paid or incurred in tax years beginning after Dec. 31, 2021	1408	5041
13207(a)	263A(d)(2)(C)	Minority and subsequent owners can expense certain costs of replanting citrus plants lost by reason of casualty	Amounts paid or incurred after Dec. 22, 2017 and before Dec. 23, 2027	1411	5042

Act §	Code §	Topic	Effective Date	Analy-sis ¶	Com Rep ¶
13221(a)	451(b)	Income inclusion for tax purposes can't be later than when included for certain financial reporting purposes	Tax years beginning after Dec. 31, 2017	1406	5043
13221(b)	451(c)	Accrual basis taxpayers may defer inclusion of advance payments in income to the end of year after year of receipt if so deferred for financial reporting	Tax years beginning after Dec. 31, 2017	1407	5043
13221(d)	None	Accrual basis taxpayers may defer inclusion of advance payments in income to the end of year after year of receipt if so deferred for financial reporting	Tax years beginning after Dec. 31, 2017	1407	5043
13221(d)	None	Income inclusion for tax purposes can't be later than when included for certain financial reporting purposes	Tax years beginning after Dec. 31, 2017	1406	5043
13221(e)	None	Income inclusion for tax purposes can't be later than when included for certain financial reporting purposes	Tax years beginning after Dec. 31, 2017	1406	5043
13301(a)	163(j)	Deduction for net business interest is limited to 30% of adjusted taxable income, with indefinite carryover	Tax years beginning after Dec. 31, 2017	1003	5044
13301(b)(1)	381(c)(20)	Deduction for net business interest is limited to 30% of adjusted taxable income, with indefinite carryover	Tax years beginning after Dec. 31, 2017	1003	5044
13301(b)(2)	382(d)(3)	Deduction for net business interest is limited to 30% of adjusted taxable income, with indefinite carryover	Tax years beginning after Dec. 31, 2017	1003	5044

Act §	Code §	Topic	Effective Date	Analy-sis ¶	Com Rep ¶
13301(b)(3)	382(k)(1)	Deduction for net business interest is limited to 30% of adjusted taxable income, with indefinite carryover	Tax years beginning after Dec. 31, 2017	1003	5044
13302(a)(1)	172(a)	NOL deduction is limited to 80% of taxable income	Losses arising in tax years beginning after Dec. 31, 2017	1001	5045
13302(a)(2)	172(b)(2)	NOL deduction is limited to 80% of taxable income	Losses arising in tax years beginning after Dec. 31, 2017	1001	5045
13302(a)(3)	172(d)(6)(C)	NOL deduction is limited to 80% of taxable income	Losses arising in tax years beginning after Dec. 31, 2017	1001	5045
13302(b)(1)	172(b)(1)(A)	NOLs can't be carried back, but can be carried forward indefinitely	NOLs arising in tax years ending after Dec. 31, 2017	1002	5045
13302(b)(2)	172(b)(1)	NOLs can't be carried back, but can be carried forward indefinitely	NOLs arising in tax years ending after Dec. 31, 2017	1002	5045
13302(c)(1)	172(b)(1)(B)	NOLs can't be carried back, but can be carried forward indefinitely	NOLs arising in tax years ending after Dec. 31, 2017	1002	5045
13302(c)(2)(A)	172	NOLs can't be carried back, but can be carried forward indefinitely	NOLs arising in tax years ending after Dec. 31, 2017	1002	5045
13302(d)(1)	172(b)(1)(C)	NOLs can't be carried back, but can be carried forward indefinitely	NOLs arising in tax years ending after Dec. 31, 2017	1002	5045
13302(d)(2)	172(f)	NOL deduction is limited to 80% of taxable income	Losses arising in tax years beginning after Dec. 31, 2017	1001	5045
13303(a)	1031(a)(1)	Like-kind exchanges are limited to exchanges of real estate	Exchanges completed after Dec. 31, 2017	1503	5046
13303(b)(1)(A)	1031(a)(2)	Like-kind exchanges are limited to exchanges of real estate	Exchanges completed after Dec. 31, 2017	1503	5046

Act §	Code §	Topic	Effective Date	Analy-sis ¶	Com Rep ¶
13303(b)(1)(B)	1031(i)	Like-kind exchanges are limited to exchanges of real estate	Exchanges completed after Dec. 31, 2017	1503	5046
13303(b)(2)	1031(e)	Like-kind exchanges are limited to exchanges of real estate	Exchanges completed after Dec. 31, 2017	1503	5046
13303(b)(3)	1031(e)	Like-kind exchanges are limited to exchanges of real estate	Exchanges completed after Dec. 31, 2017	1503	5046
13303(b)(4)	1031(h)	Like-kind exchanges are limited to exchanges of real estate	Exchanges completed after Dec. 31, 2017	1503	5046
13304(a)(1)(A)	274(a)(1)(A)	Business deduction is denied for entertainment expenses	Amounts incurred or paid after Dec. 31, 2017	1005	5047
13304(a)(1)(B)	274(a)(1)	Business deduction is denied for entertainment expenses	Amounts incurred or paid after Dec. 31, 2017	1005	5047
13304(a)(1)(C)	274(a)(2)	Business deduction is denied for entertainment expenses	Amounts incurred or paid after Dec. 31, 2017	1005	5047
13304(a)(2)(A)(i)	274(d)	Business deduction is denied for entertainment expenses	Amounts incurred or paid after Dec. 31, 2017	1005	5047
13304(a)(2)(A)(ii)	274(d)	Business deduction is denied for entertainment expenses	Amounts incurred or paid after Dec. 31, 2017	1005	5047
13304(a)(2)(B)	274(l)	Business deduction is denied for entertainment expenses	Amounts incurred or paid after Dec. 31, 2017	1005	5047
13304(a)(2)(C)	274(n)	Business deduction is denied for entertainment expenses	Amounts incurred or paid after Dec. 31, 2017	1005	5047
13304(a)(2)(D)	274(n)(1)	Business deduction is denied for entertainment expenses	Amounts incurred or paid after Dec. 31, 2017	1005	5047

Act §	Code §	Topic	Effective Date	Analy-sis ¶	Com Rep ¶
13304(a)(2)(E)	274(n)(2)	Business deduction is denied for entertainment expenses	Amounts incurred or paid after Dec. 31, 2017	1005	5047
13304(a)(2)(F)	7701(b)(5)(A)(iv)	Business deduction is denied for entertainment expenses	Amounts incurred or paid after Dec. 31, 2017	1005	5047
13304(b)(1)	274(n)(2)	Expenses for employer-operated eating facilities are only 50% deductible through 2025, then become nondeductible	Amounts incurred or paid after Dec. 31, 2017, and before Jan. 1, 2026	1006	5047
13304(c)(1)(B)	274(a)(4)	Employers can't deduct cost of providing qualified transportation fringes and other transportation benefits	Amounts incurred or paid after Dec. 31, 2017	1007	5047
13304(c)(2)	274(l)	Employers can't deduct cost of providing qualified transportation fringes and other transportation benefits	Amounts incurred or paid after Dec. 31, 2017	1007	5047
13304(d)(2)	274(o)	Expenses for employer-operated eating facilities are only 50% deductible through 2025, then become nondeductible	Amounts incurred or paid after Dec. 31, 2017, and before Jan. 1, 2026	1006	5047
13305(a)	199	Domestic production activity deduction (DPAD) is repealed	Tax years beginning after Dec. 31, 2017	1004	5048
13306(a)(1)	162(f)	Denial of deduction for fines, penalties, etc., is broadened	Amounts paid or incurred on or after Dec. 22, 2017	1008	5049
13306(b)(1)	6050X	Information reporting requirements are added for government and other agencies that receive fines, penalties, etc., of $600 or more for law violations	Amounts paid or incurred on or after Dec. 22, 2017	1009	5049

Act §	Code §	Topic	Effective Date	Analysis ¶	Com Rep ¶
13307(a)	162(q)	Business expense deduction is barred for settlement of sexual abuse or harassment suit that's subject to nondisclosure agreement	Amounts paid or incurred after Dec. 22, 2017	1010	5050
13308(a)	162(e)(2)	Business expense deduction for lobbying local governments is repealed	Amounts paid or incurred on or after Dec. 22, 2017	1011	5051
13308(a)	162(e)(7)	Business expense deduction for lobbying local governments is repealed	Amounts paid or incurred on or after Dec. 22, 2017	1011	5051
13309(a)	1061	Certain gains from partnership profits interests held in connection with performance of investment services are short-term capital gains if held for 3 years or less	Tax years beginning after Dec. 31, 2017	1502	5052
13310(a)	274(j)(3)(A)	Cash, gift cards, and other nontangible personal property don't qualify as employee achievement awards	Amounts paid or incurred after Dec. 31, 2017	2605	5053
13311(a)	162(a)	$3,000 deduction for living expenses of members of Congress is eliminated	Tax years beginning after Dec. 22, 2017	511	NONE
13313(a)	1044	Tax-free rollover of publicly traded securities gain into "specialized small business investment companies" is repealed	For sales after Dec. 31, 2017	1507	5056
13313(b)	1016(a)(23)	Tax-free rollover of publicly traded securities gain into "specialized small business investment companies" is repealed	For sales after Dec. 31, 2017	1507	5056

Act §	Code §	Topic	Effective Date	Analy-sis ¶	Com Rep ¶
13314(a)	1221(a)(3)	Patents, inventions, certain models or designs, and secret formulas or processes are excluded from the definition of a capital asset	Dispositions after Dec. 31, 2017	1504	5057
13314(b)	1231(b)(1)(C)	Patents, inventions, certain models or designs, and secret formulas or processes are excluded from the definition of a capital asset	Dispositions after Dec. 31, 2017	1504	5057
13401(a)	45C(a)	Orphan drug credit is reduced to 25% of qualified clinical testing expenses	Tax years beginning after Dec. 31, 2017	1015	5058
13401(b)	280C(b)	Reduced orphan drug credit election is available to avoid having to reduce any deduction or charge to capital account for qualified clinical testing expenses	Tax years beginning after Dec. 31, 2017	1016	5058
13402	47(a)	Credit for qualified rehabilitation expenditures is limited to certified historic structures and has to be taken ratably over 5 years	Amounts paid or incurred after Dec. 31, 2017	1014	5059
13402(b)(1)(A)	47(c)(1)	Credit for qualified rehabilitation expenditures is limited to certified historic structures and has to be taken ratably over 5 years	Amounts paid or incurred after Dec. 31, 2017	1014	5059
13402(b)(1)(B)	47(c)(2)(B)(iv)	Credit for qualified rehabilitation expenditures is limited to certified historic structures and has to be taken ratably over 5 years	Amounts paid or incurred after Dec. 31, 2017	1014	5059

Act §	Code §	Topic	Effective Date	Analysis ¶	Com Rep ¶
13402(c)	None	Credit for qualified rehabilitation expenditures is limited to certified historic structures and has to be taken ratably over 5 years	Amounts paid or incurred after Dec. 31, 2017	1014	5059
13403(a)(1)	45S	Employers are allowed a credit for paid family and medical leave	Wages paid in tax years beginning after Dec. 31, 2017 and before Jan. 1, 2020	1013	5060
13403(b)	38(b)(37)	Employers are allowed a credit for paid family and medical leave	Wages paid in tax years beginning after Dec. 31, 2017 and before Jan. 1, 2020	1013	5060
13403(c)	38(c)(4)(B)(ix)	Employers are allowed a credit for paid family and medical leave	Wages paid in tax years beginning after Dec. 31, 2017 and before Jan. 1, 2020	1013	5060
13403(d)(1)	280C(a)	Employers are allowed a credit for paid family and medical leave	Wages paid in tax years beginning after Dec. 31, 2017 and before Jan. 1, 2020	1013	5060
13403(d)(2)	6501(m)	Employers are allowed a credit for paid family and medical leave	Wages paid in tax years beginning after Dec. 31, 2017 and before Jan. 1, 2020	1013	5060
13404(a)	54	New tax-credit and direct-pay bonds may not be issued	Bonds issued after Dec. 31, 2017	1702	5061
13404(a)	54A	New tax-credit and direct-pay bonds may not be issued	Bonds issued after Dec. 31, 2017	1702	5061
13404(a)	54B	New tax-credit and direct-pay bonds may not be issued	Bonds issued after Dec. 31, 2017	1702	5061
13404(a)	54C	New tax-credit and direct-pay bonds may not be issued	Bonds issued after Dec. 31, 2017	1702	5061
13404(a)	54D	New tax-credit and direct-pay bonds may not be issued	Bonds issued after Dec. 31, 2017	1702	5061

Act §	Code §	Topic	Effective Date	Analysis ¶	Com Rep ¶
13404(a)	54E	New tax-credit and direct-pay bonds may not be issued	Bonds issued after Dec. 31, 2017	1702	5061
13404(a)	54F	New tax-credit and direct-pay bonds may not be issued	Bonds issued after Dec. 31, 2017	1702	5061
13404(a)	54AA	New tax-credit and direct-pay bonds may not be issued	Bonds issued after Dec. 31, 2017	1702	5061
13404(b)	6431	New tax-credit and direct-pay bonds may not be issued	Bonds issued after Dec. 31, 2017	1702	5061
13404(c)(1)	1397E	New tax-credit and direct-pay bonds may not be issued	Bonds issued after Dec. 31, 2017	1702	5061
13501(a)	864(c)(8)	Treatment of gain or loss of foreign person from sale or exchange of partnership interests	Sales and exchanges after Nov. 26, 2017	2304	5062
13501(b)	1446(f)	Treatment of gain or loss of foreign person from sale or exchange of partnership interests	Sales, exchanges or dispositions after Dec. 31, 2017	2304	5062
13502(a)	743(d)(1)	Mandatory basis adjustment upon transfers of partnership interests amended	Transfers of partnership interests after Dec. 31, 2017	902	5063
13503(a)	704(d)	Basis reduction for partnership charitable contributions amended	Partnership tax years beginning after Dec. 31, 2017	903	5064
13504(a)	708(b)(1)	Repeal of partnership technical termination rule	Partnership tax years beginning after Dec. 31, 2017	901	5065
13511(a)	805(b)(4)	Operations loss deduction for life insurance companies repealed	For losses arising in tax years beginning after Dec. 31, 2017	2402	5066
13511(b)(1)	810	Operations loss deduction for life insurance companies repealed	For losses arising in tax years beginning after Dec. 31, 2017	2402	5066
13511(b)(2)	844	Operations loss deduction for life insurance companies repealed	For losses arising in tax years beginning after Dec. 31, 2017	2402	5066

Act §	Code §	Topic	Effective Date	Analysis ¶	Com Rep ¶
13511(b)(3)	381(d)	Operations loss deduction for life insurance companies repealed	For losses arising in tax years beginning after Dec. 31, 2017	2402	5066
13511(b)(4)	805(a)(4)(B)(ii)	Operations loss deduction for life insurance companies repealed	For losses arising in tax years beginning after Dec. 31, 2017	2402	5066
13511(b)(5)	805(a)(5)	Operations loss deduction for life insurance companies repealed	For losses arising in tax years beginning after Dec. 31, 2017	2402	5066
13511(b)(7)	953(b)(1)(B)	Operations loss deduction for life insurance companies repealed	For losses arising in tax years beginning after Dec. 31, 2017	2402	5066
13512(a)	806	Small life insurance company deduction repealed	Tax years beginning after Dec. 31, 2017	2403	5067
13512(b)(1)	453B(e)(3)	Small life insurance company deduction repealed	Tax years beginning after Dec. 31, 2017	2403	5067
13513(a)	807(f)(1)	Repeal of ten-year spread for life insurance companies' reserve changes	Tax years after Dec. 31, 2017	2405	5068
13514(a)	815	Tax on distributions to stock life insurance company shareholders from a pre-1984 policyholders' surplus account is repealed; phased inclusion of remaining balance of policyholders' surplus account is provided	Tax years beginning after Dec. 31, 2017	2407	5069
13514(b)	801(c)	Tax on distributions to stock life insurance company shareholders from a pre-1984 policyholders' surplus account is repealed; phased inclusion of remaining balance of policyholders' surplus account is provided	Tax years beginning after Dec. 31, 2017	2407	5069

Act §	Code §	Topic	Effective Date	Analysis ¶	Com Rep ¶
13514(d)	None	Tax on distributions to stock life insurance company shareholders from a pre-1984 policyholders' surplus account is repealed; phased inclusion of remaining balance of policyholders' surplus account is provided	Tax years beginning after Dec. 31, 2017	2407	5069
13515(a)	832(b)(5)(B)	Increase from 15% to 25% of the proration rules for property and casualty insurance companies	Tax years after Dec. 31, 2017	2408	5070
13516(a)	847	Elective deduction of discounted loss reserve amounts for insurance companies — and related special estimated tax payment rules — are repealed	Tax years beginning after Dec. 31, 2017	2410	5071
13517(a)(1)	807(c)	Rules on computation of life insurance tax reserves amended	Tax years beginning after Dec. 31, 2017	2406	5072
13517(a)(2)	807(d)	Rules on computation of life insurance tax reserves amended	Tax years beginning after Dec. 31, 2017	2406	5072
13517(a)(3)	807(e)	Rules on computation of life insurance tax reserves amended	Tax years beginning after Dec. 31, 2017	2406	5072
13517(a)(4)	7702	Rules on computation of life insurance tax reserves amended	Tax years beginning after Dec. 31, 2017	2406	5072
13518(a)	812	Definition of "company's share" and "policyholder's share" amended for determining insurance company dividends received deduction and reserves	Tax years beginning after Dec. 31, 2017	2401	5073
13519(a)(1)	848(a)(2)	Amortization period for insurance companies' capitalized policy acquisition expenses increased to 15 years from 10 years	Tax years beginning after Dec. 31, 2017	2404	5074

Act §	Code §	Topic	Effective Date	Analysis ¶	Com Rep ¶
13519(a)(2)	848(c)(1)	Amortization period for insurance companies' capitalized policy acquisition expenses increased to 15 years from 10 years	Tax years beginning after Dec. 31, 2017	2404	5074
13519(a)(3)	848(c)(2)	Amortization period for insurance companies' capitalized policy acquisition expenses increased to 15 years from 10 years	Tax years beginning after Dec. 31, 2017	2404	5074
13519(a)(4)	848(c)(3)	Amortization period for insurance companies' capitalized policy acquisition expenses increased to 15 years from 10 years	Tax years beginning after Dec. 31, 2017	2404	5074
13519(b)	848(b)(1)	Amortization period for insurance companies' capitalized policy acquisition expenses increased to 15 years from 10 years	Tax years beginning after Dec. 31, 2017	2404	5074
13520(a)	6050Y	Tax reporting requirements added for policy sales and death benefits paid under life insurance contracts	Reportable policy sales and reportable death benefits paid after Dec. 31, 2017	1506	5075
13520(c)(1)	6724(d)	Tax reporting requirements added for policy sales and death benefits paid under life insurance contracts	Reportable policy sales and reportable death benefits paid after Dec. 31, 2017	1506	5075
13520(c)(2)	6047(g)	Tax reporting requirements added for policy sales and death benefits paid under life insurance contracts	Reportable policy sales and reportable death benefits paid after Dec. 31, 2017	1506	5075
13521(a)	1016(a)(1)	Cost of insurance adjustment to the basis of life insurance or annuity contracts is retroactively eliminated	For transactions entered into after Aug. 25, 2009	1505	5075

Act §	Code §	Topic	Effective Date	Analy-sis ¶	Com Rep ¶
13522(a)	101(a)	Exceptions to life insurance transfer-for-value rule don't apply to life settlement transactions	Transfers after Dec. 31, 2017	601	5075
13522(b)	101(a)(1)	Exceptions to life insurance transfer-for-value rule don't apply to life settlement transactions	Transfers after Dec. 31, 2017	601	5075
13523(a)	846(c)(2)	Modification of discounting rules for unpaid losses when determining property and casualty insurance companies' income	Tax years beginning after Dec. 31, 2017	2409	5078
13523(b)	846(d)(3)	Modification of discounting rules for unpaid losses when determining property and casualty insurance companies' income	Tax years beginning after Dec. 31, 2017	2409	5078
13523(c)	846(e)	Modification of discounting rules for unpaid losses when determining property and casualty insurance companies' income	Tax years beginning after Dec. 31, 2017	2409	5078
13523(e)	846	Modification of discounting rules for unpaid losses when determining property and casualty insurance companies' income	Tax years beginning after Dec. 31, 2017	2409	5078
13531(a)	162(r)	Deduction of FDIC premiums is phased out for banks with assets over $10 billion, eliminated at $50 billion	Tax years beginning after Dec. 31, 2017	1012	5079
13532(a)	149(d)(1)	Exclusion of interest on advance refunding bonds is repealed	Advance refunding bonds issued after Dec. 31, 2017	1701	5080
13532(b)(1)	149(d)(2)	Exclusion of interest on advance refunding bonds is repealed	Advance refunding bonds issued after Dec. 31, 2017	1701	5080
13532(b)(1)	149(d)(3)	Exclusion of interest on advance refunding bonds is repealed	Advance refunding bonds issued after Dec. 31, 2017	1701	5080

Act §	Code §	Topic	Effective Date	Analy-sis ¶	Com Rep ¶
13532(b)(1)	149(d)(4)	Exclusion of interest on advance refunding bonds is repealed	Advance refunding bonds issued after Dec. 31, 2017	1701	5080
13532(b)(1)	149(d)(6)	Exclusion of interest on advance refunding bonds is repealed	Advance refunding bonds issued after Dec. 31, 2017	1701	5080
13541(a)	1361(c)(2)(B)(v)	Expansion of qualifying beneficiaries of Electing Small Business Trusts (ESBTs)	Jan. 1, 2018	802	5081
13542(a)	641(c)(2)(E)	Charitable deductions of Electing Small Business Trusts (ESBTs)	Tax years beginning after Dec. 31, 2017	803	5082
13543(a)	481(d)	Treatment of revocations of S corporation elections	Dec. 22, 2017	801	5083
13543(b)	1371(f)	Treatment of revocations of S corporation elections	Dec. 22, 2017	801	5083
13601(a)(1)	162(m)(4)	Performance-based compensation and commissions are made subject to $1 million deduction limit	Tax years beginning after Dec. 31, 2017	2601	5084
13601(b)(1)	162(m)(3)(A)	Definition of "covered employee" who's subject to $1 million compensation deduction limit is expanded	Tax years beginning after Dec. 31, 2017	2603	5084
13601(b)(2)	162(m)(3)(B)	Definition of "covered employee" who's subject to $1 million compensation deduction limit is expanded	Tax years beginning after Dec. 31, 2017	2603	5084
13601(b)(3)	162(m)(3)(C)	Definition of "covered employee" who's subject to $1 million compensation deduction limit is expanded	Tax years beginning after Dec. 31, 2017	2603	5084
13601(c)	162(m)(2)	Definition of "publicly held corporation" subject to $1 million compensation deduction limit is expanded	Tax years beginning after Dec. 31, 2017	2602	5084

Act §	Code §	Topic	Effective Date	Analysis ¶	Com Rep ¶
13601(d)	162(m)(4)	Definition of "covered employee" who's subject to $1 million compensation deduction limit is expanded	Tax years beginning after Dec. 31, 2017	2603	5084
13602(a)	4960	Excise tax imposed on tax-exempt organizations that pay excess compensation	For tax years beginning after Dec. 31, 2017	2501	5085
13603(a)	83(i)	Employees can elect to defer income from option or RSU stock for up to five years after vesting	Stock attributable to options exercised, or restricted stock units settled, after Dec. 31, 2017	2604	5086
13603(b)(1)	3401(i)	Withholding is required at highest individual rate when stock subject to Code Sec. 83(i) election is included in income	Stock attributable to options exercised, or restricted stock units settled, after Dec. 31, 2017	2607	5086
13603(b)(2)	3402(t)	Withholding is required at highest individual rate when stock subject to Code Sec. 83(i) election is included in income	Stock attributable to options exercised, or restricted stock units settled, after Dec. 31, 2017	2607	5086
13603(c)(1)(A)	422(b)	Employees can elect to defer income from option or RSU stock for up to five years after vesting	Stock attributable to options exercised, or restricted stock units settled, after Dec. 31, 2017	2604	5086
13603(c)(1)(B)(i)	423(b)(5)	Employees can elect to defer income from option or RSU stock for up to five years after vesting	Stock attributable to options exercised, or restricted stock units settled, after Dec. 31, 2017	2604	5086

Act §	Code §	Topic	Effective Date	Analy-sis ¶	Com Rep ¶
13603(c)(1)(B)(ii)	423(d)	Employees can elect to defer income from option or RSU stock for up to five years after vesting	Stock attributable to options exercised, or restricted stock units settled, after Dec. 31, 2017	2604	5086
13603(c)(2)	409A(d)(7)	Employees can elect to defer income from option or RSU stock for up to five years after vesting	Stock attributable to options exercised, or restricted stock units settled, after Dec. 31, 2017	2604	5086
13603(d)	6051(a)(16)	Form W-2 must include information about deferrals and inclusions under Code Sec. 83(i)	Stock attributable to options exercised, or restricted stock units settled, after Dec. 31, 2017	2606	5086
13603(d)	6051(a)(17)	Form W-2 must include information about deferrals and inclusions under Code Sec. 83(i)	Stock attributable to options exercised, or restricted stock units settled, after Dec. 31, 2017	2606	5086
13603(e)	6652(p)	Penalty imposed for employer's failure to notify employee that stock is eligible for Code Sec. 83(i) election	Failures after Dec. 31, 2017	2608	5086
13604	4985(a)(1)	Excise tax on stock compensation of insiders in expatriated corporations increased	Corporations first becoming expatriated corporations after Dec. 22, 2017	2205	5087
13611(a)	408A(d)(6)(B)(iii)	Special rule allowing recharacterization of Roth IRA contributions and traditional IRA contributions does not apply to conversion contributions to a Roth IRA	Tax years after Dec. 31, 2017	2701	5088

Act §	Code §	Topic	Effective Date	Analy-sis ¶	Com Rep ¶
13612	457(e)(11)(B)	Accrual limit for length of service award plans is increased from $3,000 to $6,000	Tax years beginning after Dec. 31, 2017	2703	5089
13613	402(c)(3)	Rollover period for plan loan offset amounts is extended from 60 days, to tax return due date	Tax years beginning after Dec. 31, 2017	2702	5090
13701(a)	4968	New excise tax imposed on investment income of private colleges and universities	Tax years beginning after Dec. 31, 2017	2502	5091
13702(a)	512(a)(6)	Tax-exempt organizations' unrelated business taxable income calculated separately for each trade or business	For tax years beginning after Dec. 31, 2017	2503	5092
13703(a)	512(a)(7)	Tax-exempt organizations' unrelated business taxable income increased by disallowed fringe benefit expenses	For amounts paid or incurred after Dec. 31, 2017	2504	5093
13704(a)	170(l)(1)	Charitable deduction is denied for contributions to a college or university in exchange for athletic event seating rights	Contributions in tax years beginning after Dec. 31, 2017	513	5007
13705(a)	170(f)(8)(D)	Donee-reporting exception to substantiation requirement for charitable contributions is retroactively repealed	Contributions made in tax years beginning after Dec. 31, 2016	515	5007
13801(a)	263A(f)	Production period for beer, wine, distilled spirits won't include their aging period under the UNICAP interest capitalization rules for the next 2 calendar years	For interest costs paid or accrued in calendar years beginning after Dec. 31, 2017 and before Jan. 1, 2020	1410	5096

Act §	Code §	Topic	Effective Date	Analy-sis ¶	Com Rep ¶
13822(a)	4261(e)(5)	Payments for aircraft management services are exempted from excise taxes on taxable air transportation	For amounts paid after Dec. 22, 2017	2901	5105
13823(a)	1400Z-1	Chief executive officers of a state can designate low-income communities as Qualified Opportunity Zones	Dec. 22, 2017	1704	5106
13823(a)	1400Z-2	Gains invested in a Qualified Opportunity Fund can be temporarily deferred and permanently excluded if the investment in the Fund is held for 10 years	Dec. 22, 2017	1703	5106
13823(b)	1016(a)(38)	Gains invested in a Qualified Opportunity Fund can be temporarily deferred and permanently excluded if the investment in the Fund is held for 10 years	Dec. 22, 2017	1703	5106
14101(a)	245A	Deduction allowed for dividends received by a corporate U.S. shareholder from a specified 10% owned foreign corporation under participation exemption system	Distributions made after Dec. 31, 2017	1901	5107
14101(b)(1)	246(c)(1)	Deduction allowed for dividends received by a corporate U.S. shareholder from a specified 10% owned foreign corporation under participation exemption system	Distributions made after Dec. 31, 2017	1901	5107
14101(b)(2)	246(c)(5)	Deduction allowed for dividends received by a corporate U.S. shareholder from a specified 10% owned foreign corporation under participation exemption system	Distributions made after Dec. 31, 2017	1901	5107

Act §	Code §	Topic	Effective Date	Analy-sis ¶	Com Rep ¶
14101(d)	904(b)(5)	Dividends allowed as a Code Sec. 245A DRD are not treated as foreign source income for purposes of the FTC limitation	Deductions for tax years ending after Dec. 31, 2017	1902	5107
14102(a)	1248	Amounts treated as dividends under Code Sec. 1248 and Code Sec. 964(e) are treated as dividends for purposes of the Code Sec. 245A DRD	Sales or exchanges after Dec. 31, 2017	1904	5108
14102(b)(1)	961(d)	Basis of stock in specified 10% owned foreign corporation reduced to the extent of Code Sec. 245A DRD in determining loss on disposition	Distributions made after Dec. 31, 2017	1903	5108
14102(c)	964(e)(4)	Amounts treated as dividends under Code Sec. 1248 and Code Sec. 964(e) are treated as dividends for purposes of the Code Sec. 245A DRD	Sales or exchanges after Dec. 31, 2017	1904	5108
14102(d)(1)	91	Transferred loss amount included in income upon transfer of foreign branch assets to a specified 10% owned foreign corporation	Transfers after Dec. 31, 2017	1905	5108
14102(d)(1)	91(e)	Transferred loss amount included in income upon transfer of foreign branch assets to a specified 10% owned foreign corporation	Transfers after Dec. 31, 2017	1905	5108
14102(e)(1)	367(a)(3)	Repeal of active trade or business exception under Code Sec. 367	Transfers after Dec. 31, 2017	2203	5108
14103(a)	965(a)	Pre-2018 accumulated deferred foreign income must be included in Subpart F income upon transition to a participation exemption system	Last tax year of a deferred income corporation beginning before Jan. 1, 2018	1906	5109

Act §	Code §	Topic	Effective Date	Analy-sis ¶	Com Rep ¶
14103(a)	965(b)	Foreign E&P deficits reduce the pre-2018 accumulated deferred foreign income included in Subpart F	Last tax year of a deferred income corporation beginning before Jan. 1, 2018	1907	5109
14103(a)	965(c)	Deduction for pre-2018 accumulated deferred foreign income; disallowance of foreign tax credit for deducted portion; recapture for expatriated entities	Last tax year of a deferred income corporation beginning before Jan. 1, 2018	1908	5109
14103(a)	965(d)	Pre-2018 accumulated deferred foreign income must be included in Subpart F income upon transition to a participation exemption system	Last tax year of a deferred income corporation beginning before Jan. 1, 2018	1906	5109
14103(a)	965(e)	Pre-2018 accumulated deferred foreign income must be included in Subpart F income upon transition to a participation exemption system	Last tax year of a deferred income corporation beginning before Jan. 1, 2018	1906	5109
14103(a)	965(f)	Foreign E&P deficits reduce the pre-2018 accumulated deferred foreign income included in Subpart F	Last tax year of a deferred income corporation beginning before Jan. 1, 2018	1907	5109
14103(a)	965(g)	Deduction for pre-2018 accumulated deferred foreign income; disallowance of foreign tax credit for deducted portion; recapture for expatriated entities	Last tax year of a deferred income corporation beginning before Jan. 1, 2018	1908	5109
14103(a)	965(h)	A U.S. shareholder may elect to pay the net tax liability for pre-2018 accumulated deferred foreign income in installments	Last tax year of a deferred income corporation beginning before Jan. 1, 2018	1909	5109

Act §	Code §	Topic	Effective Date	Analysis ¶	Com Rep ¶
14103(a)	965(i)	S corporation shareholders may elect to defer net tax liability for accumulated deferred foreign income until a triggering event	Last tax year of a deferred income corporation beginning before Jan. 1, 2018	1910	5109
14103(a)	965(j)	S corporation shareholders may elect to defer net tax liability for accumulated deferred foreign income until a triggering event	Last tax year of a deferred income corporation beginning before Jan. 1, 2018	1910	5109
14103(a)	965(k)	Six year statute of limitation for assessment of net tax liability due to pre-2018 accumulated deferred foreign income	Last tax year of a deferred income corporation beginning before Jan. 1, 2018	1911	5109
14103(a)	965(l)	Deduction for pre-2018 accumulated deferred foreign income; disallowance of foreign tax credit for deducted portion; recapture for expatriated entities	Last tax year of a deferred income corporation beginning before Jan. 1, 2018	1908	5109
14103(a)	965(m)	Pre-2018 accumulated deferred foreign income excluded for purposes of REIT gross income tests; election provided to include that amount in REIT income over eight years	Last tax year of a deferred income corporation beginning before Jan. 1, 2018	1912	5109
14103(a)	965(n)	Election not to take pre-2018 accumulated deferred foreign income into account for NOL purposes	Last tax year of a deferred income corporation beginning before Jan. 1, 2018	1913	5109
14103(a)	965(o)	Pre-2018 accumulated deferred foreign income must be included in Subpart F income upon transition to a participation exemption system	Last tax year of a deferred income corporation beginning before Jan. 1, 2018	1906	5109

Act §	Code §	Topic	Effective Date	Analy-sis ¶	Com Rep ¶
14201(a)	951A	U.S. shareholders of CFCs must include their global intangible low-taxed income (GILTI) in gross income	Tax years of foreign corporations beginning after Dec. 31, 2017	2001	5110
14201(b)(1)	960(d)	80% deemed paid foreign tax credit available for global intangible low-taxed income	Tax years of foreign corporations beginning after Dec. 31, 2017	2003	5110
14201(b)(2)(A)	904(d)(1)	Separate foreign tax credit basket for global intangible low-taxed income (GILTI)	Tax years of foreign corporations beginning after Dec. 31, 2017	2004	5110
14201(b)(2)(B)	904(d)(2)(A)(ii)	Separate foreign tax credit basket for global intangible low-taxed income (GILTI)	Tax years of foreign corporations beginning after Dec. 31, 2017	2004	5110
14201(b)(2)(C)	904(c)	Separate foreign tax credit basket for global intangible low-taxed income (GILTI)	Tax years of foreign corporations beginning after Dec. 31, 2017	2004	5110
14202(a)	250	Domestic corporations allowed deduction for foreign-derived intangible income and global intangible low-taxed income	Tax years beginning after Dec. 31, 2017	2002	5111
14211(a)(3)	954(a)(5)	Foreign base company oil-related income not included in foreign base company income	Tax years of foreign corporations beginning after Dec. 31, 2017	2104	5112
14211(b)(3)	954(g)	Foreign base company oil-related income not included in foreign base company income	Tax years of foreign corporations beginning after Dec. 31, 2017	2104	5112
14212(a)	955	Previously excluded Subpart F income withdrawn from a qualified shipping investment no longer included in U.S. shareholder's income	Tax years of foreign corporations beginning after Dec. 31, 2017	2105	5113

Act §	Code §	Topic	Effective Date	Analysis ¶	Com Rep ¶
14213(a)	958(b)	Subpart F constructive attribution rules allow downward attribution from foreign persons to related U.S. persons	The last tax year of foreign corporations beginning before Jan. 1, 2018	2102	5114
14214(a)	951(b)	Definition of U.S. shareholder of a controlled foreign corporation expanded to include 10% owner by value	Tax years of foreign corporations beginning after Dec. 31, 2017	2101	5115
14215(a)	951(a)(1)	Requirement that corporation must be controlled for 30 days before Subpart F inclusions apply is eliminated	Tax years of foreign corporations beginning after Dec. 31, 2017	2103	5116
14221(a)	936(h)(3)(B)	Limitations imposed on income shifting through intangible property transfers	Transfers in tax years beginning after Dec. 31, 2017	2202	5117
14221(b)(1)	367(d)(2)	Limitations imposed on income shifting through intangible property transfers	Transfers in tax years beginning after Dec. 31, 2017	2202	5117
14221(b)(2)	482	Limitations imposed on income shifting through intangible property transfers	Transfers in tax years beginning after Dec. 31, 2017	2202	5117
14222(a)	267A	Deduction is disallowed for certain related party amounts paid or accrued in hybrid transactions or with hybrid entities	Tax years beginning after Dec. 31, 2017	2204	5118
14223(a)(3)	1(h)(11)(C)(iii)	Surrogate foreign corporation shareholders aren't eligible for reduced dividends rate	Dividends received after Dec. 22, 2017	2206	5119
14301(a)	902	Repeal of Code Sec. 902 and other adjustments to the foreign tax credit to account for participation exemption	Tax years of foreign corporations beginning after Dec. 31, 2017	2301	5120

Act §	Code §	Topic	Effective Date	Analysis ¶	Com Rep ¶
14301(b)(1)	960	Repeal of Code Sec. 902 and other adjustments to the foreign tax credit to account for participation exemption	Tax years of foreign corporations beginning after Dec. 31, 2017	2301	5120
14301(c)(1)	78	Repeal of Code Sec. 902 and other adjustments to the foreign tax credit to account for participation exemption	Tax years of foreign corporations beginning after Dec. 31, 2017	2301	5120
14302(a)	904(d)(1)	Addition of separate foreign tax credit basket for foreign branch income	Tax years beginning after Dec. 31, 2017	2303	5121
14302(b)(1)	904(d)(2)(J)	Addition of separate foreign tax credit basket for foreign branch income	Tax years beginning after Dec. 31, 2017	2303	5121
14303(a)	863(b)	Source of income from sales of inventory determined solely on basis of production activities	Tax years beginning after Dec. 31, 2017	2305	5122
14304(a)	904(g)	Taxpayers who sustain a pre-2018 overall domestic loss can elect to recharacterize as much as 100% of U.S. source income as foreign source income	Tax years beginning after Dec. 31, 2017 and before Jan. 1, 2028	2302	5123
14401(a)	59A	Base erosion minimum tax added on payments to foreign related parties.	Base erosion payments paid or accrued in tax years beginning after Dec. 31, 2017	2201	5124
14401(b)	6038A(b)	Base erosion minimum tax added on payments to foreign related parties.	Base erosion payments paid or accrued in tax years beginning after Dec. 31, 2017	2201	5124
14401(c)	26(b)(2)	Base erosion minimum tax added on payments to foreign related parties.	Base erosion payments paid or accrued in tax years beginning after Dec. 31, 2017	2201	5124

Act §	Code §	Topic	Effective Date	Analysis ¶	Com Rep ¶
14401(d)(2)	882(a)	Base erosion minimum tax added on payments to foreign related parties.	Base erosion payments paid or accrued in tax years beginning after Dec. 31, 2017	2201	5124
14401(d)(3)	6425(c)(1)(A)	Base erosion minimum tax added on payments to foreign related parties.	Base erosion payments paid or accrued in tax years beginning after Dec. 31, 2017	2201	5124
14401(d)(4)	6655	Base erosion minimum tax added on payments to foreign related parties.	Base erosion payments paid or accrued in tax years beginning after Dec. 31, 2017	2201	5124
14501(a)	1297(b)(2)(B)	Active insurance business exception to passive foreign investment company rules requires minimum insurance liabilities amount	Tax years beginning after Dec. 31, 2017	2411	5125
14501(b)	1297(f)	Active insurance business exception to passive foreign investment company rules requires minimum insurance liabilities amount	Tax years beginning after Dec. 31, 2017	2411	5125
14502(a)	864(e)(2)	Fair market value method of interest expense allocation or apportionment repealed after 2017	Tax years beginning after Dec. 31, 2017	2306	5126
11001(a)	1(j)(2)(F)	Individual income tax rate structure replaced with 10%, 12%, 22%, 24%, 32%, 35%, and 37% tax brackets	Tax years beginning after 2017 and before 2026	101	5001
11002(d)(1)(NN)	6698(e)(1)	Chained CPI-U (C-CPI-U) replaces CPI-U in inflation adjustments of various tax parameters under the Code	Tax years beginning after Dec. 31, 2017	202	5002

Act §	Code §	Topic	Effective Date	Analysis ¶	Com Rep ¶
13201(a)(2)	168(k)(6)(C)	Elective form of bonus depreciation for specified plants is extended and increased to 100% (full expensing) with phase down deferred from 2018 to 2023	Plants planted or grafted after Sept. 27, 2017 and before Jan. 1, 2027	1204	5036
13202(b)(1)(B)	280F(d)(4)(A)	Treatment of computer equipment as listed property is ended	Property placed in service after Dec. 31, 2017	1308	5037
13204(a)(2)(A)	168(b)(3)	Eligibility of building improvements for a 15-year recovery period is expanded	Property placed in service after Dec. 31, 2017	1301	5039
13204(a)(2)(B)	168(b)(3)(G)	Eligibility of building improvements for a 15-year recovery period is expanded	Property placed in service after Dec. 31, 2017	1301	5039
13204(a)(3)(B)(ii)	168(g)(3)(B)	Eligibility of building improvements for a 15-year recovery period is expanded	Property placed in service after Dec. 31, 2017	1301	5039

¶ 6001. Code Section Cross Reference Table

Code §	Act §	Topic	Effective Date	Analysis ¶	Com Rep ¶
1(f)(2)(A)	11002(c)	Inflation adjustment of income tax brackets to be made based on chained CPI-U (C-CPI-U), instead of the CPI-U	Tax years beginning after 2017	201	5002
1(f)(3)	11002(a)	Inflation adjustment of income tax brackets to be made based on chained CPI-U (C-CPI-U), instead of the CPI-U	Tax years beginning after 2017	201	5002
1(f)(6)	11002(b)	Inflation adjustment of income tax brackets to be made based on chained CPI-U (C-CPI-U), instead of the CPI-U	Tax years beginning after 2017	201	5002
1(h)(11)(C)(iii)	14223(a)(3)	Surrogate foreign corporation shareholders aren't eligible for reduced dividends rate	Dividends received after Dec. 22, 2017	2206	5119
1(i)(1)(C)	11002(c)(2)(A)	Inflation adjustment of income tax brackets to be made based on chained CPI-U (C-CPI-U), instead of the CPI-U	Tax years beginning after 2017	201	5002
1(i)(3)(C)	11002(c)(2)(B)	Inflation adjustment of income tax brackets to be made based on chained CPI-U (C-CPI-U), instead of the CPI-U	Tax years beginning after 2017	201	5002
1(j)(1)	11001(a)	Breakpoints for imposition of 15% and 20% capital gains/ qualified dividends rates are set as statutory dollar amounts, adjusted for inflation	Tax years beginning after 2017 and before 2026	1501	5001
1(j)(1)	11001(a)	Estates and trusts income tax rate structure replaced with 10%, 24%, 35%, and 37% tax brackets	Tax years beginning after 2017 and before 2026	104	5001

Code §	Act §	Topic	Effective Date	Analy-sis ¶	Com Rep ¶
1(j)(1)	11001(a)	Individual income tax rate structure replaced with 10%, 12%, 22%, 24%, 32%, 35%, and 37% tax brackets	Tax years beginning after 2017 and before 2026	101	5001
1(j)(1)	11001(a)	Kiddie tax modified to effectively apply estates' and trusts' ordinary and capital gains rates to child's net unearned income	Tax years after 2017 and before 2026	105	5001
1(j)(2)(A)	11001(a)	Individual income tax rate structure replaced with 10%, 12%, 22%, 24%, 32%, 35%, and 37% tax brackets	Tax years beginning after 2017 and before 2026	101	5001
1(j)(2)(B)	11001(a)	Individual income tax rate structure replaced with 10%, 12%, 22%, 24%, 32%, 35%, and 37% tax brackets	Tax years beginning after 2017 and before 2026	101	5001
1(j)(2)(C)	11001(a)	Individual income tax rate structure replaced with 10%, 12%, 22%, 24%, 32%, 35%, and 37% tax brackets	Tax years beginning after 2017 and before 2026	101	5001
1(j)(2)(D)	11001(a)	Individual income tax rate structure replaced with 10%, 12%, 22%, 24%, 32%, 35%, and 37% tax brackets	Tax years beginning after 2017 and before 2026	101	5001
1(j)(2)(E)	11001(a)	Estates and trusts income tax rate structure replaced with 10%, 24%, 35%, and 37% tax brackets	Tax years beginning after 2017 and before 2026	104	5001
1(j)(2)(F)	11001(a)	Individual income tax rate structure replaced with 10%, 12%, 22%, 24%, 32%, 35%, and 37% tax brackets	Tax years beginning after 2017 and before 2026	101	5001
1(j)(3)	11001(a)	Individual income tax rate structure replaced with 10%, 12%, 22%, 24%, 32%, 35%, and 37% tax brackets	Tax years beginning after 2017 and before 2026	101	5001
1(j)(3)(A)	11001(a)	Estates and trusts income tax rate structure replaced with 10%, 24%, 35%, and 37% tax brackets	Tax years beginning after 2017 and before 2026	104	5001

Code §	Act §	Topic	Effective Date	Analysis ¶	Com Rep ¶
1(j)(4)	11001(a)	Kiddie tax modified to effectively apply estates' and trusts' ordinary and capital gains rates to child's net unearned income	Tax years after 2017 and before 2026	105	5001
1(j)(5)	11001(a)	Breakpoints for imposition of 15% and 20% capital gains/ qualified dividends rates are set as statutory dollar amounts, adjusted for inflation	Tax years beginning after 2017 and before 2026	1501	5001
1(j)(6)	11001(a)	Individual income tax rate structure replaced with 10%, 12%, 22%, 24%, 32%, 35%, and 37% tax brackets	Tax years beginning after 2017 and before 2026	101	5001
2(a)(3)	11026(a)(1)	Special "combat zone" benefits extended retroactively to members of the armed forces performing services in the Sinai Peninsula of Egypt	June 9, 2015	605	5010
11(b)	13001(a)	Reduction of corporate tax rates	Tax years beginning after Dec. 31, 2017	102	5032
23(h)(2)	11002(d)(1)(A)	Chained CPI-U (C-CPI-U) replaces CPI-U in inflation adjustments of various tax parameters under the Code	Tax years beginning after Dec. 31, 2017	202	5002
24(h)	11022(a)	Child tax credit is increased to $2,000 and expanded and a partial credit is allowed for certain non-child dependents	Tax years beginning after Dec. 31, 2017 and before Jan. 1, 2026	516	5006
24(h)	11022(a)	Qualifying child's social security number is required to claim child tax credit	Tax years beginning after Dec. 31, 2017 and before Jan. 1, 2026	518	5006
24(h)	11022(a)	Refundable portion of the child tax credit is increased to $1,400 for tax years beginning after 2017	Tax years beginning after Dec. 31, 2017 and before Jan. 1, 2026	517	5006

Code §	Act §	Topic	Effective Date	Analysis ¶	Com Rep ¶
25A(h)(1)(A)(ii)	11002(d)(1)(B)	Chained CPI-U (C-CPI-U) replaces CPI-U in inflation adjustments of various tax parameters under the Code	Tax years beginning after Dec. 31, 2017	202	5002
25A(h)(2)(A)(ii)	11002(d)(1)(B)	Chained CPI-U (C-CPI-U) replaces CPI-U in inflation adjustments of various tax parameters under the Code	Tax years beginning after Dec. 31, 2017	202	5002
25B(b)(3)(B)	11002(d)(1)(C)	Chained CPI-U (C-CPI-U) replaces CPI-U in inflation adjustments of various tax parameters under the Code	Tax years beginning after Dec. 31, 2017	202	5002
25B(d)(1)(D)	11024(b)	Saver's credit is allowed for ABLE account contributions by designated beneficiary	Tax years beginning after Dec. 22, 2017, for contributions made before Jan. 1, 2026	1602	5008
26(b)(2)	14401(c)	Base erosion minimum tax added on payments to foreign related parties.	Base erosion payments paid or accrued in tax years beginning after Dec. 31, 2017	2201	5124
32(b)(2)(B)(ii)(II)	11002(d)(1)(D)	Chained CPI-U (C-CPI-U) replaces CPI-U in inflation adjustments of various tax parameters under the Code	Tax years beginning after Dec. 31, 2017	202	5002
32(j)(1)(B)(i)	11002(d)(1)(D)	Chained CPI-U (C-CPI-U) replaces CPI-U in inflation adjustments of various tax parameters under the Code	Tax years beginning after Dec. 31, 2017	202	5002
32(j)(1)(B)(ii)	11002(d)(1)(D)	Chained CPI-U (C-CPI-U) replaces CPI-U in inflation adjustments of various tax parameters under the Code	Tax years beginning after Dec. 31, 2017	202	5002

Code §	Act §	Topic	Effective Date	Analy-sis ¶	Com Rep ¶
36B(f)(2)(B)(ii)(II)	11002(d)(1)(E)	Chained CPI-U (C-CPI-U) replaces CPI-U in inflation adjustments of various tax parameters under the Code	Tax years beginning after Dec. 31, 2017	202	5002
38(b)(37)	13403(b)	Employers are allowed a credit for paid family and medical leave	Wages paid in tax years beginning after Dec. 31, 2017 and before Jan. 1, 2020	1013	5060
38(c)(4)(B)(ix)	13403(c)	Employers are allowed a credit for paid family and medical leave	Wages paid in tax years beginning after Dec. 31, 2017 and before Jan. 1, 2020	1013	5060
38(c)(6)(E)	12001(b)(1)	Limitation on aggregate business credits is conformed to the repeal of the corporate AMT	Tax years beginning after Dec. 31, 2017	1017	5029
41(d)(1)(A)	13206(d)(1)	Code Sec. 174 research and experimental expenditures paid or incurred in tax years starting after 2021 are to be amortized over 5 years	Amounts paid or incurred in tax years beginning after Dec. 31, 2021	1408	5041
41(e)(5)(C)(i)	11002(d)(1)(F)	Chained CPI-U (C-CPI-U) replaces CPI-U in inflation adjustments of various tax parameters under the Code	Tax years beginning after Dec. 31, 2017	202	5002
41(e)(5)(C)(ii)	11002(d)(2)	Chained CPI-U (C-CPI-U) replaces CPI-U in inflation adjustments of various tax parameters under the Code	Tax years beginning after Dec. 31, 2017	202	5002
42(e)(3)(D)(ii)	11002(d)(1)(G)	Chained CPI-U (C-CPI-U) replaces CPI-U in inflation adjustments of various tax parameters under the Code	Tax years beginning after Dec. 31, 2017	202	5002

Code §	Act §	Topic	Effective Date	Analysis ¶	Com Rep ¶
42(h)(3)(H)(i)(II)	11002(d)(1)(G)	Chained CPI-U (C-CPI-U) replaces CPI-U in inflation adjustments of various tax parameters under the Code	Tax years beginning after Dec. 31, 2017	202	5002
42(h)(6)(G)(i)(II)	11002(d)(3)(A)	Chained CPI-U (C-CPI-U) replaces CPI-U in inflation adjustments of various tax parameters under the Code	Tax years beginning after Dec. 31, 2017	202	5002
42(h)(6)(G)(ii)	11002(d)(3)(B)	Chained CPI-U (C-CPI-U) replaces CPI-U in inflation adjustments of various tax parameters under the Code	Tax years beginning after Dec. 31, 2017	202	5002
45C(a)	13401(a)	Orphan drug credit is reduced to 25% of qualified clinical testing expenses	Tax years beginning after Dec. 31, 2017	1015	5058
45R(d)(3)(B)(ii)	11002(d)(1)(H)	Chained CPI-U (C-CPI-U) replaces CPI-U in inflation adjustments of various tax parameters under the Code	Tax years beginning after Dec. 31, 2017	202	5002
45S	13403(a)(1)	Employers are allowed a credit for paid family and medical leave	Wages paid in tax years beginning after Dec. 31, 2017 and before Jan. 1, 2020	1013	5060
47(a)	13402	Credit for qualified rehabilitation expenditures is limited to certified historic structures and has to be taken ratably over 5 years	Amounts paid or incurred after Dec. 31, 2017	1014	5059
47(c)(1)	13402(b)(1)(A)	Credit for qualified rehabilitation expenditures is limited to certified historic structures and has to be taken ratably over 5 years	Amounts paid or incurred after Dec. 31, 2017	1014	5059

Code §	Act §	Topic	Effective Date	Analy-sis ¶	Com Rep ¶
47(c)(2)(B)(iv)	13402(b)(1)(B)	Credit for qualified rehabilitation expenditures is limited to certified historic structures and has to be taken ratably over 5 years	Amounts paid or incurred after Dec. 31, 2017	1014	5059
53(d)(2)	12001(b)(2)	Corporate minimum tax credit (MTC) may offset regular tax liability for any tax year, and is refundable for 2018−2021	Tax years beginning after Dec. 31, 2017	304	5029
53(d)(3)	12002(b)	Corporate minimum tax credit (MTC) may offset regular tax liability for any tax year, and is refundable for 2018−2021	Tax years beginning after Dec. 31, 2017	304	5029
53(e)	12002(a)	Corporate minimum tax credit (MTC) may offset regular tax liability for any tax year, and is refundable for 2018−2021	Tax years beginning after Dec. 31, 2017	304	5029
54	13404(a)	New tax-credit and direct-pay bonds may not be issued	Bonds issued after Dec. 31, 2017	1702	5061
54A	13404(a)	New tax-credit and direct-pay bonds may not be issued	Bonds issued after Dec. 31, 2017	1702	5061
54B	13404(a)	New tax-credit and direct-pay bonds may not be issued	Bonds issued after Dec. 31, 2017	1702	5061
54C	13404(a)	New tax-credit and direct-pay bonds may not be issued	Bonds issued after Dec. 31, 2017	1702	5061
54D	13404(a)	New tax-credit and direct-pay bonds may not be issued	Bonds issued after Dec. 31, 2017	1702	5061
54E	13404(a)	New tax-credit and direct-pay bonds may not be issued	Bonds issued after Dec. 31, 2017	1702	5061
54F	13404(a)	New tax-credit and direct-pay bonds may not be issued	Bonds issued after Dec. 31, 2017	1702	5061
54AA	13404(a)	New tax-credit and direct-pay bonds may not be issued	Bonds issued after Dec. 31, 2017	1702	5061

Code §	Act §	Topic	Effective Date	Analy-sis ¶	Com Rep ¶
55(a)	12001(a)	Alternative minimum tax on corporations is repealed	Tax years beginning after 2017	303	5029
55(b)(1)	12001(b)(3)(A)	Alternative minimum tax on corporations is repealed	Tax years beginning after 2017	303	5029
55(b)(3)	12001(b)(3)(B)	Alternative minimum tax on corporations is repealed	Tax years beginning after 2017	303	5029
55(c)(1)	12001(b)(4)	Alternative minimum tax on corporations is repealed	Tax years beginning after 2017	303	5029
55(d)(2)	12001(b)(5)	Alternative minimum tax on corporations is repealed	Tax years beginning after 2017	303	5029
55(d)(3)	12001(b)(5)	Alternative minimum tax on corporations is repealed	Tax years beginning after 2017	303	5029
55(d)(4)	12003(a)	Alternative minimum tax exemption amounts for individuals increased	Tax years beginning after 2017 and before 2026	301	5029
55(d)(4)(A)(ii)	11002(d)(1)(I)	Alternative minimum tax exemption amounts for individuals increased	Tax years beginning after 2017 and before 2026	301	5029
55(d)(4)(A)(ii)	11002(d)(1)(I)	Chained CPI-U (C-CPI-U) replaces CPI-U in inflation adjustments of various tax parameters under the Code	Tax years beginning after Dec. 31, 2017	202	5002
55(e)	12001(b)(6)	Alternative minimum tax on corporations is repealed	Tax years beginning after 2017	303	5029
56(b)(1)(B)	11027(b)	7.5%-of-AGI floor for medical expense deduction is retroactively extended through 2018 and applied to all taxpayers	Tax years beginning after Dec. 31, 2016, and ending before Jan. 1, 2019	505	5011
56(b)(1)(E)	11028(c)(1)(D)	AMT adjustment for standard deduction is made retroactively inapplicable to in 2016 and 2017 to net disaster losses from 2016 disaster areas	Tax years beginning after Dec. 31, 2015, and before Jan. 1, 2018	302	5012

Code §	Act §	Topic	Effective Date	Analy-sis ¶	Com Rep ¶
56(b)(2)(C)	12001(b)(7)	Alternative minimum tax on corporations is repealed	Tax years beginning after 2017	303	5029
56(c)	12001(b)(8)(A)	Alternative minimum tax on corporations is repealed	Tax years beginning after 2017	303	5029
56(g)	12001(b)(8)(A)	Alternative minimum tax on corporations is repealed	Tax years beginning after 2017	303	5029
58(a)(3)	12001(b)(9)	Alternative minimum tax on corporations is repealed	Tax years beginning after 2017	303	5029
59(a)(1)(C)	12001(b)(3)(C)(i)	Alternative minimum tax on corporations is repealed	Tax years beginning after 2017	303	5029
59(a)(2)	12001(b)(3)(C)(ii)	Alternative minimum tax on corporations is repealed	Tax years beginning after 2017	303	5029
59(b)	12001(b)(10)	Alternative minimum tax on corporations is repealed	Tax years beginning after 2017	303	5029
59(f)	12001(b)(10)	Alternative minimum tax on corporations is repealed	Tax years beginning after 2017	303	5029
59(j)(2)(B)	11002(d)(4)	Chained CPI-U (C-CPI-U) replaces CPI-U in inflation adjustments of various tax parameters under the Code	Tax years beginning after Dec. 31, 2017	202	5002
59A	14401(a)	Base erosion minimum tax added on payments to foreign related parties.	Base erosion payments paid or accrued in tax years beginning after Dec. 31, 2017	2201	5124
61(a)(8)	11051(b)(1)(A)	Alimony won't be deductible by the payor or includible by the recipient for post-2018 divorce or separation instruments	Divorce or separation instruments executed after Dec. 31, 2018	510	5025
62(a)	11011(b)(1)	20% deduction for qualified business income	Tax years beginning after Dec. 31, 2017 and before Jan. 1, 2026	702	5003

Code §	Act §	Topic	Effective Date	Analysis ¶	Com Rep ¶
62(a)(10)	11051(b)(2)(A)	Alimony won't be deductible by the payor or includible by the recipient for post-2018 divorce or separation instruments	Divorce or separation instruments executed after Dec. 31, 2018	510	5025
62(d)(3)(B)	11002(d)(1)(J)	Chained CPI-U (C-CPI-U) replaces CPI-U in inflation adjustments of various tax parameters under the Code	Tax years beginning after Dec. 31, 2017	202	5002
63	11011(b)	20% deduction for qualified business income	Tax years beginning after Dec. 31, 2017 and before Jan. 1, 2026	702	5003
63(c)	11028(c)(1)(C)	Non-itemizers are retroactively allowed to deduct net disaster losses from 2016 disaster areas in 2016 and 2017, via enhanced standard deduction	Tax years beginning after Dec. 31, 2015, and before Jan. 1, 2018	1803	5012
63(c)(4)(B)	11002(d)(1)(K)	Chained CPI-U (C-CPI-U) replaces CPI-U in inflation adjustments of various tax parameters under the Code	Tax years beginning after Dec. 31, 2017	202	5002
63(c)(7)	11021(a)	Standard deduction is almost doubled, inflation adjustment is modified	Tax years beginning after Dec. 31, 2017, and before Jan. 1, 2026	501	5005
67(g)	11045(a)	Miscellaneous itemized deductions are disallowed	Tax years beginning after Dec. 31, 2017, and before Jan. 1, 2026	503	5019
68(b)(2)(B)	11002(d)(2)	Chained CPI-U (C-CPI-U) replaces CPI-U in inflation adjustments of various tax parameters under the Code	Tax years beginning after Dec. 31, 2017	202	5002
68(f)	11046(a)	Overall limitation on itemized deductions ("Pease limitation" or "3%/80% rule") is suspended	Tax years beginning after Dec. 31, 2017, and before Jan. 1, 2026	504	5019

Code §	Act §	Topic	Effective Date	Analy-sis ¶	Com Rep ¶
71	11051(b)(1)(B)	Alimony won't be deductible by the payor or includible by the recipient for post-2018 divorce or separation instruments	Divorce or separation instruments executed after Dec. 31, 2018	510	5025
72(t)	11028(b)(1)(A)	Penalty-free early retirement plan withdrawals may be made for 2016 disaster area victims	Dec. 22, 2017	1806	5012
78	14301(c)(1)	Repeal of Code Sec. 902 and other adjustments to the foreign tax credit to account for participation exemption	Tax years of foreign corporations beginning after Dec. 31, 2017	2301	5120
83(i)	13603(a)	Employees can elect to defer income from option or RSU stock for up to five years after vesting	Stock attributable to options exercised, or restricted stock units settled, after Dec. 31, 2017	2604	5086
91	14102(d)(1)	Transferred loss amount included in income upon transfer of foreign branch assets to a specified 10% owned foreign corporation	Transfers after Dec. 31, 2017	1905	5108
91(e)	14102(d)(1)	Transferred loss amount included in income upon transfer of foreign branch assets to a specified 10% owned foreign corporation	Transfers after Dec. 31, 2017	1905	5108
101(a)	13522(a)	Exceptions to life insurance transfer-for-value rule don't apply to life settlement transactions	Transfers after Dec. 31, 2017	601	5075
101(a)(1)	13522(b)	Exceptions to life insurance transfer-for-value rule don't apply to life settlement transactions	Transfers after Dec. 31, 2017	601	5075

Code §	Act §	Topic	Effective Date	Analy-sis ¶	Com Rep ¶
108(f)(5)	11031(a)	Exclusion for discharge of certain student loans is broadened to include discharges on account of death or disability	Discharges of indebtedness after Dec. 31, 2017 and before Jan. 1, 2026	604	5013
112	11026(a)(2)	Special "combat zone" benefits extended retroactively to members of the armed forces performing services in the Sinai Peninsula of Egypt	June 9, 2015	605	5010
125(i)(2)(B)	11002(d)(1)(L)	Chained CPI-U (C-CPI-U) replaces CPI-U in inflation adjustments of various tax parameters under the Code	Tax years beginning after Dec. 31, 2017	202	5002
132(f)(6)(A)(ii)	11002(d)(5)	Chained CPI-U (C-CPI-U) replaces CPI-U in inflation adjustments of various tax parameters under the Code	Tax years beginning after Dec. 31, 2017	202	5002
132(f)(8)	11047(a)	Exclusion for qualified bicycle commuting reimbursement suspended	Tax years beginning after Dec. 31, 2017 and before Jan. 1, 2026	603	5021
132(g)	11048	Exclusion for qualified moving expense reimbursements suspended, except for armed forces	Tax years beginning after Dec. 31, 2017, and before Jan. 1, 2026	602	5022
135(b)(2)(B)(ii)	11002(d)(1)(M)	Chained CPI-U (C-CPI-U) replaces CPI-U in inflation adjustments of various tax parameters under the Code	Tax years beginning after Dec. 31, 2017	202	5002
137(f)(2)	11002(d)(1)(N)	Chained CPI-U (C-CPI-U) replaces CPI-U in inflation adjustments of various tax parameters under the Code	Tax years beginning after Dec. 31, 2017	202	5002

Code §	Act §	Topic	Effective Date	Analysis ¶	Com Rep ¶
146(d)(2)(B)	11002(d)(1)(O)	Chained CPI-U (C-CPI-U) replaces CPI-U in inflation adjustments of various tax parameters under the Code	Tax years beginning after Dec. 31, 2017	202	5002
147(c)(2)(H)(ii)	11002(d)(1)(P)	Chained CPI-U (C-CPI-U) replaces CPI-U in inflation adjustments of various tax parameters under the Code	Tax years beginning after Dec. 31, 2017	202	5002
149(d)(1)	13532(a)	Exclusion of interest on advance refunding bonds is repealed	Advance refunding bonds issued after Dec. 31, 2017	1701	5080
149(d)(2)	13532(b)(1)	Exclusion of interest on advance refunding bonds is repealed	Advance refunding bonds issued after Dec. 31, 2017	1701	5080
149(d)(3)	13532(b)(1)	Exclusion of interest on advance refunding bonds is repealed	Advance refunding bonds issued after Dec. 31, 2017	1701	5080
149(d)(4)	13532(b)(1)	Exclusion of interest on advance refunding bonds is repealed	Advance refunding bonds issued after Dec. 31, 2017	1701	5080
149(d)(6)	13532(b)(1)	Exclusion of interest on advance refunding bonds is repealed	Advance refunding bonds issued after Dec. 31, 2017	1701	5080
151(d)(4)	11041(a)(2)	Deduction for personal exemptions for taxpayer, spouse, and dependents is suspended; return-filing and withholding requirements are modified	Tax years beginning after Dec. 31, 2017, and before Jan. 1, 2026	502	5015
151(d)(4)(B)	11002(d)(1)(Q)	Chained CPI-U (C-CPI-U) replaces CPI-U in inflation adjustments of various tax parameters under the Code	Tax years beginning after Dec. 31, 2017	202	5002

Code §	Act §	Topic	Effective Date	Analy-sis ¶	Com Rep ¶
151(d)(5)	11041(a)(2)	Deduction for personal exemptions for taxpayer, spouse, and dependents is suspended; return-filing and withholding requirements are modified	Tax years beginning after Dec. 31, 2017, and before Jan. 1, 2026	502	5015
162(a)	13311(a)	$3,000 deduction for living expenses of members of Congress is eliminated	Tax years beginning after Dec. 22, 2017	511	NONE
162(e)(2)	13308(a)	Business expense deduction for lobbying local governments is repealed	Amounts paid or incurred on or after Dec. 22, 2017	1011	5051
162(e)(7)	13308(a)	Business expense deduction for lobbying local governments is repealed	Amounts paid or incurred on or after Dec. 22, 2017	1011	5051
162(f)	13306(a)(1)	Denial of deduction for fines, penalties, etc., is broadened	Amounts paid or incurred on or after Dec. 22, 2017	1008	5049
162(m)(2)	13601(c)	Definition of "publicly held corporation" subject to $1 million compensation deduction limit is expanded	Tax years beginning after Dec. 31, 2017	2602	5084
162(m)(3)(A)	13601(b)(1)	Definition of "covered employee" who's subject to $1 million compensation deduction limit is expanded	Tax years beginning after Dec. 31, 2017	2603	5084
162(m)(3)(B)	13601(b)(2)	Definition of "covered employee" who's subject to $1 million compensation deduction limit is expanded	Tax years beginning after Dec. 31, 2017	2603	5084
162(m)(3)(C)	13601(b)(3)	Definition of "covered employee" who's subject to $1 million compensation deduction limit is expanded	Tax years beginning after Dec. 31, 2017	2603	5084

Code §	Act §	Topic	Effective Date	Analy-sis ¶	Com Rep ¶
162(m)(4)	13601(a)(1)	Performance-based compensation and commissions are made subject to $1 million deduction limit	Tax years beginning after Dec. 31, 2017	2601	5084
162(m)(4)	13601(d)	Definition of "covered employee" who's subject to $1 million compensation deduction limit is expanded	Tax years beginning after Dec. 31, 2017	2603	5084
162(o)(3)	11002(d)(6)	Chained CPI-U (C-CPI-U) replaces CPI-U in inflation adjustments of various tax parameters under the Code	Tax years beginning after Dec. 31, 2017	202	5002
162(q)	13307(a)	Business expense deduction is barred for settlement of sexual abuse or harassment suit that's subject to nondisclosure agreement	Amounts paid or incurred after Dec. 22, 2017	1010	5050
162(r)	13531(a)	Deduction of FDIC premiums is phased out for banks with assets over $10 billion, eliminated at $50 billion	Tax years beginning after Dec. 31, 2017	1012	5079
163(h)(3)(F)	11043(a)	Mortgage interest deduction acquisition debt maximum is lowered to $750,000, deduction for home equity interest is suspended	Tax years beginning after Dec. 31, 2017, and before Jan. 1, 2026	507	5017
163(j)	13301(a)	Deduction for net business interest is limited to 30% of adjusted taxable income, with indefinite carryover	Tax years beginning after Dec. 31, 2017	1003	5044
164(b)(6)	11042(a)	Itemized deduction is limited to $10,000 for SALT—combined state/local property, state/local/foreign income, and (if elected) general sales taxes	Tax years beginning after Dec. 31, 2017, and before Jan. 1, 2026	506	5016

Code §	Act §	Topic	Effective Date	Analy-sis ¶	Com Rep ¶
165(d)	11050	Gambling loss limitation is broadened: deduction for *any* expense incurred in gambling—not just gambling losses—is limited to gambling winnings	Tax years beginning after Dec. 31, 2017, and before Jan. 1, 2026	509	5024
165(h)(1)	11028(c)(1)(B)	$100 per-casualty floor on deduction is retroactively raised to $500 in 2016 and 2017 for net disaster losses from 2016 disaster areas	Tax years beginning after Dec. 31, 2015, and before Jan. 1, 2018	1802	5012
165(h)(2)(A)(ii)	11028(c)(1)(A)	10%-of-AGI casualty loss threshold is retroactively made inapplicable in 2016 and 2017 to net disaster losses from 2016 disaster areas	Tax years beginning after Dec. 31, 2015, and before Jan. 1, 2018	1801	5012
165(h)(5)	11044(a)	Personal casualty losses are nondeductible unless attributable to a federally declared disaster	Losses incurred in tax years beginning after Dec. 31, 2017, and before Jan. 1, 2026	508	5018
168(b)(2)	13203(b)	200% declining balance method of MACRS depreciation is made available for many types of MACRS farming property	Property placed in service after Dec. 31, 2017	1305	5038
168(b)(3)	13204(a)(2)(A)	Eligibility of building improvements for a 15-year recovery period is expanded	Property placed in service after Dec. 31, 2017	1301	5039
168(b)(3)(G)	13204(a)(2)(B)	Eligibility of building improvements for a 15-year recovery period is expanded	Property placed in service after Dec. 31, 2017	1301	5039
168(e)	13204(a)(1)(B)	Eligibility of building improvements for a 15-year recovery period is expanded	Property placed in service after Dec. 31, 2017	1301	5039
168(e)(3)(B)(vii)	13203(a)	Most new farming equipment and machinery is made 5-year MACRS property	Property placed in service after Dec. 31, 2017	1304	5038

Code §	Act §	Topic	Effective Date	Analysis ¶	Com Rep ¶
168(e)(3)(E)	13204(a)(1)(A)(i)	Eligibility of building improvements for a 15-year recovery period is expanded	Property placed in service after Dec. 31, 2017	1301	5039
168(e)(6)	13204(a)(4)(B)	Eligibility of building improvements for a 15-year recovery period is expanded	Property placed in service after Dec. 31, 2017	1301	5039
168(g)(1)(F)	13204(a)(3)(A)(i)	ADS depreciation for buildings (and improvements) if election is made to exempt a real property business from the business interest deduction limit	Tax years beginning after Dec. 31, 2017	1303	5039
168(g)(1)(G)	13205(a)	ADS depreciation required for 10-year-or-more MACRS property if election made to exempt farming from the business interest deduction limitation	Tax years beginning after Dec. 31, 2017	1306	5040
168(g)(2)(C)	13204(a)(3)(C)	ADS recovery period for residential rental property is shortened to 30 years	Property placed in service after Dec. 31, 2017	1302	5039
168(g)(3)(B)	13204(a)(3)(B)(i)	Eligibility of building improvements for a 15-year recovery period is expanded	Property placed in service after Dec. 31, 2017	1301	5039
168(g)(3)(B)	13204(a)(3)(B)(ii)	Eligibility of building improvements for a 15-year recovery period is expanded	Property placed in service after Dec. 31, 2017	1301	5039
168(g)(8)	13204(a)(3)(A)(ii)	ADS depreciation for buildings (and improvements) if election is made to exempt a real property business from the business interest deduction limit	Tax years beginning after Dec. 31, 2017	1303	5039
168(k)	12001(b)(13)	Corporate election trading bonus and accelerated depreciation for otherwise-deferred AMT credits is ended (conforming to repeal of corporate AMT)	Tax years beginning after Dec. 31, 2017	1210	5029, 5036

Code §	Act §	Topic	Effective Date	Analysis ¶	Com Rep ¶
168(k)	13201	Overview—Bonus depreciation is increased to 100% ("full expensing") and is extended and modified	Property placed in service after Sept. 27, 2017	1201	5036
168(k)(1)(A)	13201(a)(1)(A)	Bonus depreciation increased to 100% (full expensing) with phase down generally deferred from 2018 to 2023	Property placed in service and acquired after Sept. 27, 2017 and before Jan. 1, 2027	1203	5036
168(k)(2)(A)(i)	13201(g)(1)(C)	Qualified film, television and live theatrical productions added to "qualified property" eligible for 100% bonus depreciation (full expensing)	Property placed in service and acquired after Sept. 27, 2017 and before Jan. 1, 2027	1206	5036
168(k)(2)(A)(i)	13204(a)(4)(A)	Overview—Bonus depreciation is increased to 100% ("full expensing") and is extended and modified	Property placed in service after Sept. 27, 2017	1201	5036
168(k)(2)(A)(ii)	13201(c)(1)	Used property is allowed 100% bonus depreciation (full expensing)	Property both acquired and placed in service after Sept. 27, 2017 and before Jan. 1, 2027	1205	5036
168(k)(2)(A)(iii)	13201(b)(1)(A)(i)	$8,000 increase for "qualified property" in the first-year depreciation cap for passenger autos is extended	Property both acquired and placed in service after Sept. 27, 2017 and placed in service before Jan. 1, 2027	1208	5036
168(k)(2)(A)(iii)	13201(b)(1)(A)(i)	Bonus depreciation and other benefits for qualified property are extended	Property placed in service and acquired after Sept. 27, 2017 and before Jan. 1, 2027	1202	5036
168(k)(2)(B)(i)(II)	13201(b)(1)(A)(ii)(I)	Bonus depreciation and other benefits for qualified property are extended	Property placed in service and acquired after Sept. 27, 2017 and before Jan. 1, 2027	1202	5036

Code §	Act §	Topic	Effective Date	Analy-sis ¶	Com Rep ¶
168(k)(2)(B)(i)(III)	13201(b)(1)(A)(i)	Bonus depreciation and other benefits for qualified property are extended	Property placed in service and acquired after Sept. 27, 2017 and before Jan. 1, 2027	1202	5036
168(k)(2)(B)(ii)	13201(b)(1)(A)(i)	Bonus depreciation and other benefits for qualified property are extended	Property placed in service and acquired after Sept. 27, 2017 and before Jan. 1, 2027	1202	5036
168(k)(2)(E)(i)	13201(b)(1)(A)(i)	Bonus depreciation and other benefits for qualified property are extended	Property placed in service and acquired after Sept. 27, 2017 and before Jan. 1, 2027	1202	5036
168(k)(2)(E)(ii)	13201(c)(2)	Used property is allowed 100% bonus depreciation (full expensing)	Property both acquired and placed in service after Sept. 27, 2017 and before Jan. 1, 2027	1205	5036
168(k)(2)(E)(iii)(I)	13201(c)(3)	Used property is allowed 100% bonus depreciation (full expensing)	Property both acquired and placed in service after Sept. 27, 2017 and before Jan. 1, 2027	1205	5036
168(k)(2)(F)(iii)	13201(f)	$8,000 increase for "qualified property" in the first-year depreciation cap for passenger autos is extended	Property both acquired and placed in service after Sept. 27, 2017 and placed in service before Jan. 1, 2027	1208	5036
168(k)(2)(H)	13201(g)(2)	Qualified film, television and live theatrical productions added to "qualified property" eligible for 100% bonus depreciation (full expensing)	Property placed in service and acquired after Sept. 27, 2017 and before Jan. 1, 2027	1206	5036
168(k)(4)	12001(b)(13)	Corporate minimum tax credit (MTC) may offset regular tax liability for any tax year, and is refundable for 2018−2021	Tax years beginning after Dec. 31, 2017	304	5029

Code §	Act §	Topic	Effective Date	Analysis ¶	Com Rep ¶
168(k)(5)	13201(a)(3)(A)	Elective form of bonus depreciation for specified plants is extended and increased to 100% (full expensing) with phase down deferred from 2018 to 2023	Plants planted or grafted after Sept. 27, 2017 and before Jan. 1, 2027	1204	5036
168(k)(5)(A)	13201(b)(1)(B)	Elective form of bonus depreciation for specified plants is extended and increased to 100% (full expensing) with phase down deferred from 2018 to 2023	Plants planted or grafted after Sept. 27, 2017 and before Jan. 1, 2027	1204	5036
168(k)(5)(A)(i)	13201(a)(1)(B)	Elective form of bonus depreciation for specified plants is extended and increased to 100% (full expensing) with phase down deferred from 2018 to 2023	Plants planted or grafted after Sept. 27, 2017 and before Jan. 1, 2027	1204	5036
168(k)(6)	13201(a)(2)	Bonus depreciation increased to 100% (full expensing) with phase down generally deferred from 2018 to 2023	Property placed in service and acquired after Sept. 27, 2017 and before Jan. 1, 2027	1203	5036
168(k)(6)(C)	13201(a)(2)	Elective form of bonus depreciation for specified plants is extended and increased to 100% (full expensing) with phase down deferred from 2018 to 2023	Plants planted or grafted after Sept. 27, 2017 and before Jan. 1, 2027	1204	5036
168(k)(8)	13201(a)(3)(B)	Bonus depreciation increased to 100% (full expensing) with phase down generally deferred from 2018 to 2023	Property placed in service and acquired after Sept. 27, 2017 and before Jan. 1, 2027	1203	5036
168(k)(9)	13201(d)	Property used in certain businesses exempt from business interest limitations is excluded from 100% bonus depreciation (full expensing)	Property acquired and placed in service after Sept. 27, 2017 and before Jan. 1, 2027	1207	5036

Code §	Act §	Topic	Effective Date	Analysis ¶	Com Rep ¶
168(k)(10)	13201(e)	Bonus depreciation increased to 100% (full expensing) with phase down generally deferred from 2018 to 2023	Property placed in service and acquired after Sept. 27, 2017 and before Jan. 1, 2027	1203	5036
168(k)(10)	13201(e)	Elective form of bonus depreciation for specified plants is extended and increased to 100% (full expensing) with phase down deferred from 2018 to 2023	Plants planted or grafted after Sept. 27, 2017 and before Jan. 1, 2027	1204	5036
170(b)(1)(G)	11023(a)	Limit on an individual's contributions of cash to charitable organizations is increased from 50% to 60% of donor's contribution base	Contributions made in tax years beginning after Dec. 31, 2017, and before Jan. 1, 2026	512	5007
170(f)(8)(D)	13705(a)	Donee-reporting exception to substantiation requirement for charitable contributions is retroactively repealed	Contributions made in tax years beginning after Dec. 31, 2016	515	5007
170(l)(1)	13704(a)	Charitable deduction is denied for contributions to a college or university in exchange for athletic event seating rights	Contributions in tax years beginning after Dec. 31, 2017	513	5007
172	13302(c)(2)(A)	NOLs can't be carried back, but can be carried forward indefinitely	NOLs arising in tax years ending after Dec. 31, 2017	1002	5045
172(a)	13302(a)(1)	NOL deduction is limited to 80% of taxable income	Losses arising in tax years beginning after Dec. 31, 2017	1001	5045
172(b)(1)	13302(b)(2)	NOLs can't be carried back, but can be carried forward indefinitely	NOLs arising in tax years ending after Dec. 31, 2017	1002	5045
172(b)(1)(A)	13302(b)(1)	NOLs can't be carried back, but can be carried forward indefinitely	NOLs arising in tax years ending after Dec. 31, 2017	1002	5045

Code §	Act §	Topic	Effective Date	Analysis ¶	Com Rep ¶
172(b)(1)(B)	13302(c)(1)	NOLs can't be carried back, but can be carried forward indefinitely	NOLs arising in tax years ending after Dec. 31, 2017	1002	5045
172(b)(1)(C)	13302(d)(1)	NOLs can't be carried back, but can be carried forward indefinitely	NOLs arising in tax years ending after Dec. 31, 2017	1002	5045
172(b)(2)	13302(a)(2)	NOL deduction is limited to 80% of taxable income	Losses arising in tax years beginning after Dec. 31, 2017	1001	5045
172(d)(6)(C)	13302(a)(3)	NOL deduction is limited to 80% of taxable income	Losses arising in tax years beginning after Dec. 31, 2017	1001	5045
172(f)	13302(d)(2)	NOL deduction is limited to 80% of taxable income	Losses arising in tax years beginning after Dec. 31, 2017	1001	5045
174	13206(a)	Code Sec. 174 research and experimental expenditures paid or incurred in tax years starting after 2021 are to be amortized over 5 years	Amounts paid or incurred in tax years beginning after Dec. 31, 2021	1408	5041
179(b)(1)	13101(a)(1)	Pre-adjustment Code Sec. 179 limits raised to $1 million (annual limit on expensing) and $2.5 million (annual phase-down threshold based on investment)	Property placed in service in tax years beginning after Dec. 31, 2017	1101	5034
179(b)(2)	13101(a)(2)	Pre-adjustment Code Sec. 179 limits raised to $1 million (annual limit on expensing) and $2.5 million (annual phase-down threshold based on investment)	Property placed in service in tax years beginning after Dec. 31, 2017	1101	5034
179(b)(6)(A)	13101(a)(3)(A)(i)	Pre-adjustment Code Sec. 179 limits raised to $1 million (annual limit on expensing) and $2.5 million (annual phase-down threshold based on investment)	Property placed in service in tax years beginning after Dec. 31, 2017	1101	5034

Code §	Act §	Topic	Effective Date	Analysis ¶	Com Rep ¶
179(b)(6)(A)	13101(a)(3)(B)(i)	$25,000 per-vehicle limit on Code Sec. 179 expensing of SUVs is made adjustable for inflation	Property placed in service in tax years beginning after Dec. 31, 2017	1104	5034
179(b)(6)(A)(ii)	11002(d)(1)(R)	Chained CPI-U (C-CPI-U) replaces CPI-U in inflation adjustments of various tax parameters under the Code	Tax years beginning after Dec. 31, 2017	202	5002
179(b)(6)(A)(ii)	11002(d)(1)(R)	Pre-adjustment Code Sec. 179 limits raised to $1 million (annual limit on expensing) and $2.5 million (annual phase-down threshold based on investment)	Property placed in service in tax years beginning after Dec. 31, 2017	1101	5034
179(b)(6)(A)(ii)	13101(a)(3)(A)(ii)	Pre-adjustment Code Sec. 179 limits raised to $1 million (annual limit on expensing) and $2.5 million (annual phase-down threshold based on investment)	Property placed in service in tax years beginning after Dec. 31, 2017	1101	5034
179(b)(6)(B)	13101(a)(3)(B)(ii)	$25,000 per-vehicle limit on Code Sec. 179 expensing of SUVs is made adjustable for inflation	Property placed in service in tax years beginning after Dec. 31, 2017	1104	5034
179(d)(1)	13101(c)	Otherwise-qualifying residential property no longer excluded from section 179 property	Property placed in service in tax years beginning after Dec. 31, 2017	1103	5034
179(d)(1)(B)(ii)	13101(b)(1)	More building improvements are made eligible to be section 179 property	Property placed in service in tax years beginning after Dec. 31, 2017	1102	5034
179(f)	13101(b)(2)	More building improvements are made eligible to be section 179 property	Property placed in service in tax years beginning after Dec. 31, 2017	1102	5034
199	13305(a)	Domestic production activity deduction (DPAD) is repealed	Tax years beginning after Dec. 31, 2017	1004	5048

Code §	Act §	Topic	Effective Date	Analysis ¶	Com Rep ¶
199A(a)	11011(a)	20% deduction for qualified business income	Tax years beginning after Dec. 31, 2017 and before Jan. 1, 2026	702	5003
199A(b)	11011(a)	20% deduction for qualified business income	Tax years beginning after Dec. 31, 2017 and before Jan. 1, 2026	702	5003
199A(c)	11011(a)	Qualified business income defined	Tax years beginning after Dec. 31, 2017 and before Jan. 1, 2026	703	5003
199A(d)	11011(a)	Qualified business income defined	Tax years beginning after Dec. 31, 2017 and before Jan. 1, 2026	703	5003
199A(e)	11011(a)	20% deduction for qualified business income	Tax years beginning after Dec. 31, 2017 and before Jan. 1, 2026	702	5003
199A(f)	11011(a)	20% deduction for qualified business income	Tax years beginning after Dec. 31, 2017 and before Jan. 1, 2026	702	5003
199A(f)	11011(a)	Application of qualified business income deduction to entities	Tax years beginning after Dec. 31, 2017 and before Jan. 1, 2026	704	5003
199A(f)	11011(a)	Treatment of qualified business income from Puerto Rico sources	Tax years beginning after Dec. 31, 2017 and before Jan. 1, 2026	705	5003
199A(g)	11011(a)	Application of qualified business income deduction to entities	Tax years beginning after Dec. 31, 2017 and before Jan. 1, 2026	704	5003
213(d)(10)(B)	11002(d)(7)	Chained CPI-U (C-CPI-U) replaces CPI-U in inflation adjustments of various tax parameters under the Code	Tax years beginning after Dec. 31, 2017	202	5002

Code §	Act §	Topic	Effective Date	Analy-sis ¶	Com Rep ¶
213(f)	11027(a)	7.5%-of-AGI floor for medical expense deduction is retroactively extended through 2018 and applied to all taxpayers	Tax years beginning after Dec. 31, 2016, and ending before Jan. 1, 2019	505	5011
215	11051(a)	Alimony won't be deductible by the payor or includible by the recipient for post-2018 divorce or separation instruments	Divorce or separation instruments executed after Dec. 31, 2018	510	5025
217	11049(a)	Moving expense deduction eliminated, except for certain armed forces members	Tax year beginning after Dec. 31, 2017, and before Jan. 1, 2026	514	5023
219(b)(5)(C)(i)(II)	11002(d)(1)(S)	Chained CPI-U (C-CPI-U) replaces CPI-U in inflation adjustments of various tax parameters under the Code	Tax years beginning after Dec. 31, 2017	202	5002
219(g)(8)(B)	11002(d)(1)(S)	Chained CPI-U (C-CPI-U) replaces CPI-U in inflation adjustments of various tax parameters under the Code	Tax years beginning after Dec. 31, 2017	202	5002
220(g)(2)	11002(d)(1)(T)	Chained CPI-U (C-CPI-U) replaces CPI-U in inflation adjustments of various tax parameters under the Code	Tax years beginning after Dec. 31, 2017	202	5002
221(f)(1)(B)	11002(d)(1)(U)	Chained CPI-U (C-CPI-U) replaces CPI-U in inflation adjustments of various tax parameters under the Code	Tax years beginning after Dec. 31, 2017	202	5002
223(g)(1)(B)	11002(d)(1)(V)	Chained CPI-U (C-CPI-U) replaces CPI-U in inflation adjustments of various tax parameters under the Code	Tax years beginning after Dec. 31, 2017	202	5002
243	13002(a)	Reduction in corporate dividends received deduction	Tax years beginning after Dec. 31, 2017	103	5032

Code §	Act §	Topic	Effective Date	Analy-sis ¶	Com Rep ¶
245(c)(1)(B)	13002(b)	Reduction in corporate dividends received deduction	Tax years beginning after Dec. 31, 2017	103	5032
245A	14101(a)	Deduction allowed for dividends received by a corporate U.S. shareholder from a specified 10% owned foreign corporation under participation exemption system	Distributions made after Dec. 31, 2017	1901	5107
246(b)(3)	13002(c)	Reduction in corporate dividends received deduction	Tax years beginning after Dec. 31, 2017	103	5032
246(c)(1)	14101(b)(1)	Deduction allowed for dividends received by a corporate U.S. shareholder from a specified 10% owned foreign corporation under participation exemption system	Distributions made after Dec. 31, 2017	1901	5107
246(c)(5)	14101(b)(2)	Deduction allowed for dividends received by a corporate U.S. shareholder from a specified 10% owned foreign corporation under participation exemption system	Distributions made after Dec. 31, 2017	1901	5107
246A(a)(1)	13002(d)	Reduction in corporate dividends received deduction	Tax years beginning after Dec. 31, 2017	103	5032
250	14202(a)	Domestic corporations allowed deduction for foreign-derived intangible income and global intangible low-taxed income	Tax years beginning after Dec. 31, 2017	2002	5111
263A(d)(2)(C)	13207(a)	Minority and subsequent owners can expense certain costs of replanting citrus plants lost by reason of casualty	Amounts paid or incurred after Dec. 22, 2017 and before Dec. 23, 2027	1411	5042
263A(f)	13801(a)	Production period for beer, wine, distilled spirits won't include their aging period under the UNICAP interest capitalization rules for the next 2 calendar years	For interest costs paid or accrued in calendar years beginning after Dec. 31, 2017 and before Jan. 1, 2020	1410	5096

Code §	Act §	Topic	Effective Date	Analysis ¶	Com Rep ¶
263A(i)	13102(b)	Small business exception to UNICAP rules is expanded to apply to producers and resellers meeting the $25 million gross receipts test	Tax years beginning after Dec. 31, 2017	1404	5035
267A	14222(a)	Deduction is disallowed for certain related party amounts paid or accrued in hybrid transactions or with hybrid entities	Tax years beginning after Dec. 31, 2017	2204	5118
274(a)(1)	13304(a)(1)(B)	Business deduction is denied for entertainment expenses	Amounts incurred or paid after Dec. 31, 2017	1005	5047
274(a)(1)(A)	13304(a)(1)(A)	Business deduction is denied for entertainment expenses	Amounts incurred or paid after Dec. 31, 2017	1005	5047
274(a)(2)	13304(a)(1)(C)	Business deduction is denied for entertainment expenses	Amounts incurred or paid after Dec. 31, 2017	1005	5047
274(a)(4)	13304(c)(1)(B)	Employers can't deduct cost of providing qualified transportation fringes and other transportation benefits	Amounts incurred or paid after Dec. 31, 2017	1007	5047
274(d)	13304(a)(2)(A)(i)	Business deduction is denied for entertainment expenses	Amounts incurred or paid after Dec. 31, 2017	1005	5047
274(d)	13304(a)(2)(A)(ii)	Business deduction is denied for entertainment expenses	Amounts incurred or paid after Dec. 31, 2017	1005	5047
274(j)(3)(A)	13310(a)	Cash, gift cards, and certain other property don't qualify as employee achievement awards	Amounts paid or incurred after Dec. 31, 2017	2605	5053
274(l)	13304(a)(2)(B)	Business deduction is denied for entertainment expenses	Amounts incurred or paid after Dec. 31, 2017	1005	5047

Code §	Act §	Topic	Effective Date	Analysis ¶	Com Rep ¶
274(l)	13304(c)(2)	Employers can't deduct cost of providing qualified transportation fringes and other transportation benefits	Amounts incurred or paid after Dec. 31, 2017	1007	5047
274(n)	13304(a)(2)(C)	Business deduction is denied for entertainment expenses	Amounts incurred or paid after Dec. 31, 2017	1005	5047
274(n)(1)	13304(a)(2)(D)	Business deduction is denied for entertainment expenses	Amounts incurred or paid after Dec. 31, 2017	1005	5047
274(n)(2)	13304(a)(2)(E)	Business deduction is denied for entertainment expenses	Amounts incurred or paid after Dec. 31, 2017	1005	5047
274(n)(2)	13304(b)(1)	Expenses for employer-operated eating facilities are only 50% deductible through 2025, then become nondeductible	Amounts incurred or paid after Dec. 31, 2017, and before Jan. 1, 2026	1006	5047
274(o)	13304(d)(2)	Expenses for employer-operated eating facilities are only 50% deductible through 2025, then become nondeductible	Amounts incurred or paid after Dec. 31, 2017, and before Jan. 1, 2026	1006	5047
280C(a)	13403(d)(1)	Employers are allowed a credit for paid family and medical leave	Wages paid in tax years beginning after Dec. 31, 2017 and before Jan. 1, 2020	1013	5060
280C(b)	13401(b)	Reduced orphan drug credit election is available to avoid having to reduce any deduction or charge to capital account for qualified clinical testing expenses	Tax years beginning after Dec. 31, 2017	1016	5058
280C(c)(1)	13206(d)(2)(A)	Code Sec. 174 research and experimental expenditures paid or incurred in tax years starting after 2021 are to be amortized over 5 years	Amounts paid or incurred in tax years beginning after Dec. 31, 2021	1408	5041

Code §	Act §	Topic	Effective Date	Analysis ¶	Com Rep ¶
280C(c)(2)	13206(d)(2)(B)	Code Sec. 174 research and experimental expenditures paid or incurred in tax years starting after 2021 are to be amortized over 5 years	Amounts paid or incurred in tax years beginning after Dec. 31, 2021	1408	5041
280C(c)(2)	13206(d)(2)(D)	Code Sec. 174 research and experimental expenditures paid or incurred in tax years starting after 2021 are to be amortized over 5 years	Amounts paid or incurred in tax years beginning after Dec. 31, 2021	1408	5041
280F(a)(1)(A)	13202(a)(1)	Annual caps on depreciation of passenger automobiles are raised	Property placed in service after Dec. 31, 2017	1307	5037
280F(a)(1)(B)	13202(a)(2)(A)	Annual caps on depreciation of passenger automobiles are raised	Property placed in service after Dec. 31, 2017	1307	5037
280F(d)(4)	13202(b)(2)	Treatment of computer equipment as listed property is ended	Property placed in service after Dec. 31, 2017	1308	5037
280F(d)(4)(A)	13202(b)(1)(B)	Treatment of computer equipment as listed property is ended	Property placed in service after Dec. 31, 2017	1308	5037
280F(d)(7)(B)	11002(d)(8)	Chained CPI-U (C-CPI-U) replaces CPI-U in inflation adjustments of various tax parameters under the Code	Tax years beginning after Dec. 31, 2017	202	5002
280F(d)(7)(B)(i)	11002(d)(8)	Annual caps on depreciation of passenger automobiles are raised	Property placed in service after Dec. 31, 2017	1307	5037
280F(d)(7)(B)(i)	13202(a)(2)(B)(i)	Annual caps on depreciation of passenger automobiles are raised	Property placed in service after Dec. 31, 2017	1307	5037
280F(d)(7)(B)(i)(II)	13202(a)(2)(B)(ii)	Annual caps on depreciation of passenger automobiles are raised	Property placed in service after Dec. 31, 2017	1307	5037
280F(d)(7)(B)(ii)	11002(d)(8)	Annual caps on depreciation of passenger automobiles are raised	Property placed in service after Dec. 31, 2017	1307	5037

Code §	Act §	Topic	Effective Date	Analysis ¶	Com Rep ¶
367(a)(3)	14102(e)(1)	Repeal of active trade or business exception under Code Sec. 367	Transfers after Dec. 31, 2017	2203	5108
367(d)(2)	14221(b)(1)	Limitations imposed on income shifting through intangible property transfers	Transfers in tax years beginning after Dec. 31, 2017	2202	5117
381(c)(20)	13301(b)(1)	Deduction for net business interest is limited to 30% of adjusted taxable income, with indefinite carryover	Tax years beginning after Dec. 31, 2017	1003	5044
381(d)	13511(b)(3)	Operations loss deduction for life insurance companies repealed	For losses arising in tax years beginning after Dec. 31, 2017	2402	5066
382(d)(3)	13301(b)(2)	Deduction for net business interest is limited to 30% of adjusted taxable income, with indefinite carryover	Tax years beginning after Dec. 31, 2017	1003	5044
382(k)(1)	13301(b)(3)	Deduction for net business interest is limited to 30% of adjusted taxable income, with indefinite carryover	Tax years beginning after Dec. 31, 2017	1003	5044
401(a)(31)	11028(b)(1)(F)	Favorable tax treatment provided for qualified 2016 disaster area plan distributions	Dec. 22, 2017, for distributions made on or after Jan. 1, 2016, and before Jan. 1, 2018	1804	5012
402(c)(3)	13613	Rollover period for plan loan offset amounts is extended from 60 days, to tax return due date	Tax years beginning after Dec. 31, 2017	2702	5090
402(f)	11028(b)(1)(F)	Favorable tax treatment provided for qualified 2016 disaster area plan distributions	Dec. 22, 2017, for distributions made on or after Jan. 1, 2016, and before Jan. 1, 2018	1804	5012

Code §	Act §	Topic	Effective Date	Analy-sis ¶	Com Rep ¶
408A(c)(3)(D)(ii)	11002(d)(1)(W)	Chained CPI-U (C-CPI-U) replaces CPI-U in inflation adjustments of various tax parameters under the Code	Tax years beginning after Dec. 31, 2017	202	5002
408A(d)(6)(B)(iii)	13611(a)	Special rule allowing recharacterization of Roth IRA contributions and traditional IRA contributions does not apply to conversion contributions to a Roth IRA	Tax years after Dec. 31, 2017	2701	5088
409A(d)(7)	13603(c)(2)	Employees can elect to defer income from option or RSU stock for up to five years after vesting	Stock attributable to options exercised, or restricted stock units settled, after Dec. 31, 2017	2604	5086
422(b)	13603(c)(1)(A)	Employees can elect to defer income from option or RSU stock for up to five years after vesting	Stock attributable to options exercised, or restricted stock units settled, after Dec. 31, 2017	2604	5086
423(b)(5)	13603(c)(1)(B)(i)	Employees can elect to defer income from option or RSU stock for up to five years after vesting	Stock attributable to options exercised, or restricted stock units settled, after Dec. 31, 2017	2604	5086
423(d)	13603(c)(1)(B)(ii)	Employees can elect to defer income from option or RSU stock for up to five years after vesting	Stock attributable to options exercised, or restricted stock units settled, after Dec. 31, 2017	2604	5086
430(c)(7)(D)(vii)(II)	11002(d)(1)(X)	Chained CPI-U (C-CPI-U) replaces CPI-U in inflation adjustments of various tax parameters under the Code	Tax years beginning after Dec. 31, 2017	202	5002

Code §	Act §	Topic	Effective Date	Analysis ¶	Com Rep ¶
447	13102(a)(5)(C)(ii)	Gross receipts limits for cash-method use by farming C corporations (and certain partnerships) are raised to a uniform $25 million and some related rules are changed	Tax years beginning after Dec. 31, 2017	1402	5035
447(c)	13102(a)(5)(A)(i)	Gross receipts limits for cash-method use by farming C corporations (and certain partnerships) are raised to a uniform $25 million and some related rules are changed	Tax years beginning after Dec. 31, 2017	1402	5035
447(c)	13102(a)(5)(C)	Gross receipts limits for cash-method use by farming C corporations (and certain partnerships) are raised to a uniform $25 million and some related rules are changed	Tax years beginning after Dec. 31, 2017	1402	5035
447(c)(2)	13102(a)(5)(A)(ii)	Gross receipts limits for cash-method use by farming C corporations (and certain partnerships) are raised to a uniform $25 million and some related rules are changed	Tax years beginning after Dec. 31, 2017	1402	5035
447(d)	13102(a)(5)(B)	Gross receipts limits for cash-method use by farming C corporations (and certain partnerships) are raised to a uniform $25 million and some related rules are changed	Tax years beginning after Dec. 31, 2017	1402	5035
448(b)(3)	13102(a)(2)	Gross receipts limit for cash-method use by C corporations (and certain partnerships) raised to $25 million, related rules changed	Tax years beginning after Dec. 31, 2017	1401	5035

Code §	Act §	Topic	Effective Date	Analy-sis ¶	Com Rep ¶
448(c)(1)	13102(a)(1)	Gross receipts limit for cash-method use by C corporations (and certain partnerships) raised to $25 million, related rules changed	Tax years beginning after Dec. 31, 2017	1401	5035
448(c)(4)	13102(a)(3)	Gross receipts limit for cash-method use by C corporations (and certain partnerships) raised to $25 million, related rules changed	Tax years beginning after Dec. 31, 2017	1401	5035
448(d)(7)	13102(a)(4)	Gross receipts limit for cash-method use by C corporations (and certain partnerships) raised to $25 million, related rules changed	Tax years beginning after Dec. 31, 2017	1401	5035
451(b)	13221(a)	Income inclusion for tax purposes can't be later than when included for certain financial reporting purposes	Tax years beginning after Dec. 31, 2017	1406	5043
451(c)	13221(b)	Accrual basis taxpayers may defer inclusion of advance payments in income to the end of year after year of receipt if so deferred for financial reporting	Tax years beginning after Dec. 31, 2017	1407	5043
453B(e)(3)	13512(b)(1)	Small life insurance company deduction repealed	Tax years beginning after Dec. 31, 2017	2403	5067
457(e)(11)(B)	13612	Accrual limit for length of service award plans is increased from $3,000 to $6,000	Tax years beginning after Dec. 31, 2017	2703	5089
460(c)(6)(B)(ii)	13201(b)(2)(A)	Overview—Bonus depreciation is increased to 100% ("full expensing") and is extended and modified	Property placed in service after Sept. 27, 2017	1201	5036

Code §	Act §	Topic	Effective Date	Analy-sis ¶	Com Rep ¶
460(c)(6)(B)(ii)	13201(b)(2)(A)	Placed-in-service deadline for disregard of some bonus depreciation-eligible property under the percentage of completion method is extended	Property placed in service and acquired after Sept. 27, 2017 and before Jan. 1, 2027	1209	5036
460(e)(1)(B)	13102(d)(1)(A)	Gross receipts limit to qualify for small construction contract exception to percentage of completion method is raised to $25 million	Contracts entered into after Dec. 31, 2017	1405	5035
460(e)(1)(B)(ii)	13102(d)(1)(B)	Gross receipts limit to qualify for small construction contract exception to percentage of completion method is raised to $25 million	Contracts entered into after Dec. 31, 2017	1405	5035
460(e)(2)	13102(d)(2)	Gross receipts limit to qualify for small construction contract exception to percentage of completion method is raised to $25 million	Contracts entered into after Dec. 31, 2017	1405	5035
461(l)	11012(a)	Excess business loss disallowance rule replaces limitation on excess farm loss for non-corporate taxpayers for tax years beginning after Dec. 31, 2017	Tax years beginning after Dec. 31, 2017 and ending before Jan. 1, 2026	1409	5004
471(c)	13102(c)	Alternatives to inventory accounting are made available to most small businesses meeting a $25 million gross receipts test	Tax years beginning after Dec. 31, 2017	1403	5035
481(d)	13543(a)	Treatment of revocations of S corporation elections	Dec. 22, 2017	801	5083
482	14221(b)(2)	Limitations imposed on income shifting through intangible property transfers	Transfers in tax years beginning after Dec. 31, 2017	2202	5117

Code §	Act §	Topic	Effective Date	Analy-sis ¶	Com Rep ¶
512(a)(6)	13702(a)	Tax-exempt organizations' unrelated business taxable income calculated separately for each trade or business	For tax years beginning after Dec. 31, 2017	2503	5092
512(a)(7)	13703(a)	Tax-exempt organizations' unrelated business taxable income increased by disallowed fringe benefit expenses	For amounts paid or incurred after Dec. 31, 2017	2504	5093
512(d)(2)(B)	11002(d)(1)(Y)	Chained CPI-U (C-CPI-U) replaces CPI-U in inflation adjustments of various tax parameters under the Code	Tax years beginning after Dec. 31, 2017	202	5002
513(h)(2)(C)(ii)	11002(d)(1)(Z)	Chained CPI-U (C-CPI-U) replaces CPI-U in inflation adjustments of various tax parameters under the Code	Tax years beginning after Dec. 31, 2017	202	5002
529(c)(3)(C)(i)(III)	11025(a)	Tax-free 60-day rollovers from 529 plan accounts to ABLE accounts are permitted	Distributions after Dec. 22, 2017, for transfers made before Jan. 1, 2026	1603	5009
529(c)(7)	11032(a)(1)	$10,000 per year of 529 plan account funds may be used for elementary or secondary school tuition	Distributions made after Dec. 31, 2017	1604	5014
529(e)(3)(A)	11032(a)(2)	$10,000 per year of 529 plan account funds may be used for elementary or secondary school tuition	Distributions made after Dec. 31, 2017	1604	5014
529A(b)(2)	11024(a)(2)	ABLE account contribution limit is increased for contributions by account's designated beneficiary	Tax years beginning after Dec. 22, 2017, for contributions before Jan. 1, 2026	1601	5008

Code §	Act §	Topic	Effective Date	Analy-sis ¶	Com Rep ¶
529A(b)(2)(B)	11024(a)(1)	ABLE account contribution limit is increased for contributions by account's designated beneficiary	Tax years beginning after Dec. 22, 2017, for contributions before Jan. 1, 2026	1601	5008
529A(b)(7)	11024(a)(3)	ABLE account contribution limit is increased for contributions by account's designated beneficiary	Tax years beginning after Dec. 22, 2017, for contributions before Jan. 1, 2026	1601	5008
641(c)(2)(E)	13542(a)	Charitable deductions of Electing Small Business Trusts (ESBTs)	Tax years beginning after Dec. 31, 2017	803	5082
642(b)(2)(C)(iii)	11041(b)	Deduction for personal exemptions for taxpayer, spouse, and dependents is suspended; return-filing and withholding requirements are modified	Tax years beginning after Dec. 31, 2017, and before Jan. 1, 2026	502	5015
682	11051(b)(1)(C)	Alimony won't be deductible by the payor or includible by the recipient for post-2018 divorce or separation instruments	Divorce or separation instruments executed after Dec. 31, 2018	510	5025
692	11026(a)(3)	Special "combat zone" benefits extended retroactively to members of the armed forces performing services in the Sinai Peninsula of Egypt	June 9, 2015	605	5010
704(d)	13503(a)	Basis reduction for partnership charitable contributions amended	Partnership tax years beginning after Dec. 31, 2017	903	5064
708(b)(1)	13504(a)	Repeal of partnership technical termination rule	Partnership tax years beginning after Dec. 31, 2017	901	5065
743(d)(1)	13502(a)	Mandatory basis adjustment upon transfers of partnership interests amended	Transfers of partnership interests after Dec. 31, 2017	902	5063

Code §	Act §	Topic	Effective Date	Analy-sis ¶	Com Rep ¶
801(c)	13514(b)	Tax on distributions to stock life insurance company shareholders from a pre-1984 policyholders' surplus account is repealed; phased inclusion of remaining balance of policyholders' surplus account is provided	Tax years beginning after Dec. 31, 2017	2407	5069
805(a)(4)(B)(ii)	13511(b)(4)	Operations loss deduction for life insurance companies repealed	For losses arising in tax years beginning after Dec. 31, 2017	2402	5066
805(a)(5)	13511(b)(5)	Operations loss deduction for life insurance companies repealed	For losses arising in tax years beginning after Dec. 31, 2017	2402	5066
805(b)(4)	13511(a)	Operations loss deduction for life insurance companies repealed	For losses arising in tax years beginning after Dec. 31, 2017	2402	5066
806	13512(a)	Small life insurance company deduction repealed	Tax years beginning after Dec. 31, 2017	2403	5067
807(c)	13517(a)(1)	Rules on computation of life insurance tax reserves amended	Tax years beginning after Dec. 31, 2017	2406	5072
807(d)	13517(a)(2)	Rules on computation of life insurance tax reserves amended	Tax years beginning after Dec. 31, 2017	2406	5072
807(e)	13517(a)(3)	Rules on computation of life insurance tax reserves amended	Tax years beginning after Dec. 31, 2017	2406	5072
807(f)(1)	13513(a)	Repeal of ten-year spread for life insurance companies' reserve changes	Tax years after Dec. 31, 2017	2405	5068
810	13511(b)(1)	Operations loss deduction for life insurance companies repealed	For losses arising in tax years beginning after Dec. 31, 2017	2402	5066

Code §	Act §	Topic	Effective Date	Analysis ¶	Com Rep ¶
812	13518(a)	Definition of "company's share" and "policyholder's share" amended for determining insurance company dividends received deduction and reserves	Tax years beginning after Dec. 31, 2017	2401	5073
815	13514(a)	Tax on distributions to stock life insurance company shareholders from a pre-1984 policyholders' surplus account is repealed; phased inclusion of remaining balance of policyholders' surplus account is provided	Tax years beginning after Dec. 31, 2017	2407	5069
831(b)(2)(D)(ii)	11002(d)(1)(AA)	Chained CPI-U (C-CPI-U) replaces CPI-U in inflation adjustments of various tax parameters under the Code	Tax years beginning after Dec. 31, 2017	202	5002
832(b)(5)(B)	13515(a)	Increase from 15% to 25% of the proration rules for property and casualty insurance companies	Tax years after Dec. 31, 2017	2408	5070
844	13511(b)(2)	Operations loss deduction for life insurance companies repealed	For losses arising in tax years beginning after Dec. 31, 2017	2402	5066
846	13523(e)	Modification of discounting rules for unpaid losses when determining property and casualty insurance companies' income	Tax years beginning after Dec. 31, 2017	2409	5078
846(c)(2)	13523(a)	Modification of discounting rules for unpaid losses when determining property and casualty insurance companies' income	Tax years beginning after Dec. 31, 2017	2409	5078
846(d)(3)	13523(b)	Modification of discounting rules for unpaid losses when determining property and casualty insurance companies' income	Tax years beginning after Dec. 31, 2017	2409	5078

Code §	Act §	Topic	Effective Date	Analy-sis ¶	Com Rep ¶
846(e)	13523(c)	Modification of discounting rules for unpaid losses when determining property and casualty insurance companies' income	Tax years beginning after Dec. 31, 2017	2409	5078
847	13516(a)	Elective deduction of discounted loss reserve amounts for insurance companies—and related special estimated tax payment rules—are repealed	Tax years beginning after Dec. 31, 2017	2410	5071
848(a)(2)	13519(a)(1)	Amortization period for insurance companies' capitalized policy acquisition expenses increased to 15 years from 10 years	Tax years beginning after Dec. 31, 2017	2404	5074
848(b)(1)	13519(b)	Amortization period for insurance companies' capitalized policy acquisition expenses increased to 15 years from 10 years	Tax years beginning after Dec. 31, 2017	2404	5074
848(c)(1)	13519(a)(2)	Amortization period for insurance companies' capitalized policy acquisition expenses increased to 15 years from 10 years	Tax years beginning after Dec. 31, 2017	2404	5074
848(c)(2)	13519(a)(3)	Amortization period for insurance companies' capitalized policy acquisition expenses increased to 15 years from 10 years	Tax years beginning after Dec. 31, 2017	2404	5074
848(c)(3)	13519(a)(4)	Amortization period for insurance companies' capitalized policy acquisition expenses increased to 15 years from 10 years	Tax years beginning after Dec. 31, 2017	2404	5074
863(b)	14303(a)	Source of income from sales of inventory determined solely on basis of production activities	Tax years beginning after Dec. 31, 2017	2305	5122

Code §	Act §	Topic	Effective Date	Analy-sis ¶	Com Rep ¶
864(c)(8)	13501(a)	Treatment of gain or loss of foreign person from sale or exchange of partnership interests	Sales, exchanges or dispositions after Dec. 31, 2017	2304	5062
864(e)(2)	14502(a)	Fair market value method of interest expense allocation or apportionment repealed after 2017	Tax years beginning after Dec. 31, 2017	2306	5126
877A(a)(3)(B)(i)(II)	11002(d)(1)(BB)	Chained CPI-U (C-CPI-U) replaces CPI-U in inflation adjustments of various tax parameters under the Code	Tax years beginning after Dec. 31, 2017	202	5002
882(a)	14401(d)(2)	Base erosion minimum tax added on payments to foreign related parties.	Base erosion payments paid or accrued in tax years beginning after Dec. 31, 2017	2201	5124
902	14301(a)	Repeal of Code Sec. 902 and other adjustments to the foreign tax credit to account for participation exemption	Tax years of foreign corporations beginning after Dec. 31, 2017	2301	5120
904(b)(5)	14101(d)	Dividends allowed as a Code Sec. 245A DRD are not treated as foreign source income for purposes of the FTC limitation	Deductions for tax years ending after Dec. 31, 2017	1902	5107
904(c)	14201(b)(2)(C)	Separate foreign tax credit basket for global intangible low-taxed income (GILTI)	Tax years of foreign corporations beginning after Dec. 31, 2017	2004	5110
904(d)(1)	14201(b)(2)(A)	Separate foreign tax credit basket for global intangible low-taxed income (GILTI)	Tax years of foreign corporations beginning after Dec. 31, 2017	2004	5110
904(d)(1)	14302(a)	Addition of separate foreign tax credit basket for foreign branch income	Tax years beginning after Dec. 31, 2017	2303	5121

Code §	Act §	Topic	Effective Date	Analysis ¶	Com Rep ¶
904(d)(2)(A)(ii)	14201(b)(2)(B)	Separate foreign tax credit basket for global intangible low-taxed income (GILTI)	Tax years of foreign corporations beginning after Dec. 31, 2017	2004	5110
904(d)(2)(J)	14302(b)(1)	Addition of separate foreign tax credit basket for foreign branch income	Tax years beginning after Dec. 31, 2017	2303	5121
904(g)	14304(a)	Taxpayers who sustain a pre-2018 overall domestic loss can elect to recharacterize as much as 100% of U.S. source income as foreign source income	Tax years beginning after Dec. 31, 2017 and before Jan. 1, 2028	2302	5123
911(b)(2)(D)(ii)(II)	11002(d)(9)	Chained CPI-U (C-CPI-U) replaces CPI-U in inflation adjustments of various tax parameters under the Code	Tax years beginning after Dec. 31, 2017	202	5002
936(h)(3)(B)	14221(a)	Limitations imposed on income shifting through intangible property transfers	Transfers in tax years beginning after Dec. 31, 2017	2202	5117
951(a)(1)	14215(a)	Requirement that corporation must be controlled for 30 days before Subpart F inclusions apply is eliminated	Tax years of foreign corporations beginning after Dec. 31, 2017	2103	5116
951(b)	14214(a)	Definition of U.S. shareholder of a controlled foreign corporation expanded to include 10% owner by value	Tax years of foreign corporations beginning after Dec. 31, 2017	2101	5115
951A	14201(a)	U.S. shareholders of CFCs must include their global intangible low-taxed income (GILTI) in gross income	Tax years of foreign corporations beginning after Dec. 31, 2017	2001	5110
953(b)(1)(B)	13511(b)(7)	Operations loss deduction for life insurance companies repealed	For losses arising in tax years beginning after Dec. 31, 2017	2402	5066

Code §	Act §	Topic	Effective Date	Analy-sis ¶	Com Rep ¶
954(a)(5)	14211(a)(3)	Foreign base company oil-related income not included in foreign base company income	Tax years of foreign corporations beginning after Dec. 31, 2017	2104	5112
954(g)	14211(b)(3)	Foreign base company oil-related income not included in foreign base company income	Tax years of foreign corporations beginning after Dec. 31, 2017	2104	5112
955	14212(a)	Previously excluded Subpart F income withdrawn from a qualified shipping investment no longer included in U.S. shareholder's income	Tax years of foreign corporations beginning after Dec. 31, 2017	2105	5113
958(b)	14213(a)	Subpart F constructive attribution rules allow downward attribution from foreign persons to related U.S. persons	The last tax year of foreign corporations beginning before Jan. 1, 2018	2102	5114
960	14301(b)(1)	Repeal of Code Sec. 902 and other adjustments to the foreign tax credit to account for participation exemption	Tax years of foreign corporations beginning after Dec. 31, 2017	2301	5120
960(d)	14201(b)(1)	80% deemed paid foreign tax credit available for global intangible low-taxed income	Tax years of foreign corporations beginning after Dec. 31, 2017	2003	5110
961(d)	14102(b)(1)	Basis of stock in specified 10% owned foreign corporation reduced to the extent of Code Sec. 245A DRD in determining loss on disposition	Distributions made after Dec. 31, 2017	1903	5108
964(e)(4)	14102(c)	Amounts treated as dividends under Code Sec. 1248 and Code Sec. 964(e) are treated as dividends for purposes of the Code Sec. 245A DRD	Sales or exchanges after Dec. 31, 2017	1904	5108

Code §	Act §	Topic	Effective Date	Analy-sis ¶	Com Rep ¶
965(a)	14103(a)	Pre-2018 accumulated deferred foreign income must be included in Subpart F income upon transition to a participation exemption system	Last tax year of a deferred income corporation beginning before Jan. 1, 2018	1906	5109
965(b)	14103(a)	Foreign E&P deficits reduce the pre-2018 accumulated deferred foreign income included in Subpart F	Last tax year of a deferred income corporation beginning before Jan. 1, 2018	1907	5109
965(c)	14103(a)	Deduction for pre-2018 accumulated deferred foreign income; disallowance of foreign tax credit for deducted portion; recapture for expatriated entities	Last tax year of a deferred income corporation beginning before Jan. 1, 2018	1908	5109
965(d)	14103(a)	Pre-2018 accumulated deferred foreign income must be included in Subpart F income upon transition to a participation exemption system	Last tax year of a deferred income corporation beginning before Jan. 1, 2018	1906	5109
965(e)	14103(a)	Pre-2018 accumulated deferred foreign income must be included in Subpart F income upon transition to a participation exemption system	Last tax year of a deferred income corporation beginning before Jan. 1, 2018	1906	5109
965(f)	14103(a)	Foreign E&P deficits reduce the pre-2018 accumulated deferred foreign income included in Subpart F	Last tax year of a deferred income corporation beginning before Jan. 1, 2018	1907	5109
965(g)	14103(a)	Deduction for pre-2018 accumulated deferred foreign income; disallowance of foreign tax credit for deducted portion; recapture for expatriated entities	Last tax year of a deferred income corporation beginning before Jan. 1, 2018	1908	5109

Code §	Act §	Topic	Effective Date	Analysis ¶	Com Rep ¶
965(h)	14103(a)	A U.S. shareholder may elect to pay the net tax liability for pre-2018 accumulated deferred foreign income in installments	Last tax year of a deferred income corporation beginning before Jan. 1, 2018	1909	5109
965(i)	14103(a)	S corporation shareholders may elect to defer net tax liability for accumulated deferred foreign income until a triggering event	Last tax year of a deferred income corporation beginning before Jan. 1, 2018	1910	5109
965(j)	14103(a)	S corporation shareholders may elect to defer net tax liability for accumulated deferred foreign income until a triggering event	Last tax year of a deferred income corporation beginning before Jan. 1, 2018	1910	5109
965(k)	14103(a)	Six year statute of limitation for assessment of net tax liability due to pre-2018 accumulated deferred foreign income	Last tax year of a deferred income corporation beginning before Jan. 1, 2018	1911	5109
965(l)	14103(a)	Deduction for pre-2018 accumulated deferred foreign income; disallowance of foreign tax credit for deducted portion; recapture for expatriated entities	Last tax year of a deferred income corporation beginning before Jan. 1, 2018	1908	5109
965(m)	14103(a)	Pre-2018 accumulated deferred foreign income excluded for purposes of REIT gross income tests; election provided to include that amount in REIT income over eight years	Last tax year of a deferred income corporation beginning before Jan. 1, 2018	1912	5109
965(n)	14103(a)	Election not to take pre-2018 accumulated deferred foreign income into account for NOL purposes	Last tax year of a deferred income corporation beginning before Jan. 1, 2018	1913	5109

Code §	Act §	Topic	Effective Date	Analysis ¶	Com Rep ¶
965(o)	14103(a)	Pre-2018 accumulated deferred foreign income must be included in Subpart F income upon transition to a participation exemption system	Last tax year of a deferred income corporation beginning before Jan. 1, 2018	1906	5109
1016(a)(1)	13521(a)	Cost of insurance adjustment to the basis of life insurance or annuity contracts is retroactively eliminated	For transactions entered into after Aug. 25, 2009	1505	5075
1016(a)(23)	13313(b)	Tax-free rollover of publicly traded securities gain into "specialized small business investment companies" is repealed	For sales after Dec. 31, 2017	1507	5056
1016(a)(38)	13823(b)	Gains invested in a Qualified Opportunity Fund can be temporarily deferred and permanently excluded if the investment in the Fund is held for 10 years	Dec. 22, 2017	1703	5106
1031(a)(1)	13303(a)	Like-kind exchanges are limited to exchanges of real estate	Exchanges completed after Dec. 31, 2017	1503	5046
1031(a)(2)	13303(b)(1)(A)	Like-kind exchanges are limited to exchanges of real estate	Exchanges completed after Dec. 31, 2017	1503	5046
1031(e)	13303(b)(2)	Like-kind exchanges are limited to exchanges of real estate	Exchanges completed after Dec. 31, 2017	1503	5046
1031(e)	13303(b)(3)	Like-kind exchanges are limited to exchanges of real estate	Exchanges completed after Dec. 31, 2017	1503	5046
1031(h)	13303(b)(4)	Like-kind exchanges are limited to exchanges of real estate	Exchanges completed after Dec. 31, 2017	1503	5046
1031(i)	13303(b)(1)(B)	Like-kind exchanges are limited to exchanges of real estate	Exchanges completed after Dec. 31, 2017	1503	5046

Code §	Act §	Topic	Effective Date	Analysis ¶	Com Rep ¶
1044	13313(a)	Tax-free rollover of publicly traded securities gain into "specialized small business investment companies" is repealed	For sales after Dec. 31, 2017	1507	5056
1061	13309(a)	Certain gains from partnership profits interests held in connection with performance of investment services are short-term capital gains if held for 3 years or less	Tax years beginning after Dec. 31, 2017	1502	5052
1221(a)(3)	13314(a)	Patents, inventions, certain models or designs, and secret formulas or processes are excluded from the definition of a capital asset	Dispositions after Dec. 31, 2017	1504	5057
1231(b)(1)(C)	13314(b)	Patents, inventions, certain models or designs, and secret formulas or processes are excluded from the definition of a capital asset	Dispositions after Dec. 31, 2017	1504	5057
1248	14102(a)	Amounts treated as dividends under Code Sec. 1248 and Code Sec. 964(e) are treated as dividends for purposes of the Code Sec. 245A DRD	Sales or exchanges after Dec. 31, 2017	1904	5108
1274A(d)(2)	11002(d)(10)	Chained CPI-U (C-CPI-U) replaces CPI-U in inflation adjustments of various tax parameters under the Code	Tax years beginning after Dec. 31, 2017	202	5002
1297(b)(2)(B)	14501(a)	Active insurance business exception to passive foreign investment company rules requires minimum insurance liabilities amount	Tax years beginning after Dec. 31, 2017	2411	5125

Code §	Act §	Topic	Effective Date	Analy- sis ¶	Com Rep ¶
1297(f)	14501(b)	Active insurance business exception to passive foreign investment company rules requires minimum insurance liabilities amount	Tax years beginning after Dec. 31, 2017	2411	5125
1361(c)(2)(B)(v)	13541(a)	Expansion of qualifying beneficiaries of Electing Small Business Trusts (ESBTs)	Jan. 1, 2018	802	5081
1371(f)	13543(b)	Treatment of revocations of S corporation elections	Dec. 22, 2017	801	5083
1374(b)(3)(B)	12002(c)	Corporate minimum tax credit (MTC) may offset regular tax liability for any tax year, and is refundable for 2018−2021	Tax years beginning after Dec. 31, 2017	304	5029
1397E	13404(c)(1)	New tax-credit and direct-pay bonds may not be issued	Bonds issued after Dec. 31, 2017	1702	5061
1400Z-1	13823(a)	Chief executive officers of a state can designate low-income communities as Qualified Opportunity Zones	Dec. 22, 2017	1704	5106
1400Z-2	13823(a)	Gains invested in a Qualified Opportunity Fund can be temporarily deferred and permanently excluded if the investment in the Fund is held for 10 years	Dec. 22, 2017	1703	5106
1445(e)	13001(b)(3)	Reduction of corporate tax rates	Tax years beginning after Dec. 31, 2017	102	5032
1446(f)	13501(b)	Treatment of gain or loss of foreign person from sale or exchange of partnership interests	Sales, exchanges or dispositions after Dec. 31, 2017	2304	5062
2001(g)	11061(b)	Estate tax basic exclusion amount increased from $5 million to $10 million	For estates of decedents dying and gifts made after Dec. 31, 2017, and before Jan. 1, 2026	2801	5026

Code §	Act §	Topic	Effective Date	Analysis ¶	Com Rep ¶
2010(c)(3)(B)(ii)	11002(d)(1)(CC)	Chained CPI-U (C-CPI-U) replaces CPI-U in inflation adjustments of various tax parameters under the Code	Tax years beginning after Dec. 31, 2017	202	5002
2010(c)(3)(C)	11061(a)	Estate tax basic exclusion amount increased from $5 million to $10 million	For estates of decedents dying and gifts made after Dec. 31, 2017, and before Jan. 1, 2026	2801	5026
2032A(a)(3)(B)	11002(d)(1)(DD)	Chained CPI-U (C-CPI-U) replaces CPI-U in inflation adjustments of various tax parameters under the Code	Tax years beginning after Dec. 31, 2017	202	5002
2201	11026(a)(4)	Special "combat zone" benefits extended retroactively to members of the armed forces performing services in the Sinai Peninsula of Egypt	June 9, 2015	605	5010
2503(b)(2)(B)	11002(d)(1)(EE)	Chained CPI-U (C-CPI-U) replaces CPI-U in inflation adjustments of various tax parameters under the Code	Tax years beginning after Dec. 31, 2017	202	5002
3401(a)(1)	11026(a)(5)	Special "combat zone" benefits extended retroactively to members of the armed forces performing services in the Sinai Peninsula of Egypt	Remuneration paid after Dec. 22, 2017	605	5010
3401(i)	13603(b)(1)	Withholding is required at highest individual rate when stock subject to Code Sec. 83(i) election is included in income	Stock attributable to options exercised, or restricted stock units settled, after Dec. 31, 2017	2607	5086

Code §	Act §	Topic	Effective Date	Analy- sis ¶	Com Rep ¶
3402(a)(2)	11041(c)(1)	Deduction for personal exemptions for taxpayer, spouse, and dependents is suspended; return-filing and withholding requirements are modified	Tax years beginning after Dec. 31, 2017, and before Jan. 1, 2026	502	5015
3402(f)(1)	11041(c)(2)(B)	Deduction for personal exemptions for taxpayer, spouse, and dependents is suspended; return-filing and withholding requirements are modified	Tax years beginning after Dec. 31, 2017, and before Jan. 1, 2026	502	5015
3402(m)(1)	11011(b)(4)	20% deduction for qualified business income	Tax years beginning after Dec. 31, 2017 and before Jan. 1, 2026	702	5003
3402(t)	13603(b)(2)	Withholding is required at highest individual rate when stock subject to Code Sec. 83(i) election is included in income	Stock attributable to options exercised, or restricted stock units settled, after Dec. 31, 2017	2607	5086
3405	11028(b)(1)(F)	Favorable tax treatment provided for qualified 2016 disaster area plan distributions	Dec. 22, 2017, for distributions made on or after Jan. 1, 2016, and before Jan. 1, 2018	1804	5012
4161(b)(2)(C)(i)(II)	11002(d)(11)	Chained CPI-U (C-CPI-U) replaces CPI-U in inflation adjustments of various tax parameters under the Code	Tax years beginning after Dec. 31, 2017	202	5002
4253(d)	11026(a)(6)	Special "combat zone" benefits extended retroactively to members of the armed forces performing services in the Sinai Peninsula of Egypt	June 9, 2015	605	5010

Code §	Act §	Topic	Effective Date	Analysis ¶	Com Rep ¶
4261(e)(4)(A)(ii)	11002(d)(1)(FF)	Chained CPI-U (C-CPI-U) replaces CPI-U in inflation adjustments of various tax parameters under the Code	Tax years beginning after Dec. 31, 2017	202	5002
4261(e)(5)	13822(a)	Payments for aircraft management services are exempted from excise taxes on taxable air transportation	For amounts paid after Dec. 22, 2017	2901	5105
4960	13602(a)	Excise tax imposed on tax-exempt organizations that pay excess compensation	For tax years beginning after Dec. 31, 2017	2501	5085
4968	13701(a)	New excise tax imposed on investment income of private colleges and universities	Tax years beginning after Dec. 31, 2017	2502	5091
4980I(b)(3)(C)(v)(II)	11002(d)(12)	Chained CPI-U (C-CPI-U) replaces CPI-U in inflation adjustments of various tax parameters under the Code	Tax years beginning after Dec. 31, 2017	202	5002
4985(a)(1)	13604	Excise tax on stock compensation of insiders in expatriated corporations increased	Corporations first becoming expatriated corporations after Dec. 22, 2017	2205	5087
5000A(c)	11081	Shared responsibility payment (penalty) eliminated after 2018	Months beginning after Dec. 31, 2018	401	5028
5000A(c)(3)(D)(ii)	11002(d)(1)(GG)	Chained CPI-U (C-CPI-U) replaces CPI-U in inflation adjustments of various tax parameters under the Code	Tax years beginning after Dec. 31, 2017	202	5002
6012(f)	11041(e)	Deduction for personal exemptions for taxpayer, spouse, and dependents is suspended; return-filing and withholding requirements are modified	Tax years beginning after Dec. 31, 2017, and before Jan. 1, 2026	502	5015

Code §	Act §	Topic	Effective Date	Analy-sis ¶	Com Rep ¶
6013(f)(1)	11026(a)(7)	Special "combat zone" benefits extended retroactively to members of the armed forces performing services in the Sinai Peninsula of Egypt	June 9, 2015	605	5010
6038A(b)	14401(b)	Base erosion minimum tax added on payments to foreign related parties.	Base erosion payments paid or accrued in tax years beginning after Dec. 31, 2017	2201	5124
6039F(d)	11002(d)(13)	Chained CPI-U (C-CPI-U) replaces CPI-U in inflation adjustments of various tax parameters under the Code	Tax years beginning after Dec. 31, 2017	202	5002
6047(g)	13520(c)(2)	Tax reporting requirements added for policy sales and death benefits paid under life insurance contracts	Reportable policy sales and reportable death benefits paid after Dec. 31, 2017	1506	5075
6050X	13306(b)(1)	Information reporting requirements are added for government and other agencies that receive fines, penalties, etc., of $600 or more for law violations	Amounts paid or incurred on or after Dec. 22, 2017	1009	5049
6050Y	13520(a)	Tax reporting requirements added for policy sales and death benefits paid under life insurance contracts	Reportable policy sales and reportable death benefits paid after Dec. 31, 2017	1506	5075
6051(a)(16)	13603(d)	Form W-2 must include information about deferrals and inclusions under Code Sec. 83(i)	Stock attributable to options exercised, or restricted stock units settled, after Dec. 31, 2017	2606	5086

Code §	Act §	Topic	Effective Date	Analysis ¶	Com Rep ¶
6051(a)(17)	13603(d)	Form W-2 must include information about deferrals and inclusions under Code Sec. 83(i)	Stock attributable to options exercised, or restricted stock units settled, after Dec. 31, 2017	2606	5086
6323(i)(4)(B)	11002(d)(1)(HH)	Chained CPI-U (C-CPI-U) replaces CPI-U in inflation adjustments of various tax parameters under the Code	Tax years beginning after Dec. 31, 2017	202	5002
6334(d)(4)	11041(d)	Deduction for personal exemptions for taxpayer, spouse, and dependents is suspended; return-filing and withholding requirements are modified	Tax years beginning after Dec. 31, 2017, and before Jan. 1, 2026	502	5015
6334(g)(1)(B)	11002(d)(1)(II)	Chained CPI-U (C-CPI-U) replaces CPI-U in inflation adjustments of various tax parameters under the Code	Tax years beginning after Dec. 31, 2017	202	5002
6343(b)	11071(a)	Extension of time limit for contesting IRS levy and for third party suits challenging levies	Levies made after Dec. 22, 2017 and certain levies made before Dec. 23, 2017	3002	5027
6425(c)(1)(A)	14401(d)(3)	Base erosion minimum tax added on payments to foreign related parties.	Base erosion payments paid or accrued in tax years beginning after Dec. 31, 2017	2201	5124
6431	13404(b)	New tax-credit and direct-pay bonds may not be issued	Bonds issued after Dec. 31, 2017	1702	5061
6501(m)	13403(d)(2)	Employers are allowed a credit for paid family and medical leave	Wages paid in tax years beginning after Dec. 31, 2017 and before Jan. 1, 2020	1013	5060

Code §	Act §	Topic	Effective Date	Analy-sis ¶	Com Rep ¶
6532(c)(1)	11071(b)	Extension of time limit for contesting IRS levy and for third party suits challenging levies	Levies made after Dec. 22, 2017 and certain levies made before Dec. 23, 2017	3002	5027
6601(j)(3)(B)	11002(d)(1)(JJ)	Chained CPI-U (C-CPI-U) replaces CPI-U in inflation adjustments of various tax parameters under the Code	Tax years beginning after Dec. 31, 2017	202	5002
6651(i)(1)	11002(d)(1)(KK)	Chained CPI-U (C-CPI-U) replaces CPI-U in inflation adjustments of various tax parameters under the Code	Tax years beginning after Dec. 31, 2017	202	5002
6652(c)(7)(A)	11002(d)(1)(LL)	Chained CPI-U (C-CPI-U) replaces CPI-U in inflation adjustments of various tax parameters under the Code	Tax years beginning after Dec. 31, 2017	202	5002
6652(p)	13603(e)	Penalty imposed for employer's failure to notify employee that stock is eligible for Code Sec. 83(i) election	Failures after Dec. 31, 2017	2608	5086
6655	14401(d)(4)	Base erosion minimum tax added on payments to foreign related parties.	Base erosion payments paid or accrued in tax years beginning after Dec. 31, 2017	2201	5124
6662(d)(1)(C)	11011(c)	20% deduction for qualified business income	Tax years beginning after Dec. 31, 2017 and before Jan. 1, 2026	702	5003
6695(g)	11001(b)	Head of household filing status added to paid preparer due diligence requirements	Tax years beginning after Dec. 31, 2017	3001	5001
6695(h)(1)	11002(d)(1)(MM)	Chained CPI-U (C-CPI-U) replaces CPI-U in inflation adjustments of various tax parameters under the Code	Tax years beginning after Dec. 31, 2017	202	5002

Code §	Act §	Topic	Effective Date	Analy-sis ¶	Com Rep ¶
6698(e)(1)	11002(d)(1)(NN)	Chained CPI-U (C-CPI-U) replaces CPI-U in inflation adjustments of various tax parameters under the Code	Tax years beginning after Dec. 31, 2017	202	5002
6699(e)(1)	11002(d)(1)(OO)	Chained CPI-U (C-CPI-U) replaces CPI-U in inflation adjustments of various tax parameters under the Code	Tax years beginning after Dec. 31, 2017	202	5002
6721(f)(1)	11002(d)(1)(PP)	Chained CPI-U (C-CPI-U) replaces CPI-U in inflation adjustments of various tax parameters under the Code	Tax years beginning after Dec. 31, 2017	202	5002
6722(f)(1)	11002(d)(1)(QQ)	Chained CPI-U (C-CPI-U) replaces CPI-U in inflation adjustments of various tax parameters under the Code	Tax years beginning after Dec. 31, 2017	202	5002
6724(d)	13520(c)(1)	Tax reporting requirements added for policy sales and death benefits paid under life insurance contracts	Reportable policy sales and reportable death benefits paid after Dec. 31, 2017	1506	5075
7345(f)(2)	11002(d)(1)(RR)	Chained CPI-U (C-CPI-U) replaces CPI-U in inflation adjustments of various tax parameters under the Code	Tax years beginning after Dec. 31, 2017	202	5002
7430(c)(1)	11002(d)(1)(SS)	Chained CPI-U (C-CPI-U) replaces CPI-U in inflation adjustments of various tax parameters under the Code	Tax years beginning after Dec. 31, 2017	202	5002
7508	11026(a)(8)	Special "combat zone" benefits extended retroactively to members of the armed forces performing services in the Sinai Peninsula of Egypt	June 9, 2015	605	5010

Code §	Act §	Topic	Effective Date	Analy-sis ¶	Com Rep ¶
7701(b)(5)(A)(iv)	13304(a)(2)(F)	Business deduction is denied for entertainment expenses	Amounts incurred or paid after Dec. 31, 2017	1005	5047
7702	13517(a)(4)	Rules on computation of life insurance tax reserves amended	Tax years beginning after Dec. 31, 2017	2406	5072
7872(g)(5)	11002(d)(14)	Chained CPI-U (C-CPI-U) replaces CPI-U in inflation adjustments of various tax parameters under the Code	Tax years beginning after Dec. 31, 2017	202	5002
9831(d)(2)(D)(ii)(II)	11002(d)(1)(TT)	Chained CPI-U (C-CPI-U) replaces CPI-U in inflation adjustments of various tax parameters under the Code	Tax years beginning after Dec. 31, 2017	202	5002
None	13514(d)	Tax on distributions to stock life insurance company shareholders from a pre-1984 policyholders' surplus account is repealed; phased inclusion of remaining balance of policyholders' surplus account is provided	Tax years beginning after Dec. 31, 2017	2407	5069
None	13402(c)	Credit for qualified rehabilitation expenditures is limited to certified historic structures and has to be taken ratably over 5 years	Amounts paid or incurred after Dec. 31, 2017	1014	5059
None	13221(d)	Accrual basis taxpayers may defer inclusion of advance payments in income to the end of year after year of receipt if so deferred for financial reporting	Tax years beginning after Dec. 31, 2017	1407	5043
None	13221(d)	Income inclusion for tax purposes can't be later than when included for certain financial reporting purposes	Tax years beginning after Dec. 31, 2017	1406	5043

Code §	Act §	Topic	Effective Date	Analy-sis ¶	Com Rep ¶
None	13221(e)	Income inclusion for tax purposes can't be later than when included for certain financial reporting purposes	Tax years beginning after Dec. 31, 2017	1406	5043
None	11028(a)	Favorable tax treatment provided for qualified 2016 disaster area plan distributions	Dec. 22, 2017, for distributions made on or after Jan. 1, 2016, and before Jan. 1, 2018	1804	5012
None	11028(b)(1)(B)	Favorable tax treatment provided for qualified 2016 disaster area plan distributions	Dec. 22, 2017, for distributions made on or after Jan. 1, 2016, and before Jan. 1, 2018	1804	5012
None	11028(b)(1)(C)	Recontributions of qualified 2016 disaster distributions and continued deferral of tax on amounts previously distributed permitted	Dec. 22, 2017	1807	5012
None	11028(b)(1)(D)	Favorable tax treatment provided for qualified 2016 disaster area plan distributions	Dec. 22, 2017, for distributions made on or after Jan. 1, 2016, and before Jan. 1, 2018	1804	5012
None	11028(b)(1)(E)	Qualified 2016 disaster distributions to be included in gross income ratably over three years	Dec. 22, 2017, for distributions made on or after Jan. 1, 2016, and before Jan. 1, 2018	1805	5012
None	11028(b)(2)	Period of time is provided, during which qualified retirement plans and IRAs can provide 2016 disaster relief before adopting retroactive 2016 disaster relief amendments	From Dec. 22, 2017 to last day of 2018 plan year	1808	5012
None	13001(d)	Normalization requirements for public utilities	Tax years beginning after Dec. 31, 2017	1309	5032

¶ 6002. Code Sections Amended by Act

Code §	Act §	Code §	Act §
1(f)(2)(A)	11002(c)(1)	54A	13404(a)
1(f)(3)	11002(a)	54AA	13404(a)
1(f)(6)	11002(b)	54B	13404(a)
1(f)(7)	11002(b)	54C	13404(a)
1(h)(11)(C)(iii)	14223(a)(1)	54D	13404(a)
1(h)(11)(C)(iii)	14223(a)(2)	54E	13404(a)
1(h)(11)(C)(iii)(II)	14223(a)(3)	54F	13404(a)
1(i)(1)(C)	11002(c)(2)(A)	54(l)(3)(B)	13404(c)(2)
1(i)(3)(C)	11002(c)(2)(B)	54	13404(a)
11(b)	13001(a)	55(a)	12001(a)
11(d)	12001(b)(11)	55(b)(1)	12001(b)(3)(A)
12(7)	12001(b)(12)	55(b)(3)	12001(b)(3)(B)
12(6)	13001(b)(2)(B)	55(c)(1)	12001(b)(4)
12(5)	13001(b)(2)(B)	55(d)(2)	12001(b)(5)(A)
12(4)	13001(b)(2)(B)	55(d)(2)(B)	12001(b)(5)(B)
23(h)(2)	11002(d)(1)(A)	55(d)(2)(C)	12001(b)(5)(B)
24(h)	11022(a)	55(d)(2)(D)	12001(b)(5)(B)
25A(h)(1)(A)(ii)	11002(d)(1)(B)	55(d)(3)	12001(b)(5)(A)
25B(b)(3)(B)	11002(d)(1)(C)	55(d)(3)(B)(i)	12001(b)(5)(C)(i)
25B(d)(1)(B)(ii)	11024(b)	55(d)(3)(B)(iii)	12001(b)(5)(C)(ii)
25B(d)(1)(C)	11024(b)	55(d)(4)	12001(b)(5)(A)
25B(d)(1)(D)	11024(b)	55(d)(4)	12003(a)
26(b)(2)(B)	14401(c)	55(d)(4)(A)(ii)	11002(d)(1)(I)
32(b)(2)(B)(ii)(II)	11002(d)(1)(D)	55(e)	12001(b)(6)
32(j)(1)(B)(i)	11002(d)(1)(D)	56(b)(1)(B)	11027(b)
32(j)(1)(B)(ii)	11002(d)(1)(D)	56(b)(2)(C)	12001(b)(7)
36B(f)(2)(B)(ii)(II)	11002(d)(1)(E)	56(b)(2)(D)	12001(b)(7)
38(b)(35)	13403(b)	56(c)	12001(b)(8)(A)
38(b)(36)	13403(b)	56(g)	12001(b)(8)(A)
38(b)(37)	13403(b)	58(a)(3)	12001(b)(9)
38(c)(4)(B)(ix)	13403(c)	58(a)(4)	12001(b)(9)
38(c)(4)(B)(x)	13403(c)	59A	14401(a)
38(c)(4)(B)(xi)	13403(c)	59(a)(1)(C)	12001(b)(3)(C)(i)
38(c)(4)(B)(xii)	13403(c)	59(a)(2)	12001(b)(3)(C)(ii)
38(c)(6)(E)	12001(b)(1)	59(b)	12001(b)(10)
41(d)(1)(A)	13206(d)(1)	59(f)	12001(b)(10)
41(e)(5)(C)(i)	11002(d)(1)(F)	59(j)(2)(B)	11002(d)(4)
41(e)(5)(C)(ii)	11002(d)(2)(A)	61(a)(10)	11051(b)(1)(A)
41(e)(5)(C)(ii)	11002(d)(2)(B)	61(a)(11)	11051(b)(1)(A)
42(e)(3)(D)(ii)	11002(d)(1)(G)	61(a)(12)	11051(b)(1)(A)
42(h)(3)(H)(i)(II)	11002(d)(1)(G)	61(a)(13)	11051(b)(1)(A)
42(h)(6)(G)(i)(II)	11002(d)(3)(A)	61(a)(14)	11051(b)(1)(A)
42(h)(6)(G)(ii)	11002(d)(3)(B)	61(a)(15)	11051(b)(1)(A)
45C(a)	13401(a)	61(a)(8)	11051(b)(1)(A)
45R(d)(3)(B)(ii)	11002(d)(1)(H)	61(a)(9)	11051(b)(1)(A)
45S	13403(a)(1) [sic]	62(a)	11011(b)(1)
47(a)	13402(a)	62(a)(10)	11051(b)(2)(A)
47(c)(1)(A)(iii)	13402(b)(1)(A)(i)	62(d)(3)(B)	11002(d)(1)(J)
47(c)(1)(B)	13402(b)(1)(A)(iii)	63(b)(1)	11011(b)(2)
47(c)(1)(B)	13402(b)(1)(A)(ii)	63(b)(2)	11011(b)(2)
47(c)(1)(C)	13402(b)(1)(A)(iii)	63(b)(3)	11011(b)(2)
47(c)(1)(D)	13402(b)(1)(A)(iii)	63(c)(4)(B)	11002(d)(1)(K)
47(c)(2)(B)(iv)	13402(b)(1)(B)	63(c)(7)	11021(a)
48(b)(3)	13102(a)(2)	63(d)(1)	11011(b)(3)
53(d)(2)	12001(b)(2)	63(d)(2)	11011(b)(3)
53(d)(3)	12002(b)	63(d)(3)	11011(b)(3)
53(e)	12002(a)	67(g)	11045(a)

Code §	Act §	Code §	Act §
68(b)(2)(B)	11002(d)(2)(A)	162(f)	13306(a)(1)
68(b)(2)(B)	11002(d)(2)(B)	162(m)(2)	13601(c)(1)
68(f)	11046(a)	162(m)(3)	13601(c)(2)
71	11051(b)(1)(B)	162(m)(3)(A)	13601(b)(1)
74(d)(2)(B)	13305(b)(1)	162(m)(3)(A)	13601(b)(3)
78	14301(c)(1)	162(m)(3)(B)	13601(b)(2)(A)
83(i)	13603(a)	162(m)(3)(B)	13601(b)(2)(B)
86(b)(2)(A)	13305(b)(1)	162(m)(3)(B)	13601(b)(3)
91	14102(d)(1)	162(m)(3)(C)	13601(b)(3)
101(a)(1)	13522(b)	162(m)(4)(B)	13601(a)(1)
101(a)(3)	13522(a)	162(m)(4)(C)	13601(a)(1)
108(f)(5)	11031(a)	162(m)(4)(D)	13601(a)(1)
118(b)	13312(a)(1)	162(m)(4)(E)	13601(a)(1)
118(b)	13312(a)(3)	162(m)(4)(F)	13601(a)(1)
118(c)	13312(a)(1)	162(m)(4)(F)	13601(d)
118(c)	13312(a)(3)	162(m)(4)(G)	13601(a)(1)
118(d)	13312(a)(2)	162(m)(5)(E)	13601(a)(2)(A)
118(d)	13312(a)(1)	162(m)(5)(G)	13601(a)(2)(B)
118(e)	13312(a)(2)	162(m)(6)(D)	13601(a)(2)(A)
121(d)(3)(B)	11051(b)(3)(A)(i)	162(m)(6)(G)	13601(a)(2)(B)
121(d)(3)(C)	11051(b)(3)(A)(ii)	162(o)(3)	11002(d)(6)
125(i)(2)(B)	11002(d)(1)(L)	162(q)	13307(a)
132(f)(6)(A)(ii)	11002(d)(5)	162(r)	13307(a)
132(f)(8)	11047(a)	162(r)	13531(a)
132(g)	11048(a)(1)	162(s)	13531(a)
132(g)(2)	11048(a)(2)	163(h)(3)(F)	11043(a)
135(b)(2)(B)(ii)	11002(d)(1)(M)	163(j)	13301(a)
135(c)(4)(A)	13305(b)(1)	164(b)(6)	11042(a)
137(b)(3)(A)	13305(b)(1)	165(d)	11050(a)
137(f)(2)	11002(d)(1)(N)	165(h)(5)	11044(a)
139G	13821(a)(1)	168(b)(2)(B)	13203(b)
139G(a)	13821(a)	168(b)(2)(C)	13203(b)
145(d)(4)	13402(b)(2)(A)	168(b)(2)(D)	13203(b)
145(d)(4)	13402(b)(2)(B)	168(b)(3)(G)	13204(a)(2)(A)
146(d)(2)(B)	11002(d)(1)(O)	168(b)(3)(G)	13204(a)(2)(B)
147(c)(2)(H)(ii)	11002(d)(1)(P)	168(b)(3)(H)	13204(a)(2)(A)
148(f)(4)(C)(xiv)	13532(b)(2)	168(b)(3)(I)	13204(a)(2)(A)
148(f)(4)(C)(xv)	13532(b)(2)	168(e)(3)(B)(vii)	13203(a)
148(f)(4)(C)(xvi)	13532(b)(2)	168(e)(3)(E)(iv)	13204(a)(1)(A)(iv)
148(f)(4)(C)(xvii)	13532(b)(2)	168(e)(3)(E)(iv)	13204(a)(1)(A)(i)
149(d)(1)	13532(a)	168(e)(3)(E)(ix)	13204(a)(1)(A)(i)
149(d)(2)	13532(b)(1)	168(e)(3)(E)(v)	13204(a)(1)(A)(i)
149(d)(3)	13532(b)(1)	168(e)(3)(E)(v)	13204(a)(1)(A)(iv)
149(d)(4)	13532(b)(1)	168(e)(3)(E)(vi)	13204(a)(1)(A)(iv)
149(d)(5)	13532(b)(1)	168(e)(3)(E)(vii)	13204(a)(1)(A)(ii)
149(d)(6)	13532(b)(1)	168(e)(3)(E)(vii)	13204(a)(1)(A)(iv)
149(d)(7)	13532(b)(1)	168(e)(3)(E)(viii)	13204(a)(1)(A)(iii)
151(d)(4)	11041(a)(1)	168(e)(3)(E)(viii)	13204(a)(1)(A)(iv)
151(d)(4)(B)	11002(d)(1)(Q)	168(e)(6)	13204(a)(1)(B)
151(d)(5)	11041(a)(2)	168(e)(6)	13204(a)(4)(B)(i)
152(d)(5)	11051(b)(3)(B)	168(e)(7)	13204(a)(1)(B)
162(a)	13311(a)	168(e)(8)	13204(a)(1)(B)
162(e)(2)	13308(a)	168(g)(1)(D)	13204(a)(3)(A)(i)(I)
162(e)(3)	13308(a)	168(g)(1)(E)	13204(a)(3)(A)(i)(II)
162(e)(4)	13308(a)	168(g)(1)(E)	13205(a)
162(e)(5)	13308(a)	168(g)(1)(F)	13205(a)
162(e)(6)	13308(a)	168(g)(1)(F)	13204(a)(3)(A)(i)(III)
162(e)(7)	13308(a)	168(g)(1)(G)	13205(a)
162(e)(8)	13308(a)	168(g)(8)	13204(a)(3)(A)(ii)

Code §	Act §	Code §	Act §
168(i)(7)(B)	13504(b)(1)	172(f)	13302(c)(2)(A)
168(k)	13201(b)(2)(B)	172(f)	13302(c)(2)(A)
168(k)(1)	13201(e)	172(f)	13302(d)(2)
168(k)(1)(A)	13201(a)(1)(A)	172(g)	13302(c)(2)(A)
168(k)(2)(A)(i)(II)	13201(g)(1)(A)	172(g)	13302(d)(2)
168(k)(2)(A)(i)(II)	13204(a)(4)(A)(i)	172(h)	13302(c)(2)(A)
168(k)(2)(A)(i)(III)	13201(g)(1)(B)	172(i)	13302(c)(2)(A)
168(k)(2)(A)(i)(III)	13204(a)(4)(A)(ii)	174	13206(a)
168(k)(2)(A)(i)(IV)	13201(g)(1)(C)	179(b)(1)	13101(a)(1)
168(k)(2)(A)(i)(IV)	13204(a)(4)(A)(iii)	179(b)(2)	13101(a)(2)
168(k)(2)(A)(i)(V)	13201(g)(1)(C)	179(b)(6)(A)	13101(a)(3)(A)(i)
168(k)(2)(A)(ii)	13201(c)(1)	179(b)(6)(A)	13101(a)(3)(B)(i)
168(k)(2)(A)(iii)	13201(b)(1)(A)(i)	179(b)(6)(A)(ii)	11002(d)(1)(R)
168(k)(2)(B)(i)(II)	13201(b)(1)(A)(ii)(I)	179(b)(6)(A)(ii)	13101(a)(3)(A)(ii)
168(k)(2)(B)(i)(III)	13201(b)(1)(A)(i)	179(b)(6)(B)	13101(a)(3)(B)(ii)
168(k)(2)(B)(ii)	13201(b)(1)(A)(i)	179(d)(1)	13101(c)
168(k)(2)(B)(ii)	13201(b)(1)(A)(ii)(II)	179(d)(1)(B)	13101(b)(1)
168(k)(2)(E)(i)	13201(b)(1)(A)(i)	179(f)	13101(b)(2)
168(k)(2)(E)(ii)	13201(c)(2)	199A	11011(a)
168(k)(2)(E)(iii)(I)	13201(c)(3)	199	13305(a)
168(k)(2)(F)(iii)	13201(f)	213(d)(10)(B)(ii)	11002(d)(7)
168(k)(2)(H)	13201(g)(2)	213(f)	11027(a)
168(k)(3)	13204(a)(4)(B)(ii)	215	11051(a)
168(k)(4)	12001(b)(13)	217(k)	11049(a)
168(k)(5)(A)	13201(b)(1)(B)	219(b)(5)(C)(i)(II)	11002(d)(1)(S)
168(k)(5)(A)(i)	13201(a)(1)(B)	219(f)(1)	11051(b)(3)(C)
168(k)(5)(F)	13201(a)(3)(A)	219(g)(3)(A)(ii)	13305(b)(1)
168(k)(6)	13201(a)(2)	219(g)(8)(B)	11002(d)(1)(S)
168(k)(8)	13201(a)(3)(B)	220(f)(7)	11051(b)(3)(D)
168(k)(9)	13201(d)	220(g)(2)	11002(d)(1)(T)
170(b)(1)(G)	11023(a)	221(b)(2)(C)	13305(b)(1)
170(b)(1)(H)	11023(a)	221(f)(1)(B)	11002(d)(1)(U)
170(b)(2)(D)(iv)	11011(d)(5)	222(b)(2)(C)	13305(b)(1)
170(b)(2)(D)(iv)	13305(b)(2)	223(f)(7)	11051(b)(3)(E)
170(b)(2)(D)(v)	11011(d)(5)	223(g)(1)(B)	11002(d)(1)(V)
170(b)(2)(D)(v)	13305(b)(2)	243(a)(1)	13002(a)(1)
170(b)(2)(D)(vi)	13305(b)(2)	243(c)	13002(a)(3)
170(b)(2)(D)(vi)	11011(d)(5)	243(c)(1)	13002(a)(2)(A)
170(f)(8)(D)	13705(a)	243(c)(1)	13002(a)(2)(B)
170(f)(8)(E)	13705(a)	245A	14101(a)
170(l)(1)	13704(a)(1)	245(a)(10)(C)	14301(c)(3)
170(l)(2)(B)	13704(a)(2)	245(a)(4)	14301(c)(2)
172(a)	13302(a)(1)	245(c)(1)(B)	13002(b)(1)
172(b)(1)(A)(i)	13302(b)(1)(A)	245(c)(1)(B)	13002(b)(2)
172(b)(1)(A)(ii)	13302(b)(1)(B)	246A(a)(1)	13002(d)(1)
172(b)(1)(B)	13302(b)(2)	246A(a)(1)	13002(d)(2)
172(b)(1)(B)	13302(c)(1)	246(a)(1)	14101(c)(1)
172(b)(1)(C)	13302(b)(2)	246(b)(1)	11011(d)(2)
172(b)(1)(C)	13302(d)(1)	246(b)(1)	13305(b)(1)
172(b)(1)(D)	13302(b)(2)	246(b)(1)	14202(b)(2)(A)
172(b)(1)(E)	13302(b)(2)	246(b)(1)	14202(b)(2)(B)
172(b)(1)(F)	13302(b)(2)	246(b)(3)(A)	13002(c)(1)
172(b)(2)	13302(a)(2)	246(b)(3)(B)	13002(c)(2)
172(d)(6)(A)	13302(a)(3)	246(c)(1)	14101(b)(1)
172(d)(6)(B)	13302(a)(3)	246(c)(5)	14101(b)(2)
172(d)(6)(C)	13302(a)(3)	247	13821(b)(1)
172(d)(7)	13305(b)(3)	247(a)	13821(b)
172(d)(8)	11011(d)(1)	250	14202(a)
172(d)(9)	14202(b)(1)	263A(b)(2)	13102(b)(2)

Code §	Act §	Code §	Act §
263A(d)(2)(C)	13207(a)	280F(a)(1)(A)(iv)	13202(a)(1)(D)
263A(f)(4)	13801(a)(1)	280F(a)(1)(B)(ii)	13202(a)(2)(A)
263A(f)(4)	13801(a)(2)	280F(d)(4)(A)(iii)	13202(b)(1)(A)
263A(f)(5)	13801(a)(1)	280F(d)(4)(A)(iv)	13202(b)(1)(C)
263A(f)(5)(B)(ii)	13801(b)	280F(d)(4)(A)(iv)	13202(b)(1)(B)
263A(i)	13102(b)(1)	280F(d)(4)(A)(v)	13202(b)(1)(C)
263A(j)	13102(b)(1)	280F(d)(4)(B)	13202(b)(2)
267A	14222(a)	280F(d)(4)(C)	13202(b)(2)
274(a)	13304(c)(1)(A)	280F(d)(7)(A)	13202(a)(2)(B)(i)
274(a)(1)	13304(a)(1)(B)	280F(d)(7)(B)	11002(d)(8)
274(a)(1)(A)	13304(a)(1)(A)	280F(d)(7)(B)(i)(II)	13202(a)(2)(B)(ii)
274(a)(2)(C)	13304(a)(1)(C)	367(a)(3)	14102(e)(1)
274(a)(4)	13304(c)(1)(B)	367(a)(3)	14102(e)(1)
274(d)	13304(a)(2)(A)(ii)(I)	367(a)(4)	14102(e)(1)
274(d)	13304(a)(2)(A)(ii)(II)	367(a)(4)	14102(e)(2)(A)
274(d)(2)	13304(a)(2)(A)(i)	367(a)(4)	14102(e)(2)(B)
274(d)(3)	13304(a)(2)(A)(i)	367(a)(5)	14102(e)(1)
274(d)(4)	13304(a)(2)(A)(i)	367(a)(6)	14102(e)(1)
274(j)(3)(A)	13310(a)(1)	367(d)(2)(D)	14221(b)(1)
274(j)(3)(A)(i)	13310(a)(2)	381(c)(20)	13301(b)(1)
274(j)(3)(A)(i)(I)	13310(a)(2)	381(d)	13511(b)(3)
274(j)(3)(A)(i)(II)	13310(a)(2)	382(d)(3)	13301(b)(2)
274(j)(3)(A)(i)(III)	13310(a)(2)	382(k)(1)	13301(b)(3)
274(j)(3)(A)(ii)	13310(a)(2)	382(l)(3)(B)(iii)	11051(b)(3)(F)
274(j)(3)(A)(ii)	13310(a)(3)	402(c)(3)	13613(b)(1)
274(j)(3)(A)(iii)	13310(a)(2)	402(c)(3)(A)	13613(b)(2)
274(l)	13304(a)(2)(B)	402(c)(3)(C)	13613(a)
274(l)	13304(c)(2)	408A(c)(3)(D)(ii)	11002(d)(1)(W)
274(n)	13304(a)(2)(C)	408A(d)(6)(B)(iii)	13611(a)
274(n)(1)	13304(a)(2)(D)	408(d)(6)	11051(b)(3)(G)
274(n)(2)	13304(a)(2)(E)(iii)	409A(d)(7)	13603(c)(2)
274(n)(2)	13304(a)(2)(E)(iv)	422(b)	13603(c)(1)(A)
274(n)(2)	13304(b)(3)	423(b)(5)	13603(c)(1)(B)(i)
274(n)(2)	13304(b)(4)	423(d)	13603(c)(1)(B)(ii)
274(n)(2)(B)	13304(a)(2)(E)(i)	430(c)(7)(D)(vii)(II)	11002(d)(1)(X)
274(n)(2)(B)	13304(b)(2)	447(c)	13102(a)(5)(A)(i)
274(n)(2)(B)	13304(b)(1)	447(c)(2)	13102(a)(5)(A)(ii)
274(n)(2)(C)	13304(a)(2)(E)(ii)	447(d)	13102(a)(5)(C)(ii)
274(n)(2)(C)	13304(b)(2)	447(d)	13102(a)(5)(C)(i)
274(n)(2)(C)	13304(a)(2)(E)(ii)	447(e)	13102(a)(5)(C)(i)
274(n)(2)(D)	13304(a)(2)(E)(ii)	447(e)	13102(a)(5)(C)(ii)
274(n)(2)(D)	13304(b)(2)	447(f)	13102(a)(5)(B)
274(n)(2)(E)	13304(a)(2)(E)(ii)	447(f)	13102(a)(5)(C)(ii)
274(o)	13304(d)(1)	447(g)	13102(a)(5)(C)(ii)
274(o)	13304(d)(2)	447(h)	13102(a)(5)(C)(i)
274(p)	13304(d)(1)	447(i)	13102(a)(5)(C)(i)
280C(a)	13403(d)(1)	448(c)	13102(a)(1)
280C(b)(3)	13401(b)	448(c)(4)	13102(a)(3)
280C(b)(4)	13401(b)	448(d)(7)	13102(a)(4)
280C(c)(1)	13206(d)(2)(A)	451(b)	13221(a)
280C(c)(2)	13206(d)(2)(C)	451(c)	13221(a)
280C(c)(2)	13206(d)(2)(B)	451(c)	13221(b)
280C(c)(2)	13206(d)(2)(D)	451(d)	13221(a)
280C(c)(3)	13206(d)(2)(C)	451(d)	13221(b)
280C(c)(3)(B)(ii)(II)	13001(b)(1)(A)	451(e)	13221(a)
280C(c)(4)	13206(d)(2)(C)	451(e)	13221(b)
280F(a)(1)(A)(i)	13202(a)(1)(A)	451(f)	13221(a)
280F(a)(1)(A)(ii)	13202(a)(1)(B)	451(f)	13221(b)
280F(a)(1)(A)(iii)	13202(a)(1)(C)	451(g)	13221(a)

Code §	Act §	Code §	Act §
451(g)	13221(b)	641(c)(2)(E)	13542(a)
451(h)	13221(a)	642(b)(2)(C)(iii)	11041(b)
451(h)	13221(b)	682	11051(b)(1)(C)
451(i)	13221(a)	691(c)(4)	13001(b)(2)(F)
451(i)	13221(b)	704(d)	13503(a)(1)
451(j)	13221(b)	704(d)	13503(a)(2)
451(k)	13221(b)	704(d)(3)	13503(a)(3)
453A(c)(3)	13001(b)(2)(C)	708(b)(1)	13504(a)(1)
453B(e)(2)(B)	13512(b)(1)	708(b)(1)(A)	13504(a)(1)
453B(e)(3)	13512(b)(1)(B)	743(d)(1)	13502(a)
457(e)(11)(B)(ii)	13612(a)	743(e)(4)	13504(b)(2)
457(e)(11)(B)(iii)	13612(b)	743(e)(5)	13504(b)(2)
457(e)(11)(B)(iv)	13612(c)	743(e)(6)	13504(b)(2)
460(c)(6)(B)(ii)	13201(b)(2)(A)	743(e)(7)	13504(b)(2)
460(e)(1)(B)	13102(d)(1)(A)	801(a)	13001(b)(2)(G)(ii)
460(e)(1)(B)(ii)	13102(d)(1)(B)	801(a)(2)	13001(b)(2)(G)(i)
460(e)(2)	13102(d)(2)	801(a)(2)(C)	13512(b)(3)
460(e)(3)	13102(d)(2)	801(c)	13514(b)
460(e)(4)	13102(d)(2)	804	13512(b)(4)
460(e)(5)	13102(d)(2)	805(a)(4)(B)(i)	13512(b)(5)
460(e)(6)	13102(d)(2)	805(a)(4)(B)(ii)	13511(b)(4)
461(l)	11012(a)	805(a)(4)(B)(ii)	13512(b)(5)
465(c)(7)(D)(v)(II)	13512(b)(2)	805(a)(4)(B)(iii)	13512(b)(5)
469(i)(3)(F)(iii)	13305(b)(1)	805(a)(4)(B)(iv)	13512(b)(5)
469(i)(3)(F)(iii)	14202(b)(3)	805(a)(5)	13511(b)(5)
471(c)	13102(c)	805(b)(2)(A)(iii)	13512(b)(6)
471(d)	13102(c)	805(b)(2)(A)(iii)	13512(b)(6)
481(d)	13543(a)	805(b)(2)(A)(iv)	13511(b)(6)
482	14221(b)(2)	805(b)(2)(A)(iv)	13512(b)(6)
512(a)(6)	13702(a)	805(b)(2)(A)(v)	13512(b)(6)
512(a)(7)	13703(a)	805(b)(4)	13511(a)
512(d)(2)(B)	11002(d)(1)(Y)	805(b)(5)	13511(a)
513(h)(2)(C)(ii)	11002(d)(1)(Z)	806	13512(a)
527(b)	13001(b)(2)(D)(ii)	807(c)	13517(a)(1)
527(b)(2)	13001(b)(2)(D)(i)	807(d)(1)	13517(a)(2)(C)
529A(b)(2)	11024(a)(2)	807(d)(1)	13517(a)(2)(A)
529A(b)(2)(B)	11024(a)(1)	807(d)(2)	13517(a)(2)(A)
529A(b)(7)	11024(a)(3)	807(d)(2)	13517(a)(2)(C)
529(c)(3)(C)(i)	11025(a)	807(d)(3)(A)(iii)	13517(a)(2)(D)
529(c)(3)(C)(i)(I)	11025(a)	807(d)(3)(A)(iv)(I)	13517(a)(2)(E)
529(c)(3)(C)(i)(II)	11025(a)	807(d)(3)(A)(iv)(II)	13517(a)(2)(F)
529(c)(3)(C)(i)(III)	11025(a)	807(d)(3)(B)(i)	13517(a)(2)(G)
529(c)(7)	11032(a)(1)	807(d)(3)(B)(ii)	13517(a)(2)(H)
529(e)(3)(A)	11032(a)(2)	807(d)(4)	13517(a)(2)(B)
535(b)(1)	14301(c)(4)	807(d)(4)	13517(a)(2)(A)
535(c)(5)	13001(b)(5)(B)	807(d)(5)	13517(a)(2)(A)
537(b)(4)	13302(c)(2)(B)	807(d)(6)	13517(a)(2)(B)
545(b)(1)	14301(c)(4)	807(e)(2)	13517(a)(3)(B)
594(a)	13001(b)(2)(E)	807(e)(2)	13517(a)(3)(A)
613A(d)(1)(B)	13305(b)(5)	807(e)(2)	13517(a)(3)(C)
613A(d)(1)(C)	13305(b)(5)	807(e)(3)	13517(a)(3)(B)
613A(d)(1)(C)	11011(d)(4)	807(e)(4)	13517(a)(3)(B)
613A(d)(1)(D)	11011(d)(4)	807(e)(5)	13517(a)(3)(B)
613A(d)(1)(E)	11011(d)(4)	807(e)(5)	13517(a)(3)(A)
613A(d)(1)(E)	13305(b)(5)	807(e)(6)	13517(a)(3)(B)
613A(d)(1)(F)	11011(d)(4)	807(e)(6)	13517(a)(3)(D)
613A(d)(1)(F)	13305(b)(5)	807(e)(7)	13517(a)(3)(B)
613(a)	11011(d)(3)	807(f)(1)	13513(a)
613(a)	13305(b)(4)	808(g)	13517(b)(1)

Code §	Act §	Code §	Act §
810	13511(b)(1)	861(a)(2)(B)	13002(e)(1)
811(d)(1)	13517(b)(2)	863(b)	14303(a)
812	13518(a)	864(c)(1)(A)	13401(a)(2)(A)
814(f)(1)	14301(c)(5)(B)	864(c)(1)(A)	13501(a)(2)(A)
814(f)(1)(B)	14301(c)(5)(A)	864(c)(1)(B)	13401(a)(2)(B)
815	13514(a)	864(c)(1)(B)	13501(a)(2)(B)
817A(e)(2)	13518(b)	864(c)(8)	13401(a)(1)
831(b)(2)(D)(ii)	11002(d)(1)(AA)	864(c)(8)	13501(a)(1)
831(b)(3)	13511(b)(2)(B)	864(e)(2)	14502(a)
831(e)(1)	13001(b)(2)(H)	865(h)(1)(B)	14301(c)(6)
831(e)(2)	13001(b)(2)(H)	877A(a)(3)(B)(i)(II)	11002(d)(1)(BB)
831(e)(3)	13001(b)(2)(H)	882(a)(1)	12001(b)(14)
832(b)(5)(B)	13515(a)	882(a)(1)	13001(b)(2)(L)
832(b)(5)(B)	13515(a)(1)	882(a)(1)	14401(d)(2)
832(b)(5)(B)	13515(a)(2)	897(a)(2)(A)	12001(b)(3)(D)
832(c)(5)	13001(b)(2)(I)	901(a)	14301(c)(7)
834(b)(1)(D)	13001(b)(2)(I)	901(e)(2)	14301(c)(8)
842(c)(1)	13512(b)(7)	901(f)	14301(c)(9)
842(c)(2)	13512(b)(7)	901(j)(1)(A)	14301(c)(10)
842(c)(3)	13512(b)(7)	901(j)(1)(B)	14301(c)(11)
844	13511(b)(2)(A)	901(k)(2)	14301(c)(12)
846(c)(2)	13523(a)	901(k)(6)	14301(c)(13)
846(d)(3)(B)	13523(b)	901(m)(1)(B)	14301(c)(14)
846(d)(3)(C)	13523(b)	902	14301(a)
846(d)(3)(D)	13523(b)	904(b)(2)(C)	13001(b)(2)(M)(i)
846(d)(3)(E)	13523(b)	904(b)(3)(D)	13001(b)(2)(M)(ii)
846(d)(3)(F)	13523(b)	904(b)(3)(E)	13001(b)(2)(M)(iii)
846(d)(3)(G)	13523(b)	904(b)(5)	14101(d)
846(e)	13523(c)	904(c)	14201(b)(2)(C)
846(f)	13523(c)	904(d)(1)(A)	14201(b)(2)(A)
846(f)(6)(A)	13517(b)(3)	904(d)(1)(B)	14201(b)(2)(A)
846(g)	13523(c)	904(d)(1)(B)	14302(a)
847	13516(a)	904(d)(1)(C)	14201(b)(2)(A)
847(9)	12001(b)(8)(B)	904(d)(1)(C)	14302(a)
848(a)(2)	13519(a)(1)	904(d)(1)(D)	14302(a)
848(b)(1)	13519(b)	904(d)(2)(A)(ii)	14201(b)(2)(B)
848(c)(1)	13519(a)(2)	904(d)(2)(A)(ii)	14302(b)(2)
848(c)(2)	13519(a)(3)	904(d)(2)(E)(i)	14301(c)(15)(A)
848(c)(3)	13519(a)(4)	904(d)(2)(E)(ii)	14301(c)(15)(B)
848(e)(1)(B)(iii)	13517(b)(4)	904(d)(2)(J)	14302(b)(1)
848(i)	12001(b)(8)(C)	904(d)(4)	14301(c)(16)(A)
851(b)	14212(b)(1)(B)	904(d)(4)	14301(c)(16)(B)
852(b)(1)	13001(b)(4)	904(d)(6)(A)	14301(c)(17)
852(b)(3)(A)	13001(b)(2)(J)	904(g)(5)	14304(a)
857(b)(3)(A)	13001(b)(2)(K)(i)	904(h)(10)(A)	14301(c)(18)
857(b)(3)(B)	13001(b)(2)(K)(i)	904(k)	14301(c)(19)
857(b)(3)(C)	13001(b)(2)(K)(i)	905(c)(1)	14301(c)(20)
857(b)(3)(C)(i)	13001(b)(2)(K)(ii)(I)	905(c)(2)(B)(i)	14301(c)(21)
857(b)(3)(C)(ii)	13001(b)(2)(K)(ii)(II)	906(a)	14301(c)(22)
857(b)(3)(C)(iv)	13001(b)(2)(K)(ii)(II)	906(b)(4)	14301(c)(23)
857(b)(3)(D)	13001(b)(2)(K)(i)	906(b)(5)	14301(c)(23)
857(b)(3)(E)	13001(b)(2)(K)(i)	907(b)(2)(B)	14301(c)(24)
857(b)(3)(E)	13001(b)(2)(K)(iii)	907(c)(3)(A)	14301(c)(25)(A)
857(b)(3)(F)	13001(b)(2)(K)(i)	907(c)(3)(B)	14301(c)(25)(B)
857(b)(3)(F)	13001(b)(2)(K)(iv)	907(c)(5)	14301(c)(26)
860E(e)(2)(B)	13001(b)(1)(B)	907(f)(2)(B)(i)	14301(c)(27)
860E(e)(6)(A)(ii)	13001(b)(1)(B)	908(a)	14301(c)(28)
861(a)(2)	13002(e)(2)(A)	909(b)	14301(c)(29)(A)
861(a)(2)	13002(e)(2)(B)	909(b)	14301(c)(29)(C)

Code §	Act §	Code §	Act §
909(b)	14301(c)(29)(D)	1016(a)(36)	13823(b)
909(b)(1)	14301(c)(29)(B)	1016(a)(37)	13823(b)
909(d)(5)	14301(c)(30)	1016(a)(38)	13823(b)
911(b)(2)(D)(ii)(II)	11002(d)(9)	1031(a)(1)	13303(a)
911(f)(1)(B)	12001(b)(3)(E)(i)(I)	1031(a)(2)	13303(b)(1)(A)
911(f)(1)(B)	12001(b)(3)(E)(i)(II)	1031(e)	13303(b)(2)
911(f)(2)(B)	12001(b)(3)(E)(ii)	1031(e)	13303(b)(3)
936(h)(3)(B)	14221(a)(3)	1031(h)	13303(b)(4)
936(h)(3)(B)(v)	14221(a)(1)	1031(i)	13303(b)(1)(B)
936(h)(3)(B)(vi)	14221(a)(2)	1031	13303(b)(5)
936(h)(3)(B)(vii)	14221(a)(2)	1044	13313(a)
951A	14201(a)	1059(b)(2)(B)	14101(c)(2)
951(a)(1)	14215(a)	1061	13309(a)(1)
951(a)(1)(A)	14212(b)(1)(A)	1061	13309(a)(2)
951(a)(3)	14212(b)(2)	1062	13309(a)(1)
951(b)	14101(e)(1)	1201	13001(b)(2)(A)
951(b)	14214(a)	1221(a)(3)	13314(a)
952(c)(1)(B)(i)	14212(b)(1)(C)	1231(b)(1)(C)	13314(b)
952(c)(1)(B)(iii)(I)	14211(b)(1)	1248(j)	14102(a)(1)
952(c)(1)(B)(iii)(II)	14211(b)(1)	1248(k)	14102(a)(1)
952(c)(1)(B)(iii)(III)	14211(b)(1)	1274A(d)(2)	11002(d)(10)
952(c)(1)(B)(iii)(IV)	14211(b)(1)	1291(g)(2)(A)	14301(c)(34)
952(c)(1)(B)(iii)(V)	14211(b)(1)	1293(f)(1)	14301(c)(35)
953(b)(1)(A)	13512(b)(8)	1293(f)(2)	14301(c)(35)
953(b)(1)(B)	13511(b)(7)	1293(f)(3)	14301(c)(35)
953(b)(1)(B)	13512(b)(8)	1297(b)(2)(B)	14501(a)
953(b)(1)(C)	13512(b)(8)	1297(f)	14501(b)
953(c)(1)(C)	14212(b)(1)(D)	1351(i)(3)	13511(b)(8)
953(d)(4)(B)(iv)(II)	14212(b)(3)	1361(c)(2)(B)(v)	13541(a)
954(a)(2)	14211(a)(1)	1371(f)	13543(b)
954(a)(3)	14211(a)(2)	1374(b)(3)(B)	12002(c)
954(a)(5)	14211(a)(3)	1374(b)(4)	13001(b)(2)(N)
954(b)(4)	14211(b)(2)(A)	1381(b)	13001(b)(2)(O)
954(b)(5)	14211(b)(2)(B)	1397E	13404(c)(1)
954(b)(6)	14211(b)(2)(C)	1400Z-1	13823(a)
954(g)	14211(b)(3)	1400Z-2	13823(a)
954(i)(5)(B)	13517(b)(5)	1445(e)(1)	13001(b)(3)(A)(i)
955	14212(a)	1445(e)(1)	13001(b)(3)(A)(ii)
957(a)	14101(e)(2)	1445(e)(2)	13001(b)(3)(B)
958(a)(1)	14301(c)(31)	1445(e)(6)	13001(b)(3)(C)(i)
958(b)	14213(a)(2)	1445(e)(6)	13001(b)(3)(C)(ii)
958(b)(4)	14213(a)(1)	1446(b)(2)(B)	13001(b)(3)(D)
959(d)	14301(c)(32)	1446(f)	13501(b)
959(e)	14301(c)(33)	1446(g)	13501(b)
960	14301(b)(1)	1551	13001(b)(5)(A)
960(b)	14301(b)(1)	1561	13001(b)(6)(A)
960(c)	14301(b)(1)	1561(a)	12001(b)(16)(B)
960(d)	14201(b)(1)	1561(a)(1)	12001(b)(16)(A)
960(e)	14301(b)(2)	1561(a)(2)	12001(b)(16)(A)
960(f)	14301(b)(2)	1561(a)(3)	12001(b)(16)(A)
961(d)	14102(b)(1)	2001(g)	11061(b)
962(a)(1)	12001(b)(15)	2010(c)(3)(B)(ii)	11002(d)(1)(CC)
964(b)	14212(b)(4)	2010(c)(3)(C)	11061(a)
964(e)(4)	14102(c)(1)	2032A(a)(3)(B)	11002(d)(1)(DD)
965	14103(a)	2503(b)(2)(B)	11002(d)(1)(EE)
970(b)	14212(b)(5)	3401(e)	11041(c)(2)(A)
1016(a)(1)	13521(a)	3401(i)	13603(b)(1)
1016(a)(23)	13313(b)(1)	3402(a)(2)	11041(c)(1)
1016(a)(23)	13313(b)(2)	3402(b)(1)	11041(c)(2)(C)

Code §	Act §	Code §	Act §
3402(b)(2)	11041(c)(2)(C)	6038(c)(1)(B)	14301(c)(36)
3402(f)	11041(c)(2)(D)	6038(c)(4)(C)	14301(c)(37)
3402(f)(1)	11041(c)(2)(B)	6039F(d)	11002(d)(13)
3402(f)(2)	11041(c)(2)(B)	6039H(e)	13821(c)(1)(B)
3402(f)(3)	11041(c)(2)(C)	6039H	13821(c)(1)(A)
3402(f)(4)	11041(c)(2)(C)	6047(g)	13520(c)(2)(A)
3402(f)(5)	11041(c)(2)(C)	6047(g)	13520(c)(2)(B)
3402(f)(7)	11041(c)(2)(C)	6047(h)	13520(c)(2)(A)
3402(g)(4)	11041(c)(2)(C)	6047(h)(4)	13520(c)(2)(C)
3402(l)(1)	11041(c)(2)(C)	6050X	13306(b)(1)
3402(l)(2)	11041(c)(2)(C)	6050Y	13520(a)
3402(m)	11041(c)(2)(E)	6051(a)(14)(B)	13603(d)
3402(m)(1)	11011(b)(4)	6051(a)(15)	13603(d)
3402(m)(1)	11051(b)(2)(B)	6051(a)(16)	13603(d)
3402(n)	11041(c)(2)(C)	6051(a)(17)	13603(d)
3402(t)	13603(b)(2)	6211(b)(4)(A)	13404(c)(3)
3405(a)(3)	11041(c)(2)(F)	6323(i)(4)(B)	11002(d)(1)(HH)
3405(a)(4)	11041(c)(2)(F)	6334(d)(4)	11041(d)
3405(a)(4)	11041(c)(2)(G)	6334(g)(1)(B)	11002(d)(1)(II)
4161(b)(2)(C)(i)(II)	11002(d)(11)	6343(b)	11071(a)
4261(e)(4)(A)(ii)	11002(d)(1)(FF)	6401(b)(1)	13404(c)(4)
4261(e)(5)	13822(a)	6425(c)(1)(A)	12001(b)(17)
4980I(b)(3)(C)(v)(II)	11002(d)(12)	6425(c)(1)(A)	13001(b)(2)(P)
4985(a)(1)	13604(a)	6425(c)(1)(A)	14401(d)(3)
5000A(c)(2)(B)(iii)	11081(a)(1)	6431	13404(b)
5000A(c)(3)(A)	11081(a)(2)(A)	6501(m)	13403(d)(2)
5000A(c)(3)(D)	11081(a)(2)(B)	6532(c)(1)	11071(b)(1)
5000A(c)(3)(D)(ii)	11002(d)(1)(GG)	6532(c)(2)	11071(b)(2)
5001(c)	13807(a)	6601(j)(3)(B)	11002(d)(1)(JJ)
5001(c)(1)	13807(c)(1)	6651(i)(1)	11002(d)(1)(KK)
5001(c)(3)	13807(c)(2)	6652(c)(7)(A)	11002(d)(1)(LL)
5001(c)(4)	13807(c)(2)	6652(p)	13603(e)
5001(d)	13807(a)	6655(e)(2)(A)	12001(b)(18)
5041(a)	13806(a)(1)	6655(e)(2)(A)(i)	14401(d)(4)(B)
5041(b)(1)	13805(a)	6655(e)(2)(B)(i)	12001(b)(18)
5041(b)(2)	13805(a)	6655(e)(2)(B)(i)	14401(d)(4)(B)
5041(c)(4)	13804(b)	6655(e)(2)(B)(iii)	14401(d)(4)(C)
5041(c)(8)	13804(a)	6655(g)(1)(A)(i)	12001(b)(19)
5041(c)(8)(A)	13804(c)(1)	6655(g)(1)(A)(i)	13001(b)(2)(P)
5041(c)(9)	13804(c)(2)	6655(g)(1)(A)(i)	14401(d)(4)(A)
5041(h)	13806(a)(2)	6655(g)(1)(A)(ii)	12001(b)(19)
5051(a)(1)	13802(a)	6655(g)(1)(A)(ii)	14401(d)(4)(A)
5051(a)(1)(C)(i)(II)	13802(c)(1)	6655(g)(1)(A)(iii)	12001(b)(19)
5051(a)(2)(A)	13802(b)(2)	6655(g)(1)(A)(iii)	14401(d)(4)(A)
5051(a)(2)(A)	13802(b)(1)	6662(d)(1)	11011(c)
5051(a)(2)(B)	13802(d)(1)(B)	6695(g)	11001(b)
5051(a)(2)(B)	13802(d)(1)(A)	6695(h)(1)	11002(d)(1)(MM)
5051(a)(2)(C)	13802(d)(1)(B)	6698(e)(1)	11002(d)(1)(NN)
5051(a)(4)	13802(c)(2)	6699(e)(1)	11002(d)(1)(OO)
5051(a)(5)	13802(d)(2)	6721(f)(1)	11002(d)(1)(PP)
5212	13808(a)	6722(f)(1)	11002(d)(1)()
5412	13803(b)	6724(d)(1)(B)(xxiv)	13520(c)(1)(A)
5414	13803(a)(1)	6724(d)(1)(B)(xxv)	13520(c)(1)(A)
5414(b)	13803(a)(2)	6724(d)(1)(B)(xxvi)	13520(c)(1)(A)
6012(f)	11041(e)	6724(d)(2)(HH)	13520(c)(1)(B)
6033(e)(1)(B)(ii)	13308(b)	6724(d)(2)(II)	13520(c)(1)(B)
6038A(b)	14401(b)(1)	6724(d)(2)(JJ)	13520(c)(1)(B)
6038A(d)(1)	14401(b)(2)	6724(d)(3)(C)	11051(b)(2)(C)
6038A(d)(2)	14401(b)(2)	6724(d)(3)(D)	11051(b)(2)(C)

Code §	Act §	Code §	Act §
7345(f)(2)	11002(d)(1)(RR)	7701(a)(17)	11051(b)(4)(B)
7430(c)(1)	11002(d)(1)(SS)	7701(b)(5)(A)(iv)	13304(a)(2)(F)
7518(g)(6)(A)	13001(b)(2)(Q)	7702(c)(3)(B)(i)	13517(a)(4)(A)
7518(g)(6)(A)	13001(b)(7)(A)	7702(f)(10)	13517(a)(4)(B)
7518(g)(6)(A)	13001(b)(7)(B)	7872(g)(5)	11002(d)(14)
7652(f)(2)	13807(b)	7874(e)(1)(B)	13001(b)(1)(C)
7701(a)(17)	11051(b)(4)(A)	9831(d)(2)(D)(ii)(II)	11002(d)(1)(TT)

¶ 6003. Act Sections Amending Code

Act §	Code §	Act §	Code §
11001(b)	6695(g)	11002(d)(10)	1274A(d)(2)
11002(a)	1(f)(3)	11002(d)(11)	4161(b)(2)(C)(i)(II)
11002(b)	1(f)(6)	11002(d)(12)	4980I(b)(3)(C)(v)(II)
11002(b)	1(f)(7)	11002(d)(13)	6039F(d)
11002(c)(1)	1(f)(2)(A)	11002(d)(14)	7872(g)(5)
11002(c)(2)(A)	1(i)(1)(C)	11002(d)(2)(A)	41(e)(5)(C)(ii)
11002(c)(2)(B)	1(i)(3)(C)	11002(d)(2)(A)	68(b)(2)(B)
11002(d)(1)(A)	23(h)(2)	11002(d)(2)(B)	41(e)(5)(C)(ii)
11002(d)(1)(AA)	831(b)(2)(D)(ii)	11002(d)(2)(B)	68(b)(2)(B)
11002(d)(1)(B)	25A(h)(1)(A)(ii)	11002(d)(3)(A)	42(h)(6)(G)(i)(II)
11002(d)(1)(BB)	877A(a)(3)(B)(i)(II)	11002(d)(3)(B)	42(h)(6)(G)(ii)
11002(d)(1)(C)	25B(b)(3)(B)	11002(d)(4)	59(j)(2)(B)
11002(d)(1)(CC)	2010(c)(3)(B)(ii)	11002(d)(5)	132(f)(6)(A)(ii)
11002(d)(1)(D)	32(b)(2)(B)(ii)(II)	11002(d)(6)	162(o)(3)
11002(d)(1)(D)	32(j)(1)(B)(i)	11002(d)(7)	213(d)(10)(B)(ii)
11002(d)(1)(D)	32(j)(1)(B)(ii)	11002(d)(8)	280F(d)(7)(B)
11002(d)(1)(DD)	2032A(a)(3)(B)	11002(d)(9)	911(b)(2)(D)(ii)(II)
11002(d)(1)(E)	36B(f)(2)(B)(ii)(II)	11011(a)	199A
11002(d)(1)(EE)	2503(b)(2)(B)	11011(b)(1)	62(a)
11002(d)(1)(F)	41(e)(5)(C)(i)	11011(b)(2)	63(b)(1)
11002(d)(1)(FF)	4261(e)(4)(A)(ii)	11011(b)(2)	63(b)(2)
11002(d)(1)(G)	42(e)(3)(D)(ii)	11011(b)(2)	63(b)(3)
11002(d)(1)(G)	42(h)(3)(H)(i)(II)	11011(b)(3)	63(d)(1)
11002(d)(1)(GG)	5000A(c)(3)(D)(ii)	11011(b)(3)	63(d)(2)
11002(d)(1)(H)	45R(d)(3)(B)(ii)	11011(b)(3)	63(d)(3)
11002(d)(1)(HH)	6323(i)(4)(B)	11011(b)(4)	3402(m)(1)
11002(d)(1)(I)	55(d)(4)(A)(ii)	11011(c)	6662(d)(1)
11002(d)(1)(II)	6334(g)(1)(B)	11011(d)(1)	172(d)(8)
11002(d)(1)(J)	62(d)(3)(B)	11011(d)(2)	246(b)(1)
11002(d)(1)(JJ)	6601(j)(3)(B)	11011(d)(3)	613(a)
11002(d)(1)(K)	63(c)(4)(B)	11011(d)(4)	613A(d)(1)(C)
11002(d)(1)(KK)	6651(i)(1)	11011(d)(4)	613A(d)(1)(D)
11002(d)(1)(L)	125(i)(2)(B)	11011(d)(4)	613A(d)(1)(E)
11002(d)(1)(LL)	6652(c)(7)(A)	11011(d)(4)	613A(d)(1)(F)
11002(d)(1)(M)	135(b)(2)(B)(ii)	11011(d)(5)	170(b)(2)(D)(iv)
11002(d)(1)(MM)	6695(h)(1)	11011(d)(5)	170(b)(2)(D)(v)
11002(d)(1)(N)	137(f)(2)	11011(d)(5)	170(b)(2)(D)(vi)
11002(d)(1)(NN)	6698(e)(1)	11012(a)	461(l)
11002(d)(1)(O)	146(d)(2)(B)	11021(a)	63(c)(7)
11002(d)(1)(OO)	6699(e)(1)	11022(a)	24(h)
11002(d)(1)(P)	147(c)(2)(H)(ii)	11023(a)	170(b)(1)(G)
11002(d)(1)(PP)	6721(f)(1)	11023(a)	170(b)(1)(H)
11002(d)(1)(Q)	151(d)(4)(B)	11024(a)(1)	529A(b)(2)(B)
11002(d)(1)(QQ)	6722(f)(1)	11024(a)(2)	529A(b)(2)
11002(d)(1)(R)	179(b)(6)(A)(ii)	11024(a)(3)	529A(b)(7)
11002(d)(1)(RR)	7345(f)(2)	11024(b)	25B(d)(1)(B)(ii)
11002(d)(1)(S)	219(b)(5)(C)(i)(II)	11024(b)	25B(d)(1)(C)
11002(d)(1)(S)	219(g)(8)(B)	11024(b)	25B(d)(1)(D)
11002(d)(1)(SS)	7430(c)(1)	11025(a)	529(c)(3)(C)(i)
11002(d)(1)(T)	220(g)(2)	11025(a)	529(c)(3)(C)(i)(I)
11002(d)(1)(TT)	9831(d)(2)(D)(ii)(II)	11025(a)	529(c)(3)(C)(i)(II)
11002(d)(1)(U)	221(f)(1)(B)	11025(a)	529(c)(3)(C)(i)(III)
11002(d)(1)(V)	223(g)(1)(B)	11027(a)	213(f)
11002(d)(1)(W)	408A(c)(3)(D)(ii)	11027(b)	56(b)(1)(B)
11002(d)(1)(X)	430(c)(7)(D)(vii)(II)	11031(a)	108(f)(5)
11002(d)(1)(Y)	512(d)(2)(B)	11032(a)(1)	529(c)(7)
11002(d)(1)(Z)	513(h)(2)(C)(ii)	11032(a)(2)	529(e)(3)(A)

Act §	Code §	Act §	Code §
11041(a)(1)	151(d)(4)	11061(a)	2010(c)(3)(C)
11041(a)(2)	151(d)(5)	11061(b)	2001(g)
11041(b)	642(b)(2)(C)(iii)	11071(a)	6343(b)
11041(c)(1)	3402(a)(2)	11071(b)(1)	6532(c)(1)
11041(c)(2)(A)	3401(e)	11071(b)(2)	6532(c)(2)
11041(c)(2)(B)	3402(f)(1)	11081(a)(1)	5000A(c)(2)(B)(iii)
11041(c)(2)(B)	3402(f)(2)	11081(a)(2)(A)	5000A(c)(3)(A)
11041(c)(2)(C)	3402(b)(1)	11081(a)(2)(B)	5000A(c)(3)(D)
11041(c)(2)(C)	3402(b)(2)	12001(a)	55(a)
11041(c)(2)(C)	3402(f)(3)	12001(b)(1)	38(c)(6)(E)
11041(c)(2)(C)	3402(f)(4)	12001(b)(10)	59(b)
11041(c)(2)(C)	3402(f)(5)	12001(b)(10)	59(f)
11041(c)(2)(C)	3402(f)(7)	12001(b)(11)	11(d)
11041(c)(2)(C)	3402(g)(4)	12001(b)(12)	12(7)
11041(c)(2)(C)	3402(l)(1)	12001(b)(13)	168(k)(4)
11041(c)(2)(C)	3402(l)(2)	12001(b)(14)	882(a)(1)
11041(c)(2)(C)	3402(n)	12001(b)(15)	962(a)(1)
11041(c)(2)(D)	3402(f)	12001(b)(16)(A)	1561(a)(1)
11041(c)(2)(E)	3402(m)	12001(b)(16)(A)	1561(a)(2)
11041(c)(2)(F)	3405(a)(3)	12001(b)(16)(A)	1561(a)(3)
11041(c)(2)(F)	3405(a)(4)	12001(b)(16)(B)	1561(a)
11041(c)(2)(G)	3405(a)(4)	12001(b)(17)	6425(c)(1)(A)
11041(d)	6334(d)(4)	12001(b)(18)	6655(e)(2)(A)
11041(e)	6012(f)	12001(b)(18)	6655(e)(2)(B)(i)
11042(a)	164(b)(6)	12001(b)(19)	6655(g)(1)(A)(i)
11043(a)	163(h)(3)(F)	12001(b)(19)	6655(g)(1)(A)(ii)
11044(a)	165(h)(5)	12001(b)(19)	6655(g)(1)(A)(iii)
11045(a)	67(g)	12001(b)(2)	53(d)(2)
11046(a)	68(f)	12001(b)(3)(A)	55(b)(1)
11047(a)	132(f)(8)	12001(b)(3)(B)	55(b)(3)
11048(a)(1)	132(g)	12001(b)(3)(C)(i)	59(a)(1)(C)
11048(a)(2)	132(g)(2)	12001(b)(3)(C)(ii)	59(a)(2)
11049(a)	217(k)	12001(b)(3)(D)	897(a)(2)(A)
11050(a)	165(d)	12001(b)(3)(E)(i)(I)	911(f)(1)(B)
11051(a)	215	12001(b)(3)(E)(i)(II)	911(f)(1)(B)
11051(b)(1)(A)	61(a)(8)	12001(b)(3)(E)(ii)	911(f)(2)(B)
11051(b)(1)(A)	61(a)(9)	12001(b)(4)	55(c)(1)
11051(b)(1)(A)	61(a)(10)	12001(b)(5)(A)	55(d)(2)
11051(b)(1)(A)	61(a)(11)	12001(b)(5)(A)	55(d)(3)
11051(b)(1)(A)	61(a)(12)	12001(b)(5)(A)	55(d)(4)
11051(b)(1)(A)	61(a)(13)	12001(b)(5)(B)	55(d)(2)(B)
11051(b)(1)(A)	61(a)(14)	12001(b)(5)(B)	55(d)(2)(C)
11051(b)(1)(A)	61(a)(15)	12001(b)(5)(B)	55(d)(2)(D)
11051(b)(1)(B)	71	12001(b)(5)(C)(i)	55(d)(3)(B)(i)
11051(b)(1)(C)	682	12001(b)(5)(C)(ii)	55(d)(3)(B)(iii)
11051(b)(2)(A)	62(a)(10)	12001(b)(6)	55(e)
11051(b)(2)(B)	3402(m)(1)	12001(b)(7)	56(b)(2)(C)
11051(b)(2)(C)	6724(d)(3)(C)	12001(b)(7)	56(b)(2)(D)
11051(b)(2)(C)	6724(d)(3)(D)	12001(b)(8)(A)	56(c)
11051(b)(3)(A)(i)	121(d)(3)(B)	12001(b)(8)(A)	56(g)
11051(b)(3)(A)(ii)	121(d)(3)(C)	12001(b)(8)(B)	847(9)
11051(b)(3)(B)	152(d)(5)	12001(b)(8)(C)	848(i)
11051(b)(3)(C)	219(f)(1)	12001(b)(9)	58(a)(3)
11051(b)(3)(D)	220(f)(7)	12001(b)(9)	58(a)(4)
11051(b)(3)(E)	223(f)(7)	12002(a)	53(e)
11051(b)(3)(F)	382(l)(3)(B)(iii)	12002(b)	53(d)(3)
11051(b)(3)(G)	408(d)(6)	12002(c)	1374(b)(3)(B)
11051(b)(4)(A)	7701(a)(17)	12003(a)	55(d)(4)
11051(b)(4)(B)	7701(a)(17)	13001(a)	11(b)

Act §	Code §	Act §	Code §
13001(b)(1)(A)	280C(c)(3)(B)(ii)(II)	13002(c)(1)	246(b)(3)(A)
13001(b)(1)(B)	860E(e)(2)(B)	13002(c)(2)	246(b)(3)(B)
13001(b)(1)(B)	860E(e)(6)(A)(ii)	13002(d)(1)	246A(a)(1)
13001(b)(1)(C)	7874(e)(1)(B)	13002(d)(2)	246A(a)(1)
13001(b)(2)(A)	1201	13002(e)(1)	861(a)(2)(B)
13001(b)(2)(B)	12(4)	13002(e)(2)(A)	861(a)(2)
13001(b)(2)(B)	12(5)	13002(e)(2)(B)	861(a)(2)
13001(b)(2)(B)	12(6)	13101(a)(1)	179(b)(1)
13001(b)(2)(C)	453A(c)(3)	13101(a)(2)	179(b)(2)
13001(b)(2)(D)(i)	527(b)(2)	13101(a)(3)(A)(i)	179(b)(6)(A)
13001(b)(2)(D)(ii)	527(b)	13101(a)(3)(A)(ii)	179(b)(6)(A)(ii)
13001(b)(2)(E)	594(a)	13101(a)(3)(B)(i)	179(b)(6)(A)
13001(b)(2)(F)	691(c)(4)	13101(a)(3)(B)(ii)	179(b)(6)(B)
13001(b)(2)(G)(i)	801(a)(2)	13101(b)(1)	179(d)(1)(B)
13001(b)(2)(G)(ii)	801(a)	13101(b)(2)	179(f)
13001(b)(2)(H)	831(e)(1)	13101(c)	179(d)(1)
13001(b)(2)(H)	831(e)(2)	13102(a)(1)	448(c)
13001(b)(2)(H)	831(e)(3)	13102(a)(2)	48(b)(3)
13001(b)(2)(I)	832(c)(5)	13102(a)(3)	448(c)(4)
13001(b)(2)(I)	834(b)(1)(D)	13102(a)(4)	448(d)(7)
13001(b)(2)(J)	852(b)(3)(A)	13102(a)(5)(A)(i)	447(c)
13001(b)(2)(K)(i)	857(b)(3)(A)	13102(a)(5)(A)(ii)	447(c)(2)
13001(b)(2)(K)(i)	857(b)(3)(B)	13102(a)(5)(B)	447(f)
13001(b)(2)(K)(i)	857(b)(3)(C)	13102(a)(5)(C)(i)	447(d)
13001(b)(2)(K)(i)	857(b)(3)(D)	13102(a)(5)(C)(i)	447(e)
13001(b)(2)(K)(i)	857(b)(3)(E)	13102(a)(5)(C)(i)	447(h)
13001(b)(2)(K)(i)	857(b)(3)(F)	13102(a)(5)(C)(i)	447(i)
13001(b)(2)(K)(ii)(I)	857(b)(3)(C)(i)	13102(a)(5)(C)(ii)	447(d)
13001(b)(2)(K)(ii)(II)	857(b)(3)(C)(ii)	13102(a)(5)(C)(ii)	447(e)
13001(b)(2)(K)(ii)(II)	857(b)(3)(C)(iv)	13102(a)(5)(C)(ii)	447(f)
13001(b)(2)(K)(iii)	857(b)(3)(E)	13102(a)(5)(C)(ii)	447(g)
13001(b)(2)(K)(iv)	857(b)(3)(F)	13102(b)(1)	263A(i)
13001(b)(2)(L)	882(a)(1)	13102(b)(1)	263A(j)
13001(b)(2)(M)(i)	904(b)(2)(C)	13102(b)(2)	263A(b)(2)
13001(b)(2)(M)(ii)	904(b)(3)(D)	13102(c)	471(c)
13001(b)(2)(M)(iii)	904(b)(3)(E)	13102(c)	471(d)
13001(b)(2)(N)	1374(b)(4)	13102(d)(1)(A)	460(e)(1)(B)
13001(b)(2)(O)	1381(b)	13102(d)(1)(B)	460(e)(1)(B)(ii)
13001(b)(2)(P)	6425(c)(1)(A)	13102(d)(2)	460(e)(2)
13001(b)(2)(P)	6655(g)(1)(A)(i)	13102(d)(2)	460(e)(3)
13001(b)(2)(Q)	7518(g)(6)(A)	13102(d)(2)	460(e)(4)
13001(b)(3)(A)(i)	1445(e)(1)	13102(d)(2)	460(e)(5)
13001(b)(3)(A)(ii)	1445(e)(1)	13102(d)(2)	460(e)(6)
13001(b)(3)(B)	1445(e)(2)	13201(a)(1)(A)	168(k)(1)(A)
13001(b)(3)(C)(i)	1445(e)(6)	13201(a)(1)(B)	168(k)(5)(A)(i)
13001(b)(3)(C)(ii)	1445(e)(6)	13201(a)(2)	168(k)(6)
13001(b)(3)(D)	1446(b)(2)(B)	13201(a)(3)(A)	168(k)(5)(F)
13001(b)(4)	852(b)(1)	13201(a)(3)(B)	168(k)(8)
13001(b)(5)(A)	1551	13201(b)(1)(A)(i)	168(k)(2)(A)(iii)
13001(b)(5)(B)	535(c)(5)	13201(b)(1)(A)(i)	168(k)(2)(B)(i)(III)
13001(b)(6)(A)	1561	13201(b)(1)(A)(i)	168(k)(2)(B)(ii)
13001(b)(7)(A)	7518(g)(6)(A)	13201(b)(1)(A)(i)	168(k)(2)(E)(i)
13001(b)(7)(B)	7518(g)(6)(A)	13201(b)(1)(A)(ii)(I)	168(k)(2)(B)(i)(II)
13002(a)(1)	243(a)(1)	13201(b)(1)(A)(ii)(II)	168(k)(2)(B)(ii)
13002(a)(2)(A)	243(c)(1)	13201(b)(1)(B)	168(k)(5)(A)
13002(a)(2)(B)	243(c)(1)	13201(b)(2)(A)	460(c)(6)(B)(ii)
13002(a)(3)	243(c)	13201(b)(2)(B)	168(k)
13002(b)(1)	245(c)(1)(B)	13201(c)(1)	168(k)(2)(A)(ii)
13002(b)(2)	245(c)(1)(B)	13201(c)(2)	168(k)(2)(E)(ii)

Act §	Code §	Act §	Code §
13201(c)(3)	168(k)(2)(E)(iii)(I)	13206(d)(2)(C)	280C(c)(2)
13201(d)	168(k)(9)	13206(d)(2)(C)	280C(c)(3)
13201(e)	168(k)(1)	13206(d)(2)(C)	280C(c)(4)
13201(f)	168(k)(2)(F)(iii)	13206(d)(2)(D)	280C(c)(2)
13201(g)(1)(A)	168(k)(2)(A)(i)(II)	13207(a)	263A(d)(2)(C)
13201(g)(1)(B)	168(k)(2)(A)(i)(III)	13221(a)	451(b)
13201(g)(1)(C)	168(k)(2)(A)(i)(IV)	13221(a)	451(c)
13201(g)(1)(C)	168(k)(2)(A)(i)(V)	13221(a)	451(d)
13201(g)(2)	168(k)(2)(H)	13221(a)	451(e)
13202(a)(1)(A)	280F(a)(1)(A)(i)	13221(a)	451(f)
13202(a)(1)(B)	280F(a)(1)(A)(ii)	13221(a)	451(g)
13202(a)(1)(C)	280F(a)(1)(A)(iii)	13221(a)	451(h)
13202(a)(1)(D)	280F(a)(1)(A)(iv)	13221(a)	451(i)
13202(a)(2)(A)	280F(a)(1)(B)(ii)	13221(b)	451(c)
13202(a)(2)(B)(i)	280F(d)(7)(A)	13221(b)	451(d)
13202(a)(2)(B)(ii)	280F(d)(7)(B)(i)(II)	13221(b)	451(e)
13202(b)(1)(A)	280F(d)(4)(A)(iii)	13221(b)	451(f)
13202(b)(1)(B)	280F(d)(4)(A)(iv)	13221(b)	451(g)
13202(b)(1)(C)	280F(d)(4)(A)(iv)	13221(b)	451(h)
13202(b)(1)(C)	280F(d)(4)(A)(v)	13221(b)	451(i)
13202(b)(2)	280F(d)(4)(B)	13221(b)	451(j)
13202(b)(2)	280F(d)(4)(C)	13221(b)	451(k)
13203(a)	168(e)(3)(B)(vii)	13301(a)	163(j)
13203(b)	168(b)(2)(B)	13301(b)(1)	381(c)(20)
13203(b)	168(b)(2)(C)	13301(b)(2)	382(d)(3)
13203(b)	168(b)(2)(D)	13301(b)(3)	382(k)(1)
13204(a)(1)(A)(i)	168(e)(3)(E)(iv)	13302(a)(1)	172(a)
13204(a)(1)(A)(i)	168(e)(3)(E)(ix)	13302(a)(2)	172(b)(2)
13204(a)(1)(A)(i)	168(e)(3)(E)(v)	13302(a)(3)	172(d)(6)(A)
13204(a)(1)(A)(ii)	168(e)(3)(E)(vii)	13302(a)(3)	172(d)(6)(B)
13204(a)(1)(A)(iii)	168(e)(3)(E)(viii)	13302(a)(3)	172(d)(6)(C)
13204(a)(1)(A)(iv)	168(e)(3)(E)(iv)	13302(b)(1)(A)	172(b)(1)(A)(i)
13204(a)(1)(A)(iv)	168(e)(3)(E)(v)	13302(b)(1)(B)	172(b)(1)(A)(ii)
13204(a)(1)(A)(iv)	168(e)(3)(E)(vi)	13302(b)(2)	172(b)(1)(B)
13204(a)(1)(A)(iv)	168(e)(3)(E)(vii)	13302(b)(2)	172(b)(1)(C)
13204(a)(1)(A)(iv)	168(e)(3)(E)(viii)	13302(b)(2)	172(b)(1)(D)
13204(a)(1)(B)	168(e)(6)	13302(b)(2)	172(b)(1)(E)
13204(a)(1)(B)	168(e)(7)	13302(b)(2)	172(b)(1)(F)
13204(a)(1)(B)	168(e)(8)	13302(c)(1)	172(b)(1)(B)
13204(a)(2)(A)	168(b)(3)(G)	13302(c)(2)(A)	172(f)
13204(a)(2)(A)	168(b)(3)(H)	13302(c)(2)(A)	172(g)
13204(a)(2)(A)	168(b)(3)(I)	13302(c)(2)(A)	172(h)
13204(a)(2)(B)	168(b)(3)(G)	13302(c)(2)(A)	172(i)
13204(a)(3)(A)(i)(I)	168(g)(1)(D)	13302(c)(2)(A)	172(f)
13204(a)(3)(A)(i)(II)	168(g)(1)(E)	13302(c)(2)(B)	537(b)(4)
13204(a)(3)(A)(i)(III)	168(g)(1)(F)	13302(d)(1)	172(b)(1)(C)
13204(a)(3)(A)(ii)	168(g)(8)	13302(d)(2)	172(f)
13204(a)(4)(A)(i)	168(k)(2)(A)(i)(II)	13302(d)(2)	172(g)
13204(a)(4)(A)(ii)	168(k)(2)(A)(i)(III)	13303(a)	1031(a)(1)
13204(a)(4)(A)(iii)	168(k)(2)(A)(i)(IV)	13303(b)(1)(A)	1031(a)(2)
13204(a)(4)(B)(i)	168(e)(6)	13303(b)(1)(B)	1031(i)
13204(a)(4)(B)(ii)	168(k)(3)	13303(b)(2)	1031(e)
13205(a)	168(g)(1)(E)	13303(b)(3)	1031(e)
13205(a)	168(g)(1)(F)	13303(b)(4)	1031(h)
13205(a)	168(g)(1)(G)	13303(b)(5)	1031
13206(a)	174	13304(a)(1)(A)	274(a)(1)(A)
13206(d)(1)	41(d)(1)(A)	13304(a)(1)(B)	274(a)(1)
13206(d)(2)(A)	280C(c)(1)	13304(a)(1)(C)	274(a)(2)
13206(d)(2)(B)	280C(c)(2)	13304(a)(2)(A)(i)	274(d)(2)

Act §	Code §	Act §	Code §
13304(a)(2)(A)(i)	274(d)(3)	13309(a)(1)	1061
13304(a)(2)(A)(i)	274(d)(4)	13309(a)(1)	1062
13304(a)(2)(A)(ii)(I)	274(d)	13309(a)(2)	1061
13304(a)(2)(A)(ii)(II)	274(d)	13310(a)(1)	274(j)(3)(A)
13304(a)(2)(B)	274(l)	13310(a)(2)	274(j)(3)(A)(i)
13304(a)(2)(C)	274(n)	13310(a)(2)	274(j)(3)(A)(ii)
13304(a)(2)(D)	274(n)(1)	13310(a)(2)	274(j)(3)(A)(iii)
13304(a)(2)(E)(i)	274(n)(2)(B)	13310(a)(2)	274(j)(3)(A)(i)(I)
13304(a)(2)(E)(ii)	274(n)(2)(C)	13310(a)(2)	274(j)(3)(A)(i)(II)
13304(a)(2)(E)(ii)	274(n)(2)(C)	13310(a)(2)	274(j)(3)(A)(i)(III)
13304(a)(2)(E)(ii)	274(n)(2)(D)	13310(a)(3)	274(j)(3)(A)(ii)
13304(a)(2)(E)(ii)	274(n)(2)(E)	13311(a)	162(a)
13304(a)(2)(E)(iii)	274(n)(2)	13312(a)(1)	118(b)
13304(a)(2)(E)(iv)	274(n)(2)	13312(a)(1)	118(c)
13304(a)(2)(F)	7701(b)(5)(A)(iv)	13312(a)(1)	118(d)
13304(b)(1)	274(n)(2)(B)	13312(a)(2)	118(d)
13304(b)(2)	274(n)(2)(B)	13312(a)(2)	118(e)
13304(b)(2)	274(n)(2)(C)	13312(a)(3)	118(b)
13304(b)(2)	274(n)(2)(D)	13312(a)(3)	118(c)
13304(b)(3)	274(n)(2)	13313(a)	1044
13304(b)(4)	274(n)(2)	13313(b)(1)	1016(a)(23)
13304(c)(1)(A)	274(a)	13313(b)(2)	1016(a)(23)
13304(c)(1)(B)	274(a)(4)	13314(a)	1221(a)(3)
13304(c)(2)	274(l)	13314(b)	1231(b)(1)(C)
13304(d)(1)	274(o)	13401(a)	45C(a)
13304(d)(1)	274(p)	13401(a)(1)	864(c)(8)
13304(d)(2)	274(o)	13401(a)(2)(A)	864(c)(1)(A)
13305(a)	199	13401(a)(2)(B)	864(c)(1)(B)
13305(b)(1)	74(d)(2)(B)	13401(b)	280C(b)(3)
13305(b)(1)	86(b)(2)(A)	13401(b)	280C(b)(4)
13305(b)(1)	135(c)(4)(A)	13402(a)	47(a)
13305(b)(1)	137(b)(3)(A)	13402(b)(1)(A)(i)	47(c)(1)(A)(iii)
13305(b)(1)	219(g)(3)(A)(ii)	13402(b)(1)(A)(ii)	47(c)(1)(B)
13305(b)(1)	221(b)(2)(C)	13402(b)(1)(A)(iii)	47(c)(1)(B)
13305(b)(1)	222(b)(2)(C)	13402(b)(1)(A)(iii)	47(c)(1)(C)
13305(b)(1)	246(b)(1)	13402(b)(1)(A)(iii)	47(c)(1)(D)
13305(b)(1)	469(i)(3)(F)(iii)	13402(b)(1)(B)	47(c)(2)(B)(iv)
13305(b)(2)	170(b)(2)(D)(iv)	13402(b)(2)(A)	145(d)(4)
13305(b)(2)	170(b)(2)(D)(v)	13402(b)(2)(B)	145(d)(4)
13305(b)(2)	170(b)(2)(D)(vi)	13403(a)(1) [sic]	45S
13305(b)(3)	172(d)(7)	13403(b)	38(b)(35)
13305(b)(4)	613(a)	13403(b)	38(b)(36)
13305(b)(5)	613A(d)(1)(B)	13403(b)	38(b)(37)
13305(b)(5)	613A(d)(1)(B)	13403(c)	38(c)(4)(B)(ix)
13305(b)(5)	613A(d)(1)(C)	13403(c)	38(c)(4)(B)(x)
13305(b)(5)	613A(d)(1)(E)	13403(c)	38(c)(4)(B)(xi)
13305(b)(5)	613A(d)(1)(F)	13403(c)	38(c)(4)(B)(xii)
13306(a)(1)	162(f)	13403(d)(1)	280C(a)
13306(b)(1)	6050X	13403(d)(2)	6501(m)
13307(a)	162(q)	13404(a)	54
13307(a)	162(r)	13404(a)	54A
13308(a)	162(e)(2)	13404(a)	54AA
13308(a)	162(e)(3)	13404(a)	54B
13308(a)	162(e)(4)	13404(a)	54C
13308(a)	162(e)(5)	13404(a)	54D
13308(a)	162(e)(6)	13404(a)	54E
13308(a)	162(e)(7)	13404(a)	54F
13308(a)	162(e)(8)	13404(b)	6431
13308(b)	6033(e)(1)(B)(ii)	13404(c)(1)	1397E

Act §	Code §	Act §	Code §
13404(c)(2)	54(l)(3)(B)	13517(a)(2)(A)	807(d)(2)
13404(c)(3)	6211(b)(4)(A)	13517(a)(2)(A)	807(d)(4)
13404(c)(4)	6401(b)(1)	13517(a)(2)(A)	807(d)(5)
13501(a)(1)	864(c)(8)	13517(a)(2)(B)	807(d)(4)
13501(a)(2)(A)	864(c)(1)(A)	13517(a)(2)(B)	807(d)(6)
13501(a)(2)(B)	864(c)(1)(B)	13517(a)(2)(C)	807(d)(1)
13501(b)	1446(f)	13517(a)(2)(C)	807(d)(2)
13501(b)	1446(g)	13517(a)(2)(D)	807(d)(3)(A)(iii)
13502(a)	743(d)(1)	13517(a)(2)(E)	807(d)(3)(A)(iv)(I)
13503(a)(1)	704(d)	13517(a)(2)(F)	807(d)(3)(A)(iv)(II)
13503(a)(2)	704(d)	13517(a)(2)(G)	807(d)(3)(B)(i)
13503(a)(3)	704(d)(3)	13517(a)(2)(H)	807(d)(3)(B)(ii)
13504(a)(1)	708(b)(1)	13517(a)(3)(A)	807(e)(2)
13504(a)(1)	708(b)(1)(A)	13517(a)(3)(A)	807(e)(5)
13504(b)(1)	168(i)(7)(B)	13517(a)(3)(B)	807(e)(2)
13504(b)(2)	743(e)(4)	13517(a)(3)(B)	807(e)(3)
13504(b)(2)	743(e)(5)	13517(a)(3)(B)	807(e)(4)
13504(b)(2)	743(e)(6)	13517(a)(3)(B)	807(e)(5)
13504(b)(2)	743(e)(7)	13517(a)(3)(B)	807(e)(6)
13511(a)	805(b)(4)	13517(a)(3)(B)	807(e)(7)
13511(a)	805(b)(5)	13517(a)(3)(C)	807(e)(2)
13511(b)(1)	810	13517(a)(3)(D)	807(e)(6)
13511(b)(2)(A)	844	13517(a)(4)(A)	7702(c)(3)(B)(i)
13511(b)(2)(B)	831(b)(3)	13517(a)(4)(B)	7702(f)(10)
13511(b)(3)	381(d)	13517(b)(1)	808(g)
13511(b)(4)	805(a)(4)(B)(ii)	13517(b)(2)	811(d)(1)
13511(b)(5)	805(a)(5)	13517(b)(3)	846(f)(6)(A)
13511(b)(6)	805(b)(2)(A)(iv)	13517(b)(4)	848(e)(1)(B)(iii)
13511(b)(7)	953(b)(1)(B)	13517(b)(5)	954(i)(5)(B)
13511(b)(8)	1351(i)(3)	13518(a)	812
13512(a)	806	13518(b)	817A(e)(2)
13512(b)(1)	453B(e)(2)(B)	13519(a)(1)	848(a)(2)
13512(b)(1)(B)	453B(e)(3)	13519(a)(2)	848(c)(1)(A)
13512(b)(2)	465(c)(7)(D)(v)(II)	13519(a)(3)	848(c)(2)(B)
13512(b)(3)	801(a)(2)(C)	13519(a)(4)	848(c)(3)(C)
13512(b)(4)	804	13519(b)	848(b)(1)
13512(b)(5)	805(a)(4)(B)(i)	13520(a)	6050Y
13512(b)(5)	805(a)(4)(B)(ii)	13520(c)(1)(A)	6724(d)(1)(B)(xxiv)
13512(b)(5)	805(a)(4)(B)(iii)	13520(c)(1)(A)	6724(d)(1)(B)(xxv)
13512(b)(5)	805(a)(4)(B)(iv)	13520(c)(1)(A)	6724(d)(1)(B)(xxvi)
13512(b)(6)	805(b)(2)(A)(iii)	13520(c)(1)(B)	6724(d)(2)(HH)
13512(b)(6)	805(b)(2)(A)(iii)	13520(c)(1)(B)	6724(d)(2)(II)
13512(b)(6)	805(b)(2)(A)(iv)	13520(c)(1)(B)	6724(d)(2)(JJ)
13512(b)(6)	805(b)(2)(A)(v)	13520(c)(2)(A)	6047(g)
13512(b)(7)	842(c)(1)	13520(c)(2)(A)	6047(h)
13512(b)(7)	842(c)(2)	13520(c)(2)(B)	6047(g)
13512(b)(7)	842(c)(3)	13520(c)(2)(C)	6047(h)(4)
13512(b)(8)	953(b)(1)(A)	13521(a)	1016(a)(1)
13512(b)(8)	953(b)(1)(B)	13522(a)	101(a)(3)
13512(b)(8)	953(b)(1)(C)	13522(b)	101(a)(1)
13513(a)	807(f)(1)	13523(a)	846(c)(2)
13514(a)	815	13523(b)	846(d)(3)(B)
13514(b)	801(c)	13523(b)	846(d)(3)(C)
13515(a)	832(b)(5)(B)	13523(b)	846(d)(3)(D)
13515(a)(1)	832(b)(5)(B)	13523(b)	846(d)(3)(E)
13515(a)(2)	832(b)(5)(B)	13523(b)	846(d)(3)(F)
13516(a)	847	13523(b)	846(d)(3)(G)
13517(a)(1)	807(c)	13523(c)	846(e)
13517(a)(2)(A)	807(d)(1)	13523(c)	846(f)

Act §	Code §	Act §	Code §
13523(c)	846(g)	13704(a)(1)	170(l)(1)
13531(a)	162(r)	13704(a)(2)	170(l)(2)(B)
13531(a)	162(s)	13705(a)	170(f)(8)(D)
13532(a)	149(d)(1)	13705(a)	170(f)(8)(E)
13532(b)(1)	149(d)(2)	13801(a)(1)	263A(f)(4)
13532(b)(1)	149(d)(3)	13801(a)(1)	263A(f)(5)
13532(b)(1)	149(d)(4)	13801(a)(2)	263A(f)(4)
13532(b)(1)	149(d)(5)	13801(b)	263A(f)(5)(B)(ii)
13532(b)(1)	149(d)(6)	13802(a)	5051(a)(1)
13532(b)(1)	149(d)(7)	13802(b)(1)	5051(a)(2)(A)
13532(b)(2)	148(f)(4)(C)(xiv)	13802(b)(2)	5051(a)(2)(A)
13532(b)(2)	148(f)(4)(C)(xv)	13802(c)(1)	5051(a)(1)(C)(i)(II)
13532(b)(2)	148(f)(4)(C)(xvi)	13802(c)(2)	5051(a)(4)
13532(b)(2)	148(f)(4)(C)(xvii)	13802(d)(1)(A)	5051(a)(2)(B)
13541(a)	1361(c)(2)(B)(v)	13802(d)(1)(B)	5051(a)(2)(B)
13542(a)	641(c)(2)(E)	13802(d)(1)(B)	5051(a)(2)(C)
13543(a)	481(d)	13802(d)(2)	5051(a)(5)
13543(b)	1371(f)	13803(a)(1)	5414
13601(a)(1)	162(m)(4)(B)	13803(a)(2)	5414(b)
13601(a)(1)	162(m)(4)(C)	13803(b)	5412
13601(a)(1)	162(m)(4)(D)	13804(a)	5041(c)(8)
13601(a)(1)	162(m)(4)(E)	13804(b)	5041(c)(4)
13601(a)(1)	162(m)(4)(F)	13804(c)(1)	5041(c)(8)(A)
13601(a)(1)	162(m)(4)(G)	13804(c)(2)	5041(c)(9)
13601(a)(2)(A)	162(m)(5)(E)	13805(a)	5041(b)(1)
13601(a)(2)(A)	162(m)(6)(D)	13805(a)	5041(b)(2)
13601(a)(2)(B)	162(m)(5)(G)	13806(a)(1)	5041(a)
13601(a)(2)(B)	162(m)(6)(G)	13806(a)(2)	5041(h)
13601(b)(1)	162(m)(3)(A)	13807(a)	5001(c)
13601(b)(2)(A)	162(m)(3)(B)	13807(a)	5001(d)
13601(b)(2)(B)	162(m)(3)(B)	13807(b)	7652(f)(2)
13601(b)(3)	162(m)(3)(A)	13807(c)(1)	5001(c)(1)
13601(b)(3)	162(m)(3)(B)	13807(c)(2)	5001(c)(3)
13601(b)(3)	162(m)(3)(C)	13807(c)(2)	5001(c)(4)
13601(c)(1)	162(m)(2)	13808(a)	5212
13601(c)(2)	162(m)(3)	13821(a)	139G(a)
13601(d)	162(m)(4)(F)	13821(a)(1)	139G
13603(a)	83(i)	13821(b)	247(a)
13603(b)(1)	3401(i)	13821(b)(1)	247
13603(b)(2)	3402(t)	13821(c)(1)(A)	6039H
13603(c)(1)(A)	422(b)	13821(c)(1)(B)	6039H(e)
13603(c)(1)(B)(i)	423(b)(5)	13822(a)	4261(e)(5)
13603(c)(1)(B)(ii)	423(d)	13823(a)	1400Z-1
13603(c)(2)	409A(d)(7)	13823(a)	1400Z-2
13603(d)	6051(a)(14)(B)	13823(b)	1016(a)(36)
13603(d)	6051(a)(15)	13823(b)	1016(a)(37)
13603(d)	6051(a)(16)	13823(b)	1016(a)(38)
13603(d)	6051(a)(17)	14101(a)	245A
13603(e)	6652(p)	14101(b)(1)	246(c)(1)
13604(a)	4985(a)(1)	14101(b)(2)	246(c)(5)
13611(a)	408A(d)(6)(B)(iii)	14101(c)(1)	246(a)(1)
13612(a)	457(e)(11)(B)(ii)	14101(c)(2)	1059(b)(2)(B)
13612(b)	457(e)(11)(B)(iii)	14101(d)	904(b)(5)
13612(c)	457(e)(11)(B)(iv)	14101(e)(1)	951(b)
13613(a)	402(c)(3)(C)	14101(e)(2)	957(a)
13613(b)(1)	402(c)(3)	14102(a)(1)	1248(j)
13613(b)(2)	402(c)(3)(A)	14102(a)(1)	1248(k)
13702(a)	512(a)(6)	14102(b)(1)	961(d)
13703(a)	512(a)(7)	14102(c)(1)	964(e)(4)

Act §	Code §	Act §	Code §
14102(d)(1)	91	14301(b)(1)	960(c)
14102(e)(1)	367(a)(3)	14301(b)(2)	960(e)
14102(e)(1)	367(a)(3)	14301(b)(2)	960(f)
14102(e)(1)	367(a)(4)	14301(c)(1)	78
14102(e)(1)	367(a)(5)	14301(c)(10)	901(j)(1)(A)
14102(e)(1)	367(a)(6)	14301(c)(11)	901(j)(1)(B)
14102(e)(2)(A)	367(a)(4)	14301(c)(12)	901(k)(2)
14102(e)(2)(B)	367(a)(4)	14301(c)(13)	901(k)(6)
14103(a)	965	14301(c)(14)	901(m)(1)(B)
14201(a)	951A	14301(c)(15)(A)	904(d)(2)(E)(i)
14201(b)(1)	960(d)	14301(c)(15)(B)	904(d)(2)(E)(ii)
14201(b)(2)(A)	904(d)(1)(A)	14301(c)(16)(A)	904(d)(4)
14201(b)(2)(A)	904(d)(1)(B)	14301(c)(16)(B)	904(d)(4)
14201(b)(2)(A)	904(d)(1)(C)	14301(c)(17)	904(d)(6)(A)
14201(b)(2)(B)	904(d)(2)(A)(ii)	14301(c)(18)	904(h)(10)(A)
14201(b)(2)(C)	904(c)	14301(c)(19)	904(k)
14202(a)	250	14301(c)(2)	245(a)(4)
14202(b)(1)	172(d)(9)	14301(c)(20)	905(c)(1)
14202(b)(2)(A)	246(b)(1)	14301(c)(21)	905(c)(2)(B)(i)
14202(b)(2)(B)	246(b)(1)	14301(c)(22)	906(a)
14202(b)(3)	469(i)(3)(F)(iii)	14301(c)(23)	906(b)(4)
14211(a)(1)	954(a)(2)	14301(c)(23)	906(b)(5)
14211(a)(2)	954(a)(3)	14301(c)(24)	907(b)(2)(B)
14211(a)(3)	954(a)(5)	14301(c)(25)(A)	907(c)(3)(A)
14211(b)(1)	952(c)(1)(B)(iii)(I)	14301(c)(25)(B)	907(c)(3)(B)
14211(b)(1)	952(c)(1)(B)(iii)(II)	14301(c)(26)	907(c)(5)
14211(b)(1)	952(c)(1)(B)(iii)(III)	14301(c)(27)	907(f)(2)(B)(i)
14211(b)(1)	952(c)(1)(B)(iii)(IV)	14301(c)(28)	908(a)
14211(b)(1)	952(c)(1)(B)(iii)(V)	14301(c)(29)(A)	909(b)
14211(b)(2)(A)	954(b)(4)	14301(c)(29)(B)	909(b)(1)
14211(b)(2)(B)	954(b)(5)	14301(c)(29)(C)	909(b)
14211(b)(2)(C)	954(b)(6)	14301(c)(29)(D)	909(b)
14211(b)(3)	954(g)	14301(c)(3)	245(a)(10)(C)
14212(a)	955	14301(c)(30)	909(d)(5)
14212(b)(1)(A)	951(a)(1)(A)	14301(c)(31)	958(a)(1)
14212(b)(1)(B)	851(b)	14301(c)(32)	959(d)
14212(b)(1)(C)	952(c)(1)(B)(i)	14301(c)(33)	959(e)
14212(b)(1)(D)	953(c)(1)(C)	14301(c)(34)	1291(g)(2)(A)
14212(b)(2)	951(a)(3)	14301(c)(35)	1293(f)(1)
14212(b)(3)	953(d)(4)(B)(iv)(II)	14301(c)(35)	1293(f)(2)
14212(b)(4)	964(b)	14301(c)(35)	1293(f)(3)
14212(b)(5)	970(b)	14301(c)(36)	6038(c)(1)(B)
14213(a)(1)	958(b)(4)	14301(c)(37)	6038(c)(4)(C)
14213(a)(2)	958(b)	14301(c)(4)	535(b)(1)
14214(a)	951(b)	14301(c)(4)	545(b)(1)
14215(a)	951(a)(1)	14301(c)(5)(A)	814(f)(1)(B)
14221(a)(1)	936(h)(3)(B)(v)	14301(c)(5)(B)	814(f)(1)
14221(a)(2)	936(h)(3)(B)(vi)	14301(c)(6)	865(h)(1)(B)
14221(a)(2)	936(h)(3)(B)(vii)	14301(c)(7)	901(a)
14221(a)(3)	936(h)(3)(B)	14301(c)(8)	901(e)(2)
14221(b)(1)	367(d)(2)(D)	14301(c)(9)	901(f)
14221(b)(2)	482	14302(a)	904(d)(1)(B)
14222(a)	267A	14302(a)	904(d)(1)(C)
14223(a)(1)	1(h)(11)(C)(iii)	14302(a)	904(d)(1)(D)
14223(a)(2)	1(h)(11)(C)(iii)	14302(b)(1)	904(d)(2)(J)
14223(a)(3)	1(h)(11)(C)(iii)(II)	14302(b)(2)	904(d)(2)(A)(ii)
14301(a)	902	14303(a)	863(b)
14301(b)(1)	960	14304(a)	904(g)(5)
14301(b)(1)	960(b)	14401(a)	59A

Act §	Code §	Act §	Code §
14401(b)(1)	6038A(b)	14401(d)(4)(A)	6655(g)(1)(A)(iii)
14401(b)(2)	6038A(d)(1)	14401(d)(4)(B)	6655(e)(2)(A)(i)
14401(b)(2)	6038A(d)(2)	14401(d)(4)(B)	6655(e)(2)(B)(i)
14401(c)	26(b)(2)(B)	14401(d)(4)(C)	6655(e)(2)(B)(iii)
14401(d)(2)	882(a)(1)	14501(a)	1297(b)(2)(B)
14401(d)(3)	6425(c)(1)(A)	14501(b)	1297(f)
14401(d)(4)(A)	6655(g)(1)(A)(i)	14502(a)	864(e)(2)
14401(d)(4)(A)	6655(g)(1)(A)(ii)		

¶ 6004. FTC 2nd ¶ s Affected by Act

FTC 2d ¶	Analysis ¶	FTC 2d ¶	Analysis ¶	FTC 2d ¶	Analysis ¶
A-1100	101 , 201	A-8101	202 , 301	D-1000	102
A-1101	101	A-8103	303	D-1003	102
A-1102	101	A-8130	303	D-1455	802
A-1103	101 , 201	A-8131	303	D-1482	802
A-1300	105	A-8134	303	D-1640	102 , 304
A-1301	105	A-8140	303	D-1657	102
A-1700	605	A-8141	303	D-1665	304
A-1703	605	A-8160	202 , 301 ,	D-1800	801
A-2500	701 , 1010		303	D-1846	801
A-2501	701	A-8161	303	D-2200	103 , 1901
A-2600	202 , 510 ,	A-8162	202 , 301	D-2201	103 , 701
	701	A-8163	202 , 301	D-2205	103
A-2601	701	A-8164	202 , 301	D-2251	701
A-2611.2	202	A-8190	303	D-2253	103
A-2621	510	A-8191:	303	D-2255	103
A-2700	701 , 1008	A-8200	303	D-2263	1901
A-2701	701	A-8201	303	D-5000	102
A-2710	503	A-8300	302	D-5008	102
A-2721	503	A-8305	302	D-6800	202
A-2722	503	A-8307	505	D-6804	2503 , 2504
A-2724.1	503	A-8400	303	D-6845	202
A-2725	503	A-8401	303	D-6847	202
A-2726	503	A-8800	304	E-1000	102
A-2730	202 , 504	A-8801	304	E-1001	102
A-2731	202 , 504	B-2140	1502	E-3300	102
A-2800	202 , 501 ,	B-2141	1502	E-3328	102
	1803	B-2142	1502	E-4800	102 , 2403
A-2801	1803	B-2143	1502	E-4801	102 , 2407
A-2803	501	B-3500	903	E-4807	2402
A-2809	202 , 501	B-3501	903	E-4831	2402
A-3500	502	B-3503	903	E-4838	2403
A-3500.1	502	B-4000	902	E-4841	2403
A-4050	516 , 517 ,	B-4009	902	E-4842	2403
	518	B-4009.1	902	E-4950	2405 , 2406 ,
A-4051	516 , 517 ,	B-4009.3	901		2408
	518	B-4300	901	E-4953	2406
A-4052	516 , 517 ,	B-4301	901	E-4956	2406
	518	B-4305	901	E-4958	2406
A-4055	517	C-1000	104 , 201	E-4959	2406
A-4059	518	C-1003	104	E-4973	2406
A-4200	202	C-1005	104 , 201	E-4975	2406
A-4226	202	C-2200	502	E-4982	2405
A-4240	202	C-2206	502	E-5300	2407
A-4248.1	202	C-2206.1	502	E-5301	2407
A-4400	202	C-2300	803	E-5500	102 , 202 ,
A-4417	202	C-2301	803		2409 , 2410
A-4450	202 , 1602	C-5400	510	E-5501	102
A-4451.1	202	C-5433	510	E-5503	202
A-4453	1602	C-5700	803	E-5504	102
A-4500	202	C-5701	803	E-5566	2409
A-4517.1	202	C-7000	104 , 201	E-5569	2409
A-4700	1603 , 1604	C-7002	104	E-5570	2409
A-4711	1604	C-7004	104 , 201	E-5593	2410
A-4721	1603	C-9500	102	E-5598	2408
A-4740	1601 , 1603	C-9563	102	E-5605	102
A-4744.2	1601 , 1603	C-9650	605	E-6100	102
A-8100	202 , 303	C-9651	605	E-6102	102

FTC 2d ¶	Analysis ¶	FTC 2d ¶	Analysis ¶	FTC 2d ¶	Analysis ¶
E-6520	1912	H-1453	202	I-3060	1503
E-6600	102 , 1912	H-1464	202	I-3061	1503
E-6609	102	H-1821	1006	I-3062	1503
E-10200	102	H-2200	202	I-3063	1503
E-10201	102	H-2217.1	202	I-3064	1503
E-10300	102	H-2400	202	I-3064.1	1503
E-10301	102	H-2461.3	202	I-3065	1503
F-5700	1908	H-2973	2604	I-3065.1	1503
F-5730	2205	H-3100	605	I-3065.2	1503
F-5731	2205	H-3106	605	I-3067	1503
F-6100	2203	H-3109	605	I-3089	1503
F-6128	1905	H-3109.1	605	I-3090	1503
F-6129	1905	H-3112	605	I-3091	1503
F-6500	2202	H-3200.29	2604	I-3091.1	1503
F-7000	1003	H-3327	1804 , 1807	I-3092	1503
F-7001	1003	H-3339.1	2703	I-3093	1503
F-7012	1003	H-3776	2601 , 2602 ,	I-3094	1503
F-7200	1003		2603	I-3500	2204
F-7201	1003	H-3777	2602	I-3790	1507
F-7203	1003	H-3780	2603	I-3791	1507
F-7363	1003	H-3781.1	2601	I-3792	1507
G-1200	901	H-3782	2601	I-3793	1507
G-1224	901	H-3783	2601	I-5100	102 , 1501
G-2050	1401 , 1403	H-4425	605	I-5110	1501
G-2069	1401 , 1405	H-4447	605	I-5110.1	1501
G-2073	1401	H-4475	101	I-5110.2	1501
G-2078	1401	H-4483	101	I-5110.3	1501
G-2089.1	1403	H-4485	502 , 701	I-5115.5	2206
G-2185	801	H-4492	502	I-5117	102
G-2471	1406 , 1407	H-4505	502	I-6600	1504
G-2540	1407	H-4511	701	I-6601	1504
G-2548.1	1407	H-4530	101	I-9000	1504
G-2596	1407	H-4542	101	I-9008	1504
G-3100	1210	H-4953	2406	J-1335	102
G-3143	1210	H-4956	2406	J-1360	102
G-3210	1405	H-4958	2406	J-1410	510
G-4018	2202	H-4959	2406	J-1413	510
G-4051	2202	H-4973	2406	J-1451	202
G-4201	2201	H-4975	2406	J-2900	202
G-4554	2202	H-7750	202	J-2989	202
G-5000	1403	H-7751.2H	202	J-3050	202
G-5005A	1403	H-9211	1804 , 1807	J-3053	202
G-5450	1404	H-11000	1805	J-3150	202
G-5479	1404	H-11102	1806	J-3155	202
G-5479.1	1404	H-11110	1806	J-3186	202
G-6000	102	H-11400	1804	J-3500	202
G-6317	102	H-11406.3	1804 , 1807	J-3506	202
G-6450	2403	H-11415	2702	J-3650	1701
G-6498	2403	H-11452	2702	J-3660	1701
G-6501	2403	H-11472	1804 , 1807	J-3661	1701
H-1225	202	H-12200	202	J-4001	1406
H-1231	202	H-12215	202	J-4100	202
H-1326	202	H-12217	202	J-4163	202
H-1332.1	202	H-12217.2	202	J-4700	601
H-1349	202	H-12290	202 , 2701	J-4730	601
H-1349.20	202	H-12290.7	202	J-4737	601
H-1350	202	H-12290.10	202	J-4800	2406
H-1350.14	202	H-12290.22	2701	J-4812	2406
H-1450	202	I-3050	1503	J-5300	1505

FTC 2d ¶	Analysis ¶	FTC 2d ¶	Analysis ¶	FTC 2d ¶	Analysis ¶
J-5307	1505	L-3100	1408	L-9400	1301 , 1302 ,
J-8576	1804	L-3101	1408		1303 , 1306
J-8600	101	L-3114	1408	L-9402	1301 , 1302 ,
J-8600.1	101	L-3114.1	1408		1303 , 1306
J-8602	101	L-3117	1408	L-9403	1301 , 1302
J-8617	101	L-3118	1408	L-9900	202 , 1101 ,
J-9000	101	L-3119	1408		1102 , 1103 ,
J-9001	101	L-3120	1408		1104
K-2000	505	L-3121	1408	L-9901.1	1102
K-2002	505	L-3122	1408	L-9907	1101
K-2100	202	L-3123	1408	L-9907.1	202 , 1101 ,
K-2141.1	202	L-3124	1408		1104
K-3000	513	L-3125	1408	L-9907.2	1104
K-3100	513	L-3126	1408	L-9922	1102 , 1103
K-3670	512 , 803	L-3127	1408	L-9922.1	1103
K-3671	512 , 803	L-3130	1408	L-9923.1	1102
K-3672	803	L-3131	1408	L-10000	202 , 1209
K-3700	512	L-3600	514	L-10002	1308
K-3830	701	L-3630	514	L-10004	202 , 1307
K-3832	701	L-4325	1004	L-10004.1A	1209
K-3900	515	L-4326	1004	L-10004.4	1209
K-3938	515	L-5600	1408	L-10400	901
K-4000	506	L-5613	1408	L-10401	901
K-4001	506	L-5616	1408	L-15200	1013 , 1017 ,
K-4500	506	L-5618	1408		1210
K-4502	506	L-5620	1408	L-15201	1013
K-4504	506	L-5621	1408	L-15202	1017
K-4506	506	L-5623	1408	L-15213	1210
K-4700	506	L-5900	1410	L-15300	1408
K-4701	506	L-5932	1410	L-15308	1408
K-5000	1003	L-8200	1301 , 1302 ,	L-15400	1408
K-5360	1003		1304	L-15406	1408
K-5470	507	L-8206	1304	L-15407	1408
K-5471	507	L-8208	1301	L-15500	202
K-5485	507	L-8208.1	1301	L-15511	202
K-5488	507	L-8208.2	1301	L-15530	1702
K-5490	507	L-8208.5	1301	L-15547	1702
K-5500	202	L-8210	1302	L-15550	1702
K-5502	202	L-8211	1302	L-15560	1702
K-5512	1003	L-8900	1301 , 1305	L-15570	1702
K-6000	510	L-8912	1305	L-15580	1702
K-6001	510	L-8917	1301	L-15586	1702
L-1900	202	L-9300	1309	L-15590	1702
L-1911	202	L-9301	1309	L-15593	1702
L-2000	511	L-9310	1202 , 1203 ,	L-15607	1702
L-2014	511		1204 , 1205 ,	L-15615	1015 , 1016
L-2100	1005		1206 , 1207 ,	L-15617	1015 , 1016
L-2101	1005		1208 , 1209	L-15620	1015 , 1016
L-2123	1005	L-9311.1	1203	L-15680	202
L-2124	1005	L-9311.1A	1204	L-15689.2	202
L-2125	1005	L-9312	1202 , 1206 ,	L-15700	202
L-2135	1005 , 1006		1207 , 1208 ,	L-15722	202
L-2141	1006		1209	L-15727	202
L-2149	1005	L-9312.1	1208	L-16000	202
L-2300	2605	L-9314	1205	L-16006.2	202
L-2316	2605	L-9314.1	1205	L-16100	1014
L-2400,	1011	L-9315	1202	L-16103	1014
L-2407		L-9316	1202 , 1209	L-16106	1014
L-2700	1009	L-9316.1	1202 , 1209	L-16113	1014

FTC 2d ¶	Analysis ¶	FTC 2d ¶	Analysis ¶	FTC 2d ¶	Analysis ¶
L-16300	1014	O-2400	1903 , 1906 ,	S-1106.1	3001
L-16301	1014		1907 , 1909 ,	S-1700	502
L-16480	1702		2001 , 2002 ,	S-1800	605
M-1600	508		2103	S-1808	605
M-1900	508 , 1801 ,	O-2404	2103	S-3150	2606
	1802 , 1803	O-2422	1903	S-3152	2606
M-1901	508 , 1802 ,	O-2470	1906 , 1907 ,	S-3584.1	202
	1803		1909 , 2002	S-3649.5	202
M-1907	508 , 1801	O-2520	1906 , 1907 ,	S-5320	102 , 303
M-2100	508		1909	S-5325	102 , 303
M-4100	701	O-2660	2104	S-5342	303
M-4109	701	O-2710	1906 , 1907 ,	S-6000	202
M-4200	1001		1909	S-6009	202
M-4200.1	1001	O-2740	2105	S-8000	605
M-4300	1002	O-2800	1904	S-8007	605
M-4301	1002	O-4000	1908 , 2302	T-4000	1911
M-4304	1002	O-4300	2004 , 2303	T-4200	1911
M-4307	1002	O-4400	102 , 1902 ,	T-4221.1	3101
M-4308	1002		1913	T-6600	102 , 303
M-4311	1002	O-4404.6	102	T-6605.1	102 , 303
M-4314	1002	O-4700	1905 , 2302	U-1267	202
M-4330	1002	O-4706	1905	U-1268	202
M-4331	1002	O-4720	2302	V-1750	202
M-4400	1001	O-4721	2302	V-1752	202
M-4401	1001	O-4800	1904 , 2301	V-1762	202
M-6100	509	O-4804	2301	V-1763.2	202
M-6102.1	509	O-4816.1	1904	V-1800	202
N-1010	1402	O-4900	2003 , 2301	V-1805	202
N-1036	1402	O-4903	2301	V-1811	202
N-1039	1402	O-4904	2301	V-1816	202
N-1040	1402	O-4907	2301	V-1818	202
N-1073	1002	O-10600	102 , 2304	V-2150	701
N-1081	1411	O-10602	102	V-2159	701
N-1082	1411	O-10610	2304	V-2530	202
N-1300	1409	O-10900	103 , 2305	V-2538	202
N-1331	1409	O-10928	103	V-2630	202 , 3001
N-1333	1409	O-10962	2305	V-2671	202
N-1336	1409	O-11100	2306	V-2677.1	3001
N-1339.1	1409	O-11108	2306	V-2700	202
N-1360	1304	O-11119	2306	V-2716	202
N-1361	1304	O-11650	202	V-2717	202
N-1362	1304	O-11652	202	V-2718	202
N-2403	701	O-13000	102	V-2719	202
N-2446	701	O-13035	102	V-3500	202
O-1000	2302	O-13039	102	V-3507	202
O-1100	202	O-13055	102	V-3900	202 , 401
O-1102	202	P-1700	1703	V-3901	401
O-1546	2202	Q-5000	202	V-3905	401
O-1660	103	Q-5002	202	V-3906	401
O-1661	103	R-5200	202	V-3907	202 , 401
O-2200	2411	R-5204	202	V-5100	3002
O-2202	2411	R-7000	605	V-5126	3002
O-2300	1906 , 1907 ,	R-7009	2801	V-5127	3002
	1909 , 2001 ,	R-7011	605	V-5200	202 , 502
	2002 , 2101 ,	R-7100	202	V-5232	202
	2102	R-7101	202 , 2801	V-5233	202
O-2303	2101	R-7107	2801	V-5236	502
O-2331	2102	R-9551	2801	V-6400	202
		S-1100	3001	V-6440	202

FTC 2d ¶	Analysis ¶	FTC 2d ¶	Analysis ¶	FTC 2d ¶	Analysis ¶
V-6445	202	W-5033	605	W-5103	202
W-2750	202	W-5100	202 , 2901	W-5131	2901
W-2752	202	W-5101	202	W-5134	2901
W-5000	605				

¶ 6005. USTR ¶ s Affected by Act

USTR ¶	Analysis ¶	USTR ¶	Analysis ¶	USTR ¶	Analysis ¶
14	101	1324.06	1006	1724.434	1002
14.08	101 , 1501	1324.08	202	1724.436	1002
14.09	105	1374	202	1724.437	1002
14.13	104	1464.01	202	1744	1408
14.085	2206	1474.01	202	1744.02	1408
24.02	605	1494.03	1701	1794.01	202 , 1101 ,
54AA4	1702	1514	202 , 502		1104
114.01	102	1624.040	1010	1794.02	1102 , 1103
114.02	303	1624.0091	2601 , 2602 ,	1994	1004
234	202		2603	2134	505
244	516 , 517 ,	1624.0092	2601	2134.14	505
	518	1624.141	511	2134.075	202
244.02	517	1624.157	202	2154	510
25A4.02	202	1624.388	1008 , 1009	2174	514
25B4	202 , 1602	1624.395	1011	2194.01	202
324.01	202	1634	1003	2194.02	202
36B4.06	202	1634.052	507	2204.01	202
384.01	1013	1634.054	1003	2214.01	202
384.02	1017	1634.058	1003	2234.03	202
414.01	1408	1644	506	2434.01	103
414.02	202	1654.300	508	2434.03	103
414.04	1015 , 1016	1654.304	508 , 1801 ,	2434.04	103 , 701 ,
424.50	202		1802 , 1803		1901
424.76	202	1654.350	508	2434.05	103
45C4	1015 , 1016	1654.500	509	263A4	1404
45R4.02	202	1674.033	1408	263A4.02	1404
474	1014	1684.01	1304 , 1305 ,	263A4.11	1410
534	304		1309	263A4.15	1002
544	1702	1684.02	1301 , 1302	263A4.157	1411
54A4	1702	1684.03	1301 , 1302 ,	2674	2204
54B4	1702		1303 , 1304 ,	2744.01	1005 , 1006
54C4	1702		1306	2744.09	2605
54D4	1702	1684.026	1202 , 1205 ,	2744.015	1005
54E4	1702		1206 , 1207 ,	280C4	1015 , 1016 ,
54E4.01	1702		1208 , 1209		1408
54F4	1702	1684.027	1202 , 1209	280F4	202 , 1209 ,
554	202 , 303	1684.072	901		1307 , 1308
554.01	202 , 301 ,	1684.0253	1203	3674.02	1905 , 2203
	303	1684.0254	1204	3674.03	2202
564	303	1684.0271	1208	3814	1003
564.01	303	1684.0281	1209	3814.01	1003
564.02	302 , 505	1684.0293	1210	3814.02	1003
564.03	303	1704	515	3824.01	1003
594	202	1704.05	512 , 803	4014.172	1804 , 1807
624	701	1704.06	701	4024.02	1805
624.02	202	1704.13	512	4024.03	1805
624.04	510	1704.38	513	4024.04	1804 , 1807 ,
634	202 , 501 ,	1704.50	515		2702
	701 , 1803	1724	1001	4034.04	1804 , 1805 ,
674	503	1724.12	701		1807
684	202 , 504	1724.20	1001	4084.03	1804 , 1807
714	510	1724.30	1002	408A4	202 , 2701
724.22	1806	1724.31	1002	409A4.02	2604
784	1908 , 2301	1724.33	1002	4234.02	2604
1014	601	1724.35	1002	4304.03	202
1124	605	1724.39	1002	4464.07	1403
1254.05	202	1724.42	1002	4464.225	801

USTR ¶	Analysis ¶	USTR ¶	Analysis ¶	USTR ¶	Analysis ¶
4474	1402	8634.02	2305	22,014	605
4484	1401 , 1405	877A4	202	25,034eg	202
4514.011	1406 , 1407	8824	102	26,314eg	2801
4514.166	1407	9014	1908 , 2302	34,014.17	605
4514.191	1407	9024	1908 , 2301	34,024.10	701
453A4	102	9024.02	2301	34,024.13	101
453B4	2403	9044	1902 , 2004	34,024.25	101
4574	2703	9044.01	102 , 1905 ,	34,024.26	101
4604.001	1210		2302 , 2303	34,054	1804
4604.12	1405	9114.12	202	34,064	101
4614.78	1409	9414	1909	41,614exc	202
4714.15	1403	9514	1906 , 1907 ,	42,534.08	605
4824.01	2202		1909 , 2001 ,	42,614.01exc	202
4824.04	2202		2002 , 2103	49,80I4	202
4824.065	2201	9514.01	2101	49,854	2205
5124	202 , 2503 ,	9524	1906 , 1907 ,	49,854.01	2205
	2504		1909 , 2001 ,	50,00A4.2	202 , 401
5134	2504		2002	60,124	502
5274	102	9544	1906 , 1907 ,	60,134.01	605
5294	1603		1909 , 2104	60,39F4	202
5294.02	1603 , 1604	9544.05	2104	60,514	2606
529A4	1601 , 1603	9554	2105	63,234.16	202
613A4	701	9584.01	2102	63,314.05	202 , 502
6414.08	803	9604	1908 , 2003 ,	63,354.04	3002
6424.01	502		2301	63,354.06	3002
6424.02	803	9604.03	2301	64,254	102 , 303
6824	510	9614.02	1903	64,314	1702
6914.07	102	9644.05	1904	65,014	1911
6924	605	10,164	1505 , 1703	65,324.04	3002
7044.10	903	10,314	1503	66,014	202
7064.02	901	10,314.02	1503	66,514.01	202
7074.02	1502	10,314.04	1503	66,524	202
7084	901	10,444	1507	66,554	102 , 303
7434.01	901 , 902	12,014	102	66,554.02	303
8014	102 , 2407	12,214.45	1504	66,624.03	701
8064	2403	12,314.14	1504	66,954	202
8074	2405 , 2406	12,484	1904	66,954.01	3001
8104	2402 , 2403	12,714	1406	66,984	202
8154	2407	12,714.03	202	66,994	202
8314	202	12,974	2411	67,214	202
8324.01	2408	13,614.03	802	67,224	202
8324.02	102	13,714.04	801	73,454	202
8344	102	13,744.01	102 , 304	74,304.01	202
8464	2409	13,814	102	75,084	605
8474	2410	14,454.02	102	75,184	102
8524.10	102	15,514.01	102	77,024.05	2406
8564	1912	15,614	102	78,744	1908
8574	1912	20,014.01	2801	78,724.201	202
8574.01	102	20,104eg	202 , 2801	98,314	202
8614.11	103	20,32A4eg	202		

¶ 6006. Pension Analysis ¶ s Affected by Act

PCA ¶	Analysis ¶	PCA ¶	Analysis ¶	PCA ¶	Analysis ¶
28,512	1804 , 1807	32,807.3	1804 , 1807	35,223	2701
32,101	1805	32,816	2702	40,440.1	2703
32,203	1806	32,853	2702	55,676	1804
32,211	1806	32,873	1804 , 1807		

¶ 6007. Pension & Benefits Explanations ¶ s Affected by Act

PE ¶	Analysis ¶	PE ¶	Analysis ¶	PE ¶	Analysis ¶
72-4.22	1806	402-4.03	1805	408A4	2701
132-4.08	603	402-4.04	1804 , 1807	408-4.03	1804 , 1807
401-4.172	1804 , 1807	403-4.04	1804 , 1805 ,	3405-4	1804
402-4.02	1805		1807		

¶ 6008. Estate Planning Analysis ¶ s Affected by Act

EPTC/EPA ¶	Analysis ¶	EPTC/EPA ¶	Analysis ¶	EPTC/EPA ¶	Analysis ¶
44,910	2801	45,102	2801	45,108	2801
				46,092	2801

¶ 6009. Catalyst ¶ s Affected by Act

Catalyst ¶	Analysis ¶	Catalyst ¶	Analysis ¶	Catalyst ¶	Analysis ¶
103:106	1405	124:270	1908 , 2206	209:135	901
104:140	2202	124:280	2205	210:130	902
104:146	2202	127:110	2203	210:140	901
104:199	1904	127:120	2203	217:122	1502
104:200	2004	127:140	2202	217:156	901
104:201	1905	127:163	1905	218:100	901
105:120	1005 , 2204	127:190	1908 , 2206	219:171	2801
105:183	2102	128:261	1003	251:100	801
106:200	1003	129:150	2203	251:160	801
107:185	2206	129:170	2202	252:160	802
107:190	103	129:176	2202	252:190	801
107:193	1901 , 1902	129:190	1905	252:200	801
107:222	1904	129:200	1908 , 2206	252:220	801
108:104	1005	129:260	1904	252:230	801
108:105	1004	129:300	1904	253:157	503
108:210	103	132:110	1904	254:102	802
109:100	103	132:130	1908 , 2206	254:180	801
112:100	103	135:160	1003	402:145	901
112:110	103	135:171	1002	402:190	1304
113:100	2301	135:310	2402	402:195	1301
113:120	1904	135:312	2405	402:200	1305
113:121	2301	135:313	2407	402:205	1301
113:130	1904	135:382	1002	402:280	1308
113:135	2301	136:102	1002	402:282	1307
113:160	1904	136:110	1003	402:310	1303 , 1306
113:170	1904	136:211	1002 , 1003	402:313	1302
113:172	2301	136:351	1002	403:100	1201 , 1202 , 1203
113:210	1904	137:271	1003	403:105	1004
113:212	2301	142:100	303	403:115	1101
113:216	2301	142:102	301	403:120	1102 , 1103
114:152	2604	142:110	303	403:130	1101
114:153	2601 , 2602 , 2603	142:120	303	403:134	1104
114:204	103	142:130	303	403:180	1201 , 1202 , 1203
115:181	1504	142:140	303	403:187	1204
115:205	2601 , 2602 , 2603	142:150	303	403:190	1201 , 1202 , 1203 , 1206 , 1207 , 1208
118:110	2203	142:160	303	403:200	1201 , 1202
118:115	1905 , 2004 , 2303	142:170	303	403:207	1209 , 1307
118:140	2202	142:174	103	403:209	1014
118:148	2202	142:180	303 , 1001	403:210	1201 , 1202 , 1203
118:180	1904	142:181	1002	403:212	1004
118:200	1908 , 2206	142:184	1003	403:220	1201 , 1202 , 1203
120:120	1908 , 2206	142:190	303	404:182	2404 , 2409
120:130	2205	142:194	1004	406:120	1101 , 1102 , 1103
122:120	2203	142:210	303 , 304		
122:130	2203	142:220	303	406:123	1201 , 1202 , 1203
122:150	1908 , 2206	142:230	303		
122:190	1904	152:143	2408	406:140	1305
122:220	2202	154:125	1008	406:144	1301
122:228	2202	154:130	1005	406:150	1304
124:120	2203	154:133	1008 , 1011	406:170	1302 , 1303 , 1306
124:130	2203	202:202	1502		
124:200	303	203:134	901		
124:210	2202	203:170	903		
124:219	2202	204:164	901		
		205:117	901		
		209:112	1502		
		209:120	903		

Catalyst ¶	Analysis ¶	Catalyst ¶	Analysis ¶	Catalyst ¶	Analysis ¶
406:182	1014	755:103	1401	2103:101	2101
406:234	508	755:150	2204	2103:102	2001 , 2103
406:250	303	756:186	1411	2103:121	103
406:279	2004 , 2301 ,	756:194	1405	2103:173	2409
	2303	758:122	1405	2104:100	1906 , 1907 ,
425:140	514	758:170	1005 , 1210		1909 , 1911
425:150	1408	758:211	1405	2104:101	2101
501:144	1503	762:208	503	2104:102	2001 , 2103
501:180	1504	2001:102	2202	2104:110	1907 , 1909 ,
501:182	2305	2001:111	2202		1911 , 2403
501:192	1503	2001:145	2202	2104:130	2403
501:201	2204	2001:191	2201	2104:131	2406 , 2409
502:113	1504	2101:100	1906 , 1907 ,	2104:134	2409
502:141	1504		1909 , 1911	2106:100	2206
502:161	303 , 1501	2001 , 2101		2106:130	2301
502:162	102	2101:102	2103	2106:134	2004 , 2303
502:163	301 , 1501	2101:111	2101	2106:140	1904
502:182	1002	2101:130	1906 , 1907 ,	2106:146	2301
502:195	1504		1909 , 1911	2106:160	1904
502:198	303	2101:132	2104	2106:170	1904
504:131	1505	2101:140	1906 , 1907 ,	2107:114	2411
504:135	1507		1909 , 1911	2110:100	1902 , 1908 ,
505:100	1503	2101:141	2001 , 2103		2301 , 2303
505:110	1503	2101:145	2105	2110:104	2003
508:175	901	2101:160	1906 , 1907 ,	2110:106	2004
510:104	508		1909 , 1911	2110:116	2301
511:100	1507	2101:170	1908	2110:130	2004 , 2303
511:163	1507	2101:171	2003 , 2301	2110:141	2101
552:113	1912	2102:100	1906 , 1907 ,	2110:142	2301
552:121	1002		1909 , 1911	2110:153	2301
552:140	2503	2102:101	2101	2110:180	2302
753:110	1401	2102:102	2001 , 2103	2110:190	1905
753:145	1408	2103:100	1906 , 1907 ,	2110:224	2301
754:102	1401		1909 , 1911		
754:130	1401 , 1402				

¶ 6010. Table of Action Alert Items

Date	Action	Topic	Analysis ¶
90 days after date of enactment	If a chief executive officer of a state doesn't request a 30-day extension, the chief executive officer has until Mar. 22, 2018 to nominate a census tract as a QO Zone and to notify IRS.	Chief executive officers of a state can designate low-income communities as Qualified Opportunity Zones	1704

¶ 6011. Committee Report Finding Table

Com Rept ¶	Act Sec.	Act Sec. Title	PDF Page
¶ 5001	11001	MODIFICATION OF RATES	191 to 200
¶ 5002	11002	INFLATION ADJUSTMENTS BASED ON CHAINED CPI	204 to 205
¶ 5003	11011	DEDUCTION FOR QUALIFIED BUSINESS INCOME	205 to 224
¶ 5004	11012	LIMITATION ON LOSSES FOR TAXPAYERS OTHER THAN CORPORATIONS	238 to 239
¶ 5005	11021	INCREASE IN STANDARD DEDUCTION	201 to 202
¶ 5006	11022	INCREASE IN AND MODIFICATION OF CHILD TAX CREDIT	225 to 227
¶ 5007	11023	INCREASED LIMITATION FOR CERTAIN CHARITABLE CONTRIBUTIONS	
	13704	REPEAL OF DEDUCTION FOR AMOUNTS PAID IN EXCHANGE FOR COLLEGE ATHLETIC EVENT SEATING RIGHTS	
	13705	REPEAL OF SUBSTANTIATION EXCEPTION IN CASE OF CONTRIBUTIONS REPORTED BY DONEE	263 to 273
¶ 5008	11024	INCREASED CONTRIBUTIONS TO ABLE ACCOUNTS	325 to 329
¶ 5009	11025	ROLLOVERS TO ABLE PROGRAMS FROM 529 PROGRAMS	252 to 255
¶ 5010	11026	TREATMENT OF CERTAIN INDIVIDUALS PERFORMING SERVICES IN THE SINAI PENINSULA OF EGYPT	330 to 331
¶ 5011	11027	TEMPORARY REDUCTION IN MEDICAL EXPENSE DEDUCTION FLOOR	276 to 277
¶ 5012	11028	RELIEF FOR 2016 DISASTER AREAS	332 to 335
¶ 5013	11031	TREATMENT OF STUDENT LOANS DISCHARGED ON ACCOUNT OF DEATH OR DISABILITY	246 to 248
¶ 5014	11032	529 ACCOUNT FUNDING FOR ELEMENTARY AND SECONDARY EDUCATION	281 to 282
¶ 5015	11041	SUSPENSION OF DEDUCTION FOR PERSONAL EXEMPTIONS	202 to 204
¶ 5016	11042	LIMITATION ON DEDUCTION FOR STATE AND LOCAL, ETC. TAXES	259 to 261
¶ 5017	11043	LIMITATION ON DEDUCTION FOR QUALIFIED RESIDENCE INTEREST	256 to 258
¶ 5018	11044	MODIFICATION OF DEDUCTION FOR PERSONAL CASUALTY LOSSES	261 to 262
¶ 5019	11045	SUSPENSION OF MISCELLANEOUS ITEMIZED DEDUCTIONS	273 to 276
¶ 5020	11046	SUSPENSION OF OVERALL LIMITATION ON ITEMIZED DEDUCTIONS	255 to 256

Com Rept ¶	Act Sec.	Act Sec. Title	PDF Page
¶ 5021	11047	SUSPENSION OF EXCLUSION FOR QUALIFIED BICYCLE COMMUTING REIMBURSEMENT	282 to 283
¶ 5022	11048	SUSPENSION OF EXCLUSION FOR QUALIFIED MOVING EXPENSE REIMBURSEMENT	286
¶ 5023	11049	SUSPENSION OF DEDUCTION FOR MOVING EXPENSES	278 to 279
¶ 5024	11050	LIMITATION ON WAGERING LOSSES	262
¶ 5025	11051	REPEAL OF DEDUCTION FOR ALIMONY PAYMENTS	277
¶ 5026	11061	INCREASE IN ESTATE AND GIFT TAX EXEMPTION	307 to 316
¶ 5027	11071	EXTENSION OF TIME LIMIT FOR CONTESTING IRS LEVY	329 to 330
¶ 5028	11081	ELIMINATION OF SHARED RESPONSIBILITY PAYMENT FOR INDIVIDUALS FAILING TO MAINTAIN MINIMUM ESSENTIAL COVERAGE	323 to 324
¶ 5029	12001	REPEAL OF TAX FOR CORPORATIONS	
	12002	CREDIT FOR PRIOR YEAR MINIMUM TAX LIABILITY OF CORPORATIONS	
	12003	INCREASED EXEMPTION FOR INDIVIDUALS	317 to 323
¶ 5032	13001	21-PERCENT CORPORATE TAX RATE	
	13002	REDUCTION IN DIVIDEND RECEIVED DEDUCTIONS TO REFLECT LOWER CORPORATE INCOME TAX RATES	341 to 346
¶ 5034	13101	MODIFICATIONS OF RULES FOR EXPENSING DEPRECIABLE BUSINESS ASSETS	372 to 375
¶ 5035	13102	SMALL BUSINESS ACCOUNTING METHOD REFORM AND SIMPLIFICATION	375 to 381
¶ 5036	13201	TEMPORARY 100-PERCENT EXPENSING FOR CERTAIN BUSINESS ASSETS	346 to 357
¶ 5037	13202	MODIFICATIONS TO DEPRECIATION LIMITATIONS ON LUXURY AUTOMOBILES AND PERSONAL USE PROPERTY	357 to 360
¶ 5038	13203	MODIFICATIONS OF TREATMENT OF CERTAIN FARM PROPERTY	360 to 362
¶ 5039	13204	APPLICABLE RECOVERY PERIOD FOR REAL PROPERTY	362 to 367
¶ 5040	13205	USE OF ALTERNATIVE DEPRECIATION SYSTEM FOR ELECTING FARMING BUSINESSES	367 to 370
¶ 5041	13206	AMORTIZATION OF RESEARCH AND EXPERIMENTAL EXPENDITURES	423 to 425
¶ 5042	13207	EXPENSING OF CERTAIN COSTS OF REPLANTING CITRUS PLANTS LOST BY REASON OF CASUALTY	370 to 372
¶ 5043	13221	CERTAIN SPECIAL RULES FOR TAXABLE YEAR OF INCLUSION	425 to 429
¶ 5044	13301	LIMITATION ON DEDUCTION FOR INTEREST	385 to 392

Com Rept ¶	Act Sec.	Act Sec. Title	PDF Page
¶ 5045	13302	MODIFICATION OF NET OPERATING LOSS DEDUCTION	393 to 394
¶ 5046	13303	LIKE-KIND EXCHANGES OF REAL PROPERTY	394 to 397
¶ 5047	13304	LIMITATION ON DEDUCTION BY EMPLOYERS OF EXPENSES FOR FRINGE BENEFITS	402 to 407
¶ 5048	13305	REPEAL OF DEDUCTION FOR INCOME ATTRIBUTABLE TO DOMESTIC PRODUCTION ACTIVITIES	400 to 402
¶ 5049	13306	DENIAL OF DEDUCTION FOR CERTAIN FINES, PENALTIES, AND OTHER AMOUNTS	430 to 431
¶ 5050	13307	DENIAL OF DEDUCTION FOR SETTLEMENTS SUBJECT TO NONDISCLOSURE AGREEMENTS PAID IN CONNECTION WITH SEXUAL HARASSMENT OR SEXUAL ABUSE	431
¶ 5051	13308	REPEAL OF DEDUCTION FOR LOCAL LOBBYING EXPENSES	399 to 400
¶ 5052	13309	RECHARACTERIZATION OF CERTAIN GAINS IN THE CASE OF PARTNERSHIP PROFITS INTERESTS HELD IN CONNECTION WITH PERFORMANCE OF INVESTMENT SERVICES	416 to 423
¶ 5053	13310	PROHIBITION ON CASH, GIFT CARDS, AND OTHER NON-TANGIBLE PERSONAL PROPERTY AS EMPLOYEE ACHIEVEMENT AWARDS	407 to 408
¶ 5055	13312	CERTAIN CONTRIBUTIONS BY GOVERNMENTAL ENTITIES NOT TREATED AS CONTRIBUTIONS TO CAPITAL	397 to 398
¶ 5056	13313	REPEAL OF ROLLOVER OF PUBLICLY TRADED SECURITIES GAIN INTO SPECIALIZED SMALL BUSINESS INVESTMENT COMPANIES	412 to 413
¶ 5057	13314	CERTAIN SELF-CREATED PROPERTY NOT TREATED AS A CAPITAL ASSET	413 to 414
¶ 5058	13401	MODIFICATION OF ORPHAN DRUG CREDIT	433 to 434
¶ 5059	13402	REHABILITATION CREDIT LIMITED TO CERTIFIED HISTORIC STRUCTURES	435 to 436
¶ 5060	13403	EMPLOYER CREDIT FOR PAID FAMILY AND MEDICAL LEAVE	443 to 444
¶ 5061	13404	REPEAL OF TAX CREDIT BONDS	459 to 462
¶ 5062	13501	TREATMENT OF GAIN OR LOSS OF FOREIGN PERSONS FROM SALE OR EXCHANGE OF INTERESTS IN PARTNERSHIPS ENGAGED IN TRADE OR BUSINESS WITHIN THE UNITED STATES	509 to 512
¶ 5063	13502	MODIFY DEFINITION OF SUBSTANTIAL BUILT-IN LOSS IN THE CASE OF TRANSFER OF PARTNERSHIP INTEREST	512 to 513
¶ 5064	13503	CHARITABLE CONTRIBUTIONS AND FOREIGN TAXES TAKEN INTO ACCOUNT IN DETERMINING LIMITATION ON ALLOWANCE OF PARTNER'S SHARE OF LOSS	513 to 515

Com Rept ¶	Act Sec.	Act Sec. Title	PDF Page
¶ 5065	13504	REPEAL OF TECHNICAL TERMINATION OF PARTNERSHIPS	415 to 416
¶ 5066	13511	NET OPERATING LOSSES OF LIFE INSURANCE COMPANIES	464 to 465
¶ 5067	13512	REPEAL OF SMALL LIFE INSURANCE COMPANY DEDUCTION	465 to 466
¶ 5068	13513	ADJUSTMENT FOR CHANGE IN COMPUTING RESERVES	466 to 467
¶ 5069	13514	REPEAL OF SPECIAL RULE FOR DISTRIBUTIONS TO SHAREHOLDERS FROM PRE-1984 POLICYHOLDERS SURPLUS ACCOUNT	467 to 469
¶ 5070	13515	MODIFICATION OF PRORATION RULES FOR PROPERTY AND CASUALTY INSURANCE COMPANIES	469 to 470
¶ 5071	13516	REPEAL OF SPECIAL ESTIMATED TAX PAYMENTS	473 to 476
¶ 5072	13517	COMPUTATION OF LIFE INSURANCE TAX RESERVES	476 to 479
¶ 5073	13518	MODIFICATION OF RULES FOR LIFE INSURANCE PRORATION FOR PURPOSES OF DETERMINING THE DIVIDENDS RECEIVED DEDUCTION	479 to 482
¶ 5074	13519	CAPITALIZATION OF CERTAIN POLICY ACQUISITION EXPENSES	482 to 483
¶ 5075	13520	TAX REPORTING FOR LIFE SETTLEMENT TRANSACTIONS	
	13521.	CLARIFICATION OF TAX BASIS OF LIFE INSURANCE CONTRACTS	
	13522	EXCEPTION TO TRANSFER FOR VALUABLE CONSIDERATION RULES	483 to 486
¶ 5078	13523	MODIFICATION OF DISCOUNTING RULES FOR PROPERTY AND CASUALTY INSURANCE COMPANIES	470 to 473
¶ 5079	13531	LIMITATION ON DEDUCTION FOR FDIC PREMIUMS	410 to 412
¶ 5080	13532	REPEAL OF ADVANCE REFUNDING BONDS	458 to 459
¶ 5081	13541	EXPANSION OF QUALIFYING BENEFICIARIES OF AN ELECTING SMALL BUSINESS TRUST	517
¶ 5082	13542	CHARITABLE CONTRIBUTION DEDUCTION FOR ELECTING SMALL BUSINESS TRUSTS	518
¶ 5083	13543	MODIFICATION OF TREATMENT OF S CORPORATION CONVERSIONS TO C CORPORATIONS	382 to 384
¶ 5084	13601	MODIFICATION OF LIMITATION ON EXCESSIVE EMPLOYEE REMUNERATION	486 to 491
¶ 5085	13602	EXCISE TAX ON EXCESS TAX-EXEMPT ORGANIZATION EXECUTIVE COMPENSATION	491 to 494
¶ 5086	13603	TREATMENT OF QUALIFIED EQUITY GRANTS	494 to 503

Com Rept ¶	Act Sec.	Act Sec. Title	PDF Page
¶ 5087	13604	INCREASE IN EXCISE TAX RATE FOR STOCK COMPENSATION OF INSIDERS IN EXPATRIATED CORPORATIONS	503 to 508
¶ 5088	13611	REPEAL OF SPECIAL RULE PERMITTING RECHARACTERIZATION OF ROTH CONVERSIONS	288 to 291
¶ 5089	13612	MODIFICATION OF RULES APPLICABLE TO LENGTH OF SERVICE AWARD PLANS	306 to 307
¶ 5090	13613	EXTENDED ROLLOVER PERIOD FOR PLAN LOAN OFFSET AMOUNTS	294 to 296
¶ 5091	13701	EXCISE TAX BASED ON INVESTMENT INCOME OF PRIVATE COLLEGES AND UNIVERSITIES	552 to 555
¶ 5092	13702	UNRELATED BUSINESS TAXABLE INCOME SEPARATELY COMPUTED FOR EACH TRADE OR BUSINESS ACTIVITY	545 to 548
¶ 5093	13703	UNRELATED BUSINESS TAXABLE INCOME INCREASED BY AMOUNT OF CERTAIN FRINGE BENEFIT EXPENSES FOR WHICH DEDUCTION IS DISALLOWED	408 to 410
¶ 5096	13801	PRODUCTION PERIOD FOR BEER, WINE, AND DISTILLED SPIRITS	519 to 520
¶ 5104	13821	MODIFICATION OF TAX TREATMENT OF ALASKA NATIVE CORPORATIONS AND SETTLEMENT TRUSTS	531 to 534
¶ 5105	13822	AMOUNTS PAID FOR AIRCRAFT MANAGEMENT SERVICES	534 to 537
¶ 5106	13823	OPPORTUNITY ZONES	537 to 540
¶ 5107	14101	DEDUCTION FOR FOREIGN-SOURCE PORTION OF DIVIDENDS RECEIVED BY DOMESTIC CORPORATIONS FROM SPECIFIED 10-PERCENT OWNED FOREIGN CORPORATIONS	595 to 600
¶ 5108	14102	SPECIAL RULES RELATING TO SALES OR TRANSFERS INVOLVING SPECIFIED 10-PERCENT OWNED FOREIGN CORPORATIONS	601 to 606
¶ 5109	14103	TREATMENT OF DEFERRED FOREIGN INCOME UPON TRANSITION TO PARTICIPATION EXEMPTION SYSTEM OF TAXATION	606 to 621
¶ 5110	14201	CURRENT YEAR INCLUSION OF GLOBAL INTANGIBLE LOW-TAXED INCOME BY UNITED STATES SHAREHOLDERS	635 to 645
¶ 5111	14202	DEDUCTION FOR FOREIGN-DERIVED INTANGIBLE INCOME AND GLOBAL INTANGIBLE LOW-TAXED INCOME	622 to 627
¶ 5112	14211	ELIMINATION OF INCLUSION OF FOREIGN BASE COMPANY OIL RELATED INCOME	631
¶ 5113	14212	REPEAL OF INCLUSION BASED ON WITHDRAWAL OF PREVIOUSLY EXCLUDED SUBPART F INCOME FROM QUALIFIED INVESTMENT	631

Com Rept ¶	Act Sec.	Act Sec. Title	PDF Page
¶ 5114	14213	MODIFICATION OF STOCK ATTRIBUTION RULES FOR DETERMINING STATUS AS A CONTROLLED FOREIGN CORPORATION	633 to 634
¶ 5115	14214	MODIFICATION OF DEFINITION OF UNITED STATES SHAREHOLDER	634
¶ 5116	14215	ELIMINATION OF REQUIREMENT THAT CORPORATION MUST BE CONTROLLED FOR 30 DAYS BEFORE SUBPART F INCLUSIONS APPLY	634
¶ 5117	14221	LIMITATIONS ON INCOME SHIFTING THROUGH INTANGIBLE PROPERTY TRANSFERS	661 to 662
¶ 5118	14222	CERTAIN RELATED PARTY AMOUNTS PAID OR ACCRUED IN HYBRID TRANSACTIONS OR WITH HYBRID ENTITIES	662 to 663
¶ 5119	14223	SHAREHOLDERS OF SURROGATE FOREIGN CORPORATIONS NOT ELIGIBLE FOR REDUCED RATE ON DIVIDENDS	664
¶ 5120	14301	REPEAL OF SECTION 902 INDIRECT FOREIGN TAX CREDITS DETERMINATION OF SECTION 960 CREDIT ON CURRENT YEAR BASIS	628 to 629
¶ 5121	14302	SEPARATE FOREIGN TAX CREDIT LIMITATION BASKET FOR FOREIGN BRANCH INCOME	630
¶ 5122	14303	SOURCE OF INCOME FROM SALES OF INVENTORY DETERMINED SOLELY ON BASIS OF PRODUCTION ACTIVITIES	629 to 630
¶ 5123	14304	ELECTION TO INCREASE PERCENTAGE OF DOMESTIC TAXABLE INCOME OFFSET BY OVERALL DOMESTIC LOSS TREATED AS FOREIGN SOURCE	622
¶ 5124	14401	BASE EROSION AND ANTI-ABUSE TAX	649 to 660
¶ 5125	14501	RESTRICTION ON INSURANCE BUSINESS EXCEPTION TO PASSIVE FOREIGN INVESTMENT COMPANY RULES	669 to 672
¶ 5126	14502	REPEAL OF FAIR MARKET VALUE METHOD OF INTEREST EXPENSE APPORTIONMENT	672

INDEX

References are to paragraph numbers

A

Abandonment of property
. research and development expenses, amortization of 1408

ABLE accounts for the disabled or blind
. contribution limits increased for contributions by beneficiary 1601
. new advantages added by TCJA, client letter regarding 3224
. saver's credit allowed for contributions by designated beneficiary 1602
. tax-free 60-day rollovers from qualified tuition programs permitted 1603

Accounting methods
. expanded use of cash basis accounting method 1401
. . client letter regarding 3214
. gross receipts limits for farming corporations 1402
. income inclusion for tax purposes can't be later than when included for certain financial reporting purposes 1406
. inventory accounting alternatives available to small businesses meeting gross receipts test 1403
. treatment of adjustments resulting from S corporation election revocations 801

Accrual basis
. advance payments
. . deferral of income inclusion to end of year after year of receipt if deferred for financial reporting purposes 1407

Active conduct of trade or business
. transfers to foreign corporations, repeal of active trade or business exception to recognition of gain 2203

Adjusted gross income
. 10%-of-AGI threshold retroactively made inapplicable to net disaster losses from 2016 disaster areas 1801
. medical expense deduction
. . 7.5%-of-AGI floor retroactively extended through 2018 and applied to all taxpayers 505

Adjusted net capital gain
. maximum zero rate amount 1501
. statutory dollar amounts, breakpoints for imposition of 15% and 20% rates set as . . . 1501

Advance payments
. accrual basis taxpayers

Advance payments—Cont'd
. *accrual basis taxpayers —Cont'd*
. . deferral of income inclusion to end of year after year of receipt if deferred for financial reporting purposes 1407

Advance refunding bonds
. exclusion of interest repealed 1701

Affiliated groups
. accumulated deferred foreign income, pre-2018
. . foreign E&P deficits reduce income included in Subpart F 1907
. FDIC premiums deduction phased out for banks with assets over $10 billion, eliminated at $50 billion 1012

Affordable Care Act
. elimination of "individual mandate" after 2018 401
. . client letter regarding 3211

Aircraft
. bonus depreciation 1202
. management services, payments for exempted from excise taxes on taxable air transportation 2901

Alaska Native Settlement Trusts
. assignments to not included in income, and contribution deductions allowed 3102

Alcoholic beverages
. beer, wine, distilled spirits
. . production period won't include aging period for UNICAP interest capitalization rule purposes for next two years 1410

Alimony
. not deductible by payor and not taxable to recipient, post-2018 divorces and separations 510
. . client letter regarding 3220

Alternative depreciation system (ADS)
. farmers and farming
. . ADS depreciation required for 10-year-or-more MACRS property if election made to exempt the business from interest deduction limitation 1306
. nonresidential real property
. . electing real property trade or business 1303
. . recovery period is 40 years for 1302
. qualified improvement property
. . electing real property trade or business 1303

Alternative depreciation system (ADS)—Cont'd

. qualified leasehold improvement, qualified restaurant property and qualified retail improvement property, 39-year recovery period for 1301

. residential rental property

. . electing real property trade or business 1303

. . recovery period is 30 years for 1302

Alternative minimum tax (AMT)

. corporate AMT repeal 303

. . client letter regarding 3209

. . tax liability limitation on aggregated business credits conformed to 1017

. . trading bonus and accelerated depreciation for otherwise-deferred AMT credits ended (conforming to repeal of corporate AMT) 1210

. exemption amounts increased for individuals 301

. . client letter regarding 3209

. individual AMT, temporarily eased; client letter regarding 3209

. minimum tax credit (MTC) offsets regular tax liability for any tax year, and refundable for 2018-2021 304

. standard deduction adjustment

. . doesn't apply to increase in standard deduction attributable to net disaster losses from 2016 disaster areas 302

Amortization

. insurance company policy acquisition expenses, capitalized

. . period increased to 15 years from 10 years 2404

. research and experimental expenditures

. . amortization over five years, amounts paid or incurred after 2021 1408

AMT. See Alternative minimum tax (AMT)

Annuity contracts

. cost of insurance adjustment to basis of, retroactively eliminated 1505

Armed forces

. moving expenses

. . deduction eliminated, except for certain members of armed forces 514

. . reimbursements, exclusion for suspended except for certain members of armed forces 602

. Sinai Peninsula retroactively made hazardous duty area for armed forces member tax benefits 605

Assignments of income

. to Alaska Native Settlement Trusts 3102

Athletic events

. colleges and universities

. . no charitable deduction allowed for contributions in exchange for seating rights . . 513

Athletic facilities, on-premises

. tax-exempt organizations' UBTI 2504

Automobiles

. depreciation of passenger autos

. . annual caps raised 1307

. . $8,000 increase in first-year depreciation cap extended 1208

B

Banks

. FDIC premiums deduction phased out for banks with assets over $10 billion, eliminated at $50 billion 1012

Base erosion minimum tax

. foreign related parties, added on payments to 2201

Basis for gain or loss

. life insurance or annuity contract

. . mortality, expense, or other reasonable charges, no adjustment made for . . . 1505

. partnerships and partners

. . partner's distributive share of losses, basis reduction for partnership charitable contributions amended 903

. . transfers of partnership interests, mandatory basis adjustment upon amended 902

Bicycles

. commuting expense reimbursement, exclusion for suspended 603

Blind. See "ABLE accounts for the disabled or blind"

Bonds

. advance refunding bonds, exclusion of interest repealed 1701

. tax credit bonds

. . new bonds may not be issued 1702

Bonus depreciation. See "Depreciation"

Buildings

. improvements

. . depreciation, eligibility for 15 year recovery period expanded 1301

. . Section 179 property, more improvements made eligible to be 1102

Business credits

. tax liability limitation on aggregate credits conformed to repeal of corporate AMT . . 1017

Business expenses

. employer-operated eating facilities, expenses only 50% deductible through 2025, then become nondeductible 1006

. entertainment expense deduction denied . . 1005

. lobbying local government, deduction for repealed 1011

. performance-based compensation and commissions are made subject to $1 million deduction limit 2601

Business expenses—Cont'd
. *performance-based compensation and commissions are made subject to $1 million deduction limit—Cont'd*
.. definition of "covered employee" subject to compensation deduction limit is expanded 2603
.. definition of "publicly held corporation" subject to $1 million compensation limit is expanded 2602
. qualified transportation fringes and other transportation benefits, employers can't deduct costs of providing 1007
. settlement of sexual abuse or harassment suit subject to nondisclosure agreement, deduction barred for 1010

Business property
. capital gain-ordinary loss rule 1504
. property exempt from business interest limitations excluded from 100% bonus depreciation 1207

Business tax changes
. overview, TCJA provisions
.. client letter regarding 3202

C

Canadian residents
. partial child tax credit, qualification for . . . 516

Capital assets
. exclusion of patents, models, and secret formulas or processes from 1504

Capital gain-ordinary loss rule
. business property 1504

Capital gains and losses. See also "Adjusted net capital gain"
. partnership profits interests held in connection with performance of investment services
.. gains from are short-term capital gains if held for 3 years or less 1502
. Qualified Opportunity Fund
.. gains invested in can be temporarily deferred and permanently excluded if investment is held for ten years 1703

Capitalization. See "Uniform capitalization rules"

Cash method of accounting
. C corporations
.. gross receipts limit raised to $25 million 1401
... client letter regarding 3214
... farming corporations 1402

Casualty losses. See also "Disaster losses"
. citrus plants, minority and subsequent owners can expense certain costs of replanting 1411
. personal
.. client letter regarding 3222

Casualty losses. See also "Disaster losses"—Cont'd
. *personal —Cont'd*
.. nondeductible unless attributable to federally declared disaster 508

C corporations
. cash-method use by, gross receipts limit raised to $25 million 1401
. treatment of adjustments by eligible terminated S corporation 801

Change of accounting method
. research and development expenses, amortization of 1408
. treatment of adjustments by eligible terminated S corporation 801

Charitable contributions
. to Alaska Native Settlement Trusts, deduction for 3102
. college or university athletic event seating rights in exchange for contribution, deduction denied for 513
. electing small business trusts (ESBTs), deduction limitation 803
. limit on individual's deduction for cash contributions increased from 50% to 60% of donor's contribution base 512
. partner's distributive share of losses, basis reduction for partnership charitable contributions amended 903
. substantiation requirement
.. donee reporting exception retroactively repealed 515

Child tax credit
. increased to $2,000 and expanded 516
. qualifying child
.. social security number required to claim credit 518
. refundable portion increased to $1,400 for tax years beginning after 2017 517
. TCJA doubles the credit and allows a new lower credit for other dependents; client letter regarding 3221

Civic groups
. contributions by in a capacity other than as a shareholder are not nontaxable contributions to capital 3101

Client letters
. ABLE accounts for the disabled or blind, new account advantages added by TCJA . . 3224
. alimony not deductible by payor and not taxable to recipient
.. post-2018 divorces and separations 3220
. bonus depreciation 3212
. business tax changes, overview of TCJA provisions on 3202
. child tax credit doubled and allowance of a new lower credit for other dependents 3221

Client letters—Cont'd

. corporate AMT repealed and individual AMT temporarily eased 3209

. corporate income tax rate reduced to 21% 3208

. estate and gift tax exemption doubled to $11.2 million per person 3215

. foreign tax, overview of provisions in TCJA 3204

. home equity loan interest deduction eliminated 3216

. home mortgage interest deductibility, maximum debt lowered 3216

. "individual mandate" eliminated starting in 2019 for individuals failing to maintain minimum essential coverage 3211

. individuals, overview of provisions of TCJA affecting 3201

. individual tax rate brackets, modification of 3208

. like-kind exchange nonrecognition rules limited to real estate 3217

. new employer credit for paid family and medical leave 3219

. orphan drug credit, changes to 3219

. partnerships, overview of TCJA provisions on 3203

. pass-through income, overview of TCJA provisions on 3203

. personal casualty and theft loss deductions, TCJA severely cuts 3222

. "qualified business income" ("pass-through" income), 20% deduction for 3213

. Qualified Opportunity Funds, tax benefits for investments in 3218

. qualified tuition programs (QTPs)

. . $10,000 per year of 529 plan account funds can be used for elementary or secondary school tuition 3223

. rehabilitation credit, changes to 3219

. retirement plans, overview of changes in the TCJA 3205

. S corporations, overview of TCJA provisions on 3203

. Section 179 expensing election 3212

. state and local tax deduction, $10,000 aggregate limit on 3210

. sunset provisions under Tax Cuts and Jobs Act (TCJA) 3207

. tax accounting methods, rules governing 3214

. tax-exempt organizations, TCJA provisions on 3206

Colleges and universities

. athletic event seating rights, in exchange for contributions, no deduction allowed 513

. private institutions, new excise tax imposed on investment income 2502

Combat zone

. Sinai Peninsula retroactively made qualified hazardous duty area for tax benefit purposes 605

Commissions

. performance-based compensation and commissions are made subject to $1 million deduction limit 2601

Commuting expenses

. bicycle commuting reimbursement, exclusion for suspended 603

Compensation for personal services. See "Performance-based compensation"

Computers

. listed property treatment ended for computer equipment 1308

. Section 179 property, otherwise-qualifying property no longer excluded from 1103

Computer software

. amortization of research and development expenditures 1408

Congress

. $3,000 deduction for living expenses of members eliminated 511

Consumer price indexes. See also "Indexing for inflation"

. Chained Consumer Price Index for All Urban Consumers (C-CPI-U)

. . inflation adjustment of income tax brackets based on 201

. . replaces CPI-U in inflation adjustments of tax parameters 202

Contributions to capital

. contributions by a customer or potential customer, or by a government entity or civic group in capacity other than as a shareholder

. . not nontaxable contributions to capital 3101

Controlled corporations

. dividends-received deduction, reduction in 103

Controlled foreign corporations (CFCs)

. constructive attribution rules

. . downward attribution from foreign persons to related U.S. persons 2102

. Subpart F income

. . active insurance business exception to PFIC rules requires minimum insurance liabilities amount 2411

. . constructive attribution rules

. . . downward attribution from foreign persons to related U.S. persons allowed 2102

. . foreign base company oil related income not included in foreign base company income 2104

. . foreign E&P deficits reduce pre-2018 accumulated deferred foreign income included in Subpart F 1907

Controlled foreign corporations (CFCs)— Cont'd

. *Subpart F income — Cont'd*

. . previously excluded Subpart F income withdrawn from, no longer included in U.S. shareholder's income 2105

. . requirement that corporation must be controlled for 30 days before inclusions apply eliminated 2103

. U.S. shareholders

. . definition expanded to include 10% owner by value 2101

. . election to pay net tax liability for pre-2018 accumulated deferred foreign income in installments 1909

. . gross income, U.S. shareholders must include global intangible low-taxed income (GILTI) in 2001

. . inclusion of pre-2018 accumulated deferred foreign income in Subpart F income 1906

Corporations. See also "C corporations"; "Publicly-traded corporations"

. alternative minimum tax repeal 303

. . tax liability limitation on aggregate business credits conformed to 1017

. . trading bonus and accelerated depreciation for otherwise-deferred AMT credits ended (conforming to repeal of corporate AMT) 1210

. base erosion minimum tax

. . foreign related parties, added on payments to 2201

. dividends-received deduction, reduction in 103

. domestic corporations

. . deduction allowed for foreign-derived intangible income and global intangible low-taxed income 2002

. minimum tax credit (MTC)

. . offsets regular tax liability for any tax year, and refundable for 2018-2021 304

. tax rates, reduction in 102

. . client letter regarding 3208

Cost of living adjustments. See "Indexing for inflation"

Credits. See "Tax credits"

Customers

. contributions by customer or potential customer in capacity other than as a shareholder are not nontaxable contributions to capital 3101

D

Death benefits

. reporting requirements added for benefits paid under life insurance contracts 1506

Debt-financed portfolio stock

. dividends-received deduction for dividends from 103

Decedents

. exclusion for discharge of student loans broadened to include discharge on account of death 604

Deductions. See also "Itemized deductions"; "Taxes, deductible"

. business interest, limitation on 1003

. casualty losses, personal

. . nondeductible unless attributable to federally declared disaster 508

. . . client letter regarding 3222

. clinical testing expenses

. . reduced orphan drug credit election available to avoid having to reduce any deduction or charge to capital account for clinical testing expenses 1016

. disaster losses

. . 10%-of-AGI threshold retroactively made inapplicable to net disaster losses from 2016 disaster areas 1801

. . $100 per-casualty floor retroactively raised to $500 for net disaster losses from 2016 disaster areas 1802

. . non-itemizers retroactively allowed to deduct net disaster losses from 2016 disaster areas 1803

. earnings stripping rules repealed 1003

. employer-operated eating facilities, expenses only 50% deductible through 2025, then become nondeductible 1006

. entertainment expenses, deduction denied for 1005

. FDIC premiums deduction phased out for banks with assets over $10 billion, eliminated at $50 billion 1012

. fines, penalties, etc., denial of deductions for broadened 1008

. gambling losses 509

. home equity interest deduction suspended 507

. insurance companies

. . elective deduction of discounted loss reserve amounts--and related special estimated tax payment rules--repeal of 2410

. . life insurance companies

. . . repeal of operations loss deduction . . . 2402

. . . small life insurance company deduction repealed 2403

. lobbying local government, business expense deduction for repealed 1011

. mortgage interest deduction acquisition debt maximum lowered 507

. moving expense deduction eliminated, except for armed forces members 514

. performance-based compensation and commissions are made subject to $1 million deduction limit 2601

Deductions

Deductions. See also "Itemized deductions"; "Taxes, deductible"—Cont'd

. *performance-based compensation and commissions are made subject to $1 million deduction limit—Cont'd*

. . definition of "covered employee" subject to compensation deduction limit expanded 2603

. . definition of "publicly held corporation" subject to $1 million compensation limit expanded 2602

. "qualified business income." See "Qualified business income (QBI)"

. qualified transportation fringes and other transportation benefits, employers can't deduct costs of providing 1007

Deferral of income

. accumulated deferred foreign income, pre-2018

. . foreign E&P deficits reduce income included in Subpart F 1907

. Qualified Opportunity Fund, gains invested in can be temporarily deferred and permanently excluded if investment is held for ten years 1703

. under Section 83(i) election

. . employees can election to defer income from option or RSU stock for up to five years after vesting 2604

. . employer's failure to notify employee that stock is eligible for Section 83(i) election, penalty 2608

. . Form W-2 must include information about deferrals and inclusions under Section 83(i) 2606

Deferred taxes

. reserves for

. . public utilities, normalization requirements for 1309

Dependents

. child tax credit for

. . partial child tax credit allowed for certain non-child dependents 516

. . TCJA doubles the child tax credit and allows a new lower credit for other dependents; client letter regarding 3221

. personal exemption for, suspension of 502

Deposit insurance

. FDIC premiums deduction phased out for banks with assets over $10 billion, eliminated at $50 billion 1012

Depreciation. See also "Alternative depreciation system (ADS)"

. automobiles, passenger

. . annual caps raised 1307

. . $8,000 increase in first-year depreciation cap extended 1208

. bonus depreciation

. . automobiles

. . . $8,000 increase in first-year depreciation cap for passenger autos extended . . . 1208

Depreciation. See also "Alternative depreciation system (ADS)"—Cont'd

. *bonus depreciation —Cont'd*

. . business property exempt from business interest limitations excluded from 100% bonus depreciation 1207

. . . client letter regarding 3212

. . extended for qualified property 1202

. . film, television, and theatrical productions added to "qualified property" eligible for 100% bonus depreciation 1206

. . increased to 100% (full expensing) and extended and modified 1201

. . phase-down of 100% depreciation generally deferred from 2018 to 2023 1203

. . placed in service deadline extended . . . 1209

. . plants bearing fruit or nuts, elective form of depreciation

. . . extended and increased to 100% (full expensing), phase-down deferred from 2018 to 2023 1204

. . trading bonus and accelerated depreciation for otherwise-deferred AMT credits ended (conforming to repeal of corporate AMT) 1210

. . used property allowed 100% depreciation (full expensing) 1205

. building improvements, eligibility for 15 year recovery period expanded 1301

. farmers. See "Farmers and farming"

Direct-pay tax credit bonds

. new bonds may not be issued 1702

Disability and disabled persons. See "ABLE accounts for the disabled or blind"; "Qualified disability trusts"

. exclusion for discharge of student loans broadened to include discharge on account of disability 604

Disaster losses

. deductions

. . AMT standard deduction adjustment doesn't apply to increase in standard deduction attributable to net disaster losses from 2016 disaster areas 302

. . non-itemizers retroactively allowed to deduct net disaster losses from 2016 disaster areas 1803

. . $100 per-casualty floor retroactively raised to $500 for net disaster losses from 2016 disaster areas 1802

. . 10%-of-AGI threshold retroactively made inapplicable to net disaster losses from 2016 disaster areas 1801

Disaster relief

. qualified 2016 disaster distributions from qualified plans

. . aggregate distributions may not exceed $100,000 1804

. . favorable tax treatment 1804

. . no withholding on 1804

Disaster relief—Cont'd
. *qualified 2016 disaster distributions from qualified plans — Cont'd*
. . penalty-free early retirement plan withdrawals for 2016 disaster victims 1806
. . recontributions and continued deferral on amounts previously distributed permitted
. . . . 1807
. . three-year ratable inclusion rule 1805
. . 2016 disaster area, defined 1804
. time permitted for qualified retirement plans and IRAs to provide 2016 disaster relief before adopting retroactive 2016 amendments 1808

Discharge of indebtedness
. student loans
. . exclusion for discharge of certain loans broadened to include discharge on account of death or disability 604

Dispositions of property
. research and development expenses, amortization of 1408

Dividends
. foreign corporations
. . surrogate corporation shareholders not eligible for reduced rate on dividends 2206
. statutory dollar amounts, breakpoints for imposition of 15% and 20% rates set as . . . 1501

Dividends-received deduction
. corporate deduction, reduction in 103
. insurance companies
. . definition of "company's share" and "policyholder's share" amended 2401
. U.S. corporation, dividends received from 10% owned foreign corporation
. . amounts treated as dividends under Sections 1248 and 964(e) treated as dividends for 245A DRD purposes 1904
. . basis of stock in foreign corporation reduced to extent of Section 245A DRD in determining loss on disposition 1903
. . deduction allowed by U.S. shareholder under participation exemption system 1901
. . foreign source income for purposes of FTC limitation, dividends allowed as Section 245A DRD not treated as 1902

Domestic production activities deduction
. repealed 1004

E

Earned income
. threshold for refundable child tax credit . . . 517

Education expenses
. $10,000 per year of 529 plan funds may be used for elementary or secondary school tuition 1604
. . client letter regarding 3223

Elderly. See "Older taxpayers"

Electing small business trusts (ESBTs)
. charitable deductions of 803
. qualifying beneficiaries, expansion of 802

Elections. See also "Section 83(i) election"; "Section 179 expensing election"
. corporate election trading bonus and accelerated depreciation for otherwise-deferred AMT credits ended (conforming to repeal of corporate AMT) 1210
. orphan drug credit
. . reduced credit election available to avoid having to reduce any deduction or charge to capital account for clinical testing expenses 1016
. Qualified Opportunity Fund investments
. . gains can be temporarily deferred and permanently excluded if investment is held for ten years 1703
. real estate investment trusts
. . eight-year period, pre-2018 accumulated foreign income taken into account over
. . . . 1912

Employees
. achievement awards
. . cash, gift cards, and other nontangible personal property don't qualify as 2605
. definition of "covered employee" subject to $1 million compensation deduction limit is expanded 2603

Employee stock options
. Section 83(i) election
. . employees can election to defer income from option or RSU stock for up to five years after vesting 2604
. . employer's failure to notify employee that stock is eligible for election, penalty
. . . . 2608
. . Form W-2 must include information about deferrals and inclusions under Section 83(i) 2606
. . withholding required at highest individual rate when stock subject to election is included in income 2607

Employers
. family and medical leave, paid, credit for
. . . . 1013
. penalty for failure to notify employee that stock is eligible for Section 83(i) election . . 2608
. qualified transportation fringes and other transportation benefits
. . no deduction allowed for 1007

Entertainment expenses
. business deduction denied 1005

ESBTs. See "Electing small business trusts (ESBTs)"

Estates and trusts. See also "Estate tax"
. personal exemption for, suspension of 502

Estates and trusts. See also "Estate tax"— Cont'd

. tax rate structure replaced with 10%, 24%, 35% and 37% tax brackets 104

Estate tax

. basic exclusion amount increased from $5 million to $10 million 2801

. exemption doubled to $11.2 million per person; client letter regarding 3215

Estimated taxes

. insurance companies

. . elective deduction of discounted loss reserve amounts--and related special estimated tax payment rules--repeal of 2410

Excise taxes

. aircraft management services, payments for exempted from taxes on taxable air transportation 2901

. expatriated corporations

. . stock compensation of insiders, excise tax increased 2205

. investment income of private colleges and universities, tax imposed on 2502

. tax-exempt organizations, excess compensation paid by 2501

Exclusions

. bicycle commuting expenses, exclusion for reimbursement suspended 603

. discharge of indebtedness income

. . student loans, exclusion for discharge broadened to include discharge on account of death or disability 604

. moving expense reimbursements

. . suspension of exclusion, except for armed forces members 602

. Qualified Opportunity Fund, gains invested in can be temporarily deferred and permanently excluded if investment is held for ten years 1703

Exemptions

. alternative minimum tax exemption amount for individuals increased 301

Expatriation rules

. expatriated corporations

. . specified stock compensation of insiders, excise tax increased 2205

. recapture of pre-2018 accumulated deferred foreign income deduction for expatriated entities 1908

Expensing

. citrus plants, minority and subsequent owners can expense certain costs of replanting 1411

Exploration expenditures

. amortization of research and development expenditures 1408

F

Fair market value

. interest expense allocation or apportionment repealed after 2017 2306

Family and Medical Leave Act (FMLA)

. employers allowed credit for paid leave . . 1013

Farmers and farming

. cash-method use by C corporations, gross receipts limits raised to uniform $25 million 1402

. depreciation

. . ADS depreciation required for 10-year-or-more MACRS property if election made to exempt the business from interest deduction limitation 1306

. . MACRS 200% declining balance method made available for many types of farming property 1305

. . new farming equipment and machinery, five-year recovery period 1304

. disallowance of excess farm losses

. . excess business loss disallowance replaces, non-corporate taxpayers, tax years beginning after 2017 1409

. net operating losses, two-year carryback allowed 1002

FDIC premiums

. deduction phased out for banks with assets over $10 billion; eliminated at $50 billion 1012

Filing requirements

. based solely on standard deduction for tax years from 2018-2025 502

Films

. added to "qualified property" eligible for 100% bonus depreciation 1206

Financial statements

. income inclusion for tax purposes can't be later than when included for certain financial reporting purposes 1406

Fines

. denial of deduction for broadened 1008

. reporting by government agencies 1009

Foreign base company oil related income

. not included in foreign base company income, controlled foreign corporations 2104

Foreign branches

. separate FTC baskets for 2303

. . transferred loss amount included in income upon transfer of foreign branch assets to specified 10%-owned foreign corporation 1905

Foreign corporations. See also "Controlled foreign corporations (CFCs)

. dividends received deduction, reduction in 103

. partnership interests, treatment of gain or loss from sale of 2304

Foreign corporations. See also "Controlled foreign corporations (CFCs)—Cont'd
. specified foreign corporation
. . defined 1906
. . transfer of foreign branch assets to, transferred loss amount included in income upon 1905
. surrogate corporation shareholders not eligible for reduced rate on dividends 2206
. transfers to
. . repeal of active trade or business exception to recognition of gain 2203
. U.S. shareholders, deduction allowed for dividends received by
. . specified 10% owned foreign corporation under participation exemption system, from 1901
. . . amounts treated as dividends under Sections 1248 and 964(e) treated as dividends for 245A DRD purposes 1904
. . . basis of stock reduced to extent of Section 245A DRD in determining loss on disposition 1903
. . . not treated as foreign source income for FTC limitation purposes 1902

Foreign income
. accumulated deferred foreign income, pre-2018
. . deduction for pre-2018 accumulated deferred foreign income 1908
. . election not to take into account for NOL purposes 1913
. . foreign E&P deficits reduce income included in Subpart F 1907
. . installments, U.S. shareholder election to pay net tax liability in 1909
. . REIT election to take into account over eight years 1912
. . REIT gross income tests, excluded from 1912
. . S corporation shareholder election to defer net tax liability for accumulated deferred income until triggering event 1910
. . six year statute of limitation for assessment of net tax liability due to 1911
. . Subpart F income, pre- 2018 accumulated deferred foreign income included in . . 1906

Foreign sales corporations (FSCs)
. dividends-received deduction 103

Foreign source income
. taxpayer sustaining pre-2018 ODL election to recharacterize as much as 100% of U.S. source income as 2302

Foreign tax credit
. disallowance for pre-2018 accumulated deferred foreign income deduction 1908
. dividends, deemed-paid credit
. . repeal of Section 902 and other adjustments to FTC to account for participation exemption 2301

Foreign tax credit—Cont'd
. foreign branch income
. . separate FTC basket for, addition of . . . 2303
. global intangible low-taxed income (GILTI)
. . 80% deemed paid credit 2003
. . separate basket for 2004

Foreign taxes
. itemized deduction limited to $10,000 for combined state/local property, state/local/foreign income, and general sales tax 506
. overview of provisions in TCJA, client letter regarding 3204

Forms
. W-2. See "Wage and tax statement (Form W-2)"

Fringe benefits
. employer-operated eating facilities, expenses only 50% deductible through 2025, then become nondeductible 1006
. exempt organizations' UBTI increased by disallowed fringe benefits 2504
. qualified transportation fringes and other transportation benefits, employers can't deduct costs of providing 1007

G

Gain or loss
. partnership interests, sale or exchange of
. . treatment of gain or loss of foreign person 2304

Gambling and gaming
. loss limitation broadened; deduction for any expense incurred in gambling limited to gambling winnings 509

Gift tax
. exemption doubled to $11.2 million per person 2801
. . client letter regarding 3215

Global intangible low-taxed income (GILTI)
. domestic corporations allowed deduction for 2002
. 80% deemed paid foreign tax credit 2003
. foreign tax credit basket, separate 2004
. gross income, U.S. shareholders of CFCs include GILTI in 2001

Governmental entities
. contributions by in a capacity other than as a shareholder are not nontaxable contributions to capital 3101
. fines, penalties, etc. owed to
. . denial of deduction broadened for 1008
. . information reporting requirements 1009

Gross income. See also "Adjusted gross income"
. three-year ratable inclusion rule
. . qualified 2016 disaster distributions . . . 1805

Gross income. See also "Adjusted gross income"—Cont'd

. U.S. shareholders of CFCs must include global intangible low-taxed income (GILTI) in 2001

Gross receipts test

. cash method use by C corporations, gross receipts limit raised to $25 million 1401

. . farming corporations 1402

. inventory accounting alternatives available to small businesses meeting gross receipts test 1403

. small construction contract exception to percentage-of-completion method

. . gross receipts limit raised to $25 million 1405

. UNICAP rules, small business exception expanded to apply to producers and resellers meeting gross receipts test 1404

H

Hazardous duty areas

. Sinai Peninsula retroactively made, for armed forces tax benefits 605

Head of household

. status as, paid preparer due diligence requirements 3001

Health and accident insurance

. elimination of "individual mandate" after 2018 401

. . client letter regarding 3211

Historic structures

. credit for rehabilitation expenditures limited to certified structures, and has to be taken ratably over 5 years 1014

Holding period

. partnership profits interests held in connection with performance of investment services

. . gains from are short-term capital gains if held for three years or less 1502

. Qualified Opportunity Fund

. . gains invested in can be temporarily deferred and permanently excluded if investment is held for ten years 1703

Home equity indebtedness

. deduction for interest on suspended 507

. . client letter regarding 3216

Household property

. Section 179 property, otherwise-qualifying property no longer excluded from 1103

Hybrid transactions

. related party amounts paid or accrued in, or with hybrid entities

. . deduction disallowed 2204

I

Improvements. See "Qualified improvement property"

Income. See also "Global intangible low-taxed income (GILTI)"; "Qualified business income (QBI)"

. foreign-derived intangible income

. . domestic corporations allowed deduction for 2002

. inclusion for tax purposes can't be later than when included for certain financial reporting purposes 1406

Income effectively connected with U.S. business

. partnership interests, treatment of gain or loss of foreign person from sale or exchange 2304

Indexing for inflation

. chained-CPI-U, based on 201; 202

. child tax credit, refundable portion of 517

. Section 179 expensing election limits . . . 1101

. . sport utility vehicles 1104

. standard deduction based on chained-CPI-U 501

Indian tribal governments

. business expense deduction for lobbying local governments repealed 1011

Individual retirement accounts (IRAs)

. rule allowing recharacterization of Roth and traditional IRA contributions

. . does not apply to conversion contributions to a Roth IRA 2701

. time permitted to provide 2016 disaster relief before adopting retroactive 2016 amendments 1808

Individual taxpayers

. casualty and theft loss deductions, TCJA severely cuts personal deductions; client letter regarding 3222

. charitable contributions of cash, deduction limitation increased from 50% to 60% of donor's contribution base 512

. disaster losses

. . non-itemizers retroactively allowed to deduct net disaster losses from 2016 disaster areas 1803

. . $100 per-casualty floor retroactively raised to $500 for net disaster losses from 2016 disaster areas 1802

. itemized deductions. See "Itemized deductions"

. overview of the provisions of the TCJA affecting; client letter regarding 3201

. tax rate structure replaced with 10%, 12%, 22%, 24%, 32%, 35%, and 37% tax brackets 101

. . client letter regarding 3208

Inflation adjustments. See "Indexing for inflation"

Insurance companies. See also "Life insurance companies"
. amortization of capitalized policy acquisition expenses
. . period increased to 15 years from 10 years 2404
. dividends received deduction
. . definition of "company's share" and "policy-holder's share" amended for purposes of determining 2401
. net operating losses
. . two-year carryback, 20-year carryforward 1002
. passive foreign investment companies (PFICs)
. . active insurance business exception to PFIC rules requiring minimum insurance liabilities amount 2411
. property and casualty companies
. . proration rules, increased from 15% to 25% 2408
. . unpaid losses, modification of discounting rules for 2409
. reserves
. . definition of "company's share" and "policy-holder's share" amended for purposes of determining 2401
. . discounted loss reserve amounts
. . . elective deduction of, and related special estimated tax payment rules, repealed 2410

Intangible property or rights. See also "Global intangible low-taxed income (GILTI)"
. employee achievement awards not qualifying as nontangible personal property 2605
. transfers, income shifting through
. . limitations imposed on 2202

Interest. See also "Production period interest"
. advance refunding bonds, exclusion of interest repealed 1701
. allocation or apportionment of interest expense
. . assets, adjusted bases of 2306
. . fair market value method repealed after 2017 2306
. business interests deduction limited to 30% of adjusted taxable income 1003
. carryforward of disallowed interest 1003
. earnings stripping rules repealed 1003
. home equity interest deduction suspended 507
. mortgage interest deduction acquisition debt maximum lowered 507

Inventions
. capital assets, exclusions from definition of 1504

Inventories
. accounting alternatives available to small businesses meeting gross receipts test 1403
. source of income from sales determined solely on basis of production activities 2305

Investment income
. private colleges and universities, new excise tax imposed on 2502

Investments
. Qualified Opportunity Fund
. . gains invested in can be temporarily deferred and permanently excluded if investment is held for ten years 1703

Investment services
. partnership profits interests held in connection with performance of investment services
. . gains from are short-term capital gains if held for three years or less 1502

Itemized deductions
. miscellaneous, disallowed 503
. overall limitation ("Pease limitation" or "3%/80% rule") suspended 504
. 7.5%-of-AGI floor retroactively extended through 2018 and applied to all taxpayers 505
. taxes
. . limited to $10,000 for combined state/local property, state/local/foreign income, and general sales tax 506

K

Kiddie tax
. modified to apply estates' and trusts' ordinary and capital gains rates to child's net unearned income 105

L

Land
. research and development expenses, amortization of 1408

Length of service award plans
. accrual limit increased from $3,000 to $6,000 2703

Lessees
. of aircraft, payments for management services exempted from taxes on taxable air transportation 2901

Levy and distraint
. extension of time limit for contesting IRS levy and for third party suits challenging levies 3002

Life insurance companies
. operations loss deduction repealed 2402
. policyholder surplus accounts
. . phased inclusion of remaining balance of 2407
. . pre-1984 accounts, tax on distributions to shareholders repealed 2407
. reserves
. . computation rules amended 2406
. . ten-year spread for changes, repeal of . . 2405

Life insurance companies—Cont'd

. small life insurance company deduction repealed 2403

Life insurance contracts

. cost of insurance adjustment to basis of, retroactively eliminated 1505

. life settlement transactions

. . transfer-for-value rule, exceptions to don't apply 601

. reportable policy sale, defined 601

. tax reporting requirements, policy sales and death benefits paid under 1506

Like-kind exchanges

. limited to exchanges of real estate for exchanges after 2017 1503

. . client letter regarding 3217

Listed property

. computer equipment, listed property treatment ended 1308

Loans. See "Plan loans"; "Student loans"

Lobbying activities

. business expense deduction for lobbying local government repealed 1011

Long-term contracts

. small construction contract exception to percentage-of-completion method

. . gross receipts limit raised to $25 million 1405

Losses

. farm losses, limitation on excess

. . excess business loss disallowance replaces, non-corporate taxpayers

. . . tax years beginning after 2017 1409

. gambling loss limitation broadened 509

Low-income communities

. state chief executive officers can designate communities as Qualified Opportunity Zones 1704

M

Managerial services

. aircraft management services, payments for exempted from taxes on taxable air transportation 2901

Meals and lodging

. employer-operated eating facilities, expenses only 50% deductible through 2025, then become nondeductible 1006

Medical expenses

. 7.5%-of-AGI floor on deduction retroactively extended through 2018 and applied to all taxpayers 505

Mexican residents

. partial child tax credit, qualification for . . . 516

Mines and minerals

. exploration expenses, amortization of research and development expenditures 1408

Minimum tax credit (MTC)

. offsets regular tax liability for any tax year, and refundable for 2018-2021 304

Miscellaneous itemized deductions

. disallowed 503

Models or designs

. capital assets, exclusions from definition of 1504

Modified accelerated cost recovery system (MACRS)

. alternative depreciation system recovery period for residential rental property shortened to 30 years 1302

. farmers and farming

. . ADS depreciation required for 10-year-or-more MACRS property if election made to exempt the business from interest deduction limitation 1306

. . new farming equipment and machinery, 5-year MACRS property 1304

. . 200% declining balance method made available for many types of MACRS farming property 1305

. public utility property, normalization requirements for 1309

Mortality tables

. life insurance company reserves, computation rules 2406

Mortgages

. interest deductibility, maximum debt lowered 507

. . client letter regarding 3216

Motor vehicle dealers

. business property exempt from business interest limitations excluded from 100% bonus depreciation 1207

Motor vehicles. See "Automobiles"; "Sport utility vehicles (SUVs)"

Moving expenses

. deduction eliminated, except for armed forces members 514

. exclusion for expense reimbursements suspended, except for armed forces members 602

MTC. See Minimum tax credit (MTC)

N

Net operating losses (NOLs)

. carrybacks and carryovers

. . indefinite carryforward, repeal of carryback 1002

. conforming changes to other NOL rules 1002

. deductions

Net operating losses (NOLs)—Cont'd
. *deductions* — *Cont'd*
. . foreign income, pre-2018 accumulated deferred
. . . election not to take into account for NOL purposes 1913
. . life insurance companies, removal of prohibition on deduction 2402
. . taxable income, limited to 80% of 1001

NOL. See Net operating losses (NOLs)

Nonresident aliens
. ESBTs, potential current beneficiaries of . . 802
. partnership interests, treatment of gain or loss from sale of 2304

O

ODL. See Overall domestic loss (ODL)

Oil and gas
. foreign base company oil related income
. . not included in foreign base company income, controlled foreign corporations 2104

Operating losses. See "Net operating losses (NOLs)"

Original use requirement
. bonus depreciation, qualified property . . . 1205

Orphan drug credit
. client letter regarding 3219
. qualified clinical testing expenses, reduced to 25% of 1015
. reduced credit election available to avoid having to reduce any deduction or charge to capital account for clinical testing expenses
. . . . 1016

Overall domestic loss (ODL)
. taxpayers who sustain pre-2018 ODL may elect to recharacterize U.S. source income as foreign source income 2302

P

Paid family and medical leave
. new employer credit for 1013
. . client letter regarding 3219

Parking facilities
. tax-exempt organizations' UBTI increased by disallowed fringe benefits 2504

Partnerships
. interests in
. . gain or loss of foreign person from sale or exchange of interest 2304
. . partner's distributive share of losses, basis reduction for partnership charitable contributions amended 903
. . profits interests held in connection with performance of investment services
. . . gains from are short-term capital gains if held for three years or less 1502

Partnerships—Cont'd
. *interests in* —*Cont'd*
. . transfer of, mandatory basis adjustment upon amended 902
. overview of provisions in the TCJA, client letter regarding 3203
. technical termination rule, repeal of 901

Passive foreign investment companies (PFICs)
. active insurance business exception to PFIC rules requiring minimum insurance liabilities amount 2411

Pass-through income. See "Qualified business income (QBI)"

Patents
. capital assets, exclusions from definition of
. . . . 1504

Penalties
. denial of deduction for broadened 1008
. employers
. . failure to notify employee that stock is eligible for Section 83(i) election 2608
. "individual mandate" eliminated starting in 2019 for individuals failing to maintain minimum essential coverage 401
. . client letter regarding 3211
. reporting by government agencies 1009
. tax return preparers
. . head of household filing status added to preparer due diligence requirements
. . . . 3001

Pension and profit-sharing plans
. qualified 2016 disaster distributions from qualified plans
. . aggregate distributions may not exceed $100,000 1804
. . favorable tax treatment 1804
. . no withholding on 1804
. . penalty-free early retirement plan withdrawals for 2016 disaster victims 1806
. . recontributions and continued deferral of tax on amounts previously distributed permitted 1807
. . three-year ratable inclusion rule 1805
. . 2016 disaster area, defined 1804
. retirement plan changes in the TCJA, overview of
. . client letter regarding 3205
. time permitted to provide 2016 disaster relief before adopting retroactive 2016 amendments 1808

Performance-based compensation
. made subject to $1 million deduction limit, publicly held corporations 2601
. . definition of "covered employee" subject to compensation deduction limit expanded 2603
. . definition of "publicly held corporation" subject to compensation deduction limit expanded 2602

Personal

Personal exemptions
. deductions for taxpayer, spouse, and dependents
    suspended 502

Phase-out rules
. child tax credit, increase in threshold amount
    for phaseout 516
. . client letter regarding 3221
. FDIC premiums deduction phased out for
    banks with assets over $10 billion, elimi-
    nated at $50 billion 1012
. passenger autos, $8,000 increase for "qualified
    property" in first-year depreciation cap
    1208
. "qualified business income" ("pass-through" in-
    come), 20% deduction for; client letter re-
    garding 3213
. Section 179 expensing election, limit raised to
    $2.5 million (annual phase-down threshold)
    1101

Placed in service
. bonus depreciation
. . bonus depreciation increased to 100% and ex-
    tended and modified 1201
. . passenger autos, $8,000 increase for "quali-
    fied property" in first-year depreciation
    cap 1208
. . placed in service deadline extended . . . 1209
. . qualified property, bonus depreciation and
    other benefits extended for 1202

Plan loans
. rollover period for offset amounts extended
    from 60 days, to tax return due date . . 2702

Plants and shrubs
. bonus depreciation, elective form of
. . extended and increased to 100% (full expens-
    ing), phase-down deferred from 2018 to
    2023 1204
. citrus plants, minority and subsequent owners
    can expense certain costs of replanting
    1411

Prizes and awards
. length of service award plans
. . accrual limit increased from $3,000 to $6,000
    2703

**Production activities. See also "Domestic pro-
    duction activities deduction"**
. inventory sales, source of income from deter-
    mined solely on basis of production activi-
    ties 2305
. UNICAP rules, small business exception ex-
    panded to apply to producers and resellers
    meeting gross receipts test 1404

Production period interest
. production period for beer, wine, distilled spir-
    its
. . won't include aging period for interest capi-
    talization rule purposes for next two years
    1410

Property taxes
. itemized deduction limited to $10,000 for com-
    bined state/local property, state/local/foreign
    income, and general sales tax 506

Property transfers
. to foreign corporations, repeal of active trade
    or business exception to recognition of gain
    2203

Publicly-held corporations
. performance-based compensation and commis-
    sions are made subject to $1 million deduc-
    tion limit 2601
. . definition of "covered employee" subject to
    compensation deduction limit expanded
    2603
. . definition of "publicly held corporation" sub-
    ject to compensation deduction limit ex-
    panded 2602

Publicly-traded securities
. tax-free rollover of gain from into "specialized
    small business investment companies" re-
    pealed 1507

Public utilities
. business property exempt from business interest
    limitations excluded from 100% bonus de-
    preciation 1207
. normalization requirement for public utility
    property 1309

Puerto Rico
. qualified business income from Puerto Rican
    sources, treatment of 705

Q

Qualified business income (QBI)
. overview 701
. provisions in the TCJA, client letter regarding
    3203
. Puerto Rico sources, qualified business income
    from 705
. qualified business income defined 703
. treatment by entities 704
. 20% deduction for 702
. . client letter regarding 3213

Qualified business unit (QBU)
. foreign tax credit
. . foreign branch income, separate FTC basket
    for, addition of 2303

Qualified disability trusts
. personal exemptions 502

Qualified improvement property
. building improvements
. . ADS depreciation 1303
. . eligibility for 15 year recovery period ex-
    panded 1301
. . Section 179 property, more improvements eli-
    gible to be 1102

Qualified Opportunity Fund

. gains invested in can be temporarily deferred and permanently excluded if investment is held for ten years 1703

. . client letter regarding 3218

Qualified Opportunity Zones

. chief executive officers of states can designate low-income communities as 1704

Qualified residence interest

. mortgage interest deduction acquisition debt maximum lowered 507

Qualified tuition programs (QTPs)

. $10,000 per year of 529 plan funds may be used for elementary or secondary school tuition 1604

. . client letter regarding 3223

. tax-free 60-day rollovers to ABLE accounts are permitted 1603

R

Rates of tax. See "Tax rates"

Real estate

. like-kind exchange rules limited to, for exchanges after 2017 1503

. . client letter regarding 3217

Real estate investment trusts (REITs)

. pre-2018 accumulated deferred foreign income exclusion, gross income test 1912

. taxable income, computation of

. . eight-year period, election to take income into account over 1912

Recapture

. of pre-2018 accumulated deferred foreign income deduction for expatriated entities 1908

Recognition of gain or loss

. transfers to foreign corporations, repeal of active trade or business exception to recognition of gain 2203

Rehabilitation credit

. limited to certified historic structures and has to be taken ratably over five years 1014

. . client letter regarding 3219

Reimbursed expenses

. bicycle commuting expenses, exclusion for suspended 603

. moving expenses

. . exclusion for suspended, except for armed forces members 602

REITs. See "Real estate investment trusts (REITs)"

Related parties

. foreign, base erosion minimum tax added on payments to 2201

. hybrid transactions, amounts paid or accrued in, or with, hybrid entities

. . deduction disallowed 2204

Relief provisions. See "Disaster relief"

Reports and reporting

. Alaska Native Settlement Trusts, deductible contributions to 3102

. government and other agencies

. . fines, penalties, and other amounts of $600 or more for law violations 1009

. life insurance contracts, policy sales and death benefits paid under 1506

Research and experimental expenditures

. amortization over five years, amounts paid or incurred after 2021 1408

. foreign expenditures, amortization over fifteen years 1408

Research credit

. amortization of research and development expenses, effect on credit 1408

Resellers

. UNICAP rules, small business exception expanded to apply to producers and resellers meeting gross receipts test 1404

Reserves

. insurance companies

. . discounted loss reserve amounts

. . . elective deduction of, and related special estimated tax payment rules, repealed 2410

. . life insurance companies

. . . changes, repeal of ten-year spread for 2405

. . . computation rules amended 2406

. pubic utilities

. . deferred taxes, reserves for, normalization requirements 1309

Residential property

. Section 179 property, otherwise-qualifying property no longer excluded from 1103

Restitution payments

. denial of deduction for fines, penalties, etc., exception for amount constituting restitution 1008

. reporting by government agencies 1009

Restricted stock

. settlement of restricted stock units under Section 83(i) election

. . employees can elect to defer income from option or RSU stock for up to five years after vesting 2604

. . employer's failure to notify employee that stock is eligible for Section 83(i) election, penalty 2608

. . Form W-2 must include information about deferrals and inclusions under Section 83(i) 2606

. . withholding required at highest individual rate when stock subject to Section 83(i) election is included in income 2607

Retirement of property

. research and development expenses, amortization of 1408

Revocation

. treatment of adjustments resulting from revocation of S corporation election of eligible terminated S corporation 801

Rollovers

. plan loan offset amounts, rollover period extended from 60 days, to tax return due date 2702

. of publicly traded securities gain into "specialized small business investment companies," tax-free treatment repealed 1507

. qualified tuition programs, 60-day rollovers to ABLE accounts are permitted 1603

. repayment of qualified 2016 disaster distribution treated as direct rollover 1807

Roth IRAs

. rule allowing recharacterization of Roth and traditional IRA contributions

. . does not apply to conversion contributions to a Roth IRA 2701

. three-year ratable inclusion of income rules 1805

S

Sale-leaseback transactions

. elimination of rule 1205

Sales or exchanges

. capital assets, exclusions from definition of 1504

. inventory

. . source of income from sales determined solely on basis of production activities 2305

. partnership interests

. . gain or loss of foreign person, treatment of 2304

Saver's credit

. ABLE contributions by designated beneficiary, credit allowed for 1602

Schools

. elementary or secondary school tuition

. . $10,000 per year of 529 plan account funds can be used for 1604

. . . client letter regarding 3223

S corporations

. installments, election to pay deferred tax liability in 1910

. overview of provisions in the TCJA, client letter regarding 3203

. shareholders

. . election to defer net tax liability for accumulated deferred foreign income until triggering event 1910

S corporations—Cont'd

. *shareholders —Cont'd*

. . ESBTs, charitable deduction limitation . . 803

. . ESBTs, expansion of qualifying beneficiaries of 802

. treatment of adjustments resulting from revocation of election 801

Secret formulas or processes

. capital assets, exclusions from definition of 1504

Section 83(i) election

. employee deferral of income from option or RSU stock for up to five years after vesting 2604

. Form W-2 must include information about deferrals and inclusions under Section 83(i) 2606

. penalty for employer's failure to notify employee that stock is eligible for 2608

. withholding required at highest individual rate when stock subject to election is included in income 2607

Section 179 expensing election

. building improvements eligible for 1102

. . client letter regarding 3212

. pre-adjustment limits raised to $1 million (annual limit on expensing) and $2.5 million (annual phase-down threshold) 1101

. residential property, otherwise-qualifying property no longer excluded 1103

. sport utility vehicles (SUVs)

. . $25,000 per-vehicle limit made adjustable for inflation 1104

Section 529 plans. See "Qualified tuition programs (QTPs)"

Services income

. "qualified business income" ("pass-through" income), 20% deduction for; client letter regarding 3213

Settlement

. sexual abuse or harassment suit subject to nondisclosure agreement

. . business expense deduction barred for . . 1010

Shipping

. qualified shipping investment

. . previously excluded Subpart F income withdrawn from, no longer included in U.S. shareholder's income 2105

Sinai Peninsula

. retroactively made hazardous duty area for armed forces member tax benefits 605

Social security numbers. See "Taxpayer identification numbers"

Software development

. specified R & E expenditures subject to capitalization 1408

Source of income

. inventory sales, source of income from determined solely on basis of production activities 2305

. taxpayer sustaining pre-2018 ODL may elect to recharacterize as much as 100% of U.S. source income as foreign source income 2302

Specialized small business investment companies

. tax-free rollover of publicly traded securities gain into repealed 1507

Specified 10% owned foreign corporations

. transfer of foreign branch assets to, transferred loss amount included in income upon 1905

Sport utility vehicles (SUVs)

. Section 179 expensing election

. . $25,000 per-vehicle limit made adjustable for inflation 1104

Spouses

. personal exemption for, suspension of 502

Standard deduction

. AMT adjustment for

. . doesn't apply to increase in standard deduction attributable to net disaster losses from 2016 disaster areas 302

. basic standard deduction almost doubled, inflation adjustment is modified 501

. net disaster losses from 2016 disaster areas, non-itemizers retroactively allowed to deduct via enhanced standard deduction 1803

State and local governments

. chief executive officers of states can designate low-income communities as Qualified Opportunity Zones 1704

. lobbying local government, business expense deduction for repealed 1011

State and local taxes

. itemized deduction limited to $10,000 for combined state/local property, state/local/foreign income, and general sales tax 506

. . client letter regarding 3210

Statute of limitations

. assessment of net tax liability due to pre-2018 accumulated deferred foreign income

. . six years after return 1911

Stock

. performance of services, transfers in connection with

. . employees can election to defer income from option or RSU stock for up to five years after vesting 2604

. . employer's failure to notify employee that stock is eligible for Section 83(i) election, penalty 2608

. . Form W-2 must include information about deferrals and inclusions under Section 83(i) 2606

Stock—Cont'd
. *performance of services, transfers in connection with —Cont'd*

. . withholding required at highest individual rate when stock subject to Section 83(i) election is included in income 2607

Stockholders

. controlled foreign corporations

. . U.S. shareholder

. . . definition expanded to include 10% owner by value 2101

. life insurance companies, stock

. . pre-1984 policyholders surplus account

. . . tax on distributions to shareholders repealed; phased inclusion of remaining balance is provided 2407

Stock life insurance companies

. pre-1984 policyholders surplus account

. . tax on distributions to shareholders repealed; phased inclusion of remaining balance is provided 2407

Structural components

. building improvements

. . Section 179 property, more improvements eligible to be 1102

Student loans

. exclusion for discharge of certain loans broadened to include discharge on account of death or disability 604

Subpart F income. See also "Controlled foreign corporations (CFCs)"

. active insurance business exception to PFIC rules requiring minimum insurance liabilities amount 2411

. downward attribution rules

. . stock owned by foreign person treated as owned by a U.S. person 2102

. foreign E&P deficits reduce pre-2018 accumulated deferred foreign income included in Subpart F 1907

. participation exemption system, transition to 1906

. pre-2018 accumulated deferred foreign income included in 1906

Sunset provisions

. under Tax Cuts and Jobs Act (TCJA), client letter regarding 3207

T

Taxable income

. net operating loss deduction limited to 80% of 1001

Tax credits. See also "Business credits"; "Child tax credit"; "Foreign tax credit"; "Orphan drug credit"; "Rehabilitation credit"

. paid family and medical leave, employer credit for 1013

Tax credits. See also "Business credits"; "Child tax credit"; "Foreign tax credit"; "Orphan drug credit"; "Rehabilitation credit"—Cont'd

. trading bonus and accelerated depreciation for otherwise-deferred AMT credits ended (conforming to repeal of corporate AMT)
. . . . 1210

Taxes, deductible

. itemized deduction limited to $10,000 for combined state/local property, state/local/foreign income, and general sales tax 506
. . client letter regarding 3210

Tax-exempt organizations

. excess compensation payments, excise tax imposed on 2501
. TCJA provisions on, client letter regarding
. . . . 3206
. unrelated business taxable income
. . calculated separately for each trade or business 2503
. . disallowed fringe benefit expenses, UBTI increased by 2504

Tax-free bonds. See "Bonds"

Tax-free exchanges. See "Like-kind exchanges"

Taxpayer identification numbers

. child tax credit for qualifying child without a social security number 516
. . client letter regarding 3221

Tax rates

. estates and trusts, new tax rate table for . . . 104
. foreign corporations
. . surrogate corporation shareholders not eligible for reduced rate on dividends 2206
. income tax
. . corporations, reduction in rates 102
. . . client letter regarding 3208
. individual, 10%, 12%, 22%, 24%, 32%, 35%, and 37% tax brackets 101
. . client letter regarding 3208
. withholding
. . stock subject to Section 83(i) election is included in income, withholding required at highest individual rate when 2607

Tax return preparers

. head of household filing status added to preparer due diligence requirements . . 3001

Television

. productions added to "qualified property" eligible for 100% bonus depreciation 1206

Termination

. partnership technical termination rule, repeal of
. . . . 901

Termination of employment

. plan loan offset amounts, rollover period extended from 60 days, to tax return due date
. . . . 2702

Theatrical productions

. live productions added to "qualified property" eligible for 100% bonus depreciation
. . . . 1206

Third parties

. suits challenging IRS levies, extension of time limit for 3002

Transfers

. intangible property, income shifting through
. . limitations imposed on 2202

Transportation

. other benefits
. . employers can't deduct cost of 1007
. qualified bicycle commuting reimbursement
. . deducting expenses 1007
. qualified transportation fringes
. . no deduction allowed for expenses of . . 1007
. . tax-exempt organizations' UBTI 2504

Trusts. See "Estates and trusts"

U

Uniform capitalization rules

. production period for beer, wine, distilled spirits
. . won't include aging period for UNICAP interest capitalization rule purposes over next two years 1410
. small business exception expanded to apply to producers and resellers meeting gross receipts test 1404

Unrelated business taxable income (UBTI)

. tax-exempt organizations
. . disallowed fringe benefit expenses, increased by 2504
. . trade or business, UBTI calculated separately for each 2503

Used property

. bonus depreciation, allowed 100% (full expensing) 1205

U.S. shareholder's income

. CFC shareholders must include global intangible low-taxed income (GILTI) in gross income 2001
. qualified shipping investment
. . previously excluded Subpart F income withdrawn from, no longer included in
. . . . 2105
. requirement that corporation must be controlled for 30 days before Subpart F inclusions apply eliminated 2103

U.S. source of income

. taxpayers sustaining pre-2018 ODL may elect to recharacterize U.S. source income as foreign source income 2302

W

Wage and tax statement (Form W-2)
. Section 83(i), form must include information
   about deferrals and inclusions under . . 2606

Withholding
. compensation for personal services
. . modification of individual withholding rates
   102
. . modification of rules due to suspension of
   personal exemptions 502

Withholding—Cont'd
. *compensation for personal services* —*Cont'd*
. . reduction in withholding on distributions or
   dispositions of USRPIs 102

. . stock subject to Section 83(i) election included in income, withholding required at
   highest individual rate when 2607

. partnership interest, sale or exchange by foreign
   person 2304